THE ESSEN
MONSTER
MOVIE GUIDE

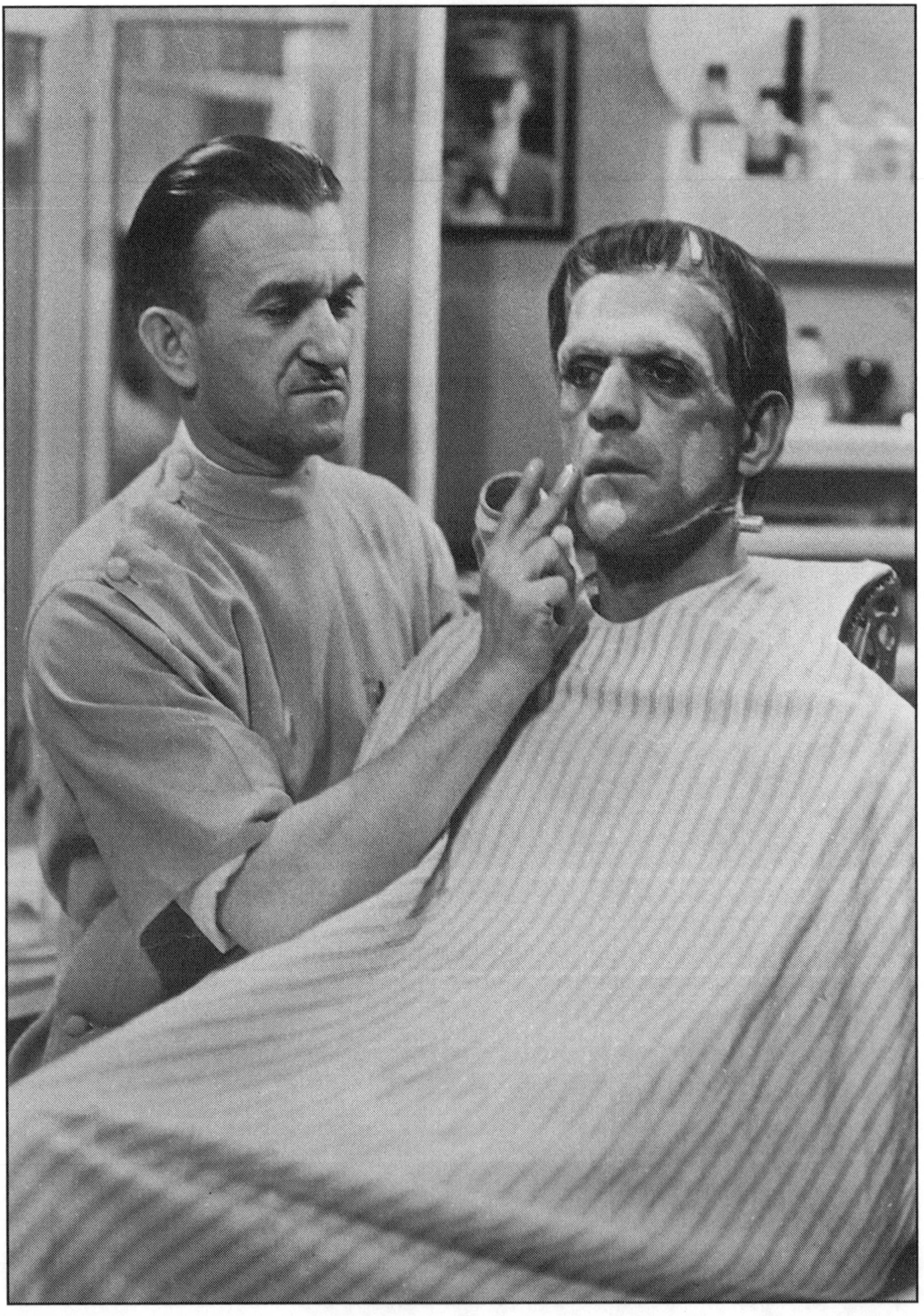

A Century of Creature Features on Film, TV and Video

STEPHEN JONES

Introduction by FORREST J ACKERMAN

TITAN BOOKS

**For my 'Three Musketeers':
Randy, Kim and Baz,
without whom this book would
have been much shorter.**

THE ESSENTIAL MONSTER MOVIE GUIDE
ISBN 1 85286 935 6

Published by
Titan Books
A division of
Titan Publishing Group Ltd
144 Southwark St
London
SE1 0UP

First edition October 1999
10 9 8 7 6 5 4 3 2 1

A CIP catalogue record for this title is available from the British Library.

Printed and bound in Great Britain by MPG Books Ltd, Victoria Square, Bodmin, Cornwall.

Page 2: Make-up artist Jack P. Pierce transforms Boris Karloff into the Monster for Frankenstein *(1931).*

CONTENTS

MONSTER MOSAIC

by Forrest J Ackerman

'Mr Filmonster'

I've had seventy-seven years of filmic fears in my life... and still haven't had enough.

A Man of Parts

When I was fifteen years old I went on Christmas Day 1931 to the first showing in San Francisco of something called...*Frankenstein*. Frankenstein? Who he? What kind of a name was that? It might as well have been Woolworth or Farnsworth for all it conveyed to me; Scaramouche would have sounded scarier. I hadn't yet learned of the book by that English teenager named Mary Shelley, but the advertising was, you should excuse the expression, a 'dead' giveaway: 'The Man Who Made a Monster'.

In front of the picture palace stood a sinister white ambulance. Inside the lobby, two nurses were in attendance. As the film unwound, the daylight scenes were in sunny amber, night scenes in pale blue, eerie scenes (of which there were plenty) a creepy green, and the pyro-climactic windmill death sequence in fiery red.

I staggered out of the theatre an addled adolescent. I had seen forty-nine dinosaurs in the film of Sir Arthur Conan Doyle's *The Lost World*; I had ventured 20,000 leagues under the sea to *The Mysterious Island*; I had accompanied *The Thief of Bagdad* to the land of living forest treemen, beneath the sea to grapple with the giant spider, into the rocky cavern of the fire-breathing dragon, on the wings of a flying horse to the moon; I had seen a second fabulous fire-breathing dragon, the Fafnir of Fritz Lang's *Siegfried*; I had stared in awe at least four of the 1,000 faces of Lon Chaney — Erik, *The Phantom of the Opera*; Quasimodo, *The Hunchback of Notre Dame*; the pale-faced mad scientist of *The Monster*; and the ghoulish caped creature of *London After Midnight* — but my bulging eyes had never before beheld anything like Jack Pierce's macabre masterpiece: Boris Karloff as the Frankenstein Monster. That body which, according to its maker, Henry Frankenstein (Colin Clive), had never lived, had been pieced together with bodies taken 'from the graves, the gallows — anywhere' onto which he turned 'the Great Ray that first brought life into the world', and when the wrist of the cadaver on Kenneth Strickfaden's electrical table moved, Dr Frankenstein knew what it felt like to be God...and the audience and I knew what it felt like to be in the presence of a horror scientifilm classic.

During one of the most frightening moments in the film, a woman in the audience screamed, jumped up out of her seat and ran up the aisle and out the theatre! In those days they didn't turn on the lights at the end of a showing and shoo patrons out of the theatre; one could stay as long as one liked and see a picture over and over. I stayed a second time. And got my first experience of movie hype: at exactly the same spot in the film, the same lady screamed, jumped up and ran up the aisle out of the theatre! Talk about theatrics!

It has been said there has never been a day since that, along with *King Kong*, it has not been playing somewhere in the world. However, when I visited China last year I learned that one billion two hundred million people had not yet seen *Frankenstein* — nor for that matter *Dracula* — so one can but conjecture how many people on the planet still have a terrifying treat in store.

I didn't dream back in 1931 that I would live to see so many sequels and spin-offs of Mary Shelley's Monster — a *Bride*, a *Son*, a *Daughter*, a *Ghost*, a *House*, an *Evil*, a *Teenage*, an *Unbound*, a *Curse* and worse, even a *Young Frankenstein* and a gay one, a Spanish, a German, a Japanese — more than 130 to date! In 1971, Mexico spawned *Santo contra la Hija de Frankestein*. Ten years earlier, in 1961, when I was but forty-five, I saw the Mexican *Orlak, el Infierno de Frankenstein*. I have forgotten the plot but fortunately(?) I recorded at the time that 'Dr Carlos Frankenstein brings an executed murderer back to life to help him in his experiments.' 1818: the birth of Frankenstein; this year, 1999, a literary legend is 181 years old and still going strong.

I have over 150 different editions of the book, the most unusual being the 1877 copy retitled *The Man Demon*. Since the first 'different' printing I acquired nearly seventy years ago, I have never seen another called other than by the name of the maker of the Monster. Perhaps one day the film-makers will run out of titles and think of calling the *nth* remake...*The Man Demon*.

A terrifying thought. I have a copy of *Frankenstein* containing the signature of Willis O'Brien and was told that following the success of his *The Lost World* he was contemplating making an animated Frankenstein! The question arises: if there had been a 1926 or '27 stop-motion model version of the film, would Boris Karloff ever have made the 1931 version?! And if Karloff had never been 'discovered' for the part by James Whale, would he have gone on to his whale of a career as mummies, Jekyll/Hyde, Fu Manchu, co-starring roles with Bela Lugosi, *et al*? I'm afraid to look into that alternate universe and perhaps discover no Boris. Why, there might not ever have even been a Forrest as we know me!

Forrest J Ackerman.

Vamp Until Ready

1931 was a double treat year for me — and the world. I also saw *Dracula* for the first time. It would not be the last — nor of his *Son* or *Father* or *Daughter* or *Brides* or *Lovers* or *Niece* or *Widow* (Sylvia 'Emmanuelle' Kristel) or *Dog* or *Doll* or *Coffin* or *Curse* or *House* (what a ghast cast in the latter: Lon Chaney Jr, John Carradine, Lionel Atwill, Glenn Strange, Onslow Stevens, Skelton Knaggs). Distinguished actor Francis Lederer essayed the role of the thirsty Count in *The Return of Dracula*, and Lugosi starred in *The Return of the Vampire*. Bela was back for the last time impersonating his legendary vampire in 1952 in *My Son the Vampire*, the American title for the variously-known British production *Mother Riley Meets the Vampire* or *Vampire Over London*, with the then popular British female impersonator comedian Arthur Lucan.

Vampire films date as far back as 1913. There have been French, German, Japanese, Spanish, Italian, Mexican, Malayan, Hungarian (silent), Romanian and even Turkish vampires. Not to overlook the gay versions *Gayracula* and *Does Dracula Really Suck?*, the inevitable *Blacula* (spawning *Blackenstein*, *Dr. Black Mr. Hyde* and so on) and, for the hearing impaired, *Deafula*. I kid you not. What — so far there hasn't been an Invisiblack Man? The Hunchblack of Notre Dame? The Creature from the White Lagoon? There's been *The Vampire of the Opera*. The twenty-first century is looming large before us — there's a new hundred years of fun and fears ahead.

As I transfer these words to my weirdprocessor, on the third finger of my left hand is Bela Lugosi's Dracula ring, last worn by him in (Abbott and Costello) *Meet Frankenstein*, and before that seen on the famous fingers of John Carradine and Lon Chaney Jr. I could, if I wished, go to my entranceway closet and withdraw the cape I saw Lugosi wearing on stage in 1932, giving one of his 1,000 live performances, before wearing it for the last time in the infamous *Plan 9 from Outer Space*.

Some years ago on a European vacation I took with me six copies of the ring and, before I left France, Germany, Italy, Spain and Luxembourg, I decided which fantasy film fan or Dracula devotee would appreciate one the most and gave it to them as a parting present. In London, with one left, I met...Christopher Lee. At the time he was on his second or third Dracula portrayal so — who else? The day after meeting him I went to his apartment door, knocked and only expected to hand him the ring and depart. Instead, he grabbed me by the hand, pulled me into the room, ran over to his library, drew down a copy of *Dracula* from a shelf, turned to a significant page, removed a sword from a wall and began waving it about dramatically (the sword, not the wall) while he theatrically read a page from Bram Stoker's masterpiece. It was a memorable extemporaneous performance. For the next several Hammer Dracula films he wore the ring. He recently transferred it to a lucky fan living in England.

All vampires have not been *doppelgängers* or descendants of Dracula. French *femme fatale* Anne Parillaud has played a mouth-watering naked vampire-to-die-for in *Innocent Blood*, a John Landis film in which, in one of the six cameos he has given me, I have my car stolen by a vampire. Ingrid Pitt has been seen (all of her curvaceous figure) as a beauteous lesbian pulchrinude in *The Vampire Lovers*, the late Caroll Borland in her youth played a female vampire in *Mark of the Vampire* (Tod Browning's remake of *London After Midnight*), and the late Klaus Kinski enhanced the talking version of *Nosferatu*. I named a young New York stage actor 'Zandor Vorkov' for his role in *Dracula vs. Frankenstein* (in which I, in one of my more than fifty cameos to date, am killed by the Frankenstein Monster). Come to think of it, I have played *Bela Lugosi himself*, in his Dracula cape standing frozen as a statue in front of the Hollywood Wax Museum, before coming to life and leaping off the pedestal and running for my undead life when the five-storeys tall Playmate comes down the Tinsel Town boulevard in *Attack of the 60 Foot Centerfold*. The comic book character I created in 1969, Vampirella, now exists as a Corman/Showtime telefilm; she's a blood-sucking, shape-changing beauty (with a shape like Talisa Soto, who needs to change?) from the planet of blood, Drakulon. Czech actress Florence Marly portrayed Velena, a sanguinary siren from the planet Centurion in *Queen of Blood*; in the climax I am holding her eggs, unaware that when they hatch they will suck humans dry. I befriended Florence during the making of this film and was at her funeral when she was laid to rest atop a cemetery in a golden casket. It was one of Basil (Sherlock Holmes) Rathbone's final films and was directed by fantasy-oriented Curtis (*Night Tide*) Harrington.

Brazil: *Love That Vampire*. France: *The Nude Vampire*. Germany: *The Vampire Happening*. Italy: *The Vampire and the Ballerina*. Japan: *Lake of Dracula*. Malaya: *Sumpah Pontianak*. Mexico: *The World of the Vampires*. Spain: *A Vampire for Two*.

Incidental intelligence: The noted female science fiction author Leigh Brackett co-scripted *The Vampire's Ghost*. The pioneering science fiction and *Weird Tales* author Edmond Hamilton wooed and won her, his conquest being abetted by the borrowing from me of a book Leigh wanted desperately to read: *The Worm Ouroboros* by E.R. Eddison.

Richard Matheson's vampire classic *I am Legend* is still scheduled for a third try before the cameras, hoping to capture the soul of the story.

Many hundreds of vampire films have sanguinised the silver screen. As early as 1914 *Vasco, the Vampire* was seen (but not heard) on the silent screen. Andy Warhol did one with Dracula, Dracula met Billy the Kid, Carmilla, Count Yorga, *Fright Night*, *House of Dark Shadows*, *The Hunger* (Catherine Deneuve), *Jonathan*, *The Last Man on Earth* (Vincent Price), *The Legendary Curse of Lemora*, *Love at First Bite*, *Martin*, *Vampyres* and scores more have all carried on the Transylvanian tradition...although nowadays script writers are inclined to break with tradition and fudge ways for the undead to do their dastardly deeds even during daylight, as in *A Polish Vampire in Burbank*. The vampiriclimax of the latter is unusual; when the young boy vampire goes bravely out into the sun's death rays to take his undead sweetheart in his arms as, to schmaltzy violins, they both lose their flesh and become fondly embracing skeletons.

Mexico got in on the act in the 1960s with *El Baron Brakola* and *Santo y el Tesoro de Dracula*. Highlight of the latter has Count Alucard duplicating Draculean damsels with a bat-ring.

We were treated to *Vampiros Lesbos* via a German-Spanish collaboration also known as *Vampyros Lesbos die Erbin des Dracula* and *Las Vampiras*.

Cinematic involvement with the undead made a living for Lugosi, Lee and Peter Cushing. It is a little-known fact that at one time the highly respected fantasy author Fritz

Leiber (Jr, son of the Senior Shakespearean actor) was being groomed for a screen role as Dracula and a continuing career late in life as a contender in the horror film genre. The ill-fated project got as far as a cold reading of the script, with Caroll Borland and myself lending our voices. Leiber's appearance as the Lovecraftian character in *Equinox* testifies to the role he could have played in macabre movies in an alternate universe.

Their Night to Howl

The lycanthrope began to lope through monster movies in 1935 in the feral form of Henry Hull as the *WereWolf of London* and his lupine adversary, the Swedish character actor Warner (Charlie Chan) Oland. Six years later, lycanthrope Larry Talbot made his début in Universal's *The Wolf Man* and a new character and series were born. Lon Chaney Jr found his niche in the horror genre, a niche that he scratched in *Frankenstein Meets the Wolf Man, House of Frankenstein, House of Dracula* and (Abbott and Costello) *Meet Frankenstein.* With the benefit of make-up maestro Jack Pierce's transformation, he played the hirsute horror to the hilt in the company of monster movie greats Claude Rains, Lionel Atwill, George Zucco, John Carradine, Maria Ouspenskaya, Glenn Strange, Evelyn Ankers and even Boris Karloff. Fans of the unfortunate Larry Talbot were happy for him when, in 1945, he was finally cured of his curse (*House of Dracula*) — but three years later, without any explanation, he was back at his machinations in the Abbott and Costello spoof (which Chaney Jr hated, claiming the comedic pair made clowns out of respected monster characters).

Dying of half-a-dozen diseases, any one of which would have proven fatal, Wolf Man Creighton (Lon Jr) Chaney nobly donated his body to the University of Southern California Medical School for research for the benefit of humanity. There is an unconfirmed rumour that his head, like that of Timothy Leary, has been preserved, although for what reason it is difficult to imagine. I'm inclined to doubt it, else we'd have the basis for a true-life horror story.

I played myself, identified with a couple of issues of *Famous Monsters of Filmland* behind my back, in Joe Dante's *The Howling*, which continued to howl through sequel after sequel, one being made in Romania.

Brazil gave us *O Coronel e o Lobisomen* (the 'Wolfman', as distinguished from Lon Chaney Jr's *The Wolf Man*).

Hammer Films introduced Oliver Reed into the horror genre with feral ferocity in *The Curse of the Werewolf*, from the novel *The Werewolf of Paris* by Guy Endore. Endore had

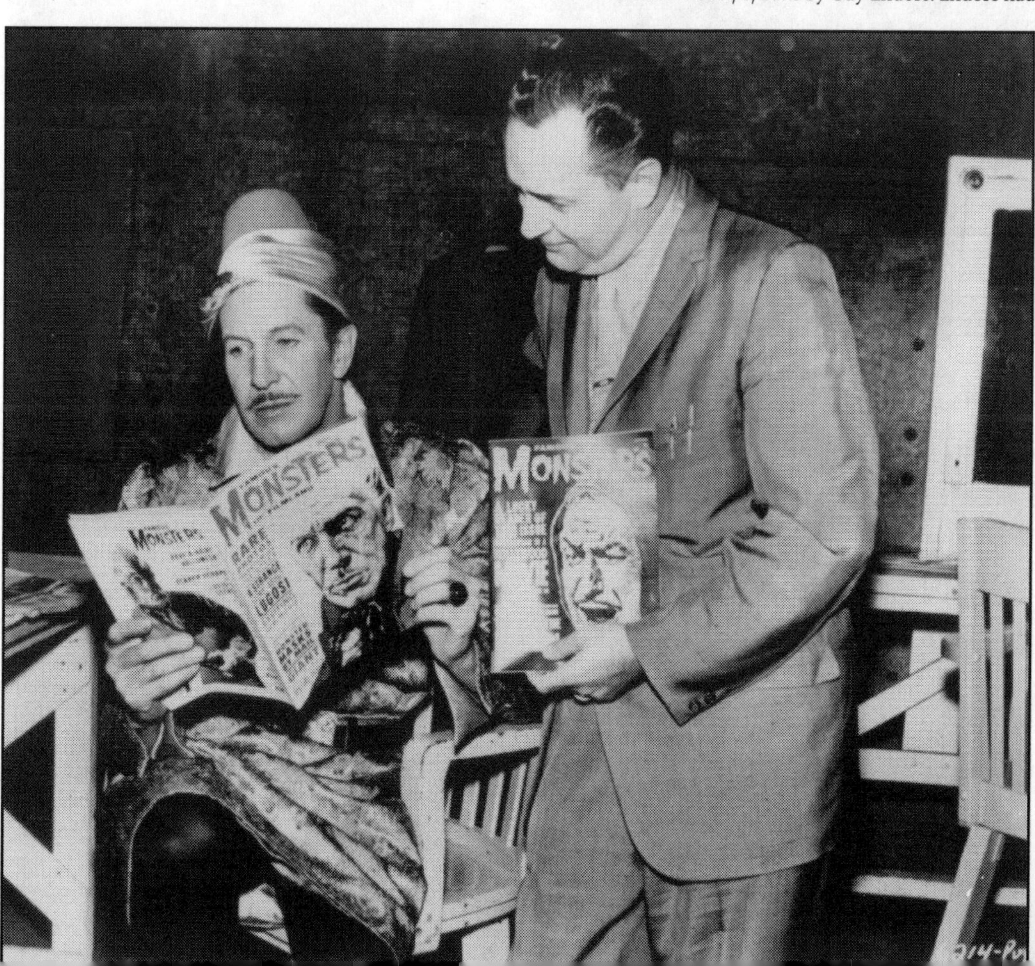

Forry meets Vincent Price behind-the-scenes on The Raven *(1963).*

Forry and Hugh Hefner.

always been a mysterious figure to me since as a kid I read a sci-fi story by him in *Blue Book Magazine* (the title eludes my eighty-two year-old memory, but I seem to recall 'skies' being part of it). I finally had the pleasure of meeting Endore at the funeral of cameraman Karl (*Metropolis, Mad Love*) Freund. I presume you will be disappointed that I don't describe him to you; I'm disappointed myself. I simply seem to recall an undistinguished gentleman of average height in a business suit. If I'd known one day it would be important, I would have made notes.

Incidental intelligence: for one magic hour of my life every word that came out of the mouth of Boris Karloff, I put into it. I was present when he recorded the Decca album I scripted, *An Evening with Boris Karloff and His Friends*. I had used the fancy term for werewolf — lycanthrope — and he was uncertain how to pronounce it, so the spotlight was on me. I suddenly realised that though he had portrayed the Frankenstein Monster, the insidious Dr Fu Manchu, been a ghoul and Dr Jekyll and Mr Hyde, he had never been called upon to play a werewolf. So I spoke up and he continued with his classic recording.

In Spain, Paul Naschy transmogrified himself into a lycanthrope in 1967 in *Frankenstein's Bloody Terror* (shot in 3-D, a version of which I saw in my native Horrorwood twenty-five years or so ago, but even with glasses it was flat), its instant success with Spanish audiences inspiring a sequel, *Nights of the Werewolf*, almost before the year was through. To date Naschy has made a spate of follow-ups, no less than eleven Waldemar Daninsky terror tales altogether: *Frankenstein's Bloody Terror, Nights of the Werewolf, Dracula vs. Frankenstein, The Fury of the Wolfman, The Werewolf vs. the Vampire Woman, Dr. Jekyll and the Werewolf, Curse of the Devil, Night of the Howling Beast, The Craving, La Bestia y la Espada Mágica* and *Licantropo el Asesino de la Luna Llena*. In the course (or curse) of his lycanthropic depredations, Waldemar Daninsky meets (and naturally defeats) an abominable snowman (yeti), the monster-making Wolfstein family, a mummy(!) and vampires. *The Fury of the Wolfman* is notable for its opening narration, a Hispanic adaptation of Curt Siodmak's legendary poem:

Even a man who is pure in heart
And says his prayers by night,
May become a wolf when the wolfbane blooms
And the autumn moon is bright.

In Spain it became:

When the heliotrope begins growing among rough rocks
And the full moon shines at night,
In a certain area of the Earth
A man turns into a wolf.

Presumably it rhymed in Spanish.

Zombies, White and Otherwise

Bela Lugosi had three outstanding roles: Count Dracula. Broken-necked Ygor. And 'Murder' Legendre — the star of *White Zombie*.

There have been astro-zombies, Karloff as *The Walking Dead*, Bogie himself as the boogeyman in *The Return of Doctor X*, Curtis Harrington's telefilm *The Dead Don't Die* with the late Reggie Nalder (who got his face scarred attempting to save the life of his brother from a fire) and Yvette Vickers (whom I met and befriended at a party in Harrington's unusual Hollywood home), *The Dead One*, *Death Warmed Up*, *Disciple of Death*, *The Ghoul* (Karloff, Thesiger, Sir Cedric Hardwicke), *Horror of the Zombies*, *Revolt of the Zombies* (miserable 1936 poverty-row bomb), *I Walked with a Zombie* (Val Lewton classic), *Night of the Living Dead* (considered the seminal modern-day zombie film), the late David Bruce, who visited the Ackermansion shortly before his death, as *The Mad Ghoul* in Jack Pierce make-up, *Raiders of the Living Dead* (Zita Johann out of retirement after fifty years to play a librarian), *Phantasm* (introducing my dear friend Angus Scrimm as 'The Tall Man'), *Plan 9* from you know where, *Orgy of the Dead* (Ed Wood!), *Zombies on Broadway* (embarrassing spoofola for poor Bela)... well, I'm not going to attempt to list every zombie film ever made. I'll just admit that I play the lead zombie smashing down a door in *Return of the Living Dead Part II* and then hastily depart the scene before Murder Legendre gets me!

Stars of Wrap Parties

'He went for a little walk.' A simple enough statement. Six words that might have been spoken by Fred Astaire or Cary Grant — right? — in a sophisticated love romance, and no one would have any reason to remember them today.

But in 1943, eleven years after they had been spoken, as editor of the *Ft. MacArthur Bulletin* I found myself interviewing the actor who made them immortal in the history of horror:

Bramwell Fletcher.

It is 1932 and Universal Studios has released its successor to *Dracula* and *Frankenstein*: *The Mummy*.

Imhotep (Boris Karloff), dead 3,700 years in the sands of ancient Egypt, is a mummy that has been unearthed by a 1921 British expedition which discovers a secret tomb where the sorcerer was buried alive for sacrilegiously attempting to bring back to life his lover, Princess Anck-es-en-Amon (Zita Johann). Foolhardy Fletcher, alone with the coffin of the Mummy, unleashes the power of the Scroll of Thoth...and dies laughing hysterically in an insane asylum, his mind having snapped when the Mummy, with infinitesimal slowness, dust and pieces of its shroud falling from its desiccated body, opens its eyes and, tortoise-slow, moves silently toward the unsuspecting researcher.

Bramwell Fletcher, in 1943 army uniform, laughed when I told him he should have been turned down for duty in World War Two on grounds of insanity; he sure convinced me in the picture that he had gone stark staring mad!

Forry and Steven Spielberg.

In the film, Edward Van Sloan (veteran of *Frankenstein* and *Dracula*), David Manners (the young hero) and director Karl Freund were all intimately involved with the production. Not to overlook the legendary eight-hour make-up of Jack Pierce. Actually, Pierce did two make-ups, the second one being eleven years later in the film when Imhotep appears as the mysterious Ardath Bey, the living mummy with the face whose skin resembles an ancient parchment.

I'd like to interrupt the plot for a moment to speak about David Manners, who sadly died at the end of 1998. He made thirty-seven films in six years. Last year, an admirer who had corresponded with him for twenty-two years, and was about to visit him for the first time, told me that he had spoken on the phone with Manners, who said, 'You better hurry up, there's not much left of me.' He was apparently a sweet old man who was ready to meet his Maker.

But back to the plot. Ardath Bey's mission impossible: to revive his ancient love. This he cannot do because she has been reincarnated as Zita Johann. None less than Katharine Hepburn(!) was originally wanted for Zita's role, but 'Electric Kate' was not available at the time. Several sequences were shot of Zita's reincarnating lives through the ages, but evidence of their existence exists only in rare stills. Missing scenes have been restored to *Frankenstein, King Kong, Metropolis, Things to Come* and *Lost Horizon*; one wishes (in fact more than one!) the same would be done with *The Mummy*.

Originally the film was to be known as *Cagliostro*, then began shooting as *Im-Ho-Tep*. Little did I dream when fifteen year-old me sat spellbound by its first showing that, as I write this account of it, I would be wearing on the middle finger of my left hand Boris Karloff's own scarab ring from the film. How do I come to have it? Did Mr Karloff give it to me? Did I purchase it at auction? None of the foregoing. A fan of mine, Philip J. Riley, moved to Los Angeles from the East coast and became devoted to the cause of increasing the holdings of the Ackermuseum. In the window of an antique shop in the seashore city of Ocean Park he spied a ring that looked somehow hauntingly familiar. It was not identified as being a movie prop. He came back to my place, sifted through my stills and, lo!, there upon Karloff's finger was the Mummy ring! He promptly went back to the shop and purchased it before someone alerted the manager to the treasure he had. I will be grateful to Philip Riley for the next 3,700 years.

On the last day of September 1997, in Universal Studios' 'Conan' auditorium, as thousands cheered, the Mummy's daughter, Sara Karloff-Sparkman, sparkling like the jewel she is, stood on the stage as a mummy shambled out and presented her with a framed portrait of her illustrious father as Imhotep, now available (in the company of Lugosi's Dracula, Karloff's Frankenstein Monster, Chaney Jr's Wolf Man and Chaney Sr's Phantom of the Opera) as a thirty-two cent postage stamp for normal one ounce usage. Director John Landis (*An American Werewolf in London, Innocent Blood*) made the introductory speech on this memorable occasion; Joe Dante, Ron Borst and Kevin J. Burns were among the filmonster fans in the audience and Burns bought up $700 worth of the stamps and ancillary items.

At the conclusion of the original *Mummy*, Karloff is struck down by a bolt from the statue of an Egyptian god. The four sequels that followed were pale imitations, mainly memorable for the introduction of the famous 'tanna leaves', nine of which, if I recall correctly, were needed to bring a mummy back to life. Post-Karloff mummies were Tom Tyler and Lon Chaney Jr as Kharis rather than Imhotep. George Zucco, John Carradine and Turhan Bey were variously involved in the nefarious doings of the bandaged badman. The quartet was known as *The Mummy's Hand, The Mummy's Tomb, The Mummy's Ghost* and *The Mummy's Curse*, but after four films proved to be tomb much.

Finally, in 1955, Kharis underwent a slight name change to Klaris in *Abbott and Costello Meet the Mummy*, and after that could have only been a bit player as he was blown to bits by dynamite.

Mexico got into the Mummy act in 1957 with *La Momia Azteca* and for the next seven years there was a spate of Mexi-mummy pix: *Attack of the Mayan Mummy, Curse of the Aztec Mummy, Face of the Screaming Werewolf* (Lon Chaney Jr as the shaggy lycanthrope; mummy scenes spliced in from *Attack*), *The Robot*(!) *vs. the Aztec Mummy* and *The Wrestling Women*(!) *vs. the Aztec Mummy*. Sorry, folks, my eighty-two year-old stomach is too 'weaque' to critique these masterpieces for you.

Hammer Films colourfully climbed aboard the mummy bandage-wagon in 1959 with Christopher Lee inheriting the wrappings of Kharis.

Michael Rennie, the aristocratic alien of the classic *The Day the Earth Stood Still*, returned as an evil alien in *Dracula vs. Frankenstein* in 1969, intent on ruling our world with the help of Dracula! the Frankenstein Monster! the Wolf Man! and the Mummy! The Mummy dukes it out with the Wolf Man and loses to his adversary when the lucky lycanthrope pulls a fasty and sets him on fire.

None less than Charlton Heston went a round with a mummy eleven years later in *The Awakening*. *Blood from the Mummy's Tomb* was based on Bram Stoker's supernatural novel *The Jewel of Seven Stars*. As was, incidentally, *The Awakening* and the more recent *Bram Stoker's Legend of the Mummy*.

My client Jerome Bixby ('It's a *Good* Life') scripted *The Volcano Man*, which reached the screen in 1958 as *Curse of the Faceless Man*: a mummified man, merely 2,000 years old this time, is buried in the lava of the eruption of Mount Vesuvius and brought back to life by Jerry Bixby.

A Night of Magic. Now who would suspect that behind this title lies a...mummy musical! Lee Harris, narrator of the Ed Wood documentary *Flying Saucers Over Hollywood*, in which I appear together with Maila 'Vampira' Nurmi, discovered this in an ad by the famous American supplier of oddball offbeat obscure videocassettes, Sinister Cinema. It is also listed in Don Willis's fine *Horror and Science Fiction Films* (The Scarecrow Press, 1972), which records that a 3,000 year-old Egyptian mummy (Marion Olive) comes to life in a sarcophagus in a man's living room and they go out on the town for a night of romance and song! Too bad Kharis didn't meet up with her!

Mummies variously known as Ank-Fen-Haris, Popoca, Prema and Serac (son of Saran Wrap?) have all shambled through: *The Curse of the Mummy's Tomb, The Monster Squad, The Mummy and the Curse of the Jackals, Mummy's Boys, The Mummy's Revenge, The Mummy's Shroud, The National Mummy, Orgy of the Dead, The Outing, Pharaoh's Curse, Tales from the Darkside The Movie, Time Walker, Voodoo*

Forry and Boris Karloff meet in 1966 at the recording of An Evening with Boris Karloff and His Friends.

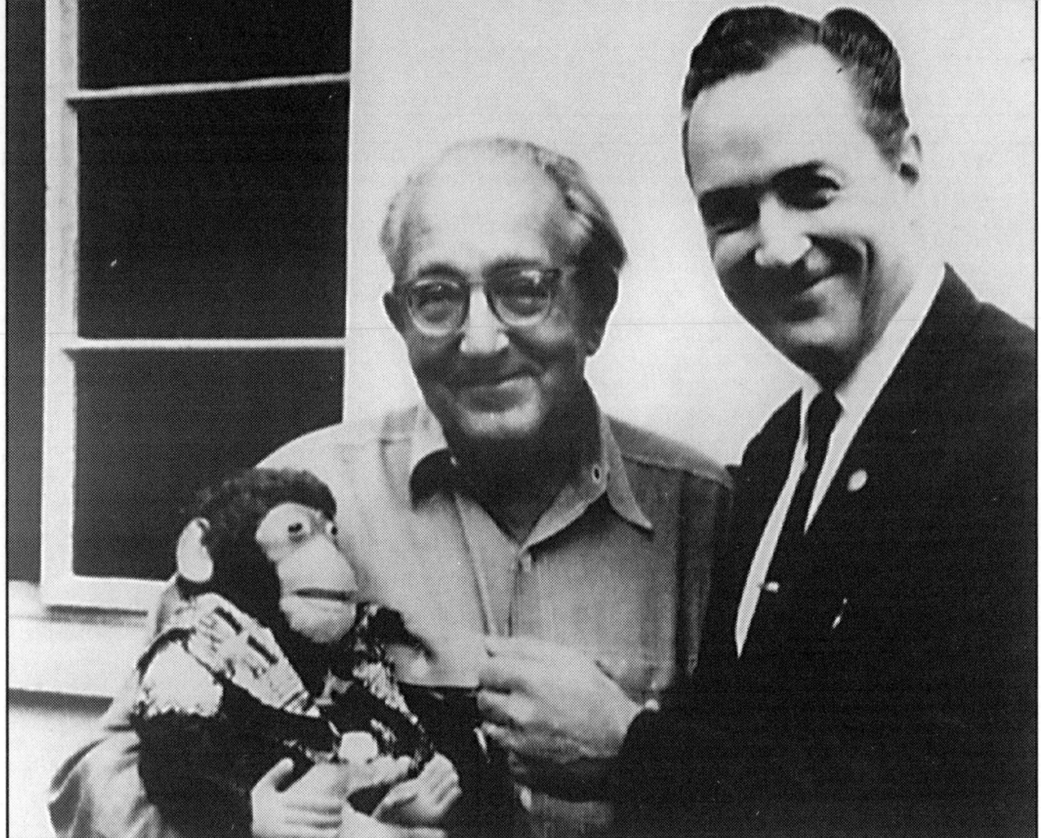

Forry and Fritz Lang.

Black Exorcist, *Waxwork* and *We Want Our Mummy*!

Involvees have ranged from David Warner to Abbott and Costello to Wheeler and Woolsey (an earlier comedy team) to John Carradine to Peter Cushing to Christopher Lee to Ed Wood and Paul Naschy.

The oldest mummy has been 4,000 years old.

Going way back to the silent days, in 1911 there were no less than three mummy films: *The Mummy*, in which one comes to life in a professor's dream...one in which a mummy is turned into a girl via electricity...and finally the predecessor of tanna leaves, a fluid that brings the dead back to life. In 1918 the great Ernst Lubitsch directed the great Emil Jannings (*Faust*, *The Blue Angel*, *Algol*) and Pola Negri in *Eyes of the Mummy Ma*, about a mummy-worshipping sect. Pola Negri? — talk about sect's appeal!

A few interesting, little-known, or unknown, facts:

Bramwell Fletcher himself created and scripted the famous sequence of the resurrected mummy sending him mad...Zita Johann became one of Fletcher's three wives (not simultaneously)...Zita left an unpublished supernatural manuscript, 'After the End', somewhat along the lines of the twice-filmed *Outward Bound* (remade as *Between Two Worlds*).

The last time I saw Virginia Christine, who played in *The Mummy's Curse* with Peter Coe, Martin Kosleck and Lon Jr (I believe she outlived them all. Tanna leaves?), it was at a Hollywood party of an Australian poet/fantasy author who had an Egyptian sarcophagus from one of the Universal Mummy films in his dying — er, living — room.

In my basement horror museum known as Grislyland (son of Disneyland), I have a very realistic mummy standing amidst the remake Blob, the Dr Lao snake, Geophagus the Earth Eater from Japanese TV, a New Zealand Feeble and other assorted monstrosities. All I know about it is that it came from Universal Studios — possibly a prop from the Abbott and Costello mummy movie? Recently, a five-and-a-half year-old boy was halfway down to Grislyland; he hesitated and decided, 'I believe I'll wait 'till I'm six.' Incidentally, reporters describing Grislyland invariably mis-spell it Grizzlyland. Un*bear*able. (That groan reached my ears.)

I have a piece of the wrapping that enshrouded Boris Karloff. I had another piece attached to a beautiful lobby-card of him in the film...but some 0%&*!! stole it — may they die of thirst in the burning sands of the Sahara desert!

Blacky La Goon

The Metaluna Mutant almost made it as the last great Universal Studios monster when it appeared in the film based on my client sci-fi author Raymond F. Jones' *This Island Earth*, but unfortunately he didn't catch on and establish himself in two or three more films. But the previous year — 1954 — a creature crawled out of a black lagoon — in 3-D — and scared the pants off panting audiences.

And became a filmonster icon in the company of the bravo band of monsterrific horror stars.

There was a creature with an atom brain, one with a blue hand, one from the haunted sea, of the walking dead, from green hell, from Highgate pond, from galaxy 27 (*Night of the Blood Beast*, an original script I agented for Martin Varno), from blood island; there've been creatures from another world (*The Crawling Eye*), creatures of evil, of destruction, that the world forgot — but never a creature as popular as the one I've nicknamed Blacky La Goon. The late Richard Carlson, star of Bradbury's 3-D classic *It Came from Outer Space*, was the lead in this one, and I have to tell you about the most amusing lunch of my life that I had with him.

It was on the famous Sunset Strip and I was invited there by Ivan Tors, who was producing the TV series *Science Fiction Theater*. I learned at that point that Carlson was actually a science fiction buff, his interest dating back to the early *Amazing Stories* magazine.

We were not offered any menus, instead we were each handed *binoculars*. The menu was on a blackboard across the room!

The original *Black Lagoon* spawned two sequels, *Revenge of the Creature* (there is no truth to the rumour he resented my calling him Blacky and sought vengeance on the Acker-monster) and *The Creature Walks Among Us*.

After the series was over, a janitor at the studio was sweeping up the remains of Blacky. Before dumping him in a trashcan, it occurred to him that his kid might like the head and claws so he took them home. The boy enjoyed scaring neighbours at Halloween for a couple of years until he outgrew what was left of Blacky and sold him to a boy down the street.

The remnants of a $35,000 cinemartifact were sold for five dollars.

I learned about it and promptly phoned the boy. 'Hey, kid, would you like to double your investment?' He laughed; he knew who I was and what I did for a dying — or living — and volunteered that one day when he got tired of it he would *give* it to me.

The time came, except when he came to my door in the evening I was out. He knew he couldn't dare simply leave it at the door, since the first filmonster fan to call on me would grab it for his collection. He would wait until the next morning.

He woke up to the realisation that he had put the Creature in the trunk of a rented car! And had returned the car without removing the Creature. Was it still there? Had someone else rented it, opened the trunk — and fainted? Or realised what a treasure they had?

Fortunately the car was still there and the fan rescued Blacky for me.

But things were looking black there for a scary while.

Beware the Hydes of March!

Fredric March garnered a coveted Oscar for his prize performance as *Dr. Jekyll and Mr. Hyde* in the Rouben Mamoulian version that established the pronunciation as 'Jee'kell'. As far as I know, Rose Hobart (March's sweetheart in the film) is the last surviving member of the cast. I had the pleasure of showing Mamoulian around the Acker-mansion at one time. I never met March, but I saw him at a distance in 1932 in an arena sequence in Cecil B. DeMille's *The Sign of the Cross*. Two years later March made such an indelible impression as Prince Sirki, Death Incarnate, in the fine fantasy *Death Takes a Holiday*, that for years I have reported the deaths of imagi-movie players as 'Prince Sirki takes...so and so.' In recent years he took Peter Cushing, my wife Wendayne and Vincent Price. At one time I had to report 'Prince Sirki takes Prince Sirki.'

The March picturisation of the famous Robert Louis Stevenson story opens with an unusual first reel wherein everything is seen through the eyes of Dr Jekyll. For some years this sequence was excised from the film, but has been restored in recent times.

Since the advent of talkies seventy-two years ago, I have heard many memorable speeches in films by Paul Muni (as Emil Zola), Boris Karloff (sympathetic scientists), Gary Cooper (Mr Deeds), Spencer Tracy, Claude Rains, James Stewart, Lord Laurence Olivier (Heathcliff) — you name 'em — but even though it's been thirteen lustrums (six-and-a-half decades) since I first heard Fredric March address his jeering colleagues, I believe I can still pretty accurately recall his words to his sceptical peers. If you ever play the picture via videocassette, check me out:

'Gentlemen: London is so full of fog that it has penetrated our minds, set boundaries for our vision. As men of science we should be curious and bold enough to peer beyond it into the many wonders it conceals. In my experiments I have found that the so-called soul of man, the human psyche, is not one but truly two. One of these strives for the nobilities of life; this we may call his good self. The other binds us with some dim animal relationship with the earth; this we call the evil. Now if we could separate these two, what heights the good in us might climb and the bad, once liberated, would vanish and trouble us no more.' Bravo, Fredric!

With Spencer Tracy in the lead role and Ingrid Bergman and Lana Turner as the luscious ladies in his life, one might expect the 1941 version to have been a winner but it was, alas, lacklustre. Tracy's make-up in no way compared to March's.

Jack Palance did a very acceptable televersion and John Barrymore still receives kudos for his silent portrayal of 1920, in which he turned into Hyde before the camera's eye without special effects by twisting and contorting his face and body as Chaney Sr might have done had he played the role. Come to think of it, why didn't he?

The Stevenson story attracted film-makers as long ago as 1908 with *The Modern*(!) *Dr. Jekyll*, 1909 (a Danish version), 1912 and 1913 (American), 1913 (a British 'Kinemacolor' version), 1914 (two versions, including *Dr. Jekyll and Mr. Hyde Done to a Frazzle*), 1920 (a comedic version with Hank Mann, the man at the controls of the 'elevated' wrecked by King Kong in the New York sequence of the original), 1920 (a second version with a dream ending) and the third attempt in '20 with Barrymore. There was another comedic version in 1925. Again in 1925, employing a set from *The Hunchback of Notre Dame*, Stan Laurel(!) appeared in *Dr. Pyckle and Mr. Pride*.

In 1953 Abbott and Costello met Dr Jekyll and Mr Hyde, played by Boris Karloff and Eddie Parker in Bud Westmore make-up. Wax figures of Dracula and the Frankenstein Monster incidentally appeared in the film. The 1963 Jerry Lewis Technicolor production *The Nutty Professor* was also inspired by Dr J and Mr H. Somewhere along the line I seem to recall a musical televersion with Kirk Douglas; not memorable.

I'm sure I've overlooked a few. Completists may want to check out Oliver Reed's interpretation in *Dr. Heckyll and Mr. Hype*, *The Two Faces of Dr. Jekyll*, *Dr. Jekyll & Sister Hyde*, *Daughter of Dr. Jekyll*, *El Hombre y la Bestia* (Argentinean), the Italian *Il Mio Amico Jekyll*, *Jekyll and Hyde Cat* (one reel 1944 colour Terrytoon featuring Mighty Mouse); Jack Benny on his TV show; *Jekyll and Hyde...Together Again*, *The Ugly Duckling*, *I, Monster*. And — are you ready for this? — he told

DON POST
STUDIOS
MONSTER MASKS
UNIVERSAL PICTURES
INC
MAKE-UP DEMONSTRATION
UNIMART IS PROUD
TO PRESENT TO YOU-
DON POST
HEAD OF DON POST STUDIOS
FOREST ACKERMAN
EDITOR OF 'MONSTER
WORLD' MAGAZINE
THOR JOHNSON
A MOST POPULAR
HORROR ACTOR

me it was his dearest wish to make his version as his final film, but failing eyesight prevented him from directing.

Who?

Fritz Lang!

Erik the Incomparable

There have been a plethora of 'Phantom' films on the shiver screen: *Phantom of the Paradise, the Red House, the Rue Morgue, the Moulin Rouge, the Convent, Soho, Fiend, Foe, Sirens, Thief, Witness, Planet, Raiders, City, Air, Empire, Chariot, Cat, Killer, Light, Crestwood, from Space, from 10,000 Leagues,* and on and on, far into the night and in the past. Herbert Lom has been the Phantom and Claude Rains has done right by him, and in recent years he's mesmerised millions of music lovers in the stage version.

But no version has ever held a candle (or a chandelier) to the definitive Lon Chaney 1925 masterpiece.

The make-up was incomparable.

The late Robert Bloch characterised it as gazing upon 'the naked face of horror.'

Weaver Wright spoke of it as 'a living death's head.'

Spencer Strong once wrote: 'His outraged visage was horror incarnate: bulging, bloodshot eyes fatigued with violet semicircles beneath them; the grotesquely exaggerated mounds of the cheekbones; the hooked-up, flaring, porcine nostrils; the rotted, jagged teeth, like the rim of an enamelled tincan top opened with a ragged knife; the scraggly strands of dead grey hair hanging like soggy serpentine from the baldspotted domed head.'

They say one picture is worth 10,000 words; it would take that many to adequately describe Chaney's master make-up.

One Halloween eve, Ray Bradbury, Robert Bloch and I sat together in Los Angeles' only silent movie theatre and thrilled and chilled again to Lon's legendary performance. At the time we didn't know what I'll now reveal. You might wonder how the chandelier sequence was accomplished, how it (apparently) fell from the ceiling and crushed a segment of the audience and the chairs beneath them. Kenneth Strickfaden was responsible for that memorable scene. He was the creator of the Frankenstein laboratory, the death-ray machine in *The Mask of Fu Manchu* and the futuristic laboratory of *Just Imagine*. I was with him in the hospital just an hour before he died. And at one time he told me: 'The seats were arranged in disarray, extras posed themselves on top of them in various mangled positions, the chandelier was lowered to within an inch of them, then it was photographed *being raised*. When it was spliced into the film, it was *run backwards!*' so that the chandelier appeared to be falling and crushing the people! What a simple, clever special effect, old timer. You did Lon justice.

In November of 1997, in Hieronymous Bosch's birth place in Holland, I relived my childhood delight in seeing *The Phantom of the Opera* for the twenty-fifth time...and the twenty-sixth...and the twenty-seventh...accompanied by a *sixty-two piece orchestra*. This was a pristine copy pieced together from the 1925 version and the 1929 version with sound and added scenes and one word spoken — though not by Lon Chaney. The magnificent colour sequence was intact, with Lon as the Masque of the Red Death in the masked ball sequence and above the Paris Opera House, his crimson-lined cape flaring in the midnight wind.

Forry and Tor Johnson on tour together in the mid-1960s.

Forry and Bobbie Bresee.

I own the cape worn by Chaney in the film and awed thoughts went through my mind as I stood on a magnificent stage built over the stables where Napoleon kept his horses when conquering the Netherlands, and I thought, 'How is it possible that I, an eighty-one year-old man, who as a ten year-old boy once saw Lon Chaney as the Phantom, am standing seventy-two years later, 6,000 miles from home, performing for television in his cape, wearing a ring with a speck of his make-up in it, gesturing in his persona?' In my time I have put an hour's worth of words into Boris Karloff's mouth for a phonograph album, played Claude Rains' Invisible Man opposite Gloria (*The Old Dark House*) Stuart before an audience at an imagi-movie convention, been a living statue of Bela Lugosi as Dracula in a film, sung a song ('Baby Face') like Al Jolson before an outdoor audience in Cheng-du (pop. 10,000,000), China — and now this immortal memory in the cloak of the grandest monster of them all, a truly humbling experience. I don't think I began to do him justice — but who could? There was only one Lon Chaney Sr; one Erik, the Phantom of the Opera.

David Bradley, who died a few days before Christmas 1997, was the movie director who discovered Charlton Heston. For many years he had remarkable New Year's parties in his Hollywood home. I was privileged to attend and

Forry and Mary Philbin, star of *The Phantom of the Opera* (1925).

met Madge Bellamy (*White Zombie*) there and Marlene Dietrich's 'Svengali', Josef von Sternberg, and silent movie star idol Francis X. Bushman, and Charlie Chaplin's widow, and Curt Siodmak and Bobbie (*Mausoleum*) Bresee, and Robert Bloch, and Curtis Harrington, Fritz Lang, ill-fated actress Jayne Mansfield, who got her head torn off in a tragic auto accident, Dr Donald Reed (creator of the Count Dracula Society), Anna (*Nana*) Sten, Kenneth (*Hollywood Babylon*) Anger, Tom and Terri Pinckard (the Pinckard Science Fiction Salon), Samson (*Inauguration of the Pleasure Dome*) DeBrier, Angelyne (Billboard Queen), Lion Feuchtwanger's widow, Celia Lovsky (Peter Lorre's widow, and Chaney's Mother in *Man of a Thousand Faces*), Brian Forbes (publisher of my *Lon of 1000 Faces!*) and dozens more. Now what has this to do with Lon Chaney? I certainly never met him there — he died in 1930. Is this the beginning of Old Timer's Disease? I know I had something in mind relating to — ah, yes! Of course! It just surfaced: among many other celebrities, I met *Mary Philbin* there, the heroine who fell at the feet of Phantom Lon, cringing in terror before the hideous visage of the unmasked horror as he roared, 'Feast your eyes, glut your soul on my accursed ugliness!' And now here was this dear little old lady, being lionised by us, over half a century later remembering little about Lon Chaney other than that 'he was a very nice man', and the same for Conrad Veidt, 'Gwynplaine', with whom she co-starred in *The Man Who Laughs*.

But, brought out of retirement, Mary Philbin had one last hurrah at the Orpheum Theater, a picture palace of yore in downtown Los Angeles where, as a teenager, I saw Sophie Tucker ('Last of the Red Hot Mamas'), Bill 'Bojangles' Robinson, Vern Coriell (Tarzan fan #1) and many other vaudevillians. One Halloween in the mid-1990s, *The Phantom of the Opera* was revived on the big screen accompanied by Korla Pandit, the famous organist. After the showing, the theatre lights went up and the spotlight illuminated a balcony where Mary Philbin stood like the Queen of England, waving her arms in appreciation at the accolading crowd below on their feet in homage. How I wish you could all have been there.

One final Phantom anecdote: I believe it was in 1965 that 1,300 avid young fans of *Famous Monsters of Filmland* wrote to me, its editor, expressing a desire to meet me. My wife and I took an 8,700 mile drive, zigging and zagging across the United States to meet as many of my fans as possible. It was gratifying to receive the appreciation rather than the feared disapproval of parents. 'We thought our boy was never even going to look at a comic book, but after he discovered your magazine he began going to the library and borrowing books by Edgar Allan Poe, Jules Verne and H.G. Wells.' I'll never forget Niles, Michigan, where we went thirty-five miles out of our way to meet a farm boy who had written that if we visited him there would be an audience of fifty.

Well, there was.

The boy and forty-nine sheep.

We arrived about one o'clock in the morning at one stop where a group of boys in their late teens were anxiously awaiting us. They took us up to their top floor and into a little movie theatre they had created. They had about nine seats that they had rescued from an abandoned theatre. They sat us in the most comfortable and doused the lights; curtains parted, another curtain rose, and they began projecting Chaney's *The Phantom of the Opera*. My wife, who had been sharing in the driving, was dead tired and fighting to keep awake. By two in the morning she was threatening to fall asleep. One of our hosts kindly brought Wendayne a cup of hot tea. I mean, it was hot. Just as Mary Philbin removed the mask from the Phantom, Wendayne fell asleep.

The boiling tea tipped into her lap.

Lon Chaney got his greatest unveiling shriek!

Quasimodo Rings the Bell

Lon Chaney as *The Hunchback of Notre Dame* inspired my best story. I've had approximately half a hundred published but 'Letter to an Angel' is the one I read when called upon to do so at a fantasy or film convention. It is about a little boy (a regular Forry Ackerman-type) in the 1920s who has a crush on Lon Chaney. He also has a humped back. He has seen Lon be legless in one film, armless in another, oriental in another, a hundred years old, even a woman (*The Unholy Three*), yet the next thing you know he's perfectly normal — even the hump is gone. What a great magician! Timmy dreams of meeting him one day and learning his secret, so he too can have a straight back. Then Lon Chaney dies. As a result of his devotion, Timmy dies too. And when he is welcomed into Heaven by the angels, he spies Lon Chaney on a golden throne with a long flowing white beard and a special effect Timmy has never seen before — a shining halo around His head. And when Timmy sits on God's lap he never even notices when the good Lord places His arm around him and the hump disappears. Adoration shining in his eyes, Timmy gasps, 'Lon Chaney!' And God smiles. I shouldn't say this, but I can't read my own story without getting a lump in my throat about the size of Timmy's hump. I'm proud to say I related the story to John Drew Barrymore one day while driving him somewhere and he confessed to getting a little tear in his eye. The late Charles Beaumont thought highly of the story and Robert Bloch, Jim Harmon, Terri Merritt-Pinckard and Ray Bradbury have also praised it. I've recorded it on audiotape and an amateur movie has been made of it. I dream of Spielberg or Landis making a half hour film of it, perennially projected around Halloween or Valentine's Day or Thanksgiving or Christmas. Ah, Rod Serling, where are you now that I need you?

Chaney Sr established the persona of Quasimodo for all time, although Charles Laughton came a close second with his remarkable portrayal in 1939. Incidentally, in the RKO version Fritz Leiber Sr, father of the famous sci-fi/fantasy author Fritz Leiber Jr (*Conjure Wife, et al*) played a role.

In the Chaney version, some of the long distance rope shots were doubled for Lon by Joe Bonomo, billed in his day as the Strongest Man in the World. I once shook hands with him in his office in New York — and couldn't type for a week afterwards.

Anthony Quinn became Quasimodo in 1956 with Gina Lollobrigida in the original Patsy Ruth Miller role. About ten years ago, before the late actress's demise, I had the pleasure of interviewing Patsy on the Universal lot in the location that was the film's Forecourt of Miracles.

A five reel version was made by Fox in 1917, and the heroine was none less than the cinema siren of her day, the legendary Theda Bara. The film was titled *The Darling of Paris*.

Quasimodo lived again in a 1937 production from India, *Nav Jawan*. Anyone know Hindu? At a guess, I imagine it might mean 'The Hunchback'.

Notre Dame has not been the sole cinematic stamping ground of hunchbacks, there's been *The Hunchback of Cedar Lodge* and *The Hunchback and the Dancer*, both silent.

There has been at least one play (which I have seen locally, with SF fan and movie actress Janet Carroll in a part). In 'showbiz' they say 'Always leave 'em laughing', so at the risk of being run out of filmonster fandom by a pack of groaning werewolves, I'll quote a punster (don't lurk at me!) who has said, 'Isn't it time they stopped portraying Quasi Modos and go all the way with a Full Modo?!'

Forgive me, Lon.

'The Eighth Wonder of the World!'

'A monster is coming! All-powerful! Listen to his roar!' Thus were my wondering sixteen year-old ears introduced over the radio in 1933 to *King Kong*.

Needless to say, I was there on opening day. And immediately sat down and wrote a raving letter to my correspondent J.R. Ayco (I never did know his first name — or, like C.L. Moore and others, is it possible a female was disguised behind the initials?). I suspect he/she was not the only one of my 127 fan friends that I wrote to in a state of ecstasy, but it was his/her response that has become legendary: 'Wasn't it great when Kong shook the men off the log and they fell into the ravine...and the giant spider got them?'

What-what-what?! Excuse my ungrammatical response, but I didn't see no spider!

Apparently, the legendary spider scene was seen in the Philippines, and not the USA or anywhere else in the world. The reason for its absence is always given as it slowed down the action of the film. I can't believe it. Now that another version may be shot, I hope they include the infamous sequence. And give living legend (ninety-one year-old) Fay Wray a part, as they did the original boy/girl team in the Christopher Reeve *Superman*. Fabulous Fay is the only player remaining alive from the original *King Kong*. At one time or another I was fortunate to meet Bruce Cabot, Robert Armstrong, Sam Hardy, co-director/producer Merian C. Cooper and the builder of Kong, Marcel Delgado. A tragedy: dear Mexican Marcel fell and hit his head toward the end of his life and wound up in a wheelchair, unaware of the fabulous prehistoric figures he had created for Willis ('O'bie') O'Brien to give, as Colin Clive said, the simulacrum of life.

When *Kong* opened at the colourful Grauman's Chinese Theater in Hollywood, the giant bust of him used in the film dominated the forecourt. Unfortunately he doesn't have his paws in cement along with Pickford, Fairbanks, Gable, Jolson, Monroe *et al*; his pawprints alone would have filled up the whole forecourt!

Inside the theatre we were treated to a stage prologue forecasting the native dance sequence on Skull Island. And in the final reel our senses reeled as the screen opened up *vertically and horizontally* to a huge square. I am aware of only two other films where this was done: *Hell's Angels* and *Portrait of Jennie*.

(Interruption. While writing this preface about *King Kong*, I just had a phone call from Bill Malone, the movie director who collaborated on the reproduction of Ultima Futura Automaton, the *Metropolis* robotrix built for me, the man who has recreated incredible likenesses for himself of Gort from *The Day the Earth Stood Still* and Robby the Robot. Bill would like to meet Fay Wray before she takes her final trip to Skull Island. I've referred him to the movie director who invited me to lunch with her about ten years ago. Good luck!).

Master animator Ray Harryhausen, successor to Willis O'Brien, always wanted to meet Fay Wray. On the occasion of the fiftieth anniversary of the film, Harryhausen and Bradbury were driven down Hollywood Blvd in style and let out in front of the Chinese theatre to the red carpet treatment. A new bust of Kong created by Rick Baker, Monster Maker, greeted the crowd; the original stood for years by a beanery on the Pacific Coast Highway until the elements finally conquered Kong. I had put a bug in the ear of the co-ordinator of the programme and when Harryhausen was called out of the audience and up on the stage, Fay Wray was there to greet him. And give him a kiss! It was the master animator's most animated moment. He must have felt as I would have if Marlene Dietrich, Sari Maritza, Simone Simon, Brigitte Bardot, Catherine Deneuve, Danielle Darrieux and Marilyn and Madonna were all rolled into one and embraced and kissed me in front of a Hollywood crowd! Wow! Kong never even got to kiss Fay — although he did divest her of half her clothing. Moviegoers only saw that scene for a short time, then it and five other sequences were censored for years. They've been put back at last, basically making Kong look more vicious than in the bowdlerised version, where he didn't drop a lady to her death from a skyscraper or squash natives in mud beneath his feet like ripe squashes.

Little known fact: Cooper and Schoedsack, co-producers, flew in one of the planes that machine-gunned Kong to his doom as he fell from atop the Empire State Building. 'Ah, the planes got him,' observes a cop. 'Oh, no,' corrects Carl Denham, 't'was Beauty killed the Beast.'

In *King Kong vs. Godzilla* (Gojira in Japan) Kong is the conqueror. Four years later, courtesy of Toho, Kong was confronted by...a robot Kong! Willis O'Brien's widow refused to see any of the ersatz Kongs.

To capitalise on the original film, *The Son of Kong* was hastily pieced together by RKO in 1933, with Robert Armstrong, Frank Reicher, Victor Wong and Noble Johnson from the original cast. For some reason, the sequel was shot under the nondescriptive title *Jamboree*. I have never seen a better short summary of the film than Donald C. Willis's: 'The son is too tame; if they had taken him to New York, he would have ridden the subway rather than wrecked it.' But it does have some nice dinosaur action and a cave bear and the climax is memorable as Kiko, son of Kong (I believe that's a moniker for him that I came up with sixty-odd years ago), goes to his death drowning while heroically holding up Carl Denham above the waves 'till his (Kiko's) last breath.

From the brother of Rod Serling of *Twilight Zone* fame, I acquired the model pteranodon that was trying to fly away with Fay Wray in *King Kong*. It arrived in the mail in a shoe box and I was so excited to think that I was the only person in the world to be in possession of this amazing cinemartifact that had been built by Marcel Delgado and animated by the wizard hands of Willis O'Brien that I wanted to hop in my car and rush to the nearest friend who would understand and appreciate my treasure. The fan's wife came to the door (a real stunner that the pteranodon would liked to have flown away with, I'm sure), but unfortunately she didn't know anything about prehistoric birds or Kongish models and she took one look at my dilapidated 'don and went screaming to her husband, 'I think Mr Ackerman is here with a *dead crow*!!!' Marcel would never have been so mortified! In the meantime, Rick Baker has meticulously reconstructed a twin pteranodon for me the way it must have looked when it was being animated for the film.

Among my Kongiana I have the gas bomb that brought down Kong on Skull Island, a native's shield, a half-eaten model man, a tree, a stegosaurus, a brontosaurus, a souvenir programme, scores of stills, a large colour reproduction of the jigsaw puzzle produced at the time, numerous lobbycards and posters both domestic and foreign (the 124-sheet from RKO's Skull Island première is particularly attractive. Joke over). And a copy of the first edition of the book signed by Fay Wray, Bruce Cabot, Mrs Max Steiner, Darlyne O'Brien, Marcel Delgado, Merian C. Cooper, Ray Harryhausen (Kong fan #1) and Ray Bradbury faking the signature of Edgar Wallace. Bids start at one million weetongs (an imaginary fannish monetary unit created by the late Big Heart Awardee Walt Liebscher).

I refuse to write about the De Laurentiis *Kong* fiasco, even if I do have an appearance in a crowd running away from Kong. I hated it; when I saw a studio advance showing, it was free — and I wanted my money back. Or should I say my monkey back. Prior to the filming, circulars were passed out by fans of the original film, pleading DON'T RAPE THE APE! De Laurentiis lent a deaf ear. Among other cardinal sins, it was a version without dinosaurs on Skull Island! Like making 'The Jolson Story' without Al's Mammy! 'The Sinatra Story' with no songs by Frank!! 'The Astaire Story' with no dances by Fred!!! 'The Ackerman Story' with no mention of sci-fi or filmonsters!!!!

I'd keep my fingers crossed for a new version — but I can't type very well that way.

The Max Steiner score adds immeasurably to the thrill of the picture and is one of the all-time imagi-movie classics.

Hey, producers: How about getting Ray Harryhausen out of retirement briefly to mastermind the spider scene? I'll volunteer to be devoured by the spider!

Frankenstein, Dracula, the Wolf Man, the Mummy, the Phantom of the Opera — when do we get King Kong on a King-size stamp? Don't, er, make it airmail!

As I leave you now to cast your ogling optics on the cinema illusions alluded to in *The Essential Monster Movie Guide*, I salute Stephen Jones and look forward to his revised edition ten or twenty years hence with an additional cast of monsterrific creatures...

Forrest J Ackerman

Dr Ackula
The Ackermonster of the (Bl)Ack Forrest
1313 Chaney Way at
Lugosi *Cross* Roads
Whollyweird Karloffornia
Untied Stakes of America

New Fears Day,
1 Janueerie, 1999

Forry in 1965 with his Collection of Life Masks of Masters of the Macabre.

ACKERMONSTER · 1965
TAKEN AT POST STUDIO
"FOR POSTERITY"
THIS COMPLETE SET OF MASKS
PRESENTED TO
DON POST
VERNE LANGDON
OCTOBER 7, 1965
DON POST · 1965
TAKEN AT POST STUDIO
"FOR POSTERITY"
MASKS ARE FIRST CAST FROM LIFE
IN MOULAGE JELLY
THEN LIQUID LAMINATED
IN FIBREGLASS

OF FORRY AND FILMONSTERS

by Stephen Jones

It has taken me two years to compile this guide to the classic monster movies of the twentieth century. However, if truth be told, I have actually been working on it for the past forty years. Ever since my mother took me to see my first film at a movie theatre when I was around six years old. It was Disney's *The Shaggy Dog* in 1959, and with its spooky museum sequence and plot about canine lycanthropy, it obviously formed the foundation for my interest in all things fantastical.

Although there was not all that much of a fantastic nature on British television in the early 1960s, I can recall watching such series as *Supercar*, *Fireball XL5*, *Pathfinders to Venus*, *The Monsters*, *Out of This World* (introduced by Boris Karloff) and, of course, *Doctor Who*. A Sunday afternoon BBC production of Charles Dickens' *Great Expectations* had me hiding behind the sofa, but it was a TV screening a few years later of the 1933 *King Kong* (still, in my opinion, one of the greatest films ever made) that cemented my love of the genre. From there it was only a short step to my local cinema and such mid-sixties double-bills as *The Face of Fu Manchu* and *City Under the Sea*, starring Christopher Lee and Vincent Price respectively, or *Dr. Who and the Daleks* and *Daleks' Invasion Earth 2150 A.D.*, both with Peter Cushing.

It should be remembered that at this time, despite the release of Universal's 'Shock Theater' packages of classic horror movies to American television in the late 1950s, horror rarely, if ever, turned up on television in the United Kingdom. In cinemas, most horror titles were given an 'X' certificate (restricting audiences to sixteen years and older), and the only way I could learn about those titles I was prevented from seeing was to rely on such American monster movie magazines (which usually arrived in Britain as ballast in ships) as *Fantastic Monsters of the Films*, *For Monsters Only*, *Modern Monsters*, *Monster Mania*, *Shriek* and Calvin T. Beck's influential *Castle of Frankenstein* (which taught me how to also appreciate films outside the genre).

I was finally able to bluff my way into my first 'X' film (Hammer's *Quatermass and the Pit*) by pretending to be two years older than I actually was, and I eventually became a member of London's Gothique Film Society (still going strong today), where I could actually meet celebrities like Christopher Lee, Terence Fisher, Mike Raven, Ray Harryhausen and William K. Everson, and catch up with some of those classic titles from the 1930s and 1940s.

However, if this book owes a debt to anyone or anything, then it has to be Forrest J Ackerman and his pun-filled monster magazine *Famous Monsters of Filmland* (along with its short-lived companion title *Monster World*). I began reading and collecting *Famous Monsters* in the mid-sixties (before I was actually old enough to legally see most of the films featured in its pages), and it not only inspired me to create my own lists of those fantasy movies I had seen — which to this day remains the basis of books such as this one — but also to turn my tiny bedroom into a mini-version of Forry's famed eighteen-room 'Ackermansion', with movie posters and lobby cards adorning the walls, and shelves filled with hand-painted Aurora model kits of the classic movie monsters in lieu of any genuine film props.

My parents, god bless them, never seriously tried to dissuade me from my odd 'hobby'. They may not have exactly understood my obsession, but (except for once forbidding me to go with my schoolfriends to see *Jason and the Argonauts*, which was playing in a somewhat unsafe borough of London), they have always given me their encouragement and support, right up to the present day and this latest volume.

I first visited the Ackermansion in Los Angeles as a teenager in the early 1970s. Although he had only that day returned from a science fiction convention in Australia, Forry gave me a personal tour of the treasure trove of more than 300,000 items it contained and I was both surprised and delighted to be invited out to lunch at his favourite House of Pies afterwards. It was extraordinary kindness to show to a young boy during his first trip to California, and I am pleased to say that we have kept in touch ever since.

From such humble beginnings a writing career was launched. I soon began contributing articles and reviews to magazines, and I had the dubious honour of 'closing out' the original run of *Famous Monsters* with my set report on the making of *Xtro* in *FM* #191 (March 1983). However, Forry had already left the title he had created by then, and the following year he invited me to become the British correspondent for the short-lived *Forrest J Ackerman's Monsterland* magazine. In 1988, I directed an interview with him in his home for a documentary for Britain's Channel Four Television. Three years later I was one of 500 people he invited to his seventy-fifth birthday party at the historic Biltmore Hotel in Los Angeles. In 1993, I was also one of his guests at the fifty-fifth Anniversary Famous Monsters World Convention held in Arlington, Virginia, and I made sure I was back for the Son of Famous Monsters World Convention in Hollywood, two years later.

Over the thirty years that we have known each other, we have met up at numerous conventions, signings and social events on both sides of the Atlantic, and he has always been more than generous when I have requested the use of stills from his legendary collection for my *Illustrated Movie Guide* series. Forry's fascinating introduction to this present volume is yet another testament to his thoughtfulness and generosity. If it wasn't for Forrest J Ackerman and *Famous Monsters of Filmland* then I doubt I would be doing what I am today. This book is therefore dedicated to both of them, and it stands as the culmination of my mis-spent youth and a life-long love of monster movies.

The other major inspiration for this particular volume is the Aurora plastic model kits which were always advertised in the back pages of *Famous Monsters* ('You'll shake! You'll tremble! You'll shudder with delight as you assemble these authentic, life-like kits of the most marvelous monsters that have thrilled and chilled audiences over the past thirty years on the "silver screen"').

Therefore, within this book you will discover reviews of films, television shows and video releases featuring Count Dracula and his fellow vampires; Frankenstein's creation and other man-made monsters; The Wolf Man and similar shape-changers; The Creature from the Black Lagoon and associated gill men; Dr Jekyll and his evil alter-ego Mr Hyde; The Phantom of the Opera and kindred masked madmen; the deformed Hunchback of Notre Dame; King Kong and related giant apes, plus various resurrected mummies and zombies, along with numerous variations, permutations and offspring from around the world. In fact, you will find all the classic movie monsters who have 'thrilled and chilled' audiences throughout the twentieth century.

As with my previous *Illustrated Movie Guide* volumes, this book is designed to be of use to both the casual viewer and the dedicated movie buff. Titles are arranged alphabetically by the whole title and reviewed under their most common usage title, with spelling and punctuation taken directly from the screen wherever possible. (Yes, it really is *Meet Frankenstein*, with the names of Bud Abbott and Lou Costello billed above the title.) The original, British or American alternative titles are cross-referenced in the index.

The year given is usually the copyright date taken from the print, with the actual release date of the version reviewed listed in parenthesis, if significantly different. Wherever such information is available, I have included the names of the director and major stars (with alternative spellings or real names in parenthesis), the production company and/or distributor, and whether the film was made in colour or black and white. Any disparity in the spelling of character names is also reflected in the text. Most reviews include a plot synopsis, along with interesting or obscure background information, and remake and sequel guides.

As well as the obvious feature-length movies, short films and cartoons, I have also listed selected episodes

Boris Karloff kills E.E. Clive in a scene cut from Bride of Frankenstein *(1935).*

The spider pit sequence censored from King Kong *(1933).*

from relevant television series and documentaries, various compilation tapes of special interest to monster fans, and as many independent video releases as I could track down. This latter area of production is one that exploded during the late 1990s as video equipment became cheaper and more sophisticated, and tapes could be sold directly through mail-order. Many of these films are distributed on a regional basis but, as always, quantity invariably does not equate with quality. Also, to help you recognise many of the names which reoccur throughout this guide, I have included mini-biographies of the key actors and technicians who worked on these productions. A complete list of biographies can be found in the personality profile index.

As always, a brief explanation of the ratings system is probably needed.

✦✦✦✦✦ = A classic!
✦✦✦✦ = Recommended.
✦✦✦ = Worth catching.
✦✦ = Average.
✦ = For completists only.
✧ = a half, which is used to give some shading to these definitions.

However, as with any at-a-glance recommendation, this ratings system unapologetically reflects my own biased tastes and opinions. Please note that these ratings should be used as a guide only. Hopefully the text will give you a better idea of just how worthwhile an entry is.

As a general criterion, if I were to base all the titles listed in this book on, for example, Orson Welles' *Citizen Kane*, then the majority of them would hardly rate more than one star. Therefore, as a rule, I have tried to take into account whether the production reviewed would appeal to the fantastic film fan and the movie monster *aficionado* in particular. It should never be forgotten that most of the titles listed in this book are supposed to be entertainments (something that far too many critics have a tendency to forget) and, as is so often the case with genre movies, a really *bad* example can still be worth watching.

I should also point out that a number of the films reviewed in this volume obviously contain adult material and may therefore not be suitable for viewers of all ages.

Obviously, it has not been possible to view every movie listed in this book, and it should be noted that readers may encounter some difficulty tracking down all the titles contained herein. Many are unfortunately lost to us, while others — especially the more obscure overseas productions which are only now coming to light in the West — have proved particularly elusive. Therefore some of the ratings are based on provisional material or contemporary references, and any reassessment will be noted in future editions.

While every effort has been made to verify the information in this book, and although the details included herein supersede all my earlier volumes, some errors are unfortunately inevitable. Given the size of this book and its schedule, I cannot claim that it is a definitive guide, but it is certainly more complete than most. I would welcome any updates or corrections c/o the publisher, and credit will be given in any subsequent printings.

Of course any book as detailed as this needs friends, and I would like to especially thank Kim Newman, Randy and Sara Broecker, Mandy Slater, Del Howison, Nicolas Barbano, David J. Skal, Ron Bonk (Salt City Productions/Salt City Home Video), Jeffrey Faoro (EI Independent Cinema), Michael Raso (EI Independent Cinema/*Alternative Cinema*), Richard J. King (Visionary Communications/Screen Edge), Jerry Feifer (Vista Street Entertainment), Ramsey Campbell, Gary Whitson (WAVE Productions), Mark W. Nelson (Scott Free), Dave Parker (Full Moon Pictures), Les Daniels, Jaime E. Jiménez (Storm Entertainment), Barry Forshaw, Tim

Lucas, Luigi Cozzi, Jo Fletcher, Ronald V. Borst (Hollywood Movie Posters), Robert M. Dowling, Jason J. Slater, Marcel Burel, Ernesto Gastaldi, Bettina Wagener (Sci-Fi), Jenny Boyce, Jonathan Clements, M.J. Simpson, Paul J. McAuley, Tom Walsh, Lisa Morton, Val and Les Edwards, Stephen Gallagher, John Landis, Al Reschke, Michael Marshall Smith, Cortlandt B. Hull, Patrick Franke (Deutsches Filmmuseum), Suzanne Coker (Regent Entertainment), Chuck Wagner, Pete Tombs, Andrew I. Porter, David J. Schow, Peter Atkins, Robert Eighteen-Bisang, Brian Mooney, Elisar Cabrera, Colin Davis, Noel O'Connor, Phill White, Frank Eisgruber, Mike Hodges, Peter Scutt, Jaap de Wreede, Diana Bilberg, Nordisk Film, Peder Pedersen, Heike Haselmayr, Jim Danforth, Gary Hill (Clein + White Inc), David Stuart Davies, Richard Newell, Dave Rogers, Patrice E. Athanasidy, Stefan Jaworzyn and David J. Howe for all their help and support in compiling what I hope you will discover is a useful and entertaining reference work.

As always, very special thanks to my hard working editors, David Barraclough, Adam ('Mr Pedantic') Newell and Gillian Christie, designer Chris Teather, Bob Kelly for the book's production, Katy Wild for looking after the project and, of course, the inimitable Forry for his introduction.

No thanks whatsoever are due to HM Customs and Excise at London Heathrow Airport (despite agreeing to copy down the credits for me), nor to the publicity office at UIP which was consistently rude and unhelpful.

I hope you will learn something from this book (I certainly did while working on it), but, more importantly, I hope you will have *fun* with it. For more than a century these movie monsters to meet them have been terrifying audiences around the world. Now it is your turn to meet them...

Stephen Jones
London, England
September, 1999

Zita Johann in her Saxon incarnation, cut from The Mummy *(1933).*

- A -

BUD ABBOTT (William Abbott) [1895-1974] and LOU COSTELLO (Louis Francis Cristillo) [1906-1959]

Abbott was the slick, thin straight man and Costello the whiny, chubby comedian, best known for taking their fast-talking vaudeville routines to Hollywood. For a decade from the early 1940s they were one of America's most popular comedy teams on radio and film. During their movie careers they encountered most of the classic screen monsters in *Meet Frankenstein* (1948), *Meet the Killer* (1949), *...Meet the Invisible Man* (1952), *Abbott and Costello Meet Dr. Jekyll and Mr. Hyde* (1953), *Abbott and Costello Meet the Mummy* (1955) and on TV's *The Colgate Comedy Hour* (1950-55). Their popularity waned after they fell out with each other, and Costello made just one solo movie, *Thirty Foot Bride of Candy Rock* (1959), before his death. In 1965 Abbott emerged from retirement to voice a cartoon version of himself in the Hanna-Barbera TV series *Abbott and Costello* (1965-67).
qv: *Africa Screams* (1949); *Fantastic Monsters of Television Land* (1999); *The World of Abbott and Costello* (1964).

ABBOTT & COSTELLO: Monster Muddled

USA, 1966. Voices: Bud Abbott, Stan Irwin, Mel Blanc, Hal Smith, Don Messick, Janet Waldo. Hanna-Barbera Productions/RKO-Jomar Productions. Colour.
Half-hour syndicated series comprising 156 five-minute cartoons. In this episode, policemen Bud (Abbott, who was having financial difficulties at the time) and Lou (Irwin) attend a costume party and meet the Frankenstein Monster, Dr Jekyll and Mr Hyde, and other actual monsters.
✦✧

ABBOTT AND COSTELLO MEET DR. JEKYLL AND MR. HYDE

USA, 1953. Dir: Charles Lamont. With: Bud Abbott, Lou Costello, Boris Karloff, Craig Stevens, Helen Westcott, Reginald Denny. Universal-International. B&W.
Slapstick version of Robert Louis Stevenson's classic story. Bud and Lou (in the fifth *Abbott and Costello Meet...* movie) play two turn-of-the-century American policemen in London who are called in by Scotland Yard to help capture a monster which is terrorising the city. Although it doesn't have the polish of earlier Abbott and Costello vehicles, Karloff adds some much-needed class as Dr Jekyll, with stuntman Eddie Parker mostly playing Mr Hyde beneath an unconvincing mask. This includes an exciting roof-top chase and a sequence in a wax museum, where two uncredited actors portray Count Dracula and the Frankenstein Monster, with the latter brought to life by electricity. Kids will enjoy it, despite originally being given an 'X' certificate by the British Board of Film Censors!
Remake: CLIMAX!: Dr. Jekyll and Mr. Hyde (qv; 1955)
✦✦

ABBOTT AND COSTELLO MEET THE MUMMY

USA, 1955. Dir: Charles Lamont. With: Bud Abbott, Lou Costello, Marie Windsor, Michael Ansara, Dan Seymour,

Stuntman Eddie Parker carries off Helen Westcott in Abbott and Costello Meet Dr. Jekyll and Mr. Hyde *(1953).*

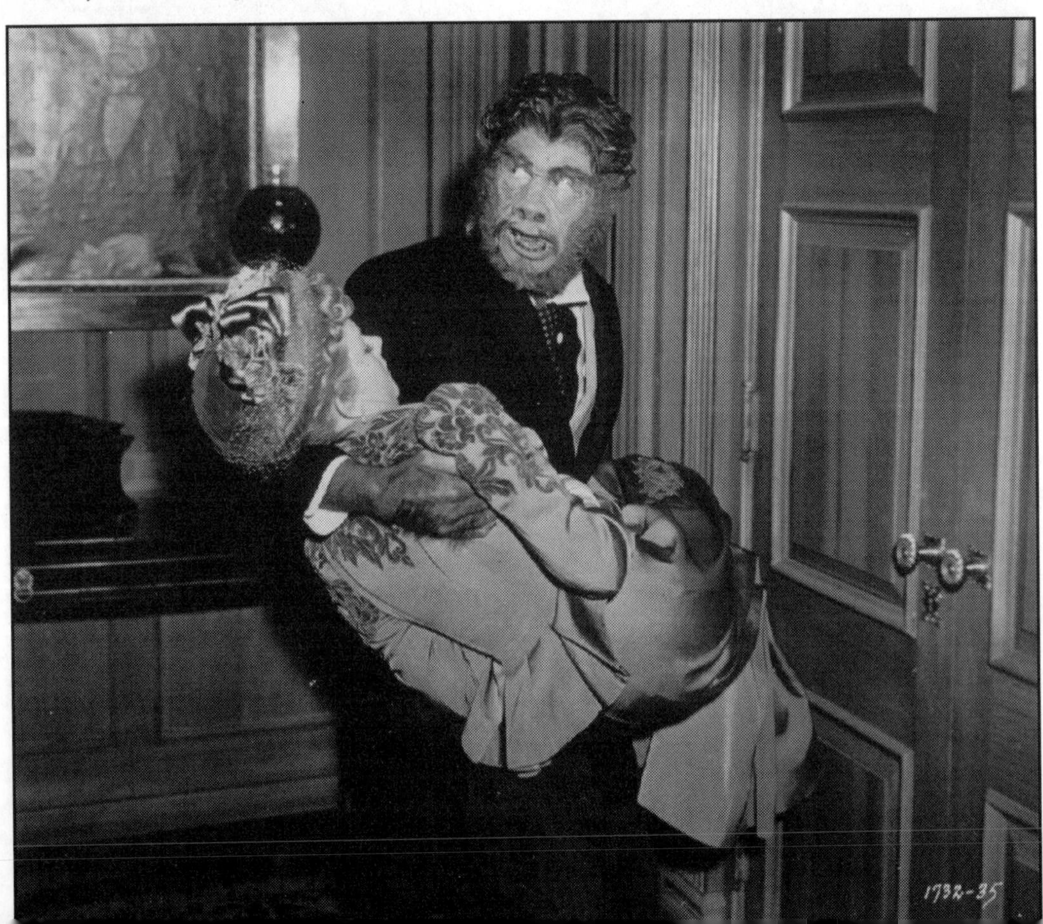

Richard Deacon. Universal-International. B&W.
Director Lamont wrings precious few laughs out of Abbott and Costello's final meeting with monsters and the comedy team's penultimate movie together. This time the ageing duo defy 'the curse of Klaris' and become involved with a disappearing body, a giant iguana(!), a pair of fake mummies (Ansara and Abbott) and the 4,000 year-old living mummy of Klaris, Prince of Evil (Edwin Parker in Bud Westmore's unconvincing suit of bandages). They are also pursued by beautiful treasure-hunter Madame Rontru (Windsor) and Semu (Deacon), the High Priest of an Egyptian cult, who are both seeking a sacred medallion.
✦✧

JOHN ABBOTT
[1905-1996]

British-born character actor with preponderant eyes. He began acting at London's Old Vic in 1935, before moving to Hollywood in 1941. His rare starring roles include the patriotic killer in *The London Blackout Murders* (1942) and an unlikely looking 400 year-old vampire in *The Vampire's Ghost* (1945).
qv: *The Cat Creature* (1973); *Cry of the Werewolf* (1944); *The Munsters: 'A Visit from Johann'* (1965); *Slapstick of Another Kind* (1982).

THE ABC COMEDY HOUR:
The Kopykats

UK/USA, 1972. With: Joe Baker, Charlie Callas, Frank Gorshin, George Kirby, Rich Little, Marilyn Michaels. ABC-TV. Colour.
Episode of this hour-long musical comedy TV show that features guest star Tony Curtis as Count Dracula meeting Gorshin, who plays both Frankenstein and his Monster.
✦

THE ABC SATURDAY SUPERSTAR MOVIE:
Daffy Duck and Porky Pig Meet the Groovie Goolies

USA, 1972. Voices: Mel Blanc, Jane Webb, Howard Morris, Larry Storch, Larry D. Mann. Filmation Associates/ Warner Bros/ABC-TV. Colour.
Hour-long series of cartoon specials (1972-73, sixteen episodes). Cousin Drac, Frankie and Wolfie from *Sabrina and the Groovie Goolies* TV series (1970-71) save a number of classic Warner Bros characters from a Phantom of the Opera-type villain. During the climax, the monsters appear in live-action.
✦✧

Mad, Mad, Mad Monsters

USA, 1972. Dir: Arthur Rankin Jr and Jules Bass. Voices: Allen Swift, Bradley Bolke, Rhoda Mann, Bob McFadden. Videocraft International/Rankin-Bass/ABC-TV. Colour.
This forty-three minute cartoon special is a semi-sequel to the same producers' 1966 movie *Mad Monster Party?*. A Karloffian Baron Henry von Frankenstein creates a mate for his Monster. With the help of jealous hunchback Igor, the Baron organises a wedding banquet for Friday the thirteenth and invites the Creature, the Invisible Man and his invisible family, the Mummy, Count Dracula and his vampiric son Boobula, and wolf man Ron Chanley. When the bride is kidnapped by giant ape Modzula, the monsters set out to rescue her. With a guest appearance by Dr Jekyll and Mr Hyde. A soundtrack album was released by RCA.
Series sequel: THE NEW SATURDAY SUPERSTAR MOVIE (qv; 1973-74)
✦✦

ABC WEEKEND SPECIALS:
Cap'n O.G. Readmore Meets Dr. Jekyll and Mr. Hyde

USA, 1986. Voices: Neil Ross, Stanley Jones, Ilene Latter, Lucille Bliss, Hal Smith. ABC Entertainment Production/ Rick Reinert Pictures/ABC-TV. Colour.
Between 1985-88, this series of cartoon specials (1977-97) featured four hour-long adventures of the eponymous literary cat and the members of his Friday Night Book Club. Travelling librarian Cap'n O.G. Readmore (Ross) and his feline friends begin reading Robert Louis Stevenson's *Strange Case of Dr. Jekyll and Mr. Hyde* until Wordsy (Jones) is sucked into the story.
Series sequel: ABC WEEKEND SPECIALS: Cap'n O.G. Readmore Meets Little Red Riding Hood (1988)
✦

ABUELITA CHARLESTÓN

Spain, 1961. Dir: Javier Setó. With: Marujita Díaz, Espartaco Santoni, Germán Cobos, Yelena Samarina, Félix Fernández, Julio Peña. Brepi Films/Producciones MD/ Edici. Colour.
Comedy musical in which a love potion transforms a man into a cat. The title translates as 'Little Grandma Charleston'.
✦

FORREST J ACKERMAN
[b 1916]

American fan and creator of the influential *Famous Monsters of Filmland* magazine. He saw his first 'imagi-movie' (Ackerman's coinage), *The Lost World*, in 1925, followed two years later by Fritz Lang's vision of one hundred years hence, *Metropolis*, which he has now seen around ninety times. Ackerman started the first science fiction club for juveniles in 1929, compiled the first list of 'scientifilms' in 1932, attended the First World Science Fiction Convention in 1939, appeared on television for the first time in 1947, created the Ackerman Science Fiction Agency in 1948, received the world's first Hugo Award in 1953, coined the ubiquitous term 'sci-fi' in 1954 and created the comic book character Vampirella. The author and editor of numerous books and magazines, he has appeared in more than fifty motion picture cameos. He lives in an eighteen-room Hollywood mansion (the former home of actor Jon Hall) filled with 300,000 pieces of memorabilia from movies and publishing and has held Open Houses approximately forty times a year since 1951.
qv: *Attack of the 60 Foot Centerfold* (1995); *Biography: 'Bela Lugosi Hollywood's Dark Prince'* (1995); *Biography: 'Boris Karloff the Gentle Monster'* (1995); *Biography: 'Lon Chaney Son of a Thousand Faces'* (1995); *Braindead* (1992); *Curse of the Queerwolf* (1987); *Dinosaur Movies* (1993); *Dracula vs. Frankenstein* (1970); *Drive-In Madness!* (1987); *Evil Spawn* (1987); *Flying Saucers Over Hollywood* (1992); *Frankenstein and Me* (1996); *From the Congo and Beyond...Hollywood Goes Ape!* (1994); *Heartstoppers* (1992); *The Howling* (1980); *Innocent Blood* (1992); *King Kong* (1976); *The Laughing Dead* (1989); *Lugosi the Forgotten King* (1985); *Mad Monster Party?* (1966); *My Lovely Monster* (1990); *My Mom's a Werewolf* (1988); *Mysteries & Scandals: 'Bela Lugosi'* (1998); *Nudist Colony of the Dead* (1991); *Queen of Blood* (1966); *Return of the Living Dead Part II* (1987); *Thriller* (1983); *Transylvania Twist* (1989); *Universal Horror* (1998); *Vampirella* (1996).

ACQUANETTA
(Burnu Davenport) [b 1920]

Although described as the 'Venezuelan Volcano' by her friend, newspaper magnate William Randolph Hearst, the exotic-looking actress (also known as Mildred Davenport) was actually born on an Arapaho Native American reservation in Wyoming. Starting out as a model in New York, she landed a small role in *Arabian Nights* (1942) before being officially 'introduced' by Universal as Paula, the Gorilla Girl in *Captive Wild Woman* (1943). She recreated that thankless role in *Jungle Woman* (1944) and worked one day on *The Mummy's Ghost* (1944) before asking the studio for a release from her contract. After retiring from the screen, she married a number of times and hosted local TV and radio shows in Arizona.

THE ADDAMS FAMILY

USA, 1964-66. Dir: Sidney Lanfield, Arthur Hiller, Jean Yarbrough, Jerry Hopper, Arthur Lubin, Nat Perrin, Sidney Salkow and Stanley Z. Cherry. With: Carolyn Jones, John Astin, Jackie Coogan, Ted Cassidy, Blossom Rock, Lisa Loring. Filmways TV Productions/ABC-TV. B&W.
Entertaining half-hour comedy TV series (sixty-four episodes) developed by David Levy and Nat Perrin, based on Charles Addams' macabre cartoon characters in *The New Yorker*. The oddball family

includes the vampiric Morticia (Jones, who also portrayed Morticia's sister Ophelia Frump in season two), her husband Gomez (Astin), Uncle Fester (Coogan), the Frankenstein Monster-like butler Lurch (Cassidy), Grandmama (Rock), the diabolical children Wednesday (Loring) and Pugsley (Ken Weatherwax), Cousin Itt (played by Felix Silla and voiced by Tony Magro) and the disembodied hand, Thing (also Cassidy). Guest stars included Fred Clark, Richard Deacon, Byron Foulger, James Flavin, Margaret Hamilton, Nestor Paiva, Eddie Quillan, Sig Ruman, Vitto Scotti, Jesse White and Robby the Robot. Pyramid Books published two novelisations in 1965 by Jack Sharkey and W.F. Miksch, respectively. *The Munsters* also débuted in 1964 and both series ended their original runs within a week of each other.

Series sequel: THE NEW SCOOBY-DOO MOVIES: Scooby-Doo Meets the Addams Family: Wednesday is Missing (qv; 1972)

Series remake: THE ADDAMS FAMILY (qv; 1973-75)

✦✦✧

AL ADAMSON (Albert Victor Adamson Jr) [1929-1995]

American writer, producer and director of numerous low-budget exploitation movies, often released under a variety of titles in versions containing differing amounts of sex and violence. His first film, in which Adamson acted under the name 'Rick Adams', was the 1955 Western *Half-Way to Hell*, but he is best known for his schlocky cult horror pictures during the 1960s and 1970s, often starring such down-on-their luck actors as John Carradine, Lon Chaney Jr, J. Carrol Naish, Russ Tamblyn and Adamson's wife, exotic dancer Regina Carrol (1944-1992). His films include *Blood of Dracula's Castle* (1967), *Dracula vs. Frankenstein* (1970), *Horror of the Blood Monsters* (1970) and *Doctor Dracula* (1977). When his career faded in the late 1970s, Adamson opened a barbecue restaurant in Santa Monica. He was apparently murdered by a builder who had been living at his California home, and his body buried in concrete under the whirlpool tub.

qv: *Blood of Ghastly Horror* (1972); *Brain of Blood* (1971).

THE ADDAMS FAMILY

USA/UK, 1973-74. Dir: Charles A. Nichols. Voices: Ted Cassidy, Jackie Coogan, Cindy Henderson, Jodie Foster, Janet Waldo, Lennie Weinrib. Hanna-Barbera Productions/NBC-TV. Colour.

Cartoon TV series about the spooky family, which ran for sixteen half-hour episodes. Based on the look of Charles Addams' cartoons in *The New Yorker* (animated in Britain by Halas & Batchelor), each week the oddball family travelled in their haunted motor home to a different American city. Only Coogan and Cassidy returned from the original series. Pugsley was voiced by an eight year-old Foster and Pat Harrington Jr, while Ocho the pet octopus was added to the family.

Series sequel: HALLOWEEN WITH THE ADDAMS FAMILY (qv; 1977)

Series remake: THE ADDAMS FAMILY FUNHOUSE (qv; 1978)

✦✧

THE ADDAMS FAMILY

USA, 1991. Dir: Barry Sonnenfeld. With: Anjelica Huston, Raul Julia, Christopher Lloyd, Elizabeth Wilson, Christina Ricci, Judith Malina. Paramount. Colour.

Enjoyable box office hit based on Charles Addams' wonderfully macabre cartoons, which also inspired the popular TV series (1964-66). The minor story involves the return of Uncle Fester (Lloyd), who could be an impostor attempting to inherit the Addams Family fortune. Ignore the plot and just sit back and enjoy the constant barrage of black humour. As the vampiric Morticia Addams, Anjelica Huston stars in the role she was born to play. With Julia as Gomez, Ricci as a wonderful Wednesday, Jimmy Workman as Pugsley, Malina as Granny, Carel Struycken as the Frankenstein Monster-like butler Lurch, magician Christopher Hart as Thing and Sally Jessy Raphael as herself. M.C. Hammer contributed the rap theme song. David Levey, who created the original TV series, sued. Scholastic published a juvenile novelisation by Stephanie Calmenson, a young adult version by Elizabeth Faucher and an illustrated adaptation by Jordan Horowitz.

Sequel: ADDAMS FAMILY VALUES (qv; 1993)

Remake: THE ADDAMS FAMILY (qv; 1992-93)

✦✦✦✧

THE ADDAMS FAMILY

USA, 1992-93. Dir: Ray Patterson, Robert Alvarez, Don Lusk and Carl Urbano. Voices: John Astin, Ruth Buzzi, Carol Channing, Jim Cummings, Rip Taylor, Marcia Wallace. H-B Production Company/Fil-Cartoons/ABC-TV. Colour.

Half-hour TV cartoon series which retains the style of Charles Addams' original illustrations. Astin recreates his role as Gomez from the original series.

Series remake: THE NEW ADDAMS FAMILY (qv; 1998)

✦✧

THE ADDAMS FAMILY FUNHOUSE

USA, 1978. With: Jack Riley, Liz Torres, Stubby Kaye, Butch Patrick, Pat McCormick. CBS-TV. Colour.

Ill-advised special based on the creepy characters created by Charles Addams, including Gomez (Riley), Morticia (Torres), Uncle Fester (Kaye), Pugsley (Patrick, from TV's *The Munsters* [1964-66]) and Lurch (McCormick).

Remake: THE ADDAMS FAMILY (qv; 1992-93)

✦

ADDAMS FAMILY REUNION

USA, 1998. Dir: Dave Payne. With: Daryl Hannah, Ed Begley Jr, Ray Walston, Kevin McCarthy, Estelle Harris, Tim Curry. Saban Entertainment/Warner Bros. Colour.

Disappointing direct-to-video entry in the series based on the characters created by cartoonist Charles Addams. This time spooky family Gomez (Curry), Morticia (Hannah), Uncle Fester (Pat Thomas), Wednesday (Nicole Fugère, who recreated the role in TV's *The New Addams Family* [1998]), Pugsley (Jerry Messing) and butler Lurch (Carel Struycken, returning from the previous two films) travel to a luxury hotel for Dr Phillip Adams' (Begley Jr) family reunion and attempt to prevent Grandpa and Grandma Addams (McCarthy and Harris) from changing into normal people. Despite the usual macabre touches, this is just not very funny. With Alice Ghostley as Granny and Phil Fondacaro as Cousin Itt, plus an uncredited Clint Howard. Special make-up and creature effects designed by John Carl Buechler. The video also includes Strate Vocalz performing the famous theme song.

Sequel: THE NEW ADDAMS FAMILY (qv; 1998)

✦✧

ADDAMS FAMILY VALUES

USA, 1993. Dir: Barry Sonnenfeld. With: Anjelica Huston, Raul Julia, Christopher Lloyd, Joan Cusack, Christina Ricci, Carol Kane. Paramount. Colour.

The original director and stars are reunited for this delightful sequel to *The Addams Family* (1991), once again based on the bizarre cartoons by Charles Addams. When the vampiric Morticia (Huston) gives birth to moustachioed baby Pubert Pendragon Addams III, the macabre family is joined by a serial killer nanny (Cusack) who has designs on Uncle Fester's (Lloyd) fortune. Ricci steals the film as the deadpan Wednesday when she and Pugsley (Jimmy Workman) are shipped off to the cheery Chippewa summer camp. Kane plays Granny, Carel Struycken recreates his role as Lurch, and director Sonnenfeld has a cameo as the father of Wednesday's weedy boyfriend (David Krumholtz). With Peter MacNicol and Peter Graves. Todd Strasser wrote the Pocket Books novelisation.

Sequel: ADDAMS FAMILY REUNION (qv; 1998)

✦✦✦✧

ADDICTED TO MURDER

USA, 1995 (1996). Dir: Kevin J. Lindenmuth. With: Mick McCleery, Laura McLauchlin, Sasha Graham, Gordon Linzner, Candice Meade, Bernadette Pauley. Kevin J. Lindenmuth/Brimstone Productions/Screen Edge. Colour.

Independent shot-on-video release, co-scripted by Lindenmuth and Tom Piccirilli and told through a series of taped interviews and

monochrome flashbacks. Haunted by a childhood encounter with the undead Rachel (McLauchlin), New York serial killer Joel Winter (McCleery) meets vampire woman Angie (Graham) at a bar called The Hungry and enters into a symbiotic relationship with her — he supplies the blood she needs, while she proves to be the ideal immortal victim for his homicidal cravings. After the girl (Jolee Becker) he attempts to have a normal relationship with is killed, Joel stakes and decapitates his undead mentor. With small press magazine editor Linzner as a clinical psychologist.
Sequel: ADDICTED TO MURDER: TAINTED BLOOD (qv; 1998)
✦✧

ADDICTED TO MURDER: TAINTED BLOOD
USA, 1998. Dir: Kevin J. Lindenmuth. With: Sasha Graham, Sarah K. Lippmann, Mick McCleery, Ted Grayson, Cloud Michaels, Robbi Firestone. Kevin Lindenmuth/Brimstone Productions. Colour.
Many of the original cast return for this prequel to the 1995 independent video release. Vampire Angie (Graham) searches for her renegade sister Rachel (Laura McLauchlin), who is changing unworthy humans into members of the undead. One of these 'tainted' candidates is psychopath Joel Winter (McCleery), who is travelling to New York City. With special appearances by actor/film-maker Joel D. Wynkoop and veteran director Ted V. Mikels (*The Astro-Zombies* [1968], etc) as vampire expert Jonas Collins. Music by Alucarda.
✦✧

THE ADDICTION
USA, 1994 (1995). Dir: Abel Ferrara. With: Lili Taylor, Christopher Walken, Annabella Sciorra, Edie Falco, Paul Caldaron, Fredro Starr. Fast Films/October Films. B&W.
Director Ferrara self-financed this pretentious $500,000 movie that equates vampirism with heroin addiction. After being bitten in a dark alley by sensuous vampire Casanova (Sciorra), New York philosophy student Katherine Conklin (Taylor) discovers that she has been transformed into one of the undead. As her thirst grows, she begins to take the blood of her victims by using a syringe and receives advice from experienced vampire Peina (a cameo by Walken).
✦✧

THE ADULT VERSION OF JEKYLL & HIDE
USA, 1971 (1972). Dir: L. Ray Monde (Lee Raymond and Byron Mabe). With: Jack Buddliner, Jane Tsentas, Rene Bond, Jennifer Brook, Linda McDowell, Harry Schwatz. Entertainment Ventures. Colour.
Softcore version of Robert Louis Stevenson's story, scripted by cinematographer Robert Birch. When Dr Christopher Leader (Buddliner) discovers the handwritten diary of Dr Jekyll in an antique bookstore, he uses it to create a potion that transforms him into a rapist and murderer. When the potion becomes too strong, he turns into the beautiful blonde Miss Hide (Tsentas) who seduces his nurse (future porn star Bond). With two Victorian flashback sequences featuring the original Mr Hyde. Co-produced by David F. Friedman.
Remake: DR. SEXUAL AND MR. HYDE (qv; 1971)
✦

THE ADVENTURES OF A TWO-MINUTE WEREWOLF
USA, 1985. Dir: Mark Cullingham. With: Knoul Johnson, Julia Reardon, Melba Moore, Lainie Kazan, Cindy Deardorf. ABC-TV. Colour.
Fifty minute special, originally shown in two parts on 'ABC's Weekend Specials'. A thirteen year-old boy (Johnson), who is a horror film fan, periodically changes into a werewolf (make-up by Ron Figuly) for two minutes. Helped by his friend (Reardon) and a gypsy fortune teller (Kazan), the boy finally gets his transformations under control and catches the crooks really responsible for a series of thefts he's accused of.
✦✦

THE ADVENTURES OF FU MANCHU:
The Master Plan
USA, 1956. With: Glen Gordon, Lester Matthews, Clark Howat, Carla Balenda, Laurette Luez, John George. Republic Pictures. B&W.
Syndicated half-hour TV series (thirty-nine episodes) based on the characters created by Sax Rohmer and starring Gordon as the eponymous mad scientist opposed by Sir Dennis Nayland-Smith (Matthews) and Dr John Petrie (Howat). In this episode, Fu Manchu resurrects Adolf Hitler from the dead.
Series remake: THE FACE OF FU MANCHU (1965)
✦✧

THE ADVENTURES OF JONNY QUEST:
The Curse of Anubis
USA, 1964. Dir: William Hanna and Joseph Barbera. Voices: Tim Matheson, Don Messick, Mike Road, Danny Bravo, Vic Perrin. Hanna-Barbera Productions/ABC-TV. Colour.
Half-hour cartoon TV series (1964-65, twenty-six episodes), developed by artist Doug Wildey, featuring the adventures of eleven year-old Jonny (Matheson), his scientist father Dr Benton Quest (Messick), bodyguard Roger 'Race' Bannon (Road), mystic Indian boy Hadji (Bravo) and their bulldog Bandit (Messick). In this episode, when Dr Quest and his companions investigate the Lost City of Ghiva they are menaced by a living mummy.
✦✦✧
Werewolf of the Timberland
USA, 1964 (1965). Dir: William Hanna and Joseph Barbera. Voices: Tim Matheson, Don Messick, Mike Road, Danny Bravo, Doug Young. Hanna-Barbera Productions/ABC-TV. Colour.
Jonny and Hadji uncover a gold smuggling operation in the Canadian backwoods guarded by a giant wolf.
Series remake: THE FUNTASTIC WORLD OF HANNA-BARBERA: THE ADVENTURES OF JONNY QUEST (qv; 1985)
✦✦

THE ADVENTURES OF SHIRLEY HOLMES:
The Case of the Mystery Child
Canada, 1996. Dir: Gary Harvey. With: Meredith Henderson, John White, Kevin McNulty, Ian D. Clark, Elizabeth Shepherd, James Martin. Winchester Television/Forefront Entertainment/Credo Entertainment/YTV. Colour.
Half-hour children's TV series (1996-), created by Ellis Iddon and Phil Meagher, about a young girl (Henderson) who follows in the footsteps of her ancestor, Sherlock Holmes. In this episode, when a famous archaeologist friend of her grandmother Peggy (Shepherd) dies, Shirley investigates an Egyptian curse and discovers the mummy of a boy-king buried in a graveyard.
✦✦✧

THE ADVENTURES OF SINBAD:
The Beast of Basra
South Africa/Canada/USA, 1997. Dir: Terry Ingram. With: Zen Gesner, George Buza, Tim Progosh, Oris Erhuero, Mariah Shirley, Laurens Chillers. Rukhs II Productions/Atlantis Films/All American Television/Global/WGN Television. Colour.
Cheap-looking, hour-long syndicated TV series (1996-98, forty-two episodes), about the magical adventures of a young Sinbad (Gesner) and his crew. In this episode, a werewolf (Keith Grenville) terrorising the port of Basra bites Sinbad's friend Doubar (Buza) on the hand, passing on the curse to the unsuspecting sailor. Scripted by creator/co-executive producer Ed Naha.
✦✦

THE ADVENTURES OF SUPERBOY:
Jackson and Hyde
USA, 1990 (1991). Dir: John Huneck. With: Gerard Christopher, Stacy Haiduk, Peter Jay Fernandez, Robert Levine, Heather Ehlers, Juice Newton. Cantharus Productions/Lowry Productions/Alexander & Ilya Salkind. Colour.
Surprisingly dark syndicated half-hour adventures (1990-92, forty-eight episodes) of the Boy of Steel (co-producer Christopher) and Lana Lang (Haiduk), who work for Capital City's Bureau for

Extranormal Matters. In this episode, when an old elixir apparently turns Bureau Chief C. Dennis Jackson (Levine) into a super-strong killer, only Superboy can stop him. From the producers of the *Superman* movies, based on the DC Comics characters.
✦✧

Metamorphosis
USA, 1992. Dir: Robert Wiemer. With: Gerard Christopher, Stacy Haiduk, Peter Jay Fernandez, Robert Levine, Roddy Piper, Robin O'Dell. Cantharus Productions/Lowry Productions/Alexander & Ilya Salkind. Colour.
When Lana joins a new health club, she discovers that its owner Adrian Temple (Piper) is a modern-day vampiric alchemist who remains young by draining the youth from his victims.
✦✦

Werewolf
USA, 1990 (1991). Dir: Bryan Spicer. With: Gerard Christopher, Stacy Haiduk, Peter Jay Fernandez, Robert Levine, Paula Marshall, Robert Winston. Cantharus Productions/Lowry Productions/Alexander & Ilya Salkind. Colour.
Scripted by Toby Martin. Christina Riley (Marshall) is cursed with lycanthropy and convinces Clark Kent/Superboy to investigate Canaris (Winston), an expert on the occult who she claims is a werewolf. As usual, this was filmed at Florida's Universal Studios, where the show's climax is set.
✦✦

THE ADVENTURES OF SUPERMAN:
(UK: aka SUPERMAN)
The Ghost Wolf
USA, 1952 (1953). Dir: Lee Sholem. With: George Reeves, Phyllis Coates, Jack Larson, John Hamilton, Robert Shayne, Stanley Andrews. ABC Production. B&W.
Syndicated half-hour TV series (1952-58, 104 episodes) based on the DC Comics character. *The Daily Planet* reporters Clark Kent/Superman (Reeves), Lois Lane (Coates) and Jimmy Olsen (Larson) travel to Canada to investigate reports of a werewolf that has caused lumberjacks working on the newspaper's timber reserve to quit their jobs.
Series remake: THE NEW ADVENTURES OF SUPERMAN (1966-67)
✦✧

THE ADVENTURES OF THE SPIRIT
USA, 1963. Dir: Don Glut. With: Don Glut, Glenn Strange, Billy Knaggs, Bob Burns, Dick Andersen, Jim Harmon. Colour.
Amateur twelve minute serial, shot on 16mm in five episodes ('The Phantom Avenger', 'Fangs of Death', 'It Lives Again!', 'Frankenstein's Fury' and 'Human Targets') featuring pulp and comic book heroes the Spirit (Glut), Superman (Burns), the Phantom Avenger (Andersen) and the Shadow (Harmon). This is only listed here because it marks Glenn Strange's return to the role of the Frankenstein Monster, revived by Dr Frankenstein (Knaggs) to battle the Spirit and Superman. It was a sequel to the equally amateur *Monster Rumble* (1961). Glut's numerous other home movies include *Dragstrip Dracula* (1962), *Frankenstein Meets Dracula* (1957), *The Frankenstein Story* (1958), *I Was a Teenage Vampire* (1958), *Return of the Wolf Man* (1957), *Revenge of Dracula* (1958), *The Teenage Frankenstein* (1959), *Teenage Frankenstein Meets Teenage Werewolf* (1959) and *Teenage Werewolf* (1959).
✦

THE ADVENTURES OF TINTIN:
(USA: THE NEW ADVENTURES OF TINTIN)
Prisoners of the Sun
France/Canada, 1992. Dir: Stéphane Bernasconi. Voices: Colin O'Meara, David Fox, Wayne Robson, John Stocker, Dan Hennessey, Susan Roman. Ellipse Programme/Nelvana/Home Box Office/Media Participations/The Family Channel/M6/The Global Television Network/FR3. Colour.
Two-part episode of the half-hour cartoon TV series based on ten *Tintin* books by Belgian cartoonist Hergé (Georges Remi). This story was previously filmed in 1969 as *Tintin et le Temple du Soleil*. When seven archaeologists discover an ancient Peruvian mummy, they unknowingly release a mysterious curse. Journalist Tintin (O'Meara), Captain Haddock (Fox) and their dog Snowy travel to South America to rescue Professor Calculus (Robson) from a lost race of Incas.
✦✦

AFI'S 100 YEARS...100 MOVIES:
Out of Control
USA, 1998. Dir: Richard Schickel. Turner Network Television. B&W/Colour.
Hour-long TV show (ten episodes) directed, produced and written by Schickel and narrated by James Woods, celebrating the American Film Institute's '100 Years...100 Movies'. This includes clips from *Frankenstein* (1931), *Jaws* (1975), *King Kong* (1933), *The Manchurian Candidate* (1962), *Psycho* (1960), *The Silence of the Lambs* (1991), *Sunset Blvd.* (1950) and many other movies featuring 'monsters' and 'freaks of nature'.
✦✦✧

AFRICA SCREAMS
USA, 1949. Dir: Charles Barton. With: Bud Abbott, Lou Costello, Clyde Beatty, Frank Buck, Max Baer, Buddy Baer. Nasbro Pictures/Nassour Studios/United Artists. B&W.
New York booksellers Buzz Johnson (Abbott) and Stanley Livington (Costello) join an unscrupulous African safari, organised by Diana Emerson (Hillary Brooke), which is secretly searching for a fortune in diamonds. This low-budget juvenile comedy also includes lion tamer Beatty and 'Bring 'em Back Alive' hunter Buck. With two Stooges, Shemp Howard and Joe Besser, an intelligent gorilla and a briefly seen Kong-size giant ape.
✦✧

AFROS, MACKS IN ZODIACS
USA, 1995. With: Rudy Ray Moore. Something Weird Video/Jhyma's Funkay Partay Productions. Colour.
Rudy Ray Moore (*Dolemite* [1974], etc) hosts this enjoyable video compilation of 1960s and early 1970s blaxploitation trailers that includes *Blacula* (1972), *Dr. Black Mr. Hyde* (1975) and *Scream Blacula Scream* (1973), amongst numerous others.
✦✦✦

AFTER DEATH: ZOMBIE 4
(Orig: OLTRA LA MORTE)
Italy/Philippines, 1988. Dir: Clyde Anderson (Claudio Fragasso). With: Chuck Peyton, Alex McBride, Jim Gaines, Lorenzo Piani, Cristina Caporilli (Candice Daly), Alan Collins (Luciano Pigozzi). Flora Film. Colour.
Unofficial, shot-on-video follow-up to *Zombie 3* (1987). A voodoo *Book of the Dead* revives a horde of flesh-eating zombies (led by Romano Puppo) on a remote tropical island.
✦

AGATHA CHRISTIE'S POIROT:
(USA: MYSTERY!)
The Adventure of the Egyptian Tomb
UK, 1993. Dir: Peter Barber-Fleming. With: David Suchet, Hugh Fraser, Pauline Moran, Rolf Saxon, Oliver Pierre, Bill Bailey. London Weekend Television/ITV. Colour.
This episode of the hour-long series (1989-) is based on Agatha Christie's 1924 story 'The Adventure of the Egyptian Tomb'. Following the death of her archaeologist husband, Lady Willard (Anna Cropper) asks diminutive Belgian detective Hercule Poirot (Suchet) to investigate the curse of Men-her-Ra, while a jackal-headed figure of Anubis prowls the desert.
✦✦✧

AGENTE SEGRETO 777 OPERAZIONE MISTERO
Italy, 1965. Dir: Henry Bay (Enrico Bomba). With: Mark Damon, Mary Young, Seyna Seyn, Lewis Jourdan, Stanley Kent. Protor Films. Colour.
One of numerous James Bond-style thrillers churned out in Italy during the mid-1960s. In this one, Secret Agent 777 (Damon) is on the trail of Professor Keller, who has discovered a method for returning the dead to life.
✦✧

AHKEA KHOTS
South Korea, 1961. Dir: Yongmin Lee. With: Yechoon Lee, Chimi Kim. Sunglim Film. B&W.
Chimi Kim is the vampiric 'Bad Flower' of the title in this South Korean imitation of Hammer's *Dracula* (1958).
✦

AIP: FAST AND FURIOUS
USA, 1985. SF Rush Video/Trailers on Tape. B&W/Colour.
Hour-long video compilation of thirty-three American International Pictures trailers dating from the 1950s to the 1970s. This includes everything from *I Was a Teenage Frankenstein* (1957) to *The Return of Count Yorga* (1971), along with Beach Party and Roger Corman previews. Narrated by TV horror host Ernie ('Ghoulardi') Anderson.
Sequel: AIP VOL II: THE COOL AND THE CRAZY (1986)
✦✦✦

AIRPLANE II THE SEQUEL
USA, 1982. Dir: Ken Finkleman. With: Robert Hays, Julie Hagerty, Lloyd Bridges, Chad Everett, William Shatner, Raymond Burr. Paramount. Colour.
This futuristic sequel to *Airplane* (1980) has little in common with the first film except an attempt by writer/director Finkleman to recreate the rapid-fire humour of the original and reunite as many cast members as possible. Test pilot Ted Striker (Hays) escapes from a mental asylum and boards a commercial shuttle flight to the Moon that he believes will suffer a computer malfunction. With clips from *The Hunchback of Notre Dame* (1923) and an incredible cast of guest stars that includes Chuck Connors, Peter Graves, Sonny Bono, John Dehner, Rip Torn, Kent McCord, John Vernon, Richard Jaeckel, John Larch, Herve Villechaize, Sandahl Bergman and Leon Askin.
✦✦

AKAZUKIN CHACHA
(USA: aka RED HOOD CHACHA)
Japan, 1994. Voices: Masami Suzuki, Shingo Katori, Noriko Hidaka, Mayumi Akado, Taiki Matsuno, Noriko Namiki. Colour.
Anime TV series loosely inspired by the Little Red Riding Hood fairytale. Akazukin Chacha (Suzuki) is a little red-hooded girl who can transform into a super-powered fighter and has magical powers which she cannot always control. Her best friend is Riiya, the werewolf boy (Katori), while Shiine (Hidaka) is another boy with magical abilities who wants Chacha.
✦✧

AKIRA KUROSAWA'S DREAMS
(Orig: YUME)
Japan/USA, 1990. Dir: Akira Kurosawa. With: Akira Terao, Mitsuko Baisho, Mieko Harada, Chishu Ryu, Hisashi Igawa, Mitsunori Isaki. Akira Kurosawa USA/ Warner Bros. Colour.
Eight fantasy vignettes as 'dreamed' by the eighty year-old director. 'The Tunnel' segment features a platoon of living-dead soldiers awaiting orders from their officer, who must come to terms with his guilt for surviving the battle in which they died. Other stories involve mutated plants, immortal horned demons and a snow fairy. With Martin Scorsese as Van Gogh and presented by Steven Spielberg. Inoshiro Honda (*Godzilla King of the Monsters!* [1954], etc] was creative consultant.
✦✦✧

AKUMULATOR 1
Czech Republic, 1994. Dir: Jan Sverak. With: Petr Forman, Edita Brychta, Zdenek Sverak. Heureka Film. Colour.
Arty feature in which a man becomes an energy vampire, sapping the life-force from everything around him and leaving behind a world populated by the *alter egos* of his victims.
✦

ALABAMA'S GHOST
USA, 1972. Dir: Frederic Hobbs. With: Christopher Brooks, E. Kerrigan Prescott, Lani Freeman, Pierre LePage, The Turk Murphy Jazz Band. Ellman/Bremson International. Colour.
Billed as 'A super hip horror movie', this regional blaxploitation release was written, produced and directed by Hobbs. Brooks plays a janitor who discovers a magician's costume hidden beneath a night club. When he tries it on, he turns into Alabama, King of the Cosmos, and tours with a rock group. It also includes voodoo ceremonies, a vampire woman and a ghost.
✦

ALFRED HITCHCOCK HOUR:
The Monkey's Paw: A Retelling
USA, 1965. Dir: Robert Stevens. With: Collin Wilcox-Horne, Leif Erickson, Lee Majors, Jane Wyatt, Zolya Talma. Shamley Productions/Alfred Hitchcock/MCA-TV/ CBS-TV. B&W.
Hour-long anthology TV series (1962-65, ninety-three episodes) introduced by Alfred Hitchcock. In this variation of W.W. Jacobs' story, set in the Bahamas, a strange woman gives a couple on holiday a monkey's paw that will grant them three wishes.
Episode remake: THE MONKEES: The Monkees Paw (qv; 1968)
✦✦

ALFRED HITCHCOCK PRESENTS:
The Greatest Monster of Them All
USA, 1960 (1961). Dir: Robert Stevens. With: Richard Hale, Robert H. Harris, Sam Jaffe, William Redfield, Meri Wells. Shamley Productions/Alfred Hitchcock/MCA-TV/NBC-TV. B&W.
Half-hour anthology TV series (1955-62, 268 episodes) introduced by Alfred Hitchcock. In this episode, scripted by Robert Bloch and based on his story 'The Cloak' (which he also adapted for *The House That Dripped Blood* [1970]), a failed horror star attempts to make a comeback in a low-budget vampire movie. When he buys a cloak that originally belonged to a member of the undead, he discovers its power.
✦✦

Museum Piece
USA, 1961. Dir: Paul Henreid. With: Larry Gates, Myron McCormick, Bert Convy, Edward Platt, Tom Gilleran, Charles Meredith. Shamley Productions/Alfred Hitchcock/MCA-TV/NBC-TV. B&W.
A visitor (McCormick) to a private museum learns how the skeleton of the District Attorney (Platt), who unjustly convicted the curator's (Gates) son (Convy) of murder, is displayed as a specimen. Hitchcock does his introduction with an Egyptian mummy.
Series sequel: ALFRED HITCHCOCK PRESENTS (qv; 1985-88)
✦✦✧

ALFRED HITCHCOCK PRESENTS:
Night Creatures
Canada/USA, 1988 (1989). Dir: Richard J. Lewis. With: Brett Cullen, Louise Vallance, Michael Rhoades, Jason Blicker, Ray James. A.H.F./Paragon/Michael Sloan Productions/MCA-TV/USA Network. Colour.
Episode of the revival anthology TV series (1985-88, eighty episodes), hosted by Alfred Hitchcock in colourised footage from the original 1955-65 shows. In this half-hour pilot, written by executive producer Michael Sloan, female reporter Holly (Vallance) suffers from a recurring dream of a demonic horseman. When she meets heavy metal vampire singer Adam Lust/Martin LeCross (Rhoades), her nightmares come true. Music by Disaster Area. The ending was left open for a never-continued series.
✦✧

ALIAS JOHN PRESTON
UK, 1955. Dir: David MacDonald. With: Betta St. John, Alexander Knox, Christopher Lee, Sandra Dorne, Patrick Holt, Betty Ann Davies. Danziger Productions/Associated Artists. B&W.
As the title character, Lee (in his first horror film) stars as a man troubled by a series of recurring nightmares in which he murders a young woman. He consults a psychiatrist (Knox) who uncovers his Jekyll and Hyde-type personality. With John Longden and Bill Fraser.
✦✧

ALICE IN HOLLYWEIRD
(aka ALICE IN HOLLYWOOD)
USA, 1992. Dir: F. (Fred) J. Lincoln. With: Francesca Lé, Tianna Taylor, Teri Diver, Peter North, Marc Wallice, Cassidy. Zane Entertainment Group. Colour.
Hardcore fantasy in which an 'innocent' young woman (Lé) rents a room in a strange boarding house whose inhabitants also include Dracula (North), James Bond and a genie — all of whom are either actors living out their roles or outpatients from a mental institution.
✦

ALIEN DEAD
(aka IT FELL FROM THE SKY)
USA, 1978 (1980). Dir: Fred Olen Ray. With: Buster Crabbe (Clarence Linden Crabbe), Raymond Roberts, Linda Lewis, Mike Bonavia, John Leirier, Rich Vogan. Firebird International. Colour.
Veteran serial star Crabbe (*Flash Gordon* [1936], etc) returns to the screen for the last time as Sheriff Kowalski, who battles a houseboat full of blood-drinking teenage zombies, the result of a crashed meteorite. Ray made his directorial début with this low-budget mess, filmed on 16mm for $12,000 in Florida. All the characters' names are associated with Roger Corman movies.
✦

ALIEN VAMPIRE BABY BREEDERS
USA, 1997. Dir: Geoffrey de Valois. With: Mihaella Stoicova, Elaine Juliette Williamson, Shyler, Robin Sheridan. Digital Entertainment Group/Salt City Home Video. Colour.
One of a series of softcore *Vampire Raw Footage* videos that includes behind-the-scenes nude and erotic sequences from *Vampire Centerfolds* (1995) and *The Vampire Conspiracy* (1995). In this tape, kinky vampire aliens impregnate helpless nude college girls in high-tech bondage orgies!
✦

WILLIAM ALLAND
[1916-1997]

American producer and actor. He began his career with Orson Welles' Mercury Theater on stage and radio, narrating as well as appearing as the enquiring reporter in *Citizen Kane* (1941). After returning from World War Two, he became staff producer for Universal-International in 1952, and was responsible for such films as *It Came from Outer Space* (1953), *Creature from the Black Lagoon* (1954), *Revenge of the Creature* (1955), *The Creature Walks Among Us* (1955), *This Island Earth* (1955) and *The Mole People* (1956), among many others.
qv: *100 Years of Horror: 'Dinosaurs'* (1996); *100 Years of Horror: 'Gory Gimmicks'* (1996); *100 Years of Horror: 'Mutants'* (1996).

ALLEGRO NON TROPPO
Italy, 1976 (1977). Dir: Bruno Bozzetto. With: Maurizio Nichetti, Nestor Garay, Maurizio Micheli, Maria Luisa Giozannina. Bruno Bozzetto Films/Speciality Films. Colour/B&W.
Feature length cartoon parody of Walt Disney's *Fantasia* (1940), with live-action framing sequences in black and white. The best episodes involve the evolution of life that begins in a Coke bottle left behind by astronauts (to Ravel's 'Bolero'), and a cat reliving its memories in a bombed-out house ('The Sad Waltz'). A hunchbacked character called Frankenstein enters a castle dungeon to create an ending for the film.
✦✦✦

ALLEN AND ROSSI MEET DRACULA AND FRANKENSTEIN
USA, 1974. With: Marty Allen, Steve Rossi. Colour.
The two TV comedians meet the titular monsters.
✦

ALL GIRL VAMPIRE CATFIGHTS
USA, 1997. Dir: Geoffrey de Valois. With: Joan A. Teeter, Heather LeMire, Liddy Roley, Barbara Savage, Kathy Arianoff. Digital Entertainment Group/Salt City Home Video. Colour.
Another in the series of softcore *Vampire Raw Footage* videos that includes behind-the-scenes nude and erotic sequences. This one features naked female vampire catfights!
✦

THE ALL NEW ADVENTURES OF LAUREL AND HARDY — FOR LOVE OR MUMMY
South Africa/USA, 1998 (1999). Dir: Larry Harmon and John Cherry. With: Bronson Pinchot, Gailard Sartain, F. Murray Abraham. Larry Harmon Pictures Corporation/ Mummy Productions/Coast Entertainment. Colour.
Ill-advised attempt to create a new franchise with the lookalike nephews of comedy duo Stan and Ollie (Pinchot and Sartian) on the trail of a reanimated 3,000 year-old mummy that has chosen Ollie's girlfriend for its bride. With Abraham as a museum curator.
✦✧

THE ALL NEW POPEYE HOUR:
Dr. Junior and Mr. Hyde
USA, 1978. Dir: Alex Lovy. Voices: Daws Butler, Virginia McSwain, Allan Melvin, Jack Mercer, Marilyn Schreffler, Jo Anne Worley. Hanna-Barbera Productions/King Features Syndicate/CBS-TV. Colour.
The further hour-long TV cartoon adventures (1978-80) of Popeye the Sailorman (Mercer) and his friends, executive produced by William Hanna and Joseph Barbera.
✦✧

Popeye Goes to Hollywood
USA, 1978. Dir: Alex Lovy. Voices: Daws Butler, Virginia McSwain, Allan Melvin, Jack Mercer, Marilyn Schreffler, Jo Anne Worley. Hanna-Barbera Productions/King Features Syndicate/CBS-TV. Colour.
In this seven minute cartoon, while competing with Popeye for a job as stuntman at Bigdome Studios, the scheming Bluto (Melvin) disguises himself as a King Kong-like ape and picks Olive (Schreffler) up in his giant paw.
✦✧

Popeye Meets the Blutostein Monster
USA, 1978. Dir: Alex Lovy. Voices: Daws Butler, Virginia McSwain, Allan Melvin, Jack Mercer, Marilyn Schreffler, Jo Anne Worley. Hanna-Barbera Productions/King Features Syndicate/CBS-TV. Colour.
When Olive is kidnapped by the Blutostein monster, Popeye has to rescue her from the castle of the creature's creator, Viktor (Butler).
✦✧

The Terrifying Transylvanian Trek
USA, 1978. Dir: Alex Lovy. Voices: Daws Butler, Virginia McSwain, Allan Melvin, Jack Mercer, Marilyn Schreffler, Jo Anne Worley. Hanna-Barbera Productions/King Features Syndicate/CBS-TV. Colour.
Popeye and Olive meet Dracula (Melvin), Vampetta (Schreffler) and the Frankenstein Monster (Melvin) while searching for treasure in the Count's castle.
Series remake: POPEYE (1980)
✦✧

ALOHA LITTLE VAMPIRE STORY
(USA: aka ALOHA THE LITTLE VAMPIRE)
Hong Kong, 1987. Dir: Ng Yinn-Jiann (Ng See-Yuen). With: Law Yoi, Lee Ting-Hing, Chen Yu-Chiao. Pan-Asia Video. Colour.
Comedy featuring a family of hopping vampires, including little Hsiu Long who runs away from home and cures his bruised human friend. When a gangster's brother becomes a caped bloodsucker, Hsiu is his only cure.
✦

AMAZING STORIES:
Mummy, Daddy
USA, 1985. Dir: William Dear. With: Tom Harrison, Bronson Pinchot, Brion James, Tracey Walter, Larry A.

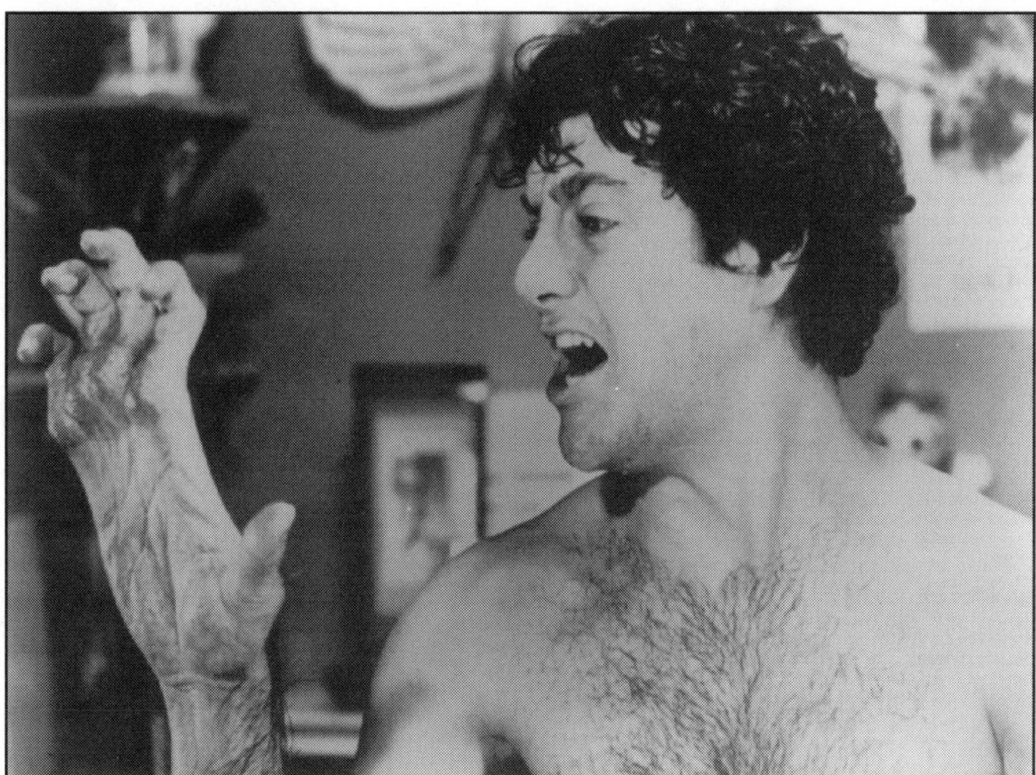

David Naughton begins to transform into An American Werewolf in London *(1981).*

Hankin, Lucy Lee Flippen. Amblin Entertainment/ Universal/NBC-TV. Colour.
Disappointing half-hour anthology TV series (1985-87, forty-five episodes), executive produced by Steven Spielberg, that takes its title from the world's first science fiction pulp magazine. In this comedy episode, based on a story by Spielberg, actor Harold (Harrison) is on location in the Southern swamps for a movie entitled *The Mummy's Kiss* when he is mistaken for real Egyptian mummy Ra-Amin-Ka (Michael Zand, in make-up created by Greg Cannon) while rushing to his pregnant wife. This episode also appeared as part of the 1987 compilation movie *Amazing Stories*. Opening narration by Ray Walston.
✦✦

AMAZING STORIES
USA, 1987. Dir: Steven Spielberg, William Dear and Robert Zemeckis. With: Kevin Costner, Casey Siemaszko, Tom Harrison, Bronson Pinchot, Christopher Lloyd, Scott Coffey. Amblin Entertainment/Universal. Colour.
Compilation of three episodes from executive producer Steven Spielberg's disappointing TV series (1985-87), linked by the turning pages of a book. 'The Mission' (1985) is a mawkish tale of a damaged World War Two bomber and a trapped tailgunner who are saved by a set of cartoon wheels! 'Mummy, Daddy' (1985) is much more fun as movie mummy Harold (Harrison) meets real Egyptian mummy Ra-Amin-Ka (Michael Zand) while rushing through the Southern swamps to his wife, who is about to give birth. Mick Garris, Tom McLoughlin and Bob Gale scripted 'Go to the Head of the Class' (1986) in which two high school students use witchcraft to revenge themselves on their hated teacher (Lloyd). The final episode works best, thanks to Stan Winston's impressive disembodied head effects. With Kiefer Sutherland, Brion James and Mary Stuart Masterson. Five more compilations followed. The first two stories were novelised by Steven Bauer in *Steven Spielberg's Amazing Stories* volumes I and II.
✦✦✧

AMAZING STORIES
Hong Kong, 1993 (1994). Dir: Ma Kam. Tai Seng Video. Colour.
Anthology movie featuring three supernatural tales. In the middle episode, a fanged vampire woman confronts a vampire-witch who has a prior claim on one of her victims. The two other stories involve ghosts seeking revenge.
✦

AN AMERICAN WEREWOLF IN LONDON
UK, 1981. Dir: John Landis. With: David Naughton, Jenny Agutter, Griffin Dunne, John Woodvine, Brian Glover, Lila Kaye. PolyGram Pictures/Lycanthrope Films. Colour.
Slightly overrated blend of horror and humour that is never entirely successful because of a weak plot and the absence of any real shocks. Despite the dire warnings of the locals in The Slaughtered Lamb pub, two American tourists on vacation in England go walking on the moors at night and are attacked by a monstrous beast (Paddy Ryan). Jack Goodman (Dunne) is killed and his friend, David Kessler (Naughton), badly wounded. Awakening in a London hospital, David is plagued by bizarre nightmares and visited by his dead friend Jack, who warns him that he is starting to turn into a werewolf... The comedy is most effective when David's victims return to haunt him. Rick Baker's bone-crunching transformation effects are superb (if overlong) and won the first Academy Award for Best Make-up Effects, but the animatronic werewolf used during the climax looks like a shaggy dog. Director Landis makes good use of his London locations, and stages an impressive multiple car crash in Piccadilly Circus. This has some wonderful moments and a great

soundtrack that features such songs as 'Bad Moon Rising', 'Moondance' and 'Blue Moon'. With Frank Oz and Rik Mayall.
Sequel: AN AMERICAN WEREWOLF IN PARIS (qv; 1997)
✦✦✦✦

AN AMERICAN WEREWOLF IN PARIS
France/Luxembourg/USA/Holland, 1997. Dir: Anthony Waller. With: Tom Everett Scott, Julie Delpy, Vince Vieluf, Phil Buckman, Julie Bowen, Pierre Cosso. Stonewood Communications/Hollywood Pictures Company/J&M Entertainment/Cometstone Pictures/Avrora Media/Delux Productions/Buena Vista Pictures Distribution. Colour.
Based on characters created by John Landis, this belated sequel to *An American Werewolf in London* (1981) attempts to recreate the original's mix of humour and horror. Andy (Scott), Brad (Vieluf) and Chris (Buckman) are a trio of typical backpacking American college graduates on a daredevil tour of Europe. Descending on Paris for some serious fun, Andy finds himself bungee jumping off the Eiffel Tower to save the suicidal Serafine (Delpy). Soon they all become involved with a sinister cult of skinhead lycanthropes led by the evil Claude (Cosso). Subsequently infected by the werewolf virus and haunted by his undead victims, Andy sets out to stop Claude and his pack of Gallic monsters from massacring a church full of tourists. The film eschews the complicated make-up effects of the first film for unconvincing CGI werewolves, created by Santa Barbara Studios. Director/co-writer/executive producer Waller (who replaced Marco Brambilla before shooting began) has a cameo as a metro driver.
✦✦✧

AMOURS COLLECTIVES
France, 1976. Dir: Jean-Pierre Bouyxou. With: Jean-Pierre Bouyxou, Willy Braque, Catherine Castel, Alban Ceray, Jackie Dartois, Jean Rollin. Colour.
Low budget sex film supervised by French director Rollin (under the name Michel Gand). He also appears in the film under his occasional pseudonym, Michel Gentil, the Vampire.
✦

ANAK PONTIANAK
Malaya, 1958. Dir: Ramon Estella. With: Hasimah, Haj Sattar, Dayang Sofia, Jins Sashudin, Kemat bin Hassan. Shaw. B&W.
Sequel to *Sumpah Pontianak* (1958). The son of the vampire turns up in this fourth entry in the popular 'Pontianak' series. This also includes a bodiless creature (a *Polong*) and a snake devil (a *Hnatu*).
Sequel: PONTIANAK KEMBALI (qv; 1963)
✦✧

ANASTASIA
USA, 1997. Dir: Don Bluth and Gary Goldman. Voices: Meg Ryan, John Cusack, Kelsey Grammer, Christopher Lloyd, Hank Azaria, Bernadette Peters. Twentieth Century Fox/Fox Family Films. Colour.
Impressive cartoon musical based on the romanticised story of the Princess Anastasia (Ryan), supposedly the last surviving member of Russia's Romanov family, which was destroyed through a curse by the evil Rasputin (Lloyd, in a role perfect for Christopher Lee). Ten years after the Revolution, Anastasia teams up with con-men companions Dimitri (Cusack) and Vladimir (Grammer) to travel to Paris where she will be reunited with her grandmother (Angela Lansbury). However, the long-dead Rasputin is revived by sorcery as a decaying zombie and together with his comic bat companion Bartok (Azaria) and some demonic servants, he sets out to destroy them all. This includes excellent visuals, perfect voice characterisations and some nice songs by Lynn Ahrens and Stephen Flaherty. With Kirsten Dunst as the voice of young Anastasia.
✦✦✦✦

THE ANCINES WOODS
(Orig: EL BOSQUE DE ANCINES/EL BOSQUE DEL LOBO. USA: aka THE WOLF FOREST)
Spain, 1968 (1969). Dir: Pedro Olea. With: (José) Luis López Vazquez, Amparo Soler Leal, Antonio Casas, Nuria Torray, Alfredo Mayo, John Steiner. Amboto. Colour.
Award-winning thriller, based on Galician folklore and the novel *L'Uomo Lupo di Galicia* by Carlos Martinez Barbeto. An epileptic serial killer (comedian Vasquez in a dramatic role) is believed by the locals to be a werewolf. In the end he is caught in a wolf trap.
✦✧

DER ANDERE
Germany, 1912. Dir: Max Mack. With: Albert Bassermann, Emmerich Hanus, Reilly Ridon, Hanni Weisse, Leon Rosemann, Otto Collot. Vitascope. B&W.
Silent drama based on the play by Paul Lindau, about a man who develops a murderous alter-ego. The title translates as 'The Other'.
Remake: THE MAN WITHIN (qv; 1930)
✦

ANDHERI RAAT MEIN DIYA TERE HAATH MEIN
India, 1986. Dir: Dada Kondke. With: Dada Kondke. Colour.
Low-budget Hindi horror in which a mad scientist creates a monster, Big John, who wears tennis shoes. The creature goes on a rampage, killing a girl with an umbrella and battling a group of 1970s-style pimps.
✦

ANEMIA
Italy, 1986. Dir: Alberto Abruzzese and Achille Pisanti. With: Hans Zischler, Gioia Maria Scola, Gérard Landry. RAI-TV. Colour.
Political satire in which Umberto (German actor Zischler), the forty year-old leader of Italy's Communist Party, becomes a bloodsucker after reading the morbid memoirs of his mysterious grandfather. Based on the novel by Abruzzese.
✦

ANGEL
USA, 1999. With: David Boreanaz, Charisma Carpenter, Glenn Quinn, Elisabeth Rohm, James Masters. Twentieth Century Fox/Mutant Enemy/Kuzui Enterprises/Sandollar Television/The WB Network. Colour.
Hour-long spin-off series from *Buffy the Vampire Slayer* (1996-), also created by executive producer Joss Whedon, in which the eponymous 244 year-old tortured vampire (Boreanaz) moves to Los Angeles, where he teams up with Cordelia (Carpenter) and demonic guardian angel Doyle (Quinn) to save the souls of others. Other *Buffy* regulars occasionally guest star in various episodes. A series of tie-in novels was published by Pocket Books.
✦✦✦✧

ANGELES Y QUERUBINES
Mexico, 1972. Dir: Rafael Corkidi. With: Ana Luisa Peluffo, Helena Rojo, Jorge Humberto Robles, David Silva, Roberto Canedo, Cecilia Pezet. Cine Producciones. Colour.
This anthology movie includes three stories, the middle one about vampire bride Angela (Rojo).
✦

ANGELIC FRANKENSTEIN
USA, 1964. Dir: Bob Mizer. With: Ray Greig, Earl Dean. Athletic Models Guild. B&W.
Six minute gay short in which Frankenstein (Greig) creates a perfect male (Dean) who rebels when taught how to use a gun. This was apparently sold through magazines.
✦

ANGEL OF THE NIGHT
(Orig: NATTENS ENGEL)
Denmark, 1998. Dir: Shaky Gonzales. With: Thomas Villum Jensen, Maria Karlsen, Mette Louise Holland, Ulrich Thomsen, Karin Rørbech, Erik Holmey. Wise Guy Productions/Nordisk Film Biografdistribution. Colour.
This black comedy is apparently Denmark's first vampire movie. Rebecca (Karlsen) inherits her grandfather's old house and decides to explore with her fiancé Mads (Jensen) and best friend Charlotte

(Holland). When they find the eponymous book inside a crypt, it turns out to be a journal written by her grandfather, Rico Mortiz (Holmey), who is really a centuries-old vampire. Discovering the skeleton of a giant bat in a stone sarcophagus, Rebecca reawakens the bloodsucker during an occult ritual, but is finally forced to destroy her undead ancestor with a wooden stake.

✦✧

THE ANGRY BEAVERS:

The Day the World Got Really Screwed Up!

USA, 1998. Dir: Michael R. Gerard and Patty Shinagawa. Voices: Nick Bakay, Richard Horvitz, Tom Kane, Peter Graves, Adrienne Barbeau, William Schallert. Nickelodeon/Gunther-Wahl Productions. Colour.

Children's cartoon TV series (1996-) created by Mitch Schauer about a pair of beavers who usually end up arguing with each other. This hilarious Halloween special is a twenty-three minute sci-fi spoof narrated by Graves in which Daggett (Horvitz) and Norbert (Bakay) go Trick or Treating. They end up at the house of 'B' movie actor Oxnard Montalvo (Kane), where they team up with their he-man hero, his girlfriend Toluca Lake (Barbeau) and Dr Cowtiki (Schallert) to battle Oxnard's manservant Mann Servante (Jonathan Haze, sounding like Lon Chaney Jr), along with his various movie monster props (including a Golem, mummy, werewolf, hunchback and zombie), which are controlled by an evil vampiric alien intelligence (John Byner) from another dimension. Just look at that voice cast!

✦✦✦✧

Guess Who's Stumping to Dinner?

USA, 1997. Dir: Michael R. Gerard and Bobtown Productions. Voices: Nick Bakay, Richard Horvitz, Tom Cane (Tom Kane), Charlie Brissette, Leyla Hoyle. Nickelodeon/Gunther-Wahl Productions. Colour.

In this eleven minute episode, Daggett becomes jealous of Norbert's new friend, a tree stump. They all watch an old black and white horror movie on TV entitled *Curse of the Mummy's Curse*.

✦✦✧

ANIMANIACS:

(aka STEVEN SPIELBERG PRESENTS ANIMANIACS)

Brain Meets Brawn

USA/Japan/South Korea, 1994. Dir: Michael Gerard. Voices: Maurice LaMarche, Rob Paulsen. Warner Bros/ Amblin Entertainment/Fox Kids Network/The WB Network. Colour.

In this segment of the Emmy Award-winning musical cartoon TV series (1993-95, seventy-eight episodes), intelligent laboratory mice Pinky (Paulsen) and The Brain (LaMarche) use Doctor Jekyll's formula to turn the latter into a giant green Mr Hyde monster. Brain then has the strength to stop Big Ben at 4.00pm, thereby creating a permanent English tea-time that will allow them to take over the world. The series was executive produced by Steven Spielberg.

✦✦✦✧

Draculee, Draculaa

USA/Japan, 1993. Dir: Michael Gerard and Byron Vaughns. Voices: Rob Paulsen, Jess Harnell, Tress MacNeille. Warner Bros/Amblin Entertainment/Fox Kids Network/The WB Network. Colour.

In 1930, cartoonists created the Warner Bros, Yakko (Paulsen) and Wakko (Harnell), and their sister Dot (MacNeille). Totally out of control, they were captured and locked away in the studio water tower until they finally escaped. In this episode, the trio end up in Transylvania ('Home of Terror'), where their mad antics drive a green-faced Count Dracula batty. With a guest appearance by the Tasmanian Devil. A 1994 show also included a brief Dracula opening.

✦✦✦

The Girl With the Googily Goop

USA/South Korea/Thailand, 1996 (1997). Voices: Rob Paulsen, Jess Harnell, Tress MacNeille. Warner Bros/ Amblin Entertainment/Fox Kids Network/The WB Network. Colour.

Seven minute werewolf segment, preceded by a song reference to the 'Hunchback of Notre Damey'.

✦✦

Moon Over Minerva

USA/South Korea/Japan/Thailand, 1993. Voices: Rob Paulsen, Jess Harnell, Tress MacNeille. Warner Bros/ Amblin Entertainment/Fox Kids Network/The WB Network. Colour.

Halloween werewolf segment of the comedy cartoon.

✦✦

Phranken-Runt

USA/Japan, 1993. Dir: Michael Gerard. Voices: Rob Paulsen, Jess Harnell, Tress MacNeille, Frank Welker, Sherri Stoner, Nathan Ruegger. Warner Bros/Amblin Entertainment/Fox Kids Network/The WB Network. Colour.

Rita the cat has to prevent a mad female Dr Phrankenstein and her rat creation Mr Squeak from attempting to transplant the brain of Runt the dog into monster-dog Scout. With a guest appearance by the Animaniacs.

Series sequels: ANIMANIACS: I'M MAD (1994) and PINKY AND THE BRAIN (qv; 1995-98)

✦✦

EVELYN ANKERS
[1918-1985]

Chilean-born British leading lady who made her film début in 1933 and moved to Hollywood in 1940. For a decade she was Universal's leading horror heroine in such films as *The Wolf Man* (1941), *The Ghost of Frankenstein* (1942), *Captive Wild Woman* (1943), *The Mad Ghoul* (1943), *Son of Dracula* (1943) and *Jungle Woman* (1944) before she married actor Richard Denning (1914-1998), moved to Hawaii and all but retired from the screen.

ANNA AND ELIZABETH

(Orig: ANNA UND ELISABETH)

Germany, 1933. Dir: Frank Wisbar (Wysbar). With: Dorothea Wieck, Hertha Thiele, Mathias Wieman, Maria Wanck, Carl Ballhaus, Willy Kaiser-Heyl. Kollektiv Film/Terra Film. B&W.

This drama from the director of *Devil Bat's Daughter* (1946), etc apparently involves returning the dead to life.

✦

ANNABEL LEE

USA, 1969. Dir: Ron Morante. Narrator: Vincent Price. Warner Bros. Colour.

Ten minute short based on the Edgar Allan Poe poem, about a dead woman calling her lover back to the grave. Director Morante uses retouched photographs to tell the story, aided by Price's eerily effective narration.

✦✦✦

ANOTHER WORLD

USA, 1996. With: Les Brandt, Nancy Frangione, Anna Kathryn Holbrook, Mark Pinter, Diego Serrano, Paul Michael Valley. Procter & Gamble Productions/NBC-TV. Colour.

In this episode of the daily hour-long TV soap-opera (1964-99), orderly Thomás Rivera (Serrano) is bitten on the neck by a hospital patient claiming to be a vampire.

✦✧

ANYBODY ANYWAY

(aka ANY BODY...ANY WAY/BEHIND LOCKED DOORS)

USA, 1968 (1973). Dir: Charles Romine. With: Joyce Denner, Eve Reeves, Daniel Garth, Ivan Hagar, Irene Lawrence, Andrea Beatrice. SHB/Distribpix/Box Office International. Colour.

When their car runs out of petrol, Anne and Terry (Denner and Reeves) are held captive in a hilltop mansion by mad scientist Mr Bradley (Garth) and his sinister sister Mina, who are experimenting with creating the perfect love-mate. In the end, Bradley's preserved victims apparently return to life and attack him in his burning cellar. This low-budget sexploitation movie was cut by eight minutes in Britain.

✦

A*P*E
(USA: aka ATTACK OF THE GIANT HORNY GORILLA/ HIDEOUS MUTANT)
Korea/USA, 1976. Dir: Paul Leder. With: Rod Arrants, Joanna De Varona, Alex Nicol, Francis Lee (Lee Hoon), Alice Wu, Joseph P. Hill. Lee Ming Film Company/Jack H. Harris/Worldwide Entertainment Corporation. Colour.
Originally titled *The New King Kong* before RKO brought a $1,500,000 lawsuit, the ads warned 'Not to be confused with *King Kong*'. There wasn't much chance of that with this Korean cheapie, originally released in terrible 3-D. A captured thirty-six-foot high ape (a man in a gorilla suit) escapes, battles a giant Great White shark, lays waste to a couple of Korean cities and kidnaps American movie star Marilyn Baker (De Varona) before being killed by Korean and American armed forces. From the father of future director Mimi Leder (*Deep Impact* [1998], etc), who reputedly also worked on this film.
✦

THE APE MAN
(UK: LOCK YOUR DOORS)
USA, 1943. Dir: William Beaudine. With: Bela Lugosi, Louise Currie, Wallace Ford, Henry Hall, Minerva Urecal, Emil Van Horn. Favorite Films/Banner Productions/ Monogram. B&W.
Incredibly, this is probably director William 'One Shot' Beaudine's most coherent movie, filmed under the title *The Gorilla Strikes* and originally set to co-star Amelita Ward (who ended up in Universal's *Jungle Captive* [1945] instead). Hiding out in his basement with the help of his ghost-hunting sister Agatha Brewster (Urecal), missing mad scientist Dr James Brewster (sixty year-old Lugosi in possibly his most thankless role) uses a serum to turn himself into an apeman in this poverty row quickie. He then sends his fake-looking pet gorilla (Van Horn) out to murder young women and uses their spinal fluid to become human again. With Currie and Ford as a pair of likeable reporters, and a recurring comedy relief character (Ralph Littlefield), who at the end reveals that he's the author of the picture! Produced by 'Jungle' Sam Katzman and Jack Dietz, and based on the story 'They Creep in the Dark' by Karl Brown. The following year Lugosi starred in Monogram's *Return of the Ape Man*, which is not a sequel to anything.
✦✧

AQUÍ HUELE A MUERTO...(¡PUES YO NO HE SIDO!)
Spain, 1989. Dir: Álvaro Sáenz de Heredia. With: Martes y Trece (José María Yuste and Millán Salcedo), Paul Naschy (Jacinto Molina), Ana Álvarez, Raúl Fraire, Pilar Alcón. Colour.
Comedy/horror film starring the comic duo Martes and Trece. Naschy turns up as a Comisario who disguises himself as a werewolf.
✦

ARE YOU AFRAID OF THE DARK?:
The Tale of the Dark Dragon
Canada/USA, 1993. Dir: D.J. MacHale and Jacques Payette. With: Chuck Campbell, Cara Pifko, Eleanor Noble, Richard Dumont, Sean Hayes. Campfire Productions/ YTV/Cinar/Nickelodeon. Colour.
Half-hour young adult anthology TV series (1992-96, sixty-five episodes) in which the group of teenagers (Jason Alisharan, Rachel Blanchard, Ross Hull, Nathaniel Moreau, Raine Pare-Coull, Jodie Resther, Daniel De Santo, Joanna Garcia, Jacob Tierney and Codie Wilbee) who make up The Midnight Society tell each other spooky stories around a campfire. In this episode, when crippled high school student Keith Saunders (Campbell) takes Sardo's magic potion to bring out the best in himself, he discovers it releases his darker side as he begins to transform into a monster. This also includes a monstrous bunny.
✦✦

The Tale of the Full Moon
Canada/USA, 1993. Dir: Ron Oliver and Jacques Payette. With: Dominic Zamprogna, Jesse Lauendel, Peter Colvey, Ellen Cohen, Carl Alacchi. Campfire Productions/YTV/ Cinar/Nickelodeon. Colour.
A boy who finds lost pets suspects that a werewolf living in his neighbourhood is dating his mother.
✦✦

The Tale of the Guardian's Curse
Canada/USA, 1994. Dir: D.J. MacHale and Jacques Laberge. With: Danny Cooksey, Martin Doyle, Vanessa King, James W. Carroll, Maha Rouabhia. Campfire Productions/YTV/Cinar/Nickelodeon. Colour.
When a brother and sister discover an ancient serum for eternal life, they accidentally bring an Egyptian mummy back from the dead.
✦✦

The Tale of the Midnight Madness
Canada/USA, 1993. Dir: D.J. MacHale and Jacques Payette. With: Eddie Robinson, Melanie Wiesenthal, Aron Tager, Harry Standjosfski, Chris Hyerdahi. Campfire Productions/YTV/Cinar/Nickelodeon. Colour.
A failing movie theatre is saved by a strange old man and his unusual black and white vampire movie.
✦✦

The Tale of the Nightly Neighbors
Canada/USA, 1992. Dir: Jacques Payette. With: Suzanna Shebib, Noah A. Godfrey, Carl Alacchi, Françoise Robertson, Johnny Morina, Mark Camacho. Campfire Productions/YTV/Cinar/Nickelodeon. Colour.
A young girl is convinced that the new neighbours are vampires.
✦✦

The Tale of the Night Shift
Canada/USA, 1995 (1996). Dir: J.D. MacHale and Jacques Laberge. With: Kathleen Fee, Irene Contogiorgis, Tyrone Benskin, David Siscoe, Richard Azimov, Elisha Cuthbert. Campfire Productions/YTV/Cinar/Nickelodeon. Colour.
Two boys discover that the night shift at a hospital consists of vampires.
✦✦

The Tale of the Twisted Claw
Canada/USA, 1992. Dir: J.D. MacHale and Jacques Payette. With: Maxwell Medeiros, Noah Plener, Ann Page, Linda Smith, Paul Stewart, Gordon Masten. Campfire Productions/YTV/Cinar/Nickelodeon. Colour.
As a Halloween treat, a woman who is rumoured to be a witch gives two boys a vulture's claw that grants wishes in this variation on the story 'The Monkey's Paw' by W.W. Jacobs.
✦✦

SAMUEL Z. ARKOFF
[b 1918]

American producer who co-founded American International Pictures in 1956 with James H. Nicholson. AIP was responsible for such classic drive-in movies as *I Was a Teenage Frankenstein* (1957), *I Was a Teenage Werewolf* (1957) and Roger Corman's colourful Edgar Allan Poe series of the 1960s. After the partnership broke up in 1971, Arkoff went on to executive produce *Blacula* (1972), *Scream Blacula Scream* (1973) and many other films. His autobiography, *Flying Through Hollywood By the Seat of My Pants* (with Richard Trubo), was published in 1992.
qv: *Heartstoppers* (1992); *Runaway Daughters* (1994).

EL ARMA SECRETA
Mexico, 1992. Dir: Sergio Goyri. With: Sergio Goyri, Rafael Inclán, Augustín Bernal, Telly Filippini, Rodolfo Rodriguez, Alfonso Munguia. Goyri & Asociados/Video Producciones de Tijuana/Baja Films. Colour.
Comedian Inclán plays the last living Frankestein (*sic*), who uses a brain and other body parts to create his super-strong Monster (Bernal), complete with neck-bolts. The title of this low-budget, direct-to-video release translates as 'The Secret Weapon'.
✦

ARMY OF DARKNESS
USA, 1992 (1993). Dir: Sam Raimi. With: Bruce Campbell, Embeth Davidtz, Marcus Gilbert, Ian Abercrombie, Richard Grove, Timothy Patrick Quill. Dino De Laurentiis Communications/Renaissance Pictures. Colour.

Actually titled *Bruce Campbell vs. Army of Darkness* on print. In this third *Evil Dead* movie, Ash (in yet another interpretation of the character by co-producer Campbell) is thrown back in time to medieval England, where he sets out on a quest to recover an occult book, the dreaded *Necronomicon*, and ends up defending a castle against an army of the dead (great stop-motion animation and KNB make-up effects). Co-writer/director Raimi plays this episode more for slapstick humour than horror, and the video version features a different (and better) ending from the 1993 release print. With Bridget Fonda, Patricia Tallman and Theodore Raimi, plus directors Harley Cokliss, William Lustig, Bernard Rose and Sam Raimi. Danny Elfman contributed a 'March of the Dead' theme.

✦✦✦✧

ROBERT ARMSTRONG
(Donald Robert Smith) [1890-1973]

Tough-talking American actor, best remembered for his role as producer Carl Denham in both *King Kong* (1933) and *The Son of Kong* (1933).

qv: *Gang Busters* (1942); *The Mad Ghoul* (1943); *Mighty Joe Young* (1949).

THE ARRIVAL

USA, 1990. Dir: David Schmoeller. With: John Saxon, Joseph Culp, Robin Frates, Robert Sampson, Geoff Mansen, Michael J. Pollard. Del Mar Entertainment/ Rapid. Colour.

This predictable science fiction/horror thriller from the creator of the *Puppet Master* series should not be confused with the big budget 1996 movie of the same title. An old man (Sampson) is possessed by an unseen alien from a crashed meteor. It turns him into a vampire serial killer (Culp) who grows younger with each victim. Genre veteran Saxon plays an FBI investigator, there's another oddball cameo by Pollard, and appearances by Schmoeller as a doctor, fellow director Stuart Gordon as a biker and his wife Carolyn Purdy-Gordon as a complaining wino. See *The Hidden* (1987) instead. Music by Richard Band.

✦✧

EL ASESINATO EN LOS ESTUDIOS

Mexico, 1944. With: Fu Manchu (David T. Bamberg). B&W.

One of a series of crime thrillers starring British-born stage magician Bamberg, who took the name Fu Manchu because of the oriental make-up he wore for his stage show. When a murder occurs in a studio where Bamberg is scheduled to make a film, the magician investigates. This also includes scenes of a horror film being shot at the same location involving a Frankenstein-like Monster. The title translates as 'Murder in the Studios'.

✦

JACK ASHER
[1916-1994]

British cinematographer and colour expert, who began his career working for Gainsborough in 1930. He photographed *The Curse of Frankenstein* (1957) and several other seminal Hammer horrors.

qv: *The Brides of Dracula* (1960); *Dracula* (1958); *The Mummy* (1959); *The Revenge of Frankenstein* (1958); *The Two Faces of Dr. Jekyll* (1960).

ASTRO BOY:
Colosso
(Orig: TETSUWAN ATOMA: Franken)

Japan, 1963. Dir: Osamu Tezuka. Voices: Billie Lou Watt, Ray Owens, Gilbert Mack, Peter Fernandez. Mushi Productions/Video Promotions/NBC Films. B&W.

Half-hour syndicated cartoon TV series (1963-66, 104 out of 193 episodes dubbed into English), based on the popular Japanese comic book created by Tezuka and previously adapted as a live-action TV series in 1959-60 (which apparently included an episode featuring the Frankenstein Monster). Set in the year 2003, Dr Boynton/Dr Tenma (Owens) creates the eponymous robotic hero (Watt) shortly after his own son is killed in a car crash. In this episode, a giant robot named Colosso (Franken in the original version) malfunctions and is used by a criminal to rob banks until defeated by Mighty Atom/Astro Boy.

Episode remake: ASTRO BOY: Frankenstein (qv; 1980)

✦✧

ROY ASHTON
[1909-1995]

Australian-born make-up artist who began at Hammer Films by assisting Phil Leakey on *Dracula* (1958) before becoming the studio's chief make-up man from 1959 to 1966, where he created many of the monsters in such films as *The Mummy* (1959), *The Curse of the Werewolf* (1960), *The Two Faces of Dr. Jekyll* (1960), *The Phantom of the Opera* (1962) and *The Plague of the Zombies* (1966). In later years he also created make-ups for such anthology movies as *Tales from the Crypt* (1972), *Vault of Horror* (1973) and *The Monster Club* (1980).

qv: *Asylum* (1972); *The Brides of Dracula* (1960); *The Curse of the Mummy's Tomb* (1964); *Dracula Prince of Darkness* (1965); *Dr. Terror's House of Horrors* (1965); *The Evil of Frankenstein* (1964); *Frankenstein: The True Story* (1973); *The Kiss of the Vampire* (1962); *Legend of the Werewolf* (1974); *The Reptile* (1966); *The Ugly Duckling* (1959).

JOHN ASTIN
[b 1930]

American character actor often associated with weird roles, including Gomez in *The Addams Family* TV series (1964-66) and its various cartoon and live-action spin-offs.

qv: *The Addams Family* (1992-93); *Attack of the Killer Tomatoes: 'Frankenstem'* (1990); *Attack of the Killer Tomatoes: 'Spatula, Prinze of Dorkness'* (1990); *Circle of Fear: 'The Graveyard Shift'* (1973); *Eerie Indiana: 'Mr Chaney'* (1992); *Eerie Indiana: 'Zombies in P.J.S'* (1992); *Gremlins 2 The New Batch* (1990); *Halloween With the Addams Family* (1977); *Killer Tomatoes Eat France!* (1991); *The New Addams Family: 'Grandpapa Addams Comes to Visit'* (1998); *The New Scooby-Doo Movies: 'Scooby-Doo Meets the Addams Family: Wednesday is Missing'* (1972); *Night Life* (1989); *Rod Serling's Night Gallery: 'The Girl with the Hungry Eyes'* (1972); *Runaway Daughters* (1994); *The Silence of the Hams* (1993); *Teen Wolf Too* (1987).

ASTRO BOY:
Frankenstein
(Orig: TETSUWAN ATOM)

Japan, 1980. Dir Osamu Tezuka. Colour.

Remake (1980-81, fifty-two episodes) of the 1963-66 cartoon TV series created by Tezuka, and dubbed into different English versions for the Canadian and Australian markets.

✦

THE ASTRO-ZOMBIES
(aka THE SPACE VAMPIRES/SPACE ZOMBIES)

USA, 1968. Dir: Ted V. Mikels (Theodore Vincent Mikacevich). With: Wendell Corey, John Carradine, Tom Pace, Joan Patrick, Tura Satana, Rafael Campos. Ram Ltd-T.V. Mikels/Jack H. Harris Enterprises/Geneni Film Distributors. Colour.

'See berserk human transplants!' Corey (in one of his last films) plays CIA chief Holman pursuing Mexican-looking foreign agents led by ex-stripper and Russ Meyer star Satana. They are both after Carradine's mad Dr DeMarco who, along with his hunchbacked assistant Franchot (William Bagdad), is using stolen body parts to create an army of Astro-Zombies (actors wearing silly-looking skeleton masks). Carradine spends most of the film explaining to his deformed helper what's happening while his first zombie experiment (Rod Wilmoth), given a psychopath's brain by mistake, is tearing people apart. Made on a minuscule budget and written by Mikels and actor Wayne M. Rogers (Trapper in TV's *M*A*S*H* [1972-85]),

who also co-executive produced.
✦

ANG ASWANG
Philippines, 1932. B&W.
Based on ancient folklore, this was apparently the first Filipino sound movie. The title translates as 'The Vampire'.
✦

ASWANG
Philippines, 1992. Dir: Peque Gallaga and Lore Reyes. With: Alma Moreno, Aiza Seguerra, Aljon Jimenez, John Estrada, Manilyn Reynes, Janice de Belen. Good Harvest/ Regal Films. Colour.
Drama in which the shapeshifting vampire of the title appears as a mysterious young woman (Moreno) who lives on the edge of a forest, an old crone (Lilia Cuntapay) who appears and disappears, and as a large snake.
✦

ASYLUM
(USA: aka HOUSE OF CRAZIES)
UK, 1972. Dir: Roy Ward Baker. With: Peter Cushing, Britt Ekland, Herbert Lom, Patrick Magee, Barry Morse, Barbara Parkins. Amicus/Harbor. Colour.
All-star episodic horror thriller, scripted by Robert Bloch and based on his own short stories. When Dr Martin (Robert Powell) arrives to take up a new post at a remote private asylum, he must first discover the identity of the now-insane head of the institution, Dr Starr. 'Frozen Fear' is fun as Sylvia Syms' neatly wrapped severed limbs take voodoo revenge on her husband Richard Todd and his lover Parkins; Cushing adds dignity to 'The Weird Tailor' (previously adapted in 1961 by Bloch for TV's *Thriller*), trying to bring his dead son back to life with a magic suit; Ekland and Charlotte Rampling share a psychological secret in 'Lucy Comes to Stay'; however, 'Mannikins of Horror' fails to overcome the low budget, as Lom's homicidal homunculi are revealed as clumsy-looking toys filled with human viscera. With a nice shock ending and solid support from James Villiers and Geoffrey Bayldon. Bantam Books published a novelisation by William Johnston.
✦✦✦

AT DAWN THEY SLEEP
USA, 1999. Dir: Brian Paulin. With: Brian Paulin. Morbid Vision Films. Colour.
Ambitious independent film by Massachusetts writer/director/actor Paulin. When angels declare war on the human race, they begin infecting mortal men with a vampire virus until the demon world decides to put an end to their plans.
✦✧

ATOM AGE VAMPIRE
(Orig: SEDDOK L'EREDE DI SATANA. UK: SEDDOK)
Italy, 1960. Dir: Anton Giulio Majano. With: Alberto Lupo, Susanne Loret, Sergio Fantoni, Franca Parisi, Ivo Garrani, Andrea Scotti. Lion's Films/Topaz Film-Corp. B&W.
Despite the title, this is not really a vampire movie but an imitation of Georges Franju's classic *Eyes Without a Face* (1959). When Professor Levin (Lupo) restores the horribly scarred face of car accident victim Jeanette (Loret), he becomes infatuated with the blonde stripper. The doctor then periodically transforms himself (through stop-motion photography!) into a scaly-faced monster and kills women for their glands to keep his patient looking beautiful. Apparently some scenes were filmed in two versions, with more topless nudity for a European release. Richard McNamara directed the English-language version. Many reference works still erroneously credit Mario Bava (instead of Mario Fava) as the producer.
✦✦✧

THE ATOMIC BRAIN
(aka MONSTROSITY)
USA, 1963 (1964). Dir: Joseph (V.) Mascelli. With: Marjorie Eaton, Frank Gerstle, Frank Fowler, Erika (Erica) Peters, Judy Bamber, Lisa Lang. Emerson Film Enterprises/ Cinema Venture. B&W.
Mascelli, the cinematographer of *The Incredibly Strange Creatures Who Stopped Living and Became Mixed-Up Zombies!!?* (1963) and other Ray Dennis Steckler movies, turned director for this low-budget horror film about a mad doctor hired by a wealthy widow to transfer her brain into a younger body. During a test run, the incompetent doctor and his mutant assistant turn two girls into scientific zombies and transplant a cat's brain into a third. The electrical effects were created by Kenneth Strickfaden (*Frankenstein* [1931], etc). Co-starring Xerxes the Cat.
✦

ATTACK OF THE FLESH DEVOURING SPACE WORMS FROM OUTER SPACE
USA, 1998. Dir: Mike A. Martinez. With: David Wood, Barbara Jurgens, George N. Thompson, Brandon Baca, Brian Klapstein, Greg S. Campbell. Scythe Productions. Colour.
Hour-long comedy made on video by a group of teenagers for around $100. The co-writer/director/cinematographer/editor describes it as a parody-satire of Lucio Fulci zombie films.
✦

ATTACK OF THE GIANT LEECHES
(aka ATTACK OF THE GIANT LEACHES/THE GIANT LEECHES. UK: DEMONS OF THE SWAMP)
USA, 1959. Dir: Bernard L. Kowalski. With: Ken Clark, Yvette Vickers, Gene Roth, Jan Shepard, Tyler McVey, Bruno Ve Sota. Balboa/American International Pictures. B&W.
A bunch of swamp dwellers living near Cape Canaveral are menaced by intelligent, bloodthirsty giant leeches (obviously divers in unconvincing rubber suits) in this $70,000 cheapie from executive producer Roger Corman. His brother Gene produced. The title is misspelled on the TV version distributed by Wade Williams.
✦✧

ATTACK OF THE KILLER TOMATOES: Spatula, Prinze of Dorkness
USA, 1990. Voices: John Astin, Chris Guzek, Kath Souci, Neil Ross, Thom Bray, Cam Clark. Fox Kids Network/Four Square Productions/Akom Productions/ Marvel Productions. Colour.
Half-hour children's cartoon TV series (1990-92, twenty-one episodes), based on the *Attack of the Killer Tomatoes* films, about giant mutant tomatoes which can change into human form and want to rule the world. In this episode, using the powers of Dracula, the evil Dr Putrid T. Gangreen (Astin, recreating his movie role) creates a horde of vampire tomatoes. Other episodes include 'Tomato from the Black Lagoon', 'Frankenstem Tomato' and 'Phantomato of the Opera'.
✦✧

ATTACK OF THE MAYAN MUMMY
Mexico/USA, 1957/64. Dir: Jerry Warren (and Rafael López Portillo). With: Nina Knight, Richard Webb, Bruno Ve Sota, George Mitchell, John Burton, Steve Conte. Medallion. B&W.
Producer/director Warren's tedious and confusing reworking of footage from *La Momia Azteca* (1957), the first in Portillo's Aztec Mummy series. Although the screenplay is credited to Gilbert Solar (Gilberto Martinez Solares) and Alfred Salimar (Alfredo Salazar), the static American-shot sequences include excruciatingly long conversations between a sceptical Los Angeles newspaper editor (Ve Sota) and Dr Frederick Munson (Mitchell). Relying on narration, Warren doesn't even bother to dub most of what little remains of the original film (about a reincarnated princess and an archaeological expedition menaced by an ugly 2,000 year-old Aztec [now Mayan] mummy). Terrible!
✦

ATTACK OF THE PUPPET PEOPLE
(aka FANTASTIC PUPPET PEOPLE)
USA, 1958. Dir: Bert I. Gordon. With: John Agar, John

Hoyt, June Kennedy, Michael Mark, Jack Kosslyn, Marlene Willis. American-International Pictures. B&W.
Not quite as bad as you'd expect for a film produced and directed by Gordon, who was also responsible for the original story and special effects. Hoyt plays crazy old doll-maker Mr Franz, who shrinks people down to miniature size and keeps them in glass tubes, only letting them out to have rock 'n' roll parties. Hero Bob Wesley (Agar) takes his date to see Gordon's *The Amazing Colossal Man* (1957) and later beats up a marionette of Dr Jekyll (created by Paul Blaisdell, who also fabricated most of the giant props). The screenplay, by George Worthing Yates, is better than most fifties AIP low budgeters and the special effects are pretty good as well, even if the ending appears somewhat rushed and unconvincing. With Gordon's daughter, Susan.
✦✦

ATTACK OF THE ROBOTS

(Orig: CARTAS BOCA ARRIBA/CARTES SUR TABLE) Spain/France, 1966. Dir: Jess (Jesús) Franco. With: Eddie Constantine, Françoise Brion, Fernando Rey, Alfredo Mayo, Sophie Hardy, Marcelo Arroita Jáuregui. Hesperia Films/ Speva Films/Ciné-Alliance/American International. B&W.
Secret agent Al Peterson/Al Pereira (Constantine) investigates a series of bizarre VIP murders and uncovers a plot by the diabolical Sir Percy (Rey) and Lady Cecilia (Brion) to create an army of zombiefied killers in sunglasses from kidnap victims with a certain blood-type. The director has a cameo as a pianist in a go-go bar. Planned colour sequences were apparently abandoned due to budget problems.
Sequel: LES EBRANLEES (1972)
Remake: VIAJE A BANKOK ATAÚD INCLUIDO (1985)
✦

ATTACK OF THE 60 FOOT CENTERFOLD

USA, 1995. Dir: Fred Olen Ray. With: J.J. North, Tammy Parks, John Lazar, Jay Richardson, Ross Hagen, Michelle Bauer (Michelle McClellan). New Horizons. Colour.
Lame, low-budget comedy in which pin-up model Angel Grace (North) asks a doctor (Lazar) to enhance her breasts with an experimental formula. She subsequently starts growing out of control, and ends up fighting another giant woman (Parks) on Hollywood Boulevard. Along with the cheap-looking effects there are cameos by Russ Tamblyn, Stanley Livingston, Tommy Kirk(!) as a drunken redneck, George Stover, Jim Wynorski and Forrest J Ackerman dressed as Dracula.
✦

LIONEL ATWILL [1885-1946]

'The maddest doctor of them all', British stage actor Atwill went to Hollywood in 1932, where he was usually cast as stocky villains, police inspectors or burgomasters. Known as 'Pinky' by his associates, the actor liked to attend murder trials and drive around Hollywood in a bullet-riddled Rolls Royce. He was memorable as the mad sculptor in *Mystery of the Wax Museum* (1932), the one-armed Inspector Krogh in *Son of Frankenstein* (1939) and as Moriarty in *Sherlock Holmes and the Secret Weapon* (1942). After denying accusations of showing pornographic movies and holding sex orgies at his home, the actor confessed and was sentenced to five years' probation for perjury. Atwill was later absolved of his conviction, but his career never really recovered and he died three years later, leaving behind a young wife and a new son.
qv: *Doctor X* (1932); *Frankenstein Meets the Wolf Man* (1943); *The Ghost of Frankenstein* (1942); *House of Dracula* (1945); *House of Frankenstein* (1944); *Man Made Monster* (1941); *Mark of the Vampire* (1935); *The Vampire Bat* (1933).

Howard Vernon prepares to show another victim why he is called The Awful Dr. Orlof *(1961).*

AUR KAUN

India, 1979. Dir: Tulsi Ramsay and Shyam Ramsay. With: Sachin, Rajni Sharma, Padmini Kapila, Roopesh Kumar, Sudhir, Vimal Sahu. Ramsay Pictures. Colour.

Mona is a woman who returns from the dead to continue her affair with the son of a landowner. The title of this Hindi film translates as 'Who Else?'.

✦

THE AVENGERS:
Never, Never Say Die

UK, 1967. Dir: Robert Day. With: Patrick Macnee, Diana Rigg, Christopher Lee, Jeremy Young, Patricia English, David Kernan. Associated British Corporation Television Films/ITV. Colour.

Sophisticated hour-long TV series (1961-69, 161 episodes) which teamed debonair investigator John Steed (Macnee) with a succession of partners (Ian Hendry, Honor Blackman, Diana Rigg and Linda Thorson). In this episode, when the corpse of a hit-and-run victim gets up and walks out on Steed and Emma Peel (Rigg, in the role originally given to Elizabeth Shepherd), their investigations lead to a top-secret project where robot duplicates created by Professor Frank N. Stone (Lee) are replacing humans.

Series sequel: THE NEW AVENGERS (qv; 1976-77)
Series remake: THE AVENGERS (1998)

✦✦✦

THE AVENGING HAND

UK, 1915. Dir: Charles Calvert. With: Dorothy Bellew, Sydney Vautier, Douglas Payne. Cricks. B&W.

Silent thriller in which a mummy's stolen hand is used to commit murder.

✦

AVENTURA AL CENTRO DE LA TIERRA

Mexico, 1963 (1966). Dir: Alfredo B. Crevenna. With: Kitty De Hoyos, Javier Solis, Columba Dominguez, José Elias Moreno, David Reynoso, Carlos Cortez. Producciones Sotomayor/Columbia. B&W.

This low-budget adventure is inspired by Jules Verne's classic 1864 novel *Journey to the Centre of the Earth*. An expedition discovers a subterranean world where they encounter dinosaurs, a giant spider, a cyclops and a race of hairy vampire bat monster-men with hypnotic powers. Possibly filmed as early as 1957 on location in the Cacahuamilpa caverns, it includes stock footage from *One Million B.C.* (1940), *Unknown Island* (1948) and *La Edad de Piedra* (1962).

Remake: WHERE TIME BEGAN (qv; 1976)

✦✧

THE AWAKENING

UK/Egypt, 1980. Dir: Mike Newell. With: Charlton Heston, Susannah York, Jill Townsend, Stephanie Zimbalist, Patrick Drury, Bruce Myers. Solofilm/Orion Pictures/EMI Films/British Lion. Colour.

Most mummy films are pretty boring, but this is worse than most. Based on Bram Stoker's short novel *The Jewel of Seven Stars* (which was previously filmed by Hammer in 1971 as *Blood from the Mummy's Tomb*, although the producers apparently didn't know about it), Heston stars as obsessed archaeologist Matthew Corbeck, who believes that his daughter Margaret (Zimbalist) is the reincarnation of 3,800 year-old evil Egyptian Queen Kara. In fact, he's right, as she proves by killing off most of the cast in various bloody ways. Despite an impressive budget, Jack Cardiff's beautiful cinematography and unusual Egyptian locations, it took no less than three scriptwriters to cobble this nonsense together. A novelisation was written by R. Chetwynd-Hayes.

Remake: BRAM STOKER'S LEGEND OF THE MUMMY (qv; 1997)

✦✦

THE AWFUL DR. ORLOF

(Orig: GRITOS EN LA NOCHE/L'HORRIBLE DOCTEUR ORLOF. UK: THE DEMON DOCTOR)

Spain/France, 1961 (1962). Dir: Jess Frank (Jesús Franco). With: Howard Vernon (Mario Lippert), Diana Lorys, Conrad Sanmartin (Conrado San Martin), Richard Valley (Ricardo Valle), Mary Silvers (Maria Silver), Perla Cristal. Hispamer/Eurociné/Sigma III. B&W.

Franco's first horror hit (supposedly based on one of his pseudonymous 'David Kuhne' novels) is yet another reworking of *Eyes Without a Face* (1959), as turn-of-the-century mad surgeon Dr Orlof (Vernon) attempts to restore the features of his horribly disfigured daughter Melissa (Lorys) through gory skin grafts. He uses his brother Marius/Morpho (Valley) as a blind zombie slave to kidnap women to use in his experiments. The French print apparently contains more nudity.

Sequel: DR. ORLOFF'S MONSTER (qv; 1964)

✦✦✧

BABES OF WOLFGANG
USA, circa 1992. Star Data. Colour.
Hardcore independent video about a woman with a werewolf husband who sleeps too much. When he wakes up and discovers her having sex with a woman who sells erotic toys, he joins in the action.
✦

BACK FROM HELL
(aka DEMON APOCALYPSE)
USA, 1992. Dir: Matt Jaissle. With: Shawn Scarbrough, Larry DuBois. Kashmir. Colour.
Low-budget deal-with-the-Devil story that also involves a possessed cop, zombies and plenty of gore. Written, produced, directed and photographed by the 'multi-talented' Jaissle, who also composed the music.
✦

BACK TO LIFE AFTER 2000 YEARS
(UK: THE ROMAN'S AWAKENING)
France, 1910. Pathé. B&W.
Thirteen minute silent short in which an ancient Roman is brought back to life to tour modern Rome.
✦

BACK TO THE USSR
(Orig: TAKAISIN RYSSIIN)
Finland, 1992. Dir: Jari Halonen. With: Taisto Reimaluoto, Jorma Tommila, Rose-Marie Precht. Mondo Furioso Filmproductions. Colour.
Low-budget political black comedy about the meeting between a failed drunken worker, Reima, and vampiric communist icon Lenin. The film apparently explores the bloodsucking tendencies between the suicidal Reima's capitalist homeland and his communist ideal.
✦

BAD BLOOD
UK/Romania, 1999. Dir: Tim Fywell. With: Alex Jennings, Lia Williams, Steven Mackintosh, Emilia Fox, Kelly Hunter, Taro J. Sherabayani. Carlton Television/ITV. Colour.
Overwrought TV mini-series scripted by Tony Marchant and shown in three one-hour episodes. Desperate to have a child, infertile British heart surgeon Joe Harker (Jennings) and his wife Nina (Williams) travel to Romania, where they adopt three year-old Valentin (Sherabayani) from his creepy dying Grandmother (Ileana Iordache). This results in Joe apparently being possessed by evil as he contaminates the blood of his patient Renfield (Trevor Martin) and is pursued by ex-priest Stephen Irving (Mackintosh), who believes that Harker is a murderer.
✦✦✧

BAD MOON
Canada/USA, 1996. Dir: Eric Red. With: Mariel Hemingway, Michael Paré, Mason Gamble, Ken Pogue, Hrothgar Mathews, Johanna Marlowe Lebovitz. Morgan Creek Productions/Warner Bros. Colour.
Based on Wayne Smith's novel *Thor*, which is named after the faithful German Shepherd who lives with successful Seattle lawyer Janet (Hemingway) and her ten year-old son Brett (Gamble). When Janet's moody photojournalist brother Ted (Paré) returns from the Nepal jungle and parks his trailer on her property, the clever canine soon suspects that he is the werewolf (created by Steve Johnson and played by stunt co-ordinator Ken Kirzinger) who is terrorising the local community. At just over seventy minutes long, this is a major disappointment from writer/director Red, who co-scripted *Near Dark* (1987). With a clip from *WereWolf of London* (1935) on TV.
✦✧

BADSHAH
(aka BADSHAH DAMPATI)
India, 1954. Dir: Amiya Chakravarty. With: K.N. Singh, Usha Kiron, Pradeep, Agha, Ulhas. B&W.
Hindi version of Victor Hugo's *The Hunchback of Notre Dame*, with Ulhas as the disfigured bellringer who helps a young woman.
Remake: THE HUNCHBACK OF NOTRE-DAME (qv; 1956)
✦

THE BAD SISTER
UK, 1983. Dir: Laura Mulvey and Peter Wollen. With: Dawn Archibald, Isabel Dean, Kevin McNally, Matyelock Gibbs, Hugh Millais, Neil Cunningham. Moving Picture Company/Channel Four Television/Modelmark. Colour.
Made-for-TV movie, shot entirely on video. Archibald plays Jane, a Scottish girl living in London, who sets out on a dream-like journey to discover her secret past and the cause of her mother's mysterious death. Based on a novel by Emma Tennant, this is arty for art's sake. Slow-moving, confusing and pretentious, only the recurring vampire motif holds any interest.
✦

RICK BAKER
[b 1950]

American make-up artist, inspired by *Famous Monsters of Filmland* and Dick Smith. He assisted Smith on *The Exorcist* (1973) and won Academy Awards for his work on *An American Werewolf in London* (1981) and *The Nutty Professor* (1996). He has portrayed numerous apes on the screen, most notably in the ill-conceived remake of *King Kong* (1976).
qv: *Body Bags* (1993); *Ed Wood* (1994); *The Frankenstein File: How Hollywood Made a Monster* (1999); *The Funhouse* (1981); *Gremlins 2 The New Batch* (1990); *Heartstoppers* (1992); *The Howling* (1980); *The Incredible Melting Man* (1978); *Mighty Joe Young* (1998); *Modern Vampires* (1998); *Monster By Moonlight: The Immortal Saga of the Wolf Man* (1999); *Mummy Dearest: A Horror Tradition Unearthed* (1999); *Octaman* (1971); *She's Alive: Creating the Bride of Frankenstein* (1999); *Tanya's Island* (1980); *Thriller* (1983); *Werewolf* (1987); *Werewolf* (1987-88); *Wolf* (1994).

ROY WARD BAKER
[b 1916]

Competent British director, who made films for both Hammer and Amicus. Among his best work are *Quatermass and the Pit* (1967), *The Vampire Lovers* (1970) and *Dr. Jekyll & Sister Hyde* (1971).
qv: *Asylum* (1972); *Flesh and Blood: The Hammer Heritage of Horror* (1994); *The Legend of the 7 Golden Vampires* (1974); *The Monster Club* (1980); *100 Years of Horror: 'Blood-Drinking Beings'* (1996); *100 Years of Horror: 'Dracula and His Disciples'* (1996); *100 Years of Horror: 'Dr. Jekyll and Mr. Hyde'* (1996); *Scars of Dracula* (1970); *Vault of Horror* (1973).

JOHN L. BALDERSTON
[1889-1954]

American screenwriter who began on Broadway adapting Hamilton Deane's British version of *Dracula* in 1927 and had his own success the following year as the co-author of *Berkeley Square* with J.C. Squire. His credits on *Frankenstein* (1931) and *Dracula's Daughter* (1936) are based on unused outlines, but he did script *Dracula* (1931), *The Mummy* (1933) and *Bride of Frankenstein* (1935). In the early 1950s Balderston claimed his conception of Frankenstein's Monster had been unfairly exploited by Universal and successfully sued the studio.
qv: *Dracula* (1982); *Mad Love* (1935).

BANDH DARWAZA
India, 1990. Dir: Tulsi Ramsay and Shyam Ramsay. With: Hashmat Khan, Manjeet Kular, Kunika, Satish Kaul,

Anita Sareen, Vijayendra. Ramsay Films/GVi/Gurpreej Video International. Colour.
Epic two-and-a-half hour Hindi vampire musical with totally inappropriate songs. A group of evil acolytes resurrect a demonic red-eyed vampire (Anirudh Agarwal) so that he can revenge himself on the family that originally destroyed him. The film owes much to the Hammer style, and after a superbly atmospheric opening sequence there are some very effective horror scenes, impressive gore and several martial arts battles. The title translates as 'Closed Door'.
✦✦✦✧

B&W HORROR AND SF TRAILERS #1
USA, circa 1990. Cinemacabre Video. B&W.
Compiled by George Stover, this video collection of trailers includes Universal's *Dracula* (1931) and *Frankenstein* (1931), both containing brief scenes not in the final release prints, and the red-tinted staking sequence from *The Return of Dracula* (1957).
✦✦✧

BANGLOW 666
India, 1990. Priwa International. Colour.
This apparently includes more Indian vampires.
✦✧

THE BARE BREASTED COUNTESS
(Orig: LA COMTESSE NOIRE/LA COMTESSE AUX SEINS NUS/LES AVALEUSES. USA: aka EROTIKILL/THE LOVES OF IRINA)
France/Belgium/Portugal, 1973. Dir: J. (James) P. Johnson (Jesús Franco). With: Lina Romay (Rosa Maria Almirall), Alice Arno (Marie-France Broquet), Jack Taylor (George Brown Randall/Grek Martin), Monica Swinn (Monika Swuine), Luis Barboo, Gilda Arancio. Eurociné/Les Films Marc/Brux International Pictures. Colour.
The Countess Irina Karlstein (Romay) is a mute bisexual vampire who kills her lovers through fellatio. She eventually drowns herself in a bath of blood to be with her telepathic lover Baron Von Rathnoy (Taylor), who she emasculated. Various permutations of this Franco mess exist, ranging from a straight horror film without much sex to a hardcore version. The director also photographed, scripted and edited the film, as well as appearing (under the name 'Jess Franck') as forensic surgeon Dr Roberts who, along with the blind Dr Orloff (French critic Jean-Pierre Bouyxou), discovers the Countess' secret.
✦

BARON BLOOD
(Orig: GLI ORRORI DEL CASTELLO DI NORIMBERGA/ BARON VAMPIRE. USA: aka THE TORTURE CHAMBER OF BARON BLOOD)
Italy/West Germany, 1972. Dir: Mario Bava. With: Joseph Cotten, Elke Sommer, Massimo Girotti, Rada Rassimov (Rosalba Neri/Sarah Bay), Antonio Cantáfora, Humi Raho. Leone International/Cinevision/American International. Colour.
One of the best of Bava's latter-day movies, shot on location in Austria under the title *The Thirst of Baron Blood*. When government historian Eva (Sommer) and last male descendant Peter (Cantáfora) recite a witch's curse, they revive horribly deformed sixteenth century torturer Baron Otto von Kleist. The Baron buys back his own castle at auction and is soon up to his old tricks again until he is dispatched by his victims, reanimated from the dead by a magic amulet. Veteran Cotten plays the Baron mostly in a wheelchair (it is unlikely that he also appears under the scarred make-up), while Rassimov/Bay has a fine cameo as a medium. Scenes of Eva being pursued by the Baron through the foggy streets have a wonderfully atmospheric quality that rate alongside some of Bava's best work. Lamberto Bava was assistant director, and Stelvio Cipriani's score was replaced with one by Les Baxter on some English-language prints. With Alan Collins (Luciano Pigozzi) as yet another creepy caretaker.
✦✦✦

EL BARON BRAKOLA
(aka SANTO CONTRA EL BARON BRAKOLA)
Mexico, 1965. Dir: José Diaz Morales. With: Santo (Rodolfo Guzmán Huerta), Fernando Osés, Andrea Palma, Mercedes Carreno, Antonio de Hud, Susana Robles. Filmica Vergara/Columbia. B&W.
Santo the Mexican wrestler, also known as 'El Enmascarado de Plata' (The Man in the Silver Mask), battles the Dracula-like Baron Brakola (co-writer Osés, looking very much like Bela Lugosi on the poster art) and his vampire brides.
Sequel: LA INVASIÓN DE LOS MARCIANOS (1966)
✦✧

BARRY McKENZIE HOLDS HIS OWN...
UK/France/Australia, 1974 (1975). Dir: Bruce Beresford. With: Barry Crocker, Barry Humphries, Donald Pleasence, Ed Devereaux, Dick Bentley, Frank Windsor. Reg Grundy/EMI Film Distributors. Colour.
The second Barry McKenzie film, based on the cartoon strip in *Private Eye* magazine. Barry (Crocker) and his Australian pals uncover a plot by the sinister Erich Count Plasma (Pleasence) to kidnap the Queen of England so that she can be used to promote the Transylvanian tourist industry. A bad taste comedy, with copious vomiting, a bloody kung fu battle, a vampire staked with a sharpened French loaf and a hunchbacked assistant named Dorothy (Robert Gillespie). Humphries plays the dreadful Edna Everage as well as several other characters, and a number of veteran British comedians (Tommy Trinder, Derek Guyler, Arthur English, Roy Kinnear and John Le Mesurier) are totally wasted. With Clive James, Andrew Lodge, Katya Wyeth and Little Nell.
✦✧

JOHN BARRYMORE (John Blythe) [1882-1942]

Acclaimed American stage and screen actor, the brother of Ethel (1879-1959) and Lionel Barrymore (1878-1954), and father of John Barrymore Jr (b 1932). A popular matinée idol renowned for his 'great profile', he delighted in playing bizarre characters, including the eponymous *Dr. Jekyll and Mr. Hyde* in the 1920 version. Unfortunately, his career ultimately floundered amongst alcoholism and self-parody in films such as *The Invisible Woman* (1941).

RALPH BATES [1940-1991]

Likeable British leading man who Hammer Films unsuccessfully tried to promote as a new horror star in the early 1970s. Despite giving solid performances in a number of films, including *Taste the Blood of Dracula* (1969) and *Dr. Jekyll & Sister Hyde* (1971), his movie career quickly floundered and he moved to TV, where he remained until his untimely death.
qv: *The Horror of Frankenstein* (1970); *Lust for a Vampire* (1970).

BATMAN
(aka AN EVENING WITH BATMAN AND ROBIN)
USA, 1943. Dir: Lambert Hillyer. With: Lewis Wilson, Douglas Croft, J. Carrol Naish, Shirley Patterson, Charles Middleton, Charles C. Wilson. Columbia. B&W.
Frenetic fifteen episode serial with such chapter titles as 'The Electrical Brain', 'The Mark of the Zombies' and 'The Living Corpse', based on the popular comic book character created by Bob Kane. Wilson makes a laconic Bruce Wayne/Batman, but this long serial is spiced up by Naish's outrageous performance as Japanese spy Dr Daka, who is hiding out in a waxworks tour depicting war-time atrocities committed against prisoners of war by 'the slinty eyed Japs' (certain scenes and dialogue referring to the Japanese were cut or re-dubbed for the 1990 reissue on video). With a diabolical machine that turns his victims into radio-controlled zombies, and a pit full of alligators, Daka is after radium to power his death ray. The complete serial was released as a four-hour feature in 1965.
Sequel: BATMAN AND ROBIN (1949)
✦✦✧

BATMAN:
The Penguin's Nest/The Bird's Last Jest
USA, 1966. Dir: Murray Golden. With: Adam West, Burt Ward, Alan Napier, Neil Hamilton, Stafford Repp, Burgess Meredith. Greenway Productions/Twentieth Century-Fox Television/ABC-TV. Colour.
Half-hour cult crime-fighting TV series (1966-68, 120 episodes) based on the DC Comics characters Batman (West) and Robin (Ward). In this two-part episode, the Penguin (Meredith) opens a restaurant so he can forge the signatures of millionaires. With Vito Scotti, and Ted Cassidy as Lurch (from *The Addams Family* [1964-66]) in a brief guest appearance in the window of a building the Dynamic Duo are scaling. West and Ward recreated their characters for a sixteen episode cartoon series in 1977.
Series sequel: BATMAN (1966)
Series remake: THE NEW ADVENTURES OF BATMAN (1977)
✦✦

BATMAN DRACULA
USA, 1964. Dir: Andy Warhol. With: Jack Smith, Naomi Levine, Baby Jane Holzer. Film-maker's Cooperative. B&W.
Smith portrays the Count in this two hour underground film directed by cult favourite Warhol.
✦

BATMAN FIGHTS DRACULA
Philippines, 1967. Dir: Leody M. Diaz. With: Jing Abalos, Dante Rivero, Vivian Lorrain, Ramon D'Salva. Lea/ Fidelis. Colour.
The title probably says it all: Batman (Abalos) fights Dracula (Rivero) in this obscure, low-budget rip-off.
✦

BATMAN: THE ANIMATED SERIES:
Avatar
USA, 1994. Dir: Kevin Altieri. Voices: Kevin Conroy, Bob Hastings, Efrem Zimbalist Jr, David Warner, Helen Slater, Nichelle Nichols. Warner Bros/Fox Kids Network. Colour.
Nicely stylised half-hour cartoon TV series (1992-94, seventy episodes), based on the DC Comics characters. This episode, scripted by Michael Reaves, opens with a prologue set in Egypt in 1898. A scroll stolen in Gotham City leads immortal Middle Eastern sorcerer Ra's al Ghul (Warner) to a lost Egyptian temple where, along with Batman (Conroy) and his estranged daughter Talia (Slater), he encounters 3,000 year-old vampiric zombie queen Thoth-Khepera (Nichols) and her pool of slimy green horrors. Series theme by Danny Elfman.
✦✦✦
Moon of the Wolf
USA, 1992. Dir: Dick Sebast. Voices: Kevin Conroy, Bob Hastings, Robert Costanzo, Efrem Zimbalist Jr, Harry Hamlin, Janet May. Warner Bros/Fox Kids Network. Colour.
This episode is scripted by Len Wein and based on his 1974 *Batman* comic book story. The evil Professor Milo (Treat Williams) creates an illegal steroid derivative that has the side effect of transforming athlete Anthony Romulus (Hamlin) into a powerful werewolf that is forced to battle Batman.
✦✦✦
On Leather Wings
USA, 1992. Dir: Kevin Altieri. Voices: Kevin Conroy, Bob Hastings, Lloyd Bochner, Clive Revill, Marc Singer, Rene Auberjonois. Warner Bros/Fox Kids Network. Colour.
When a bat-like figure attacks a security guard, Batman is blamed and detective Harvey Bullock (Robert Costanzo) heads a task-force to capture the Dark Knight. However, the real culprit is Dr Kirk Langstrom (Singer), who is stealing the chemicals he needs for his experiments with a Jekyll and Hyde-type serum that transforms him into Man-Bat — a half-man, half-bat creature.
Episode sequel: BATMAN: THE ANIMATED SERIES: Terror in the Sky (qv; 1992)
✦✦
Terror in the Sky
USA, 1992. Dir: Boyd Kirkland. Voices: Kevin Conroy, Bob Hastings, Lloyd Bochner, Marc Singer. Warner Bros/Fox Kids Network. Colour.
When Batman suspects that Dr Langstrom (Singer) has used his serum to transform into the monstrous Man-Bat again, he discovers that it is actually Langstrom's wife, Francine, who has accidentally taken the formula as part of one of her father's experiments.
Series sequel: THE ADVENTURES OF BATMAN & ROBIN (1994-95)
✦✦

THE BAT PEOPLE
USA, 1974. Dir: Jerry Jameson. With: Stewart Moss, Marianne McAndrew, Michael Pataki, Paul Carr, Arthur Space, Robert Berk. American International. Colour.
Originally announced as *It's Alive* and *It Lives By Night*. When a biologist (Moss) is bitten by vampire bats, he turns into a briefly seen man-size bat monster created by Stan Winston. A low-key horror movie in which Pataki stands out as a sleazoid cop who blows his own head off when attacked by bats.
✦✧

BATTLE IN HELL
Hong Kong, 1989. Dir: Girgo Fan, Ji Rao Fan and Yen Hua. With: Zhong Xiu-Fang, Bao Ling-Yan, Ji Rao Fan. Colour.
Cantonese film in which two Mongolian sisters commit suicide when their father's army is defeated by the invading Chinese. Centuries later, their spirits are revived as deadly vampires.
✦✧

MARIO BAVA
[1914-1980]

Italian director and cinematographer, and father of Lamberto Bava (b 1944). He entered the industry by assisting his father, former cameraman Eugenio Bava, who was head of the optical effects department at Instuto Luce. Bava became a director of photography in 1939, working alongside G.W. Pabst, Roberto Rossellini and Raoul Walsh before teaming up with Riccardo Freda to make *The Devil's Commandment* (1956), the first Italian horror film since the silent era. He took over the direction when Freda suddenly quit the project, an uncredited role he repeated on several other movies before his 'official' directorial début, *Black Sunday* (1960), which made a star out of Barbara Steele. Boris Karloff played his only movie vampire in Bava's *Black Sabbath* (1963), reportedly the director's own personal favourite film. Unfortunately, most of his movies were extensively re-edited and re-scored for American and British release and he died of a heart attack just days after a medical check-up found him perfectly healthy.
qv: *Baron Blood* (1972); *Hercules in the Haunted World* (1961); *Planet of the Vampires* (1965).

LES BAXTER
[1922-1996]

American composer and jazz musician who worked with Nat King Cole, Mel Tormé and others. As American International Pictures' in-house composer he created the music for Roger Corman's Edgar Allan Poe series and re-scored many of Mario Bava's movies for American release.
qv: *Baron Blood* (1972); *The Beast Within* (1982); *Black Sabbath* (1963); *Black Sunday* (1960); *The Bride and the Beast* (1957); *Cliffhangers: 'The Curse of Dracula'* (1979); *Cry of the Banshee* (1970); *Dracula '79* (1979); *The Ghost in the Invisible Bikini* (1966); *The Loves of Dracula* (1979); *Pharaoh's Curse* (1956); *Tales of Terror* (1962); *Voodoo Island* (1957); *The World of Dracula* (1979).

BAYWATCH NIGHTS:
Night Whispers
USA, 1996. With: David Hasselhoff, Angie Harmon, Donna D'Errico, Eddie Cibrian, Dorian Gregory, Felicity Waterman. The Baywatch Nights Production Company/ Tower 12 Productions/All American Fremantle International/UPN. Colour.

It's probably not Jon Hall inside the monster suit in The Beach Girls and the Monster *(1964).*

Hour-long, 'adult' spin-off (1995-97, forty-four episodes) from the popular *Baywatch* (1989-) TV series that was revised from straight detective plots into a supernatural show during its second and final season. Mitch Buchannon (co-executive producer Hasselhoff) and Ryan McBride (Harmon) run a private investigation agency that becomes involved in various bizarre cases, aided by enigmatic expert on the occult Diamont Teague (Gregory). In this episode, Ryan witnesses the brutal murder of a late-night jogger in a nearby park and convinces Mitch that Francesca Bryce (Waterman), the female suspect being held by the police, is really a modern-day vampire.
✦✧

THE BEACH GIRLS AND THE MONSTER

(aka MONSTER FROM THE SURF)
USA, 1964. Dir: Jon Hall. With: Jon Hall, Sue Casey, Walker Edmiston, Arnold Lessing, Elaine Dupont, Dale Davis. American Academy/US Films. B&W/Colour.
Filmed under the title *Surf Terror*, this laughably inept beach party/ monster movie marked the ignominious return of forties star Hall. He plays oceanographer Otto Lindsay, who likes to dress up as a seaweed-covered gill man and kill bikini-clad teens. As if that wasn't bad enough, the running time is padded out with dancing and surfing (the latter sequences in colour). With music by Frank Sinatra Jr, plus the Watusi dancing girls from Hollywood's famed Whiskey A-Go-Go nightclub.
✦

BEAST CITY

(Orig: INMA DAITOSHI)
Japan, 1996-97. Dir: Shinichi Watanabe. Voices: Ayane Ishizuka, Mizuki Hayama, Yu Keijo. Naomi Hayakawa/ Comstock/Anime 18. Colour.
Direct-to-video, two-part anime release ('Vampire Madonna'/'Beast City') in which three sexy vampire women from the planet Draculon drink the blood of teenage boys.
✦

THE BEASTMASTER

USA, 1982. Dir: Don Coscarelli. With: Marc Singer, Tanya Roberts, Rip Torn, John Amos, Josh Milrad, Rod Loomis. Leisure Investment Company. Colour.
Juvenile sword and sorcery adventure, co-written and directed by twenty-nine year-old Coscarelli (*Phantasm* [1979], etc). It's overlong at nearly two hours, but Singer makes a likeable barbarian hero, Dar, who can talk with the animals. His quest brings him into contact with busty ex-*Charlie's Angels* star Roberts as slave girl Kiri, Torn's evil high priest Maax, zombie guards in bondage gear, a trio of witches, a 'seeing' ring and, best of all, a race of giant vampire creatures (led by Daniel Zormeier). An odd mixture of violence and cuteness. Two sequels followed.
Sequel: BEASTMASTER 2 THROUGH THE PORTAL OF TIME (1991)
✦✦✧

BEASTMASTER THE EYE OF BRAXUS

USA, 1995 (1996). Dir: Gabrielle Beaumont. With: Marc Singer, Tony Todd, Keith Coulouris, Sandra Hess, Lesley-Anne Down, David Warner. MCA Television/Universal. Colour.
Bottom-of-the-barrel syndicated TV movie (called *Beastmaster III: The Eye of Braxus* on the end titles). Dar (Singer, thirteen years after he first played the character) and his animal friends team up with bodyguard Seth (Todd), warrior woman Shada (Hess) and a wise-cracking witch (an embarrassing Down) to battle evil wizard Lord

Agon (Warner, slumming again), who uses his powers to suck the life-force out of others in order to prolong his own existence as he seeks the Key of Braxus (a silly-looking demon created by Chiodo Bros Productions). With Casper van Dien and Patrick Kilpatrick.

✦

THE BEAST MUST DIE
(USA: aka BLACK WEREWOLF)
UK, 1974. Dir: Paul Annett. With: Calvin Lockhart, Peter Cushing, Charles Gray, Anton Diffring, Marlene Clark, Ciaran Madden. Amicus Productions/British Lion. Colour.
Horror whodunit, loosely based on the story 'There Shall Be No Darkness' by James Blish. This begins like a James Bond adventure, but soon settles down as six people trapped in an isolated house are killed off by one of their own number, who also happens to be a werewolf. Big game hunter Tom Newcliffe (Lockhart) wants the creature as a trophy and uses Pavel's (Diffring) sophisticated monitoring devices to track the beast. Among the suspects are Cushing's unconvincing Germanic doctor, horror veteran Gray and Michael Gambon. This includes a thirty second 'werewolf break' in which the audience is invited to guess the identity of the werewolf, as explained in the opening narration by an uncredited Valentine Dyall. Produced by Max J. Rosenberg and Milton Subotsky.

✦✦✧

BEASTS:
What Big Eyes
UK, 1976. Dir: Donald McWhinnie. With: Patrick Magee, Madge Ryan, Michael Kitchen. ATV/ITV. Colour.
Fourth of six hour-long plays, shot on video and written by Nigel Kneale. A strange pet shop owner (Magee) takes delivery of a consignment of Hungarian wolves to prove his theory about werewolves and the origin of the Little Red Riding Hood legend.

✦✧

THE BEAST WITHIN
USA, 1982. Dir: Philippe Mora. With: Ronny Cox, Bibi Besch, Paul Clemens, Don Gordon, R.G. Armstrong, L.Q. Jones. Bernhard-Katzka/United Artists. Colour.
Old-fashioned monster movie, scripted by Tom Holland (*Fright Night* [1985], etc) from the novel by Edward Levy and set in the Deep South. The vengeful spirit of a man chained in a cellar possesses his teenage offspring, Michael MacCleary (Clemens). When the moon rises, the boy sheds his skin and becomes a were-cicada (created by Thomas R. Burman), revenging himself on those who incarcerated his father. Some of the characters are named after those in H.P. Lovecraft's stories. With Logan Ramsey. Music score by Les Baxter.

✦✦✦

WILLIAM BEAUDINE
[1892-1970]

American director who began his career in the silent era as an assistant to D.W. Griffith and worked with such stars as Mary Pickford. Nicknamed 'One Shot' for obvious reasons, he churned out numerous low-budget movies between the 1940s and 1960s, many starring Bela Lugosi, John Carradine or the East Side Kids. He ended his career directing episodes of TV's *The Green Hornet* (1966-67).
qv: *The Ape Man* (1943); *Bela Lugosi Meets a Brooklyn Gorilla* (1952); *Billy the Kid Versus Dracula* (1965); *The Face of Marble* (1946); *Jesse James Meets Frankenstein's Daughter* (1965); *The Living Ghost* (1942); *Voodoo Man* (1944).

BEAUTIFUL NUDE MALIBU CHEERLEADERS
USA, 1997. Dir: Geoffrey de Valois. With: Elaine Juliette Williamson. Digital Entertainment Group/Salt City Home Video. Colour.
Part of a series of softcore *Vampire Raw Footage* videos that includes behind-the-scenes nude and erotic sequences from *The Vampire Conspiracy* (1995). Williamson and a group of Malibu State cheerleaders audition, rehearse and perform their topless routines.

✦

BEAUTY AND THE BEAST
USA, 1961 (1963). Dir: Edward L. Cahn. With: Joyce Taylor, Mark Damon, Eduard Franz, Michael Pate, Merry Anders, Walter Burke. Harvard Film Corporation/United Artists. Colour.
One of veteran director Cahn's last films (he died the same year it was released), this colourful fairy-tale is surprisingly adult in tone. George Bruce and Orville H. Hampton's screenplay ('As suggested by the ancient legend') is set in Italy during the Middle Ages, where young maid Althea (Taylor) travels to a neighbouring duchy. There she discovers that her fiancé Duke Eduardo (Damon) suffers the ancient curse of an entombed sorcerer that transforms him into a werewolf-like beast (make-up created by veteran Jack Pierce and Ernie Young) at each sundown until he can be cured by love. With some nice villainy from Pate and Burke.
Remake: BEAUTY AND THE BEAST (1966)

✦✦✧

BECAUSE THE DAWN
USA, 1988. Dir: Amy Goldstein. With: Edwige Sandy Gray, Gregory St. John. Colour.
Rambling, arty, forty-five minute short about modern New York girl Marie who also happens to be a centuries-old lesbian vampire. Her jaded existence leads her to sing the blues, pose for a photographer, and ride in a mystical horse and carriage through Times Square. Music by Sting (Gordon Sumner).

✦✧

BEDTIME WITH ROSIE
UK, 1974. Dir: Wolf Rilla. With: Una Stubbs, Diana Dors, Johnny Briggs, Margaret Lewis, Ned Lynch, Nicky Henson. FPD. Colour.
Sex comedy that includes a nightmare sequence involving a vampire.

✦

THE BEETLE
UK, 1919. Dir: Alexander Butler. With: Leal Douglas, Fred Morgan, Maudie Dunham. Barker. B&W.
The soul of an Egyptian princess is reincarnated in a beetle and seeks revenge. This silent film is probably based on the 1897 novel by Richard Marsh.

✦

BEETLEBORGS: CURSE OF THE SHADOW BORG
USA/Japan, 1996. Dir: Gabbe Torres and John Putch. With: Wesley Barker, Herbie Baez, Shannon Chandler, Billy Forester, Vivian Smallwood, Kim Delgado. Renaissance-Atlantic Films/Toei Company/Bugboy Productions/Saban Entertainment/Fox Kids Network. Colour.
Video compilation of six episodes from TV's *Big Bad BeetleBorgs* (1996-97) series, featuring three typical young kids Drew (Barker), Roland (Baez) and Jo (Chandler). They are given the power to transform into the eponymous comic book superheroes by the ghostly Flabber (Forester, looking like a blue Jay Leno) who lives in a haunted house along with the Frankenbeans Monster (David H. Fletcher), Count Fangula the vampire (Joe Hackett), Mums the mummy (Blake Torney) and Wolfgang the werewolf (Frank Tahoe, voiced by Scott Page-Pagter).

✦✧

BEETLEBORGS METALLIX
USA/Japan, 1997-98. With: Wesley Barker, Herbie Baez, Brittany Konarzewski, Billy Forester, Vivian Smallwood, Kim Delgado. Saban Entertainment/Renaissance-Atlantic Films/Toei Company/Bugboy Productions/Fox Kids Network. Colour.
This retitled second season (thirty-five episodes) of the children's TV series *Big Bad BeetleBorgs* adds the female Little Ghoul (Lina Godouse) to the line-up of monsters — Mums the mummy (Blake Torney), the Frankenbeans Monster (David Fletcher), Count Fangula the vampire (Joe Hackett) and Wolfgang the werewolf (Frank Tahoe). The evil Crustaceans, Nukus (Christopher Cho) and Horribelle

(Claudine Barros), use the drawings of criminal cartoonist Les Fortunes (Marshal Hilton) to create creatures to battle the new-look BeetleBorgs — Platinum Purple, Titanium Silver and Chromium Gold. Episode titles include 'The Curse of the Mummy's Mommy', 'Son of Frankenbeans', 'Super Fang' and 'Wolfie's Wild Ride'.
✦✧

BEETLEBORGS: METALLIX — THE MOVIE
USA/Japan, 1997 (1998). Dir: Jim Mathers. With: Wesley Barker, Herbie Baez, Brittany Konarzewski, Billy Forester, Channe Nolen, Vivian Smallwood. Saban Entertainment/Renaissance-Atlantic Films/Toei Company/Bugboy Productions/Fox Kids Network. Colour.
Video compilation of episodes ('Crush of the Crustaceans', 'Metallix Rising' and 'Battle Station Alert') from the second season of the *Big Bad BeetleBorgs* TV series. With the Magnavors defeated and sent back to the comic book world forever, Drew (Barker), Roland (Baez) and Jo (Konarzewski) have their superpowers stolen by the evil Nukus (Christopher Cho), Overlord of the Second Dimension. While the children learn how to transform into talking bugs, the horned villain melts Flabber (Forester) and helps cartoonist Les Fortunes (Marshal Hilton) escape from the Charterville Prison for the Criminally Insane.
✦✧

BEETLEBORGS: THE VAMPIRE FILES
USA/Japan, 1997. Dir: Gabbe Torres and John Putch. With: Wesley Barker, Herbie Baez, Shannon Chandler, Billy Forester, Vivian Smallwood, Kim Delgado. Renaissance-Atlantic Films/Toei Company/Bugboy Productions/Saban Entertainment/Fox Kids Network. Colour.
When Prince Vlad the Impaler, Commissioner of Vampires, arrives at Hillhurst and threatens Count Fangula (Joe Hackett) with eternal retirement unless he starts acting like a blood-drinking member of the undead, Flabber (Forester) and the children pretend to be Fangula's victims. This video compilation includes the episode 'Fangula's Last Bite' from TV's *Big Bad BeetleBorgs* (1996-97) series.
✦✦

BEFORE I HANG
USA, 1940. Dir: Nick Grindé. With: Boris Karloff, Evelyn Keyes, Bruce Bennett (Herman Brix), Edward Van Sloan, Ben Taggart, Pedro de Cordoba. Columbia. B&W.
The weakest of Karloff's short series of mad doctor movies for Columbia. This time he's Dr John Garth, convicted of a mercy killing and sentenced to death by hanging. Continuing his experiments in prison, he creates a serum that prevents him from ageing. However, because he uses the blood of a convict, he is transformed into a homicidal maniac. It's an easy role for Karloff, and he turns in the film's best performance, rubbing his rubber-gloved hands together or absently twisting his handkerchief before strangling a victim. There's also good support from Van Sloan as his colleague Dr Howard in this otherwise workmanlike thriller. It was cut by nine minutes when originally released in Britain.
✦✦

BELA LUGOSI MEETS A BROOKLYN GORILLA
(aka THE BOYS FROM BROOKLYN. UK: THE MONSTER MEETS THE GORILLA)
USA, 1952. Dir: William Beaudine. With: Bela Lugosi, Duke Mitchell, Sammy Petrillo, Charlita, Muriel Landers, Ramona the Chimp. Jack Broder Productions/Realart. B&W.
This is actually *worse* than the legendary *Plan 9 from Outer Space* (1958)! Lugosi (who only receives billing in the title) is reunited with director William 'One Shot' Beaudine (following *The Ape Man* [1943]). He plays the sick-looking Dr Zabor, an insanely jealous mad scientist living on a tropical island. When Mitchell and irritating eighteen year-old Petrillo (who look and act exactly like Dean Martin and Jerry Lewis, respectively) crash their plane on the island, Zabor plans to use a serum he has created to turn Sammy into a gorilla (Ray 'Crash' Corrigan, as usual). Associate produced by Herman Cohen, this was filmed in less than two weeks. When producer Hal Wallis threatened to sue over their impersonation of his box office stars, Mitchell and Petrillo's brief movie partnership was over.
✦

BELA LUGOSI SPOTLIGHT
USA, 1999. With: Bela Lugosi, Art Baker, Milton Burle, Mae Questel. VideoSteve. B&W.
Feature-length video compilation covering the actor's career from 1931-58, including thirty uncut trailers, 1950s TV promos for *Shock Theater*, the 1933 short *Hollywood on Parade No.8*, Lugosi's appearance on TV's *You Asked for It* (1953), and various newsreel interviews.
✦✦✦

RALPH BELLAMY
[1904-1991]

American actor who went from playing boring leading men to become an accomplished character actor in his later years.
qv: *The Ghost of Frankenstein* (1942); *Lugosi the Forgotten King* (1985); *100 Years of Horror: 'Bela Lugosi'* (1996); *100 Years of Horror: 'Boris Karloff'* (1996); *100 Years of Horror: 'Frankenstein and Friends'* (1996); *100 Years of Horror: 'Werewolves'* (1996); *The Twilight Zone: 'Monsters!'* (1986); *The Wolf Man* (1941).

LA BELLE CAPTIVE
France, 1983. Dir: Alain Robbe-Grillet. With: Daniel Mesguich, Gabrielle Lazure, Cyrielle Claire, Daniel Emilfork, François Chaumette. Argos. Colour.
Inspired by Rene Magritte's famous painting, from which it takes its title. Lazure stars as Marie-Ange, a mysterious vampire-woman who hires a private detective.
✦✧

LIONEL BELMORE
[1867-1953]

British character actor in Hollywood from the late 1920s. Often cast as portly burgomasters.
qv: *Frankenstein* (1931); *The Ghost of Frankenstein* (1942); *Son of Frankenstein* (1939); *The Vampire Bat* (1933).

JAMES BERNARD
[b 1925]

British film composer, a protégé of Benjamin Britten. He started by composing music for BBC radio plays and began his long association with Hammer Films on *The Quatermass Experiment* (1954). His many memorable scores for the studio include *The Curse of Frankenstein* (1957), *Dracula* (1958), *The Kiss of the Vampire* (1962), *Dracula Prince of Darkness* (1965), *The Plague of the Zombies* (1966), *Frankenstein Created Woman* (1966), *Dracula Has Risen from the Grave* (1968), *Frankenstein Must Be Destroyed* (1969), *Taste the Blood of Dracula* (1969), *Scars of Dracula* (1970), *Frankenstein and the Monster from Hell* (1973) and *The Legend of the 7 Golden Vampires* (1974). His new symphony to accompany *Nosferatu* (1922) was premièred in 1997.
qv: *Flesh and Blood: The Hammer Heritage of Horror* (1994); *Hammer A-Z* (1997); *Hammer the Studio That Dripped Blood!* (1987); *Torture Garden* (1967); *Universal Horror* (1998).

MICHAEL BERRYMAN
[b 1948]

Bizarre-looking, bald-headed American character actor who made his début in *One Flew Over the Cuckoo's Nest* (1975) but is best known for his portrayals of cannibals, mutants and psychopaths. The Rondo Hatton of the 1980s and 1990s.
qv: *Honey, I Shrunk the Kids: 'Honey, Let's Trick or Treat'* (1998); *Love and Curses: 'Bride of the Wolfman'* (1991); *Saturday the 14th Strikes Back* (1988); *Tales from the Crypt: The Reluctant Vampire* (1991); *Teenage Exorcist* (1991); *Weird Science* (1985).

WILLIE BEST
[1916-1962]

Pop-eyed black comedian (also billed as Sleep 'n' Eat) who made a career out of playing frightened manservants.
qv: *The Face of Marble* (1946); *The Ghost Breakers* (1940); *Mummy's Boys* (1936).

¡LAS BESTIAS DEL TERROR!
(aka SANTO CONTRA LAS BESTIAS DEL TERROR)
Mexico/USA, 1972. Dir: Alfredo B. Crevenna. With: Santo (Rodolfo Guzmán Huerta or Eric del Castillo), Elsa Cardenas, El Enmascarado Negro, Victor Junco, Antonio de Hud, Alma Ferrari. Peliculas Latinoamericanas/Azteca Films. Colour.
When yet another mad scientist brings the dead back to life, Santo the silver masked wrestler battles the beasts of terror. Partially filmed in Florida.
Sequel: SANTO CONTRA LA MAGIA NEGRA (qv; 1972)
✦

LA BESTIA Y LA ESPADA MÁGICA
(aka OOKAMI-OTOKO TO SAMURAI)
Spain/Japan, 1983. Dir: Jacinto Molina. With: Paul Naschy (Jacinto Molina), Shigeru Amachi, Beatríz Escudero, Junko Asahina, Violeta Cela, Yoko Fuji. Acònito Films/Amachi/Cinema International Corporation. Colour.
This tenth outing for Waldemar Daninsky (Naschy) features El Hombre Lobo in sixteenth century Japan. After a holy man unsuccessfully tries to lift his curse, Daninsky goes on a murderous rampage until the woman he loves kills him with a silver sword. It includes a sequence in which the werewolf wrestles a tiger. Produced, written and directed by Naschy under his real name, this was filmed as *La Bestia y los Samurais*.
Sequel: LICANTROPO EL ASESINO DE LA LUNA LLENA (qv; 1996)
✦✧

MARTINE BESWICKE
[b 1941]

Exotic-looking sixties Bond girl (*From Russia With Love* [1963]; *Thunderball* [1965]) and Hammer starlet, also known as Martine Beswick. She made a sexy female Jack the Ripper in *Dr. Jekyll & Sister Hyde* (1971), but her career took a dive after she moved to America.
qv: *Flesh and Blood: The Hammer Heritage of Horror* (1994); *The Offspring* (1986); *100 Years of Horror: 'Dinosaurs'* (1996); *100 Years of Horror: 'Dr. Jekyll And Mr. Hyde'* (1996); *Trancers II* (1990).

BETTY BOOP, M.D.
USA, 1932. Dir: Dave Fleischer. Voices: Mae Questel. Fleischer/Paramount. B&W.
Six minute cartoon in which Betty Boop's elixir 'Jippo' has various effects on those who drink it, including turning one man into Fredric March's Mr Hyde. Produced by Max Fleischer.
Sequel: BETTY BOOP'S BAMBOO ISLE (1932)
✦✦

BETTY BOOP'S MUSEUM
USA, 1932. Dir: Dave Fleischer. Voices: Mae Questel. Fleischer/Paramount. B&W.
Five minute cartoon set in a museum that contains animal skeletons, a spooky portrait and a 1,000 year-old mummy that comes to life. Produced by Max Fleischer.
Sequel: BETTY BOOP'S KER-CHOO (1932)
✦✦

BETTY BOOP'S PENTHOUSE
USA, 1933. Dir: Dave Fleischer. Voices: Mae Questel, Jack Mercer. Fleischer/Paramount. B&W.
Six minute cartoon in which Betty is menaced by a Frankenstein-like monster. When she sprays him with her perfume, the creature is transformed into a dancing flower! Produced by Max Fleischer. This was hand-coloured in Korea for TV's *The Betty Boop Show* (1971) and included in the 1970s compilation feature *The Betty Boop Follies*.
Sequel: SNOW WHITE (1933)
✦✦✧

BILLY BEVAN
(William Bevan Harris) [1887-1957]

Australian-born comedian who arrived in Hollywood during the 1920s and became one of Mack Sennett's troupe. He often appeared in small roles as jocular policemen, barkeeps or air-raid wardens.
qv: *Dracula's Daughter* (1936); *Dr. Jekyll and Mr. Hyde* (1941); *The Man Who Wouldn't Die* (1942); *The Return of the Vampire* (1943).

BEVERLY HILLS BODY$NATCHERS
USA, 1989 (1990). Dir: Jon Mostow. With: Vic Tayback, Frank Gorshin, Rodney Eastman, Warren Selko, Art Metrano, Seth Jaffe. Busybody Productions/Hess-Kallberg Associates/McGuffin Productions/Shapiro Glickenhaus Entertainment. Colour.
Teen comedy in which brothers Freddie and Vincent (Eastman and Selko) start work in the Mafia-run Greener Pastures Funeral Home and discover that a greedy mortician (Tayback) and a crazy doctor (Gorshin) have invented a serum for bringing the dead back to life for profit. It's not nearly as funny as it should be.
✦✧

BEVERLY HILLS VAMP
USA, 1988. Dir: Fred Olen Ray. With: Britt Ekland, Eddie Deezen, Tim Conway Jr, Jay Richardson, Michelle Bauer (Michelle McClellan), Robert Quarry. Austin Enterprises/American-Independent. Colour.
Awful, low-budget horror comedy from prolific co-producer/director Ray. A trio of nerdy would-be film-makers arrive in Hollywood and visit a Beverly Hills bordello run by vampire Madam Cassandra (Ekland) and her three undead hookers. It's just another excuse for the director to include a succession of naked breasts. Deezen's impersonation of Jerry Lewis continues to be as irritating as the original, while guest star Quarry (playing a priest in a wheelchair) is a long way from the relative sophistication of the *Count Yorga* films.
✦

BEWITCHED
USA, 1945. Dir: Arch Oboler. With: Phyllis Thaxter, Edmund Gwenn, Henry H. Daniels Jr, Horace (Stephen) McNally, Minor Watson, Addison Richards. Loew's Incorporated/Metro-Goldwyn-Mayer. B&W.
Based on Oboler's radio play 'Alter Ego'. This bizarre stylised thriller stars Thaxter as Joan Ellis, a woman with a dual personality whose evil side (voiced by Audrey Totter) forces her to kill. During the climax, Joan is hypnotised and the two personalities confront each other!
✦✧

BEWITCHED
(Orig: GU)
Hong Kong/Thailand, 1981. Dir: Kuei Chih-Hung (Kwei Chi-Hung/Gui Zhihong/Zi Hong). With: Wang Chin Sang, Ai Fei, Lily Chan (Chen Lili), Fanny (Fen Ni), Melvin Wong (Kam Sun). Shaw Brothers. Colour.
A man (Fei) from Hong Kong visiting Thailand falls under the spell of a young witch (Chan) and every full moon is forced to kill until his own daughter becomes a victim. A police inspector (Wong) investigating the case also falls under the woman's charm and calls in an exorcist to combat the evil.
Sequel: MO (1983)
✦✧

BEWITCHED AREA OF 1000 YEARS
Hong Kong, 1991. World Video. Colour.

When Shu Mei's possessed father bites her, she is transformed into a vampiric were-snake.
✦

TURHAN BEY
(Turhan Selahattin Sahultavey Bey) [b 1920]

Austrian-born Turkish actor. He quickly established himself as an exotically handsome leading man in Hollywood while many established stars were away serving in World War Two. He later became a freelance photographer for soft-porn magazines and moved back to Vienna, only returning to acting in the mid-1990s.
qv: *Captive Wild Woman* (1943); *The Climax* (1944); *The Mad Ghoul* (1943); *The Mummy's Tomb* (1942); *Murder, She Wrote* (1995); *100 Years of Horror: 'Boris Karloff'* (1996); *100 Years of Horror: 'Mad Doctors'* (1996); *100 Years of Horror: 'Mummies'* (1996); *100 Years of Horror: 'Phantoms'* (1996); *100 Years of Horror: 'Zombies'* (1996); *Universal Horror* (1998).

THE BEYOND
(Orig: ...E TU VIVRAI NEL TERRORE! L'ALDILA. USA: aka 7 DOORS OF DEATH)
Italy/USA, 1981. Dir: Lucio Fulci. With: Katherine (Catriona) MacColl, David Warbeck, Sarah Keller, Antoine Saint John, Veronica Lazar, Al Cliver (Pier Luigi Conti). Fabrizio de Angelis/Fulvia Film/Aquarius Productions. Colour.
Director Fulci combines Lovecraftian concepts (*The Book of Eibon*) with elements from *The Sentinel* (1976) to create another incoherent narrative as the dead return to life when one of the seven gateways to Hell is opened during the renovation of an old Louisiana hotel. Although the pre-credits sequence is promising, the film soon falls apart due to abrupt gaps in the plot and a lack of logic. Warbeck makes an unconvincing doctor, and a few atmospheric sequences are lost amongst the banal dialogue, poor dubbing and out-of-focus photography. Watch for the hospital sign that reads 'Do Not Entry'! When originally released in America in 1983, ten minutes were cut and Fulci was credited as 'Louis Fuller'. A comic strip version was published in the 1990s by Blackest Heart Media, which included a CD of the score.
✦✧

BEYOND REALITY:
The Passion
Canada/USA, 1993. Dir: Bruce Pittman. With: Shari Belafonte, Carl Marotte, Leon Pownall, Nikki de Boer, Sam Malkin. Paragon Entertainment/Glen Warren Productions/Four Point Entertainment/USA Network. Colour.
Half-hour TV series (1991-93, forty-four episodes) created by Richard Manning and Hans Beimler, in which para-psychologist Dr Laura Wingate (Belafonte) and Professor J.J. Stillman (Marotte) originally investigated supposedly actual cases of the paranormal. However, in this episode from the fictionalised third season, a mysterious stranger reveals to Stillman how his great grandfather, J. Baker MD (also played by Marotte), helped destroy a vampiric Jack the Ripper and his beautiful victim in 1888 London. Written by Marc Scott Zicree.
✦✦✧

BEYOND TERROR
(Orig: MÁS ALLA DEL TERROR)
Spain, 1979. Dir: Thomas Aznar. With: Francisco Sanchez Grajera, Raquel Ramirez, Emilio Siegrist, Antonio Siegrist, Antonio Jabalera, Alexia Loreto, David Forrest. Cinevision. Colour.
Teenage drug-addicted murderers are attacked by ghosts and mouldering zombies seeking revenge in an old monastery.
✦✧

BIG BAD BEETLEBORGS
USA/Japan, 1996-97. With: Wesley Barker, Herbie Baez, Shannon Chandler, Brittany Konarzewski, Billy Forester, Vivian Smallwood. Renaissance-Atlantic Films/Toei Company/Bugboy Productions/Saban Entertainment/Fox Kids Network. Colour.
Half-hour children's superhero TV series (fifty-two episodes). While visiting the haunted Hillhurst House, three typical average young kids Drew (Barker), Roland (Baez) and Jo (Chandler/Konarzewski) free the ghostly Flabber (Forester) who gives them the power to transform into their favourite comic book superheroes, the BeetleBorgs. Along with the Frankenbeans Monster (David H. Fletcher), Count Fangula the vampire (Joe Hackett), Mums the mummy (Blake Torney) and Wolfgang the werewolf (Frank Tahoe, voiced by Scott Page-Pagter), they battle evil villains Vexor (Rick Tane, voiced by Joey Pal), Jara (Balinda English), Noxic (Michi Yahato/Lee Whey) and Typhus (Kyle Jordan) and their bizarre Magnavors, who are also released from the comics.
✦✧

Fangs Over Charterville
USA/Japan, 1996. Dir: Bob Allen. With: Wesley Barker, Herbie Baez, Shannon Chandler, Billy Forester, Vivian Smallwood, Kim Delgado. Renaissance-Atlantic Films/Toei Company/Bugboy Productions/Saban Entertainment/Fox Kids Network. Colour.
In this episode, local bullies Van (Patrick Seaborn) and Trip (Todd Hurst) are transformed by Count Fangula into vampires until a kiss changes them back.
✦✧

She Wolf
USA/Japan, 1997. Dir: Brian Thomas Jones. With: Billy Forester, Wesley Barker, Herbie Baez, Brittany Konarzewski, Channe Nolen, Vivian Smallwood. Renaissance-Atlantic Films/Toei Company/Bugboy Productions/Saban Entertainment/Fox Kids Network. Colour.
When Wolfgang bites villainess Jara during the full moon, she is transformed into a she-wolf.
✦✧

Something Fishy
USA/Japan, 1997. Dir: Worth Keeter. With: Wesley Barker, Herbie Baez, Brittany Konarzewski, Billy Forester, Channe Nolen, Vivian Smallwood. Renaissance-Atlantic Films/Toei Company/Bugboy Productions/Saban Entertainment/Fox Kids Network. Colour.
Drew, Roland and Jo find they cannot convince even friendly ghost Flabber or the monsters that Charterville Charlie — a green-scaled gill man with smelly breath (voiced by Dave Hallow) — has emerged from the local lake. Other episode titles include 'Never Cry Werewolf', 'The Hunchback of Hillhurst', 'Bye, Bye Frankie', 'Operation Frankenbeans', 'The Curse of Mums' Tomb', 'Bride of Frankenbeans' and 'Norman Nussebaum: Vampire Hunter'.
Series sequel: BEETLEBORGS METALLIX (qv; 1997-98)
✦✧

THE BIG EASY:
Vamps Like Us
USA, 1997. Dir: Vern Gillum. With: Tony Crane, Susan Walters, Barry Corbin, Eric George, Faber Dewar, Fabiana Udenio. ITC Distribution/Grosso-Jacobson Productions/PolyGram/USA Network. Colour.
Hour-long TV series (1996-97) based on the 1987 movie of the same title, created by co-executive producer Daniel Petrie Jr. Laconic homicide detective Remy McSwain (Crane) and assistant District Attorney Anne Osborne (Walters) investigate crime in a steamy New Orleans. In this episode, when a writer of books about the occult is found dead and drained of blood in a local cemetery, Remy and Anne encounter the Goth members of a self-styled vampire cult and a very human murderer.
✦✦

BIGFOOT AND WILDBOY:
The Eye of the Mummy
USA, 1979. Dir: Leslie H. Martinson. With: Ray Young, Joseph Butcher, Yvonne Regaldo, Al Wyatt Jr, John Harding, Bob Hoy. Sid and Marty Krofft/ABC-TV. Colour.
Half-hour, live action spin-off (1977-79, twenty episodes) from *The*

Krofft Supershow (1976-77) about a legendary missing link creature (Young) and the abandoned boy (Butcher) he raised in the wilderness of the Pacific Northwest. In this episode, mad scientist Dr Zorkin reanimates a powerful mummy using a ruby embedded in its forehead.
✦✧

Return of the Vampire

USA, 1979. With: Ray Young, Joseph Butcher, Yvonne Regaldo, Al Wyatt Jr, Deborah Ryan. Sid and Marty Krofft/ABC-TV. Colour.

Bigfoot, Wildboy and forest ranger's daughter Cindy (Regaldo) encounter a vampire Countess (Ryan) who is accidentally freed by two treasure hunters.
✦✧

BIG MAN ON CAMPUS

(aka THE HUNCHBACK OF UCLA. UK: THE HUNCHBACK HAIRBALL OF L.A.)

USA, 1989. Dir: Jeremy Kagan. With: Allan Katz, Corey Parker, Cindy Williams, Melora Hardin, Jessica Harper, Tom Skerritt. Vestron Pictures. Colour.

Likeable teen comedy in which ugly lovesick hunchback Bob (scriptwriter Katz) is discovered living in a University clock tower and is entrusted to the care of students Cathy (Hardin) and Alex (Parker), sympathetic psychologist Dr Richard Webster (Skerritt) and speech therapist Dr Diane Girard (Williams). With Gerrit Graham and Armin Shimerman. Produced by Arnon Milchan.
✦✦✧

BIG MEAT EATER

Canada, 1982 (1984). Dir: Chris Windsor. With: George Dawson, Big Miller, Andrew Gillies, Stephen Dimopoulous, Georgina Hegedos, Ida Carnevali. BCD Entertainment Corporation/New Line. Colour.

Low-budget comedy/horror/musical set in the small town of Burquitlam during the 1950s. A pair of aliens in a flying saucer resurrect murdered Mayor Carmine Rigatoni (Howard Taylor) from the dead so that they can tap into the radioactive gasses created by the septic tank in Bob Sanderson's (Dawson) butcher's shop. The zombie mayor replaces his severed hand with a kitchen whisk while cast members launch into incongruous song and dance numbers for no apparent reason. With Canadian jazz musician Miller as Abdullah, the massive meat eater and murderer.
✦✧

BIG WOLF ON CAMPUS

Canada, 1999. With: Brandon Quinn, Danny Smith, Rachelle LeFevre, Natalie Vander, Dom Di Roser, Rob De Leeuw. Telescene/Fox Family Channel. Colour.

Half-hour (twenty-two episodes) TV sitcom, created by Peter Knight and Christopher Briggs, about Pleasantville High School senior Tommy Dawkins (Quinn) who is bitten by a wolf while on a camping trip and transforms into a pointy-eared lycanthrope during extreme situations. Along with his geeky Goth friend Merton Dingle (Smith) he attempts to keep his new life secret from his girlfriend Stacey (LeFevre) and his parents (Jane Wheeler and Alan Fawcett). Anybody remember *Teen Wolf* (1985)?
✦✧

BIKINI BEACH

USA, 1964. Dir: William Asher. With: Frankie Avalon, Annette Funicello, Martha Hyer, Don Rickles, Harvey Lembeck, John Ashley. American International Pictures. Colour.

The third in AIP's successful Beach Party series. When Dee Dee (Funicello) falls for The Potatoe Bug (Avalon), Frankie (also Avalon) challenges the British pop star to a drag race. The supporting cast includes series regulars Candy Johnson and Jody McCrea, Keenan Wynn and his intelligent ape Clyde (Janos Prohaska), Timothy Carey as the psychopathic South Dakota Slim, Little Stevie Wonder, The Pyramids, The Exciters Band, and a cameo by Boris Karloff as the Art Dealer. With *Famous Monsters of Filmland* competition winner Val Warren as a briefly-seen teenage werewolf monster in a pool hall.

Sequel: PAJAMA PARTY (1964)
✦✦

DAS BILDNIS DER DORIAN GRAY

(aka DIE MARQUISE DE SADE)

West Germany/Switzerland/Portugal, 1976. Dir: Jess (Jesús) Franco. With: Lina Romay (Rosa Maria Almirall), Monica Swinn (Monika Swuine), Ramón Ardid, Martine Stedil, Peggy Markoff, Ronald Weiss. Elite-Film/Avis Film. Colour.

There's not much of Oscar Wilde's story left in this typical Franco mess, apparently available in both hardcore and softcore versions. Following a visit by an American journalist (Swinn), the reclusive Doriana Gray (Romay) discovers that she is some kind of sex vampire, telepathically connected to her twin sister (also Romay) hidden away in a psychiatric hospital run by the mysterious Dr Orloff. This was apparently sold under the export titles *Dirty Dracula* and *Ejaculations*.
✦

BILLY THE KID AND THE GREEN BAIZE VAMPIRE

UK, 1985. Dir: Alan Clarke. With: Phil Daniels, Alun Armstrong, Bruce Payne, Louise Gold, Eve Ferret, Richard Ridings. ITC Entertainment/Zenith Productions. Colour.

Borderline fantasy/musical about snooker! Daniels plays dislikeable working class hero Billy Kidd who challenges middle class world champion Maxwell Randall (Armstrong) — who likes to live and dress as a vampire for no apparent reason — to a final, deciding match. The songs are terrible, the characters unsympathetic and the direction reflects all the worse excesses of music videos. Even the climactic revelation that Randall possesses real supernatural powers can't save this from being a disaster. With Don Henderson, Zoot Money and Caroline Quentin.
✦

BILLY THE KID MEETS THE VAMPIRES

USA, 1991. Dir: Steve J. Postal. With: Michael K. Saunders, Jeff Michaels, Angela Shepard, Linda R. Wasserman, Sonia Sutton, Maurice S. Postal. Steve Postal Productions. Colour.

Sixth in the low-budget horror/comedy series from independent Florida *auteur* Postal who, as usual, photographed, directed, co-edited, co-executive produced and co-scripted! The extra-terrestrial ghost of Billy the Kid (Saunders) returns from the vampire planet Sirius II to vacation in the haunted honeymoon cottage belonging to peeping-tom monster-landlord B.J. Smith (Maurice Postal). Smith, who bought the house from Dracula, sends five beautiful bloodthirsty vampire bitches to bug Billy. You probably think I'm making this up...

Sequel: THE CURSE OF THE HOUSE SURGEON (qv; 1991)
✦

BILLY THE KID VERSUS DRACULA

USA, 1965. Dir: William Beaudine. With: John Carradine, Chuck Courtney, Melinda Plowman, Virginia Christine, Walter Janowitz, Bing Russell. Embassy Pictures/Circle Productions. Colour.

Classic grade 'Z' horror/Western has fifty-nine year-old Carradine recreating his Dracula role in the movies for the first time since *House of Dracula* (1945). Actually, it's better than expected. Veteran director William 'One Shot' Beaudine (making his penultimate film) does his best with a weak script, using clever lighting effects to add extra menace to Carradine's smooth-talking, top-hatted vampire (who happily walks around in broad daylight!). The Count poses as the uncle of ranch owner Betty Bentley (Plowman) until dispatched by her foreman (Courtney), who turns out to be reformed outlaw Billy the Kid. Although the production values are bottom-of-the-barrel (including a particularly fake-looking bat), this is worth watching for Carradine's remarkable, over-the-top performance and such old-time Western performers as Virginia Christine, Harry Carey Jr and Roy Barcroft. Not released in Britain until 1974.
✦✧

BINBINING TSUPER-MAN

Philippines, circa 1985. Dir: Ben Feleo. With: Miguel Rodriguez, Panchito, Babalu, Jaime Fabregas, Rose Ann Gonzales. Shining Star. Colour.

Comedy in which an alien revives a cemetery full of zombies who can turn into bats and cats to battle the eponymous superhero.
✦

BIOGRAPHY:
Bela Lugosi Hollywood's Dark Prince
USA, 1995 Dir: Kevin Burns. With: Bela Lugosi Jr, Ray Walston, Martin Landau, Ronald V. Borst, Forrest J Ackerman, Robert Wise. Twentieth Century Fox/Van Ness Films/Twentieth Television/A&E Network. Colour/B&W.
Excellent hour-long documentary, written by David J. Skal, that looks at the life and career of the actor whose name became synonymous with Dracula. With many rare photographs, clips and trailers from such movies as *The Ape Man* (1943), *The Body Snatcher* (1945), *Bride of the Monster* (1954), *Chandu the Magician* (1932), *Dracula* (1931), *Frankenstein Meets the Wolf Man* (1943), *Glen or Glenda* (1953), *Hollywood on Parade No.8* (1933), *The Invisible Ray* (1936), *Mark of the Vampire* (1935), (Abbott and Costello) *Meet Frankenstein* (1948), *The Midnight Girl* (1925), *Murders in the Rue Morgue* (1932), *Plan 9 from Outer Space* (1958), *Renegades* (1930), *The Return of the Vampire* (1943), *The Silent Command* (1923), *Son of Frankenstein* (1939), *White Zombie* (1932) and *Wild Company* (1930), plus *Intimate Interviews* (1932) with Dorothy West, TV's *You Asked for It* (1953), rare newsreel footage and colour home movies. Interviewees include Lugosi's friend Dick Sheffield. Narrated by Richard Kiley and hosted by Peter Graves.
✦✦✦✦

Boris Karloff the Gentle Monster
USA, 1995. Dir: Kevin Burns. With: Sara Karloff, Ronald V. Borst, Bela Lugosi Jr, Roddy McDowall, Forrest J Ackerman, Robert Wise. Twentieth Century Fox/ Van Ness Films/Twentieth Television/A&E Network. Colour/B&W.
Another excellent hour-long documentary, written and co-produced by David J. Skal, that looks at the life and career of Boris Karloff, with many rare photographs, clips and trailers from *The Bells* (1926), *Black Sabbath* (1963), *The Body Snatcher* (1945), *Bride of Frankenstein* (1935), *Business and Pleasure* (1931), *The Cabinet of Dr. Caligari* (1919), *The Climax* (1944), *The Comedy of Terrors* (1963), *Dracula* (1931), *Frankenstein* (1931), *Frankenstein 1970* (1958), *The Ghoul* (1933), *His Majesty the American* (1919), *House of Frankenstein* (1944), *House of Rothschild* (1934), *The Invisible Ray* (1936), *The Mummy* (1933), *Night Key* (1937), *The Raven* (1963), *Sharp Shooters* (1928), *Son of Frankenstein* (1939), *Targets* (1967), such TV shows as *The Entertainers* (1965) with Karloff and Carol Burnett, *Heart of Darkness* (1958) featuring Karloff and McDowall, *The Lux Show Starring Rosemary Clooney* (1957), *This is Your Life* (1958), *Thriller* (1960-62) and a Ronson Comet lighter commercial, plus colour home movie footage (including candid behind-the-scenes shots of the actor as the Monster in *Son of Frankenstein*). Other interviewees include his friend and biographer Cynthia Lindsay, co-star Anna Lee, Carol Burnett, his agent and friend Arthur Kennard and Peter Bogdanovich. Narrated by Peter Graves and hosted by Jack Perkins.
✦✦✦✦✧

Lon Chaney Son of a Thousand Faces
USA, 1995. Dir: Kevin Burns. With: Bob Kokai, Ron Chaney, Ronald V. Borst, Forrest J Ackerman, Carla Laemmle, Sara Karloff. Twentieth Century Fox/ Van Ness Films/Twentieth Television/A&E Network. Colour/B&W.
An excellent hour-long look at the life and career of Chaney Jr, written by David J. Skal. With clips from several Lon Chaney Sr films, plus *Of Mice and Men* (1939), *Witchcraft* (1964), and TV's *Route 66*: 'Lizard's Leg and Owlet's Wing' (1962) and *Tales of Tomorrow*: 'Frankenstein' (1952), and trailers for *The Alligator People* (1959), *Dracula vs. Frankenstein* (1970), *Frankenstein Meets the Wolf Man* (1943), *The Ghost of Frankenstein* (1942), *House of Frankenstein* (1944), *Man of a Thousand Faces* (1957), (Abbott and Costello) *Meet Frankenstein* (1948), *The Mummy's Tomb* (1942), *Son of Dracula* (1943) and *The Wolf Man* (1941). This also includes interviews with biographer Kokai, grandson Ron Chaney, and actresses Elena Verdugo, Patricia Morison and Beverly Garland, among others. Introduced by Peter Graves and narrated by Richard Kiley.
✦✦✦✦

PAUL BIRCH
[1912-1969]

Stocky American character actor who, as the vampiric alien Mr Johnson, apparently didn't endear himself to the cast and crew of *Not of This Earth* (1957).

DER BISS
West Germany/USA, 1985. Dir: Marianne Enzenberger. With: Marianne Enzenberger, Marianne Rosenberg, Rosa von Praunheim, Ulrike Buschbauer. Marianne Enzenberger. Colour.
When a Berlin woman is bitten in New York by a Greenwich Village vampire, she flies back to Germany as one of the undead. The title translates as 'The Bite'.
✦

WHIT BISSELL
(Whitner Bissell) [1914-1996]

Dependable, although somewhat stuffy American character actor who often turned up as a scientist (either the mad or sane variety) and other authority figures in movies. On TV he played General Heywood Kirk in *Time Tunnel* (1966-67).
qv: *Creature from the Black Lagoon* (1954); *A Double Life* (1947); *I Was a Teenage Frankenstein* (1957); *I Was a Teenage Werewolf* (1957); *The Man from U.N.C.L.E.: 'The Bat Cave Affair'* (1965); *Monster on the Campus* (1958).

BITE!
(aka BITE — THE FIRST BLOOD)
USA, 1991. Dir: Scotty Fox. With: Alicyn Sterling, P.J. Sparx (P.J. Sparxx/P.J. Carrington), Buck Adams, Randy West, Alexandra Quinn (Alexandria Quinn/Dianne Stewart), Lorraine Day. Legend Video. Colour.
Porno vampire comedy shot on video and available in both hard- and softcore versions. When the vampiric Colin 'Count' Bramberg (Adams) bites Victoria (Sterling) three times, she is transformed into one of the undead. After staking the Count, Victoria uses her new hypnotic powers to seduce and bite everyone around her, including her roommate Christine (newcomer Sparx), until she meets her match with another vampire (Mike Horner).
✦

A BITE OF LOVE
Hong Kong/UK, 1990. Dir: Stephin Shin. With: George Lam, Rosamund Kwan Chi-Lam, Tsui Siu-Keung. D&B Films. Colour.
Vampiric aristocrat Duke Lee (pop star Lam) only drinks animal blood to survive. When he uses his own immortal blood to save a fatally injured little boy, Lee is kidnapped by a dying Triad heroin dealer (Siu-Keung) who is transformed into a powerful undead adversary. With a clip from *Fright Night* (1985) playing on a TV in a video store.
✦✦

BIZARRE'S DRACULA
USA, 1995. With: Ariana, Scott Baker, Hank Armstrong, Summer Cummings, Ivy English, Nicole London. EI Independent Video. Colour.
Low-budget fetish and S&M video with vampires.
Sequel: BIZARRE'S DRACULA 2 (qv; 1995)
✦

BIZARRE'S DRACULA 2
USA, 1995. With: Nicole London, Anna Malle. EI Independent Video. Colour.
More low-budget fetish and S&M with the undead.
✦

BJ AND THE BEAR:
A Coffin with a View
USA, 1978 (1979). With: Greg Evigan, Sam, Claude Akins,

Mills Watson, Pamela Helmsley, John Carradine. Glen A. Larson/Universal/NBC-TV. Colour.
Inspired by the movie *Every Which Way But Loose* (1978), this hour-long TV series (1978-81) is about an independent trucker, Billy Joe McKay (Evigan), and his travelling companion Bear, a chimp (Sam). In this episode, they get involved with transporting the coffin of the vampire-like Paul Desmond (George Lazenby) along with his creepy caretaker (Carradine).
Series sequel: LOBO (1979-81)
✦✦

BLACK CAT
India, 1959. Dir: N.A. Ansari. With: N.A. Ansari, Balraj Sanhi, Johnny Walker, Shammi, Sheila Kashmiri, Minu Kumtaz. Sippy Films. B&W.
Two-and-a-half hour Hindi crime thriller which apparently includes elements of Robert Louis Stevenson's *Strange Case of Dr. Jekyll and Mr. Hyde*.
✦

THE BLACK CAULDRON
USA, 1985. Dir: Ted Berman and Richard Rich. Voices: John Hurt, Grant Bardsley, Susan Sheridan, Freddie Jones, Nigel Hawthorne, Arthur Malet. Walt Disney Productions/Silver Screen Partners II. Colour.
Disney's first feature-length cartoon to be shot in 70mm since *Sleeping Beauty* (1959), this attempt to squeeze Lloyd Alexander's excellent 'The Chronicles of Prydain' trilogy into just eighty minutes is ultimately disappointing. When the evil Horned King (Hurt) carries off clairvoyant pig Henwen so that he can locate the all-powerful Black Cauldron, pig-keeper Taran (Bardsley) teams up with a cowardly creature named Gurgi (John Byner), the self-opinionated Princess Eilonwy (Sheridan) and the minstrel Fflewddur (Hawthorne) to rescue the animal and prevent the birth of the 'cauldron-born' — a supernatural army of warriors raised from the dead. Despite taking five years to make and costing $25,000,000, this was not a box office hit.
✦✦✧

BLACK DEMONS
(Orig: DEMONI 3)
Italy/Brazil, 1991 (1992). Dir: Umberto Lenzi. With: Keith Van Hoven, Joe Balogh, Sonia Curtis, Philip Murray (Philip Munroe), Juliana Texeira, Maria Alves. Filmirage/ Filmakers. Colour.
Under its original title, this was a sequel in name only to Lamberto Bava's two *Demons* movies (1985/1987). Dick (Van Hoven), his sister Jessica (Curtis) and her boyfriend Kevin (Balogh) are a trio of American tourists in Rio de Janeiro who encounter Macumba voodoo. When their jeep breaks down near an old cemetery, they are menaced by six slimy zombie slaves who were murdered one hundred years before.
✦✧

BLACKENSTEIN
(aka BLACK FRANKENSTEIN)
USA, 1972. Dir: William A. (Al) Levey. With: John Hart, Ivory Stone, Liz Renay, Roosevelt Jackson, Andrea King, Nick Bolin. Exclusive International/L.F.G. Films. Colour.
Feeble attempt to cash-in on the blaxploitation market of the early 1970s. The white Dr Stein (Hart) experiments on a black Vietnam war veteran (Joe DeSue), using an experimental DNA formula to attach new limbs to his body. But a jealous lab assistant swaps the formula, resulting in a crazed monster with a square afro who kills women and eats their intestines. In the end the creature is torn apart by Los Angeles police dogs. The laboratory equipment was originally created by Ken Strickfaden for Universal's *Frankenstein* (1931). A sequel announced in 1976, *Black Frankenstein Meets the White Werewolf*, was thankfully never made.
✦

BLACK LIMELIGHT
(aka FOOTSTEPS IN THE SAND)
UK, 1938. Dir: Paul Stein. With: Raymond Massey, Joan Marion, Walter Hudd, Henry Oscar, Elliott Mason, Coral Browne. Associated British-Pathé/Alliance. B&W.
Creaky whodunit, based on the play by Gordon Sherry. A full moon murderer suffers from nyctalopia and can see in the dark.
✦✧

BLACK MAGIC WITH BUTCHERY
(Orig: NAO MO. USA: aka BLACK MAGIC WITH BUDDHA) Hong Kong, 1983 (1989). Dir: Lo Lieh (Law Lit). With: Lo Lieh (Law Lit), Candy Yu, Chaun Koon Tai, Chau Sing. Colour.
A pair of jungle explorers discover a mummy in a lost temple, they remove its brain and return to Hong Kong. When they use it in black magic ceremonies, the brain goes on a killing spree!
✦✧

BLACK MOON
USA, 1934. Dir: Roy William Neill. With: Jack Holt, Fay Wray, Dorothy Burgess, Cora Sue Collins, Arnold Korff, Lumsden Hare. Columbia. B&W.
American businessman Stephen Lane (wooden hero Holt) travels to the Caribbean island of St. Christopher where he discovers that his wife Juanita (Burgess), who has gone native and been put into a zombiefied state by the voodoo drums, is preparing to sacrifice their young daughter Nancy (Collins) at the urging of the local witch doctor. Wray plays Lane's faithful secretary Gail, who is in love with her boss. Based on the novel by Clements Ripley, this jungle adventure is dated and pretty offensive today. Future director Edward Bernds was the sound engineer, but that doesn't prevent the microphone shadow from repeatedly appearing in shot.
✦✦

THE BLACK ROOM
USA, 1981 (1984). Dir: Norman Thaddeus Vane and Elly Kenner. With: Stephen Knight, Cassandra Gaviola, Jimmy Stathis, Clara Perryman, Charlie Young, Linnea Quigley. Lancer Productions/Vestron. Colour.
Low-budget story about an incestuous brother and sister (Knight and Gaviola) who rent out a room in their Beverly Hills mansion to a couple cheating on each other. The voyeuristic brother is a modern-day vampire, who suffers from a rare form of anaemia and needs fresh blood to survive. Too timid to touch his victims, he relies on medical transfusions to control his hereditary illness.
✦✧

BLACK SABBATH
(Orig: I TRE VOLTI DELLA PAURA/LES TROIS VISAGES DE LA PEUR)
Italy/France/USA, 1963. Dir: Mario Bava. With: Boris Karloff, Mark Damon, Michèle Mercier, Susy (Susi) Andersen, Lidia Alfonsi, Jacqueline Pierreux (Jacqueline Soussard). Emmepi Cinematografica/Galatea Film/ Cinématográfica Lyre/American International Pictures. Colour.
Originally called *The Three Faces of Fear*, AIP changed the title to cash-in on the success of their earlier Bava release, *Black Sunday* (1960). They also cut four minutes, changed the order of the episodes, and added a jokey Les Baxter score and scenes of Karloff linking the three stories in his best *Thriller* manner. 'The Drop of Water' by Anton Chekhov is an effective tale of a murderous ghost, while 'The Telephone' by 'F.G. Snyder' is a confusing story about a man returning from the dead for revenge. However, it is the last and longest episode — based on 'The Wurdalak' by Alexei Tolstoy — which is the real winner. Karloff is marvellously evil as Gorca, a Balkan hunter, who becomes a curly-haired vampire (a *Wurdalak*) forced to drink the blood of those he loves most. Bava's jokey final shot, revealing Karloff riding a rocking horse in a studio setting, only appears in the original version. This is worth catching for the final episode alone.
✦✦✦

BLACK SUNDAY
(Orig: LA MASCHERA DEL DEMONIO. UK: THE MASK OF SATAN/REVENGE OF THE VAMPIRE)
Italy, 1960. Dir: Mario Bava. With: Barbara Steel (Barbara

Barbara Steele with one of her victims in *Black Sunday* (1960).

Steele), John Richardson, Andrea Checchi, Ivo Garrani, Arturo Dominici, Enrico Olivieri. Galatea/Jolly Film. B&W.
Based on Nikolai Gogol's story 'The Vij'. English actress Steele became a cult star in the dual roles of heroine Katia and Princess Asa, the latter a seventeenth century witch accidentally released from her tomb by a drop of blood. With the aid of her vampire helper (Dominici), she plans to replace Katia, who is her exact double. Atmospherically photographed by co-writer/director Bava, it begins with a great scene in which a spiked mask is hammered onto Asa's face. The AIP version replaced Roberto Nicolosi's moody score with an inferior one by Les Baxter. American audiences were given a card with the word 'spell' on it, to chant when they became frightened. It was banned in Britain until 1968, when it was finally released in a cut version.
Remake: DEMONS 5: DEVIL'S VEIL (qv; 1990)
✦✦✦✦✦

BLACULA
USA, 1972. Dir: William Crain. With: William Marshall, Denise Nicholas, Vonetta McGee, Gordon Pinsent, Thalmus Rasulala, Emily Yancy. American International Productions. Colour.
From its prologue set in 1780 Transylvania, where an evil Count Dracula (Charles Macauley) bites and then imprisons African prince Mamuwalde (Marshall, who portrays the vampire with dignity), director Crain's film rises above its blaxploitation roots and is much better than it deserves to be. Finally released from his coffin in 1970s Los Angeles, Blacula seduces Tina (McGee), the reincarnation of his lost wife Luva. With Elisha Cook (Jr) as a hook-handed morgue attendant (a role Martin Kosleck also tested for), songs performed by The Hues Corporation and a great cartoon title sequence. Samuel Z. Arkoff was executive producer. Producer Paul Nobert and Dimension Productions announced *Black Dracula* the same year, but it was never made.
Sequel: SCREAM BLACULA SCREAM (qv; 1973)
✦✦✦

BLADE
USA, 1998. Dir: Stephen Norrington. With: Wesley Snipes, Stephen Dorff, Kris Kristofferson, N'Bushe Wright, Udo Kier, Traci Lords. New Line Cinema/Amen Ra Films/ Imaginary Forces. Colour.
Fast, flashy and violent action film based on the Marvel Comics character created by Marv Wolfman and Gene Coon. Co-producer Snipes stars as Blade, a half-vampire half-human killing machine whose search for the vampire who attacked his mother is secondary only to his search for a permanent cure to his hunger for human blood. Using weapons created by his human mentor Abraham Whistler (Kristofferson) and aided by haematologist Dr Karen Jansen (Wright), Blade confronts renegade vampire Deacon Frost (Dorff), who has taken control of The Council of Vampires. Frost plans to create a vampire Apocalypse and needs only the blood of Blade to fulfil the divine prophecy. A surprise box office hit from the director of *Death Machine* (1994), a sequel was quickly put into development and the original ending is included in supplementary material on the DVD. Stan Lee was co-executive producer. The novelisation was written by Mel Odom.
✦✦✦✧

BLAKES 7:
Duel
UK, 1978. Dir: Pennant Roberts. With: Gareth Thomas, Sally Knyvette, Paul Darrow, Jan Chappell, Michael Keating, Isla Blair. BBC-TV. Colour.
Hour-long TV series (1978-81, fifty-two episodes), created by Terry Nation and shot on video and film, about a band of intergalactic outlaws battling a totalitarian Federation. The first and second seasons of this sub-*Star Wars* show featured the Mutoids — humans adapted to live on an artificial blood-serum or the blood of the Federation's enemies. They are first introduced in this episode, in which Blake (Thomas), Jenna (Knyvette) and Travis (Stephen Greif) are transported to an alien planet where they are forced to fight each other to the death. All three Mutoids episodes are scripted by Nation.
✦✧

Pressure Point
UK, 1979. Dir: George Spenton Foster. With: Gareth Thomas, Sally Knyvette, Paul Darrow, Jan Chappell, Michael Keating, Jane Sherwin. BBC-TV. Colour.
In this episode, Blake sets out to cripple the Federation's central

computer and once again confronts the blood-drinking Mutoids.
✦✧

Project Avalon

UK, 1978. Dir: Michael E. Briant. With: Gareth Thomas, Sally Knyvette, Paul Darrow, Jan Chappell, Michael Keating, David Jackson. BBC-TV. Colour.

Using a captured resistance leader (Julia Vidler) as bait, Travis sets a trap to capture Blake on an ice-planet. Glynis Barber plays the principal blood-drinking Mutoid who aids him. With a silly-looking robot, and Jacqueline Pearce as sexy villain Servalan.
✦✧

Sarcophagus

UK, 1980. Dir: Fiona Cumming. With: Paul Darrow, Jan Chappell, Michael Keating, Steven Pacey, Josette Simon, Peter Tuddenham. BBC-TV. Colour.

When the *Liberator* comes across a craft floating in space, a centuries-old vampiric alien uses Cally's (Chappell) body to drain the life-force from the crew. Scripted by Tanith Lee, who was also responsible for 'Dayna's Song' heard in this episode.
✦✦

PAUL BLAISDELL [1929-1983]

Low budget monster-maker who made memorable contributions to a number of movies in the mid-to-late 1950s. He appeared inside his cheaply-created monster suits in such cult favourites as *It Conquered the World* (1956), *The She-Creature* (1956), *Voodoo Woman* (1956), *Invasion of the Saucermen* (1957) and *The Ghost of Dragstrip Hollow* (1959). After Blaisdell publicly badmouthed *Famous Monsters of Filmland*, publisher James Warren blacklisted his name from the magazine. The effects designer retaliated by creating his own magazine with Bob Burns, but *Fantastic Monsters of the Films* ran for only seven issues in the early 1960s. He died in obscurity at the age of fifty-three after a long illness.

qv: *Attack of the Puppet People* (1958); *Cat Girl* (1957); *How to Make a Monster* (1958); *Invisible Invaders* (1959); *It! The Terror from Beyond Space* (1958); *Not of This Earth* (1957).

ROBERT BLOCH [1917-1994]

American author who began corresponding with H.P. Lovecraft while still a teenager and became a prolific pulp magazine writer in the 1930s and 1940s. As a scriptwriter he often adapted his own work for radio, television and movies, but he will always be identified with his 1959 novel *Psycho* and Alfred Hitchcock's movie version released the following year.

qv: *Alfred Hitchcock Presents: 'The Greatest Monster of Them All'* (1960); *Asylum* (1972); *The Cat Creature* (1973); *Darkroom: 'The Boogeyman Will Get You'* (1981); *The Dead Don't Die* (1974); *Fear in the Dark* (1991); *The Horror of It All* (1983); *The House That Dripped Blood* (1970); *Star Trek: 'Catspaw'* (1967); *Tales from the Darkside: 'Beetles'* (1987); *Tales from the Darkside: 'A Case of The Stubbons'* (1984); *Thriller: 'The Weird Tailor'* (1961); *Torture Garden* (1967).

BLONDE HEAVEN

USA, 1994 (1996). Dir: Ellen Cabot (David DeCoteau). With: Julie Strain, Raelyn Saalman, Michelle Bauer (Michelle McClellan), Joe Estevez, Alton Butler, Jason Clow. Torchlight Entertainment/New City Releasing/ Cinemax. Colour.

Near-hardcore erotic horror movie, eventually released directly to cable TV. Set in 1992, a Los Angeles coven of vampires seduce their victims by changing shape (and sometimes sex) until their leader Illyana (Strain) falls in love with Angie (newcomer Saalman), a would-be actress/waitress. This has plenty of female nudity, some stupid comedy, but little in the way of plot, acting or originality.
✦

BLOOD!

USA, 1974. Dir: Andy Milligan. With: Allen Berendt, Hope Stansbury, Eve Crosby, Patti Gaul, Michael Fischetti, Pamela Adams. Damiano Films/Kent/Bryanston. Colour.

More low-budget nonsense from photographer/writer/director Milligan, filmed on Staten Island in ten days for the princely sum of $20,000. Set in 1899, Dracula's daughter Regina (Stansbury) meets Dr Lawrence Orlovski (Berendt), the son of Larry Talbot, the Wolf Man. They get married, move to America and attempt to raise flesh-eating plants to cure their respective curses. They needn't have bothered.
✦

BLOOD

UK, 1999. Dir: Charly Cantor. With: Adrian Rawlins, Lee Blakemore, Phil Cornwell, Nicolas Harvey, Paul Herzberg, Elizabeth Marmur. Cantor-Markham Productions/Omni International/Yorkshire Media Production Agency. Colour.

Low-budget vampire thriller filmed in Yorkshire. Created for Project Elixir twenty years ago by Dr Carl Dyson (Rawlins) and his colleagues, Lix (newcomer Blakemore) is an artificially-created woman whose blood has a powerful narcotic effect on those who drink it. However, for every pint of blood she loses, she must drink nine pints of human blood to survive.
✦✧

BLOOD & DONUTS

Canada, 1995. Dir: Holly Dale. With: Gordon Currie, Justin Louis, Helene Clarkson, Fiona Reid, Frank Moore, David Cronenberg. Daban Films/The Feature Film Project/Malofilm International/Live. Colour.

Low-budget urban vampire comedy in which the undead Boya Zsekely (Currie) awakens from a twenty-five year sleep in Toronto, drinks rat blood and meets bored cashier Molly (Clarkson) in a run-down donut shop. Pursued by his would-be bride (Reid) and a local crime boss (a surprise cameo by Cronenberg), he saves the life of a friendly cab driver (Louis) in this meandering story. Producer Steve Hoban was also responsible for John Fawcett's vampire-oriented short *Half Nelson* (1993).
✦✧

BLOOD AND ROSES

(Orig: ET MOURIR DE PLAISIR/IL SANGUE E LA ROSA) France/Italy, 1960. Dir: Roger Vadim. With: Mel Ferrer, Elsa Martinelli, Annette Vadim (Annette Stroyberg), Marc Allégret, Alberto Bonucci, R.J. Chauffard. Paramount/Les Films EGE Documento. Colour/B&W.

Fairly bloodless version of 'Carmilla' by J. Sheridan Le Fanu (Le Vanu [*sic*] in the credits!). Stroyberg (then married to co-writer/director Vadim) stars as Carmilla, who is obsessed with her vampire ancestor Mircalla. At a masked ball, she seduces and bites her cousin's fiancée, Georgia Monteverdi (Martinelli). It contains some wonderfully bizarre black and white dream sequences, but the English-language version (with dubbing supervised by Edgar G. Ulmer's daughter Arianné) removed most of the lesbian subtext from this otherwise slow-moving horror movie. A novelisation by Robin Carlisle was published by Hillman.

Remake: CRYPT OF HORROR (qv; 1964)
✦✦✧

BLOOD BATH

(aka TRACK OF THE VAMPIRE)

USA, 1966. Dir: Jack Hill and Stephanie Rothman. With: William Campbell, Marissa (Marrisa) Mathes, Linda (Lori) Saunders, Sandra Knight, Carl Schanzer, Biff Elliot. American International Pictures. B&W.

Filmed in atmospheric Venice, California. Campbell plays macabre artist Antonio Sordi, possessed by a fifteenth century vampire ancestor who paints his victims and then dunks them in a vat of boiling wax. In the end, the wax-coated corpses come back to life and kill him. Roger Corman fired writer/producer Hill and replaced him with Rothman, who was given all Hill's footage (including that from Michael Roadel's Yugoslavian film, *Operacija Ticijan* [1962]) and told to shoot new material with Sandra Knight. The result is a hallucinatory, impressionistic horror film which is a perfect companion piece to Corman's beatnik classic *A Bucket of Blood* (1959). This includes

AIP regulars Jonathan Haze and Sid Haig, and scenes of a wax-covered Patrick Magee (uncredited) from the 1965 Yugoslavian footage (finally released as *Portrait in Terror*). *Star Wars* (1977) producer Gary Kurtz recorded the sound.
✦✦✦

THE BLOOD BEAST TERROR
(USA: aka THE VAMPIRE-BEAST CRAVES BLOOD)
UK, 1967. Dir: Vernon Sewell. With: Peter Cushing, Robert Flemyng, Wanda Ventham, Vanessa Howard, David Griffin, Glynn Edwards. Tigon British. Colour.
Cushing stars in the thankless role of nineteenth century police inspector Quennell investigating a series of bizarre deaths. It turns out that Flemyng's Professor Mallinger has created a giant blood-sucking moth that seduces its prey in the guise of a beautiful woman (Ventham)! Basil Rathbone was originally signed to play the mad doctor, but died before filming began. During a student play, Cushing watches a parody of his Frankenstein role when the corpse of a train accident victim is revived by electricity. British comedian Roy Hudd livens things up as a morgue attendant, but Sewell's direction is, at best, workmanlike. Apparently, Cushing considered this his worst film.
✦✦

THE BLOOD DEMON
(Orig: DIE SCHLANGENGRUBE UND DAS PENDEL. USA: aka CASTLE OF THE WALKING DEAD/CURSE OF THE WALKING DEAD/THE TORTURE CHAMBER OF DR. SADISM)
West Germany, 1967. Dir: Harold (Harald) Reinl. With: Christopher Lee, Lex Barker, Karin Dor, Carl Lange, Vladimir Medar, Christiane Ruecker. Constantin Film/ New Realm. Colour.
Supposedly based on Edgar Allan Poe's 'The Pit and the Pendulum', Lee stars as the evil Count Regula who was dismembered for killing twelve virgins. Now he's been resurrected and is ready to claim his thirteenth victim and become immortal. Lee walks through his role as the undead Count, but ex-Tarzan Barker makes a solid hero. The period setting is enhanced by striking colour photography and imaginative production design, but the weak script lets the side down.
✦✦✧

THE BLOOD DRINKERS
(USA: aka VAMPIRE PEOPLE)
Philippines/USA, 1966. Dir: Gerardo de Leon. With: Amelia Fuentes, Ronald Remy, Eddie Fernandez, Eva Montez, Celia Rodriguez, Paquito Salcedo. Cirio H. Santiago Productions/Hemisphere Pictures. Colour.
When he discovers that Christina, the girl he loves, is dying, bald-headed vampire Dr Marco (Remy) pursues her twin sister so that he can transplant her heart into his beloved. The undead aristocrat is aided by his sexy assistant Tanya (Montez), hunchbacked dwarves and a trained bat called Basra. Fuentes plays the twins and also turned up as a vampire in the same director's *Creatures of Evil* four years later. This is an odd mixture of real colour and tinted black and white footage, based on a Filipino *komiks* series. In America, audiences were given free packets of Green Blood as a promotional gimmick.
✦✧

BLOODEATERS
(Orig: FOREST OF FEAR. USA: aka TOXIC ZOMBIES)
USA, 1980 (1984). Dir: Charles (Chuck) McCrann. With: Charles Austin, Beverly Shapiro, Dennis Helfend, Paul Haskin, John Amplas, Kevin Hanlon. CM Productions/ Parker National. Colour.
Low-budget thriller shot on 16mm in Pennsylvania by writer/director/producer McCrann. When an experimental herbicide being used by government agents is sprayed over people harvesting a marijuana crop, it turns them into homicidal flesh-eating zombies who start killing people with machetes.
✦✧

BLOOD FEAST
USA, 1963. Dir: Herschell G. (Gordon) Lewis. With: Thomas Wood (William Kerwin), Mal Arnold, Connie Mason, Lyn Bolton, Scott H. Hall, Toni Calvert. Box Office Spectaculars. Colour.
'Nothing So Appalling in the Annals of Horror!' claimed the ads for what is generally regarded as the first gore movie. After making a number of nudie films, director Lewis (who is also credited for the music, photography and special effects) branched out into horror with this ludicrous tale of Fuad Ramses (the mad-looking Arnold), an Egyptian caterer living in Miami, who worships an ancient goddess and cuts up women for their body parts. When he sets his sights on his next victim (June 1963 *Playboy* playmate Mason), a moronic detective (Wood) saves her just in time and Ramses is crushed to death in a garbage truck. This was shot in nine days and cost less than $70,000. Despite their amateurishness, the gore scenes are quite explicit for the time. Produced by David F. Friedman. *Blood Diner* (1987) was an unofficial sequel. Lewis' script was published by Malibu Graphics in 1991.
✦

BLOOD FOR DRACULA
(Orig: DRACULA CERCA SANGUE DI VERGINE E...MORI DI SETE!!!/DRACULA VUOLE VIVERE...CERCA SANGUE DI VERGINE!)
Italy/France, 1974. Dir: Paul Morrissey (and Anthony M. Dawson/Antonio Margheriti). With: Joe Dallesandro, Udo Kier, Vittorio De Sica, Arno Juerging (Jürging), Maxime McKendry, Milena Vukotic. Compagnia Cinematográfica Champion/EMI/Bryanston Pictures. Colour.
Filmed in English, three of the stars from *Flesh for Frankenstein* (1973) are reunited in this companion movie from the same writer/director(s). Because of a shortage of victims in Romania, a dying Dracula (Kier) and his secretary Anton (Juerging) load up their vintage car with the Count's coffin on top and head off to Catholic Italy in search of 'wirgin's' blood. They end up at the villa of an impoverished aristocrat (veteran director De Sica) and his four unmarried daughters. Unfortunately, the vampire throws up every time he does not get the pure stuff. Roman Polanski turns up in an uncredited cameo as a game-playing villager, and in the bloody finale, Dracula has his arms and legs hacked off by an axe-wielding, revolutionary gardener (an unlikely Dallesandro) before being staked. Special effects by Carlo Rambaldi. Although advertised in America as *Andy Warhols Dracula* and *Andy Warhols Young Dracula*, Warhol was actually never directly involved with this horror comedy.
✦✦✧

BLOOD FREAK
(aka BLOOD FREAKS)
USA, 1971 (1974). Dir: Steve Hawkes and Brad F. Grinter. With: Steve Hawkes, Dana Cullivan, Heather Hughes, Bob Currier, Larry Wright, Randy Grinter Jr. Preacher Man Company/Variety Fair/Sampson Motion Picture Production Company/Reel Movies. Colour.
Florida biker Herschell (co-director Hawkes) is transformed by drugs into a bloodsucking monster with a turkey head. After killing some hippies and a drug dealer, he turns to religion in this god-awful Christian gore film with an all-a-dream ending. Brad Grinter, who also plays the chain-smoking narrator, directed the dreadful *Flesh Feast* (1970) which starred Veronica Lake and also featured Heather Hughes.
✦

BLOOD FROM THE MUMMY'S TOMB
UK, 1971. Dir: Seth Holt (and Michael Carreras). With: Andrew Keir, Valerie Leon, James Villiers, Hugh Burden, George Coulouris, Mark Edwards. Hammer Films/EMI Film Productions. Colour.
Christopher Wicking's literate script, based on Bram Stoker's 1903 novel *The Jewel of Seven Stars*, is an odd blend of the supernatural and suburbia. At the exact moment when archaeologist Professor Julian Fuchs (the excellent Keir, who took over from Peter Cushing after one day's shooting when the latter's wife died) discovers the ancient tomb of evil Egyptian Queen Tera, his daughter Margaret is born. Years later, an obsessed Fuchs believes that Margaret (Leon) has been possessed by Tera as the members of his original expedition

are killed off through the relics they possess. Maverick director Holt died of a heart attack a week before the end of the six-week shoot, and although Carreras completed the filming, Holt apparently kept his concept for the movie in his head. The uneven editing, dream-like flashbacks and enigmatic sequences are a result of this (and the fact that some of the footage Holt shot doesn't fit into the finished film). With Rosalie Crutchley, Aubrey Morris, James Cossins, Tamara Ustinov and Edwards as a doomed hero named Tod Browning.
Remake: THE AWAKENING (qv; 1980)
✦✦✦✦

BLOOD HUNTER
USA, 1996. Dir: Jack Shrum and Chuck Ellis. With: Jack Shrum, Chuck Ellis, Cynthia Hudson. Cabin Productions. Colour.
Low-budget independent vampire movie, shot in Kentucky and Nebraska and released directly to video. Viktor (co-director Shrum) is a Russian vampire who emerges from the caves beneath Kentucky after several centuries to become a car mechanic in a junkyard. When he starts killing the (mostly deserving) locals, the town sheriff (co-director Ellis) sets out to stake the undead émigré.
✦

BLOOD IN THE NIGHT
USA, 1993. Dir: Lincoln Kupchak. With: Reggie Athnos, Mark Moyer, Laird Scott, Bonita Walker, Michael Bradberry, Gina Altizer. Rivers of Blood Productions. Colour.
Low-budget independent video in which inexperienced young vampire Veronique (Athnos) travels to America, pursued by her vengeful cousin Vladius (Scott).
✦

BLOOD KISS
USA, 1999. Dir: Michael W. Johnson. With: Steve Lee, Jeff Murphy, Amanda Murphy, Michael W. Johnson, Lisa Kosse, Melinda Shaffer. Nightmare Productions. Colour.
Independent video release in which Murphy plays Danny Dodd, whose wife was murdered and daughter Trudy (Murphy) abducted by vampire Adam Mortis (Lee) sixteen years earlier. Now it appears that Mortis is back in town with a beautiful woman who protects and serves her undead lover.
✦

THE BLOODLESS VAMPIRE
Philippines/USA, 1965. Dir: Michael du Pont. With: Charles Macauley, Helen Thompson. Journey Productions. B&W.
There is some doubt as to whether this Filipino vampire movie was ever completed or released. Macauley later played Dracula in *Blacula* (1972).
✦

BLOODLUST
USA, 1968. Karma. Colour.
Twenty minute psychedelic horror film. Escaping from the police, a pair of hippie girls discover an old house. They have sex and smoke marijuana and one of the girls is attacked by a vampire, who bites her neck. This apparently has a shock ending.
✦

BLOODLUST
(Orig: MOSQUITO DER SCHAENDER)
Switzerland, 1976. Dir: Marijan Vajda. With: Werner Pochath, Ellen Umlauf, Birgit Zamulo, Gerhard Ruhnke, Peter Hamm, Charly Hiltl. Monarex/EI Independent Cinema. Colour.
In this nihilistic, low-budget horror film, an abused young German book-keeper (Pochath) breaks into mortuaries and mutilates the corpses, drinking their blood through a pipette and signing his name 'Mosquito'. The deaf and dumb vampire also steals the body of an unbalanced girl (Umlauf) who he secretly loved, and is finally arrested for murdering a young couple in the woods. The title on the 1999 video box is *Bloodlust The Vampire of Nuremberg*.
✦✧

BLOODLUST
(Orig: LE CAS ÉTRANGE DE DR. JEKYLL ET DE MISS OSBOURNE/DR. JEKYLL ET LES FEMMES. UK: BLOODBATH OF DR JEKYLL/BLOOD OF DR. JEKYLL. USA: aka DR. JEKYLL AND HIS WOMEN. UK/USA: aka THE EXPERIMENT)
France, 1979 (1981). Dir: Walerian Borowczyk. With: Udo Kier, Marina Pierro, Patrick Magee, Gisèle Préville, Howard Vernon (Mario Lippert), Clément Harari. Whodunit Productions/Allegro Productions/Multimedia. Colour.
Polish director Borowczyk's highly erotic and violent retelling of Robert Louis Stevenson's story, filmed in English. At a dinner party to celebrate his engagement to Miss Fanny Osbourne (fashion model Pierro), Dr Henry Jekyll (Kier) immerses himself in a bathtub full of chemicals and emerges as the immoral Mr Hyde (Gérard Zalcberg). After an orgy of perverse sex and gratuitous gore, Jekyll's fiancée also bathes in the chemicals and gives herself over to Hyde before they escape together in a carriage, licking each other's wounds. This was veteran horror star Magee's last film.
Remake: DR. JEKYLL AND MR. HYDE (qv; 1980)
✦✧

BLOOD LUST
UK, 1980. Dir: Russell Gay. Harrison Marks Company/ Mistral Films. Colour.
Billed as 'The First Sex Horror Movie' (it obviously wasn't), this Super-8mm softcore short was sold through magazines. Vampire Carmilla rises from her grave and seduces teenage virgin Jennifer who she then presents to her master, Count Dracula, Prince of Darkness and Lord of Depravity. They end up in a three-way until Jennifer's boyfriend turns up, equipped with a flaming stake and crucifix, to save her from her undead lovers.
✦

BLOODLUST
Australia, 1991 (1992). Dir: Richard Wolstencroft and Jon Hewitt. With: Jane Stuart Wallace, Kelly Chapman, Robert James O'Neill, Phil Motherwell, Paul Moder, James Young. Windhover Productions. Colour.
This crude black comedy claims to be 'the sickest movie ever made'. Three psychotic killers who think they are vampires (Wallace, Chapman and O'Neill) steal $3,000,000 from a drug dealer and are pursued by religious fanatics, comedy-relief cops and gangsters to a derelict house in the country. This includes multiple stakings, necrophilia, foot fetishism, castration, coke-sniffing and softcore sex. Prints were apparently seized by British customs. Music by Revolting Cocks, Pailhead, Lead Into Gold and 1000 Homo DJs.
✦

BLOODLUST SUBSPECIES III
Romania/USA/Spain, 1993. Dir: Ted Nicolaou. With: Anders Hove, Denice Duff, Kevin Blair, Melanie Shatner, Pamela Gordon, Michael Dellafemina. Full Moon Entertainment/Paramount. Colour.
Second sequel to *Subspecies* (1990), executive produced by Charles Band and again written and atmospherically directed by Nicolaou. Rebecca (Shatner), Mel (Blair) and Police Lt Marin (Ion Haiduc) attempt to destroy evil vampire Radu Vladislas (Hove) and his wizened witch mummy (Gordon) and rescue Michelle (Duff). Filmed back-to-back with *Bloodstone Subspecies II* (1993), this overcomes its low budget thanks to unusual Transylvanian locations, serious performances and impressive make-up effects. With more neat stop-motion demons created by David Allen.
Sequel: SUBSPECIES 4 BLOODSTORM (qv; 1998)
✦✦✧

BLOOD MANIAC
Hong Kong, 1986. Dir: Tong Wai-Sing. With: Ching Wong-Mui, Min Fung-Fun, Wai Lan, Ko Ling. Colour.
A recently married man (Lan) is possessed by the spirit of his dead Satanist brother and creates a telepathic link with a zombie buried in the back garden. In the end, his new wife (Mui) gives birth to a fanged monster that tears its way out of her stomach.
✦

BLOODY NASTY

USA, 1989 (1992). Dir: Richard Gabai and Robert Strauss. With: Todd McCammon, Catherine McGuinness, Allison Barron, Richard Gabai, Troy Donahue, Linnea Quigley. Interstellar Films. Colour.

Dire low budget horror comedy in which an energy force from an exploding plane revives dead graverobber Roy Flowers (McCammon), who is also possessed by the spirit of Luis 'Blade' Orlando (Richard B. Rifkin). Quigley turns up as Miami psychic stripper Wanda Dance. This is so bad that it was apparently never officially released in America.

✦

BLOOD OF DRACULA

(UK: BLOOD IS MY HERITAGE)

USA, 1957. Dir: Herbert L. Strock. With: Sandra Harrison, Louise Lewis, Gail Ganley, Jerry Blaine, Heather Ames, Malcolm Atterbury. Carmel Productions/American International Pictures. B&W.

A companion piece to producer Herman Cohen's teen Frankenstein and werewolf entries (made the same year), this should really have been called *I Was a Teenage Vampire*. Nancy Perkins (Harrison) is transformed into an ugly, pointy-eared monster wearing a prerequisite fifties tight sweater when she is hypnotised with an old Carpathian amulet by evil girls' school teacher Miss Branding (Lewis). Hero Blaine sings 'Puppy Love'. This has nothing to do with Dracula and was titled *Blood of the Demon* in Canada.

✦✧

BLOOD OF DRACULA'S CASTLE

(aka DRACULA'S CASTLE)

USA, 1967 (1969). Dir: Al Adamson (and Jean Hewitt). With: John Carradine, Paula Raymond, Alex D'Arcy, Robert Dix, Gene O'Shane, Barbara Bishop. Paragon Pictures/A&E Film Corporation/Crown International. Colour.

Probably one of producer/director Adamson's better low-budget efforts (which isn't saying much!). At least the script makes some sense, and the cast actually give performances for a change. This could be because Hewitt helped (uncredited) with the direction and Laszlo Kovacs and Vilmos Zsigmond handled the photography. Shot on the Charles Manson ranch, veterans D'Arcy and Raymond play the Count and Countess Townsend (in fact, Dracula), who keep a stock of half-naked girls chained up in their desert castle for nourishment. George the butler (a slyly humorous performance by Carradine) sacrifices them now and then to the great god Luna. Add Dix as Johnny, a psychopathic full moon killer attempting to learn the secret of immortality, Mango the hulking hunchback (Ray Young), and production manager John Cardos as a security guard, and you have a trash classic. Jayne Mansfield was originally set to star in the Raymond role, while a proposed sequel, *Dracula's Coffin*, was never made. The retitled American TV version apparently includes extra footage.

✦✧

BLOOD OF GHASTLY HORROR

(aka THE FIEND WITH THE ELECTRONIC BRAIN/MAN WITH THE SYNTHETIC BRAIN/PSYCHO-A-GO-GO)

USA, 1972. Dir: Al Adamson. With: John Carradine, Kent Taylor, Tommy Kirk, Regina Carrol, Roy Morton, Tracey Robbins. TAL/Independent-International. Colour.

Okay, pay attention: producer/director Adamson originally made this in 1965 as *Psycho-a-Go-Go*, with Morton as a zombiefied killer with an electronic control device in his head. New scenes were added in 1969 and it was released as *The Fiend With the Electronic Brain*. More scenes were added in 1972 and the title changed again (it later turned up on American TV and in Britain as *Man With the Synthetic Brain*). Whatever the title, it is still an incomprehensible mess. Carradine plays the mad Dr Vanard, experimenting with human guinea pigs. Taylor is another mad scientist out to revenge his son's death using a disfiguring serum and a green-tinged monster. And ex-Disney star Kirk appears as a befuddled police detective who vomits when he discovers a severed head in a box. Filmed in 'Chill-O-Rama'.

✦

THE BLOOD OF NOSTRADAMUS

(Orig: LA SANGRE DE NOSTRADAMUS)

Mexico, 1960 (1962). Dir: Frederick (Federico) Curiel. With: Germán Robles, Julio Aleman, Domingo Soler, Aurora Alvarado, Manver (Manuel Vergara), Manuel Casanueva. Estudios America/American International. B&W.

A sequel to *The Genii of Darkness* (1960), and the last of four features cut down from a twelve-part Mexican serial and released directly to TV in America. Robles stars as the bearded vampire descendant of the sixteenth century prophet Nostradamus. He is pursued by Professor Duran (Soler) and the police, who are armed with silver bullets, and in the end he is staked after causing a total eclipse of the moon! This includes the episodes 'El Aparecido en el Convento', 'El Ave Negra' and 'La Ultima Victima'. The English-language version was produced by K. (Kenneth) Gordon Murray and directed by Stim (Stem) Segar.

✦✧

BLOOD OF THE VAMPIRE

UK, 1958. Dir: Henry Cass. With: Donald Wolfit, Barbara Shelley, Vincent Ball, Victor Maddern, William Devlin, Andrew Faulds. Artistes Alliance Production/Eros Films. Colour.

Gruesome horror movie scripted by Hammer veteran Jimmy Sangster, and probably the best production from the team of Robert S. Baker and Monty Berman (the latter also responsible for the excellent colour photography). Actor/manager Sir Donald Wolfit must have needed the cash to have agreed to play the villainous Dr Callistratus, revived from the dead and experimenting with the blood of the inmates of an insane asylum in order to stay alive. Director Cass, who usually handled Shakespearean plays at the Old Vic theatre, includes plenty of sleazy torture and murder, and Maddern is great as Carl, the doctor's mute hunchbacked assistant. With John Le Mesurier, Bernard Bresslaw and Milton Reed (Reid). Extra scenes of actresses Barbara Burke and Mary Marshall chained up in the basement wearing low-cut blouses were apparently shot for a European version.

✦✦✦

BLOOD REINCARNATION

(Orig: YIN-YANG CHIEH)

Hong Kong, 1974. Dir: Ting Shan-Hsi. With: Shih Tien, Shirley Huang (Huang Sha-Li), Chiang Nan, Meng Li, Yang Chung, Tang Pao-Yun. Fong Ming. Colour.

Anthology movie featuring three stories. In the first ('The Treasure'), a new-born baby is possessed by the spirit of a woman seeking vengeance, while the second ('The Wanton') is about a mischievous water spirit. In the third segment, 'Lau Tin Sok', the eponymous acupuncturist (Chung) is executed for a crime he didn't commit and revived by a spell for seven days so that he can revenge himself on the man who framed him.

✦✧

BLOOD RELATIONS

(Orig: BLOEDVERWANTEN/LES VAMPIRES EN ONT RAS LE BOL)

Netherlands/France, 1977. Dir: Wim Lindner. With: Maxim Hamel, Gregoire Aslan, Sophie Deschamps, Robert Dalban, Eddie Constantine, Ralph Arliss. Jaap van Rij Filmproductie/CTIS. Colour.

Horror comedy based on a story by Dutch author 'Belcampo' (Herman P. Schoenfeld Wichers). A young nurse (Deschamps) suspects that the hospital's blood plasma supply is being stolen by a vampire doctor (Hamel) and his undead policeman son (Arliss). Inspired by an old vampire movie, she tries to destroy them by injecting herself with holy water, but ends up becoming another refined bloodsucker. Cult favourite Constantine (*Alphaville* [1965], etc) plays a priest.

✦✦

BLOODSCENT

USA, 1995. Dir: Bill Randolph. With: Mandy Leigh, Julie T. Wallace, Bill Randolph, Laura Hamilton, Sarah McCormick, George Frich. In-House Productions. Colour.

Low-budget vampire video with Randolph as the undead St. Germaine.
✦

BLOOD SLAVES OF THE VAMPIRE WOLF
USA, 1996. Dir: Conrad Brooks. With: Conrad Brooks, Jennifer Knight, Michael Hooker, Annette Perez, Don Miller, Joe Estevez. Psycho Cinema Pictures. Colour.
Shot on video in ten days at Quality Studios and dedicated to the memory of Ed Wood (who never made anything as bad as this). An unlikely British police inspector in Los Angeles (Hooker, who can't even remember his lines) attempts to track down one hundred year-old vampire Selina Yarnall (Knight), her mute assistant Monk (producer/director Brooks) and their monstrous zombie/vampire/werewolf slave, Antonio (scriptwriter Miller), who are draining the blood from hookers and homeless people in Hollywood. With a truly irritating synthesiser score, stock footage from *The Torture Zone* (1968), a trailer for *WereWolf of London* (1935) on TV, numerous stupid in-jokes and a bizarre walk-on by Estevez, most home movies are technically more competent than this apparently improvised mess.
✦

THE BLOOD SPATTERED BRIDE
(Orig: LA NOVIA ENSANGRENTADA. USA: aka BLOODY FIANCEE/TILL DEATH DO US PART)
Spain, 1972. Dir: Vincent (Vicente) Aranda. With: Simon Andreu, Maribel Martin, Alexandra Bastedo, Dean Selmier, Rosa Ma Rodrigues, Monserrat Julio. Morgana Films/Europix International. Colour.
Yet another version of J. Sheridan Le Fanu's classic story 'Carmilla'. Bastedo plays enigmatic 200 year-old vampire Mircalla Karstein/Carmilla (discovered naked and buried in the sand) who seduces frigid newly-wed Susan (Martin) and turns her against her new husband (Andreu). In the end, the man tears the hearts out of both women when he finds them sleeping together in Mircalla's coffin. The climax was cut for British and American release prints.
Remake: CARMILLA (qv; 1973)
✦✦

BLOODSTONE SUBSPECIES II
Romania/USA/Spain, 1993. Dir: Ted Nicolaou. With: Anders Hove, Denice Duff, Kevin Blair, Melanie Shatner, Pamela Gordon, Michael Denish. Full Moon Entertainment/Paramount. Colour.
Writer/director Nicolaou's atmospheric sequel to his *Subspecies* (1990), again executive produced by Charles Band. Now a vampire, Michelle (Duff) asks for help from her sister Rebecca (Shatner) to escape evil vampire Radu Vladislas (Hove) and his wizened witch mummy (Gordon) and keep the Bloodstone out of their hands. With brief stop-motion demons created by David Allen. This was filmed back-to-back with the second sequel and 'Rated "R" for Vampire Violence' in America.
Sequel: BLOODLUST SUBSPECIES III (qv; 1993)
✦✦✧

BLOOD SUCKERS
(Orig: LA ISLA DE LA MUERTE/DAS GEHEIMNIS DER TODESINSEL. USA: ISLAND OF DEATH/ISLAND OF THE DOOMED/MAN-EATER OF HYDRA)
Spain/West Germany, 1965 (1966). Dir: Mel Welles (Ernst von Theumer). With: Cameron Mitchell, Kay Fisher (Kai Fischer), Elisa Montes, George (Jorge) Martin, Matilde (Muñoz) Sampedro, Ralph (Rolf von) Naukoff. Orbita/Tefi/Allied Artists/Chevron Pictures. Colour.
Mitchell stars as insane botanist Baron von Weiser, who feeds guests on his island retreat to a vampire tree he has created. The blood-soaked finale has hero David Moss (Martin) using an axe to hack away at the tree's pulsating tentacles as the Baron is destroyed by his own creation. Apparently Sylvia Miles dubbed the voice of an old lady.
✦✦

BLOODSUCKERS FROM OUTER SPACE
USA, 1984 (1987). Dir: Glen Coburn. With: Thom Meyers, Laura Ellis, Dennis Letts, Big John Brigham, Pat Paulsen, Chris Heldman. One-of-Those Productions/Reel Movies International. Colour.
Low-budget science fiction spoof, filmed in Texas. An airborne alien virus turns members of the local farming community into blood-drinking zombies. This results in the creatures retaining their original personalities after they've become the walking dead. The outbreak of blood-spewing is not helped by a group of incompetent scientists, an ineffectual President of the United States (comedian Paulsen) and a nuclear-mad American general.
✦✧

BLOODSUCKING PHARAOHS IN PITTSBURGH
USA, 1988 (1991). Dir: Alan Smithey (Dean Tschetter). With: Jake Dengel, Joe Sharkey, Susann Fletcher, Beverly Penberthy, Shawn Elliott, Jane Esther Hamilton (Veronica Hart). Saratoga Film Corp/Night Mare Home Video/Paramount. Colour.
Comedy horror film originally announced as a remake of *Blood Feast* (1963) and filmed under the title *Picking Up the Pieces*. A detective's daughter teams up with two cops to investigate members of an Egyptian cannibalistic cult who are looking for eternal life in Pittsburgh. Special make-up effects created by Tom Savini.
✦

BLOOD THIRST
Philippines/USA, 1965 (1971). Dir: Newt Arnold. With: Robert Winston, Yvonne Nielson, Judy Dennis, Vic Diaz, Katherine Henryk, Eddie Infante. Chevron/Paragon/Journey. B&W.
Filmed under the title *The Horror from Beyond*. Winston plays wise-cracking New York detective Adam Rourke, who travels to the Philippines and uncovers a cult of blood-drinking sun worshippers led by an ageless vampire priestess and her monstrous servant. In the end, the vampire is burned to death and reverts to her centuries-old self.
✦✧

BLOODTHIRSTY
USA, 1992. Dir: Robert Guy Barrows. With: Ascello Charles, Winston McDaniel, Lia Marino, Stefanie Roumeliotes, Nicole Zafrano, Josh Barrows. Barrows Productions. Colour.
Low-budget thriller in which an accident in a virologist's laboratory turns people into crazy blood-drinkers.
✦✧

BLOOD THIRSTY
USA, 1998. Dir: Jeff Frey. With: Monique Parent, Leslie Danon, Julie Strain. RAMM Entertainment. Colour.
A young woman develops a fetish for drinking blood from the veins of her roommate.
✦

THE BLOOD THIRSTY DEAD
(Orig: FEI SHI. USA: aka REVENGE OF THE CORPSE)
Hong Kong, 1981. Dir: Sun Chung. With: Pai Piao, Lo Lieh (Law Lit). Shaw Brothers. Colour.
Low-budget Hong Kong zombie movie.
✦

BLOOD TIES
USA, 1991. Dir: Jim McBride. With: Harley Venton, Patrick Bauchau, Kim Johnson-Ulrich, Michelle Johnson, Bo Hopkins, Michael C. Gwynne. Richard and Esther Shapiro Entertainment/Fox Network. Colour.
Pilot TV movie, stylishly directed by co-producer McBride. Likeable reporter Harry Martin (Venton) is related to a powerful family of 'Carpathians' (vampires) based in Long Beach, California, and headed by traditionalist Eli Chelarin (Bauchau). Harry teams up with district attorney Amy Lauren (Johnson-Ulrich) to help young Texan Cody Puckett (Jason London) revenge the death of his parents by fanatical SCAV (Southern Coalition Against Vampirism) hunters. With Grace Zabriskie. Produced by Gene Corman and released on video in 1993 in a slightly different version.
✦✦✦

BLOOD WATERS OF DR. Z
(Orig: ZAAT. USA: aka ATTACK OF THE SWAMP CREATURE/HYDRA/THE LEGEND OF THE ZAAT MONSTER)
USA, 1972 (1975). Dir: Don Barton (Arnold Stevens). With: Dave Dickerson, Sanna Ringhaver, Paul Galloway, Gerald Cruse, Marshall Grauer, Wade Popwell. Horizon Films/ Cougar/Capital/Barton Films. Colour.
'Filmed entirely on location in Florida', this low-budget scaly monster movie is inspired by the real-life 'walking catfish' phenomenon which hit the area in the late sixties. Mad scientist Dr Leopold (Grauer) attempts to create an army of killer-catfish and tests his new serum on himself. He turns into a vampiric fish monster (played by Popwell) who kills his former associates and sets about finding a mate. Ultra-cheap regional thrills. This was re-released in 1985 as *Attack of the Swamp Creatures* with new cast and production credits.
✦

THE BLOODY VAMPIRE
(Orig: EL CONDE FRANKENHAUSEN/EL VAMPIRO SANGRIENTO)
Mexico, 1961 (1963). Dir: Michael Morata (Miguel Morayta). With: Begoña Palacios, Erna Martha Bauman, Raul Farell, Bertha Moss, Carlos Agosti, Francisco A. Cordova. Pelicula Mexicana/Tele Talia Films/ Internacional Sono-Film/Clasa-Mohme/American International. B&W.
Filmed back-to-back with *Samson vs. the Vampire Women* (1961). Count Caliostro and his group of Mexican vampire hunters convince Caliostro's daughter to disguise herself as a serving girl to gain entrance to the mansion of the undead Count Frankenhausen (Agosti). There she discovers a torture chamber and an evil housekeeper before the glowing-eyed vampire turns into a giant bat and defeats his enemies! This includes a great-looking slow-motion sequence featuring a carriage driven by Death. The English-language version was produced by K. (Kenneth) Gordon Murray and directed by Manuel San Fernando.
Sequel: THE INVASION OF THE VAMPIRES (qv; 1961)
✦✦✧

BLUE DEMON CONTRA CEREBROS INFERNALES
(aka BLUE DEMON VS. EL CRIMEN/EL CEREBRO INFERNAL)
Mexico, 1967 (1968). Dir: Chano Urueta. With: Blue Demon (Alejandro Muñoz), David Reynoso, Ana Martin, Victor Junco, Barbara Angeli, Noé Murayama. Estudios America/Cinematográfica RA. Colour.
The eponymous blue-clad hero battles a gang of zombie-like women who are killing scientists and male wrestlers and stealing their brain cells with the help of Dr Sanders (Junco). Co-scripted by ex-wrestler Fernando Osés. The title translates as 'Blue Demon versus the Infernal Brain'.
Sequel: BLUE DEMON CONTRA LAS DIABOLICAS (1967)
✦

BLUE DEMON EL DEMONIO AZUL
(aka EL DEMONIO AZUL)
Mexico, 1963. Dir: Chano Urueta. With: Blue Demon (Alejandro Muñoz), Rosa Ma. (María) Vázquez, Jaime Fernández, Mario Orea, Cesar Gay, Fernando Osés. Filmica Vergara/Columbia. B&W.
In his third film, wrestling hero the Blue Demon stars in three episodes ('El Demonio Azul', 'El Aullido Macabro' and 'La Furia de la Bestia'), helping a professor battle a furry-faced werewolf (with a Tarzan-like cry) that is terrorising the countryside. They discover that a mad scientist living in an old castle is using a formula to transform himself and a wrestling opponent of the Blue Demon into wolfmen. The music score is taken from Hammer's *Dracula* (1958). With Lobo Negro (Guillermo Hernández).
Sequel: BLUE DEMON VS. EL PODER SATANICO (1964)
✦✦

THE BLUE JEAN MONSTER
(Orig: ZHUO NIU ZI KU DE ZHONG KUI)
Hong Kong, 1990. Dir: Jimmy Li (Kai Ming Lai). With: Shing Fui-On, Amy Yip, Pauline Wong, Gloria Yip. Golden Harvest/Diagonal Pictures/Paragon Films. Colour.
Horror comedy about cop Tsu Hsaing (On) who is killed during a bank robbery. Revived by an electrical storm, he becomes an indestructible zombie seeking revenge who needs to recharge himself regularly with electricity to survive.
✦✧

THE BLUE LAMP IN A WINTER NIGHT
Hong Kong, 1985. Dir: Yao Feng-Pan. Colour.
Turn-of-the-century story about a love triangle. The Temple Kai Yuen is haunted by a mouldy-faced old vampire woman and beautiful ghost Chinn Chinn. The shape-changing vampire turns into a giant before the possibly-all-a-dream ending.
✦

BLUES BROTHERS 2000
Canada/USA, 1998. Dir: John Landis. With: Dan Aykroyd, John Goodman, Joe Morton, J. Evan Bonifant, The Blues Brothers Band, Aretha Franklin. Universal. Colour.
Belated sequel to the 1980 comedy hit. Forget the plot, there isn't one — Elwood Blues (Aykroyd, looking pretty good) gets out of prison and decides to reassemble the old band — and sit back and enjoy the fabulous musical numbers. This includes a green-faced zombie dance number, skeletal Ghost Riders in the sky, 130 year-old voodoo queen Mousette (Erykah Badu) and an even bigger car crash than in the original. With cameos by Frank Oz, B.B. King, Wilson Pickett, Steve Lawrence, James Brown, Eric Clapton, Bo Diddley, Isaac Hayes, Dr John, Billy Preston, Jimmie Vaughan, Steve Winwood and numerous others.
✦✦✧

THE BLUE SEXTET
USA, 1971. Dir: David E. Durston. Unisphere. Colour.
Sex film written and directed by Durston, about a man who makes 8mm movies, one of which includes Dracula-like vampires chasing naked women through a dungeon.
✦

BODY BAGS
(aka JOHN CARPENTER PRESENTS BODY BAGS)
USA, 1993. Dir: John Carpenter and Tobe Hooper (and Larry Sulkis). With: John Carpenter, Robert Carradine, Alex Datcher, Stacy Keach, David Warner, Deborah Harry. Showtime Networks. Colour.
Gory all-star cable TV horror anthology, hosted by Carpenter's comedy zombie morgue attendant (in make-up co-created by Rick Baker). The three very predictable stories involve a woman's (Datcher) first frightening night on the job at 'The Gas Station', an experimental cure for baldness that has unfortunate side-effects on Richard Cobritz's (Keach) 'Hair', and a baseball player (Mark Hamill) who is possessed by a serial killer's 'Eye' after a transplant operation. Despite the remarkable supporting cast that includes Twiggy (Lesley Hornby), veteran John Agar, Tom Arnold, Tobe Hooper (who also directed the third segment), Wes Craven, Sam Raimi, David Naughton, (George) Buck Flower, Sheena Easton, Roger Corman and Charles Napier, this should have been much better considering the talent involved. Sulkis directed the linking sequences.
✦✦✧

DeWITT BODEEN
[1908-1988]

American screenwriter, best known for his work on such classy Val Lewton 'B' pictures as *Cat People* (1942), *The Seventh Victim* (1943) and *The Curse of the Cat People* (1944).

THE BODY BENEATH
USA/UK, 1971. Dir: Andy Milligan. With: Gavin Reed, Jackie Skarvellis, Berwick Kaler, Susan Heard, Richmond

Ross, Emma Jones. World Video Pictures/Cinemedia Films/Nova International. Colour.
More rubbish from Staten Island's writer/producer/director Milligan, who also photographed it on 16mm on location in London's Highgate Cemetery. Reed portrays the Reverend Algernon Ford, the leader of a family of nineteenth century vampires based at Carfax Abbey. He kidnaps a pregnant relative (Skarvellis) to continue the bloodline. Only the creepy Kaler stands out in another Milligan gorefest which is, if possible, even more amateurish than usual. This was originally on an incredible double-bill with the same director's *Guru the Mad Monk* (1970).
✦

BODY DOUBLE

USA, 1984. Dir: Brian De Palma. With: Craig Wasson, Gregg Henry, Melanie Griffith, Deborah Shelton, Guy Boyd, Dennis Franz. Delphi Productions II/Columbia. Colour.
De Palma's complex thriller borrows plot elements from Hitchcock's *Rear Window* (1954) and *Vertigo* (1958), as voyeuristic unemployed actor Jake Scully (Wasson) is duped into witnessing a murder. The film opens with him being fired by director Rubin (Franz) from a low-budget vampire movie called *Vampire's Kiss* (later the title of a 1988 movie starring Nicolas Cage). With Barbara Crampton, Brinke Stevens, and porn stars Annette Haven, Linda Shaw and Lisa Berenger.
✦✦✦

BONE CHILLERS:
Edgar Allan Poe-Session

USA, 1996. Dir: Willard Carroll. With: Linda Cardellini, Saadia Persad, Esteban Powell, John Patrick White, Charles Fleischer, Dave Ruby. Silverman-Hyperion Productions/ABC-TV. Colour.
Half-hour TV show (twelve episodes) created by Adam Rifkin, based on the series of young adult horror books by Betsy Haynes and Daniel Weiss, which follows the adventures of students Fitzgerald 'Fitz' Charleston Crump (White), Lexi Orwell (Persad), Brian Hoseapple (Powell) and Sarah Moss (Cardellini) at Smiley Heights' spooky Edgar Allan Poe High School. In this episode, when the zombie-like Principal Pussman (Arthur Burghardt) replaces a bust of Poe with his own likeness, the ghostly poet possesses Brian. Film fan Fitz watches *White Zombie* (1932) on TV. With Loren Rubin as TV horror host Igor Von Ghoulie and Carl V. Dupré as the Zombie Twins.
✦✦

Franken-Turkey

USA, 1996. Dir: Valerie Breiman. With: Linda Cardellini, Saadia Persad, Esteban Powell, John Patrick White, Charles Fleischer, Dave Ruby. Silverman-Hyperion Productions/ABC-TV. Colour.
In an attempt to save Gobbles the school turkey from becoming Thanksgiving dinner, the four schoolfriends create a decoy which is accidentally given monstrous life by a lightning bolt. This features Fitz watching *Frankenstein's Brother-in-Law* (with a midget Monster) on TV.
✦✦✧

Full Moon Goon

USA, 1996. Dir: Christopher Coppola. With: Linda Cardellini, Saadia Persad, Esteban Powell, John Patrick White, Charles Fleischer, Dave Ruby. Silverman-Hyperion Productions/ABC-TV. Colour.
When Sarah falls for the mysterious motorcycle-riding Lobo (Jim Griffin), she is transformed into a werewolf by her lycanthropic boyfriend. This episode reuses Curt Siodmak's verse from *The Wolf Man* (1941) and features series semi-regular Laraine Newman as the mild-mannered Miss Dewberry.
✦✦

Mr. Fitz & Dr. Hyde

USA, 1996. Dir: Richard Elfman. With: Linda Cardellini, Saadia Persad, Esteban Powell, John Patrick White, Charles Fleischer, Dave Ruby. Silverman-Hyperion Productions/ABC-TV. Colour.
Looking for a new science project, Fitz convinces the school's creepy janitor Arnie (Fleischer) to open the old chemistry laboratory and discovers the scientific diary of Dr Jacob Hyde. However, when he drinks Hyde's distillation X 279, Fitz is transformed into the mad doctor (Vincent Schiavelli), who continues to work on his secretion of pure evil.
✦✦

Mummy Dearest

USA, 1996. Dir: Richard Elfman. With: Linda Cardellini, Saadia Persad, Esteban Powell, John Patrick White, Charles Fleischer, Dave Ruby. Silverman-Hyperion Productions/ABC-TV. Colour.
A student production of *Antony and Cleopatra* suffers from disappearing actors and a living mummy (Doug Jones) that is looking for a bride with the aid of his jackal-headed servants.
✦✧

Teacher Creature

USA, 1996. Dir: Rif Coogan. With: Linda Cardellini, Saadia Persad, Esteban Powell, John Patrick White, Charles Fleischer, Dave Ruby. Silverman-Hyperion Productions/ABC-TV. Colour.
When substitute science teacher Mr Batrachian mistakenly eats some toxic waste-contaminated frog's eggs, he begins to transform into a green-skinned amphibian monster.
✦✧

THE BONEYARD

USA, 1990. Dir: James Cummins. With: Ed Nelson, Deborah Rose, Norman Fell, Jim Eustermann, Denise Young, Phyllis Diller. Backbone/Cori Films/Prism. Colour.
Low-budget chiller filmed for $850,000 in North Carolina by writer/director Cummins. Based on the Chinese legend of the *kyoshi*, a pair of 300 year-old flesh-eating ghoul children escape to an old city morgue where they attack and infect others. While suicidal 300 pound psychic Alley Cates (Rose) and stuffy cop Jersey Callum (veteran Nelson) investigate, night-shift receptionist Miss Poopinplatz (Diller *sans* wig) is transformed into a ten-foot undead monster and her pet poodle Floofsoms becomes a creature from Hell.
✦✧

BONGO WOLF'S REVENGE

USA, 1970. Dir: Tom Baker. With: Bongo Wolf (William Donald Grollman).
Short film in which the drummer-lecturer pays a visit to the Count Dracula Society.
✦

LA BONNE DAME

France, 1966. Dir: Pierre Philippe. With: Valeska Gert, Constantin Nepo. SOFAC.
Twenty-five minute short featuring vampires. Narrated by Germaine Kerjean.
✦

BOO

USA, 1932. Dir: Albert DeMond. Universal. B&W.
Nine minute Universal Brevity comedy short featuring re-edited clips from *The Cat Creeps* (1930), *Frankenstein* (1931) and, surprisingly, *Nosferatu* (1922).
✦

THE BOOK TOWER:
Vampire Master

UK, 1979. Dir: Richard Callanan. With: Mark Miwurdz, Gerry Cowan, Dean Manning, Helen Stockdale. Yorkshire Television/ITV. Colour.
Magazine TV show, hosted by Miwurdz, which dramatises extracts from children's books. The first programme included a scene from Virginia Ironside's eponymous volume.
✦

THE BOOKWORM

USA, 1939. Dir: Isadore (Friz) Freleng. Metro-Goldwyn-Mayer. Colour.
Seven minute cartoon that includes a *Dr. Jekyll and Mr. Hyde* sequence, plus Edgar Allan Poe's 'The Raven' and the three witches from Shakespeare's *Macbeth*.

Sequel: THE BOOKWORM TURNS (qv; 1940)
✦✦

THE BOOKWORM TURNS
USA, 1940. Dir: Hugh Harman. Metro-Goldwyn-Mayer. Colour.
Seven minute cartoon sequel to *The Bookworm* (1939), in which Mr Hyde works a machine that transfers the Bookworm's mind into the body of a stupid raven.
✦✧

BOOS IN THE NIGHT
USA, 1950. Dir: I. (Isadore) Sparber. Famous Studios/ Paramount. Colour.
Eight minute musical cartoon in the *Screen Songs* series. During the song 'Pack Up Your Troubles', Frankenstein's Monster and a Peter Lorre-type character discover an old house haunted by ghosts.
Sequel: FIESTA TIME (1950)
✦✦

BORDELLO OF BLOOD
(aka TALES FROM THE CRYPT PRESENTS BORDELLO OF BLOOD)
Canada/USA, 1996. Dir: Gilbert Adler. With: Dennis Miller, Erika Eleniak, Angie Everhart, Chris Sarandon, Corey Feldman, John Kassir. Universal. Colour.
Following *Demon Night* (1995), this disappointing second movie spin-off from the *Tales from the Crypt* TV series (1989-96), is based on an unproduced script by Bob Gale and Robert Zemeckis. Comedian Miller is likeable as wisecracking private eye Rafe Guttman, whose search for the missing brother of Katherine Verdoux (Eleniak) leads him to a funeral home that doubles as a bordello of sexy vampires run by the undead Lilith (model Everhart) and televangelist Reverend Current (Sarandon). With Aubrey Morris, Phil Fondacaro, an uncredited cameo by Whoopi Goldberg, and William Sadler as a mummy and Sheila Mills as the Bride of Frankenstein in the framing sequences featuring the Crypt Keeper (voiced as usual by Kassir).
✦✦✧

CAROLL BORLAND
[1914-1994]

American actress and author, also known as Carol Borland. A friend and protégé of Bela Lugosi, she appeared with him as Luna, the vampire woman, in Tod Browning's *Mark of the Vampire* (1935).
qv: *Lugosi the Forgotten King* (1985); *100 Years of Horror: 'Bela Lugosi'* (1996); *100 Years of Horror: 'Dracula and His Disciples'* (1996); *100 Years of Horror: 'Scream Queens'* (1996); *The South Bank Show: 'Dracula'* (1993).

BORN OF THE WIND
USA, 1961. Dir: Mike Kuchar. Film-maker's Coop. Colour.
Twenty minute underground film in which a scientist restores a mummy to life. Produced by Mike and George Kuchar.
✦

BOSKO'S MECHANICAL MAN
USA, 1933. Dir: Hugh Harman. Voices: Carmen Maxwell, Rochelle Hudson. Harman-Ising/Warner Bros. B&W.
Six minute *Looney Tunes* cartoon drawn by Friz (Isadore) Freleng and Thomas McKimson. When Honey (Hudson) makes Bosko (Maxwell) do the dishes, he builds a robot called Frankensteen, which goes on the rampage until he inserts a record of 'Mary Had a Little Lamb' into it. This was Bosko's last film for Warners, although he survived for another five years at MGM.
Sequel: BOSKO'S PARLOR PRANKS (1934)
✦✧

BOSKO THE DRAWBACK
USA, 1933. Dir: Hugh Harman. Voices: Carmen Maxwell. Harman-Ising/Warner Bros. B&W.
Seven minute *Looney Tunes* cartoon in which Bosko (Maxwell) leads his football team to victory against opponents whose players include the Hunchback of Notre Dame and the Four Horsemen of the Apocalypse.
Sequel: BOSKO THE SPEED KING (1933)
✦✧

ROB BOTTIN
[b 1959]

American make-up effects artist and protégé of Rick Baker. As a teenager he assisted his mentor on *Star Wars* (1977) and *The Incredible Melting Man* (1978), before moving on to such New World releases as *Piranha* (1978) and *Humanoids from the Deep* (1980). Bottin created the werewolf transformations for Joe Dante's *The Howling* (1980) and the incredible alien shape-shifter effects for John Carpenter's *The Thing* (1982). He won an Academy Award for his work on *Total Recall* (1990).
qv: *Legend* (1985); *King Kong* (1976); *Tanya's Island* (1980).

BOUND
USA, 1996. Dir: The Wachowski Brothers (Larry Wachowski and Andy Wachowski). With: Jennifer Tilly, Gina Gershon, Joe Pantoliano, John (P.) Ryan, Christopher Meloni, Richard C. Sarafian. Dino De Laurentiis Company/Summit Entertainment/Newmarket Capital Group/Gramercy Pictures. Colour.
Sexy, stylish crime thriller that revolves around $2,000,000 stolen by gangster's girlfriend Violet (Tilly) and her tattooed ex-con lover Corky (Gershon) from hot-headed Mafia hood Caesar (Pantoliano). With a brief clip from *Night of the Living Dead* (1968) on TV.
✦✦✦

BOWERY AT MIDNIGHT
USA, 1942. Dir: Wallace Fox. With: Bela Lugosi, John Archer, Wanda McKay, Tom Neal, Dave O'Brien, Wheeler Oakman. Monogram/Astor Pictures. B&W.
One of Monogram's better low-budget outings (which isn't saying much), produced by 'Jungle' Sam Katzman and Jack Dietz. Lugosi stars as homicidal genius Karl Wagner, a college professor by day and a gangster by night, who uses a Bowery soup house as his cover. The real horror element comes from an old mad doctor-type who somehow brings Lugosi's victims back to life as zombies. It doesn't make a lot of sense.
✦✧

THE BOWERY BOYS MEET THE MONSTERS
USA, 1954. Dir: Edward Bernds. With: Leo Gorcey, Huntz Hall, Laura Mason, Ellen Corby, Lloyd Corrigan, John Dehner. Allied Artists. B&W.
'B' movie comedy in the long-running Bowery Boys series. The boys approach the creepy Gravesend family about using their old dark house as a playground for local kids. Pretty soon a mad doctor (Dehner) wants to put Gorcey's brain into Cosmos the gorilla, Hall is turned into a werewolf, and they get involved with Gorog the robot, a carnivorous plant and even a vampire (Paul Wexler). Like the rest of the series, you have to be a fan.
Sequel: JUNGLE GENTS (1954)
✦

BOY GOD
(aka STONE BOY)
Philippines, 1983 (1986). Dir: J. Erastheo Cuenco. With: Nino Muhlach, Jimi Melendrez, Isabel Rivas, Cecille Castillo. Video City/Cinex/D'Wonder Films. Colour.
Outlandish, low-budget children's monster movie. When a mad German scientist starts dumping chemicals into the water supply, he creates various monsters, including a winged vampire, a trio of werewolf sisters with furry tails, a two-headed monster and a cannibalistic Cyclops. Only Rocco, the limestone-like son of an immortal, can defeat the scientist's plans. With a sorcerer who shoots rays and a vaporising machine.
✦

LES BOWIE
[1913-1979]

British special effects technician who had a knack of making something out of nothing. Bowie first worked with Hammer Films on *The Quatermass Experiment* (1955), for which he was given a budget of £30, and he ended up winning an Academy Award for his work on *Superman* (1978).

qv: *Casino Royale* (1967); *The Curse of Frankenstein* (1957); *The Curse of the Werewolf* (1960); *Doctor Blood's Coffin* (1961); *Dracula A.D. 1972* (1972); *Dracula Prince of Darkness* (1965); *The Evil of Frankenstein* (1964); *Frankenstein Created Woman* (1966); *Grip of the Strangler* (1958); *The Kiss of the Vampire* (1962); *The Legend of the 7 Golden Vampires* (1974); *The Mummy's Shroud* (1967), *The Plague of the Zombies* (1966); *The Reptile* (1966); *The Satanic Rites of Dracula* (1973); *Vampire Circus* (1971).

PETER BOYLE
[b 1933]

Former monk who became a dependable character actor in offbeat movies. He played the singing and dancing Monster in *Young Frankenstein* (1974).

BOY MEETS WORLD: Who's Afraid of Cory Wolf?
USA, 1994. Dir: David Trainer. With: Ben Savage, William Daniels, Betsy Randle, Will Friedle, Rider Strong, William Russ. Touchstone Television/Michael Jacobs Productions/ ABC-TV. Colour.

Half-hour comedy TV series (1993-). On Halloween night, thirteen year-old Cory (Savage) goes through the normal teenage changes and is convinced that he is turning into a werewolf (he even sees his lycanthropic reflection in a mirror). With a special appearance by Phyllis Diller as clairvoyant Madame Ouspenskaya!

✦✦

THE BOY WHO CRIED WEREWOLF
USA, 1973. Dir: Nathan H. Juran. With: Kerwin Mathews, Elaine Devry, Robert J. Wilke, Scott Sealey, Bob Homel, Jack Lucas. RKF/Universal. Colour.

The star and director of *The 7th Voyage of Sinbad* (1958) are reunited with this unatmospheric chiller. When Roger Bridgestone (Mathews) is bitten by a werewolf (Paul Baxley) and turns into one himself when the moon is full, no one believes his twelve year-old son Richie (Sealey) except a commune of Jesus-freaks. In the end, the werewolf is impaled on a broken crucifix. Actor Homel also scripted. Make-up effects by Tom Burman.

✦✧

THE BRAHMIN'S MIRACLE
France, 1908. Pathé. Colour.

Silent short in which a magician transforms a mummy into a girl as part of his act.

✦

BRAINDEAD
(USA: DEAD ALIVE)
New Zealand, 1992. Dir: Peter Jackson. With: Timothy Balme, Diana Peñalver, Elizabeth Moody, Ian Watkin, Stuart Devenie, Brenda Kendall. WingNut Films/New Zealand Film Commission/Avalon/NFU Studios/ PolyGram. Colour.

Outrageously gory horror/comedy from thirty-one year-old co-writer/director Jackson, set in 1957 New Zealand. While spying on her son Lionel (comedian Balme) and his new Spanish girlfriend Paquita (Peñalver) at the zoo, insufferably possessive mother Vera (Moody) is bitten by a stop-motion Sumatran rat-monkey from Kong's Skull Island and transformed into a voracious cannibal zombie. Soon the plague spreads, and various townsfolk are transformed into the flesh-eating dead before they are finally chopped to pieces by Lionel in the over-the-top climax. With the director as an undertaker's assistant and a brief cameo by the ubiquitous Forrest J Ackerman.

✦✦✦

BRAIN OF BLOOD
(USA: aka THE BRAIN/THE CREATURE'S REVENGE/THE UNDYING BRAIN)
USA/Philippines, 1971. Dir: Al Adamson. With: Grant Williams, Kent Taylor, John Bloom, Regina Carrol, Vicki Volante, Angelo Rossitto. Phil-Am Enterprises/ Hemisphere Pictures. Colour.

As if Eddie Romero's series of Filipino *Blood Island* movies weren't bad enough, the producers hired Al Adamson to make his own contribution to the mad doctor genre. The result is predictably terrible. Taylor stars as Dr Lloyd Trenton, whose experiments with brain transplanting result in Gor (Bloom), an ugly pinhead monster. Meanwhile, Dorro (Rossitto), his sadistic dwarf assistant, torments the women they keep chained in the cellar for their blood. With Zandor Vorkov (Roger Engell) and guest star Reed Hadley. It was also released in Canada under the title *Brain Damage*.

✦

BRAINSTORM
USA, 1983. Dir: Douglas Trumbull. With: Christopher Walken, Natalie Wood, Louise Fletcher, Cliff Robertson, Jordan Christopher, Alan Fudge. Metro-Goldwyn-Mayer/United Artists. Colour.

Filmed in 70mm, this was nearly abandoned due to the suspicious drowning of star Natalie Wood in 1981. It was successfully completed by producer/director Trumbull two years later. Experiments by a group of scientists with a virtual reality recorder result in some unexpected side-effects and a vision of Heaven. With a clip from *Dr. Jekyll and Mr. Hyde* (1931) on TV and a music score by James Horner.

✦✦✧

THE BRAIN THAT WOULDN'T DIE
USA, 1960 (1962). Dir: Joseph Green. With: Herb (Jason) Evers, Virginia Leith, Leslie Daniel, Adele Lamont, Bonnie Sharie, Paula Maurice. Rex Carlton/American International Pictures. B&W.

Filmed under the title *The Head That Wouldn't Die* in New York in 1959, this sleazy exploitation horror thriller stars Evers as an obsessed surgeon who accidentally decapitates his fiancée in a car accident. He keeps her head alive while searching for a big-breasted stripper or photographic model whose body he can use for a transplant. During the gory climax, the mutant pinhead monster (seven-foot, eight-inch Eddie Carmel) he keeps locked in the closet escapes and bites a chunk out of his throat. With plenty of footage of ugly, near-naked women, and Sammy Petrillo (*Bela Lugosi Meets a Brooklyn Gorilla* [1952], etc) as a photographer.

✦✦

BRAM STOKER'S COUNT DRACULA
(Orig: EL CONDE DRÁCULA/NACHTS, WENN DRACULA ERWACHT/IL CONTE DRACULA. USA: COUNT DRACULA)
Spain/West Germany/Italy/Liechtenstein, 1970. Dir: Jess (Jesús) Franco. With: Christopher Lee, Herbert Lom, Klaus Kinsky (Kinski), Frederick (Fred) Williams, Maria Rohm, Soledad Miranda (Soledad Redon Bueno). Fénix Films/ Corona-Filmproduktion/Filmar Compagnia Cinematográfica/Towers of London. Colour.

Despite aspirations to be a definitive version of the novel, this is ultimately let down by the low budget. However, Lee plays Dracula the way Bram Stoker described him, and has more to do than in the Hammer sequels. He starts out as an older man with white hair and a moustache who gets younger after drinking blood. In the end, Dracula is set on fire in his coffin and tossed over a castle wall. When on screen, Lee dominates with just his presence, but there's good support from Lom as Professor Van Helsing (a role originally announced for Vincent Price) and Kinski as a surprisingly subdued Renfield. Unfortunately, it's written (under his usual pseudonym 'Peter Welbeck') and produced by Harry Alan Towers, and while this is one of director Franco's most assured films (he also turns up as Van Helsing's butler), he nearly ruins everything with his relentless

zooms and pans. With Paul Müller, Jack Taylor (George Brown Randall/Grek Martin), Teresa Gimpera, and Emma Cohen as another vampire. At one time, AIP was going to release this in America under the title *Dracula '71*. Pedro Portabella's *Cuadecuc (Vampir)* (1970) includes rare behind-the-scenes footage of the making of this film.
Remake: DRACULA (qv; 1972)
✦✦✧

BRAM STOKER'S DRACULA

USA, 1992. Dir: Francis Ford Coppola. With: Gary Oldman, Winona Ryder, Anthony Hopkins, Keanu Reeves, Richard E. Grant, Cary Elwes. Columbia/American Zoetrope/Osiris Films. Colour.
Originally announced as *Bram Stoker's Dracula: The Untold Story*, co-producer/director Coppola's overblown if visually striking $47,000,000 movie was touted as the first faithful screen adaptation of Stoker's novel and the most erotic interpretation to date. It is certainly one of the most tedious. In a prologue lifted from Richard Matheson's 1972 version and set in 1462, the wife (Ryder) of a long-haired Vlad (a miscast Oldman) drowns herself after being falsely told that her husband perished driving the Turkish invaders from his land. Renouncing God, the prince drinks blood and vows that he will rise from his own death to take revenge through the powers of darkness. In 1897, Dracula travels to London to seduce Mina Harker (Ryder again), who he believes to be the reincarnation of his eternal love. However, an enigmatic Abraham Van Helsing (Hopkins, who also appears as a priest in the opening scenes), Jonathan Harker (the terrible Reeves), Dr Jack Seward (Grant), Lord Arthur Holmwood (Elwes) and the Texan Quincey P. Morris (Bill Campbell) are around to try and stop the amorous vampire and his mad servant Renfield (musician Tom Waits). With laughable British accents, flashy Academy Award-winning special make-up effects (by Greg Cannom) and a complete lack of any sense of evil, this is yet another big-budget horror film made by people who don't really care for them. With Florina Kendrick, Michaela Bercu and Monica Bellucci as Dracula's vampiric brides. There was a novelisation by Fred Saberhagen and screenwriter James V. Hart, a graphic novel adaptation, and *Bram Stoker's Dracula: The Film and the Legend* was an official behind-the-scenes look at the production that included the script. *The Van Helsing Chronicles* is the title of the long-announced sequel to star Hopkins.
Remake: DRACULA (qv; 1994)
✦✦✦

WALTER BRANDI
(Walter Bigari) [1928-1996]

Italian leading man, also known as Walter Brandt, who appeared as a bloodsucker in a number of atmospheric vampire movies in the early 1960s. He later became a producer and died in near-poverty from leukaemia.
qv: *The Devil's Wedding Night* (1973); *King of Kong Island* (1968); *The Playgirls and the Vampire* (1960); *The Slaughter of the Vampires* (1962); *Terror Creatures from the Grave* (1965); *The Vampire and the Ballerina* (1960).

BRAM STOKER'S LEGEND OF THE MUMMY

(aka BRAM STOKER'S THE MUMMY)
USA, 1997 (1998). Dir: Jeffrey Obrow. With: Louis Gossett Jr, Amy Locane, Eric Lutes, Mark Lindsay-Chapman, Richard Karn, Lloyd Bochner. Goldbar Entertainment/Unapix Films/A-Pix Entertainment. Colour.
Made on an obviously shoestring budget, this third screen adaptation of Stoker's novel *The Jewel of Seven Stars* is even more incompre-

Christopher Lee puts the bite on Soledad Miranda in Bram Stoker's Count Dracula *(1970).*

hensible than the 1971 Hammer version. When Egyptologist Abel Trelawney (veteran Bochner) is struck down in his San Francisco home, his daughter Margaret (Locane) calls on art historian Robert Wyatt (Lutes) for help. Together with Trelawney's former partner John Corbeck (a tired-looking Gossett Jr with a laughable British accent), Wyatt discovers that various members of the household are being killed off by a mummy in the basement, while 3,000 year-old Egyptian Queen Tera (Rachel Naples) attempts to reincarnate her spirit inside Margaret's body. With Aubrey Morris (who was also in *Blood from the Mummy's Tomb* [1971]) and a wasted Victoria Tennant.
✦

THE BRAND OF SATAN

USA, 1917. Dir: George Archainbaud. With: Montagu Love, Gerda Holmes, Evelyn Greeley. Peerliss-World. B&W.
Silent melodrama about a strangler with a split personality. Scripted by J.P. Looney!
✦

BREAKFAST WITH DRACULA: A VAMPIRE IN MIAMI

Italy/USA, 1993. Dir: Fabrizio de Angelis. With: David Warbeck. Colour.
Warbeck portrays the Sheriff in this obscure Italian movie which has apparently never been released.
✦

BERNARD BRESSLAW [1933-1993]

British comedy actor, originally considered for the role of the Creature in Hammer's *The Curse of Frankenstein* (1957). A regular of the *Carry On* series.
qv: *Blood of the Vampire* (1958); *Carry On Christmas* (1969); *Carry On Screaming* (1966); *Morgan a Suitable Case for Treatment* (1966); *The Ugly Duckling* (1959); *Vampira* (1974).

SHANE BRIANT [b 1946]

Unmemorable British actor in several Hammer films before he subsequently moved to Australia.
qv: *Captain Kronos Vampire Hunter* (1972); *Frankenstein and the Monster from Hell* (1973).

THE BRIDE

France/UK, 1985. Dir: Franc Roddam. With: Sting (Gordon Sumner), Jennifer Beals, Geraldine Page, Clancy Brown, Anthony Higgins, David Rappaport. Columbia/ Delphi II Productions/Colgems Productions. Colour.
Romantic fable which, after a superb creation sequence, almost picks up where *Bride of Frankenstein* (1935) ended. Although overlong and slow in places, this remains an impressive version of Mary Shelley's classic, thanks to the stunning photography, atmospheric French locations, beautiful set design and strong casting: Sting's Baron Charles Frankenstein grows more monstrous as Brown's sympathetic creature Viktor becomes more human, thanks to the guidance of friendly dwarf Rinaldo (Rappaport). The eccentric supporting cast includes Page as a housekeeper, Alexei Sayle and Phil Daniels as comic villains, Quentin Crisp as the Baron's assistant Dr Zahlus, plus Veruschka, Cary Elwes, Tim Spall, Ken Campbell, Guy Rolfe and Tony Haygarth. Only Beals disappoints as the Monster's mate, Eva. Vonda N. McIntyre wrote the novelisation, and there were also illustrated adaptations by Elizabeth Levi and Les Martin (L.M. Schulman).
✦✦✦

THE BRIDE AND THE BEAST

(aka QUEEN OF THE GORILLAS)
USA, 1957 (1958). Dir: Adrian Weiss. With: Lance Fuller, Charlotte Austin, Johnny Roth, William Justine, Jeanne Gerson, Steve Calvert. Adrian Weiss/Allied Artists. B&W.
Laughably cheap gorilla movie scripted by none other than Edward D. Wood Jr (*Plan 9 from Outer Space* [1958], etc) and filmed under the title *Queen of the Gorillas*. During their honeymoon to Africa, big game hunter Dan (Fuller) discovers that his new bride Laura (Austin) is the reincarnation of a prehistoric love of amorous ape Spanky (Calvert in a monkey suit). In the end, she reverts to her animal state and disappears into the African jungle to live with others of her kind. This is padded with plenty of safari stock footage from *Man-Eater of Kumaon* (1948), and includes Ray 'Crash' Corrigan as another gorilla and a music score by Les Baxter.
✦

BRIDE OF CHUCKY

Canada/USA, 1998. Dir: Ronny Yu. With: Jennifer Tilly, Brad Dourif, Katherine Heigl, John Ritter, Nick Stabile, Alexis Arquette. Universal. Colour.
With this belated follow-up to *Child's Play 3* (1991), Hong Kong director Yu attempts to resurrect the franchise about the eponymous demonic doll (created by Kevin Yagher and voiced as usual by Dourif). Still possessed by the soul of serial killer Charles Lee Ray, the ravaged Chucky is revived by voodoo and teams up with his sexy psychopath girlfriend Tiffany (Tilly), who is electrocuted in the bath and reincarnated in a bridal doll. Only the soul-transferring amulet buried with Ray's human remains can allow the couple to possess the bodies of a pair of eloping teenagers. This includes numerous horror film in-jokes and clips from *Bride of Frankenstein* (1935) on TV. With music by Judas Priest, White Zombie, Slayer, Monster Magnet and Screamin' Cheetah Wheelies. A sequel entitled *Seed of Chucky* was announced in 1999.
✦✦✧

BRIDE OF FRANKENSTEIN

USA, 1935. Dir: James Whale. With: (Boris) Karloff, Colin Clive, Valerie Hobson, Elsa Lanchester, Una O'Connor, Ernest Thesiger. Universal. B&W.
Finally convinced by Universal to make a sequel to his *Frankenstein* (1931), director Whale created this classic black comedy (filmed under the titles *The Return of Frankenstein* and *Frankenstein Lives Again!*). It benefits from a higher budget, excellent photography, an inventive script (co-writer John L. Balderston threatened to disown the film — he wrote it as a satire) and a superb cast: Karloff recreates his role as the sympathetic Monster (in Jack P. Pierce's modified make-up), discovered still living in the ruins of the burned-out mill, who learns to talk, drink and smoke; Ernest Thesiger's marvellous Dr Septimus Pretorius (originally to have been played by Bela Lugosi or Claude Rains), with his bottled homunculi and a predilection for gin ('It's my only weakness'); and Lanchester, who appears as both creator Mary Shelley during the opening sequence and the shock-haired mate for the Monster (a role originally considered for Brigitte Helm). With solid support from Clive (who survives as Henry Frankenstein from the previous film), O'Connor's comedy relief Minnie, Dwight Frye's hunchbacked Karl, E.E. Clive's Burgomaster, O.P. Heggie's blind Hermit, and Mary Gordon, Walter Brennan, John Carradine and Billy Barty in small roles. Franz Waxman's memorable score was later reused in Universal's *Flash Gordon* serials. Fifteen minutes were cut after previews (including the Monster killing the Burgomaster and Karl's murder of his rich uncle) and a happy ending — in which Henry and Elizabeth survive the laboratory explosion — was added. It was novelised by Michael Egremont (Michael Harrison) in 1936, by Carl Dreadstone (Ramsey Campbell) in 1977, and as a juvenile by Carl R. Green and William R. Sanford (William Reynolds) in 1985. Edited by Philip J. Riley, MagicImage Filmbooks published the script in 1989. Anne Rice scripted a proposed remake for Universal in 1992 and in 1999 producers Brian Grazer and Sean Daniel (*The Mummy* [1999], etc) announced another remake set in the near future.
Sequel: SON OF FRANKENSTEIN (qv; 1939)
Remake/sequel: THE BRIDE (qv; 1985)
✦✦✦✦✦

BRIDE OF RE-ANIMATOR

(UK: RE-ANIMATOR 2)
USA, 1989 (1990). Dir: Brian Yuzna. With: Bruce Abbott, Claude Earl Jones, Fabiana Udenio, David Gale, Kathleen Kinmont, Jeffrey Combs. Wildstreet. Colour.
Disappointing 'B' movie sequel to Stuart Gordon's inventive *Re-*

Elsa Lanchester rejects Boris Karloff in Bride of Frankenstein *(1935).*

Animator (1985). Directed by the producer of the earlier film, it picks up where the original left off, with Herbert West (Combs) and Dan Cain (Abbott) back at Miskatonic University using spare body parts to create life instead of trying to reanimate it. Returning from the first film, Gale as the still-living decapitated head of Dr Hill (now with added bat wings!) is wasted. However, the creation of the Bride (Kinmont) almost recaptures the magic of James Whale's 1935 classic and Screaming Mad George's special effects are impressive, if predictable. This doesn't have much to do with H.P. Lovecraft's original novella. With Johnny Legend (Martin Margulies). It was heavily cut by the censor in Britain.

✦✦✧

BRIDE OF THE GORILLA

USA, 1951. Dir: Curt Siodmak. With: Barbara Payton, Lon Chaney, Raymond Burr, Tom Conway, Paul Cavanagh, Woody Strode. Jack Broder Productions/Realart. B&W.

Writer/director Siodmak and Chaney Jr are reunited from *The Wolf Man* (1941) for this silly murder mystery. Rubber plantation manager Barney Chavez (Burr) murders his boss (Cavanagh), marries his young widow (Payton) and is then cursed by an old witch woman. He begins to act like a gorilla until the local police chief Taro (Chaney) tracks him down and kills him. Herman Cohen was assistant producer. With Ray 'Crash' Corrigan in yet another ape suit.

✦✧

THE BRIDE'S INITIATION

USA, 1976. Dir: Duncan Stewart. With: Carol Connors, Constance Murray, Ambrosia, Candida Robbins, Mark Brock, Tony Manhall. VCX. Colour.

More hardcore antics, as a semen-drinking Dracula kidnaps and seduces a pair of newly-weds. In the end, the Count turns gay and goes off with the detective investigating the couple's disappearance. This also includes an ugly witch, female vampires and the cannibalism of genitalia.

✦

THE BRIDES OF DRACULA

UK, 1960. Dir: Terence Fisher. With: Peter Cushing, Freda Jackson, Martita Hunt, Yvonne Monlaur, Miles Malleson, Henry Oscar. Hotspur Films/Hammer Films/Universal-International. Colour.

Despite the title, Christopher Lee didn't want to repeat his role as the Count from *Dracula* (1958), so three scriptwriters (including Jimmy Sangster) cobbled together this atmospheric sequel which once again stars Cushing as Doctor Van Helsing. Set at the end of the nineteenth century, the opening narrative explains that, although Dracula is dead, his disciples live on. When naïve French schoolteacher Marianne Danielle (Monlaur) releases the Baron Meinster (forty year-old David Peel) from his mother's chains, little does she realise that she has set free a vampire to prey upon a nearby school for girls. Director Fisher gives the film a fairy-tale quality, and the best scenes include Van Helsing burning a vampire's bite from his neck; the mad Greta (Jackson) crawling over the grave of a recent victim, willing the new vampire to rise from the dead; and a great climax where a blazing mill forms the shadow of a cross. With Hammer veteran Michael Ripper, and Andree Melly as a seductive female vampire. Monarch published the paperback novelisation by Dean Owen (Dudley Dean McGaughy).

✦✦✦

THE BRIDES WORE BLOOD
(aka BLOOD BRIDE)

USA, 1982 (1984). Dir: Robert R. Favorite. With: Dolores Heisel. Favorite/Regal. Colour.

A vampiric demon plans to impregnate an unsuspecting blonde (Heisel) in this low-budget chiller, filmed in Jacksonville, Florida. Director Favorite apparently manages to botch most scenes, including the vampire's death-by-sunlight transformation.

✦

THE BRIGHTON STRANGLER

USA, 1945. Dir: Max Nosseck. With: John Loder, June Duprez, Michael St. Angel, Rose Hobart, Miles Mander, Ian Wolfe. RKO Radio Pictures. B&W.

Low-budget thriller in which an English actor (Loder) is caught during the Nazi blitz on London. When the smoke clears, he is presumed dead. In fact, he has taken on the personality of the killer he portrayed in a play. Thanks to a sympathetic performance by Loder and some imaginative camerawork this is a fun, if unremarkable, 'B' movie.

✦✦

BRIMSTONE:
Poem

USA, 1998. Dir: Felix Enriquez Alcalá. With: Peter Horton, John Glover, Teri Polo, Roger Yuan, Ntare Mwine, Rosalind Chao. Warner Bros Television/Fox Network. Colour.

Dark and moody hour-long supernatural TV series (1998-99, thirteen episodes), created by co-executive producers Ethan Reiff and Cyrus Voris. After being damned for murdering the man who raped his wife, police detective Ezekiel Stone (co-producer Horton) makes a deal with the Devil (a witty Glover) to return to Earth fifteen years later and recover 113 escaped souls from Hell. In this episode, Stone travels to Los Angeles' Chinatown district, where he has to track down a 1,000 year-old serial killer who is stealing the blood of his virgin victims to complete an epic love poem. Series theme composed by Peter Gabriel.

✦✦✦

BRING ME THE VAMPIRE

(Orig: ÉCHENME AL VAMPIRO)

Mexico/Venezuela, 1961 (1964). Dir: Alfredo B. Crevenna. With: (Alfonso) 'Pompin' Iglesias, María Eugenia San Martin, Carlos Riquelme, Hector Godoy, 'Mantequilla' (Fernando Soto), 'Borolas' (Joaquin Garcia Vargas). Producciones Rosas Priego/Estudios America/Clasa-Mohme/American International. B&W.

Old dark house comedy in three episodes, possibly filmed as early as 1959. A group of misfits have to stay in the Black Castle for a month so that they can inherit a possible fortune. This includes a mad killer, disappearing bodies and a fake vampire ('Mantequilla'). The sequel explains everything away with a happy ending. With Yerye Beirute. The English-language version was produced by K. (Kenneth) Gordon Murray and directed by Manuel San Fernando.

Sequel: LA CASA DE LOS ESPANTOS (qv; 1961)

✦

BRITANNIA HOSPITAL

UK, 1982. Dir: Lindsay Anderson. With: Leonard Rossiter, Graham Crowden, Joan Plowright, Jill Bennett, Marsha Hunt, Malcolm McDowell. EMI Films. Colour.

This dark satire caused an outcry in Britain when first released. Director Anderson concludes the loose trilogy he began with *If...* (1968) and *O Lucky Man!* (1973), set in an anarchic near-future during street riots and a visit by the Queen Mother to a run-down hospital. Crowden's delightfully mad Professor Millar and his assistant Macmillan (Bennett) are secretly creating a patchwork monster with the head of TV reporter Mick Travis (McDowell, recreating his role from the previous two films) and enough gore to rival *Re-Animator* (1985). In the end, Millar reveals his Genesis project — a giant living brain. The impressive supporting cast includes Mark Hamill(!), Robin Askwith, Peter Jeffrey, Fulton Mackay, Dandy Nichols, Vivian Pickles, Valentine Dyall, Roland Culver and guest appearances by Alan Bates and Arthur Lowe (in one of his last roles). A bitter attack on British politics and the collapse of the National Health Service, this was a box office flop. Music by Alan Price.

✦✦✦✦

BROTHER, CAN YOU SPARE A DIME?

UK, 1975. Dir: Philippe Mora. Goodtimes/Visual Programme Systems. B&W.

Documentary about the American Depression, from the director of two of the worst *Howling* sequels. This includes clips from *King Kong* (1933). Produced by David Puttnam.

✦✦✧

CONRAD BROOKS
(Conrad Biedrzycki/Bederski) [b 1931]

American supporting actor and sometimes director who has fashioned a career-of-sorts out of his association with Edward D. Wood Jr.
qv: *Blood Slaves of the Vampire Wolf* (1996); *Conrad Brooks Meets the Werewolf* (1993); *Curse of the Queerwolf* (1987); *Ed Wood* (1994); *Ed Wood Look Back in Angora* (1994); *Flying Saucers Over Hollywood* (1992); *The Haunted World of Ed Wood* (1996); *The Ironbound Vampire* (1997); *Night of the Ghouls* (1959); *On the Trail of Ed Wood* (1992); *Plan 9 from Outer Space* (1956); *A Polish Vampire in Burbank* (1983).

MEL BROOKS
(Melvin Kaminsky) [b 1926]

Unsubtle American comedy writer/producer/director/actor who began his career in television. Following the success of *The Producers* (1967), his career has been hit-or-miss, although *Young Frankenstein* (1974) remains a high point. His production company is responsible for much more interesting films, such as *The Elephant Man* (1980).
qv: *Dracula Dead and Loving It* (1995); *Everyman: 'The True Story of Frankenstein'* (1986); *Get Smart* (1965-70); *High Anxiety* (1977); *The Silence of the Hams* (1993).

RICOU BROWNING
[b 1930]

American stunt man and second unit director. A former Olympic swimmer, he played the Gill Man for the underwater sequences in *Creature from the Black Lagoon* (1954), *Revenge of the Creature* (1955) and *The Creature Walks Among Us* (1955).
qv: *The Colgate Comedy Hour: Abbott and Costello* (1953).

TOD BROWNING
(Charles Albert Browning) [1880-1962]

American writer, producer and director. After running away to join the circus in 1896, he became a clown for the Ringling Brothers and performed a 'Hypnotic Living Corpse' act before appearing in vaudeville. Following his role as a comic undertaker in D.W. Griffith's *Scenting a Terrible Crime* (1913), he moved to Hollywood where he made his directorial début with the two-reel comedy *The Lucky Transfer* (1915). Other shorts and stints both in front and behind the camera on *Intolerance* (1916) led to his feature début, *Jim Bludso* (1917). Despite problems with the studios because of his alcoholism, Browning made his comeback with *The Unholy Three* (1925), starring Lon Chaney Sr. Together they collaborated on a series of successful pictures, including *The Unknown* (1927), *London After Midnight* (1927), *West of Zanzibar* (1928) and a sound remake of *The Unholy Three* (1930) prior to Chaney's premature death. Browning had a hit with *Dracula* (1931), but his career went into a terminal slide with *Freaks* (1932), *Mark of the Vampire* (1935), *The Devil-Doll* (1936) and *Miracles for Sale* (1939). He retired in 1942 and later died of the same throat cancer as Chaney without ever giving a major interview about his career.

DAVID BRUCE
(Marden McBroom) [1914-1976]

Lightweight leading man, groomed for stardom at Warner Bros in the late 1930s, before becoming a contract player at Universal during the 1940s. *The Mad Ghoul* (1943) was a rare starring role.
qv: *The Mummy's Ghost* (1944).

THE BRUTE MAN

USA, 1946. Dir: Jean Yarbrough. With: Rondo Hatton, Tom Neal, Jan Wiley, Jane Adams, Donald MacBride, Peter Whitney. Producers Releasing Corporation/Pathé

Industries. B&W.
Almost a prequel to the previously-released *House of Horrors* (1946), which also featured Hatton as The Creeper. When handsome football hero Hal Moffat (Fred Coby) is disfigured in a chemical explosion, he is transformed into a hulking murderer (Hatton, in make-up created by Jack P. Pierce). He befriends beautiful blind piano teacher Helen Paige (Adams), who eventually betrays him to a pair of comedy relief cops (Whitney and MacBride). Director Yarbrough makes the mistake of revealing The Creeper's disfigured features too early, thus lessening their impact, while Hatton's attempts to create sympathy for his character fail with his wooden delivery of the monosyllabic dialogue. It was the actor's last film — he died two months after completing it at the age of fifty-one from a heart condition brought on by his acromegaly. Universal decided not to release the film and sold it on to PRC in America and Grand National in Britain. Although it runs only fifty-eight minutes, it seems much longer. With Tristram Coffin.
✦✧

BUBBLE GUM CRISIS 5: MOONLIGHT RAMBLER
(USA: aka BUBBLE GUM CRISIS 5)
Japan, 1988 (1991). Dir: Masami Obari. Voices: Yoshiko Sakakibara, Kinuko Oomori, Masayoshi Sogabe, Y. Mizutani. Artmic/Youmex/AIC/AnimEigo/Anime Projects. Colour.
Forty-five minute anime based on an original story by Toshimichi Suzuki in which a series of vampire killings in MegaTokyo turn out to be the work of pleasure-model android Sylvie. She is taking the blood to save her fellow sexaroid Anri, who was injured in their escape from a space station and requires the transfusions to remain functional.
✦✧

BUCK ROGERS
(aka DESTINATION SATURN/PLANET OUTLAWS)
USA, 1939. Dir: Ford Beebe and Saul Goodkind. With: Larry (Buster) Crabbe, Constance Moore, Jackie Moran, Jack Mulhall, Anthony Warde, Philson Ahn. Universal/ Filmcraft. B&W.
Made between the second and final *Flash Gordon* serials, Crabbe stars as yet another space hero, this time based on the character created by Philip Francis Nowlan in the pulp magazines and comic strips. Buck Rogers (Crabbe) and his teenage companion Buddy Wade (Moran) have been in suspended animation since their airship crashed. Rescued in the year 2240, they agree to help Dr Huer (C. Montague Shaw) and Wilma Deering (Moore) in their fight against Killer Kane (Warde) and his electronic zombies. Over twelve chapters, with such titles as 'Revolt of the Zuggs', 'Bodies Without Minds' and 'A Prince in Bondage', Buck and his companions fly around in unconvincing model spaceships, ride in an underground shuttle car, escape a disolvo-ray and encounter the monstrous Zuggs — servants of the Saturnians. With props and music borrowed from various Universal productions, this was released in different feature versions in 1953 and 1965.
Remake: BUCK ROGERS IN THE 25TH CENTURY (1979)
✦✦✦

BUCK ROGERS IN THE 25TH CENTURY:
Space Vampire
USA, 1980. Dir: Larry Stewart. With: Gil Gerard, Erin Gray, Tim O'Connor, Christopher Stone, Nicholas Hormann, Lincoln Kilpatrick. Universal/Glen A. Larson Productions/Bruce Lansbury Productions/NBC-TV. Colour.
Hour-long TV series (1979-81, thirty-seven episodes), based on the comic strip character. In 1987 NASA launched the last of America's deep space probes. In a freak mishap, *Ranger 3* and its pilot Captain William 'Buck' Rogers (Gerard) are blown out of their trajectory into an orbit which freezes his life-support systems and returns Rogers to Earth 500 years later. In one of the better episodes, Buck must save Wilma Deering (Gray) from becoming the next victim of The Vorvon, an alien soul-stealing Nosferatu that wants to turn her into one of the living dead. With Mel Blanc as the voice of robot Twiki, and opening narration by an uncredited William Conrad.
✦✦✧

BUENAS NOCHES, SEÑOR MONSTRUO
Spain, 1982. Dir: Antonio Mercero. With: Regalíz, Paul Naschy (Jacinto Molina), Luis Escobar, Fernando Bilbao, Andrés Mejuto, Guillermo Montesinas. José Frade Productions. Colour.
Musical comedy featuring the Regalíz group of child actors, with Naschy as a character named H.L. (a parody of J.R. in TV's *Dallas* [1978-91]) who also appears as a werewolf (not Waldemar Daninsky). This also includes Count Draculin (M.A. Valerro), Quasimodo (Montesinas), the Frankenstein Monster (Bilbao) and his creator (Mejuto). The title translates as 'Good Evening, Mr Monster'.
✦✧

BUFFY THE VAMPIRE LAYER
USA, circa 1996. Dir: Jack Stephen. With: Kristi Myst (Tina Harlow/Pamela Sanderson), Mila, Sahara Sands, Randi Storm, Randi Rage, Jack Stephen. Cinderella Distributors. Colour.
One of a series of hardcore comedies featuring Buffy (Myst), who in this video is summoned to Transylvania by the evil lawyer/vampire Count Hymie, also known as 'The Impaler'.
✦

BUFFY THE VAMPIRE SLAYER
USA, 1992. Dir: Fran Rubel Kuzui. With: Kristy Swanson, Donald Sutherland, Rutger Hauer, Luke Perry, Paul Reubens, Michele Abrams. Twentieth Century Fox/ Sandollar/Kuzui. Colour.
A nice idea from writer Joss Whedon. Valley Girl cheerleader Buffy (Swanson) discovers she is the Slayer, the reincarnation of a long line of young women whose destiny is to track down and destroy vampires. With the help of her mentor Merrick (a dignified Sutherland) and the local weirdo (Perry), she sets out to confront the King of the Undead, Lothos (a foppish performance by Hauer), and his wise-cracking henchman Amilyn (great support from an unrecognisable Reubens, aka Pee-Wee Herman). Unfortunately, director Kuzui doesn't have the lightness of touch the material needs and totally misjudges the climax where the vampire hordes attack the high school prom. With Candy Clark and Natasha Gregson Wagner. Richie Tankersly Cusick wrote the novelisation for Pocket Books.
Sequel: BUFFY THE VAMPIRE SLAYER (qv; 1996)
✦✦✧

BUFFY THE VAMPIRE SLAYER
USA, 1996. Dir: Charles Martin Smith and John T. Kretchmer. With: Sarah Michelle Gellar, Nicholas Brendon, Alyson Hannigan, Charisma Carpenter, Anthony Stewart Head, Brian Thompson. Twentieth Century Fox/Mutant Enemy/Kuzui Enterprises/Sandollar Television/The WB Network. Colour.
Improved sequel to the 1992 film and the pilot TV movie for the subsequent series (also shown in two parts as 'Welcome to the Hellmouth' and 'The Harvest'). When Slayer Buffy Summers (the very likeable Gellar) moves to Sunnydale, she learns from her 'Watcher' Rupert Giles (Head) that the town is a centre of mystical energy. She teams up with new friends Willow Rosenberg (Hannigan) and Xander Harris (Brendon) to battle the demonic nosferatu-like Master (Mark Metcalf) and his army of vampires, who are preparing for 'The Harvest', when they plan to open the Hellmouth and rule the world. Fun, fast-paced and scary. A second theatrical *Buffy* movie starring the TV cast was announced in 1999.
Sequel: BUFFY THE VAMPIRE SLAYER (qv; 1996-)
✦✦✦✧

BUFFY THE VAMPIRE SLAYER
USA, 1996- . With: Sarah Michelle Gellar, Nicholas Brendon, Alyson Hannigan, Charisma Carpenter, David Boreanaz, Anthony Stewart Head. Twentieth Century Fox/Mutant Enemy/Kuzui Enterprises/Sandollar Television/The WB Network. Colour.
This fast, fun and frightening TV series created by executive producer Joss Whedon is one of the best genre shows on TV. In every generation there is a chosen one. She alone will stand against the

vampires, the demons and the forces of darkness. Buffy Summers (Gellar) is the Slayer who goes to the high school in Sunnydale, a town built over the mouth of Hell. Aided by Willow Rosenberg (Hannigan), Xander Harris (Brendon), Cordelia Chase (Carpenter), her 'Watcher' Rupert Giles (Head) and the undead Angel (Boreanaz), she battles all manner of monsters (special make-up effects created by John Vulich and Optic Nerve Studios) in each hour-long episode. With Seth Green as Willow's werewolf boyfriend Oz, Kristine Sutherland as Buffy's mother Joyce, Eliza Dushku as renegade Slayer Faith, Blanca Lawson as Caribbean Slayer Kendra, Mark Metcalf as the vampiric Master, Robia LaMorte as techno-pagan Miss Calendar, James Marsters as Spike, Juliet Landau as Drusilla, K. Todd Freeman as Mr Trick, Harry Groener as the scheming Mayor Richard Wilkins III, Alexis Denisof as replacement 'Watcher' Wesley Wyndam-Pryce, Emma Caulfield as demon witch Anya, Marc Blucas as teaching assistant Riley Finn and Armin Shimerman as Principal Snyder. Cast members selected their all-time favourite music videos on the 1998 MTV Halloween special, *Videos That Don't Suck*, which also included a behind-the-scenes look at the series, and Gellar hosted the 1999 season finale of *Saturday Night Live*. There are numerous novelisations and tie-in books available.

✦✦✦✦

Beauty and the Beasts

USA, 1998. Dir: James Whitmore Jr. With: Sarah Michelle Gellar, Nicholas Brendon, Alyson Hannigan, Charisma Carpenter, David Boreanaz, Seth Green. Twentieth Century Fox/Mutant Enemy/Kuzui Enterprises/Sandollar Television/The WB Network. Colour.

A series of gruesome murders in Sunnydale are blamed on werewolf Oz until it is discovered that jealous science student Pete (Jason Patrick White) is using a potion to turn himself into the kind of man he things his submissive girlfriend Debbie (Danielle Weeks) wants him to be. The climax features a battle between the transformed Rage Monster and the lycanthrope, until Angel escapes after spending centuries in Hell and arrives to sort things out.

✦✦✧

Dead Man's Party

USA, 1998. Dir: James Whitmore Jr. With: Sarah Michelle Gellar, Nicholas Brendon, Alyson Hannigan, Charisma Carpenter, David Boreanaz, Seth Green. Twentieth Century Fox/Mutant Enemy/Kuzui Enterprises/Sandollar Television/The WB Network. Colour.

Buffy returns to Sunnydale to discover that a glowing-eyed Nigerian demon mask belonging to her mother is bringing the recently dead back to life as homicidal zombies.

✦✦

Go Fish

USA, 1998. Dir: David Semel. With: Sarah Michelle Gellar, Nicholas Brendon, Alyson Hannigan, Charisma Carpenter, David Boreanaz, Anthony Stewart Head. Twentieth Century Fox/Mutant Enemy/Kuzui Enterprises/Sandollar Television/The WB Network. Colour.

The Sunnydale High sports coach Carl Marin (Charles Cyphers) uses an experimental DNA process to create a champion swim-team. Unfortunately, Buffy and her friends discover that it has the side-effect of turning team members into monstrous gill men. With Conchata Ferrell.

✦✦✦

Inca Mummy Girl

USA, 1997. Dir: Ellen S. Pressman. With: Sarah Michelle Gellar, Nicholas Brendon, Alyson Hannigan, Charisma Carpenter, David Boreanaz, Anthony Stewart Head. Twentieth Century Fox/Mutant Enemy/Kuzui Enterprises/Sandollar Television/The WB Network. Colour.

When a cursed seal is broken at the museum, the vampiric mummy of a beautiful Inca princess (Ara Celi) is returned to life. Masquerading as South American exchange student Ampata Gutierrez living in Buffy's house, she needs to suck out the life-force of her victims to survive.

✦✦✧

Killed by Death

USA, 1998. Dir: Deran Sarafian. With: Sarah Michelle Gellar, Nicholas Brendon, Alyson Hannigan, Charisma Carpenter, David Boreanaz, Anthony Stewart Head. Twentieth Century Fox/Mutant Enemy/Kuzui Enterprises/Sandollar Television/The WB Network. Colour.

While recovering in hospital from the flu, Buffy has a vision of Der Kindestod (James Jude Courtney), a hideous creature which is invisible to adults and sucks the life out of sick children.

✦✦✧

Lie to Me

USA, 1997. Dir: Joss Whedon. With: Sarah Michelle Gellar, Nicholas Brendon, Alyson Hannigan, Charisma Carpenter, David Boreanaz, Anthony Stewart Head. Twentieth Century Fox/Mutant Enemy/Kuzui Enterprises/Sandollar Television/The WB Network. Colour.

Billy Fordham (Jason Behr), an old schoolfriend of Buffy's, is apparently transferred to Sunnydale High. It turns out that he is a wannabe vampire who is prepared to trade the life of The Slayer in return for immortality as one of the undead. This includes clips from the 1972 *Dracula* featuring Jack Palance being shown in a vampire Goth club.

✦✦✦✧

Phases

USA, 1998. Dir: Bruce Seth Green. With: Sarah Michelle Gellar, Nicholas Brendon, Alyson Hannigan, Charisma Carpenter, David Boreanaz, Anthony Stewart Head. Twentieth Century Fox/Mutant Enemy/Kuzui Enterprises/Sandollar Television/The WB Network. Colour.

When Willow discovers that the werewolf (played by Keith Campbell, in make-up by Todd McIntosh) terrorising Sunnydale is her boyfriend Oz, Buffy must save the reluctant lycanthrope from werewolf hunter Cain (Jack Conley).

✦✦✧

Some Assembly Required

USA, 1997. Dir: Bruce Seth Green. With: Sarah Michelle Gellar, Nicholas Brendon, Alyson Hannigan, Charisma Carpenter, David Boreanaz, Anthony Stewart Head. Twentieth Century Fox/Mutant Enemy/Kuzui Enterprises/Sandollar Television/The WB Network. Colour.

In this Frankenstein-inspired episode, when Chris Epps (Angelo Spizzirri), a member of the school Science Fair, brings his dead brother Daryl (Ingo Neuhaus) back to life after a car crash, the reanimated football star wants a girlfriend created from body parts stolen from the cemetary and Cordelia's head.

Series sequel: ANGEL (qv; 1999-)

✦✦✦

BUGS:

Renegades

UK, 1997. Dir: Matthew Evans. With: Craig McLachlan, Jaye Griffiths, Jesse Birdsall, Jan Harvey, Paula Hunt, Robert Morgan. Carnival Films/BBC-TV. Colour.

Hour-long hi-tech TV show (1995-), created by series consultant Brian Clemens and written by Stephen Gallagher. In this episode, Ed (McLachlan), Ros Henderson (Griffiths) and Nick Beckett (Birdsall) must stop their friend, Bureau of Weapons chief Roland Blatty (Morgan), and two others who have been reactivated as super-strong zombies by a sentient computer virus that is attempting to steal four program disks to reboot itself.

✦✦✧

BUGS BUNNY'S HOWL-OWEEN SPECIAL

USA, 1977. Dir: David Detiege (and Friz [Isadore] Freleng, Chuck [Charles M.] Jones, Abe Levitow, Robert McKimson and Maurice Noble). Voices: Mel Blanc, June Foray. Warner Bros/CBS-TV. Colour.

Half-hour cartoon special that includes confusing new bridging animation featuring Bugs Bunny, Witch Hazel, Dr Jekyll and his green-skinned alter-ego, plus clips from *A-Haunting We Will Go* (1966), *Broomstick Bunny* (1956), *Hyde Go Tweet* (1959), *Scaredy Cat* (1948) and *Transylvania 6-5000* (1963), with Sylvester, Tweetie, Daffy, Speedy and Porky.

✦✦

BUNNICULA, THE VAMPIRE RABBIT

USA, 1982. Dir: Charles A. Nichols. Voices: Jack Carter, Howard Morris, Pat Peterson, Alan Young, Janet Waldo, Alan Dinehart. Ruby-Spears Enterprises/ABC-TV. Colour.

Half-hour cartoon special based on the popular children's book by Deborah and James Howe. A cute rabbit found in a shoe box turns out to be the eponymous Romanian rabbit who drains tomatoes of their juices.

✦✦

BUREAU OF ALIEN DETECTORS:
Twinkle, Twinkle

USA, 1996. Voices: Bree Anderson, G. Gordon Baer, Reuben Daniels, Sammy Lane, Michael McConnohie, Walter Rego. A Joint Venture/Saban International/UPN Kids. Colour.

Half-hour children's TV cartoon series (thirteen episodes). Led by Sgt Ben Packer and psychic communicator Casey Taylor, BAD is an elite group of top secret, trained professionals backed up by super technology and high-tech weapons that has the ability to detect extraterrestial beings. Together they have only one mission; to confront, control and contain all alien encounters. In this two-part episode, invading Martians resurrect the dead of Earth's wars and transform them into a zombie army to conquer the world.

✦✧

BURNED TO LIGHT

Luxembourg/USA, 1999. Dir: Elias Merhige. With: John Malkovich, Willem Dafoe, Udo Kier, Cary Elwes, Catherine McCormack, Eddie Izzard. Saturn Films/BBC Films/Lions Gate Films. Colour.

$10,000,000 fictionalised look at the lengths F.W. Murnau (Malkovich) went to lend authenticity to his *Nosferatu* (1922). Demanding utter realism, the director hires real vampire/actor Max Shreck (Dafoe) to star in his film. Originally announced under the title *Shadow of the Vampire*, this was co-produced by Nicholas Cage (*Vampire's Kiss* [1988], etc).

✦✦✧

THE BURNING ZONE:
Faces In The Night

USA, 1996. Dir: Scott Brazil. With: Jeffrey Dean Morgan, Michael Harris, James Black, Tamlyn Tomita, Marc Poppel, Alicia Coppola. Universal/Sandstar Productions/UPN. Colour.

Short-lived, hour-long, disease-of-the-week TV series (1996-97, nineteen episodes) created by Coleman Luck. A team of bio-specialists battle a secret organisation, The Dawn (who want to eradicate mankind from the Earth), and various outbreaks of weird and bizarre diseases. In this episode, when a full-moon serial murderer who calls himself 'The Werewolf Killer' kidnaps Dr Kimberly Shiroma (Tomita), the bio-crisis team attempt to identify the murderer by cloning his features from his DNA.

✦✦✧

BYRON'S EVIL

UK, 1972. Dir: Andrew Sinclair. With: Oliver Reed. Lee International Films. Colour.

This was apparently never completed after shooting was halted when the production ran into financial problems. Reed played the title role and also appeared as the Frankenstein Monster.

✦

CAFE FLESH
USA, 1982. Dir: Rinse Dream (Stephen Sayadian). With: Pia Snow (Michelle Bauer/Michelle McClellan), Marie Sharp, Andrew Nichols, Paul McGibboney, Robert Dennis, Becky Savage. Caribbean/VCA Pictures. Colour.
Flashy, erotic science fiction film, set in the post-holocaust 'mutant universe' five years after a nuclear war. The few remaining Sex Positives are forced to perform for the Sex Negatives in the Café Flesh. This includes Nichols as Max, a vampiric emcee (with a mock-Lugosi accent), and a performer with fangs. Snow was the July 1981 *Penthouse* Pet before she became scream queen Bauer. Released in both hard- and softcore versions, from the director of *Dr. Caligari* (1989).
Sequel: CAFE FLESH 2 (1997)
✦✧

EDWARD L. CAHN
[1899-1963]
Prolific, if undistinguished American director and producer who began his career at Universal during the 1920s.
qv: *Beauty and the Beast* (1961); *Creature With the Atom Brain* (1955); *Curse of the Faceless Man* (1958); *The Four Skulls of Jonathan Drake* (1959); *Invisible Invaders* (1959), *It! The Terror from Beyond Space* (1958), *Zombies of Mora Tau* (1957).

A CALL FROM THE DEAD
USA, 1915. With: Ethyle Cooke, Justus Barnes, Boyd Marshall, Thomas Curran. Thanhouser. B&W.
Fifteen minute silent short in which a man's corpse revenges itself on his murderer.
✦

BRUCE CAMPBELL
[b 1958]
American leading man and producer, best known for his portrayal of the long-suffering Ash in Sam Raimi's trilogy, *The Evil Dead* (1982), *Evil Dead II* (1987) and *Army of Darkness* (1992). On TV he played the eponymous Western hero in *The Adventures of Brisco County, Jr.* (1993-4) before being put under contract by Disney.
qv: *The Dead Next Door* (1989); *The Demolitionist* (1995); *Filmhouse Fever* (1986); *From Dusk Till Dawn 2: Texas Blood Money* (1998); *Sundown The Vampire in Retreat* (1988); *Waxwork II: Lost in Time* (1991).

CAMPFIRE TALES
USA, 1990 (1991). Dir: William Cooke and Paul Talbot. With: Gunnar Hansen, David Avin, L.E. Campbell, Jeff Jordan, H. Ray York, M.R. Smith. Crimson Productions. Colour.
Low-budget anthology movie in which a bearded drifter (Hansen) tells a group of kids four campfire stories about a hook-handed serial killer ('The Hook'), bad marijuana that turns people into mush ('Overtoke'), a demonic Satan (*sic*) Claus ('The Fright Before Christmas') and zombie pirates that rise from the sea ('Skull & Crossbones'). With clips from *Reefer Madness* (1936), *The Terror* (1963) and *Witchcraft Through the Ages* (1918/21). Not to be confused with a 1996 anthology movie with the same title.
✦✧

THE CANDIDATE
(aka PARTY GIRLS FOR THE CANDIDATE)
USA, 1964. Dir: Robert Angus. With: Mamie Van Doren, June Wilkinson, Ted Knight, Eric Mason, Rachel Roman. Cosnat Productions/Morgan. B&W.
Exposé of political corruption in Washington DC. At a party, people wearing Frankenstein and other monster masks (created by Ellis Burman) try to frighten the guests. Cinematography by the great Stanley Cortez.
✦

CANNIBAL HOOKERS
USA, 1987. Dir: Donald Farmer. With: Mayra Grant, Sheila Best, Matt Borlenchi, Gary J. Levinson. Camp Video. Colour.
Shot-on-video horror about two sorority pledges who have to dress up as hookers on Hollywood Boulevard. While the guys watch clips from *Curse of the Screaming Dead* (1982), the girls become flesh-eating zombies. With producer Levinson as Lobo, this was shot at Ted V. Mikels' castle in Hollywood by the director of *Vampire Cop* (1988).
✦

CAPE CANAVERAL MONSTERS
USA, 1960. Dir: Phil Tucker. With: Scott Peters, Linda Connell, Jason Johnson, Katherine Victor, Gary Travis, Frank Smith. CCM. B&W.
More low-budget ineptitude from the director of the infamous *Robot Monster* (1953). Two disembodied aliens arrive on Earth and cause a car to crash. They then possess a pair of dead bodies they have reanimated (Johnson and Victor) in an attempt to sabotage the American space programme. Star Connell's father, Merle, was the cinematographer.
✦

CAPTAIN BARBELL
Philippines, 1986. Dir: Leroy Salvador. With: Edu Manzano, Herbert Bautista, Lea Salonga, Dennis Da Silva, Ruel Vernal, Sharon Cuneta. Viva Films. Colour.
Cut-price children's superhero fantasy about a young boy, Tengteng, who can transform into superhero Captain Barbell (Manzano). He battles a vampire-werewolf who can fly and wears a cape, until the monster is impaled on a cross. The Captain also encounters a spider woman and her monster assistants, alien woman Darna (Cuneta) and some ghostly electrical beings.
Sequel: ANG PAGBABALIK NI PEDRO PENDUKO (qv; 1994)
✦

CAPTAIN KRONOS VAMPIRE HUNTER
UK, 1972 (1974). Dir: Brian Clemens. With: Horst Janson, John Carson, Shane Briant, Caroline Munro, John Cater, Ian Hendry. Hammer Films/EMI. Colour.
This was the first and, regrettably, only film in a proposed series created by writer/director Clemens (TV's *The Avengers* [1961-69], etc) and filmed under the title *Kronos*. It's a heady blend of Hammer vampires, comic book violence, spaghetti Westerns, heroic fantasy and offbeat comedy. Swashbuckling soldier of fortune Captain Kronos (German actor Janson, dubbed by Julian Holloway), hunchback assistant Prof Hieronymous Grost (Cater) and busty gypsy Carla (Munro) must discover the identity of a vampire (a relation to the Karnstein family) who steals youth instead of blood. Could it be guest stars Carson, Hendry or Wanda Ventham (from *The Blood Beast Terror* [1967], etc)? The direction is sometimes unsure, but there's plenty of new vampire lore and some stunning visuals. Fontana Books published the novelisation by Hugh Enfield under the title *Kronos*, the character continued his exploits in a series of comic strips in the first three issues of *The House of Hammer* magazine (1976), and the film itself was adapted in the retitled *House of Horror* no.20 (1978).
✦✦✦✦

CAPTAIN YAGIT
Philippines, circa 1985. Dir: Angel Labra. With: Cachupoy, Luis Gonzales, Redford White, Gladys Mercado, Max Alvarado, Bamba. Horizon Films. Colour.
Low-budget fantasy in which an alien from a flying fireball gives a man (White) a medallion that enables him to transform into the eponymous superhero. When a second, cyborg-looking alien raises the dead from a cemetery, Captain Yagit battles the zombies. With an appearance by Superman in a dream sequence and John Williams' score from *Superman* (1978) used uncredited throughout.
✦

CAPTIVE WILD WOMAN

USA, 1943. Dir: Edward Dmytryk. With: Acquanetta (Burnu Davenport), Evelyn Ankers, John Carradine, Milburn Stone, Lloyd Corrigan, Martha MacVicar (Vickers). Universal. B&W.

First announced in 1941, Universal tried to boost its failing horror cycle with this thriller starring Carradine as the mad Dr Sigmund Walters, who injects Cheela the ape (Ray 'Crash' Corrigan in a monkey suit) with glandular extractions from a sick girl (MacVicar). The ape is transformed into a beautiful woman (Acquanetta, making her 'official' screen début as 'The Gorilla Girl') who Walters christens Paula Dupree. Unfortunately, she periodically reverts back to her animal state (make-up by Jack Pierce) and is finally shot to death saving the life of animal trainer Fred Mason (Stone, who later played Doc on TV's *Gunsmoke* [1955-75]), whom she loves. This includes plenty of stock footage from *The Big Cage* (1933) featuring Clyde Beatty (who gets a special credit for his 'co-operation and inimitable talent'). With Fay Helm, Paul Fix and an uncredited Turhan Bey, who supplied the closing narration.

Sequel: JUNGLE WOMAN (qv; 1944)

✦✦

CAPULINA CONTRA LAS MOMIAS

(aka CAPULINA ENTRE LAS MOMIAS/EL TERROR DE GUANAJUATO)

Mexico, 1972 (1973). Dir: Alfredo Zacharias. With: Gaspar Henaine 'Capulina', Jacqueline Voltaire, Enrique Panton, Freddy Fernandez. Estudios America/Producciones Zacarias/Panorama Films/Azteca Films. Colour.

Popular moustachioed musical comedian 'Capulina' (Henaine) made his film début in 1945 and first began meeting monsters as part of the comedy team Viruta (Marco Antonio Campos) and Capulina in *Se los Chupo la Bruja* (1957) and *Muertos de Miedo* (1957). He even teamed up with Santo in 1968 (*Santo contra Capulina*). Here he finds himself dreaming that a mad scientist restores the mummies of Guanajuato to life. This apparently started out as a three-part TV mini-series.

Sequel: CAPULINA VS. LOS MONSTRUOS (qv; 1972)

✦✧

CAPULINA CONTRA LOS VAMPIROS

Mexico, 1972 (1973). Dir: René Cardona. With: Gaspar Henaine 'Capulina', Rosa Mendoza, Juan Gallardo, Carlos Agosti, Aurelio Perez ('Chori'), Jacqueline Andere. Producciones Zacarias/Clasa-Mohme. Colour.

Silly comedy starring the moustachioed 'Capulina' (Henaine), who hides in a suit of armour from the hordes of big-fanged vampires pursuing him. In the end, the toothless undead drink milk from baby-bottles. Directed by horror veteran Cardona.

Sequel: CAPULINA CONTRA LAS MOMIAS (qv; 1972)

✦✧

CAPULINA VS. LOS MONSTRUOS

(aka CAPULINA CONTRA LOS MONSTRUOS)

Mexico, 1972. Dir: Miguel Morayta. With: Gaspar Henaine 'Capulina', Irlanda Mora, Gloriella, Hector Andremar, Salvador Zea, Marco Contreras. Estudios America/ Producciones Zacarias/Panorama Films/Azteca Films. Colour.

More humour from the moustachioed comedian 'Capulina' (Henaine) when he helps a group of children battle a vampire (Zea), a werewolf (Contreras), a mummy (Juan Garza), the Frankenstein Monster (Guillermo Amador) and Mr Hyde. Don't they ever get tired of this plot in Mexico?

✦✧

CARESS OF THE VAMPIRE

USA, 1997. Dir: Frank Terranova. With: Paulina Monet, Jessica English, Darien Price, Joe Moller, Moe Noodleman, Bob Gonzo. Brain Escape Pictures/Terranova, Light & Magic/EI Independent Cinema. Colour.

Independent softcore video shot in New Jersey. While two detectives investigate the series of killings she is responsible for, alien lesbian vampire Seth decides that her next victim will be the divorcee who has just moved in next door. There's not much of a plot amongst the topless nudity. Although this is under an hour long, the tape is padded out with thirty-five minutes of sleazy behind-the-scenes footage. *Caress of the Vampire 2* (1997) is a sequel in name only.

Sequel: CARESS OF THE VAMPIRE 3 LUST OF THE NIGHT STALKER (qv; 1998)

✦

RENÉ CARDONA (Sr)
[1906-circa 1970s]

Cuban-born Mexican actor-turned-director, whose prolific output encompasses five decades of horror and fantasy films South of the Border. These include several titles featuring Santo, the Silver-Masked Wrestler. His less-talented son René Cardona Jr followed in his footsteps as a writer/director.

qv: *Capulina Contra los Vampiros* (1972); *La Invasión de los Muertos* (1972); *The Macabre Trunk* (1936); *Las Mujeres Panteras* (1966); *La Mujer Murciélago* (1967); *El Museo del Crimen* (1944); *Santo Contra el Espectro del Estrangulador* (1963); *Santo Contra el Estrangulador* (1963); *Santo Contra los Cazadores de Cabezas* (1969); *Santo en la Venganza de la Momia* (1969); *Santo y el Tesoro de Dracula* (1967); *The Wrestling Women vs. the Aztec Mummy* (1964); *The Wrestling Women vs. the Killer Robot* (1968).

CARESS OF THE VAMPIRE 3 LUST OF THE NIGHT STALKER

(aka CARESS OF THE VAMPIRE 3: VAMPIRE LUST)

USA, 1998 (1999). Dir: Mario Cimadevilla. With: Danni D'Vine, Sabrina Sidoti. Brain Escape Pictures/Salt City Home Video/Draculina Cine/EI Independent Cinema. Colour.

Originally announced as *Caress: The Hunted*, this direct softcore video sequel to the 1997 original features more gratuitous nudity and simulated sex. Undercover Florida police officer Kathy has a series of lesbian encounters with prostitutes while she is hunting for 200 year-old alien vampire serial killer Lette. This is even more amateurish than the first one, from which it repeats an entire sequence despite being under an hour long. The tape also includes five minutes of naked audition footage.

✦

CARESS OF THE VAMPIRE 2 TEENAGE GHOUL GIRL A GO-GO

USA, 1997. Dir: The People at Severed Lips Recordings. With: Ruby Honeycat, William Hellfire, Mikey Ovum, Matt Icklan. Brain Escape Pictures/Severed Lips Recordings/EI Independent Cinema. Colour.

Billy the vampire turns the town's teens into bloodsuckers in this cheap-looking independent video, filmed in a house in New Jersey. Lesbians, gays, a vampire rock band and foot fetishist Dr Acula (Icklan) are all featured in this failed attempt to create a no-budget cult classic.

✦

VERONICA CARLSON
(Veronica Mary Glazier) [b 1944]

British actress and former model who played the innocent blonde heroine in the Hammer movies *Dracula Has Risen from the Grave* (1968), *Frankenstein Must Be Destroyed* (1969) and *The Horror of Frankenstein* (1970).

qv: *Fangs: A History of Vampires in the Movies* (1992); *Flesh and Blood: The Hammer Heritage of Horror* (1994); *100 Years of Horror: 'Baron Frankenstein'* (1996); *100 Years of Horror: 'Dracula and His Disciples'* (1996); *This is Your Life: 'Christopher Lee'* (1974); *Vampira* (1974).

CARMILLA

Spain, 1973. Dir: Jaime Picas. With: Marisa Paredes, Maria Enriquetta Caballeira.

Spanish TV adaptation of J. Sheridan Le Fanu's 1871 novella, with Paredes as the vampiric Carmilla.

Remake: CARMILLA LE COEUE PÉTRIFIÉ (qv; 1988)

✦

CARMILLA

USA, 1994 (1998). Dir: Jay Lind. With: Maria Pechukas, Julie Teachey, Colleen Van Ryan, Amanda Lauren Lind, Jasmine St. James, Mandy Leigh. Evil Clown Productions/ Draculina Cine/Salt City Home Video. Colour.

Written and directed by Lind, this independent erotic video release updates J. Sheridan Le Fanu's 1871 novella to modern-day Long Island, New York. The undead Carmilla/Madelaine (Pechukas) is preying on the upscale teenagers who populate the town in which she lives.

Remake: VAMPIRE CARMILLA (qv; 1999)

✦

CARMILLA LE COEUE PÉTRIFIÉ

France, 1988. Dir: Paul Planchon. With: Aurelle Doazan, Emmanuelle Meyssignac, Yvette Stahl, Paulette Schlegel, Roland Kieffer, André Pomarat. FR3 Alsace. Colour.

Hour-long TV adaptation of the story by J. Sheridan Le Fanu, with Meyssignac as the vampiric Carmilla.

Remake: NIGHTMARE CLASSICS: Carmilla (qv; 1989)

✦✧

CARNE DE TU CARNE

Colombia, 1984. Dir: Carlos Mayolo. With: Adriana Herran, David Guerrero, José Angel. Producciones Visuales. Colour.

Muddled political satire from Colombia, about a wealthy family involved in incest and vampirism in 1956. The film is dedicated to Roman Polanski and Roger Corman.

✦

CARNIVAL OF SOULS

(aka CORRIDORS OF EVIL)

USA, 1962. Dir: Herk Harvey. With: Candace Hilligoss, Sidney Berger, Herk Harvey, Frances Feist, Dan Palmquist, Bill de Jarnette. Harcourt/Herts-Lion International. B&W.

Shot in and around Lawrence, Kansas, for just $30,000 by director/producer Harvey, who is also featured as The Man, a pasty-faced zombie/spectre who haunts organist Mary Henry (Hilligoss) when she is drowned in a car accident and then mysteriously revived in a dream-like half-world. As the story unfolds, the low budget, amateur performances and offbeat locations (the haunting pavilion filled with the dancing dead) give the film an almost surreal quality. Reissued in 1989 in a version that restored nine minutes of explanatory footage originally cut by the distributor and subsequently released on video with a new introduction by Harvey (who died in 1996), this remains a real oddity with some genuinely unnerving moments.

Remake: CARNIVAL OF SOULS (qv; 1998)

✦✦✦✧

CARNIVAL OF SOULS

(aka WES CRAVEN PRESENTS CARNIVAL OF SOULS)

USA, 1998 (1999). Dir: Adam Grossman. With: Bobbie Phillips, Larry Miller, Cleavant Derricks, Paul Johansson, Anna Kristin McKown, Shawnee Smith. Trimark Pictures/Chicagowest Entertainment. Colour.

Creepy, atmospheric reworking of the 1962 original in which the line between reality and nightmare blurs for bar owner Alex Grant (Phillips) as she is menaced by demonic clown Louis Seagram (a genuinely disturbing performance by comedian Miller), who she witnessed murdering her mother twenty years previously. After apparently crashing her car into the river, Grant finds herself drawn to a dream-like carnival populated by the living dead and Clive Barker-inspired monsters. Original co-star Sidney Berger appears in a cameo. Wes Craven and Anthony Hickox were among the executive producers.

✦✦✦

CAROL BURNETT SHOW

USA, 1972. With: Carol Burnett, Vincent Price, Harvey Korman, Vicki Lawrence. CBS-TV. Colour.

Hour-long entertainment TV series that includes the comedy sketch 'House of Terror', in which Dr Frankenstein (Price) plans to use the parts of his new bride (Burnett) to restore his mother's youth. His artificially-created hunchbacked assistant Igor (Korman) falls in love with the woman and refuses to help complete the experiment.

✦✧

JOHN CARRADINE
(Richmond Reed Carradine) [1906-1988]

Cadaverous American actor with a sonorous voice who had a life-long admiration for the works of William Shakespeare. Also known as John Peter Richmond, he began his career as a painter and sculptor working on set designs for Cecil B DeMille. After small roles in *The Invisible Man* (1933) and *Bride of Frankenstein* (1935), Carradine was reduced to playing a grade 'B' bogeyman in such 1940s fodder as *Captive Wild Woman* (1943), *Revenge of the Zombies* (1943), *Voodoo Man* (1944), *The Mummy's Ghost* (1944) and *The Face of Marble* (1946). Much of his best work was done for director John Ford, and he still managed to make a respectable Dracula in both *House of Frankenstein* (1944) and *House of Dracula* (1945) before ending up in such dross as *Billy the Kid Versus Dracula* (1965) and *Nocturna* (1979). The father of five sons (including actors David, Keith and Robert) and with several failed marriages behind him, Carradine worked to pay the bills. He continued to turn up in films after his death via stock footage.

qv: *The Astro Zombies* (1968); *BJ and the Bear: 'A Coffin With a View'* (1978); *Blood of Dracula's Castle* (1967); *Blood of Ghastly Horror* (1972); *The Cat Creature* (1973); *Doctor Dracula* (1977); *Dr. Terror's Gallery of Horrors* (1966); *Evils Of The Night* (1983); *Evil Spawn* (1987); *Frankenstein Island* (1981); *Hillbillys in a Haunted House* (1967); *The Horror of It All* (1983); *Horror of the Blood Monsters* (1970); *House of Dracula's Daughter* (1973); *The House of Seven Corpses* (1973); *House of the Black Death* (1966); *The Howling* (1980); *Invisible Invaders* (1959); *Jungle Woman* (1944); *Lights Out: 'The Meddlers'* (1951); *Lugosi the Forgotten King* (1985); *Mary, Mary, Bloody Mary* (1975); *Matinee Theater: 'Dracula'* (1956); *McCloud: McCloud Meets Dracula* (1977); *The Monster Club* (1980); *The Mummy and the Curse of the Jackals* (1969); *Munster, Go Home!* (1966); *The Munsters* (1965-67); *The Night Strangler* (1972); *100 Years of Horror: 'Bela Lugosi'* (1996); *100 Years of Horror: 'Dracula and His Disciples'* (1996); *100 Years of Horror: 'Mummies'* (1996); *100 Years of Horror: 'Mutants'* (1996); *Pacto Diabólico* (1968); *Peggy Sue Got Married* (1986); *Rod Serling's Night Gallery: 'The Big Surprise'* (1971); *La Señora Muerte* (1968); *Shock Waves* (1976); *Thriller: 'Masquerade'* (1961); *The Tomb* (1985); *Las Vampiras* (1968); *Vampire Hookers* (1978); *The Vampire Interviews* (circa 1990s); *Young Frankenstein* (1974).

MICHAEL CARRERAS
[1927-1994]

Son of Sir James Carreras (1909-1990), who founded Hammer Films, he worked as an executive producer for the studio until he took control from 1971 until 1979. As a producer, director and writer for Hammer (sometimes under the pseudonyms 'Henry Younger' or 'Michael Nash') he worked on such films as *The Ugly Duckling* (1959), *The Two Faces of Dr. Jekyll* (1960), *The Curse of the Mummy's Tomb* (1964) and *Blood from the Mummy's Tomb* (1971).

qv: *Flesh and Blood: The Hammer Heritage of Horror* (1994); *Hammer: The Studio That Dripped Blood* (1987); *The Mummy* (1959); *100 Years of Horror: 'Dracula and His Disciples'* (1996); *100 Years of Horror: 'Dr. Jekyll and Mr. Hyde'* (1996); *100 Years of Horror: 'Mummies'* (1996); *100 Years of Horror: 'Mutants'* (1996).

CARRY ON CHRISTMAS

UK, 1969. Dir: Ronnie Baxter. With: Sidney James, Terry Scott, Charles Hawtrey, Hattie Jacques, Barbara Windsor, Frankie Howerd. Thames Television/ITV. Colour.

Hour-long TV special, broadcast on Christmas Eve and based on the popular series of comedy films. In this reworking of Charles Dickens' *A Christmas Carol*, recorded in front of a live audience, Ebenezer Scrooge (James) is visited by the Spirit of Christmas Past (Hawtrey),

who introduces him to Dr Frank N. Stein (Scott), his Monster (Bernard Bresslaw, finally playing the role his agent turned down for Hammer's *The Curse of Frankenstein* [1957]) and a friendly Count Dracula (Peter Butterworth).
✦✦

CARRY ON SCREAMING

UK, 1966. Dir: Gerald Thomas. With: Harry H. Corbett, Kenneth Williams, Jim Dale, Charles Hawtrey, Fenella Fielding, Joan Sims. Anglo Amalgamated. Colour.
The vampish Valeria (Fielding) and her reanimated brother Dr Orlando Watt (Williams) are using their Frankenstein-like monster Odbodd (Tom Clegg) to kidnap nubile young girls so they can petrify them (literally!) into show window mannequins. When the creature loses a finger, it grows into Odbodd Jr (Billy Cornelius, voiced by director Thomas). Because Sidney James was unavailable, Corbett stepped into the role of the bumbling policeman, Detective Sergeant Sidney Bung, who is transformed by a potion into a fanged Mr Hyde-like monster. With Bernard Bresslaw as the Karloffian butler Sockett, Peter Butterworth, Jon Pertwee, Frank Forsyth and a mummy named Rubbatiti (Denis Blake). This was the twelfth in the long-running British comedy series (1958-1992) and one of the best.
✦✦✧

LA CASA DE LOS ESPANTOS

Mexico/Venezuela, 1961 (1964). Dir: Alfredo B. Crevenna. With: María Eugenia San Martin, Carlos Riquelme, Hector Godoy, (Alfonso) 'Pompin' Iglesias, José Jasso. Estudios America/Rosas Priego/Clasa-Mohme. B&W.
This haunted house comedy is a sequel to Crevenna's *Bring Me the Vampire* (1961), also filmed in three episodes, and features many of the same cast and crew members. The prospective inheritors of a fortune return to the Black Castle against their will because the mad murderer ('Mantequilla') from the previous film failed to find the treasure. This includes more ghosts and a talking head on a plate. In the end, it all turns out to have been a hoax.
✦✧

THE CASE OF BECKY

USA, 1915. Dir: Frank Reicher. With: Blanche Sweet, James Neill, Carlyle Blackwell, Theodore Roberts. Lasky/Paramount. B&W.
Silent drama based on the play by Edward Locke and directed by Reicher, who went on to become a solid supporting player in *King Kong* (1933) and numerous other movies. A woman's evil dual personality is released by hypnotism.
Remake: THE CASE OF BECKY (qv; 1921)
✦

THE CASE OF BECKY

USA, 1921. Dir: Chester M. Franklin. With: Constance Binney, Glenn Hunter, Frank McCormack, Montagu Love, Margaret Seddon, Jane Jennings. Paramount/Realart. B&W.
Silent remake of the 1915 film, also based on the play by Edward Locke. A hypnotist creates a woman's evil dual personality, but it is eventually destroyed by another hypnotist.
✦

CASE OF THE FULL MOON MURDERS

(aka SEX ON THE GROOVE TUBE. UK: CASE OF THE SMILING STIFFS)
USA, 1971 (1973). Dir: Sean S. Cunningham. With: Fred Lincoln, Ron Browne, Cathy Walker, Harry Reems, Sheila Stuart, Jean Jennings. Seaburg/Lobster Enterprises/Dana Films. Colour.
Hard- and softcore feature from Cunningham, the producer of *The Last House on the Left* (1972) and director of *Friday the 13th* (1980), filmed in Florida. This is a *Dragnet*-style parody of sex films, with a female vampire (Walker) who kills by fellatio. Reems went on to star in the legendary *Deep Throat* (1972). It was edited by future director Steve Miner (*House* [1985], etc).
✦

THE CASE OF THE STUTTERING PIG

USA, 1937. Dir: Frank Tashlin. Voices: Mel Blanc. Warner Bros. B&W.
Seven minute *Looney Tunes* cartoon. Porky and Petunia Pig are menaced in an old dark house by scheming lawyer Goodwill, who uses a Jekyll and Hyde formula to transform himself into a monster. He attempts to kidnap the pigs so that he can steal their uncle's inheritance. Not as good as it might have been, though some scenes may frighten very young children.
Sequel: PORKY'S HERO AGENCY (1937)
✦✧

CASINO ROYALE

UK, 1967. Dir: John Huston, Ken Hughes, Val Guest, Robert Parrish and Joe McGrath. With: Peter Sellers, Ursula Andress, David Niven, Orson Welles, Joanna Pettet, Daliah Lavi. Columbia. Colour.
Over two hours of sci-spy mayhem. Ian Fleming's first James Bond novel was the only one not owned by the Saltzman and Broccoli partnership. Columbia kept the title, threw out the plot and turned it into an all-star hit-and-miss comedy. When Sir James Bond (Niven) is called out of retirement to battle SMERSH, he encounters a Caligari-ish spy school run by a Dr Strangelove-like administrator (Ronnie Corbett), and Dave Prowse in his first appearance as the Frankenstein Monster. This took two years and five directors to make (but still needed Val Guest to return and shoot extra sequences with cinematographer Nicolas Roeg). With Woody Allen as the surprise villain, Deborah Kerr, William Holden, Charles Boyer, John Huston as 'M', Kurt Kasznar, George Raft as himself, Jean-Paul Belmondo, Jacqueline Bisset, cameos by Peter O'Toole and racing driver Stirling Moss, and Dusty Springfield singing Burt Bacharach's wonderful 'Look of Love'.
✦✦✦

CASPER:

The Scummies

USA, 1997. Dir: Marija Miletic Dail. Voices: Joe Alaskey, Jess Harnell, Joe Nipote, Malachi Pearson, Dan Castellaneta. Universal Cartoon Studios/Amblin Television/Harveytoons/Fox Family Channel. Colour.
Emmy award-winning half-hour cartoon TV series (1996-97, fifty-two episodes). Based on characters created in 1945 by Joseph Oriolo and Sy (Seymour) Reit for Harvey Comics, it is filled with numerous in-jokes and inspired by the 1995 movie. Kat and her father, ghost psychiatrist Dr Harvey, live in an old house haunted by Casper the Friendly Ghost and his trio of mischievous uncles, Stretch, Stinkie and Fatso. This episode is set at the thirteenth annual Scummy Awards presented from Pasascreama and features spoofs of various TV themes, including zombie horse *Mr. Dead*, and there's a ghostly Frankenstein Monster in the audience.
✦✦

Spooky and Poil Meet the Monsters

USA, 1996. Dir: Alfred Ginemo. Voices: Joe Alaskey, Brad Garrett, Joe Nipote, Malachi Pearson, Dan Castellaneta, Miriam Flynn. Universal Cartoon Studios/Amblin Television/Harveytoons/Fox Family Channel. Colour.
In this Halloween episode, Spooky answers an ad to haunt a creepy castle and tries to convince his ghostly girlfriend Poil that the other inhabitants include the Universal Frankenstein Monster, a Lugosi-like Count Dracula, a Chaney Jr Wolf Man, the Creature and a Karloff-voiced Mummy. The Invisible Man turns up at the end.
✦✦

The Trick's a Treat

USA, 1996. Dir: Alfred Gimeno. Voices: Joe Alaskey, Jess Harnell, Joe Nipote, Malachi Pearson, Dan Castellaneta. Universal Cartoon Studios/Amblin Television/Harveytoons/Fox Family Channel. Colour.
When Kat is tricked by Casper into holding a rival Halloween party, Amber and her friends set out to prove there are no real spooks at Whipstaff Manor and encounter the Ghostly Trio, Frankenstein's Monster (in a nice *Young Frankenstein* [1974] gag), Count Dracula, the Wolf Man, and the Mummy. There's also a brief shot of the Creature. These latter two episodes are also available on video as part of the 1997 *The Spooktacular New Adventures of Casper* compilation series.
✦✧

Frentenstein's Monster grabs Evangélina Elizondo in Castle of the Monsters *(1957).*

TED CASSIDY
[1932-1979]

Hulking American actor and prolific cartoon voice who portrayed the butler Lurch on TV's *The Addams Family* (1964-66).
qv: *The Addams Family* (1973-75); *Batman: 'The Penguin's Nest/The Bird's Last Jest'* (1966); *Fangface* (1978); *The Flintstones Meet Rockula and Frankenstone* (1979); *Frankenstein Jr. and the Impossibles* (1966-67); *Halloween With the Addams Family* (1977); *The New Scooby-Doo Movies: 'Scooby-Doo Meets the Addams Family: Wednesday is Missing'* (1972); *Shindig* (1965).

CAST A DEADLY SPELL

USA, 1991. Dir: Martin Campbell. With: Fred Ward, David Warner, Julianne Moore, Clancy Brown, Alexandra Powers, Charles Hallahan. HBO Pictures/Pacific Western. Colour.

Made-for-cable TV movie filmed under the title *Lovecraft*. It is set in 1948 Los Angeles where everybody uses magic except for Ward's hardboiled private detective H. Phillip ('Phil') Lovecraft, who is looking for a stolen copy of the *Necronomicon*. Along the way he encounters a unicorn, gremlins, a zombie bouncer (Jaime Cardrichie) and living dead construction workers, a runic oatmeal demon, a vampire hooker, a werewolf suspect (Jim Eustermann), a friendly voodoo witch, and a living gargoyle sent by evil sorcerer Amos Hackshaw (Warner) who wants to bring the ancient Old Ones back to Earth. With nice attention to period detail. Produced by Gale Anne Hurd.

Sequel: WITCH HUNT (qv; 1994)

✦✦✦✧

EL CASTILLO DE LAS MOMIAS DE GUANAJUATO

Mexico, 1972. Dir: Tito Novaro. With: Superzán, Blue Angel, 'Tinieblas' (Manuel Leal), Zulma Faiad, Maria Salome, Tito Novaro. Producciones Filmicas Agrasanchez. Colour.

The third in this mummy series, and a sequel to *Robo de las Momias de Guanajuato* (1972). A trio of wrestling heroes investigate the castle of the Aztec mummies of Guanajuato and battle mad scientist Dr Dallier and his dwarfish henchmen.

Sequel: LAS MOMIAS DE SAN ANGEL (qv; 1973)

✦

CASTLE OF BLOOD

(Orig: DANZA MACABRA/LA LUNGA NOTTE DEL TERRORE/LA DANSA MACABRE. UK: CASTLE OF TERROR)

Italy/France, 1964. Dir: Anthony Dawson (Antonio Margheriti) (and Sergio Corbucci). With: Barbara Steele, George Rivière, Margrete Robsahm (Margaret Robsham), Henry Kruger, Montgomery Gleen (Silvano Tranquili), Sylvia Sorent(e). Vulsinia Films/Unidis/Jolly/Léo Lax/ Ulysee/Woolner Bros. B&W.

Supposedly based on Edgar Allan Poe's 'Dance Macabre'. While interviewing Poe (Kruger) in London, journalist Alan Foster (Rivière) accepts a wager by Poe and Sir Thomas Blackwood that he can't spend 'The Night of the Dead' in a castle from which previous visitors have never returned. During his stay, the writer encounters Elisabeth Blackwood (Steele) and other blood-drinking ghosts who re-enact their deaths once a year at midnight. The European version apparently includes a brief topless shot of Sorente and more of Steele's minor lesbian scenes with Robsahm. Director Margheriti liked it so much he remade it in colour six years later.

Remake: WEB OF THE SPIDER (qv; 1970)

✦✦✧

CASTLE OF BLOODY LUST
(Orig: IM SCHLOSS DER BLÜTEN BEGIERDE. USA: aka CASTLE OF THE CREEPING FLESH)
West Germany, 1967 (1968). Dir: Percy G. Parker (Adrian Hoven). With: Janine Reynaud, Jan Hendricks, Howard Vernon (Mario Lippert), Elvira Berndorff, Michel Lemoine, Pier A. Caminneci. Aquila Film Enterprises. Colour.
Gothic horror movie in which hedonistic Baron Brack (Lemoine) arrives at the castle of reclusive scientist Count von Saxon (Vernon) and rapes his daughter Elena (Berndorff). The Count then kills the baron's lover (Claudia Butenuth) and attempts to revive his dead daughter through a heart transplant. This apparently includes shots of actual open-heart surgery.
✦

CASTLE OF THE MONSTERS
(Orig: EL CASTILLO DE LOS MONSTRUOS)
Mexico, 1957. Dir: Julián Soler. With: 'Clavillazo' (Antonio Espino), Evangélina Elizondo, Carlos Orellana, Guillermo Orea, Germán Robles. Producciones Sotomayor/Columbia. B&W.
Just what we needed, a Mexican version of (Abbott and Costello) *Meet Frankenstein* (1948). Comedians 'Clavillazo' and Elizondo play newly-weds trapped in a castle with a mad scientist who has created his own versions of a werewolf, a mummy, the Creature from the Black Lagoon (La Bestia de la Laguna Seca), Frentenstein's (*sic*) Monster and a vampire (Robles, in a cameo parodying his character Count Lavud from *The Vampire* and *The Vampire's Coffin*, both made the same year). This also includes a gorilla.
Remake: FRANKENSTEIN, EL VAMPIRO Y CIA (qv; 1961)
✦✧

CASUAL RELATIONS
USA, 1973. Dir: Mark Rappaport. With: Sis Smith, Mel Austin, Paula Barr, Adrienne Claiborne, Peter Campus, Alan Dahl. Rappaport. Colour/B&W.
Independent feature that looks at the confusion of modern life in a single day. It includes a spoof film-within-a-film entitled *A Vampire's Love*. Editor/writer/producer/director/distributor Rappaport opens and closes his film with footage from Murnau's *Nosferatu* (1922).
✦

CATCH US IF YOU CAN
(USA: HAVING A WILD WEEKEND)
UK, 1965. Dir: John Boorman. With: The Dave Clark Five, Barbara Ferris, David Lodge, Robin Bailey, Yootha Joyce, David De Keyser. Warner Bros/Anglo Amalgamated. B&W.
Swinging sixties musical comedy featuring pop group The Dave Clark Five as disillusioned stuntmen searching for a dream island. In one scene, film buff Guy (Bailey) dresses up as the Frankenstein Monster and helps the boys escape from police at a movie masquerade party. This marked Boorman's début as a feature film director. With Ronald Lacey and Michael Gwynn.
✦✧

THE CAT CREATURE
USA, 1973. Dir: Curtis Harrington. With: Meredith Baxter, David Hedison, Gale Sondergaard, Stuart Whitman, John Carradine, Renne Jarrett. Screen Gems/ABC-TV. Colour.
Enjoyable TV movie, scripted by Robert Bloch as a homage-of-sorts to Val Lewton's *Cat People* (1942). An Egyptian mummy is accidentally revived and takes the form of a blood-drinking black cat hypnotically controlling the minds of its victims while trying to recover the ancient amulet that can destroy it. 'B' movie thrills, held together by a stylish script, low-key direction and a classic cast that includes such genre veterans as Sondergaard (in only her second film since the 1940s, after being blacklisted during the communist witch-hunts in Hollywood), Carradine, Keye Luke, Kent Smith (the star of the original *Cat People*, etc), Milton Parsons and John Abbott, plus Peter Lorre Jr (actually actor Eugene Weingand, who was not related to Lorre and was apparently taken to court for using the late actor's name illegally).
✦✦✧

CAT GIRL
UK, 1957. Dir: Alfred Shaughnessy. With: Barbara Shelley, Robert Ayres, Kay Callard, Ernest Milton, Lilly Kann, Jack May. Insignia Films/Anglo Amalgamated/American International Pictures. B&W.
The first of several horror films Shelley made over the following decade. As Leonora Brandt, she is called back to the ancestral mansion by her crazy uncle Edmund (Milton), who tells her that because of the family's 700 year-old curse (never fully explained) her soul will possess the body of an escaped leopard. She uses her power to kill her cheating husband (May) and threaten the wife of the doctor she loves. After a chase through the back streets of London's East End, Leonora dies at the same moment the leopard is killed. Low-budget chills that borrow heavily from Val Lewton's *Cat People* (1942). Apparently, close-up shots of the character in cat-form featured Paul Blaisdell in a mask (also seen briefly at the climax of *How to Make a Monster* [1958]) and were inserted into the American version by AIP.
✦✦

CAT LIVING TEN TIMES
(USA: aka DEVIL CAT)
Hong Kong, 1992. Dir: Lee Leung (Xen Chu-Lung). With: Wong Mai-Shi, Chu Ping-Fun, Chui Shin-Ha, Yeung Chi-Fu. World Video. Colour.
Ling, a beautiful silver-haired woman, transforms into a deadly cat monster to revenge herself on a family whose ancient ancestor Chow Sung raped an innocent young girl.
✦✧

THE CATMAN OF PARIS
USA, 1946. Dir: Lesley Selander. With: Carl Esmond, Lenore Aubert, Adele Mara, Douglass Dumbrille, Gerald Mohr, John Dehner. Republic. B&W.
Esmond portrays brilliant but controversial author Charles Regnier, who suffers from blackouts after visiting the Orient and is convinced that he must be the murderous killer stalking the streets of turn-of-the-century Paris. In fact, it turns out to be his friend (Dumbrille) who, when the stars are right, turns into a briefly-glimpsed lycanthropic killer (Robert J. Wilke) that appears every 300 years and is on its ninth and last incarnation. The top-hatted were-creature is pretty effective (in make-up by Bob Mark), and Western director Selander (*The Vampire's Ghost* [1945], etc) creates an effective transformation scene in this otherwise plodding thriller. With Anthony Caruso and Fritz Feld.
✦✧

CAT PEOPLE
USA, 1942. Dir: Jacques Tourneur. With: Simone Simon, Kent Smith, Tom Conway, Jane Randolph, Jack Holt, Elizabeth Russell. RKO Radio. B&W.
The first in producer Val Lewton's series of classy low-budget 'B' movies for RKO is a dark thriller about New York artist Irena Dubrovna (Simon), who believes that she will transform into a were-panther when her passion is aroused. After marrying naval architect Oliver Reed (Smith), she attracts the attention of psychiatrist Dr Judd (Conway) and it appears that her fears may have some basis in the legend of a mythical Serbian race of cat people. Director Tourneur's expert use of light and shadow creates some memorably suggestive sequences, including the pursuit of heroine Alice Moore (Randolph) through Central Park at night, ended by the jolting relief of a bus pulling up alongside her; Alice treading water in a basement pool while something unseen prowls in the shadows; a cartoon dream sequence; and Irena's meeting with a mysterious feline woman (Russell), who calls her 'sister'. *Cat People* cost just $134,000 to make and grossed more than $4,000,000, helping to save RKO from bankruptcy. However, the studio insisted on inserting a shot of a black panther, while Lewton and Tourneur were content to keep audiences guessing. With Alan Napier.
Sequel: THE CURSE OF THE CAT PEOPLE (qv; 1944)
Remake: CAT PEOPLE (qv; 1982)
✦✦✦✦✧

CAT PEOPLE
USA, 1982. Dir: Paul Schrader. With: Nastassia (Natassja) Kinski, Malcolm McDowell, John Heard, Annette O'Toole,

Ruby Dee, Ed Begley Jr. RKO-Universal/Charles Fries. Colour.
In 1963, Amicus producers Milton Subotsky and Max J. Rosenberg had talked about a remake of Val Lewton's 1942 original and Subotsky revived the idea in the mid-1970s as a 3-D production (he also sued to have his name credited on this version). In 1978, French director Roger Vadim also became briefly involved with the project. This flashy, highly sexual, but misguided $15,000,000 remake was scripted by Alan Ormsby (*Children Shouldn't Play With Dead Things* [1972], etc). It follows DeWitt Bodeen's original story quite closely and even unwisely tries to recreate some of the classic set-pieces. Irena Gallier (Kinski, who unsuccessfully asked for her nude scenes to be removed), the orphaned daughter of a European circus family, comes to live with her long-lost clergyman brother Paul (McDowell) in New Orleans. He tries to convince her that they can only mate with each other because they are both members of a race of shape-changing felines (make-up created by Tom Burman), who can transform into black leopards (from the inside!) when sexually aroused and return to their own form by consuming human flesh. This includes a great-looking stylised prologue, created by visual effects supervisor Albert Whitlock. With early appearances from John Larroquette and Ray Wise. Music score by Giorgio Moroder and a hit theme song by David Bowie. Gary Brandner (*The Howling*, etc) wrote the novelisation. Will Smith's production company Overbrook Entertainment and Universal announced another remake in 1999, to be scripted by Rafael Moreu (*The Rage: Carrie 2* [1999]) and set in contemporary New York.
✦✦✧

THE CAT WOMAN
USA, 1988. Dir: John Leslie. With: Kathleen Jentry, John Leslie, Joey Silvera, Alexa Parks, Lauryl Canyon, Veronica Hall. Louie T. Beagle Productions/VCA Pictures. Colour.
Loose hardcore reworking of Val Lewton's *Cat People* (1942), co-scripted, edited and directed by co-star Leslie (who also plays harmonica on the soundtrack!). Photographer Jennifer (Jentry) is told by the King of the Cats (Leslie) that beneath her human form she is turning into a sensuous cat creature. Winner of the 1988 Adult Video News Award for Best Video.
Sequel: CURSE OF THE CAT WOMAN (qv; 1991)
✦

IL CAV. COSTANTE NICOSIA DEMONIACO OVVERO DRACULA IN BRIANZA
Italy, 1975. Dir: Lucio Fulci. With: Lando Buzzanca, Sylva Koscina, Rossano Brazzi, Moira Orfei, John Steiner, Christa Linder. Titanus/Coralta Cinematográfica. Colour.
Vampire sex comedy from director Fulci, better known for his zombie movies. While on a trip to Romania, an entrepreneur (Sicilian comic Buzzanca) is bitten by Count Dragulescu (Steiner). Fearing that he has been 'infected' by homosexuality, the businessman discovers that drinking blood heightens his sexual prowess. Scripted by future director Pupi Avati; with Italian star Cicciolina (Ilona Staller).
✦

CAVE OF THE LIVING DEAD
(Orig: DER FLUCH DER GRÜNEN AUGEN)
West Germany/Yugoslavia, 1964 (1966). Dir: Akos von Ratony. With: Adrian Hoven, Karin Field, Carl Moehner, Erika Remberg, Wolfgang Preiss (Lupo Prezzo), Emmerich Schrenck. Objektiv/Triglav/Trans-Lux. B&W.
Interpol Inspector Doren (Hoven) and a witch discover that vampire Professor Adelsberg (Preiss) and his secretary Karin (Field) are transforming missing girls into the living dead in a secret cave beneath an old castle. In the end, the vampire turns into a skeleton and then explodes. Executive produced by Richard Gordon and filmed in English.
✦✧

CEMETERY MAN
(Orig: DELLAMORTE DELLAMORE. USA: aka DEMONS '95)
Italy/France, 1993 (1996). Dir: Michele Soavi. With: Rupert Everett, François Hadji-Lazaro, Anna Falchi, Stefano Masciarelli, Mickey Knox, Fabiana Formica. Audifilm-Urania Film/October Films. Colour.
Based on the novel by Tiziano Sclavi, this surprisingly ambitious zombie movie stars an impressive Everett as Francesco Dellamorte, the caretaker of the bizarre Buffalora graveyard (a great-looking set) where the dead return to life seven days after having been interred. His moronic assistant Gnaghi (Hadji-Lazaro) talks with the severed head of a female zombie (Formica) in his TV set. With Finnish-born Falchi playing three different women named Laura. Although the gore effects are sometimes unconvincing, this mostly succeeds in overcoming the restrictions of the genre.
✦✦✦✧

CENSORED SCENES FROM KING KONG
UK, 1974. BBC-TV. Colour.
Howard Schuman's drama was banned from TV, although the author adapted it for the London stage in 1978.
✦✦

CHABELO Y PEPITO VS. LOS MONSTRUOS
(aka CHABELO Y PEPITO CONTRA LOS MONSTRUOS)
Mexico, 1973. Dir: José Estrada. With: Xavier López 'Chabelo', Martin Ramos 'Pepito', Silvia Pasquel. Alameda Films/El Patrocino De EN. Colour.
Yet another Mexican multi-monster marathon. This one features the comedy team of 'Chabelo' and 'Pepito' confronting Frankenstein's Monster, a werewolf, the Mummy, Mr Hyde, the Creature from the Black Lagoon and a gorilla. Most of the 'monsters' are Don Post masks!
✦

CHAMELEONS
USA, 1992. Dir: John Leslie. With: Deidre (Diedre) Holland, Ashlyn Gere, Rocco (Siffredi), Jon Dough, P.J. Sparxx (P.J. Carrington), Mickey Ray. Louie T. Beagle Productions/VCA Pictures. Colour.
A seemingly ordinary couple (Holland and Rocco) are really psychic sex vampires who have the power to assume the identity of anyone they choose. However, whenever they steal someone's appearance, they also steal their life-force in this hardcore feature that includes Gere as a woman who accidentally discovers the couple's secret and wants it for herself.
✦

CHAMELEONS: NOT THE SEQUEL
USA, 1992. Dir: John Leslie. With: Diedre (Deidre) Holland, Ashlyn Gere, Fawn Miller, P.J. Sparxx (P.J. Carrington), Sunset Thomas, Tracey Wynn. Louie T. Beagle Productions/ VCA Pictures. Colour.
Hardcore fantasy in which Holland, Gere and Rocco Siffredi play sexual vampires with the ability to assume the physical characteristics of both sexes. In the end, the various couplings turn out to have been orchestrated by Siffredi's character to replenish his own life-force.
✦

THE CHAMPIONS:
The Body Snatchers
UK, 1969. Dir: Paul Dickson. With: Stuart Damon, Alexandra Bastedo, William Gaunt, Anthony Nicholls, Bernard Lee, Ann Lynn. ITC/ITV. Colour.
Hour-long TV series (1968-69, thirty episodes), created by Monty Berman and Dennis Spooner, about a trio of super-powered heroes working for international criminal investigation agency Nemesis. In this episode, scripted by Terry Nation, Craig Stirling (Damon), Sharron Macready (Bastedo) and Richard Barrett (Gaunt) investigate a secret laboratory containing the frozen body of an American General beneath a cemetery in north Wales.
✦✦

CHANGELING 2: THE REVENGE
(Orig: FA SEMPRE, FINO ALLA MORTE. USA: aka UNTIL DEATH)
Italy, 1987. Dir: Lamberto Bava. With: Gioia Scola, David Brandon, Giuseppe De Sando, Roberto Pedicini, Marco

Vivio, Urbano Barberini. Reteitalia/Dania/Devon. Colour.
Horror thriller in which a woman (Scola) and her lover poison and then bury her still-living husband. Six years later she is haunted by a handyman (Brandon) who is the reincarnation of her dead spouse. Meanwhile, her young son (Vivio) is having bad dreams about maggot-filled zombies. Despite the title, this has nothing to do with Peter Medak's superior ghost story *The Changeling* (1979).
✦✧

LON CHANEY
(Leonidas Chaney) [1883-1930]

'The Man of a Thousand Faces' was the son of Colorado deaf-mutes who learned the art of mime through his parents. After a stint with his younger brother's travelling theatre, he entered motion pictures in 1912 working in one-reel comedies. He appeared in more than one hundred before joining Universal in 1914, when his career began to take off. It was with *The Miracle Man* (1919) that he became one of the most sought-after character actors in the industry once he strapped his legs up behind his knees to play the part of 'Frog', a fake amputee. He was famous for his incredible — and often painful — physical make-ups in such films as *A Blind Bargain* (1922), *The Hunchback of Notre Dame* (1923), *The Monster* (1925), *The Unholy Three* (1925), *The Phantom of the Opera* (1925), *The Unknown* (1927), *London After Midnight* (1927) and *West of Zanzibar* (1928), most notably in collaboration with director Tod Browning. They made one sound film together, a remake of *The Unholy Three* (1930), before Chaney died of throat cancer at the age of forty-seven. He was portrayed by James Cagney in the 1957 biopic *Man of a Thousand Faces*.

LON CHANEY JR
(Creighton Chaney) [1906-1973]

The son of Lon Chaney, who attempted to dissuade his son from entering the acting profession. He started as an extra and stunt man in movies before appearing in minor roles in a number of films, including *A Scream in the Night* (1935) and the serial *Undersea Kingdom* (1936). Finally forced by the industry to assume his father's name, and despite an acclaimed performance as Lenny in *Of Mice and Men* (1939), Chaney Jr was groomed as a horror star by Universal. They made him the monster in such films as *Man Made Monster* (1941), *The Ghost of Frankenstein* (1942), *Son of Dracula* (1943) and a series of *Mummy* sequels. His one genuine creation was Lawrence Talbot, the cursed lycanthrope of *The Wolf Man* (1941) and its sequels. Alcoholism eventually destroyed his career, and he ended his days playing pathetic retreads of his Lenny role in such grade 'Z' productions as *Hillbillys in a Haunted House* (1967) and *Dracula vs. Frankenstein* (1970). Roger Smith played him in *Man of a Thousand Faces* (1957).

qv: *Biography: 'Lon Chaney Son of a Thousand Faces'* (1995); *Bride of the Gorilla* (1951); *The Colgate Comedy Hour: Abbott And Costello* (1951); *Dr. Terror's Gallery of Horrors* (1966); *Face of the Screaming Werewolf* (1960); *Frankenstein Meets the Wolf Man* (1943); *Ghost Catchers* (1944); *House of Dracula* (1945); *House of Frankenstein* (1944); *House of the Black Death* (1966); *Indestructible Man* (1955); (Abbott and Costello) *Meet Frankenstein* (1948); *The Mummy's Curse* (1944); *The Mummy's Ghost* (1944); *The Mummy's Tomb* (1942) *100 Years of Horror: 'Phantoms'* (1996); *The Pat Boone Show* (circa 1959); *Route 66: 'Lizard's Leg and Owlet's Wing'* (1962); *Tales of Tomorrow: 'Frankenstein'* (1952).

CHANOC CONTRA EL TIGRE Y EL VAMPIRO
Mexico, 1971. Dir: Gilberto Martinez Solares. With: Tin-Tan (Germán Valdés), Gregorio Casals, Aurora Cavel, Lina Marin, Marisa, Carlos Nieto. Cinematográfica RA/Azteca. Colour.
More comic strip vampires from Mexico, as the eponymous jungle hero (Casals) and comedian Tin-Tan (who died in 1973) battle the twin foes of the title.
Sequel: CHANOC CONTRA LOS DEVOURADORES DE HOMBRES (1971)
✦

CHANOC Y EL HIJO DEL SANTO CONTRA LOS VAMPIROS ASESINOS
Mexico, 1981. Dir: Rafael Peréz Grovas. With: Gregorio Casals, El Hijo del Santo (Jorge Guzman), Santo (Eric del Castillo or Rodolfo Guzmán Huerta). Colour.
Comic book jungle hero Chanoc (Casals) and La Hija de Santo (The Son of Santo) team up to battle vampires. Santo Sr (who died in 1984) turns up briefly to pass the baton on to his less impressive offspring.
Sequel: EL HIJO DEL SANTO EN FRONTERA SIN LEY (1982)
✦

BEN CHAPMAN
[1908-1991]

Tahiti-born American actor who was executive producer on *Donovan's Brain* (1953) and also donned the Gill Man costume for the land scenes in *Creature from the Black Lagoon* (1954).

CHAPPAQUA
USA, 1966 (1967). Dir: Conrad Rooks. With: Jean-Louis Barrault, Conrad Rooks, William S. Burroughs, Allen Ginsberg, Ravi Shankar, Ornette Coleman. Conrad Rooks Productions. B&W/Colour.
1960s psychedelica from writer, producer and director Rooks. He also plays a top-hatted, Lugosi-voiced Dracula who bites a woman's neck and hangs around in a coffin. Music by Shankar.
✦

CHARLIE CHAN AT THE OPERA
USA, 1936. Dir: H. Bruce Humberstone. With: Warner Oland, Boris Karloff, Keye Luke, Charlotte Henry, Thomas Beck, Margaret Irving. Twentieth Century-Fox. B&W.
Among the better entries in the long-running series (1931-1949) based on Earl Derr Biggers' famous detective. The opening credits proclaim 'Warner Oland vs. Boris Karloff', and although Oland puts an extra spark of humour into his role as the wily sleuth, Karloff gives a surprisingly routine performance as Graville, an escapee from an insane asylum and the suspected murderer of a famous prima donna and her admirer. Director Humberstone handles Oscar Levant's *Carnival* opera sequences well, but he brings little atmosphere to the rest of the film. The solid supporting cast includes series regular Luke as Lee Chan and William Demarest as a sceptical police sergeant.
Sequel: CHARLIE CHAN AT THE OLYMPICS (1937)
✦✦✧

CHARLIE CHAN IN EGYPT
USA, 1935. Dir: Louis King. With: Warner Oland, Pat Paterson, Thomas Beck, Rita Cansino (Rita Hayworth), Stepin Fetchit, Jameson Thomas. Fox Film. B&W.
One of the most atmospheric entries in the series (1931-1949) based on the books by Earl Derr Biggers. The philosophical Chan (Swedish-born Oland) investigates some stolen artefacts, a mummified murder victim, secret tombs and ancient Egyptian curses. Director King gives the mystery the feel of a horror film with the discovery of the mummified corpse by a giant X-ray machine and the killer hidden beneath an Egyptian head-dress. The suspects include a sixteen year-old Cansino as Nayda the servant and an unbilled Frank Reicher as a doctor. As Snowshoes, mumbling black comedian Stepin Fetchit supplies the comedy relief. The music score was taken from *Chandu the Magician* (1932).
Sequel: CHARLIE CHAN IN SHANGHAI (1935)
✦✦✧

LES CHARLOTS CONTRE DRACULA
(aka LES CHARLOTS CHEZ DRACULA JUNIOR)
France, 1980. Dir: Jean-Pierre Desagnat. With: Les Charlots, Amelie Prevost, Andreas Voutsinas, Gerard Jugnot, Vincent Martin, Dora Doll. Planfilm/Belstar Productions/Stephan Films/Films de la Tour. Colour.
French spoof in which Dracounet, the son of Dracula, dreams of

being a vampire just like his father. However, Dracounet can't become one of the undead until he can find a woman, who is the double of his late mother, to give him a cursed potion to drink. The three-member Les Charlots ('Charlot' being the nickname of Charlie Chaplin in France) were a sixties group famous for their parodies of well-known songs.
✦

CHARMED:
Feats of Clay
USA, 1998 (1999). Dir: Kevin Inch. With: Shannen Doherty, Holly Marie Combs, T.W. King, Dorian Gregory, Alyssa Milano, Victor Browne. Aaron Spelling Television/ The WB Network. Colour.
Hour-long TV series (1998-), created by co-executive producer Constance M. Burge, about the three Halliwell sisters, Prue (Doherty), Piper (Combs) and Phoebe (Milano), who discover the *Book of Shadows* in the attic of their grandmother's San Francisco home and use it to obtain the magic they were destined to have. Despite being threatened by warlocks, the trio of witches use their powers to help Prue's police detective boyfriend Andrew 'Andy' Trudeau (King) to solve crimes of a paranormal nature. In this episode, Phoebe's ex-boyfriend Clay (Browne) turns up with a stolen and cursed Egyptian urn.
✦✦✧

I've Got You Under My Skin
USA, 1998. Dir: John T. Kretchmer. With: Shannen Doherty, Holly Marie Combs, T.W. King, Dorian Gregory, Alyssa Milano, Michael Philip. Aaron Spelling Television/ The WB Network. Colour.
While Piper worries about her powers and Prue has problems with Andy, Phoebe meets Stefan (Philip), a photographer who remains youthful by draining the life-force through the eyes of young women. A series of tie-in novels were published by Pocket Books.
✦✦✧

CHEHRE PE CHERHA
India, 1979. Dir: Raj Tilak. With: Sanjeev Kumar, Rekha, Vinod Mehra, Sulakshna Pandit, Shatrughan Sinra, Amjad Khan. Tilak Movies. Colour.
Anachronistic low-budget version of *Dr. Jekyll and Mr. Hyde* that closely follows the 1941 and 1960 movie adaptations. Although set in the nineteenth century, Dr Vincent (Kumar) recounts his ability to transform into the drooling Mr Blackstone (make-up created by Mike Westmore) into a tape recorder! This also includes red plastic telephones, a pair of bikini-clad disco dancers and the monster riding a motorbike! The title translates as 'Face to Face'.
✦

LE CHEVALIER DE LA NUIT
France, 1953. Dir: Robert Darlène. With: Jean-Claude Pascal, Renée Saint-Cyr, Gregoire Aslan, Max Dalban, Louis de Funes. Telouet/Zodiaque. B&W.
Supernatural thriller about an old man who has discovered a method of separating his good and evil personalities. The title translates as 'The Knight of the Night'.
✦

THE CHILD
(aka KILL AND GO HIDE!/ZOMBIE CHILD)
USA, 1973 (1977). Dir: Robert Voskanian. With: Laurel Barnett, Rosalie Cole, Frank Janson, Richards Hanners, Ruth Ballan, Blossom Bing Jong. Panorama Films/Valiant International/Boxoffice International Pictures. Colour.
Set in the 1930s. Housekeeper Alicianne (Barnett) discovers that Rosalie (Cole), an eleven year-old girl who lives in the woods with her widower father, uses her supernatural powers to control cannibalistic zombies from a nearby cemetery to revenge herself on those she feels were responsible for the death of her mother.
✦✦

THE CHILDREN
USA, 1980. Dir: Max Kalmanowicz. With: Martin Shaker, Gil Rogers, Gale Garnett, Jessie Abrams, Tracy Griswold, Joy Glaccum. Albright/World Northal. Colour.
A radioactive cloud released from a nuclear power plant transforms a bus full of children into murderous zombies whose black finger-nailed touch is death. The only way to defeat the stiff-armed, living-dead kids is to cut their hands off. In the end, ex-country singer Garnett ('We'll Sing in the Sunshine', etc) gives birth to a mutant baby.
✦✧

CHILDREN OF THE DARK
USA, 1994. Dir: Michael Switzer. With: Peter Horton, Tracy Pollan, Roy Dotrice, Bill Smitrovich, Natalija Nogulich, Eric Pierpoint. Multimedia Motion Pictures/ Steve Krantz Productions. Colour.
TV movie 'inspired by actual events'. Two young girls affected by a rare genetic disorder will die if they are exposed to sunlight. But the locals soon have them singled out as vampires and force the family to leave town. With Ramon Bieri.
✦✧

CHILDREN OF THE NIGHT
USA, 1990 (1992). Dir: Tony Randel. With: Karen Black, Peter DeLuise, Ami Dolenz, Maya McLaughlin, Evan MacKenzie, Garrett Morris. Fangoria Films/Columbia TriStar Video. Colour.
Black plays Karen Thompson, the undead mother of Cindy (McLaughlin), who together plan to infest the small town of Allburg with their blood-drinking habits. David Sawyer is Romanian vampire high priest Vlado Czakyr who keeps the town's children suspended in an underwater crypt as emergency rations. Despite a confusing storyline, director Randel (*Hellbound Hellraiser II* (1988), etc) makes the slimy special effects watchable.
✦✧

CHILDREN OF THE NIGHT
(Orig: HIJOS DE LA NOCHE)
Mexico, 1997. Dir: Sebastián Pérez. With: Lucio Gutiérrez, Bárbara Ruiz, Iván Suárez, Marcos Villaseñor, Carlos Luna, Daniel Rodríguez. Producciones Tikal. B&W/ Colour.
Low-budget vampire movie that includes a cameo by the director/co-editor.
✦✧

CHILDREN SHOULDN'T PLAY WITH DEAD THINGS
(UK/USA: aka REVENGE OF THE LIVING DEAD)
USA, 1972. Dir: Benjamin (Bob) Clark. With: Alan Ormsby, Valerie Mamches, Jeffrey Gillen, Anya Ormsby, Paul Cronin, Jane Daly. Midnight Owl Production/Geneni Film Distributing/Brandywine/Motionarts. Colour.
Filmed for just $70,000, this stylish shocker is obviously influenced by George A. Romero's *Night of the Living Dead* (1968). But these zombies are much scarier — straight out of the pages of an EC comic! Ormsby (who also co-scripted as 'Alan Ormack' and was responsible for the gory make-up) gives a wonderfully camp performance as the nasty director of a theatrical troupe, who brings his actors to a deserted island cemetery where their experiments with witchcraft raise the flesh-eating dead. Although it builds slowly, there are some nice touches of humour and the scares are very effective. *Children Shouldn't Play With Dead Things Again* was a sequel announced in the 1990s.
✦✦✦

CHILLERS
USA, 1988. Dir: Daniel Boyd. With: Jesse Emery, Marjorie Fitzsimmons, Laurie Pennington, Jim Wolff, David Wohl. Big Pictures/Raedon Entertainment/Troma. Colour.
Independent horror anthology movie, made in West Virginia by thirty-three year-old college professor Boyd. Five people miss their bus and pass the time by telling each other scary stories. A girl's boyfriend turns out to be a white-eyed ghost with a head wound; an adult camp leader is really a crazy killer; a woman meets a TV news reporter who is a vampire; a young man can wish people from the obituary columns back to life, and a female student is possessed by a Native American spirit. When the next bus turns up it takes them all to Hell.
✦✧

THE CHILLING

(aka GAMMA 693)
USA, 1989 (1992). Dir: Deland Nuse and Jack A. Sunseri. With: Linda Blair, Dan Haggerty, Troy Donahue, Jack A. De Rieux, Ron Vincent, Michael Jacobs. Hemdale. Colour.
Unconvincing low-budget chiller set on Halloween. Lightning revives a group of cryogenically-frozen bodies as green flesh-eating zombies in Kansas City. Haggerty plays Sergeant Vince Marlow, who battles the foil-wrapped living dead.
✦✧

THE CHINESE CAT

(aka CHARLIE CHAN IN MURDER IN THE FUN HOUSE/ CHARLIE CHAN IN THE CHINESE CAT/MURDER IN THE FUN HOUSE)
USA, 1944. Dir: Phil Rosen. With: Sidney Toler, Benson Fong, Joan Woodbury, Mantan Moreland, Weldon Heyburn, Ian Keith. Monogram. B&W.
Low-budget murder mystery in which Charlie Chan (Toler), on the trail of the eponymous statue containing an uncut diamond, tracks a murderer to his hideout in an old fun house, surrounded by such spooky props as dancing skeletons, mummies and zombie-like figures.
Sequel: BLACK MAGIC (1944)
✦✧

A CHINESE GHOST STORY

(Orig: QIAN NU YOU HUN/SIEN NUI YAU WAN)
Hong Kong, 1987. Dir: Ching Siu-Tung (Cheng Xiu-Dong). With: Leslie Cheung (Leslie Cheung Kwok-Wing), Joey Wang (Wang Tsu-Hsien/Wang Zu-Xian/Wong Ki-Chang), Wo Ma (Wu Ma/Yuen Wah/Ng Ma-Wu), Liu Zhaoming (Lau Siu-Ming), Lin Wei, Xue Zhilan. Film Workshop/ Cinema City. Colour.
Produced by Tsui Hark (Xu Ke) and based on Pu Songling's much-filmed novel *The Magic Sword*, this wonderfully inventive fantasy combines martial arts action, comedy, horror and stunning special effects. Pop star Cheung stars as Lin Choi Sin/Neng, a young debt collector who awakens in the haunted Lan Ro Temple and falls in love with a beautiful ghost, Lit Siu Seen/Siusin (Wang). However, aided by sardonic Taoist priest Yen Che-Hsia (Ma), he soon ends up battling thieves, reanimated corpses and an androgynous 1,000 year-old tree demon (Zhaoming), before the whole thing climaxes up with a battle in Hell. Forget the plot, just sit back and enjoy this non-stop adventure. Winner of the main prize at the 1987 Brussels Film Festival for its special effects.
Sequel: A CHINESE GHOST STORY II (qv; 1990)
Remake: A CHINESE GHOST STORY: THE TSUI HARK ANIMATION (qv; 1997)
✦✦✦

A CHINESE GHOST STORY: THE TSUI HARK ANIMATION

(Orig: SIU-SIN/XIAOQUIN)
Hong Kong, 1997 (1998). Dir: Andrew Chen. Voices: Jan Lam Hoi-Fung, Nicky Wu Chi-Lung, Anita Yuen Wing-Yee, Sylvia Chang Ai-Chia, Raymond Wong Lau-Man, Samo Hung Kam-Po (Hung Kam-Bo/Hong Jin-Baoh). Lighthouse Entertainment/Tai Seng Video. Colour.
Big-budget musical cartoon version of the classic 1987 fantasy film, written and produced by Hark (Xu Ke). Lowly tax collector Neng (voiced by Hoi-Fung in the Cantonese version and Chi-Lung in the Mandarin edition) wanders the countryside with his dog Solid Gold (Tsui Hark) and encounters beautiful young ghost Shine (Wing-Yee/Ai-Chia), who is supposed to be collecting his soul for her demonic mistress, Madame Trunk (Kelly Chan Wai-Lum/Yon Fan).
✦✦

A CHINESE GHOST STORY II

(Orig: QIAN NU YOU HUN II: REN JIAN DAO/SIEN NUI YAU WAN II: YAN GAAN DO)
Hong Kong, 1990. Dir: Ching Siu-Tung (Cheng Xiu-Dong). With: Leslie Cheung (Leslie Cheung Kwok-Wing), Joey Wang (Wang Tsu-Hsien/Wang Zu-Xian/Wong Ki-Chang),

Valerie Mamches doesn't listen when told that Children Shouldn't Play With Dead Things *(1972).*

Wo Ma (Wu Ma/Yuen Wah/Ng Ma-Wu), Michelle Li, Jacky Cheung (Cheung Hok-Yau), Waise Lee. Film Workshop/ Golden Princess Film Production. Colour.
Slightly disappointing sequel to the 1987 original. After a recap of the first film, the story of debt collector Neng (pop star Leslie Cheung) continues when he returns home to find his village full of cannibals. Thrown into jail by mistake and facing execution, he escapes and takes refuge from a storm in an old house. With help again from Master Yan (Ma), he teams up with warrior-magician monk Autumn Leaf (Jacky Cheung) and Wind (Wang), a woman who looks like his lost love Siusin (also Wang), to battle Lau Shun's evil High Priest (really a giant centipede) and his zombie slaves. Produced by Tsui Hark (Xu Ke).
Sequel: A CHINESE GHOST STORY III (1991)
✦✦✧

CHINESE MAGIC
UK, 1900. Dir: Walter R. Booth. Paul. B&W.
Two minute silent short in which a Chinese conjurer transforms himself into a giant bat.
✦

THE CHIPMUNKS GO TO THE MOVIES: Kong!
USA, 1990. Dir: Don Spenser. Voices: Ross Bagdasarian (Jr), Janice Karman, Frank Welker, Dody Goodman, Thom(as) Watkins. Bagdasarian Productions/Ruby-Spears Productions/DIC/NBC-TV. Colour.
Short-lived half-hour cartoon TV series (1990-91) featuring singing chipmunks Alvin (Bagdasarian), Simon (also Bagdasarian) and Theodore (Karman), created in the 1950s by singer/songwriter Ross Bagdasarian Sr and Janice Karman. In this episode, Alvin is a Broadway producer looking for a huge attraction. He finds it in Theodore's friend Kong, a giant ape. The credit sequence spoofs a number of movies, including *Frankenstein* (1931).
✦✧

CHIQUIDRACULA
(aka EL EXTERMINADOR NOCTURO)
Mexico, 1985 (1986). Dir: Julio Aldama. With: Carlitos Espejel 'Resortes', Ana Luisa Peluffo, Teresita Velasquez, Luis Manuel Pelayo, 'El Comanche', Bruno Rey. Agrasanchez/ Impulsora Mexicana. Colour.
While inside Mexico City's Wax Museum, a little boy day-dreams that he is a vampire. When he later imagines he sees a priest with fangs, he disguises himself as the eponymous character. The title translates as 'Little Dracula'.
✦✧

CHOPPER CHICKS IN ZOMBIETOWN
USA, 1989 (1990). Dir: Dan Hoskins and Rodney McDonald. With: Jamie Rose, Catherine Carlen, Lycia Naff, Vicki Frederick, Don Calfa, Kristina Loggia. Chelsea Partners/Triax Entertainment/Troma. Colour.
Low-budget rip-off of *The Magnificent Seven* (1960), with a gang of seven leather-clad biker babes, The Cycle Sluts, protecting the desert town of Zariah and a bunch of blind orphans from an army of cannibalistic zombies (make-up effects by Edward French), created by mad mortician Ralph Willum (Calfa) to mine radioactive materials. Despite midget (Ed Gale) abuse, this would have been a lot funnier with better acting, more imaginative direction and tighter editing. It's still better than most Troma pick-ups, which isn't saying much. Featuring an early appearance by Billy Bob Thornton.
✦✦

CHOSEN SURVIVORS
USA/Mexico, 1974. Dir: Sutton Roley. With: Jackie Cooper, Bradford Dillman, Richard Jaeckel, Alex Cord, Diana Muldaur, Pedro Armendariz Jr. Metromedia Producers Corporation/Alpine/Churubusco Studios/Cinerama/ Columbia. Colour.
Filmed under the title *The Bat*. A group of 'B' movie stars, trapped more than 1,700 feet beneath the desert during a thermonuclear test, battle against a plague of starving vampire bats. TV movie-type thrills.
✦✦

VIRGINIA CHRISTINE [1920-1996]

American character actress and wife of actor Fritz Feld (1900-1993). She portrayed the reincarnated Princess Ananka in *The Mummy's Curse* (1944).
qv: *Billy the Kid Versus Dracula* (1965); *The Scooby-Doo and Scrappy-Doo – Puppy Hour* (1982-83).

CHRONIQUE DE VOYAGE
France, 1970. Dir: Robert de Laroche. With: Marc Olivier Cayre, Claude Moro, Francine Roussel.
Surreal half-hour short, which includes the heroine in the clutches of a vampire. Narrated by Fabien Roy.
✦

CHU-CHIN-CHOW
UK, 1934. Dir: Walter Forde. With: George Robey, Anna May Wong, Fritz Kortner, John Garrick, Pearl Argyle, Jetsam. Gainsborough/Gaumont-British. B&W.
Musical/comedy version of the Arabian Nights fantasy of Ali Baba and the Forty Thieves, co-scripted by Sidney Gilliat and based on the operetta by Oscar Asche (previously filmed in 1924). Dependable comedy actor (Sir) George Robey uses his talents as a music hall entertainer to play Ali Baba, who steals the loot of the villainous Abu Hassan (Kortner). The words 'Open-O-Sesamee' control zombie-like slaves who turn a giant wheel to open a cave's secret entrance. Wong plays a spy of Hassan's who betrays him when he humiliates her, the greedy Caliph (Francis L. Sullivan) is found hanged and quartered, and Dennis Hoey turns up as a thief.
✦✦

C.H.U.D. II BUD THE CHUD
USA, 1988 (1989). Dir: David Irving. With: Brian Robbins, Bill Calvert, Tricia Leigh Fisher, Robert Vaughn, Gerrit Graham, Larry Cedar. MCEG/Lightning Pictures/Vestron Pictures. Colour.
Spoof semi-sequel to *C.H.U.D.* (1984), scripted by Ed Naha under the W.C. Fields-inspired pseudonym 'M. Kane Jeeves' and directed by actress Amy's brother. Graham has some fun as Bud, the last cannibal zombie created by a crazy American general (Vaughn, in one of his worst performances). When he is stolen and revived by a trio of teenagers, the whole town soon becomes infected with the zombie virus. A typical teen comedy, only worth catching for cameos by Bianca Jagger, Larry Linville, Norman Fell, June Lockhart, Clive Revill and an uncredited Robert Englund.
✦✧

A CHUMP AT OXFORD
USA, 1939 (1940). Dir: Alfred Goulding. With: Stan Laurel, Oliver Hardy, Forrester Harvey, Wilfred Lucas, Forbes Murray, Frank Baker. Hal Roach Studios/United Artists. B&W.
One of the last of a number of comedy shorts made by Laurel and Hardy at Hal Roach Studios between 1927-1940. Originally produced as a 'streamlined feature' running for forty-two minutes, a twenty minute prologue (in which the comedy team pose as a maid and butler) was added for simultaneous European release. When the duo travel to Oxford to get an education, an accidental blow on the head turns Stanley into brilliant scholar and athlete Lord Paddington. This features a fake ghost (Eddie Borden) in a maze and an early appearance by Peter Cushing as a vengeful young student. Silent star Harry Langdon was one of the screenwriters.
✦✦✦

CIAO MASCHIO
(Orig: REVE DE SINGE. USA/UK: aka BYE BYE MONKEY)
Italy/France/USA, 1978. Dir: Marco Ferreri. With: Gérard Depardieu, James Coco, Marcello Mastroianni, Geraldine Fitzgerald, Gail Lawrence (Abigail Clayton), Mimsy Farmer. Giorgio Nocella/Maurice Bernart. Colour.
Downbeat black comedy about a group of outcasts living in a Manhattan over-run by a plague of rats. As the odd Lafayette, who

works in a wax museum, a pre-superstar Depardieu adopts a baby chimpanzee discovered near the corpse of King Kong (apparently left over from Dino De Laurentiis' 1976 remake). This was filmed in English by Italian director Ferreri (*La Grande Bouffe* [1973], etc) on location in New York.
✦

CIGARETTE CHARLIE
East Germany, 1962. Dir: Katia Georgi and Klaus Georgi. DEFA. Colour.
Anti-smoking cartoon short in which the eponymous corpse sits up in his coffin and asks for one more cigarette.
✦

CIRCLE OF FEAR: The Graveyard Shift
USA, 1973. Dir: Don McDougall. With: John Astin, Patty Duke Astin, Joe Renteria, Douglas Henderson, Don 'Red' Barry, Paul Picerni. Screen Gems/William Castle/Colex Enterprises/Columbia/NBC-TV. Colour.
The title and format of *Ghost Story* (1972) were dropped after fourteen episodes, but the TV series continued under this title for the remaining nine shows. William Castle was executive producer, Jimmy Sangster and Seeleg Lester were story consultants and Richard Matheson developed the show for TV. In this spoof episode, set in a condemned film studio, a couple find themselves haunted by the ghosts of various movie characters. With I. Stanford Jolley as a wolfman, Hal Bokar as an apeman and executive producer Castle playing the studio head, Mr Fillmore.
✦✦

THE CITY OF GHOSTS
Hong Kong, circa 1980s. Long Shore Pictures. Colour.
Comedy/horror based on a poem by Li Bai and set in Feng Dou, a 'ghost city' on the edge of Hell that only emerges at night. A general uses hopping vampires (called 'zombies') to carry opium, but in the end a Taoist priest defeats them with lightning.
✦✧

CITY OF THE LIVING DEAD
(Orig: LA PAURA NELLA CITTÀ DEI MORTI VIVENTI. USA: THE GATES OF HELL)
Italy/USA, 1980. Dir: Lucio Fulci. With: Christopher George, Katriona (Catriona) MacColl, Carlo De Mejo, Antonella Interlenghi, Giovanni Lombardo Radice, Janet Agren. Dania Film/Medusa Distribuzione/National Cinematográfica. Colour.
New York reporter Peter Bell (George) rescues medium Mary Woodhouse (MacColl) from being buried alive and together they travel to the town of Dunwich, Massachusetts, which is populated by the ancestors of the Salem witch burners. There, ghostly flesh-eating zombies are controlled by the spirit of local priest Father William Thomas (Luciano Rossi) who hanged himself and thereby opened the gates of Hell, allowing the dead to walk the Earth. Despite its low budget and enigmatic ending, several clever set pieces and the unexpected deaths of major characters help make this one of Fulci's most stylish films. With Michele Soavi. *The Gates of Hell II: Dead Awakening* (1997) was an independent 'Fulci-inspired' sequel released directly to video.
✦✦✦

CITY OF THE VAMPIRES
USA, 1994. Dir: Ron Bonk. With: Matthew Jason Walsh, Anne-Marie O'Keefe, Pam Simmons, Noel Bonk. Salt City Video Productions. Colour.
Independent shot-on-video production. When they take a wrong turn, Sam Helling (Walsh) and his girlfriend Christine (O'Keefe) find themselves lost in the city of Braddock. There they encounter a horror so unspeakable that Sam flees, leaving Christine to her fate. A month later, and on the verge of suicide, he decides to go back and retrace his steps, and in doing so he discovers the lair of the undead and learns exactly what happened to Christine on that fateful night.
✦

CITY OF THE WALKING DEAD
(Orig: INCUBO SULLA CITTÀ CONTAMINATA/LA INVASIÓN DE LOS ZOMBIES ATOMICOS. UK: NIGHTMARE CITY)
Italy/Spain, 1980 (1983). Dir: Umberto Lenzi. With: Hugo Stiglitz, Laura Trotter, Maria Rosaria Omaggio, Francisco Rabal, Mel Ferrer, Sonia Viviani. Dialchi Film/Lotus Film International/21st Century. Colour.
Stiglitz plays reporter Dean Miller, who goes to the airport to meet a professor. But when the plane lands it is full of bloodthirsty zombies who might be the result of a nuclear accident. Poor old Mel Ferrer stands around looking worried as a military general while the vampiric ghouls transform their victims and lead a full-scale assault on the city. With plenty of gore and cheap-looking make-up effects, these zombies are every bit as mobile as the humans, even using machine guns to kill soldiers. In the end, Miller's wife (Trotter) falls out of a helicopter and when he wakes up from his nightmare the story begins again...
✦✦

CITY OF WOMEN
(Orig: LA CITTÀ DELLE DONNE/LA CITE DES FEMMES)
Italy/France, 1980. Dir: Federico Fellini. With: Marcello Mastroianni, Anna Prucnal, Bernice Stegers, Iole Silvani, Donatella Damiani, Ettore Manni. Opera Film Produzione/Gaumont/Franco Rossellini. Colour.
One of Fellini's lesser films. While travelling on a train, Snàporaz (Mastroianni) goes on a dream-quest across the countryside, where he encounters various women in sexual situations, including one wearing a Frankenstein Monster mask.
✦✦

CITY UNDER THE SEA
(USA: WAR-GODS OF THE DEEP)
UK, 1965. Dir: Jacques Tourneur. With: Vincent Price, David Tomlinson, Tab Hunter, Susan Hart, John Le Mesurier, Henry Oscar. Anglo Amalgamated/American International Pictures. Colour.
After *The Tomb of Ligeia* (1964), Roger Corman didn't want to direct any more of AIP's Edgar Allan Poe adaptations, so this became veteran Tourneur's last movie (he died in 1977). Inspired by Poe's poem 'City in the Sea', this underrated juvenile fantasy/adventure features a group of smugglers kept alive for more than one hundred years in the lost underwater city of Lyonesse off the Cornish coast. Price gives an excellent performance as the Captain (his body eventually withers away when exposed to sunlight) who uses a lost race of gill men as his slaves. Tomlinson and his pet rooster Herbert supply the comedy relief.
✦✦✧

CLASSIC HORROR TRAILERS
USA, circa 1990- . Sinister Cinema. B&W/Colour.
Sinister Cinema has released many of these value-for-money video compilations, each containing more than twenty trailers from the 1950s, 1960s and 1970s for such films as *The Beast Must Die* (1974), *Blacula* (1972), *Blood of Dracula* (1957), *Blood of Dracula's Castle* (1967), *Blood of the Vampire* (1958), *Count Yorga, Vampire* (1970), *Fangs of the Living Dead* (1968), *The Fearless Vampire Killers* (1966), *Frankenstein's Bloody Terror* (1967), *The Haunted Strangler* (1958), *House of Dark Shadows* (1970), *I Bury the Living* (1958), *I, Monster* (1971), *The Monster of Piedras Blancas* (1958), *My Son the Vampire* (1952), *Old Dracula* (1974), *Pharaoh's Curse* (1956), *The Return of Count Yorga* (1971), *The Return of Dracula* (1957), *Scream Blacula Scream* (1973), *The Velvet Vampire* (1971), *Werewolf in a Girls' Dormitory* (1961), *Werewolves on Wheels* (1971), *Young Frankenstein* (1974), *Zombies of Mora Tau* (1957) and hundreds of other titles.
✦✦✦

THE CLEARING
Russia/USA, 1991. Dir: Vladimir Alenikov. With: George Segal, Tamara Tana, Nikolai Kochegarov, Victor Repnikov, Natalia Silantyeva. Kodiak Films/Odessa Studios/Sovampex/Astral. Colour.
Set in eleventh century Russia, when a Pagan 'Summer Moon' fertility ritual results in the death of a woman. Grigory, the village Chief-

tain (a miscast Segal) blames the death on a werewolf, but Christian priest Father Agafangel (Kochegarov) suspects that local witch Feofania (Tana) is to blame. In the end, despite the supernatural elements, it turns out to be a straightforward murder mystery.
✦✧

BRIAN CLEMENS
[b 1931]

British writer and producer who set the style with some of the best episodes of TV's *The Avengers* (1961-69). Although much of his other work has never risen above TV movie-quality, he did script two of Hammer's most imaginative projects, *Dr. Jekyll & Sister Hyde* (1971) and *Captain Kronos Vampire Hunter* (1972), the latter also marking his sole directorial credit.
qv: *Bugs* (1995- 99); *The New Avengers: 'The Eagle's Nest'* (1976).

CLEOPATRA

(Orig: CLÉOPÂTRE. UK: CLEOPATRA'S TOMB/ROBBING CLEOPATRA'S TOMB)
France, 1899. Dir: Georges Méliès. With: Georges Méliès. Star Film. B&W.
Early silent short in which Cleopatra, Queen of the Nile, is raised from the dead.
✦

CLEOPATRA'S BONDAGE REVENGE

(aka BONDAGE REVENGE)
USA, 1985. With: Pia Snow (Michelle Bauer/Michelle McClellan). Colour.
When a professor and his female assistant accidentally revive the mummy of the Queen of the Nile, she instructs them in the Egyptian arts of bondage and discipline in this hardcore video.
✦

CLIFFHANGERS:
The Curse of Dracula

USA, 1979. Dir: Kenneth Johnson, Jeffrey Hayden, Sutton Roley and Richard Milton. With: Michael Nouri, Carol Baxter, Stephen Johnson, Bever-Leigh Banfield, Louise Sorel, Antoinette Stella. Universal/NBC-TV. Colour.
Shown in twenty minute episodes, this was one-third of a weekly TV show celebrating the old movie serials, created by executive producer Kenneth Johnson. Nouri portrays an urbane and sophisticated Dracula who teaches night-school at San Francisco's South Bay College while battling Mary Gibbons (Baxter) and Van Helsing's grandson Kurt (Johnson), who are attempting to track down the Count's boxes of sacred earth and destroy them along with his undead followers. The TV series began with Chapter Six and was cancelled after ten episodes. Les Baxter co-composed the music score. Episodes were later edited together to create the TV movies *Dracula '79* (1979) and *The Loves of Dracula* (1979), while all ten episodes were compiled into a two-hour movie, *The World of Dracula* (1979).
✦✦

THE CLIMAX

USA, 1944. Dir: George Waggner. With: Susanna Foster, Turhan Bey, Boris Karloff, Gale Sondergaard, June Vincent, Thomas Gomez. Universal. Colour.
This Technicolor melodrama was Universal's attempt to follow-up the success of *Phantom of the Opera* (1943), which also starred Foster and utilised the same sets. In his first film for two years, Karloff does his best with the poorly-written role of Dr Fredrick Hohner, the Vienna opera house physician who ten years before strangled the woman he loved (Vincent) because her singing career was coming between them. Now he keeps her mummified body in a secret crypt and uses hypnotism to prevent a young singer, Angela Klatt (Foster), who sounds just like his murdered love, from performing. Co-scripted by Curt Siodmak and based on a play by Edward Locke (previously filmed by Universal in 1930 in sound and silent versions), producer/director Waggner (who replaced Arthur Lubin before shooting began) creates some striking moments, but the film concentrates too much on the opera set-pieces and romantic sub-plot instead of the horror. The original trailer includes some alternate takes and a couple of shots of Karloff that do not appear in the release print. Florence Jay Lewis wrote the hardcover novelisation.
✦✦✧

CLIMAX!:
Dr. Jekyll And Mr. Hyde

USA, 1955. With: Michael Rennie, Sir Cedric Hardwicke, Mary Sinclair, Lowell Gilmore. CBS-TV. B&W.
Live, hour-long version of Robert Louis Stevenson's story, adapted by Gore Vidal. Following the death of Mr Hyde (Rennie), Utterson (Hardwicke) reads the journal of Dr Jekyll and discovers his dark secret. Music score by Jerry Goldsmith. Series hosted by William Lundigan.
Episode remake: MATINEE THEATER: Dr. Jekyll and Mr. Hyde (qv; 1957)
✦✧

COLIN CLIVE
(Colin Clive-Greig) [1900-1937]

Sensitive French-born British stage actor who was in Hollywood from 1930. His friend James Whale cast him as an hysterical Henry Frankenstein ('It's alive!') in both *Frankenstein* (1931) and *Bride of Frankenstein* (1935), but rumours of alcoholism and bisexuality plagued the actor. Following his premature death, his ashes remained unclaimed. He was played by Matt McKenzie in *Gods and Monsters* (1998).
qv: *Mad Love* (1935).

E.E. CLIVE
[1879-1940]

Busy British character actor who arrived in Hollywood late in life and ended up playing fussy butlers and burgomasters.
qv: *Bride of Frankenstein* (1935); *Dracula's Daughter* (1936), *Tarzan Escapes* (1936).

CLIVE BARKER'S A-Z OF HORROR:
The Kingdom of the Dead

UK/USA, 1997. Dir: Ann Hawker and Mike Ibeji. With: Clive Barker, George A. Romero, John Russo, Russ(ell) Streiner, Bill Hinzman, Marilyn Eastman. BBC/A&E Network. Colour.
Series of six (originally ten, before re-editing) half-hour TV documentaries, filmed in 1995 and presented by Barker. This episode includes 'Z' for 'Zombie' and looks at the making of the cult classic *Night of the Living Dead* (1968), featuring numerous clips and interviews with cast and crew members, including Karl Hardman, Kyra Schon and Judy O'Dea. Other episodes were titled 'American Psycho' (Ed Gein and *Psycho* [1960]), 'Beyond Good and Evil' (with Ira Levin and Barbara Steele), 'Broken Homes' (with John Carpenter), 'The Devil You Know' (the making of *The Exorcist* [1973]), and 'A Fate Worse Than Death' (*The Crow* [1994]). BBC Books published a tie-in volume.
✦✦✦

A CLOCKWORK ORANGE

UK, 1971. Dir: Stanley Kubrick. With: Malcolm McDowell, Patrick Magee, Adrienne Corri, Miriam Karlin, Michael Bates, Warren Clarke. Polaris Productions/Warner Bros. Colour.
Based on the novel by Anthony Burgess, Kubrick's disturbing masterpiece follows the violent exploits of malcontent Alex DeLarge (McDowell) and his gang, the Droogs, in a not-too-distant future when law and society have completely broken down. In one scene, Alex imagines himself as a vampire. The film caused an outcry when first released, and due to a number of copycat attacks was withdrawn from distribution in Britain by Kubrick until after his death in 1999. With Aubrey Morris, Anthony Sharp, Margaret Tyzack, Steven Berkoff, David Prowse, Virginia Wetherell and Katya Wyeth. A photo-scriptbook was published by Ballantine in 1972.
✦✦✦✦✦

CLOSE ENCOUNTER OF THE VAMPIRE
(Orig: JIANGSHI PAPA. USA: aka HEY, GHOST!)
Hong Kong/Taiwan, 1986. Dir: Yuen Wo-Ping. With: Leung Ka-Yan, Yuen Cheung-Yan, Yuen Sun-Yi, Yeun Yat-Choch, Jan Chi-Jing, Lee Jok-Wai. Feiteng Film Company/ Chou Ling Kong. Colour.

Horror comedy set in medieval China. Three incompetent exorcists unsuccessfully attempt to destroy a hopping vampire with a bizarre array of weapons, while a group of orphans are menaced by a young vampire. In the end, the undead Mandarin is struck by lightning and explodes.

Sequel: VAMPIRES STRIKE BACK (qv; 1988)

✦✧

THE CLOWN AT MIDNIGHT
Canada/USA, 1998 (1999). Dir: Jean Pellerin. With: James Duval, Sarah Lassez, Tatyana Ali, Melissa Galianos, Margot Kidder, Christopher Plummer. Winnipix Clown/ GFT/Paquin Entertainment. Colour.

Pointless direct-to-video slasher film scripted by special effects supervisor Kenneth J. Hall (Hal Kennedy) and filmed in Winnipeg, Manitoba. A group of teen drama students (one of whom is a Lon Chaney Sr fan!) find themselves trapped in an old theatre owned by kindly Mr Caruthers (Plummer) and being killed-off by a homicidal Pagliacci clown. Meanwhile, the miserable Kate (Lassez) keeps getting psychic flashbacks to the murder of her opera diva mother in the same theatre fifteen years before. As drama teacher Ellen Gibby, Kidder (following her much-publicised breakdown) gets axed in the head.

✦✧

CLUB VAMPIRE
USA, 1998. Dir: Andy Ruben. With: John Savage, Ross Malinger, Starr Andreeff, Michael Anderson. Concorde/ New Horizons. Colour.

Erotic direct-to-video vampire thriller in which a woman is drawn into the mysterious realm of the undead who inhabit an underground nightclub.

✦✧

COED VAMPIRE SEX SLAVES
USA, 1997. Dir: Geoffrey de Valois. With: Joan A. Teeter, Anastasia Alexander, Aleandre Scully, Catherine Hart. Digital Entertainment Group/Salt City Home Video. Colour.

One of a series of softcore *Vampire Raw Footage* videos that includes behind-the-scenes nude and erotic sequences. *Penthouse* and *Playboy* models Alexander and Scully are bound and chained with sorority girl Hart by Vampire Mistress Teeter in her dungeon from Hell.

✦

HERMAN COHEN
[1928-1985]

American producer and writer who crossed teenagers with horror and discovered a drive-in gold mine.

qv: *Bela Lugosi Meets a Brooklyn Gorilla* (1952); *Blood of Dracula* (1957); *Bride of the Gorilla* (1951); *The Horror of It All* (1983); *Horrors of the Black Museum* (1959); *How to Make a Monster* (1958); *I Was a Teenage Frankenstein* (1957); *I Was a Teenage Werewolf* (1957), *Konga* (1960).

COITUS INTERRUPTUS
Taiwan, 1988. Colour.

Hardcore sex comedy that includes a hopping ghost, a trio of spooks and an apparently fake fanged vampire in a cape who turns out to be real. This also features a hopping vampire movie on TV.

✦

THE COLGATE COMEDY HOUR:
Abbott and Costello
USA, 1951. With: Bud Abbott, Lou Costello, Sidney Fields, Lon Chaney, Lonnie Burr. NBC-TV. B&W.

Hour-long comedy TV series (1950-55). Chaney Jr recreates his role as the Frankenstein Monster in a sketch featuring the popular duo looking for treasure in a haunted house (incorporating routines from [Abbott and Costello] *Meet Frankenstein* [1948]), and dances during a musical number at the end of the show.

✦✦

(aka Abbott and Costello Meet the Creature/Meet the Monsters)
USA, 1953. With: Bud Abbott, Lou Costello, Glenn Strangle (Strange), Ricou Browning. NBC-TV. B&W.

Bud and Lou visit the Universal property department (complete with dummies of Dracula, Mr Hyde and a gorilla), where Lou recreates some of the best comedy routines from (Abbott and Costello) *Meet Frankenstein* (1948) and encounters the Invisible Man, the Creature from the Black Lagoon (Browning) and Frankenstein's Monster (Strange, whose name was apparently misspelled on the end credits).

✦✦✧

MADELEINE COLLINSON and MARY COLLINSON
[b 1952]

Playboy's first twin playmates (October 1970), the eighteen year-old Maltese-born sisters appeared as seductive vampire Frieda and virtuous heroine Maria, respectively, in Hammer's *Twins of Evil* (1971).

COMEDY DRACULA
(aka COMEDY DRACULLA)
India, circa 1980s. With: Farhana Khan, Rauf Lala, Shazad Raza. Colour.

Filmed stage comedy that includes a cackling caped Dracula (Raza) who turns up near the end with big removable fangs.

✦

COME RUBAMMO LA BOMBA ATOMICA
Italy, 1966 (1967). Dir: Lucio Fulci. With: Franco Franchi, Ciccio Ingrassia, Julie Menard (Ann Menard), Eugenia Litrel, Gianfranco Marici, Franco Bonvicini. Five-Fono Roma/Copro. Colour.

One of numerous James Bond-inspired films produced in Italy during the 1960s, this one happens to be directed by Fulci (*Zombie* [1979], etc). Set in the Egyptian desert, the comedy duo of Franco and Ciccio become involved with mad scientist Dr Si, who is attempting to revive mummies with atomic energy. This includes characters named James Bomb (Adham), Modesty Bluff (Litrel) and Derek Flit (Bonvicini). The titles translates as 'How to Steal an Atomic Bomb'.

✦

THE COMIC
USA, 1969. Dir: Carl Reiner. With: Dick Van Dyke, Michele Lee, Mickey Rooney, Cornel Wilde, Pert Kelton, Steve Allen. Columbia. Colour.

As self-destructive screen comedian Billy Bright, Van Dyke recreates John Barrymore's version of *Dr. Jekyll and Mr. Hyde* (1920) in a black and white silent spoof entitled *Dr. Jerk and Mr. Hyde*. With movie veterans Fritz Feld, Mantan Moreland, Jeff Donnell and director Reiner in supporting roles.

✦✦

COMING SOON
USA, 1982 (1983). Dir: John Landis. With: Jamie Lee Curtis. Universal. Colour/B&W.

Hour-long compilation of classic Universal trailers, featuring those for most of the studio's monster series plus, among others, Hammer's *The Evil of Frankenstein* (1964), *King Kong vs. Godzilla* (1963), Hitchcock's six minute trailer for *Psycho* (1966; which includes a tour of the Bates house and motel), and a preview for *The Wolf Man* (1941) that contains a few clips of the scene of Lon Chaney Jr wrestling a bear which was cut from the final film. Scripted/co-produced by Mick Garris and hosted by scream queen Curtis from the Universal backlot.

✦✦

THE COMPANY OF WOLVES

UK, 1984. Dir: Neil Jordan. With: Angela Lansbury, David Warner, Micha Bergese, Sarah Patterson, Graham Crowden, Brian Glover. Palace Pictures/ITC. Colour.

Stories within dreams are the basis for this great-looking, if overrated, werewolf tale, co-scripted by Angela Carter from her own stories. Anton Furst's highly atmospheric set designs are remarkable, and the animatronic transformation effects (created by Peter McDonald, Alan Whibley and Christopher Tucker) are impressive. Although Jordan's direction shows all the imagination and flair promised by *Angel* (1982), the actual tales themselves are little more than vignettes, and logic and plot are often sacrificed for surreal imagery and nightmare scares. In her attic bedroom, pre-pubescent Rosaleen (newcomer Patterson, who unfortunately cannot act) dreams of a magical world inspired by the fairy-tale of Little Red Riding Hood, where young girls should beware of men whose eyebrows meet in the middle and of wolves who are hairy on the inside. An uncredited Terence Stamp turns up as the Devil in a white Rolls Royce.

✦✦✦✧

CONDEMNED TO LIVE

USA, 1935. Dir: Frank Strayer. With: Ralph Morgan, Pedro De Cordoba, Maxine Doyle, Russell Gleason, Mischa Auer, Lucy Beaumont. Invincible Pictures/Chesterfield Motion Pictures. B&W.

From the director of *The Vampire Bat* (1933) comes another low-budget, independent movie filmed on the Universal backlot. A woman (Barbara Bedford) bitten by a giant vampire bat in Africa gives birth to a baby that grows up into kindly Professor Paul Kristan (Morgan). Years later, he is unknowingly transformed under the influence of the full moon into the vampire killer terrorising a European village. His faithful hunchbacked servant, Zan (Auer), knows his secret and disposes of the victims in a hidden pit.

✦✦

CONFESSIONS OF A MALE ESCORT

(Orig: OBSZÖNITÄTEN)

West Germany, 1971 (1975). Dir: Alois Brummer. With: Stefan Grey, Sandra Reni, Miriam Moor, Kurt Grosskurth (Großkurth), Johan (Johannes) Buzalski, Eva Karinka. Brummer-Film-Produktion. Colour.

Softcore comedy set in a spooky old castle. This includes a vampire, a zombie and a proposed penis transplant!

✦

CONQUEST

(Orig: MACE IL FUORILEGGE/LA CONQUISTA DE LA TIERRA PERDIDA/EL BARBARO)

Italy/Spain/Mexico, 1980 (1983). Dir: Lucio Fulci. With: George Rivero, Andrew (Andrea) Occhipinti, Conrado (Corrado) San Martin, Violeta Cela, José Gras Palau, Sabrina Sellers (Sabrina Siani). Clemi Cinematográfica/ Golden Sun/Producciones Esme/Conquest Films/United Film Distribution Company. Colour.

Silly heroic fantasy adventure in which dim-witted barbarian Ilias (Occhipinti), armed with a magic bow and arrows, sets out on a quest to destroy the evil sorceress Ocron (Sellers, dressed only in a metal mask, leather G-string and a python). Along the way he is helped by Maxz (Rivero), and together they must battle Ocron's army of wolfmen, swamp zombies and the metallic demon Zora. Obviously made on a very low budget, Fulci throws in every possible cliché in a vain attempt to enliven a terrible script and unconvincing special effects.

✦

CONQUEST OF THE EARTH

USA, 1980. Dir: Sidney Hayers, Sigmund Neufeld Jr and Barry Crane. With: Kent McCord, Barry Van Dyke, Robyn Douglass, Lorne Greene, Robert Reed, Fred Holliday. Universal/Glen A. Larson Productions/ABC-TV. Colour.

Senseless feature-length compilation of two episodes from the short-lived 1980 TV series *Galactica 1980* ('Galactica Discovers Earth' and 'The Night the Cylons Landed'). When the spaceship *Battlestar Galactica* finally reaches Earth, Commander Adama (Greene) sends two emissaries, Capt Troy (McCord) and Lt Dillon (Van Dyke), to observe mankind. Teaming up with reporter Jamie Hamilton (Douglass), they discover that humanoid Cylon Andromus (Roger Davis) and his companion Centurion Andromidus (Neil Zeunik) have crashed nearby in their damaged war machine. While the Galacticans are looking for survivors, the two Cylons are given a ride to a Halloween party by a couple dressed as a vampire (Lara Parker from TV's *Dark Shadows*) and a clown (William Daniels). With Wolfman Jack as himself, Peter Mark Richman, Brion James and brief appearances by John Colicos (as Baltar) and Richard Lynch. Scripted by executive producer Glen A. Larson.

✦✧

CONRAD BROOKS MEETS THE WEREWOLF

USA, 1993. Dir: David Nelson. With: David Nelson, Conrad Brooks, Henry Brooks, Ted Brooks. Nelson. Colour.

The three Brooks (Bederski/Biedrzycki) brothers were all in Ed Wood's *Jailbait* (1954). They are reunited in this senseless mess, shot on tape in Baltimore, in which a laughing Conrad chases a werewolf (Nelson) through a Jewish cemetery in Baltimore and repeatedly runs the creature over in his car. The video release includes outtakes and interviews.

✦

GARY CONWAY
(Gareth Carmody) [b 1938]

Lightweight American leading man who played the ugly monster in *I Was a Teenage Frankenstein* (1957) and *How to Make a Monster* (1958). After moving to TV during the sixties (*Land of the Giants* [1968-69], etc), he returned to movies the following decade.

TOM CONWAY
(Thomas Sanders) [1904-1967]

Urbane, Russian-born British leading man, the brother of George Sanders (1906-1972). He played the Falcon's brother on screen from 1942-46 and brought style to three of Val Lewton's best: *Cat People* (1942), *I Walked With a Zombie* (1943) and *The Seventh Victim* (1943). His career declined during the 1950s, and after years of ill-health he died nearly destitute.

qv: *Bride of the Gorilla* (1951).

JACKIE COOGAN
[1914-1984]

American actor and former child star of the silent era who portrayed Uncle Fester on TV's *The Addams Family* (1964-66).

qv: *The Addams Family* (1973-75); *Dr. Heckyl & Mr. Hype* (1980); *Halloween With the Addams Family* (1977); *The New Scooby-Doo Movies: 'Scooby-Doo Meets the Addams Family: Wednesday is Missing'* (1972); *The Phantom of Hollywood* (1974).

ELISHA COOK JR
[1903-1995]

Weaselly American character actor, best remembered as the neurotic gunsel Wilmer in *The Maltese Falcon* (1941). He lent welcome support to a number of horror films, invariably ending up as a victim.

qv: *Blacula* (1972); *Dead of Night* (1976); *Hellzapoppin'* (1941); *Messiah of Evil* (1973); *The Night Stalker* (1971); *Salem's Lot* (1979); *Voodoo Island* (1957).

O CORONEL E O LOBISOMEN

Brazil, 1978 (1979). Dir: Alcino Diniz. With: Mauricio do Valle, Maria Claudia, Tonico Pereira. Alcino Diniz/ Embrafilme. Colour.

Sex comedy in which a military man dreams of a werewolf (played by Pereira). Based on the novel by J.C. de Carvalho. The title translates as 'The Colonel and the Wolfman'.

✦

MERIAN C. COOPER [1893-1973] and ERNEST B. SCHOEDSACK [1893-1979]

American producer-director team who started out making adventure documentaries and are justly remembered for *King Kong* (1933) and its less successful sequel, *The Son of Kong* (1933). Together they also collaborated on *The Most Dangerous Game* (1932), *She* (1935) and *Mighty Joe Young* (1949), while separately Cooper produced *The Phantom of Crestwood* (1932) and former cameraman Schoedsack directed *Dr. Cyclops* (1940). Cooper won a Special Academy Award in 1952 'for his many innovations and contributions to the art of the motion picture.'

ROGER CORMAN [b 1926]

Prolific American producer, director and distributor, best remembered for his drive-in exploitation movies of the 1950s and his series of Edgar Allan Poe adaptations with Vincent Price for AIP during the 1960s. He gave many actors and film-makers their early breaks, most notably through the creation of New World Pictures in 1970. Never one to allow art to get in the way of commerce, his 1990 autobiography is aptly titled *How I Made a Hundred Movies in Hollywood and Never Lost a Dime.*
qv: *Body Bags* (1993); *Death Race 2000* (1975); *Dracula Rising* (1992); *Frankenstein Unbound* (1990); *The Horror of It All* (1983); *The Howling* (1980); *Humanoids From the Deep* (1980); *The Little Shop of Horrors* (1960); *Not of This Earth* (1957); *100 Years of Horror: 'Blood-Drinking Beings'* (1996); *100 Years of Horror: 'Boris Karloff'* (1996); *100 Years of Horror: 'Girl Ghouls'* (1996); *100 Years of Horror: 'Gory Gimmicks'* (1996); *100 Years of Horror: 'Mutants'* (1996); *100 Years of Horror: 'Scream Queens'* (1996); *Queen of Blood* (1966); *Runaway Daughters* (1994); *Tales of Terror* (1962); *The Wasp Woman* (1959).

THE CORPSE

(USA: CRUCIBLE OF HORROR)
UK, 1969 (1972). Dir: Viktors Ritelis. With: Michael Gough, Yvonne Mitchell, Olaf Pooley, Sharon Gurney, Simon Gough, David Butler. London Cannon/Abacus/Grand National Film Distributors. Colour.
Filmed under the title *The Velvet House*. This low-budget chiller stars Gough as the tyrannical stockbroker Walter Eastwood, who is apparently murdered by his wife (Mitchell) and daughter (Gurney), but whose body keeps popping up in unexpected locations until he attacks his daughter and finally resumes his place at the breakfast table. Screenwriter Pooley appears as an inquisitive neighbour, and his wife Gabrielle Beaumont produced.
✦✦

THE CORPSE DRIVERS OF XIANGXI

China, 1957. Dir: Wang Tin-lam. B&W.
This apparently features the hopping corpses of Chinese legend.
✦

THE CORPSE VANISHES

(UK: THE CASE OF THE MISSING BRIDES)
USA, 1942. Dir: Wallace Fox. With: Bela Lugosi, Luana Walters, Tristram Coffin, Elizabeth Russell, Minerva Urecal, Kenneth Harlan. Monogram. B&W.
Lugosi plays mad orchid lover Dr Lorenz, who sleeps in a coffin and kidnaps young brides from the wedding altar to take to his underground laboratory, where he uses their blood to keep his aged wife, the Countess (Val Lewton favourite Russell), eternally young. He's assisted by Urecal's sinister old housekeeper, Frank Moran as her hulking idiot son and Angelo Rossitto playing his usual sadistic dwarf. Lugosi mugs his way through more low-budget madness produced by 'Jungle' Sam Katzman and Jack Dietz. Not released in Britain until 1946.
✦✧

STANLEY CORTEZ (Stanislaus Kranz) [1908-1997]

Superlative American cinematographer, the brother of actor Ricardo (1899-1977). In Hollywood since the silent era, he could always be relied upon to illuminate the bleakest concept.
qv: *The Candidate* (1964); *The Ghost in the Invisible Bikini* (1966); *The Neanderthal Man* (1953); *They Saved Hitler's Brain* (1963).

COSTINHA CONTRA O KING MONG

Brazil. With: Costinha.
Spoof of *King Kong* (1933) featuring comedian Costinha.
✦

COUNT DRACULA

UK, 1977. Dir: Philip Saville. With: Louis Jourdan, Frank Finlay, Susan Penhaligon, Judi Bowker, Mark Burns, Jack Shepherd. BBC-TV/WNET-13. Colour.
Billed as 'A Gothic romance', this made-for-TV movie is overlong at two-and-a-half hours (it was originally shown in three parts). Despite that, it's a fairly faithful adaptation of the Bram Stoker novel (and even includes the scene of Dracula crawling head-first down a castle wall), but the mix of film and video gives the production an uneven quality. Jourdan is too debonair as the Count, although director Saville manages to include a few Hammer-type shock moments and there's solid support from Finlay's Van Helsing and Shepherd's Renfield. With Susie Hickford, Belinda Meuldijk and Sue Vanner as the Count's undead brides, whose baby-eating antics were cut from American prints. Corgi Books published a novelisation by scriptwriter Gerald Savory. A $3,000,000 cartoon version with character designs by Frank Frazetta had been announced in 1976 by Orsatti Productions but was never made.
Remake: DRACULA (qv; 1979)
✦✦

COUNT DUCKULA

UK, 1987-89. Dir: Chris Randall. Voices: David Jason, Jack May, Brian Trueman, Jimmy Hibbert, Barry Clayton. Cosgrove Hall Productions/Pearson Television International/Thames Television. Colour.
Half-hour children's cartoon TV series featuring the adventures of the eponymous vegetarian vampire duck (Jason), reanimated by his manservant Igor (May) and clumsy housekeeper Nanny (Trueman), set in and around the flying Castle Duckula in Transylvania. With Touser the werewolf and vampire-hunter Dr Von Goosewing (Hibbert). Additional voices are by Ruby Wax.
✦✦

Hunchbudgie of Notre Dame

UK, 1988. Dir: Chris Randall. Voices: David Jason, Jack May, Brian Trueman, Jimmy Hibbert, Barry Clayton. Cosgrove Hall Productions/Pearson Television International/Thames Television. Colour.
While the green-faced Count Duckula studies art in Paris, Nanny paints the Eiffel Tower pink.
✦✧

No Sax Please We're Egyptian

UK, 1987. Dir: Chris Randall. Voices: David Jason, Jack May, Brian Trueman, Jimmy Hibbert, Barry Clayton. Cosgrove Hall Productions/Pearson Television International/Thames Television. Colour.
When Count Duckula learns about his ancestors from his manservant Igor, he travels to Egypt in search of a mystic saxophone and encounters a pair of High Priests who want to raise the mummy of their Pharaoh from the dead.
✦✧

The Zombie Awakes

UK, 1989. Dir: Chris Randall. Voices: David Jason, Jack May, Brian Trueman, Jimmy Hibbert, Barry Clayton. Cosgrove Hall Productions/Pearson Television International/Thames Television. Colour.

Louis Jourdan as TV's romantic Count Dracula *(1977).*

The mad Caligari-like Dr Quackbrain and his one hundred year-old zombie slave Morpheus use a machine to bring to life the dreams of Count Duckula, Nanny and Igor.
✦✦✧

COUNTER DESTROYER

Hong Kong, 1987. Dir: Edgar Jere. With: Cynthia Rose, Tony Job, Harriet Brown, Bob Poe. Thomas Tang/Filmark International/TransWorld Video. Colour.
Comedy horror about a female screenwriter who gives birth to the monstrous son of a long finger-nailed vampire, while a Taoist priest battles a pair of hopping vampires.
✦

COUNT EROTICO — VAMPIRE

USA, 1971. Dir: Tony Teresi. With: John Peters, Mary Simon, Paul Robinson, Keith Erickson. Lobo Productions. Colour.
Hardcore comedy/vampire movie in which the wife of Count Erotica fails to get her undead husband to come out of his coffin and ends up having sex with the family cretin (Erickson).
✦

COUNTESS DRACULA

UK, 1970. Dir: Peter Sasdy. With: Ingrid Pitt, Nigel Green, Sandor Elès, Maurice Denham, Lesley-Anne Down, Patience Collier. Hammer Films/Rank Film Distributors. Colour.
Despite the title, this is in fact based on the real-life exploits of Erzsébet/Elizabeth Báthory (1560-1614). Eighteenth century Hungarian Countess Elisabeth Nadasdy (a dubbed Pitt) bathes in the blood of virgins to regain her youth. The excellent Green is her devoted servant Captain Dobi, who helps her obtain victims. A slow moving historical drama from Hammer, with very little horror (except for a nasty stabbing) and a climactic wedding that is pure melodrama. A good cast, including Peter Jeffrey, overact dreadfully. Michel Parry wrote the novelisation.
✦✦

COUNT TICKULA

USA, 1990. Dir: Tony Sinclair. Sinclair Blue Productions. Colour.
'Adults only' tickling video from writer/director Sinclair. The eponymous fanged and caped vampire holds captive the naked young girls of a village and tickles to death his victims who are chained up in a dungeon.
✦

COUNT YORGA, VAMPIRE

(aka THE LOVES OF COUNT IORGA, VAMPIRE)
USA, 1970. Dir: Bob Kelljan (Robert Kelljchian). With: Robert Quarry, Roger Perry, Michael Murphy, Michael Macready, Donna Anders, Judith Lang. Erica Productions/American International. Colour.
Shot under the title *Vampyre* for just $64,000, this was originally planned as a sex film. Set in contemporary Los Angeles, a group of friends fall under the influence of suave Bulgarian vampire, Count Yorga, who is guarded by his hulking manservant Brudah (Edward Walsh) and keeps his three undead 'brides' in the cellar. Former child star Quarry is impressive as Yorga, portraying the vampire with wit and intelligence, while writer/director Kelljan makes the most of the low budget to create some striking vampire attacks. Actor/producer Macready used his father, veteran actor George Macready, to narrate the opening and closing scenes. In the end almost everyone ends up dead (or undead).
Sequel: THE RETURN OF COUNT YORGA (qv; 1971)
✦✦✦

THE CRAVING

(Orig: EL RETORNO DEL HOMBRE LOBO)
Spain, 1980. Dir: Jack (Jacinto) Molina. With: Paul Naschy (Jacinto Molina), Julia Saly, Silvia Aguilar, Azucena Hernandez, Narciso Ibáñez Menta, Beatriz Elorietta. Dalmata Films. Colour.
Sequel to *Night of the Howling Beast* (1975). Naschy's ninth movie as El Hombre Lobo, Waldemar Daninsky, which he also directed and scripted under the name Jack Molina. The wolfman is revived when two grave robbers remove a silver cross from his heart, and he is soon settling an old score with the undead Countess Elizabeth Bathory (Saly) and her female vampires. The scenes of the vampire women have an imaginative, dream-like quality that is missing from the rest of the movie. This was a major box-office flop in Spain.
Sequel: LA BESTIA Y LA ESPADA MÁGICA (qv; 1983)
✦✧

> **HAZEL COURT**
> **[b 1926]**
>
> Red-haired British leading lady and former Rank starlet. She made her movie début in 1944 and brought a strong independence to her roles in a number of horror films for Hammer and Roger Corman during the late 1950s and early 1960s. She married actor/director Don Taylor (1920-1998) and moved to America to become a sculptor.
> qv: *The Curse of Frankenstein* (1957); *Doctor Blood's Coffin* (1961); *Flesh and Blood: The Hammer Heritage of Horror* (1994); *100 Years of Horror: 'Baron Frankenstein'* (1996); *100 Years of Horror: 'Mad Doctors'* (1996); *100 Years of Horror: 'Girl Ghouls'* (1996); *100 Years of Horror: 'Scream Queens'* (1996).

THE CRAZY PROFESSOR

Philippines, 1985. Dir: Ben Feleo. With: Dolphy, Alma Moreno, Aga Muhlach, Janice de Belen, Panchito, Babalu. RVQ/Trigon Video Colour.
Musical comedy in which college Professor Frank Einstein creates a serum that can bring the dead back to life. He also produces a potion that transforms a man into a hog and another that when applied to tennis shoes enables basketball players to jump incredibly high (just like in Disney's *The Absent Minded Professor* [1961]).
✦

CRAZY SAFARI

Hong Kong/South Africa, 1990 (1991). Dir: Billy Chan (Lo Weng-Tung) (and Jamie Uys). With: Lam Ching-Ying (Lin Zheng-Ying), N!Xau, Sam Christopher Chan, Peter Chan, Jumbo. Win's Movie Productions/Samico Films. Colour.
Wild horror comedy variation on *The Gods Must Be Crazy* (1980) that begins with a short documentary detailing the differences between Western and Asian vampires. A magical priest, HiSing (Ching-Ying), and his young ward Leo (Sam Christopher Chan) are returning to Hong Kong with the revived body of a fifteenth century mummified vampire purchased at a Sotheby's auction in England. However, the plane runs out of fuel and is forced to land in the South African jungle. While the two heroes are trying to escape the wild animals, the vampire falls from the sky and is immediately hailed as a god by the local natives. The climax involves a battle between the hopping vampire and a superhuman African zombie (Jumbo), while the spirit of Bruce Lee(!) is transferred from a photo into the native chief (N!Xau).
✦✦

CREATURE FROM THE BLACK LAGOON

USA, 1954. Dir: Jack Arnold (and Charles S. Welbourne). With: Richard Carlson, Julia Adams (Julie Adams/Betty May Adams), Richard Denning, Antonio Moreno, Nestor Paiva, Whit Bissell. Universal-International. B&W.
The first, and best, of Universal's trilogy featuring the prehistoric Gill Man (make-up by Bud Westmore and Jack Kevan), discovered in the Amazon jungle by a team of scientists. Director Arnold uses the atmospheric studio jungle backlot and 3-D process as effectively as his more usual desert setting to create a sense of unease. The excellent underwater photography (directed by Welbourne) exploits our fear of what might wait just below the surface, while scenes of Adams and the Creature swimming together contain heavy sexual overtones. Although Glenn Strange was originally considered for the role, Ricou Browning played the Creature in the water and Ben Chapman portrayed it on land. The film was novelised by Vargo Statten (John Russell Fearn) in 1954, and again under the 'Carl

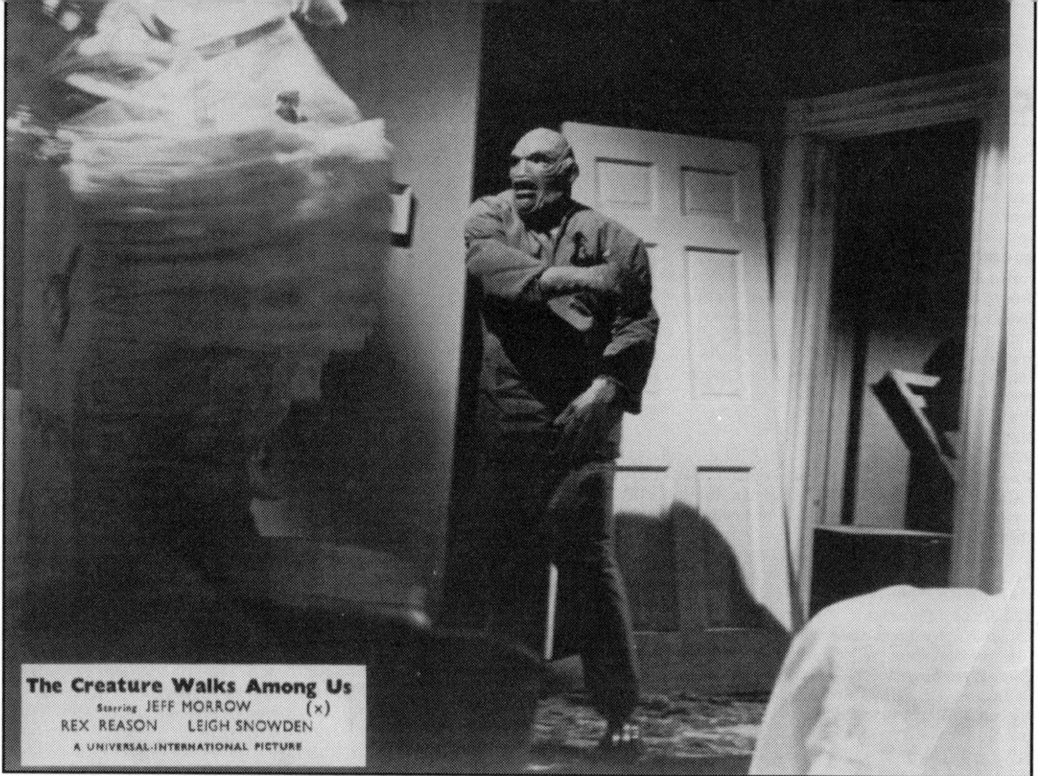

Don Megowan as the surgically-altered Gill Man in The Creature Walks Among Us *(1955).*

Dreadstone' house name in 1977. John Carpenter was linked with an early 1990s remake, while a decade previously Universal planned a 3-D remake to be directed by Arnold and executive produced by John Landis from a script by Nigel Kneale. Rick Baker would have created the Creature. In the end, the studio decided to back *Jaws 3-D* (1983) instead!

Sequel: REVENGE OF THE CREATURE (qv; 1955)

✦✦✦✦✧

CREATURE OF THE WALKING DEAD

(Orig: LA MARCA DEL MUERTO)

Mexico/USA, 1960/63. Dir: Frederic Corte (Fernando Cortés). With: Rock Madison (Fernando Casanova), Ann Wells (Sonia Furio), George Todd, Willard Gross, Bruno Ve Sota, Katherine Victor. Alameda Films/ADP Productions/ Medallion TV Enterprises. B&W.

Cheapo producer Jerry Warren added new footage (directed by Richard Wallace) for the American release of this Mexican horror film. Scientist Martin (Madison) revives his dead grandfather, the mad Dr John Malthus (also Madison), only to discover that the living corpse kills for the blood transfusions it needs to remain youthful-looking. Like Warren's other abominations, this is a mess. The original Mexican cast included Pedro de Auguillón, Aurora Alvarado, Rosa María Gallardo and Hortensia Santoveña.

✦

CREATURES OF EVIL

(Orig: DUGO NG VAMPIRA. USA: aka CURSE OF THE VAMPIRES)

Philippines/USA, 1970. Dir: Gerardo de Leon. With: Amelia Fuentes, Romeo Vasques, Eddie Garcia, Johnny Monteiro, Rosario del Pilar, Mary Walter. Sceptre Industries/Hemisphere Pictures. Colour.

Director de Leon and star Fuentes are reunited from *The Blood Drinkers* (1966) for this unusual vampire thriller, shot in vibrant colour. A brother (Garcia) and sister (Fuentes) return to their father's estate, only to discover that he keeps their dead mother (Walter) — now a vampire — chained in a basement crypt, where he periodically whips her. When the brother also becomes a vampire, it ends in tragedy for everyone. More a soap opera than a horror film, this family saga also includes a couple of ghosts and plenty of religious symbolism.

✦✧

THE CREATURE WALKS AMONG US

USA, 1955. Dir: John Sherwood. With: Jeff Morrow, Rex Reason, Leigh Snowden, Gregg Palmer, Maurice Manson, James Rawley. Universal-International. B&W.

The sequel to *Revenge of the Creature* (1955), this final episode in Universal's Gill Man trilogy reunites Morrow and Reason, the stars of *This Island Earth* (1955). Morrow plays the insanely jealous Dr William Barton, who captures the Creature (Ricou Browning) and transports him to Florida. Horribly burned by accident, the Creature's gills are removed and, through a delicate operation, it is transformed into a rubber-suited mutant monster (Don Megowan) before breaking out of its compound and returning to the sea. Although not up to the standard of the previous two films, director Sherwood does his best with the lightweight material, helped by good-looking photography and a strong cast of contract players.

✦✦✧

CREATURE WITH THE ATOM BRAIN

USA, 1955. Dir: Edward L. Cahn. With: Richard Denning, Angela Stevens, Michael Granger, Linda Bennett, Harry Lauter, Tristram Coffin. Columbia/Clover Productions. B&W.

Scripted by Curt Siodmak (*Donovan's Brain*, etc). Denning plays pipe-smoking police doctor Chet Walker who discovers that ex-Nazi scientist Professor Steigg (Gregory Gay) is replacing dead gangster's brains with atomic energy and turning them into radioactive zombie killers. Despite a few eerie shots, this is more low-budget madness from producer 'Jungle' Sam Katzman.

✦✦✧

THE CREEPER

USA, 1948. Dir: Jean Yarbrough. With: Eduardo Ciannelli, Onslow Stevens, June Vincent, Ralph Morgan, Janis Wilson, John Baragrey. Twentieth Century-Fox/Reliance

Pictures. B&W.
Apparently, this was the only serious horror film released in America in 1948. It's an obvious attempt by Twentieth Century-Fox's 'B' movie unit, Reliance, to re-create the success of Val Lewton's low-budget horrors over at RKO. Unfortunately, director Yarbrough is unable to make much of the flimsy material and contract cast. When Dr Jim Borden (Stevens) experiments on himself with a new serum derived from West Indian cats, his hand transforms into a fluffy claw which he uses to kill his enemies. Top-billed Ciannelli looks menacing in the red-herring role of Dr Van Glock, and this is worth catching if only to see nervous heroine Nora (Wilson), who suffers from nightmares and a fear of cats, shoot hero Dr John Reade (Baragrey) by mistake! With Philip Ahn.
✦✦

THE CREEPS

USA, 1997. Dir: Charles Band. With: Rhonda Griffin, Justin Lauer, Bill Moynihan, Kristin Norton, Phil Fondacaro, Jon Simanton. Tanna Productions/Full Moon Pictures. Colour.
Silly, low-budget comedy/horror thriller filmed in 3-D but released flat on video. A librarian (Griffin) and a video store manager/part-time detective (Lauer) attempt to stop a mad doctor (the irritating Moynihan) from using his 'Archetype Inducer' machine on stolen copies of first editions and original manuscripts to bring life to such literary creations as the Werewolf (Jon Simanton), the Mummy (Joe Smith), Frankenstein's Monster (Thomas Wellington) and Dracula (Fondacaro, who brings surprising dignity to the role). However, as a result of a problem in the process, when they materialise they are just three feet tall (special make-up effects created by Atlantic West Effects). Produced and directed by Band, this also includes some unnecessary nudity.
✦✧

CREEPSHOW

USA, 1982. Dir: George A. Romero. With: Hal Holbrook, Adrienne Barbeau, Fritz Weaver, Leslie Nielsen, Carrie Nye, Viveca Lindfors. Laurel Entertainment/Warner Bros. Colour.
Overlong anthology film based on an original screenplay by Stephen King, which in turn was inspired by the EC horror comics of the 1950s. A fine cast is wasted in weak stories about zombie patriarch Dead Nate (John Amplas) returning from the grave to collect a gruesome cake ('Father's Day'); a backwoods farmer (King himself) possessed by alien plant life from a meteorite ('The Lonesome Death of Jody Verrill'); a pair of living-dead corpses (Gaylen Ross and Ted Danson!) returning from a watery grave for revenge ('Something to Tide You Over'); Henry Northup (Holbrook) discovering an Arctic monster in a crate dating from 1834 ('The Crate'); and the reclusive Upson Pratt (E.G. Marshall) besieged by a horde of killer cockroaches ('They're Creeping Up on You'). The linking story ('Voodoo Doll') contains some nice cartoon animation, and Tom Savini's special make-up effects are pretty gruesome. It should all have worked better than it does. With Savini as a garbage man, King's son Joe, Bingo O'Malley and an uncredited Tom Atkins. A graphic novel adaptation, illustrated by Berni Wrightson, was published by Plume/New American Library.
Sequel: CREEPSHOW 2 (qv; 1987)
✦✦✧

CREEPSHOW 2

USA, 1987. Dir: Michael Gornick. With: Lois Chiles, George Kennedy, Dorothy Lamour, Tom Savini, Domenick John, Philip Dore. Laurel Entertainment/New World Pictures. Colour.
This cheap-looking follow-up to *Creepshow* (1982) is based on three stories by Stephen King and scripted by George A. Romero. However, the blame for this shambles should rest with cinematographer Gornick, making his début as a director, and producer Richard P. Rubinstein. The first tale ('Old Chief Wood'nhead'), about a cigar store wooden Indian (Dan Kamin) that comes to life to avenge a murder, also includes equally wooden performances by veterans Kennedy and Lamour (her last film). The second story ('The Raft') features a group of teenagers who are menaced by a monster that resembles a floating garbage bag on a mountain lake. The final episode ('The Hitchhiker'), originally set to star Barbara Eden, involves a zombie hitchhiker (Tom Wright) who seeks revenge after being killed by a hit-and-run motorist (Chiles), and includes a cameo by King as a truck driver. The stories are linked by The Creep (Savini, voiced by Joe Silver) and some terrible cartoon sequences.
✦✧

CREEPY CLASSICS

USA, 1987. Dir: Pamela Page. With: Vincent Price. The Carter Companies/Fox Lorber Associates/Archive Film. Colour/B&W.
Produced exclusively as a promotional item for Hallmark (with a special trivia card included in each video box), this half-hour tape features Price introducing quite lengthy clips and trailers from inside a movie theatre. These include *Attack of the Puppet People* (1958), *Dr. Terror's House of Horrors* (1965), *I Was a Teenage Werewolf* (1957) and *Night of the Living Dead* (1968).
✦✧

CREEPY TALES

USA, 1988-89 (1995). Dir: John P. Fedele and Michael (L.) Raso. With: Director Tex, David Weber, John Sanders, David Munro, Kathy Heidenger, Tex Joe Bob Young. The EI Brothers Production Company/O'Gore Productions/Swiss Home Video. Colour/B&W.
Fourth volume in a series of video compilations, featuring two half-hour episodes of the late night New Jersey cable TV series *The Meadowlands Showcase Presents*. The 1989 Halloween show is presented by horror host Angus (Weber) and includes three short films: the uncredited *Evil Vision* (which includes clips from *Night of the Living Dead* [1968] on TV), The Cramps music video 'Garbage Man' and Pete Jacelone's *The Day the Shopping Carts Came to Life*. Angus and co-host Emily (Heidenger) then present the cablecast for 31 October 1988, which was only shown once due to its graphic nature. This features the uncredited *Tag You're It!*, a slightly longer version of *Evil Vision* and Timothy O'Rawe's *A Halloween Tale*, which is loosely based on Charles Dickens' *A Christmas Carol*: a neighbourhood grouch who hates children and hates Halloween is visited by four spirits of Halloween past — Dracula, a werewolf, a Karloffian Frankenstein Monster and a zombie — who teach her a series of bloody lessons.
✦

ALFREDO B. CREVENNA [1914-1996]

German-born Mexican director whose credits encompass more than 140 films, including several of Santo's later adventures.
qv: *Aventura al Centro de la Tierra* (1963); *¡Las Bestias del Terror!* (1972); *Bring Me the Vampire* (1961); *La Casa de los Espantos* (1961); *La Dinastia Dracula* (1978); *La Huella Macabra* (1962); *Las Muñecas del King Kong* (1978); *Santo Contra la Magia Negra* (1972).

CRIME DOCTOR'S COURAGE

USA, 1945. Dir: George Sherman. With: Warner Baxter, Hillary Brooke, Jerome Cowan, Robert Scott, Lloyd Corrigan, Emory Parnell. Columbia. B&W.
In 1943, Columbia began a series of ten films based on Max Marcin's successful radio show, *Crime Doctor*. Baxter starred in them all as amnesia victim Dr Ordway, who becomes a leading criminal psychologist before discovering he was once a gang leader himself. In this mystery/thriller his investigations into a possible homicidal maniac lead to the Braggas (Anthony Caruso and Lupita Tovar [star of the 1931 Spanish-language *Dracula*]), a mysterious Spanish dance team who are suspected of being 300 year-old vampires. It's all explained scientifically in the end.
Sequel: CRIME DOCTOR'S WARNING (1945)
✦✦

CROCODILE MOTHER

Thailand, circa 1980s. Colour.
Low-budget mix of horror and softcore sex, about a jealous woman

who transforms into a crocodile to kill her rival. In the end she is destroyed by lightning, but leaves behind two eggs...
✦

CRISWELL
(Charles Jeron Criswell King) [1907-1982]

American TV psychic popular during the 1950s. A friend and supporter of Edward D. Wood Jr, he was played by Jeffrey Jones in Tim Burton's *Ed Wood* (1994).
qv: *Ed Wood Look Back in Angora* (1994); *Night of the Ghouls* (1959); *Orgy of the Dead* (1965); *Plan 9 from Outer Space* (1958).

CRONOS
(Orig: LA INVENCIÓN DE CRONOS)
Mexico, 1992 (1994). Dir: Guillermo del Toro. With: Federico Luppi, Ron Perlman, Claudio Brook, Margarita Isabel, Tamara Shanath, Daniel Gimenez Cacho. Producciones Iguana/Ventana Films/October Films. Colour.
An imaginative and stylish reworking of the vampire legend by twenty-seven year-old writer/director del Toro, who made it for just $2,000,000. When elderly antiques dealer Jesús Gris (Argentinean actor Luppi) discovers the ancient mechanical Cronos device, the creation of a sixteenth century alchemist, it reveals the secret of eternal life to him. However, as part of his transformation he becomes infected with a craving for human blood and only his mute granddaughter (Isabel) can help him. Together they are pursued by the psychopathic Angel de la Guardia (Perlman), who wants the device for his dying industrialist uncle, Dieter (genre veteran Brook). This won multiple awards.
✦✦✦✧

THE CROSS OF SEVEN JEWELS
(Orig: LA CROCE DALLE 7 PIETRE/CROCIFISSO DI SETTE GIOIELLOS)
Italy, 1986. Dir: Marco Antonio Andolfi. With: Eddy Endolf (Marco Antonio Andolfi), Annie Belle, Gordon Mitchell, Paolo Florino, Giorgio Ardisson, Zaira Zoccheddu. Gino Serra Pictures. Colour.
While on his way to Rome, a jewelled crucifix belonging to Italian Marco/Michael (Endolf) is stolen by a motorcycle gang. This results in him periodically transforming into a hairy naked werewolf. If that wasn't bad enough, his attempts to recover the talisman through the criminal underworld lead to encounters with a Satanic priest (Mitchell) possessed by a bestial demon, the leader of the Sicilian Mafia (Ardisson), and a medium dressed in black lingerie! It doesn't make a great deal of sense, and writer/editor/director/star Andolfi was also responsible for the laughable special effects.
✦

CRUISE INTO TERROR
USA, 1978. Dir: Bruce Kessler. With: Dirk Benedict, Frank Converse, John Forsythe, Christopher George, Lynda Day George, Jo Ann Harris. Aaron Spelling Productions/ABC-TV. Colour.
Silly all-star TV movie in which the passengers and crew aboard a luxury cruise ship bound for Mexico discover an ancient Egyptian sarcophagus that contains a legendary evil said to return every 1,000 years to bring about Armageddon. Veteran Ray Milland is the archaeologist who raises the hidden relic from the sea, while ageing hero Hugh O'Brien plays the ship's Captain, who has to keep his passengers safe from sharks, storms and a secret servant of the malevolent force. With Lee Meriwether, Roger E. Mosley, Stella Stevens and Marshall Thompson in a brief cameo.
✦✦

LA CRUZ DEL DIABLO
Spain, 1974. Dir: John Gilling. With: Carmen Sevilla, Adolfo Marsillach, Emma Cohen, Ramiros Oliveros, Eduardo Fajardo, Mónica Randall. Bulnes. Colour.
Based on the writings of nineteenth century Spanish poet Gustavo Adolfo Bácquer, the script is co-credited to Jacinto Molina (aka Paul Naschy), although it was extensively rewritten by British director Gilling (*The Plague of the Zombies* [1966], etc), who retired to live in Spain and whose last film this is. Experimenting with drugs to overcome his writer's block, Alfred Dawson (Oliveros) is investigating local folklore when he experiences visions of a beautiful Beatriz (Cohen) and his world begins to disintegrate around him. The undead Templar Knights appear in a dream sequence, thus making this an unofficial addendum to the Amando de Ossorio's 'Blind Dead' series. The title translates as 'Cross of the Devil'.
✦✧

CRY OF THE BANSHEE
UK, 1970. Dir: Gordon Hessler. With: Vincent Price, Essy Persson, Hugh Griffith, Elisabeth Bergner, Patrick Mower, Hilary Dwyer. American International Pictures. Colour.
This was AIP's attempt to recreate the success of *Witchfinder General* (1968). However, director Hessler is not in the same class as Michael Reeves. Set in sixteenth century England, Price (in supposedly his one hundredth movie) stars as Lord Edward Whitman who destroys a local witchcraft cult. In revenge, the coven's leader Oona (seventy-two year-old veteran Bergner) curses Whitman and sends a sidhé, a shape-changing demonic spirit (Mower), to destroy him and his family. In the 'twist' ending, the powers of evil triumph. Despite John Coquillion's atmospheric photography and a music score by Les Baxter, this remains merely an average chiller. With Sally Geeson, Michael Elphick and Robert Hutton. Terry Gilliam animated the opening credits.
✦✦

CRY OF THE WEREWOLF
USA, 1944. Dir: Henry Levin. With: Nina Foch, Stephen Crane, Osa Massen (Ase Madsen), Blanche Yurka, Barton MacLane, John Abbott. Columbia. B&W.
Atmospheric murder mystery in which Foch stars as Celeste La Tour, High Priestess of the Troiga gypsy tribe, who believes that she has inherited lycanthropic powers and can turn into a werewolf to protect her mother's secret temple in New Orleans. With Crane as Bob, the dumb hero, Massen as hypnotised heroine Elsa, and a great uncredited supporting cast that includes Abbott, Fritz Leiber and Milton Parsons as yet another undertaker. Filmed under the title *Daughter of the Werewolf*, this actually started out as the sequel to *The Return of the Vampire* (1943).
✦✦✧

CRYPT OF DARK SECRETS
USA, 1976. Dir: Jack Weis. With: Ronald Tanet, Maureen Ridley, Wayne Mack, Butch Benit, Maureen Chan, Herbert G. Jahncke. Weis. Colour.
From the director of *Mardi Gras Massacre* (1976) comes this low-budget voodoo thriller also filmed in New Orleans. When Vietnam veteran Ted Watkins is murdered for the money he keeps hidden in his island home, he is revived from the dead by nude voodoo priestess Damballa, who can transform into a snake. The swamp witch also does a dance on top of a smoking mummy case in this regional rarity.
✦

CRYPT OF HORROR
(Orig: LA CRIPTA E L'INCUBO/LA MALDICIÓN DE LOS KARNSTEIN. USA: TERROR IN THE CRYPT)
Italy/Spain, 1964. Dir: Thomas Miller (Camillo Mastrocinque). With: Christopher Lee, Audrey Amber (Adriana Ambesi), Ursula Davis (Pier Anna Quaglia), José Campos, Vera Valmont, Nela Conjú. MEC Cinematográfica/ Hispamer Films/American International Pictures. B&W.
An uncredited reworking of J. Sheridan Le Fanu's 'Carmilla', with Lee as Count Ludwig Karnstein. Karnstein believes that his daughter Laura (Amber) is the reincarnation of the dead witch Sheena, who is murdering members of his cursed family. In fact, her friend Lyuba (Davis) is revealed as the vampiric killer. Despite all the usual genre trappings, director Mastrocinque lacks the style of Bava and Freda, and any attempt at eroticism is lost in the muddled script.
Remake: MYSTERY AND IMAGINATION: Carmilla (qv; 1966)
✦✧

CRYPT OF THE LIVING DEAD
(Orig: LA TUMBA DE LA ISLA MALDITA. USA: aka HANNAH QUEEN OF THE VAMPIRES/YOUNG HANNAH QUEEN OF THE VAMPIRES. UK: aka VAMPIRE WOMAN) Spain/Turkey/USA, 1972 (1973). Dir: Ray Danton (and Julio Salvador). With: Andrew Prine, Teresa Gimpera, Patty (Paty) Shepard, Frank (Francisco) Braña, Daniel Martin, Mark Damon. Orbita Films/Filmax/Atlas Films/Coast Industries. Colour.
Atmospheric night sequences and unusual Turkish locations make this an interesting vampire thriller. 700 year-old undead queen Hannah (Gimpera), the bride of Louis VII, is resurrected on Vampire Island. Another bloodsucker, burned to a crisp, continues to attack villagers during the climax. The American version apparently includes additional footage directed by actor-turned-director Danton and produced by writer Lou Shaw.
✦✦

CRY UNCLE
(UK: SUPER DICK)
USA, 1971. Dir: John G. Avildsen. With: Allen Garfield (Allen Goorwitz), Madeleine Le Roux, Devin Goldenberg, David Kirk, Sean Walsh, Pamela Gruen. Cry Uncle Productions/Crest Films. Colour.
Based on the novel *Lie a Little, Die a Little* by Michael Brett. Overweight New York private detective Jake Masters (comedian Garfield) is hired to clear an elderly millionaire (Kirk) suspected of the murder of a cocktail waitress who was blackmailing him. This softcore spoof includes *Bride of Frankenstein* (1935) on TV as an important plot device. Director Avildsen (*Rocky* [1976], etc) was also the cinematographer and editor. With Paul Sorvino as an airport cop and production manager Lloyd Kaufman as a hippie on LSD. It was cut by ten minutes when released in Britain in 1973.
✦✧

CRY WOLF
UK, 1980. Dir: Leszek Burzynski. With: Paul Maxwell, Rosalind Ayres, Stephen Greif, James Bree, Chris Fairbank, Gabrielle Daye. Picture Partnership Productions/ Paramount. B&W.
For this enjoyable thirty-two minute pastiche of British horror films, the producers persuaded cinematographer Robert Krasker (*The Third Man* [1949], etc) out of retirement one last time (he died the following year) to successfully duplicate the black and white look of the 1950s. Stan Hey's screenplay is a reasonably amusing spoof on werewolf films, as animal research scientist Dr Jack Russell (Maxwell) drinks a cup of tea accidentally laced with a canine serum by his assistant Maria Moore (Ayres). When Jack starts transforming into a werehound and stealing tins of dog food, a Romanian expert on lycanthropy, Professor Ion Porphiriou (Greif), decides to track him down. This reuses Leith Stevens' music score from *War of the Worlds* (1953).
✦✦

CUADECUC (VAMPIR)
(USA: aka VAMPIR)
Spain, 1970. Dir: Pedro Portabella. With: Christopher Lee, Herbert Lom, Soledad Miranda (Soledad Redon Bueno), Fred (Frederick) Williams, Jack Taylor (George Brown Randall/Grek Martin), Maria Rohm. Films 69 Barcelona. B&W.
Running just over an hour, this tedious experimental film uses electronic effects instead of natural sound (such as the incongruous noise of a jet plane over scenes of a funeral hearse) to accompany rare footage of cast members joking around behind-the-scenes on Jesús Franco's *Bram Stoker's Count Dracula* (1970). The grainy black and white cinematography also doesn't help.
✦

A CULPA
Portugal, 1981. Dir: A. Victorino d'Almeida. With: Sindey Felipe, Estrella Novais, Mario Vergas, Marillia Gama, Riu Mendes, Paula Guedes. Colour.
Portuguese film about a male werewolf.
✦

CULT OF THE COBRA
USA, 1955. Dir: Francis D. Lyon. With: Faith Domergue, Richard Long, Marshall Thompson, Kathleen Hughes, William Reynolds, Jack Kelly. Universal-International. B&W.
Despite the low budget and contract cast, director Lyon brings a nice *film noir* look to this enjoyable slice of fifties hokum. Sultry Domergue plays Lisa, the Asian high priestess of the Lamiates, who can transform into a deadly cobra. She travels to America to revenge herself on five GIs (future TV stars Long, Thompson, Reynolds, Kelly and David Janssen) who photographed the secret ritual of her cult of snake-worshippers. 'B' movie favourite Thompson gets the role of his career as Domergue's insanely jealous boyfriend. Credited as 'Jack Halloran', Edward Platt (from TV's *Get Smart* [1965-70], etc) turns up as a high priest.
✦✦✦

CULT OF THE DAMNED
(Orig: LA ISLA DE LOS MUERTOS/LA MUERTE VIVIENTE. USA: aka CULT OF THE DEAD/ISLE OF THE SNAKE PEOPLE/SNAKE PEOPLE)
Mexico/USA, 1968 (1971). Dir: John (Juan) Ibañez (and Jack Hill). With: Boris Karloff, Julissa, Charles (Carlos) East, Ralph (Rafael) Bertrand, Judy Carmichael (July Marichael), Tongolele (Yolanda Montes). Filmica Vergara/Columbia/Parasol/Cineplex. Colour.
The first of four movies Karloff made towards the end of his life for Mexican producer Luis Enríque Vergara. In this muddled mix of sex and sadism, an obviously ill-looking Karloff plays Dr Carl Van Molder who, in the guise of mysterious high priest Damballah, controls a voodoo cult that creates blood-drinking zombies on the South Seas island of Koabia. Even a silly narration can't make sense of the muddled plot. Karloff's scenes were shot separately in Hollywood (by Hill, who also scripted) and later edited into the rest of the movie. When Columbia disowned the film, it was finally released directly to American TV in 1971 (with direction credited to 'Henry Verg') before going straight to (heavily cut) video in Britain in 1988. An embarrassing end to a great career.
✦

CURADOS DE ESPANTOS: SE LES METIO EL DIABLO
Mexico, 1990. Dir: Adolfo Martinez Solares. With: Alfonso Zayas, Roberto 'Flaco' Guzman, Lina Santos, Cesar Bono, Rene 'Tun Tun' Ruiz, Claudio Sorel. Filmoimagen/ Televicine. Colour.
Comedy in which old vampire Vladimir (Guzman) is discovered mummified in a Mexican pyramid. After drinking the blood of a nurse to become young again, he flies off in human form but keeps crashing into obstacles. He becomes intoxicated on the blood of a drunken woman and catches fire in the sun's rays. In the end, two infant twins sport vampire fangs. Co-scripted by the director and his father, veteran Gilberto Martinez Solares.
✦

FEDERICO CURIEL
[1916-1985]

Mexican journeyman director of Germán Robles' vampiric *Nostradamus* series and more than a decades' worth of Santo adventures.
qv: *The Blood of Nostradamus* (1960); *The Curse of Nostradamus* (1960); *The Genii of Darkness* (1960); *El Imperio de Dracula* (1966); *Las Momias de Guanajuato* (1970); *The Monsters Demolisher* (1960); *Santo Contra el Cerebro Diabolico* (1961); *La Sombra del Murciélago* (1966); *Las Vampiras* (1968); *La Venganza de las Mujeres Vampiro* (1969).

CURSE OF DRACULA
USA, 1956. Dir: Tony (Anthony) Brzezinski. Adventure Film Productions. B&W.
Amateur Dracula film shot on 8mm by teenager Brzezinski and his

Christopher Lee as the scarred Creature in The Curse of Frankenstein *(1957).*

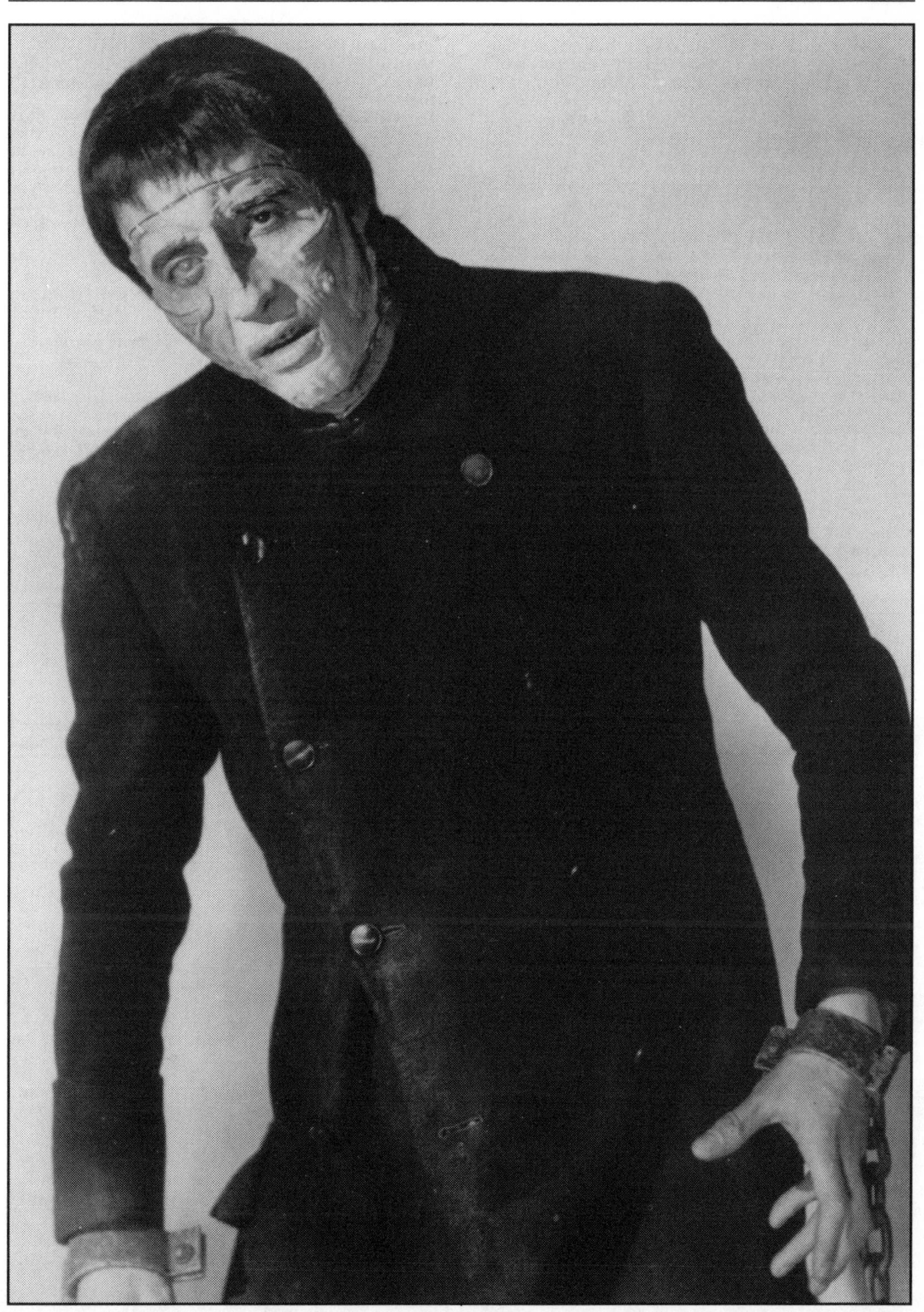

fellow students in Riverside, California. A sequel, *Black Inferno*, was made the same year, and Brzezinski followed them with a feature-length version of *Dracula* and *Horrors of Frankenstein*. The director ended up making explicit hardcore movies such as *Dr. Sexual and Mr. Hyde* (1971).
✦

THE CURSE OF FRANKENSTEIN
UK, 1957. Dir: Terence Fisher. With: Peter Cushing, Hazel Court, Robert Urquhart, Christopher Lee, Valerie Gaunt, Noel Hood. Hammer Films/Warner Bros. Colour.
Originally conceived by Milton Subotsky and Max J. Rosenberg (who later founded Amicus Productions), this was the film that launched the Hammer house of horror and made the names of Cushing, Lee and director Fisher synonymous with the horror genre. Jimmy Sangster's Gothic screenplay returns to Mary Shelley's original novel (with added gore and sex) as Baron Victor Frankenstein (Cushing) tries to convince his jailers that the murders for which he's been condemned to death were committed by a monster he created in his laboratory. Lee's features as the Creature are mostly hidden beneath Phil Leakey's scarred make-up (Universal controlled the rights to their traditional image) and he plays the role simply as a homicidal maniac, lacking any of the subtlety of Karloff's performance. However, it is Cushing who dominates the film as the obsessed and uncaring Victor, and it was his character who became the focus of the sequels. Made for just $250,000, it grossed millions. This was novelised by John Burke in 1966 as part of *The Hammer Horror Omnibus*, published by Pan Books, and adapted into comic strip format in *The House of Hammer* nos.2 and 3 (1976).
Sequel: THE REVENGE OF FRANKENSTEIN (qv; 1958)
Remake: MATINEE THEATER: Frankenstein (qv; 1957)
✦✦✦✧

THE CURSE OF KING TUTANKHAMEN'S TOMB
(USA: THE CURSE OF KING TUT'S TOMB)
UK/Egypt, 1980. Dir: Peter Leacock. With: Robin Ellis, Harry Andrews, Angharad Rees, Wendy Hiller, Eva Marie Saint, Raymond Burr. HTV/Columbia/ITV/NBC-TV. Colour.
This melodramatic TV movie, based on the book *Behind the Mask of Tutankhamen* by Barry Wynne, attempts to blend fact with fiction. In November 1922, archaeologist Howard Carter (Ellis, in a role originally intended for Ian McShane until the latter broke his leg on location) and his patron Lord Carnarvon (Andrews) discover the lost tomb of an ancient Egyptian Pharaoh. But soon rumours of a curse and impending tragedy threaten to tarnish their triumph. The British print was shorter than the American TV version, which was shown in two parts, with Barbara Murray's role as Giovanna cut entirely and a narration by Paul Scofield used to cover the gaps. This also includes Tom Baker, and a badly miscast Burr as the villainous Jonash Sabastian.
✦✦

THE CURSE OF NOSTRADAMUS
(Orig: LA MALDICIÓN DE NOSTRADAMUS)
Mexico, 1960 (1961). Dir: Frederick (Federico) Curiel. With: Germán Robles, Julio Aleman, Domingo Soler, Aurora Alvarado, Manver (Manuel Vergara), Manuel Casanueva. Estudios America/American International. B&W.
In 1959, Robles starred in a twelve-part serial (each segment running twenty-five minutes) which was re-edited into four features and released by American International directly to TV in America. In this first episode, Robles plays the bearded vampire descendant of the sixteenth century prophet Nostradamus. He kills two colleagues of Professor Duran (Soler) and kidnaps the professor's daughter (Alvarado) before escaping through a maze of underground tunnels. There's even a hunchbacked assistant. Like most Mexican features of this period, it comprises of three episodes ('El Dedo del Destino', 'El Libro de los Siglos' and 'Las Victimas de la Noche') because many independent film-makers were restricted by the unions from producing full-length movies. The English-language version is produced by K. (Kenneth) Gordon Murray and directed by Stim (Stem) Segar.
Sequel: THE MONSTERS DEMOLISHER (qv; 1960)
✦✧

CURSE OF THE AZTEC MUMMY
(Orig: LA MALDICIÓN DE LA MOMIA AZTECA)
Mexico, 1957 (1961). Dir: Rafael (López) Portillo. With: Ramón Gay, Rosita Arenas, Crox Alvarado, Luis Aceves Castañeda, Jorge Mondragón, Angelo de Steffani. Cinematográfica Calderón/American International. B&W.
Sequel to *La Momia Azteca* (1957), once again scripted by Alfred (Alfredo) Salazar and featuring many of the same cast and crew. The evil Dr Krupp/The Bat (Castañeda) kidnaps and hypnotises Flora (Arenas), the reincarnation of the Aztec princess Xochitl, to discover the whereabouts of the lost treasure guarded by Popoca, the ugly living mummy. He is once again opposed by Dr Armada (Gay) and his assistant (Alvarado), who is secretly the wrestling hero El Angel. Also with Mexican wrestlers 'Murciélago Velazquez' (Jesús Velazquez), Enrique y Añez, 'Lobo Negro' (Guillermo Hernández), Alberto y Añez, Firpo Segura and Sergio y Añez. The English-language version was produced by K. (Kenneth) Gordon Murray and directed by Paul Nagle (Nagel).
Sequel: THE ROBOT VS THE AZTEC MUMMY (qv; 1957)
✦

CURSE OF THE BLACK WIDOW
(aka LOVE TRAP)
USA, 1977. Dir: Dan Curtis. With: Tony Franciosa, Donna Mills, Patty Duke Astin, June Lockhart, June Allyson, Jeff Corey. Dan Curtis Productions/ABC-TV. Colour.
Made by director/executive producer Curtis (TV's *Dark Shadows* [1966-71], etc) as a contractual obligation to ABC, this originally started out as a Harlan Ellison project entitled *Dark Destroyer*. No trace of Ellison's original remains in this silly story about a mysterious woman who, during the cycle of the full moon, can turn into a blood-drinking giant spider because of a Native American curse. Franciosa makes a likeable private detective, and there's good support from veteran Corey as an old medicine man and Vic Morrow as a disbelieving detective. Also with Roz Kelly and Sid Caesar. Unfortunately, it is let down by a weak script and unconvincing special effects.
✦✦

CURSE OF THE BLUE LIGHTS
(aka BLUE LIGHTS)
USA, 1988 (1990). Dir: John Henry Johnson. With: Brent Ritter, Bettina Julius, Kent E. Fritzell, Willard Hall, Andy Asbury, George Schanze. Blue Lights/Tamarack Productions/Magnum Entertainment. Colour.
Low-budget independent horror movie set in Dudley, Colorado. The Ghoul Clan led by Loath (Ritter) plan to use dissolved human bodies to revive the legendary petrified Muldoon Man (Schanze). This also includes a witch (Julius) and several slimy zombies. Scripted, produced, directed, photographed and edited by the 'multi-talented' Johnson.
✦

THE CURSE OF THE CAT PEOPLE
USA, 1944. Dir: Gunther V. (Von) Fritsch and Robert Wise. With: Simone Simon, Kent Smith, Jane Randolph, Ann Carter, Eve March, Julia Dean. RKO Radio. B&W.
A marvellously poetic sequel-of-sorts from producer Val Lewton and screenwriter DeWitt Bodeen to their *Cat People* (1942). A psychological study of a lonely child's fantasy world, seven year-old Amy (Carter) is the daughter of Oliver and Alice Reed (Smith and Randolph), who conjures up Oliver's first wife, the dead Irena (Simon), as an imaginary companion. When Amy visits 'The Witch's House' down the street, where a half-crazed old actress (Dean) recounts to her a nightmarish version of *The Legend of Sleepy Hollow*, Irena apparently saves her from the woman's psychologically disturbed daughter (the wonderful Elizabeth Russell), who believes that Amy has stolen her mother's affection. Fritsch was replaced by Wise (making his directorial début) when he fell behind schedule. Lewton originally wanted to call the film *Amy and Her Friend*, but the studio insisted on a more commercial title. With Sir Lancelot.
✦✦✦✦

CURSE OF THE CAT WOMAN
USA, 1991. Dir: John Leslie. With: Selena Steele, Raven,

Rocco Siffredy (Siffredi), Patricia Kennedy, Racquel Darrian, Zara Whites. Louie T. Beagle Productions/VCA Pictures. Colour.
Porn star-turned-director/writer/editor Leslie's hardcore follow-up his *The Cat Woman* (1988), also shot on video. Steele and Raven play sisters Raquel and Veronica who compete with each other to become the reincarnated Supreme One, the leader of a feline-like race who hang out in a bizarre nightclub. With Marc Wallice, Jamie Gillis (who was also assistant director), Randy Spears, Tom Byron and T.T. Boy.
✦

THE CURSE OF THE CRYING WOMAN
(Orig: LA MALDICIÓN DE LA LLORONA)
Mexico, 1961 (1963). Dir: Raphael (Rafael) Baledón. With: Rosita Arenas, Abel Salazar, Rita Macedo, Carlos Lopes (López) Moctezuma, Henry (Enrique) Lucero, Mario Sevilla. Cinematográfica ABSA/Clasa-Mohme/American International. B&W.
First filmed in 1933, this was the fifth movie based on the Mexican legend about a ghostly crying woman, La Llorona. When Emily (Arenas) visits her Aunt Thelma (Macedo), the latter turns out to be a black-eyed vampire woman who, along with her horribly scarred homicidal servant Fred (Lucero), attempts to revive the mummified corpse of her mistress, the wailing witch. While Emily develops a thirst for blood because of a family curse, her husband Herbert (producer Salazar) encounters rubber bats in the bell tower, his wife's insane Uncle Daniel, voodoo dolls, hypnosis, sadistic whippings and a pack of vicious dogs. The couple finally escape as the house of horror collapses around them. A flashback sequence (in negative) includes clips from Salazar's *The Man and the Monster* (1958), *The Witch's Mirror* (1960) and *The World of the Vampires* (1960). The English-language version was produced by K. (Kenneth) Gordon Murray and directed by Stim (Stem) Segar.
Remake: SANTO Y MANTEQUILLA NÁPOLES EN LA VENGANZA DE LA LLORONA (1973)
✦✦

CURSE OF THE DEVIL
(Orig: EL RETORNO DE WALPURGIS. USA: aka THE BLACK HARVEST OF COUNTESS DRACULA)
Spain/Mexico, 1973. Dir: Charles Aured (Carlos Aured/ Carlos A. Alonso). With: Paul Naschy (Jacinto Molina), Fay (Fabiola) Falcón, Vidal Molina, May Oliver (Maritza Olivares), María Silva, Ana Farra. Lotus Films/Scorpio (Producciones Escorpion)/Atlas International/Goldstone Films. Colour.
Naschy's seventh outing as El Hombre Lobo (following *Dr. Jekyll and the Werewolf* [1971]). In a new origin story, he plays sixteenth century Hungarian inquisitor Irineus Daninsky, cursed by the Satanic Countess Elisabeth Bathory (Paty Shepard) as she burns at the stake. Centuries later, his descendant Waldemar (also Naschy) is seduced by a gypsy woman (Oliver) and turned into a werewolf, until he is finally staked with a silver dagger by his lover (Falcón).
Sequel: NIGHT OF THE HOWLING BEAST (qv; 1975)
✦✧

CURSE OF THE DOLL PEOPLE
(Orig: LOS MUÑECOS INFERNALES)
Mexico, 1960 (1961). Dir: Benito Alazarki. With: Elvira Quintano, Raymond (Ramón) Gay, Robert (Roberto) G. Rivera, Quintin Bulnes, Alfonso Arnold, Jorge Mondragon. Cinematográfica Calderón/American International. B&W.
Haitian sorcerer Zandor (Bulnes) uses voodoo to bring dolls (midgets in masks and dark suits) to life and revenge himself upon those who witnessed a forbidden ceremony and stole his sacred idol. He is assisted by scruffy-looking zombie Sabud, which sleeps in an Egyptian sarcophagus and is ultimately decapitated by a car before being burned. The English-language version was produced by K. (Kenneth) Gordon Murray and directed by Paul Nagle (Nagel).
✦✧

CURSE OF THE FACELESS MAN
USA, 1958. Dir: Edward L. Cahn. With: Richard Anderson, Elaine Edwards, Adele Mara, Luis Van Rooten, Gar Moore, Felix Locher. Vogue Pictures/United Artists. B&W.
'Entombed for Eaons... Turned to Stone... Seeking Women — Women — Women!' screamed the ads. In fact, the faceless creature is a slave named Quintilius (played by both Bob Bryant and Charles Gemora), a 2,000 year-old Etruscan mummy discovered in the ruins of Pompeii. He returns to life and carries off artist Tina Enright (Edwards), who is the reincarnation of his lost love. Handsome Dr Paul Mallon (Anderson) tries to stop him, and in the end the mummy dissolves in the sea. Made on a shoestring budget and scripted by science fiction author Jerome Bixby, who provides a logical explanation for the mummy's reanimation. Narrator Morris Ankrum has to explain to the audience what is happening.
✦✧

THE CURSE OF THE HOUSE SURGEON
USA, 1991. Dir: Steve J. Postal. With: Kendrick Kaufman, Jennifer Tuck, Angela Shepard, Mikki Rohyans, Angel Langley, Maurice Postal. Steve Postal Productions. Colour.
Based on Rudyard Kipling's story 'The House Surgeon', this is the seventh in the low-budget horror/comedy series from Florida *auteur* Steve Postal featuring Maurice Postal as the monster-landlord B.J. Smith. When cousins Phyllis and Kim invite house surgeon Dr Moore to exorcise the evil spirits from Smith's haunted honeymoon cottage, ghosts, zombies, vampires and the Green Monster turn up from outer space to create mayhem. As usual, Postal photographed, directed, co-edited, co-executive produced and co-scripted!
✦

THE CURSE OF THE LIVING CORPSE
USA, 1964. Dir: Del Tenney. With: Helen Waren, Roy R. Scheider, Margo Hartman, Hugh Franklin, Robert Milli, Candace Hilligoss. Iselin-Tenney/Twentieth Century-Fox. B&W.
Filmed in Stamford, Connecticut. Scheider (*Jaws* [1975], etc) makes his screen début in this low-budget melodrama, written, produced and directed by drive-in theatre owner Tenney as a co-feature to his equally terrible *The Horror of Party Beach* (1964). Set in nineteenth century New England, a tyrannical millionaire who was afraid of premature burial apparently returns from the dead as a masked killer to revenge himself in various gory ways on the family members who ignored the terms of his will. Richard Burton and Elizabeth Taylor apparently attended the New York première as a joke. When originally released, audience members were asked to sign a 'Fright Release'.
✦

THE CURSE OF THE MUMMY'S TOMB
UK, 1964. Dir: Michael Carreras. With: Terence Morgan, Fred Clark, Ronald Howard, Jeanne Roland, George Pastell, Jack Gwillim. Hammer Films/Columbia. Colour.
This second entry in Hammer's unrelated Mummy series is set in the 1920s when, ignoring the warnings of Hashmi Bey (Pastell), crass American showman Alexander King (played with gusto by veteran Clark) ships the sarcophagus of young Pharaoh Ra-Antef to London for display. But soon the mummy (stuntman Dickie Owen under Roy Ashton's bandages) is brought back to life and used as an instrument of revenge by his High Priest brother, Adam Beauchamp/Be (Morgan), who is cursed to live through the centuries for killing his sibling. This allows for some particularly atmospheric scenes on fog-shrouded streets and a climax that takes place in the sewers below the city. Entertainingly written (under the pseudonym 'Henry Younger'), produced and directed by Carreras, this is strictly 'B' movie chills. With Michael Ripper. In America, the first 10,000 patrons to see the film received a set of black stamps. This was novelised by John Burke in 1966 as part of *The Hammer Horror Omnibus*, published by Pan Books.
✦✦

CURSE OF THE QUEERWOLF
USA, 1987. Dir: Mark Pirro. With: Michael Palazzolo, Taylor Whitney, Kent Butler, Sharon Alsina, Cynthia Brownell, Darwyn Carson. Pirromount Pictures/Raedon. Colour.
'Even a wrist that is strong and firm and holds up straight by day,

may become limp when the moon is full and the Queerwolf comes your way.' From camera operator/editor/co-producer/writer/director Pirro (who also scripted *My Mom's a Werewolf* [1988], etc), comes this inventive, often offensive, low-budget spoof, filmed in Santa Barbara on Super-8mm. Sleazy, homophobic macho man Larry Smalbut (Palazzolo) is bitten on the behind by a good-looking woman he picks up in a bar, who turns out to be a man. Larry becomes a 'Dickenthrope', taking on stereotypical gay characteristics during the nights of the full moon, and can only be killed with a silver dildo. A gypsy sees the sign of the 'Pansygram' in his palm, and in the end he is cured by a 'Fagxorcist'! With cameos by Forrest J Ackerman and Conrad Brooks as therapy patients who come to nasty ends, and numerous dead dog jokes.

✦✧

CURSE OF THE SCREAMING DEAD
(aka CURSE OF THE CANNIBAL CONFEDERATES)
USA, 1982 (1984). Dir: Tony Malanowski. With: Steve Sandkuhler, Christopher Gummer, Rebecca Bach, Mimi Ishikawa, Judy Dixon. Little Warsaw/Troma/Mogul. Colour.

A voodoo curse causes the theft of a diary from a Confederate graveyard to raise the flesh-eating dead in this amateurish, low-budget gore film shot in Maryland.

✦

CURSE OF THE SWAMP CREATURE
USA, 1966. Dir: Larry Buchanan. With: John Agar, Francine York, Shirley McLine, Bill Thurman, Jeff Alexander, Carl Duggan. Azalea Pictures/American International. Colour.

Shot on 16mm and costing around $25,000, this was one of a series of seven low-budget AIP movies directed by Texas-based Buchanan and released directly to TV in America. Geologist Mr Rogers (Agar) and con artiste Brenda (McLine) discover that balding mad doctor Simon (Alexander) is experimenting on the local 'natives' in the Florida Everglades. In the end, he turns Brenda into an unconvincing fish-woman (played by Thurman, who also turns up as a murdered oilman). As with some of the other Buchanan cheapies, the bald-headed gill men have ping-pong ball eyes.

✦

CURSE OF THE UNDEAD
(aka MARK OF THE WEST)
USA, 1959. Dir: Edward Dein. With: Eric Fleming, Michael Pate, Kathleen Crowley, John Hoyt, Bruce Gordon, Edward Binns. Universal-International. B&W.

Filmed under the title *Affairs of a Vampire*, this surprisingly cerebral horror/Western features a suavely menacing Pate as hired gunslinger Drake Robey, revealed to be Don Drago Robles, who took his own life after murdering his brother and returned as one of the undead. Fleming's sanctimonious Preacher Dan finally saves ranch owner Dolores Carter (Crowley) from the vampire's spell by killing the black-clad bloodsucker with a bullet incorporating a crucifix. With Edwin Parker.

✦✦✦

DAN CURTIS
[b 1928]

American producer and director who first found success with his daily Gothic soap opera *Dark Shadows* (1966-71), which he spun off into two feature films, *House of Dark Shadows* (1970) and *Night of Dark Shadows* (1971), and briefly remade in 1990-91. His TV movies *The Night Stalker* (1971) and *The Night Strangler* (1972) led to the *Kolchak: The Night Stalker* series (1974-75), and he also remade such classics as *The Strange Case of Dr. Jekyll and Mr. Hyde* (1967), *Dracula* (1972) and *Frankenstein* (1973).

qv: *Curse of the Black Widow* (1977); *Dark Shadows: Behind the Scenes* (1991); *Dead of Night* (1976); *The Norliss Tapes* (1973); *Scream of the Wolf* (1974); *Trilogy of Terror* (1975); *Trilogy of Terror II* (1996).

THE CURSE OF THE VAMPIRE
(Orig: AQUELARRE DE VAMPIROS/LA LLAMADA DEL VAMPIRO)
Spain, 1971 (1973). Dir: Joseph de Lacy (José Maria Elorietta). With: Diana Sorel, Nicholas Ney, Beatriz Lacy, Ines Skorpio, Loretta Tovar, Rosario Royo. Sesena Film/Arco Films. Colour.

Dr Greta Metterlich (Lacy) and her assistant Erika (Sorel) are invited to stay at the sinister lake-side mansion of Carl von Rysselbert (Ney). He turns out to be a vampire who, under the influence of the full moon, puts the bite on Erika and attacks the doctor before being staked.

✦

PETER CUSHING
[1913-1994]

Probably remembered as the screen's greatest monster hunter, this British actor made his Hollywood début in the late 1930s before becoming a star with his portrayal of Winston Smith in BBC-TV's 1955 adaptation of *Nineteen Eighty-Four*. With Hammer's *The Curse of Frankenstein* (1957), Cushing and Christopher Lee became the Karloff and Lugosi of their generation and, like Karloff, Cushing was a quiet gentleman who could play noble heroes and arrogant villains with equal skill. A genuine horror icon, among his most popular roles were Baron Frankenstein, Professor Van Helsing, Sherlock Holmes, Doctor Who and Grand Moff Tarkin in *Star Wars* (1977). *Peter Cushing: An Autobiography* was published in 1986 and *Past Forgetting: Memoirs of the Hammer Years* appeared in 1988.

qv: *Asylum* (1972); *The Beast Must Die* (1974); *The Blood Beast Terror* (1967); *The Brides of Dracula* (1960); *A Chump at Oxford* (1939); *Dracula* (1958); *Dracula A.D. 1972* (1972); *Dr. Terror's House of Horrors* (1965); *Everyman: 'The True Story of Frankenstein'* (1986); *The Evil of Frankenstein* (1964); *Flesh and Blood: The Hammer Heritage of Horror* (1994); *Frankenstein and the Monster from Hell* (1973); *Frankenstein Created Woman* (1966); *Frankenstein Must Be Destroyed* (1969); *Hammer the Studio That Dripped Blood!* (1987); *Horror Express* (1972); *The House That Dripped Blood* (1970); *I, Monster* (1971); *Incense for the Damned* (1970); *The Legend of the 7 Golden Vampires* (1974); *Legend of the Werewolf* (1974); *Madhouse* (1974); *The Morecambe & Wise Show* (1980); *The Mummy* (1959); *Mystery on Monster Island* (1982); *The New Avengers: 'The Eagle's Nest'* (1976); *100 Years of Horror: 'Dracula and His Disciples'* (1996); *One More Time* (1970); *Peter Cushing: A One-Way Ticket To Hollywood* (1988); *The Revenge of Frankenstein* (1958); *The Satanic Rites of Dracula* (1973); *Scream and Scream Again* (1969); *Shock Waves* (1976); *Tales from the Crypt* (1972); *Tender Dracula* (1974); *This is Your Life: 'Christopher Lee'* (1974); *Twins of Evil* (1971); *The Vampire Interviews* (circa 1990s); *The Vampire Lovers* (1970); *The World of Hammer: 'Hammer Stars: Peter Cushing'* (1990).

THE CURSE OF THE WEREWOLF
UK, 1960. Dir: Terence Fisher. With: Clifford Evans, Oliver Reed, Yvonne Romain, Catherine Feller, Anthony Dawson, Richard Wordsworth. Hammer Films/Universal-International. Colour.

Scripted by John Elder (producer Anthony Hinds) and loosely based on the 1933 novel *The Werewolf of Paris* by Guy Endore, Hammer's version of the werewolf myth is set in an unconvincing eighteenth century Spain. The rape of a mute servant girl (Romain) by a pathetic beggar (Wordsworth) results in the birth of Leon (twenty-two year-old Reed), who in later life is cursed with lycanthropy. In the end, he is killed with a silver bullet fired by his step-father, Don Alfredo Carido (Evans). Fisher's direction lacks the sparkle of some of his previous films, but there's a fine supporting cast and excellent werewolf make-up (created by Roy Ashton), which is only revealed in close-up during the final few minutes. Banned in Spain until 1976, the film was cut in both Britain and America during its original release. Recent video and TV prints have restored the missing footage. With Warren Mitchell, George Woodbridge, Peter Sallis and

Oliver Reed suffers The Curse of the Werewolf *(1960).*

Michael Ripper. Artist John Bolton and writer Steve Moore adapted this into comic strip format for *The House of Hammer* no.10 (1978).
✦✦✦✧

CURSE OF THE WICKED WIFE
(aka WICKED WIFE)
Hong Kong, 1984. Dir: Wong King-Fang. Colour.
When twins are separated at birth, one goes to live with a rich family, the other with a poor family. There are subplots involving a vampire and an evil land-owner who kills his victims with 'death bugs'. The climax has the heroine spewing up all kinds of insects!
✦✧

CURSE OF THE ZOMBI
Hong Kong/Thailand, 1989. Dir: Hao Lee. With: Shaojun Lau, Xiao Yan-Ze. Ferreira/Tain Seng Video. Colour.
An archaeologist (Lau) and his wife (Yan-Ze) go on a working vacation to the jungles of Thailand, where a jealous rival convinces evil sorcerer Shin to animate a murderous flying zombie. This fun horror fantasy also includes fake ghosts and a witch who puts an invincible spell on the hero.
✦✧

CYBER CITY OEDO 808 FILE-3 BLOODLUST
(Orig: CYBER CITY OEDO 808 DATA-3 KURENAI NO BAITAI. USA: aka CYBER CITY OEDO 808 FILE-3)
Japan 1995. Dir: Yoshiaki Kawajiri. Voices: Hiroya Ishimaru, Kaneto Shiozawa, Tessho Genda, Norio Wakamoto. Madhouse/Japan Home Video/Manga Video/ Manga Corps. Colour.
Forty-nine minute anime video in which an androgynous martial arts expert, Benten, battles innocent cyborg vampire Remi, who is collecting blood for his evil master.
✦✦

CYBILL:
Virgin, Mother, Crone
USA, 1995. Dir: Robert Berlinger. With: Cybill Shepherd, Christine Baranski, Tom Wopat, Dedee Pfeiffer, Alicia Witt, Alan Rosenberg. YBYL Productions/Jay Daniel Productions/Chuck Lorre Productions/River Siren Productions/Carsey Werner/Paramount/CBS-TV. Colour.
In the opening sequence of this sophisticated half-hour comedy sitcom series (1995-98), actress Cybill (who also executive produced) has a problem playing the victim of an amorous vampire. When Rachel (Pfeiffer) announces that she is pregnant, Cybill suddenly realises that she is going to become a grandmother. With guest appearances by Tim Matheson and an uncredited Robert Wagner and Stefanie Powers.
✦✦✦✧

-D-

DAFFY DUCK'S QUACKBUSTERS

USA, 1987. Dir: Chuck (Charles M.) Jones, Friz (Isadore) Freleng, Robert McKimson, Greg Ford and Terry Lennon. Voices: Mel Blanc, Roy Firestone, B.J. Ward. Warner Bros. Colour.

Feature-length cartoon spoof of *Ghostbusters* (1984), in which Daffy Duck inherits millions of dollars and sets up a ghost-exterminating agency. With cameos by Porky Pig, Sylvester the Cat, Tweety Pie and a guest appearance by Bugs Bunny. Besides new cartoon shorts *The Night of the Living Duck* and *The Duxorcist*, this also includes (uncredited) sequences taken from earlier cartoons, including *Hyde and Go Tweet* (1959), in which Tweety Pie periodically turns into a monstrous canary after swallowing Dr Jekyll's formula, *The Abominable Snow Rabbit* (1961) and *Transylvania 6-500* (1963), amongst others.

✦✦✧

ALBERT S. D'AGOSTINO
[1893-1970]

American art director at Universal during the 1930s and responsible for redressing his sets from *The Magnificent Ambersons* (1942) at RKO Radio for Val Lewton's series of stylish shockers in the forties.
qv: *Cat People* (1942); *Curse of the Cat People* (1944); *Dracula's Daughter* (1936); *Isle of the Dead* (1945); *I Walked With a Zombie* (1943); *The Thing from Another World* (1951); *The WereWolf of London* (1935); *Zombies on Broadway* (1945).

JOE DALLESANDRO
[b 1948]

American actor of limited range who started his career in films for Andy Warhol's resident film-maker Paul Morrissey.
qv: *Blood for Dracula* (1974); *Flesh for Frankenstein* (1973).

JOE D'AMATO
(Aristide Massaccesi) [1935-1999]

Prolific Italian producer, director and cinematographer who worked under a number of pseudonyms (David Hills, Michael Holloway etc) on everything from hardcore porno to hardgore horror.
qv: *Death Smiles on a Murderer* (1972); *The Devil's Wedding Night* (1973); *Erotic Nights of the Living Dead* (1979); *Killing Birds* (1988); *Return from Death* (1991).

DAMN YANKEES

(UK: WHAT LOLA WANTS)

USA, 1958. Dir: George Abbott and Stanley Donen. With: Tab Hunter, Gwen Verdon, Ray Walston, Russ Brown, Shannon Bolin, Jean Stapleton. Warner Bros. Colour.

Colourful adaptation of Abbott's Broadway musical based on the novel *The Year the Yankees Lost the Pennant* by Douglass Wallop. The Devil (Walston) and his temptress Lola (Verdon) rejuvenate a baseball fan into a star player (Hunter) to beat the New York Yankees. During one of Walston's songs, a vampire is briefly seen. With choreography by Bob Fosse and such classic songs as '(You Gotta Have) Heart' and 'Whatever Lola Wants' by Richard Adler and Jerry Ross.

✦✦✦

DANCE OF THE DAMNED

(aka HALF LIFE)

USA, 1988 (1989). Dir: Katt Shea Ruben. With: Starr Andreeff, Cyril O'Reilly, Deborah Ann Nassar, Maria Ford, Athena Worthy, Tom Ruben. New Classics/Concorde/ Virgin Vision. Colour.

When suicidal stripper Jodie Kurtz (Andreeff) goes home with a tall dark stranger (O'Reilly), she discovers he's an outcast vampire who wants her to describe to him all the pleasures he misses, like the feel of sunlight on the skin. A low-budget attempt to do something different with the genre, directed by ex-actress and Roger Corman protégé Ruben. Corman executive produced.

Remake: TO SLEEP WITH A VAMPIRE (qv; 1992)

✦✧

MARK DAMON
(Alan Harris) [b 1933]

American actor who started his career as a young lead for American International Pictures and others before becoming a successful producer.
qv: *Agente Segreto 777 Operazione Mistero* (1965); *Beauty and the Beast* (1961); *Black Sabbath* (1963); *Crypt of the Living Dead* (1972); *The Devil's Wedding Night* (1973).

DANCE OF THE VAMPIRES

(USA: THE FEARLESS VAMPIRE KILLERS)

UK, 1966 (1967). Dir: Roman Polanski. With: Jack MacGowran, Sharon Tate, Alfie Bass, Ferdy (Ferdinand) Mayne, Terry Downes, Fiona Lewis. Metro-Goldwyn-Mayer. Colour.

Often very amusing, but oddly downbeat horror comedy, co-scripted, starring and directed by Polanski. Fearless vampire killers Professor Abronsius (MacGowran) and his faithful assistant Alfred (Polanski) travel to Transylvania to stay in the castle of the sinister Count Von Krolock (Mayne), who they suspect is a vampire terrorising the local villagers. The dance of the title is a marvellously macabre set-piece. In America, the film was cut by at least ten minutes, re-edited, re-dubbed and released with a new animated title sequence. Polanski unsuccessfully asked for his name to be removed from the credits. With a Jewish vampire (Bass, who replaced Akim Tamiroff when the latter was taken ill), a gay vampire (Iain Quarrier) and Polanski's wife, Sharon Tate. Fangs by Dr Ludwig Von Krankheit. In 1997, Polanski created a musical stage version of the film that played in Vienna.

✦✦✦✦

DANDY DUST

UK/Austria, 1998. Dir: A. Hans Scheirl. With: A. Hans Scheirl, Suzie Krüger, Leonora Rogers-Wright, Tres Trash Temperilli. Colour.

Low-budget multimedia underground film. Set in organic cyberspace, director Scheirl plays Dandy, a transgendered cyborg who crash-lands on a planet where twin scientists remove his H-memory, making him a natural member of the chemo-sexual structure. However, Dandy is soon haunted by strange creatures, including his former self, Supermother Cyniborg, his eighteenth century aristocratic father and a dusty living mummy.

✦

DANGER ISLAND

(aka THE PRESENCE)

USA, 1992. Dir: Tommy Lee Wallace. With: Lisa Banes, Richard Beymer, Maria Celedonio, Gary Graham, Kathy Ireland, Joe Lara. National Broadcasting Company/Von Zerneck-Sertner Films/Vidmark. Colour.

Average pilot TV movie, filmed in Hawaii as *The Island*. A group of evacuees escaping a revolution crash their plane near a tropical island. The survivors discover a secret scientific research facility, abandoned for more than fifteen years, where genetic experiments by the military result in mutant gill man transformations (created by Make-up Effects Unlimited). With June Lockhart (who also narrates).

✦✦

DANGEROUS SEDUCTRESS

Indonesia, 1993. Dir: John Miller. With: Amy Weber, Tonya Offer, Kristin Anin, Joseph Cassano. Midnight Video. Colour.

Following a shoot-out between the police and a gang of crooks, spilled blood resurrects The Evil Queen (a topless Weber). She pos-

sesses Susan (Offer), the American sister of a fashion model who carelessly reads aloud an incantation from a Sumatran book of black magic, and soon the sexy blonde succubus is sent out to inhale the blood of her victims. This low-budget hilarity ends with a magic duel.
✦✧

THE DANNY KAYE SHOW
USA, 1966. With: Danny Kaye, Harvey Korman, Joyce Van Patten, Fred Gwynne. Dena Productions/CBS-TV. Colour.
Hour-long musical comedy sketch show (1963-67). In this episode, Gwynne appears as Herman Munster.
✦✧

ROYAL DANO
[1922-1994]

Cadaverous American character actor, the poor man's John Carradine.
qv: *House II The Second Story* (1987), *Messiah of Evil* (1973); *Moon of the Wolf* (1972).

DANSE MACABRE
(aka DANCE MACABRE/PHANTOM OF MANHATTAN/ TERROR OF MANHATTAN)
USA/Russia, 1991. Dir: Greydon Clark. With: Robert Englund, Michelle Zeitlin, Marianna Moen, Julene Renee, Nina Goldman, Irina Davidoff. Breton Films/Lenfilm/ 21st Century Film Corp. Colour.
Originally announced as *Phantom of the Opera 2*, a sequel to the 1989 film, this direct-to-video release finally emerged as a straight slasher movie, with students at a Russian dance academy being killed off through a number of gruesome methods. With Englund in the dual role of an American choreographer and an unconvincing crippled ballerina! Co-executive produced by the legendary Harry Alan Towers.
✦

RAY DANTON
[1931-1992]

American actor and director who also found work in Europe.
qv: *Crypt of the Living Dead* (1972); *Deathmaster* (1972).

ALEX D'ARCY
(Alexander Sarruf) [1908-1996]

Egyptian-born actor who turned into a fuzzy-faced monster in *Horrors of Spider Island* (1959) and portrayed the Count in *Blood of Dracula's Castle* (1967).
qv: *Way...Way Out* (1966).

DARK CITY
Australia, 1997 (1998). Dir: Alex Proyas. With: Rufus Sewell, Kiefer Sutherland, Jennifer Connelly, Richard O'Brien, Ian Richardson, William Hurt. Dark City Productions/New Line Cinema/Mystery Clock. Colour.
An intriguing and stylish science fiction thriller, announced under the titles *Dark World* and *Dark Empire*. Framed as a serial killer, John Murdoch (Sewell), discovers through the help of the strange Dr Schraber (Sutherland), that he and everyone else are living in a wonderfully *noir*-ish city in outer space. Here, a dying race of alien 'Strangers' (who look like Clive Barker creations) possess and reanimate the bodies of the dead and stop time so that they can change people's identities around. With the help of policeman Frank Bumstead (Hurt) and the mental powers he now possesses, Murdoch sets out to discover the truth. With Bruce Spence and John Bluthal.
✦✦✦✦

DARKNESS
(aka DARKNESS THE VAMPIRE CUT)
USA, 1992 (1994). Dir: Leif Jonker. With: Gary Miller, Michael Gisick, Cena Donham, Randall Aviks, Steve Brown, Lisa Franz. Leif Jonker/Norseman Film/Film Threat Video/Screen Edge. Colour.
Inspired by George A. Romero's *Dawn of the Dead* (1978) and filmed over three years on murky Super-8mm in Wichita, Kansas, by writer/director/producer Jonker for just $6,000, this gory direct-to-video release is billed as 'The Ultimate in Vampire Horror'. Six teenage friends returning from a concert and a dedicated young vampire hunter (Miller) encounter long-haired vampire leader Liven (Aviks), who plans to conquer mankind with his legion of undead bloodsuckers. The climactic meltdown sequence apparently set a world record for exploding heads! A longer 'Vampire Cut' was released in 1998, and a sequel, *Darkness 2 The Day of Shadows*, has been announced.
✦

THE DARK POWER
USA, 1985. Dir: Phil Smoot. With: Lash LaRue (Alfred LaRue), Anna Lane Tatum, Cynthia Balley, Mary Dalton, Paul Holman, Cynthia Farbman. New Vision/Triad/ Magnum. Colour.
Shot in North Carolina for just $160,000, this low-budget horror thriller marks the return of veteran Western star LaRue (then in his eighties!). He plays a ranger out to defeat four ancient Mexican sorcerers, who return from the dead to kill a group of teenagers living in a house built on their sacred land. Filmed without much style or originality, the aged LaRue appears hardly capable of cracking his legendary whip, while the zombie villains go through a number of Three Stooges routines. Despite some gratuitous nudity and impressive gore effects, this remains a regional curio. LaRue also appeared in *Alien Outlaw* (1985) for the same director.
✦

DARK ROMANCES VOLUME I
USA, 1986 (1989). Dir: Mark Shepard. With: Julie Carlson, Elizabeth Morehead, Robert Rothman, Ron Rolek, Brinke Stevens, Dawn Wildsmith. Nightfall Productions/Salt City Home Video. Colour.
Video compilation of two erotic horror stories, both featuring scream queen Stevens as evil seductress Diana, and originally made for cable TV. 'Born Evil' is about Justine (Carlson), the star at the Grand Guignol theatre in Paris, who undergoes hypnosis to cure her violent psychosis. In the shorter 'Listen to Midnight', alcoholic photographer Todd encounters an underage model who turns out to be a vampire. With a clip from *The Little Shop of Horrors* (1960) on TV. A further five stories were released as *Dark Romances Volume II* (1986).
✦

DARKROOM:
The Boogeyman Will Get You/Uncle George
Canada/USA, 1981. Dir: John McPherson and Rick Rosenthall. With: Helen Hunt, Randolph Powell, Quinn Cummings, Arlen Dean Snyder, Gloria DeHaven, R.G. Armstrong. Universal/ABC-TV. Colour.
Short-lived (1981-82, seven episodes), hour-long anthology TV series, hosted by James Coburn. In the first of the two stories in this episode, DiDi Lawrence (Cummings) believes that Philip Ames (Powell), the mystery man pursuing her sister Nancy (Hunt), is a vampire. In fact, the twist is he turns out to be a werewolf. Scripted by Robert Bloch and based on his own story. Claude Akins, June Lockhart and Dub Taylor starred in the second segment. Jeffrey Bloom was executive story consultant.
✦✧

DARK ROSE: FEEDIN' AND BREEDIN'
USA, 1998. Dir: Jason Liquori. With: Laura Lee, Michelle Pfeifer. Hocus Focus Productions. Colour.
Independent spoof shot in New York, New Jersey and Connecticut, and released directly to video. The eponymous heroine (Lee) reveals her secret past while she battles an Italian vampire clan, led by the undead Rosalin and Jaqueline (both played by former model Pfeifer), who destroyed her family and are now unleashing their terror on an unsuspecting group of college co-eds.
✦

DARK SHADOWS
USA, 1966-71. Dir: Lela Swift, John Sedwick, John Weaver,

Sean Dhu Sullivan, Penberry Jones, Henry Kaplan and Dan Curtis. With: Joan Bennett, Jonathan Frid, Lara Parker, David Selby, Kathryn Leigh Scott, Grayson Hall. Dan Curtis Productions/ABC-TV. B&W/Colour.
Five-days-a-week, half-hour supernatural TV soap opera, created by executive producer Dan Curtis (who also handled the special effects) and shot on video. This clocked up an incredible 1,225 episodes and two movie spin-offs during its five year run. Set in the small fishing village of Collinsport, Maine, the ever more complicated plots travel back to the late eighteenth century and even into parallel time! During the 1967 season, the show introduced 175 year-old reluctant vampire Barnabas Collins (Frid); Jeremiah Collins (Anthony George) and Josette du Pres (Scott) both became zombies in 1968; and Robert Rodan joined the cast the same year in the role of Adam, created from corpses by Dr Eric Lang (Addison Powell) and brought to life by Dr Julia Hoffman (Hall) and Barnabas, who shared a psychic link with the creature. A mate was also created for Adam, 'cleverly' named Eve (Marie Wallace). Donald Briscoe played Chris Jennings who, along with his ancestor Quentin Collins (Selby), transformed into a werewolf (both played by stunt double Alex Stevens, in make-up created by Vincent Loscalzo) in the confusing 1968-69 season. In 1970, Jeb Hawkes (Christopher Pennock) raised an army of zombies to kidnap Julia and bury Quentin, and Pennock also portrayed scientist Cyrus Longworth, whose experiments with a potion that can separate a person's good and evil natures resulted in him transforming into the slick John Yaeger before he was killed by Barnabas. With various other vampires and numerous ghosts, voodoo, witches and the disembodied head of Judah Zachery (Michael McGuire). Among the many series regulars (who often played different roles in different story arcs) were Thayer David, Roger Davis, Kate Jackson, Keene Curtis, Dana Elcar, Marsha Mason (as Audrey the Leviathan Vampire Girl), Kenneth McMillan and Abe Vigoda. The show is available on video on 196 tapes containing five episodes each. There are thirty-two novelisations by Marilyn Ross (William Edward Daniel Ross) and various tie-in books.
Series remakes: HOUSE OF DARK SHADOWS (qv; 1970) and DARK SHADOWS (qv; 1990-91)
✦✧

DARK SHADOWS
USA, 1990 (1991). Dir: Dan Curtis. With: Ben Cross, Jean Simmons, Roy Thinnes, Barbara Steele, Joanna Going, Jim Fyfe. Dan Curtis Productions/MGM-UA/NBC-TV. Colour.
TV movie pilot for the briefly revived series (1990-91). Horror icon Steele plays Dr Julia Hoffman, a medical researcher trying to cure vampire Barnabas Collins (Cross). This comprises the first four episodes, originally shown in two one-hour episodes over two nights on American TV.
Sequel: DARK SHADOWS (qv; 1990-91)
✦✦

DARK SHADOWS
USA, 1990-91. Dir: Dan Curtis, Armand Mastroianni, Paul Lynch, Rob Bowman and Mark Sobel. With: Ben Cross, Barbara Blackburn, Jim Fyfe, Barbara Steele, Roy Thinnes, Jean Simmons. MGM-UA/Dan Curtis Productions/NBC-TV. Colour.
This confusing hour-long remake of the original Gothic soap opera, created by executive producer by Dan Curtis, lasted just twelve episodes (including the pilot movie) before ending on a cliff-hanger. Cross replaces Jonathan Frid as reluctant vampire Barnabas Collins, veteran Simmons is Collinwood matriarch Elizabeth Collins Stoddard and cult horror star Steele plays Dr Julia Hoffman, the only person who can save Barnabas from his 'curse'. The storyline oscillates between contemporary times and the 1790s, with many of the cast playing dual roles. Featuring more vampires, witches, ghosts and time-travel. With Lysette Anthony, Joanna Going, Joseph Gordon-Levitt, Veronica Lauren, Ely Pouget, Michael T. Weiss, Stefan Gierasch and Adrian Paul.
✦✦

DARK SHADOWS: BEHIND THE SCENES
USA, 1991. With: Jonathan Frid, David Selby, Joan Bennett, Kate Jackson, Lara Parker, Kathryn Leigh Scott. MPI Home Video. Colour.
Feature-length video history of the popular TV Gothic soap opera, which covers both the original series (1966-71) and the short-lived revival (1990-91). Includes rare footage, an interview with original star Jonathan Frid and commentary by creator Dan Curtis. Other MPI video releases include *The Best of Dark Shadows* (a half-hour compilation), *Dark Shadows Bloopers*, *Dark Shadows Music Videos*, *Dark Shadows The 25th Anniversary* and *The Resurrection of Barnabas Collins* (a summary of the series' first year and the first five Barnabas episodes). Numerous books, soundtracks and audio tapes also exist.
✦✧

DARKSIDE BLUES
Japan, 1994. Dir: Nobuyasu Furkukawa. Voices: Natsuki Akira, Nozomu Sasaki, Kotono Mitsuishi, Hideyuki Hori, Maki Kachisa, Kôichi Yamadera. Toho/Akita Shoten/JC Staff/Manga Corps. Colour.
Anime created by Hideyuki Kikuchi and Yuho Ashibe in which vampiric stranger Darkside (Akira) arrives in a horse-drawn coach from another dimension to save the inhabitants of a future world ruled by the Hogetsu family's all-powerful Persona Century Corporation.
✦✧

DARKSTALKERS
USA, 1996. Graz Entertainment/Capcom Production. Colour.
Syndicated half-hour cartoon TV series (thirteen episodes), loosely based on the 1994 video arcade game and CD-ROM. Harry Gomori lives with cat woman Felicia, and their monster companions include Morrigan the succubus and the vampire Demitri, who is controlled by evil alien Pyron.
Remake: VAMPIRE HUNTER (qv; 1997)
✦

DARK UNIVERSE
USA, 1993. Dir: Steve Latshaw. With: Blake Pickett, Cherie Scott, John Maynard, Steve Barkett, Joe Estevez, William Grefe. Sharan/American Independent Pictures. Colour.
Low-budget variation on *First Man Into Space* (1958) and *The Incredible Melting Man* (1977), based on a story by executive producer Fred Olen Ray. After re-entry into the Earth's atmosphere, a space pilot (Barkett) transforms into a mutant and drains his victims' blood of red cells. With a matte painting by Jim Danforth. Co-produced by Jim Wynorski.
✦✧

THE DARLING OF PARIS
USA, 1917. Dir: J. Gordon Edwards. With: Theda Bara, Glen White, Walter Law, Herbert Hayes, Miss Carey Lee, Alice Gale. Fox. B&W.
Five-reel silent drama based on the novel *Notre-Dame de Paris* by Victor Hugo. Legendary screen 'vamp' Bara is miscast as innocent gypsy girl Esmeralda, who is put on trial and tortured for a crime she didn't commit. White plays a non-deformed Quasimodo who rescues her in the end. It was subsequently re-released with new footage in 1917 and again in 1919, the latter featuring a different ending in which Quasimodo kills a priest and Esmeralda is executed. Future director Phil Rosen (*Spooks Run Wild* [1941], etc) was the cinematographer.
Remake: ESMERALDA (qv; 1922)
✦

DARNA
Philippines, 1991. Dir: Joel Lamangan. With: Rachel Alejandro, Herbert Bautista, Jimmy Santos, Ruby Rodriguez, Nanette Medved, Dennis Padilla. Viva Films. Colour.
One of a series of films based on the 1950s *komiks* character created by artist Mars Ravelo. Narda, a junior reporter living in a Manila ghetto, is given a magic pearl by an angel in a cave. Whenever she swallows the pearl and says the name 'Darna!', Narda changes into the flying super-heroine in a skimpy red costume (Medved). In this low-budget adventure, snake-haired villainess Valentina (from *Valentina* [1989]) teams up with devilish industrialist Dominico

Lipollico, whose potion transforms a prim schoolteacher into an *aswang*, a bat-winged bloodsucker that attacks children.
Sequel: DARNA! ANG PAGBABALIK (1993)
✦✧

DARNA AT DING
Philippines, 1984. Dir: J. Erastheo Navoa. With: Vilma Santos, Nino Muhlach, Marissa Delgado, Ike Lozada, Max Alvarado, Paquito Diaz. D'Wonder Films. Colour.
Based on the 1950s *komiks* character created by Mars Ravelo, with Santos playing bikini-clad superwoman Darna for the ninth time. In this serial-like story, she battles a mad giant German scientist who reanimates the dead as drooling zombies and a voodoo priestess who conjures up a death-ray robot and an evil Darna double.
✦

DARNA, KUNO...?
Philippines, 1985. Dir: Luciano B. Carlos. With: Dolphy, Lotis Key, Celia Rodriguez, Marissa Delgado, Ruel Vernal, Bella Flores. Regal Films. Colour.
The further adventures of Mars Ravelo's *komiks* character. Having borrowed the magic jewel from a pregnant(!) Darna, whenever Darno says 'Darna, Kuno!' she turns into a bikini-clad superwoman. While she battles giant singing horses, winged female vampires and a witch who kidnaps brides and keeps them frozen, the original Darna confronts a shape-shifting hag who entices children into her cave so that she can turn them into cookies and bake them. Some aliens with ray-guns also turn up. And you thought Mexican movies were weird...
✦✧

DARWAZA
India, 1978. Dir: Tulsi Ramsay and Shyam Ramsay. With: Sameer Khan, Imtiaz, Anil Dhawan, Shamlee, Trilok Kapoor, Shakti Kapoor. Kiran Ramsay. Colour.
With a running time of more than two hours, this epic Hindustani horror film marked the financial comeback of the Ramsay family after their previous film, *Andhera* (1975), nearly resulted in bankruptcy. When a Thakur kills a priest of Kali, he is cursed by the goddess and transformed into a werewolf-like creature (Trilok Kapoor) who becomes addicted to a serum created by a mad doctor. The title translates as 'The Door'.
✦✧

DAUGHTER OF DARKNESS
USA/Hungary, 1989 (1990). Dir: Stuart Gordon. With: Anthony Perkins, Mia Sara (Sara Pocciello), Robert Reynolds, Dezsu Garas, Jack Coleman, Erika Bodnar. King Phoenix Entertainment/Accent Entertainment/CBS-TV. Colour.
This first TV movie from director Gordon (*Re-Animator* [1985], etc) is something of a disappointment. Plagued by recurring nightmares, a young American girl (Sara) travels to Ceausescu's Romania to discover the father she's never known. He turns out to be Anton Crainic (Perkins), a 200 year-old vampire who helps her escape from the undead survivors of his ancient family. This lacks much of the style and humour Gordon has brought to his other projects.
✦✦

DAUGHTER OF DRACULA
(Orig: LA FILLE DE DRACULA/LA FILHA DE DRACULA) France/Portugal, 1972. Dir: Jess (Jesús) Franco. With: Britt Nichols, Anne Libert (Josiane Gibert), Alberto Dalbes, Howard Vernon (Mario Lippert), Daniel J. (Jerome) White, Fernando Bilbao. Comptoir Français du Film Production/ Interfilme. Colour.
Another shoddy sex/horror cheapie from Franco, the last in a loosely connected trilogy featuring many of the same characters and actors. Following the death of Baron Karlstein/Dracula (Vernon), Luisa Karlstein (Nichols) learns from her dying grandmother (Carmen Carbonnel) that she is the daughter of the vampire and is given the key to the chapel. With Lina Romay (Rosa Maria Almirall), and Franco as a caretaker. This was apparently mostly improvised by cast and crew.
✦

DAUGHTER OF DR. JEKYLL
USA, 1957. Dir: Edgar G. Ulmer. With: John Agar, Gloria Talbott, Arthur Shields, John Dierkes, Martha Wentworth, Mollie McCart. Film Ventures/Allied Artists. B&W.
Low-budget nonsense from legendary director Ulmer (*The Black Cat* [1934], etc). Heroine Janet Smith (Talbott) returns to her ancestral home with stony-faced fiancé George Hastings (Agar) only to learn that she is the daughter of the infamous Dr Jekyll. A series of full-moon murders points to the girl as the killer, until it is revealed that the kindly Dr Lomas (Shields) has hypnotised her and turns himself into a scientifically-created werewolf (played by Michael Fox). He is finally staked to death by the angry villagers (cut from the British print). This poverty-row quickie was produced and written by Jack Pollexfen. With clips from *Frankenstein* (1931). The TV version also apparently includes footage from *Frankenstein 1970* (1958) in a nightmare sequence.
✦✧

DAUGHTERS OF DARKNESS
(Orig: LE ROUGE AUX LÈVRES/BLUT AN DEN LIPPEN. USA: aka CHILDREN OF THE NIGHT)
Belgium/France/West Germany/Italy, 1971. Dir: Harry Kümel. With: Delphine Seyrig, Andréa Rau, John Karlen, Danièlle Ouimet, Paul Esser, Georges Jamin. Showking/ Ciné Vog/Maya Film/Roxy Films/Mediterranea/Target International. Colour.
Stylish, sensual, erotic chiller, filmed under the title *Erzebeth*. Newlyweds Valerie (Ouimet) and Stefan Chiltern (Karlen) stay at an out-of-season seaside hotel in Ostend and are seduced by Seyrig's stunning thirties-looking Countess Elizabeth (Erzsebeth) Bathory and her companion/lover Ilona (Rau). Despite several bloody deaths, director Kümel never quite reveals if the Countess is really a centuries-old vampire. The film combines moments of great visual poetry with camp splendour, resulting in an almost dream-like intensity. The American version was re-edited by Fima Noveck, and original release prints excluded a postscript featuring Ouimet.
✦✦✦✦

DAWN
UK, 1990. Dir: Niall Johnson. With: Elizabeth Rees, Geoff Sloan, Craig Johnson, Kate Jones Davies, David Steadman, Louise Murray. Shooting Gallery Productions. Colour.
Low-budget horror film, shot on video in Bristol with all the style and sophistication of the worst TV soap opera. Sloan plays Louis, a 200 year-old fangless vampire who seduces and impregnates a woman (Rees) before she stakes him at sunrise. Too much talk and clumsy action scenes can be blamed on director Johnson, who also produced, scripted and co-edited. Songs by Mesh.
✦

DAWN OF THE DEAD
(aka ZOMBIE/ZOMBIE: DAWN OF THE DEAD. UK: aka ZOMBIES)
USA, 1978. Dir: George A. Romero. With: David Emge, Ken Foree, Scott H. Reiniger, Gaylen Ross, David Crawford, David Early. Dawn Associates/Laurel Group Productions. Colour.
Written, edited and directed by Romero (who has a cameo in the opening scenes as a TV director), his enjoyable, action-packed follow-up to *Night of the Living Dead* (1968) follows four survivors who take over a Philadelphia shopping mall and secure it against cannibalistic zombies until it is invaded by a gang of bikers. With gory make-up special effects created by Tom Savini (who also appears as a motorcycle raider), an original music score by The Goblins and script consultant Dario Argento (who supervised the European version), and casting by actor John Amplas (Romero's *Martin* [1976], etc). Filmed under the title *Dawn of the Living Dead*, this was made for just $1,500,000. A novelisation by Romero and Susanna Sparrow was published by St. Martin's Press.
Sequel: DAY OF THE DEAD (qv; 1985)
✦✦✦✧

DAWN OF THE MUMMY
Egypt/Italy/USA, 1980 (1981). Dir: Frank (Farouk) Agrama (and Armand Weston). With: Brenda King, Barry

A messed-up zombie awakens to the *Dawn of the Dead* (1978).

Sattels, George Peck, John Salvo, Ibrahm Kahn, Joan Levy. Harmony Gold. Colour.
This amateurish, low-budget chiller features a ten-foot tall mummy returning from the tomb to revenge itself on grave robbers and menace a group of New York fashion models. The 3,000 year-old mummy also happens to lead an army of blood-drinking zombies, which results in the usual close-up shots of neck-munching. Some impressive make-ups and an eerie music score can't overcome the hysterical acting. From the director of *Queen Kong* (1976), who took over from Armand Weston.
✦✧

THE DAY IT CAME TO EARTH

USA, 1979. Dir: Harry (Z.) Thomason. With: Wink Roberts, Roger Manning, Bob Ginnaven, Delight De Bruine, Rita Wilson, George Gobel. Rainbow/Atlas. Colour.
Low-budget obscurity filmed in 1977 in Little Rock, Arkansas. Set in the 1950s, a strange meteorite crashes into a lake and reanimates the drowned body of underworld informant Lou Jacoby (Ed Love). The reanimated zombie (who looks exactly like a man in a rubber mask) then sets out to revenge himself on the gangsters who killed him. This might have been intended as a comedy, but it's hard to tell. Actress Wilson later married Tom Hanks, while the director and his wife went on to help Bill Clinton become President.
✦

DAY OF THE DEAD

USA, 1985. Dir: George A. Romero. With: Lori Cardille, Terry Alexander, Joe Pilato, Richard Liberty, Howard Sherman, Jarlath Conroy. Laurel/UFDC. Colour.
Writer/director Romero's third *Dead* movie (following *Night of the Living Dead* [1968] and *Dawn of the Dead* [1978]). A small group of survivors — both military and scientific — hold out beneath ground while flesh-eating zombies control the world above. As the others fight amongst themselves, Liberty's insane Dr Logan (called 'Frankenstein' by the other characters) experiments on the brains of the living dead in an attempt to control them. Budget cuts at the last minute prevented this from concluding the series. However, it is filled with strong performances (particularly Cardille's tough heroine), improved zombie make-up and gore effects by Tom Savini, a great music score by John Harrison and some nice offbeat humour. In 1988, Simon & Schuster published a novelisation by Romero and the series original co-creator, John Russo.
✦✦✦✦

DEAD & BURIED

USA, 1981. Dir: Gary A. Sherman. With: James Farentino, Melody Anderson, Jack Albertson, Dennis Redfield, Nancy Locke Hauser, Lisa Blount. Ronald Shusett Productions/ Avco Embassy Pictures. Colour.
In his last role, Albertson plays mad mortician G. William Dobbs who revives the dead without their hearts (make-up effects designed by Stan Winston) in the small New England town of Potters Bluff. Farentino is perplexed local sheriff Dan Gillis who discovers his own wife Janet (Anderson) is a zombie, and there's support from Robert Englund, Bill Quinn, Lisa Marie and Michael Pataki. Apparently, gore reshoots were required. From the director of *Death Line* (1972) and credited to scriptwriters Ronald Shusett and Dan O'Bannon (who apparently denies his involvement), the creators of *Alien* (1979). Chelsea Quinn Yarbro wrote the novelisation from Warner Books.
✦✦

THE DEAD DON'T DIE

USA, 1974 (1975). Dir: Curtis Harrington. With: George Hamilton, Linda Cristal, Joan Blondell, Ralph Meeker, James McEachin, Ray Milland. Douglas S. Cramer Co/ NBC-TV. Colour.
Wonderfully enjoyable TV movie, scripted by Robert Bloch and based on his pulp horror/detective story. Special guest star Milland plays master villain Varek, who is bringing the dead back to life in 1930s Chicago in an attempt to rule the world. The film may have a poverty row look, but Harrington's direction is atmospheric, there's an impressive zombie attack in a graveyard and the dream 'B' movie cast includes genre veterans Reggie Nalder (as a revived corpse), Milton Parsons and Yvette Vickers.
✦✦✦✧

DEAD HEAT

USA, 1988. Dir: Mark Goldblatt. With: Treat Williams, Joe Piscopo, Darren McGavin, Lindsay Frost, Vincent Price, Keye Luke. Helpern-Meltzer/New World Pictures. Colour.
Underrated horror/action thriller. Williams and comedian Piscopo play a pair of tough Los Angeles cops investigating a series of zombie heists. They uncover a plot by Price's sinister scientist Arthur P. Loudermilk to create a rich man's resurrection machine. In an enjoyable plot twist, Roger Mortis (Williams) is killed and his coroner girlfriend (Clare Kirkconnell) uses the machine to allow him twelve hours to track down his killers as his revived body begins to fall apart. Editor-turned-director Goldblatt gives the film a high budget gloss and includes some exciting action sequences, while cameos from genre villains McGavin, Price and Luke add to the fun. With Robert Picardo, Dick Miller, and a clip from *D.O.A.* (1950) on TV.
✦✦✦✧

DEAD IS DEAD

USA, 1992. Dir: Mike Stanley. With: Mike Stanley, Connie Cocquyt, Rob Binge, Dave Hildwein. Video Outlaw/ Tempe Video. Colour.
Low-budget video production filmed under the title *Just Add Water* by star/writer/producer/director/editor Stanley. A bad batch of the drug Doxital brings the dead back to life as homicidal zombies.
✦

DEAD KIDS

(USA: STRANGE BEHAVIOUR. UK: aka HUMAN EXPERIMENTS. USA/UK: aka SMALL TOWN MASSACRE)
New Zealand, 1981. Dir: Michael Laughlin. With: Michael Murphy, Louise Fletcher, Dan Shor, Fiona Lewis, Arthur Dignam, Dey Young. Gupta Film Services/Flavius Films/ Endeavour Productions/Bannon Glen/South Street Films/ Fay Richwhite/Hemdale. Colour.
Low-budget chiller scripted by director Laughlin and associate producer Bill Condon (*Gods and Monsters* [1998], etc). In the small Illinois town of Galesburg, sexy mad scientist Dr Gwen Parkinson (Lewis) and her supposedly dead mentor Dr LeSange (Dignam) are conducting conditioning experiments on local college students and turning them into zombie killers to revenge themselves on the parents. One of the murderers (Marc McClure) wears a creepy Tor Johnson mask. With veterans Scott Brady and Charles Lane, special make-up effects by Craig Reardon and music by Tangerine Dream. David Hemmings was co-executive producer.
✦✦✧

DEADLINE

(USA: aka ANATOMY OF A HORROR)
Canada, 1980. Dir: Mario Azzopardi. With: Stephen Young, Sharon Masters, Marvin Goldhar, Jeannie Elias, Cindy Hinds, Phillip Leonard. Horror Picture Films/ ACFC. Colour.
Young portrays horror novelist and screenwriter Steven Lessey (based on you-know-who), who is driven insane by his success and family problems. He eventually writes this film and then kills himself! Co-writer/director Azzopardi visualises a number of extracts of Lessey's work, including a mutant baby, a mad Nazi scientist using the sound of a punk band to make people explode and, best of all, vampire nuns.
✦✦✧

DEADLOCK

USA, 1997. Dir: Stuart Chapin. With: Aaron Hendry, Michelle Beauchamp, Anthony DeLongis, Stuart Chapin, Vanessa Chapin, Derek Lebrero. Sick Puppy Productions/ Bonneville Worldwide Entertainment. Colour.
A newly-wed couple meet the newly dead after they buy a home that is a gateway to another dimension.
✦✧

DEADLY FRIEND

USA, 1986. Dir: Wes Craven. With: Matthew Laborteaux, Kristy Swanson, Michael Sharrett, Anne Twomey, Anne Ramsey, Richard Marcus. Pan Arts/Layton/Warner Bros. Colour.
Neat little horror thriller, scripted by Bruce Joel Rubin and based on Diana Henstell's novel *Friend*. When budding mad scientist Paul Conway (the likeable Laborteaux) moves into a new neighbourhood with his friendly robot, he falls in love with girl next door Sam (Swanson). However, when she is killed in an accident, he implants the robot's brain into her skull and she returns to a form of semi-life — only now she's a homicidal zombie bent on revenge. The teenage cast work well, particularly Swanson as the confused corpse, and it ends with a nice *frisson* as Paul decides that if at first you don't succeed... With the voice of Charles Fleischer.
✦✦✧

DEADLY LOVE

Canada, 1995. Dir: Jorge Montesi. With: Susan Dey, Stephen McHattie, Eric Peterson, Julie Khaner, Robert S. Woods, Jean LeClerc. Power Pictures Corporation/Victor Television/Alexander-Enright & Associates/ABC Distribution Company. Colour.
Made-for-cable TV movie based on the novel *Love Bite* by Sherry Gottlieb in which the vampiric Rebecca Barnes (Dey), seeking a companion to share her secret, falls for a cop (McHattie) on the trail of a serial killer whose victims die from unusual neck wounds.
✦✦

DEADLY NEIGHBOR

USA, 1991. Dir: Donald M. Dohler. With: Don Leifert, George Stover, Lydia Laurans. VCI. Colour.
Low-budget, independent production filmed in Milford, Delaware, under the title *Fiend*. Suburban music teacher Mr Longfellow (Leifert) is really a resurrected corpse who is killing off local women. Sometimes he glows red and talks to his cat.
✦

DEAD MATE

(Orig: GRAVEROBBERS)
USA, 1988 (1989). Dir: Straw Weisman. With: Elizabeth Mannino, David Gregory, Adam Wahl, Lawrence Bockius, Judith Mayes, Kelvin Keraga. Prism Entertainment/ Filmas Around the World/Jaylo International Films. Colour.
Originally to be directed by Andy Milligan, this low-budget, direct-to-video black comedy was filmed in the towns of Rhinebeck and Reed Hook, New York, for just $137,000. Newly-wed waitress Nora (Mannino) discovers that her mortician husband Henry (Gregory) and his creepy chauffeur Morley (mime artist Keraga) are the leaders of a group of high-tech necrophiliacs who electrically reanimate the corpses of high school cheerleaders. Produced by Lew Mishkin, son of the legendary producer-distributor William.
✦

THE DEAD MATTER

USA, 1998. Dir: Edward Douglas. With: Kenlyn Creech, Chris Robichaud, Jeff Kasunic, Tracy Brown. Entity Pictures/Salt City Home Video. Colour.
Low-budget independent video about a group of friends who discover a mystical relic that reveals a world of vampires and the living dead.
✦

DEAD MEN DON'T DIE

USA, 1990. Dir: Malcolm Marmorstein. With: Elliott Gould, Melissa Anderson, Mark Moses, Mabel King, Jack Betts, Philip Bruns. Waymar Productions. Colour.
Lame, low-budget comedy written and directed by Marmorstein. When TV news anchor Barry Barron (Gould, who mugs outrageously) is murdered by cocaine dealers, he is revived by cleaning lady/voodoo priestess Chafuka (King) as her immortal zombie. As the bodies pile up and then keep disappearing, several more zombies are raised from the dead before the climactic car chase and happy ending. With George 'Buck' Flower.
✦✧

DEAD MEN TELL NO TALES

UK, 1938. Dir: David MacDonald. With: Emlyn Williams, Marius Goring, Hugh Williams, Lesley Brook, Sara Seeger.

British National/Alliance. B&W.
A hunchbacked headmaster with a split personality commits a series of diabolical murders until he cuts his own throat with a piece of glass. Co-scripted by star Williams and based on the book *The Norwich Victims* by Francis Beeding.
✦✧

DEAD MEN WALK
(aka CREATURE OF THE DEVIL)
USA, 1943. Dir: Sam Newfield. With: George Zucco, Mary Carlisle, Nedrick Young, Dwight Frye, Fern Emmett, Robert Strange. Producers Releasing Corporation. B&W.
George Zucco, in a dual role, plays a vampiric black magician determined to kill his kindly twin brother, who is a doctor. They are eventually both destroyed by fire. The evil Zucco is aided by Zolor the hunchback (a sick-looking Frye, in his final horror movie — he died of a heart attack the same year). This is an incomprehensible mess!
✦✧

THE DEADNESS OF DAD
UK, 1997 (1998). Dir: Philippa Cousins. With: Rhys Ifan, Lisa Palfrey, Paul Jones. Celtic Productions/BBC Wales. Colour.
Award-winning twenty-five minute short, scripted by Stephen Volk (*Gothic* [1986], etc) and filmed in Wales for $60,000. Set in 1965, a seven year-old schoolboy (Jones) becomes convinced that his father (Ifan), who was run over by a bus, has returned from the grave. In fact, it is his uncle Dai (also Ifan) who has come to console his Mam (Palfrey).
✦✦✧

THE DEAD NEXT DOOR
USA, 1989. Dir: J.R. Bookwalter. With: Scott Spiegel, Peter Ferry, Bogdan 'Don' Pecic, Michael Grossi, Jolie Jackunas, Robert Kokai. Amsco Studios/The Suburban Tempe Co/ Screen Edge. Colour.
Low-budget, hour-long independent zombie movie edited, written, produced and directed by a teenage Bookwalter, who was also responsible for the music and appears in a cameo. Shot in 1986 on Super-8mm for $100,000, it was partially financed by an uncredited Sam Raimi. In Akron, Ohio, 'Zombie Squad' soldiers battle reanimated flesh-eating corpses infected with a laboratory virus and encounter the members of a bizarre religious cult who use human sacrifices to feed the walking dead. Some of the characters are named after horror film celebrities, such as Carpenter, Savini and Raimi (Ferry, apparently dubbed by Bruce Campbell who supervised the audio post-production). With silly gore effects and a clip from *The Evil Dead* (1982) on TV.
✦✧

DEAD NUDE SORORITY GIRLS
USA, 1997. Dir: Geoffrey de Valois. With: Liddy Roley, Barbara Savage. Digital Entertainment Group/Salt City Home Video. Colour.
One of a series of softcore *Vampire Raw Footage* videos that includes behind-the-scenes nude and erotic sequences. Sorority girls become involved in vampire sex.
✦

DEAD OF NIGHT
USA, 1976 (1977). Dir: Dan Curtis. With: Ed Begley Jr, Patrick Macnee, Anjanette Comer, Elisha Cook Jr, Horst Buchholz, Joan Hackett. Dan Curtis Productions/ABC-TV. Colour.
Three more scripts by Richard Matheson for a proposed *Dead of Night* series were incorporated into this second made-for-TV movie (following *Trilogy of Terror* [1975]). 'Second Chance' is adapted from a time travel story by Jack Finney, while 'Bobby' is an original reworking of W.W. Jacobs' 'The Monkey's Paw' as a mother (Hackett) performs a ritual to bring her drowned son (Lee Montgomery) back to life (it was filmed again by Curtis for *Trilogy of Terror II* [1996]). The middle episode is based on Matheson's own short story, 'No Such Thing as a Vampire': Professor Gheria (Macnee) and his beautiful wife Alexis (Comer) live in an old mansion. One night she is attacked by a vampire — or is she? A young doctor (Buchholz) is called, and the denouement is fairly predictable.
✦✦

DEAD OF NIGHT
USA, 1997. Dir: Kristoffer Tabouri. With: John Enos, Kathleen Kinmont, Robert Knepper. Playboy Entertainment Group. Colour.
Erotic thriller in which a detective becomes determined to stop a pair of immortal killers who feed on the blood of their sexual partners. Produced by Andrew Stevens.
✦✧

THE DEAD ONE
USA, 1960 (1961). Dir: Barry Mahon. With: Linda Ormond, John Mackay, Clyde Kelley, Darlene Myrick, Monica Davis. Mardi Gras Productions/Favorite Films. Colour.
'See Exotic Rituals Bring the Dead to Life' promised the ads for this rarely-seen low-budget voodoo thriller, shot in and around New Orleans by Errol Flynn's former agent and prolific 'adult's only' film-maker Mahon (*The Beast That Killed Women* [1965], etc). Returning to the family plantation in Louisiana, newly-weds Linda and John Mackay (Ormond and Mackay) discover that John's cousin Monica (Davis), scared of losing her inheritance, has raised her brother Jonas from the dead and ordered him to kill the new bride. The ugly zombie (Kelley) wears an evening suit and murders Bella Bella the belly dancer (Myrick) by mistake, before Monica is shot to death by the police and Jonas disintegrates in the rays of the sun.
✦

THE DEAD PIT
USA, 1989. Dir: Brett Leonard. With: Jeremy Slate, Danny Gochnauer, Steffen Gregory Foster, Cheryl Lawson, Geha Getz, Joan Bechtel. Cornerstone Production Company/ Skouras Pictures. Colour.
Impressive low-budget début from the director of *The Lawnmower Man* (1992) and *Virtuosity* (1995). When an earthquake opens up his sealed subterranean laboratory after twenty years, living-dead surgeon Dr Colin Ramzi (Gochnauer) transforms the mentally ill patients and staff at the State Institution into brain-eating zombies. In the end, the scientifically-created walking dead are dissolved by holy water(!). Newcomer Lawson plays psychic amnesiac Jane Doe and was reputedly doubled by porno star Shauna McCullough for the topless scenes.
✦✦✧

DEADTIME STORIES
(UK: FREAKY FAIRY TALES)
USA, 1985 (1986). Dir: Jeffrey S. Delman. With: Scott Valentine, Nicole Picard, Catheryn De Prume, Melissa Leo, Michael Mesmer, Brian DePersia. Scary Stuff/Cinema Group/Bedford Entertainment. Colour.
Low-budget horror anthology, shot over four years in Greenwich, Connecticut. The linking story, 'The Boy Who Cried Monster', has an uncle (Mesmer) recounting a trio of gruesome fairy-tales to his nephew (DePersia). In the second story, 'Little Red Runninghood', a young woman (Picard) in a red jogging outfit picks up some medicine for her grandmother but is mistakenly given the medication for a man suffering from lycanthropy. Changing into a wolf (Matt Mittler in special make-up effects created by Ed French), he tries to get the medication back but is finally stabbed through the neck with a silver cake knife. The other episodes are 'Peter and the Witches' and 'Goldi Lox and the Three Baers', featuring Valentine and De Prume, respectively.
✦✧

DEAFULA
USA, 1975. Dir: Peter Wechsberg. With: Peter Wechsberg, James Randall, Dudley Hemstreet, Lee Darrel, Gary R. Holmstrom, Katherine Wilson. Signscope/Holmstrom. B&W.
Writer/director Wechsberg, who is deaf, stars as theology student Steve Adams, infected before birth by Dracula (Holmstrom). He peri-

odically grows fangs, a big nose and turns into Deafula, until finally destroyed by religious symbols while trapped by the police in a church. What makes this low-budget vampire pic almost unique is that it was filmed entirely in sign language (with a minimal voice-over commentary) for the hearing-impaired. It also includes a hunchbacked assistant with tin-can hands.

✦

DEATH BECOMES HER

USA, 1992. Dir: Robert Zemeckis. With: Goldie Hawn, Bruce Willis, Meryl Streep, Isabella Rossellini, Ian Ogilvy, Adam Storke. Universal. Colour.

Unfunny big-budget horror comedy in which a pair of Hollywood rich bitches (Hawn and Streep) are given eternal beauty by a devilish Beverly Hills witch (Rossellini in a fun cameo). Willis plays the pathetic plastic surgeon caught between the two bickering zombie babes. Cinematographer Dean Cundey ensures that it looks good, while Dick Smith and his team contribute some truly remarkable make-up effects: Streep walks around with her head on backwards, while Hawn has a hole blown clear through her stomach. Unfortunately, Zemeckis' direction doesn't have the lightness of touch this unpleasant film cries out for. With Sydney Pollack. The ending was re-shot just prior to release.

✦✧

DEATH CURSE OF TARTU

(UK: aka CURSE OF DEATH)

USA, 1966. Dir: William Grefé. With: Fred Pinero, Babette Sherrill, Mayra Christine, Sherman Hayes, Gary Holtz, Maurice Stewart. Thunderbird International/Falcon Productions. Colour.

Filmed on location in the Florida Everglades. A group of boring archaeology students are killed by a mummified Seminole witch doctor (an effective-looking Doug Hobart) who rises from the dead and transforms himself into a shark, a snake and an alligator to revenge himself on the desecrators of his tomb. He finally disappears beneath the quicksand. Writer/director Grefé pads out the slim storyline with interminable treks through the undergrowth, accompanied by an irritating music score and numerous screams.

✦✧

DEATHDREAM

(UK: DEAD OF NIGHT)

Canada, 1972. Dir: Bob Clark. With: John Marley, Lynn Carlin, Henderson Forsyth, Richard Backus, Anya Ormsby, Jane Daly. Night Walk/Impact Quadrant Films/ Entertainment International. Colour.

Slow-moving, low-budget chiller filmed under the titles *The Night Walk*, *The Night Andy Came Home* and *The Veteran* in Florida for $250,000. In this uncredited version of W.W. Jacobs' 'The Monkey's Paw', Christine Brooks (Carlin) refuses to believe that her soldier son Andy (Backus) has been killed in action (presumably in Vietnam). She is convinced that he cannot die and he will return home. He does, as a living corpse (make-up effects by screenwriter Alan Ormsby and assistant Tom Savini) who chokes the family dog to death, murders his girlfriend at the drive-in, and uses a syringe to obtain the blood he needs to survive. John Cardos was the production manager and author Peter James was co-executive producer. This won a couple of awards at European film festivals in 1975.

✦✧

DEATH HOUSE

USA, 1988. Dir: John Saxon (and Fred Olen Ray). With: John Saxon, Dennis Cole, Tane McClure, Anthony Franciosa, Michael Pataki, Ron O'Neal. Action International. Colour.

Director Saxon plays a government official who is using a behaviour-modification drug to transform prison inmates into scientifically-created killer zombies in this low-budget thriller.

✦

DEATHMASTER

USA, 1972. Dir: Ray Danton. With: Robert Quarry, Bill Ewing, Brenda Dickson, John Fielder, Betty Anne Rees, William Jordan. RF Productions/World Entertainment Productions/American International Pictures. Colour.

Filmed under the title *Khorda*, the name of the long-haired, bearded vampire played by associate producer Robert (Count Yorga) Quarry, whose coffin is washed ashore in southern California. He becomes a guru to a group of hippies before turning them into the undead in this dated film directed by ex-actor Danton, also responsible for *Crypt of the Living Dead* (1972).

✦✧

DEATH MOON

USA, 1978. Dir: Bruce Kessler. With: Robert Foxworth, Joe Penny, Barbara Trentham, Dolph Sweet, Charles Haid, France Nuyen. EMI Televison Programs/Roger Gimbel/ CBS-TV. Colour.

TV movie filmed on the island of Kauai in Hawaii. Vacationing businessman Jason Palmer (Foxworth) inherits a Polynesian curse that turns him into an impressive looking homicidal werewolf (make-up by Bob Dawn and Michael Westmore) under the influence of the full moon. He is eventually shot to death in a cave before the predictable twist ending.

✦✦

DEATH RACE 2000

USA, 1975. Dir: Paul Bartel. With: David Carradine, Simone Griffeth, Sylvester Stallone, Mary Woronov, Roberta Collins, Martin Kove. New World Pictures. Colour.

Enjoyable futuristic road movie, co-scripted by Robert Thom and Charles B. Griffith (based on an original story, 'The Racer', by Ib Melchior) and produced by Roger Corman. In Mr President's fascist United Provinces of America, five teams enter the twentieth Annual Transcontinental Road Race from New York to New Los Angeles, scoring points for the quickest time and each person they hit and kill along the route. Carradine stars as masked champion racer 'Frankenstein', who has supposedly been rebuilt after surviving repeated crashes in his car, The Monster. However, a pre-stardom Stallone steals the film as his rival, the manic Machine Gun Joe Viterbo. Featuring comic book characters and mayhem, with cameos by Joyce Jameson, director Bartel as a doctor, John Landis as a mechanic and Harriet White Medin as Madame President. Lewis Teague and Charles B. Griffith directed the second units. Some scenes were later reused in *Hollywood Boulevard* (1976). In 1999 Paramount announced a remake entitled *Death Race 3000* to be directed by Paul Anderson and star Tom Cruise.

✦✦✦

DEATH ROW DINER

USA, 1988. Dir: D. Wood. With: Jay Richardson, Michelle McClellan (Michelle Bauer), John Content, Tom Schell, Dennis Mooney, Frank Sarcinello Jr. Camp. Colour.

When an unjustly executed movie executive is brought back from the dead by a freak electrical storm, he soon begins exacting his revenge.

✦✧

DEATH SMILES ON A MURDERER

(Orig: LA MORTE HA SORRISO ALL'ASSASSINO)

Italy, 1972. Dir: Aristide Massaccesi (Joe D'Amato). With: Ewa Aulin, Klaus Kinski, Angela Bo, Sergio Doria, Attilio Dottesio, Giacomo Rossi Stuart. Dany Film/Avco Embassy. Colour.

Confusing Italian horror thriller set in turn-of-the-century Germany. Dr Sturges (Kinski) reanimates the dead using an ancient Inca formula he discovers engraved on the back of a medallion. With a hunchback, several razor killings and Aulin (*Candy* [1968], etc) as Greta, who appears as a decomposing corpse.

✦

DEATHSTALKER II DUEL OF THE TITANS

(aka EL CAZADOR II)

USA/Argentina, 1986 (1987). Dir: Jim Wynorski. With: John Terlesky, Monique Gabrielle, John La Zar, Toni Naples, Maria Socas, Marcos Wolinsky. Concorde/New Horizons/Vestron Video. Colour.

Low-budget sword and sorcery sequel to *Deathstalker* (1983). The eponymous barbarian hero (Terlesky) battles evil sorcerer Jarek (La Zar), who raises Sultana (Naples) from the dead and creates a evil vampiric double of sexy heroine Evie (*Penthouse* Pet Gabrielle). With zombies, pig-men, and wrestler Queen Kong (Deanna Booher). Executive produced by Roger Corman, this includes clips from the first film, scenes from *The Terror* (1963) and ends with outtakes. Two more sequels followed.

Sequel: DEATHSTALKER III THE WARRIORS FROM HELL (1988)

✦✦

DEATH WARMED UP

New Zealand, 1984. Dir: David Blyth. With: Michael Hurst, Margaret Umbers, David Letch, William Upjohn, Norelle Scott, Gary Day. Tucker Production Company/ New Zealand Film Commission. Colour.

Sub-Cronenberg tale of illegal brain operations and mutant zombies created by the demented Dr Archer Howell (Day), who menaces two teenage couples on a remote island. Unfortunately, Blyth's film is all style and no substance, and the thin script remains standard mad scientist stuff with extra gore and black humour. Letch stands out as Spider, the leader of the punk zombies, and Bruno Lawrence plays hunchback Tex Monroe, whose brain explodes. Winner of the Grand Prix at the 1984 International Festival of Fantasy and Science Fiction Films in Paris. Star Hurst is now better known for his role as Iolaus on TV's *Hercules the Legendary Journeys* (1995-99).

✦✧

YVONNE DE CARLO (Peggy Middleton) [b 1922]

Canadian-born Hollywood leading lady. Best known as Lily Munster in TV's *The Munsters* (1964-66).

qv: *Here Come the Munsters* (1995); *Munster, Go Home!* (1966); *The Munster's Revenge* (1981); *Nocturna* (1979).

DEF BY TEMPTATION

USA, 1990. Dir: James Bond III. With: James Bond III, Kadeem Hardison, Bill Nunn, Samuel L. Jackson, Minnie Gentry, Cynthia Bond. Bonded Enterprises/Orpheus Pictures/Troma. Colour.

Uneven horror comedy, billed as 'The black rap chiller thriller of the decade'. A young country preacher (Bond III) visits New York and is tempted by a sexy vampiric demon (an excellent début by Bond). The humour sits uneasily with the gore and some of the performances leave much to be desired, however this remains an enjoyable chiller written, produced, co-executive produced, music supervised, directed and starring the obviously 'multi-talented' Bond III. With special guest appearances by singers Freddie Jackson, Najee and Melba Moore.

✦✦✧

DEFENDERS OF THE EARTH: The Mind Warriors

USA, 1986. Dir: Ray Lee and John Gibbs. Voices: William Callaway, Adam Carl, Ron Feinberg, Buster Jones, Loren Lester, Peter Mark Richman. King Features Entertainment/ Marvel Productions. Colour.

Half-hour cartoon TV series set in 2015AD and based on characters created by Alex Raymond and Lee Falk. Flash Gordon, the twenty-seventh Phantom, Mandrake the Magician and Lothar team up with their four teenage offspring to defeat the evil plans of Ming the Merciless. In this episode, a computer combined with an imagination device conjures up a Frankenstein Monster, a witch, demons and skeletal warriors. Stan Lee wrote the main title lyrics. This is included on the video compilation *Defenders of the Earth: The Story Begins* (1986).

✦✦

THE DEMOLITIONIST

USA, 1995. Dir: Robert Kurtzman. With: Nicole Eggert, Bruce Abbott, Susan Tyrrell, Peter Jason, Richard Grieco, Sarah Douglas. Planet Productions/Le Monde Entertainment Sales/A-Pix Entertainment. Colour.

Set in the near future. When undercover Metro City cop Alyssa Lloyd (Eggert) is killed by psycho gang leader Mad Dog (Grieco), Professor Jack Crowley (Abbott) brings her back to life as a leather-clad zombie avenger, The Demolitionist. Not quite as much fun as it could have been, but director Kurtzman handles the comic book plot with style, helped by an exploitation cast that includes Heather Langenkamp, Jack Nance, Tom Savini, Reggie Bannister and an uncredited Bruce Campbell as a biker.

✦✦✧

GERARDO DE LEON [1913-1981]

Filipino director of *Terror is a Man* (1959) and *The Mad Doctor of Blood Island* (1969), also responsible for two vampire movies: *The Blood Drinkers* (1966) and *Creatures of Evil* (1970).

MARCEL DELGADO [1902-1976]

Mexican-born model-maker who began his career by collaborating with stop-motion animator Willis H. O'Brien on *The Lost World* (1925). They continued to work together on *King Kong* (1933), *The Song of Kong* (1933), *Mighty Joe Young* (1949) and a number of unrealised projects.

THE DEMON AND THE MUMMY

USA, 1975. Dir: Don Weis and Don McDougall. With: Darren McGavin, Simon Oakland, Andrew Prine, Keenan Wynn, Ramon Bieri, Pippa Scott. Universal/Francy Productions/ABC-TV. Colour.

TV movie compilation of two episodes from *Kolchak: The Night Stalker* (1974-75). When Chicago reporter Carl Kolchak (McGavin) investigates a number of fatal heart attacks among male college students, he discovers they are caused by a 10,000 year-old Sumerian succubus ('Demon in Lace'). At the same time, Kolchak also uncovers a plot to sacrifice young hotel executive Pepe Torres (Erik Estrada) and briefly revive the mummy of an ancient Aztec sorcerer ('Legacy of Terror'). With Jackie Vernon, Carolyn Jones, Sorrell Booke, Victor Campos and Milton Parsons.

✦✦✧

DEMON COP

USA, 1990 (1991). Dir: Rocco Karega and Hal Miles (and Fred Olen Ray). With: Theresa Fenneaux, Ray Klein, Julia Westland, Tony Zotta, Rocco Karega, Cameron Mitchell. American-Independent Productions. Colour.

Writer/co-director Karega plays Edward Thurman, a police officer in Colorado Springs, who contracts a rare blood disease that periodically transforms him into a demonic beast with an insatiable urge to kill. Low-budget chills, with veteran Mitchell as 'special guest star'. Filmed under the title *The Curse of Something Bestial*.

✦

DEMON HUNTER (Orig: CAZADOR DE DEMONIOS)

Mexico, 1983 (1985). Dir: Gilberto De Anda. With: Rafael Sánchez Navarro, Tito Junco, Roxana Chávez, Roberto Montiel, Ruby Re, Jorge Russek. Raul De Anda/ Cinematográfica Intercontinental. Colour.

Slow and talky horror thriller. When a husband kills the Chihuahua medicine man he believes responsible for the death of his wife and unborn child, the Native Mexican's evil spirit returns from the grave and transforms into a giant werewolf (Juan Duarte) to kill its victims. A young doctor (Montiel), the local police chief (Navarro) and a priest (Junco, to whose memory the film is dedicated) team up to hunt the creature down with a silver dagger and silver bullets.

✦

DEMON OF PARADISE

USA/Philippines, 1987. Dir: Cirio H. Santiago. With: Kathryn Witt, William Steis, Leslie Huntly, Laura Banks,

Fred(erick) Bailey. Santa Fe Productions/Concorde. Colour.
Scripted by co-star Bailey. Dynamite fishing by drug dealers in an Hawaiian lagoon awakens Akusa, a legendary rubber gill man. Is it a missing link between reptiles and primates or just a mutation? Who cares?
✦

DEMON QUEEN
USA, 1986 (1987). Dir: Donald Farmer. With: Mary Fanaro, Dennis Stewart, Cliff Dance. Mogul/Camera. Colour.
Low-budget video release in which a vampiric woman seduces and then kills her victims.
✦

DEMONS 5: DEVIL'S VEIL
(Orig: LA MASCHERA DEL DEMONIO/SABBAH, LA MASCHERA DEL DEMONIO. USA: aka THE MASK OF SATAN) Italy, 1990. Dir: Lamberto Bava. With: Debora Kinski, Eva Grimaldi, Giovanni Guidelli, Michele Soavi, Piero Nomi, Stanko Molnar. Reitalia/Anfri/TVE/Beta Film/SFP/RTP. Colour.
Director Bava's reworking of his father Mario's classic *Black Sunday* (1960), based in turn on Nikolai Gogol's story 'The Vij'. This time four young couples (including actor/director Soavi) discover the frozen body of vampire/witch Anibas (Grimaldi) during a skiing trip. After the spiked mask is removed from her face, only a pair of young lovers (Kinski and Guidelli) and a blind priest can defeat the sorceress' evil powers. Grimaldi (in a dual role) is no match for Barbara Steele in the original, and Lamberto proves (as if we didn't know) that he has none of his father's talent. Music by Simon Boswell.
✦✧

DEMONSOUL
UK, 1995. Dir: Elisar C. Kennedy (Elisar Cabrera). With: Kerry Norton, Daniel Jordan, Eileen Daly, Janine Ulfane, Drew Rhys-Williams, R.J. Bell. Vista Street Entertainment/Gothic Film Production. Colour.
Set in London, this low-budget, shot-on-video production was written, produced and directed by Kennedy/Cabrera in just thirteen days. Erica Steele (Norton) is troubled by bizarre nightmares of a childhood encounter and visits scheming hypnotherapist Dr Charles Bucher (Jordan). Following the doctor's regression therapy, Erica is soon possessed by the spirit of a demon vampire, thanks to lesbian disciple Selena (Daly) and her hooded monks. With magazine editor Allan Bryce as a doctor.
✦

DEMONWARP
USA, 1988. Dir: Emmett Alston. With: George Kennedy, David Michael O'Neill, Pamela Gilbert, Billy Jacoby, Colleen McDermott, Hank Stratton. Vidmark Entertainment/Design Projects. Colour.
George Kennedy's career hits rock-bottom with this direct-to-video nonsense, based on a story by effects creator John Buechler. The cast wanders interminably through the backwoods as Kennedy searches for his missing daughter, kidnapped by a Bigfoot monster. Meanwhile, a group of teen campers encounter wizards, zombie slaves, alien monsters and a spaceship. It was made for just $250,000. With Michelle Bauer (Michelle McClellan).
✦

DEMON WIND
USA, 1990. Dir: Charles Philip Moore. With: Eric Larson, Francine Lapensee, Rufus Norris, Sandra Margot, Tiffany Million, Mindy McEnnan. Demon Wind Productions/ United Filmmakers/Prism Entertainment. Colour.
Low-budget video release filmed in 1989. A group of teenagers discover an old isolated farmhouse that is a gateway to Hell. They also encounter various demons and zombies. The video box is in 3-D.
✦

DENDAM PONTIANAK
Malaya, 1957. Dir: B.N. Rao. With: Maria Menado, Puteh Lawak, S.M. Wahid, Mustapha Maarof, Salmah Ahmad, Rahimah Alias. Keris Films. B&W.
Sequel to the popular *Pontianak* (1956). Menado returns as the vampire, out for revenge.
Sequel: SUMPAH PONTIANAK (qv; 1958)
✦✧

SUSAN DENBERG (Dietlinde Ortrun Zechner) [b 1944]

Polish-born model/actress and *Playboy* centrefold (August 1966) who was cast by Hammer as the reanimated Christina, possessed by the soul of her unjustly executed boyfriend, in *Frankenstein Created Woman* (1966). She subsequently appeared in the *Star Trek* episode 'Mudd's Women' (1966) before suffering mental health problems connected with drug abuse. Following a newspaper interview with her in 1975, reports of her premature death remain unsubstantiated.

AMANDO DE OSSORIO [b 1925]

Spanish writer/director best known for his quartet of 'Blind Dead' films: *Tombs of the Blind Dead* (1971), *Return of the Evil Dead* (1973), *Horror of the Zombies* (1974) and *Night of the Seagulls* (1975).
qv: *Malenka The Niece of the Vampire* (1968); *Man Hunter* (1980); *Night of the Sorcerers* (1973).

DES VOIX DANS LA NUIT: Succubus
France/UK, 1991. Dir: Patrick Dromgoole. With: Barry Foster, Lyndsey Baxter, Jeremy Gilley, Aurore Clément. Hamster Productions/TF1. Colour.
The first of six hour-long episodes in this French TV series. Divorcé Mike (Foster) and his teenage son Mark move to an old, isolated monastery in Provence, where the suicides of a number of novices are reputed to be linked to a vampiric demon that seduces male virgins.
✦✧

A DEUSA DE MARMORE — ESCRAVA DO DIABO
Brazil, 1978. Dir: Rosangela Maldonado. With: Rosangela Maldonado, José Mojica Marins, Joao Paulo, Luandy Maldonado, Anadir Goe, Anita Nunes. Panorama do Brazil. Colour.
Maldonado wrote, produced, directed and starred in this sex/horror movie. She plays a 2000 year-old woman whose deal with the Devil means she will always remain young by sucking the life-force out of her victims with a fatal kiss during sex. In the end, she reverts to her real age when confronted by a cross. This includes Marins, better known as Coffin Joe/Zé do Caixão.
✦✧

LES DEUX ORPHELINES VAMPIRES
(USA: LOST IN NEW YORK)
France/USA, 1995. Dir: Jean Rollin. With: Alexandra Pic, Isabelle Teboul, Bernard Charnacé, Brigitte Lahaie, Tina Aumont, Martin Snaric. Les Films ABC/Lincoln Publishing/Francam Inter Service. Colour.
Filmed for just $700,000, which was writer/director/executive producer Rollin's biggest budget ever. Based on Rollin's 1993 novel, Louise (Pic) and Henriette (Teboul) are two blind girls at an orphanage who have the power to see at night because they are vampires. They play in the local cemetery, tell each other arty stories and meet a bat-winged vampire woman in an old crypt, before finally drowning themselves in a lake. The title translates as 'The Two Vampire Orphans'.
✦✧

THE DEVIL & THE GHOSTBUSTER
Taiwan, 1986. Dir: Lu Twai Xeng. Citymax/Rainbow Video. Colour.
Comedy horror with a troupe of hopping vampires, flying ghosts, exorcism dolls and a supernatural earthquake. Not to be confused with a 1989 film of the same title.
✦✧

THE DEVIL BAT

(aka DEVIL BATS/KILLER BATS)
USA, 1940. Dir: Jean Yarborough (Yarbrough). With: Bela Lugosi, Suzanne Kaaren, Dave O'Brien, Guy Usher, Yolande Mallott, Donald Kerr. Producers Releasing Corporation. B&W.
Lugosi portrays the mad Dr Carruthers, who creates a pair of gigantic vampire bats to destroy those he believes have cheated him. The bats are attracted to their victims by a pungent aftershave lotion! Lugosi goes over the top and everything else is rock-bottom.
Sequel: DEVIL BAT'S DAUGHTER (qv; 1946)
Remake: THE FLYING SERPENT (1945)
✦✧

DEVIL BAT'S DAUGHTER

USA, 1946. Dir: Frank Wisbar (Wysbar). With: Rosemary LaPlanche, John James, Michael Hale, Molly Lamont, Nolan Leary, Monica Mars. Producers Releasing Corporation/Pathé Industries. B&W.
Talky, low-budget sequel to *The Devil Bat* (1940). LaPlanche (who was Miss America of 1941) plays the daughter of the late Dr Carruthers (Bela Lugosi in the previous film), who is convinced by a scheming psychiatrist (Eddie Kane) that she is possessed by her dead father and has committed murder. In the end, the hero proves not only her innocence but, in a cheat twist, that of her father as well! With a few distorted clips from the earlier movie, none of which feature Lugosi.
✦

DEVIL CURSE

(Orig: MENG GUI ZHOU)
Hong Kong, 1992. Tai Seng Video. Colour.
Supernatural comedy that includes a possessed woman who transforms into a big-fanged vampire.
✦✧

DEVIL DESIGN

Hong Kong, 1987. Dir: Yuen Cheung-Yan. With: Ko Sun-Chu, Sui Kim, Chung Long. Colour.
A group of retreating Mongolian soldiers are slaughtered in a cemetery by reanimated zombies. The leader (Sun-Chu) is possessed by a demon and leads an attack on a nearby Chinese village.
✦✧

DEVIL HUNTER YOHKO

(Orig: MAMONO HUNTER YOHKO. UK: DEVIL HUNTER YOKO)
Japan, 1990 (1992). Dir: Katsuhisa Yamada. Voices: Aya Hisakawa, Yuji Mitsuya, N. Matsui, Mika Doi, Mugibito, K. Yamaguchi. Toho/Japan Computer System/Mad House/AD Vision/Western Connection. Colour.
Forty-three minute anime in which sixteen year-old Yohko Mano (Hisakawa) discovers from her grandmother that she is the 108th Devil Hunter and it is her family's sworn duty to slay demons. She starts by preventing her fellow student Reiko (Matsui), a vampire, from becoming the Black Queen of evil and bringing her demon-brothers into the mortal world.
✦✦

THE DEVIL'S COMMANDMENT

(Orig: I VAMPIRI. UK: LUST OF THE VAMPIRE)
Italy, 1956 (1960). Dir: Richard (Riccardo) Freda (and Mario Bava). With: Gianna Maria Canale, Carlo D'Angelo, Dario Michaelis, Antoine Balpêtré, Renato Tontini, Paul Müller. Titanus/Athena Cinematográfica/BP Productions/RCIP. B&W.
This marked the beginning of the Italian horror film renaissance. Loosely based on the Elizabeth (Erzsebeth) Bathory legend, mad Professor Du Grande (Balpêtré) uses the blood of female victims to restore youth to his beloved Countess (Miss Italy finalist Canale). It was photographed in CinemaScope by Bava, who completed the twelve days filming when director Freda walked off the production. Because of added bath murders and rape scenes, this was originally released as an 'adults only' feature in America with Al Lewis (TV's *The Munsters* [1964-66], etc) in the new footage directed by Ron(ald) Honthaner.
✦✦✧

THE DEVIL'S DAUGHTER

(Orig: POCOMANIA)
USA, 1939. Dir: Arthur Leonard. With: Nina Mae McKinney, Hamtree Harrington, Jack Carter, Ida James, Willa Mae Lane, Emmett Lawrence. Lenwal. B&W.
George Terwilliger reworked his script for *Love Wanga* (1935) as this obscure voodoo movie, filmed in Jamaica. When Miss Isabel (McKinney) feels cheated out of a banana plantation, she uses drugs and superstition to turn the owner into a 'zombie'.
✦

THE DEVIL'S MISTRESS

USA, 1966 (1968). Dir: Orville Wanzer. With: Arthur Resley, Joan Stapleton, Forrest Westmoreland, Douglas Warren, Oren Williams, Robert Gregory. Emerson/Holiday/WGW Pictures. Colour.
Low-budget Western about vampiric Indian half-caste Liah (Stapleton) who uses her magic powers to revenge herself on the four outlaws who killed her strange husband and raped her. In the end, her dead spouse returns to life.
✦✧

DEVILS OF DARKNESS

UK, 1964. Dir: Lance Comfort. With: William Sylvester, Hubert Noel, Carole Gray, Tracy Reed, Diana Decker, Rona Anderson. Planet Films. Colour.
Contemporary vampire thriller set in France. When a young British holiday-maker is killed in a Breton village on All Souls' Eve, his two companions and American Paul Baxter (Sylvester) investigate the mysterious death. Noel plays Count Sinistre, the leader of a local vampire cult. A dull plot, abrupt ending and complete lack of chills make this one to miss.
✦✧

DEVIL SOULS

USA, 1994 (1997). Dir: Jeffery Scott Buckles. With: Kory L. Andrew, Curtis Huskins, Denise Gross, Debbie Cable, Jeff Buckles, David Daniel Sr. Jeffery Scott Buckles/Horror International Picture Productions/Brain Escape Pictures/Swiss Home Video. Colour.
Low-budget anthology, shot on video in Tennessee and Virginia. The Devil (co-writer/producer Andrew) offers a young married couple the use of a magical green 'wishing stone', but first he tells them the stories that go along with it: when an archaeologist uncovers a 3,000 year-old tomb containing the stone, he sets loose a living mummy; a hiker finds the stone in the woods and wishes his companion back as a zombie; and a woman watches a movie on TV called *Curse of the Bloodsuckers* and wishes she was a vampire. When the Devil leaves the couple the stone on a trial basis, the husband turns his friend into a demon from Hell. As Satan's army of monsters grows, a group of hunters encounter a werewolf in the woods. This totally amateurish production is nowhere near as interesting as it sounds.
✦

THE DEVIL'S PLAYTHING

(Orig: DER FLUCH DER SCHWARZEN SCHWESTERN/LA SECTE DE L'HORREUR. USA: aka REVENGE OF THE BLACK SISTERS/VAMPIRE ECSTASY/VEIL OF BLOOD)
West Germany, 1973. Dir: Joseph W. Sarno. With: Nadia Sentowa, Unte Syring, Marie Forså, Nico Wolf, Ulrite Butz, Flavia Reyt. Monarex/Saya Film/Leisure Time/El Independent Cinema. Colour.
Erotic vampire thriller from legendary sex director Sarno, filmed in English. Helga (Swedish actress Forså), Monica and Donna arrive for the reading of a family will at a creepy castle in the German mountains. Along with Dr Julia Malenka (Syring), who is an expert on local superstitions, and her brother Peter (Wolf), they discover that stern housekeeper Wanda (Sentowa) is the leader of a coven of naked lesbian priestesses who are using orgiastic rites to prepare for

the reincarnation of Baroness Danielle Varga, a vampire burned at the stake 400 years before.
✦✦

THE DEVIL'S SKIN

Singapore, 1970. With: Ingrid Hu, Meng Li, Sun Tao. Cathay Productions. Colour.
A fairy vixen duels with a vampire.
✦

DEVIL STORY

(Orig: IL ETAIT UNE FOIS..LE DIABLE)
France, 1986 (1987). Dir: Bernard Launois. With: Pascal Simon, Marcel Portier, Vèronique Renaud, Catherine Day, Nicole Dessailly, Christian Paumelle. Condor Films/ Launois/Commodore Films. Colour.
Low-budget gore film involving a living Egyptian mummy that raises a Nazi zombie from its coffin. This also includes a possessed horse and a ghost ship.
✦

DEVIL'S VINDATA

Hong Kong/Thailand, 1986 (1991). Dir: Liu Kuo-Shin (L. Chang-Xu). With: Cheung Man, Chow Ken-Bo, Fung Sui-Fang. Rising Sun Films/High Grow Films. Colour.
The title is supposed to be *Devil's Vendetta*! After devouring the pulsating heart offered by a hypnotised Buddhist monk, the Devil turns into a beautiful demoness named Twiggy. Sucked into the afterlife, she transforms into a giant cockroach and then decides to become a fanged vampire. This also includes some little hopping vampires.
✦

THE DEVIL'S WEDDING NIGHT

(Orig: IL PLENILUNIO DELLE VERGINI)
Italy, 1973. Dir: Paul Solvay (Paolo Solvay/Luigi Batzella). With: Mark Damon, Sarah Bay (Rosalba Neri/Rada Rassimov), Miriam Barrios (Esmeralda Barros), Frances Davis (Francesca Romana Davila), Stan Papps (Xiro Papas), Alexander Getty. Virginia Cinematográfica/Dimension Pictures. Colour.
Supposedly based on the original story 'The Brides of Countess Dracula' by producer Ralph Zucker and Ian Danby. Twin brothers Karl and Franz Schiller (both played by Damon) search a castle in Transylvania for the legendary Nibelungen ring. After twenty-five years, on the night of the first full moon, it has the power to evoke a witches' Sabbath where the local virgins are sacrificed to celebrate the wedding of a now-vampirised Franz to the undead Countess del Vries/Countess Dracula (Bay, who takes her clothes off a lot). Photographed by 'Michael Holloway' (Joe D'Amato/Aristide Massaccesi); Walter Brandt (Walter Brandi/Walter Bigari) was the production manager.
✦✧

THE DEVIL TO PAY

USA, 1920. Dir: Ernest C. Warde. With: Roy Stewart, Robert McKim, Fritzi Brunette, George Fisher, Evelyn Selbie, Joseph J. Dowling. Brunton Films. B&W.
Silent drama in which a man (Stewart), hanged for a crime he did not commit, is brought back to life by a doctor (Mark Fenton) and haunts the wealthy banker (McKim) who framed him, until the latter commits suicide.
✦

DEVIL WOLF OF SHADOW MOUNTAIN

USA, 1964. Dir: Gary Kent. With: Johnny Cardoz, Gary Kent, Gene Pollock. Principle Productions. B&W.
When American Cavalry trooper Aven Hunter (Cardoz) drinks from the tracks of a wolf in a stream, he is transformed into a werewolf. In the end, he is dispatched with a silver bullet. The script by co-star Pollock was based on an original idea by John 'Bud' Cardos, who was supposed to play the werewolf and claims that it was never made.
✦

DHANWAN

(aka MAZDOOR KI BETI)
India, 1937. Dir: Premankur Atorthy. With: Ratanbai, Hafeesjee. Imperial. B&W.
Hindi drama inspired by the novel *Notre-Dame de Paris* by Victor Hugo. Other versions were filmed in India in 1946, 1981 and 1993.
Remake: THE HUNCHBACK OF NOTRE DAME (qv; 1939)
✦

DIAL 666 FOR LUST

USA, 1991. Dir: Jane Waters. With: Taylor Wayne, Cameo (Kelly Page/Katrina Cameo/Kameo), Cal Jammer, Biff Malibu, Ron Jeremy, Mike Horner. AFV Releasing. Colour.
A female vampire (Wayne, who also scripted) advertises through the personal columns in this hardcore feature. When her victims dial 666-Lust, she appears in a leather bikini and they have sex before she kills them. Jeremy plays a vampire-hunting doctor and this also includes an uncredited Sharon Kane.
✦

DICK TRACY'S G-MEN

USA, 1939. Dir: William Witney and John English. With: Ralph Byrd, Irving Pichel, Ted Pearson, Phyllis Isley (Jennifer Jones), Walter Miller, George Douglas. Republic Pictures. B&W.
Third and probably best of Republic's four serials starring Byrd as the square-jawed detective hero of Chester Gould's comic strip. Over fifteen fast-paced chapters, Tracy battles master spy Zarnoff (the wonderful Pichel), who in the opening scenes is brought back from the dead by an ancient drug after being executed in the gas chamber. In the end, Zarnoff is poisoned by drinking from an arsenic well. With Ed Parker, Milton Frome and Tris(tram) Coffin. A two hour cut-down version was produced for TV in 1973.
Sequel: DICK TRACY VS. CRIME, INC. (1941)
✦✦✧

DIDDLED!

UK, 1912. Dir: C. Calvert. Cricks and Martin. B&W.
Eight minute silent short in which a man disguises himself as a mummy to fool a professor.
✦

DIE HARD ANGELS

(Orig: DAI HADO ENJERUSU)
Japan, 1992. Dir: Arthur Mitsuga Sawada. With: Naomi Akimoto, Y. Hoshi. Colour.
A group of female commandos confront evil criminals Zombie Man and Zombie Woman.
Sequel: DIE HARD ANGELS: PROJECT ZOMBIE ANNIHILATION (qv; 1993)
✦

DIE HARD ANGELS: PROJECT ZOMBIE ANNIHILATION

(Orig: DAI HADO ENJERUSU: KIKEN NI DAKARETA ONNATACHI)
Japan, 1993. Dir: Arthur Mitsuga Sawada. With: Naomi Akimoto. Colour.
Sequel to *Die Hard Angels* (1992), in which the female fighters battle flesh-eating zombies.
✦

DIE HARD DRACULA

USA/Czech Republic, 1998. Dir: Howard Stanton. With: Gary Hurst, Mark Woodley, Stan Ferguson, George Lava, Maria Ortega, Lida Habas. PH Productions. Colour.
Comedy that spoofs both the action-adventure genre and vampire movies.
✦

DILBERT:
Elbonian Trip

USA, 1999. Voices: Daniel Stern, Chris Elliott, Larry Miller, Gordon Hunt, Jackie Hoffman. Global/United Media/Idbox/Columbia TriStar/UPN. Colour.
Half-hour cartoon TV series (1999-) based on the comic strip created by co-executive producer Scott Adams. With Dilbert's new prod-

uct, the Gruntmaster 6000, ready to go into production, Dilbert, Wally and Alice travel to a manufacturing plant in the fourth-world country of Elbonia, where infants, animals and even corpses work in the sweatshops. Meanwhile, Dilbert's dog creates chaos when he arrives as the American diplomat to Elbonia.
✦✦✦

LA DINASTIA DRACULA

(aka DRACULA '87)
Mexico, 1978. Dir: Alfredo B. Crevenna. With: Fabiano Forte (Fabian), Sylvia Manrique, Ruben Rojo, Magda Guzman, Erika Carlson, Roberto Nelson. Conacite Dos/ Eagle Video. Colour.
Following the execution of a Satanist by the Inquisition, the story moves to the late nineteenth century when a shape-changing witch (Carlson) removes the stake from the long-haired vampire (Nelson) and together they plot to take possession of a hacienda in a small provincial town. Low-budget thrills with sixties teenage heart-throb Fabian as Dracula, who can appear in a burst of flame, turn into a paper bat, and is finally destroyed by a priest with a crucifix.
✦

DINNER WITH A VAMPIRE

(Orig: A CENA CON IL VAMPIRO/DINNER WITH THE VAMPIRE/PRANZO CON VAMPIRO. USA: aka HAVING SUPPER WITH A VAMPIRE)
Italy, 1987 (1988). Dir: Lamberto Bava. With: George Hilton, Patrizia Pellegrino, Riccardo Rossi, Valeria Milillo, Yvonne Scio, Isabel Russinova. Dania-Devon/ Reteitalia/Surf Film. Colour.
Unimaginative TV comedy/horror thriller from co-writer/director Bava, filmed in English. Three girls and a boy are invited by famous horror film director Karl Yurek (Hilton) to make a movie at his eerie castle. However, their host is revealed to be a 2,000 year-old vampire and he challenges the teenagers to find a way to kill him and finally end his boring, centuries-old existence. There's also a hunchbacked servant and a *Dorian Gray* plot-twist involving the destruction of an old black and white film taken in the 1920s of the vampire being accidentally released from his tomb.
✦✦

DINOSAUR!

USA, 1985. Dir: Robert Guenette. With: Christopher Reeve. Phillips-Mark Productions/Robert Guenette Productions/Vestron Video. Colour/B&W.
Hour-long, Emmy Award-winning docudrama about dinosaurs, hosted by Reeve. It includes some superb original stop-motion animation by Phil Tippett and clips from *Caveman* (1981), *King Kong* (1933), *The Lost World* (1925), *Planet of Dinosaurs* (1978) and *When Dinosaurs Ruled the Earth* (1969). Endorsed by the National Education Association of America.
✦✦✦✦

DINOSAUR MOVIES

USA, 1993. Dir: Donald F. Glut. With: Don (Donald F.) Glut, Christy Block, Forrest J Ackerman, Jim Danforth, Ray Harryhausen. Popcorn Pictures/Simitar. Colour/ B&W.
Feature-length video, written, directed and co-hosted by 'Dinosaur' Don Glut who, along with Block, introduces a superb selection of rare clips, trailers and interviews covering cartoons, silent movies, enlarged lizards, stop-motion animation (by far the longest segment), Harryhausen, more recent titles, puppets and men-in-suits. This includes trailers for *King Kong* (1933) and *The Son of Kong* (1933), with Ackerman showing off some of the original models in his collection, plus fascinating extracts from *Flying Elephants* (1927), *His Prehistoric Past* (1914), *One Million AC/DC* (1969), *The Secret of the Loch* (1934), Glut's own amateur production *Son of Tor* (1964), and *The Three Ages* (1923), amongst many others. As an added bonus, this also features Winsor McCay's full 1914 version of *Gertie*, along with Willis O'Brien's 1915 short *The Dinosaur and the Missing Link* and all his surviving footage from *Creation* (1930-31). Co-executive produced by Jim Steranko. 'Dedicated to Willis O'Brien (1886-1962)'.
✦✦✦✦

DISCIPLE OF DEATH

UK, 1972. Dir: Tom Parkinson. With: Mike Raven (Austin Churton Fairman), Ronald Lacey, Stephen Bradley, Marguerite Hardiman, Betty Alberge, Nicholas Amer. Chromage Productions/Allan King Associates/Target International Pictures. Colour.
Amateurish, low-budget Gothic horror film, shot on Super-16mm and set in eighteenth century Cornwall. When secret lovers Julia (awful newcomer Hardiman) and Ralph (Bradley) accidentally spill a drop of blood on the grave of a suicide, they revive the evil Stranger (a melodramatic Raven, in his last role). With his living dead slaves (who include Louise Jameson and Virginia Wetherell) and a demonic dwarf (Rusty Goffe), the zombie sorcerer searches for a willing virgin sacrifice to Satan who will release him from eternal damnation. Unfortunately, the film eventually collapses into lame comedy and bizarre fantasy from which it never really recovers. Raven also co-produced and co-scripted under his real name, and several sequences were apparently cut by the British censor prior to release.
✦✧

THE DISEMBODIED

USA, 1957. Dir: Walter Grauman. With: Paul Burke, Allison Hayes, John E. Wengraf, Eugenia Paul, Jack Marston, Paul Thompson. Allied Artists. B&W.
Originally announced as *Voodoo Girl* and *Vampire Girl*. For fans of Hayes, this perhaps proves even more than her role in *Attack of the 50ft Woman* (1958) that she couldn't act. Here she plays the sultry Tonda, clothed in little more than a belt and dagger, who sets out to seduce movie-maker Tom (Burke), attempts to murder her jungle doctor husband (Wengraf) with a doll fetish, and shows off her hip-jiggling voodoo dance with the local natives. There are even touches of soul transference and zombies, but they can't save this low-budget bore, filmed on a minimum of sets.
✦

DIVERSIONS

UK, 1976. Dir: Derek Ford. With: Heather Deeley, Gilly Sykes, Timothy Blackstone, Tony Kenyon, Derek Martin, Tim Burr. Blackwater Film Productions. Colour.
Low-budget sex film written and directed by Ford, which includes two women on a train ride fantasising about having sex with a vampire.
✦

THE DIVINE ENFORCER

USA, 1991. Dir: Robert Rundle. With: Michael Foley, Don Stroud, Carrie Chambers, Erik Estrada, Jan-Michael Vincent, Judy Landers. Prism Entertainment. Colour.
Only the exploitation cast makes this psycho thriller worth watching. Chambers plays a woman with psychic powers who is linked with a 'vampire' serial killer (Stroud). With Jim Brown and Robert Z'Dar.
✦✧

DOCTOR BLOOD'S COFFIN

UK, 1961. Dir: Sidney J. Furie. With: Kieron Moore, Hazel Court, Ian Hunter, Gerald C. Lawson, Kenneth J. Warren, Andy Alston. Caralan/United Artists. Colour.
Low-budget horror chiller set in a small Cornish village. Moore plays Peter Blood, a mad doctor transplanting the hearts of living (but 'worthless') bodies into corpses to bring them back to life. Nothing very exciting happens until the climax, when a green-faced rotting zombie (Paul Stockman) takes grisly revenge. From the Canadian director of *The Snake Woman* (1961) and *Lady Sings the Blues* (1972). Nick (Nicholas) Roeg was the camera operator.
✦✦

DOCTOR DRACULA

USA, 1977 (1981). Dir: Paul Aratow and Al Adamson. With: John Carradine, Donald Barry, Larry Hankin, Susan McIver, Geoffrey Land, Regina Carrol. Independent-International/Rafael Film Associates. Colour.
Psychiatrist Anatol Gregorio (Land) is really Count Dracula, who thwarts the Satanic plans of the occult Society of the Bleeding Rose, or The Evil Ones, headed by Radcliffe (Carradine) and Dr John

Wainwright (Hankin), a hypnotist who believes he is the reincarnation of Svengali. The Count is finally blown to pieces by a woman (McIver) whose mother is now Dracula's undead bride. Apparently this is a re-edited version of Aratow's *Lucifer's Women* (1974), with extra footage directed by Adamson and shot by Gary Graver. It's still pretty terrible. Self-styled Satanist Anton (Szandor) LeVey was the technical advisor for the Black Mass scenes.

✦

DOCTOR FRANKEN

USA, 1980. Dir: Marvin J. Chomsky and Jeff Lieberman. With: Robert Vaughn, Robert Perault, David Selby, Teri Garr, Josef Sommer, Cynthia Harris. Titus-Janus/NBC-TV. Colour.

TV movie pilot, filmed in 1979 as *The Franken Project* and 'suggested' by Mary Shelley's novel. Vaughn plays Dr Arno Franken, a direct descendant of the legendary Dr Frankenstein, who works as a New York surgeon and builds a creature (Perault) out of spare organs. Despite an open ending, the ugly photography and downbeat story ensured this never became a regular series.

✦

DOCTOR GORE

(aka THE BODY SHOP)

USA, 1972 (1974). Dir: J.G. 'Pat' Patterson. With: J.G. Patterson, Jenny Driggers, Roy Mehaffey, Linda Fiele, Jan Benfield, Candy Furr. Metrolina/Studio 1/Video Communications/Paragon Video Productions. Colour.

Tormented by the death of his wife, crazy paediatrician Dr Don Brandon (director Patterson, also responsible for the make-up effects) decides to create the perfect mate. Along with his mute, hunchbacked assistant Greg (Mehaffey), he kills a number of women and uses their body parts to produce a perfect woman, Anitra (Driggers), who he brings to life. However, when she discovers other men, she hitches a ride with a stranger while the mad doctor languishes in an asylum. Filmed in Milwaukee by one-time North Carolina TV host and spook show presenter Patterson, who died in 1974. The 1980s video release includes an introduction by Herschell Gordon Lewis, who had worked with the director.

✦

DOCTOR PENETRATION

USA, 1986. Dir: Alex DeRenzy. With: Stacey Donovan, Melissa, Taija Rae, Lois Ayres, Sher St. Clair, Britanny Stryker. Gregory Dark/Hustler Video. Colour.

Hardcore horror spoof as the eponymous mad scientist (William Lee) and his assistant Igor (St. Clair) use the Neuro-sexual Fantasy Soul Stealer machine to absorb the sexual fantasies of their guests and turn them into zombies. In the end, the doctor is killed by his Lobster Monster (Dick Rambone).

✦

DOCTOR TICKLESTEIN

USA, 1989. Dir: Tony Sinclair. Sinclair Blue Productions. Colour.

Another 'adults only' tickling video from writer/director Sinclair.

Sequel: SON OF TICKLESTEIN (qv; 1990)

✦

DOCTOR VAMPIRE

(Orig: JIANG SHI YI SHENG)

Hong Kong/UK, 1990. Dir: Lu Jian-Ming (Jamie Luk Kam-Ming/Q. Xen-Lee) and Martin Sullivan. With: Guo Jin-En (Bowie Lam), Chan Ya-Lun (Ellen Chan), Peter Kjaer. Golden Harvest/Paragon Films. Colour.

Stranded when his car breaks down in the country, a young surgeon (Jin-En) visiting Britain stumbles across a brothel run by vampires and is subsequently bitten by the undead Cora (Ya-Lun). However, the couple fall in love and are pursued to Hong Kong by the girl's evil bloodsucking pimp (Kjaer). The vampires in this frenetic horror comedy are the traditional kind, not the hopping variety.

✦✧

DOCTOR WHO:

The Brain of Morbius

UK, 1975 (1976). Dir: Christopher Barry. With: Tom Baker, Elisabeth Sladen, Philip Madoc, Colin Fay, Cynthia Grenville, Gilly Brown. BBC-TV. Colour.

The BBC's longest-running science fiction TV show (1963-89, 701 episodes), with several actors portraying the eponymous Time Lord who travels through time and space with various companions in the TARDIS, which looks like a police telephone box from the outside. In this four-part story, written by Robin Bland (Terrance Dicks), the Doctor (Baker) and his companion Sarah Jane Smith (Sladen) discover that the TARDIS has been diverted to a planet where mad scientist Solon (Madoc) and his misshapen assistant Condo (Fay) have created a patchwork body out of alien parts. The crowning achievement will be the Doctor's head, which will house the brain of a renegade Time Lord. W.H. Allen published a novelisation by Dicks in 1977 and a junior novelisation followed from the same author in 1980.

✦✦✧

The Chase

UK, 1965. Dir: Richard Martin. With: William Hartnell, William Russell, Jacqueline Hill, Maureen O'Brien, Hywel Bennett, Peter Purves. BBC-TV. B&W.

The Daleks use their own machine to pursue the TARDIS across time and space in six linked episodes, written by Terry Nation. In the fourth story, 'Journey Into Terror', the Doctor (Hartnell) and his companions Vicki (Maureen O'Brien), Ian Chesterton (Russell) and Barbara Wright (Hill) land in a 'haunted' Gothic castle where they are menaced by Count Dracula (Malcolm Rogers), a Karloff-like Frankenstein Monster (John Maxim) and a ghostly Grey Lady (Roslyn De Winter), who all turn out to be robots in a 1996 amusement attraction, Frankensteins (*sic*) House of Horrors. With Purves in two roles and clips of The Beatles singing 'Ticket to Ride'. This was novelised by John Peel in 1989.

✦✦

The Claws of Axos

UK, 1971. Dir: Michael Ferguson. With: Jon Pertwee, Katy Manning, Nicholas Courtney, Peter Bathurst, Paul Grist, Bernard Holley. BBC-TV. Colour.

Four-part story produced under the title *The Vampire from Space*. The Earth is visited by an organic spacecraft containing beautiful golden aliens, the Axons. Although the visitors offer an end to the world's food shortage, the Doctor (Pertwee) and Jo Grant (Manning) discover that they are in fact hideous tentacled parasites intent on draining the planet of all its energy. A novelisation by Terrance Dicks was published in 1977.

✦✦✧

The Curse of Fenric

UK, 1989. Dir: Nicholas Mallett. With: Sylvester McCoy, Sophie Aldred, Dinsdale Landen, Alfred Lynch, Nicholas Parsons, Tomek Bork. BBC-TV. Colour.

Four-part story in which the Doctor (McCoy) and Ace (Aldred) return to World War Two Whitby (shades of Stoker's *Dracula*!), where they encounters the vampiric Haemovores and cursed Vikings. The video release apparently includes extra footage cut from the TV version. A novelisation from Ian Briggs was published in 1990.

✦✦

The Greatest Show in the Galaxy

UK, 1988. Dir: Alan Wareing. With: Sylvester McCoy, Sophie Aldred, T.P. McKenna, Jessica Martin, Ricco Ross, Ian Reddington. BBC-TV. Colour.

In this four-part story, the Doctor (McCoy) and Ace (Aldred) visit the renowned Psychic Circus on the planet Segonax, where they meet such other visitors as pompous explorer Captain Cook (McKenna), circus fan Whizzkid (Gian Sammarco), masked biker Nord (Daniel Peacock) and punk werewolf Mags (impressionist Martin). The Doctor eventually discovers that the sinister Chief Clown (Reddington) and his deadly troupe of robot clowns are controlled by the evil Gods of Ragnarok. With veteran comedienne Peggy Mount in a cameo. A novelisation by Stephen Wyatt appeared in 1989.

✦✦

Inferno

UK, 1970. Dir: Douglas Camfield. With: Jon Pertwee, Caroline John, Nicholas Courtney, Olaf Pooley,

Christopher Benjamin, Derek Newark. BBC-TV. Colour.
Seven-part story in which a power fluctuation in the TARDIS console transports the time-travelling Doctor (Pertwee) and Liz Shaw (John) to a parallel Earth, where they discover a fascist government attempting to drill through the planet's crust. This releases a heat-based substance that transforms those who come into contact with it into werewolf-like beastmen. A novelisation by Terrance Dicks was published in 1984.
✦✦✧

Planet of Evil
UK, 1975. Dir: David Maloney. With: Tom Baker, Elisabeth Sladen, Frederick Jaeger, Ewen Solon, Prentis Hancock, Graham Weston. BBC-TV. Colour.
Four-part story in which the Doctor (Baker) and his companion Sarah Jane Smith (Sladen) land on the planet Zeta Minor, where the members of a geological expedition are being killed off by an energy monster and Professor Sorenson (Jaeger) is transforming into an anti-matter werewolf. Terrance Dicks' novelisation was published in 1977.
✦✧

Pyramids of Mars
UK, 1975. Dir: Paddy Russell. With: Tom Baker, Elisabeth Sladen, Bernard Archard, Michael Sheard, George Tovey, Peter Copley. BBC-TV. Colour.
Four-part story in which the TARDIS transports the Doctor (Baker) and Sarah Jane Smith (Sladen) to England in 1911. There they discover jackal-headed alien god Sutekh is using a zombie archaeologist (Archard) and an army of robotic mummies to build a rocket so that he can escape after 7,000 years imprisonment from beneath an Egyptian pyramid and destroy the Earth. A novelisation by Terrance Dicks was published in 1976.
✦✦✧

State of Decay
UK, 1980. Dir: Peter Moffatt. With: Tom Baker, Lalla Ward, Matthew Waterhouse, Emrys James, Rachel Davies, William Lindsay. BBC-TV. Colour.
Four-part story, written by Terrance Dicks, in which the TARDIS lands on an unnamed medieval planet in E-Space ruled by 1,000 year-old vampires Aukon (James), Camilla (Davies) and Zargo (Lindsay). They await the arising of a giant buried entity, the Great Vampire, banished there by the Time Lords. But when the Doctor (Baker) sends a spaceship into the heart of the creature, the trio of vampires are reduced to dust. A novelisation by Dicks appeared in 1982.
✦✦✧

The Stones of Blood
UK, 1978. Dir: Darrol Blake. With: Tom Baker, Mary Tamm, Susan Engel, Beatrix Lehmann, Nicholas McArdle, Elaine Ives-Cameron. BBC-TV. Colour.
Four-part story in which the Doctor (Baker) and Romana (Tamm), while searching for the third segment of the Key of Time on Earth, encounter a blood-drinking Druid circle of stones, the Orgi, controlled by pagan aliens. Terrance Dicks' novelisation was published in 1980.
✦✧

The Talons of Weng-Chiang
UK, 1977. Dir: David Maloney. With: Tom Baker, Louise Jameson, John Bennett, Michael Spice, Christopher Benjamin, Trevor Baxter. BBC-TV. Colour.
Surprisingly horrific Holmesian adventure as the Doctor (Baker) and Leela (Jameson) travel back to gas-lit Victorian London. There they team up with police pathologist Professor Litefoot (Baxter) and theatre owner Henry Gordon Jago (Benjamin) to prevent fifty-first century war criminal Magnus Greel, alias the ancient Chinese god Weng-Chiang (Spice), who feeds on the life-force of his victims, from recovering his lost time cabinet. Scriptwriter Robert Holmes takes his inspiration from Fu Manchu, the Phantom of the Opera and Jack the Ripper. This six-part story (written under the working title *The Talons of Greel*) also features Greel's evil dwarf homunculus Mr Sin (Deep Roy), who has the brain of a pig, and giant rats living in the London sewers. A novelisation by Terrance Dicks was published in 1977.
Series sequel: DOCTOR WHO (qv; 1996)
✦✦✦

DOCTOR WHO
Canada/USA/UK, 1996. Dir: Geoffrey Sax. With: Paul McGann, Eric Roberts, Daphne Ashbrook, Sylvester McCoy, Yee Jee Tso, John Novak. BBC Worldwide/MCA Television. Colour.
This impressive TV movie, based on the classic BBC TV show (1963-89), should have become a series. The seventh incarnation of the time-travelling Doctor (McCoy) arrives in San Francisco on the eve of the Millennium and is killed, regenerating into the likeable McGann (mirrored by clips from *Frankenstein* [1931] on TV). Teaming up with Dr Grace Holloway (Ashbrook), he must stop the reanimated Master (a nicely evil Roberts) from stealing his body and destroying space and time. Although Matthew Jacobs' script misses a few beats, it is basically a new origin story (for the American audience), stylishly photographed and directed, and featuring some impressive set designs and CGI effects. A novelisation by Gary Russell and a scriptbook were published by BBC Books. Another *Doctor Who* movie was announced in 1999, to be directed by Paul Anderson (*Event Horizon* [1997], etc).
✦✦✦✧

DOCTOR X
USA, 1932. Dir: Michael Curtiz (Mihaly Kertesz). With: Lionel Atwill, Fay Wray, Lee Tracy, Preston Foster, John Wray, Harry Beresford. First National Pictures/ Vitaphone. Colour and B&W.
During each full moon, a crazed cannibalistic strangler, who eats human glands, creates a functioning hand out of synthetic flesh (make-up created by Max Factor Co). Is it the mysterious Dr Xavier (Atwill, in a rare starring role)? His devoted daughter Joanna (Wray), who screams every time she finds her father lurking around their lonely cliff-top mansion? Or perhaps it's one of the sinister scientists (Foster, Wray, Beresford and Arthur Edmund Carewe), who all have something to hide? It adds up to a wonderfully gruesome pulp horror thriller, although the comedy antics of Tracy's wise-cracking reporter hero Lee Taylor almost ruin the genuine chills. With regular Laurel and Hardy foil Mae Busch as a speakeasy Madame. Filmed simultaneously in two different versions, in monochrome and the two-strip Technicolor process, the latter was restored in 1985 by UCLA Film Archives.
✦✦✦✧

DOCUMENT OF THE DEAD
USA, 1989. Dir: Roy Frumkes. With: George A. Romero, Richard Rubinstein, Tom Savini, John Amplas, Gahan Wilson, Steve (Stephen R.) Bissette. Ray Frumkes Production/Studio Entertainment/The School of Visual Arts. Colour.
This overlong, rambling, pseudo-intellectual documentary about George A. Romero started out as a student film that Frumkes made around the shooting of *Dawn of the Dead* (1978), while the director was still studying at New York's School of Visual Arts. Here he supplements his original film interviews with Romero, Savini, Amplas and Rubinstein with new video commentary by Romero and artists Wilson and Bissette. This includes clips from *Night of the Living Dead* (1968), *Martin* (1976) and *Monkey Shines* (1988), plus a spoof *Fantastic Voyage* (1966) commercial that Romero made in the 1960s. Narrated by Susan Tyrrell, it was released on DVD in 1998 in a 'special edition' with supplemental material, including deleted interview footage with Adrienne Barbeau, Romero and Savini.
✦✧

DOES DRACULA REALLY SUCK?
(aka DRACULA AND THE BOYS/DRACULA...DOES HE?/ DRACULA SUCKS)
USA, 1969. Colour.
Hardcore gay vampires.
✦

DONA MACABRA
Mexico, 1986. Dir: Roberto Gavaldon. With: Marga López, Hector Suarez, Carmen Montejo, Carmen Salinas, Luis Alarcon, Ricardo Cortez. Roberto Gavaldon/Azteca. Colour.

1-7
109-190.

Horror comedy in which a mad doctor keeps a bizarre wax museum in the cellar of the home of two old ladies. Along with a live leopard and a man in an ape suit, the underground hideaway also includes a wax figure of the Frankenstein Monster.
✦✧

DON DRACULA
(aka OSAMU TEZUKA'S DON DRACULA)
Japan, 1982. Dir: Masamune Ochiai. Voices: Kenji Utsumi, Saeko Shimazu, Takao Oyama, Junpei Takiguchi, Masaru Tanaka. Tezuka Productions. Colour.
Half-hour anime adaptation of Osamu Tezuka's popular manga serial in *Shonen Champion Comics*. Although seven episodes were made, only four were shown on Japanese TV, with the full series subsequently released directly to video. Dracula (Utsumi, who also voiced the character in *Dracula: Sovereign of the Damned* [1980]), his daughter Chocola (Shimazu) and their servant Igor (Oyama) leave Transylvania for Tokyo, where the Count has trouble finding enough victims. Chocola attempts to help her father, although it interferes with her studies at night-school, as their arch-enemy Dr Van Helsing (Takiguchi) arrives in the city. This also apparently involves Dorian Gray (Tanaka).
✦✦

DOS FANTASMAS Y UNA MUCHACHA
Mexico, 1958. Dir: Rogelio A. Gonzalez. With: 'Tin-Tan' (Germán Valdés), Ana L. (Luisa) Peluffo, Manuel 'Loco' Valdés, Luis Aldas, Miguel Manzano. Producciones Sotomayor. B&W.
The musical adventures of a pair of ghosts who disappear when they sneeze and who can turn into skeletons. This includes a scene being filmed on a movie set which features the Frankenstein Monster, a werewolf, a mummy and a gill man. The title translates as 'Two Ghosts and a Girl'.
✦

A DOUBLE LIFE
USA, 1947. Dir: George Cukor. With: Ronald Colman, Signe Hasso, Edmond O'Brien, Shelley Winters, Ray Collins, Philip Loeb. Kanin Productions. B&W.
Enjoyable psychological horror drama for which Colman won an Academy Award for his portrayal of Broadway star Anthony John, unhinged by his stage role as Othello, who gradually sinks deeper into madness and murder. Stylishly directed by Cukor, from a fine script by Ruth Gordon and Garson Kanin. Veteran actor Walter Hampden was brought in to help Colman with his Shakespeare. With Whit Bissell. Manly Wade Wellman wrote the novelisation.
✦✦✦

DOUBLE TROUBLE
USA, 1967. Dir: Norman Taurog. With: Elvis Presley, Annette Day, John Williams, Yvonne Romain, Chips Rafferty, Michael Murphy. Metro-Goldwyn-Mayer. Colour.
A teenage heiress (Day) falls for pop star Guy Lambert (Presley) while he's performing in London. In real-life, Elvis never visited England. He sings 'Old MacDonald' and 'Long Legged Girl'. This includes characters in Dracula, Frankenstein Monster and Phantom of the Opera masks.
✦✦

DOUG:
Doug's Bloody Buddy
USA, 1994. Voices: Billy West, Constance Shulman, Doug Preis, Alice Playten, Fred Newman, Becca Lish. Nickelodeon-Elipse/Jumbo Pictures/Walt Disney. Colour.
Half-hour cartoon TV series (1991-94, fifty-two episodes), created by Jim Jinkins, about the adventures of eleven year-old Doug Funnie (West) and his dog Porkchop. In this Halloween episode, while Doug and his friends speculate about the identity of the vampiric Bat Master at school, all the evidence points to his blue-skinned best friend Skeeter Valentine (Newman) being the Bluffington bloodsucker. It also includes a video game featuring the Frankenstein Monster and the Mummy, and a teacher who dresses up as one of the undead and reads to the class from *Dracula*. This episode is available on the video *Brand Spanking New! Doug: The Vampire Caper*, which includes a Scooby-Doo spoof opening. A tie-in book was published in 1997.
Series sequel: BRAND SPANKING NEW! DOUG (1996-99)
✦✦

Bela Lugosi as the Count in Dracula *(1931).*

DOW HOUR OF GREAT MYSTERIES:
The Inn of the Flying Dragon
UK, 1960. With: Farley Granger, Barry Morse, Hugh Griffith, Michael Shillo, Macha Meril. B&W.
Based on the 1872 story 'The Room in the Dragon Volant' by J. Sheridan Le Fanu.
Remake: THE INN OF THE FLYING DRAGON (qv; 1978)
✦✧

DOWN AND DIRTY
USA, circa 1969. Colour.
Man encounters a cult of Satanists who watch a film with a werewolf in it.
✦

THE D.P. MAN
USA, 1992. Dir: Jim Enright. With: Jonathan Morgan, Ron Jeremy, Francesca Lé, Pearl Joyce, Teri Diver, P.J. Sparxx (P.J. Carrington). Fat Dog Productions. Colour.
When the Baron's niece, Fran Frankenstein (Joyce), returns to the family castle, she ends up creating her own double-endowed Monster (Jonathan Morgan) from her uncle's notes and spare body parts. This hardcore spoof of *Young Frankenstein* (1974) also includes a parody of the scene with the blind hermit (Patricia Kennedy).
Sequel: THE D.P. MAN PART 2 (qv; 1992)
✦

THE D.P. MAN PART 2
USA, 1992 (1993). Dir: Jim Enright. With: Jonathan Morgan, Tiffany Mynx (Tiffany Minx), P.J. Sparxx (P.J. Carrington), Ron Jeremy, Pearl Joyce, Francesca Lé. Fat Dog Productions. Colour.
Hardcore sequel involving Frankenstein's niece Fran (Joyce) and her double-donged creation.
✦

DRACULA
USA, 1931. Dir: Tod Browning. With: Bela Lugosi, Helen Chandler, David Manners, Dwight Frye, Edward Van Sloan, Herbert Bunston. Universal. B&W.
Originally billed as 'The strangest love story of all', this slow moving, stagey version of Bram Stoker's 1897 novel (previously filmed as *Nosferatu* [1922]) was released on St. Valentine's Day, 1931. After playing the Count in the hit stage production since 1927 (alongside Van Sloan), this was forty-nine year-old Hungarian actor Bela Lugosi's (Bela Blasko) first starring role in Hollywood (replacing Lon Chaney Sr, who died before shooting began). Based on the play by Hamilton Deane and John L. Balderston, the script by Garrett Fort (and Dudley Murphy and Browning) still has its moments, but looks quite dated today, thanks to Karl Freund's static cinematography. Despite Frye's manic Renfield, Van Sloan's dignified Van Helsing and the Count's seductive trio of vampire wives (Dorothy Tree, Cornelia Thaw and Jeraldine Dvorak), the film is dragged down by Lugosi's hammy performance, the weak love interest between Manners' John Harker and Chandler's insipid Mina, and the climactic staking of the Count off-screen. However, along with Universal's *Frankenstein* the same year, this started the horror boom of the 1930s. With the director in a small role as a Harbour Master. The long-lost original epilogue by Van Sloan, telling the audience that vampires really do exist, was included in the 1999 DVD release along with an unnecessary new alternative score performed by The Kronos Quartet and composed by Philip Glass. Crestwood House published a juvenile novelisation by Ian Thorne in 1977, and the script appeared as part of the MagicImage Filmbooks series in 1990.
Sequel: DRACULA'S DAUGHTER (qv; 1936)
Remake: DRACULA (qv; 1931)
✦✦✦✧

DRACULA

USA, 1931. Dir: George Melford. With: Carlos Villar (Carlos Villarías/Carlos Villarías Llano), Lupita Tovar, Barry Norton, Pablo Alvarez Rubio, Eduardo Arozamena, José Soriano Viosca. Universal. B&W.

While Tod Browning was shooting his much more famous version starring Bela Lugosi, Universal decided to make a simultaneous Spanish-language version at night using the same sets and script, but with a different cast and crew. American director Melford (Valentino's *The Sheik* [1921], etc) actually improved upon Browning's version — it is better paced and more imaginatively photographed (by George Robinson), while thirty-eight year-old Villar makes an impressive, bestial Conde Drácula. With Rubio playing a sly Renfield and Arozamena as an erudite Professor Van Helsing. Although the movie follows the Browning version very closely, there are still many major differences in the way certain scenes were filmed and new sequences were added. Interestingly, some of Browning's alternative takes (including long shots of Lugosi) were used as stock footage. Lost for many years, an almost complete print turned up in the late 1970s and it was fully restored in 1990. This was released on video in 1992 with a special introduction by Tovar.

Remake: DRAKULA ISTANBUL'DA (qv; 1952)

♦♦♦♦

DRACULA

(USA: HORROR OF DRACULA)

UK, 1958. Dir: Terence Fisher. With: Peter Cushing, Christopher Lee, Michael Gough, Melissa Stribling, Carol Marsh, Olga Dickie. Hammer Films/Universal-International. Colour.

Following its success with *The Curse of Frankenstein* (1957), Hammer revived another classic horror character with this first colour version of Bram Stoker's novel. Jimmy Sangster's action-packed script is a definite improvement over previous adaptations, helped by lavish sets, stylish direction and — pretty daring for a fifties film — strong sexual and graphic overtones. Cushing gives one of his finest performances as a dynamic Van Helsing and Lee became an instant sex symbol as the demonic Count. Although a little slow in places, the climactic duel remains a masterpiece of modern horror cinema. A Gothic fairy-tale with John Van Eyseen as Jonathan Harker and Valerie Gaunt as Dracula's single vampire 'bride', plus solid support from Charles Lloyd Pack, George Woodbridge, Miles Malleson and Geoffrey Bayldon. This was adapted into comic strip format by Paul Neary in *The House of Hammer* no.1 (1976).

Sequels: THE BRIDES OF DRACULA (qv; 1960) and DRACULA PRINCE OF DARKNESS (qv; 1965)

Remake: PLAYHOUSE: MYSTERY AND IMAGINATION: Dracula (qv; 1968)

♦♦♦♦♦

DRACULA

(USA: aka BRAM STOKER'S DRACULA)

UK/Yugoslavia/USA, 1972 (1973). Dir: Dan Curtis. With: Jack Palance, Simon Ward, Nigel Davenport, Pamela Brown, Fiona Lewis, Penelope Horner. Dan Curtis Productions/Latglen/CBS-TV. Colour

Underrated adaptation of Bram Stoker's novel, originally made for American TV but released theatrically (in a cut version) overseas. The script, by Richard Matheson, borrows heavily from Hammer's 1958 film but, probably because of its small screen origins, concentrates on the Count's Byronic qualities instead of his bloodletting. Palance, not the most subtle of actors, gives one of his better performances as a more human Dracula, motivated as much by love as bloodlust. Davenport's Dr Van Helsing is perhaps a little too dynam-

Carlos Villar about to put the bite on Carmen Guerrero in the Spanish-language Dracula *(1931).*

ic and Lewis far too voluptuous as Lucy Westenra, but overall this is a particularly effective version of the story thanks to excellent colour photography and stylish period setting. With Sarah Douglas, Barbara Lindley and Virginia Wetherall as Dracula's wives.
Remake: PURPLE PLAYHOUSE: Dracula (qv; 1973)
✦✦✦✧

DRACULA
UK/USA, 1979. Dir: John Badham. With: Frank Langella, Laurence Olivier, Donald Pleasence, Kate Nelligan, Trevor Eve, Jan Francis. Mirisch/Universal. Colour.
Langella recreates his Broadway hit role in this overblown version of the much-filmed novel. Director Badham makes it look atmospheric and hauntingly beautiful, helped by a big budget, superb production design and a lush John Williams score, but it's all so *boring*. Pleasence is fine as Dr Seward and Tony Haygarth makes a nicely maniacal Renfield; however, Olivier's performance as Van Helsing sounds more like a homage to Peter Sellers' Inspector Clouseau, Nelligan and Eve fail to bring any spark to their respective roles of Lucy and Jonathan Harker, and the best scene in the movie (and the only one to inspire even a shiver of fear) is when Van Helsing confronts his red-eyed vampiric daughter Mina (Francis) in an old mine shaft.
Remake: NOSFERATU THE VAMPYRE (qv; 1979)
✦✦✧

DRACULA
USA, 1982. With: Frank Langella. Home Box Office. Colour.
Langella recreates his role as the Count for this cable TV restaging of the hit 1977 Broadway revival of the Hamilton Deane and John L. Balderston play, with sets and costumes designed by Edward Gorey.
Remake: BRAM STOKER'S DRACULA (qv; 1992)
✦✦✧

DRACULA
Thailand, circa 1986. Extra Times Promotions. Colour.
Comedy in which constantly cackling vampire 'Dachoora' sleeps in a coffin, wears a metal plate over his heart as protection against wooden stakes, and is quickly revived by a drop of blood.
✦

DRACULA
Cuba, circa 1990. Dir: Lima. Noel Lima.
One minute cartoon in which the Count is more batty than usual.
✦

DRÁCULA
Venezuela, circa 1992. Dir: Humberto Morales. With: Astrid Carolina Herrera, Aroldo Betancourt, Julie Restifo, Erick Noriega, Rodolfo Drago. Marte Television. Colour.
Over-the-top TV movie in which Dracula's coffin appears in a swamp. Soon the Count is vampirising the local women, while a priest and the Commandant of the National Guard battle a growing hoard of zombie-vampires.
✦

DRACULA
Italy, 1994 (1995). Dir: Mario Salieri. With: Selen, Jean-Yves Le Castel, Ron Jeremy, Roberto Malone, Deborah Wells, Joy Karins. 999 Black and Blue Productions. Colour.
Impressive-looking, hour-long hardcore version, shot on video and obviously inspired by the success of Francis Ford Coppola's 1992 adaptation. After an opening sequence set in 1453 Romania in which Vlad Dracul (uncredited non-porn actor Enzo Montefusco) is killed in battle with the Turks and his widow Elisabetta poisons herself after being tortured and raped, the action moves briefly to 1887 London, where Sandy (a reincarnated Elisabetta) and other members of her family travel to Transylvania to claim their inheritance of Dracula's castle. However, a murderous coachman (a sleazy Jeremy!) murders Sandy and her sister, and almost everyone ends up having sex with hypnotic vampires before Vlad finally rises from his tomb at the end. The various sex scenes are unimaginatively staged and lack any sense of eroticism, and it appears that director Salieri was more interested in the story's Gothic trappings than in titillating his audience.
Remake: DRACULA (qv; 1998)
✦

DRACULA
USA, 1998. Dir: Anthony Kane. With: Karen Black. Pandora Pictures/Monarex. Colour.
Written and directed by Kane and filmed in and around Los Angeles and Palm Springs.
Remake: DRAKULA (qv; 1998)
✦

DRACULA A.D. 1972
UK, 1972. Dir: Alan Gibson. With: Christopher Lee, Peter Cushing, Stephanie Beacham, Christopher Neame, Michael Coles, Marsha Hunt, Caroline Munro. Hammer Films/Warner Bros. Colour.
Originally announced as *Dracula Chelsea '72* and filmed under the title *Dracula Today*, the sixth in Hammer's Dracula series updates the Count to 1970s swinging Chelsea. It actually works surprisingly well, thanks to Gibson's stylish direction, good production values and the opportunity, fourteen years after the original, to see Lee and Cushing (as Van Helsing's grandson, Lorrimer) once again pitted against each other. The dialogue and lifestyle of the overage hippies was already dated when the film was released and is simply an embarrassment. However, there's a great pre-credits flashback sequence, solid support by Coles as baffled police inspector Murray and some nice original touches (such as Neame's vampiric Johnny Alucard coming to a nasty end in the shower). Music by San Francisco band Stoneground (who replaced Rod Stewart and The Faces).
Sequel: THE SATANIC RITES OF DRACULA (qv; 1973)
✦✦✦

DRACULA & COMPANY
(Orig: DRACULA TAN EXARCHIA)
Greece, 1983. Dir: Nikos Zervos. With: Kostas Soumas, Yannis Panousis, Vangelis Contronis. Allagi Films. Colour.
Set in Athens, where a reincarnated Dracula and his servant dig up the bodies of famous musicians to construct, Frankenstein-like, a superhuman rock star. The final half of the film apparently consists of the creature's performance.
✦

DRACULA AND SON
(Orig: DRACULA, PÈRE ET FILS. USA: aka DRACULA FATHER & SON)
France, 1976 (1979). Dir: Eduard Molinaro (Édouard Molinaro). With: Christopher Lee, Bernard Menez, Marie-Hélène Breillat, Catherine Breillat, Jean-Claude Dauphin, Anna Gaël. Gaumont International/Production 2000/ Quartet Films/Water Bearer Films. Colour.
Three years after he quit playing the Count for Hammer, Lee appeared as grey-haired vampire Count Poitevin (not Dracula) in this comedy from the director of *La Cage aux Folles* (1978). Fleeing with his son Ferdinand (Menez) from communist Transylvania, the undead aristocrat travels to London and becomes a star of vampire movies, while his son arrives in Paris, where his exists in abject poverty. Molinaro's film was a clever inspiration for *Love at First Bite* (1979), but the re-edited and re-dubbed version originally released in America is a travesty. Loosely based on the novel *Paris-Vampire* by Claude Klotz.
✦✦✧

DRACULA BITES THE BIG APPLE
USA, 1979. Dir: Richard Wenk. With: Peter Lowey. Home Box Office. Colour.
Half-hour comedy short, filmed for $12,000 on 16mm from the director of *Vamp* (1986).
✦✧

DRACULA BLOWS HIS COOL
(Orig: GRAF DRACULA BEIßT JETZT AUCH IN OBERBAYERN/GRAF DRACULA IN OBERBAYERN. UK:

DRACULA SUCKS)
West Germany, 1979 (1982). Dir: Carlo Ombra (Carl Schenkel). With: Johnny Garco (Gianni Garko), Betty Vergès, Bea Fiedler, Giacomo Rizzo, Ralph Walter (Ralf Wolter), Linda Grondier. Lisa/Barthonia Film Production/ Martin Films. Colour.
Silly sex comedy in which a group of *Playboy* models turn Castle Dracula into a hotel and disco — until the Count (Garco, who also appears as Stan, the fashion photographer hero) and his vampire mistress Countess Olivia (Vergès) show up. More knockabout humour than horror, although there are a couple of atmospheric moments amongst the nudity. For some reason, all the terrible disco songs are in English. With Ellen Umlaüf as Ellen Van Helsing. This was originally going to be called *Dracula Sucks* in America until the producers found out about the 1979 porno film with the same title.
✦

DRACULA CINEMATIC SCRAPBOOK
(UK: DRACULA)
USA, 1990 (1991). Dir: Ted Newson. Robert T. Newsom/ Heidelberg Films/Rhino Video. Colour/B&W.
Hour-long video compilation that features all the Universal and Hammer vampire trailers (with behind-the-scenes footage from *Dracula A.D. 1972* [1972], narrated by Orson Welles), plus scenes from *Nosferatu* (1922) and *Uncle Was a Vampire* (1959). Other trailers, presented chronologically, include *Billy the Kid versus Dracula* (1965), *Blacula* (1972), *Blood of Dracula* (1957), *Bram Stoker's Count Dracula* (1970), *Love at First Bite* (1979), *Mark of the Vampire* (1935; in which Lugosi speaks to the audience), *One More Time* (1970; with Christopher Lee), *Plan 9 from Outer Space* (1958), *The Return of Dracula* (1957) and *Vampire Over London* (1952). Rhino has also produced equally fascinating tapes based around Frankenstein and the Wolf Man.
✦✦✦

DRACULA DAY
UK, 1997. Dir: Peter Wells. With: Thane Bettany, Tony Delicata, Caroline McKellar. Peter Wells. Colour.
Twelve minute 16mm short, written and directed by Wells, in which a group of twelve year-old children from the north of England go on a school trip to the town of Whitby to meet Count Dracula.
✦✧

DRACULA DEAD AND LOVING IT
USA, 1995. Dir: Mel Brooks. With: Leslie Nielsen, Peter MacNicol, Steven Weber, Amy Yasbeck, Lysette Anthony, Harvey Korman. Castle Rock Entertainment/Gaumont/ Brooksfilms/Columbia. Colour.
Silly, but often funny and faithful spoof of Francis Ford Coppola's overblown 1992 version. Nielsen stars as a slapstick Count, with MacNicol as a manic Renfield, Anthony as a very sexy Lucy and producer/director/co-writer Brooks doing his usual Jewish *schtik* as Van Helsing. Only Weber disappoints as a low-key Jonathan Harker. The production values are excellent, although this also uses stock footage from *Mutiny on the Bounty* (1962) and Roger Corman's *The Premature Burial* (1962)! With cameos by Clive Revill as a gravedigger and Brooks' wife Anne Bancroft as a gypsy.
✦✦✦

DRACULA EXOTICA
(UK: LOVE AT FIRST GULP)
USA, 1980 (1981). Dir: Warren Evans. With: Jamie Gillis, Samantha Fox, Vanessa Del Rio, Mark Dexter, Erik Edwards, Gordon G. Duvall. Fat Bat Company/ Entertainment Ventures/VCA Pictures. Colour.
Gillis repeats his role as the Count from *Dracula Sucks* (1979) in this vampire movie available in both hard- and softcore versions. This time, cursed by his own remorse to become one of the undead, Dracula falls in love with FIB agent and assassin Sally (Fox) who is the reincarnation of the virgin Surka (also Fox) he raped 400 years before. Pursued by the FIB, Russian spies and a vampirised cop (Dexter), Dracula and Sally finally consummate their passion for each other before both turning into doves and flying off into the sunset! With Del Rio as the Count's undead secretary and Denise Sloan and Dianna Sloan as Dracula's vampire wives.
✦

Veronica Carlson and Christopher Lee in a posed shot from Dracula Has Risen from the Grave *(1968).*

DRACULA HAS RISEN FROM THE GRAVE
UK, 1968. Dir: Freddie Francis. With: Christopher Lee, Rupert Davies, Veronica Carlson, Barbara Ewing, Barry Andrews, Ewan Hooper, Michael Ripper. Hammer Films/ Warner-Pathe. Colour.
The third entry in Hammer's Dracula series and a direct sequel to *Dracula Prince of Darkness* (1965). The overtly religious script by John Elder (Anthony Hinds) has Lee's demonic-looking Count acting as a catalyst when he commands a weak-willed priest (a dubbed Hooper) and others to take revenge on Davies' Catholic Monsignor, who has exorcised Dracula's castle. Director Francis (who replaced Terence Fisher when the latter broke his leg before filming began) wisely keeps the Count in the background and concentrates on the violence and sexuality of the myth. This includes a memorable sequence in which Dracula rips a wooden stake from his bleeding chest when the hero (Andrews) can't finish the required prayer because of his lack of faith!
Sequel: TASTE THE BLOOD OF DRACULA (qv; 1969)
✦✦✧

DRACULA IN THE MOVIES
USA, 1992. Dir: Sandy Oliveri. Film Shows/Goodtimes Video. Colour/B&W.
Accurately billed as 'Highlights of over fifty years of vampire films', and only spoiled by some intrusive captions, this hour-long video compilation includes trailers from *Atom Age Vampire* (1960), *Black Sunday* (1960), *Blacula* (1972), *Blood of Dracula* (1957), *The Brides of Dracula* (1960), *Captain Kronos Vampire Hunter* (1972), *Count Dracula and His Vampire Bride* (1973), *Count Yorga, Vampire* (1970), *The Devil's Wedding Night* (1973), *Dracula* (1931), behind-the-scenes footage of *Dracula A.D. 1972* (1972), *Dracula Has Risen from the Grave* (1968), *Dracula Prince of Darkness* (1965), *Dracula's Daughter* (1936), *The Fearless Vampire Killers* (1966), *Frankenstein's Bloody Terror* (1967), *Horror of Dracula* (1958), *Horroritual* (1972), *House of Dark Shadows* (1970), *House of Dracula* (1945), *House of Frankenstein* (1944), *The Kiss of the Vampire* (1962), *Lust for a Vampire* (1970), Bela Lugosi in specially-shot footage promoting *Mark of the Vampire* (1935), (Abbott and Costello) *Meet Frankenstein* (1948), *Nosferatu* (1922), *Queen of Blood* (1966), *The Return of Dracula* (1957), *The Return of the Vampire* (1943), *Scars of Dracula* (1970), *Son of Dracula* (1943), *Taste the Blood of Dracula* (1969), *The Vampire* (Mexico, 1957), *The Vampire-Beast Craves Blood* (1967), *The Vampire Lovers* (1970) and *The Vampire's Coffin* (1957), plus a 1952 newsreel interview with Lugosi.
✦✦✧

DRACULA PRINCE OF DARKNESS
UK, 1965. Dir: Terence Fisher. With: Christopher Lee, Barbara Shelley, Andrew Keir, Francis Matthews, Suzan Farmer, Charles Tingwell, Thorley Walters. Seven Arts-Hammer Film/Associated British-Pathe. Colour.
It was seven years before Hammer made a direct sequel to their box office hit *Dracula* (this movie begins with a reprise of the closing minutes of the 1958 film), and it became one of the top fifteen commercial releases of 1966. The script by 'John Sansom' (Jimmy Sangster and Anthony Hinds) is not particularly original — on a visit to the Carpathian mountains a group of travellers are forced to spend the night in an eerie castle — and it is left to director Fisher to build the tension slowly (Dracula isn't resurrected until about a third of the way into the film). Once his body has been reconstituted from the blood of a sacrificial victim, Lee doesn't have any dialogue as the Count, but imbues the character with a powerful sense of evil. Cushing's presence as Van Helsing is sorely missed, but Keir gives strong support as the larger-than-life vampire-hunting monk, Father Sandor, and Barbara Shelley makes a demonic creature of the night. It was filmed back-to-back with *Rasputin the Mad Monk* (1965), using many of the same sets and cast members. With Philip Latham as Klove, and George Woodbridge. Cut-out fangs were given away to

male audience members in America. This was novelised by John Burke in 1967 as part of Pan Books' *The Second Hammer Horror Film Omnibus*, and adapted into comic strip format for *The House of Hammer* no.6 (1977), with art by John Bolton. Father Shandor was given his own adventures, also illustrated by Bolton, in three subsequent issues of the magazine.
Sequel: DRACULA HAS RISEN FROM THE GRAVE (qv; 1968)
✦✦✦

DRACULA PRISONER OF FRANKENSTEIN
(Orig: DRACULA CONTRA FRANKENSTEIN/DRACULA CONTRA EL DOCTOR FRANKENSTEIN/DRACULA LE PRISONNIER DE FRANKENSTEIN. USA/UK: THE SCREAMING DEAD)
Spain/France/Liechtenstein, 1972. Dir: Jess (Jesús) Franco. With: Howard Vernon (Mario Lippert), Dennis Price, Genevieve Deloir, Josiane Gibert (Anne Libert), Albert (Alberto) D'Albes, Mary Francis (Paca Gabaldon). Fénix Films/Prodif Ets/Comptoir Français du Film Production/ Interfilme. Colour.
The first of three films by Franco, loosely connected by many of the same characters and actors. Dr Frankenstein (a sick-looking Price, dubbed by a younger voice) and his mute servant Morpho (Luis Barboo) revive a green-faced Dracula (Vernon) so that together with his vampire brides they can create an undead army to conquer the world. Fernando Bilbao plays a Karloff-like Frankenstein Monster, and Dr Seward (D'Albes), a gypsy witch and a mangy werewolf (Brandy) are also involved. This was supposedly a homage to director James Whale, but it is simply more tedious ineptitude from director Franco and another nail in the coffin of Dennis Price's career. It exists in various inept versions, and the English-language print was directed by Richard McNamara. With Britt Nickols (Nichols) as Lady Dracula.
Sequel: THE EROTIC RITES OF FRANKENSTEIN (qv; 1972)
✦

DRACULA RISES FROM THE COFFIN
Republic of Korea, 1982. Dir: Lee Hyoung-Pyo. With: Kang Yong-Suk, Park Yang-Rae. Tai Chang Inc. Colour.
Apparently inspired by Hammer's *The Legend of the 7 Golden Vampires* (1974). Dracula is obsessed with a young student and follows her back to Korea, where he appears at the girl's wedding. However, her husband and a Buddhist monk defeat the Count with some spiritual kung fu.
✦

DRACULA RISING
USA/Bulgaria, 1992. Dir: Fred Gallo. With: Christopher Atkins, Stacey Travis, Doug Wert, Tara McCann, Vessela Karlukovska, Nikolai Sotirov. Pacific Trust/New Horizons. Colour.
Los Angeles art historian Theresa (Travis) travels to a monastery in eastern Europe where she discovers she was burned at the stake 500 years before for being a witch. She once again finds herself caught up in the rivalry between her old lover, Vlad (Atkins) — the son of an undead Vlad the Impaler (Zahari Vatahov) — and the evil Alec (Wert), two monks who are now both vampires. The flashy special effects finale seems out of place. Produced by Roger Corman.
✦✧

THE DRACULA SAGA
(Orig: LA SAGA DE LOS DRÁCULA. USA: SAGA OF THE DRACULAS/THE DRACULA'S SAGA/DRACULA — THE BLOODLINE CONTINUES)
Spain, 1972. Dir: León Klimovsky. With: Tina Sainz, Tony Isbert, Narciso Ibañez Menta, Cristina Suriani, Maria Kosti, Helga Liné (Helga Lina Stern). Profilmes. Colour.
Set in contemporary Hungary, where the Count's pregnant granddaughter, Berta (Sainz), returns to the ancestral castle to meet Dracula (Menta) and her (undead) family. Repelled by the blood she is forced to drink, she attempts to kill the unborn child she is carrying, the last heir to the aristocratic title. An interesting idea, which also features a monstrous cyclopic child and music by J. Sebastian Bach.
✦✧

DRACULA'S DAUGHTER
USA, 1936. Dir: Lambert Hillyer. With: Otto Kruger, Gloria Holden, Marguerite Churchill, Edward Van Sloan, Gilbert Emery, Irving Pichel. Universal. B&W.
It took five years for Universal to get around to producing this direct sequel to *Dracula* (1931), credited to Bram Stoker's story 'Dracula's Guest' but in fact based on an original screenplay by Garrett Fort. The year before it was made, the studio announced Bela Lugosi, Boris Karloff and Colin Clive as the stars, to be directed by James Whale. Although the others dropped out, Lugosi was paid a $4,000 retainer (more than he received for *Dracula*!). Even though he never appeared in the final movie, Lugosi did visit the set for publicity purposes. Screenwriter R.C. Sheriff and director Edward Sutherland were also paid off by the studio before filming commenced. The story begins only moments after the original ends, with the police discovering the body of Renfield and arresting Professor von (*sic*) Helsing (Van Sloan, reprising his role) for murder! It's a great idea, but the film soon begins to drag when the Count's body (an obvious wax figure) is stolen by his daughter, Countess Marya Zaleska (twenty-seven year-old Holden), who wants to escape her vampiric heritage but is forced to drink the blood of young female models. Weak leads Kruger and Churchill replaced Cesar Romero and Jane Wyatt when shooting was delayed, Pichel plays the Countess' macabre servant, Sandor, and there's a great supporting cast (including Nan Grey, Hedda Hopper, E.E. Clive, Billy Bevan, Halliwell Hobbes and Edgar Norton). However, director Hillyer (better known for his Westerns) fails to bring any sparkle to the proceedings, and this remains only an interesting curio. A belated novelisation appeared in 1977 by Carl Dreadstone/E.K. Leyton (Ramsey Campbell), and a juvenile version by Carl R. Green and William R. Sanford (William Reynolds) was published in 1985.
Sequel: SON OF DRACULA (qv; 1943)
✦✦✧

DRACULA'S DOG
(UK: ZOLTAN...HOUND OF DRACULA)
USA, 1977. Dir: Albert Band (Alfredo Antonini). With: Michael Pataki, Reggie Nalder (Alfred Reginald Natzick), José Ferrer, Jan Shutan, Libbie Chase, John Levin. Vic Cinema. Colour.
Directed by producer Charles Band's French-born father, Albert (*I Bury the Living* [1958], etc), this low-budget horror film has a wonderfully silly premise: Dracula's vampire dog and his undead servant Veidt Smit (the creepy looking Nalder) escape from their Transylvanian tomb and travel to modern Los Angeles to find the Count's last living relative, Michael Drake (Pataki). Although scenes of a pack of vampire dogs attacking Drake's all-American family are laughable, much of the photography is too dark and Ferrer's career hits rock-bottom as Van Helsing-type vampire hunter Inspector Branco, this is still an enjoyable time-waster. Ken Johnson wrote the novelisation.
✦✧

DRACULA '79
USA, 1979. Dir: Jeffrey Hayden and Kenneth Johnson. With: Michael Nouri, Carol Baxter, Stephen Johnson, Bever-Leigh Banfield, Antoinette Stella, Mark Montgomery. Universal/NBC-TV. Colour.
One hour compilation of the first four episodes (chapters 6-9) of TV's *Cliffhangers* serial, *The Curse of Dracula*, created by executive producer Kenneth Johnson. Nouri plays an urbane and sophisticated Dracula teaching night classes about European history in San Francisco. Meanwhile, Mary Gibbons (Baxter) and the grandson of Professor Van Helsing (Johnson) attempt to track down the Count's boxes of sacred earth and destroy them. Les Baxter co-composed the music score. *The World of Dracula* (1979) was another compilation from the serial.
Sequel: THE LOVES OF DRACULA (qv; 1979)
✦✧

DRACULA'S GREAT LOVE
(Orig: EL GRAN AMOR DEL CONDE DRACULA. UK: DRACULA'S VIRGIN LOVERS. USA: aka CEMETERY GIRLS/ COUNT DRACULA'S GREAT LOVE/VAMPIRE PLAYGIRLS).

Spain, 1972 (1974). Dir: J. (Javier) Aguirre. With: Paul Naschy (Jacinto Molina), Haydée Politoff, Rossana Yanni (Yanny), Mirta Miller, Vic Winner (Victor Alcazar), Ingrid Garbo. Janus Films/Eva Films/International Amusement Corporation/Motion Picture Marketing. Colour.
Spanish horror star Naschy co-scripted and stars as Dr Wendell Marlow, really Count Dracula, who runs a strange nursing home near his Transylvanian castle and turns a group of unwary travellers into vampires. He falls in love with virgin Karen (Politoff), and wants to use her in an attempt to bring his dead daughter Countess Rhonda back to life. When she refuses, he becomes probably the first Dracula to commit suicide with a stake in the heart!
✦✧

DRACULA'S HAUNTED CASTLE
USA, 1995. Dir: Ray Spencer and Jos Claesen. With: Arthur Mallet. Showscan Productions/New Wave Entertainment. Colour.
After a warning from the Count's butler (Mallet), this novelty short combines Showscan images with motion simulation as it takes the viewer on a high-speed roller-coaster ride tour through the haunted corridors of Dracula's castle, encountering sword-wielding skeletons, ghosts, guillotines and open coffins.
✦✦✦

DRACULA: SOVEREIGN OF THE DAMNED
(Orig: YAMI NO TEIKOKU KYUKETSUKI DRACULA. UK: DRACULA: VAMPIRE EMPEROR OF DARKNESS)
Japan, 1980 (1983). Dir: Minoru Okazaki. Voices: Kenji Utsumi, Hiroko Suzuki, Kazuyuki Sogabe, Yasuo Hisamatsu. Toei Animation Co/TV Asahi/Harmony Gold/Northstar Entertainment. Colour.
Full-length anime made for TV and based on Marvel Comics' *The Tomb of Dracula* series. Set in modern-day London, after Dracula's (Utsumi) half-mortal baby son Janus (Sogabe) is accidentally killed by a Satanist and restored to life by Heaven, the Count loses his evil personality and sets out to rediscover his vampiric side again. This features colourful, if static, animation and a complicated plot for children. The English-language version was written and directed by Robert Barron.
✦✧

DRACULAS RING
Denmark, 1978. Dir: Flemming La Cour. With: Bent Børgesen, Brita Fogsgaard, Søren Steen, Ejner Hans Jensen, Gitte Herman, Mary C. Collieri. Danmarks Radio. Colour.
Seven-part TV mini-series in which three tourists discover Dracula's coffin in Malta. They steal his ring as a souvenir, which results in the moustachioed Count (Børgesen) returning to life and pursuing the perpetrators back home to Denmark. Each episode of this amateurish series apparently features a cameo by a locally famous media personality.
✦

DRACULA SUCKS
(aka DRACULA'S BRIDE/LUST AT FIRST BITE/THIS VAMPIRE SUCKS)
USA, 1979. Dir: Philip Marshak (Philip Morris). With: Jamie Gillis, Annette Haven, John Leslie, Serena, Detlef van Berg (Reggie Nalder/Alfred Reginald Natzick), Kay Parker. First International Pictures/MR Productions/ Kodiak Films. Colour.
All-star (including John Holmes, Paul Thomas, and Seka making her début) porno adaptation of the story, released in both hard- and softcore versions. A virtual scene-for-scene remake of the 1930 movie, the soundtrack borrows snippets of dialogue (including Bela Lugosi's voice) from old radio shows. A pseudonymous Nalder makes a creepy Dr Van Helsing, Gillis is surprisingly effective as Dracula and McGoogle Schlepper (Richard Bulik) is the most manic Renfield since Dwight Frye. *Idol of Fire* was a photo-magazine version published by Dolphin, and a novelisation by Maxwell Kearney appeared in Britain in 1981. Numerous clips from this film turn up in *I'll Suck You Dry* (1982).
Remake: DRACULA (qv; 1982)
✦✧

DRACULA'S WEDDING DAY
USA, 1967. Dir: Mike Jacobson. Film-maker's Cooperative. Tinted.
Silent five minute underground film, shot on 16mm and tinted purple, in which Dracula leads his bride into a cave at sunset.
✦

DRACULA'S WIDOW
USA, 1988 (1989). Dir: Christopher Coppola. With: Sylvia Kristel, Josef Sommer, Lenny von Dohlen, Marc Coppola, Stefan Schnabel, Rachel Jones. De Laurentiis Entertainment/HBO Home Video. Colour.
Any promise of an erotic twist on the legend with the casting of ex-Emmanuelle Kristel is quickly forgotten in this dire vampire movie, which remained on the shelf for a couple of years following the collapse of De Laurentiis' movie empire. Kristel plays Dracula's widow, Vanessa, transported to America in a crate for a vampire exhibition being mounted by a strange young man, Raymond Everett (von Dohlen), in his run-down Hollywood wax museum. Meanwhile, Victor Helsing (Schnabel as the grandson of Dr Van Helsing) is hot on the trail of the vampire. Not very much happens, although Kristel gets to wear some sexy outfits while the film runs its tedious course. Co-writer/director Coppola (the twenty-five year-old nephew of Francis Ford) can't seem to decide if this is meant to be a horror film or a comedy. Instead, it's simply a bore. With George Stover and clips from *Nosferatu* (1922).
✦✧

DRACULA (THE DIRTY OLD MAN)
USA, 1969. Dir: William Edwards. With: Vince Kelley, Ann Hollis, Libby Caculus, Joan Pickett, Bill Whitton, Sue Allen. Whit Boyd Productions. Colour.
Produced, written and directed by Edwards, this silly softcore sex comedy has Count Alucard (Kelley with a funny Lugosi-like accent) and his werewolf/jackalman assistant Dr Irving Jekyll (Whitton, in make-up by Tony Tierney) kidnapping naked virgins and chaining them up in a cave. This was apparently shot as a straight horror movie, then redubbed into a comedy with narration by Ron Scott. It's still pretty terrible.
✦

DRACULA THE SERIES
Luxembourg/Canada, 1990-91. Dir: Allan Eastman, Alan King, Randy Bradshaw, Rene Bonniere, Jeff Woolnough, Michael Sloan and Allan Kroeker. With: Geordie Johnson, Jacob Tierney, Joe Roncetti, Mia Kirshner, Bernard Behrens, Kim Coates. Dracula Productions/Homescreen Entertainment/Cinexus/Famous Players/RHI Entertainment/Blair Entertainment/Action Media Group. Colour.
Short-lived (twenty-one episodes), half-hour syndicated TV series, with Johnson as Alexander Lucard, a contemporary business tycoon who is really a blond Dracula and transforms into a bat. The Count and his zombie slaves are opposed by three typical teens, Max Townsend (Tierney), his brother Chris (Roncetti) and college student Sophie Metternich (Kirshner), along with Uncle Gustav (Behrens), the great-grandson of Professor Van Helsing. With Geraint Wyn Davies (*Forever Knight* [1992-96], etc) as semi-regular Klaus, Gustav's vampiric son.
✦✦

DRACULA UNLEASHED
USA, 1994. David Marsh/Viacom New Media. Colour.
A CD-ROM interactive horror movie for PCs. Using video clips and graphics, you travel through nineteenth century London as Alexander Morris, investigating the strange circumstances surrounding the death of your brother. The clues and objects you gather lead you to Count Dracula and his vampires. In 1996, Jeff Goldblum played Count Dracula opposite Isabella Rossellini's Lady Cadaver in *Goosebumps: Escape from Horrorland*, an interactive computer game from DreamWorks.
✦✦

DRACULA VS. FRANKENSTEIN
(Orig: EL HOMBRE QUE VINO DEL UMMO/DRACULA JAGT

FRANKENSTEIN/LOS MONSTRUOS DEL TERROR. USA: aka ASSIGNMENT TERROR)
Spain/West Germany/Italy, 1969 (1971). Dir: Tulio Demichelli (and Hugo Fregonese). With: Michael Rennie, Karin Dor, Craig Hill, Paul Naschy (Jacinto Molina), Patty Sheppard (Paty Shepard), Angel de Pozo. Producciones Jaime Prades/Eichberg-Film/International Jaguar/ Monarch. Colour.
The sequel to *Nights of the Werewolf* (1968). Michael (*The Day the Earth Stood Still* [1951], etc) Rennie's last film stars him as Dr Odo Varnoff, the leader of a group of aliens who have travelled from their dying planet, Ummo, to resurrect the world's legendary monsters — Count Waldemar Daninsky the werewolf (Naschy, who again wrote the script under his real name), Dracula (de Pozo), Frankenstein's creature (Fernando Bilbao) and the Mummy (Gene Reyes) — and conquer the Earth. Plans to feature a Golem were dropped because of lack of money. In the end, El Hombre Lobo is shot to death by his lover, reanimated lab assistant Maleva (Dor). Filmed in just six days, the whole thing moves at a leaden pace, and Universal learned to stop doing this sort of thing twenty-five years earlier. Despite the title, Dracula and the Frankenstein Monster never actually meet! Argentinean director Fregonese (who was married to actress Faith Domergue) quit towards the end of production and was replaced by Demichelli, while the English-language version was directed by Peter Riethof.
Sequel: THE FURY OF THE WOLFMAN (qv; 1970)
✦

DRACULA VS. FRANKENSTEIN
(aka BLOOD OF FRANKENSTEIN/SATAN'S BLOOD FREAKS/ THEY'RE COMING TO GET YOU. UK: aka REVENGE OF DRACULA)
USA, 1970. Dir: Al Adamson. With: J. Carrol Naish, Lon Chaney, Zandor Vorkov (Roger Engell), Anthony Eisley, Regina Carrol, Greydon Clark. Independent-International. Colour.
Feeble, seventy year-old, wheelchair-bound veteran Naish (*House of Frankenstein* [1944], etc) came out of retirement to play Dr Durea (actually the last Frankenstein) experimenting with blood in an attempt to cure his crippled legs. He is aided by such side-show horrors as Groton (a mute, pathetic-looking Chaney Jr), who is turned by an injection of blood serum into a mad axe-wielding zombie wearing a rubber werewolf mask, and Grazbo the sadistic dwarf (Angelo Rossitto). Russ Tamblyn (as a biker) and Jim Davis are special guest stars. Forrest J Ackerman plays Dr Beaumont, who is crushed to death by a puffy Frankenstein Monster (John Bloom). Former stockbroker Engel (re-named 'Zandor Vorkov' by technical consultant Ackerman) appears as a hammy Dracula who has a ring that zaps people — including ageing hippy hero Mike Howard (Eisley). The electronic equipment was originally created by Ken Strickfaden for *Bride of Frankenstein* (1935). This was another mess from director Adamson, who shot it over a couple of years (originally as *Blood Freaks* and *The Blood Seekers* in 1969). It marked a tragic end to the careers of both Naish and Chaney Jr.
✦

DRACULITO, MON SAIGNEUR
France, 1992. Dir: France-Hélène Joubaud. Colour.
Half-hour children's cartoon TV series (twenty-six episodes). The title translates as 'Dracula, My Lord'.
✦✧

DRAGON AGAINST VAMPIRE
(USA: aka CLOSE ENCOUNTER OF THE VAMPIRE/DRAGON VS VAMPIRE)
Hong Kong, 1985. Dir: Lionel Leung. With: Elton Chong, Carrie Lee, Martin Kim, Robin See, Oliver Cheng, Irene Kong. Saturn Productions. Colour.
Three comic grave robbers meet a vampire and the lone survivor teams up with an old Shaolin wizard who lives in an underground cave. A restaurant owner is decapitated and his daughter possessed, while the vampire has his secrets tattooed on his back. An incoherent mess with music by an uncredited Tangerine Dream!
✦

DRAK PACK
USA, 1980-82. Dir: Chris Cuddington and Steve Lumley. Voices: Jerry Dexter, Bill Callaway, Hans Conried, Chuck McCann, Julie McWhirter, Don Messick. Hanna-Barbera/ CBS-TV. Colour.
Half-hour cartoon TV series in which Drak Jr (Dexter), Frankie Frankenstein (Callaway) and Howler (also Callaway), the teenage sons of famous monsters, become heroes and foil Dr Dred (Conried) and his Organisation of Generally Rotten Endeavours (OGRE), whose members include Mummy Man (McCann), Toad (Messick), Fly (also Messick) and Vampira (McWhirter).
✦✧

DRAKULA
(aka DRAKULA HALÁLA)
Hungary/Austria, 1921. Dir: Lajthay Károly. With: Paul Askenas, Lene Myl (Margit Lux). Magyar Film. B&W.
Despite unsubstantiated rumours of F.W. Murnau's *The Twelfth Hour* (1920), this is now probably the first known movie inspired by Bram Stoker's novel. Directed by Transylvanian-born Károly, it premièred in Vienna in February 1921 (preceding Murnau's *Nosferatu* by more than a year). Closer in theme to *The Cabinet of Dr. Caligari* (1919), this is set in and around an Alpine asylum. While visiting her dying adopted father in the mental hospital, sixteen year-old Mary Land (Myl) meets her old music instructor, a once famous composer who has gone mad and claims to be the immortal Drakula (a demonic-looking Askenas). After being attacked by two patients who think they are doctors and saved from an operation on her eyes, Mary dreams about being abducted by Drakula and taken back to his castle, where she is escorted by his twelve wives to a black magic marriage ceremony. Mary wakes up from her nightmare and, in the end, Drakula is shot dead by another patient. A paperback novelisation, *The Death of Drakula* by Pánczél Lajos, was published in 1924, a year after the movie opened in Hungary. This is now apparently a lost film.
Remake: NOSFERATU (qv; 1922)
✦

DRAKULA
USA/France/Austria, 1998. Dir: Steve Bennett. With: Steve Bennett, Stephen Hubbard, Tevania Tranberg-Bennett, Sarah Beston. Iron Fist Motion Pictures. Colour.
Low-budget horror film produced, written, directed and starring Bennett. Filming started on Halloween 1997 in Boston, Massachusetts. The following year, Twentieth Century Fox announced an animated musical version of *Dracula* to be scripted by Joss Whedon (TV's *Buffy the Vampire Slayer* [1996-], etc).
✦✧

DRAKULA ISTANBUL'DA
Turkey, 1952 (1953). Dir: Mehmet Muhtar. With: Annie Ball, Cahit Irgat, Ayfer Feray, Bülent Oran, Atif Kaptan, Kemal Emin Bara. And Film/Erman Film. B&W.
The first non-Western version of the story is obviously inspired by Hollywood's various adaptations. This is a grim but surprisingly faithful interpretation of Bram Stoker's uncredited novel and *Kazikli Voyvoda* (*The Impaling Voivode*) by Ali Riza Seyfioglu. The familiar prologue sequence is set in 1938 Romania with only a single vampire bride, a hunchback servant and a wall-crawling Count. Instead of London the action then moves to contemporary Istanbul as Dracula (an eerily effective Kaptan with fangs) pursues a dancer (Ball) while others try to stop him. The vampire is finally staked and then beheaded (off-screen).
Remake: MATINEE THEATER: Dracula (qv; 1956)
✦✦

DRAKULITA
Philippines, 1969. Dir: Consuelo P. Osorio. With: Rossana Ortiz, Lito Legaspi, Gina Laforteza, Joseph Gallego, Rebecca Rocha. RJF Brothers. Colour.
Ortiz stars as a vampire in this Filipino haunted house comedy.
✦

DR. BLACK MR. HYDE
(aka THE WATTS MONSTER)

USA, 1975 (1976). Dir: William Crain. With: Bernie Casey, Rosalind Cash, Marie O'Henry, Milt Kogan, Stu Gilliam, Ji-Tu Cumbuka. Charles Walker-Manfred Bernhard Productions/Dimension Pictures. Colour.
In 1972, Christopher Lee announced that a film company wanted him to star opposite Sammy Davis Jr in a blaxploitation movie entitled *Dr Black and Mr White*. This version, from the director of the superior *Blacula* (1972), features Casey as Dr Henry Pride. While working in a free clinic doing kidney research, he develops a drug that changes him into an albino monster who murders Los Angeles prostitutes. He is finally shot off the top of the Watts Towers by the police. Make-up effects created by Stan Winston.
✦✧

DR. CRIPPEN LEBT
West Germany, 1957. Dir: Erich Engels. With: Elisabeth Müller, Peter van Eyck, Fritz Tillmann, Katarina Mayberg, Howard Vernon (Mario Lippert), Inge Meysel. Europa. B&W.
The English murderer is apparently brought back from the dead in this obscure thriller. The title translates as 'Dr Crippen Lives'.
✦✧

DR. DEVIL AND MR. HARE
USA, 1964. Dir: Robert McKimson. Voices: Mel Blanc. Warner Bros. Colour.
Seven minute *Merrie Melodies* cartoon. In an attempt to get rid of the Tasmanian Devil, Bugs Bunny disguises himself as a physician, maternity ward nurse, psychiatrist and mad doctor. As the latter, he creates a Frankenstein Monster which ends up attacking both of them. Bugs sings 'By a Waterfall' from *Footlight Parade* (1933).
Sequel: FALSE HARE (1964)
✦✦✧

DREAM DEMON
UK, 1988. Dir: Harley Cokliss. With: Kathleen Wilhoite, Jemma Redgrave, Timothy Spall, Jimmy Nail, Susan Fleetwood, Mark Greenstreet. Palace Pictures/Filmscreen/ British Screen/Spectrafilm. Colour.
Despite being scripted by Christopher Wicking, this is a ludicrous British attempt to recreate the success of *A Nightmare on Elm Street* (1984) on a minuscule budget. As her marriage to a Falklands War hero approaches, socialite Diana Markham (Redgrave, making her movie début) begins to suffer from bizarre and horrifying nightmares in her London apartment. Meeting American Jenny Hoffman (Wilhoite) doesn't help, while two clichéd tabloid reporters, Peck and Paul (Spall and Nail), are transformed into slimy zombies who still pursue her through her dreams. With a script that is all over the place and a climax that makes no sense, this is a good example of how not to make a horror movie. As a result, Anne Billson's novelisation didn't appear until 1989.
✦

THE DREAM OF A PAINTING
USA, 1914. With: William Francey, Louise Fazenda, Gale Henry. Joker/Universal. B&W.
Silent short in which a man dreams an Ancient Egyptian princess steps out of a painting.
✦

DREAM ON:
Finale With a Vengeance
USA, 1995. Dir: Ron Walotzky. With: Brian Benben, Chris Demetral, Denny Dillon, Wendie Malick, Dorien Wilson, Michael McKean. MTE/St. Clare Entertainment/Home Box Office. Colour.
In this final episode of the half-hour adult comedy/fantasy TV series (1990-96, 118 episodes), created by Marta Kauffman and David Crane and co-executive produced by John Landis, publishing editor Martin Tupper (Benben) is about to re-marry his ex-wife Judith (Malick) when he discovers that her frozen husband Dr Richard Stone may be revived. This includes clips from *House of Frankenstein* (1944), *The Invisible Man* (1933), *The Invisible Woman* (1941) and *Frankenstein* (1931). With special guest stars Tippi Hedren and William Schallert.
✦✦✦

For Richard or for Poorer
USA, 1992. Dir: Peter Baldwin. With: Brian Benben, Chris Demetral, Denny Dillon, Wendie Malick, Dorien Wilson, Jack Blessing. MTE/Kevin Bright Productions/St. Clare Entertainment/Home Box Office. Colour.
Martin attempts to seduce his ex-wife Judith after her husband forgets their wedding anniversary. With numerous clips from *The Wolf Man* (1941), plus *It's a Wonderful Life* (1946) and (Abbott and Costello) *Meet Frankenstein* (1948).
✦✦✧

The Son Also Rises
USA, 1992. Dir: Betty Thomas. With: Brian Benben, Chris Demetral, Denny Dillon, Wendie Malick, Dorien Wilson, Bryn Erin. MTE/Kevin Bright Productions/St. Clare Entertainment/Home Box Office. Colour.
Martin is disturbed when he discovers that his thirteen year-old son Jeremy (Demetral) has some condoms hidden in his room. With numerous clips from *Bride of Frankenstein* (1935) and *Frankenstein* (1931).
✦✦✦✧

DREAMSCAPE
USA, 1983 (1984). Dir: Joseph Ruben. With: Dennis Quaid, Max Von Sydow, Christopher Plummer, Eddie Albert, Kate Capshaw, David Patrick Kelly. Bella Productions/ Zupnik-Curtis Enterprises. Colour.
Inventive $8,000,000 fantasy/adventure, co-scripted by Chuck Russell and directed with style by Ruben, that surprisingly failed at the box office. When scientist Dr Paul Novotny (Von Sydow) invents a machine that can project someone's consciousness into another person's dreams, creepy spy boss Bob Blair (Plummer) decides to use it for his own ends. Likeable psychic Alex Gardner (Quaid) has to enter the nuclear nightmares of the President of the United States (Albert), which include some post-holocaust zombies, to stop hired assassin Tommy Ray Glatman (Kelly), who is also in the dreamscape and has the power to transform into a murderous Snakeman (Larry Cedar). This includes great make-up effects created by Craig Reardon and Greg Cannom, stop-motion effects by James R. Aupperle and visual effects by Peter Kuran. With George Wendt as horror writer Charlie Prince (get it?).
✦✦✦

CARL THEODOR DREYER (1889-1968)
Danish writer, producer and director of the dream-like *Vampyr* (1931-32). His *Day of Wrath* (1943), about an old woman accused of being a witch, is much better.

DR. FRANKENSTEIN ON CAMPUS
(UK: FRANKENSTEIN ON CAMPUS)
Canada, 1970. Dir: Gil Taylor. With: Robin Ward, Kathleen Sawyer, Austin Willis, Sean Sullivan, Ty Haller, Tony Moffat-Lynch. Astral Films/Agincourt/Medford. Colour.
Possibly filmed as early as 1967 under the title *Flick*. With the help of a mysterious professor (Sullivan), Viktor Frankenstein IV (Ward) creates lethal mind-control tablets which he uses to revenge himself on those students who tormented him. In the end, Viktor is revealed to be an artificial creature.
✦✧

DR. HACKENSTEIN
USA, 1987 (1989). Dir: Richard Clark. With: David Muir, Stacey Travis, Catherine Davis Cox, Dyanne DiRosario, John Alexis, William Schreiner. Marketing Media/Vista Street Films. Colour.
Gory, direct-to-video horror comedy. Set in 1912, Dr Elliott Hackenstein (Muir) keeps the head of his decapitated wife (Sylvia Lee Baker) alive. When three young women accidentally run their car off the road, they take refuge in his house over night and each just happens to have the parts he needs to complete his experiments

and create a new body for his wife. With cameo appearances by Phyllis Diller and the husband and wife team of Logan and Anne Ramsey (in one of her last performances), who turn up as comic grave robbers.
✦✧

DR. HECKYL & MR. HYPE

USA, 1980 (1981). Dir: Charles B. Griffith. With: Oliver Reed, Sunny Johnson, Maia Danziger, Virgil Frye, Mel Welles (Ernst von Theumer), Jackie Coogan. Cannon Films. Colour.
Unfunny horror comedy ('with apologies to Robert Louis Stevenson') written and directed by Griffith with a leaden touch. Grotesque chiropodist Dr Henry Heckyl (Reed in make-up by Steve Neill) uses a slimming potion created by Dr Vince Hinkle (Welles) to transform himself into handsome lady killer (literally!) Mr Hype. However, the results are only temporary. With Corinne Calvet, Dick Miller and Lucretia Love.
✦

DRILLER

USA, 1984 (1985). Dir: Joyce James. With: Taija Rae, Dick Howard, George Payne, Renee Summers, Peter Jay, Angelique. Abelard Productions/VCA Pictures. Colour.
Hardcore horror spoof of Michael Jackson's *Thriller* (1983), featuring singing/dancing rock star Mr J as a werewolf monster (Carson Pyle) who emerges from the TV set of the teenage Louisa (Rae) and has sex using his corkscrew penis. In the end, it all turns out to have been a dream about to come true. This also includes Quazi-modo, a Peter Lorre-voiced hunchback, some ghoul girls and a zombie orgy. From the producer of *Cafe Flesh* (1982).
✦

DRIVE-IN MADNESS!

(aka SCREEN SCARIES)
USA, 1987. Dir: Tim Ferrante. With: James Karen, Sam Sherman, Forrest J Ackerman, Bobbie Bresse, Linnea Quigley, George A. Romero. Imagine. Colour/B&W.
Video compilation of exploitation trailers that includes *Horror of the Blood Monsters* (1970, narrated by Brother Theodore), *Night of the Living Dead* (1968), AIP's *Queen of Blood/Blood Bath* (1966) double-bill and *Vampyres* (1974), along with interviews with Tom Savini, John Russo and Russell Steiner, amongst others. This was also released in a cut-down version on Simitar Video.
✦✦✦

DRIVER DUG, FALDER RIM

Denmark, 1984 (1985). Dir: Irene Werner Stage. With: Mika Heilman, Aslak Stage, Frits Helmuth, Poul Dissing, Georgios Marinos, Merete Axelberg. Statens Filmcentral. Colour.
Forty-two minute short, shot on 16mm. In this fairy-tale fantasy, a young girl (Heilman) encounters a boy (Stage) who can transform into a wolf. After they compete with each other in an archery competition, she uses the bow she wins to kill him. Narrated by Vibeke Trokmarr.
✦

DR. JECKEL & MS. HIDE

(aka THE STRANGE CASE OF DR. JECKEL & MS. HIDE)
USA, 1990. Dir: Michael Craig. With: Ashlyn Gere, Champagne, Madison (Madison Stone), Celia Young, Mike Horner, Peter North. Las Vegas Video. Colour.
Hardcore version of Stevenson's story, in which Dr Jeckel (Horner) invents a formula that will halt the effects of ageing. Unfortunately, it has a side effect that results in him periodically changing into Ms Hide (Gere), with all the predictable results.
✦

DR. JEKYL AND MR. ZIP

(aka HAPPY HOOLIGAN IN DR. JEKYL AND MR. ZIP)
USA, 1920. Dir: Bill (William C.) Nolan. International Film Services/Goldwyn-Bray Comic. B&W.
Six minute silent cartoon featuring comic strip hobo Happy Hooligan, created by Burr Opper. Animated by Walter Lantz.
Sequel: HAPPY HOOLIGAN IN OIL (1920)
✦

DR. JEKYLL AND MR. HYDE

(aka THE MODERN DR. JEKYLL)
USA, 1908. Dir: Col. William N. Selig. Selig Polyscope Company. B&W.
Possibly the earliest film adaptation of Robert Louis Stevenson's 1886 novella *Strange Case of Dr. Jekyll and Mr. Hyde* was made in 1897. However, its existence can no longer be confirmed, making this now apparently lost thirteen minute silent short the first known movie version and the first American horror film. Selig based his one-reel condensation on the 1897 play by Luella Forepaugh and George F. Fish, and the film is divided into four acts, which include the rising and falling of a theatre curtain and long shots of the stage. After Dr Jekyll (an anonymous actor) transforms into the monstrous Mr Hyde, he attacks the vicar's daughter Alice, kills her father, and in the form of Hyde finally takes his and Jekyll's lives with poison. There is also some question as to whether *The Modern Dr. Jekyll* was a 1909 re-release title for this film, or was a new comedic version also made by Selig.
Remake: DR. JEKYLL AND MR. HYDE (qv; 1909)
✦

DR. JEKYLL AND MR. HYDE

(Orig: DEN SKÆBNESVANGRE OPFINDELSE. USA: aka JEKYLL AND HYDE)
Denmark, 1909 (1910). Dir: August Blom. With: Alwin Neuss, Emilie Sannom, Holger Pedersen, Ella La Cour, Victor Fabian, Rigmor Jerichau. Nordisk Films Kompagni/Great Northern Film Company. B&W.
Fairly faithful, seventeen minute silent version of Stevenson's story, starring German-born actor Neuss as Dr Jekyll and the bestial Mr Hyde. The doctor also turns his old servant into a monkey-like creature. In the end, Jekyll is shot and dies in the arms of his fiancée, Maud, after taking the antidote. It all turns out to have been a dream. Now apparently a lost film, the original title translates as 'The Fatal Invention'.
Remake: THE DUALITY OF MAN (qv; 1910)
✦

DR. JEKYLL AND MR. HYDE

USA, 1912. Dir: Lucius Henderson. With: James Cruze, Marguerite Snow, Harry Benham. Thanhouser Film Corporation. B&W.
Fifteen minute silent short filmed in New Rochelle, New York, and based on Thomas Russell Sullivan's 1887 stage version of Robert Louis Stevenson's story starring Richard Mansfield. Future director Cruze appears as Dr Jekyll opposite his wife, Snow, who is billed as the 'Minister's Daughter'. After turning into a curly-haired Hyde (apparently also sometimes played by Benham), he attacks his fiancée and her father (Benham again). Discovering that he has used the last of his potion and will remain as Hyde forever, he takes poison and his body is discovered in its transformed state.
Remake: DR. JEKYLL AND MR. HYDE (qv; 1913, IMP/Universal)
✦✧

DR. JEKYLL AND MR. HYDE

USA, 1913. Dir: Herbert Brenon (and King Baggot). With: King Baggot, Jane Gail, Matt Snyder, Howard Crampton, William Sorelle. Independent Moving Picture Company/Universal. B&W.
Thirty-three minute silent adaptation of Stevenson's story, apparently co-directed by Baggot, who was Universal's top box office star of the year. When he runs out of the chemicals he needs to change back into Jekyll (Baggot), Hyde is discovered dead on the floor of his laboratory. Removing the blanket that covers his body, Alice (Gail) reveals the corpse of her beloved doctor. The first of three versions made in 1913, this was probably re-released by Universal in 1915 and formed the basis of the 1932 comedy short *Dr. Jekyll's Hide*.
Remake: DR. JEKYLL AND MR. HYDE (qv; 1913, Kineto-Kinemacolor)
✦✧

Brandon Hurst plots with John Barrymore in Dr. Jekyll and Mr. Hyde *(1920).*

DR. JEKYLL AND MR. HYDE
UK, 1913. Kineto-Kinemacolor Company. Colour.
Rarely screened half-hour silent adaptation of Robert Louis Stevenson's story. This was apparently the first-ever horror film made in colour (not tinted by hand), using a system of two interlocked double-speed projectors fitted with revolving red and green filters.
Remake: DR. JEKYLL AND MR. HYDE (qv; 1913, Vitascope)
✦

DR. JEKYLL AND MR. HYDE
USA, 1913. Dir: Max Mack. With: Albert Basserman. Vitascope. B&W.
The third silent version of Stevenson's story filmed in 1913.
Remake: DR. JEKYLL AND MR. HYDE (qv; 1914)
✦

DR. JEKYLL AND MR. HYDE
USA, 1914. Starlight. B&W.
Misguided silent comedy version of Robert Louis Stevenson's story. Apparently the critical response was so poor that it was withdrawn from theatres after only two performances.
Remake: EL SELTSAMER FALL (qv; 1914)
✦

DR. JEKYLL AND MR. HYDE
USA, 1920. With: Hank Mann. Arrow Film Corporation. B&W.
Another failed attempt to create a silent comedy out of Stevenson's story, with Mann as both Jekyll and Hyde. It was reportedly only shown three times before being withdrawn from distribution.
Remake: WHEN QUACKEL DID HYDE (qv; 1920)
✦

DR. JEKYLL AND MR. HYDE
USA, 1920. Dir: John S. Robertson. With: John Barrymore, Brandon Hurst, Martha Mansfield, Charles Lane, Cecil Clovelly, Nita Naldi. Famous Players-Lasky Corporation/ Paramount-Artcraft. Tinted.
The first great American horror movie, based on Robert Louis Stevenson's 1886 novella *Strange Case of Dr. Jekyll and Mr. Hyde*, and also on the Richard Mansfield play and Oscar Wilde's 1891 novel *The Picture of Dorian Gray*. Thirty-eight year-old Barrymore's maniacally leering Hyde grows progressively more hideous with each transformation. The actor, who was at the height of his fame, transformed his Great Profile by physically distorting his features, the use of camera dissolves and a minimum of make-up. In a remarkable climactic scene, Barrymore portrays a man-sized spider with Hyde's head that crawls across Jekyll's bed in a bizarre waking nightmare. In the end, Jekyll swallows poison as he is changing. When this was later reissued as a half-hour abridgement with narration for the TV series *Silents Please* (aka *The History of the Motion Pictures*) both of the female lead characters were renamed.
Remake: DR. JEKYLL AND MR. HYDE (qv; 1920, Louis B. Mayer/Pioneer)
✦✦✦✧

DR. JEKYLL AND MR. HYDE
USA, 1920. (Dir: Charles J. Hayden.) With: Sheldon Lewis, Alexander Shannon, Dora Mills Adams, Gladys Field, Harold Forshay, Leslie Austin. Louis B. Mayer Productions/Pioneer Film Corporation. B&W.
Producer Mayer's attempt to cash-in on Paramount's classic adaptation of the Stevenson story, filmed the same year starring John Barrymore. This shoddy forty minute silent version, set in modern day New York, stars silent serial star Lewis as Dr Jekyll and a purse-snatching Mr Hyde. Finally condemned to the electric chair for his crimes, Jekyll awakens to discover that it was all a dream. Writer/director Hayden had his name removed from the credits, while Lewis recreated his role in a 1929 sound short.
Remake: DR. PYCKLE AND MR. PRIDE (qv; 1925)
✦

DR. JEKYLL AND MR. HYDE
USA, 1925. Standard Cinema Corporation. B&W.

Apparently another silent comedy version of Robert Louis Stevenson's *Strange Case of Dr. Jekyll and Mr. Hyde*. This could be the same films as Standard's other spoof, *Dr. Pyckle and Mr. Pride*, made the same year.
Remake: DR. JEKYLL AND MR. HYDE (qv; 1929)
✦

DR. JEKYLL AND MR. HYDE
USA, 1929. With: Sheldon Lewis. B&W.
Early sound short based on the Stevenson story, with Lewis recreating his portrayal of Jekyll and Hyde from the 1920 Pioneer feature.
Remake: DR. JEKYLL AND MR. HYDE (qv; 1931)
✦

DR. JEKYLL AND MR. HYDE
USA, 1931 (1932). Dir: Rouben Mamoulian. With: Fredric March, Miriam Hopkins, Rose Hobart, Holmes Herbert, Halliwell Hobbes, Edgar Norton. Paramount. B&W.
Originally to have starred Irving Pichel in the title roles, March won the Academy Award for Best Actor for his dual portrayal of Jekyll and Hyde. The Neanderthal-like Mr Hyde took make-up artist Wally Westmore three hours to create, and Armenian-born director Mamoulian achieved the stunning transformations through the use of coloured filters and light sensitive make-up. Hyde becomes progressively more bestial and decadent, but the scene of him trampling a small child apparently only appears in a specially posed publicity still and was never filmed. According to some references, R.L. Stevenson, the nephew of Robert Louis Stevenson, appears in a small uncredited role. A shortened version of the film was re-issued in 1935 (after the introduction of Will Hays' Motion Picture Production Code two years earlier), and all prints were withdrawn when MGM bought up the rights in 1941 so that it wouldn't compete with their remake. It was finally rediscovered in the early 1970s and almost twenty minutes of missing footage has now been restored. March went on to recreate his roles on radio's *The Theatre Guild on the Air* in 1950. The movie was recreated with frame blow-ups in a volume of Richard J. Anobile's *The Film Classics Library* in the 1970s.
Remake: DR. JEKYLL AND MR. HYDE (qv; 1941)
✦✦✦✦✦

DR. JEKYLL AND MR. HYDE
USA, 1941. Dir: Victor Fleming. With: Spencer Tracy, Ingrid Bergman, Lana Turner, Donald Crisp, Ian Hunter, Barton MacLane. Metro-Goldwyn-Mayer. B&W.
MGM bought up the rights to the 1931 Paramount version and removed it from distribution for nearly three decades. Tracy (in make-up created by Jack Dawn) replaced Robert Donat before production began in the title roles, and gives an excellent performance in this otherwise dark, psychological version of Robert Louis Stevenson's classic tale. Although originally cast to type as Beatrix and Ivy respectively, Bergman and Turner decided to swap roles to great effect. This includes an incredibly Freudian dream sequence, impressive transformation effects (sixty seconds took five hours to film) and a great supporting cast, including C. Aubrey Smith, Billy Bevan, Frederic Warlock and Forrester Harvey. Tracy recreated his roles on *Lux Radio Theatre* the same year. Although a movie tie-in paperback of Stevenson's short novel was published in 1941, the film was also belatedly novelised by Horace J. Elias in 1974.
Remake: SUSPENSE: Dr. Jekyll and Mr. Hyde (qv; 1949)
✦✦✦✧

DR. JEKYLL AND MR. HYDE
UK/USA, 1973. Dir: David Winters (David Weizer). With: Kirk Douglas, Susan George, Susan Hampshire, Stanley Holloway, Donald Pleasence, Michael Redgrave. Timex/ Winters-Rosen Productions/NBC-TV. Colour.
All-singing and dancing shot-on-video TV movie of Robert Louis Stevenson's story, scored by Lionel Bart, Mel Mandell and Norman Sachs. Douglas is surprisingly effective in the dual musical roles. In 1976, comedian Peter Cook announced *Dr. Jekyll and Mrs. Hyde*.
Remake: THE EROTIC DR. JEKYLL (qv; 1975)
✦✦✧

Fredric March as the latter in Dr. Jekyll and Mr. Hyde *(1931).*

DR. JEKYLL AND MR. HYDE
(USA: MYSTERY!: DR. JEKYLL AND MR. HYDE)
UK, 1980. Dir: Alastair Reid. With: David Hemmings, Lisa Harrow, Ian Bannen, Clive Swift, Diana Dors, Leo McKern. BBC-TV. Colour.
Uninspired TV movie, based on the story by Robert Louis Stevenson and shot on videotape. Hemmings stars as the doctor experimenting with a potion that splits his dual nature. With a young Toyah Wilcox as Janet, the maid.
Remake: DR. JEKYLL AND MR. HYDE (qv; 1986)
✦✦

DR. JEKYLL AND MR HYDE
Australia, 1986. Dir: Warwick Gilbert and Geoff Collins. Voices: Max Meldrum, David Nettheim, John Ewart, Carol Adams, Simeon Hawkins, Philip Hinton. Burbank Films. Colour.
Fifty minute children's cartoon that takes some minor liberties with Stevenson's story. However, it still has some effective moments, and is notable for having two different actors voice Jekyll and Hyde (Meldrum and Nettheim, respectively).
Remake: STRANNAYAR ISTORIYAR DOKTORA DZEHEKILA I MISTERA KHAIDA (qv; 1986)
✦✧

DR. JEKYLL AND MR. HYDE DONE TO A FRAZZLE
USA, 1914. With: Charlie De Forrest. Crystal-Superba/ Warner Features/Lubin. B&W.
Fifteen minute silent comedy based on Robert Louis Stevenson's story, with De Forrest playing both Jekyll and Hyde.
Remake: DR. JEKYLL AND MR. HYDE (qv; 1920, Arrow Film Corporation)
✦

DR. JEKYLL AND MR. MOUSE
USA, 1947. Dir: William Hanna and Joseph Barbera. Metro-Goldwyn-Mayer. Colour.
Eight minute *Tom and Jerry* cartoon, nominated for an Academy Award, in which Jerry tries to poison Tom and instead creates a mouse with super-strength. When the cat tries the potion on himself, he shrinks down to miniature proportions.
Sequel: SALT WATER TABBY (1947)
✦✦

DR. JEKYLL AND MS. HYDE
Canada/USA, 1995. Dir: David Price. With: Sean Young, Tim Daly, Lysette Anthony, Harvey Fierstein, Stephen Tobolowsky, Jeremy Piven. Savoy Pictures/Rastar/Leider-Shapiro. Colour.
Tasteless, misogynistic comedy misfire from director Price, 'suggested' by Stevenson's novel. Dr Jekyll's great-grandson, Dr Richard Jacks (Daly), works for a perfume company and inherits his ancestor's notebooks. Combining Jekyll's research with his own formulas for a perfume fragrance, Jacks drinks the potion and periodically transforms (thanks to Kevin Yagher's make-up and visual effects by Dream Quest Images) into his alter-ego, the charming and ambitious Helen Hyde (Young). With time rapidly running out, Jacks must find an antidote to prevent Helen from possessing his body forever, and convince his girlfriend Sarah (Anthony) that he's not actually a cross-dresser. Despite extensive re-editing, this is still not very funny. Most of Robert Wuhl's performance ended up on the cutting room floor. It includes clips from Barrymore's *Dr. Jekyll and Mr. Hyde* (1920) on TV.
✦

DR. JEKYLL & SISTER HYDE
UK, 1971. Dir: Roy Ward Baker. With: Ralph Bates, Martine Beswick (Martine Beswicke), Gerald Sim, Lewis Fiander, Susan Brodrick, Dorothy Alison. Hammer Films/ EMI Film Productions. Colour.
Hammer's third variation on Stevenson's story (following *The Ugly Duckling* [1959] and *The Two Faces of Dr. Jekyll* [1960]) is one of the studio's best latter efforts, thanks to an inventive twist by screenwriter Brian Clemens (TV's *The Avengers* [1961-69], etc). This time, Dr Henry Jekyll (Bates) turns into a female Hyde (Beswick), who

David Hemmings as the former in TV's Dr. Jekyll and Mr. Hyde *(1980).*

becomes Jack the Ripper to obtain female hormones to continue the experiments. Grave robbers Burke and Hare (Ivor Dean and Tony Calvin) are also thrown in for good measure. Always-dependable director Baker handles the killings effectively, and there's some sly humour (Jekyll unconsciously making advances to Hyde's boyfriend) and atmospheric fog-shrouded alleyways. With Paul Whitsun-Jones, Philip Madoc and Virginia Wetherell. American posters included a warning to parents.
Remake: EL HOMBRE Y LA BESTIA (qv; 1972)
✦✦✦

DR. JEKYLL AND THE WEREWOLF
(Orig: DOCTOR JEKYLL Y EL HOMBRE LOBO)
Spain, 1971 (1972). Dir: Leon Kaminsky (León Klimovsky). With: Paul Naschy (Jacinto Molina), Shirley Corrigan, Jack Taylor (George Brown Randall/Grek Martin), Marta (Mirta) Miller, Barta Barri, Luis Induñi. Filmaco/Arturo Gonzalez/Briteway Associates/International Cine Film Corporation. Colour.
Sixth in the series and the sequel to *The Werewolf vs. the Vampire Woman* (1970). El Hombre Lobo Waldemar Daninsky (Naschy) rescues a young woman, Justine (Corrigan), from attackers and discovers she is in love with the grandson of Dr Jekyll (Taylor). The young doctor has rediscovered his ancestor's formula and uses it on Daninsky to finally cure his affliction. Unfortunately, the doctor's jealous assistant Sandra (Miller) increases the dosage and turns the wolfman into a monstrous new version of Mr Hyde! Originally filmed in 70mm. Announced in 1972, *A Study in Identity*, which was set to pit Sherlock Holmes against a killer who used Dr Jekyll's formula, was another unfilmed project.
Sequel: CURSE OF THE DEVIL (qv; 1973)
✦✧

DR. JEKYLL LIKES 'EM HOT
(Orig: IL DOTTORE JEKILL JR./DOTTOR JEKYLL E IL GENTILE SIGNORA)
Italy, 1978 (1979). Dir: Steno (Stefano Vanzina). With: Paolo Villaggio, Edwige Fenech, Gianrico Tedeschi, Gordon Mitchell, Paolo Paoloni. Koral-Medusa/Medusa Distribuzione. Colour.
This crazy sex comedy from veteran director Steno has the grandson of Dr Jekyll (Villaggio) working for an evil multi-national corporation (run by Mitchell) and discovering his ancestor's serum in the basement of a London townhouse. When his employers decide to use the Queen of England for an advertising campaign, the young doctor drinks his grandfather's concoction. However, the potion has gone stale, and instead of turning evil he becomes mankind's benefactor. In the downbeat ending the villains win.
✦✧

DR. JEKYLL'S DUNGEON OF DEATH
USA, 1979 (1982). Dir: James Wood. With: James Mathers, John Kearney, Dawn Carver Kelly, Nadine Kalmes, Jake Pearson, Tom Nicholson. Rochelle Productions/Group One International. Colour.
Scripted by star Mathers and supposedly based on Robert Louis Stevenson's story! Along with his lobotomised sister Hilda (Kalmes) and moronic assistant Boris (Pearson), Dr Henry Jekyll (Mathers, who seems to think he's Orson Welles), the sadistic great-grandson of Dr Jekyll, tests out an aggression serum that turns his subjects into killing machines. This no-budget production, filmed in Nevada and supposedly set in 1958 San Francisco, is padded out with interminable footage of violent martial arts fights. In the end, Jekyll goes mad and everyone else ends up dead. You can blame the awful performances, tedious direction and dark photography on editor/photographer/producer/director Wood.
✦

DR. JEKYLL'S HIDE
USA, 1932. Dir: Albert De Mond. Snappy/Universal. B&W.
Comedy short made up of footage from the studio's 1913 version of *Dr. Jekyll and Mr. Hyde* starring King Baggot, released to capitalise on the Paramount version.
✦

DR. JERKYL'S HIDE
USA, 1954. Dir: Friz (Isadore) Freleng. Voices: Mel Blanc, Stan Freberg. Warner Bros. Colour.
Seven minute *Looney Tunes* cartoon, and a follow up to *Tree for Two* (1952) with dogs Alfie (aka Spike) and Chester picking on Sylvester the cat. However, Sylvester has just swallowed Dr Jekyll's formula and periodically turns into a sabre-toothed monster whenever he is alone with Alfie. The first in a trio of *Jekyll and Hyde* cartoons from director Freleng.
Sequel: BY WORD OF MOUSE (1954)
✦✦✧

DR. LOVE AND HIS HOUSE OF PERVERSIONS
(aka DR. LOVE).
USA, 1978. Dir: Robert Michaels. With: Bobby Astyr, Mary Stuart, Samantha Fox, Margo Barnett, Mark Anthony, Susie Gold. VCA Pictures. Colour.
Hardcore comedy in which frigidity expert Dr Franken Schlong (Astyr) creates a well-endowed monster in his laboratory with the help of a female assistant. Finally, the monster blows up and the film ends with the caption 'To be continued'.
✦

DROOPY MASTER DETECTIVE:
Queen of the Mutant Weirdo Vampires
USA/Philippines/Australia, 1993. Dir: Joanna Romersa

and Ray Patterson. Voices: Charlie Adler, Teresa Ganzel, William Callaway, Don Messick, Frank Welker. Hanna-Barbera Cartoons/Turner Entertainment/Fox Kids Network. Colour.
Cartoon TV series (1993-94, thirteen episodes) featuring Tex Avery's dour dog detective (Messick) and his son Dripple (Adler) investigating bizarre crimes. In this seven minute episode, they travel to Transylvania to discover who is trying to kill the star of the eponymous 'B' movie musical. The half-hour show also features the adventures of Screwball Squirrell (also Adler). Additional guest voices in the series include Rene Auberjonois, Hamilton Camp, Nancy Cartwright, Bud Cort, Jim Cummings, Tim Curry, June Foray, Phil Hartman, Tony Jay, Arte Johnson, Kenneth Mars, Alan Oppenheimer, Gary Owens, Clive Revill, Sally Struthers and Paul Winchell. Executive produced by Joseph Barbera.
✦✧

DR. ORLOFF'S MONSTER

(Orig: EL SECRETO DEL DR. ORLOFF)
Spain, 1964. Dir: Jess Frank (Jesús Franco). With: Agnès Spaak, Joseph Raven (José Rubio), Perla Cristal, Patrick Long (Pastor Serrador), Hugh White (Hugo Blanco), Mike Arnold (Marcelo Arroita Jáuregui). Leo Films/Nueva Films/American International. B&W.
Franco's first semi-sequel to *The Awful Dr. Orlof* (1961). Dr Conrad Fisherman (Arnold), a mad disciple of Dr Orloff, kills and then transforms the corpse of his adulterous brother Andros (White) into a radio-controlled zombie. Using supersonic beams, the doctor orders the creature to destroy his unfaithful wife Inglud (Cristal) and various strippers. The director has a cameo playing the piano in a nightclub and is also credited with writing the novel under his pen name 'David Khunne'. In France, Italy and West Germany this was released as a Dr Jekyll movie!
Sequel: THE DIABOLICAL DR. Z (1965)
✦

DR. PYCKLE AND MR. PRIDE

USA, 1925. Dir: Joe Rock. With: Stan Laurel. Standard Cinema Corporation/FBO. B&W.
Twenty minute silent comedy in which Stan Laurel spoofs John Barrymore's version of *Dr. Jekyll and Mr. Hyde* (1920). Laurel's Mr Pride is a mischievous joker who tweaks noses and kicks innocent bystanders. Filmed on the same set as the Lon Chaney Sr version of *The Hunchback of Notre Dame* (1923).
Remake: DR. JEKYLL AND MR. HYDE (qv; 1925)
✦✧

DR. SATAN

(aka EL DOCTOR SATAN)
Mexico, 1966. Dir: Miguel Morayta. With: Joaquin Cordero, Alma Delia Fuentes, José Galvez, Judith Azcarraga, Gina Romano, Carlos Agosti. Producciones Espada/Pelicula/Clasa-Mohme. B&W.
While plotting to take over the world, the glowing-eyed Dr Satan (Cordero) revives a trio of zombie slaves who sleep in coffins, keeps women chained up in a cave, and conjures up an impressive winged devil in a cemetery.
Sequel: DR. SATAN Y LA MAGIA NEGRA (qv; 1967)
✦✧

DR. SATAN Y LA MAGIA NEGRA

Mexico, 1967. Dir: Rogelio A. Gonzalez Jr. With: Joaquin Cordero, Sonia Furio, Noe Murayama, Aurora Clavel, Luz Ma. (Maria) Aguilar, Carlos Agosti. Producciones Espada/Bruckner. Colour.
Attempting to discover a formula for transforming base metals into gold, the caped Dr Satan (Cordero) and his female zombies become involved with a vampire (Murayama). With wrestlers Nathanael Leon 'Frankenstein' and Guillermo Hernández 'Lobo Negro'.
✦✧

DR. SEXUAL AND MR. HYDE

USA, 1971. Dir: Anthony Brzezinski. With: Cindy Hopkins. Colour.
Hardcore version filmed on 16mm, in which an old doctor is transformed into a young stud. Written, directed and produced by Brzezinski, who as a teenager made an amateur film entitled *The Mysterious Dr. Jekyll* in the early 1960s. In 1972, *Dr. Jekyll and Miss Hyde, Dr. Jekyll and Mrs Hyde, Dr. Jekyll and Mistress Hyde* and the Italian *The Niece of Dr. Jekyll* were all announced but never made. *Naughty Dr. Jekyll* (aka *Dirty Dr. Jekyll*) was announced the following year, but again it was never produced.
Remake: THE MAN WITH 2 HEADS (qv; 1971)
✦

DR. SHRINKER:
King Kong

USA, 1976. Dir: Jack Regas. With: Jay Robinson, Billy Barty, Ted Eccles, Susan Lawrence, Jeff McCay. Sid and Marty Krofft/ABC-TV. Colour.
Fifteen minute segment (sixteen episodes), broadcast as part of *The Krofft Supershow* (1976-77), about three teenagers who are marooned on a Pacific island and shrunk down to miniature size by the eponymous mad scientist (Robinson) and his assistant Hugo (Barty). In this episode, Dr. Shrinker sends out a monkey to capture Brad (Eccles), B.J. (Lawrence) and Gordie (McCay), but the ape helps the shrinkies to escape.
✦

DR. STRANGE

USA, 1978. Dir: Philip DeGuere. With: Peter Hooten, Clyde Kusatsu, Jessica Walter, Eddie Benton, Philip Sterling, John Mills. Universal/CBS-TV. Colour.
Terrible TV pilot movie, based on the Marvel Comics character. Sceptical young psychiatrist Dr Stephen Strange (a wooden Hooten) is chosen by ageing sorcerer Lindmer (veteran Mills in one of his most embarrassing roles) to carry on the battle against evil through the use of magic. Walter has some fun as their adversary, Morgan LeFay, who has been granted power over men's souls. With Michael Ansara and clips from (Abbott and Costello) *Meet Frankenstein* (1948) on TV. Stan Lee was a consultant.
✦

DR. TERROR'S GALLERY OF HORRORS

(aka ALIEN MASSACRE/THE BLOOD SUCKERS/GALLERY OF HORROR/RETURN FROM THE PAST)
USA, 1966 (1967). Dir: David L. Hewitt. With: Lon Chaney, John Carradine, Rochelle Hudson, Roger Gentry, Ron Doyle, Karen Joy. Borealis Enterprises/Dorad Corporation/American General Pictures. Colour.
Inept five-part horror anthology, shot on cardboard sets and featuring the same small group of performers, plus stock footage from various AIP Poe movies. Carradine introduces the segments and plays seventeenth century warlock Tristram Halbin, whose mysterious timepiece is discovered by a writer and his wife in 'The Witches (*sic*) Clock'. A series of baffling murders in turn-of-the-century London are blamed on the undead in 'King Vampire'; a dead man (Vic McGee) returns from the tomb to revenge himself on his unfaithful wife and assistant in 'Monster Raid'; in 'The Spark of Life', set in Scotland, poor old Chaney Jr plays Dr Mendell (he still had worse roles to come), a contemporary of Dr Frankenstein, who with the help of two medical students (one of whom is named 'Cushing' [Doyle]) uses electricity to bring a crazed murderer back to life; and Mitch Evans plays the eponymous 'Count Alucard' ('Count Dracula' in the end credits) who is defeated by a werewolf Jonathan Harker (Gentry) in a silly recreation of the opening chapters from Bram Stoker's novel. Based on original stories by Russ Jones and filmed in 'Totalvision'.
✦

DR. TERROR'S HOUSE OF HORRORS

USA, 1943. National Roadshow. B&W.
The producers of this compilation roadshow movie edited together sequences from five independent films, including Carl Dreyer's *Vampyr* (1931-32), *The Living Dead* (Germany, 1932; aka *Unheimliche Geschichten/Histoires Extraordinaires*), two Bela Lugosi features (*White Zombie* [1932] and *The Return of Chandu* [1934]) and the 1936 version of *The Golem*.
✦

DR. TERROR'S HOUSE OF HORRORS
UK, 1965. Dir: Freddie Francis. With: Christopher Lee, Roy Castle, Peter Cushing, Max Adrian, Ann Bell, Michael Gough. Amicus Productions/Regal Films International. Colour.
The first of the Amicus anthology films and the movie that established the company as a serious rival to Hammer. On a railway journey, the mysterious Dr Schreck (Cushing) introduces himself to his five travelling companions and offers to tell their fortunes with his Tarot cards. Predictably, each of the stories (scripted by co-producer Milton Subotsky back in 1948 for a proposed TV series) leads to death. The first involves Scottish architect James Dawson (Neil McCallum), who discovers the coffin of a 200 year-old werewolf whose spirit is protected by his lycanthropic wife Deirdre (Ursula Howells). The other tales are about an intelligent vine, a voodoo god and a crawling hand. In the final story, American doctor Bob Carroll (Donald Sutherland) is convinced by another doctor, Blake (Adrian), that his French bride Nicolle (Jennifer Jayne) is a vampire and it is his duty to destroy her by driving a stake through her heart. The twist is that Blake is the real vampire. With disc jockey Alan Freeman, Jeremy Kemp, Peter Madden, Katy Wild, Bernard Lee, Kenny Lynch, Judy Cornwall and Frank Forsyth. A novelisation by John Burke was published in 1965 by Pan Books.
✦✦✧

DR. TYCKLE & MISTER TIED
USA, 1989. Dir: Tony Sinclair. Sinclair Blue Productions. Colour.
'Adults only' video that apparently combines writer/director Sinclair's two favourite themes of bondage and tickling.
✦

DR. ZITBAG'S TRANSYLVANIAN PET SHOP
UK/France, 1994. Dir: Tony Barnes. Voices: Nicolette McKenzie, Christian Rodska, Kerry Shale. TFI/Le Centre National de la Cinématographic/PMMP/Carlton Television/Transylvanian Pets/ITV. Colour.
Twenty minute children's cartoon TV series in which second-class mad scientist Dr Sidney Zitbag uses his Monsterfication Machine to create monstrous pets. This also features Horrorfido the skeleton dog, and various vampire locals.
✦

THE DUALITY OF MAN
UK, 1910. Wrench. B&W.
Ten minute silent short, and the first British film based on Robert Louis Stevenson's *Strange Case of Dr. Jekyll and Mr. Hyde*. Dr Jekyll's potion turns him into the evil Mr Hyde, who robs a group of gamblers. As Jekyll, he is confronted by his fiancée and her father, killing the latter after changing back to Hyde again. When the police enter the room, Hyde drinks poison. This is now apparently a lost film.
Remake: DR. JEKYLL AND MR. HYDE (qv; 1912)
✦

DUCK TALES:
Dr. Jekyll and Mr. McDuck
USA/South Korea, 1987. Dir: Terence Harrison. Voices: Peter Cullen, Jim Cummings, Dick Gautier, Joan Gerber, Alan Oppenheimer, Alan Young. The Walt Disney Company/Walt Disney Television Animation. Colour.
Half-hour syndicated children's cartoon TV series (1987-88, sixty-five episodes) based on the comic books illustrated by Carl Barks. In this episode, Scrooge McDuck (Young) and his nephews Huey, Dewey and Louie (all voiced by Russi Taylor) enlist the aid of Sherlock Holmes when they visit London to discover a cure for a potion that turns people into uncontrollable spenders.
✦✧
Ducky Horror Picture Show
USA/South Korea, 1987. Dir: Terence Harrison. Voices: Peter Cullen, Jim Cummings, Dick Gautier, Joan Gerber, Alan Oppenheimer, Alan Young. The Walt Disney Company/Walt Disney Television Animation. Colour.
Uncle Scrooge opens up his mansion to the Monsters Unanimous Convention, which includes Drakeula, Mr Wolf, the Quackenstein Monster and his Bride, the Mummy, Quackimodo, the Creature from the Blue Lagoon, the Blob and giant ape Ping Pong. Meanwhile, Huey, Dewey and Louie watch a black and white Frankenstein movie at Uncle Scrooge's Monster Movie Marathon. This episode is also available on the Disney video *Monster Bash*.
Series sequel: DUCK TALES: TIME IS MONEY (1988)
✦✦

DUE SOUTH:
Mojo Rising
Canada, 1998. Dir: Bruce Pittman. With: Paul Gross, Callum Keith Rennie, Beau Starr, Camilla Scott, Ramona Milano, Tony Craig. Screen Ventures XXVII Productions/Pro Sieben Media/BBC/Baton/Alliance /CTV/CBS-TV. Colour.
Hour-long comedy detective series (1994-98, sixty-seven episodes) created by Paul Haggis, in which straight-laced RCMP Constable Benton Fraser (Gross) finds himself and his wolf-dog Diefenbaker (played by 'Draco') assigned to the Chicago police force and new partner Detective Stanley Raymond Kowalski (Rennie). In this episode, an apparently dead voodoo priest revives and walks out of the morgue when Fraser and Kowalski become involved with Haitian magic and a battle between the forces of good and evil. With guest stars Salome Bey and Maury Chaykin.
✦✦✧

THE DUNGEONMASTER
(UK: RAGEWAR)
USA, 1985. Dir: Charles Band, David Allen, Steve Ford, John Carl Buechler, Rosemarie Turko, Peter Monoogian and Ted Nicolaou. With: Jeffrey Byron, Richard Moll, Leslie Wing, Gina Calabrese, Danial Dion, Bill Bestolarides. Empire Pictures/Ragewar Productions. Colour.
Announced as *Digital Knights*, and filmed in 1983, seven directors each contribute an episode showcasing their special effects skills. The simplistic storyline has computer genius Paul Bradford (Byron) selected by the Satanic Mestema (Moll) as a worthy opponent. He is transported into an alternate dimension, along with his girlfriend Gwen Rogers (Wing), who is the prize in seven challenges. In director Turko's episode, 'Ice Gallery', Paul and Gwen find themselves in an alien museum. When Mestema turns up the temperature, frozen figures of a werewolf (Kenneth J. Hall [Hal Kennedy] in his own make-up), Jack the Ripper, Genghis Khan and a mummy (Jack Reed) come to life and menace the pair. Buechler's 'Demons of the Dead' is about an unconvincing demon, Ratspit, that commands an army of zombies. Other episodes feature a stop-motion giant, a skid-row slasher, an angel, post-holocaust warriors and the rock band W.A.S.P. With Sal and Phil Fondacaro. Produced by Charles Band.
Sequel: PULSEPOUNDERS (1988)
✦✧

MICHAEL DUNN
(Gary Neil Miller) [1934-1973]

Talented American dwarf actor who always gave performances of stature. A semi-regular on TV's *The Wild Wild West* (1965-69) as diminutive mad scientist Dr Miguelito Loveless, he was too often trapped in films like *The Werewolf of Washington* (1973), *Frankenstein's Castle of Freaks* (1973) and *The Mutations* (1973).
qv: *Murders in the Rue Morgue* (1971).

THE DUST OF EGYPT
USA, 1915. Dir: George D. Baker. With: Edith Storey, Antonio Moreno, Hughie Mack, Naomi Childers, Charles Brown, Cissy Fitzgerald. Vitagraph. B&W.
Six-reel silent drama, based on the play by Alan Campbell, in which an archaeologist dreams a long-dead Egyptian princess back to life.
✦

THE EARTH DIES SCREAMING

UK, 1964. Dir: Terence Fisher. With: Willard Parker, Virginia Field, Dennis Price, Thorley Walters, Vanda Godsell, Anna Palk. Lippert/Twentieth Century-Fox. B&W.

Low-budget science fiction movie in which American test pilot Jeff Nolan (Parker) discovers that silly-looking alien robots have invaded the Earth, killing most of the population with poison gas. A handful of survivors gather in a small British village and prepare to fight to stay alive, while victims of the invaders are revived as blank-eyed zombies. Despite the clichés and cheap-looking special effects, Hammer veteran Fisher manages to create a few creepy moments during the short running time.

✦✦

EARTH FINAL CONFLICT:
Avatus

Canada/USA, 1998. Dir: Neill Fearnley. With: Robert Leeshock, Lisa Howard, Von Flores, Richard Chevolleau, David Hemblen, Leni Parker. Lost Script II Productions/ Atlantis Films/Tribune Entertainment/Roddenberry-Kirschner Productions/CTV/Tele München Gruppe/ Polygram Television International. Colour.

Hour-long TV series (1997-) originally created by Gene Roddenberry in 1976. Leeshock plays bodyguard Liam Kincaid, a man who is more than human, caught in the struggle between the alien Taelons (also known as the 'Companions') and the human Resistance. In this episode, Augur (Chevolleau) taps into the Taelon Commonality and inadvertently transforms Da'an (Parker) into a monstrous vampiric Avatus that absorbs the life-force of his victims. With Howard in a dual role as fighter pilot US Marine Captain Lili Marquette and Augur's computer-simulated version of the magical Jeannie from *I Dream of Jeannie* (1965-70).

✦✦

Anthony Perkins is balancing on the Edge of Sanity *(1988).*

ED AND HIS DEAD MOTHER

(aka BON APPETIT, MAMA)

USA, 1992 (1994). Dir: Jonathan Wacks. With: Ned Beatty, Steve Buscemi, Miriam Margolyes, John Glover, Eric Christmas, Rance Howard. ITC Entertainment/Cinemax. Colour.

Offbeat, low-budget horror comedy, released directly to cable TV, in which depressed hardware store owner Ed Chilton (Buscemi) pays sleazy cryogenics salesman A.J. Pattle (Glover) to reanimate his long-dead mother Mabel (Margolyes). She's supposed to stay in the refrigerator and eat bugs to remain reanimated, but insects just don't seem to satisfy her any more...

✦✦

EDGE OF SANITY

Hungary/UK/USA, 1988. Dir: Gérard Kikoine. With: Anthony Perkins, Glynis Barber, Sarah Maur-Thorp, David Lodge, Ben Cole, Jill Melford. Allied Vision/August Entertainment. Colour.

Filmed under the title *Dr. Jekyll and Mr. Hyde: A Journey Into Fear*, this very sleazy version of Robert Louis Stevenson's story (the author doesn't even get a credit!) combines Hyde's exploits with those of Jack the Ripper. French porno director Kikoine obviously has problems with the 1880s setting, not helped by Perkins' over-the-top performance as the drug-crazed scientist Henry Jekyll, who murders prostitutes as Jack Hyde. Originally, this apparently had hardcore inserts. Co-produced by the legendary Harry Alan Towers and co-executive produced by his actress wife, Maria Rohm.

Remake: NIGHTMARE CLASSICS: The Strange Case of Dr. Jekyll and Mr. Hyde (qv; 1989)

✦

EDISON'S FRANKENSTEIN

USA, 1990. Dir: Robert David. B&W.

Short film which uses still photographs to reconstruct Edison's 1910 *Frankenstein*.

✦

EDWARD PENISHANDS

USA, 1991. Dir: Paul Norman. With: Sikki Nixx, Jeanna Fine, Ashley Nicole, Jamie Lee, Dominique Simone, John Dough. Video Team/Pleasure. Colour.

Clever hardcore parody of Tim Burton's 1990 movie. A saleslady of marital aids (Alexandria Quinn) discovers artificial man Edward (Nixx in make-up closely resembling Johnny Depp's original), the possessor of the titular appendages. She takes him home, where he falls in love with her daughter (Fine).
Sequel: EDWARD PENISHANDS PART 2 (qv; 1991)
✦✧

EDWARD PENISHANDS PART 3
USA, 1991. Dir: Paul Norman. With: Sikki Nixx, Fred Lincoln, Monique Hall, Teri Diver, Bianca Trump, K.C. Williams. Video Team/Pleasure. Colour.
The second hardcore sequel to the 1991 original. An ageing Edward (Lincoln) reminisces about the sexual exploits of his younger self (again played by Nixx). A compilation entitled *Best of Edward Penishands* appeared in 1993.
✦

EDWARD PENISHANDS PART 2
USA, 1991. Dir: Paul Norman. With: Angela Summers, Sikki Nixx, April Rayne, Madison (Madison Stone), Jamie Lee, K.C. Williams. Video Team/Pleasure. Colour.
'He's back and he's got something up his sleeves.' Nixx recreates his role as the artificial man with the well-endowed digits in this hardcore sequel.
Sequel: EDWARD PENISHANDS PART 3 (qv; 1991)
✦

EDWARD SCISSORHANDS
USA, 1990. Dir: Tim Burton. With: Johnny Depp, Winona Ryder, Dianne Wiest, Anthony Michael Hall, Vincent Price, Alan Arkin. Twentieth Century Fox. Colour.
Delightful *Frankenstein*-inspired fantasy starring Depp as an artificial man with scissorhands created by a kindly inventor (Price, in his last feature film role). Following his creator's untimely death, Edward is rescued from his Gothic hiding place by Avon lady Peg Boggs (Wiest) and introduced to suburbia, where he finds both romance and tragedy. Music by Danny Elfman.
✦✦✦✦

EDWARD II
UK, 1991. Dir: Derek Jarman. With: Steven Waddington, Kevin Collins, Andrew Tiernan, John Lynch, Dudley Sutton, Tilda Swinton. Working Title/British Screen/BBC Films. Colour.
Jarman's typically overblown adaptation of the 1592 play by Christopher Marlowe, about the downfall of the eponymous British monarch (Waddington) who was openly gay. In one scene, Queen Isabella (Swinton) turns into a vampire and bites out the throat of her victim (Jerome Flynn). With Nigel Terry, and Annie Lennox singing Cole Porter's 'Ev'ry Time We Say Goodbye'.
✦✦

ED WOOD
USA, 1994. Dir: Tim Burton. With: Johnny Depp, Martin Landau, Sarah Jessica Parker, Patricia Arquette, Jeffrey Jones, G.D. Spradlin. Touchstone Pictures. B&W.
Co-producer/director Burton's $18,000,000 tribute to cross-dressing Hollywood maverick Edward D. Wood Jr (exuberantly portrayed by Depp), which lovingly recreates his surprisingly loyal friends and the shooting of some of his memorable movie disasters (*Glen or Glenda* [1953], *Bride of the Monster* [1954], *Plan 9 from Outer Space* [1958], etc). Landau justifiably won the Academy Award for Best Supporting Actor for his bravura performance as an old, embittered, drug-addicted Bela Lugosi (in Oscar-winning make-up designed by Rick Baker) who watches *White Zombie* (1932) on TV with 'Eddie' while complaining about Boris Karloff. With Jones as 'clairvoyant' Criswell, Lisa Marie as TV horror host Vampira, George 'The Animal' Steele (Jim Myers) as Tor Johnson, Bill Murray as Bunny Breckinridge and Conrad Brooks as a bartender. It may take a few liberties with the facts, but this biopic is funny, occasionally touching and sometimes just plain unbelievable.
✦✦✦✦

ED WOOD LOOK BACK IN ANGORA
USA, 1994. Dir: Ted Newsom. With: Conrad Brooks, Dolores Fuller, Joe Robertson, Mrs Kathy Wood, Edward D. Wood Jr, Criswell (Charles Jeron Criswell King). Rhino Home Video. Colour/B&W.
Entertaining documentary that uses clips, trailers, rare behind-the-scenes footage and interviews to tell the story of Hollywood maverick Edward D. Wood Jr. This includes material from such Wood projects as the test reel for Fred Olen Ray's *Beach Blanket Bloodbath* (1978, featuring Forrest J Ackerman), *The Bride and the Beast* (1957), *Bride of the Monster* (1954), *Crossroads Avenger* (a 1953 TV pilot), an alternate shot from *Glen or Glenda* (1953), *Jail Bait* (1954), behind-the-scenes footage of *Orgy of the Dead* (1965), *Plan 9 from Outer Space* (1958), *Pretty Models All in a Row* (1969, aka *Love Feast/The Photographer*), *The Sinister Urge* (1960) and *The Violent Years* (1956). Narrated by Gary Owens, this also features Timothy Farrell and a brief newsreel interview with Bela Lugosi.
✦✦✧

EERIE INDIANA:
America's Scariest Home Video
USA, 1991. Dir: Sam Pillsbury. With: Omri Katz, Justin Shenkarow, Mary-Margaret Humes, Francis Guinan, Julie Condra, Tony Jay. Hearst Entertainment/Unreality Inc/ Cosgrove Meurer Productions/NBC-TV. Colour.
Joe Dante was creative consultant for this short-lived (1991-92, nineteen episodes), half-hour TV series set in the town of Eerie, Indiana (population 16,661, including Elvis living on the paper round and Bigfoot eating out of the trash), the centre of weirdness for the entire planet. Clips of Bela Lugosi from *White Zombie* (1932), a Mexican Aztec mummy movie, *Nosferatu* (1922) and zombies from *Night of the Living Dead* (1968) turn up in the original opening sequence. In this Halloween episode, when the younger brother of Marshall Teller's (Katz) friend Simon Holmes (Shenkarow) plays with the TV remote control, he changes places with long-dead horror star Boris von Orloff (Jay) who is appearing as the bandaged lead in the Halloween movie *Bloody Revenge of the Mummy's Curse*. After some channel hopping, the Mummy finally ends up in a beach party movie! Created by Karl Schaefer and producer José Rivera.
✦✦

Mr. Chaney
USA, 1992. Dir: Mark Goldblatt. With: Omri Katz, Justin Shenkarow, Mary-Margaret Humes, Francis Guinan, Julie Condra, Jason Marsden. Hearst Entertainment/Unreality Inc/Cosgrove Meurer Productions/NBC-TV. Colour.
Thirteen year-old Marshall wins the Harvest King lottery and solves the mystery of Eerie's wolf(man). With John Astin in the recurring role of Bartolemew J. Radford, owner of The World of Stuff general store.
✦✦✧

Zombies in P.J.s
USA, 1992. Dir: Bob Balaban. With: Omri Katz, Justin Shenkarow, Mary-Margaret Humes, Francis Guinan, Julie Condra, Jason Marsden. Hearst Entertainment/Unreality Inc/Cosgrove Meurer Productions/NBC-TV. Colour.
In return for their souls, Hellish advertising executive The Donald (Rene Auberjonois) turns the inhabitants of Eerie into shopping zombies while they sleep. With John Astin as Mr Radford.
Series sequel: EERIE INDIANA 'THE OTHER DIMENSION' (qv; 1998)
✦✧

EERIE INDIANA 'THE OTHER DIMENSION':
Nightmare on Eerie Street
Canada, 1998. Dir: René Bonnière. With: Bill Switzer, Daniel Clark, Deborah Odell, Bruce Hunter, Lindy Booth, Neil Crone. Eerie Corporation/Global/Power Pictures/ Saban International. Colour.
Based on the short-lived TV series *Eerie Indiana* (1991-92) created by Karl Schaefer and José Rivera. Mitchell Taylor (Switzer) and his friend Stanley (Clark) live in Eerie, Indiana, the most 'normal' town in the country, until they are contacted via an inter-dimensional TV signal by Marshall and Simon, who warn them that the weirdness is spilling out into their world through multi-channel satellite dishes. Now the boys are hunting down whatever weirdness got through from the

'other' Eerie and collecting the evidence. In this episode, Mitchell and Stanley have to escape nightmare zombies and prevent The Sandman from putting the whole of Eerie to sleep through his broadcasts on radio station W-Y-R-D. With Bruce Hunter as Edward Taylor, owner of The World of Stuff general store.
✦✦

EGYPTIAN MELODIES
USA, 1931. Dir: Wilfred Jackson. Walt Disney/Columbia. B&W.
Seven minute *Silly Symphonies* cartoon in which a spider investigates the spooky tunnels beneath a sphinx and discovers dancing mummies and ranks of marching hieroglyphics.
Sequel: IN A CLOCK STORE (1931)
✦✦

THE EGYPTIAN MUMMY
USA, 1913. Kalem. B&W.
Eight minute silent comedy about a man who impersonates an Egyptian mummy in a sarcophagus.
✦

THE EGYPTIAN MUMMY
USA, 1914. Dir: Lee Beggs. With: Billy Quirk, Constance Talmadge, Joel Day. Vitagraph. B&W.
Silent short in which a living mummy acts as a matchmaker between two lovers.
✦

8 HEADS IN A DUFFEL BAG
USA, 1997. Dir: Tom Schulman. With: Joe Pesci, Andy Comeau, Kristy Swanson, Todd Louiso, George Hamilton, Dyan Cannon. Orion Pictures/Rank Film Distributors. Colour.
Screwball black comedy in which medical student Charlie (newcomer Comeau) arrives in Mexico for a vacation with his girlfriend Laurie (Swanson) and her dysfunctional parents Dick and Annette (Hamilton and Cannon). He discovers that due to a mix-up at the airport, his luggage contains eight decapitated heads which were being transported across country by psychotic New Jersey gangster Tommy (Pesci). In a nightmare sequence, Tommy dreams that the severed heads come to life in a motel and sing 'Mr Sandman' just before he is attacked by their headless corpses (special make-up effects created by Greg Cannom). With David Spade.
✦✦✧

EJACULA
USA, 1994. Dir: Max Bellocchio. With: Ron Jeremy, Patricia Kennedy, Rocco Siffredi, Lynn LeMay. VCA Pictures. Colour.
Hardcore spoof, with Kennedy as the vampiric Ejacula.
Sequel: EJACULA 2 (qv; 1994)
✦

EJACULA 2
USA, 1994. Dir: Max Bellocchio. With: Ron Jeremy, Patricia Kennedy, Rocco Siffredi, Lynn LeMay. VCA Pictures. Colour.
Hardcore sequel, filmed back-to-back with the first film, in which a group of vampire hunters interrupt an undead orgy. With Jeremy as the worm-eating hunchback Delfi.
✦

THE ELEVENTH DIMENSION
USA, 1915. With: William E. Welsh, Howard Crampton, Allen Holubar, Frances Nelson. IMP/Universal. B&W.
Twenty-five minute silent drama in which a mad professor attempts to revive a body to prove his theory of life after death. Written and produced by Raymond L. Shrock.
✦

EL FANG-DANGO
USA, circa 1970s. Dir: Tony deNonno. With: Tony Travis, Chris Jones, Susan Rockower. Showtime Network. B&W.
Fourteen minute made-for-TV short. In this silent movie-style comedy, Travis plays Dracula with fang-ache.
✦

THE ELIMINATOR
UK, 1996. Dir: Enda Hughes. With: Barry Wallace, Michael Hughes, Mik Duffy. Cousins Pictures. Colour.
Ultra-low-budget independent spoof, shot for less than $5,000 on 16mm over two years in Northern Ireland by twenty-two year-old writer/director/cinematographer/editor Hughes. When Stone, a maverick member of The Organisation, is murdered by his cyborg commander Hawk, he returns from the grave with an army of zombies seeking revenge.
✦

ELIXIR OF LIFE
USA, 1916. Dir: Allen Curtis. With: William (Billy) Franey, Gale Henry, Lillian Peacock. Joker/Universal. B&W.
Eleven minute silent comedy in which the eponymous potion returns a mummy to life and turns sausages back into live dogs.
✦

ELLERY QUEEN:
The Adventure of the Pharaoh's Curse
USA, 1975. Dir: Seymour Robbie. With: Jim Hutton, David Wayne, Tom Reese, John Hillerman, Ken Swofford. Fairmont-Foxcroft Productions/Universal/NBC-TV. Colour.
Hour-long TV series (1975-76, twenty-two episodes) developed by Richard Levinson and William Link, based on the characters created by author 'Ellery Queen' (Frederic Dannay and Manfred Bennington Lee). In this episode, mystery writer Ellery Queen (Hutton) and his police inspector father Richard (Wayne) investigate the seven owners of an ancient sarcophagus who have all died under mysterious circumstances.
✦✦

ELUSIVE SONG OF THE VAMPIRE
Taiwan, 1987. Dir: Lu Bin (Takako Shira). With: He Hong-Tong, Zi Quiang-Qu, Chu Hong. Colour.
This confused story is set in ancient China. Xiao Fan (Hong-Tong) discovers that his home is haunted by a quartet of hopping vampires/zombies and enlists the aid of a kung fu sorcerer to banish them. Meanwhile, the transvestite king (Quiang-Qu) steals the soul of castle priestess Xiao Cui (Hong) and refuses to return it until she can replace it with the soul of a male virgin. Events then get even more complicated...
✦✧

ELVIRA MISTRESS OF THE DARK
USA, 1988. Dir: James Signorelli. With: Elvira (Cassandra Peterson), W. Morgan Sheppard, Daniel Greene, Susan Kellermann, Jeff Conaway, Edie McClurg. New World Pictures/NBC Productions. Colour.
Totally unfunny horror comedy based around vampiric TV movie hostess Elvira, who learns that she has inherited a spooky old mansion. What might have been a fun variation on the old dark house plot is ruined by the low-brow humour (numerous breast jokes) and Peterson's minimal talents as an actress. Only Sheppard makes any effort as her evil great uncle, Vincent Talbot, who turns into a spell-casting demon to gain a recipe book of magic.
✦✧

EMBRACE THE DARKNESS
USA, 1998. Dir: Kelley Cauthen. With: Kevin Spirtas, Madison Clark, Angelia High, Brad Bartram, Colleen McDermott, Cliff Potts. Mystique Fims/Playboy Home Video/Eros Collection. Colour.
Softcore erotic vampire thriller from Playboy, set in contemporary Los Angeles. When the sensitive undead Galen (TV soap actor Spirtas) falls in love with performance artist Jennifer (Clark), his companion, wild bisexual bloodsucker Miranda (High), also seduces their new mortal neighbour. After Galen turns the dying Jennifer into one of his own kind, he commits suicide by exposing himself to the rays of the sun.
✦✦

EMERGENCY! LIVING DEAD IN TOKYO BAY
(USA: aka BATTLE GIRL: TOKYO CRISIS WARS)
Japan, circa 1990s. Dir: Gaira (Kazuo Komizu). With: Cutei Suzuki, Kenzi Ohtsuki, Kera. Daiei Studios. Colour.
When a meteorite crashes into Tokyo Bay, it results in DNA gas being accidentally released that reanimates the dead as flesh-eating zombies. Keiko (female wrestler Suzuki), the daughter of a missing military scientist, uses a sexy hi-tech battle-suit created by her father to try and stop the insane General Hugioka (Ohtsuki), who is attempting to create an invincible army of mutant zombie/human hybrids to aid him in his plans for world domination.
✦✧

EMMERDALE
UK, 1989-90. Dir: David Richards, Stephen Butcher, Sue Butterworth and Tim Dowd. With: Sheila Mercier, Frederick Pyne, Ronald Magill, Arthur Pentelow, Frazer Hines, Jean Rogers. Yorkshire Television/ITV. Colour.
Long-running half-hour soap opera (1972-) created by Kevin Laffan and set in a farming community in north Yorkshire. In a story arc running over Christmas and the New Year, The Woolpack pub owner Amos (Magill) is inspired by a set of plastic fangs and decides to adapt his own version of *Dracula* for the New Year village show. Death-obsessed Bill Whiteley (Teddy Turner) wants to play the Prince of Darkness and wears a set of fake fangs, but his rival Seth Armstrong (Stan Richards) dresses up as Dracula for a New Year's Eve party and portrays the Count on stage.
✦✧

ENCOUNTER AT RAVENSGATE
Australia, 1987 (1988). Dir: Rolf de Heer. With: Steven Vidler, Celine Griffin, Ritchie Singer, Vince Gil, Saturday Rosenberg, Max Cullen. Hemdale/International Film Management. Colour.
This begins slowly, with various odd occurrences in a remote farming community, but the final explanation involving extraterrestrial encounters and murderous human zombies is lost amongst the flashy visuals and the complex relationships.
✦✦

ENCOUNTER IN THE THIRD DIMENSION
USA, 1999. Dir: Ben Stassen. With: Stuart Pankin, Elvira (Cassandra Peterson), Harry Shearer, Andrea Thompson. N Wave Pictures/Sony IMAX. Colour.
Forty-five minute IMAX short, in which The Professor (Pankin) and his cute flying saucer (also voiced by Pankin) attempt to create their own 3-D effects and along the way supply a history of 3-D movies with clips. Their biggest success is presenting the vampy Elvira in 3-D and a roller coaster ride to the stars. Narrated by Shearer.
✦✦✦

ENCOUNTER OF THE SPOOKY KIND
(Orig: GWAI CHUK GWAI/GUI DA GUI. USA: aka SPOOKY ENCOUNTER)
Hong Kong, 1980 (1982). Dir: Samo Hung Kam-Po (Hung Kam-Bo/Hong Jin-Baoh). With: Samo Hung (Samo-Hung Kam-Po/Hung Kam-Bo/Hong Jin-Baoh), Wu Ma (Wo Ma/Yuen Wah/Ng Ma-Wu), Wong Har, Yuen Biao, Chung (Cheung) Fat, Chan Lung. Golden Harvest/Bo Ho Film/Rainbow Video. Colour.
One of the first and most successful Hong Kong horror/kung fu fantasies. Following a nightmare involving a pair of cannibalistic spirits and being tricked into a fake seance by his friends, 'Courageous' Cheung (director/star/co-writer/action choreographer Samo Hung) is framed for the apparent murder of his unfaithful wife by a local magistrate. After meeting the warrior-sorcerer Tsui (Fat), who tries to protect him, he encounters a blind hopping vampire while spending a night in a temple, sleeps with a wormy zombie and is attacked by a trio of evil spirits before he helps Tsui defeat his older brother, the wizard Chin Hoi (Lung), in a magic dual. With Lam Ching-Ying (Lin Zheng-Ying) as a police captain. Produced by Raymond Chow.
Sequel: ENCOUNTER OF THE SPOOKY KIND II (qv; 1989)
✦✦✧

ENCOUNTER OF THE SPOOKY KIND II
(Orig: GUI YAO GUI. USA: aka SPOOKY ENCOUNTERS 2)
Hong Kong, 1989 (1990). Dir: Ricky Lau (Ricky Hui/Xu Guan-Ying). With: Ricky Lau (Ricky Hui/Xu Guan-Ying), Samo Hung (Samo Hung Kam-Po/Hung Kam-Bo/Hong Jin-Baoh), Meng Hoi, Lam Ching-Ying (Lin Zheng-Ying). Boho Films/Long Shong Pictures/Golden Harvest. Colour.
After a nightmare prologue that includes a pair of hopping vampires, a wanderer named Po (Hung) helps a young ghost woman. They battle an evil priest who raises mummy-like corpses and a pair of zombies filled with cockroaches in this belated action-packed comedy sequel to the 1980 hit.
✦✦

ENCULELA
France, circa 1990s. Vanessa. Colour.
Hardcore film about a female vampire and her coffin-bound followers.
✦

LA ENDEMONIADA
Mexico, 1967. Dir: E.G. Muriel. With: Libertad Leblanc, Enrique Rocha, Rogelio Guerra, Carlos Cortez. Cima Films. Colour.
A woman shares a psychic link with a cloaked vampire who can turn into a bat.
✦

ENGELBERT HUMPERDINCK
USA, 1970. With: Engelbert Humperdinck (Gerry Dorsey), Jerry Lewis. ABC-TV. Colour.
Hour-long musical comedy TV show. In one sketch, Dr Frankenstein (Lewis) creates a monster (singer Humperdinck) which behaves like Jerry Lewis.
✦

ENSIGN PULVER
USA, 1964. Dir: Joshua Logan. With: Robert Walker Jr, Burl Ives, Walter Matthau, Tommy Sands, Millie Perkins, Kay Medford. Warner Bros. Colour.
Disappointing sequel to *Mister Roberts* (1955) in which Walker Jr takes over Jack Lemmon's Oscar-winning role as the eponymous seaman. Ives' Captain Morton keeps screening a film for the crew entitled *Young Dr Jekyll Meets Frankenstein* (which combines scenes from *The Walking Dead* [1936] with new footage). This includes early appearances by Larry Hagman, Al Freeman Jr, James Farentino, James Coco and Jack Nicholson.
✦✧

ER:
Ghosts
USA, 1996. Dir: Richard Thorpe. With: Anthony Edwards, George Clooney, Sherry Stringfield, Noah Wyle, Julianna Margulies, Eriq La Salle. Warner Bros Television/Constant C Productions/Amblin Television/NBC-TV. Colour.
Halloween episode of the popular ensemble medical TV series (1994-) created by co-executive producer Michael Crichton. It opens with a Trick or Treat shooting victim in Frankenstein Monster make-up going wild in the emergency room. With William Schallert.
✦✦✦✧
Masquerade
USA, 1998. Dir: Steve De Jarnatt. With: Anthony Edwards, George Clooney, Noah Wyle, Julianna Margulies, Gloria Reuben, Eriq La Salle. Warner Bros Television/Constant C Productions/Amblin Television/NBC-TV. Colour.
Nurse Carole Hathaway (Margulies) surprises Dr Doug Ross (Clooney) by pretending to be a vampire at the beginning of this Halloween episode.
✦✦✦

ERECTION
Italy, circa 1988. Guido Manuli. Colour.
Short film that includes a Frankenstein Monster rising to the occasion.
✦

THE EROTIC DR. JEKYLL
(aka THE AMAZING DR. JEKYLL)
USA, 1975 (1976). Dir: T. McCoy. With: Harry Reems, C.J. Laing, Bobby Astyr, Terri Hall, Susan Sparkle, Zebedy Colt. AB Entertainment/Webster. Colour.
Hardcore version of Robert Louis Stevenson's story featuring Dr Jekyll and his hunchbacked assistant.
Remake: BLOODLUST (qv; 1979)
✦

EROTIC ENCOUNTERS OF THE FOURTH KIND
(Orig: THE SPACE ORGAN/WHAM-BAM-THANK YOU, SPACEMAN)
USA, 1975. Dir: W (William). A. (Al) Levey. With: Dyanne Thorne, Ann Gaybis, Jay Rasumny, Chet Norris, Maria Arnold. Marketta/Malibu Video. Colour.
A softcore science fiction comedy starring Thorne (*Ilsa She Wolf of the SS* [1973], etc). Two aliens arrive on Earth with phalluses where their noses should be. This includes an actor playing Dracula on a movie set.
✦

EROTIC NIGHTS OF THE LIVING DEAD
(Orig: LE NOTTE EROTICHE DEI MORTE VIVENTI/LA REGINA DEGLI ZOMBI. USA: aka SEXY EROTIC LOVE)
Italy, 1979 (1980). Dir: Joe D'Amato (Aristide Massaccesi). With: Laura Jimenez (Laura Gemser/Moira Chen), George Eastman (Luigi Montefiori), Dirce Funari, Mark Shannon (Manlio Cersosimo). Cine International/Mondial/Film Superstore. Colour.
Softcore horror set on the supposedly uninhabited Cat Island, where the dead rise as maggoty zombies who attack the living. Only a bullet in the brain or a voodoo charm can stop these walking corpses. This also apparently exists in a version with hardcore inserts, and was filmed back-to-back with D'Amato's *Porno Holocaust* (1979) and *Voodoo Baby* (1980).
✦

THE EROTIC RITES OF FRANKENSTEIN
(Orig: LES EXPÉRIENCES ÉROTIQUES DE FRANKENSTEIN/LA MALDICIÓN DE FRANKENSTEIN. UK: aka THE CURSE OF FRANKENSTEIN)
France/Spain/Portugal, 1972. Dir: Jess (Jesús) Franco. With: Denis (Dennis) Price, Howard Vernon (Mario Lippert), Anne Libert (Josiane Gibert), Britt Nichols (Brit Nicols), Albert (Alberto) Dalbes, Luis Barboo. Comptoir Français du Film Production/Fénix-Film. Colour.
Franco's equally incomprehensible sequel to *Dracula Prisoner of Frankenstein* (1972). An ill-looking Price returns briefly as Dr Frankestein (*sic*), giving his silver-skinned creation (Fred Harrison [Fernando Bilbao]) the ability to speak before being killed by blind bird-woman Melissa (Libert) and her servant Caronte (Barboo). She then takes the Monster back to her living dead master, Count Cagliostro (Vernon), who uses his mental powers to enslave Frankestein's daughter Vera (Béatrice [Beatriz] Savon) and forces her to create a female creature which he can mate with the Monster to propagate a new master race. With Britt Nichols playing Abigail/Madame Orloff. Franco's attempts to recreate the Hammer style fail miserably, although this mess is occasionally punctuated by flashes of wild imagination. Lina Romay (Rosa Maria Almirall) makes her film début as gypsy girl Esmeralda, but only in the Spanish version, and director Franco turns up as Frankenstein's assistant Morpho.
Sequel: DAUGHTER OF DRACULA (qv; 1972)
✦

ESCALA EN HI-FI
Spain, 1963. Dir: Isidoro Martinez Ferry. With: Arturo Fernandez, Cassen, Germaine Damar, José Rubio, Manuel Zargo, Dorothy Peterson. Documento/Izaro. Colour.
This musical comedy includes a nightmare sequence set in Count Dracula's castle.
✦

ESMERALDA
France, 1906. Dir: Alice Guy-Blanché and Victorin Jasset. With: Denise Becker, Henri Vorins. Gaumont. B&W.
This ten minute silent short was the first screen version of Victor Hugo's 1831 novel *Notre-Dame de Paris*. With Vorins as Quasimodo, the hunchbacked bellringer, and Becker as the eponymous gypsy dancing girl.
Remake: THE HUNCHBACK (qv; 1909)
✦

ESMERALDA
UK, 1922. Dir: Edwin J. Collins. With: Sybil Thorndike, Booth Conway, Arthur Kingsley, Annesley Hely. Master. B&W.
This silent drama in the *Tense Moments from Master Plays* series is based on the novel *Notre-Dame de Paris* by Victor Hugo and features Conway as the hunchback Quasimodo and Thorndike as the eponymous gypsy dancer.
Remake: THE HUNCHBACK OF NOTRE DAME (qv; 1923)
✦

EL ESPIRITU DE LA COLMENA
(USA/UK: aka THE SPIRIT OF THE BEEHIVE)
Spain, 1973. Dir: Victor Erice. With: Fernando Fernan Gomez, Teresa Gimpera, Ana Torrent, Isabel Telleria, Miguel Picazo, José Villasante. Elias Querejeta PC. Colour.
Delightful childhood fantasy. In 1940, the Universal *Frankenstein* (*El Dr. Frankenstein, Autor del Monstruo* [1931]) is shown in a small Castillian village. After the screening, young Ana (Torrent) believes her sister Isabel (Telleria) when the latter tells her the Monster is a real spirit. When she becomes lost in the woods, Ana imagines that the Karloffian Frankenstein Monster (Villasante) is coming for her.
✦✦✦✧

HARRY J. ESSEX
[1910-1997]

A former reporter for *The New York Daily Mirror* who in 1935 sold his story 'The Electric Man' to Universal; the studio eventually filmed it as *Man Made Monster* (1941). In later years he became a director of low budget 'B' movies, but he will always be remembered as the creator of the *Creature from the Black Lagoon* (1953).
qv: *Octaman* (1971).

THE ETERNAL
USA/Ireland, 1998 (1999). Dir: Michael Almereyda. With: Christopher Walken, Alison Elliott, Jared Harris, Lois Smith, Jason Miller. Trimark Pictures. Colour.
Low-budget direct-to-video release from the director of *Nadja* (1994), filmed under the titles *The Mummy* and *Trance*. American couple Nora (Elliott) and Jim (Harris) find themselves trapped in the ancestral Irish mansion with their mad Uncle Bill (Walken), who is trying to revive a 2,000 year-old shape-shifting Druid witch (also Elliott).
✦✧

ETERNAL DESIRES
USA, 1995. Dir: Kenneth Bush. With: Rachel Moriello, Niki Sullivant, Gabriel Biderman, Judith Durkee, Jonny Law, Chris Danko. Jade Films. Colour.
Arty independent vampire movie, filmed on murky 16mm in New Hampshire and released directly to video. When student Allison is fatally injured during a midnight visit to a graveyard, she is carried off by one hundred year-old vampire Lord Christopher, whose bite brings her back as one of the undead. She starts wearing black clothes and attacks her friend Kristin, who is soon cutting up the local boys for their blood. This romantic Goth film also includes a whipping scene and headache-inducing montages.
✦

ETERNITY
USA, 1990. Dir: Scotty Fox. With: Tracey Adams, Sunny McKay, Rayne (Rayne Dawn), Ashlyn Gere, Randy West, Peter North. Sin City Video. Colour.

Hardcore feature in which Adams plays a psychic vampire who must have sex with men and women to drain their life-force and retain her youthful appearance.
✦

CLIFFORD EVANS
[1912-1985]

Welsh stage actor, in films since 1936. As the fanatical vampire hunter Professor Zimmer, he proved himself a worthy stand-in for Professor Van Helsing in Hammer's *The Kiss of the Vampire* (1962). **qv:** *The Curse of the Werewolf* (1960).

AN EVENING WITH KITTEN

USA, 1983. Dir: Les Barnum. With: Kitten (Francesca) Natividad, Kerry Angerman, Kathy Clark, John Baron, Gerald Frank. Kitten and Kompany/Rhino Video. Colour.
Half-hour video burlesque revue, in which the big-breasted star drinks an Incredible Bulk formula, is imagined by a fan as Miss Milky Way, and meets a bearded Count after reading *The Annotated Dracula*. The mind boggles!
✦

EVERY HOME SHOULD HAVE ONE

(USA: THINK DIRTY)
UK, 1970. Dir: Jim Clark. With: Marty Feldman, Judy Cornwell, Shelly Berman, Julie Ege, Patrick Cargill, Jack Watson. Example Productions/British Lion. Colour.
Dated comedy which marked pop-eyed comedian Feldman's first starring movie role. As a day-dreaming advertising executive who is obsessed with sex, he imagines himself as a vampire battling the Frankenstein Monster, a hedonistic Pan and a cartoon Superman pitted against Batman (Dinsdale Landen) in one of several sequences created by the Richard Williams Studio. Norwegian-born Ege (*The Mutations* [1973], etc) makes her movie début naked.
✦✧

EVERYMAN:
The True Story of Frankenstein

(USA: BIOGRAPHY: The True Story of Frankenstein)
UK, 1986. Dir: Alan Lewens. With: Brian Aldiss, Mel Brooks, Peter Cushing. Everyman/BBC Wales. Colour.
Disappointing hour-long documentary, featuring clips from *Bride of Frankenstein* (1935), *Frankenstein* (1910 and 1931), *Frankenstein Conquers the World* (1964), *Frankenstein's Daughter* (1958), *The Horror of Frankenstein* (1970), *Jesse James Meets Frankenstein's Daughter* (1965), *The Revenge of Frankenstein* (1958), *The Terminator* (1984) and *Young Frankenstein* (1974). There is also a 'dramatised collage' of Mary Shelley's story featuring Christopher Guard as Dr Frankenstein, Clive Russell as The Creature and Sylvestra Le Touzel as Mary. Other interviewees include literary critic Rosemary Jackson, film historian Philip Strick, Robert Oppenheimer and the voice of Boris Karloff.
✦✦

EVIL BLACK MAGIC

(Orig: CHU NU DE YOU HUO)
Hong Kong, 1991. Dir: Meng-Hwa Ho. Hong Kong Films. Colour.
Sex and horror film that features a sorcerer who raises the corpse of a woman and drives a spike through the top of her head to control her, a ghost woman who revives some dead dwarves, and a vampire woman in the shower.
✦

EVIL CAT

Hong Kong, 1986. Dir: Dennis Yu (Yun Kong-Yu). With: Lau Kar-Leung (Liv Chia-Liang), Tang Lai-Ying, Mark Cheng (Hao Nan-Cheng), Wong Ching (Wong Ching-Jing/ Lau Sze-Yu), Stuart Ong. Dennis Yu/Cinema City/ Rainbow Video. Colour.
A blood-drinking cat creature with nine lives reappears every fifty years to possess the living. The super-strong feline (Taiwanese actress Tsui Suk-Woon) wreaks havoc and destroys a police station. This was titled *Devil Cat* on advertising material.
✦✧

EVIL CLUTCH

(Orig: CLUTCH — IL BOSCO/NOTTE NEL BOSCO/PRESA TENACE. USA: aka HORROR QUEEN)
Italy, 1988 (1989). Dir: Andreas Marfori. With: Coralina C. (Cataldi) Tessoni, Diego Ribon, Elena Cantarone, Luciano Crovato, Stefano Molinari. Fomar Film/Centro Sperimentale/Eagle Pictures/Troma. Colour.
Inspired by the *Evil Dead* films. A young couple vacationing in the Alps find themselves in a haunted forest and encounter fanged female demon Arva (Cantarone) and a zombie, amongst other gory horrors.
✦✧

EVIL OF DRACULA

(Orig: CHI O SUU BARA)
Japan, 1974 (1975). Dir: Michio Yamamoto. With: Toshio Kurosawa, Yunosuke Ito, Kunie Tanaka, Katsuhiko Sasaki, Shin Kishida, Mariko Mochizuki. Toho/UPA Productions of America. Colour.
The third and last of director Yamamoto's series of Western-style vampire films for Toho. A new professor of psychology (Kurosawa) arrives to teach at a remote girl's school and discovers that the Principal (Tanaka) and his wife are really a pair of 200 year-old vampires preying on pupils who scratch themselves on a rose thorn. The undead pair also prolong their existence by wearing the faces of their victims. When the Principal is finally staked with a red-hot poker, both vampires are reduced to skeletons. Despite the title, this has nothing to do with Dracula.
✦✦✧

THE EVIL OF FRANKENSTEIN

UK, 1964. Dir: Freddie Francis. With: Peter Cushing, Peter Woodthorpe, Sandor Eles, Kiwi Kingston, Duncan Lamont, Katy Wild. Hammer Films/Universal-International. Colour.
The third and probably weakest in Hammer's Frankenstein series. Director Francis took over from Terence Fisher for this one entry and consequently Cushing's Baron appears more humane. This time the real villain is Woodthorpe's drunken hypnotist, Zoltan, who uses the revived Monster (ex-wrestler Kingston, in make-up by Roy Ashton that closely resembled Karloff's original) to revenge himself on the authorities of Carlstaad. The screenplay by John Elder (Anthony Hinds) contains few surprises and has no connection with the previous films, while a confused flashback sequence only adds to the muddled narrative. When released to American TV in 1968, NBC included extra sequences filmed at Universal Studios (featuring William Phipps, Steven Geray, Patrick Horgan, Tracy Stratford and Maria Palmer), in which the mute beggar girl meets the Monster as a child. Even more confusing, scenes from *The Evil of Frankenstein* also turn up in *Kiss of Evil*, the NBC-TV version of Hammer's *The Kiss of the Vampire* (1962).
Sequel: FRANKENSTEIN CREATED WOMAN (qv; 1966)
✦✦

EVILS OF THE NIGHT

(aka SPACE MONSTERS)
USA, 1983 (1984). Dir: Mardi Rustam. With: Neville Brand, Aldo Ray, Julie Newmar, John Carradine, Tina Louise, Karrie Emerson. Lightning/Mars Productions/ Aquarius Releasing. Colour.
Brand (in his last role) and Ray play two crazed garage mechanics who abduct teenage girls to keep evil alien vampires (Carradine, Newmar and Louise) supplied with fresh blood for their dying planet. With Dawn Wildsmith and porno stars Amber Lynn, Jerry Butler and Crystal Breeze (Lisa Breeze). Low-budget thrills, but just look at that exploitation cast!
✦

EVIL SPAWN

(USA: aka ALIVE BY NIGHT/DEADLY STING. UK: METAMORPHOSIS)
USA, 1987 (1988). Dir: Kenneth J. Hall (Hal Kennedy) (and Fred Olen Ray). With: Bobbie Bresee, Drew Godderis, John Terence, Donna Shock (Dawn Wildsmith), Jerry Fox, John

Peter Cushing is back in the lab in The Evil of Frankenstein *(1964).*

Carradine. BB Entertainment/Mogul/American Independent Pictures. Colour.
Unofficial, low-budget reworking of *The Wasp Woman* (1959), filmed under the title *Wasp*. Produced by Frank Bresee and starring his wife Bobbie as ageing Hollywood movie actress Lynn Roman, who uses a special serum created by the mad Dr Zeitman (a frail-looking Carradine, in one of his last roles) and his equally loony assistant Evelyn (Shock) to make her young again. The only side effect is that she occasionally changes into a murderous giant insect. Forrest J Ackerman turns up briefly as a pool man. This direct-to-video feature was shot on 16mm. In the late 1980s, star Bresee was so embarrassed by the original video cassette of this film that she offered to tape over copies with a re-edited and re-recorded version free of charge! Uncredited executive producer Fred Olen Ray later reworked most of the movie into Ted Newsom's equally awful *The Alien Within* (1990), with added footage of Gordon Mitchell.
✦

EVIL SPIRITS IN THE HOUSE
USA, 1990. Dir: Steve J. Postal. With: Larry Wallace, Jennifer Filkins, Angela Shepard, Dawn Chappel, Maurice Postal. Steve Postal Productions. Colour.
Second in the low-budget horror comedy video series from Florida *auteur* Postal who edited, photographed, directed, co-produced and co-scripted! When a bank embezzler and his daughter hide out in the honeymoon cabin belonging to landlord-monster B.J. Smith (Maurice Postal), their attempts to contact the spirit world raise a vampire (Chappel), resulting in torture and death.
Sequel: VAMPIRES FROM OUTER SPACE (qv; 1990)
✦

THE EVIL TOUCH:
Dear Beloved Monster
Canada/Australia, 1973. With: Ray Walston, Alistair Duncan, Jan Kingsbury, Mark Hashfield. Amalgamated Pictures/OLOLA Productions/Allied Artists. Colour.
Half-hour syndicated anthology TV series (1973-74, twenty-six episodes), hosted by Anthony Quayle. In this episode, a Nobel Prize-winning scientist (Walston) is implicated when he creates a creature that becomes a murderer.
✦✧

The Fans
Canada/Australia, 1973. Dir: Vic Morrow. With: Vic Morrow, Alfred Sandor, Enid Lorimer, Queenie Ashton. Amalgamated Pictures/OLOLA Productions/Allied Artists. Colour.
Morrow stars as horror actor Purvis Green, famous for his Dracula-type roles. He is kidnapped by two old women who eventually impale him on a sword.
✦✧

THE EVIL WITHIN
(Orig: BABY BLOOD)
France, 1990. Dir: Alain Robak. With: Emmanuelle Escourrou, Jean-Francois Gallotte, Christian Sinniger, Roselyn Geslot, Francois Frapier, Thierry LePortier. Partners Productions/Exo7 Productions/Miramax/A-Pix Entertainment. Colour.
Offbeat black comedy in which an ancient, bloodthirsty parasite forms itself into a phallus and penetrates the womb of pregnant gap-toothed circus girl Yanka (Escourrou). When it talks to her telepathically (voiced by an uncredited Gary Oldman!) and demands to be born, she is driven mad and forced to kill to obtain the male blood she needs to feed her growing 'baby'.
✦✧

EXORCIST MASTER
Hong Kong, 1992 (1993). Dir: Wu Ma (Wo Ma/Yuen Wah/Ng Ma-Wu). With: Wu Ma (Wo Ma/Yuen Wah/Ng Ma-Wu), Lam Ching-Ying (Lin Zheng-Ying). Gold Leaf Film/Network Kingdom Video. Colour.
Horror comedy in which Vatican-trained Chinese priest Father Wu (director Ma) and Master A-Chiou (Ching-Ying) battle a British priest who was killed by a falling cross in a churchyard and has been resurrected as a vampire. This also includes a group of apparently fake hopping vampires.
✦✧

THE EXPLOITS OF ELAINE

USA, 1914-15. Dir: Louis J. Gasnier and George B. Seitz. With: Pearl White, Arnold Daly, Creighton Hale, Sheldon Lewis, William Riley Hatch, Floyd Buckley. Star Company/ Pathé. B&W.

Fourteen episode silent serial, with such chapter titles as 'The Twilight Sleep', 'The Poisoned Room', 'The Death Ray', 'The Blood Crystals' and 'The Devil Worshippers'. Chapter six is entitled 'The Vampire', in which master villain Perry Bennett, aka the Clutching Hand (Lewis), tries to drain the blood from heroine Elaine Dodge (White) through a hypodermic needle.

Sequels: THE NEW EXPLOITS OF ELAINE (1915) and THE CLUTCHING HAND (1936)

✦✧

EXTREME HEAT

USA, 1987. Dir: Scotty Fox. With: Sheena Horne, Marisa Betancourt, Bionca (Bionica Bradley), Jessica Wylde. Moonlight Entertainment. Colour.

Hardcore spoof of *The Nutty Professor* (1963), in which a scientist's serum turns him into Bobby Lust.

✦

THE EYE OF COUNT FLICKENSTEIN

USA, 1966. Dir: Tony Conrad. B&W.

Short underground flicker film which includes a brief Dracula parody.

✦

EYES ARE UPON YOU

USA, 1997. Dir: David A. Goldberg. With: Brinke Stevens, Tom Savini, Edward Lee Vincent, Zander Teller, Sam Nicotero. EI Independent Cinema. Colour.

Low-budget video apparently featuring lesbian vampires.

✦

THE EYES OF THE MUMMY MA

(Orig: DIE AUGEN DER MUMIE MA/DIE MUMIA MA) Germany, 1918. Dir: Ernst Lubitsch. With: Pola Negri, Emil Jannings, Harry Liedtke, Max Lawrence, Margarethe Kupfer. PAG-Union/Paramount. B&W.

Fifty-five minute silent drama in which Jannings plays Ma, a religious fanatic and the leader of an Egyptian sect of mummy-worshippers who attempts to frighten a woman (Negri) to death through hypnotism and appearing as an apparition. From the director of such sophisticated comedies as *Ninotchka* (1939) and *Heaven Can Wait* (1943).

✦

THE FACE AT THE WINDOW

Australia, 1919. Dir: Charles Villiers. With: Agnes Dobson, D.B. O'Connor, Claud Turton, Collet Dobson. D.B. O'Connor Feature Films. B&W.

Silent murder mystery based on the play by F. Brooke Warren.

Remake: THE FACE AT THE WINDOW (qv; 1920)

✦

THE FACE AT THE WINDOW

UK, 1920. Dir: Wilfred Noy. With: C. Aubrey Smith, Gladys Jennings, Jack Hobbs, Charles Quatermaine, Ben Field, Simeon Stuart. British Actors/Phillips. B&W.

Second silent adaptation of the play by F. Brooke Warren, previously filmed in Australia in 1919. The victims of a murderer are distracted by a hideous face peering through the window. In the end, a corpse is revived long enough to identify its killer.

Remake: THE FACE AT THE WINDOW (qv; 1932)

✦✧

THE FACE AT THE WINDOW

UK, 1932. Dir: Leslie S. Hiscott. With: Raymond Massey, Isla Bevan, Eric Maturin, Claude Hulbert, Henry Mollison, A. Bromley Davenport. Real Art/RKO Radio Pictures. B&W.

Based on F. Brooke Warren's stage play, previously filmed in Australia in 1919 and Britain in 1920. A hideous face distracts the victims of a murderer. In the end, a corpse is brought back from the dead long enough to identify the killer.

Remake: THE FACE AT THE WINDOW (qv; 1939)

✦✦

Robert Shayne and John Carradine look upon The Face of Marble *(1946).*

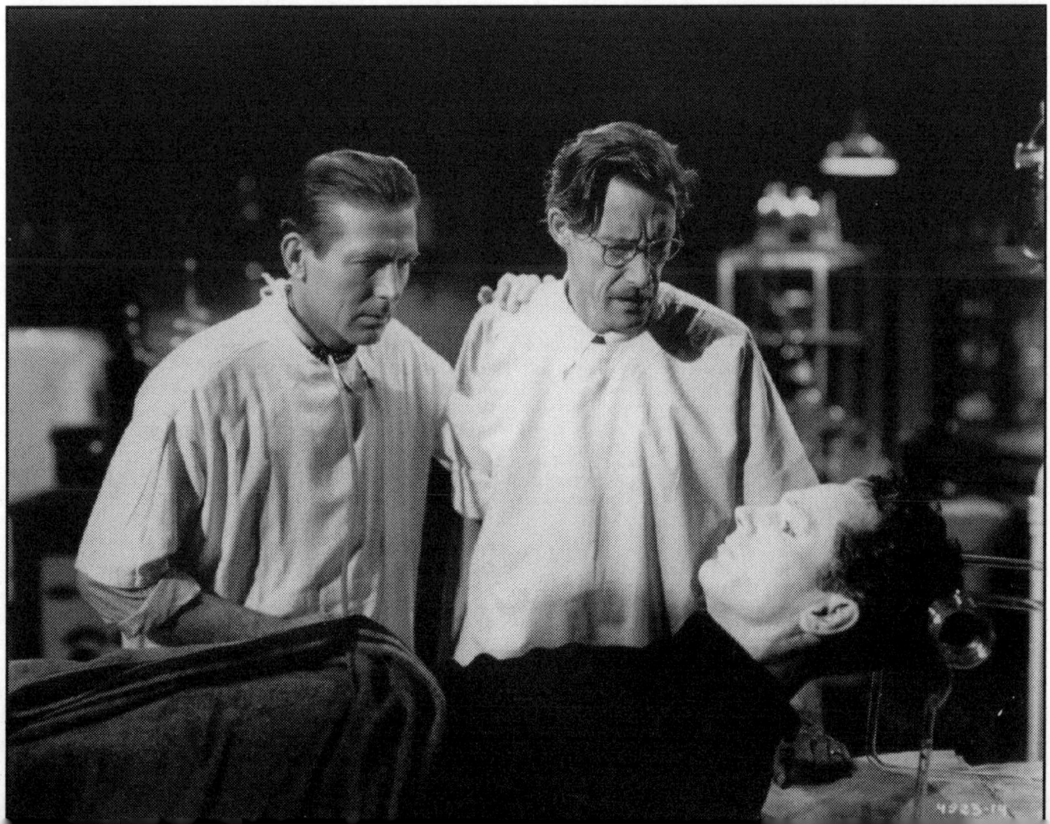

THE FACE AT THE WINDOW

UK, 1939. Dir: George King. With: Tod Slaughter, Marjorie Taylor, John Warwick, Aubrey Mallalieu, Robert Adair, Wallace Evenett. British Lion/Ambassador. B&W.

The fourth version of F. Brooke Warren's stage play (previously filmed in 1919, 1920 and 1932) and one of Tod Slaughter's best horror melodramas. Set in 1880, the Parisian location is hardly convincing, but the star gives a marvellous, barnstorming performance as the lecherous Chevalier del Gardo, who is also a grisly knife murderer known as Le Loup (The Wolf). He is aided by his hideous half-brother (Harry Terry), whose bestial face appears at the window to hold the victim's attention. Director King also throws in white slavery and a mad professor (Evenett) involved with electrical experiments to revive the dead.

✦✦✦

THE FACE OF DARKNESS

UK, 1976 (1977). Dir: Ian F.H. Lloyd. With: Lennard Pearce, John Bennett, David Allister, Roger Bizley, Gwyneth Powell, Jonathan Elsom. Cromdale Films. Colour.

When his wife is killed by terrorists, a politician (Pearce) uses his occult knowledge to resurrect a man (Allister) buried alive during the Spanish Inquisition so that he can commit a murder which will force the British Government to reintroduce the death penalty. At least it's under an hour long.

✦✧

THE FACE OF MARBLE

USA, 1946. Dir: William Beaudine. With: John Carradine, Claudia Drake, Robert Shayne, Maris Wrixon, Willie Best, Thomas E. Jackson. Monogram. B&W.

Mad Professor Randolf (Carradine) experiments with reviving the dead, but his victims quickly expire again with rigid faces. When he resuscitates a Great Dane, the dog becomes a semi-transparent vampire and walks through walls with a ghostly woman. This is actually better-than-expected low-budget Monogram madness that also

features an evil housekeeper (Rosa Rey), voodoo rituals and the usual comedy relief from Best.
✦✦

FACE OF THE SCREAMING WEREWOLF
(Orig: LA CASA DEL TERROR)
Mexico/USA, 1960 (1965). Dir: Gilbert Solar (Gilberto Martinez Solares) (and Jerry Warren). With: Landa Varle (Yolanda Varela), Lon Chaney, Raymond Gaylord (Rámon Gay), D.W. Barron (Alfred Wally Barron), Germán Valdés 'Tin-Tan', Yerye Beirute. Diana Films/Clasa-Mohme/ Azteca/ADP International Picture. B&W.
An incomprehensible mess, credited to screenwriters Solar and Alfred Salimar (Alfredo Salazar), and re-edited and dubbed into English by Warren (who also incorporated some footage from *La Momia Azteca* [1957]). The original version is a musical/comedy/horror film in which a mad professor (Beirute, who looks just like Boris Karloff) uses a secret laboratory in a wax museum for his experiments to reanimate stolen bodies. When he steals an Egyptian mummy, he uses the blood of a comic relief caretaker ('Tin-Tan') and a stray lightning bolt to bring it back to life. Under the influence of the full moon, the mummy promptly changes into a werewolf (a non-speaking Chaney Jr, recreating two of his most famous roles). The werewolf (make-up by Roman Juarez) kidnaps a woman and climbs up the outside of a skyscraper before being destroyed in a fire. This also includes another mummy and a reincarnated princess. Mexican comedy star Valdés was almost totally cut out of the American version! Although highly unlikely, the possibility that in 1957 Edward D. Wood Jr was involved with filming the climactic footage of Chaney in werewolf make-up, scaling the outside of an apartment block, remains tantalisingly unsubstantiated.
✦✧

FADE TO BLACK
USA, 1980. Dir: Vernon Zimmerman. With: Dennis Christopher, Tim Thomerson, Gwynne Gilford, Normann Burton, Linda Kerridge, Morgan Paull. Leisure Investment/Movie Ventures/American Cinema. Colour.
Christopher plays crazy film buff Eric Binford, who kills off those people he doesn't like by taking on the persona of his favourite movie characters. These include Richard Widmark's psychotic Tommy Udo from *Kiss of Death* (1947), Hopalong Cassidy, the Mummy and Count Dracula. With Marilyn Monroe look-alike Kerridge, Mickey Rourke as a young punk, a clip from *Night of the Living Dead* (1968) and a climax set on the roof of Mann's Chinese Theater in Hollywood. Pinnacle Books published the novelisation by Ron Renauld.
✦✧

THE FAMOUS ADVENTURES OF MR. MAGOO:
(aka MR. MAGOO LITERARY CLASSICS)
Sherlock Holmes/Doctor Frankenstein
USA, 1965. Dir: Abe Levitow. Voices: Jim Backus. Columbia/UPA/NBC-TV. Colour.
Hour-long cartoon TV show (1964-65) in which the near-sighted character created by Milfred Kaufman and John Hubley in 1949 portrays different literary or historical characters every week. Magoo (Backus) plays a bumbling Dr Watson in the first half-hour story, while in the second Frankenstein's Monster escapes and plans to create an army of monsters until a repentant Mr Magoo/Dr Frankenstein blows up the laboratory. Both these episodes were later included in the compilation feature film *Mr. Magoo, Man of Mystery* (1967).
Series sequel: WHAT'S NEW MR. MAGOO? (1977-78)
✦✦

FANGFACE
USA, 1978-79. Dir: Rudy Larriva. Voices: Frank Welker, Bart Braverman, Susan Blu, Jerry Dexter, Allan Melvin, Ted Cassidy. Ruby-Spears Enterprises/Filmways/ABC-TV. Colour.
Half-hour cartoon TV series which is very similar to *Scooby Doo Where Are You!* (1969-72). Every 400 years a baby werewolf is born to the Fangsworth family. So when the moon (or a picture of it!) shines on Sherman Fangsworth (Welker), known to his friends as Fangs, he changes into Fangface until the sun can change him back. Teaming up with three daring teenagers, Kim (Blu), Biff (Dexter) and Puggsy (Braverman), together they investigate the supernatural. The opening sequence includes a living mummy. Executive produced by Joe Ruby and Ken Spears.
✦✧
A Creep from the Deep
USA, 1978. Dir: Rudy Larriva. Voices: Frank Welker, Bart Braverman, Susan Blu, Jerry Dexter, Allan Melvin, Ted Cassidy. Ruby-Spears Enterprises/Filmways/ABC-TV. Colour.
In this episode, Fangface and his friends arrive on a Mexican island, where they encounter the underwater Mummy of Molezuma who guards a cursed sunken treasure.
✦✧
Where's the Wolf, That's the Werewolf
USA, 1978. Dir: Rudy Larriva. Voices: Frank Welker, Bart Braverman, Susan Blu, Jerry Dexter, Allan Melvin, Ted Cassidy. Ruby-Spears Enterprises/Filmways/ABC-TV. Colour.
The gang investigate a werewolf that is setting all the wolves free from a safari park.
Series sequel: THE PLASTIC MAN COMEDY-ADVENTURE SHOW: Fangface & Fangpuss (qv; 1979-80)
✦✧

FANGS: A HISTORY OF VAMPIRES IN THE MOVIES
USA, 1992. Dir: Bruce G. Hallenbeck. With: Veronica Carlson. European Film Production/Pagan Video/EI Independent Cinema. Colour/B&W.
Ex-Hammer scream queen Carlson (*Dracula Has Risen from the Grave* [1968], etc) hosts this hour-long documentary on vampire movies with some poor-looking clips and trailers from *Black Sunday* (1960), *The Last Man on Earth* (1961), Murnau's *Nosferatu* (1922) and various Hammer titles.
✦✧

FANNY HILL MEETS DR. EROTICO
USA, 1967. Dir: Barry Mahon. With: Sue Evans. Chancellor. Colour.
Nudie sequel to *Fanny Hill Meets Lady Chatterley* (1967). Fanny Hill (Evans) discovers that Dr Erotico has created a monster in his castle laboratory. When she accidentally brings the creature to life, it falls in love with her before being burned to death by the villagers.
Sequel: FANNY HILL MEETS THE RED BARON (1968)
✦

EL FANTASMA DE LA OPERETA
Argentina, 1955. Dir: Enrique Carreras. With: Amelita Vargas, Alfredo Barbieri, Tono Andreu, Gogo Andreu, Iñez Fernandez. Belgrano/Cine Argentine. B&W.
A horror comedy that includes a vampire and a Frankenstein-like monster. Not to be confused with the 1959 Mexican movie with the same title.
✦

EL FANTASMA DE LA OPERETA
Mexico, 1959 (1960). Dir: Fernando Cortes. With: Germán Valdés 'Tin-Tan', Ana Luisa, Peluffo, Manuel 'Loco' Valdés, Vitola, Marcelo. Brooks/Azteca. B&W.
Not to be confused with the 1955 Argentinean film, this horror spoof involves comedian 'Tin-Tan' with ghosts and a group of opera phantoms.
✦✧

FANTASMAGORIE
France, 1962. Dir: Patrice Molinard. With: Edith Scob, Venantino Venantini, Jean Henry.
Short film with vampires.
✦

FANTASTIC DINOSAURS OF THE MOVIES
USA, 1990 (1992). Dir: Sandy Oliveri. Film Shows/ Goodtimes Home Video. Colour/B&W.

Compiled and edited by Oliviri, this includes a short documentary about dinosaurs, a behind-the-scenes look at the making of *The Golden Voyage of Sinbad* (1973), and more than thirty trailers from such dinosaur and dragon movies as *The Giant Claw* (1957), *Jack the Giant Killer* (1961), *Jason and the Argonauts* (1963), *King Dinosaur* (1955), a re-release double bill of *King Kong/The Son of Kong* (both 1933), *King Kong vs. Godzilla* (1963), *The Land Unknown* (1957), *The Loch Ness Horror* (1982), *One Million Years B.C.* (1966), *Reptilicus* (1962), *Rodan* (1956), *The 7th Voyage of Sinbad* (1958), *Valley of the Dragons* (1961) and *When Dinosaurs Ruled the Earth* (1969), amongst others.

✦✦✦

THE FANTASTIC JOURNEY:
Funhouse

USA, 1976 (1977). Dir: Art Fisher. With: Jared Martin, Carl Franklin, Ike Eisenmann, Katie Saylor, Roddy McDowall, Mel Ferrer. Columbia/Bruce Lansbury Productions/NBC-TV. Colour.

Short-lived, hour-long TV series (ten episodes) about a party of adventurers, lost in the Devil's Triangle and trapped in a dimension with beings from the future and other worlds, who journey through zones of time back to their own period. In this episode, the travellers encounter a bizarre carnival run by Marcus Apollonius (Ferrer), an ancient Greek sorcerer who, along with his female companion (Mary Frann), was cursed with lycanthropy for challenging the gods. Apollonius attempts to possess the body of scientist Jonathan Willoway (McDowall) to escape his imprisonment.

✦✦

FANTASTIC MONSTERS OF TELEVISION LAND

USA, 1999. With: Bud Abbott, Lou Costello, Fred Gwynne, Danny Kaye, Frank Shuster, Johnny Wayne. VideoSteve. B&W.

Two hour video compilation that includes Gwynne as Herman Munster on a 1966 episode of the *The Danny Kaye Show*, the unaired fifteen minute pilot film *My Fair Munster* (1964), TV promos for *The Addams Family* (1964-66) and *The Munsters* (1964-66), CBS-TV promos and trailer for *Munster, Go Home!* (1966), the 1953 episode of *The Colgate Comedy Hour* in which Abbott and Costello meet the Creature from the Black Lagoon (Ricou Browning) and Frankenstein's Monster (Glenn Strange), and the 1966 TV special *Wayne and Shuster Take an Affectionate Look at the Monsters*.

✦✦✦

FANTASY GIRLS

USA, 1988. Dir: John Stagliano. With: Brandy Alexandre (Alexander), Belladonna, Kathleen Gentry, Buddy Love, Tom Byron, Jesse Adams. Caballero. Colour.

This episodic hardcore feature includes a sequence in a movie theatre where a woman asks a man dressed like Dracula to bite her. Later, two Texas cowboys in Los Angeles follow a mysterious Rolls Royce to an apartment house, where they meet the Count and become involved in an orgy.

✦

FANTASY ISLAND:
Aphrodite/Dr. Jeckyll and Miss Hyde

USA, 1980. Dir: Rod Holcomb. With: Ricardo Montalban, Herve Villechaize, George Maharis, Rosemary Forsyth, Don Stroud, Britt Ekland. Columbia/Spelling-Goldberg Productions/ABC-TV. Colour.

Long-running anthology TV series (1978-84, 157 episodes), created by Gene Levitt, in which visitors spend $50,000 to live out their wildest fantasies on the secluded island of the mysterious Mr Roarke (Montalban) and the diminutive Tatoo (Villechaize, who committed suicide in 1993). In this episode's second story, a female psychiatrist attempts to discover the genesis of evil.

✦✧

Best Seller/The Tomb

USA, 1978. Dir: George McCowan. With: Ricardo Montalban, Herve Villechaize, Desi Arnaz Jr, Barry Sullivan, David Opatoshu, Gloria DeHaven. Columbia/Spelling-Goldberg Productions/ABC-TV. Colour.

In this episode's second story, an archaeologist is searching for the cursed tomb of King Tut's brother.

✦✧

The Experiment/The Proxy Billionaire

USA, 1981. Dir: Richard Benedict. With: Ricardo Montalban, Herve Villechaize, James Broderick, Robert Goulet, Britt Ekland, Troy Donahue. Columbia/Spelling-Goldberg Productions/ABC-TV. Colour.

In this episode's first story, a scientist wants to succeed with his experiments to raise the dead. With Woody Strode.

✦✧

The Lady and the Monster/The Last Cowboy

USA, 1981. Dir: Don Chaffey. With: Ricardo Montalban, Herve Villechaize, Lynda Day George, William Smith, Stuart Whitman, Diane Baker. Columbia/Spelling-Goldberg Productions/ABC-TV. Colour.

In the first story of this Halloween episode, Dr Carla Frankenstein (George) visits her disgraced ancestor's castle where she discovers his gentle Monster (Smith).

✦✧

Man-Beast/Ole Island Oprey

USA, 1981. With: Ricardo Montalban, Herve Villechaize, David Hedison, Wendy Schaal, Carol Lynley, Anne Francis. Columbia/Spelling-Goldberg Productions/ABC-TV. Colour.

In this episode's first story, an accountant is haunted by a recurring nightmare about a werewolf.

✦✧

Vampire/The Lady and the Longhorn

USA, 1978. Dir: Arnold Laven. With: Ricardo Montalban, Herve Villechaize, Robert Reed, Eva Gabor, Jack Elam, Lloyd Bochner. Columbia/Spelling-Goldberg Productions/ABC-TV. Colour.

In the first story of this episode, an actor about to play Dracula wants to become a real vampire to impress the woman he loves.

Series remake: FANTASY ISLAND (1998)

✦✧

FANTASY MISSION FORCE

Hong Kong, 1984. Dir: Chu Yen-Ping. With: Jackie Chan, Chang Ling, Wang Yu, Lin Ching-Hsia (Venus Lin). Cheung Ming Film/ZIV International/All Seasons. Colour.

Action comedy about soldiers of fortune trying to rescue a group of generals held captive by the Japanese in Word Ward Two. This includes an incongruous sequence set in a haunted house with real ghosts and vampire-like men with fangs.

✦✦

FASCINATION

France, 1979. Dir: Jean Rollin. With: Franka Maï, Brigitte Lahaie, Fanny Magier, Muriel Montossé, Sophie Noel. Comex Productions/Films ABC/Consortium Europeen Cinematographique. Colour.

After making a number of hardcore movies, Rollin returned to the horror genre with this story set in the early twentieth century about a cult of wealthy blood-drinking women led the bisexual Elisabeth (Maï) and Eva (Lahaie). They meet in a remote château and ritually slaughter and devour men. Problems arise when Elisabeth falls in love with their next victim, escaping thief Mark (Jean-Marie Lemaire). As usual, the visuals far outstrip the storyline and performances.

✦✦

FATAL EXPOSURE

(aka MANGLED ALIVE)

USA, 1989. Dir: Peter B. Good. With: Blake Bahlen, Ena Henderson, Julie Austin, Dan Schmale, Renee Cline, Gary Wise. Tapeworm Video. Colour.

Low-budget independent horror film made by a Herschell Gordon Lewis fan in Alabama. The blood-drinking great grandson of Jack the Ripper photographs his victims and seeks the perfect woman to continue the family line.

✦

FATHER, SANTA KLAUS HAS DIED

Russia, 1992. Dir: Eugeny Yufit. With: Anatoly Egorov, Ivan Ganzha, Ljudmila Kozlovskava, Vlaery

Krishtapenco, Maxim Gribov. Lenfilm/ES. B&W.
Poetic, almost silent art film which marks the début of director Yufit. Loosely based on Alexei Tolstoy's story 'The Vampire Family' ('The Wurdalak'), it apparently includes elements of horror, science fiction, bondage and humour.
✦✧

FEAR IN THE DARK
UK/USA, 1991. Dir: Dominic Murphy. With: John Carpenter, Clive Barker, Wes Craven, Dario Argento, Robert Bloch, Barbara Steele. Classic Films/NBD Entertainment/A&E Network/Channel Four Television. Colour.
Intelligent, hour-long TV documentary that examines what scares movie audiences. This includes several sequences from *Nosferatu* (1922), clips from *Vampyres* (1974) and other films, plus interviews with directors William Friedkin, John McNaughton and Brian Yuzna, designer Saul Bass, novelist James Herbert, critic and author Kim Newman, writer Julian Petley, psychoanalyst Dr Glen Wilson, and a number of silly horror film fans. Narrated by Christopher Lee.
✦✦✦

FEARLESS FOSDICK PUPPET SHOW:
(aka FEARLESS FOSDICK IN)
Batula
USA, 1952. With: The Mary Chase Marionettes. Louis G. Cowan, Inc/NBC-TV. B&W.
The twelfth and last in the TV series of half-hour marionette adventures, produced by Charles Buggenheim and based on Al Capp's dumb comic strip detective. In this episode, Fosdick encounters a vampire who is stealing men's toupees.
✦
Frank N. Stein
USA, 1952. With: The Mary Chase Marionettes. Louis G. Cowan, Inc/NBC-TV. B&W.
In this sixth episode in the series, Fosdick creates a monster in his laboratory who goes on a rampage through the city.
✦
Mr. Ditto
(aka Fearless Fosdick is Mr. Ditto)
USA, 1952. With: The Mary Chase Marionettes. Louis G. Cowan, Inc/NBC-TV. B&W.
In this fourth episode, Fosdick is blamed for a series of crimes committed by Mr Ditto, a gangster who can assume the features of anyone.
✦

FEARLESS FRANK
USA, 1967 (1969). Dir: Philip Kaufman. With: John Voigt, Monique Van Vooren, Severn Darden, Joan Darling, Lou Gilbert, Nelson Algren. Jeriko Film/American International Pictures. Colour.
Filmed in Chicago under the title *Frank's Greatest Adventure*. When naïve country boy Frank (Voigt) is murdered by gangsters, he is revived by the Good Doctor (Darden) and becomes a bullet-proof crime fighter with the ability to fly. However, the Good Doctor's evil brother, Claude (also Darden), creates False Frank (also Voigt), a Frankenstein Monster-like double. The two Franks battle each other until they find themselves taking on the other's characteristics. Director Kaufman moved on to bigger and better things.
✦✧

THE FEARLESS KUNG FU ELEMENTS
Hong Kong, 1983. Dir: Tsai Ku. With: Chan Hsang-Lin, Wei Tse-Yun, Cen Hsing, Sma Yu-Jiau, Lin Wi-Wa, Lung Shao. Wang Hsia-Ts/Wang Ai-Ching/Chen Jou/Ocean Shores Video. Colour.
Kung fu fantasy which involves a vampiric fox woman who sucks blood in her human form to replenish her life-force. This also features other monsters and magical transformations.
✦✧

FEAR OF THE MUMMY
(Orig: YAMI NI HIKARU ME)
Japan, 1958. B&W.
Possibly compiled from a TV series. A scientist uses a serum to reanimate a disfigured Egyptian mummy in a sarcophagus. The mummy kills another scientist, breaks out of a wooden cage and dresses in everyday clothes. With a flashback to ancient Egypt, just like in the classic Universal film.
✦

FEMALE MERCENARIES ON ZOMBIE ISLAND
USA, 1998. Dir: Gary Whitson. With: Pamela Sutch, Tina Krause, Laura Giglio, Kathy Steel, Sydney Nice, Dawn Murphy. WAVE Productions/ShockOrama Pictures/EI Independent Cinema. Colour.
Shot under the more appropriate title *Bimbo Warriors on Zombie Island*, this low-budget video release from co-writer/director/editor Whitson is set in the year 2008, after the impact of an asteroid has killed most of the Earth's population. While some survivors have reverted back to more primitive lifestyles, a female mad doctor (Sutch) experiments with brain transplants and rules what remains with her army of mini-skirted warrior women and a small group of electronically-controlled cannibal zombies. This overlong tape includes the usual mild bondage and nudity, along with mud wrestling(!) and some unconvincing gore effects. It ends on a cliff-hanger with the threat that *The Mad Doctor of Zombie Island* is coming soon!
✦

FEMPYRE
USA, 1999. With: Dawn Murphy. WAVE Productions. Colour.
More fetishism and vampires from the low-budget New Jersey video company.
✦

FERAT VAMPIRE
(Orig: UPIR Z FERATU)
Czechoslovakia, 1982. Dir: Juraj Herz. With: Jiri Menzel, Dagmar Veskrnova, Jana Brezkova, Jan Schmid, Petr Cepek. Barrandov. Colour.
Director Herz parodies the horror genre with this story about a car which runs on the blood of its driver. Loosely based on a story by Roald Dahl.
✦✧

THE FERRET
USA, 1915. Dir: Rupert Julian. With: Rupert Julian, Elsie Jane Wilson, 'Doc' Crane. Universal. B&W.
A doctor with a split personality can change his features. This silent drama is directed by and stars Julian, who also helmed Chaney Sr's *The Phantom of the Opera* (1925).
✦

FIEND
(aka DEADLY NEIGHBOR)
USA, 1980. Dir: Don Dohler. With: Don Leifert, Richard Nelson, Elaine White, George Stover, Greg Dohler. Cinema Enterprises/Force Video/Prism Entertainment/VCI Video. Colour.
Low-budget thrills from Baltimore in which a legendary supernatural creature inhabits the body of a resurrected corpse, Dorian/Mr Longfellow (Leifert), who strangles a number of people and absorbs the energy of his female victims to survive. In the end, Dorian's body quickly decomposes when he is stabbed to death with a sword. From the director of *The Alien Factor* (1979).
✦

FIEND WITHOUT A FACE
UK, 1958. Dir: Arthur Crabtree. With: Marshall Thompson, Kynaston Reeves, Kim Parker, Stanley Maxted, Terence Kilburn, Peter Madden. Producers Associates/Eros Films. B&W.
From the producers of *First Man Into Space* (1958), this cheap-looking science fiction/horror thriller features the same imported American star (Thompson) and benefits from an imaginative script by Herbert J. Leder, based on the story 'The Thought Monster' by Amelia Reynolds Long. Set in Canada, locals living near an atomic air force base are being killed off by invisible mind vampires created

by a scientist's brain-boosting experiments. Crabtree's workmanlike direction keeps the action moving, and the incredible climax involves an attack by flying stop-motion brains attached to spinal cords. Executive produced by Richard Gordon. In 1995 a remake was announced by Norman J. Warren!
✦✦✧

FIGURES FROM EARTH
(Orig: CHUT SI KEI BING/CHU SHI QI BING)
Hong Kong, 1988. Dir: Gin Luang. With: He Mei-Wei, Feng Cui-Fan, Wan Xiu-Liang. Taylor Film & Video. Colour.
Two comedy undercover agents (Cui-Fan and Xiu-Liang) trying to capture grave robbers in feudal China are mummified by a professional demon hunter. 500 years later they are reanimated in contemporary Hong Kong and encounter an evil vampire-witch (Mei-Wei) from their own time who attacks her victims during oral sex.
✦✧

FILM BUFF
USA, 1994 Dir: Jim Enright. With: Chasey Laine (Chasey Lain), Tera Heart, Tiffany Mynx (Tiffany Minx), Norma Jeane, Joey Silvera, Tom Byron. Wicked Pictures. Colour.
This hardcore feature stars Laine in a number of sequences that spoof famous scenes in silent, biker, prison and vampire movies.
✦

FILMHOUSE FEVER
USA, 1986. Dir: Domonic Paris. With: Steve Buscemi, Mojo Nixon. Vestron Video. Colour.
Comedy compilation of scenes and trailers from the director of *Last Rites* (1980). Movie fans Tony (Buscemi) and Vinnie (Nixon) become excited about a 'B' movie marathon on TV. This includes clips from various obscure movies by Al Adamson, H.G. Lewis and even a Sam Raimi short featuring Bruce Campbell. In the end, the rest of the audience turn out to be zombies.
✦✧

FINAL CURTAIN
USA, 1957. Dir: Edward D. Wood Jr. With: James 'Duke' Moore, Dudley Manlove, Jeannie Stevens. Atomic Productions. B&W.
Twenty minute short written, produced and directed by the legendary Ed Wood, this was a pilot episode for a projected TV series called *Portraits in Terror*. After the last performance of a horror play, a vampire actor (Moore) wanders through the empty theatre, compelled by a strange force to seek an unknown object. Narrated by Manlove, with Stevens as a female vampire. This was apparently the script Bela Lugosi was reading when he died. Footage from this film later turned up in Wood's *Night of the Ghouls* (1959).
✦

JON FINCH
[b 1942]

Likeable British leading man who got his start with Hammer before starring in such films as Polanski's *Macbeth* (1971), Hitchcock's *Frenzy* (1972) and *The Final Programme* (1973). After being taken ill on set, he was replaced in *Alien* (1979) by John Hurt. The actor made a belated return to genre films in the 1994 Lovecraft adaptation *Lurking Fear*.
qv: *The Horror of Frankenstein* (1970); *The Vampire Lovers* (1970).

FINGERS AT THE WINDOW
USA, 1942. Dir: Charles Lederer. With: Lew Ayres, Laraine Day, Basil Rathbone, Walter Kingsford, Miles Mander, Charles D. Brown. Metro-Goldwyn-Mayer. B&W.
Enjoyable comedy horror thriller. Ayres and Day are reunited from MGM's popular *Dr. Kildare* series (1937-47) to play fast-talking actor Oliver Duffy and scatty heroine Edwina Brown. They team up to track down smooth villain Dr Santelle (Rathbone) who is impersonating the head of an asylum and turning the patients (including an uncredited Milton Parsons) into mad zombie axe murderers programmed to kill anyone who knows his real identity. Atmospheric direction along with a slick script and likeable performances make this a minor gem. With James Flavin.
✦✦✧

FIRST MAN INTO SPACE
UK, 1958. Dir: Robert Day. With: Marshall Thompson, Marla Landi, Bill Edwards, Robert Ayres, Bill Nagy, Carl Jaffe. Metro-Goldwyn-Mayer/Producers Associates. B&W.
Low-budget science fiction/horror film that owes quite a lot to Hammer's *Quatermass* movies. Shot under the title *Satellite of Blood* and based on an original story by Wyott Ordung, Edwards plays test pilot Lieutenant Dan Prescott, the first man into space, whose ship passes through a cloud of radioactive meteorite dust. He returns to Earth as an ugly monster craving human blood. Imported American star Thompson is his stuffy brother, Air Force Commander Chuck Prescott, and only Roger Delgado stands out in a brief comedy cameo. The sets look cheap and most of the 'special effects' are stock footage. Richard Gordon was executive producer.
✦✧

THE FIRST VAMPIRE IN CHINA
(Orig: MAO SHAN XIAO TANG)
Hong Kong, 1986. Dir: Huang Ying. With: Wang Lung-Wei, Huang Cheng-Li, Yi Yuen. Eternal Film. Colour.
Comedy horror with a great opening sequence in which a dead wizard-warlord is resurrected during a strange celestial configuration. Along with an army of Moon-worshipping hopping vampires, who revive when their hanging coffins are disturbed, the undead general attempts to kill the heroine because his son wants her. This also includes a zombie rooster and a mass attack by vampire bats.
✦✧

TERENCE FISHER
[1904-1980]

British director who entered the film industry at the age of twenty-eight. As part of a training scheme run by the Rank Organisation, Fisher directed his first film in 1947, and he began his association with Hammer Films three years later. Such early projects for the studio as *Stolen Face* (1952), *Four Sided Triangle* (1953) and *Spaceways* (1953) were indicative of the course his career would take after the success of *The Curse of Frankenstein* (1957), which was scripted by Jimmy Sangster. Fisher and Sangster continued to work together on *Dracula* (1958), *The Revenge of Frankenstein* (1958), *The Mummy* (1959), *The Man Who Could Cheat Death* (1959) and *The Brides of Dracula* (1960). However, following the poor box-office performance of *The Phantom of the Opera* (1962), Hammer dropped its star director, although he periodically returned to the studio to direct *The Gorgon* (1964), *Dracula Prince of Darkness* (1965), *Frankenstein Created Woman* (1966), *The Devil Rides Out* (1967), *Frankenstein Must Be Destroyed* (1969) and *Frankenstein and the Monster from Hell* (1973). He always brought integrity and an uncomplicated style to his best work in the horror genre.
qv: *The Curse of the Werewolf* (1960); *The Earth Dies Screaming* (1964); *The Horror of It All* (1963); *The Two Faces of Dr. Jekyll* (1960).

FIST OF THE NORTH STAR
USA/Japan, 1995. Dir: Tony Randel. With: Gary Daniels, Costas Mandylor, Chris Penn, Isako Washio, Leon 'Vader' White, Malcolm McDowell. Overseas Filmgroup/Toei Video/First Look Pictures/Ozla Pictures/Zeta Entertainment/Neo Motion Pictures. Colour.
Post-apocalyptic fantasy/adventure scripted by Peter Atkins and director Randel (who previously worked together on *Hellbound Hellraiser II* [1988]) and based on the Japanese graphic novel *Hokuto No Ken* by Buronson and Tetsuo Hara (filmed in 1986 as a cartoon feature). Mystical martial arts warrior Kenshiro (Daniels), known as Fist of the North Star, wanders through a devastated wasteland searching for his evil brother Lord Shin (Mandylor), Master of the Southern Cross, who has stolen his girlfriend (Washio). With Melvin Van Peebles, Downtown Julie Brown, Clint Howard, and McDowell's character as a zombie in a nightmare sequence.
✦✧

THE FLAMING SIGNAL

USA, 1933. Dir: C.E. (Edward) Roberts and George Jeske. With: Marcelene Day, John David Horsley, Carmelita Geraghty, Noah Beery, Henry B. Walthal(l), Mischa Auer. William Berke Productions/Imperial. B&W.

Serial-like thrills as pilot Jim Robbins (Horsley) and his wonder dog Flash crash their aeroplane off the coast of uncharted Tabu Island. They soon find themselves caught up in a confrontation between the white settlers and the islanders. When high priest Manu (Auer) is shot by brutal German trader Otto von Krantz (Beery), he is apparently revived from the dead by the natives' supernatural rituals.

✦✧

FLESH AND BLOOD: THE HAMMER HERITAGE OF HORROR

USA/UK, 1994. Dir: Ted Newsom. With: Peter Cushing, Christopher Lee, Roy Ward Baker, James Bernard, Martine Beswicke, Joe Dante. Heidelberg Films/Bosustow Media Group/BBC-TV. Colour/B&W.

Written, co-produced and directed by Newsom, this atrocious TV documentary about the Hammer heritage of horror, originally shown in two fifty minute segments, is incompetently made. It includes interviews with various cast and crew (including Veronica Carlson, Michael Carreras, Hazel Court, Freddie Francis, Val Guest, Ray Harryhausen, Anthony Hinds, Andrew Keir, Francis Matthews, Christopher Neame, Caroline Munro, Ferdy Mayne, Jimmy Sangster and even Raquel Welch), sub-standard clips and trailers (with material from the BBC-2 documentary *Hammer the Studio That Dripped Blood!* [1987], TV's *Tales of Frankenstein* [1958] and *The Mystery of the Mary Celeste/Phantom Ship* [1936] with Bela Lugosi), plus home movie footage taken behind-the-scenes on *Dracula Prince of Darkness* (1965). Depressingly, it also marks the final pairing of Lee and Cushing, who teamed up again after twelve years to record the narration. Too ill to watch the programme, eighty-one year-old Peter Cushing OBE died of cancer before the second instalment was transmitted in Britain. Joe Dante, Bill Kelley and Roy Skeggs were associate producers. The 1999 video release from Anchor Bay was apparently remastered and is an improvement.

✦

FLESH FOR FRANKENSTEIN

(Orig: IL MOSTRO É IN TAVOLA...BARONE FRANKSTEIN/ CARNE PER FRANKENSTEIN/DE LA CHAIR POUR FRANKENSTEIN. USA: aka FRANKENSTEIN/THE FRANKENSTEIN EXPERIMENT)

Italy/France, 1973. Dir: Paul Morrissey (and Anthony M. Dawson/Antonio Margheriti). With: Joe Dallesandro, Dalila di Lazzaro, Monique Van Vooren, Udo Kier, Arno Juerging (Jürging), Aleksic Miomir. Carlo Ponti/ Compagnia Cinematográfica Champion/EMI/Bryanston Pictures. Colour.

From the same writer/director(s) as *Blood for Dracula* (1974), this adaptation of the Mary Shelley novel has little to recommend it. Kier's Baron Frankenstein spends most of the film explaining how brilliant he is and trying to create the 'Serbian ideal' of a super-race by mating his male and female monsters (Carlo Mancini and Srdjan Zelenovic), until his entrails end up impaled on a pole. Juerging plays his assistant Otto, while Dallesandro's Brooklyn-accented shepherd seems totally out of place amongst the incestuous sex, gratuitous gore and black humour (nearly ten minutes were cut in Britain). Most of the characters end up either strangled or decapitated as Frankenstein's two children begin work on their own creation. Originally released in the uneven 3-D Spacevision process, this was advertised in America as *Andy Warhols Frankenstein*.

Remake: FRANKENSTEIN: THE TRUE STORY (qv; 1973)

✦✧

FLESH FOR FRANKENSTEIN

USA, 1987. Dir: Bill Blackman. With: Dana Lynn, Nikki Knight (Knights), Ebony Ayes, Amy Berens. Mark Curtis/ Video Exclusives. Colour.

Hardcore horror feature in which Dr X creates Frankenstein, who he sends out to bring back women for himself and his assistant, Igor.

✦

THE FLINTSTONE COMEDY SHOW: THE FRANKENSTONES

(aka BACK TO BEDROCK/THE FLINTSTONES FAMILY ADVENTURE HOUR)

USA, 1980-81. Dir: Gordon Hunt. Voices: Henry Corden, Ruta Lee, Charles Nelson Reilly, Paul Reubens, Zelda Rubenstein, Frank Welker. Hanna-Barbera Productions/ NBC-TV. Colour.

Fifteen minute segment of the ninety minute cartoon TV show featuring the Flintstone's new neighbours, the Frankenstones, who consist of father Frank (Reilly), his wife Hidea (Lee), son Freaky (Reubens), daughter Atrocia (Rubenstein) and dog Rockjaw (Welker).

Series sequel: WIND-UP WILMA (1981)

✦✦

THE FLINTSTONES:

(aka THE FLINTSTONES COMEDY HOUR/THE FLINTSTONES SHOW/FRED FLINTSTONE AND FRIENDS)

Alvin Brickrock Presents

USA, 1962 (1961). Dir: William Hanna and Joseph Barbera. Voices: Alan Reed, Mel Blanc, Jean Vander Pyl, Bea Benaderet, John Stephenson, Hal Smith. Hanna-Barbera Productions/Screen Gems/ABC-TV. Colour.

Hugely popular half-hour cartoon TV series (1960-66, 166 episodes) that spawned various spin-off shows and TV specials plus two live-action movies. It follows the adventures of Fred (Reed) and Wilma (Vander Pyl) Flintstone and their neighbours Barney (Blanc) and Betty (Bea Benaderet/Gerry Johnson) Rubble, two modern Stone Age families. In this episode, detective fiction fan Fred suspects that his new neighbour, the Alfred Hitchcock-like Alvin Brickrock (Elliott Field), is a serial wife-killer. When Fred and Barney sneak into Brickrock's basement looking for evidence, the creepy archaeologist shows them his 2,000 year-old mummy and mastodon skeleton. There's even a neat, Hitchcock-style twist ending.

✦✦✦

Fred Goes Ape

USA, 1966. Dir: William Hanna and Joseph Barbera. Voices: Alan Reed, Mel Blanc, Jean Vander Pyl, Gerry Johnson, Don Messick. Hanna-Barbera Productions/ABC-TV. Colour.

When Fred mistakenly takes Goosepimple's Pepstone Pills to stop himself sneezing, he turns into an ape.

✦✧

The Gruesomes

USA, 1965 (1964). Dir: William Hanna and Joseph Barbera. Voices: Alan Reed, Mel Blanc, Jean Vander Pyl, Gerry Johnson, Don Messick, Howard Morris. Hanna-Barbera Productions/ABC-TV. Colour.

Fred and Barney encounter Weirdly Gruesome (Morris) and the rest of his Addams-like family: his wife Creepella (Naomi Lewis) and son Goblin (Messick), who move into spooky Tombstone Manor next door.

Episode sequel: THE FLINTSTONES: The Hatrocks and the Gruesomes (qv; 1965)

✦✧

The Hatrocks and the Gruesomes

USA, 1965. Dir: William Hanna and Joseph Barbera. Voices: Alan Reed, Mel Blanc, Jean Vander Pyl, Gerry Johnson, Don Messick, Howard Morris. Hanna-Barbera Productions/ABC-TV. Colour.

When Fred's hillbilly relations the Hatrocks come to stay in Bedrock, they nearly eat Fred and Wilma out of house and home. Fred calls on the Gruesomes to scare them off, but when that doesn't work, the Flintstones, Rubbles and Gruesomes don Beatles-like wigs and drive them away with 'bug' music.

✦✧

Monster Fred

USA, 1964. Dir: William Hanna and Joseph Barbera. Voices: Alan Reed, Mel Blanc, Jean Vander Pyl, Gerry Johnson, Don Messick, Harvey Korman. Hanna-Barbera Productions/ABC-TV. Colour.

Fred gets hit on the head by a bowling ball and thinks he's a baby. Barney takes him to Dr Len Frankenstone (Alan Melvin), who ends up accidentally swapping Fred's personality with Dino and then again with Barney.

✦✧

The Split Personality
USA, 1960. Dir: William Hanna and Joseph Barbera. Voices: Alan Reed, Mel Blanc, Jean Vander Pyl, Bea Benaderet, Howard McNear. Hanna-Barbera Productions/Screen Gems/ABC-TV. Colour.
When Fred accidentally hits himself on the head with a bottle, he regains consciousness as Frederick, a highbrow sophisticate who upsets all of Bedrock with his refined manners.
Series sequels: A MAN CALLED FLINTSTONE (qv; 1966) and THE PEBBLES AND BAMM-BAMM SHOW (1971-72)
✦✧

THE FLINTSTONES MEET ROCKULA AND FRANKENSTONE
USA, 1980. Dir: Ray Patterson. Voices: Gay Autterson, Mel Blanc, Ted Cassidy, Casey Kasem, Don Messick, Jean Vander Pyl. Hanna-Barbera Productions/NBC-TV. Colour.
Fifty-minute cartoon TV special in which the Flintstones and Rubbles win a free trip on a game show to visit Castle Rockula in Rocksylvania. There they meet a Peter Lorre-voiced Igor (Messick) and attend a Monster Bash costume ball. Dressed as a vampire and Monster respectively, Fred (Henry Corden) and Barney (Blanc) discover a secret laboratory and accidently revive the Frankenstone Monster (Cassidy) who in turn wakes up the vampiric Count Rockula (John Stephenson) after 500 years. When Rockula decides to make Wilma (Vander Pyl) his bride, he has to make her a widow first. Barney gets to wear a werewolf mask and Wilma dresses up as a mummy. William Hanna and Joseph Barbera were executive producers.
Sequel: FRED'S FINAL FLING (1980)
✦✦

THE FLINTSTONES' NEW NEIGHBORS
USA, 1980. Dir: Carl Urbano. Voices: Gay Autterson, Mel Blanc, Henry Corden, Jim McGeorge, Julie McWhirter, Jean Vander Pyl. Hanna-Barbera Productions/NBC-TV. Colour.
Half-hour cartoon TV special in which Fred Flintstone's (Corden) new neighbours are the Frankenstones, a family of friendly monsters consisting of father Frank (John Stephenson), 'Bride' Oblivia (Pat Parris), teenage daughter Hidea (McWhirter) and young son Stubby (Jim MacGeorge).
Sequels: THE FLINTSTONES MEET ROCKULA AND FRANKENSTONE (qv; 1980) and THE FLINTSTONE COMEDY SHOW: THE FRANKENSTONES (qv; 1980-81)
✦✦

FLYING SAUCERS OVER HOLLYWOOD
(aka THE ED WOOD STORY: THE PLAN 9 COMPANION)
USA, 1992 (1995). Dir: Mark Patrick Carducci. With: Gregory Walcott, Harry Thomas, Carl Anthony, Conrad Brooks, Paul Marco, Mrs Tom Mason. Atomic Pictures/ MPI Home Video. Colour/B&W.
An affectionate made-for-video look at the life and career of Edward D. Wood Jr through film clips, 8mm home movies and interviews with the surviving cast and crew members of *Plan 9 from Outer Space* (1958), plus Maila Nurmi, Valda Hansen, Stephen Apostoloff, Drew Friedman, Rudolph Grey, Harry Medved, Sam Raimi, Joe Dante, Tony Randel, Gary Gerani, Scott Spiegel, Forrest J Ackerman, Bill Warren, Eric Caidin and others. This also includes a tribute to Tor Johnson, a look at the Don Post Studios (with Verne Langdon and Don Post Jr), and a tour of the tiny Quality Studios, where 'Eddie' filmed his most (in)famous movie. Narrated by Lee Harris and produced by Wade Williams. Valda Hansen died in 1993 and writer/ director Carducci committed suicide in 1997.
✦✦✦

FOG FOR A KILLER
(USA: aka OUT OF THE FOG)
UK, 1962. Dir: Montgomery Tully. With: David Sumner, Susan Travers, James Hayter, Jack Watson, George Woodbridge, Michael Ripper. Eternal. B&W.
An ex-convict (Sumner) is suspected of being a full-moon serial killer in this minor British thriller.
✦✧

NINA FOCH
[b 1924]

Dutch-born American actress who made her movie début as a teenager opposite Bela Lugosi in *The Return of the Vampire* (1943).
qv: *Cry of the Werewolf* (1944) *I Love a Mystery* (1945); *100 Years of Horror: 'Dracula and His Disciples'* (1996); *100 Years of Horror: 'Girl Ghouls'* (1996); *100 Years of Horror: 'Werewolves'* (1996); *Shadow Chasers* (1985-86); *Universal Horror* (1998).

FOLLOW ME
(USA: THE PUBLIC EYE)
UK, 1971 (1972). Dir: Carol Reed. With: Mia Farrow, Topol, Michael Jayston, Margaret Rawlings, Annette Crosbie, Dudley Foster. Universal/Rank. Colour.
Romantic comedy scripted by Peter Shaffer and based on his one-act play *The Public Eye*. Topol plays Julian Cristoforou, an eccentric private detective who falls in love with the woman he is following (played by Farrow). This includes a fake double bill at a cinema (*Werewolves from Mars/Bloodsuckers from Venus*) with clips from Hammer's *The Evil of Frankenstein* (1964) and *Frankenstein Created Woman* (1966).
✦

FOLLOW THAT BIRD
(aka SESAME STREET PRESENTS: FOLLOW THAT BIRD)
Canada/USA, 1985. Dir: Ken Kwapis. With: Carroll Spinney, Jim Henson, Frank Oz, Richard Hunt, Kathryn Mullen, Jerry Nelson. Warner Bros/Children's TV Workshop/World Film Services. Colour.
Cute musical mix of muppets, live action and cartoon animation, based on the characters created by Jim Henson and Frank Oz for the young children's PBS-TV series *Sesame Street* (1969-). When six year-old Big Bird (Spinney) is placed in a foster home with a family of Dodos, he decides to walk all the way back to Sesame Street and encounters various friends along the way. This also includes guest stars Paul Bartel, Sandra Bernhard, John Candy, Chevy Chase, Joe Flaherty, Waylon Jennings and Dave Thomas, voices by Laraine Newman, Eddie Deezen and Sally Kellerman, and Count von Count, the monocled vampiric puppet (performed by Nelson) from the TV show.
✦✦

FOLLOW THAT GOBLIN!
UK/Israel, 1992. Dir: Jonathan Lubell. Voices: Daniel Diker, Chaya Golinkin. One Eighty One Productions/ Scopus Films. Colour.
This half-hour clay animation short for children follows the adventures of Gerbert Goblin and features a fairground haunted house that includes the Frankenstein Monster-like Frankie, a vampire, wolf man, mummy, hunchback, gorgon, witch and various ghosts.
✦✧

FOOLS
USA, 1970. Dir: Tom Gries. With: Jason Robards, Katherine Ross, Scott Hylands, Roy C. Jenson, Mark Bramhall, Marc Hannibal. Translor/Cinerama. Colour.
Romantic drama in which Robards plays waning horror film star Matthew South, who watches himself as a vampire in one scene.
✦

DICK FORAN
(Nicholas Foran) [1910-1979]

Rugged American leading man who, as archaeologist Steven Banning, escaped *The Mummy's Hand* (1940) but succumbed in *The Mummy's Tomb* (1942).

FORCED NIGHTMARE
(Orig: HUA GUI LU XING TUAN)
Hong Kong, 1992. Dir: Lau Sze-Yu (Wong Ching-Jing/Wong Ching). With: Lam Ching-Ying (Lin Zheng-Ying), Sandra

The EDISON KINETOGRAM

VOL. 2 MARCH 15, 1910 No. 4

SCENE FROM

FRANKENSTEIN

FILM No. 6604

EDISON FILMS RELEASED FROM MARCH 16 TO 31 INCLUSIVE

Ng, Yau Kin Kowk, Charlie Chao. Grand March Movie Production/Golden Princess Amusement/World Video. Colour.
Comedy horror in which a group of bus passengers, having been killed in a crash, are possessed by ghosts from a graveyard and turn into flesh-eating zombies. The ghost of a psychic (Ng) calls on a priest (Ching-Ying) with his ecto-detector to defeat the leader of the ghouls, who is caped and fanged like a vampire.
✦✧

FORCE OF NATURE
USA, 1999. Dir: Barbara Kopple. Sci-Fi Channel/USA Network. Colour.
TV series that retells the werewolf myth from a woman's point of view.
✦✦

FOREVER EVIL
USA, 1987. Dir: Roger Evans. With: Charles Trotter, Howard Jacobsen, Red Mitchell, Tracey Huffman, Kent Johnson, Diane Johnson. FrameWork/B&S/United. Colour.
Independent, low-budget horrors, released directly to video and apparently produced by a group of Texas special effects designers. While on vacation, several people are trapped in a secluded cabin by a cult who worship a Lovecraft-inspired god and their zombie killer (Kent Johnson).
✦

FOREVER KNIGHT
Canada/USA, 1992-96. With: Geraint Wyn Davies, Catherine Disher, Nigel Bennett, John Kapelos, Deborah Duchêne, Gary Farmer. Paragon Entertainment/Tele-München/Glen-Warren Great Entertainment/TriStar. Colour.
Belated hour-long spin-off TV series (seventy episodes) from the TV movie *Nick Knight* (1989), originally shown on CBS-TV and syndicated for its second and third seasons, where it also appeared on the USA Network. Davies replaces Rick Springfield as the angst-ridden vampire brought across in 1228. Having preyed on humans for their blood, he now wants to be mortal again, to repay society for his sins. As a Toronto homicide detective who works the night-shift, he lives in a steel-shuttered loft. With Disher as Dr Natalie Lambert, the medical examiner who knows his secret, Kapelos as his partner Detective Schanke, Duchêne as the undead owner of the vampire nightclub The Raven, and Bennett as his evil nemesis, Lacroix. The final season also introduced Nick's new partner Tracy Vedder (Lisa Ryder) and her irresponsible vampire boyfriend, Vachon (Ben Bass). Created by James D. Parriott and Barney Cohen.
✦✦

GARRETT FORT
[1898-1945]

American screenwriter who worked on the scripts for *Dracula* (1931), *Frankenstein* (1931) and *Dracula's Daughter* (1936), along with such other horror titles as *The Devil-Doll* (1936), *Among the Living* (1941) and *The Man in Half Moon Street* (1944).
qv: *Made for Love* (1926).

FORTUNE HUNTERS
(aka GANDY GOOSE IN FORTUNE HUNTERS)
USA, 1946. Dir: Connie Rasinski. Voices: Arthur Kay. Terrytoons/Twentieth Century-Fox. Colour.
Six minute Paul Terry cartoon in which Gandy Goose (Kay) dreams that a fortune teller guides him to his grandfather's haunted house where he is pursued by ghosts and the Frankenstein Monster. The footage of the Monster is colourised from *G-Man Jitters* (1939), and several sequences from this film were later re-used in Mannie Davis' *Seeing Ghosts* (1947).
Sequel: IT'S ALL IN THE STARS (1946)
✦✦

Charles Stanton Ogle as the first Frankenstein *(1910).*

FOUR SHALL DIE
(aka CONDEMNED MEN)
USA, 1940. Dir: Leo C. Popkin. With: Mantan Moreland, Dorothy Dandridge, Niel Webster, Reggie (Reginald) Fenderson, Jessie (Jess) Lee Brooks, Jack Carr. Million Dollar Pictures/Toddy. B&W.
Low-budget, all-black horror comedy that apparently involves 'zombies', with seventeen year-old Dandridge making an early appearance.
✦✧

THE FOUR SKULLS OF JONATHAN DRAKE
USA, 1959. Dir: Edward L. Cahn. With: Eduard Franz, Valerie French, Grant Richards, Henry Daniell, Paul Cavanagh, Howard Wendell. Vogue Pictures/United Artists. B&W.
Scripted by Orville H. Hampton (*The Snake Woman* [1961], etc). 180 years ago Dr Emil Zurich (veteran Daniell) had his head sewn onto the body of an Amazonian witch-doctor. With the aid of his zombie servant Zutai (Paul Wexler), whose mouth is sewn shut, Zurich continues the Drake family curse by ensuring that each male member is decapitated at the age of sixty and the head then shrunken. With Lumsden Hare.
✦✦

THE FOX WOMAN
USA, 1915. Dir: Lloyd Ingraham. With: Signe Auen (Seena Owen), Elmer Clifton, Teddy Sampson. Majestic/Mutual. B&W.
Forty-five minute silent adaptation of the story by John Luther Long. A man's soul is restored when a vampiric were-fox (Auen) is killed.
✦

FREDDIE FRANCIS
[b 1917]

Academy Award-winning British cinematographer who never managed to bring the same skills to directing Hammer's Frankenstein and Dracula series or his anthology films for Amicus. He also directed *Legend of the Werewolf* (1974) and *The Ghoul* (1975) for Tyburn Films, run by his son Kevin (b 1944).
qv: *Dracula Has Risen from the Grave* (1968); *Dr. Terror's House of Horrors* (1965); *The Evil of Frankenstein* (1964); *Flesh and Blood: The Hammer Heritage of Horror* (1994); *100 Years of Horror: 'Baron Frankenstein'* (1996); *100 Years of Horror: 'Dracula and His Disciples'* (1996); *Son of Dracula* (1974); *Tales from the Crypt* (1972); *Tales from the Crypt: 'Last Respects'* (1996); *Torture Garden* (1967); *The Vampire Happening* (1971).

JESÜS FRANCO
(Jesús Franco Manera) [b 1930]

Spanish film-maker who has made nearly 200 movies in all genres, many in a bewildering array of soft- and hardcore versions under various pseudonyms (Clifford Brown, Jess Franco, A.M. Frank, Jess Frank, J.P. Johnson, Franco Manera etc). Although he entered the European film industry in the early fifties, he made his horror début in 1961 with *The Awful Dr. Orlof.* Despite being shot quickly and often ineptly (Franco's over-reliance on crash zooms quickly becomes irritating), the director and his films have achieved something of a cult status amongst many revisionist film critics.
qv: *Attack of the Robots* (1966); *The Bare Breasted Countess* (1973); *Das Bildnis der Dorian Gray* (1976); *Bram Stoker's Count Dracula* (1970); *Daughter of Dracula* (1972); *Dracula Prisoner of Frankenstein* (1972); *Dr. Orloff's Monster* (1964); *The Erotic Rites of Frankenstein* (1972); *Lust for Frankenstein* (1997); *Man Hunter* (1980); *La Mansión de los Muertos Viventes* (1982); *Marie-Cookie and the Killer Tarantula* (1998); *El Misterio del Castillo Rojo* (1972); *The Oasis of the Living Dead* (1981); *Revenge in the House of Usher* (1983); *La Tumba de los Muertos Vivientes* (1981); *Vampiresas 1930* (1960); *Vampiros Lesbos* (1970); *Virgin Among the Living Dead* (1971).

FRANKENHOOKER
USA, 1990. Dir: Frank Henenlotter. With: James Lorinz, Patty Mullen, Shirley Stoler, Louise Lasser, Charlotte Helmkamp, Lia Chang. Shapiro Glickenhaus Entertainment. Colour.
Sleazy black comedy from co-writer/director Henenlotter (the *Basket Case* series, etc), filmed under the title *Frankenstein '90*. When do-it-yourself mad scientist Jeffrey Franken (Lorinz) accidentally runs over his fiancée Elizabeth Shelley (Mullen) with a remote-controlled lawnmower(!), he keeps her head alive and begins to stitch her body back together with parts taken from Times Square hookers. In the end, the sum of the parts take their revenge. The outrageous make-up effects created by Gabe Bartalos add to the fun. With quite a bit of nudity and a cameo by veteran TV horror host John Zacherle as a TV weatherman.
✦✦✧

FRANKENHUNTER, QUEEN OF THE PORNO ZOMBIES
USA, 1989. With: Heather Hunter. Colour.
Hardcore feature starring Hunter, who is also in *Frankenhooker* (1990).
✦

FRANKENSTEIN
USA, 1910. Dir: J. Searle Dawley. With: Charles Stanton Ogle, Augustus Phillips, Mary Fuller. Edison Film Company. B&W.
After numerous stage versions, this first short movie adaptation of Mary Shelley's 1818 novel is quite faithful to the story. Obsessed with creating the perfect human being, young medical student Dr Frankenstein (Phillips) produces a Monster (Ogle) from a cauldron of fiery chemicals. Standing before a mirror, the misshapen creature vanishes as it is finally defeated by its creator's better nature. This is now available from Incredibly Strange Filmworks as a twelve minute video with music soundtrack, along with a 150-page book. *Edison's Frankenstein* (1990) recreates the film in still photographs.
Remake: LIFE WITHOUT SOUL (qv; 1915)
✦✧

FRANKENSTEIN
USA, 1931. Dir: Robert Florey. With: Bela Lugosi, Edward Van Sloan, Dwight Frye. Universal. B&W.
Apparently lost twenty minute test reel with Lugosi playing the Monster. It was adapted by Garett Fort and Robert Florey, and photographed by Paul Ivano on the *Dracula* (1931) sets in June 1931. Universal didn't like the Golem-type make-up Lugosi and Jack Pierce designed, and the actor (whose name appears prominently on the pre-release poster) was reputedly not happy that the Monster was a non-speaking role. Although originally set to direct *Frankenstein* (1931), Florey was replaced by James Whale and his significant contributions to the final script went uncredited (except in his native France). Other cast members would have included Leslie Howard as Henry Frankenstein and Bette Davis as his fiancée Elizabeth.
✦

FRANKENSTEIN
USA, 1931. Dir: James Whale. With: Colin Clive, Mae Clarke, John Boles, Boris Karloff, Dwight Frye, Edward Van Sloan. Universal. B&W.
Director Whale's dark, Gothic version of Mrs Percy B. Shelley's classic novel has some nice moments of humour and, along with *Dracula* (1931) from the same studio, kicked off the first great horror cycle. Still memorable for Clive's manic Henry Frankenstein ('It's alive!') and Frye's demented hunchback, Fritz. After Bela Lugosi and John Carradine both reputedly turned the role down because it involved no dialogue, the Monster (created by make-up artist Jack Pierce) made a star of forty-four year-old Karloff, who brought a unique child-like pathos to the role. In the 1980s it was re-released in its full version, which included the Monster throwing little Maria (Marilyn Harris) into the river to see if she would float like the flowers. With Lionel Belmore as the Burgomaster, and electrical equipment created and operated by Frank Graves, Kenneth Strickfaden and Raymond Lindsay. Some original release prints were apparently tinted green. Universal filmed two endings and, following previews, decided to use the one where Henry survives. Crestwood House published a juvenile novelisation by Ian Thorne in 1977, the film was recreated by Richard J. Anobile with frame blow-ups in a 1974 volume, and the original shooting script was published by MagicImage Filmbooks in 1989. A sequel announced in 1933, *The Return of Frankenstein*, stayed on the studio's tentative schedule until 1935.
Sequel: BRIDE OF FRANKENSTEIN (qv; 1935)
Remake: EL SUPERLOCO (qv; 1936)
✦✦✦✦

FRANKENSTEIN
USA, 1940. Dir: Glenn Alvey. Pixilated Pictures. B&W.
This is a real rarity: the earliest known amateur Frankenstein film (apparently a remake of the 1931 version), distributed through the Interstate Theatre Circuit in Texas.
Remake: TALES OF TOMORROW: Frankenstein (qv; 1952)
✦

FRANKENSTEIN
West Germany, 1965. Dir: Julian Beck and Judith Malina. With: Julian Beck, The Living Theatre Company.
Film record of the Berlin performance of *Frankenstein* by The Living Theatre Company. Co-directed by actor Beck (*Poltergeist II The Other Side* [1986], etc), who also stars as Dr Frankenstein.
Remake: PLAYHOUSE: MYSTERY AND IMAGINATION: Frankenstein (qv; 1968)
✦

FRANKENSTEIN
UK, 1969. Dir: Alan Harrison. Sheffield Polytechnic. B&W.
Twenty-five minute 16mm reconstruction of scenes from James Whale's 1931 version, including the creation sequence and the fiery climax. Made and performed by students at the Sheffield College of Art.
Remake: THE HORROR OF FRANKENSTEIN (qv; 1970)
✦

FRANKENSTEIN
USA, 1973. Dir: Glenn Jordan. With: Robert Foxworth, Susan Strasberg, Heidi Vaughn, Bo Svenson, John Karlen, Philip Bourneuf. Dan Curtis Productions/ABC-TV. Colour.
Miserable TV movie adaptation of Mary Shelley's novel, shot on video and originally shown in two parts on *ABC Wide World of Entertainment*. Foxworth overacts as Victor Frankenstein and he's not helped by a lacklustre supporting cast, dire script, awful music score and unimaginative direction. Only Svenson (billed as 'The Giant') gives a reasonable performance as the sympathetic creature. With Rosella Olson as the Monster's bride. Yet another version of the story we could have done without. Low on horror, high on angst.
Remake: FLESH FOR FRANKENSTEIN (qv; 1973)
✦

FRANKENSTEIN
(aka FRANKENSTEIN, UNE HISTOIRE D'AMOUR)
France, 1974. Dir: Bob Thénault. With: Gérard Benard, Karin Petersen, François Lugagne, Bernard Mesguich, Gérard Boucaron, Nicolas Silberg. 3e Chaîne. Colour.
Ninety-five minute TV movie of Mary Shelley's novel, in which Benard portrays Victor Frankenstein and the Monster's features are never revealed.
Remake: VICTOR FRANKENSTEIN (qv; 1976)
✦✦

FRANKENSTEIN
(Orig: KYOFU DENSETSU: KAIBUTSU! FRANKENSTEIN. USA: aka MYSTERY! FRANKENSTEIN — LEGEND OF TERROR)
Japan, 1981 (1984). Dir: Yugo SeriKawa. Voices: Nachi Nozawa, Mami Koyama, Michimasa Komatsu, Satoshi Toyama, Ichiro Nagai, Minori Matsushima. Aoi Productions/Toei Animation/Terebi (TV) Asahi/Harmony

Boris Karloff makes an impressive entrance in Frankenstein *(1931).*

310

Gold. Colour.
Set in north Wales, this feature-length cartoon made for TV is apparently based on Mary Shelley's novel and the Marvel Comics series. Working from his father's notes, Dr Victor Frankenstein (Nozawa) creates a Monster, Franken (Komatsu), who is subsequently disfigured by a lightning bolt. Befriended by Victor's father, the creature saves the daughter (Koyama) of his creator from a bear before committing suicide. The English-language version is dubbed by other voices.
Remake: FRANKENSTEIN (qv; 1984)
✦✧

FRANKENSTEIN
(USA: BROADWAY ON SHOWTIME: FRANKENSTEIN)
UK, 1984. Dir: James Ormerod. With: Robert Powell, Carrie Fisher, David Warner, John Gielgud, Terence Alexander, Susan Wooldridge. Yorkshire Television. Colour.
Another TV movie version (shot on video) of the story, adapted by Victor Gialanella from his short-lived Broadway stage play. This adds nothing to previous adaptations and, although Warner gives his scarred creature (complete with cropped hair) an air of pathos, most of the performances are disappointing (especially Wooldridge). With Powell as Victor Frankenstein, Gielgud as the blind hermit De Lacey, Fisher (doing a passable English accent) as Elizabeth, and Edward Judd giving the film's best performance as a grave robber axed to death by the Monster. Almost everyone ends up dead at the finish. Mary Shelley isn't even credited!
Remake: FRANKENSTEIN 90 (qv; 1984)
✦✧

FRANKENSTEIN
(aka FRANKENSTEIN A CINEMATIC SCRAPBOOK)
USA, 1990 (1991). Dir: Ted Newsom. Robert T. Newsom/ Heidelberg Films/Rhino Home Video. B&W/Colour.
Hour-long compilation written and directed by Newsom that includes chronological clips and trailers from all the Universal and Hammer Frankenstein films (including *The Revenge of Frankenstein* [1958] in which Peter Cushing speaks to the audience), plus numerous other movies (from *I Was a Teenage Frankenstein* [1957] to *Young Frankenstein* [1974]), news clips of Boris Karloff as the Monster at a 1941 celebrity baseball match, and Glenn Strange playing the Monster on TV's *Colgate Comedy Hour* (1953) featuring Abbott and Costello. Titled *Frankenstein A Cinematic Scrapbook* on the video box from Rhino, who have also released equally fascinating tapes based around Dracula and the Wolf Man.
✦✦✦

FRANKENSTEIN
(UK: FRANKENSTEIN — THE REAL STORY)
UK/USA/Poland, 1992 (1993). Dir: David Wickes. With: Patrick Bergin, John Mills, Randy Quaid, Lambert Wilson, Fiona Gillies, Jacinta Mulcahy. Turner Pictures/ David Wickes/TNT. Colour.
This overlong, made-for-cable TV movie is not quite the definitive version the producers would have you believe. After creating various animal hybrids in his laboratory, Bergin's boring Professor Victor Frankenstein uses obscure science to birth his fully-grown Monster (a sympathetic Quaid, in effective make-up created by Image Animation's Mark Coulier) in a tank of chemicals containing the 'elements of life'. When the creature is revived by an electrical accident, it shares a symbiotic relationship with its creator. After the aborted birth of a female companion (the film's best sequence), the Monster revenges itself on Frankenstein's family, until the two nemeses finally destroy each other on the Arctic ice. With Mills as the blind hermit and Michael Gothard in one of his last roles (he committed suicide in 1993) as the ship's bosun.
Remake: MARY SHELLEY'S FRANKENSTEIN (qv; 1994)
✦✦

FRANK ENSTEIN
USA, 1992. Dir: Douglas Richards. Voices: Laura Gabriel, David Nettheim, Lee Perry, Alan Glover. International Family Classics II/Holric Entertainment Group/INI Entertainment Group. Colour.
Hour-long children's cartoon supposedly based on Mary Shelley's novel. TV news researcher Libby becomes involved with the mad Dr Max Enstein, his dim-witted bionic Monster, Frank, and their attempts to regain a stolen computer disc containing the plans for a water-powered car.
✦

FRANKENSTEIN
(aka BUCK ADAMS' FRANKENSTEIN)
USA, 1994. Dir: Buck Adams. With: Buck Adams, Rebecca Wild, Felecia, Anna Malle, Brittany O'Connell, Lady Berlin. Sin City Video. Colour.
Hardcore version inspired by the Kenneth Branagh film, with director Adams as Frankenstein.
✦

FRANKENSTEIN
USA, 2000. Dir: Dave Carson and Brent Maddock. Universal Pictures Animation & Visual Effects/Industrial Light & Magic. Colour.
In 1998, Universal and ILM started production on this $80,000,000 full-length computer-created cartoon sequel for release on Halloween 2000. Originally announced as *Frankenstein and the Wolf Man* and referred to as *The Untitled CGI Monster Project* during filming, the script by Carson, Maddock and S.S. Wilson is set in eastern Europe during the nineteenth century and follows Dr Pretorious' attempts to rediscover the secret of Frankenstein's experiments. The mad scientist must locate the remaining electrode from the neck of the long-lost Karloffian Monster so that he can further his own researches into 'improving' another artificial creation called Novo. The Wolf Man is also involved.
✦✦✧

FRANKENSTEIN AND ME
Canada/USA, 1996. Dir: Robert Tinnell. With: Jamieson Boulanger, Myriam Cyr, Louise Fletcher, Burt Reynolds, Ricky Mabe, Ryan Gosling. Mojave Frankenstein Productions/Melenny Productions/Malofilm Communications. Colour.
Filmed under the title *Mojave Frankenstein*, this charming children's film set in the early 1970s involves twelve year-old monster movie fan Earl Williams (Boulanger) and his friends, who discover Frankenstein's original Monster (special make-up effects created by Ted Haines) at a travelling carnival in the Mojave desert and attempt to revive it. It also features fun fantasy recreations of classic horror movie scenes (including a werewolf, Dracula [Conner van Deer] and his three vampire 'brides', and a mummy), *Night of the Living Dead* (1968) playing at a drive-in, *Dark Shadows* (1966-71) and *The Devil Bat* (1940) on TV, copies of *Famous Monsters of Filmland* and an uncredited Forrest J Ackerman as a priest!
✦✦✧

FRANKENSTEIN AND THE MONSTER FROM HELL
UK, 1973 (1974). Dir: Terence Fisher. With: Peter Cushing, Shane Briant, Madeline Smith, John Stratton, Bernard Lee, Clifford Mollison. Hammer Films/Avco Embassy. Colour.
The sixth and last in Hammer's Frankenstein series marks a return to form for the studio. Despite the low budget, obvious care was taken with the casting, design and photography. Making a superb entrance, Cushing returns as the obsessed Baron Frankenstein (aka Dr Victor), his hands horribly burned, who is helped by Dr Simon Helder (Briant) to create a new Monster (Dave Prowse, in an unconvincing body suit created by Eddie Knight) from the lunatic inhabitants of Carlsbad's asylum for the criminally insane. The script by John Elder (Anthony Hinds) works on several levels and this is a fitting end to both the series and the career of director Fisher (who died in 1980). With Charles Lloyd-Pack, and Patrick Troughton as a bodysnatcher.
✦✦✦

THE FRANKENSTEIN COMPLEX
(aka THE FRANKENSTEIN SYNDROME)
USA, 1991 (1992). Dir: Larry Fessenden. With: Miriam

Heavy-Lovie, Stephen Ramsey, David Van Tieghem, Richard Topol, Ashley Arcement. Glass Eye Pix. Colour.
Canadian director Fessenden attempts to make a serious statement about his opposition to scientific experimentation in this obscure movie. While researching skin grafts in his isolated country mansion, obsessed scientist Geoffrey Gaines uses various animals for his vivisection experiments. Meanwhile, his artist wife Lillian becomes involved with sympathetic environmentalist Alex Vine, who is investigating the bizarre animal deaths in the area.
✦

FRANKENSTEIN CONQUERS THE WORLD
(Orig: FURANKENSHUTAIN TAI BARAGON)
Japan/USA, 1964 (1965). Dir: Inoshiro Honda. With: Nick Adams, Tadao Takashima, Kumi Mizuno, Yoshio Tsuchiya, Takashi Shimura, Haruo Nakajima. Toho/ Henry G. Saperstein Enterprises/American International Pictures. Colour.
A boy eats the radioactive heart of the Frankenstein Monster and begins to grow into an ugly giant who watches Japanese teenagers do the twist! Stealing Willis O'Brien's concept of a fifty-foot tall Frankenstein Monster from his proposed *King Kong vs Frankenstein* (aka *King Kong vs Prometheus*), Toho pitted their towering version of Mary Shelley's creation against a fire-breathing prehistoric reptile called Baragon (played by stuntman Nakajima in a silly-looking rubber suit). With a giant crawling hand and imported American actor Adams looking confused. The original ending, with the Monster being dragged into the sea by a bizarre giant octopus (which walks on land!), was replaced in Western prints with an alternative sequence in which the Monster is killed when a mountain collapses.
Sequels: WAR OF THE GARGANTUAS (qv; 1966) and DESTROY ALL MONSTERS (1968)
✦✦

FRANKENSTEIN CREATED WOMAN
UK, 1966. Dir: Terence Fisher. With: Peter Cushing, Susan Denberg, Thorley Walters, Robert Morris, Duncan Lamont, Peter Blythe. Hammer Films/Associated British-Pathe. Colour.
This fourth outing for Cushing's Baron (following *The Evil of Frankenstein* [1964]) marks the welcome return of director Fisher, but the screenplay by John Elder (producer Anthony Hinds), originally written in 1958, seems unsure of how to vary the formula. As a result, Frankenstein and his bumbling assistant Dr Hertz (Walters) are experimenting with cryogenic suspension when they end up transplanting the soul of a young man (Morris) falsely executed for murder into the corpse of the once-crippled Christina Kleve (twenty-two year-old August 1966 *Playboy* centrefold Denberg). He/she then revenges herself on the real killers. For a change, Frankenstein survives at the end to continue his experiments.
Sequel: FRANKENSTEIN MUST BE DESTROYED (qv; 1969)
✦✦✧

FRANKENSTEIN '80
(Orig: MOSAICO)
Italy/West Germany, 1972. Dir: Mario Mancini. With: John Richardson, Gordon Mitchell, Renato Romano, Xiro Papas (Ciro Papa), Dalila Parker (Dalila Di Lazzaro), Bob Fiz. MGD Film Productions/MPI. Colour.
A combination of police procedural and horror film, this dark and ugly contemporary reworking of Mary Shelley's novel is merely an excuse for a series of sleazy murders. While attempting to discover who stole the transplant serum that could have saved his sister's life on the operating table, newspaper reporter Karl (Richardson) learns that misguided surgeon-turned-pathologist Dr Otto Frankenstein (Mitchell) has created a patchwork creature named Mosaic (Papas, who was subsequently killed in a car accident) from various body parts. The rapist monster goes on a gory rampage, killing various naked hookers and strippers, and eventually hacking his creator to death, before a built-in rejection mechanism causes his brain to disintegrate after forty-eight hours. This includes footage of actual transplant surgery and special effects created by Carlo Rambaldi.
✦

THE FRANKENSTEIN FILES: HOW HOLLYWOOD MADE A MONSTER
USA, 1999. Dir: David J. Skal. With: Rudy Behlmer, Paul M. Jensen, Gregory W. Mank, Donald F. Glut, Bob Madison, Rick Baker. Universal Studios Home Video. Colour/B&W.
Forty-five minute documentary, written and narrated by Skal and released as a supplement to the DVD of *Frankenstein* (1931). This looks at the history of Mary Shelley's Monster from page to stage to screen, focusing primarily on the 1931 film, with an overview of the classic Universal cycle. It includes the long-missing 'Now I know what it feels like to be God!' line deleted by censors, restored here for the first time by Universal. With numerous clips, the 1938 and 1951 re-release trailers, the short film *Boo!* (1933), plus interviews with film historian Ivan Butler (a member of Hamilton Deane's original *Frankenstein* stage company), Universal Studios archivist Jan-Christopher Horak, Sara Karloff, Dwight D. Frye and Bill Condon.
✦✦✦✧

FRANKENSTEIN GENERAL HOSPITAL
USA, 1988. Dir: Deborah Roberts. With: Mark Blankfield, Leslie Jordan, Jonathan Farwell, Kathy Shower, Hamilton Mitchell, Irwin Keyes. New Star Entertainment. Colour.
Silly *Young Frankenstein*-type spoof. Dr Bob Frankenstein (Blankfield, doing a Gene Wilder impersonation), the great-great-grandson of the original, creates a new Monster (Keyes) in his monochromatic laboratory beneath General Hospital. With a few laughs, some mild nudity, a framed photo of Colin Clive, *Studs* TV presenter Mark DeCarlo and a cameo by singer Bobby 'Boris' Pickett.
✦✧

FRANKENSTEIN ISLAND
USA/Mexico, 1981. Dir: Jerry Warren. With: Robert Clarke, Steve Brodie, Cameron Mitchell, Robert Christopher, Tain Bodkin, Patrick O'Neil. Chriswar/Jerry Warren. Colour.
Several 'B' movie stars turn up in the worst film of their careers, the last to be produced and directed by legendary low-budget veteran Warren (who died in 1988). It's difficult to decide if this is meant to be funny or not. Clarke heads a group of balloonists who crash on a mysterious island populated by bikini-clad warrior women descended from aliens! Frankenstein's great-great-granddaughter, Sheila (Katherine Victor!), is also around trying to keep her 200 year-old husband alive by experimenting on zombie captives, while the Karloffian Monster escapes from beneath the sea. It all turns out to have been a dream...or was it? With a wasted Mitchell playing a Poe-quoting sailor, Brodie as a yo-ho-ho pirate and Andrew Duggan in a brief cameo as a navy officer. Scenes of John Carradine's superimposed ghost of Dr Frankenstein talking rubbish were obviously filmed earlier.
✦

FRANKENSTEIN — ITALIAN STYLE
(Orig: FRANKENSTEIN ALL'ITALIANA/PRENDIMI, STRAZIAMI, CHE BRUCIO DI PASSIONE!)
Italy, 1975. Dir: Armando Crispino. With: Gianrico Tedeschi, Ninetto Davoli, Jenny Tamburi, Anna Mazzemauro, Aldo Maccione, Lorenzo Guerrieri. Filmex/ Euro International/RPA. Colour.
Comedy sexploitation version of *Young Frankenstein* (1974). Professor Frankenstein (Tedeschi) creates a well-endowed Monster (Maccione) that ends up servicing his assistant Igor (Davoli), wife (Tamburi) and servant (Mazzemauro) before the scientist transplants his creation's penis onto himself.
Remake: SEVIMLI FRANKESTAYN (qv; 1975)
✦

FRANKENSTEIN JR. AND THE IMPOSSIBLES
(aka THE SPACE GHOST/FRANKENSTEIN JR. SHOW)
USA, 1966-67. Dir: William Hanna and Joseph Barbera (and Charles A. Nichols). Voices: Dick Beals, Ted Cassidy, Paul Frees, Don Messick, Hal Smith, John Stephenson. Hanna-Barbera Productions/CBS-TV. Colour.
Half-hour cartoon TV show (nineteen episodes) which includes an eight minute *Frankenstein Jr.* segment and another about a rock band who transform into secret champions for the fight for justice. Young

boy genius Buzz (Beals) and his scientist father, Dr Conroy (Stephenson), create a thirty-foot tall crime-fighting robot called Frankenstein Jr (Cassidy), controlled by Buzz when he says 'Allakazoom!' into his radar ring. Frankenstein Jr cartoons were later recycled in *The Space Ghost/Frankenstein Jr. Show* (1976) and the syndicated TV series *Hanna-Barbera's World of Super Adventures* (1980).
✦✧

FRANKENSTEIN, LA VERITABLE HISTOIRE
France, circa 1981. Dir: Roland Portiche. B&W.
Experimental short which is apparently a homage to James Whale's *Frankenstein* (1931).
✦

FRANKENSTEIN MEETS THE SPACEMONSTER
(aka MARTE INVADE A PUERTO RICO. UK: DUEL OF THE SPACE MONSTERS)
USA, 1965. Dir: Robert Gaffney. With: Marilyn Hanold, Jim (James) Karen, Lou Cutell, Nancy Marshall, David Kerman, Robert Reilly. Vernon Films/Seneca/Futurama Entertainment/Allied Artists. B&W.
Dr Adam Steele (Karen) creates an astronaut, Colonel Frank Saunders (Reilly), out of corpses and machinery. However, when his brain is damaged by the henchmen of sexy alien Princess Marcuzan (Hanold), who are kidnapping Earth women, Saunders is transformed into a monster. In the end, 'Frankenstein' battles the space creature Mull before destroying both the aliens and himself with a laser. Padded with plenty of documentary space footage, this was filmed under the title *Operation San Juan* (apparently without synchronised sound) in Puerto Rico and New York for just $67,000. With incredible sixties songs by The Distant Cousins and The Poets. Original American audiences were offered 'space shield eye protectors' to prevent their abduction into outer space.
✦✧

Bela Lugosi vs Lon Chaney Jr in Frankenstein Meets the Wolf Man *(1943).*

FRANKENSTEIN MEETS THE WOLF MAN
USA, 1943. Dir: Roy William Neill. With: Lon Chaney, Ilona Massey (Ilona Hajmassy), Patric Knowles, Bela Lugosi, Lionel Atwill, Maria Ouspenskaya. Universal. B&W.
The forties horror boom was already failing when Universal decided to make this sequel to *The Wolf Man* (1941) and *The Ghost of Frankenstein* (1942), originally titled *Wolf Man Meets Frankenstein* by scriptwriter Curt Siodmak and atmospherically directed by 'B' movie veteran Neill. Chaney Jr recreates his role as the doomed lycanthrope Lawrence Talbot from the former film, while a frail-looking Lugosi takes over as Frankenstein's creation (a role he originally turned down in 1931), with more than a little help from stunt doubles Eddie Parker and Australian Gil Perkins. His stiff portrayal makes more sense when you realise that all references to the Monster's blindness (as a result of a brain transplant in the previous film) and his ability to speak were cut from the release print. After a great opening sequence in which the Wolf Man is accidentally revived by two grave robbers, Talbot travels to Transylvania in the hope of discovering a cure for his affliction in the journals of Dr Frankenstein. Instead, he discovers the Monster. The two creatures eventually confront each other until they are washed away by an exploded dam. This was the first time that audiences saw Chaney change from a man into a wolf — in *The Wolf Man*, he only transformed from a wolf into a man. The impressive supporting cast includes Atwill as the Mayor, Ouspenskaya as the gypsy Maleva, Dennis Hoey as a police inspector, Dwight Frye, Harry Stubbs and Jeff Corey as villagers, Martha MacVicar (later Martha Vickers) in her screen début as a victim of the Wolf Man, and Massey as Elsa, the daughter of Frankenstein. This was belatedly adapted as a juvenile novel by Ian Thorne in 1981, and MagicImage Filmbooks published the script in 1990.
Sequel: HOUSE OF FRANKENSTEIN (qv; 1944)
✦✦✦

FRANKENSTEIN MUST BE DESTROYED
UK, 1969. Dir: Terence Fisher. With: Peter Cushing, Simon Ward, Veronica Carlson, Thorley Walters, Freddie Jones, Maxine Audley. Hammer Films/Warner Bros-Seven Arts.

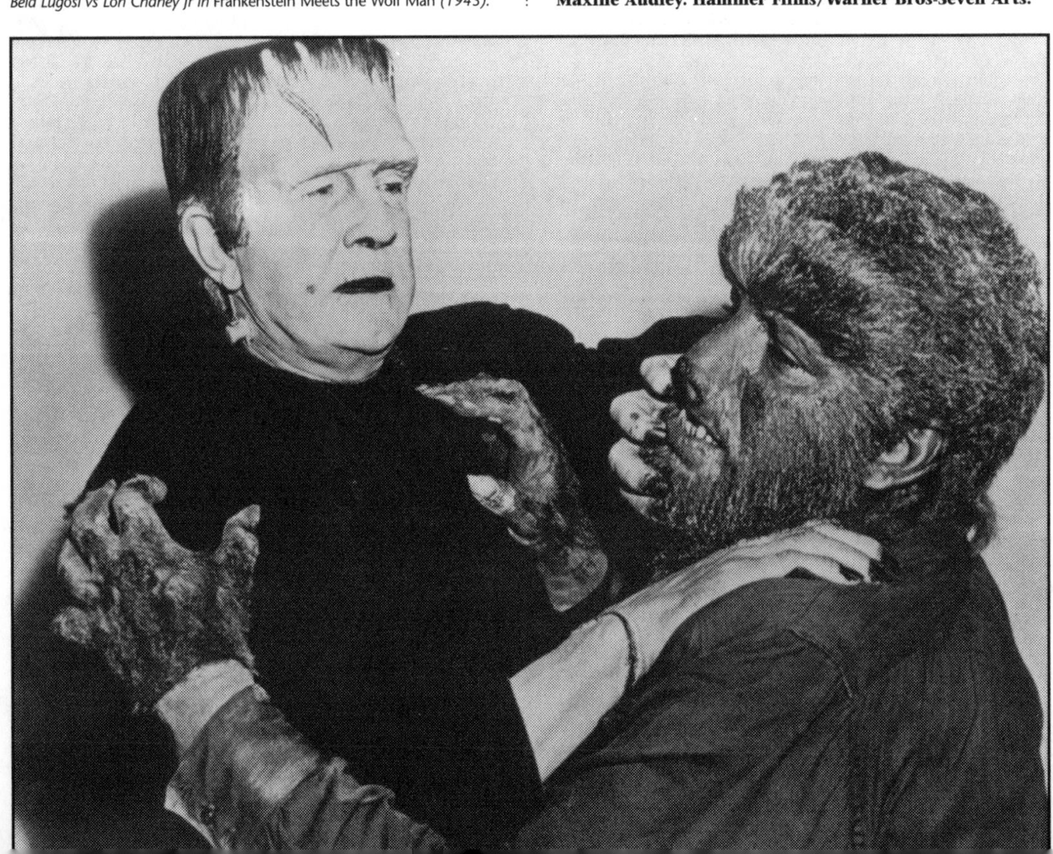

Colour.
Unpleasant fifth entry in Hammer's Frankenstein series. Assistant director Bert Batt's ill-judged screenplay presents Cushing's Baron as a totally irredeemable character — the film's true monster. His blackmailing of the hapless Karl Holst (Ward, making his film début) and rape of Anna Spengler (Carlson) — originally cut from American release prints — results in the sadistic destruction of the young couple. Jones brings some much-needed sympathy to the film as the tragic Dr Brandt, who awakens to discover his brain has been transplanted into another body, and veterans Walters and Geoffrey Bayldon as policemen add a welcome touch of comedy to their investigations of the gory killings.
Sequel: FRANKENSTEIN AND THE MONSTER FROM HELL (qv; 1973)
✦✦

FRANKENSTEIN 1970
USA, 1958. Dir: Howard W. Koch. With: Boris Karloff, Tom Duggan, Jana Lund, Donald Barry, Charlotte Austin, Irwin Berke. Allied Artists. B&W.
Karloff returns to the saga as the crazy, crippled Baron Victor. So that he can afford a shiny new atomic reactor, the Baron allows an American TV crew to film a special celebrating the 230th(!) anniversary of Frankenstein at his castle in Germany. But the Nazi-hating Baron kills cast and crew members to restore vital organs to the body of his great-great-grandfather's preserved Monster (Mike Lane). In the end, they are both destroyed in a laboratory explosion and it is revealed that the creature has the features of a younger Victor (also Karloff). Co-scripted by George Worthing Yates, it was filmed in CinemaScope under the titles *Frankenstein 1960* and *Frankenstein 1975*. Scenes from this film were later edited into a dream sequence in TV prints of *Daughter of Dr. Jekyll* (1957).
✦✦

FRANKENSTEIN 90
France, 1984. Dir: Alain Jessua. With: Jean Rochefort, Eddy Mitchell, Fiona Gélin, Herma Vos, Ged Marlon, Serge Marquand. AJ Films/TF 1 Films/AMLF. Colour.
Contemporary reworking of Mary Shelley's *Frankenstein* which mixes horror and humour. Cybernetics genius Victor Frankenstein (Rochefort) equips his Monster, Frank (Mitchell), with a microprocessor for a brain. But when the scientist creates a sexy mate from the bodies of murdered disco dancers, the ugly creature prefers the doctor's gentle girlfriend Elizabeth (Gélin).
Remake: FRANKENSTEIN (qv; 1992)
✦✧

FRANKENSTEIN OF SUNNYBROOK FARM
USA, 1971. Dir: William Rotsler.
Underground short in which two nudists watch the psychedelic film of the title.
✦

FRANKENSTEIN REBORN!
Romania/USA, 1998. Dir: Julian Breen. With: Jaason Simmons, Ben Gould, Haven Burton, Ethan Wilde, George Calin, Oana Stefanescu. Tanna Productions/Full Moon Pictures. Colour.
The second of executive producer Charles Band's *Filmonsters!*, a proposed series of thirteen films aimed at teenagers. When her parents are killed, thirteen year-old Anna Frankenstein (Burton) goes to live with her uncle, Baron Victor (Simmons), in his castle. With the help of Thomas (Gould), she discovers that Frankenstein and his assistant Ludwig (Calin) have brought to life a hideous creature (Wilde in make-up created by Mark Williams) which they have constructed from corpses. When the Monster escapes into the woods, Anna befriends it. In the end, both Monster and creator are destroyed by fire. At forty-five minutes long, this is just another variation on the usual story. Mary Shelley isn't even credited.
✦✧

FRANKENSTEIN'S AUNTIE
Czechoslovakia/West Germany, 1986 (1987). Dir: Juraj Jakubisko. With: Viveca Lindfors, Ferdy (Ferdinand) Mayne, Jacques Herlin, Flavio Bucci, Gerhard Karzel, Eddie Constantine. Beta Film/Slovensky Film. Colour.
Children's TV series (thirteen episodes) in which veteran Lindfors portrays the title character, with Mayne as Count Dracula, Bucci as a werewolf, Herlin as Igor and Karzel as Albert, Frankenstein's sympathetic Monster. In some European countries this was also edited into a ninety minute movie.
✦✧

FRANKENSTEIN'S BABY
UK, 1990. Dir: Robert Bierman. With: Nigel Planer, Kate Buffery, Yvonne Bryceland, William Armstrong, Sian Thomas, Gillian Raine. BBC-TV. Colour.
Blackly comic TV movie, written by Emma Tennant. When Paul Hocking (Planer) quarrels with his girlfriend Jane (Buffery) about when they should start a family, Dr Eva Frankenstein (Bryceland) overhears their argument and offers her own, unique solution.
✦✧

FRANKENSTEIN'S BLOODY TERROR
(Orig: LA MARCA DEL HOMBRE LOBO. USA: aka MARK OF THE WOLFMAN. UK: HELL'S CREATURES)
Spain, 1967 (1971). Dir: Henry L. Egan (Enrique [López] Eguilúz). With: Paul Naschy (Jacinto Molina), Diane Konopka (Dianik Zurakowska), Rossana Yanni (Rossana Yanny), Julián Ugarte, Michael Manz (Manuel Manzanaque), Joseph Morton (José Nieto). DC Films/ Maxper/Independent-International. Colour.
American audiences were promised a free burial to anyone who died of fright during performances of this film — a pretty safe bet. When gypsies steal the silver dagger impaling his body, the werewolf Count Imre Wolfstein is revived and bites his descendant, Count Waldemar Daninsky (Naschy, who also scripted under his real name). Now a werewolf (El Hombre Lobo) himself, Daninsky appeals to a pair of weird occultists, Janos and Wandessa Mikelhov (Ugarte and Aurora de Alba), for help to end his curse. Unfortunately, they turn out to be vampires. The film ends with a fight to the death between the two wolfmen, and Daninsky is killed by a silver bullet fired by a woman who loves him (Konopka). Originally released in Spain in 3-D, this was a box office smash there and led to a series of films with Naschy as Daninsky. Dr Frankenstein (who changes into a werewolf!) only appears in artist Gray Morrow's cartoon prologue for the American version, which was totally re-edited (by F. Neumann) and released in 'Super 70mm Chill-O-Rama'.
Sequel: NIGHTS OF THE WEREWOLF (qv; 1968)
✦✧

FRANKENSTEIN'S CASTLE OF FREAKS
(Orig: IL CASTELLO DELLA PAURA/TERROR! IL CASTELLO DELLE DONNE MALEDETTE. USA: aka HOUSE OF FREAKS)
Italy, 1973. Dir: Robert H. Oliver (Gianni Vernuccio). With: Rossano Brazzi, Michael Dunn, Edmund Purdom, Christiane Royce (Krista Roker), Gordon Mitchell, Alan Collins (Luciano Pigozzi). Classic Film International/ Cinerama. Colour.
Sleazy sex and horror film featuring *South Pacific* (1958) star Brazzi (sounding like a cross between Chico Marx and Bela Lugosi) as Count Frankenstein. He brings caveman Goliath (Loren Ewing) back from the dead with his electric accumulator and gives him the brain of a young girl. With poor three-feet four-inch Michael Dunn (who died in 1973) as Genz the Evil Dwarf, Gordon Mitchell as Igor, and Boris Lugosi (Salvatore Baccaro) playing Ook the Neanderthal Man.
✦

FRANKENSTEIN'S CAT
(aka MIGHTY MOUSE IN FRANKENSTEIN'S CAT)
USA, 1942. Dir: Mannie Davis. Voices: Tom Morrison. Terrytoons/Twentieth Century-Fox. Colour.
Ten minute Paul Terry cartoon in which the super-powered Mighty Mouse (Morrison) — originally called Supermouse — battles a monster cat and knocks his head off, freeing a kidnapped baby bird.
Sequel: HE DOOD IT AGAIN (1943)
✦✦

FRANKENSTEIN'S DAUGHTER

USA, 1958. Dir: Richard Cunha. With: John Ashley, Sandra Knight, Donald Murphy, Sally Todd, Harold Lloyd Jr, Felix Locher. Astor Pictures/Layton Film Productions. B&W.

Murphy is wonderful as arrogant scientist Oliver Frank (really the grandson of Frankenstein), who needs fresh organs to create the perfect being. Meanwhile, he uses a drug to periodically turn teenager Trudy Morton (Knight) into a monster with big teeth and ping-pong ball eyes, and creates his own female creature ('Frankenstein's daughter!') using the body of murdered good-time girl Suzy Lawler (Todd). In the end, Trudy's boyfriend Johnny (Ashley) throws acid in Frankenstein's face while the monster (former Wallace Beery stand-in Henry Wilson, in make-up created by Harry Thomas) accidentally sets itself on fire! With Robert Dix, George Barrows, and Page Cavanaugh and his Trio (who sing 'Daddy-Bird' and 'Special Date'). An underrated schlock classic, this was originally co-billed with the same director's *Missile to the Moon* (1958).

✦✦✧

FRANKENSTEIN'S GREAT-AUNT TILLIE

Mexico, 1983 (1985). Dir: Myron J. Gold. With: Donald Pleasence, Yvonne Furneaux, June Wilkinson, Aldo Ray, Zsa Zsa Gabor, Rod Colbin. Tillie Productions/Filmier/ Video City. Colour.

Comedy set in the Transylvanian town of Mucklefugger, written, produced and directed by Gold. When the town council plan to repossess the Frankenstein family mansion for non-payment of taxes, Pleasence's Victor Jr, his buxom companion (Wilkinson) and his youthful-looking 109 year-old great-aunt (Furneaux) arrive to search for the family fortune and become involved with women's emancipation. With a green-faced Monster (Miguel Angel Fuentes) who looks like Herman Munster. Filmed in English, this was apparently cut down from a TV mini-series and includes outtakes from the longer version at the end.

✦

FRANKENSTEIN SINGS

(aka MONSTER MASH THE MOVIE)

USA, 1994. Dir: Joel Cohen and Alec Sokolow. With: Ian Bohen, Candace Cameron, Sarah Douglas, John Kassir, Bobby Pickett, Adam Shankman. The Greenhouse Film Group/Spelling Entertainment Group/The Brae Group. Colour.

Likeable comedy based on the 1967 stage musical *I'm Sorry the Bridge is Out, You'll Have to Spend the Night* by Sheldon Allman and musician Bobby 'Boris' Pickett (and including his classic song 'Monster Mash'). When their car breaks down, teenagers Scott (Bohen) and Mary (Cameron) find themselves forced to spend Halloween night in the castle of Dr Victor Frankenstein (Pickett, doing his Karloff imitation), along with hunchbacked assistant Igor (Kassir), a green-faced Monster (Deron McBee), Count Dracula (Anthony Crivello) and his undead bride Natasha (Douglas), Wolfgang the werewolf (Shankman), the mummy of Elvis (E. Aron Price), and a chorus of three sexy dancing Draculettes (Linda Cevallos, Carrie Ann Inaba and Daryl Richardson). With Mink Stole and Jimmie Walker. A cartoon feature based on Pickett's *Monster Mash* was announced in 1998.

✦✦✧

FRANKENSTEIN'S PLANET OF MONSTERS

USA, 1993. Dir: Brad Anderson. With: Mike Brunelle. Nomad. Colour.

Forty-five minute amateur production, produced, directed, edited and photographed by Anderson and sold through the mail from Massachusetts. Three female astronauts and their floating cyborg head land on a barren planet controlled by the Frankenstein Monster (co-producer/writer Brunelle). They are befriended by a wolfman and attacked by various monsters (people in masks). About as good as you would expect.

✦

FRANKENSTEIN: THE COLLEGE YEARS

USA, 1991. Dir: Tom Shadyac. With: William Ragsdale, Christopher Daniel Barnes, Larry Miller, Andrea Elson, Voreaux White, Patrick Richwood. FNM Films/Spirit Productions/Twentieth Century Fox. Colour.

Enjoyable made-for-cable TV movie, in which college medical students Mark and Jay (Ragsdale and Barnes) discover the late Professor Lippzigger's experiments with transplant tissue rejection involved Victor von Frankenstein's original Karloffian Monster (Vincent Hammond). When the creature is accidentally revived with electricity, they pass him off as a foreign exchange student named Frank N. Stein and sign him up for the campus football team when an ambitious professor (Miller) starts to suspect the truth. With likeable characters and a lack of nerdiness, this is better than most teen comedies. It also includes a TV clip from *Reptilicus* (1962) and the Monster hip-hop dancing.

✦✦✧

FRANKENSTEIN: THE TRUE STORY

UK, 1973. Dir: Jack Smight. With: James Mason, Leonard Whiting, David McCallum, Jane Seymour, Nicola Pagett, Michael Sarrazin. Universal/NBC-TV. Colour.

Impressive three-hour adaptation by Christopher Isherwood and Don Bachardy, first shown as part of *NBC's World Premiere Movie* and given a cinema release in Britain in a shortened version. The original splits neatly into two parts: the first stays fairly faithful to Mary Shelley's novel, with Whiting's Victor Frankenstein creating a sympathetic creature (Sarrazin) whose body slowly begins to decay. However, the second half is an outlandish sequel, with Mason's power-mad mesmerist, Dr Polidori, controlling Prima, a homicidal female monster (Seymour). The all-star cast includes McCallum as Frankenstein's mentor Henry Clerval, plus Michael Wilding, Clarissa Kaye, Agnes Moorehead, Margaret Leighton, Ralph Richardson, John Gielgud and Tom Baker. The screenplay was published by Avon Books.

Remake: FRANKENSTEIN (qv; 1974)

✦✦✦✦

FRANKENSTEIN UNBOUND

USA/Italy, 1990. Dir: Roger Corman. With: John Hurt, Raul Julia, Bridget Fonda, Catherine Rabett, Jason Patric, Michael Hutchence. Twentieth Century-Fox/Mount Company. Colour.

In 1985, TriStar announced *Roger Corman's Frankenstein* from a script by Wes Craven. It was never made but, after nearly twenty years, Corman returned to directing with this silly science fiction adventure, based on the novel by Brian W. Aldiss. New Los Angeles scientist Joseph Buchanan (Hurt) messes around with space and time while creating a death ray in 2031 and is sucked through a cloud vortex back to 1817 Switzerland where the mad Dr Frankenstein (Julia, rising above the material) and his ugly but misunderstood Monster (Nick Brimble, in make-up created by Nick Dudman) co-exist with their creator, Mary Shelley (Fonda). The film is not helped by the risible dialogue, hammy performances, confusing dream sequences and terribly limp performances by rock star Hutchence as Lord Byron and Patric as Percy Shelley. However, despite being cut by twenty minutes in America, this still remains a low-budget delight. Welcome back Roger!

✦✦✧

FRANKENSTYMIED

USA, 1961. Dir: Jack Hannah. Voices: Grace Stafford. Walter Lantz Productions/Universal-International. Colour.

Six minute *Woody Woodpecker* cartoon in which the character is pursued by Franky, a mechanical chicken-plucker created by a mad scientist.

Sequel: BUSMAN'S HOLIDAY (1961)

✦✧

FRANKENTICKLE

USA, circa 1980s. With: Deacon Blue, Anthony Lawton. California Star. Colour.

'Adults only' tickling video. Dr Frankentickle (Blue) and the Monster (Lawton) he created enjoy tickling young girls.

✦

FRANKENWEENIE

USA, 1984. Dir: Tim Burton. With: Shelley Duvall, Daniel Stern, Barret Oliver, Joseph Maher, Roz Braverman, Paul

Bartel. Walt Disney Productions. B&W.
A follow-up to his equally offbeat *Vincent* (1982), twenty-five year-old Burton designed and directed this twenty-seven minute short, using stylised sets and black and white photography to faithfully pay homage to James Whale's original (even Kenneth Strickfaden's electrical apparatus was dusted off for use again). This time the Frankensteins are a contemporary middle-class family whose dog Spaŕky is accidentally killed by a car. Inspired by his science teacher (a nice cameo by Bartel) and experiments with a dead frog, their ten year-old son Victor (Oliver) digs up his canine pet and uses electricity to bring it back to life in his bedroom laboratory — with problematic results. Never quite as amusing nor as inventive as it might have been, this remains a beautifully crafted, one-joke idea.
✦✦✦

FRANKESTEIN, EL VAMPIRO Y CIA
Mexico, 1961 (1963). Dir: Benito Alazraki (Carlo J. Arconti). With: Manuel 'Loco' Valdés, José Jasso, 'Borolas' (Joaquin Garcia Vargas), Martha Elena Cervantes, Nora Veyrán, Roberto G. Rivera. Cinematográfica Calderón. B&W.
After *Castle of the Monsters* (1957), here's another Mexican version of (Abbott and Costello) *Meet Frankenstein* (1948). The comedy team of 'Loco' Valdés and José Jasso are employed to deliver wax figures of the Frankestein (*sic*) Monster and a vampire (Quintin Bulnes) to a mysterious castle. When the figures come to life, the vampire tries to convince female scientist Dr Sofia (Veyrán) to transplant Valdés' brain into the Monster so that it can conquer America! This also includes a wolfman who is trying to destroy the other monsters.
Remake: LEENA MEETS FRANKENSTEIN (qv; 1993)
✦

FRANKIE STEIN'S ROBOT
UK, 1998. Dir: Alex Kirby. With: Bill Oddie, Tom Moore, Peter Holdway, Fiona McArthur, Janet Henfrey. London Weekend Television/ITV. Colour.
Oddie narrates this twenty minute TV comedy, made as part of the European Broadcasting Union's children's drama exchange initiative. When schoolboy scientist Frankie (Moore) builds Robert the robot (Holdway), things don't turn out quite the way he hoped.
✦

FRANKY AND HIS PALS
USA, 1992. Dir: Gerald Cormier. With: Eric Weathersbee, Jerry Cormier Jr, Keith Lack, Wilson Smith, Richard Sumner, Phil Rabin. Shasta Motion Pictures. Colour.
Dire shot-on-video adult comedy that involves the vampiric Drak (Cormier Jr) with a Mohawk haircut, Humper the hunchback (make-up creator Lack), Wolfie the gay wolfman (Smith), a Mummy (Sumner) with a creature living in its stomach, and the flatulent Franky Monster (Weathersbee), who all live in a cave. When these friendly creatures invade the nearby town of French Gulch, they discover a cache of hidden gold which pays the locals' back taxes. In the end, the monsters disappear in a time machine created by the Mad Inventor (Mr 'C').
✦

FREAKAZOID!:
(aka STEVEN SPIELBERG PRESENTS FREAKAZOID!)
The Cloud
USA/Korea, 1995. Dir: Scott Jeralds. Voices: Paul Rugg, Edward (Ed) Asner, John P. McCann, Tress MacNeille, David Kaufman, Googy Gress. Warner Bros/Amblin Entertainment/Kids WB Network. Colour.
Half-hour comedy cartoon TV series (1995-97, twenty-four episodes) filled with in-jokes. Computer nerd Dexter Douglas (Kaufman) is sucked into cyberspace and emerges as the crazy costumed blue-skinned superhero (co-producer Rugg). In this eleven minute segment, Freakazoid and 'B' movie scientist Professor Heiney investigate a spooky cloud that is transforming the citizens of Schnitzel into clown zombies. With Joe Leahy as Our Announcer. Executive produced by Spielberg.
✦✦✧
House of Freakazoid
USA/Korea, 1996. Dir: Scott Jeralds. Voices: Paul Rugg, Edward (Ed) Asner, John P. McCann, Tress MacNeille, David Kaufman, Googy Gress. Warner Bros/Amblin Entertainment/Kids WB Network. Colour.
Eight-minute episode, in which Dexter meets Lonnie Tallbutt, who happens to be a werewolf.
✦✦✧
Tomb of Invisibo
USA/Korea, 1997. Dir: Rich Arons and Peter Shin. Voices: Paul Rugg, Edward (Ed) Asner, John P. McCann, Tress MacNeille, David Kaufman, Googy Gress. Warner Bros/Amblin Entertainment/Kids WB Network. Colour.
Fourteen minute segment in which the red-clad superhero and police Sgt Mike Cosgrove (Asner) battle an invisible 3,000 year-old Egyptian prince (Corey Burton, sounding like Vincent Price) who is accidentally released from his sarcophagus and attempts to drain the city's electrical power into his magic sceptre. With John Rhys Davies as Professor Beasthead.
✦✦✧

FREAKY STORIES:
The Vampire
Canada, 1997. Dir: Steve E. Schnier. Voices: Susan Roman. Big-Time Talking Pictures/Flextech Television/Canal Famille/Decode Entertainment/Vujadé Entertainment/ YTV. Colour.
TV series of four minute cartoons created by Steve Schnier and John A. Delmage featuring 'true stories' that happened to friends-of-friends. In this episode, Jerry believes that Mr Alucard, who lives in a spooky old house and works as the head waiter in a restaurant, is really a vampire. He's right.
✦✦

RICCARDO FREDA
[b 1909]

Egyptian-born Italian director, considered second only to Mario Bava for his contributions to the history of Italian horror. Although Freda made his directing début in 1942, it was only in 1956 that he came up with the idea of reviving the moribund Italian horror genre with *The Devil's Commandment*. However, when he walked off the production, it was completed by Bava. Under the pseudonyms Robert Hampton and Richard Freda, Freda went on to make such uneven films as *Caltiki the Immortal Monster* (1959), *The Witch's Curse* (1962), *The Horrible Dr. Hichcock* (1962), *The Ghost* (1963) and the gratuitous *Murder Obsession* (1980).

KARL FREUND
[1890-1969]

Czechoslovakian-born German cinematographer and director who shot *The Golem* (1920), *Der Januskopf* (1920) and *Metropolis* (1926) before moving to Hollywood, where he photographed *Dracula* (1931) and *Murders in the Rue Morgue* (1932). His brief stint as a director encompassed two classic horror movies, *The Mummy* (1933) and *Mad Love* (1935), before he moved to television and created the multi-camera technique for shooting sitcoms.

JONATHAN FRID
[b 1924]

Canadian actor best known for his portrayal of vampire Barnabas Collins in the Gothic TV soap opera *Dark Shadows* (1966-71) and the first spin-off movie, *House of Dark Shadows* (1970). His other horror credits include the TV movie *The Devil's Daughter* (1972) and Oliver Stone's *Seizure* (1974).
qv: *Dark Shadows: Behind the Scenes* (1991).

FRIDAY THE 13TH PART VI JASON LIVES
(UK: JASON LIVES FRIDAY THE 13TH PART VI)
USA, 1986. Dir: Tom McLoughlin. With: Thom Mathews, Jennifer Cooke, David Kagen, Renee Jones, Kerry Noonan,

Darcy DeMoss. Terror, Inc./Paramount. Colour.
Although there's nothing particularly original here, at least thanks to writer/director McLoughlin (*One Dark Night* [1982], etc) this is both fun and looks good. Much of the expected gore is missing (it could have been a TV movie) as mass murderer Jason Voorhees (C.J. Graham) is revived by a bolt of lightning in a wonderfully atmospheric opening sequence. Now a hockey-masked zombie, he menaces a group of young children and their teenage supervisors at Camp Crystal. This sixth entry adds little to the waning series except a much-needed supernatural element. Songs by Alice Cooper (Vince Furnier). It was given a pointless title change in Britain.
Sequel: FRIDAY THE 13TH PART VII — THE NEW BLOOD (1988)
✦✦

FRIDAY THE 13TH THE SERIES:
Bad Penny
Canada/USA, 1989. Dir: William Fruet. With: Robey, Steve Monarque, Chris Wiggins, Sean McCann, John Bourgeois, Ed Setrakian. Paramount/Triumph Entertainment Corporation/Hometown Films. Colour.
Syndicated anthology TV series (1987-90, seventy-two episodes) about Ryan Dallion (John D. Le May), Micki Foster (Robey) and Jack Marshak (Wiggins) who must retrieve the cursed objects sold from antique store Curious Goods. For the third and final season, Micki and Jack team up with new partner Johnny Ventura (Monarque). Executive produced by Frank Mancuso Jr, this had nothing in common with the movie series of the same title. In this episode, a corrupt cop discovers the cursed coin that nearly killed Micki (in 'Tails I Live, Heads You Die' [1988]) and accidentally brings his dead partner back to life.
✦✦
The Baron's Bride
Canada/USA, 1987 (1988). Dir: Bradford May. With: John D. Le May, Robey, Chris Wiggins, Tom McCamus, Kevin Bundy, Susannah Hoffmann. Paramount/Variety Artists/ Lexicon Productions/Hometown Films. Colour/B&W.
A cape transforms its wearer, Frank Edwards (McCamus), into one of the undead and sends Micki and Ryan back through time to London's Whitechapel on 12 March 1875 (in atmospheric black and white), where they team up with unlikely writer Abraham Stoker (Bundy) to save Micki, who is under the spell of the vampire. No prizes for guessing which book the adventure inspires Bram to write. With Diana Barrington as another vampire.
✦✦✦
Bottle of Dreams
Canada/USA, 1988. Dir: Mac Bradden. With: John D. Le May, Robey, Chris Wiggins, Elais Zarou, R.G. Armstrong, Lazar Rockwood. Paramount/Variety Artists/Hometown Films. Colour/B&W.
In this end of season framing episode, Micki and Ryan are trapped by the evil spirit of Uncle Lewis Vandredi (Armstrong) inside the vault with an Egyptian artefact that causes them to re-experience some of their most horrific encounters with the supernatural (including scenes from 'The Baron's Bride' [1987], with new sequences that change the ending of that episode).
✦✦✧
The Butcher
Canada/USA, 1989. Dir: Francis Delia. With: John D. Le May, Robey, Chris Wiggins, Nigel Bennett, Julius Harris, John Gilbert. Paramount/Triumph Entertainment Corporation/Hometown Films. Colour.
A magic amulet reanimates a Nazi zombie that hunts down a group of World War Two survivors, including Jack Marshak.
✦✦✧
Epitaph for a Lonely Soul
Canada/USA, 1989. Dir: Allan Kroeker. With: Robey, Steven Monarque, Chris Wiggins, Neil Munro, Monika Schnarre, Barclay Hope. Paramount/Triumph Entertainment Corporation/Hometown Films. Colour.
A crazed mortician uses a cursed antique embalming instrument to bring the corpse of a beautiful woman back to life. When she spurns his advances, he digs up another body...
✦✦✧
Master of Disguise
Canada/USA, 1988. Dir: Tom McLoughlin. With: John D. Le May, Robey, Chris Wiggins, John Bolger, Hrant Alianak, Chapelle Jaffe. Paramount/Triumph Entertainment Corporation/Hometown Films. Colour.
Micki becomes involved with a murderous movie actor named 'William Pratt' (Bolger) who periodically mixes the blood of his victims with the magical make-up kit once owned by assassin John Wilkes Booth to transform his horrific features into a handsome mask.
✦✦
Midnight Riders
Canada/USA, 1989 (1990). Dir: Allan Eastman. With: Robey, Steven Monarque, Chris Wiggins, Dennis Thatcher, Andrea Roth, David Orth. Paramount/ Triumph Entertainment Corporation/Hometown Films. Colour.
During a rare planetary conjunction, a dead motorcycle gang return to life and Jack meets his long-lost father.
✦✦
Night Prey
Canada/USA, 1989. Dir: Armand Mastroianni. With: Robey, Steven Monarque, Chris Wiggins, Michael Burgess, Eric Murphy, Genevieve Langlois. Paramount/Triumph Entertainment Corporation/Hometown Films. Colour.
Having spent twenty years obsessively hunting vampire Evan Van Hellier (Murphy) who took his new wife Michele (Langlois), Kurt Backman (Burgess) steals the Cross of Fire, a cursed silver crucifix and relic from the Crusades, which needs a human sacrifice before it can destroy the undead. An unusually sexual episode for this series, it features a climactic duel between two vampires and a surprise ending.
✦✦✦
Repetition
Canada/USA, 1989 (1990). Dir: William Fruet. With: Robey, Steven Monarque, Chris Wiggins, David Ferry, Kate Trotter, Vicki Wauchope. Paramount/Triumph Entertainment Corporation/Hometown Films. Colour.
When a newspaper reporter accidentally kills a little girl with his car, he attempts to use a cursed cameo locket to bring her back to life.
✦✦
Scarlet Cinema
Canada/USA, 1989. Dir: David Winning. With: John D. Le May, Robey, Chris Wiggins, Jonathan Wise, John Graham, Peter Messaline. Paramount/Triumph Entertainment Corporation/Hometown Films. Colour.
College student Darius Pogue (Wise) is obsessed with the classic horror film *The Wolf Man* (1941). When he steals an antique movie camera with supernatural powers, he discovers a way to become the werewolf he always wished he could be.
✦✦✦
The Sweetest Sting
Canada/USA, 1988 (1989). Dir: David Winning. With: John D. Le May, Robey, Chris Wiggins, Art Hindle, David Palffy, Tim Webber. Paramount/Triumph Entertainment Corporation/Hometown Films. Colour.
Micki and Ryan discover that murderous beekeeper McCabe (Hindle) uses a magical hive to create vampire bees whose sting imparts immortality through a physical transference. Special honey made from blood is periodically needed to rejuvenate the new bodies.
✦✦✧
Tails I Live, Heads You Die
Canada/USA, 1988. Dir: Mark Sobel. With: John D. Le May, Robey, Chris Wiggins, Colin Fox, Bill Macdonald, Allen Stewart-Coates. Paramount/Triumph Entertainment Corporation/Hometown Films. Colour.
The leader of an occult sect uses a magical coin to raise a trio of dead Satanists (as scary-looking zombies) so that together they can invoke the Devil. When Micki is unexpectedly killed, she is revived by the coin.
Episode sequel: FRIDAY THE 13TH THE SERIES: Bad Penny (qv; 1989)
✦✦✦

FRIGHT
(USA: aka NIGHT LEGS)
UK, 1971. Dir: Peter Collinson. With: Susan George, Honor Blackman, Ian Bannen, John Gregson, George Cole, Dennis Waterman. Fantale Films/British Lion. Colour.
Unpleasant slasher film in which immature babysitter Amanda (George) is menaced by slobbering escaped lunatic Brian (Bannen). The team of screenwriter Tudor Gates and producers Harry Fine and Michael Style fail to recreate the look of their Hammer productions (*The Vampire Lovers* [1970], etc) and a cast of fine British character actors look justifiably embarrassed. As Amanda's boyfriend Chris, Waterman meets a nasty end when he is battered to death. With Maurice Kaufmann, Roger Lloyd Pack and scenes from *The Plague of the Zombies* (1966) on TV.
✦✧

FRIGHT NIGHT
USA, 1985. Dir: Tom Holland. With: Chris Sarandon, William Ragsdale, Amanda Bearse, Stephen Geoffreys, Roddy McDowall, Jonathan Stark. Vista Organization/ Delphi IV Productions/Columbia. Colour.
Screenwriter Holland (*The Beast Within* [1982], etc) makes his directorial début with this horror comedy. When young Charley Brewster (Ragsdale) suspects his suave next-door neighbour Jerry Dandridge (a likeable Sarandon) is a vampire, the only person to believe him is ham horror actor Peter Vincent (a fun cameo by McDowall). Dandridge's undead assistant Evil Ed (Geoffreys) transforms from a vampire into a werewolf (created by Steve Johnson) before being staked to death by Vincent, while Dandridge turns into a bat-creature (courtesy of Randy Cook). This features excellent make-up effects and an exciting climax. However, some sequences seem a bit extreme when compared to the jokiness of the first half. With a clip from *The Premature Burial* (1962). Forrest J Ackerman supplied the movie props. Splatterpunks John M. Skipp and Craig Spector wrote the novelisation.
Sequel: FRIGHT NIGHT PART 2 (qv; 1988)
✦✦✦

FRIGHT NIGHT PART 2
USA, 1988. Dir: Tommy Lee Wallace. With: Roddy McDowall, William Ragsdale, Traci Lin, Julie Carmen, Jonathan Gries, Russell Clark. Vista Organization/ Columbia. Colour.
Okay sequel to *Fright Night* (1985). Three years after destroying the undead next door, Charley Brewster (Ragsdale) is just getting over the experience when Regine (Carmen), the seductive sister of the original vampire, turns up for revenge. With the help of failed TV horror host Peter Vincent (McDowall), Charley has to learn to believe in the undead again before he can destroy them. In one scene, wisecracking vampire Louie (Gries) transforms into a werewolf (make-up effects by Greg Cannom and others) to scale the apartment of Charley's new girlfriend (Lin). Another uneven mixture of horror and humour, but likeable characters and impressive special effects make this an entertaining follow-up.
✦✦✧

FROM DUSK TILL DAWN
USA/Mexico, 1995 (1996). Dir: Robert Rodriguez. With: Harvey Keitel, George Clooney, Quentin Tarantino, Juliette Lewis, Ernest Liu, Salma Hayek. Miramax/ Dimension Films/A Band Apart/Los Hooligans Productions. Colour.
Co-executive producer Tarantino's first script was transformed by director Rodriguez into a fast-paced, violent action movie. After a blood-drenched hold-up, the psychotic bank robbing Gecko brothers, Seth and Richard (Clooney and Tarantino), kidnap preacher Jacob Fuller (Keitel), his son Scott (Liu) and dysfunctional daughter Kate (Lewis) and flee with them across the border to Mexico. Then, in a surprise plot twist, they all end up at the Titty Twister bar, where they have to defend themselves against an army of shape-changing vampires led by undead stripper Santanico Pandemonium (a wasted Hayek). The script is uneven, but the performances, music score, special effects and action sequences make this a lot of fun. With a great cast that includes Cheech Marin in three roles, Fred Williamson, Tom Savini, Michael Parks and a wasted John Saxon. The script was published by Faber and Faber in 1996 with a foreword by Clive Barker, and *Full Tilt Boogie* (1997) is a feature-length behind-the-scenes documentary about the making of the film. Two video sequels followed.
Sequels: FROM DUSK TILL DAWN: THE HANGMAN'S DAUGHTER (qv; 1998) and FROM DUSK TILL DAWN 2: TEXAS BLOOD MONEY (qv; 1998)
✦✦✦✧

FROM DUSK TILL DAWN: THE HANGMAN'S DAUGHTER
USA, 1998 (1999). Dir: P.J. Pesce. With: Sonia Braga, Rebecca Gayheart, Michael Parks, Jordana Spiro, Marco Leonardi, Orlando Jones. Miramax/Dimension Films/A Band Apart Productions/Los Hooligans. Colour.
Parks is the only actor who returns from the original in this prequel to the 1995 film. Set in the 1800s, outlaw Johnny Madrid escapes the noose and runs off with the hangman's daughter, who is destined to become Santanico Pandemonium, the queen of the vampires. A small party of missionaries join together with the bandit to fight against the bloodsuckers who are besieging them. Quentin Tarantino and Robert Rodriguez (who co-scripted with his cousin Alvaro) are among the co-executive producers.
✦✦

FROM DUSK TILL DAWN 2: TEXAS BLOOD MONEY
South Africa/USA, 1998 (1999). Dir: Scott Spiegel. With: Robert Patrick, Muse Watson, Brett Harrelson, Bo Hopkins, Raymond Cruz, Duane Whitaker. Miramax/ Dimension Films/A Band Apart Productions/Los Hooligans. Colour.
The second direct-to-video follow-up to the 1995 original, but the first to be released. A band of robbers assembled by Buck (Patrick) plan a $5,000,000 bank heist, not knowing that their leader Luther (co-writer Whitaker) has been bitten by Razor Eddie (Danny Trejo, the only actor to return from the original), the undead tattooed bartender of the Titty Twister. As more members of the gang are turned into vampires, the robbery itself ends up as a Mexican stand-off between the bloodsuckers and the forces of law led by Sheriff Otis Lawson (Hopkins), with Buck caught in the middle. This features Bruce Campbell and Tiffany Amber-Thiesen in a fun opening sequence which has nothing to do with the rest of the movie. Director/co-writer Spiegel (who appears in a cameo) uses a number of arty subjective shots, including one from inside a vampire's mouth! Quentin Tarantino and Robert Rodriguez were among the co-executive producers.
✦✦

FROM THE CLOUD TO THE RESISTANCE
(aka DALLA NUBE ALLA RESISTENZA)
Italy/France/West Germany/UK, 1979. Dir: Jean-Marie Straub and Danièle Huillet. With: Olimpia Carlisi, Guido Lombardi, Gino Felici Lauricella, Lori Pelosini, Walter Pardini, Ennio Lauricella. Straub-Huillet/RAI-TV/ Channel 2/INA/Janus Film und Fernsehen/Artificial Eye. Colour.
This features six episodic dialogues between figures in Greek mythology and a tale set in modern times, split into two parts and based on the books *Dialoghi con Leucò* and *La Luna e I Falò* by Cesare Pavese. In the fourth episode, set in a cave, two hunters (Andrea Bacci and Lori Cavalini) decide to bury the werewolf they have just killed in case it is still partly human.
✦

FROM THE CONGO AND BEYOND...HOLLYWOOD GOES APE!
USA, 1994. Dir: Donald F. Glut. With: Bob Burns, Ashley Austin, Forrest J Ackerman, Ray Harryhausen, George E. Turner. Popcorn Pictures/Simitar. Colour/B&W.
Hosted by associate producer Burns (TV's *The Ghost Busters* [1975-76], etc) and Austin, this entertaining feature-length video documentary tells you everything you need to know about apes and apemen in the movies (and the people who played them). This

includes clips and trailers from *Africa Screams* (1949), *The Ape Man* (1943), *Bela Lugosi Meets a Brooklyn Gorilla* (1952), *The Bowery Boys Meet the Monsters* (1954), *The Bride and the Beast* (1957), *Bride of the Gorilla* (1951), *Captive Wild Woman* (1943), *King Kong* (1933), *Konga* (1960), *Master Minds* (1949), *The Mighty Gorga* (1969), *Mighty Joe Young* (1949), *Monster on the Campus* (1958), *The Son of Kong* (1933) and *Teenage Zombies* (1957), amongst numerous others. Dedicated to Charles Gemora (1903-61).
✦✦✦✧

THE FROZEN DEAD

UK, 1967. Dir: Herbert J. Leder. With: Dana Andrews, Anna Palk, Karel Stepanek, Kathleen Breck, Basil Henson, Philip Gilbert. Goldstar/Seven Arts. Colour.
Low-budget horror thriller with imported American star Andrews as Nazi scientist Dr Norborg, attempting to revive an army of top Nazis frozen at the end of World War Two and hidden in caves. He also keeps the severed head of a female victim (Breck) alive in a box. With Edward Fox in a small role as a murderous zombie.
✦✧

FROZEN SCREAM

USA, 1980. Dir: Frank Roach. With: Renee Harmon, Lynne Kocol. Platinum/VEC/Continental. Colour.
Obscure, low-budget movie in which a cop and his girlfriend discover that a mad doctor and his nurse (producer Harmon) freeze their victims and use prefrontal lobotomies to turn them into bug-eyed zombies. The extensive narration attempts to explain the plot.
✦

DWIGHT FRYE
[1899-1943]

American character actor and accomplished concert pianist who began his career on Broadway. Arriving in Hollywood in 1930, his portrayal of the memorable fly-eating Renfield in *Dracula* (1931) quickly resulted in Frye being typecast as madmen and hunchbacked assistants, notably the sadistic Fritz in *Frankenstein* (1931) and the ghoulish Karl in *Bride of Frankenstein* (1935). His appearance was cut from *Son of Frankenstein* (1939). Unable to find regular dramatic work, he was reduced to playing a voyeur in a stag film. At the time of his death, the actor was working nights designing bombsights to support his family. His death certificate listed his profession as 'tool designer'.
qv: *Dead Men Walk* (1943); *Frankenstein* (1931, test reel); *Frankenstein Meets the Wolf Man* (1943); *The Ghost of Frankenstein* (1942); *The Vampire Bat* (1933)

F TROOP:
V is for Vampire

USA, 1966. With: Forrest Tucker, Larry Storch, Ken Berry, Melody Patterson, Frank de Kova, Vincent Price. Warner Bros/ABC-TV. Colour.
Half-hour comedy TV show (1965-66, sixty-five episodes) set in the old West. In this episode, Price plays Dracula's cousin, actor Count Sforza (with a Bela Lugosi accent!), who had to leave Transylvania because he couldn't stand the sight of blood. Now on a theatrical tour of America, he arrives at Fort Courage driving a hearse and pretty soon Sergeant Morgan O'Rourke (Tucker) and Corporal Randolph Agarn (Storch) are getting out the garlic...
✦✦✧

FULL ECLIPSE

USA, 1993 (1994). Dir: Anthony Hickox. With: Mario Van Peebles, Patsy Kensit, Bruce Payne, Anthony John Denison, Jason Beghe, Paula Marshall. Home Box Office/ Tapestry Films/Citadel Entertainment. Colour.
Silly made-for-cable-TV movie with great action scenes, co-written and co-executive produced by Richard Christian Matheson. Van Peebles plays a Los Angeles cop, who discovers that psychologist Adam Garou (Payne) is the immortal leader of an elite secret squad within the police department who are injecting themselves with a serum, enabling them to transform into super-strong werewolf vigilantes. Unfortunately, Garou's final transmutation into a huge werewolf (created by Alterian Studios) looks more like a big bear.
✦✦✧

LUCIO FULCI
[1927-1996]

Italian film-maker who directed everything from comedies and musicals to Westerns and psychological thrillers. Best known for the gory *Zombie* (1979), an unofficial 'sequel' to George Romero's *Dawn of the Dead* (1978), he followed it with *City of the Living Dead* (1980), *The Beyond* (1981) and *The House by the Cemetery* (1982). Fulci continued his proclivity for violence in such films as *The Black Cat* (1980), *New York Ripper* (1982) and the self-indulgent *Nightmare Concert* (1990). Because of ill-health he was replaced during production on *Zombie 3* (1987) by Bruno Mattei, and he died a few days before he was due to start directing *Wax Mask* (1996) for producer Dario Argento.
qv: *Il Cav. Costante Nicosia Demoniaco Ovvero Dracula in Brianza* (1975); *Come Rubammo la Bomba Atomica* (1966); *Conquest* (1980); *House of Clocks* (1989); *Manhattan Baby* (1982).

FULL MOON HIGH

USA, 1981 (1986). Dir: Larry Cohen. With: Adam Arkin, Roz Kelly, Ed McMahon, Joanne Nail, Bill Kirchenbauer, Kenneth Mars. Filmways Pictures/Larco. Colour.
Rarely-seen low-budget comedy, written, produced and directed by Cohen with tax-shelter money. When likeable 1950s high school student Tony Walker (Arkin, from TV's *Chicago Hope* [1994-], etc) visits Romania with his CIA father (McMahon), he is bitten by a werewolf (make-up by Rick Baker alumnus Steve Neill). Doomed by a curse to remain young and wander all over the world, he returns to Full Moon High twenty years later masquerading as his own son, but soon has problems adjusting to his new surroundings. With Elizabeth Hartman as another werewolf, Alan Arkin as a crazy psychiatrist, Pat Morita, Laureen (*sic*) Landon and Julius W. Harris.
✦✧

FULL TILT BOOGIE

USA/Mexico, 1997 (1998). Dir: Sarah Kelly. With: George Clooney, Quentin Tarantino, Juliette Lewis, Fred Williamson, Robert Rodriguez. Miramax. Colour.
Feature-length behind-the-scenes documentary about the making of *From Dusk Till Dawn* (1995), with footage of Clooney and Tarantino having fun on the set, an early interview with director Rodriguez, and Tarantino at a *Fangoria* convention. This also includes numerous clips from the film.
✦✦✧

JOHN P. FULTON
[1902-1965]

American special visual effects pioneer. At Universal since 1930, he created such memorable highlights for the studio as invisible men and man-into-wolf and man-into-bat transformations. He later won several Academy Awards for his work on *The Ten Commandments* (1956) and others.
qv: *Bride of Frankenstein* (1935); *Dracula's Daughter* (1936); *Frankenstein* (1931); *Frankenstein Meets the Wolf Man* (1943); *Ghost Catchers* (1944); *Hellzapoppin'* (1941); *House of Dracula* (1945); *House of Frankenstein* (1944); *Man Made Monster* (1941); *The Mummy's Curse* (1944); *Son of Dracula* (1943); *Son of Frankenstein* (1939); *WereWolf of London* (1935); *The Wolf Man* (1941).

THE FUNHOUSE

USA, 1981. Dir: Tobe Hooper (and Gregory Goodell and Andrew Laszlo). With: Cooper Huckabee, Miles Chapin, Largo Woodruff, Sylvia Miles, William Finley, Kevin Conway. Mace Neufeld Productions/Universal. Colour.
Disappointing horror thriller from director Hooper (*The Texas Chain Saw Massacre* [1974], etc) which apparently had a troubled production. It begins promisingly with a *Psycho* (1960) in-joke and the build

up to a Ray Bradbury-ish carnival and freak show, but soon deteriorates when a group of dislikable teenagers are trapped in a funhouse with a mutated monster (created by Rick Baker and Craig Reardon) and its murderous father (Conway). The mutant (played by mime artist Wayne Doba) dresses up as Universal's Frankenstein Monster. It is left to a brief cameo by Finley as Marco the Magnificent and newcomer Elizabeth Berridge as young heroine Amy to brighten an otherwise dull film. With Herb Robins (*The Worm Eaters* [1977], etc) and a clip from *Bride of Frankenstein* (1935). The American cable TV version apparently includes restored footage. Dean R. Koontz wrote the novelisation under the pseudonym 'Owen West'.
✦✦

THE FUNTASTIC WORLD OF HANNA-BARBERA: THE ADVENTURES OF JONNY QUEST: Vikong Lives

USA, 1985 (1986). Dir: Ray Patterson. Voices: Scott Menville, Don Messick, Sonny Granville Van Dusen, Rob Paulsen, Georgi Irene. Hanna-Barbera Productions. Colour.

This half-hour syndicated cartoon TV series (thirteen episodes) revives the original 1964-65 show. In this episode, eleven year-old Jonny (Menville), his father Dr Benton Quest (Messick), Roger 'Race' Bannon (Van Dusen), Hadji (Paulsen) and Bandit the dog (Messick) discover a frozen giant ape while on a Scandinavian archaeological expedition. Guest voices include Rene Auberjonois, Roger C. Carmel, Darryl Hickman, Keye Luke, George Takei, Jeffrey Tambor and Les Tremayne.

Series remakes: JONNY'S GOLDEN QUEST (1993) and JONNY QUEST THE REAL ADVENTURES (qv; 1996)
✦✦

THE FURY OF THE WOLFMAN

(Orig: LA FURIA DEL HOMBRE LOBO)
Spain, 1970 (1974). Dir: José María Zabalza (and Enrique López Eguiluz). With: Paul Naschy (Jacinto Molina), Perla Cristal, Verónica Luján, Mark Stevens, Michael Rivers, Diana Montes. Plata Films/Maxper/Avco Embassy Pictures. Colour.

Having plundered Universal's *House of Frankenstein* (1944) as the inspiration for the previous instalment, *Dracula vs. Frankenstein* (1969), this fourth entry in the El Hombre Lobo series uses *WereWolf of London* (1935) as its inspiration. Professor Waldemar Daninsky (Naschy) is the only surviving member of an expedition to Tibet. Attacked and bitten by a werewolf, he returns to civilisation where he kills his unfaithful wife and her lover before apparently being electrocuted. Daninsky is revived by vengeful female scientist Ilona (Argentinean actress Cristal), who he jilted, and she dominates his mind along with those of the mutant plant men that she and the masked Dr Wolfstein keep in the cellar of her castle. In the end, Daninsky is forced to battle his zombie wife Eva (Luján), who Ilona has also turned into a werewolf, before he is killed with a silver bullet. According to Naschy, this dull entry reuses footage from the first in the series, *Frankenstein's Bloody Terror* (1967), because the director was always drunk and his final cut was too short!

Paul Naschy reveals The Fury of the Wolfman *(1970).*

Sequel: THE WEREWOLF VS. THE VAMPIRE WOMAN (qv; 1970)
✦

FUTURESHOCK

USA, 1993. Dir: Eric Parkinson, Francis Sassone and Matt Reeves. With: Vivian Schilling, Scott Thompson, Sam Clay, Martin Kove, Bill Paxton, Brion James. Paradise/Park-Place Entertainment/Hemdale Home Video. Colour.

Compilation of three short films, linked by a psychiatrist (Kove) listening to the stories from his patients. Schilling (who also scripted her segment) stars in 'Jenny Porter' as the eponymous woman terrified by a prowler. In the other two episodes, made by UCLA students in 1988 and 1992 respectively, a con man (Paxton) moves in with a morgue attendant (Thompson) in 'The Roommate', and a photographer (Clay) has a phobia of death in the comic episode 'Mr. Petrified Forest'. With Sidney Lassick, James Karen, Rick Rossovich and Julie Strain as a stripper, plus clips from *Howling II Stirba — Werewolf Bitch* (1984) and *The Return of the Living Dead* (1984) on TV.
✦✦

GABRIEL KNIGHT: THE BEAST WITHIN
USA, 1996. Dir: Will Binder. With: Dean Erickson, Joanne Takahashi, Peter Jozef Lucus, Andrea Martin, Nicholas Worth, Russell Mitchell. Sierra On-Line. Colour.
Gothic CD-ROM interactive horror movie in which Gabriel Knight (Erickson) investigates a werewolf. This even includes a specially-composed gypsy opera. A novelisation, written by the game's creator, Jane Jensen, was published in 1998.
✦✦

GADGET BOY'S ADVENTURES IN HISTORY: Gadget-Stein
France/USA, 1997 (1998). Dir: Pascal Morelli and Charlie Sansonetti. Voices: Don Adams, Maurice LaMarche, Tara Charendoff, Louise Vallance. DIC Entertainment/M6/ National Education Association/The History Channel. Colour.
Half-hour cartoon TV series (twenty-six episodes), a spin-off from *Inspector Gadget* (1982-85) and *Gadget Boy and Heather* (1995) and featuring the eponymous juvenile bionic secret agent (Adams), Agent Heather (Charendoff) and mechanical canine G-9. In this episode, the evil Spyder (Vallance) travels back in time to Lake Geneva, Switzerland, in 1816. There she uses her new metaboliser helmet to get Mary Shelley to imagine some monster warriors (including a werewolf, mummy, giant ape and 'Bride'), which menace Percy B. Shelley, Lord Byron and Gadget Boy (who thinks he is at a costume party). Meanwhile, her vulture sidekick Boris (LaMarche) is forced to write the novel *Frankenstein* with Spyder as the hero.
✦✧

GALACTICA 1980: (UK: BATTLESTAR GALACTICA) The Night the Cylons Landed
USA, 1980. Dir: Sigmund Neufield Jr and Barry Crane. With: Kent McCord, Barry Van Dyke, Robyn Douglass, Lorne Greene, Patrick Stuart, William Daniels. Universal/ Glen A. Larson Productions/ABC-TV. Colour.
Short-lived hour-long TV series (ten episodes) set thirty years after *Battlestar Galactica* (1978-79), when the space fleet has finally reached Earth. Galactican warriors Troy (McCord) and Dillon (Van Dyke) team up with Earth reporter Jamie Hamilton (Douglass) to observe mankind. In this two-part episode, humanoid Cylon Andromus (Roger Davis) and his companion Centurion Andromidus (Neil Zeunik) crash their war machine on Earth. While looking for a radio transmitter to contact the Cylon fleet, they are given a ride to a Halloween party by a couple dressed as a vampire (Lara Parker from *Dark Shadows* [1966-71]) and a clown (Daniels). With Wolfman Jack as himself, Peter Mark Richman, Bernie Hamilton and a live-action dancing Scooby-Doo! This was also released as part of the feature compilation *Conquest of the Earth* (1980). Written by executive producer Glen A. Larson.
✦✦

THE GAMES OF THE COUNTESS DOLINGEN OF GRATZ (Orig: LES JEUX DE LA COMTESSE DOLINGEN DE GRATZ)
France, 1980. Dir: Catherine Binet. With: Michel Lonsdale, Carol Kane, Katia Wastchenko, Robert Stephens, Marina Vlady, Marilu Marini. Les Films du Nautile/Prospectacle/Perec/Zajdermann. Colour.
Based on the book by Unica Zurn and a chapter from Bram Stoker's *Dracula*. A young woman, Louise (Kane), suspects a family friend of being a vampire.
✦

THE GAMMA PEOPLE
UK, 1955. Dir: John Gilling. With: Paul Douglas, Eva Bartok, Leslie Phillips, Walter Rilla, Philip Leaver, Martin Miller. Warwick Films/Columbia. B&W.
Two British journalists (Douglas and Phillips) find themselves trapped in a small Eastern European country run by mad scientist Dr Boronski (Rilla), who is using gamma rays to turn children into geniuses. Unfortunately, his failures are roaming the countryside as scary-looking murderous zombies. This is an odd blend of political propaganda, spy thriller, science fiction adventure and comedy (Phillips' silly-ass Englishman) from co-writer/director Gilling (Hammer's *The Plague of the Zombies* [1966], etc).
✦✧

GANG BUSTERS
USA, 1942. Dir: Ray Taylor and Noel Smith. With: Kent Taylor, Irene Harvey, Ralph Morgan, Robert Armstrong, Richard Davies, Joseph Crehan. Universal. B&W.
Thirteen chapter serial based on the factual radio show. Professor Mortis (Morgan), the head of an organisation called The League of Murdered Men, uses capsules to bring supposedly executed criminals back to life. In the end, he is killed by a speeding subway train while trying to escape. Forde Beebe was associate producer.
✦✦

GANJA & HESS (aka BLACK EVIL/BLACK OUT: THE MOMENT OF TERROR/BLACK VAMPIRE/BLOOD COUPLE/DOUBLE POSSESSION/DRACULA — UP IN HARLEM)
USA, 1973. Dir: Bill Gunn. With: Duane Jones, Marlene Clark, Leonard Jackson, Mabel King, Bill Gunn, Sam Waymon. Kelly-Jordan Enterprises/Heritage Enterprises. Colour.
This arty, elliptical vampire movie, shot in New York under the title *Vampires of Harlem*, is a welcome attempt to get away from the blaxploitation cycle of the early seventies. Jones (*Night of the Living Dead* [1968], etc) plays Dr Hess Green, a wealthy anthropologist who becomes a vampire when he's stabbed with an ancient Myrthian bone dagger by his unbalanced research assistant George Meda (writer/director Gunn). He turns his attacker's wife Ganja (Clark) into a vampire before finally committing suicide in the shadow of a cross. Filmed on 16mm for $300,000, this has been reissued under several different titles in America (and credited to Russian-born editor F.H. Novikov [Fima H. Noveck] on the revised 1974 version released as *Blood Couple* or *Double Possession*). See the original instead, which was released on video in a special 'restored director's cut' in 1998.
✦✦✦

THE GARDEN
Canada, 1990. Dir: Will Dixon. With: Jan Rubes, Scott Bremner, Benjamin Woolf, Erin Reesor, Lee Henderson, Jason Ward. Garden Productions/Saskatchewan Television Network/Heartland Motion Pictures. Colour.
Forty-seven minute children's TV film in which three young friends believe that the strange old man (Rubes) living next door to Jess (Bremner) is really a vampire who killed and buried a local boy in his garden. However, when they eventually befriend him, they discover that he is just lonely and misses his dead wife. Together they dress up as vampires to scare off a gang of local bullies who want to destroy his prized plot.
✦✦

GARDEN OF THE DEAD (UK: TOMB OF THE UNDEAD)
USA, 1972. Dir: John Hayes. With: Duncan McLeod, John Dennis, John Dullaghan, Lee Frost, Lewis Sterling, Marland Procktor. Millenium Productions/Entertainment Pyramid. Colour.
Prisoner's wife Carol (Susan Charney), Dr Saunders (McLeod) and Sergeant Jablonsky (Dennis) are trapped in an isolated American prison camp when spilled formaldehyde causes convicts executed after a failed escape attempt to rise from the grave as bloodthirsty zombies. The walking dead can only be destroyed by a shotgun blast at point blank range or concentrated light, which causes them to turn green and decompose. This low-budget chiller is just fifty-nine minutes long.
✦

GARGOYLES:
Eye of the Beholder
USA, 1995. Voices: Thom Adcox Hernandez, Jeff Bennett, Keith David, Bill Fagerbakke, Salli Richardson, Jonathan Frakes, Frank Welker. Buena Vista Television/ABC-TV. Colour.
Half-hour children's cartoon TV series (1994-96, sixty-five episodes). Stone by day, warriors by night, the Gargoyles were betrayed by the humans they had sworn to protect and frozen in stone by a magic spell for 1,000 years. Now in Manhattan, the spell is broken and they live again. In this Halloween episode, Gargoyle leader Goliath (David) and police detective Elisa Maza (Richardson) discover that the fiancée of the evil David Xanatos (Frakes) is transformed into a werewolf by a mystical jewel.
✦✦✧
Mark of the Panther
USA, 1995 (1996) Dir: Dennis J. Woodyard. Voices: Brigitte Bako, LeVar Burton, Keith David, Nichelle Nichols, Salli Richardson, Frank Welker. Buena Vista Television/ABC-TV. Colour.
In this episode, Goliath, his daughter Angela (Bako) and Elisa travel to Africa where they battle the evil Anansi (Burton), a giant spider god, and encounter a pair of were-panthers.
Series sequel: GARGOYLES: THE GOLIATH CHRONICLES (1996-97)
✦✦✧

THE GATE
Canada, 1986 (1987). Dir: Tibor Takacs. With: Stephen Dorff, Louis Tripp, Christa Denton, Ingrid Veninger, Kelly Rowan, Jennifer Irwin. New Century/Vista. Colour.
Fun, low-budget horror thriller in which a group of kids accidentally open a supernatural gateway to Hell in their backyard. Their subsequent attempts to thwart the powers of darkness are hampered by a variety of demons (including some created through excellent stop-motion effects by Randy Cook) and the reanimated corpse of a construction worker (Carl Kraines, in special make-up by Craig Reardon).
Sequel: GATE II (1989)
✦✦

THE GATE OF THE HELL
Hong Kong, 1981. Dir: Lu Pao-Lun. With: Tsui Hsin-Yu, Chang Ming-Ting, Li Ying, Li Tao-Hung, Warrick Evens, Ema Emily. Ie Loong/Wild West Video/Ocean Shores Video. Colour.
Horror comedy in which the skeleton of a vampire reconstitutes its flesh in an old house in the New Territories. Soon all the heroine's friends have been turned into bloodsuckers. With an unrelated prologue involving a flying skull and an it-was-all-a-dream ending.
✦✧

TUDOR GATES
[b 1930]

British scriptwriter who worked on *Danger: Diabolik* (1967) and *Barbarella* (1967) before writing Hammer's 'Karnstein Trilogy': *The Vampire Lovers* (1970), *Lust for a Vampire* (1970) and *Twins of Evil* (1971).
qv: *Fright* (1971); *Hammer A-Z* (1997).

VALERIE GAUNT
[b 1933]

British actress of the fifties, who was cast as the ill-fated Justine in Hammer's *The Curse of Frankenstein* (1957) after producer Anthony Hinds saw her screaming in a TV play. She subsequently turned up as the Count's single sexy 'bride' in *Dracula* (1958).

GAYRACULA
USA, 1983. Dir: Roger Earl. With: Tim Kramer, Douglas Poston, Steve Collins, Ray Medina, Max Cooper. Marathon/HIS Video. Colour.
Hardcore gay movie filmed on 35mm. In eighteenth century Transylvania the Marquis de Suede turns Gaylord into a vampire. Now in present-day Los Angeles, the homosexual vampire is sinking more than his teeth into his male victims.
✦

RAMÓN GAY
[1917-1960]

Mexican actor, also billed as Raymond Gay and Raymond Gaylord, who appeared in *La Momia Azteca* (1957), *Curse of the Aztec Mummy* (1957) and *The Robot vs the Aztec Mummy* (1957), as well as other Mexican monster movies. He was shot to death by a jealous husband.
qv: *Attack of the Mayan Mummy* (1957/64); *Curse of the Doll People* (1960); *Face of the Screaming Werewolf* (1960).

DO GAZ JAMEEN KE NEECHE
India, 1972. Dir: Tulsi Ramsay and Shyam Ramsay. With: Surendra Kumar, Pooja, Imtiaz, Shobhana, Satyendra Kapoo, Smita Mayank. Ramsay Films. Colour.
When a scheming woman murders her rich young husband, he is chemically revived as a zombie seeking revenge. At over two hours long, this Hindustani film includes the obligatory musical numbers and ran into censorship problems in India. The title translates as 'Crime Does Not Pay'.
✦✧

GEEK MAGGOT BINGO
USA, 1983. Dir: Nick Zedd. With: Robert Andrews, Brenda Bergman, Richard Hell, Donna Death, (John) Zacherle, Bob Martin. Weirdo Films/Penetration. Colour.
Zedd follows up his directing début on *They Eat Scum* (1979) with this horror spoof featuring the mad doctor Frankenberry (Andrews), his hunchback assistant (Bruno Zeus), a female vampire (Death) and a two-headed Formaldehyde Man (Tyler Smith, in make-up created by him and Ed French) brought to life through 'chemosynthetic regeneration'. Shot on 16mm on obviously cardboard sets, this includes some nudity. With a guest appearance by Martin, the then-editor of *Fangoria*, while TV horror host Zacherley is shown sleeping during the breaks.
✦

DE GENERAZIONE
Italy, 1994. Dir: Antonio Antonelli, Asia Argento, Piergiorgio Bellocchio, Eleonora Fiorini, Alex Infascelli, Antonio Manetti, Marco Manetti, Andrea Maulà, Andrea Prandstraller, Alberto Taraglio and Alessandro Valori. With: Asia Argento, Corrado Guzzanti, Alessandro Haber, Pietro Jona, Pierfrancesco Loche, Antonio Manetti. Mox & Fox/Notorius. Colour.
Allegorical ten-part anthology movie produced by a group of young Italian film-makers. The various episodes include one about an invisible man and another entitled 'Just Another Vampire Story'. With the voice of Dario Argento.
✦

THE GENII OF DARKNESS
(Orig: NOSTRADAMUS, EL GENIO DE LAS TINIEBLAS)
Mexico, 1960 (1962). Dir: Frederick (Federico) Curiel. With: Germán Robles, Julio Aleman, Domingo Soler, Aurora Alvarado, Manver (Manuel Vergara), Fanny Schiller. Estudios America/American International. B&W.
A sequel to *The Monsters Demolisher* (1960), and the third of four features cut down from a twelve-part Mexican serial and released directly to American TV. Robles stars as the bearded vampire descendant of Nostradamus who falls in love, while his nemesis Professor Duran (Soler) steals the ashes of the original Nostradamus from a crypt in the forest. This includes the episodes 'El Genio de las Tinieblas', 'Mas alla de la Vida' and 'El Hijo de la Noche'. The English-language version was produced by K. (Kenneth) Gordon Murray and directed by Stim (Stem) Segar.
Sequel: THE BLOOD OF NOSTRADAMUS (qv; 1960)
✦✧

GENTLEMAN JEKYLL AND DRIVER HYDE
Canada, 1950. International. B&W.
Eight minute documentary about safe driving.
✦

JOSEPH GERSHENSON
[b 1904]

Russian-born music director who conducted (often uncredited) many of Universal's scores during the 1940s and 1950s.
qv: *Abbott and Costello Meet Dr. Jekyll and Mr. Hyde* (1953); *Abbott and Costello Meet the Mummy* (1955); *Creature from the Black Lagoon* (1954); *The Creature Walks Among Us* (1955); *Curse of the Undead* (1959); *Man of a Thousand Faces* (1957); *Monster on the Campus* (1958); *Revenge of the Creature* (1955); *The World of Abbott and Costello* (1964).

GET ALONG, LITTLE ZOMBIE
USA, 1946. Dir: Edward Bernds. With: Hugh Herbert, Christine McIntyre, Dick Curtis, Jessie Arnold, Dudley Dickerson, Jack Roper. Columbia. B&W.
Obscure twenty minute comedy short from the regular Three Stooges director.
✦✧

THE GETAWAY
USA, 1994. Dir: Roger Donaldson. With: Alec Baldwin, Kim Basinger, Michael Madsen, Jennifer Tilly, Richard Farnsworth, James Woods. Largo International/JVC Entertainment. Colour.
This stylish crime thriller is a remake of Sam Peckinpah's 1972 film starring Steve McQueen and Ali MacGraw. When Carol McCoy (Basinger) makes a deal to break her husband Doc (Baldwin) out of prison, the couple agree to become involved in a dangerous heist that goes wrong. In one scene, Madsen and Tilly's characters watch Lon Chaney Jr's Wolf Man in a clip from (Abbott and Costello) *Meet Frankenstein* (1948) on TV.
✦✦✧

GET SMART:
House of Max
USA, 1969 (1970). Dir: Tony Leader. With: Don Adams, Barbara Feldon, Edward Platt, Charles Bateman, Hedley Mattingly, Marcel Hillaire. Talent Associates/Norton Simon/CBS-TV. Colour.
Two-part episode of the half-hour TV sci-spy spoof (1965-70, 138 episodes), created by Buck Henry and Mel Brooks. CONTROL Agent 86, Maxwell Smart (Adams), is sent to London to help Scotland Yard's Inspector Sparrow (Mattingly) catch a killer whose murders are a copy of those committed by the original Jack the Ripper. Their investigations lead them to a sinister wax museum, where the mad Professor Duval (Hillaire) brings the wax figures to life, including a werewolf (George Sawaya) and W.C. Fields (Bill Oberlin).
✦✦✧

The Mummy
USA, 1966 (1967). Dir: Earl Bellamy. With: Don Adams, Barbara Feldon, Edward Platt, Laurie Main, Lisa Gaye, Marc London. Talent Associates/Norton Simon/NBC-TV. Colour.
Maxwell Smart discovers a plot by KAOS agents to smuggle themselves into the country in Egyptian sarcophagi, then use the same mummy cases to transport kidnapped CONTROL agents out again.
✦✦

Shock it to Me
USA, 1969. Dir: Jay Sandrich. With: Don Adams, Barbara Feldon, Edward Platt, Tom Poston, Sid Haig, Milton Parsons. Talent Associates/Norton Simon/NBC-TV. Colour.
In this episode, KAOS mad scientist Dr Eric Zharko (Poston) revives dead agents with his stolen electrical apparatus and plans to put Maxwell Smart and Agent 99 (Feldon) into suspended animation. With Haig as Bruce the hunchback and horror veteran Parsons as Mr Obler, the morgue attendant.
✦✦✧

The Wax Man
USA, 1967 (1968). Dir: James Komack. With: Don Adams, Barbara Feldon, Edward Platt, Richard Devon, Robert Ridgely, Robert Lussier. Talent Associates/Norton Simon/NBC-TV. Colour.
Devon plays a KAOS agent and the sinister owner of a wax museum, who sends apparently living figures of the Frankenstein Monster and Dracula (Ridgely) after Maxwell Smart and Agent 99.
✦✦

Weekend Vampire
USA, 1965. Dir: Bruce Bilson. With: Don Adams, Barbara Feldon, Edward Platt, Martin Kosleck, Ford Rainey, Roger Price. Talent Associates/Norton Simon/NBC-TV. Colour.
Maxwell Smart and Agent 99 investigate a series of vampire-like killings of CONTROL agents. They turn out to be the work of the diabolical Dr Drago (horror veteran Kosleck) and his double-barrelled flute, which shoots poisoned ice-pellets into the jugular. The series was briefly revived in 1995 with Adams reprising his role.
Series sequel: THE NUDE BOMB (1980)
✦✦

THE GHOST BREAKERS
USA, 1940. Dir: George Marshall. With: Bob Hope, Paulette Goddard, Richard Carlson, Paul Lukas, Willie Best, Anthony Quinn. Paramount. B&W.
Based on the play *The Ghost Breaker* by Paul Dickey and Charles W. Goddard (previously filmed in 1914 and 1922), this atmospheric follow-up to Paramount's *The Cat and the Canary* (1939) reunites stars Hope and Goddard in a comedy thriller involving gangsters, ghosts, red herrings and a scary zombie (Noble Johnson). When he becomes involved in a murder investigation, radio columnist Larry Lawrence (a wise-cracking Hope in top form) accompanies Mary Carter (Goddard) to spooky Castillo Maldito off Cuba to claim her inheritance. Director Marshall plays the mystery elements straight, and there's great support from an eye-rolling Best, Lukas as a Lugosi-like villain, Quinn in an early dual role and Virginia Brissac as the zombie's eerie mother.
Remake: SCARED STIFF (qv; 1953)
✦✦✦✦

THE GHOST BRIGADE
(aka THE KILLING BOX)
USA, 1993. Dir: George Hickenlooper. With: Adrian Pasdar, Corbin Bernsen, Martin Sheen, Cynda Williams, Ray Wise, Alexis Arquette. Fred Kuehnert/MPCA. Colour.
During the American Civil War, a Union general (Sheen) wants to discover who is slaughtering soldiers on both sides of the battlefield. Captain Harling (Pasdar), Confederate prisoner Strayn (Bernsen) and slave Rebecca (Williams) find that a brigade of zombie soldiers is responsible. Edited by cult director Monte Hellman.
✦✦

THE GHOST BUSTERS:
Dr. Whatshisname
USA, 1975. Dir: Norman Abbott. With: Forrest Tucker, Larry Storch, Bob Burns, Bernie Kopell, Bill Engesser. Filmation Associates/Incorporated Television Company/CBS-TV. Colour.
Shot-on-video half-hour comedy TV series (fifteen episodes) about the members of Ghost Busters Inc — Jake Kong (Tucker), Eddie Spenser (Storch) and the beanie-wearing Tracy the Gorilla (Burns) — who are given their assignments on a self-destructing tape by the mysterious Mr Z. In this episode, Kong and Spencer encounter the ghosts of Dr Frankenstein (Kopell) and his Monster (Engesser), who are searching for the world's most gullible brain. Naturally, they decide Spencer's is perfect to transplant into the Monster.
✦✧

Hyde and Go Seek
USA, 1975. Dir: Norman Abbott. With: Forrest Tucker, Larry Storch, Bob Burns, Severn Darden, Joe E. Ross. Filmation Associates/Incorporated Television Company/CBS-TV. Colour.
The ghost of Dr Jekyll (Darden) needs to sacrifice a man with no personality, like Spenser, to rid himself of the caveman-like Mr Hyde (Ross).
✦✧

Vampire's Apprentice
USA, 1975. With: Forrest Tucker, Larry Storch, Bob Burns. Filmation Associates/Incorporated Television Company/ CBS-TV. Colour.
Kong and Spenser become involved with the undead.
✦✧

Who's Afraid of the Big Bad Wolf
USA, 1975. Dir: L.A. Peerce. With: Forrest Tucker, Larry Storch, Bob Burns, Dodo Denney, Lennie Weinrib. Filmation Associates/Incorporated Television Company/ CBS-TV. Colour.
The ghosts of a gypsy (Denney) and a werewolf (Weinrib) search for an amulet owned by Spencer that can lift the lycanthropic curse.
✦✧

The Worthless Gauze
USA, 1975. With: Forrest Tucker, Larry Storch, Bob Burns. Filmation Associates/Incorporated Television Company/ CBS-TV. Colour.
Tracy the ape is mistaken for a mighty sorcerer by an Egyptian queen and her living mummy who are seeking the secret of immortality. Other episodes guest-starred Jim Backus, Billy Barty, Johnny Brown, Ted Knight and Huntz Hall.
Series sequel: GHOSTBUSTERS (qv; 1986-87)
✦✧

GHOSTBUSTERS
(aka THE ORIGINAL GHOSTBUSTERS)
USA, 1986-87. Voices: Pat Fraley, Peter Cullen, Alan Oppenheimer, Susan Blu, Linda Gary, Erik Gunden. Filmation Associates/Tribune Broadcasting. Colour.
Syndicated half-hour cartoon series based on the live-action series *The Ghost Busters* (1975), in which Jake Kong Jr (Fraley), Eddie Spenser Jr (Cullen) and Tracy the genius ape (Lou Scheimer), along with their pink vampire bat Belfry, battle metal-masked villain Prime Evil (Oppenheimer) and his all-ghoul band (including the ghostly Mysteria and Fangster the werewolf). Each episode ends with an educational message. Not to be confused with the cartoon series *The Real Ghostbusters* (1986-88), based on the hit 1984 movie.
✦✦

GHOSTBUSTING
(Orig: ZHUAGUI TEGONGDUI)
Hong Kong, 1987. Dir: Chao Chen-Kuo. With: David Tao, Fong Cheng, Chang Fei, Chen Shin, An An, Fong Fon-Fon. Long Shong Pictures/Cinema City/Rainbow Video. Colour.
Horror comedy in which the vampire Black Cloud sleeps in an Egyptian-looking sarcophagus and plots to turn doctor's wife Hsiao-Chen, who he hypnotically controls, into his Queen of the Night. In the end, her husband and a boy with psychic powers use a soul-stealing ray to destroy the vampire and other revellers at a costume party dressed as the Frankenstein Monster, a werewolf, witches and gremlins.
✦✧

GHOST BUSTING
(Orig: HUAGUI YOUXIAN GONGSI)
Hong Kong, 1989. Dir: Wong Ching (Wong Ching-Jing/Lau Sze-Yu). With: Sandra Ng, Lolanto Chan. Grand March Movie Company/Tai Seng Video. Colour.
Horror comedy set in a school for exorcists. Among the many monsters the students encounter are a gay bloodsucker and a caped vampire queen who can shoot rays. Both undead creatures can also transform into cartoon winged bat-demons.
✦✦

GHOST CATCHERS
USA, 1944. Dir: Edward F. Cline. With: Ole Olsen, Chic Johnson, Gloria Jean, Martha O'Driscoll, Leo Carrillo, Andy Devine. Universal. B&W.
Shot under the title *High Spirits*. The vaudevillian comedy team of Olsen and Johnson attempt to combine the zany humour of their *Hellzapoppin'* (1941) and *Crazy House* (1943) with ghosts and gangsters. The duo play the owners of a nightclub who investigate the 'haunted' house next door and uncover a cellar full of pre-Prohibition booze. Despite some nice John P. Fulton special photographic effects and a wonderful swing version of 'Quoth the Raven' (by Paul F. Webster and Harry Revel), the plot simply stops too often for another silly gag or a musical number. With Carrillo apparently wearing a Kharis the mummy mask, Devine dressed as a horse, seventh-billed Lon Chaney Jr totally wasted in a bear costume, Jack Norton as a tipsy ghost, Tor Johnson (with hair!) as a gangster, Mel Tormé as a drummer, plus future producer/director Jerry Warren, midget Billy Curtis and Kay Harding in bit parts. Olsen and Johnson made just one more movie together.
✦✧

GHOST FEVER
USA/Mexico, 1986 (1987). Dir: Alan Smithee (Lee Madden). With: Sherman Hemsley, Luis Avalos, Jennifer Rhodes, Deborah Benson, Pepper Martin, Diana Brookes. Infinite/Miramax. Colour.
Slapstick comedy starring Hemsley and Avalos as two bumbling cops caught up in a supernatural mystery. A Haitian voodoo curse turns an evil slave owner (Martin) into a vampire who then haunts a Georgia cemetery and creates zombies in his torture dungeon. Filmed in 1984 and extensively re-shot and re-edited, director Madden had his name removed from the credits. With veteran Myron Healey and a guest appearance by boxer 'Smokin'' Joe Frazier. Who says they don't make them like Monogram anymore?
✦✧

GHOST GUARDING TREASURE
Hong Kong, circa 1990. Colour.
When a sorcerer makes a horde of hopping vampires disappear, an undead little boy and his big-fanged mother are among those who remain behind.
✦

GHOST HOSPITAL
Hong Kong, 1988. Dir: Yu Kong-Yun (Dennis Yu). With: Choy King-Fei, Leung Sui-Long, Kwan Hoi-San, Cook Fung. Colour.
A patient in a cursed hospital is transported in his sleep to another dimension where exorcist priests battle hopping zombies.
✦

THE GHOST IN THE INVISIBLE BIKINI
USA, 1966. Dir: Don Weis. With: Tommy Kirk, Deborah Walley, Basil Rathbone, Patsy Kelly, Susan Hart, Boris Karloff. American International Pictures. Colour.
This mindless AIP comedy/horror/musical variation on their *Beach Party* series was filmed under various titles, including *Slumber Party in Horror House, Bikini Party in a Haunted House, Beach Party in a Haunted House* and *Pajama Party in a Haunted House*. In what look like tacked-on sequences, Karloff plays Hiram Stokely (billed as 'The Corpse' in the credits), who is told by his dead girlfriend (Hart) that he must do a good deed to go to Heaven. This involves helping Kirk and his teenage friends stop scheming lawyer Reginald Ripper (Rathbone) killing the heirs to a hidden fortune. It all ends with a frenetic chase through a chamber of horrors that includes a dummy of the Frankenstein Monster. With veterans Kelly, Jesse White and Francis X. Bushman, Harvey Lembeck as Eric von Zipper, Nancy Sinatra (who sings), some unconvincing monsters and a gorilla. Not released in Britain until 1989. You've got to see it to believe it! Photographed by the great Stanley Cortez.
Sequel: BACK TO THE BEACH (1987)
✦✦

GHOSTLY LOVE
(Orig: QIAN YUNYU QING)
Hong Kong, 1990. Dir: Wu Kuo-Ren (Cheung Kit). With: Hui Tien-Chee, Emily Chu, Lam Wei, Mark Long. Pan-Asia Video. Colour.
Softcore fantasy involving a vampiric ghost woman who must marry the ghost king, who sucks the blood from virgins to maintain his strength. This also includes a line of hopping vampire women.
✦✧

THE GHOST MONSTER

USA, 1966. Dir: Ralph Bakshi. Voices: Herschel Bernardi, Lionel Wilson. Terrytoons/CBS Films/Twentieth Century-Fox. Colour.

Series of eight minute TV cartoons (twenty-six episodes) featuring The Mighty Heroes — Strong Man, Cuckoo Man, Tornado Man, Rope Man and Diaper Man. In this episode the unlikely crime fighters battle the Ghost Monster, which returns to the peaceful town of Goodhaven every hundred years to terrorise the inhabitants. The creature lives in an old haunted house, and its horrible helpers include a plague of bats and silly yellow 'werewolves' (which look more like demons). In 1970 this was one of several episodes also released to movie theatres in America.

✦✧

THE GHOST OF DRAGSTRIP HOLLOW

USA, 1959. Dir: William Hole Jr. With: Jody Fair, Martin Braddock, Russ Bender, Jack Ging, Leon Tyler, Paul Blaisdell. American International Pictures/Alta Vista. B&W.

Sequel to *Hot Rod Gang* (1958), filmed under the title *The Haunted Hot Rod*. When forced to vacate their club because of money difficulties, various drag-racing teens and their girlfriends turn up in monster costumes for a rock 'n' roll Halloween party in an abandoned old house. Among them are a teenager dressed as the Frankenstein Monster and Paul Blaisdell, who is revealed as himself in the costume he created for *The She-Creature* (1956). With music by The Renegades.

✦

THE GHOST OF FRANKENSTEIN

USA, 1942. Dir: Erle C. Kenton. With: Lon Chaney, Sir Cedric Hardwicke, Ralph Bellamy, Lionel Atwill, Bela Lugosi, Evelyn Ankers. Universal. B&W.

The fourth entry in Universal's Frankenstein cycle (following *Son of Frankenstein* [1939]) reduces the series to the level of a formula horror thriller utilising the studio's contract players. Hardwicke's Ludwig, the second son of Frankenstein (he also plays his father's ghost), is totally overshadowed by Atwill's mad Dr Theodor Bohmer and Lugosi's resurrected Ygor. Between them, they rescue the Monster from the lime pit and restore his strength. Chaney Jr plays Frankenstein's creation as a dumb brute, despite a failed attempt to recapture Karloff's pathos in a scene where he kidnaps a little girl (Janet Ann Gallow). In the end, Frankenstein is tricked into transplanting Ygor's brain into the Monster. With Barton Yarborough, Dwight Frye, Holmes Herbert, Lionel Belmore, Lawrence Grant, Brandon Hurst and Eddie Parker doubling for Chaney. A juvenile novelisation by Carl R. Green and William R. Sanford (William Reynolds) was published in 1985, and editor Philip J. Riley included the script in his series of Universal Filmbooks for MagicImage in 1990.

Sequel: FRANKENSTEIN MEETS THE WOLF MAN (qv; 1943)

✦✦✦

GHOST'S HOSPITAL

Hong Kong, 1989. Dir: Tony Lu-Yung. World Video. Colour.

Horror comedy in which hopping vampires break out of jail and the police trail some escaped ghosts to a local hospital, where they are harassing the patients. This also includes a fake vampire.

✦

GHOSTS THAT STILL WALK

USA, 1977 (1978). Dir: James T. Flocker. With: Ann Nelson, Matt Boston, Jerry Jensen, Caroline Howe, Phil Catalli, Rita Crafts. Flocker/Gold Key Television. Colour.

Silly supernatural TV movie. While his astral body is elsewhere, a boy is possessed by the spirit of a Native American mummy that kills the members of the youngster's family to preserve its secret. In one scene, a number of desert boulders threaten his grandparents in their motor home.

✦✧

Lon Chaney Jr hands Janet Ann Gallow to Olaf Hytten in The Ghost of Frankenstein *(1942).*

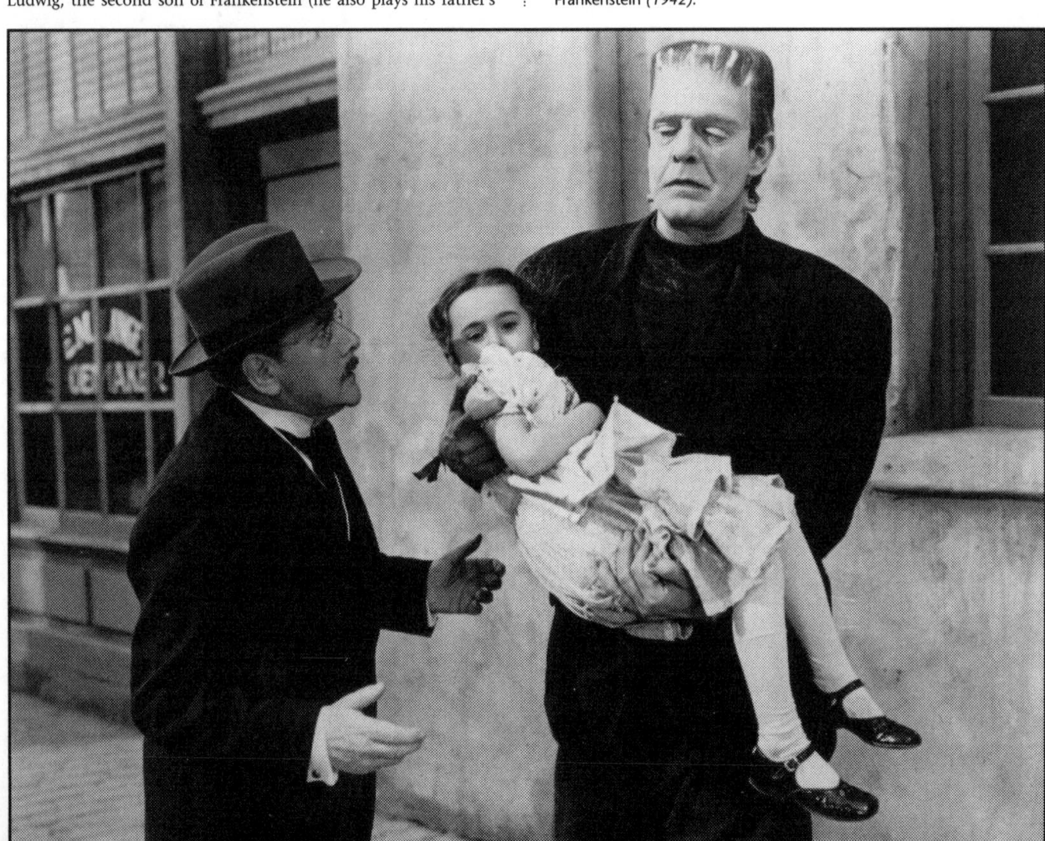

GHOST STORIES: GRAVEYARD THRILLER

USA, 1986. Dir: Lynn Silver. With: Bob Jenkins, Ralph Lucas, Laura Kay, Sandra McLees, Maria Hayden, Jules Anton. High Ridge/Alamance/Vestron. Colour.

Set in Tuesday Hill Boneyard, the Graveyard Keeper (Jenkins) is the host for five horror stories. These include a tale about the offspring of a woman and rats ('Where Have You Been Billy Boy, Billy Boy?'), a psycho killer ('Mr Fox') and a woman who returns from the grave to play a ghost ('Buried Alive'). In 'Hunting Werewolves for Uncle Jack', a man befriends the Frankenstein Monster and is attacked by a werewolf and a sphinx, while 'Reunion' is yet another variation on 'The Monkey's Paw' with Anton as a living corpse. At least it's under an hour long.

Remake: SEE HEAR!: The Monkey's Paw (qv; circa 1989)

✦

GHOST STORY:

Alter-Ego

USA, 1972. Dir: David Lowell Rich. With: Helen Hayes, Geoffrey Horne, Gene Andrusco, Michael-James Wixted, Colin Wilcox-Horne, Charles Aidman. Columbia/William Castle/NBC-TV. Colour.

Short-lived anthology TV series developed by Richard Matheson, produced by William Castle and introduced by Sebastian Cabot as Winston Essex. After fourteen episodes Cabot was dropped and the title changed to *Circle of Fear* for a further nine shows. In this episode scripted by D.C. Fontana, when a lonely young boy, Davey (Andrusco), conjures up an imaginary playmate across his chessboard, he creates an evil counterpart — a psychic vampire that wants to destroy the boy's favourite teacher.

✦✦

Cry of the Cat

USA, 1972. Dir: Arnold Laven. With: Doug McClure, Lauri Peters, Mariette Hartley, Jackie Cooper, Don 'Red' Barry, Clint Richie. Columbia/William Castle/NBC-TV. Colour.

Rodeo star Dan Hollis (McClure) discovers that his fiancée Mariah (Peters) has the power to transform into a deadly cougar.

✦✧

The Dead We Leave Behind

USA, 1972. Dir: Paul Stanley. With: Jason Robards, Stella Stevens, Jack Kelly, John McLiam, Skip Ward, Burt Smidt. Columbia/William Castle/NBC-TV. Colour.

When a husband (Robards) accidentally kills his selfish, TV-addicted wife (Stevens) and subsequently murders her lover (Kelly), evil spirits possess the TV set and show his victims returning from the dead.

✦✦✧

Elegy for a Vampire

USA, 1972. Dir: Don McDougall. With: Marilyn Mason, Hal Linden, Mike Farell, John Milford, Arthur O'Connell, Sheila Larken. Columbia/William Castle/NBC-TV. Colour.

Shortly after the death of a college professor who had been researching the origins of vampirism, campus girls are found murdered with all the blood drained from their bodies.

Series sequel: CIRCLE OF FEAR (qv; 1973)

✦✦

GHOST STORY OF KAM PIN MUI

(Orig: LIAO ZHAI JIN PING MEI)

Hong Kong, 1991. Dir: Richard Yang. With: Chan Pui-Ki, Wu Ma (Wo Ma/Yuen Wah/Ng Ma-Wu), McLaren Lu. Colour.

Softcore Cantonese horror about a quartet of sexy female vampires and their ghostly family who haunt the village of Kam Pin Mui.

✦✧

GHOST WRITER

USA, 1989. Dir: Kenneth J. Hall (Hal Kennedy). With: Audrey Landers, Judy Landers, Jeff Conaway, Anthony Franciosa, David Doyle, Joey Travolta. Rumar Films/LBC Communications/Prism Entertainment. Colour.

Tabloid writer Angela Reid (Audrey Landers) discovers that after supposedly committing suicide in 1962, movie star Billie Blaine (Judy Landers) still haunts the beach house she was murdered in. She torments her killer by appearing as a vampire in a coffin, and as Elsa Lanchester's Bride of Frankenstein at the Movieland Wax Museum's Chamber of Horrors. Co-produced by David DeCoteau and featuring John Matuszak, Dick Miller, Kenneth Tobey and George 'Buck' Flower, this was presented by the two stars' mother, Ruth.

✦

THE GHOUL

UK, 1933. Dir: T. Hayes Hunter. With: Boris Karloff, Cedric Hardwicke, Ernest Thesiger, Dorothy Hyson, Anthony Bushell, Kathleen Harrison. Gaumont-British Picture Corp. B&W.

This old dark house thriller, based on the novel by Frank King, was thought a lost film for many years until a print was discovered in Czechoslovakia in 1969. Returning to his homeland for the first time in twenty-four years, British-born Karloff is given little to do except stagger around in bizarre make-up as Egyptologist Professor Morlant, who returns from the grave to recover an occult jewel, 'The Eternal Light', that has been stolen. Despite a little too much comedy relief from Harrison, there's good support from Hardwicke and Thesiger as a couple of creepy characters and Ralph Richardson making his movie début.

Remake: WHAT A CARVE UP! (1961)

✦✦✧

GHOULIES

USA, 1984 (1985). Dir: Luca Bercovici. With: Peter Liapis, Lisa Pelikan, Keith Joe Dick, Michael Des Barres, Jack Nance, Mariska Hargitay. Ghoulies Productions/Empire Productions. Colour.

Enjoyable supernatural thriller executive produced by Charles Band. When Jonathan Graves (Liapis) returns to his family's old mansion with a group of friends, he is soon conjuring up demons and familiars (the Ghoulies of the title) before his sorcerer father Malcolm (Des Barres) returns from the grave and they uses their powers to prove who is the better wizard. Des Barres makes a wonderful villain, his face decaying while he tries to explain to his son why they might have been friends, but John Buechler's puppet Ghoulies look terrible. Despite the low budget, director Bercovici creates some interesting characters and offbeat humour. With Bobbie Bresee, Jason Scott Lee and Tamara De Treaux as a Satanic midget. Three direct-to-video sequels followed.

Sequel: GHOULIES II (1987)

✦✦✧

GHOUL SCHOOL

USA, 1990. Dir: Timothy O'Rawe. With: Bill Friedman, Scott Gordon, Paul Venier, Nancy Sirianni, Jackie 'the Joke Man' Martling, Joe Franklin. Hollywood Home Entertainment. Colour.

Direct-to-video horror spoof filmed in Wayne, New Jersey, and set in a high school where a toxic leak in the boiler room turns the swim team into blue-faced, fanged, flesh-eating zombies. Executive produced by David DeCoteau, this also apparently includes future porno star Savannah (Shannon Wilsey).

✦

GHOUL SEX SQUAD

(Orig: JIANGSHI YANTAN/GYONSI YIM TAM. USA: aka LOVE STORIES OF THE LIVING DEAD)

Hong Kong/Taiwan, 1991. Sin City Video/Threat Theatre/Taboo Video. Colour.

Hardcore Cantonese horror comedy in which a traveller removes the spells from the foreheads of five hopping vampires (*gyonshee*), who have not been buried properly, and they return from the grave seeking revenge.

✦

GIANT FROM THE UNKNOWN

USA, 1957 (1958). Dir: Richard E. Cunha. With: Edward Kemmer, Sally Fraser, Buddy Baer, Morris Ankrum, Bob Steele, Joline Brand. Screencraft Enterprises/Astor. B&W.

Professional boxer Baer portrays Spanish conquistador Vargas, who is revived by a bolt of lightning in twentieth century California. A mineralogist (Kemmer) teams up with an archaeologist (Ankrum, giving the film's only decent performance) and his daughter (Fraser)

to protect the superstitious townsfolk from the murderous menace. The giant's quite effective make-up was created by veteran Jack Pierce. Shot in just six days for $55,000, producer Arthur P. Jacobs went on to make *Planet of the Apes* (1968), while director/photographer Cunha was responsible for the low-budget gem *Frankenstein's Daughter* (1958).
✦✧

ALAN GIBSON
[1938-1987]

Canadian-born director and former actor who worked on Hammer's TV series *Journey to the Unknown* (1968-69) before moving into movies in the early 1970s, updating the Count into contemporary times with *Dracula A.D. 1972* (1972) and *The Satanic Rites of Dracula* (1973).
qv: *Orson Welles' Great Mysteries: 'The Monkey's Paw'* (1973).

GIDGET:
A Hard Day's Night

USA, 1965. With: Sally Field, Don Porter, Betty Conner, Peter Deuel (Pete Duel), Lynette Winter, Mike Nader. Columbia/Colex Enterprises/ABC-TV. Colour.
This episode of the comedy TV show (thirty-two episodes), based on the popular series of movies about Californian teen Francine 'Gidget' Lawrence (Field), apparently features a werewolf.
Series sequel: GIDGET GROWS UP (1970)
Series remake: THE NEW GIDGET (1986-88)
✦

GIDGET GETS MARRIED

USA, 1971 (1972). Dir: E.W. Swackhamer. With: Michael Burns, Monie Ellis, Don Ameche, Joan Bennett, Macdonald Carey, Corrine Camacho. Universal. Colour.
Second TV movie continuation of the sixties film series, as Burns and Ellis play young newly-weds in Glossop, Maryland. Paul Lynde impersonates various movie characters, including Count Dracula. It's terrible.
Sequel: THE ABC SATURDAY SUPERSTAR MOVIE: Gidget Makes the Wrong Connection (1972)
✦

GILLIGAN'S ISLAND:
And Then There Were None

USA, 1966. Dir: Jerry Hopper. With: Bob Denver, Alan Hale (Jr), Jim Backus, Natalie Schafer, Tina Louise, Russell Johnson. Gladasya-United Artists Television/CBS-TV. Colour.
Half-hour comedy TV series (1964-67, ninety-eight episodes), created and produced by Sherwood Schwartz, who also co-wrote the famous theme song 'The Ballad of Gilligan's Isle' with George Wyle. The crew and passengers on a three-hour pleasure cruise aboard the *S.S. Minnow* are caught in a storm and shipwrecked on an uncharted desert island. In this episode, when the other six castaways begin to disappear one by one, Gilligan (Denver) dreams that he is Dr Jekyll, on trial in a Victorian Court for murder. He transforms into a hairy, fanged Mr Hyde at the mention of various foods. With Dawn Wells.
✦✧

Up at Bat

USA, 1966. Dir: Jerry Hopper. With: Bob Denver, Alan Hale (Jr), Jim Backus, Natalie Schafer, Tina Louise, Russell Johnson. Gladasya-United Artists Television/CBS-TV. Colour.
Gilligan is bitten on the neck by a bat while exploring a cave. Positive he is going to turn into one of the undead, he goes to the other side of the island where he dreams he is a Lugosi-like vampire and Ginger is his bloodsucking companion in 1895 Transylvania, pursued by the Professor (Johnson) as Sherlock Holmes and the Skipper (Hale) as Watson. This episode also manages to spoof the *Batman* (1966-68) TV series!
✦✧

Boris Karloff is resurrected as The Ghoul *(1933).*

Voodoo

USA, 1966. Dir: George M. Cahan. With: Bob Denver, Alan Hale (Jr), Jim Backus, Natalie Schafer, Tina Louise, Russell Johnson. Gladasya-United Artists Television/CBS-TV. Colour.
When Gilligan discovers native artefacts in a cave, the Skipper believes they are sacred and shouldn't be touched. After the other Castaways remove the objects, they react in pain when a native witch doctor (Eddie Little Sky) sticks pins in dolls he's made of each of them. Because the Professor doesn't believe in witchcraft, he is turned into a zombie. A cartoon TV series followed in the 1970s, along with two TV movies.
Series sequel: THE NEW ADVENTURES OF GILLIGAN (1974-75)
✦✧

JOHN GILLING
[1912-1984]

British writer and director who began his career in the late 1940s scripting *The Greed of William Hart* (1948) and such early Hammer thrillers as *The Man in Black* (1950) and *Room to Let* (1950). He directed Bela Lugosi in *Mother Riley Meets the Vampire* (1952) before moving on to more interesting projects like *The Gamma People* (1955) and *The Flesh and the Fiends* (1959). He later returned to Hammer to direct *The Plague of the Zombies* (1966), *The Reptile* (1966) and *The Mummy's Shroud* (1967) before relocating to Spain, where he ended his career with the 'Blind Dead' coda *La Cruz del Diablo* (1974).

THE GIRL WITH THE HUNGRY EYES

USA, 1993 (1995). Dir: Jon Jacobs. With: Christina Fulton, Isaac Turner, Leon Herbert, Bret Carr, Susan Rhodes. Eden West/Penn/Columbia-TriStar Video. Colour.
Low-budget vampire movie 'inspired' by the 1949 short story by Fritz Leiber (to whom the film is dedicated), previously adapted for a 1972 episode of TV's *Rod Serling's Night Gallery*. When she discovers that her fiancé is cheating on her, fashion model Louise Balfour (Fulton) hangs herself at Miami's The Tides Hotel in 1937. She is mysteriously revived fifty-six years later in the derelict building as a vampire. Trendy Cuban fashion photographer Carlos (Turner) is obsessed with her and she becomes his new lingerie model, working only at night.
✦✦

G-MAN JITTERS
(aka GANDY GOOSE IN G-MAN JITTERS)

USA, 1939. Dir: Eddie Donnelly. Voices: Arthur Kay. Terrytoons/Twentieth Century-Fox. B&W.
Seven minute Paul Terry cartoon, in which Gandy Goose (Kay) dreams he is a detective investigating a haunted house. He is pursued by Dracula, the Frankenstein Monster and ghosts. Colourised footage from this film later turned up in *Fortune Hunters* (1946) and *King Tut's Tomb* (1950).
Sequel: A BULLY ROMANCE (1939)
✦✧

G-MEN VS. THE BLACK DRAGON
(aka BLACK DRAGON OF MANZANAR)

USA, 1943. Dir: William Witney. With: Rod Cameron, Roland Got, Constance Worth, Nino Pipitone, C. Montague Shaw, George J. Lewis. Republic. B&W.
Fifteen chapter serial in which Cameron plays Rex Bennett, a government agent on the trail of evil Japanese saboteur Haruchi (Pipitone), who is smuggled into the United States in a state of suspended animation in a mummy case. This also involves explosive paint and a death ray that can destroy aircraft. It was released as a feature in 1966.
Sequel: SECRET SERVICE IN DARKEST AFRICA (1943)
✦✦

GODS AND MONSTERS

USA, 1998. Dir: Bill Condon. With: Ian McKellen, Brendan Fraser, Lynn Redgrave, Lolita Davidovich, Kevin J.

O'Connor, David Dukes. Overseas Filmgroup/First Look Pictures/Regent Entertainment/Showtime Networks/ Lion's Gate Films. Colour.
Despite winning numerous awards, including the Academy Award for Best Adapted Screenplay, this film version of Christopher Bram's superior 1995 gay novel *Father of Frankenstein* is overlong and occasionally plodding. Set in Hollywood in 1957, heterosexual gardener Clayton Boone (an unexpectedly impressive Fraser) finds himself befriending retired film director James Whale (McKellen, giving an excellent, Oscar-nominated performance), who recalls his experiences in the First World War and subsequent film career through a series of sensory flashbacks triggered by a recent stroke. This includes numerous clips from *Bride of Frankenstein* (1935), an impressive recreation of the 'unveiling' scene from that film (featuring Arthur Dignam as Ernest Thesiger, Matt McKenzie as Colin Clive and Amir Aboulela as a briefly-seen Frankenstein Monster), and a fictitious encounter between Whale, Elsa Lanchester (Rosalind Ayers) and the elder Boris Karloff (Jack Betts) at a garden party. Redgrave's ludicrous over-the-top performance as Whale's fiercely protective housekeeper Hannah was also nominated for an Academy Award. From the director of *Candyman Farewell to the Flesh* (1995), Clive Barker was co-executive producer.
✦✦✦

GODZILLA KING OF THE MONSTERS
UK, 1998. Dir: Nick Freand Jones. With: Alex Cox, Jun Fakuda, Dean Devlin, Yoshio Tsuchiya, Kimi Honda, Akira Ifukube. BBC-TV. Colour/B&W.
Forty minute documentary that includes clips and trailers from numerous Godzilla and other Japanese monster movies (including *King Kong vs. Godzilla* [1963]) and TV shows, along with rare behind-the-scenes stills and footage. This also features interviews with many of the original creative people, including actor Kenji Sahara, Haruo Nakajima (who played Godzilla 1954-1975), cameraman Koichi Takano, actor Akira Kubo, director Noriaki Yuasa, producer Kazuo Tsuburaya, Kenpachiro Satsuma (who played Godzilla 1985-1995), director Roland Emmerich, designer Patrick Tatopoulos, effects producer Fiona Bull, plus Godzilla enthusiasts August Ragone and Tony Luke, writer and film historian Stuart Galbraith, and excerpts from *The Beast from 20,000 Fathoms* (1953), *Godzilla* (1998) and *King Kong* (1933).
✦✦✦

GO FOR A TAKE
UK, 1972. Dir: Harry Booth. With: Reg Varney, Norman Rossington, Sue Lloyd, Dennis Price, Julie Ege, Patrick Newell. Century Films International/Rank. Colour.
Wilfrid Stone (Varney) and Jack Foster (Rossington) are two gamblers on the run from gangsters who hide out in a movie studio. Not only was Price reduced to appearing in Jesús Franco movies, but he turns up as himself playing a plump Count Dracula on a film set in this dire comedy. With David Lodge, Bob Todd, Aubrey Morris and Anouska Hempel.
✦

GOGGLE WATCH:
The Horror of the House of Goggle Part 13
UK, 1998. Dir: John Morgan. With: Hilda Brand, Su Elliott, Paul Grunert, Christopher Adamson, Len Collin, Seb Craig. Granada Television/ITV. Colour.
Daily half-hour children's TV series featuring the Goggle Family who, after spending a holiday at the haunted French Chateau du Phantome, decide to turn their guest house into a themed hotel, 'Goggle House of Horror'. Son Gary (Leigh Foley) creates an android named Frankie (Richard Sinnott) in the attic for his school's science project; dad Gordon (Grunert) dresses up as Count Dracula (complete with fake fangs) and uses the ghostly Uncle Horace's (Craig) hair restorer potion to transform into a werewolf; and a pair of crooks kidnap Gran (Braid) and wrap her up like a mummy. Written by Nigel Crowle and introduced by spooky butler Cringe (Adamson), each two-part episode was followed by a phone-in holiday competition.
✦

GOKE, BODY SNATCHER FROM HELL
(Orig: KYÛKETSUKI GOKEMIDORO. USA: aka BODY SNATCHER FROM HELL/THE VAMPIRE THAT CAME FROM SPACE)
Japan, 1967. Dir: Hajime Sato. With: Teruo Yoshida, Tomomi Satô, Hideo Kô, Masaya Takahashi, Nobuo Kaneko, Eizô Kitamura. Shochiku. Colour.
The crew and passengers of a crashed airliner are terrorised by a vampiric alien that possesses the bodies of its victims by splitting their heads open and crawling into their brains! Once everyone starts arguing amongst themselves, director Sato runs out of ideas and keeps repeating scenes of Vietnam atrocities to support the film's anti-war message. Two crew members finally escape, only to discover — as in *Invasion of the Body Snatchers* (1956) — that the colonisation of the rest of the Earth is already underway. This includes imaginative scenes of birds committing suicide by smashing themselves to bloody pulp against the windows of the plane.
✦✧

GOLDEN AGE HORROR CLASSICS
USA, 1986. Sinister Cinema. B&W.
There are two hour-long volumes available on video containing fascinating trailers from the 1930s and 1940s, including *King Kong* (1933), *White Zombie* (1932) and a number of Val Lewton titles.
✦✦✦✧

GOLDEN NUN
Hong Kong, 1987. Dir: Hsu Tien-Yung. With: Land Lo, Li Tau-Hung. Colour.
Apparently good witch The Golden Nun (Lo) rescues a village carpenter (Tau-Hung) from a group of vampires.
✦

GOLIATH AND THE VAMPIRES
(Orig: MACISTE CONTRO IL VAMPIRO)
Italy, 1961 (1964). Dir: Giacomo Gentilomo (and Sergio Corbucci). With: Gordon Scott, Gianna Maria Canale, Jacques Sernas, Leonora Ruffo, Mario Feliciani, Annabella Incontrera. Ambrosiana Cinematográfica/American International Pictures. Colour.
'See: the virgin-harem of the Vampire God!' promised the ads. This violent peplum stars ex-Tarzan Scott as Italian muscleman Maciste (changed to Goliath for American audiences) in one of the best of the series. With the help of the subterranean Blue Men, he battles an army of faceless zombies controlled by shape-changing vampire Kobrak (Guido Celano). During the climax, Goliath also confronts an undead double of himself. Presented by Dino De Laurentiis.
✦✧

THE GONG SHOW MOVIE
USA, 1980. Dir: Chuck Barris. With: Chuck Barris, Robin Altman, Mabel King, Jaye P. Morgan, Buddy Didio, Murray Langston. Chuck Barris Productions/Universal. Colour.
Fictionalised behind-the-scenes look at the cult TV show (1976-80) created by Barris, which presented the often bizarre talents of 'ordinary' people searching for fame. One of the contestants in this dire comedy is Count Banjola, who dresses like Dracula and hangs upside-down while playing the banjo! With Jamie Farr, Rip Taylor, Phil Hartman, Vincent Schiavelli, Tony Randall, Harvey Lemback, 'Rosey' (Roosevelt) Grier and Kitten (Francesca) Natividad. Scripted by Robert Downey (Sr).
✦

GOOBER AND THE GHOST CHASERS:
The Haunted Wax Museum
USA, 1973. Dir: Charles A. Nichols. Voices: Jerry Dexter, Jo Ann Harris, Ronnie Schell, Alan Dinehart Jr, Alan Oppenheimer, Paul Winchell. Hanna-Barbera Productions/ABC-TV. Colour.
Twenty minute cartoon TV series (seventeen episodes) that is another variation on *Scooby Doo Where Are You!* (1969-72), starring the eponymous phantom canine (Winchell) and his trio of teen companions, Tina (Harris), Ted (Dexter) and Gillie (Schell), from *Ghost*

Chasers Magazine. In this episode, they team up with semi-regular guest stars the Partridge (Family) kids (Danny Bonaduce, Susan Dey, Suzanne Crough and Brian Forster) to investigate Willy Waxman's Wax Museum and encounter wax figures of a wolfman and Jack the Ripper. The title sequence includes a living mummy and several episodes feature a celebrity guest star. Executive produced by William Hanna and Joseph Barbera.
✦✧

Mummy Knows Best
USA, 1973. Dir: Charles A. Nichols. Voices: Jerry Dexter, Jo Ann Harris, Ronnie Schell, Alan Dinehart Jr, Alan Oppenheimer, Paul Winchell. Hanna-Barbera Productions/ABC-TV. Colour.
Goober and his friends again team up with guest stars the Partridge kids to rescue a kidnapped king and battle a pair of fake mummies.
✦✧

THE GOOD BOOK
USA, 1997. Dir: Mathew Giaquinto. With: Brian Campbell, Chris Payne, Mathew Giaquinto, Barry Gerdsen. Drop Dead. Colour.
Low-budget independent video set in a computerised near-future world run by the GVC Corporation. Emergency computer repairman Joe (Campbell) battles zombies while driving around and has visions of a Christ-like demon (co-scriptwriter Gerdsen) who tells him to destroy the Internet with a virus. Joe watches *Vampire Girlfriend Roommates 5* on pay-per-view TV, and the co-writer/director turns up crucified in flashbacks.
✦

GOOF ON THE LOOSE
USA, 1962. Dir: Ray Dennis Steckler. With: Rich Dennis. Morgan-Steckler Productions. B&W.
Comedy short from the director of *The Incredibly Strange Creatures Who Stopped Living and Became Mixed-up Zombies!!?* (1963). The Frankenstein Monster carries off a young female victim.
✦

GOOF TROOP:
Frankengoof
USA/South Korea, 1992. Dir: Carole Beers and Terrence Harrison. Voices: Charlie Adler, Nancy Cartwright, Jim Cummings, Bill Farmer, Rob Paulsen, Frank Welker. The Walt Disney Company/Walt Disney Television Animation/ABC-TV. Colour.
Syndicated half-hour children's TV cartoon series (1992-93, ninety-one episodes), based on the character who made his début in 1939. In this episode, when Goofy's (Farmer) great grand uncle Dr Frankengoof passes away, he inherits the family castle in the Old Country where he encounters Igor the caretaker and accidentally brings the green-faced Monster to life. Meanwhile, Goofy's neighbour Pete (Cummings) disguises himself as the Frankengoof Monster and is pursued by angry villagers into an old windmill. This episode is also available on the Disney video *Monster Bash.*
✦✦

GOOFY GROCERIES
USA, 1941. Dir: Robert Clampett. Warner Bros. Colour.
Seven minute *Merrie Melodies* cartoon set after hours in a grocery store, where all the characters on the packages come to life and impersonate movie and radio stars. In the end, Jack Bunny saves them from a King Kong-style ape that appears from a box of animal crackers. This features a song and dance routine based on Eubie Blake's 'I'm Just Wild About Harry'.
✦✦

GOOSEBUMPS:
Don't Wake Mummy
Canada/USA, 1996 (1997). Dir: William Fruet. Protocol Entertainment/Scholastic Productions/Saban International/Fox Kids Network. Colour.
Half-hour anthology series (1995-98, seventy episodes) based on the phenomenally successful young adult horror books by R.L. Stine. In this episode, when his mean-spirited sister Kim and her friend inadvertently release a living mummy from a sarcophagus in their basement, timid Jeff must stop the killer creature from recovering its still-beating heart and becoming human again. This also includes sequences from a black and white mummy movie on TV.
✦✦

Phantom of the Auditorium
Canada/USA, 1995. Dir: John Bell. With: Jessica Moyes, Shawn Potter, Stuart Stone, Kathryn Greenwood, Julie Annis, Philip Eddolls. Protocol Entertainment/Scholastic Productions/Saban International/Fox Kids Network. Colour.
A mystery figure in a mask terrorises Brooke Rogers (Moyes) who's playing heroine Esmeralda in a cursed school production of *The Phantom.*
✦✦

Return of the Mummy
Canada/USA, 1995. Dir: John Bell. With: Daniel De Santo, Annick Obonsawin, Elias Zarou, Afra Gouda, Gerry Mendicino, Peter Jarvis. Protocol Entertainment/ Scholastic Productions/Saban International/Fox Kids Network. Colour.
While visiting his archaeologist uncle in Egypt, young Gabe's (De Santo) totem awakens the mummy of a prince (Jarvis) who is finally reunited with his 4,000-year-old sister, Nila Rahmad (Gouda).
✦✦✧

Vampire Breath
Canada/USA, 1996. Dir: Ron Oliver. With: Zack Lipovsky, Meredith Henderson, Earl Pastko, Krista Dufresne, Nola Augustson, Robert McClure. Protocol Entertainment/ Scholastic Productions/Saban International/Fox Kids Network. Colour.
While searching for presents on the eve of their thirteenth birthday, brother and sister Fred and Cara Renfield (Lipovsky and Henderson) discover a secret underground chamber. When they uncork a bottle marked 'vampire breath', they awaken Count Nightwing (Pastko), the 650 year-old Lord of the Undead.
✦✦✧

Welcome to Dead House
Canada/USA, 1996. Dir: William Fruet. With: Amy Stewart, Ben Cook, Elizabeth Brown, Benedict Campbell, Ian D. Clark, Jessica Greco. Protocol Entertainment/ Scholastic Productions/Saban International/Fox Kids Network. Colour.
In this creepy two-part story, Amanda (Stewart) and Josh Benson (Cook) and their parents move to the town of Dark Falls, where they discover that an accident at a chemical factory three years earlier turned all the town's inhabitants into vampiric zombies who are afraid of sunlight.
✦✦✦

The Werewolf of Fever Swamp
Canada/USA, 1996. Dir: William Fruet. With: Brenden Fletcher, Maria Ricossa, Marion Bennett, Geoffrey Bowes, Michael Barry, Don Francks. Protocol Entertainment/ Scholastic Productions/Saban International/Fox Kids Network. Colour.
Two-part story in which young teenager Grady Tucker (Fletcher) sets out to discover the truth about the legend of a werewolf responsible for several disappearances and the strange old hermit (Francks) lurking around his family's new home near the swamp. In fact, the impressive-looking lycanthrope turns out to be his friend Will Blake (Barry).
✦✦✧

Werewolf Skin
(aka ULTIMATE GOOSEBUMPS: Werewolf Skin)
Canada/USA, 1997. Dir: Ron Oliver. With: Keegan MacIntosh, Nicky Guadagni, Ron Lea, James Mainprize, Terra Vanessa Kowalyk, Bucky Hill. Protocol GB Productions 3/Protocol Entertainment/Scholastic Productions/Saban International/Fox Kids Network. Colour.
Two-part story in which amateur photographer Alex Blackwell (MacIntosh) goes to stay with his relatives for a month in rural Wolf Creek and discovers that his aunt Marta (Guadagni) and uncle Colin (Lea) are werewolves (created by Ron Stefaniuk Studios) who can

only be saved by destroying the skins they shed in daylight. The ending was cut on British TV.
✦✦

GORE-MET ZOMBIE CHEF FROM HELL
USA, 1986 (1987). Dir: Don Swan. With: Theo Depuay, Kelley Kunicki, C.W. Casey, Alan Marx, Michael O'Neill, Jeff Pillars. Swan Films/Camp Video. Colour.
Direct-to-video release filmed on Super-8mm, and amateur in every way. Cursed with immortality in the fourteenth century, rebellious priest Goza the Philosopher (Depuay) and his devoted servant/cook Blozar (O'Neill) run a seaside bar and restaurant where they drink the blood of their cannibalised victims, who end up on the menu.
✦

GORE WHORE
USA, 1994. Dir: Hugh Gallagher. With: Audrey Street, Brady Debussey, D'Lana Tunnell, Paul Woodard, Sherry Lynn Garris, Jennifer Mclean. Ill-Tex. Colour.
Independent low budget video release in which private detective Chase (Debussey) is hired to track down a scientific formula stolen by reanimated hooker Dawn (Street), who needs fresh blood to survive.
✦

GOTHIC
UK, 1986. Dir: Ken Russell. With: Gabriel Byrne, Julian Sands, Natasha Richardson, Myriam Cyr, Timothy Spall, Alec Mango. Virgin Vision. Colour.
During the late 1960s, Paul McCartney announced that he was going to play Percy Shelley in a movie musical based on the occurrences at the Villa Diodati in June 1816. It probably wouldn't have been as bad as this ludicrously overwrought retelling of the events that led to Mary Shelley writing *Frankenstein*. During a crazed night, Lord Byron (Byrne), Percy Bysshe Shelley (Sands), Mary (Richardson), her step-sister Claire Clairmont (Cyr) and the blood-obsessed Dr John Polidori (Spall) tell ghost stories, indulge in drink, drugs and debauchery, and wander around the Swiss villa encountering a half-glimpsed Monster (a composite of their 'worst fears'), which has been conjured up by sex, a seance and their subconscious. Russell directs the historic histrionics at full throttle, piling each stupidity upon the next, and he's not helped by Stephen Volk's unintentionally hilarious script (which he also novelised) or the terrible performances. At least Cyr and Spall bring a pantomime exuberance to their roles. Music by Thomas Dolby.
✦✧

MICHAEL GOUGH
[b 1917]

Stuffy British stage and screen actor, equally at home in productions of Ibsen or playing sadistic madmen. Probably his finest moment was as the arrogant killer in Arthur Crabtree's *Horrors of the Black Museum* (1959), but he is now known to a whole new generation as Alfred the faithful butler in Warner Bros' series of *Batman* movies.
qv: *The Corpse* (1969); *Dracula* (1958); *Dr. Terror's House of Horrors* (1965); *Horror Hospital* (1973); *Konga* (1960); *The Little Vampire* (1985); *The Phantom of the Opera* (1962); *The Secret Files of the Spydogs* (1998-); *The Serpent and the Rainbow* (1987).

GRAMPA'S MONSTER MOVIES
USA, 1988. Dir: Peter Zasuly. With: Al Lewis. Voices: Kieth Williams. Amvest Video. Colour/B&W.
Disappointing video compilation of Universal trailers, hosted by Lewis (looking like the vampiric Grandpa from TV's *The Munsters* [1964-66]). This includes material from many of the studio's monster movies, including *Bride of Frankenstein* (1935), *The Climax* (1944), *Dracula* (1931), *Dracula's Daughter* (1936), *Frankenstein* (1931), *Frankenstein Meets the Wolf Man* (1943), *The Ghost of Frankenstein* (1942), *House of Dracula* (1945), *House of Frankenstein* (1944), (Abbott and Costello) *Meet Frankenstein* (1948), *The Mummy* (1933), *The Mummy's Curse* (1944), *The Mummy's Hand* (1940), *Phantom of the Opera* (1943), *Son of Dracula* (1943), *WereWolf of London* (1935), and *The Wolf Man* (1941), amongst many others, but there are few surprises.
✦✧

THE GRANNY
(UK: THE MATRIARCH)
USA, 1994. Dir: Luca Bercovici. With: Stella Stevens, Shannon Whirry, Sandy Helberg, Teresa Ganzel, Kedrick Wolf. Tapestry Video/WarnerVision. Colour.
When mean Granny Gargoli (Stevens) drinks an ancient elixir, she dies and revives as a homicidal zombie. She then starts killing off her family with a variety of sharp implements when they cheat the kindly Kelly (Whirry) out of her inheritance.
✦

ARTHUR GRANT
[1915-1972]

British cinematographer who, along with Jack Asher, helped to establish the look of Hammer's horrors.
qv: *Blood from the Mummy's Tomb* (1971); *The Curse of the Werewolf* (1960); *Dracula Has Risen from the Grave* (1968); *Frankenstein Created Woman* (1967); *Frankenstein Must Be Destroyed* (1969); *The Mummy's Shroud* (1967); *The Phantom of the Opera* (1962); *The Plague of the Zombies* (1966); *The Reptile* (1966); *Taste the Blood of Dracula* (1969).

MORAY GRANT
[1917-1977]

Scottish-born cinematographer who started his career in 1935 and shot several of Hammer's later films.
qv: *The Horror of Frankenstein* (1970); *I, Monster* (1971); *Scars of Dracula* (1970); *Vampire Circus* (1971); *The Vampire Lovers* (1970).

JORGE GRAU
[b 1930]

Spanish writer, director, actor, playwright and painter. He worked in radio before moving to Rome to study in film school and later worked on co-productions with Riccardo Freda and Sergio Leone.
qv: *The Legend of Blood Castle* (1972); *The Living Dead at Manchester Morgue* (1974).

GRAVEDALE HIGH
(aka RICK MORANIS IN GRAVEDALE HIGH)
USA, 1990-91. Voices: Rick Moranis, Shari Belafonte, Eileen Brennan, Georgia Brown, Tim Curry, Jonathan Winters. Hanna-Barbera Productions/NBC Productions/NBC-TV. Colour.
Half-hour cartoon TV series in which Max Schneider (Moranis) finds himself teaching at the eponymous high school for monsters. The students include vampire Vinnie Stoker (Roger Rose), werewolf Reggie Moonshroud (Barry Gordon), the snake-haired Medusa/'Duzer' (Kimmy Robertson), Frankentyke (Frank Welker), lagoon surfer Gill Waterman (Jackie Earl Haley), overweight mummy Cleofatra (Ricki Lake) and Southern zombie Belle (Belafonte).
✦✧

GRAVE OF THE VAMPIRE
(aka SEED OF TERROR)
USA, 1972. Dir: John (Patrick) Hayes. With: William Smith, Michael Pataki, Kitty Vallacher, Lyn Peters, Diane Holden, Jay Adler. Clover/Flamingo Film Productions/Ember/Entertainment Pyramid. Colour.
Based (uncredited) on the novel *The Still Life* by screenwriter David Chase. Smith plays James Eastman, the reluctant vampire offspring of the undead Charles Croydon/Caleb Croft (Pataki), who raped his mother (Vallacher) in an open grave. He sets out to find his father, who is now posing as night-school professor Adrian Lockwood, and

finally destroys him by driving a broken table leg through his heart. Despite its low budget, this at least attempts to do something different with the usual clichés. Pataki turned up as the Count in *Dracula's Dog* five years later.
✦✦

GRAVE SECRETS
USA, 1989 (1990). Dir: Donald P. Borchers. With: Paul Le Mat, Renee Soutendijk, Lee Ving, Olivia Barash, David Warner, John Crawford. Planet Productions/New Sky Communications/Shapiro-Glickenhaus Entertainment. Colour.
Alcoholic parapsychologist David Shaw (Le Mat) is hired by Iris Norwood (Dutch actress Soutendijk), the owner of a rural bed and breakfast hotel, to investigate a haunting. After the decapitated ghost possesses medium Dr Carl Farnsworth (Warner) during a seance, the body of the woman's father (Bob Herron), who had an incestuous relationship with his daughter and buried their baby alive, returns as a zombie to reclaim his dead son.
✦✦

GRAVEYARD DISTURBANCE
(Orig: DENTRO IL CIMITRIO/UNA NOTTE NEL CIMITERO) Italy, 1987. Dir: Lamberto Bava. With: Gregory Lech Thaddeus, Lea Martino, Beatrice Ring, Gianmarco Tognazzi, Karl Zinny, Lino Salemme. Reteitalia/Dania Film/Devon. Colour.
Made-for-TV movie about a group of teenagers who find themselves in a ghostly old graveyard inn. For a bet, they descend into the tunnels of Hell and meet a variety of vampires, zombies and other creatures (mostly played for laughs) until they return to confront the Grim Reaper himself. Co-writer/director Bava makes a cameo appearance as a shopkeeper, and he even includes a nod to his father's far superior *Black Sunday* (1960).
✦

GRAVEYARD SHIFT
Canada, 1986 (1987). Dir: Gerard Ciccoritti. With: Silvio Olivierio, Helen Papas, Cliff Stoker, Dorin Ferber, Lesley Kelly, Frank Procopio. Cinema Ventures/Lightshow Communications/Shapiro Entertainment. Colour.
Olivierio plays 350 year-old all-night cab driver Stephen Tsepes, who is also an urban vampire. He wants to give up his undead harem to live with Michelle (Papas), a terminally ill director of mock-Gothic rock videos. In this movie, vampirism cures cancer. With Procopio as a character named Mario Bava.
Sequel: THE UNDERSTUDY: GRAVEYARD SHIFT II (qv; 1988)
✦✧

THE GREAT BEAR SCARE
USA, 1983 (1984). Dir: Hal Mason. Voices: Tom Smothers, Louis Nye, Hans Conried, Sue Raney, Hal Smith, Lucille Bliss. DimenMark International/Family Home Entertainment/IVE International Video Entertainment. Colour.
Half-hour syndicated TV cartoon for very small children in which Ted E. Bear (Smothers) and his friends in Bearbank learn to face their fear when a vampire (Nye) leads an invasion of monsters from nearby Monster Mountain.
✦✧

GREAT BOOKS:
Dracula
USA/Romania, 1998 (1999). Dir: Trish Mitchell. With: David J. Skal, James V. Hart. CWC-Cronkite Ward Co/TLC Discovery Communications/The Learning Channel. Colour/B&W.
Hour-long literary TV documentary that looks at the writing of Bram Stoker's 1897 novel, with clips from *Bram Stoker's Dracula* (1992), *Count Dracula* (1977), *Dracula* (1931), *Nosferatu* (1922) and various Hammer films. This also includes a number of interviews plus sequences with actors portraying Stoker and Henry Irving. Narrated by Donald Sutherland.
✦✦

THE GREATEST AMERICAN HERO:
The Resurrection of Carlini
USA, 1982. Dir: Arnold Laven. With: William Katt, Connie Sellecca, Robert Culp, Andrew Robinson, Jack Magee, Timothy Carey. Stephen J. Cannell/ABC-TV. Colour.
Hour-long comedy TV series (1981-83, forty-five episodes), created by Stephen J. Cannell, in which liberal schoolteacher Ralph Hinkley (Katt) is given a red superhero suit by little green aliens. He loses the instruction book, but still teams up with FBI agent Bill Maxwell (Culp) to fight crime. In this episode, Bill is named in the will of a magician who died under mysterious circumstances and has vowed to return from the dead. With Ferdy Mayne.
✦✦

GREAT GHOST TALES:
The Monkey's Paw
USA, 1961. With: Mildred Dunnock, R.G. Armstrong, William Hansen, James Hickman. NBC-TV. Colour.
Hosted by Frank Gallop (*Light's Out* [1946-52], etc), this short-lived, half-hour anthology series (twelve episodes) was the last drama show to be presented live on American TV. In this adaptation of W.W. Jacob's classic story, a married couple are warned about the eponymous item that has the power to grant its owner three wishes.
Episode remake: YOUR JEWELER'S SHOWCASE: 'The Monkey's Paw' (qv; 1963)
✦✧

THE GREAT LONDON MYSTERY
UK, 1920. Dir: Charles Raymond. With: David Devant, Lady Doris Stapleton, Lester Gard, Lola de Liane. T&P. B&W.
De Liane plays Froggie the Vampire in this twelve-part silent serial with great chapter titles like 'The Sacred Snake Worshippers', 'The Fraudulent Spiritualistic Seance' and 'The Living Dead'. It also includes such characters as the Master Magician (Devant) and the Man Monkey (Gard).
✦

THE GREAT PIGGY BANK ROBBERY
USA, 1946. Dir: Robert Clampett. Voices: Mel Blanc. Warner Bros. Colour.
Six minute *Looney Tunes* cartoon parody of the *Dick Tracy* comic strip. After being hit on the head while reading his favourite comic book, Daffy Duck dreams he is detective Duck Twacy, menaced by various villains, including Neon Noodle (who looks exactly like Frankenstein's Monster) and Wolf Man (who has the head of a wolf). With a guest appearance by Porky Pig.
Sequel: BIRTH OF A NOTION (1947)
✦✦✦

GREMLINS 2 THE NEW BATCH
USA, 1990. Dir: Joe Dante. With: Zach Galligan, Phoebe Cates, John Glover, Robert Prosky, Robert Picardo, Christopher Lee. Amblin Entertainment/Warner Bros. Colour.
Executive producer Steven Spielberg and director Dante leave behind the atmospheric chills of *Gremlins* (1984) for a knockabout sequel which is a live-action homage to the classic Warner Bros cartoons (complete with appearances by Bugs Bunny, Daffy Duck and Porky Pig!). This time the gremlins run riot through the high-tech skyscraper of millionaire Daniel Clamp (Glover). Prosky plays vampiric TV horror host Grandpa Fred, Lee appears as the wacky Dr Catheter, and watch out for cameos by Dick Miller, Keye Luke (who died in 1991), Jerry Goldsmith, Belinda Balaski, Paul Bartel, Kenneth Tobey, John Astin, Henry Gibson, Leonard Maltin, Hulk Hogan, Dick Butkus and Bubba Smith, the voices of Howie Mandel and Tony Randall (as the 'Brain' Gremlin), plus an uncredited Dante as a TV director. With a clip from *Octaman* (1971). Special make-up effects by Rick Baker. The video and TV prints, supervised by Dante, both include alternative sequences. David Bischoff wrote the novelisation.
✦✦✦

GRIP OF THE STRANGLER
(USA: THE HAUNTED STRANGLER)
UK, 1958. Dir: Robert Day. With: Boris Karloff, Jean Kent,

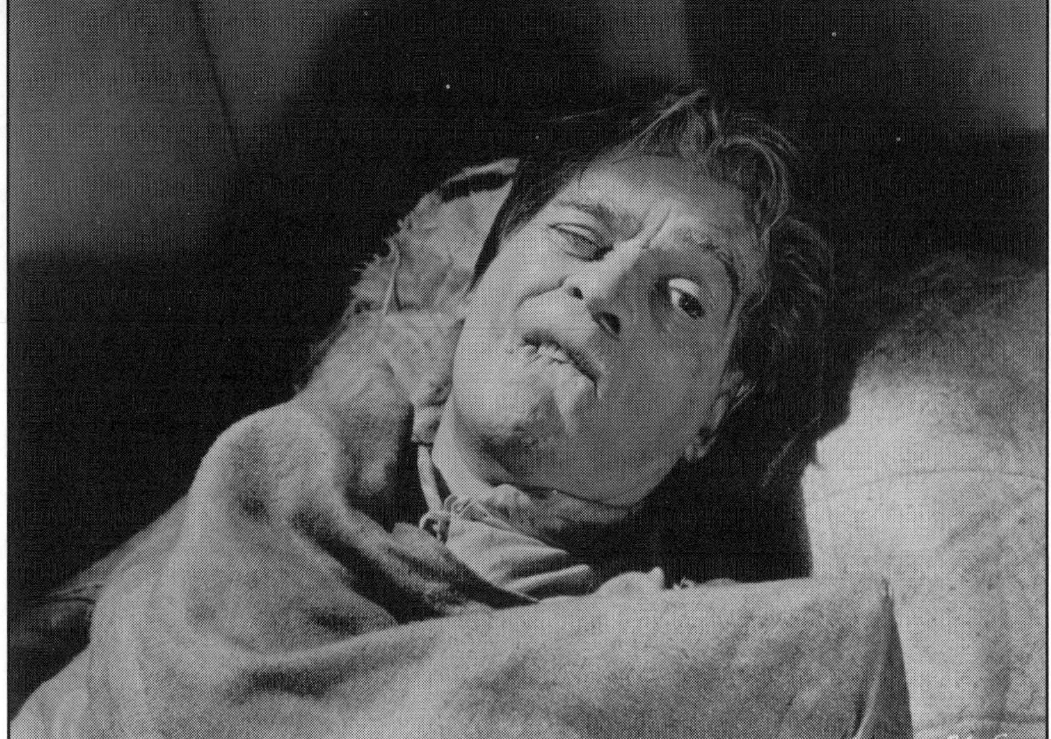

Boris Karloff discovers he is under the Grip of the Strangler *(1958).*

Elizabeth Allen, Anthony Dawson, Vera Day, Tim Turner. Eros/Producers Associates. B&W.
Filmed as *Stranglehold*, and based on the story of the same name by co-screenwriter Jan Read. Karloff plays nineteenth century novelist James Ranklin investigating the case of Edward Styles, known as the Haymarket Strangler, who was wrongly hanged twenty years earlier for five murders. Possessed by the killer's knife, Ranklin discovers that he, in fact, is the real murderer he has been searching for. Karloff creates his Jekyll and Hyde-type transformation into the Strangler simply by distorting his face. The period atmosphere is nicely recreated, but Karloff is the best thing in this cheap chiller, executive produced by Richard Gordon. From the same producer-director-star team as *Corridors of Blood* (1958). Ace Books published a novelisation by John C. Cooper.
✦✦

CHARLES B. GRIFFITH
[b 1930]

American writer and director who began his career working with Roger Corman in the 1950s. He brought a spark of anarchic originality to productions that couldn't even afford a shoestring.
qv: *Death Race 2000* (1975); *Dr. Heckyl and Mr. Hype* (1980); *The Little Shop of Horrors* (1960); *Little Shop of Horrors* (1986); *Not of This Earth* (1957); *Not of This Earth* (1988); *Not of This Earth* (1995).

HUGH GRIFFITH
[1912-1980]

A former Welsh bank clerk turned actor, Griffith later became a flamboyant supporting player and guest star in numerous British films.
qv: *Cry of the Banshee* (1970); *Dow Hour of Great Mysteries: 'The Inn of the Flying Dragon'* (1960); *Legend of The Werewolf* (1974).

THE GROOVIE GOOLIES
(aka GROOVIE GOOLIES AND FRIENDS)

USA, 1970-72. Dir: Hal Sutherland. Voices: Larry Storch, Don Messick, Howard Morris, Jane Webb, Dallas McKenna, John Irwin. Filmation Associates/CBS-TV. Colour.
Set in Humble Hall, owned by Count Dracula (Storch) and his witchy wife Hagatha (Webb), this half-hour musical cartoon series is a spin-off from *Sabrina and the Groovie Goolies* (1970-71). It features the adventures of Frankie, Wolfie and Mummy (all Morris), switchboard operator Bella La Ghostly (Webb), Boneapart the clumsy skeleton (Larry Mann), Batso (Mann), Ratzo (Storch), Hauntleroy (Mann), Dr Jekyll and Mr Hyde (Mann) and teen witch Sabrina (Webb).
Sequels: SABRINA, THE TEENAGE WITCH (1971-74) and THE ABC SATURDAY SUPERSTAR MOVIE: Daffy Duck and Porky Pig Meet the Groovie Goolies (qv; 1972)
✦✧

GROTESQUE

USA, 1987 (1988). Dir: Joseph Tornatore. With: Linda Blair, Tab Hunter, Donna Wilkes, Guy Stockwell, Luana Patten, Robert Z'Dar. United Filmmakers/Concorde. Colour.
After a young woman's family is slaughtered while they are vacationing in a remote mountain cabin, the gang of laughing punks responsible are pursued by her hunchbacked/mutant brother. A mad plastic surgeon (Hunter!) turns up at the end to surgically mutilate their bodies. This unpleasant thriller also includes Stockwell as horror movie make-up artist Orville Kruger, who creates a wolf man (Jeff Richard) and a ghoul (Don Tornatore). Blair (*The Exorcist* [1973], etc) is credited as co-associate producer.
✦

GUESS WHAT HAPPENED TO COUNT DRACULA?
(aka THE LUST OF DRACULA/THE MASTER OF THE DUNGEON).

USA, 1970. Dir: Laurence Merrick. With: Des Roberts, Claudia Barron, John Landon, Robert Branche, Frank Donato, Yvonne Gaudry. Laurence Merrick International. Colour.
Ultra-cheap *Count Yorga* imitation has Roberts (with a goatee beard and mock-Lugosi accent) giving a terrible performance as Dracula's urbane son Count Adrian, who frequents the Dracula's Dungeon nightclub and sets out to turn actress Angelica (newcomer Barron)

into his vampire bride after three bites. This includes a macumba ceremony and other sequences filmed in Hollywood's Magic Dungeon Academy, plus a hunchback (Lawrence Steinhalier) and a gorilla (Robert A. Wagner). A Frankenstein Monster (Howard A. Adams) and a mummy (Mae Adams) are also supposed to be in there somewhere. Besides a straight horror version, this was apparently released in Switzerland as the softcore *Dracula's Lüsterne Sex-vampire* with different credits. The star also arranged and scored the music, while the 'multi-talented' Merrick scripted, produced and directed.
✦

GURU THE MAD MONK

USA, 1970 (1971). Dir: Andy Milligan. With: Neil Flanagan, Paul Lieber, Jacqueline Webb, Judith Israel, Julia Willis, Ron Keith. Maipix Organisation/Nova International. Colour.
More insanity from writer/producer/director Milligan, filmed in New York City. In the name of The Lost Souls Church of Mortavia, crazed priest Father Guru (Flanagan) tortures villagers with the aid of his vampire-witch mistress Olga (Webb) and his one-eyed hunchbacked assistant Igor. At just over an hour it's still too long. This was originally co-billed with Milligan's *The Body Beneath* (1971).
✦

GUWAPINGS: THE FIRST ADVENTURE

Philippines, 1992. Dir: J.J. Reyes. With: Joey Marquez, Anjo Yllana, Erik Cayetano. Regal Films. Colour.
Horror comedy in which a group of vampires attack a house full of humans. This also apparently includes some superfluous zombies.
✦

GUYS IN GHOSTS HAND

Hong Kong, 1990. Dir: Stanley Wing-Siu (Ma Sui-Wai/Chin Sing-Wai). With: Alex Fong, Wu Ma (Wo Ma/Yuen Wah/Ng Ma-Wu), Hui Ying-Hung, Ku Feng. Colour.
The decapitated spectre of a murdered woman recruits vampires, zombies and ghosts to revenge herself on the ancestors of the man who killed her. In the end they are all defeated by exorcist priests.
✦✧

MICHAEL GWYNN
[1916-1976]

Gaunt British stage and TV actor who occasionally appeared in films. He portrayed the twisted, cannibalistic monster in Hammer's *The Revenge of Frankenstein* (1958).
qv: *Catch Us if You Can* (1965); *Scars of Dracula* (1970).

FRED GWYNNE
[1926-1993]

Lugubrious-looking American comedy actor, best known for his portrayal of the Frankenstein-like Herman Munster in TV's *The Munsters* (1964-66). Occasionally appeared in movies.
qv: *Danny Kaye Show* (1966); *Fantastic Monsters of Television Land* (1999); *Munster, Go Home!* (1966); *The Munster's Revenge* (1981); *Pet Sematary* (1989).

HABIT

USA, 1997. Dir: Larry Fessenden. With: Larry Fessenden, Meredith Snaider, Aaron Beall, Patricia Coleman, Heather Woodbury. Glass Eye Pix. Colour.

Ambitious, low-budget independent horror film in which New York bar and restaurant manager Sam (director Fessenden) meets the mysterious Anna (Snaider) at a Halloween party. She turns out to be a vampire, or does she? Despite utilising the usual clichés, the hard-drinking Sam's experiences, including bloodsucking, can all be explained by his out-of-control lifestyle.

✦✧

EL HACHA DIABOLICA

(aka SANTO CONTRA EL HACHA DIABOLICA)
Mexico, 1964. Dir: José Diaz Morales. With: Santo (Rodolfo Guzmán Huerta), Lorena Velázquez, Bety Gonzalez, Fernando Osés, Mario Sevilla, Colocho. Filmica Vergara/Columbia. B&W.

Filmed in three episodes ('El Hacha Diabolica', 'Terror en el Pasado' and 'El Discipulo de Satanas') to circumnavigate union restrictions. Santo, the silver masked wrestler, travels back in time to 1630 and teams up with his seventeenth century ancestor to battle the Satanic Black Mask (who can transform into a bat) and his enchanted axe. More Mexican madness with a demonic idol, a time-travel helmet and former Miss Mexico Velázquez as a ghost.

Sequel: PROFANADORES DE TUMBAS (1965)
Remake: SANTO Y BLUE DEMON EN EL MUNDO DE LOS MUERTOS (1969)

✦✧

HALE AND PACE

UK, 1997 (1998). Dir: Peter Orton. With: Gareth Hale, Norman Pace, Andrew Alston, Helen Barlow, Antony Carrick, Andrew Dennis. London Weekend Television/ ITV. Colour.

Half-hour TV comedy sketch show. This episode includes a (wide-screen!) spoof about the staking of Count Cleansing (Hale), the fastidious vampire.

✦✧

THE HALFBACK OF NOTRE DAME

Canada, 1995. Dir: Rene Bonniere. With: Scott Hylands, Allen Cutler, Sandra Nelson, Emmanuelle Vaugier, Gabriel Hogan, Nicole Parker. Showtime Networks/Sugar Entertainment/Hallmark Entertainment. Colour.

Taking its title from a 1923 silent short, this romantic cable TV movie features Hogan as big but clumsy 'Crazy' Craig Modeau, who plays football for Notre Dame High School but is prepared to disappoint his father, the coach (Hylands), and quit the team when he falls in love with a French exchange student named Esmeralda (Vaugier) who teaches him to play the piano. With football players named Victor and Hugo.

✦✦

HALLOWEEN NIGHT

Thailand, circa 1987. All Asian Home Video. Colour.

Not to be confused with the 1988 American movie of the same title, this horror comedy is apparently inspired by the 'Mummy, Daddy' episode of TV's *Amazing Stories* (1985). A real mummy and a fake mummy from a movie set team up on Halloween to battle a group of bumbling cops. In one sequence, the real mummy takes his human girlfriend on a motorcycle ride in the sky. This also includes a mummy movie on TV.

✦✧

THE HALLOWEEN THAT ALMOST WASN'T

USA, 1979. Dir: Bruce Bilson. With: Judd Hirsch, Mariette Hartley, Henry Gibson, John Schuck, Jack Riley, Josip Elic. Concepts Unlimited/ABC-TV. Colour.

Emmy Award-winning half-hour TV special for children. There will be no more Halloween unless Count Dracula (Hirsch), Frankenstein's Monster (Schuck), the Wolf Man (Riley), the Zombie, the Mummy (Bob [Robert] Fitch) and Igor (Gibson) can convince the Witch (Hartley) to fly over the moon.

✦✦

HALLOWEENTOWN

USA, 1998. Dir: Duwayne Dunham. With: Debbie Reynolds, Judith Hoag, Kimberly J. Brown, Joey Zimmerman, Phillip Van Dyke, Emily Roeske. Disney Enterprises/Singer White Entertainment/Disney Channel. Colour.

Made-for-cable TV movie aimed at younger children. When thirteen year-old Marnie Cromwell (Brown) discovers she is descended from a family of witches, she travels to HalloweenTown with her brother Dylan (Zimmerman) and sister Sophie (Roeske) to help their witchy Grandma (veteran Reynolds) defeat the evil warlock Calabar (Robin Thomas) who is attempting to return the powers of darkness to the colourful world of ghosts and monsters (special make-up effects created by Sota Effects, Inc). Along the way the children encounter a Frankenstein Monster (Nurmi Husa) on a bus, a zombie salesman (Kenneth Choi), a mummy getting a manicure, a werewolf hairdresser (Michael Patrick Egan), a fishy gill man on his way to the pool, a vampire (Betty Moyer) having her fang extracted and an aerobics cat-woman (Shannon Day). Former director Alfred Sole (*Tanya's Island* [1980], etc) was the production designer.

✦✦

HALLOWEEN II

USA, 1981. Dir: Rick Rosenthal. With: Jamie Lee Curtis, Donald Pleasence, Charles Cyphers, Jeffrey Kramer, Lance Guest, Pamela Susan Shoop. Dino De Laurentiis Corporation/Universal. Colour.

Disappointing sequel to *Halloween* (1978), once again produced and scripted by John Carpenter and Debra Hill who at one time considered shooting it in 3-D. This time the homicidal Shape (stunt co-ordinator Dick Warlock in a Don Post mask) pursues Laurie Strode (Curtis) to Haddonfield hospital where she is recovering from the events in the first film. Curtis and (especially) Pleasence as the obsessed Dr Sam Loomis are fine recreating their roles from the original, while Cyphers and Nancy Loomis (as a corpse) also return briefly. Unfortunately, débuting director Rosenthal turns in an unpleasant slice of stalk 'n' slash, and the film was reputedly so slow that Carpenter shot three extra scenes and re-edited the picture himself. This also includes *Night of the Living Dead* (1968) on TV. With Dana Carvey. Dennis Etchison wrote the novelisation under the pseudonym 'Jack Martin'.

Sequel: HALLOWEEN III SEASON OF THE WITCH (1982)

✦✧

HALLOWEEN WITH THE ADDAMS FAMILY

(Orig: HALLOWEEN WITH THE NEW ADDAMS FAMILY)
USA, 1977. Dir: Dennis Steinmetz. With: John Astin, Carolyn Jones, Jackie Coogan, Ted Cassidy, Henry Darrow, Patrick Campbell. Charles Fries/NBC-TV. Colour.

Disappointing revival of the hit 1960s series, based on Charles Addams' cartoons. All the original cast members except Blossom Rock are reunited when Gomez (Astin) returns home from a business trip in time to celebrate Halloween and help prevent a gang of electronics experts from stealing the family fortune. With Vito Scotti, Suzanne Krazna as Countess Dracula and Felix Silla as Cousin Itt. Shot on video, it was originally shown as a Halloween special and then reissued as a TV movie in 1980.

Sequel: THE ADDAMS FAMILY (qv; 1991)

✦✧

VICTOR (HUGO) HALPERIN [1895-19??]

Chicago-born independent director who, along with his producer-brother Edward, made a number of low-budget films from the 1920s until the early 1940s. Their concepts usually exceeded their talent.
qv: *Revolt of the Zombies* (1936); *White Zombie* (1932).

HAMMER A-Z
UK, 1997. Dir: Colin Spector. With: Bear Van Beers, Michael Ripper, Don Fearney. Sci-Fi Channel Europe. Colour.
To celebrate forty years of Hammer horror, this half-hour special looks at everything from 'Anniversary' to 'Zenith', including 'Bats', 'Kiss of Death', and 'Vamps', with brief but good-looking clips from *Blood from the Mummy's Tomb* (1971), *The Curse of Frankenstein* (1957), *Dracula* (1958), *Dracula A.D. 1972* (1972), *The Kiss of the Vampire* (1962), *Lust for a Vampire* (1970), *The Mummy's Shroud* (1967), *Scars of Dracula* (1970), *The Vampire Lovers* (1970), and numerous others, plus commentary by Ian Scoones, Aida Young, Valerie Leon, Ingrid Pitt, Roy Skeggs, camera assistant Harry Oakes, Francis Matthews, James Bernard, critic Derek Malcolm, Hammer archivist Max Decharné and Tudor Gates.
✦✦

HAMMER HOUSE OF HORROR:
Children of the Full Moon
UK, 1980. Dir: Tom Clegg. With: Christopher Cazenove, Celia Gregory, Diana Dors, Robert Urquhart, Jacob Witkin, Adrian Mann. Chips Productions/Jack Gill/ Cinema Arts International/Hammer Films/ITC Entertainment/ITV. Colour.
Hour-long anthology TV series (thirteen episodes) that failed to recapture the success of Britain's most popular horror studio. When married couple Tom and Sarah Martin (Cazenove and Gregory) are stranded in the West Country, they arrive at the home of Hungarian Mrs Ardoy (Dors) and her pack of lupine children. After Sarah is attacked by a shadowy figure, she discovers she is pregnant and her eating habits begin to change dramatically... In America, this was combined with 'Visitor from the Grave' (1980) to create a TV movie.
✦✦
Visitor from the Grave
UK, 1980. Dir: Peter Sasdy. With: Kathryn Leigh Scott, Simon MacCorkindale, Gareth Thomas, Mia Nadasi. Chips Productions/Jack Gill/Cinema Arts International/ Hammer Films/ITC Entertainment/ITV. Colour.
When an intruder is killed by a woman with a shotgun and buried by her boyfriend in the woods, he returns from the grave seeking revenge. Scripted by Hammer veteran John Elder (Anthony Hinds), it's another of those attempts-to-drive-a-wealthy-woman-mad plots. In America, this was combined with 'Children of the Full Moon' (1980) to create a TV movie.
✦✧

HAMMER THE STUDIO THAT DRIPPED BLOOD!
UK, 1987. Dir: Nick Jones and David Thompson. With: Peter Cushing, Christopher Lee, Anthony Hinds, Jimmy Sangster, Aida Young, Don Sharp. BBC-TV. Colour/B&W.
Excellent fifty minute documentary about the British studio, narrated by Charles Gray. This features numerous clips and stills (with behind-the-scenes footage of Terence Fisher directing *Stolen Face* [1952] and *Frankenstein Must Be Destroyed* [1969]) and interviews with many of the people who worked for the studio, including Michael Carreras (from 1974), composer James Bernard, James Carreras (from 1970), Ingrid Pitt and Yutte Stensgaard (from 1970), plus writer David Pirie and Hammer fan Martin Scorsese.
✦✦✦

THE HAND OF NIGHT
(USA: aka BEAST OF MOROCCO)
Morocco/UK, 1966. Dir: Fredric Goode. With: William Sylvester, Diane Clare, Alizia Gur, Edward Underdown, William Dexter, Terence De Marney. Associated British-Pathe. Colour.
An unusual blend of ghosts and vampires. After the accidental death of his family, architect Paul Carver (Sylvester) is drawn to Morocco by a death-wish. There he is tempted by the Servants of the Night, a cult of phantoms led by a beautiful princess (Gur) and her eerie servant Omar (De Marney), who want his soul. These vampires may not have fangs, but they still don't cast reflections and can be destroyed by a stake through the heart. Director Goode gives the film a bizarre, dream-like quality, aided by the unusual desert locations, and Sylvester finally proves that he really can act.
✦✦✧

THE HAND OF PLEASURE
USA, 1971. Dir: Z.G. Spencer. With: Marie Arnold. Satyr IX. Colour.
Softcore sex movie set in London, in which masked mad scientist Dr Dreadful is turning women into man-murdering love robots with his sex transference helmet. This includes the figure of a mummy in the doctor's wax museum.
✦

THE HANGING WOMAN
(Orig: LA ORGIA DE LOS MUERTOS/L'ORGIA DEI MORTI. UK: aka BEYOND THE LIVING DEAD. USA: aka BEYOND THE LIVING DEAD/BRACULA — THE TERROR OF THE LIVING DEAD!/HOUSE OF TERROR/THE RETURN OF THE ZOMBIS)
Spain/Italy, 1972 (1974). Dir: John Davidson (José Luis Merino). With: Stan Cooper (Stelvio Rosi), Vickie Nesbitt (Dianik Zurakowska), Marcella Wright (Maria Pia Conte), Catherine Gilbert, Gerald (Gerard) Tichy, Carl Mansion (Mancini). Prodimex Film/Petruka Films/International Artists. Colour.
Set in the nineteenth century Carpathians, where the mad Dr Leon (Tichy) harnesses 'nebula electricity' in his experiments to bring the dead back to life through capsules implanted in their brains. In the end, the doctor's mental control fails and he is strangled by his blind creations. Eleventh billed Paul Nash (Paul Naschy/Jacinto Molina) plays Igor, a necrophiliac hunchbacked gravedigger who is decapitated by bland hero Cooper after being revived as a zombie.
✦✧

HANNO CAMBIATO FACCIA
Italy, 1971. Dir: Corrado Farina. With: Adolfo Celi, Giuliano Disperati, Geraldine Hooper, Francesca Modigliani, Amedeo Tommasi, Rosalba Bongiovanni. Filmsettanta/Garigliano. Colour.
Allegorical fantasy with Celi (*Thunderball* [1965], etc) as engineer Giovanni Nosferatu, the powerful owner of a business empire who offers a young man (Disperati) a place on the Board of Executives if he will ruthlessly exploit his fellow workers. Heavy on the symbolism and vampire metaphors, the title translates as 'They've Changed Faces'.
✦

HAPPY CIRCUS DAYS
USA, 1942. Dir: Connie Rasinski. Terrytoons/Twentieth Century-Fox. Colour.
Paul Terry cartoon in which a little boy and his dog visit the circus where they encounter Gigantica, a giant ape which is 'taller than the Empire State Building'.
✦

HAPPY DAYS
USA, 1980. Dir: Jerry Paris. With: Henry Winkler, Marion Ross, Anson Williams, Erin Moran, Al Molinaro, Tom Bosley. Paramount/Miller-Milkis-Boyett Productions/ Henderson Production Company/ABC-TV. Colour.
Long-running half-hour comedy TV show (1974-83, 256 episodes), created by Garry Marshall and set in 1950s suburbia. In one episode, after watching *Frankenstein's Doctor* on TV, Fonzie (Winkler) dreams he meets a Count Dracula look-alike scientist (Dick Gautier) who wants to transfer his 'coolness' into a Frankenstein-like Monster named Doggie (also Winkler).
Series sequel: FONZ AND THE HAPPY DAYS GANG (1980-82)
✦✧

HAPPY GHOST
(USA: aka ABRAKADABRA/HEAVEN WIFE, HELL WIFE/LOVES OF THE LIVING DEAD)
Hong Kong, 1982 (1986). Dir: Peter Mak/Clifton Ko Chi-Sum (Mak Yai-Kit/Ho Meng-Hua). With: Annie Bai, Peter Mak (Mak Yai-Kit/Ho Meng-Hua), Raymond Wong, May Lo. Long Shong Pictures/Cinema City & Films/Rainbow

Video. Colour.
This typical Hong Kong horror comedy, the first in a mostly unrelated quartet, concerns the vampiric ghost of stripper Pinkish Red (Bai) and everyone else who died in the fire that killed her. They return through a haunted mirror so that they can revenge themselves on those responsible and attempt to exchange places with the living. One of the four heroes accidentally raises up a horde of hopping zombies from a graveyard with his Spirit Machine, and this includes an audience of zombies watching a vampire stage act in a strip club. The phantoms are finally stopped by the power of a magic symbol and the use of a hair dryer. From the director of *Mighty Peking Man* (1977).
Sequel: HAPPY GHOST II (1983)
✦✧

HAPPY HELL NIGHT
Canada/Yugoslavia, 1991 (1992). Dir: Brian Owens. With: Darren McGavin, Charles Cragin, Nick Gregory, Franke Hughes, Laura Carney, Ted Clark. Pavlina/Petersen Productions/Brisun Entertainment. Colour.
Raised from the dead during a fraternity pledge that went wrong, evil priest Malius (Cragin) escapes from an asylum after twenty-five years and starts killing college students, who go to Hell. In one bizarre scene, a statue of Christ on the cross comes alive.
✦✦

HARAM ALEK
Egypt, 1953. Dir: Issa Karama. With: Ismaïl Yassine. Studio Guiza. B&W.
Comedy in which Yassine encounters a Frankenstein-type Monster, a werewolf and a mummy. The title translates as 'Shame on You'.
✦

HARD ROCK ZOMBIES
USA, 1984 (1985). Dir: Krishna Shah. With: E.J. Curcio, Geno (Geno Andrews), Sam Mann, Mick McMains, Lisa Toothman, Jennifer Coe. Patel-Shah Film Company/Cannon. Colour.
A guitar riff revives a rock band from the dead to confront a re-animated Hitler (Jack Bliesner), a lycanthropic granny (Susan Prevatte), a murderous groupie and various masked dwarves in this low-budget mess. Special effects created by John (Carl) Buechler. Clips from this film turned up in the same director's *American Drive-In* (1985).
✦

SIR CEDRIC HARDWICKE [1893-1964]
Acclaimed British actor, knighted in 1934 for outstanding performances on the London stage, who often wasted his talents in Hollywood playing sophisticated villains. Despite his many successes, he died in near-poverty.
qv: *Climax!: 'Dr. Jekyll and Mr. Hyde'* (1955); *The Ghost of Frankenstein* (1942); *The Ghoul* (1933); *The Hunchback of Notre Dame* (1939); *The Outer Limits: 'The Forms of Things Unknown'* (1964).

THE HARDY BOYS/NANCY DREW MYSTERIES:
The Hardy Boys and Nancy Drew Meet Dracula
USA, 1977. Dir: Joseph Pevney. With: Shaun Cassidy, Parker Stevenson, Janet Louise Johnson, Edmund Gilbert, Lisa Eilbacher, Lorne Greene. Glen A. Larson Productions/Universal/ABC-TV. Colour.
Hour-long children's TV series (1977-78, forty-six episodes) based on the popular books created by Franklin W. Dixon and Carolyn Keene (Edward Stratemeyer and Harriet Adams, etc). In this two-part juvenile mystery, Frank and Joe Hardy (Stevenson and Cassidy) and Nancy Drew (Johnson) visit a Transylvanian rock festival in Castle Dracula. Richard Kiel (Jaws in *Moonraker* [1979], etc) plays a bouncer who looks like the Frankenstein Monster. With Paul Williams and Leon Askin.
✦✦

The Mystery of King Tut's Tomb
USA, 1977. With: Shaun Cassidy, Parker Stevenson, Janet Louise Johnson, Edmund Gilbert, Lisa Eilbacher, Taryn Power. Glen A. Larson Productions/Universal/ABC-TV. Colour.
While sightseeing in Egypt, the boys wind up accused of purse-snatching and have to find the real culprit. With Cesare Danova. Other episodes guest-starred Reggie Nalder ('The Mystery of the Haunted House' [1977]) and Casey Kasem and J.D. Cannon (the two-part 'Mystery of the Hollywood Phantom' [1977]).
Series remake: THE HARDY BOYS (1995)
✦✦

HARE CONDITIONED
USA, 1945. Dir: Charles M. (Chuck) Jones. Voices: Mel Blanc. Warner Bros. Colour.
Seven minute *Looney Tunes* cartoon in which Bugs Bunny is chased around a department store until he scares the manager by doing an impersonation of the 'horrible Frankencense Monster'.
Sequel: HARE TONIC (qv: 1945)
✦✦

HARE REMOVER
USA, 1945 (1946). Dir: Frank Tashlin. Voices: Mel Blanc. Warner Bros. Colour.
Seven minute *Merrie Melodies* cartoon in which Elmer Fudd invents a serum to turn Bugs Bunny into a monster. When it doesn't work, Bugs tries it on Elmer. With a reference to the 1941 *Dr. Jekyll and Mr. Hyde*.
Sequel: RHAPSODY RABBIT (1946)
✦✦

HARE TONIC
USA, 1945. Dir: Charles M. (Chuck) Jones. Voices: Mel Blanc, Arthur Q. Bryan. Warner Bros. Colour.
Seven minute *Looney Tunes* cartoon in which Bugs Bunny impersonates Dr Killpatient and the Frankenstein Monster to torment Elmer Fudd, who is convinced he has 'rabbititus' and is turning into a rabbit.
Sequel: BASEBALL BUGS (1946)
✦✦

CURTIS HARRINGTON [b 1928]
American director responsible for bringing style and sophistication to low-budget projects. A friend of James Whale, he began his career in avant-garde film-making, which directly influenced his feature début, *Night Tide* (1961). After making the best he could from *Queen of Blood* (1966), Harrington moved into television with such movies as *The Cat Creature* (1973) and *The Dead Don't Die!* (1975).
qv: *The Horror of It All* (1983); *The World of Gods and Monsters: A Journey With James Whale* (1999).

HART TO HART:
Murder Wrap
USA, 1981. With: Robert Wagner, Stefanie Powers, Lionel Stander, John McMartin, Fiona Lewis, Thaao Penghlis. Columbia/Rona II/Spelling-Goldberg Productions/ABC-TV. Colour.
Popular hour-long TV mystery series (1979-84, 110 episodes) created by Sidney Sheldon, about the eponymous husband and wife team of amateur sleuths. In this episode, millionaires Jonathan (Wagner) and Jennifer (Powers) investigate the death of a noted archaeologist by an apparently walking mummy that is missing from a museum. Tom Mankiewicz was creative consultant.
✦✦

HATYARIN
India, 1991. Dir: Vinod Talwar. With: Jamuna, Deepak Prashar, Amita Nangia, Javed Khan, Shree Pradha, Rajesh Vivek. Sohal Productions. Colour.
Horror film with songs, in which Jamuna portrays the eponymous big-fanged vampire woman who lures virgin brides away from their wedding parties into the forest. There they are trapped in the branches of a living tree and sacrificed over the open grave of a demonic magician who needs their blood to live again. With a nightmare sequence involving a graveyard full of zombies.
✦✦

RONDO HATTON [1894-1946]

Monosyllabic American actor (to use the term loosely) who suffered from the disfiguring disease of acromegaly, reputedly after being exposed to German poison gas in France during World War One. Universal somewhat tastelessly cast him as a deformed killer in several low-budget horror movies, most notably as a character called The Creeper in three otherwise unconnected productions: *The Pearl of Death* (1944), *House of Horrors* (1946) and *The Brute Man* (1946). **qv:** *The Hunchback of Notre Dame* (1939); *The Jungle Captive* (1944); *The Spider Woman Strikes Back* (1945).

THE HAUNTED CASTLE

(Orig: LE MANOIR DU DIABLE. UK/USA: aka THE DEVIL'S CASTLE/THE DEVIL'S MANOR/THE MANOR OF THE DEVIL) France, 1896. Dir: Georges Méliès. With: Georges Méliès. Robert-Houdin/Pathé/Star. B&W.

One of film pioneer Méliès' short (two minutes) trick films. A bat flies around a medieval castle and turns into the Devil (portrayed by the director). He then conjures up a parade of ghosts, skeletons and witches from a magic cauldron until one holds up a crucifix and Mephistopheles disappears in a puff of smoke.

✦

THE HAUNTED COP SHOP

(Orig: MENG GUI CHA GUAN)
Hong Kong, 1985 (1987). Dir: Jeffrey Lau (Jeffrey Lau Chan-Wai/Liu Zhen-Wei). With: Jacky Cheung (Cheung Hok-Yau), Hui Gon-Ying, Wo Fung, Chan Kai-Chia. Colour.

Silly horror comedy set in a local Hong Kong police station that is haunted by vampire-ghost General Issey and the phantoms of other Japanese soldiers who committed suicide after World War Two. This also includes some bloodsuckers who awaken during an afternoon solar eclipse.

Sequel: THE HAUNTED COP SHOP II (qv; 1986)

✦✧

THE HAUNTED COP SHOP II

(Orig: MENG GUI XUE TANG)
Hong Kong, 1986 (1988). Dir: Jeffrey Lau (Jeffrey Lau Chan-Wai/Liu Zhen-Wei). With: Zhang Xueyou, Ricky Hoi, Su Jiabao, Wen Liyan, Lin Jian-Ming, Jeffrey Lau (Jeffrey Lau Chan-Wai/Liu Zhen-Wei). In-Gear Films/ World Video/Threat Video. Colour.

Improved comedy sequel to the 1985 original that features non-stop action. This includes various vampires, a horde of cannibalistic zombies and a werewolf cop. The lead female vampire (Jiabao) is finally destroyed by the hero urinating into a pool and completing an electrical circuit!

✦✦

THE HAUNTED CURIOSITY SHOP

UK, 1901. Dir: Walter R. Booth. Paul. B&W.

Silent trick short in which a woman is transformed into a mummy and then into a skeleton, only the top half of a woman crosses a room, and three gnomes turn into one.

✦

HAUNTED HONEYMOON

UK/USA, 1986. Dir: Gene Wilder. With: Gene Wilder, Gilda Radner, Dom DeLuise, Jonathan Pryce, Paul L. Smith, Peter Vaughan. Orion Pictures. Colour.

Director/co-writer/star Wilder's unfunny attempt to make a 1930s old dark house murder mystery for contemporary audiences. He obviously has great affection for the genre and although the film is a faithful recreation of the period and style, almost every gag, incident and character is taken from other movies (with the funniest sequence lifted from *Murder, He Says* [1945]). Neurotic radio broadcaster Larry Abbott (Wilder) and his fiancée Vickie Pearle (Radner) arrive at the spooky Abbott mansion, where the entire family has gathered to celebrate their wedding. However, Great Aunt Kate (DeLuise in drag) has decided to change her will in Larry's favour and claims that one of her relations is the werewolf (Will Keaton) seen prowling the grounds. As the bodies begin to pile up, Larry and Vickie set out to discover the identity of the murderer. Despite Smith's passable impersonation of Orson Welles, the supporting cast (including Bryan Pringle and Eve Ferret) is grievously wasted.

✦✧

HAUNTED NIGHTS

USA, 1993. Dir: Jim Enright and Jace Rocker. With: Jonathan Morgan, Steven St. Croix, Celeste, Britt Morgan, Mystica, Sahara (Sahara Sands). Wicked Pictures. Colour.

Hardcore sequel to *Arabian Nights* (1993), once again featuring private dicks Sam J. Flywheel (Morgan) and Roscoe (St. Croix, doing an imitation of Jerry Lewis) in a porno pastiche of the Hope and Crosby *Road* movies. This time Roscoe and Flywheel investigate a missing heiress at Castle McAngus in Scotland and encounter the evil Lord and Lady McAngus (Randy Spears and Morgan), the insect-eating butler Benson (Marc Wallice), exchange student/werewolf Albert Frankenstein (T.T. Boy), the spooky Lorna Doone (Celeste), a mad scientist (Ron Jeremy) experimenting with brain transplants, and a gorilla (Jake Williams). This won the Adult Video News Award for Best Shot-on-Video Feature of 1993.

✦

HAUNTED SUMMER

USA, 1988. Dir: Ivan Passer. With: Philip Anglim, Laura Dern, Alice Krige, Eric Stoltz, Alex Winter, Peter Berling. Cannon Films. Colour.

Based on the novel by Anne Edwards, this was originally announced in 1986 with John Huston directing. It is one of two films released in the same year inspired by the events of June 1816 which led up to Mary Godwin/Shelley (Krige) writing *Frankenstein*. Also enjoying a stay at the Villa Diodati are a bisexual Lord Byron (Anglim), Claire Clairmont (Dern), Percy Bysshe Shelley (Stoltz) and Dr John Polidori (Winter). Music by Christopher Young.

✦✧

THE HAUNTED WORLD OF ED WOOD

(aka THE HAUNTED WORLD OF EDWARD D. WOOD JR.) USA, 1996. Dir: Brett Thompson. With: Dolores Fuller, Conrad Brooks, Loretta King, Paul Marco, Lyle Talbot, Maila Nurmi (Vampira). Wood-Thomas Pictures/ Englewood Entertainment. Colour.

The Ed Wood cult continues with this documentary that includes new interviews with those who knew the director, plus clips from his work (including cut scenes from *Glen or Glenda* [1953] and a 1948 Betty Crocker TV commercial). Along with footage from the archives of Bela Lugosi Jr (who blames Wood for ruining his father's career), this was ninety-three year-old veteran Talbot's last screen appearance (he died the same year).

✦✦✧

HAVE YOU GOT ANY CASTLES?

USA, 1938. Dir: Frank Tashlin. Voices: Mel Blanc. Vitaphone/Warner Bros. Colour.

Seven minute *Merrie Melodies* cartoon about a number of book characters coming to life and singing the title song and 'Old King Cole' (both from *Varsity Show* [1937]) plus 'Swing for Sale'. Includes Frankenstein's Monster, Mr Hyde, the Phantom of the Opera and Fu Manchu. With reused sequences from *Clean Pastures* (1937).

✦✦✦

HAWAII FIVE-O:

(aka McGARRETT)
Death Mask
USA, 1978. Dir: Ralph Levy. With: Jack Lord, Marsha Mercant, Tim Thomerson, Robert Ellerstein, Cyd Charisse, Rory Calhoun. CBS Entertainment/Leonard Freeman Production/CBS-TV. Colour.

Long-running hour-long police TV series (1968-80, 268 episodes) created by executive producer Leonard Freeman and set on Hawaii. In this episode, a thief dies under a curse when King Tut's mask is stolen and Detective Steve McGarrett (Lord) investigates.

✦✦

LINDA HAYDEN
(Linda Higginson) [b 1951]

British actress who appeared in a number of horror films during the 1970s but never quite achieved scream queen status.
qv: *Madhouse* (1974); *Taste the Blood of Dracula* (1969); *Vampira* (1974).

THE HEAD
(Orig: DIE NACKTE UND DER SATAN)
West Germany, 1959 (1962). Dir: Victor Trivas. With: Horst Frank, Karin Kernke, Helmut Schmid, Michel Simon, Paul Dahlke, Dietter Eppler. Trans-Lux Pictures/ Prism/Wolfgang Hartwig/Rapid Film. B&W.
Sleazy, low-budget horror thriller in which French actor Simon plays Professor Dr Abel (*sic*), who has invented 'Serum-Z', which he uses to keep a dog's severed head living. However, his new co-worker, the scientifically-created mad genius Dr Ood (Frank), decapitates the doctor and keeps his head alive with the serum. He also transplants the head of beautiful hunchbacked nurse Irene (Kernke) onto the body of Lilly the stripper (Christiane Maybach)! This was director Trivas' last film. Art director Hermann Warm also designed the expressionist sets for *The Cabinet of Dr. Caligari* (1919).
✦✧

HEARTSTOPPER
USA, 1989 (1992). Dir: John A. Russo. With: Kevin Kindlin, Moon Zappa, Tom Savini, Michael J. Pollard. Thinker Productions/Tempe Video. Colour.
Low-budget vampire thriller, written and directed by Russo (co-creator of *Night of the Living Dead* [1968]) and based on his 1983 novel *The Awakening*. Hanged for being a vampire during the American Revolution, Tory physician Benjamin Latham (Kindlin) is accidentally resurrected in modern-day Pittsburgh and uses a scalpel to take blood from his victims. Co-star Savini plays an obsessed cop and supplied the make-up effects, while Pollard turns up in an amusing cameo as an odd vampire expert.
✦✧

Horst Frank reduces Michel Simon to just The Head *(1959).*

HEARTSTOPPERS
USA, 1992. With: George Hamilton, Wes Craven, John Landis, Rick Baker, Samuel Z. Arkoff, Charles Band. Colour/B&W.
Feature-length TV documentary in which a smirking Hamilton (who dresses up as Dracula) hosts and narrates a look at Hollywood horror movies, with segments devoted to vampires, AIP, William Castle and *Night of the Living Dead* (1968), amongst others. This features numerous clips and trailers, including *An American Werewolf in London* (1981), *Black Sunday* (1960), *Blood of Dracula* (1957), *Bram Stoker's Dracula* (1992), *Bride of Frankenstein* (1935), *Buffy the Vampire Slayer* (1992), *Creature from the Black Lagoon* (1954), *Death Becomes Her* (1992), *Dracula* (1958), *Dracula's Great Love* (1972), *Dr. Jekyll and Mr. Hyde* (1920), *Elvira Mistress of the Dark* (1988), *Frankenstein Meets the Wolf Man* (1943), *The Howling* (1980), *How to Make a Monster* (1958), *The Hunchback of Notre Dame* (1923), *Innocent Blood* (1992), *I Was a Teenage Werewolf* (1957), *King Kong* (1933), *The Little Shop of Horrors* (1960), *Love at First Bite* (1979), *Meridian* (1990), *Nosferatu* (1922), *Pet Sematary* (1989), *The Phantom of the Opera* (1925), *The Son of Kong* (1933), *Transylvania Twist* (1989) and *The Vampire Bat* (1933), plus interviews with creature effects designers Tom Woodruff and Alec Gillis, scream queens Gail Harris and Deborah Dutch, irritating horror host Elvira, Jim Wynorski, George Romero and Forrest Ackerman.
✦✦

THE HEATHCLIFF AND DINGBAT SHOW: DINGBAT AND THE CREEPS
USA, 1980-81. Voices: Frank Welker, Don Messick. Ruby-Spears Productions/ABC-TV. Colour.
Half-hour cartoon TV series (twenty-seven episodes) which includes the lazy orange cat (Mel Blanc) of comic-strip fame and four-minute episodes of *Dingbat and the Creeps*, featuring the eponymous vampire bat dog (*vampira dogus scaredy catus*), voiced by Welker, and his monstrous friends Nobody the pumpkin and Sparerib the skeleton (both Messick) from Transylvania.
Series sequel: THE HEATHCLIFF AND MARMADUKE SHOW: DINGBAT AND THE CREEPS (qv; 1981-82)
✦

THE HEATHCLIFF AND MARMADUKE SHOW: DINGBAT AND THE CREEPS
USA, 1981-82. Voices: Frank Welker, Don Messick. Ruby-

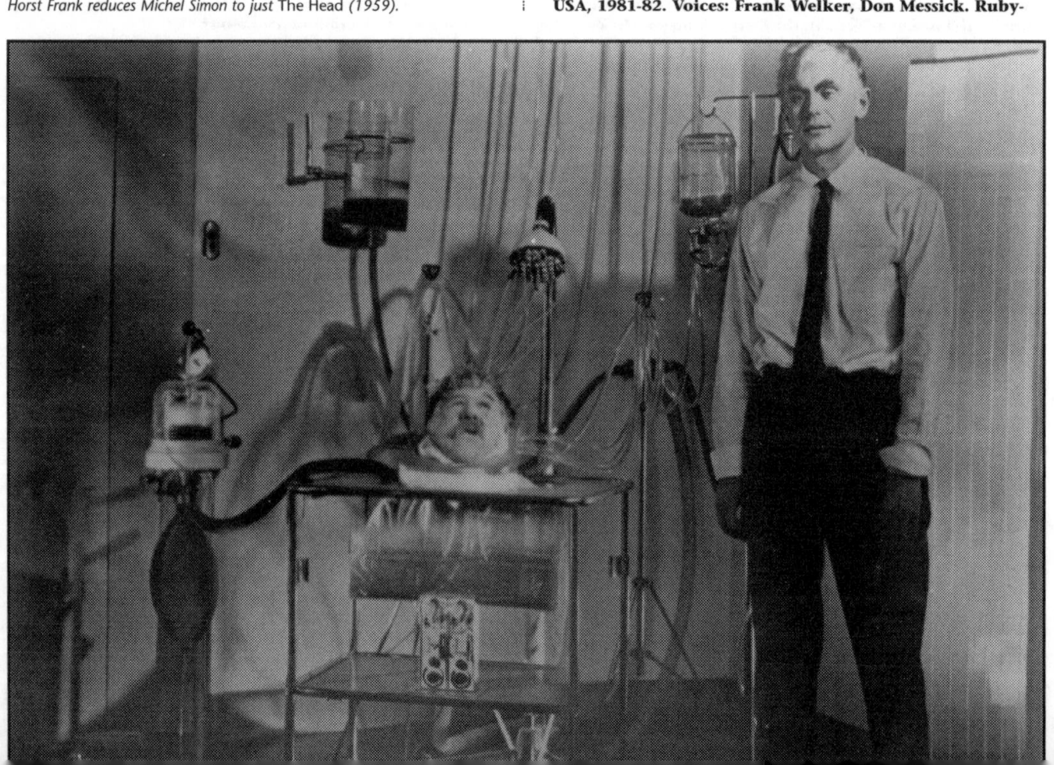

Spears Productions/ABC-TV. Colour.
More TV cartoon adventures of the orange cat (Mel Blanc), plus Brad Anderson's comic-strip great Dane, Marmaduke (Paul Winchell). This also includes alternating episodes of *Dingbat and the Creeps*, once again featuring the vampire bat dog (Welker) and his friends Nobody and Sparerib (both Messick).
Series sequel: HEATHCLIFF AND THE CATILLAC CATS (1984-85)
✦

HEAVY METAL
Canada/USA/UK, 1981. Dir: Gerald Potterton (and Harold Whitaker, Jimmy T. Murikami, Pino Van Lamsweerde, Jack Stokes, Paul Sabella, Julian Szuchopa, Barrie Nelson, Brian Larkin and John Bruno). Voices: John Candy, Joe Flaherty, Eugene Levy, Harold Ramis, Richard Romanos, John Vernon. Columbia. Colour.
Uneven full-length cartoon anthology inspired by *Heavy Metal* magazine and based on original art and stories by Richard Corben, Angus McKie, Dan O'Bannon, Thomas Warkentin and Berni Wrightson, amongst others. Each of the eight stories is dominated by Lochnar, a glowing green sphere that is the sum of all evils throughout the universe. In O'Bannon's 'B.17' segment (designed by Mike Ploog), the pilot of the eponymous bomber is menaced by his zombiefied crew. When he parachutes onto a desert island, he discovers that he has not left the walking dead behind. Music by Elmer Bernstein, Black Sabbath, Blue Oyster Cult, Cheap Trick, Devo, Donald Fagin, Don Felder, Grand Funk Railroad, Sammy Hagar, Journey, Nazareth, Stevie Nicks, Riggs and Trust.
✦✦✧

HEBA THE SNAKE WOMAN
UK, 1915. Excelsior. B&W.
Sixteen minute silent short in which an Aztec princess transforms into a snake and kills a doctor.
✦

O.P. HEGGIE
[1879-1936]

Australian stage actor in Hollywood since the late 1920s. As the blind hermit in *Bride of Frankenstein* (1935), he saw potential intelligence in the Monster.

HELLGATE
South Africa, 1989 (1990). Dir: William A. (Al) Levey. With: Ron Palillo, Abigail Wolcott, Carel Trichardt, Petrea Curran, Evan J. Klisser, Joanne Ward. Ghost Town Film Management/Distant Horizon/Anant Singh/New World Pictures. Colour.
Amateurish, low-budget horror movie in which director Levey turns up as a talking head in a refrigerator. In an exhibition ghost town supposedly set in California, two 'teenage' couples encounter a zombie girl (Wolcott) killed by bikers in the 1950s, her deranged father and his glowing crystal which can revive the dead. Most of the plot doesn't make sense, the cinematography is ugly, none of the cast can act, and the pseudo-fifties soundtrack soon becomes simply irritating.
✦

HELLO AGAIN
USA, 1987. Dir: Frank Perry. With: Shelley Long, Judith Ivey, Gabriel Byrne, Corbin Bernsen, Sela Ward, Austin Pendleton. Buena Vista/Touchstone/Silver Screen Partners III. Colour.
Desperately unfunny comedy. A year after she chokes to death on a chicken bone, housewife Lucy Chadman (Long) is brought back to life by her sister's magic spell. She soon discovers that things have changed and that her husband (Bernsen) is particularly surprised to see her. This could have been fun, but unfortunately neither producer/director Perry nor star Long have the lightness of touch to make it work.
✦✧

HELLO, DRACULA
(aka HELLO DRACULAR)
Taiwan/Hong Kong, 1985. Dir: Henry Wu-Leung (Leung Tung-Ni). With: Kim To, Lam Kwong, Wong Chun-Yu, Puon Sam (Pan San). Kinco Films/Sunny Video. Colour.
A dead body on its way to the sacred burial ground is reanimated by hopping child-vampire Konsi and becomes Dracula. The local officials recruit three vampire hunters from Europe while a gang of children on unicycles battle the undead. This includes a musical dance number with some friendly vampires, a vampire baseball game and the Count being blown up by a vampire child wearing a belt of dynamite!
✦✧

HELL'S FIRE
USA, 1934. Dir: Ub Iwerks. Voices: Jane Withers. Celebrity Pictures/Metro-Goldwyn-Mayer. Colour.
Seven minute *Willie Whopper* cartoon, about the little boy who tells lies. It features Rasputin, the Devil, Cerberus and Dr Jekyll and Mr Hyde.
Sequel: ROBIN HOOD JR. (1934)
✦✦

HELLZAPOPPIN'
USA, 1941. Dir: H.C. Potter. With: Ole Olsen, Chic Johnson, Martha Raye, Hugh Herbert, Jane Frazee, Mischa Auer. Universal/Mayfair. B&W.
'Any similarity between *Hellzapoppin'* and a motion picture is purely coincidental' warns the opening caption of this near-plotless musical comedy based on the successful Broadway stage revue. The comedy duo of Olsen and Johnson try to help their friend Jeff (Robert Paige) put on a backyard show and win the hand of heiress Kitty (Frazee). Along the way there's a sequence set in Hell, *Citizen Kane* (1941) and *Here Comes Mr. Jordan* (1941) gags, John P. Fulton's invisible effects, a talking bear and an appearance by the Universal Frankenstein Monster (played by actor-stuntman Dale Van Sickel). With Elisha Cook Jr, Shemp Howard and midgets Angelo Rossitto (as a devil) and Billy Curtis.
✦✦✦

HELTER SKELTER
UK, 1949. Dir: Ralph Thomas. With: Carol Marsh, David Tomlinson, Mervyn Johns, Peter Hammond, Richard Hearne, Terry-Thomas. Gainsborough. B&W.
Comedy set in a haunted castle. With clips from *Would You Believe It!* (1929) and a great supporting cast that includes Jimmy Edwards, Glynis Johns, Valentine Dyall, Dennis Price, Harry Secombe, and Wilfred Hyde White as Dr B. Jekyll and Mr Hyde.
✦✧

HENSHIN NINJA ARASHI
Japan, 1972. With: Eisei Amamoto, Kenji Ushio. Ishinomori Productions/Toei. Colour.
Children's TV series created by Shotaro Ishinomori. Set in samurai times, Henshin ninja ('Transforming ninja') Arashi and his long-lost brother Tsukinowa ('Moon Mask') battle robot-like villain Majin Sai and the Hell Priest, who has called up such creatures as a patchwork Frankenstein Monster (named 'Franken'), Dracula, Wolf Man, Mummy Man, Sphinx and Witch Gorgon. After Majin Sai is defeated, Satan (Amamoto) himself attempts to conquer Japan until the classic creatures are destroyed by a laser eye-beam.
✦✧

HOLMES HERBERT
(Edward Sanger) [1882-1956]

British supporting actor in Hollywood, often cast as authority figures. **qv:** *Dr. Jekyll and Mr. Hyde* (1931); *The Ghost of Frankenstein* (1942); *Mark of the Vampire* (1935); *The Mummy's Curse* (1944); *Son of Dr. Jekyll* (1951); *The Undying Monster* (1942).

HERCULES IN THE HAUNTED WORLD
(Orig: ERCOLE AL CENTRO DELLA TERRA. UK: HERCULES IN THE CENTER OF THE EARTH)

Italy, 1961 (1963). Dir: Mario Bava. With: Reg Park, Christopher Lee, Leonora (Eleonara) Ruffo, Giorgio Ardisson, Franco Giacobini, Marisa Belli. SPA Cinematográfica/Woolner Brothers. Colour.
Probably the best of the Italian musclemen (*peplum*) movies. Hercules (British strongman and former Mr Universe Park) and Theseus (Ardisson) must travel to Hades to save the soul of Daianara (Ruffo), put under a spell by vampire-like villain Licho (Lee, dubbed by someone else, but still impressive). Along the way they have to overcome unconvincing stone giant Procrustes, a flying army of the dead and a lake of boiling lava. There's too much comedy, but co-writer/photographer/director Bava gives the film a wonderful fairy-tale quality.
✦✦✦

HERCULES, PRISONER OF EVIL
(Orig: URSUS E IL TERRORE DEI KIRGHISI)
Italy/Tunisia, 1964 (1967). Dir: Anthony Dawson (Antonio Margheriti) (and Ruggero Biola/Ruggero Deodato). With: Reg Park, Mireille Granelli, Ettore Manni, Maria Teresa Orsini, Furio Meniconi, Lilly Mantovani. Adelphia Compagnia Cinematográfica/Ambrosiana Cinematográfica/Royale Sodifilm/American International. Colour.
Ursus (Park), renamed Hercules in the English dubbed version, is the leader of the Circassians, oppressed by the Great Khan. Each night, evil sorceress Princess Anniko (Granelli) uses a magical wine to transform Hercules into a cloaked, werewolf-like monster known as The Falcon, who then kills his own people, including women and children. A horror *peplum* apparently made for Italian TV, from the director of *Castle of Blood* (1964).
✦✧

HERCULES THE LEGENDARY JOURNEYS: HERCULES IN THE UNDERWORLD
New Zealand/USA, 1994. Dir: Bill L. Norton. With: Kevin Sorbo, Anthony Quinn, Tawny Kitaen, Marlee Shelton, Cliff Curtis, Jeorge Gonzales. Universal/Renaissance Pictures. Colour.
Hercules (Sorbo) crosses the River Styx and goes to Hell to battle disgusting-looking zombies, recapture the three-headed Cerubus for Hades (Mark Ferguson), and bring his wife Deianeira (Kitaen) back from the dead in this, the darkest and most violent of the five *Action Pack* pilot TV movies. With some impressive make-up effects by KNB EFX Group and visual effects created by VCE/Peter Kuran. Series regular Michael Hurst turns up here as both an early victim and Charon the Boatman. Sam Raimi was executive producer.
✦✦✦✧

HERCULES THE LEGENDARY JOURNEYS:
Mummy Dearest
New Zealand/USA, 1996. Dir: Anson Williams. With: Kevin Sorbo, Robert Trebor, Galyn Gorg, John Watson, Mark Newnham, Alan de Malmanche. MCA Television/Pacific Renaissance Pictures/The WB Network. Colour.
Hour-long TV series (1995-99, 110 episodes), loosely based on Greek mythology and old movie plots. Hercules (a likeable Sorbo) journeys the Earth battling the minions of his wicked stepmother Hera, powerful Queen of the Gods. This episode is directed by the *Happy Days* (1974-84) star and a disclaimer reads 'Any similarity between our Mummy and the foot dragging classic we all know and love is purely intentional'. When Salmonius (Trebor) decides to open a 'House of Horrors' waxworks, little does he realise that the centre-piece of his exhibit is the scary living mummy (Newnham) of an ancient Egyptian Pharaoh. Co-executive produced by Sam Raimi.
✦✦✦✧

HERE COME THE MUNSTERS
USA, 1995. Dir: Robert Ginty. With: Edward Herrmann, Veronica Hamel, Robert Morse, Christine Taylor, Mathew Botuchis, Troy Evans. MTE/Bodega Bay/St. Clare Entertainment/Fox Broadcasting/Fox Network. Colour.
Thirty years after the original series, this likeable TV movie, co-executive produced by John Landis, recounts a new origin story of the Munster family. Driven out of present-day Transylvania by a mob of torch-wielding peasants, the Frankenstein Monster-like Herman (Herrmann, doing an extraordinary impersonation of the late Fred Gwynne), vampiric Lily (Hamel), Grandpa (Morse) and wolf boy Eddie (Botuchis, who gets to transform into a pint-sized werewolf) emigrate to America. Upon their arrival, they discover that Herman's sister Elsa (Judy Gold, looking like the Bride of Frankenstein) is in a coma and learn from their normal-looking niece Marilyn (Taylor) that Elsa's husband Norman Hyde (Max Grodenchik) has been transformed into obnoxious right-wing politician Brent Jekyll (Jeff Trachta), who is using a platform of racial intolerance to get elected. Despite the disappointing script and low budget, director Ginty ensures that the film looks superb, the stars all fit perfectly into their roles and the character make-up effects are remarkably re-created by Steve Johnson's XFX company. There is also fun support from Mary Woronov as a nosy neighbour, special appearances by original cast members Yvonne De Carlo, Al Lewis, Butch Patrick and Pat Priest as a weird family group, and clips from Universal's original *Frankenstein* (1931).
Sequel: THE MUNSTERS' SCARY LITTLE CHRISTMAS (qv; 1996)
✦✦

HERE'S BOOMER:
Camityville's Boomer
USA, 1982. Dir: Larry Stewart. With: Rick Lohman, Forbesy Russell, Allan Arbus, Victor Buono, Richard Moll, Terry Hart. A.C. Lyles Productions/DWP Productions/Paramount/NBC-TV. Colour.
Half-hour TV series (1980-82) created by Don Balluck, A.C. Lyles, Leon Tokatyan and Diana Bell Tokatyan. In this episode, young couple Peter and Bonnie (Lohman and Russell) and their talking dog Boomer take shelter from a thunderstorm in the home of Dr Frankenstein (Buono), where they discover his laboratory and encounter his friendly grey-faced 'Monster' (Moll).
✦✧

GORDON HESSLER
[b 1930]

German-born journeyman director who began his career as a story editor and producer on TV's *Alfred Hitchcock Presents* (1955-1962). After being fired by American International Pictures from *De Sade* (1969), he went on to make *The Oblong Box* (1969), *Scream and Scream Again* (1969), *Cry of the Banshee* (1970) and *Murders in the Rue Morgue* (1971) for them, before returning to television.
qv: *House of Dracula's Daughter* (1973); *Kiss Meets the Phantom of the Park* (1978); *100 Years of Horror: 'Mad Doctors'* (1996); *100 Years of Horror: 'Zombies'* (1996).

ANTHONY HICKOX
[b 1959]

British writer, producer and director, the son of director Douglas Hickox (1929-1988), who has a genuine visual flair and a love of horror, but is often let down by weak scripts. He usually has cameos in his own films and starred in *Lobster Man from Mars* (1989).
qv: *Full Eclipse* (1993); *Return of the Living Dead III* (1993); *Sundown The Vampire in Retreat* (1988); *Waxwork* (1988); *Waxwork II Lost in Time* (1991).

THE HIDDEN ROOM:
Dream of the Wolf
Canada/USA, 1991. Dir: Jorge Montesi. With: Adam Arkin, Laurie Paton, Anthony Sherwood, Ron Lea, Asia Vieira, John Boylan. Hidden Room Productions/Chesler Perlmutter Productions/Lifetime Television. Colour.
Half-hour anthology TV series (1991-93, thirty-three episodes). This episode features Patrick McGrath's adaptation of Scott Bradfield's oblique werewolf story. Businessman Larry Chambers (Arkin from *Full Moon High* [1981], etc) dreams of being a wolf, much to the consternation of his unfaithful wife (Paton) and exasperated employers. Introduced by Mimi Kuzyk as The Woman in the Hidden Room.
✦✧

HIGH ANXIETY

USA, 1977. Dir: Mel Brooks. With: Mel Brooks, Madeline Kahn, Cloris Leachman, Harvey Korman, Ron Carey, Dick Van Patten. Twentieth Century-Fox/Crossbow Productions. Colour.

Silly comedy thriller dedicated to Alfred Hitchcock, in which co-writer/producer/director/star Brooks spoofs a number of the Master of Suspense's movies (including several sequences from *Vertigo* [1958], the shower scene in *Psycho* [1960] and an attack of *The Birds* [1963]). When psychiatrist Dr Richard H. Thorndyke (Brooks), who suffers from a fear of heights, takes over the running of The Psycho Neurotic Institute for the Very, *Very* Nervous, he begins to suspect that his predecessor was murdered. In one scene, the scheming Dr Montague (Korman) wears false fangs and pretends to be a vampire to scare a patient (Ron Clark) who dreams about werewolves. With future director Barry Levinson as a bellboy. Ace Books published a novelisation by Robert H. Pilpel.

✦✦✧

HIGHCLIFF MANOR

USA, 1979. Dir: Nick Havinga. With: Shelley Fabares, Stephen McHattie, Eugenie Ross-Leming, Christian Marlowe, Harriet White Medin. TAT Productions/NBC-TV. Colour.

Four-part, half-hour Frankenstein spoof, shot on video. Scientist Frances (Ross-Leming) creates her own Monster lover named Bram (Marlowe) in a basement laboratory.

✦

HIGHLANDER:

The Beast Below

France/Canada/USA, 1993. Dir: Daniel Vigne. With: Adrian Paul, Alexandra Vandernoot, Stan Kirsch, Dee Dee Bridgewater, Christian Van Acker, Werner Stocker. Gaumont Télévision/RTL Plus/Rysher Distribution/ Reteitalia Productions/Amuse Video/TF1/USA Network. Colour.

Hour-long syndicated TV show (1992-98, 119 episodes), a spin-off from the movie series and based on the character created by Gregory Widen. Paul plays Duncan MacLeod, a 400 year-old Immortal born in the Highlands of Scotland. There are others like him — some good, some evil. For centuries he has battled the forces of darkness, with holy ground his only refuge. He cannot die unless you take his head, and with it his power. In the end, there can be only one. In this episode, apparently inspired by *The Phantom of the Opera*, a scheming opera singer attempts to convince Darius (Stocker), a slow-witted Immortal living in the catacombs under the Paris Opera House, to murder her rival. With theme music by Queen ('Princes of the Universe').

✦✦

The Modern Prometheus

France/Canada/USA, 1997. Dir: Adrian Paul. With: Adrian Paul, Jim Byrnes, Jonathan Firth, Barbara Keogh. Gaumont Télévision/Filmline International/Rysher Entertainment/M6/Reteitalia. Colour.

When the protégé of Jim Dawson (Byrnes) dies because of the influence of an immortal Lord Byron (Firth), MacLeod is forced to confront the decadent poet-turned-rock star, whose lifestyle is out of control. With Keogh as Mary Shelley.

✦✦

Pharaoh's Daughter

France/Canada/USA, 1994. Dir: Dennis Berry. With: Adrian Paul, Stan Kirsch, Michel Modo, Jim Byrnes, Nia Peeples, James Faulkner. Gaumont Télévision/Rysher TPE/M6/Reteitalia/USA Network. Colour.

Duncan MacLeod releases Cleopatra's Immortal handmaiden (Peeples) from inside an Egyptian sarcophagus in modern-day Paris. Although he tries to befriend her, she is obsessed with revenging herself on the Roman she believes was responsible for her queen's death 2,000 years before.

✦✧

The Vampire

France/Canada/USA, 1994. Dir: Dennis Berry. With: Adrian Paul, Jim Byrnes, Jeremy Brudenell, Trevor Peacock, Denis Lill, Nathalie Presles. Gaumont Télévision/Rysher TPE/M6/Reteitalia/USA Network. Colour.

In modern-day Paris, Immortal Duncan MacLeod once again confronts Nicholas Ward (Brudenell), an Immortal serial killer who 200 years before (shown in flashback) used a pincer device to create the mark of the vampire to cover up his murders.

Series sequel: HIGHLANDER THE ANIMATED SERIES (1994-95)

✦✦✦

HIGH PLAINS DRIFTER

USA, 1972. Dir: Clint Eastwood. With: Clint Eastwood, Verna Bloom, Marianna Hill, Mitchell Ryan, Jack Ging, Stefan Gierasch. Malpaso/Universal. Colour.

Eastwood's second film as both star and director owes much to his 'spaghetti Westerns' with Sergio Leone, but with one major difference — here, the whip-wielding Stranger who rides out of the desert haze and into the town of Lago turns out to be a murdered Marshall who has returned from the grave for revenge on his trio of killers and the town that wouldn't help him. Eastwood's sure direction results in some striking visuals, while Ernest Tidyman's enigmatic script neatly integrates the supernatural elements with the existential Western theme. With Geoffrey Lewis, Richard Bull, John Hillerman and midget Billy Curtis as Mordecai Fortune. The novelisation by screenwriter Tidyman appeared in 1973.

✦✦✦✧

HIGH SPIRITS

Ireland/UK, 1988. Dir: Neil Jordan. With: Peter O'Toole, Daryl Hannah, Steve Guttenberg, Beverly D'Angelo, Jennifer Tilly, Peter Gallagher. Vision PDG/Palace Productions. Colour.

Filmed under the title *Ghost Tours* and billed as a supernatural comedy, this old-fashioned farce from writer/director Jordan (*The Company of Wolves* [1984], etc) is simply not very funny. O'Toole tries hard as Peter Plunkett, the alcohol-sodden owner of a run-down Irish castle hotel who unsuccessfully attempts to convince a group of unpleasant American tourists that it is full of (fake) spooks. It therefore comes as a surprise to everyone when Plunkett's zombie ancestors climb out of their crypts and the 200 year-old ghost of Mary (Hannah) falls in love with visitor Jack (Guttenberg). Thanks to Anton Furst's spectacular castle design and Derek Meddings' impressive optical effects the film looks great, but the actors are bogged down by the clichéd script (which an uncredited Michael McDowell also worked on) and Jordan's leaden direction. With Liam Neeson as a murderous ghost, and Ray MacAnally as the zombie leader.

✦✦

THE HIGHWAYMAN:

Billionaire Body Club

USA, 1988. Dir: Ivan Nagy. With: Sam Jones, Mark 'Jacko' Jackson, Jane Balder, Tim Russ, Cindy Morgan, Kim Johnston Ulrich. Glen Larson Productions/Twentieth Century Fox/NBC-TV. Colour.

Short-lived TV series (1987-88, ten episodes) set in a dystopian near-future where the Mad Max-looking Highwayman (Jones) and Australian sidekick Jetto (Jackson) work for a super-secret organisation policing the highways of a decaying America in an atomic truck filled with gadgets. In this episode, a young cop teams up with The Highwayman to investigate reports of a modern-day vampire. Instead, they discover a thriving black market in spare body parts. Title sequence narrated by an uncredited William Conrad.

✦✧

HIGHWAY TO HEAVEN:

I Was a Middle-Aged Werewolf

USA, 1987. Director: Michael Landon. With: Michael Landon, Victor French, Eldon Ratcliff, Granville Van Dusen, Nancy Frangione, Devon Odessa. Michael Landon Productions/NBC-TV. Colour.

Hour-long fantasy TV series (1984-88, 111 episodes) in which probationary angel Jonathan Smith (Landon) is sent to Earth to earn his wings and teams up with ex-cop Mark Gordon (French) to help people sort their lives out. In this Halloween episode, writer/direc-

tor Landon reprises his role from *I Was a Teenage Werewolf* (1957) to aid a young boy in defending himself against a group of bullies.
✦✧

HI HONEY, I'M HOME:
Grey Skies
USA, 1991. Dir: Doug Rogers. With: Susan Cella, Charlotte Booker, Stephen Bradbury, Pete Benson, Julie Benz, Eric Kushnick. Nickelodeon/ABC-TV. Colour.
Half-hour comedy TV series (1991-92, thirteen episodes) about a fictional 1950s sitcom family, the Neilsens, who are relocated to 1990s suburban New Jersey after their show is cancelled. Each episode usually features a cameo by a character from another cancelled programme. The vampiric Grandpa Munster (Al Lewis) makes an appearance in this episode, in which Honey Neilsen (Booker) tries to cheer up her depressed husband Lloyd (Bradbury) when he can't get a job in the real world.
✦✧

THE HILARIOUS HOUSE OF FRIGHTENSTEIN
Canada, 1970-72. Dir: Riff Markowitz. With: Vincent Price, Billy Van, Rais Fishka, Professor Julius Sumner Miller, Joe Torby, Guy Big. CHCH-TV. Colour.
Syndicated, one-hour TV musical comedy show hosted by Price, in which vampiric mad scientist Count Frightenstein (Van, who also played six other roles) and his assistant Igor (professional wrestler Fishka) are exiled from Transylvania when they fail to bring a Karloff-like Monster (named Brucie!) to life. The Count also imitates the Wolf Man. In America this was re-edited into a repetitive, five-days-a-week, half-hour TV series from 1974-75 (130 episodes). With Wolfman Jack.
✦✧

HILLBILLYS IN A HAUNTED HOUSE
USA, 1967. Dir: Jean Yarbrough. With: Ferlin Husky, Joi Lansing, Don Bowman, John Carradine, Lon Chaney, Basil Rathbone. Woolner Bros. Colour.
A sequel to *Las Vegas Hillbillys* (1966), this country music horror comedy was filmed under the title *Ghost Party*. A trio of would-be music stars (Husky, Lansing and Bowman) on their way to Nashville spend the night in a spooky old mansion being used by an atom spy ring. Dragon Lady Madame Wong (Linda Ho) tries to scare them away with fake ghosts and a gorilla (George Barrows). The three horror stars are grievously wasted: Carradine and a feeble-looking Rathbone (in his last role) turn up as scientists Dr Himmel and Gregor, respectively, while Chaney Jr plays their drunken assistant. With guest appearances by singers Merle Haggard, Sonny James and Molly Bee, several irritating songs, a real ghost and a dummy of a werewolf. This was also the last feature film from veteran director Yarbrough, who must have thought he was back working with the Bowery Boys.
✦✧

HILL STREET BLUES:
Film at Eleven
USA, 1981. Dir: Georg Stanford Brown. With: Daniel J. Travanti, Michael Conrad, Michael Warren, Bruce Weitz, Charles Haid, Veronica Hamel. MTM Productions/NBC-TV. Colour.
Popular hour-long ensemble police TV series (1981-87, 145 episodes), created by Michael Kozoll and executive producer Steven Bochco. In this episode, Detective Mick Belker (Weitz) arrests Kevin Herman Dracula (Mark Metcalf), who has to be subdued with crucifixes and subsequently dies in custody.
✦✦✦✧

LAMBERT HILLYER
[1893-1969]

American director, best known for his 'B' Westerns dating back to the silent era, but also remembered for his two 1936 productions for Universal, *Dracula's Daughter* and *The Invisible Ray*, and the serial *Batman* (1943).

ANTHONY HINDS
[b 1922]

British writer and producer, the son of Hammer's co-founder William Hinds (aka Will Hammer, 1887-1957). Along with Michael Carreras, he was responsible for defining 'Hammer Horror' during the 1950s and early 1960s before becoming one of the studio's most prolific scriptwriters under the pseudonym 'John Elder'.
qv: *The Brides of Dracula* (1960); *The Curse of Frankenstein* (1957); *The Curse of the Werewolf* (1960); *Dracula* (1958); *Dracula Has Risen from the Grave* (1968); *Dracula Prince of Darkness* (1965); *The Evil of Frankenstein* (1964); *Flesh and Blood: The Hammer Heritage of Horror* (1994); *Frankenstein and the Monster from Hell* (1973); *Frankenstein Created Woman* (1966); *Hammer House of Horror: 'Visitor from the Grave'* (1980); *Hammer the Studio that Dripped Blood!* (1987); *Journey to the Unknown* (1968-69); *The Kiss of the Vampire* (1962); *Legend of the Werewolf* (1974); *The Mummy's Shroud* (1966); *The Phantom of the Opera* (1962); *100 Years of Horror: 'Zombies'* (1996); *The Reptile* (1966); *The Revenge of Frankenstein* (1958); *Scars of Dracula* (1970); *Taste the Blood of Dracula* (1969).

HIROKU KAIBYODEN
Japan, 1969. Dir: Tokuzo Tanaka. With: Kojiro Hongo, Naomi Kobayashi, Mitsuyo Kamei, Matsuhiro Toura, Koichi Uenoyama, Akane Kawasaki. Daiei. Colour.
Based on the Japanese legend of the ghost cat (*bakeneko mono*) of Nabeshima — previously filmed as *Nabeshima Kaibyoden* (1949). Set in the eighteenth century castle of Lord Nabeshima (Uenoyama), a ghost-cat with supernatural powers transforms itself into a fanged female demon that drinks the blood of its victims until it is finally impaled by a samurai warrior (Hongo).
✦✦

HIS EGYPTIAN AFFINITY
USA, 1915. Dir: A.E. Christie. With: Victoria Forde, Eddie Lyons. Nestor/Universal. Colour.
Fifteen minute silent comedy about a 3,000 year-old princess returned to life, who meets her reincarnated lover. They are then both pursued by the reincarnated son of a sheikh.
✦

LAS HISTORIAS DE PLINIO:
El Hombre Lobo
Spain, 1970. Dir: Antonio Jimenez Rico. Colour.
Werewolf episode of a Spanish TV series.
✦

HITLER, A FILM FROM GERMANY
(Orig: HITLER, EIN FILM AUS DEUTSCHLAND)
West Germany/UK/France, 1977 (1980). Dir: Hans-Jürgen Syberberg. With: Harry Baer (Bär), Heinz Schubert, Peter Kern, Hellmut Lange, Rainer von Artenfels, Martin Sperr. TMS/Solaris/Westdeutscher. Colour.
Originally shown on German TV in four parts, this seven hour dramatisation of Hitler's rise to power apparently includes scenes of Hitler as Frankenstein. With music by Wagner, Mozart and Beethoven. Distributed in cinemas by Francis Ford Coppola.
✦✧

HALLIWELL HOBBES
(Herbert Hobbes) [1877-1962]

British all-purpose character actor in Hollywood.
qv: *Dracula's Daughter* (1936); *Dr. Jekyll and Mr. Hyde* (1931); *Six Hours to Live* (1932); *The Undying Monster* (1942).

HOCUS POCUS
USA, 1993. Dir: Kenny Ortega. With: Bette Midler, Sarah Jessica Parker, Kathy Najimy, Omri Katz, Thora Birch, Vinessa Shaw. Walt Disney Pictures. Colour.
Enjoyable musical comedy, co-scripted by Mick Garris. A trio of evil witches, Winifred (Midler), Sarah (Parker) and Mary (Najimy),

hanged in Salem 300 years before for stealing the life-force from children, are accidentally conjured up on Halloween. With the help of a boy who the sisters have transformed into an immortal black cat (voiced by Norbert Weisser), a trio of youngsters (Katz, Birch and Shaw) steal the witches' book of spells in an attempt to destroy the supernatural siblings before sunrise. This also includes a helpful zombie (Doug Jones) and an uncredited Penny Marshall.
✦✦✦✧

VALERIE HOBSON [1917-1998]

Bland British leading lady who went to Hollywood as a teenager in the 1930s. After appearing in such Universal productions as *The Mystery of Edwin Drood* (1935), *Bride of Frankenstein* (1935) and *WereWolf of London* (1935), she returned to Britain and retired from the screen in the mid-fifties to marry Conservative member of Parliament John Profumo, who was later disgraced in a sex scandal. Her distinctive scream was apparently re-used by Universal for years. qv: *Life Returns* (1934).

GLORIA HOLDEN [1908-1991]

British actress who moved to Hollywood and portrayed the Count's tortured offspring, Countess Marya Zaleska, in *Dracula's Daughter* (1936).

HOLE IN THE MOON
(Orig: HOR B'LEVANA)
Israel, 1964. Dir: Uri Zohar. With: Dahn Ben Amotz, Ze'ev Berlinski, Christiane Dancourt, Daphne Eilat, Israel Gurion, Uri Zohar. Geva Film. B&W.
This Hebrew-language film apparently includes a spoof of *King Kong* (1933).
✦✧

HOLLOW-MY-WEANIE, DR. FRANKENSTEIN
USA, 1969. Colour.
Gay porno movie in which Dr Frankenstein and his hunchbacked assistant create a well-endowed Monster in their basement laboratory. This was apparently also advertised as *Frankenstein De Sade*.
✦

HOLLYWOOD CAPERS
USA, 1935. Dir: Jack King. Warner Bros. B&W.
Seven minute *Looney Tunes* cartoon set in a movie studio. When Beans the cat enters the set of a Frankenstein movie, he accidentally brings the mechanical Monster to life. The creature causes havoc amongst the crew until Beans chops him up with the blades of a wind machine. With a guest appearance by Porky Pig as the production assistant.
Sequel: GOLD DIGGERS OF '49 (1935)
✦✧

HOLLYWOOD DINOSAUR CHRONICLES
USA, 1987. With: Doug McClure. Rhino Video. Colour/B&W.
Forty-two minute video documentary about dinosaur movies, hosted by McClure. It includes clips from *King Kong* (1933).
✦✦

HOLLYWOOD DINOSAURS
USA, 1991. Dir: Ted Newsom. Fireworks Home Video/ Video Treasures. Colour/B&W.
Hour-long video documentary that includes extensive clips from *The Lost World* (1925), Willis O'Brien's test footage for *Creation* (1930-31), plus trailers for *Frankenstein Conquers the World* (1964), *King Kong* (1933), *King Kong vs. Godzilla* (1963) and numerous other dinosaur and giant monster movies. Narrated by Reid Richmond.
✦✦✦

HOLLYWOOD ON PARADE NO.8
USA, 1933. Dir: Lewis Lewyn. With: Eddie Borden, Mae Questel, Bela Lugosi, Rex Bell, Dorothy Burgess, George Sidney. Lewyn/Paramount. B&W.
Ten minute novelty short, filmed in Charles Pressley's Motion Picture Museum and Hall of Fame in Hollywood. Borden visits a wax museum where the exhibits come to life. In a brief sequence, visitor Questel, dressed as Betty Boop, sings 'My Silent Love'. The wax figure of Lugosi, in his Dracula costume, comes to life and bends towards her throat, warning: 'Boop! You have booped your last boop!' This also includes Gayne Whitman as Chandu the Magician and silent Lubitsch star Marie Prevost as a harem girl. The eighth in a series of twenty-four shorts produced by Paramount between 1932-33.
✦✧

HOLLYWOOD REVIEW OF 1929
USA, 1929. Dir: Charles Reisner. With: Conrad Nagel, Jack Benny, John Gilbert, Norma Shearer, Joan Crawford, Bessie Love. Metro-Goldwyn-Mayer. B&W/Colour.
All-star musical and comedy revue which was designed to introduce MGM's silent movie stars to the talkies. Co-hosted by Nagel and Benny, one sequence includes Gus Edwards singing 'Lon Chaney Will Get You if You Don't Watch Out', with people wearing various Chaney horror make-ups. With Lionel Barrymore, Laurel and Hardy, Nils Asther and Buster Keaton, amongst others.
✦✧

HOLLYWOOD SHUFFLE
USA, 1987. Dir: Robert Townsend. With: Robert Townsend, Anne-Marie Johnson, Starletta DuPois, Helen Martin, Keenan Ivory Wayans, Damon Wayans. Conquering Unicorn/Goldwyn. Colour.
This autobiographical comedy was apparently filmed for just $100,000. Co-writer/director Townsend plays a struggling young black actor trying to avoid stereotyping in Hollywood. It includes a clip from *Attack of the Street Pimps*, a spoof movie featuring zombie pimps.
✦✦✧

HOLLYWOOD STEPS OUT
USA, 1941. Dir: Fred (Tex) Avery. Warner Bros. Colour.
Seven minute *Merrie Melodies* cartoon in which the Frankenstein Monster dances a conga in a posh Hollywood nightclub. With caricatures of Boris Karloff, Peter Lorre, the Three Stooges, Humphrey Bogart, George Raft, James Cagney, Clark Gable, Bing Crosby, Johnny Weissmuller, Groucho Marx and numerous other movie stars.
✦✦✦

HOLLYWOOD UNCENSORED
USA, 1987. Dir: James Forsher. With: Douglas Fairbanks Jr, Peter Fonda, Mamie Van Doren, Martin Scorsese, Carroll Baker, Eli Wallach. IVE. B&W/Colour.
Hosted by Fairbanks Jr and Fonda, this feature-length documentary looks at movie censorship and includes the 'cut' scenes from *King Kong* (1933), but not the infamous spider pit sequence. Scorsese discusses Michael Powell's *Peeping Tom* (1960) and Van Doren reminisces about working with Albert Zugsmith.
✦✦

HOLMES AND YOYO:
The Last Phantom
USA, 1976. Dir: Jack Arnold. With: Richard B. Shull, John Schuck, Andrea Howard, Bruce Kirby, Augie Tribach, Stefan Gierasch. Universal/ABC-TV. Colour.
Half-hour comedy TV series (thirteen episodes), created by Jack Sher and Lee Hewitt, about Detective Alexander Holmes (Shull), a cop who gets prototype robot Gregory 'Yoyo' Yoyonovich (Schuck) as his new partner. In this episode, the mismatched pair suspect either an actor, a make-up artist or a stunt man of having attempted to murder the movie producer who fired them all. A sad comedown for the director of *Creature from the Black Lagoon* (1954), etc.
✦✧

EL HOMBRE QUE VOLVIO DE LA MUERTE
Mexico, 1990. Dir: Raul Araiza. With: Olivia Collins,

Rodolfo de Anda, Aaron Hernan, Bruno Rey. Televicine/Mex-American Home Video. Colour.
Based on a story by Narciso Ibañez Serrador. A wife discovers that her dead husband has returned from the grave.
✦

SETH HOLT [1923-1971]

Palestinian-born British director who began his career as an editor and associate producer at Ealing Studios. He made two stylish psychological thrillers for Hammer, *Taste of Fear* (1960) and *The Nanny* (1965), before his premature death during the production of *Blood from the Mummy's Tomb* (1971).

EL HOMBRE Y LA BESTIA

(aka EL EXTRAÑO CASO DEL HOMBRE Y LA BESTIA/EL SENSACIONAL Y EXTRAÑO CASO DEL HOMBRE Y LA BESTIA)
Argentina, 1951. Dir: Mario Soffici. With: Mario Soffici, Ana Maria Campoy, Olga Zubarry, José Cibrian, Rafael Frontura. Argentina Sono Films. B&W.
Co-writer/producer/director Soffici stars as Dr Enrique Jekyll, who quits his job in a Buenos Aires hospital to continue his hedonistic experiments with a drug which suppresses all moral and social inhibitions. However, he apparently transforms into a sympathetic Mr Hyde in this contemporary version of Robert Louis Stevenson's *Strange Case of Dr. Jekyll and Mr. Hyde.*
Remake: SHADA KALO (qv; 1953)
✦✧

EL HOMBRE Y LA BESTIA

Mexico, 1972. Dir: Julian Soler. With: Enrique Lizalde, Sasha Montenegro, Julian Pastor, Carlos López Moctezuma, Eduardo Noriega, Nancy Compare. Estudios America. Colour.
A doctor (Lizalde) creates a serum that changes him into a murderous big-nosed brute in this faithful, if talky, period version of the short novel by 'Louis Stevenson' (*sic*). After he strangles the nightclub singer who was attempting to blackmail him, and beats to death her male accomplice, the doctor cannot prevent himself from transforming. He kills his own manservant and attempts to force his fiancée to drink the potion before she finally shoots him to death.
Remake: DR. JEKYLL AND MR. HYDE (qv; 1973)
✦✦

O HOMEN LÔBO

Brazil, 1971. Dir: Raffaele Rossi. With: Raffaele Rossi, Claudia Cerine, Lino Braga, Juliana Pitelli, Toni Cardi, Osmano Cardoso. Pinheiro-Filmes. Colour.
A scientist (Braga) accepts the blame for the actions of his adopted son Roberto (Rossi), who becomes a werewolf at the onset of adolescence. A heavy-handed allegory of paternal responsibility, written, directed and edited by star Rossi. The title translates as 'The Wolf Man'.
✦

HOMUNCULUS

(aka DIE GEBURT DES HOMUNCULUS/DIE RACHE DES HOMUNCULUS)
Germany, 1916. Dir: Otto Rippert. With: Olaf Fönss, Friedrich Kuehne, Ernst Ludwig, Albert Paul, Lore Rueckert, Max Ruhbeck. Deutsche-Bioscop. B&W.
Six-part silent serial (401 minutes) in which Danish star Fönss portrays a 'perfect' man created by a scientist (Kuehne). When the creature discovers that he has no soul, he revenges himself on mankind as a tyrant, relentlessly pursued by his creator, until destroyed by a bolt of lightning. This was reissued in 1920 by Decla-Bioscop in a three-part condensed (275 minutes) version.
✦✦

HONEY, I SHRUNK THE KIDS:

Honey, Let's Trick or Treat
Canada/USA, 1998. Dir: Stuart Gordon. With: Peter Scolari, Barbara Alyn Woods, Hillary Tuck, Thomas Dekker, George Buza, Michael Berryman. Disney/ Plymouth Productions/St. Clare Entertainment/Buena Vista Television. Colour.
Hour-long syndicated comedy TV series (1996-) based on the 1989 hit film and characters created by Stuart Gordon, Brian Yuzna and co-executive producer Ed Naha. In this Halloween episode, Wayne Szalinski (Scolari) invents a device designed to scan images and project them as four-dimensional characters. When a book of urban legends is accidentally scanned, the neighbourhood is soon overrun with materialising myths. Diane Szalinski (Woods) dresses up as Xena and has a sword fight with a hook-handed killer (Berryman), while a 'haunted' house includes a fake vampire and werewolf, a real zombie, and Nick Szalinski (Dekker) wrapped up like a mummy. John Landis was another executive producer.
✦✦✧

Honey, The Garbage Took Us Out
Canada/USA, 1998. Dir: Scott McGinnis. With: Peter Scolari, Barbara Alyn Woods, Hillary Tuck, Thomas Dekker, Bruce Jarchow, Dylan Neal. Disney/Plymouth Productions/St. Clare Entertainment/Buena Vista Television. Colour.
Jealous of his son Nick's hero-worship of eco-warrior Roger Persimmons, Wayne attempts to solve the world's environmental problems by inventing RIP — Refuse Ingesting Protozoa. Unfortunately, after consuming three tons of toxic waste, RIP mutates and turns everyone who comes into contact with it into garbage-eating zombies. John Landis directed the third season premier (1999) involving time travel and a Soviet plot in the 1960s to turn American teenagers into zombies.
✦✦✧

HOORAY FOR HOLLYWOOD

USA, 1970. Dir: Grey Lockwood. With: Don Adams, Don Rickles, Charlton Heston. Youngstreet Productions/ Stacey Productions/ABC-TV. Colour.
Hour-long special featuring a comedy sketch in which co-producer/co-writer/star Adams (TV's *Get Smart* [1965-70], etc) plays Dr Frankenstein, who temporarily cures hunchback Egor (Rickles). Narrated by Heston.
✦✧

THE HORNY VAMPIRE

USA, circa 1970s. Dir: Sven Christian (Ray Dennis Steckler). With: Victor Alexander. Something Weird Video. Colour.
Only around forty minutes survives of this hardcore horror comedy in which two vampire Counts stalk around Las Vegas (often in full daylight!) searching for victims. One is successful while the other (Alexander) only gets to watch.
✦

THE HORRIBLE DR. HICHCOCK

(Orig: L'ORRIBILE SEGRETO DEL DR. HICHCOCK/ RAPTUS: THE SECRET OF DR. HICHCOCK. UK: THE TERROR OF DR. HICHCOCK/RAPTUS: THE TERROR OF DR. HICHCOCK)
Italy, 1962 (1964). Dir: Robert Hampton (Riccardo Freda). With: Barbara Steele, Robert Flemyng, Montgomery Glenn (Silvano Tranquili), Teresa Fitzgerald (Maria Teresa Vianello), Harriet White (Harriet White Medin), Spencer Williams. Panda Film/Sigma III Corporation. Colour.
A minor classic, shot in only sixteen days as a bet by Freda. Set in London in 1885, English actor Flemyng plays Dr Bernard Hichcock who is only sexually aroused by necrophilia. Having accidentally killed his first wife Margaretha (Fitzgerald) with an overdose of drugs, his new wife Cynthia (Steele) is menaced by her ghostly predecessor, who has returned from the grave seeking blood. Director Freda uses the colour photography to create some wonderful images, and Steele has never looked better as the put-upon heroine. Scenes of Flemyng fondling dead female bodies were cut from the film's original release in both American and British prints (which are significantly different).
Sequel: THE GHOST (1963)
✦✦✦✧

HORRIBLE HORROR

USA, 1986. Dir: David Bergman. With: Zacherley (John Zacherle). Movietime/Bergman-Harris/Goodtimes Home Video. Colour/B&W.

Value-for-money video collection of trailers, out-takes and genre clips, presented by manic 1950s TV horror host Zacherley from his movie dungeon. This includes rare footage of Karloff and Lugosi, clips and trailers for *The Ape Man* (1943), *Carnival of Souls* (1962), *King of the Zombies* (1941), *Monster on the Campus* (1958), *Night of the Living Dead* (1968) and TV's *Tales of Frankenstein* (1958), plus, most interesting of all, several out-takes from (Abbott and Costello) *Meet Frankenstein* (1948). The 1999 video *Zacherle Archives* includes footage from four of the New York horror host's TV shows (1958-59).

✦✦✦

HORRIBLE HYDE

USA, 1915. Dir: Jerold T. Hevener. With: Jerold T. Hevener, Eva Bell. Lubin. B&W.

Hevener both directs and stars as an actor who poses as Mr Hyde to scare people in this silent comedy short, loosely suggested by Robert Louis Stevenson's story.

✦

THE HORRIBLE SEXY VAMPIRE

(Orig: EL VAMPIRO DE LA AUTOPISTA)

Spain, 1970 (1973). Dir: Jim Delavena (Arthur Davidson/José Luis Madrid). With: Waldemar Wohfahrt (Wolfgang Wohlfahrt), Patricia Loran, Barta Barry, Luis Iduñi, Adela Tauler, Joe Camroy (Anastasio Campoy). Cinefilms/Delta Films/Paragon. Colour.

Wohfahrt stars as Count Adolf Oblensky, the last of the von Winninger family, who must spend the night with his lover Marianne (Loran) in the cursed ancestral castle to claim his inheritance. They are haunted by his ancestor, the invisible vampire Baron von Winninger, who likes to strangle his naked victims.

✦

HORROR EXPRESS

(Orig: PANICO EN EL TRANSIBERIANO)

Spain/UK, 1972. Dir: Gene (Eugenio) Martin. With: Christopher Lee, Peter Cushing, Telly Savalas, Alberto de Mendoza, Silvia Tortosa, Julio Peña. Grande Films/Bemar. Colour.

Enjoyable horror/science fiction thriller, apparently only made because the producer owned the model train from *Nicholas and Alexandra* (1971). Set in the early twentieth century, arrogant anthropologist Sir Alexander Saxton (Lee) returns with an archaeological specimen of early man he has discovered in the icy mountains of China. However, after his find is loaded upon the Trans-Siberian Express, it turns out that the creature is possessed by a million year-old alien who absorbs brains and possesses bodies. While Saxton teams up with old rival Dr Wells (Cushing), the alien works its way through the other passengers: a Rasputin-like monk (de Mendoza), a Russian count (Jorge Rigaud) and his beautiful wife (Tortosa), a police captain (Peña) and Savalas in a lively cameo as a mad Cossack. The glowing-eyed alien is used effectively, and the exciting climax features a train full of blank-eyed zombies.

✦✦✦

HORROR HEAVEN

West Germany, 1984. Dir: Jörg Buttgereit. With: Daktari Lorenz, Peter Pynthetic, Johannes Willes, Arnold Reisse, Hagen Liebing, Jörg Buttgereit. J.B. Films. Colour.

Twenty-five minute compilation of amateur shorts, shot on 8mm by the director of *Nekromantik* (1987), which include a mummy and Godzilla.

✦

HORROR HIGH

(aka TWISTED BRAIN)

USA, 1974. Dir: Larry N. Stouffer. With: Pat Cardi, Austin Stoker, Rosie Holotik, John Niland, Joye Hash, 'Mean' Joe Greene. Crown International. Colour.

Working as a high school laboratory assistant, teenage nerd Vernon Potts (Cardi), known as 'the Creeper' to his class-mates, discovers a formula that changes him into a hairy-faced, bow-legged monster. He uses his new-found strength to kill his enemies until the police (all played by American pro-football players) blast him to death with a shotgun. In the opening scene, the students in an English class are watching a version of Stevenson's *Dr. Jekyll and Mr. Hyde* (heard off-screen). Filmed on 16mm.

✦

HORROR HOSPITAL

(USA: aka COMPUTER KILLERS/DOCTOR BLOODBATH)

UK, 1973. Dir: Antony Balch. With: Michael Gough, Robin Askwith, Vanessa Shaw, Ellen Pollock, Skip Martin, Dennis Price. Noteworthy Films. Colour.

Amateurish horror movie co-scripted and directed by independent distributor Balch, a former collaborator with William S. Burroughs. Songwriter Jason Jones (Askwith) and Judy Peters (the awful Shaw) stay at a health hotel run by the horribly disfigured Dr Storm (Gough), who is experimenting with brain operations and electronically-controlled zombies. With Martin as Frederick, a rebellious dwarf, and guest star Price as Mr Pollack, a camp travel agent for Hairy Holidays. Produced by Richard Gordon and released as *Frankenstein's Horror-Klinik* in Germany and *La Griffe de Frankenstein* in France.

✦

THE HORROR OF FRANKENSTEIN

UK, 1970. Dir: Jimmy Sangster. With: Ralph Bates, Kate O'Mara, Veronica Carlson, Dennis Price, Graham James, Bernard Archard. Hammer Films/EMI Film Productions. Colour.

Co-scripted, produced and directed by Sangster, this ill-advised comedy remake of *The Curse of Frankenstein* (1957) has nothing to do with Hammer's series starring Peter Cushing. Bates is a totally unsympathetic Victor Frankenstein who creates a Monster (six-foot, seven-inch David Prowse) that is a mindless killer. With Price as a fawning grave robber who gets his wife (Joan Rice) to do all the digging and Jon Finch as a police inspector.

Remake: LADY FRANKENSTEIN (qv; 1971)

✦✦

THE HORROR OF IT ALL

UK, 1963. Dir: Terence Fisher. With: Pat Boone, Erica Rogers, Dennis Price, Andree Melly, Valentine Dyall, Jack Bligh. Lippert/Twentieth Century-Fox. B&W.

Clean-cut crooner Boone (who sings the dreadful title song) stars in this horror comedy as American salesman Jack Robinson, who falls in love with plump Cynthia Marley (Rogers). He is invited back to her ancestral old dark house to meet the rest of the relatives, who include her undead-looking sister Natalia (Melly, who played a real vampire in *The Brides of Dracula* [1960]), crazy actor Cornwallis (Price), Muldoon the madman locked in the basement (Archie Duncan) and Reginald Marley (Dyall), the sepulchral head of the family. Scripted by horror author Ray Russell, this was similar to William Castle's *The Old Dark House* (1962) and is probably director Fisher's worst film. It wasn't released in Britain for three years.

✦

THE HORROR OF IT ALL

USA, 1983. Dir: Gene Feldman. With: Rouben Mamoulian, Roger Corman, John Carradine, Robert Bloch, Curtis Harrington, Gloria Stuart. Wombat Productions/PBS-TV. Colour/B&W.

Forty-five minute documentary about the fascination of horror films, written, co-produced and directed by Feldman and narrated by José Ferrer. This includes fascinating interviews with directors Mamoulian, Corman and Harrington; producer Herman Cohen; actors Carradine, Stuart and Dana Andrews; and writer Bloch. With behind-the-scenes footage at New World (including shots of future directors Tony Randell and Carl Buechler), and the Haunted Mansion at Long Beach, New Jersey. Universal films are only illustrated with stills, but there are some great clips from *The Bat Whispers* (1930), *Black Sunday* (1960), *Bluebeard* (1944), *The Body Snatcher* (1945), *The Cabinet of Dr. Caligari* (1919), *The Cat and the Canary*

(1927), *Curse of the Demon* (1957), *Dementia 13* (1963), *Dr Jekyll and Mr Hyde* (1920 and 1931 versions), *Ghidrah the Three-Headed Monster* (1964), *The Golem* (1920), *Horror of Dracula* (1958), *King Kong* (1933), *The Mad Monster* (1942), *Metropolis* (1926), *Nosferatu* (1922), *The Phantom of the Opera* (1925), *Svengali* (1931), *The Vampire Bat* (1933) and *White Zombie* (1932). Forrest J Ackerman, Samuel Z. Arkoff, Martine Beswicke and Alex and Richard Gordon are among those thanked in the credits.
✦✦✦✧

THE HORROR OF PARTY BEACH

USA, 1964. Dir: Del Tenney. With: John Scott, Alice Lyon, Allan Laural, Eulabelle Moore, Marilyn Clarke, Agustin Mayor. Iselin-Tenney/Twentieth Century-Fox. B&W.

Teen horror movie with rock-bottom production values, filmed over two weeks in Stamford, Connecticut, by two drive-in theatre owners (under the shooting title *Invasion of the Zombies*). While a group of overaged teenagers swing to the music of the Del-Aires ('You're Not a Summer Love', 'The Zombie Stomp', etc), radioactive waste dumped in the ocean turns old skeletons into silly-looking amphibian sea creatures (stunt man Robin Boston Barron in a couple of monster suits). They go on the rampage, attacking the members of a slumber party, local drunks and girls out for kicks, until a scientist destroys them with sodium. Billed as 'The first horror monster musical!', it was co-billed with Tenney's equally bad *The Curse of the Living Corpse* (1964). A photo-strip magazine appeared from Warren Publishing the same year.
✦

HORROR OF THE BLOOD MONSTERS

(aka CREATURES OF THE PREHISTORIC PLANET/ CREATURES OF THE RED PLANET/THE FLESH CREATURES/FLESH CREATURES OF THE RED PLANET/ HORROR CREATURES OF THE PREHISTORIC PLANET/ SPACE MISSION OF THE LOST PLANET/VAMPIRE MEN OF THE LOST PLANET)

USA, 1970 (1972). Dir: Al Adamson. With: John Carradine, Robert Dix, Vicki Volante, Joey Benson, Jennifer Bishop, Bruce Powers. Independent-International. Colour.

Another mess from producer/director Adamson. When Earth is invaded by alien vampires (not seen), testy scientist Dr Rynning (Carradine) leads a low-budget space mission to a new galaxy, where they land on a planet poisoned by 'chromatic radiation'. This is just a cheap explanation for Adamson's use of colour-tinted dinosaur footage from *One Million B.C.* (1940), *Unknown Island* (1948) and a black and white Filipino movie with snake men, bat demons and claw creatures. They even advertised the process as 'Spectrum X'! With tacky-looking special effects created by David L. Hewitt and camerawork by William (Vilmos) Zsigmond.
✦

HORROR OF THE ZOMBIES

(Orig: EL BUQUE MALDITO. USA: aka THE CURSED SHIP)

Spain, 1974. Dir: Amando de Ossorio. With: Maria Perschy, Jack Taylor (George Brown Randall/Grek Martin), Barbara Rey, Carl Leonard (Carlos Lemos), Manuel de Blas, Blanca Estrada. Ancla Century Films/ Belen Films/Independent-International. Colour.

A follow-up to *Return of the Evil Dead* (1973), this third entry in Ossorio's Blind Dead series is all at sea. A boat full of bikini-clad fashion models and their male companions encounter a strange ship in the fog. When they investigate, they are attacked by the mummified, bloodlusting Templarios Knights.

Sequel: NIGHT OF THE SEAGULLS (qv; 1975)
✦✧

HORROR RISES FROM THE TOMB

(Orig: EL ESPANTO SURGE DE LA TUMBA)

Spain, 1972. Dir: Carlos Aured (Carlos A. Alonso). With: Paul Naschy (Jacinto Molina), Vic Winner (Victor Alcazar), Emma Cohen, Helga Liné (Helga Lina Stern), Cristina Suriani, Betsabe Ruiz. Profilmes/Jeme Films/ Avco Embassy. Colour.

Scripted by Naschy under his real name. Two fifteenth century sorcerers (Naschy and Suriani) are brought back from the dead and reunited with their severed heads. They tear the hearts out of their hypnotised victims, and the corpses then return as creepy looking zombies. Naschy portrays both the evil knight, Alaric de Marnac, and his modern descendant.

Sequel: LATIDOS DE PANICO (qv; 1983)
✦✧

HORRORITUAL

USA, 1972. With: Barry Atwater. Warner Bros. Colour.

Three minute promotional film made to be shown with the American release of *Dracula A.D. 1972* (1972). Atwater (from *The Night Stalker* [1971], etc) stars as a vampire in this comedy short. From his coffin he invites members of the audience to repeat the oath to 'call back Dracula' and become honorary members of the Count Dracula Society. Free cards were given away at the box office reading 'I've been to a Horroritual with Dracula'.
✦

THE HORROR SHOW

USA, 1979. Dir: Richard Schickel. With: Anthony Perkins, Boris Karloff, Bela Lugosi, Charles Laughton, Claude Rains, Lon Chaney Sr. Universal. Colour/B&W.

Made-for-TV documentary celebrating 'sixty magical years of movie monsters' from Universal studios. Hosted by Perkins and including clips of all the above plus Lon Chaney Jr, John Barrymore, Vincent Price, Christopher Lee, Bette Davis, Janet Leigh, Lee Remick, Robert Shaw, Charlton Heston and many others from *Dracula* (1931), *Frankenstein* (1931), *Phantom of the Opera* (1943), *Psycho* (1960), etc. Produced, written and directed by Schickel.
✦✦

HORRORS OF THE BLACK MUSEUM

UK, 1959. Dir: Arthur Crabtree. With: Michael Gough, June Cunningham, Graham Curnow, Shirley Ann Field, Geoffrey Keen, Gerald Andersen. Anglo Amalgamated. Colour.

In this wonderfully sleazy thriller, Gough plays arrogant crime author Edmond Bancroft, who kills his female victims in a variety of gruesome ways while he taunts the police with his newspaper articles about the murders. Bancroft also turns his assistant into a monstrous Jekyll and Hyde-type killer with a serum he creates in his basement wax museum. Directed by the workmanlike Crabtree (*Fiend Without a Face* [1958], etc) and produced by the legendary Herman Cohen, this includes some inventive murder instruments (spiked binoculars, ice tongs, a guillotine/bed) and a climax set in a funfair. Filmed in CinemaScope, and originally released in America in 'HypnoVista', which referred to a tagged-on thirteen minute prologue about hypnotism.
✦✦✧

THE HORROR STAR

(aka FRIGHTMARE/UPON A FRIGHTMARE)

USA, 1981. Dir: Norman Thaddeus (Vane). With: Ferdinand (Ferdy) Mayne, Luca Bercovici, Jennifer Starret, Nita Talbot, Barbara Pilavin, Leon Askin. Screenwriters Production Co/VFO. Colour.

Enjoyable low-budget horror thriller. Mayne has fun with the role of Conrad Ragzoff, a horror film star who returns from the dead as a murderous zombie to revenge himself on the teenage members of The Horror Film Society, who stole his body. Dressed in his vampire cloak, Ragzoff stalks around an old mansion using his supernatural mental powers to kill off the kids (who include a young Jeffrey Combs). The horror movie memorabilia was supplied by Forrest J Ackerman.
✦✦

HORROR STORY

Spain, 1972. Dir: Manuel Esteba. With: Manuel Calatrava, Francisco Calatrava, Silvia Solar, Marta May, Rojo Fernando Ulloa, Gustavo Re. Producciones Cinematográficas Cire. Colour.

Obscure Spanish vampire comedy which apparently involves twins.
✦

HOTEL

India, 1981. Dir: Tulsi Ramsay and Shyam Ramsay. Kiran Ramsay. Colour.

When a group of unscrupulous businessmen build a hotel on the site of an old Catholic graveyard, they find themselves stalked by silent shrouded zombies, led by the corpse of an old priest, who have returned from the dead seeking revenge.

✦✧

THE HOT GIRLS

UK, 1974. Dir John Lindsay and Laurence Barnett. With: Tim Blackstone, Jan Adair, Janet Adler, Patsy Allen, Linda Benson, Eva Chatt (Ava Cadell). Baskform/New Realm. Colour.

Forty minute sexploitation docu-drama in which The Rag Dolls Agency sends its nude models out to a variety of jobs. These include Linda Remington, who poses as a vampire's victim for the cover of a book; Danish-born actress Helli Louise, who is interviewed by David McGillivray on the set of her latest film, *Lust to Kill*; and Janet Marsden having beer sprayed over her body for an advertisement. Co-director Lindsay was subsequently prosecuted (unsuccessfully) for producing obscene films.

✦

HOT LOVE

West Germany, 1987. Dir: Jörg Buttgereit. With: With: Daktari Lorenz, Marion Koob, Jörg Buttgereit, Franz Rodenkirchen, Norbert Hahnel, Simone Schulz. J.B. Films. Colour.

Twenty-six minute amateur film about a man who commits suicide and then returns from the dead seeking revenge against his ex-girlfriend. Shot on 8mm by the director of *Nekromantik* (1987).

✦

HOT WAX ZOMBIES ON WHEELS

USA, 1998. Dir: Michael Roush. With: Jill Miller, John Riann, N.A. Stewart, Randall St. George, John Rawling, Lynne Hatcher. Wax Rhapsodic. Colour.

Independent low-budget comedy horror film.

✦

JOHN HOUGH
[b 1941]

British director who began his career in television with *The Avengers* (1961-69) before concluding Hammer's 'Karnstein Trilogy' with *Twins of Evil* (1971). Following *The Legend of Hell House* (1973), he made several uneven films in America and returned to Britain to helm *Biggles* (1985), Peter Cushing's final movie.

qv: *Howling IV The Original Nightmare* (1988).

DON HOUGHTON
[1933-1991]

French-born British screenwriter, the son of novelist George W. Houghton. He began his career writing for television before scripting the final three films in Hammer's Dracula series and becoming the story editor for TV's *Hammer House of Mystery and Suspense* (1984-85). He also scripted the dialogue for two Hammer records, *Dracula* and *The Legend of the 7 Golden Vampires*.

qv: *Dracula A.D. 1972* (1972); *The Legend of the 7 Golden Vampires* (1974); *The Satanic Rites of Dracula* (1973).

HOUSE

(Orig: IE).

Japan, 1977. Dir: Nobuhiko Obayashi. With: Kimiko Ikegami, Kumiko Oba, Ai Matsubara, Miki Jinbo, Mieko Sato, Masayo Miyako. Toho. Colour.

The feature début by writer/director/producer Obayashi, who was also responsible for the special effects. Oshare and her school friends spend the summer in her aunt's house in the forest, which is filled with bizarre clocks and strange toys. During a horrific night, the house reveals its evil nature and consumes everyone. In one scene, a girl sees her reflection in a mirror transform into a fanged vampire before she bursts into flames.

✦✦

HOUSE

USA, 1985. Dir: Steve Miner. With: William Katt, George Wendt, Richard Moll, Kay Lenz, Mary Stavin, Michael Ensign. Sean Cunningham Films/New World Pictures. Colour.

First and best in an unrelated series of *House* movies. When horror author Roger Cobb (Katt) moves into his aunt's old mansion after she hangs herself, he's soon seeing her ghost and other strange creatures that populate a bedroom cupboard. He finally discovers a doorway to Hell through the bathroom cabinet and rescues his missing son from the rotting corpse of Big Ben (the excellent Moll), a Vietnam war buddy he left behind to die. This starts off as an effective haunted house chiller, but the film-makers got cold feet halfway through, adding a couple of pointless songs, some unnecessary comedy and not a lot of plot sense. Despite this, Katt and Wendt (as a nosy neighbour) are likeable, and the various monsters are quite effective. With Felix Silla. Produced by Sean S. Cunningham.

✦✦✧

THE HOUSE BY THE CEMETERY

(Orig: QUELLA VILLA ACCANTO AL CIMITERO/ FREUDSTEIN)

Italy/USA, 1982. Dir: Lucio Fulci. With: Katherine (Catriona) MacColl, Paolo Malco, Dagmar Lassander, Anja Pieroni, Giovanni Frezza, Silvia Collatina. Fulvia Film. Colour.

Over-the-top Gothic horrors from co-writer/director Fulci. Following the death of the previous occupant, academic researcher Norman Boyle (Malco), his wife Lucy (MacColl) and their young son Bob (Frezza) move into a haunted house in the small town of New Whitby, near Boston. Still alive in the cellar is a radical nineteenth century doctor, Freudstein (Giovanni de Nari), his decaying flesh kept alive by the transplanted bodies of his victims. The murders are particularly nasty, but the atmospheric story is muddled by a subplot involving the ghost of a young girl.

✦✦✧

HOUSE OF CLOCKS

(Orig: LA CASA DEL TEMPO)

Italy, 1989. Dir: Lucio Fulci. With: Paolo Bernardi, Carla Cassola, Al Cliver (Pier Luigi Conti), Francesca DeRose, Karina Huff, Keith Van Hoven. Dania/Reteitalia. Colour.

TV movie directed by Fulci for the *House of Doom* series, in which a murdered elderly couple return from the dead seeking revenge.

✦✧

HOUSE OF DARK SHADOWS

USA, 1970. Dir: Dan Curtis. With: Jonathan Frid, Grayson Hall, Joan Bennett, Kathryn Leigh Scott, Roger Davis, Nancy Barrett. Metro-Goldwyn-Mayer/Dan Curtis. Colour.

Feature version of the popular *Dark Shadows* (1966-71) daytime TV serial. Many of the original cast repeat their roles although, in this version, Barnabas Collins (Frid) is an evil vampire preying on the Collins family. Accidentally freed from his coffin by Willie Loomis (John Karlen), the 150 year-old member of the undead is convinced that his long lost love has been reincarnated in Maggie Evans (Scott). Hall plays Doctor Julia Hoffman who believes vampirism is a curable disease. In the end, Barnabas is dispatched with a crossbow bolt. When he ages, the reason he looks just like Dustin Hoffman in *Little Big Man* (1970) is because Dick Smith was responsible for both make-ups. Paperback Library published the novelisation by Marilyn Ross (William Edward Daniel Ross).

Sequel: NIGHT OF DARK SHADOWS (1971)

✦✦✧

HOUSE OF DRACULA

USÀ, 1945. Dir: Erle C. Kenton. With: Lon Chaney, Martha O'Driscoll, John Carradine, Lionel Atwill, Onslow Stevens, Glenn Strange. Universal. B&W.

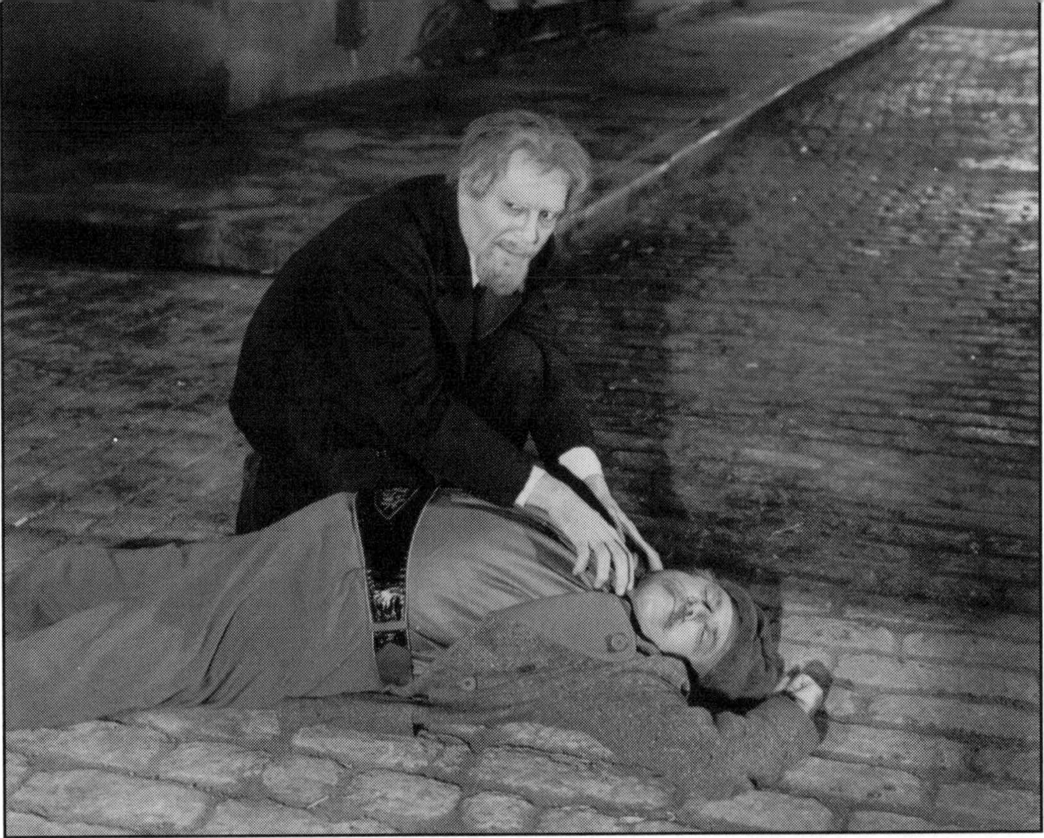

Onslow Stevens is infected with the Count's bloodlust in House of Dracula *(1945).*

This uninspired sequel to *House of Frankenstein* (1944) was originally announced as *The Wolf Man vs. Dracula* (to be produced and directed by Ford Beebe), although the two characters never actually meet in the final version. Dr Franz Edelmann (Stevens) attempts to cure the monsters with the aid of his scientifically-created mould! But Carradine's suave Count Dracula decides he enjoys being a vampire and turns Edelmann into one as well. The Jekyll and Hyde-like mad doctor tries to revive the Frankenstein Monster (Strange, who is given little to do) during the blazing climax (lifted from *The Ghost of Frankenstein* [1942]), while Lawrence Talbot (Chaney Jr) returns, with no attempt to explain how he survived a fatal shooting in the previous film, and is finally 'cured' after changing into the Wolf Man only once. Jane Adams portrays beautiful hunchbacked nurse Nina, Atwill turns up as another police inspector, Ludwig Stossel is a victim of Edelmann's transformation and Skelton Knaggs plays an angry villager. Worth catching for John P. Fulton's wonderful man-into-bat transformations. Clips from *Bride of Frankenstein* (1935) turn up in a nightmare sequence. The original trailer includes a shot of Strange's Frankenstein Monster not found in the final film and an outtake of Lon Chaney Jr from *The Ghost of Frankenstein* (1942). MagicImage published the script in 1993.
Sequel: MEET FRANKENSTEIN (qv; 1948)
✦✦✧

HOUSE OF DRACULA'S DAUGHTER

USA, 1973. Dir: Gordon Hessler. With: John Carradine, Peter Lorre Jr (Eugene Weingand), David Carradine, Lorraine Day, Broderick Crawford. Universal Entertainment. Colour.
This was either never made or never completed! The interesting cast supposedly includes Weingand, who was not related to Peter Lorre and was apparently taken to court for using the name illegally in a number of films.
✦

HOUSE OF FRANKENSTEIN

USA, 1944. Dir: Erle C. Kenton. With: Boris Karloff, Lon Chaney, John Carradine, J. Carrol Naish, Anne Gwynne, Lionel Atwill. Universal. B&W.

Entertaining sequel to *Frankenstein Meets the Wolf Man* (1943), based on a story by Curt Siodmak. Karloff's mad Dr Gustav Niemann (the brother of a former assistant to the original Dr Frankenstein) and Daniel the homicidal hunchback (Naish) escape from a prison for the criminally insane and take over a travelling carnival. Pursued by Atwill's police Inspector Arnz, they revive 'Baron Latos' (Carradine as Count Dracula, complete with top hat) before arriving at Castle Frankenstein, where they discover the Wolf Man (Chaney Jr as Lawrence Talbot, still trying to find a cure) and the Frankenstein Monster (Glenn Strange, who isn't given much to do, despite being coached in the role by Karloff). In the end, the villagers storm the castle and put a stop to it all while the Monster drags Niemann into the quicksands. Announced as *Chamber of Horrors* and *The Devil's Brood*, it was originally going to include Universal's Mummy as well. With brief appearances by George Zucco, Elena Verdugo, Sig Ruman, Frank Reicher and Brandon Hurst. The script was published as part of Philip J. Riley's Universal series for MagicImage Filmbooks in 1991.
Sequel: HOUSE OF DRACULA (qv; 1945)
Remake: HOUSE OF FRANKENSTEIN (qv; 1997)
✦✦✦

HOUSE OF FRANKENSTEIN

(aka HOUSE OF FRANKENSTEIN 1997)
USA, 1997. Dir: Peter Werner. With: Adrian Pasdar, Greg Wise, Teri Polo, C.C.H. Pounder, Miguel Sandoval, Peter Crombie. Universal Television Entertainment/Big Productions/Michael R. Joyce Productions/NBC-TV. Colour.
A series of murders in Los Angeles, attributed by the media to 'The Midnight Raptor', are actually the work of master vampire Crispian Grimes (Wise) and his werewolf assistant, Klaus. With the help of a scientist, they recover the frozen body of Frankenstein's sympathetic Creature (Crombie, who gives the only decent performance) for the opening of their nightclub, The House of Frankenstein. But when the

Monster escapes onto the streets and Grace (Polo), the woman he's just started dating, is transformed into another werewolf, Los Angeles homicide detective Vernon Coyle (Pasdar) is as confused as the viewer. Despite the impressive special make-up effects created by Peter Cannom (with Edward French and others), this three hour mini-series, shown in two parts, never overcomes the clichéd script, poor production values and terrible performances. With Richard Libertini. Titled *House of Frankenstein 1997* on the end credits.

✦

HOUSE OF HAMMER

USA, 1986. Sinister Cinema. Colour.

Two hour-long volumes are available on video containing classic Hammer trailers from the 1950s to the 1970s.

✦✦✧

HOUSE OF HAMMER

USA, 1987. SF Rush Video/Trailers on Tape. Colour.

This fourth video compilation in the hour-long *Horror/Sci-Fi* series contains excellent 35mm transfers of many of Hammer's classic trailers, along with narration on a second audio channel.

✦✦✦

THE HOUSE OF SEVEN CORPSES

USA, 1973. Dir: Paul Harrison. With: John Ireland, Faith Domergue, John Carradine, Carole (Carol) Wells, Jerry Strickler, Charles Macaulay. Television Corporation of America/International Amusement. Colour.

Not much happens until the final twenty-five minutes of this low-budget movie, filmed in Utah. While making a horror movie in an old house where seven family members mysteriously died, cast and crew are killed off by a zombie (Wells Bond) who has the confusing ability to change his appearance (Strickler) and apparently be in two places at the same time. The ghoul's first victim is Carradine, who plays creepy caretaker, Edgar Price. The ending doesn't make any sense.

✦✦

HOUSE OF THE BLACK DEATH

(aka BLOOD OF THE MAN-DEVIL)

USA, 1966 (1975). Dir: Harold Daniels (and Jerry Warren). With: Lon Chaney, John Carradine, Andrea King, Tom Drake, Delores Faith, Sabrina. Taurus Films. B&W.

Incomprehensible mess about rival warlocks, the evil devil-horned Belial De Sade (Chaney Jr) and his benign brother Andre (Carradine), who never gets out of bed. During the climax, hero Paul De Sade (Drake) turns into an ugly werewolf. Filmed in 1965 for $70,000 under the titles *Night of the Beast* and *The Widderburn Horror* (based on the novel of the same name by Lora Crozetti), an uncredited Warren was apparently called in to try and make some sense of it all! Reginald Le Borg was second unit director. With Katherine Victor and plenty of gratuitous belly-dancing.

✦

HOUSE OF THE LIVING DEAD

(Orig: SKADUWEES OOR BRUGPLAAS. USA: DOCTOR MANIAC)

South Africa, 1973. Dir: Ray Austin. With: Mark Burns, Shirley Ann Field, David Oxley, Margaret Inglis, Dia Sydow, Lynne Maree. Associated Film Producers/ Worldwide. Colour.

A nineteenth century mad scientist (Burns) experiments on his family. In the end, he is driven to his death by the stolen souls of his victims when they escape their containers.

✦

HOUSE ON BARE MOUNTAIN

USA, 1962. Dir: R.L. (Lee) Frost. With: Bob Cresse, Laine Carlin, Leticia Cooper, Laura Eden, Connie Hudson, Dan Hyland. B and M Production/Olympic International Films. Colour.

Filmed in 'Raw Color and SinScope', the ads also boasted 'Twenty

Boris Karloff threatens John Carradine in House of Frankenstein *(1944).*

Terrified Teen Lovelies Tastefully Unattired'. 'Lovable' Bob Cresse stars in drag (and also narrates) as a bootlegger who runs Granny Good's School for Good Girls. He keeps his underpaid assistant Krakow, a seven-foot tall Wolfman ('Abe Greyhound' [Hugh Cannon]), in the cellar. Meanwhile, a fake Frankenstein Monster ('Percy Frankenstein' [Warren Ames]), Dracula ('Doris Dracula' [Jeffrey Smithers]), Phantom of the Opera and another werewolf do the twist at a topless costume ball. The monster make-ups were created by Harry Thomas. This cost $72,000 and was one of the most expensive adult movies made at the time.
✦

THE HOUSE ON SKULL MOUNTAIN

USA, 1974. Dir: Ron(ald) Honthaner. With: Victor French, Janee Michelle, Jean Durand, Mike Evans, Ella Woods, Lloyd Nelson. Chocolate Chip/Pinto/Film Fund Enterprises/Twentieth Century-Fox. Colour.
When four relatives gather in the old Christophe mansion perched atop Skull Mountain to hear the reading of a will, the family servant, Thomas Petoine (Durand), uses his Haitian voodoo powers to start killing off the descendants. Petoine eventually raises the elderly Pauline Christophe (Mary J. Todd McKenzie) from the grave as a zombie, before crashing through a window to his death. Filmed in Atlanta, this includes Georgia Senator Leroy Johnson as the lawyer who reads the will.
✦✧

THE HOUSE ON TOMBSTONE HILL

(aka THE DEAD COME HOME/DEAD DUDES IN THE HOUSE)
USA, 1988. Dir: James Riffel. With: Mark Zobain, Victor Verhaeghe, Sarah Newhouse, Douglas F. Gibson, John Cerna, Naomi Kooker. October Films/Troma/AIP Home Video. Colour.
A group of friends are trapped in an isolated old mansion by the ghost of an old woman (Gibson) who starts slashing them to death with sharp objects. Her victims then return as zombies. Low-budget thrills, filmed on 16mm in Cherry Valley, New York, by twenty-eight year-old NYU graduate Riffel. Ed French created the special make-up effects.
✦

THE HOUSE THAT DRIPPED BLOOD

UK, 1970. Dir: Peter Duffell. With: Christopher Lee, Peter Cushing, Nyree Dawn Porter, Denholm Elliott, Jon Pertwee, Ingrid Pitt. Amicus. Colour.
Robert Bloch scripted four of his stories for this episodic horror thriller. After renting an old house in the country, Paul Henderson (Pertwee), one of Britain's foremost horror stars, disappears. Mr Stoker, an estate agent, relates the tragic history of the house to the investigating police inspector... In the tongue-in-cheek fourth tale ('The Cloak', previously adapted by Bloch for TV's *Alfred Hitchcock Presents* [1960]), Pertwee's unpleasant character buys an old cloak, but when his co-star Carla (Pitt) wears it she becomes a real vampire and he ends up as her victim. The other stories (about a fictional character coming to life ['Method for Murder'], a creepy wax museum ['Waxworks'] and a voodoo doll ['Sweets to the Sweet']) are also pretty good.
✦✦✦

HOUSE II THE SECOND STORY

USA, 1987. Dir: Ethan Wiley. With: Arye Gross, Jonathan Stark, Royal Dano, Lar Park Lincoln, John Ratzenberger, Dean Cleverdon. New World Pictures. Colour.
Originally subtitled *The Second Storey*, this incomprehensible follow-up to *House* (1985) has absolutely nothing to do with the earlier movie. Apparently beset with narrative and production problems (George Wendt was originally set to return from the first film), this silly horror/comedy has Dano and Cleverdon as 170 year-old zombie cowboys Gramps and Slim, searching for a magical Aztec crystal skull. Pretty soon there are timewarps turning up all over the place, and although the 'lovable' monsters are terrible, Mark Sullivan animates some excellent stop-motion dinosaurs. Two more unrelated *House* movies followed.
✦✧

THE HOWLING

USA/Canada, 1980. Dir: Joe Dante. With: Dee Wallace, Patrick Macnee, Dennis Dugan, Christopher Stone, Belinda Balaski, Kevin McCarthy. Avco Embassy Pictures/International Film Investors/Wescom Productions. Colour.
Director Dante and scriptwriters John Sayles and Terence H. Winkless turn Gary Brandner's pulp werewolf novel into a low-budget horror film buff's dream. After TV newscaster Karen White (Wallace) undergoes a terrifying ordeal while acting as a decoy to trap a sex killer known as Eddie (Robert Picardo), she consults psychoanalyst Dr George Waggner (Macnee) about her recurring nightmares. However, she soon learns that Waggner's retreat, The Colony, is a haven for a pack of modern-day werewolves (excellent make-up effects by Rob Bottin, with a little help from Rick Baker and Greg Cannom). This features clips from *The Wolf Man* (1941) and cameos by John Carradine (as werewolf Erle Kenton!), Slim Pickens, Kenneth Tobey, Roger Corman, Forrest J Ackerman, and Dick Miller as Walter Paisley. Many of the characters are named after the directors and producers of werewolf movies. Unfortunately, David Allen's stop-motion werewolves were left on the cutting room floor.
Sequel: HOWLING II STIRBA — WEREWOLF BITCH (qv; 1984)
✦✦✦✦✧

HOWLING V THE REBIRTH

Hungary/UK/USA, 1989. Dir: Neal Sundström. With: Philip Davis, Victoria Catlin, Elizabeth Shé, Ben Cole, William Shockley, Mary Stavin. Howling Productions/Allied Vision/Lane Pringle Productions/Vestron Video International/International Video. Colour.
A tired variation on Agatha Christie's *Ten Little Indians* and *The Beast Must Die* (1974) as Count Istvan (Davis) invites a group of celebrities to the opening of his family's cursed castle after five centuries. While most of the cast spend their time wandering around dark corridors, a briefly-seen werewolf begins killing them off one-by-one. Co-writer/producer Clive Turner appears in a cameo role as Ray.
Sequel: HOWLING VI THE FREAKS (qv; 1990)
✦✧

HOWLING IV THE ORIGINAL NIGHTMARE

South Africa/UK, 1988. Dir: John Hough. With: Romy Windsor, Michael T. Weiss, Antony Hamilton, Susanne Severeid, Lamya Derval, Norman Anstey. Filmtrax/Allied Vision. Colour.
Supposedly based on the novels *The Howling I, II* and *III* by Gary Brandner, this fourth in the direct-to-video series stars Windsor as Marie, a writer trapped in a small town full of werewolves (make-up effects by Steve Johnson). Although slightly better than the previous two sequels, that's not really saying much, and director Hough turns in a workmanlike job. In the end, all the werewolves are burned to death in an ancient bell tower. Produced by the infamous Harry Alan Towers.
Sequel: HOWLING V THE REBIRTH (qv; 1989)
✦✧

THE HOWLING NEW MOON RISING

(Orig: HOWLING VII MYSTERY WOMAN)
USA/UK, 1994 (1995). Dir: Clive Turner (and Roger Nall). With: Clive Turner, John Ramsden, John Huff, Elizabeth Shé, Jaqueline Armitage, Romy Walthall. Allied Vision/Allied Entertainment/New Line Home Video. Colour.
Seventh and probably worst entry yet in the low-budget, direct-to-video series, which started so promisingly back in 1980. Editor/accountant/post-production supervisor/writer/producer/director/star Turner plays Ted Smith, a drifter who arrives in the desert community of Pioneer Town. He begins working at the local bar, while a policeman and a priest investigate a number of killings which appear to have been committed by a werewolf. In an attempt to make some sense of the disparate chronology, this uses numerous clips (via flashbacks) from *Howling IV The Original Nightmare* (1988) and *Howling V The Rebirth* (1989). A totally amateurish production, filled with stupid jokes, gratuitous country and western music and non-actors who live in the real-life town built by Roy Rogers and Gene Autry back in the 1930s and 1940s. The werewolves are treated as little more than a sub-

plot (special make-up effects created by SOTA FX's Roy Knyrim and Jerry Macaluso).
✦

HOWLING VI THE FREAKS

USA/UK, 1990. Dir: Hope Perello. With: Brendan Hughes, Michele Matheson, Sean Gregory Sullivan, Antonio Fargas, Carol Lynley, Bruce Martyn Payne. Allied Lane Pringle Productions. Colour.

Sixth in the direct-to-video series, still supposedly loosely inspired by Gary Brandner's trio of books. Urbane vampire Harker (Payne) kidnaps reluctant lycanthrope Ian (Hughes) to put on show in his travelling carnival of freaks. Although nowhere near the standard of Joe Dante's first film in the series, *The Howling* (1980), this is still a huge improvement over all the other sequels, thanks to a strong storyline, the atmospheric desert setting and a stylish directing début by Perello. At the end, Harker transforms into an impressive man-size bat (make-up effects created by Steve Johnson and Todd Masters) to fight the werewolf. This also includes an alligator boy (Sullivan).

Sequel: THE HOWLING NEW MOON RISING (qv; 1994)
✦✦✧

HOWLING II STIRBA — WEREWOLF BITCH

(USA: HOWLING II YOUR SISTER IS A WEREWOLF)
UK/USA/France/Italy/Czechoslovakia, 1984 (1986). Dir: Philippe Mora. With: Christopher Lee, Annie McEnroe, Reb Brown, Marsha A. Hunt, Sybil Danning, Judd Omen. Granite Film/Cinema '84/Hemdale/Thorn EMI. Colour.

Sleazy, low-budget sequel to Joe Dante's inventive original. Following the funeral of his sister, Ben White (Brown), the brother of the heroine from *The Howling* (1980), teams up with moody occult expert Stefan Crosscoe (Lee) and insipid TV reporter Jenny Templeton (McEnroe) to travel to Transylvania and destroy the lycanthropic cult led by well-endowed witch Stirba, Queen of the Werewolves (Danning). Co-scripted by author Gary Brandner, these werewolves (make-up by Jack Bricker, Steve Johnson and Scott Wheeler) can only be killed by titanium bullets. Originally, Fritz Kiersch (*Children of the Corn* [1984], etc) was set to direct, but was replaced by French-born Mora. With Jimmy Nail, Ferdinand Mayne (as a werewolf) and a zombie dwarf. Originally re-edited by the producers, the TV version includes a new epilogue but less of Danning's blouse-busting breasts.

Sequel: THE MARSUPIALS THE HOWLING III (qv; 1987)
✦

HOWL OF THE DEVIL

(Orig: EL AULLIDO DEL DIABLO)
Spain, 1988. Dir: Jacinto Molina (Paul Naschy). With: Paul Naschy (Jacinto Molina), Caroline Munro, Howard Vernon (Mario Lippert), Serge Mills (Sergio Molina), Fernando Hilbelck, Vidal Molina. Freemont-Naschy International/Lorion Films. Colour.

Naschy not only wrote and directed, but he also portrays a number of classic horror roles as crazy actor Hector in this homage to the Universal monsters. These include Frankenstein's creation, Mr Hyde, the Phantom of the Opera, Quasimodo, Bluebeard, Fu Manchu, his zombie twin and, of course, a werewolf. A blend of horror nostalgia and explicit gore, Vernon turns up as Hector's sinister manservant Eric and Munro plays Carmen the cook. This was Naschy's first film shot in English. The ad art depicts Germán Robles' vampiric Count Lavud, Boris Karloff's Frankenstein Monster and Fredric March's Mr Hyde!
✦✧

HOW TO MAKE A MONSTER

USA, 1958. Dir: Herbert L. Strock. With: Robert H. Harris, Paul Brinegar, Gary Conway, Gary Clarke, Malcolm Atterbury, Dennis Cross. American International Pictures. B&W/Colour.

Inventive cheapie from producer Herman Cohen. Harris plays Hollywood make-up artist Pete Drummond, who gets fired when the studio decides to make rock 'n' roll films instead of *Werewolf Meets Frankenstein*. He dresses up as a caveman when he gets his revenge and uses drugged make-up to turn two actors into murderous teenage monsters (Conway, recreating his role from *I Was a Teenage Frankenstein* [1957], and Clarke, replacing Michael Landon from *I Was a Teenage Werewolf* [1957]). With a colour climax, Morris Ankrum, Robert Shayne and guest star John Ashley singing 'You've Got to Have Ee-ooo'. Spot all the old props from AIP movies.
✦✧

HOW TO SUCCEED WITH GIRLS

(aka THE PEEPING PHANTOM)
USA, 1964. Dir: Edward A. Biery. With: Paul Leder, Leon Schrier, Marrisa Mathes, Patty Leigh, Helen Goodman, Cathy Crowfoot. B&W/Colour.

Silly, low-budget comedy in which introverted salesman Harvey Brubaker (co-producer Leder) has various sexual day-dreams (in colour!) which include guest appearances (via monster masks) from Frankenstein's Monster, the Phantom of the Opera, King Kong and the Invisible Man in a mad scientist's laboratory. With Mathes (*Playboy*'s Miss June 1962) as Harvey's busty secretary and the actress now known as Rue McClanahan (TV's *The Golden Girls* [1985-92]). Filmed under the title *Harvey's Girls*.
✦

LA HUELLA MACABRA

Mexico, 1962. Dir: Alfredo B. Crevenna. With: Guillermo Murray, Rosa Carmina, Carmen Molina, Jaime Fernandez, Elsa Cardenas, José Luis Jimenez. Rosas Priego/Clasa-Mohme. B&W.

An obscure movie which apparently includes a vampire child. The title translates as 'Macabre Footsteps'.
✦

HUGO THE HUNCHBACK

USA, 1910. Selig Polyscope Company. B&W.

This silent short was another unauthorised remake of the 1906 French film, *Esmeralda*, based on the novel *Notre-Dame de Paris* by Victor Hugo.

Remake: THE LOVE OF A HUNCHBACK (qv; 1910)
✦

HUGUES-LE-LOUP

France, 1974 (1975). Dir: Michel Subiela. With: Jean-Claude Dauphin, Claude Titre, Patricia Calas, André Valmy, Bernard Charnacé. TF1. Colour.

TV movie written and directed by Subiela, originally shown as part of the series *Les Classiques de l'Étrange*. Le Comte de Nideck (Valmy), the head of an ancient family, discovers his castle in the forest is plagued by a giant werewolf. The curse is apparently cured by love. Based on the 1876 story by Émile Erckmann and Alexandre Chatrian.

Remake: HUGUES-LE-LOUP (qv; 1978)
✦✦

HUGUES-LE-LOUP

France, 1978 (1979). Dir: Paul Planchon. With: André Pomarat, Paul Sonnendrucker, Maurice Sarfati, Eric de Dadelsen, Raymond Roumegous, Marcel Spegt. FR3 Alsace. Colour.

Fifty-two minute version of the 1876 story by Émile Erckmann and Alexandre Chatrian, about a family curse and the werewolf that plagues the castle of Le Comte de Nideck (Pomarat).
✦✧

HENRY HULL
[1890-1977]

Theatrical American actor best remembered for playing the stuffy Dr Wilfrid Glendon in *WereWolf of London* (1935).

HUMANOIDS FROM ATLANTIS

USA, 1992. Dir: J.R. Bookwalter. With: James L. Edwards. Tempe Video. Colour.

Independent shot-on-video comedy release from director/producer/editor Bookwalter, in which a green-skinned gill man from Atlantis goes on a rampage in a coastal town.
✦

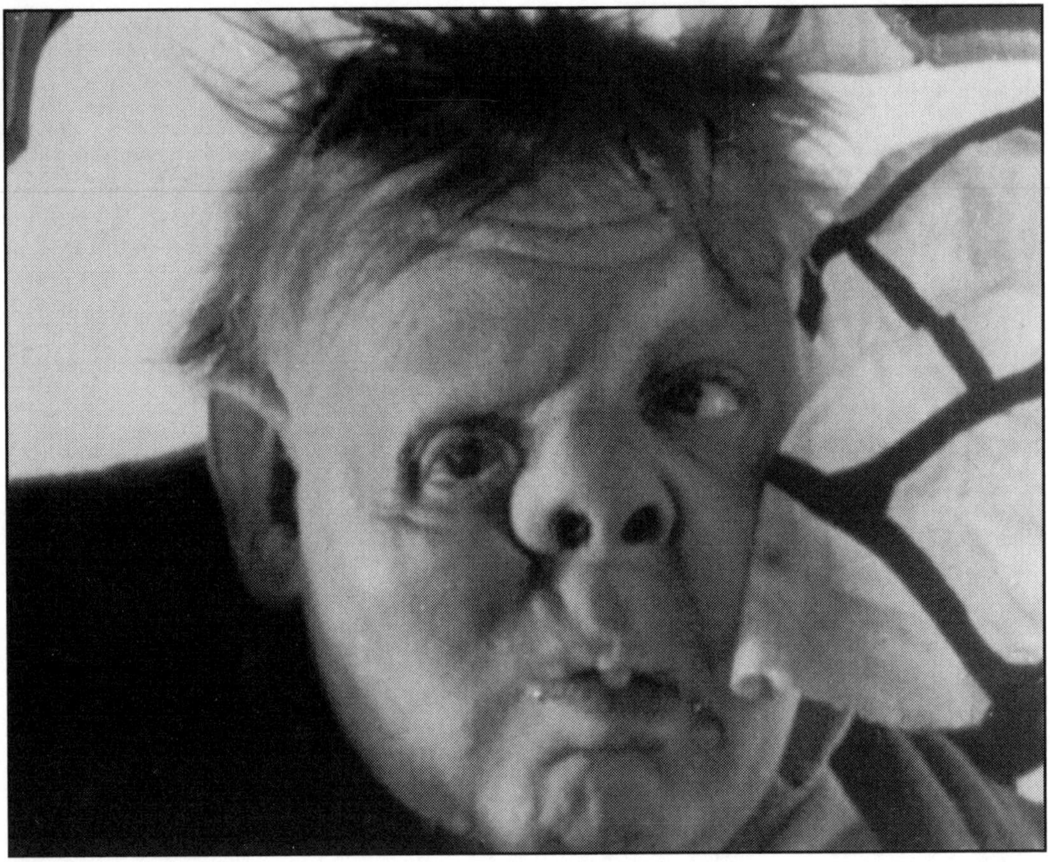

Charles Laughton as the deformed bellringer in The Hunchback of Notre Dame *(1939).*

HUMANOIDS FROM THE DEEP
(UK: MONSTER [HUMANOIDS FROM THE DEEP])
USA, 1980. Dir: Barbara Peeters. With: Doug McClure, Ann Turkel, Vic Morrow, Cindy Weintraub, Anthony Panya, Denise Galik. New World Pictures/United Artists. Colour.

DNA-created gill men from beneath the sea attack a small coastal fishing village. While McClure's local hero Jim Hill tries to stop them and redneck fisherman Hank Slattery (Morrow) blames the Native Americans, marine biologist Susan Drake (Turkel) is the scientist responsible. This is a fun monster movie, although the marauding sea creatures (designed and created by Rob Bottin) rape their female victims. It caused an outcry when the film was first released, and director Peeters claimed that producer Roger Corman had added the sex scenes after she left the project.

Remake: HUMANOIDS FROM THE DEEP (qv; 1996)

✦✦✧

HUMANOIDS FROM THE DEEP
USA, 1996. Dir: Scott Yonis. With: Robert Carradine, Emma Samms, Danielle Weeks, Clint Howard, Kaz Garas, Season Hubley. Concorde/New Horizons/Libra Pictures/ Showtime. Colour.

Inferior cable TV movie remake of the 1980 original. A single father (Carradine) and his teenage son investigate illegal toxic dumping and discover that test subjects injected with salmon DNA by a genetic scientist (Samms) have been transformed into scaly gill men, who attack the town carnival. With Bert Remsen.

✦✧

THE HUNCHBACK
USA, 1909. Dir: J. Stuart Blacktop. Vitagraph. B&W.

This silent short was an unauthorised remake of the French film *Esmeralda* (1906), also based on the novel *Notre-Dame de Paris* by Victor Hugo.

Remake: HUGO THE HUNCHBACK (qv; 1910)

✦

THE HUNCHBACK
(UK: THE HUNCHBACK OF NOTRE DAME)
USA/Hungary/Czech Republic/France, 1997. Dir: Peter Medák. With: Mandy Patinkin, Richard Harris, Salma Hayek, Edward Atterton, Benedick Blythe, Nigel Terry. Alliance Communications/Adelson-Baumgarten Productions/Turner Network. Colour.

Yet another TV movie based on the novel by Victor Hugo, set against social and political upheaval in Paris during the early sixteenth century. After Quasimodo (a sympathetic Patinkin), the deformed bellringer of Notre Dame Cathedral, is shown compassion by sensual gypsy dancing girl Esmeralda (Hayek), he rescues her from being executed for a murder committed by his guardian, the repressed Monsignor Don Frollo (a sepulchral Harris). With Jim Dale as the King of Thieves.

Remake: QUASIMODO D'EL PARIS (qv; 1999)

✦✦✧

THE HUNCHBACK OF NOTRE DAME
USA, 1923. Dir: W. (Wallace) M. Worsley. With: Lon Chaney, Patsy Ruth Miller, Ernest Torrence, Norman Kerry, Raymond Hatton, Tully Marshall. Universal. Tinted.
Chaney Sr is superb as Quasimodo, the deformed bellringer of Notre Dame Cathedral in Paris. Prevailed upon by Jehan (Brandon Hurst), the arch-deacon's evil brother, to kidnap dancing gypsy girl Esmeralda (Miller), Quasimodo fails and is sentenced to be whipped in the public square. While he is suffering under the lash, Esmeralda brings him water and from that time on he is her devoted slave. When the girl is wrongfully sentenced to death for murder, she escapes to the Cathedral and takes refuge, while Quasimodo sacrifices his life defeating Jehan and beating off the invading mob. Based on the classic 1831 novel *Notre-Dame de Paris* by Victor Hugo and set against the reign of Louis XI (Marshall), Chaney (who was secretly doubled in the climbing scenes by strongman Joe Bonomo) combines just the right amount of menace and pathos with a triumph of make-up (based on Hugo's original drawings, it took four-and-a-half hours to apply and the hump weighed forty pounds). When prevented from filming in front of the original in France, Universal reconstructed the Cathedral and all the other eight squares of buildings in their entirety on the backlot at a cost of $1,000,000 (Edgar G. Ulmer was one of the art directors), while 3,500 extras were used for the mob scenes. The movie grossed $1,500,000, a record for that time. The original roadshow running time of just over two hours was shortened for general release, and the film was cut again for its reissue in 1930.
Remake: NAV JAWAN (qv; 1937)
✦✦✦✧

THE HUNCHBACK OF NOTRE DAME
USA, 1939. Dir: William Dieterle. With: Charles Laughton, Sir Cedric Hardwicke, Thomas Mitchell, Maureen O'Hara, Edmond O'Brien, Alan Marshall. RKO Radio Pictures. B&W.
Remake of the 1923 film, set during the Middle Ages, as social change sweeps through France. Laughton gives one of his most sympathetic performances as Quasimodo, the deaf and deformed bell-ringer of Notre Dame Cathedral, although the actor apparently disagreed with make-up artist Perc Westmore, rejecting a number of designs until finally agreeing upon one which took two-and-a-half hours to apply. He is ably supported by a cast that includes Hardwicke as the scheming racist Frollo, who believes he has been bewitched by dancing gypsy girl Esmeralda (Laughton discovery O'Hara), plus George Zucco, Fritz Leiber (Sr), Arthur Hohl, George Tobias and an uncredited Rondo Hatton in the King of Fools sequence. An uncredited Jacques Tourneur reputedly handled the impressive crowd scenes and the film was co-edited by Robert Wise. This was the only film screened at the first Cannes film festival because Hitler invaded Poland the same weekend.
Remake: ROBERT MONTGOMERY PRESENTS: The Hunchback of Notre Dame (qv; 1954)
✦✦✦✧

THE HUNCHBACK OF NOTRE-DAME
(Orig: NOTRE-DAME DE PARIS)
France, 1956. Dir: Jean Delannoy. With: Gina Lollobrigida, Anthony Quinn, Jean Danet, Alain Cuny, Valentine Tessier, Danielle Dumont. Robert & Raymond Hakim/Paris Film Productions. Colour.
The first colour version of Victor Hugo's classic novel. Although Quinn makes a reasonably sympathetic Quasimodo (in disappointing make-up), he is reduced to little more than a supporting role while director Delannoy concentrates on the obvious charms of top-billed Lollobrigida's Esmeralda. Even the crowd scenes look a little thin when compared to previous versions, although Danet gives a strong performance as the villainous Phoebus de Chateaupers. Future director Jean Rollin was apparently an extra.
Remake: THE HUNCHBACK OF NOTRE DAME (qv; 1965)
✦✦

THE HUNCHBACK OF NOTRE DAME
UK, 1965. With: Peter Woodthorpe, James Maxwell, Gary Raymond, Gay Hamilton, Suzanne Neve, Alex Davion. B&W
TV version of Victor Hugo's novel with Woodthorpe as Quasimodo.
Remake: THE HUNCHBACK OF NOTRE DAME (qv; 1978)
✦✧

THE HUNCHBACK OF NOTRE DAME
UK/USA, 1978. Dir: Alan Cooke. With: Kenneth Haigh, Warren Clarke, Michelle Newell, Christopher Gable, David Rintoul, Richard Morant. BBC-TV/NBC-TV. Colour.
Shot on video, this TV movie version of Victor Hugo's novel was scripted by Robert Muller and stars Clarke as the misshapen Quasimodo (make-up by Maureen Winslade) and Newell as Esmeralda.
Remake: THE HUNCHBACK OF NOTRE DAME (qv; 1981)
✦✦

THE HUNCHBACK OF NOTRE DAME
(USA: aka HUNCHBACK)
UK/USA, 1981 (1982). Dir: Michael Tuchner. With: Anthony Hopkins, Derek Jacobi, Lesley-Anne Down, Robert Powell, John Gielgud, David Suchet. Columbia/ Rosemont/Hallmark Hall of Fame/CBS-TV. Colour.
Two-hour TV movie version of Victor Hugo's novel *Notre-Dame de Paris*, set in fifteenth century Paris. Hopkins stars as a sympathetic Quasimodo (in make-up created by Nick Malley), adopted as a baby by the calculating archdeacon of Notre Dame, Dom Claude Frollo (Jacobi). The one person who shows the deaf hunchback any kindness is the gypsy dancer Esmeralda (Down). With Gerry Sundquist, Rosalie Crutchley, Roland Culver and Tim Pigott-Smith.
Remake: THE HUNCHBACK OF NOTRE-DAME (qv; 1985)
✦✦✧

THE HUNCHBACK OF NOTRE-DAME
Australia, 1985. Dir: Warwick Gilbert and Geoff Collins. Voices: Tom Burlinson, Angela Punch McGregor, Ron Haddrick, Richard Meikle, Phillip Hinton, Ric Hutton. Burbank Films. Colour.
Fifty minute children's cartoon, adapted from the novel by Victor Hugo. Deaf and deformed bellringer Quasimodo (Burlinson) is given water by the gypsy girl Esmerelda (McGregor), even after he is ordered to kidnap her by his master, the scheming Frollo (Haddrick). When she is falsely sentenced to death for witchcraft and murder, the hunchback saves her from burning and claims sanctuary within the Cathedral's walls.
Remake: THE HUNCH BACK OF NOTRE DAME (qv; 1995 Jetlag)
✦✧

THE HUNCHBACK OF NOTRE DAME
(aka PAUL NORMAN'S HUNCHBACK OF NOTRE DAME)
USA, 1991. Dir: Paul Norman. With: Buck Adams, Kim Kataine, Alyssa Jarreau, Aja, K.C. Williams, Ron Jeremy. Pleasure Productions/Video Team. Colour.
Hardcore reworking of the story, with Adams as a hunchbacked janitor who falls in love with a stripper (Aja). Jeremy plays a sleazy strip club manager.
✦

THE HUNCH BACK OF NOTRE DAME
Japan/USA, 1995. Dir: Toshiyuki Hiruma Takashi. Voices: Tony Ail, Nathan Aswell, Cheralynn Bailey, Kathleen Barr, Gary Chalk, Lilliam Carlson. Jetlag Productions/ Goodtimes Entertainment. Colour.
Adapted from the novel by Victor Hugo, at just forty-five minutes long this cheap-looking children's musical cartoon is mercifully short. In the end, Quasimodo and Esmeralda run away together!
Remake: THE HUNCHBACK OF NOTRE DAME (qv; 1995)
✦

THE HUNCHBACK OF NOTRE DAME
USA, 1995. Dir: Bobby Hsieh. Sony Wonder/Golden Films. Colour.
With a running time of under fifty minutes, this juvenile musical cartoon is definitely sub-Disney. Fleeing the evil Jean-Claude, gypsy

Melody and her magical talking instruments take refuge in Notre-Dame Cathedral where they meet Quasimodo, who lives with a family of bats in the bell tower. In the end, the hunchback is transformed by magic. With music and inappropriate lyrics by Richard Hurwitz.
Remake: THE HUNCHBACK OF NOTRE DAME (qv; 1996)
✦

THE HUNCHBACK OF NOTRE DAME
USA/France, 1996. Dir: Gary Trousdale and Kirk Wise. Voices: Tom Hulce, Demi Moore, Tony Jay, Kevin Kline, Paul Kandel, Jason Alexander. Disney Enterprises/Buena Vista Pictures Distribution. Colour.
Despite taking more than $100,000,000 at the American box office, this Broadway-style musical (Disney's thirty-fourth full-length animated movie), inspired by Victor Hugo's novel, is not considered a success because of its adult approach. At the urging of his jokey gargoyle companions Victor (Charles Kimbrough), Hugo (Alexander) and Laverne (Mary Wickes and Jane Withers), who he brings to life in his imagination, Quasimodo (a mis-cast Hulce) defies his evil guardian, the scheming Minister of Justice Frollo (the excellent Jay), and joins the Festival of Fools. Rejected by the crowd for his looks, he is rescued by gypsy girl Esmeralda (Moore, plus Heidi Mollenhaur for the singing) and her pet goat Djali, and together they set out to save the city he loves. Narrated by Clopin, the sinister Harlequin (Kandel). With music by Alan Menken and lyrics by Stephen Schwartz, and a nice *The Wizard of Oz* (1939) gag. The opening 'The Bells of Notre Dame' sequence (animated in France) is stunning. *The Making of the Hunchback of Notre Dame* (1996) was a half-hour special on the Disney Channel hosted by Jason Alexander.
Remake: THE HUNCHBACK (qv; 1997)
✦✦✦✧

THE HUNCHBACK OF THE MORGUE
(Orig: EL JOROBADO DE LA MORGUE. USA: aka THE RUE MORGUE MASSACRES)
Spain, 1973. Dir: Javier Aguirre. With: Paul Naschy (Jacinto Molina), Rossana Yanni (Yanny), Vic Winner (Victor Alcazar), Maria Elena Arpon, Alberto Dalbes, Maria Pershy (Perschy). Eva Film/F Lara Polop/ZIV International. Colour.
Naschy (who also co-wrote the script under his real name) stars as Gotho the hunchback, who is in love with a dying girl. After her death, he steals her body and keeps it in an underground torture chamber where it is attacked by rats (in one scene, real rats are apparently set on fire and the actor suffered rodent bites). A mad scientist (Dalbes) promises to restore life to the girl in return for bodies to feed the slimy monster he has created. In the end almost everyone ends up dead, with Gotho falling into a vat of acid. Despite plenty of gratuitous gore and nudity, this is actually one of Naschy's better films.
✦✦

THE HUNGER
UK/USA, 1983. Dir: Tony Scott. With: Catherine Deneuve, David Bowie, Susan Sarandon, Cliff De Young, Beth Ehlers, Dan Hedaya. Richard Shepherd Company/Metro-Goldwyn-Mayer. Colour.
Based on Whitley Strieber's novel, Scott's movie suffers from an emphasis on style over content. Deneuve is impressive as centuries-old Egyptian vampire queen Miriam Blaylock, who seduces scientific researcher Sarah Roberts (Sarandon) when her previous companion John (rock star Bowie) begins to age rapidly. Her undead lovers — who continue to survive, no matter how mummified their bodies become — eventually revenge themselves in the horrific climax. The sex scenes between Deneuve and Sarandon are pretty steamy. With James Aubrey, Shane Rimmer, Bessie Love, Willem Dafoe, Sophie Ward and Goth group Bauhaus (who perform 'Bela Lugosi's Dead'). Special effects make-up created by Dick Smith and others.
✦✦

THE HUNGER
USA, 1993. Dir: Henri Pachard. With: Ona Zee, Rebecca Wild, Jon Dough, Meo (Cris Collins), Nikki Shane, Marc Wallice. Forbidden Films. Colour.
Zee and Dough play vampire lovers in this hardcore feature.
✦

THE HUNGER
Canada/UK/USA, 1997. Dir: Tony Scott, Jake Scott and Russell Mulcahy. With: Terence Stamp, Balthazar Getty, Amanda Ryan, Karen Black, Lena Headey, Philip Casnoff. Scott Free/Telescene/The Movie Network/Nightnote/ Showtime Networks. Colour.
Pilot cable TV movie for the half-hour erotic horror series featuring Stamp as the enigmatic Host. 'The Swords' is based on a story by Robert Aickman, about a woman (Ryan) in a Soho nightclub who can pass swords through her body. 'Ménage à Trois' is adapted from a story by F. Paul Wilson in which an aged invalid (an impressive Black) possesses the body of her nurse (Headey) so that she can obtain sexual satisfaction. 'Necros' is based on a story by Brian Lumley about a youth-devouring vampire. All three episodes have also been shown separately as part of the series. With Timothy Spall and Leonardo Cimino.
Sequel: THE HUNGER (qv; 1997-)
✦✦✧

THE HUNGER:
Clarimonde
Canada/USA, 1997. Dir: Tom Dey. With: David La Haye, Audrey Benoit, James Bradford, Sheena Larkin, Pierre Lablanc, Guy Heroux. The Movie Network/Scott Free/ Telescene/Showtime Networks. Colour.
Half-hour made-for-cable sex and horror anthology TV series (1997-), created by co-executive producer Jeff Fazio and obscurely introduced by Terence Stamp during the first season and David Bowie during the second. In this episode, based on Théophile Gautier's 1836 vampiric ghost story, young priest Romuaid (La Haye) is seduced in his dreams by the beautiful Clarimonde (Benoit).
✦

Fly by Night
Canada/USA, 1997. Dir: Pierre Dalpé. With: Giancarlo Esposito, Kim Feeney, Gouchy Boy, Éric Hoziel, Don Jordan, Bobo Vian. The Movie Network/Scott Free/ Telescene/Showtime Networks. Colour.
Based on a story by Gemma Files. Sonia (Feeney) is a traumatised ex-soldier who recognises a fellow psychiatric patient (Esposito) as being a vampire.
✦

Footsteps
Canada/USA, 1997. Dir: Jimmy Kaufman. With: Paul-Anthony Stewart, Sofia Shinas, Cédric Noël, Jean-Guy Bouchard, Doris Milmore, Emidio Michetti. The Movie Network/Scott Free/Telescene/Showtime Networks. Colour.
Based on a werewolf story by Cordwainer Bird (Harlan Ellison). A sexy shape-changer (Shinas) escapes to Paris, where she falls in love with a young man (Stewart) with powers like hers who happens to be a vegetarian.
✦

A Matter of Style
Canada/USA, 1997. Dir: John Hamilton. With: Chad Lowe, Isabelle Cyr, Marie-Josée Croze, Janine Thériault, Claudia Besso, Éric Goulem. The Movie Network/Scott Free/ Telescene/Showtime Networks. Colour.
Comedy episode based on a story by Ron Dee. When Neville Burlington (Lowe) discovers that he is now a vampire, his sexy mentor Carmilla (Cyr) attempts to instruct him in the ways of the undead, without much success.
✦✦

Necros
Canada/USA, 1997. Dir: Russell Mulcahy. With: Philip Casnoff, Céline Bonnier, Leonardo Cimino, Tony de Santis, Richard Jutras, Lida Russo. The Movie Network/ Scott Free/Telescene/Showtime Networks. Colour.
There's not much left of Brian Lumley's vampire story in this nicely directed adaptation, filmed in Montreal. While on vacation, William Cobb (Casnoff) meets a beautiful woman, Helma (Bonnier), and her aged companion Nero (Cimino), who reputedly feeds on the energy of the living. However, everything is not as it first appears...
✦✦

Red Light

Canada/USA, 1997. Dir: Christian Duguay. With: Tomas Arana, Liliana Komorowska, Vlasta Vrana, Benoît Brière, Jacklin Webb, Don Jordan. The Movie Network/Scott Free/Telescene/Showtime Networks. Colour.
Written by David Schow and based on his oblique, World Fantasy Award-winning vampire story. Top fashion model Natasha (Komorowska) believes that the cameras are stealing her soul. When the photographer (Arana) she flees to secretly takes some pictures of her, she discovers she has nothing left to give...
✦✧

HUNGRY

USA, 1992. Dir: Paul Norman. With: Alexis DeVell, Samantha Strong, Peter North, Woody Long, Alicia Rio, Shayla (Shayla LaVeaux). Sin City Video. Colour.
Hardcore feature in which a news reporter (DeVell) and a pair of cops (Jon Dough and Long) investigate a series of attacks by two nineteenth century vampires posing as gourmet caterers (Strong and North) who suck the life-force from their victims.
Sequel: HUNGRY PART 2 (qv; 1993)
✦

HUNGRY PART 2

(aka NIGHT FEAST)
USA, 1993. Dir: Paul Norman. With: Alexis DeVell, Samantha Strong, Peter North, Woody Long, Alicia Rio, Shayla (Shayla LaVeaux). Sin City Video. Colour.
This hardcore vampire sequel features most of the same cast and too much footage from the first film. Following the death of his partner, a cop (Long) teams up again with a reporter (DeVell) to track down the new wave vampires (Strong and North) responsible. With Ron Jeremy in a non-sex role.
✦

THE HUNGRY SNAKE WOMAN

(Orig: NYAI BLORONG)
Indonesia, 1987. Dir: Sisworo Gautama Putra. With: Advani Rangua, George Rudy, Suzzanna. Midnight Video. Colour.
After attempting to rape and kill his girlfriend Carlita (Rangua), Brian (Rudy) escapes into the jungle where he meets the goddess Snake Woman (Suzzanna). She promises him a fortune if he will kill three women and drink their blood. Returning to town with fangs and a cape, Brian's cannibalistic attacks are attributed to Dracula by a local newspaper before he traps the Snake Woman in her reptile form by inserting a pin in her head during sex. This ends with a magic duel between two female snake demons.
✦✧

RAYMOND HUNTLEY
[1904-1990]

British character actor who often played pompous Englishmen. He portrayed Dracula on the stage during the play's original London run in 1927.
qv: *The Mummy* (1959).

HURACÁN RAMÍREZ CONTRA LOS TERRORISTAS

Mexico, 1989. Dir: Juan Rodriguez. With: Huracán Ramírez Jr. Colour.
The son of original wrestling hero Huracán Ramírez (who began his film career in 1952) battles terrorists in this shot-on-video cheapie. A pasty-faced zombie briefly shows up in a nightmare sequence.
✦

BRANDON HURST
[1866-1947]

British actor in Hollywood since the silent era, he became a dependable character player during the 1930s and 1940s.
qv: *Dr. Jekyll and Mr. Hyde* (1920); *The Ghost of Frankenstein* (1942); *House of Frankenstein* (1944); *The Hunchback of Notre Dame* (1923); *Legally Dead* (1923); *Made for Love* (1926); *White Zombie* (1932).

HYDE AND GO TWEET

USA, 1959 (1960). Dir: Friz (Isadore) Freleng. Voices: Mel Blanc. Warner Bros. Colour.
The final seven minute *Merrie Melodies* cartoon in Freleng's Jekyll and Hyde trilogy. After swallowing Dr Jekyll's formula, Tweety Pie periodically turns into a monstrous canary, much to the consternation of Sylvester the cat.
Sequels: MOUSE GARDEN (1960) and TRIP FOR TAT (1960)
✦✦✦

HYDE AND HARE

USA, 1955. Dir: Friz (Isadore) Freleng. Voices: Mel Blanc. Warner Bros. Colour.
Seven minute *Looney Tunes* cartoon in which Bugs Bunny becomes the pet of Dr Jekyll and doesn't realise that his new owner periodically transforms into his fearsome alter-ego. After doing an impression of Liberace, Bugs drinks the formula and turns into a rabbit version of Mr Hyde. This was the second of Freleng's three Jekyll and Hyde cartoons.
Sequel: KNIGHT-MARE HARE (1955)
✦✦✧

HYDE AND SNEAK

USA, 1962. Dir: Paul J. Smith. Voices: Dal McKennon. Walter Lantz Productions/Universal. Colour.
Cartoon short in which Inspector Willoughby (McKennon) attempts to capture jewel thief Vampira Hyde, who is also a quick-change artist.
Sequel: COMING-OUT PARTY (1963)
✦✧

HYOCHO NO BIJO

Japan, 1977. Dir: Umeji Inoue. Shochiku. Colour.
TV movie based on the story 'Kyuketsuki' ('Vampire') by pseudonymous writer Edogawa Rampo (Naoto Takenaka).
✦

HYSTERICAL

USA, 1982 (1985). Dir: Chris Bearde. With: The Hudson Brothers (Bill Hudson, Mark Hudson, Brett Hudson), Charlie Callas, Bud Cort, Robert Donner. Cinema Group Venture/New World Pictures. Colour.
Unfunny horror spoof written by and starring Portland TV comedy trio the Hudson Brothers. When best-selling author Frederick Lansing (Bill Hudson) rents a haunted lighthouse in Hellview, Oregon, the vengeful ghost of Venetia (Julie Newmar) raises the one hundred year-old corpse of her lover Captain Howdy (Richard Kiel) from the sea and turns the townsfolk into zombies. Bumbling vampire-hunters Dr Paul Battan (Mark Hudson) and Fritz (Brett Hudson) are called in to investigate. Such guest stars as Murray Hamilton, Cindy Pickett, Clint Walker, Keenan Wynn, Gary Owens, John Larroquette, John Diehl, Natalie Cole and Callas (who appears as a manic Dracula in the prologue) are all wasted. This was released directly to cable TV in America.
✦✧

I BELIEVE
USA, 1917. Dir: George Loane Tucker. With: Milton Rosmer. Cosmotofilm. B&W.
In this seventy-five minute silent drama, a man who is revived from the dead has no soul.
✦

I BOUGHT A VAMPIRE MOTORCYCLE
UK, 1990. Dir: Dirk Campbell. With: Neil Morrissey, Amanda Noar, Michael Elphick, Anthony Daniels, Andrew Powell, George Rossi. Dirk Productions. Colour.
Crass, low-budget horror comedy, with more gore than wit. The irritating Morrissey plays a dispatch rider who buys a demonically possessed motorcycle that runs on blood. As it travels around Birmingham decapitating victims, only sunlight and the sign of the cross have the power to stop it. Elphick is Inspector Cleaver, with terminal garlic breath; Daniels (C3PO in the *Star Wars* series) plays a priest; and Burt Kwouk (from the *Pink Panther* films) has a pointless cameo as 'Fu King Owner' (ha-ha). The shoddy special effects were created by Bob Keen's Image Animation.
✦

I BURY THE LIVING
USA, 1958. Dir: Albert Band (Alfredo Antonini). With: Richard Boone, Theodore Bikel, Peggy Maurer, Howard Smith, Herbert Anderson, Robert Osterloh. Maxim Productions/United Artists. B&W.
If you only know director Band for the films he makes now with his producer son, Charles, check out this often quite brilliant low-budget horror movie to see what he was once capable of. Originally titled *Killer on the Wall*, Boone gives a great performance as cemetery manager Robert Kraft, who discovers that people die when he sticks the wrong pin in a map of the graveyard plots. When he decides to see if doing the reverse will have the opposite effect — bring the dead back to life — the film builds to a terrifying crescendo. Although the great-looking poster art features a zombie ('Out of a Time-rotted Tomb Crawls an Unspeakable Horror!'), it all turns out to be a plot by Bikel's character (with a silly Scottish accent). Yet despite the disappointing ending (the result of pressure from the distributor), this is still a dark, impressionistic and truly scary chiller. Make-up by Jack Pierce.
✦✦✦✦

I, DESIRE
USA, 1982. Dir: John Llewellyn Moxey. With: David Naughton, Dorian Harewood, Brad Dourif, Marilyn Jones, Barbara Stock, Arthur Rosenberg. Columbia/Green-Epstein/ABC-TV. Colour.
Surprisingly downbeat TV movie about an undead Hollywood hooker. Naughton (*An American Werewolf in London* [1981], etc) plays law student David Balsiger, who is obsessed by the knowledge that a vampire named Desire (Stock) is loose in modern-day Los Angeles. When no one will believe him, except for Dourif's odd street character, he sets about tracking the creature down — even if it means losing everything. Director Moxey did it better with *The Night Stalker* (1971), but he still handles the vampire attacks with style and flair.
✦✦

IDLE ROOMERS
USA, 1944. Dir: Del Lord. With: The Three Stooges (Jerry 'Curly' Howard, Larry Fine, Moe Howard), Duke York, Christine McIntyre, Vernon Dent. Columbia. B&W.
Seventeen minute slapstick short in which the comedy trio are working at the Hotel Snazzy-Plaza as bellboys. There they encounter a showman's latest carnival attraction — Lupe, the hunchbacked wolfman (York), who goes insane whenever he hears music.
✦✦✦

I EAT YOUR SKIN
(aka ZOMBIE)
USA, 1964 (1971). Dir: Del Tenney. With: William Joyce, Heather Hewitt, Betty Hyatt-Linton, Dan Stapleton, Walter Coy, Robert Stanton. Iselin-Tenney/Cinemation Industries. B&W.
Filmed as *Caribbean Adventure*, and then titled *Zombies* and *Voodoo Blood Bath*, this wasn't released for seven years, until producer Jerry Gross co-billed it with *I Drink Your Blood* (1971). Set on Voodoo Island in the Caribbean, author and adventurer Tom Harris (Joyce) discovers that Dr Biladeau (Stanton), who is seeking a cure for cancer, injects the natives with a radioactive snake-venom serum that transforms them into pasty-faced zombies. This is the final feature to date from the Florida-based writer/producer/director of *The Horror of Party Beach* (1964) and *The Curse of the Living Corpse* (1964). With Don Strawn's Calypso Band. William Grefé (*Death Curse of Tartu* [1966], etc) was second unit director.
✦

I HOWL AT THE MOON
Japan, 1989. Dir: Setsuko Shibunnoichi. Voices: Fumi Hirano, Toshio Furukawa, Akira Kamiya. 5-Ace/Kitty Films/Pony/AnimEigo. Colour.
Half-hour anime video about an inept cook who accidentally creates a pair of wolf men. This is available with another Shibunnoichi short, *Raging Sherbet* (1988), on the 1993 video release *Urusei Yatsura OVA 2: Raging Sherbet/I Howl at the Moon*.
✦

I LIKE BATS
(Orig: LUBIE NIETOPERZE)
Poland, 1985. Dir: Grzegorz Warchol. With: Katarzyna Walter, Marek Barbasiewicz, Malgorzata Lorentowicz, Jonasz Kofta, Edwin Petrykat, Jan Prochyra. The Polish Corporation for Film Production/Film Polski. Colour.
Walter plays busty vampire Isabella, feeding off bats in her attic. Unable to get along with humans, she eventually visits psychiatrist Dr Judd, who first locks her up and then falls in love with her. Finally they marry and her daughter has fangs.
✦

I'LL SUCK YOU DRY
USA, 1982 (1986). Dir: Stuart Koslov. With: Nina de Ponca, Taija Rae, Nina Hartley, Ron Jeremy. Afton Productions/EZSex Productions. Colour.
Hardcore feature that appears to be made up of numerous clips from *Dracula Sucks* (1979), some featuring Jaime Gillis as Dracula. In the apparently original footage, a caped, glowing-eyed vampire watches a woman have sex with a man in a skull mask.
✦

I LOVE A MYSTERY
USA, 1945. Dir: Henry Levin. With: George Macready, Nina Foch, Jim Bannon, Barton Yarborough, Carole Mathews, Lester Matthews. Columbia. B&W.
First of a trio of low-budget whodunits based on Carlton E. Morse's *I Love a Mystery* radio show of the 1940s. Detectives Jack Packard (Bannon) and Doc Young (Yarborough) investigate an ancient Tibetan cult who want to replace the decaying head of the 1,000 year-old mummy of their High Priest with Macready's. Despite the supernatural touches, it all turns out to be a murder plot with a neat twist at the end.
Sequel: THE DEVIL'S MASK (1946)
Remake: I LOVE A MYSTERY (1973)
✦✧

I MARRIED A VAMPIRE
USA, 1983 (1986). Dir: Jay Raskin. With: Brendan Hickey, Rachel Gordon, Ted Zalewski, Deborah Carroll, Temple Aaron, David Dunton. Full Moon/Troma/Starmaker. Colour.
A young woman (Gordon) living in Boston discovers that her husband, Robespierre (Hickey), is a one hundred year-old vampire having one-night stands with other women in this very unfunny, low-budget comedy shot on 16mm. It includes clips from *Vampyr* (1931-32).
✦

IMMORAL TALES
(Orig: CONTES IMMORAUX)
France, 1973 (1974). Dir: Walerian Borowczyk. With: Lise Danvers, Charlotte Alexandra, Pascale Christophe, Fabrice Luchini, Paloma Picasso, Florence Bellamy. Argos/New Line Cinema. Colour.
A collection of four erotic stories aimed at art house audiences. The third and best sequence stars Picasso's daughter Paloma as a lesbian Countess Erzsebeth Báthory, bathing in the blood of virgins to stay young. The final episode is about Lucretia Borgia (Bellamy). A fifth segment, based on *Beauty and the Beast*, was expanded by writer/director Borowczyk into *The Beast* (1974).
✦✧

I, MONSTER
UK, 1971. Dir: Stephen Weeks. With: Christopher Lee, Peter Cushing, Mike Raven (Austin Churton Fairman), Richard Hurndall, George Merritt, Kenneth J. Warren. Amicus Productions/British Lion Films. Colour.
After an uneven opening, this turns into a slow-moving but stylish adaptation of Robert Louis Stevenson's *Strange Case of Dr. Jekyll and Mr. Hyde*. Scripted by co-producer Milton Subotsky and imaginatively directed by twenty-three year-old Weeks, making his feature début. Lee gives a restrained performance as Dr Charles Marlowe, who uses himself as a guinea pig to test a new drug he believes will release his inner self. As a result, he transforms into Edward Blake, whose features grow progressively bestial the more evil he commits. With solid support from Cushing and Raven, excellent cinematography by Moray Grant, wonderfully cluttered Victorian sets designed by Tony Curtis and an atmospheric music score by Carl Davis. Filmed in 3-D, Subotsky blamed Weeks for not using the process correctly and had to edit the film down to a trim seventy-five minutes. Not released in the USA until 1973, the Italian version (*La Vera Storia del Dr Jekyll*) apparently includes at least three minutes of extra/alternative footage. With an uncredited Ian McCulloch in a crowd scene.
Remake: DR. JEKYLL & SISTER HYDE (qv; 1971)
✦✦✧

IMPAKTITA
Philippines, 1989. Dir: Teddy Chiu. With: Nida Blanca, Gloria Romero, Aga Muhlach, Richard Gomez, Jean Garcia. Regal International. Colour.
Based on the *komiks* serial by J.R. Mercado and Amoroso. A young woman discovers that she can transform into a bat-monster and revenge herself on the men who raped her.
✦

THE IMPATIENT PATIENT
USA, 1942. Dir: Norm(an) McCabe. Voices: Mel Blanc. Warner Bros. B&W.
Seven minute *Looney Tunes* cartoon, in which singing telegram Daffy Duck is suffering from hiccups and has to deliver a message from Frank N. Stein to the creepy home of Dr Jerkle. The doctor drinks a potion that turns him into a monster named Chlöe.
Sequel: THE DAFFY DUCKAROO (1942)
✦✦✧

EL IMPERIO DE DRACULA
(aka LAS MUJERES DE DRACULA)
Mexico, 1966. Dir: Federico Curiel. With: Cesar del Campo, Ethel Carrillo, Lucha Villa, Eric del Castillo, Fernando Osés, Rebeca Iturbide. Filmica Vergara/Columbia. Colour.
A young man (del Campo) is sent by his dying mother to Castle Draculstein(!) to avenge his father who was killed by the Count (del Castillo). This apparently owes much to Fisher's *Dracula Prince of Darkness* (1965), and includes a sexy vampire woman and an assistant named Igor. It was also reputedly the first Mexican horror film shot in 'maravillosos colores'. The title translates as 'The Empire of Dracula'.
✦✧

INCENSE FOR THE DAMNED
(USA: BLOODSUCKERS)
UK/Greece, 1970 (1973). Dir: Michael Burrowes (Robert Hartford-Davis). With: Patrick Macnee, Peter Cushing, Alex Davion, Johnny Sekka, Madeline Hinde, Edward Woodward. Lucinda Films/Titan International Productions/Grand National/Chevron Pictures. Colour.
Based on Simon Raven's novel *Doctors Wear Scarlet*, this muddled horror thriller was finally released after three years, following several lawsuits and with the director's name removed from the credits. What's left attempts to explain vampirism as a sexual perversion (although there is still an inexplicable supernatural element and it takes a stake through the heart to dispatch them). Macnee (TV's *The Avengers* [1961-69], etc) plays retired Major Longbow who agrees to help Penelope (Hinde) rescue her fiancé Richard Fountain (Patrick Mower) from a cult of Greek vampires. This also features William Mervyn, David Lodge, and Imogen Hassall as the sexy Chriseis, while Cushing has a brief cameo as the principal of an Oxford university.
✦✦

INCH HIGH PRIVATE EYE:
The Mummy's Curse
USA, 1973. Dir: Charles A. Nichols. Voices: Jamie Farr, Kathy Gori, Ted Knight, Bob Luttrell, Don Messick, Lennie Weinrib. Hanna-Barbera Productions/NBC-TV. Colour.
Twenty minute cartoon TV series (1973-74, thirteen episodes) about the world's biggest little detective (Weinrib), who works for the Finkerton Detective Agency and is aided by his niece Lorie (Gori), her dumb boyfriend Gator (Luttrell) and their lazy St. Bernard dog, Braveheart (Messick). In this episode, when a map revealing the location of a hidden treasure is apparently stolen by the living mummy of King Ra, Mr Finkerton (John Stephenson) uses the case as an opportunity to once again fire Inch. Joseph Barbera and William Hanna were executive producers.
✦✧

THE INCREDIBLE HULK:
Dark Side
USA, 1980. Dir: John McPherson. With: Bill Bixby, Jack Colvin, Lou Ferrigno, William Lucking, Rosemary Forsyth, Philece Sampler. Universal/CBS-TV. Colour.
Popular hour-long TV series (1977-82, eighty-five episodes) based on the Marvel Comics character. Due to an overdose of gamma radiation that altered his body chemistry, Dr David Bruce Banner (Bixby) transforms into the green-skinned Hulk (Ferrigno) whenever he grows angry or outraged. The creature is wanted for a murder he did not commit, and is pursued by investigative reporter Jack McGee (Colvin). In this episode, Banner takes an experimental drug to free him from the Hulk, but instead it releases the dark side of his personality. Developed for TV by executive producer Kenneth Johnson; creator Stan Lee was consultant.
Series sequel: THE INCREDIBLE HULK RETURNS (1988)
Series remake: THE INCREDIBLE HULK (1984-85)
✦✦✧

THE INCREDIBLE MELTING MAN
USA, 1977. Dir: William Sachs. With: Alex Rebar, Burr DeBenning, Myron Healey, Michael Alldredge, Ann Sweeny, Rainbeaux Smith. Quartet Productions/American International. Colour.
Filmed on a very low budget, this uncredited remake of *First Man Into Space* (1958) stars Rebar as Colonel Steve West, the only survivor of a space mission orbiting Saturn, who returns as a murderous blood-seeking monster until his body eventually falls apart completely. Rick Baker created the gory special make-up effects. With split-screen sequences, veteran Healey as an army general, and Jonathan Demme (who directed *The Silence of the Lambs* [1991], etc) in a small role. Presented by Max J. Rosenberg. A novelisation by Phil Smith was published in Britain.
✦✧

THE INCREDIBLY STRANGE CREATURES WHO STOPPED LIVING AND BECAME MIXED-UP ZOMBIES!!?
(aka TEENAGE PSYCHO MEETS BLOODY MARY)
USA, 1963. Dir: Ray Dennis Steckler. With: Cash Flagg (Ray Dennis Steckler), Carolyn Brandt, Brett O'Hara,

Atlas King, Sharon Walsh, Madison Clarke. Morgan-Steckler Productions/Fairway International. Colour.
Producer/director Steckler stars as unlikely teenager Jerry, hypnotised by Midway gypsy fortune teller Madam Estrella (O'Hara) into becoming a hooded homicidal maniac. She also keeps a secret room full of acid-scarred monstrosities that escape at the end, while Jerry is finally shot by the police and falls into the surf. This bottom-of-the-barrel chiller was made for $38,000 and features surprisingly imaginative photography (particularly an impressive nightmare sequence) by Joseph V. Mascelli, Laszlo Kovacs and Vilmos Zsigmond, while Brandt makes an inauspicious début as heroine Marge Neilson. The awful music was apparently released on Rel Records.
✦✧

INDESTRUCTIBLE MAN
USA, 1955 (1956). Dir: Jack Pollexfen. With: Lon Chaney, Casey Adams, Marion Carr, Ross Elliott (Elliot), Stuart Randall, Kenneth Terrell. CGK Productions/Allied Artists. B&W.
An unofficial remake of *The Walking Dead* (1936). Chaney Jr (whose twitching eyes are repeatedly shown in close-up) gives an outrageous performance in the mostly non-speaking role of 'Butcher' Benton, an executed psychopath who is accidentally brought back to life by a scientist's (Robert Shayne) electrical experiments. Now a superhuman killer impervious to bullets, Benton seeks revenge on the gang he believes double-crossed him. His face is horribly burned by a flame-thrower in the Los Angeles sewer system and he is finally killed by a massive charge of electricity. Elliott's risible *Dragnet*-style narration tries to make some sense out of this low-budget madness.
✦

THE INFERNAL TRIO
(Orig: LE TRIO INFERNAL)
France/Italy/West Germany, 1973. Dir: Francis Girod. With: Michel Piccoli, Romy Schneider, Mascha Gomska, Philippe Brizard, Francis Claude, Hubert Deschamps. Belstar Productions/Lira Films/Films 66/Fox Europa Productions/Oceania PIC/TIT Film Produktion/ Twentieth Century-Fox/Levitt-Pickman Films. Colour.
Black comedy thriller in which scheming lawyer George Sarret (Piccoli) and two German sisters Philomene and Catherine (Schneider and Gomska) use acid baths to dispose of their murder victims before claiming the insurance. In one scene, Schneider's character dresses up as Count Dracula. Based on the novel by Solange Fasquelle. Music by Ennio Morricone.
✦✧

THE INHUMAN WOMAN
(Orig: L'INHUMAINE. USA: aka THE LIVING DEAD MAN) France, 1923 (1924). Dir: Marcel L'Herbier. With: Eve Francis, Georgette LeBlanc, Jacques Catelain, Philippe Heriat. Cinégraphic. B&W.
Silent drama in which an opera singer, poisoned by a jealous Maharajah, is revived after death by an engineer's dangerous experiment.
✦

INNOCENT BLOOD
USA, 1992. Dir: John Landis. With: Anne Parillaud, Robert Loggia, Anthony LaPaglia, Don Rickles, Tony Lip, Kim Coates. Lee Rich Productions/Warner Bros. Colour.
Slick-looking but quirky blend of comedy, romance and thriller which breaks many rules of the genre. Set in Pittsburgh, a miscast Parillaud (*Nikita* [1990], etc) plays Marie, a beautiful vampire with a conscience. When she makes a mistake and allows one of her victims to transform, she teams up with undercover cop Joe Gennaro (LaPaglia) to go after undead Mafia mobster Sal 'The Shark' Macelli (Loggia) before there's an epidemic of bloodsuckers. Forrest J Ackerman makes another cameo appearance, along with Chazz Palminteri, Angela Bassett, Robert Walker (Jr) and Linnea Quigley, directors Michael Ritchie, Sam Raimi, Frank Oz and Dario Argento, and special effects wizard Tom Savini. TV clips include *Dracula* (1931 and 1958 versions), *The Beast from 20,000 Fathoms* (1953), *Phantom of the Rue Morgue* (1954) and Hitchcock's *Strangers on a Train* (1951), which result in 'cheat' credits for Christopher Lee, Peter Cushing, Bela Lugosi, Charlie Gomorra, Alfred Hitchcock and US Vice President Dan Quayle! In Australia this was retitled *A French Vampire in America*.
✦✦✧

THE INN OF THE FLYING DRAGON
(aka ONDSKANS VÄRDSHUS. UK: THE SLEEP OF DEATH) Sweden/Ireland, 1978. Dir: Calvin Floyd. With: Per Oscarsson, Patrick Magee, Marilu Tolo, Curd Jürgens (Curt Jurgens), Brendan Price, Niall Toibin. Aspekt Film/Dragon Co/Swedish Film Institute/National Film Studios of Ireland. Colour.
Loosely based on J. Sheridan Le Fanu's 1872 story 'The Room in the Dragon Volant'. Robert Tanner (Oscarsson), a young nobleman, becomes obsessed with a beautiful countess (Tolo). She is accompanied by a sinister old man, Count Nicolas de St. Alyre (Jürgens), who the superstitious locals believe is a vampire.
✦✧

INSAAN BANA SHAITAN
(aka INSAAN SHAITANI)
India, 1992. Dir: Mohan Bhakri. With: Deepark Parashar, Shree Pradha, Javed Khan, Upasana Singh, Anil Dhawan, Jagdeep. Ramakrishna Film. Colour.
Low-budget horror thriller in which a woman's murdered husband returns as a zombie seeking revenge on his wife and her lover. The title translates as 'Man Into Monster'.
✦

INSANE NUDE PSYCHO CHICKS
USA, 1997. Dir: Geoffrey de Valois. With: Heather LeMire, Shyler. Digital Entertainment Group/Salt City Home Video. Colour.
One of a series of *Vampire Raw Footage* videos that includes behind-the-scenes nude and erotic sequences. Mad psychiatrist Dr Wolfon treats the sexually obsessive nightmares of *The Vampire Conspiracy* (1995) star LeMire.
✦

IN SEARCH OF DRACULA
(Orig: PA JAKT EFTER DRACULA. UK: aka IN SEARCH OF THE REAL DRACULA)
Sweden/Transylvania, 1971. Dir: Calvin Floyd (and Tony Forsberg). With: Christopher Lee. Aspekt Film/Swedish Film Production/Swedish Television Two/Independent International. Colour.
Subtitled 'The Legend and the Vampire Tradition', this hour-long docu-drama for Swedish TV is based on the book of same title by Raymond T. McNally and Radu Florescu. Lee narrates and appears as himself, Prince Vlad Tepes and Count Dracula (in especially shot scenes) in this look at the historic facts, folklore, literature and films. With clips from *Nosferatu* (1922) and Hammer's *Scars of Dracula* (1970). The longer theatrical version apparently features material from Florescu's book *In Search of Frankenstein*, plus clips from *Dracula vs. Frankenstein* (1970).
✦✦

IN SEARCH OF DRACULA WITH JONATHAN ROSS
UK, 1996. Dir: Luke Jeans. With: Jonathan Ross, Michael Ripper. London Weekend Television/ITV. Colour.
Irreverent hour-long documentary about vampire movies (not just Dracula). Ross visits Romania and also interviews Christopher Lee, Stephanie Beacham, Richard E. Grant, Gary Oldman, Grace Jones, Jack Palance, Ingrid Pitt, author James Herbert, Sadie Frost, Francis Ford Coppola, a weird-looking Ken Russell, Bela Lugosi Jr, Princess Alexandra Caradja (who claims to be the twenty-second generation descendant of Vlad the Impaler), London Zoo's head bat-keeper Frank Wheeler, and Bram Stoker's biographer and great nephew Daniel Farson. With impressive-looking clips from *Bram Stoker's Dracula* (1992), *Carry On Screaming* (1966), *Countess Dracula* (1970), *Dracula* (1931, 1958 and 1972 versions), *Dracula A.D. 1972* (1972), *Dracula Dead and Loving It* (1995), *Dracula Has Risen from the Grave* (1968), *Dracula Prince of Darkness* (1965), *Nosferatu* (1922), *The Sat-*

anic Rites of Dracula (1973), *Scars of Dracula* (1970), *Vamp* (1986), *Vampire in Brooklyn* (1995) and *The Vampire Lovers* (1970).
✦✦✦

IN SEARCH OF HISTORY:
Legends of the Werewolves
USA, 1998. Dir: Nancy Gimbrone. With: Gary Brandner, Daniel Cohen, David J. Skal, J. Gordon Melton, Curt Siodmak, S.P. Somtow (Somtow Sucharitkul). A&E Television Networks/Weller-Grossman/History Channel. Colour.
Impressive, hour-long documentary about werewolves, both historical and fictional. Illustrated with original footage (werewolf created by John Beuchler and Magical Media Industries), clips and trailers from *Condemned to Live* (1935), *The Curse of the Werewolf* (1960), *Dracula* (1931), *Face of the Screaming Werewolf* (1960), *Frankenstein Meets the Wolf Man* (1943), *House of Frankenstein* (1944), *WereWolf of London* (1935), *The Wolf Man* (1941) and a Paul Naschy movie, plus interviews with Professor of History Ronald Hutton, Arnold W. Gurevitch MD, Professor Anthony F. McDonagh, editor/publisher Ray Ferry and Stan Lee.
✦✦✦

The Real Dracula
USA/Ireland, 1998. Dir: Charlie Ryan. With: Leslie Shepard, Dennis McIntyre, Raymond T. McNally, Norine Dresser, David J. Skal, J. Gordon Melton. A&E Television Networks/Weller-Grossman/History Channel. Colour.
Well-researched, hour-long look at the novel *Dracula*, the life of author Bram Stoker and the historical facts behind the character, illustrated with clips and trailers from *Condemned to Live* (1935), *Dracula* (both 1931 versions; 1972) and *Nosferatu* (1922), plus interviews with various authors, including Radu R. Florescu and Yaffa Weisman of the Hebrew Union College.
✦✦✦

Tom Cruise flashes his fangs in Interview With the Vampire The Vampire Chronicles *(1994).*

INSOMNIA
(Orig: INSOMNIE)
France, 1963. Dir: Pierre Etaix. With: Pierre Etaix. B&W/Colour.
Short film in which the wife of a man reading a book about vampires turns out to be one of the undead herself.
✦

THE INSPIRATIONS OF HARRY LARRABEE
USA, 1917. Dir: Bertram Bracken. With: Clifford Gray, Margaret Landis, Winifred Greenwood, William Ehfe, Frank Brownlee. General Film Company. B&W.
Forty-five minute silent drama. When a girl (Landis) is killed by a ruthless jewel thief, a playwright (Gray) restores her to life with the Pulmoter machine, invented by his scientist friend. Based on a novelette by Howard Fielding.
✦

INTERCOURSE WITH THE VAMPYRE
USA, 1994. Dir: Paul Norman. With: Rocco Siffredi, Christina Angel. Sin City Video. Colour.
Siffredi plays a hedonistic vampire in this hardcore feature.
Sequel: INTERCOURSE WITH THE VAMPYRE 2 (qv; 1994)
✦

INTERCOURSE WITH THE VAMPYRE 2
USA, 1994. Dir: Paul Norman. With: Christina Angel, Tara Monroe, Rocco Siffredi, Gerry Pike, Vixxen, Melissa Ashley. Sin City Video. Colour.
Hardcore sequel about a woman (Angel) who finds herself falling under the spell of a sensual vampire (Siffredi).
✦

THE INTERVIEW
USA, 1973. Dir: Richard Beymer. With: Joanna Bochco. Colour.
Underground short exploring how movies shape our consciousness, featuring clips from *House of Dracula* (1945).
✦

INTERVIEW WITH A VAMP
USA, 1994. Dir: Justin Case. With: Alex Jordan, Asia Carerra, Tiffany Torres (Sydney Dance), Tiffany Mynx (Tiffany Minx), Mike Horner, Ian Daniels. Realistic/ Anabolic Video. Colour.
Hardcore horror inspired by *Interview With the Vampire The Vampire Chronicles* (1994), in which vampire Louisa (Mynx), who longs for an end to her bloodsucking ways, recounts her life story to reporter David (David Hardman) in a series of sexual flashbacks involving her undead mentor, the female vampire Lestar (Jordan).
✦

INTERVIEW WITH THE VAMPIRE THE VAMPIRE CHRONICLES
UK/USA/France, 1994. Dir: Neil Jordan. With: Tom Cruise, Brad Pitt, Stephen Rea, Antonio Banderas, Christian Slater, Kirsten Dunst. The Geffen Film Company/Warner Bros. Colour.
This was originally announced in 1977, with Peter O'Toole and Jon Voight considered for the lead roles! Mick Jagger, David Bowie and John Travolta all wanted to star in it, and Elton John was asked to turn the book into a Broadway musical. It was finally scripted by Anne Rice (who initially distanced herself from the production),

based on her best-selling novel. In fact, despite being slow and uneven, director Jordan gives the film an impressive historical sweep. When River Phoenix (to whom the film is dedicated) died in 1993, Slater replaced him as journalist Daniel Malloy, who finds himself interviewing vampire Louis Pointe du Lac (Pitt) in modern-day San Francisco. Du Lac relates his own history, from when he was an eighteenth century plantation owner, depressed after the deaths of his wife and child, who was offered eternal life by the undead Lestat de Lioncourt (a wildly overacting Cruise). Eleven year-old Dunst gives a simply amazing performance as the child-vampire Claudia, and there's fun support from Banderas and Rea as evil theatrical bloodsuckers. Stan Winston created the impressive vampire make-ups and effects. The hour-long BBC documentary *Bookmark: The Vampire's Life* (1993, dir: Anand Tucker) is about author Anne Rice.
✦✦✧

IN THE GRIP OF THE VAMPIRE
USA, 1912. Gaumont. B&W.
In this silent drama, the heroine's guardian, really a super-villain called The Vampire, uses a drug to turn her into a mindless idiot. A scientist uses hypnotism to restore her sense at the end. Based on a story by Leonce Perret.
✦

IN THE HOUSE:
The Curse of Hill House
USA, 1996. With: LL Cool J, Kim Wayans, Maia Campbell, Alfonso Ribeiro. National Broadcasting Company/Quincy Jones-David Salzman Entertainment Company/Winifred Hervey Productions/UPN-TV. Colour.
Half-hour sitcom (1995-98, sixty-nine episodes) created by executive producer Winifred Hervey with rapper LL Cool J as Marion Hill, a former pro football player who co-owns a gym and shares his house with various women and children. In this Halloween episode, Marion is scared by a woman pretending to be a vampire at a party. Co-executive produced by Quincy Jones.
✦✧

INTO THE BADLANDS
USA, 1991. Dir: Sam Pillsbury. With: Bruce Dern, Mariel Hemingway, Helen Hunt, Dylan McDermott, Lisa Pelikan, Andrew Robinson. MTE/Ogiens-Kane Productions/USA Network. Colour.
Cable TV movie with a grizzled Dern as Barston, a spooky bounty hunter who narrates and links three short Western stories. In the first, a wanted gunslinger (McDermott) witnesses his own burial, while the second features Hemingway as a woman who may have imagined the wolves that attacked the cabin she's staying in. The final story involves the bounty hunter himself, as he tries to hold on to a body in an almost-deserted ghost town. In the end, Barston returns from the grave. Subtle and intelligently scripted, director Pillsbury (*The Scarecrow* [1981], etc) piles on the atmosphere thanks to the washed-out photography and a jangling music score.
✦✦✦✧

INTO THE LABYRINTH:
Dr. Jekyll and Mrs. Hyde
UK, 1982. Dir: Peter Graham Scott. With: Pamela Salem, Simon Beal, Chris Harris, Howard Goorney, June Marlow, Mhairi Harkens. HTV/ITV. Colour.
Half-hour children's fantasy TV series (1981-82, twenty-one episodes). In the third and final seven-part story, bumbling wizard Lazlo (Harris) asks Phil (Beal) to help him pursue the evil witch Belor (Salem) into Delta Time, where fictional characters can become real, and recover the magical Scarabeaus she has stolen from him. In this episode, the two magicians battle for control of London's underworld when Lazlo becomes Dr Jekyll and Belor takes on the guise of the evil Mrs Hyde.
✦✧

The Phantom of the Opera
UK, 1982. Dir: Alex Kirby. With: Pamela Salem, Simon Beal, Chris Harris, Howard Goorney, Conrad Phillips, Norman Bowler. HTV/ITV. Colour.
While Lazlo and Phil search the catacombs beneath the Paris opera house for the Scarabeaus, Belor (in the guise of a young girl) is kidnapped by the legendary Phantom (Phillips).
✦✧

INTO THE LIGHT
UK, 1999. Dir: Emma Farrell. With: Sara Bienvenue. Six Foot High Films. Colour.
Low-budget, independent feature set in modern day Manchester, as nineteenth century vampire Anne (Bienvenue) moves in with a female friend and battles to control her bloodlust. The producers sold shares in the film to the public in an attempt to complete production.
✦

INTO THE WOODS...
Finland, 1998. Dir: Tommi Salama and Matti Suksi. With: Tommi Salama, Matti Suksi, Tuomo Rämö, Minttu Tarkiainen, Jussi Honka, J.P. Jokinen. Insane Bastards Productions. Colour.
Gory half-hour comedy short, shot in English, in which a group of young survivalists encounter flesh-eating zombies in an isolated forest.
✦

LA INVASIÓN DE LOS MUERTOS
(aka BLUE DEMON Y ZOVEK EL LA INVASIÓN DE LOS MUERTOS)
Mexico, 1971 (1972). Dir: René Cardona Sr. With: Zovek (Francisco Javier Chapa del Bosque), Blue Demon (Alejandro Muñoz), Christa Linder, Raul Ramirez, Carlos Cardan, Polo Ortin. Productora Filmica Real/ Producciones Nova/Azteca Films. Colour.
This time masked Mexican wrestler Blue Demon and mystic escape artiste Professor Zovek battle a horde of zombies when a radioactive meteorite falls to Earth, revives the dead and also creates a couple of fanged beastmen. This was apparently compiled using footage from a second Zovek feature (following *El Incríeble Profesor Zovek* [1971]) after the death of del Bosque in an accident before shooting was completed. The scenes featuring the Blue Demon never interact with the Zovek footage.
Sequel: SANTO Y BLUE DEMON CONTRA DRACULA Y EL HOMBRE LOBO (qv; 1971)
✦✧

INVASION OF THE BEE GIRLS
(aka GRAVEYARD TRAMPS)
USA, 1973. Dir: Denis Sanders. With: William Smith, Anita Ford, Victoria Vetri (Angela Dorian), Cliff Osmond, Wright King, Ben Hammer. Sequoia Pictures/Centaur/ MPM. Colour.
Low-budget science fiction thriller, scripted by novelist/movie director Nicholas Meyer (*Time After Time* [1979], etc). Smith plays tough government agent Neil Agar, investigating the deaths of male research scientists from sexual exhaustion. It turns out to be a plot by a group of glamorous women in sunglasses, led by Dr Susan Harris (Ford). Through altering their cellular structure with radiation, they transform themselves into beautiful but deadly queen 'bees' with voracious sexual appetites.
✦✧

INVASION OF THE BLOOD FARMERS
USA, 1972. Dir: Ed Adlum. With: Norman Kelley, Tanna Hunter, Bruce Detrick, Paul Craig Jennings, Jack Neubeck, Richard Erickson. Ed Adlum Productions/NMD Distributing. Colour.
Laughable low-budget thriller, co-written, produced and directed by Adlum (who also scripted *Shriek of the Mutilated* [1974], etc) for just $40,000 in upstate New York. A Druid blood cult kidnap victims from a small town in an attempt to revive their ancient queen. This features terrible performances, particularly from the lisping lead villain, and a ludicrous mock-James Mason narration. The gore effects are unconvincing, and the 'songs' were apparently co-written by someone named A.J. Smut! The ads warned: 'Don't eat before you see this show and you'll have nothing to lose!!'
✦

THE INVASION OF THE VAMPIRES
(Orig: LA INVASIÓN DE LOS VAMPIROS)
Mexico, 1961 (1962). Dir: Miguel Morayta. With: Erna Martha Bauman, Rafael del Rio, Tito Junco, Fernando Soto 'Mantequilla', Bertha Moss, Carlos Agosti. Internacional Sono-Film/Tele Talia Films/Pelicula Mexicana/Azteca Films/American International. B&W.
Just try to follow the totally confusing plot of this sequel to Morayta's *The Bloody Vampire* (1961), set in the sixteenth century. Young Dr Albaran (del Rio), an associate of Count Caliostro, traces the strange deaths in a village to vampire Count Frankenhausen (Agosti, repeating his role from the previous film) and his undead daughter Countess Brunilda (Bauman). When the Count is impaled on a spear while in bat-form, his undead victims (with stakes still protruding from their chests!) attack the village and can only be stopped by the doctor's distillation of black garlic. The English-language version was produced by K. (Kenneth) Gordon Murray.
✦✦

THE INVENTORS
USA, 1934. Dir: Al Christie. With: F. Chase Taylor, Wilbur Budd Hulick, Olive Borden, Harry Short, Evelyn Dall, Lucile Watson. Educational Pictures/Christie. B&W.
Twenty-two minute comedy short based on the *Stoopnagle and Budd* radio show. Colonel Lemuel Q. Stoopnagle (Taylor) and Budd (Hulick) build a 'Stoopenstein' (Frankenstein's second cousin) out of various spare parts collected by the students at a girls' school. However, the mechanical creature goes out of control, until a bell calms him down. This short was later included in the compilation *The Sound of Laughter* (1963).
✦

INVISIBLE GHOST
USA, 1941. Dir: Joseph H. Lewis. With: Bela Lugosi, Polly Ann Young, John McGuire, Clarence Muse, Terry Walker, Betty Compson. Monogram/Banner Pictures/Astor Pictures. B&W.
Supposedly based on a true story and originally titled *Murder by the Stars* and *The Phantom Killer*, director Lewis (*Gun Crazy* [1949], etc) brings a style and sophistication to this poverty-row horror that is more than its muddled storyline deserves. Whenever kindly Mr Kessler (Lugosi) sees the wife he believes is dead (Compson), he unknowingly turns into a psychopathic killer who strangles someone in his household with his dressing gown! Incredibly, the incompetent police allow the family to continue living in the house, and even manage to execute the wrong man for the murders. With Jack Mulhall.
✦✦

INVISIBLE INVADERS
USA, 1959. Dir: Edward L. Cahn. With: John Agar, Jean Byron, Philip Tonge, Robert Hutton, John Carradine, Hal Torey. Premium Pictures/United Artists. B&W.
Despite being just over an hour long, this ludicrous low-budget science fiction/horror thriller uses voice-over narration and stock footage to fill the gaps in the plot. The Earth is invaded by invisible aliens from the Moon who possess the bodies of the recently dead. The pasty-faced walking corpses obviously inspired George Romero's zombies in *Night of the Living Dead* (1968), and Carradine has a cameo as the resurrected scientist who is the leader of the aliens. Screenwriter Samuel Newman uses some of the same character names from his *The Giant Claw* (1957), while Paul Blaisdell's monster suit from Cahn's *It! The Terror from Beyond Space* (1958) makes a brief reappearance.
✦✧

IO ZOMBO, TU ZOMBI, LEI ZOMBA
Italy, 1979. Dir: Nello Rossati. With: Duilio del Prete, Renzo Montagnani, Cochi Ponzoni, Nadia Cassini, Daniele Vargas, Tullio Solenghi. TV Cine 77. Colour.
In this lively spoof of *Dawn of the Dead* (1978), a quartet of comic flesh-eating zombies (led by Montagnani's gravedigger) are revived by voodoo. They run amok in the Italian countryside, attempting to eat unsuspecting travellers and various guests at a motel, until the army corner the living dead in a supermarket. In the end, it all apparently turns out to be a dream. The title translates as 'I am a Zombie, You Are a Zombie, She is a Zombie'.
✦✧

THE IRONBOUND VAMPIRE
USA, 1997 (1998). Dir: Karl Petry. With: Richard Matyskiel, Deana Enoches, Dennis Drenth, Conrad Brooks, Dolores Fuller, Johnny Link. Brain Escape Pictures/MVP Productions/EI Independent Cinema. Colour.
Set in the Ironbound section of Newark, New Jersey, where a retired detective-turned-author tracks down haunted vampire Thomas Lane, who was transformed on the battlefields of the First World War. This independent video release features cameos by Ed Wood veterans Brooks and Fuller (reunited for the first time on screen since *Glen or Glenda* [1953]), while the unrated version includes more scenes of lesbian seduction.
✦

ISABELL, A DREAM
Italy, 1968. Dir: Luigi Cozzi. With: Isabell Karlsson, Carla Gasperini, Anna Orban, Walter Braggian. B&W.
This nine minute short marked the professional début of twenty-one year-old Cozzi. A young man falls in love with a rainbow-like girl (Karlsson). In a dream sequence, women take over the world and hunt the few surviving males (who wear Don Post masks of Dracula, the Mummy and Frankenstein's Monster) through a forest. Footage from this also turned up in Cozzi's *Il Tunnel Sotto Il Mondo* (1969) and *Il Vicino di Casa* (1973).
✦

ISLAND OF MUTATIONS
(Orig: L'ISOLA DEGLI UOMINI PESCI. USA: ISLE OF THE FISHMEN/SCREAMERS/SOMETHING WAITS IN THE DARK)
Italy, 1979. Dir: Sergio Martino. With: Barbara Bach, Claudio Cassinelli, Richard Johnson, Beryl Cunningham, Joseph Cotten, Franco Javarone. Dania Film/Medusa. Colour.
Silly horror adventure in which shipwrecked survivors trapped on a desert island discover strange voodoo rites, the lost city of Atlantis, Johnson's hilarious mad scientist Rackman experimenting with genetic mutations, and a predictable volcanic climax. The scientifically-created gill men look pretty unconvincing. In 1980, New World Pictures added twelve minutes of new opening footage (photographed by Gary Graver) featuring Cameron Mitchell, Mel Ferrer and a living corpse (created by Chris Walas) in the Cave of the Dead, and credited it to 'Dan T. Miller' (Miller Drake).
✦✧

ISLE OF THE DEAD
USA, 1945. Dir: Mark Robson. With: Boris Karloff, Ellen Drew, Marc Cramer, Katherine Emery, Helene Thimig, Alan Napier. RKO Radio Pictures. B&W.
Unfairly neglected chiller from Val Lewton's 'B' unit at RKO, this was Karloff's second teaming with the talented producer. The actor gives a strong performance as obsessed Greek General Pherides, who believes the pagan myths that a vampire-like 'vorvolaka' is killing off the inhabitants of a plague-ridden island during the 1912 Balkan War. Despite a sometimes confusing script by Ardel Wray and an uncredited Josef Mischel, Robson's atmospheric direction, coupled with the haunting sets and an impressive cast (including Jason Robards Sr and Skelton Knaggs), make this a minor classic. Suggested by a painting by Arnold Böcklin, this was banned by the British censor for ten years.
✦✦✦✦

IT
USA/Canada, 1990. Dir: Tommy Lee Wallace. With: Dennis Christopher, Tim Curry, Olivia Hussey, Annette O'Toole, John Ritter, Richard Thomas. Lorimar/Warner Bros/ABC-TV. Colour.
Superior three hour, two-part TV movie based on the mega-novel by

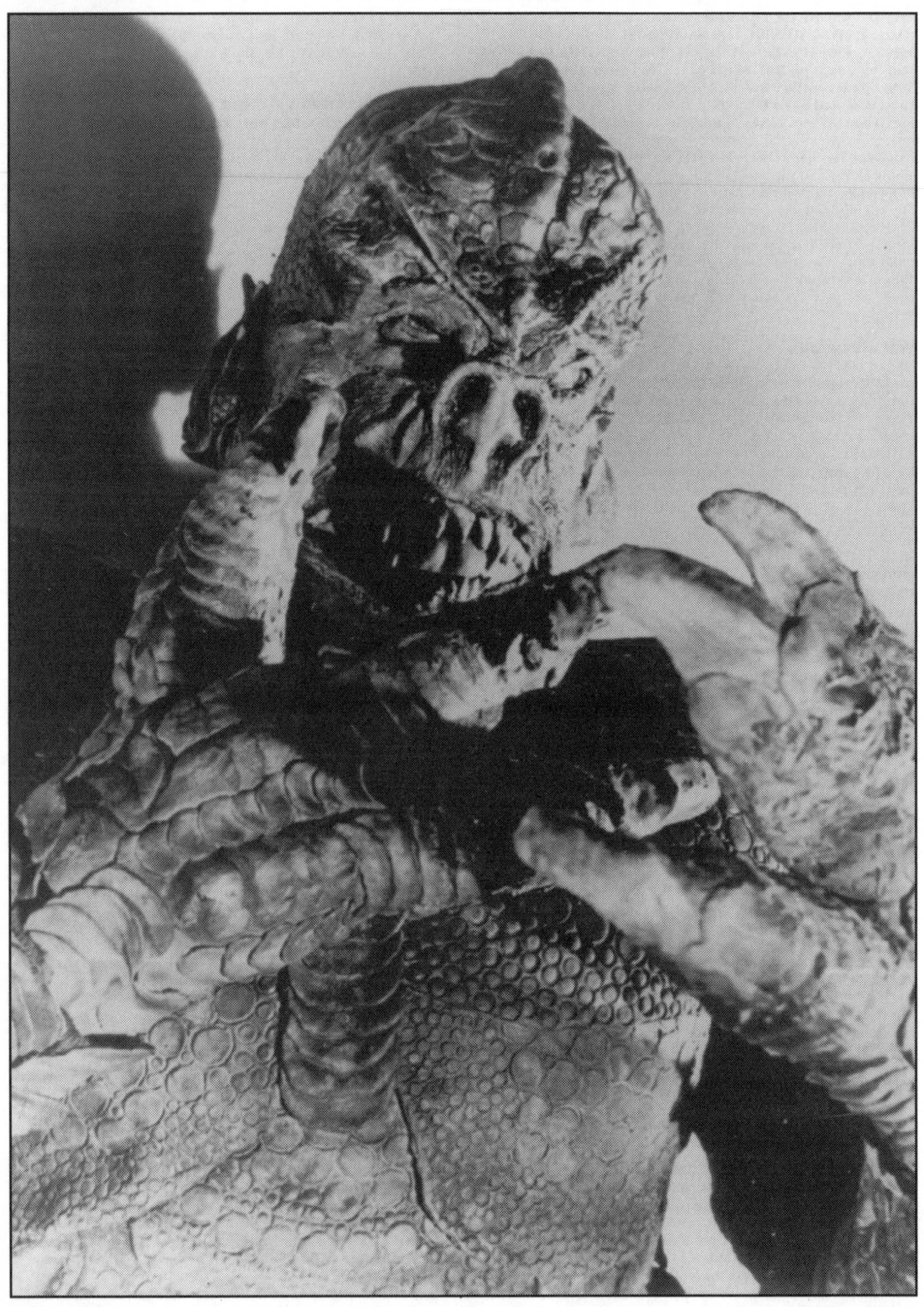

Stephen King. Every thirty years, an ancient evil returns to plague the small New England town of Derry and destroy its children. The shape-shifting monster takes the appearance of Pennywise the Clown (a nicely menacing performance by Curry), various rotting zombies, and the lycanthrope from the 1957 movie *I Was a Teenage Werewolf* (make-up created by Norman Cabrera and Jack Bricker). Disappointingly, the subterranean menace turns out to be a giant stop-motion spider (created by Gene Warren Jr and the Fantasy II effects team, and animated by Pete Kleinow). Scriptwriter Lawrence D. Cohen (*Carrie* [1976], etc) does a fine job paring down the text, but the first half works better, before too many flashbacks get in the way of the plot.
✦✦✦

IT CAME FROM HOLLYWOOD

USA, 1982. Dir: Andrew Solt and Malcolm Leo. With: Dan Aykroyd, John Candy, Cheech (Marin) and (Thomas) Chong, Gilda Radner, Don E. Carney. Strausberg-Stein/ Paramount. Colour/B&W.
Paramount apparently re-edited this routine compilation of unidentified clips and trailers, arranged under various headings, from some of Hollywood's all-time 'Golden Turkeys'. These include *Attack of the Puppet People* (1958), *The Brain That Wouldn't Die* (1960), *Creature from the Black Lagoon* (1953), *Curse of the Faceless Man* (1958), *Fiend Without a Face* (1958), *First Man Into Space* (1958), *Frankenstein and the Monster from Hell* (1973), *Frankenstein Conquers the World* (1964), *Frankenstein Meets the Spacemonster* (1965), *Frankenstein's Daughter* (1958), *The Horror of Party Beach* (1964), *The Incredible Melting Man* (1977), *The Incredibly Strange Creatures Who Stopped Living and Became Mixed-up Zombies!!?* (1963), *I Was a Teenage Frankenstein* (1957), *Plan 9 from Outer Space* (1958), *Teenage Monster* (1957), *Zombies of the Stratosphere* (1952) and numerous others. There are no rarities and few surprises (probably because Michael and Harry Medved were 'special consultants'), and the new linking material by various alumni from TV's *Saturday Night Live* (1975-) is, at best, inane. Executive producers/directors Solt and Leo apparently know nothing and care even less about their subject matter.
✦✧

I, THE VAMPIRE

(Orig: YO EL VAMPIRO)
Mexico, circa 1980s. Dir: Juan López Moctezuma. Colour.
This is an apparently unreleased film by the director of *Mary, Mary, Bloody Mary* (1975).
✦

IT! THE TERROR FROM BEYOND SPACE

USA, 1958. Dir: Edward L. Cahn. With: Marshall Thompson, Shawn Smith, Kim Spalding, Ann Doran, Dabbs Greer, Paul Langton. Vogue/United Artists. B&W.
Filmed under the title *It! The Vampire from Beyond Space*, this very effective low-budget science fiction/horror movie was probably the high point of director Cahn's career. Jerome Bixby's tight screenplay later 'influenced' everything from *Queen of Blood* (1966) to *Alien* (1979), although it in turn seems to have been 'inspired' by A.E. van Vogt's story 'The Black Destroyer'. Thompson (who also starred in *Fiend Without a Face* and *First Man Into Space* the same year) has one of his best roles as Captain Carruthers, being returned to Earth by the second Mars mission to stand trial for the murders of his entire crew. What they don't know is that the real killer — a blood-drinking scaly monster (played by Ray 'Crash' Corrigan) — has sneaked aboard and soon begins ripping up the supporting cast. Cahn wisely kept Paul Blaisdell's creature suit in the shadows for most of the movie to create a minor classic. Audiences were offered a guaranteed $50,000 'by a world-renowned insurance company' to the first person who could prove 'It' was not on Mars.
✦✦✦✧

IT WAS BEAUTY KILLED THE BEAST

USA, 1992. Dir: Scott Benson. With: Murray Spivack, Rudy Behlmer, George (E.) Turner, Linwood (G.) Dunn, Richard Edlund, Jerry Goldsmith. Turner Home Entertainment. Colour/B&W.
Interesting half-hour documentary about the making of *King Kong* (1933) which celebrates the sixtieth anniversary of the film. Among those interviewed are original sound effects technician Spivack and optical photographer Dunn. Narrated by Don Kennedy.
✦✦✦

Ray 'Crash' Corrigan inside Paul Blaisdell's suit of It! The Terror from Beyond Space *(1958).*

I WALKED WITH A ZOMBIE

USA, 1943. Dir: Jacques Tourneur. With: James Ellison, Frances Dee, Tom Conway, Edith Barrett, Christine Gordon, James Bell. RKO Radio Pictures. B&W.
The second film from producer Val Lewton's 'B' unit at RKO. The script by Curt Siodmak and Ardel Wray may be credited to a story by Inez Wallace (based on an *American Weekly* article), but this is actually a thinly-veiled reworking of *Jane Eyre* by an uncredited Lewton. When Canadian nurse Betsy (Dee, who replaced Anna Lee before filming) arrives on the Caribbean island of St. Sebastian to care for the apparently paralysed Jessica Holland (Gordon), she soon becomes involved with the local voodoo ceremonies and a mystery surrounding Jessica's haunted husband, Paul (Conway). The atmospheric walk by the two women through the sugar cane fields, their meeting with the zombie guardian Carrefour (Darby Jones), and the poetic climax when Mrs Holland's body is carried into the sea are among the high points of this minor classic. With Sir Lancelot as the calypso singer. Dimension Films announced an unnecessary remake in 1999, to be written and directed by Rob Cohen.
✦✦✦✦

I WAS A NUDE VAMPIRE MOVIE STARLET

USA, 1997. Dir: Geoffrey de Valois. With: Elaine Juliette Williamson. Digital Entertainment Group/Salt City Home Video. Colour.
Another in the series of softcore *Vampire Raw Footage* videos that includes behind-the-scenes nude and erotic sequences. Big-breasted Williamson reveals her secret desires and fantasies.
✦

I WAS A TEENAGE FRANKENSTEIN

(UK: TEENAGE FRANKENSTEIN)
USA, 1957. Dir: Herbert L. Strock. With: Whit Bissell, Phyllis Coates, Robert Burton, Gary Conway, George Lynn, John Cliff. Santa Rosa Productions/American International Pictures. B&W/Colour.
AIP's follow-up to its box office hit *I Was a Teenage Werewolf* (1957) is better than expected. Bissell stars as a stuffy Professor Frankenstein in modern Los Angeles, who creates an ugly monster (Conway) out of teenage auto wreck victims. When not ignoring his fiancée (Coates), the Professor is throwing her to the alligator he keeps in the cellar. In the end, Frankenstein decides to give his monster a new face before it electrocutes itself during the predictable climax (which is in colour!). Produced by Herman Cohen. Some sequences later turned up in AIP's *Terror from the Year 5000* (1958).
Sequel: HOW TO MAKE A MONSTER (qv; 1958)
✦✦

I WAS A TEENAGE MUMMY

USA, 1991 (1992). Dir: Christopher C. Frieri. With: Joan Devitt, Gregg Kalek, John Gonchar, Robert Reiss. Ghost Limb. B&W.
Laughable amateur production about an Egyptian boy who turns a schoolgirl (Devitt) into a murderous mummy.
✦

I WAS A TEENAGE WEREWOLF

USA, 1957. Dir: Gene Fowler Jr. With: Michael Landon, Yvonne Lime, Whit Bissell, Tony Marshall, Dawn Richard, Barney Phillips. Sunset Productions/American International Pictures. B&W.
This first feature from director Fowler Jr was filmed under the title *Blood of the Werewolf*. It was shot in seven days on a budget of $125,000 and earned more than $2,000,000 in its first year. The mad Dr Alfred Brandon (Bissell) plans to save humanity by hypnotically

Christine Gordon and Frances Dee meet Darby Jones in I Walked With a Zombie *(1943).*

regressing emotionally disturbed Tony Rivers (Landon) back to a more primitive stage of evolution. The teenage tearaway transforms into a toothy werewolf (make-up created by Philip Scheer) before being shot to death by the police. Scenes from this film also turned up in the 1973 rockumentary, *Let the Good Times Roll*. Scriptwriter 'Ralph Thornton' was actually a pseudonym for producer Herman Cohen and novelist Aben Kandel. Ken Miller sings 'Eeny, Meeny, Miney, Mo'. With Vladimir Sokoloff and Guy Williams (TV's *Lost in Space* [1965-68], etc). A cult classic, AIP's Samuel Z. Arkoff announced a remake in 1992 and even organised an open casting call in New York to find an unknown lead.
Sequel: HOW TO MAKE A MONSTER (qv; 1958)
✦✦

I WAS A TEENAGE ZOMBIE

USA, 1986 (1987). Dir: John Elias Michalakias. With: Michael Rubin, Steve McCoy, George Seminara, Peter Bush, Kevin Nagle, Cassie Madden. Periclean/Charter/ Horizon. Colour.
Terrible teen nerd horror/sex comedy originally filmed on 16mm. Radioactivity leaking into a local river turns swimmers into violent zombies. A group of teenagers try to stop the walking dead, whose ranks include an unpleasant zombie drug dealer named Mussolini. With music by Los Lobos, the Fleshtones, the Waitresses and Violent Femmes.
✦

I ZOMBIE THE CHRONICLES OF PAIN

UK, 1998. Dir: Andrew Parkinson. With: Giles Aspen, Ellen Softley, Dean Sipling, Claire Griffin, Peter Hacket, Kate Thorougood. Andrew Parkinson/Lost Films/Screen Edge. Colour.
Relentlessly downbeat and gory low-budget début by writer/director Parkinson, shot on 16mm over a four year period in London and Brighton. When student Mark (Aspen) becomes infected by the bite of a zombiefied woman (Jane Smith) he discovers in a derelict house, his mind and body start to slowly decay and like a drug addict he craves a regular supply of fresh human flesh to survive. Impressive special make-up effects by Paul Hyett.
✦✦

J'ACCUSÉ

France, 1918. Dir: Abel Gance. With: Séverin-Mars, Romuald Joubé, Marise Daouvray, Desjardins, Angele Guys. United Artists. B&W/Colour.
During the climax of this silent short, the dead of the First World War rise from their graves as a warning to the living.
Remake: J'ACCUSÉ (qv; 1938)
✦

J'ACCUSÉ

(USA: THAT THEY MAY LIVE)
France, 1938 (1939). Dir: Abel Gance. With: Victor Francen, Line Noro, Marie Lou, Reneé Devillers, Georges Saillard, Jean Louis Barrault. Forrester-Parant Productions/Arthur Mayer-Joseph Burstyn Inc. B&W.
Writer/director Gance's remake of his own 1918 anti-war short, in which Jean Diaz (Francen), the lone survivor from the last patrol wiped out at the end of the First World War, invents a formula for super-strong glass. After making a promise to his fallen comrades that there will never be another war, he learns that his invention is to be used as a weapon in a forthcoming conflict. During the climax he calls upon the forgotten dead of twenty years before to rise from their graves at Verdun to stop the living from fighting again. Apparently, real disfigured casualties from the First World War were used to portray the walking dead.
✦✦

THE JACK BENNY SHOW

USA, circa 1955. Dir: Frederick De Cordova and Ralph Levy. With: Jack Benny, Eddie 'Rochester' Anderson, Don Wilson, Dennis Day, Mary Livingstone, Mel Blanc. CBS-TV. B&W.
In one episode of the comedian's popular TV musical/variety show, Dr Jekyll (Benny) is suspected of being Mr Hyde. However, when the fanged monster is finally unmasked, he is revealed as singer Day.
✦

JACK THE BEAR

USA, 1993. Dir: Marshall Herskovitz. With: Danny DeVito, Robert J. Steinmiller Jr, Miko Hughes, Gary Sinise, Art LaFleur, Stefan Gierasch. American Filmworks/Lucky Dog/Twentieth Century Fox. Colour.
Downbeat family drama set in California in 1972, in which DeVito's alcoholic John Leary plays late-night TV horror host Al Gory. This includes clips from *Frankenstein* (1931), (Abbott and Costello) *Meet Frankenstein* (1948), *The Wolf Man* (1941) and other films. With Julia Louis-Dreyfus.
✦✧

JACK THE RIPPER

UK/USA, 1988. Dir: David Wickes. With: Michael Caine, Armande Assante, Jane Seymour, Ray McAnally, Lewis Collins, Ken Bones. Euston/Hill-O'Connor/Lorimar/ Thames Television/CBS-TV. Colour.
All-star, four-hour TV mini-series commemorating the centenary of the original Ripper murders. Although it adds nothing new to the various theories, Caine gives a strong performance as Inspector Frederick Abberline, the policeman investigating the Whitechapel slayings. As one of the suspects, Assante plays American actor Richard Mansfield, recreating his performance as Dr Jekyll and Mr Hyde on the London stage. With Susan George, Harry Andrews (who died the following year), Lysette Anthony, Michael Gothard, Ronald Hines, Edward Judd, T.P. McKenna and Gerald Sim. Narrated by an uncredited Patrick Allen. Signet published a novelisation by Mark Daniel. Caine and director Wickes were reunited for *Jekyll & Hyde* (1990).
✦✦✦

THE JAIL BREAK

(aka MIGHTY MOUSE IN THE JAIL BREAK)
USA, 1946. Dir: Eddie Donnelly. Voices: Tom Morrison. Terrytoons/Twentieth Century-Fox. Colour.
Six minute Paul Terry cartoon in which Count Dracula and the Frankenstein Monster are prisoners on Alcatraz. This was a sequel to *Mighty Mouse Meets Bad Bill Bunion* (1945).
Sequel: THE CRACKPOT KING (1946)
✦✧

JAMES HOUND: THE MONSTER MAKER

USA, 1966. Dir: Ralph Bakshi. Voices: Dayton Allen. Terrytoons/Twentieth Century-Fox. Colour.
Seven minute cartoon inspired by Ian Fleming's fictional spy, in which secret agent James Hound (Allen) short-circuits Professor Mad's army of Frankenstein Monsters.
Sequel: RAIN DRAIN (1966)
✦✧

DER JANUSKOPF

(USA: aka DR. JEKYLL AND MR. HYDE/THE HEAD OF JANUS/LOVE'S MOCKERY)
Germany, 1920. Dir: F. (Friedrich) W. (Wilhelm) Murnau. With: Conrad Veidt, Margarete Schlegel, Willy Kayser-Heyl, Margaret Kupfer, Gustav Botz, Bela Lugosi. Lipow Film/Decla-Bioscop. B&W.
Unauthorised silent version of Robert Louis Stevenson's 1886 novella *Strange Case of Dr. Jekyll and Mr. Hyde*, from the director of *Nosferatu* (1922). Subtitled *Eine Tragödie am Rande der Wirklichkeit* ('A Tragedy on the Border of Reality'), Veidt portrays the wealthy Dr Warren, who is possessed by a bust of Janus, the Roman god with two faces. As the evil Mr O'Connor, he murders a small girl and forces his fiancée into prostitution before taking his own life with poison. Lugosi appears in the role of Warren's butler in this now apparently lost film.
Remake: DR. JEKYLL AND MR. HYDE (qv; 1920, Paramount)
✦✦

JAWS OF THE JUNGLE

(aka JUNGLE VIRGIN)
Ceylon/USA, 1936. Dir: J.D. Kendis. With: Teeto, Minta, Gukar, Walla the Ape, Agena the Bear. Jay Dee Kay. B&W.
Independent feature in which a horde of giant vampire bats attack a village in Ceylon. Narrated by C. Howell.
✦

GRIFFIN JAY
[1905-1954]

American 'B' movie writer, best remembered for creating the clichés in Universal's *Mummy* sequels.
qv: *Captive Wild Woman* (1943); *Cry of the Werewolf* (1944); *Devil Bat's Daughter* (1946); *The Mummy's Ghost* (1944); *The Mummy's Hand* (1940); *The Mummy's Tomb* (1942); *The Return of the Vampire* (1943).

JEKYLL & HYDE

UK, 1990. Dir: David Wickes. With: Michael Caine, Cheryl Ladd, Joss Ackland, Ronald Pickup, Lionel Jeffries, Diane Keen. London Weekend Television/ITV. Colour.
Writer/director Wickes and star Caine are reunited from *Jack the Ripper* (1988) for this glossy two-hour TV movie, 'derived' from Robert Louis Stevenson's short novel. It attempts to make the story work for a contemporary audience, but amongst the chases and love interest, Caine's Mr Hyde (in burn-like make-up created by Image Animation) is simply a rampaging monster with none of the subtle evil the role demands. With Lance Percival, and Miriam Karlin as the scary-looking madame of a whorehouse.
Remake: MARY REILLY (qv; 1996)
✦✦

THE JEKYLL AND HYDE PORTFOLIO

(aka JEKYLL AND HYDE UNLEASHED)
USA, 1971 (1972). Dir: Eric Jeffrey Haims. With: Gray

Daniels, Mady Maguire, Sebastian Brook, John Terry, Don Greer, Rene Bond. Xerxes Productions/HMS Releasing. Colour.
This has nothing to do with the story by Robert Louis Stevenson. It's about a psychotic sex killer with a split personality killing women at a nursing school. Actor Greer also scripted the film.
✦

JEKYLL AND HYDE...TOGETHER AGAIN
USA, 1982. Dir: Jerry Belson. With: Mark Blankfield, Bess Armstrong, Krista Errickson, Tim Thomerson, Ann M. Nelson, George Chakiris. Titan/Paramount. Colour.
TV writer Belson made his directing début with this unfunny comedy starring Blankfield, who uses a cocaine-like drug to turn himself from repressed hospital surgeon Dr Jekyll into super-stud Mr Hyde. With George Wendt, Cassandra Peterson (aka Elvira), a spoof of *The Elephant Man* (1980) and Robert Louis Stevenson actually spinning in his grave.
✦

JEKYLL ISLAND
USA, 1998. Dir: Ken Dupuis. With: Brion James, Everett McGill, Finola Hughes. Artist View Entertainment. Colour.
When a senator is robbed of millions of dollars, the culprit turns out to be a famous criminologist (James) who teaches by day and becomes a master thief by night. Except for the title, this action-adventure movie has nothing to do with Robert Louis Stevenson's story.
✦✧

JESSE JAMES MEETS FRANKENSTEIN'S DAUGHTER
USA, 1965. Dir: William Beaudine. With: Narda Onyx, John Lupton, Cal Bolder, Estelita, Jim Davis, Nestor Paiva. Embassy Pictures/Circle Pictures. Colour.
Despite the title, it's actually Frankenstein's *granddaughter* Maria (Onyx) who, along with her weak brother Rudolph (Steven Geray), transplants a synthetic brain into Jesse James' sidekick Hank Tracy (Bolder) and turns him into Igor, a monster. Lupton as outlaw Jesse and Davis as a sympathetic sheriff play this as a straight Western, while Estelita's Mexican heroine Juanita has to be seen to be believed! The last film from veteran director William 'One Shot' Beaudine, this is actually slightly better than its companion feature, *Billy the Kid Versus Dracula* (1965), which is hardly a recommendation. Both movies were not released in Britain until 1974.
✦✧

THE JETSONS:
Haunted Halloween
USA, 1962. Dir: William Hanna and Joseph Barbera. Voices: Janet Waldo, Daws Butler, George O'Hanlon, Mel Blanc, Jean Vander Pyl, Penny Singleton. Hanna-Barbera Productions/ABC-TV. Colour.
The half-hour cartoon adventures (1962-63, twenty-four episodes) of twenty-first century family The Jetsons. In this episode, Dr Scarem, a mad scientist, creates a dancing Frankenstein Monster-like robot for his waxite museum collection. It also includes a dream sequence featuring George (O'Hanlon) and Jane Jetson (Singleton) as vampires, their son Elroy (Butler) as the mummy, and daughter Judy (Waldo) as a witch. With the voice of Don Messick.
Series sequel: THE JETSONS (1984)
✦✧

THE JITTERS
Canada/USA/Japan, 1988 (1989). Dir: John M. Fasano. With: Sal Viviano, Marilyn Yokuda, James Hong, Frank Dietz, Handy Atmadja, John Quincey Lee. Gaga Communications/Fascination/Skouras Pictures/Prism Entertainment. Colour.
For fans of Hong Kong hopping vampires comes this Westernised version, filmed in Toronto and set in the Los Angeles Chinatown district. It's an enjoyable, if silly, horror comedy in which murder victims are revived by Tony Yang Sr (Hong) and his son (Lee) as the pointy-eared undead *gyonsi*, to seek vengeance against a violent street gang who are looking for a hidden treasure.
✦✦

JOHNNY BRAVO:
A Wolf in Chick's Clothing
USA, 1997. Dir: Butch Hartman. Voices: Jeff Bennett, Brenda Vaccaro, Mae Whitman. Hanna-Barbera Cartoons/The Cartoon Network. Colour.
Half-hour cartoon series (thirty-nine episodes) created by twenty-six year-old animator Van Partible (who took his character's name from the title of an episode of *The Brady Bunch* [1969-74]). In this seven minute segment, the eponymous egotistical Elvis soundalike (Bennett) goes on a date with Fluffy, a woman who transforms into a werewolf under the full moon.
✦✧

NOBLE JOHNSON
[1897-1978]

Muscular American character actor. Often cast as a mute or savage, most notably as the Native Chief of Skull Island in *King Kong* (1933) and *The Son of Kong* (1933). He also menaced Bob Hope as a scary-looking zombie in the horror comedy *The Ghost Breakers* (1940).
qv: *The Mummy* (1933).

STEVE JOHNSON
[b 1960]

American special effects make-up artist. An assistant on *An American Werewolf in London* (1981) and other movies in the early 1980s, he has since graduated to creating his own monsters, most notably with the uneven *Howling* series.
qv: *Bad Moon* (1996); *Dead Heat* (1988); *Fright Night* (1985); *Here Come the Munsters* (1995); *The Howling* (1980); *Howling IV The Original Nightmare* (1988); *Howling VI The Freaks* (1990); *Howling II Stirba — Werewolf Bitch* (1984); *Innocent Blood* (1992); *Lord of Illusions* (1995) *The Munsters' Scary Little Christmas* (1996); *Necronomicon* (1993); *Pet Sematary II* (1992); *Return of the Living Dead III* (1993).

TOR JOHNSON
(Tor Johansson) [1903-1971]

Swedish-born professional wrestler who toured America as the 'Super Swedish Angel' and made his film début in the W.C. Fields comedy *The Man on the Flying Trapeze* (1935). After retiring from the ring, the bald, hulking actor became typecast as a monster, most notably in poverty-row quickies for Ed Wood Jr. He recreated his character Lobo for a series of personal appearances in Southern California during the late 1960s. Tor Johnson masks are still a popular Halloween item and he was played by George 'The Animal' Steele (Jim Myers) in *Ed Wood* (1994).
qv: *Ghost Catchers* (1944); *Night of the Ghouls* (1959); *Plan 9 from Outer Space* (1958).

JOKERS PLAYING GAMES
Hong Kong, circa 1987. Dir: Tommy Young. Lisa Mok/ Ocean Shores Video. Colour.
Horror comedy in which a man possessed by a ghost battles fake hopping vampires and zombie cops from Hell.
✦✧

JONATHAN
(aka JONATHAN, VAMPIRE STERBEN NICHT)
West Germany, 1970. Dir: Hans W. Geissendörfer. With: Jürgen Jung, Hans Dieter Jendreyko, Paul Albert Krumm, Hertha von Walther, Oskar von Schab, Ilona Grübel. Iduna Film. Colour.
Bram Stoker's *Dracula* is freely adapted by writer/director Geissendörfer as a political allegory for the rise of fascism. The eponymous hero is, of course, Jonathan Harker (Jung), a member of the peasant resistance movement who is sent by an old professor (von Schab) to destroy Krumm's Führer-like Dracula and his black-shirted thugs. The Count and his undead acolytes are finally driven into the sea and

destroyed. Cinematographer Robert (Robbi) Müller contributes remarkably fluid camerawork. Scenes of sex and violence were apparently added after release to make the film more commercial.
✦✦✦

JONATHAN OF THE NIGHT
USA, 1987. Dir: Buddy Giovinazzo. With: Don Striano, Mitch Maglio, Melissa Tait, Eric Collica, Ricky G. 2000 AD. Colour.
Ten minute short written, produced and directed by Giovinazzo (*Combat Shock* [1984], etc), designed to interest backers in a full-length feature. Unfortunately, the amateurish performances and grainy photography hardly enhance this tale of a modern-day vampire at a New York party. Music by Ricky G, who has a brief cameo as a drunken slob.
✦

JONATHAN WINTERS SHOW
USA, 1968. With: Jonathan Winters, Boris Karloff, Agnes Moorehead. CBS-TV. Colour.
Karloff's penultimate TV appearance was in this Halloween comedy special, first broadcast 30 October. He portrays a Frankenstein-like scientist and performs the song 'It Was a Very Good Year'.
✦✧

CAROLYN JONES
[1929-1983]

American leading lady of the 1950s, best remembered as the vampish Morticia Addams from TV's *The Addams Family* (1964-66).
qv: *The Demon and the Mummy* (1975); *Halloween With the Addams Family* (1977); *Kolchak: The Night Stalker: 'Demon in Lace'* (1975); *The New Scooby-Doo Movies: 'Scooby-Doo Meets the Addams Family: Wednesday is Missing'* (1972).

DARBY JONES
[1910-1986]

Black American actor who portrayed the eponymous corpse in *I Walked With a Zombie* (1943) and recreated the role in the comedy *Zombies on Broadway* (1945).
qv: *Tarzan Escapes* (1936).

DUANE JONES
[1937-1988]

Black American actor. As Ben, the hero of George Romero's *Night of the Living Dead* (1968), he meets an ironic end.
qv: *Ganja & Hess* (1973); *Night of the Day of the Dawn of the Son of the Bride of the Return of the Terror: The Revenge of the Terror of the Attack of the Evil, Mutant, Hellbound, Flesh-Eating, Subhumanoid Living Dead, Part 2* (1968/91); *To Die For* (1988); *Vampires* (1988).

FREDDIE JONES
[b 1927]

Well-respected British actor, often reduced to playing outlandish character roles. In Hammer's *Frankenstein Must Be Destroyed* (1969) he gives a remarkably sympathetic performance as a victim of a brain transplant experiment. He later portrayed the Baron himself in the musical comedy *Son of Dracula* (1973).
qv: *The Black Cauldron* (1985); *The Last Vampyre* (1992); *Neverwhere* (1996); *The Satanic Rites of Dracula* (1973); *Vampira* (1974); *Woof!* (1988-); *Young Sherlock Holmes* (1985).

JONNY QUEST THE REAL ADVENTURES:
(aka JONNY QUEST THE NEW ADVENTURES)
In the Darkness of the Moon
USA/Japan, 1996. Dir: Thomas Ray and Kunio Shimamura. Voices: R.D. Roth, George Segal, Robert Patrick, Jesse (P.) Douglas, Michael Benyaer, Frank Welker. Hanna-Barbera Cartoons/The Cartoon Network/TNT/TBS. Colour.
Half-hour cartoon TV series (sixty-five episodes), which updates the characters from *The Adventures of Jonny Quest* (1964-65). In this episode, the teenage Jonny (Roth) and Hadji (Benyaer), along with Dr Benton Quest (Segal), Roger 'Race' Bannon (Patrick), Jessie Bannon (Douglas) and Bandit the dog (Welker), leave the Quest Compound in Maine and travel to The Yukon, Canada. There they help create a scientific cure for the last member of a cursed family of werewolves. Background design by Alex Nino.
✦✧

NEIL JORDAN
[b 1950]

Irish writer and director. His high-concept horror projects include *The Company of Wolves* (1984), *High Spirits* (1988) and *Interview With the Vampire The Vampire Chronicles* (1994).

LOUIS JOURDAN
(Louis Gendre) [b 1919]

Debonair French leading man who portrayed the eponymous romantic bloodsucker in the BBC-TV movie *Count Dracula* (1977) and turned up as the evil Dr Anton Arcane in *Swamp Thing* (1981) and *The Return of Swamp Thing* (1989).

JOURNEY TO THE UNKNOWN:
Jane Brown's Body
UK/USA, 1968 (1969). Dir: Alan Gibson. With: Stefanie Powers, David Buck, Alan McNaughtan, Sarah Lawson, Arthur Pentelow, Clive Graham. Hammer Film Productions/Twentieth Century-Fox/ITV. Colour.
Disappointing hour-long anthology TV series (1968-69, seventeen episodes) created by Hammer and executive produced by former Hitchcock assistant Joan Harrison. This episode is based on a story by Cornell Woolrich. When the eponymous character (Powers) commits suicide, she is brought back to life by Dr Ian Denholt (McNaughtan) with no memory of her past. With Lewis Fiander. This episode wasn't broadcast when the series was first shown in America on ABC-TV.
✦✦

EL JOVENCITO DRACULA
Spain, 1975. Dir: Carlos Benpar (Carlos Benito Parra). With: Carlos Benpar (Carlos Benito Parra), Susanna Estrada, Victor Israel, Marina Ferri, Veronica Miriel, Norma Kerr. Los Films del Mediterraneo. Colour.
Director Benpar stars in this low-budget comedy as Jonathan, the last descendant of Count Dracula, who travels to Transylvania to claim his inheritance. But the descendant of Van Helsing is the town mayor who wants to turn Castle Dracula into a tourist attraction. With characters named after those in Bram Stoker's novel.
✦

JUGULAR WINE
USA, 1997. Dir: Blair Murphy. With: Shaun Irons, Lisa Malkiewicz, Rachelle Packer, Vladimir Kehkaial, Michael Colyar, Meghan Bashaw. Pagan Pictures/Cinequanon/ Empyre Pictures/EI Independent Cinema. Colour.
Made for just $75,000, this was reputedly given a limited theatrical release in America before going to video (titled *Jugular Wine: A Vampire Odyssey* on the box). When young anthropologist James Grace (Irons) is bitten by female vampire Alexandra while on board ship in Alaska, he begins looking for the answers that lead him towards an encounter with a heart-devouring, centuries-old monster named Legion. This arty, independent feature was produced, directed, scripted and edited by thirty year-old Murphy in such locations as Philadelphia, New Orleans, Los Angeles and Alaska. With special appearances by Marvel Comics' Stan Lee, artist Frank Miller and singer Henry Rollins, plus clips from *Nosferatu* (1922).
✦✧

RAUL JULIA
[1940-1994]

Puerto Rican actor who became a Hollywood star. He proved a worthy successor to John Astin playing an energetic Gomez Addams in *The Addams Family* (1991) and *Addams Family Values* (1993) before his untimely death after suffering a stroke.
qv: *Frankenstein Unbound* (1990).

JULIA JEKYLL AND HARRIET HYDE
UK, 1995-1998. With: Olivia Hallinan, Victoria Williams, Ian Keith, Simon Green, Ann Emery, Dale Rapley. BBC-TV. Colour.
Silly, juvenile comedy TV series. As a result of a scientific experiment, schoolgirl Julia Jekyll (Hallinan) periodically transforms into a hairy giant monster called Harriet Hyde (John Asquith).
✦

RUPERT JULIAN
[1886-1943]

American journeyman director of the silent era. His best-known credit is *The Phantom of the Opera* (1925), probably due to the input of its star, Lon Chaney Sr.
qv: *The Ferret* (1915).

JULY SPIRIT
Hong Kong, 1986. Dir: Wang Chung-Kuang. With: Tien Ping-Chun, Woo Yan-Man, Shek Fung. Cogeda Video. Colour.
Horror comedy in which a couple visit an old house haunted by the vampiric ghost of a criminal (Ping-Chun) and other supernatural creatures.
✦✧

JUMPING CORPSES
Hong Kong, circa 1989. Gordon's Film & Company/ Rainbow Video. Colour.
Horror comedy in which a fat, fake hopping vampire meets the real thing. In the end, a priest shoots lightning and makes the real vampire disappear.
✦✧

THE JUNGLE CAPTIVE
(aka WILD JUNGLE CAPTIVE)
USA, 1944 (1945). Dir: Harold Young. With: Otto Kruger, Vicky Lane, Rondo Hatton, Amelita Ward, Phil Brown, Jerome Cowan. Universal. B&W.
Sequel to *Jungle Woman* (1944), and the third and last in Universal's Paula the Ape Woman series. This time it's the turn of biochemist Dr Stendhal (Kruger) to stop reviving dead rabbits and bring Paula Dupree (Lane, taking over the thankless role from Acquanetta) back to life one last time. With the help of his demented assistant, the monstrous Moloch the Brute (non-actor Hatton, who should have remained mute), he plans to transplant the brain of his secretary (Ward, who replaced Betty Bryant when the latter couldn't find a baby-sitter!) into the mentally subnormal Ape Woman. In the end, Paula kills Stendhal before she is shot to death by Cowan's Police Inspector Harrigan. Despite the shoddy production values and lacklustre direction, Jack Pierce's make-up is still very impressive. With clips from *Jungle Woman*, *Captive Wild Woman* (1943) and *The Invisible Man* (1933). Reissued in 1952 under a different title in America, this was banned in Britain until after World War Two.
✦✧

JUNGLE WOMAN
USA, 1944. Dir: Reginald LeBorg. With: Evelyn Ankers, Acquanetta (Burnu Davenport), J. Carrol Naish, Samuel S. Hinds, Lois Collier, Milburn Stone. Universal. B&W.
Announced as *Jungle Queen* and *Jungle Girl*, this is the second and worst entry in the Paula Dupree trilogy, Universal's misguided attempt to *ape* the Val Lewton series over at RKO. Non-actress Acquanetta returns from the first film as the insanely jealous, super-strong Ape Woman, Ankers and Stone recreate their roles in cameos, and John Carradine turns up in the confusing flashback footage from the earlier film's finale. This time sympathetic scientist Dr Carl Fletcher (Naish) revives Paula Dupree but is put on trial for subsequently killing the Ape Woman with a hypodermic needle. Director LeBorg unwisely keeps Paula's transformed features (make-up by Jack P. Pierce) in shadow until the climax. With Douglass Dumbrille as the District Attorney; Julie London's scenes were cut prior to release. This includes confusing stock footage from *The Big Cage* (1933) within stock footage from *Captive Wild Woman* (1943)!
Sequel: THE JUNGLE CAPTIVE (qv; 1944)
✦

JUNOON
(USA: aka OBSESSION)
India, 1992. Dir: Mahesh Bhatt. With: Pooja Bhatt. Colour.
This is apparently a Hindi remake of *An American Werewolf in London* (1981). The title translates as 'Obsession'.
✦

KABRASTAN
India, 1989. Dir: Mohan Bhakri. MKB Films Combines. Colour.
Hindi horror film written, produced and directed by Bhakri. A subjective camera is used to represent the point-of-view of the monster in this story of heart surgeon Dr D'Souza, who steals body parts to conduct his Frankenstein-like experiments. The title translates as 'The Graveyard'.
✦

KAFTAN
India, 1990. Dir: Shree Ram Bohra. With: Jumuna. Colour.
Sleazy Hindi horror movie involving human sacrifice, Satanic rituals, a multi-armed Kali that shoots lightning bolts and a pair of female zombies. The title translates as 'The Shroud'.
✦✦

KAIBUTSU-KUN
Japan, 1968. Dir: Masaaki Osumi. Voices: Yumi Shiraishi, Hiroshi Otake, Shingo Kawamoto, Tadao Imanishi, Monori Matsujima. Studio Zero/Tokyo Movie Shinsha Company. Colour.
Cartoon series based on the popular comic books created by Fujio Fujiko. The Li'l Monster Prince/'Kaibutsu-Kun' (Shiraishi) arrives on Earth and lives with Dracula (Otake), Franken (Imanishi), a child-like Frankenstein Monster and the Wolfman (Kawamoto). With the help of their neighbour Hiroshi (Matsujima) they battle the evil BEMs. Another Japanese cartoon series, *Dr. Slump*, features various Frankenstein Monsters, including one which is also a werewolf!
✦✦

KAIBUTSU KUN, KAIBUTSU KANDO ENO SHOTAI
Japan, 1981. Dir: Hiroshi Fukutomi. Voices: Masako Nozawa, Katsue Miwa, Taroh Sagami, Kaneta Kimotsuki, Takuzoh Kamiyama, Dai Kanai. Sin-ei Doga/Toho International. Colour.
Feature-length cartoon based on the *Kaibutsu-Kun* comic strip by Fujio Fujiko. The Monster Prince Kaibutsu Kun and his monster friends Furanken, Dorakyura and Ohkami-Otoko travel to Monster Land, where they battle a huge Golem and other bizarre creatures to obtain the magical ingredients that will save their human friend Hiroshi, who has been turned to stone.
✦✧

KALABOG EN BOSYO STRIKE AGAIN
Philippines, circa 1986. Dir: Ben Feleo. With: Dolphy, Panchito, Rolly Quizon, Joyce Ann Burton, Bong Dimayacyac, Zeny Zabala. Cinema 1635/Tri-Films. Colour.
Comedy in which the mad Dr Kagaw (Jaime Fabregas) uses lightning to bring his powerful monster to life. This also includes several zombies being raised from their graves.
✦

KALIMÁN, EL HOMBRE INCREÍBLE
Mexico/Egypt, 1969 (1970). Dir: Alberto Mariscal. With: Jeff Cooper. Colour.
This epic adaptation of the popular comic book character runs over two hours and stars Cooper as the eponymous turbaned hero, an expert in mystic powers and martial arts, who battles mummies, monsters and aliens.
Sequel: KALIMÁN EN EL SINIESTRO MUNDO DE HUMANÓN (1974)
✦

KALKUT
(aka KISMET KI BHOOL)
India, 1935. Dir: D.K. Kale. With: Nyampally, Godse, Lobo. Sudha Pictures. B&W.
This Hindi film was apparently inspired by *The Mummy* (1933) and includes a prince turned into a leper by supernatural powers.
✦

KAOS
Italy, 1984. Dir: Paolo Taviani and Vittorio Taviani. With: Margarita Lozano, Claudio Bigagli, Massimo Bonetti, Franco Franchi, Ciccio Ingrassia, Biagio Barone. Filmtre/RAI Channel 1/Cinecitta. Colour.
Freely adapted from the Sicilian folk-tales of Luigi Pirandello by writers/directors the Taviani brothers. Although overlong at nearly three hours, these beautifully photographed stories have a magical, if not supernatural, atmosphere. In 'The Other Son', a mother (Lozano) spurns her son while missing his two brothers. Batà (Bigagli) turns into a 'werewolf' (without make-up) under the influence of 'Moon Sickness'. 'The Jar' is an amusing fable about a man (Franchi) trapped in a giant jar who refuses to come out. A trick gives a village their own graveyard in 'Requiem', and Pirandello (Omero Antonutti) is called back to his birthplace by the ghost/ memory of his dead mother (Regina Bianchi) in the epilogue, 'Conversing With Mother'.
✦✦✧

KARA BOGA
Turkey, 1974. Dir: Yavuz Figenli. Colour.
Vlad the Impaler is brought back to life with virgin's blood by his hunchbacked servant. As the leader of a Satanic group of black-masked villains, he ravages the countryside until he is staked and beheaded by the hero. The title translates as 'The Black Bull'.
✦

KARA MURAT
Turkey, 1973. With: Cüneyt Arkin. Colour.
Historical adventure based on a comic strip and featuring a bald-headed Vlad the Impaler, who nails the turbans to the heads of the Sultan's ambassadors and disembowels his mistress when she pretends to be pregnant. In the end, the Sultan's musketeer Kara Murat (Arkin) is sent to dispatch Vlad.
✦

KARANLIK SULAR
Turkey, 1994. Dir: E. Kutlug Ataman. With: Daniel Chace, Gonen Bozbey, Metin Uygun, Haluk Kurtoglu. Colour.
Various people are looking for fragments of an old manuscript that contains the secret of eternal life. Among them is a vampiric child, the reincarnation of the 800 year-old Empress Theodora of Byzantium. The title translates as 'The Serpent's Tale'.
✦

KARMINA
Canada, 1996. Dir: Gabriel Pelletier. With: Isabelle Cyr, Robert Brouillette, Yves Pelletier, France Castel, Gildor Roy, Raymond Cloutier. Lux Film. Colour.
French-language spoof in which 140 year-old vampire Karmina (Cyr) argues with her Transylvanian parents over marrying Vlad (Pelletier). She runs away to Montreal in search of her aunt Esmeralda (Castel), who has regained her humanity and now runs a dating agency. When a magic potion makes Karmina human again, she meets and falls in love with Philippe (Brouillette). Meanwhile, Vlad has followed her to the city and begins turning his victims into undead followers.
✦✧

KATHAVAI THATTEYA MOHINI PAYE
India, 1975. Dir: M.A. Rajaraman. With: C.R. Patiban, Sanjivirajan, Desikan, Liza. Anuradha International. Colour.
A private detective ends a cursed vampire prince's reign of terror in this Tamil horror film, apparently inspired by Bram Stoker's *Dracula*.
✦

KEDOK KETAWA
Indonesia, 1940. B&W.
Apparently inspired by Universal's *Phantom of the Opera* (1943), the title translates as 'The Laughing Mask'.
✦

BORIS KARLOFF (William Henry Pratt) [1887-1969]

'The King of Horror', British-born Karloff sailed to Canada in 1909 where he worked at a variety of menial jobs before joining a touring theatre company. After establishing himself as a popular stage villain, he arrived in Hollywood in 1917. Numerous minor appearances in movies followed before he recreated his stage role as a killer in Howard Hawks' *The Criminal Code* (1931). After being spotted by James Whale in the Universal commissary, he landed the part of the Monster in *Frankenstein* (1931) and the rest is history. A gentle man who enjoyed playing cricket and entertaining children, Karloff never minded being typecast as the bogeyman. A trouper to the end, he died of respiratory failure at the age of eighty-one. He was portrayed by both Jack Betts and Amir Aboulela in *Gods and Monsters* (1998).
qv: *Abbott and Costello Meet Dr. Jekyll and Mr. Hyde* (1953); *Before I Hang* (1940); *Bikini Beach* (1964); *Biography: 'Boris Karloff the Gentle Monster'* (1995); *Black Sabbath* (1963); *Bride of Frankenstein* (1935); *Charlie Chan at the Opera* (1936); *The Climax* (1944); *Cult of the Damned* (1968); *Everyman: 'The True Story of Frankenstein'* (1986); *Frankenstein 1970* (1958); *The Ghost in the Invisible Bikini* (1966); *The Ghoul* (1933); *Grip of the Strangler* (1958); *The Horror Show* (1979); *House of Frankenstein* (1944); *Isle of the Dead* (1945); *Jonathan Winters Show* (1968); *Madhouse* (1974); *Mad Monster Party?* (1966); *The Man They Could Not Hang* (1939); *The Mummy* (1933); *The Mummy* (1999, documentary); *100 Years of Horror: 'Boris Karloff'* (1996); *100 Years of Horror: 'Frankenstein and Friends'* (1996); *100 Years of Horror: 'Mummies'* (1996); *Red Skelton Hour* (1968); *Rivals: 'Frankenstein vs Dracula'* (1995); *Route 66: 'Lizard's Leg and Owlet's Wing'* (1962); *Shindig* (1965); *Son of Frankenstein* (1939); *Suspense: 'The Monkey's Paw'* (1949); *This is Your Life: 'Boris Karloff'* (1957); *Thriller* (1960-62); *The Torture Zone* (1968); *Transylvania Twist* (1989); *Voodoo Island* (1957); *The Universal Story* (1995); *The Venetian Affair* (1966); *The Walking Dead* (1936); *You'll Find Out* (1940).

SAM KATZMAN [1901-1973]

Prolific American producer, nicknamed 'Jungle' Sam Katzman for his series of *Jungle Jim* movies featuring Johnny Weissmuller. Through his Banner Productions, he is usually associated with Monogram's series featuring The East Side Kids and a string of poverty-row horrors starring Bela Lugosi in the early 1940s. His biggest hit was *Rock Around the Clock* (1956).
qv: *The Ape Man* (1943); *Bowery at Midnight* (1942); *The Corpse Vanishes* (1942); *Creature With the Atom Brain* (1955); *Invisible Ghost* (1941); *Lock Up Your Daughters* (1956); *The Man Who Turned to Stone* (1957); *Voodoo Man* (1944); *The Werewolf* (1956); *Zombies of Mora Tau* (1957).

ANDREW KEIR [1926-1997]

Scottish character actor. The screen's finest Professor Quatermass (in Hammer's *Quatermass and the Pit* [1967], a role he recreated for BBC Radio 3's *The Quatermass Memoirs* [1996]), and a worthy stand-in for Van Helsing as vampire hunter Father Sandor in *Dracula Prince of Darkness* (1965).
qv: *Blood from the Mummy's Tomb* (1971); *Flesh and Blood: The Hammer Heritage of Horror* (1994); *Late Night Horror: 'No Such Thing as a Vampire'* (1968).

BOB KELLJAN (Robert Kelljchian) [1930-1982]

American director who brought new energy to the vampire genre in the 1970s with *Count Yorga, Vampire* (1970), *The Return of Count Yorga* (1971), *Scream Blacula Scream* (1973) and TV's *Starsky & Hutch* episode, 'The Vampire' (1976).

ERLE C. KENTON [1896-1980]

American director and former writer for Mack Sennett. After the delirious delights of *Island of Lost Souls* (1932), he became a reliable if unremarkable director of such Universal sequels as *The Ghost of Frankenstein* (1942), *House of Frankenstein* (1944) and *House of Dracula* (1945).

JACK KEVAN

American make-up artist who created the Frankenstein Monster for the 3-D short *Third Dimensional Murder* (1940) and produced *The Monster of Piedras Blancas* (1958).
qv: *Abbott and Costello Meet Dr. Jekyll and Mr. Hyde* (1953); *Creature from the Black Lagoon* (1954); *Monster on the Campus* (1958).

ANTHONY NELSON KEYS [1913-1984]

British producer for Hammer Films since the mid-1950s. After co-scripting *Frankenstein Must Be Destroyed* (1969), he formed Charlemagne Productions with Christopher Lee in 1972. Their only film was the underrated *Nothing But the Night* (1972).
qv: *The Brides of Dracula* (1960); *The Curse of Frankenstein* (1957); *The Curse of the Werewolf* (1960); *Dracula* (1958); *Dracula Prince of Darkness* (1965); *Frankenstein Created Woman* (1966); *The Mummy* (1959); *The Mummy's Shroud* (1966); *The Plague of the Zombies* (1966); *The Reptile* (1966); *The Revenge of Frankenstein* (1958); *The Two Faces of Dr. Jekyll* (1960).

KHATRA

India, 1991. With: Rajesh Vivek. Colour.
Vivek plays a zombie who transforms himself into a hairy monster by sucking his own contaminated blood through his finger.
✦

KHOONI DRACULA

India, 1992. Harinam Singh Films. Colour.
Very low-budget Hindi horror film in which a vampire in a big hat stalks a number of scantily-clad women. He turns into an ugly monster before being beaten with strings of garlic and stabbed to death with a miniature *trishul* fork. The title translates as 'Deadly Dracula'.
✦

KID MILLIONS

USA, 1934. Dir: Roy Del Ruth. With: Eddie Cantor, Ann Sothern, Ethel Merman, George Murphy, Burton Churchill, Warren Hymer. Samuel Goldwyn. B&W/ Colour.
Typical Cantor musical comedy in which he plays Edward ('Eddie') Grant Wilson Jr, who discovers he is the lost heir of an American explorer and has inherited a $77,000,000 treasure in Egypt. While in the Chamber of the Dead, the eye-rolling comedian and his companions hide in the mummy cases and sing 'Let My People Go'. The final musical number, set in an ice cream factory, is in colour. With Stanley Fields, Edgar Kennedy and the Nicholas Brothers.
✦✦✧

UDO KIER [b 1944]

Cult German actor discovered by pop singer/director Mike Sarne in the mid-1960s. His career ranges from art house movies to exploitation sleaze, and he is one of the few actors to portray Count Dracula (*Blood for Dracula* [1974]), Baron Frankenstein (*Flesh for Frankenstein* [1973]), Dr Jekyll (*Bloodlust* [1979]) and Jack the Ripper (*Lulu* [1980]).
qv: *Blade* (1998); *Burned to Light* (1999); *Modern Vampires* (1998); *Spermula* (1975).

KILLERS FROM SPACE

USA, 1954. Dir: W. Lee Wilder. With: Peter Graves, Barbara Bestar, James Seay, Frank Gerstle, Steve Pendleton, John Merrick. Planet Filmways/RKO Radio Pictures. B&W.

More low-budget science fiction from the less talented brother of Billy Wilder. Graves plays nuclear scientist Douglas P. Martin, surgically revived from the dead by silly-looking pop-eyed aliens from Astron Delta (make-up created by Harry Thomas). Hypnotised into helping them with their planned invasion of Earth, he is taken to a cave (Bronson Cavern) full of giant lizards and insects they have created. In the end he blows them all up. Narrated by Mark Scott.

✦✧

KILLER TOMATOES EAT FRANCE!

USA, 1991 (1992). Dir: John DeBello. With: John Astin, Steve Lundquist, Angela Visser, Marc Price, Tom Katsis, Bill LaFleur. Twin Pics/KT Entertainment/Twentieth Century Fox. Colour.

Direct-to-video sequel to *Killer Tomatoes Strike Back* (1990) and the fourth in the unfunny series, subtitled 'Les Tomats Français Munch Munch'. Astin returns as the scheming Professor Gangrene who takes his shape-changing tomatoes to Paris in an attempt to conquer the world. This includes appearances by The Phantom-ato of the Opera and The Hunchback of Notre Dame (Bruno Toussaint). With Lundquist as Igor.

✦

KILLING BIRDS

(Orig: RAPTORS: GLI UCCELLI ASSASSINI. USA: DARK EYES OF THE ZOMBIES/KILLER BIRDS)
Italy/USA, 1988. Dir: Claude Milli (Claude Milliken/ Claudio Lattanzi) (and Aristide Massaccesi). With: Lara Wendel, Timothy W. Watts, Robert Vaughn, Leslie Cummins, James Villemaire, Sal Maggiore Jr. Filmirage/ Flora Film. Colour.

Filmed in Louisiana. A group of teens investigating an isolated house are killed off by freak accidents, murderous zombies and a flock of menacing birds. Produced by Massaccesi (Joe D'Amato).

✦✧

KILLING FRANKESTAYNA KARSI

Turkey, 1967. Dir: Nuri Akinci. With: Oktay Gursel, Oya Peri, Gultekin Ceylan, Ferhan Tanseli, Aynur Aydan, Yasar Sener. Omur Film. B&W.

One of a series of films based on the Italian comic book character Killing. Here, the skull-masked master criminal battles the Frankenstein Monster.

✦

THE KILLING GAME

(Orig: JEU DE MASSACRE)
France, 1967. Dir: Alain Jessua. With: Jean-Pierre Cassel, Claudine Auger, Michel Duchaussoy, Eleanore Hirt, Anna Gaylor. AJ/Francinor/LFM. Colour.

A comic strip writer bases his stories on the real life adventures of a strange young playboy. This apparently includes a scene in a cinema featuring a clip from a vampire movie.

✦

KILLING SPREE

USA, 1987 (1990). Dir: Tim Ritter. With: Asbestos Felt, Courtney Lercara, Raymond Carbone, Joel D. Wynkoop, Rachel Rutz, Bruce Paquette. Twisted Illusions. Colour.

Shot on video in Florida by twenty-one year-old Ritter. Newly-wed mechanic Tom Russo (Felt) uses a ceiling fan, a screw-driver and a lawn mower to kill the men he imagines his wife Leeza (Lercara) is having affairs with. However, his victims don't intend to remain buried in the backyard for long, and they return as zombies seeking revenge.

✦

KILLING TIME

USA, 1984. Dir: Damian Harris. With: Stephen Nichols, Del Zamora, Eric Stoltz, Michael Simms, Leslie Morris, Arvid Holmberg. Graymatter Productions. Colour.

Half-hour short, scripted by director Harris and producer Patrick Aumont (both the sons of famous actors) and loosely based on 'The Late Shift' by Dennis Etchison. Unfortunately, the original story's premise of scientifically revived zombies being used as cheap labour in Los Angeles is reduced to a vague series of encounters by horror comics illustrator Macklin (Nichols). Scenes that explained the film's ending and a cameo by Etchison as an evil doctor were cut before release.

✦✧

KILLING ZOË

France/USA, 1993 (1994). Dir: Roger Avary. With: Eric Stoltz, Jean-Huges Anglade, Julie Delpy, Gary Kemp, Bruce Ramsay, Kario Salem. Killing Zoë Productions/ October Films/Live Entertainment/PolyGram Filmed Entertainment. Colour.

Stylish if rambling heist movie, co-executive produced by Quentin Tarantino, in which American safecracker Zed (Stoltz) arrives in Paris to team up with a drug-addled gang of bank robbers led by the unpredictable Eric (Anglade). As the raid gets out of control and the death toll mounts, Zed finds himself joining forces with hostage and part-time prostitute Zoë (Delpy) to survive. With special make-up effects by Tom Savini, a surprise cameo by Ron Jeremy Hyatt, and shots of *Nosferatu* (1922) on TV intercut with a sex scene.

✦✦✦

KINDRED: THE EMBRACED

USA, 1996. Dir: Peter Medak, Ralph Hemecker, James L. Conway, Kenneth Fink and John Harrison. With: Mark Frankel, C. Thomas Howell, Kelly Rutherford, Stacy Haiduk, Erik King, Patrick Bauchau. Spelling Television/ John Leekley Productions/Republic Pictures/Fox Network. Colour.

Confusing, slow-moving TV series based on the White Wolf book and role-playing game *Vampire: The Masquerade*, created by Mark Rein-Hagen. San Francisco cop Frank Kohanek (Howell) makes an uneasy alliance with Prince of the City, Julian Luna (Frankel), the head of the shape-changing Kindred (vampire) clans, to battle the evil Brujah Clan, led by Eddie Fiori (Brian Thompson). With Jeff Kober as Daedalus, a member of the killer Nosferatu Clan, and Haiduk as vampiric nightclub owner Lily Langtry. This was cancelled after just eight shows, but the 1998 three-volume video release in America includes an exclusive unseen episode.

✦✧

STEPHEN KING
[b 1947]

American writer, the most successful horror novelist ever and now a publishing 'category' to himself. Many of his books and stories have been adapted for film and television, often by the author himself, with variable results.

qv: *Creepshow* (1982); *Creepshow 2* (1987); *It* (1990); *The Night Flier* (1997); *Pet Sematary* (1989); *Pet Sematary II* (1992); *A Return to Salem's Lot* (1987); *Salem's Lot* (1979); *Silver Bullet* (1985); *Sleepwalkers* (1992); *Sometimes They Come Back* (1991); *Tales from the Darkside The Movie* (1990).

KINGDOM IN THE SAND

(Orig: IL CONQUISTATORE DELL'ATLANTIDA)
Italy/Egypt, 1965 (1966). Dir: Alfonso Brescia. With: Kirk Morris, Luciana Gilli, Hélèn Chanel, Piero Lulli, Andrea Scotti, Mahmud El Sabba. Copro Film/PCA Produzione. Colour.

Italian *peplum* in which a mysterious scientist from Atlantis controls an army of zombies created from kidnapped Bedouins.

✦✧

KINGDOM OF SHADOWS

USA, 1998. Dir: Brett Wood. Kino on Video. B&W.

Fascinating feature-length documentary about silent horror films, illustrated with still photographs and many clips, including *The*

Fay Wray is rescued by the Eighth Wonder of the World, King Kong *(1933).*

Avenging Conscience (1914), *The Bells* (1926, with Boris Karloff), *The Cabinet of Dr. Caligari* (1919), various versions of *Dr. Jekyll and Mr. Hyde*, *Nosferatu* (1922), *Vampyr* (1931-32), *Warning Shadows* (1922) and *Witchcraft Through the Ages* (1918/21). Narrated by an enthusiastic Rod Steiger.
✦✦✧

KINGDOM OF THE VAMPIRES

USA, 1991. Dir: J.R. Bookwalter. With: Mathew Jason Walsh, Cherie Patry, Shannon Doyle. CVH/Suburban Tempe/Cinema Home Video. Colour.

Independent feature, shot on video in Medina County, Ohio. Walsh (who also scripted and composed the music) plays Jeff, a long-haired convenience store worker who also happens to be a very reluctant ninety year-old vampire. When he becomes romantically involved with a young woman, Jeff finally kills his demanding undead mother.
✦

KING DONG

(aka LOST ON ADVENTURE ISLAND/SUPERSIMIAN)
USA, 1984. Dir: Yancey Hendrieth. With: Crystal Holland, Chaz St. Peters, Mikhael, Felicia Fox, Elizabeth Davies, Dee Hendrieth. Hendrieth/Oman/Selectatape/MVC Video. Colour.

Hardcore *King Kong* pastiche, filmed on video in Honolulu. Anna (Holland) is shipwrecked on an island where she discovers an eighty-foot tall female gorilla, cannibals, warrior women and dinosaurs — these apparently include a pretty impressive stop-motion brontosaurus, tyrannosaurus and the Kong-like ape created by Magic Film Ventures. With a character named 'Dr Cronenberg' and the director in an ape suit. Another stop-motion 'King Dong' turns up briefly in the softcore *Flesh Gordon Meets the Cosmic Cheerleaders* (1989).
✦✧

KING KLUNK

USA, 1933. Dir: Walter Lantz and William Nolan. Walter Lantz/Universal. B&W.

Nine minute *Pooch the Pup* cartoon spoof on *King Kong* (1933). Adventurer Pooch's girlfriend is menaced by a dinosaur which is then bested by the eponymous giant gorilla in a boxing match before it is turned into a skeleton.
Sequel: SHE DONE HIM RIGHT (1933)
✦✦

KING KONG

USA, 1933. Dir: Ernest B. Schoedsack and Merian C. Cooper. With: Fay Wray, Robert Armstrong, Bruce Cabot, Frank Reicher, Sam Hardy, Noble Johnson. RKO Radio Pictures. B&W.

Variously entitled *Kong*, *The Beast* and *The Eighth Wonder* during filming, this is, quite simply, one of the greatest movies ever made! An expedition by film-maker Carl Denham (Armstrong) to Skull Island discovers a prehistoric world ruled over by Kong, a giant ape. When the creature is captured and brought back to New York for exhibition, it breaks loose and wrecks Manhattan, until shot down by fighter planes from the top of the Empire State Building. Although filmed in 1932, the movie was not completed until a year later due to Willis H. O'Brien's superb stop-motion effects (using Marcel Delgado's models). Based on an idea by Edgar Wallace and Merian C. Cooper, and novelised by Delos W. Lovelace in 1932 and as a juvenile by Ian Thorne in 1977. This was filmed on some of the same sets as *King of Kings* (1927) and *The Most Dangerous Game* (1932), and features a wonderful Max Steiner score. The infamous spider pit sequence (cut prior to release) is still missing from the 'restored' prints, and a colourised version was released on video in 1989. A comic book adaptation, illustrated by Alberto Giolitti, was published in 1968, *The Making of King Kong* by Orville Goldner and George E. Turner appeared in 1975, and *The Girl in the Hairy Paw* was another seventies volume about the movie edited by Ronald Gottesman and Harry Geduld. 'Scream Ann, scream for your life!'
Sequel: THE SON OF KONG (qv; 1933)
Remake: KING KONG (qv; 1976)
✦✦✦✦✦

KING KONG

India, 1962. Dir: Babubhai Mistri. With: Dara Singh, Kumkum, Chandrasekhar, Pravin Choudhury, Sheila Kashmiri, Kamal Mehra. Santosh Productions. B&W.

This two-and-a-half hour Hindi action movie features wrestler Singh as the eponymous strongman, and has nothing to do with the giant ape.

✦

KING KONG

USA, 1976. Dir: John Guillermin. With: Jeff Bridges, Charles Grodin, Jessica Lange, John Randolph, Rene Auberjonois, Ed Lauter. Paramount. Colour.

In 1972, David Allen created a stop-motion King Kong TV advertisement for Volkswagen that was better than this travesty of the 1933 classic. When Universal lost the race to produce Joseph Sargent's *The Legend of King Kong,* a period remake with stop-motion animation, producer Dino De Laurentiis (who got the idea from a poster of the original hanging in his daughter's bedroom!) churned out this overblown $24,000,000 contemporary version, originally titled *King Kong: The Legend Reborn.* Geologists searching for oil discover a prehistoric island ruled by Kong, a giant ape. Transported back to America and put on show to the public, the creature escapes and is eventually shot down by jet planes from the top of New York's World Trade Center. The terrible special effects (Kong is portrayed by Rick Baker in a monkey suit and Carlo Rambaldi's static thirty-foot high robot) incredibly won an Academy Award. Newcomer Lange gets all the worst lines in Lorenzo Semple Jr's inane script, which was based on the original movie and published by Ace Books. With Julius Harris, Jack O'Halloran, Dennis Fimple, John Agar as a City Official, and Forrest J Ackerman among the fleeing crowd of '45,000' extras at the climax. *The King Kong Story* was the official tie-in magazine from Phoebus Publishing, and *The Creation of Dino De Laurentiis' King Kong* by Bruce Bahrenburg was a sanctioned behind-the-scenes look at the production.

Sequel: KING KONG LIVES (qv; 1986)
Remake: THE MIGHTY KONG (qv; 1998)

✦✦

KING KONG ESCAPES

(Orig: KINGU KONGU NO GYAKUSHU. USA: aka KING KONG VS. MECHA-KONG)

Japan/USA, 1967 (1968). Dir: Inoshiro Honda and Arthur Rankin Jr. With: Rhodes Reason, Mie Hama, Linda Miller, Akira Takarada, Eisei Amamoto. Toho/Universal. Colour.

Toho's juvenile follow-up to *King Kong vs. Godzilla* (1963) features a man in a monkey suit battling a dinosaur (later called Gorosaurus) and a sea serpent on a prehistoric island. The evil Dr Who (Amamoto) and Madame Piranha (Hama) create a robot double, Mechakong, and the two monsters slug it out on top of the Tokyo Tower. Special effects by Eiji Tsuburaya. The original title translates as 'King Kong's Counterattack'.

Sequel: DESTROY ALL MONSTERS (1968)

✦

KING KONG LIVES

USA, 1986. Dir: John Guillermin. With: Brian Kerwin, Linda Hamilton, John Ashton, Peter Michael Goetz, Frank Maraden, Jimmie Ray Weeks. De Laurentiis Entertainment Group. Colour.

Dino De Laurentiis' delayed sequel to his 1976 remake. Ten years later, the giant ape is being kept alive by a scientist (Hamilton), who needs Kong-like plasma before she can transplant a synthetic heart into the wounded creature. By coincidence, adventurer Hank Mitchell (Kerwin) discovers a female Kong in Borneo, and everything is fine until the two apes (played by Peter Elliot and George Yiasomi) break loose and decimate the military. This ends with Kong's death (again!) and the birth of a baby Kong. More rotten special effects by Carlo Rambaldi. In 1996, Universal signed Peter Jackson to co-write and direct a new version of *King Kong* in New Zealand, which was never made.

✦✧

KING KONG'S FIST

(aka KING KONGS FAUST)

West Germany/USA, 1984. Dir: Heiner Stadler. With: Leonard Lansink, Werner Grassmann, Heinz van Nouhuys, Wim Wenders, Laslo Benedek, Bert Willis. IFP/Seybold/NDR. Colour.

The search by a reporter (Lansink) for the creator of the original King Kong's giant paw leads from the 1984 Berlin Film Festival to a man in London who has the hairy hand. This spoof of Hollywood movies includes a German-dubbed video of *King Kong* (1933) and a colourised version on TV.

✦✧

Men in monster suits battle on top of Mount Fuji in King Kong vs. Godzilla *(1963).*

Joan Woodbury and Dick Purcell (centre) are captured by the King of the Zombies *(1941).*

THE KING KONG SHOW

(aka ORIGINAL TV ADVENTURES OF KING KONG)
Japan/USA, 1966-67. Rankin-Bass/Videocraft International/ABC-TV. Colour.

Launched with a hour-long preview containing two episodes, this half-hour children's cartoon TV series (twenty-four episodes) features the once-mighty sixty-foot ape as a 'lovable' hero who teams up with Professor Bond, his son Bobby and daughter Susan to battle evil scientist Dr Who from the remote island on Mondo in the Java Sea. With character designs by Jack Davis.

✦

KING KONG VS. GODZILLA

(Orig: KINGU KONGU TAI GOJIRA)
Japan/USA, 1963. Dir: Inoshiro Honda and Thomas Montgomery. With: Michael Keith, James Yagi, Tadao Takashima, Mie Hama, Yu Fujiki, Kenji Sahara. Toho/Universal. Colour.

For many years, Willis O'Brien dreamed of filming *King Kong vs Frankenstein* (aka *King Kong vs Prometheus*), a sequel to the classic *King Kong* (1933), in which the giant ape would battle a fifty-foot tall Frankenstein monster. He reportedly cried when this was announced. When a pharmaceutical company discovers Kong on a Pacific island, he is floated back to Japan by balloons, where he ends up battling Godzilla on the top of Mount Fuji. Added American sequences only confuse things more, although Kong apparently comes out on top in both the original and American versions. As usual, Eiji Tsuburaya was in charge of the men in monster suits and toy tanks. The third Godzilla film and the first to be shot in colour.
Sequels: GODZILLA VS. THE THING (1964) and KING KONG ESCAPES (qv; 1967)

✦✦

KING OF KONG ISLAND

(Orig: EVA, LA VENERE SELVAGGIO. USA: aka EVE THE WILD WOMAN)
Italy, 1968. Dir: Robert Morris (Ralph Zucker/Mario Pupillo). With: Brad Harris, Marc Lawrence, Esmeralda Barros, Adrianna Alben, Aldo Cecconi, Mario Donatone. Three Star/Monarch. Colour.

A mad scientist's (Lawrence) plot to control huge gorillas with remote-control devices is foiled by a beautiful savage (Barros) raised by the apes and an apparent normal-sized descendant of the mighty Kong himself. Produced by Zucker/Pupillo and Walter Brandt (Walter Brandi/Walter Bigari).

✦

KING OF NEW YORK

Italy/USA, 1989. Dir: Abel Ferrara. With: Christopher Walken, David Caruso, Larry (Lawrence) Fishburne, Victor Argo, Wesley Snipes, Janet Julian. Reteitalia/Scena International/Rank Film Distributors. Colour.

Violent but downbeat thriller in which conscientious gang boss Frank White (Walken) is released from prison and ruthlessly begins wiping out the competition until the cops decide to adopt the same methods. With Steve Buscemi, Phoebe Legere, singer Freddy Jackson, and *Nos-*

feratu (1922) showing in a movie theatre. Walken's evil millionaire industrialist in *Batman Returns* (1992) was named Max Shreck, and the actor played a real vampire in Ferrara's 1994 film *The Addiction*.
✦✦✦

KING OF THE CASTLE

UK, 1977. Dir: Peter Hammond, Terry Harding and Leonard White. With: Philip Da Costa, Fulton Mackay, Milton Johns, Talfryn Thomas, Derek Smith, Jamie Foreman. HTV/ITV. Colour.

Seven-part, half-hour children's serial in which teenager Roland Wright (Da Costa) falls down the elevator shaft of the tower block in which he lives and imagines himself in a nightmarish fantasy world while waiting to be rescued. His stepmother June (Angela Richards) becomes a witch, the school bully Ripper (Foreman) is transformed into a Samurai warrior, and his headmaster Spurgeon (Mackay) becomes mad scientist Hawkspur, who has created a Frankenstein-like creature. It all turns out to be the result of a nervous breakdown.
✦✦

KING OF THE ZOMBIES

USA, 1941. Dir: Jean Yarbrough. With: Dick Purcell, Joan Woodbury, Mantan Moreland, Henry Victor, John Archer, Patricia Stacey. Monogram Pictures. B&W.

Silly, but surprisingly entertaining low-budget horror comedy from prolific director Yarbrough (who replaced Howard Bretherton before production). Patriotic Navy heroes James 'Mac' McCarthy and Bill Summers (Purcell and Archer), along with comedy relief servant Jefferson Jackson (Moreland), crash their plane on a remote West Indian island and discover caped Nazi agent Dr Miklos Sangre (Victor, in a role originally intended for Bela Lugosi or Peter Lorre!) creating an army of zombies using his hypnotic powers and voodoo rituals. In a wonderfully comic moment, the scene-stealing Moreland is transformed into a pseudo-zombie: 'I *am* a zombie!'. Incredibly, former dentist Edward Kay's music score was nominated for an Academy Award! With Guy Usher.
✦✦

KING TUT-ANKH-AMEN'S EIGHTH WIFE

(aka THE MYSTERY OF KING TUT-ANKH-AMEN'S EIGHTH WIFE)
USA, 1923. Dir: Andrew Remo. Max Cohen. B&W.

Silent drama about the curse on those who violate the tomb of the Pharaoh.
✦

KING TUT'S TOMB

(aka HECKLE AND JECKLE, THE TALKING MAGPIES, IN KING TUT'S TOMB)
USA, 1950. Dir: Mannie Davis. Terrytoons/Twentieth Century-Fox. Colour.

Seven minute Paul Terry cartoon in which an Egyptian cat dancer is magically transformed into the Frankenstein Monster (using colourised footage from *G-Man Jitters* [1939]). This also includes a flying carpet, ghosts and mummies.
Sequel: RIVAL ROMEOS (1950)
✦✧

KINGUKONGU EDO NI ARAWARETA

Japan, 1934. B&W.

Obscure adventure film with special effects created by Fuminori Ohashi. The title translates as 'King Kong Appears in Edo'.
✦

KINKY VAMPIRE SEX

USA, 1997. Dir: Geoffrey de Valois. With: Mihaella Stoicova, Shyler, Joan A. Teeter. Digital Entertainment Group/Salt City Home Video. Colour.

One of a series of *Vampire Raw Footage* videos, which also includes behind-the-scenes nude and softcore sequences from *The Vampire Conspiracy* (1995). Insane alien vampire Stoicova tortures nude college co-ed Shyler and battles to the death with 1998 Vampire Centrefold of the Year Teeter.
✦

KLAUS KINSKI (Klaus-Günther Nakszynski) [1926-1991]

Polish-born actor (sometimes mis-billed as Klaus Kinsky) who detested his career, which alternated between art films (notably with Werner Herzog) and exploitation trash. He portrayed a manic Renfield in Jesús Franco's *Bram Stoker's Count Dracula* (1970), before graduating to the vampire himself in *Nosferatu the Vampyre* (1979) and *Vampire in Venice* (1988). His autobiography *Kinski Uncut* was published in 1996.
qv: *Death Smiles on a Murderer* (1972); *Web of the Spider* (1970).

THE KISS

Canada, 1988. Dir: Pen Densham. With: Joanna Pacula, Meredith Salenger, Mimi Kuzyk, Nicholas Kilbertus, Jan Rubes, Pamela Collyer. Tri-Star Pictures/Astral Film Enterprises/Trilogy Film Production/Richard B. Lewis. Colour.

Originally announced as *The Host*. Fashion model Felice (the awful Pacula) is some kind of living dead witch attempting to pass her African powers on to her niece Amy Halloran (Salenger) with a vampiric kiss. Anyone who gets in her way dies. Director Densham can do little with the ludicrous screenplay co-written by Stephen Volk (*Gothic* [1986], etc), uneven performances, and a silly-looking cat monster and slug creature created by make-up effects supervisor Chris Walas.
✦

KISS DADDY GOODBYE

(aka REVENGE OF THE ZOMBIE/VENGEANCE OF THE DEAD/THE VENGEFUL DEAD)
USA, 1981. Dir: Patrick Regan. With: Fabian Forte, Marilyn Burns, John Cedar, Marvin Miller, Chester Grimes, Jed Mills. Bandwagon Films/Academy. Colour.

Two young children (Nell and Patrick Regan) use their psychic powers to raise their (real) father (director Regan) from the dead and send him after the bikers who killed him. With former fifties heart-throb Fabian as the new deputy sheriff investigating the macabre killings and Burns (*The Texas Chain Saw Massacre* [1974], etc) as a sympathetic member of the Board of Education.
✦✧

KISS KISS, KILL KILL

(Orig: KOMMISSAR X: JAGD AUF UNBEKANNT)
West Germany/Italy/Yugoslavia, 1965 (1966). Dir: Frank Kramer (Gianfranco Parolini). With: Tony Kendall (Luciano Stella), Brad Harris, Maria Perschy, Christa Linder, Nicola Popovic, Pino Mattei. Parnass/Metheus/Avala. Colour.

Sci-spy adventure based on the *Kommissar X* novels by Bert F. Island. In an underground complex, a drug is being used to turn people into 'zombies'. Not to be confused with the 1974 TV movie with the same title.
✦✧

KISS MEETS THE PHANTOM OF THE PARK

(aka KISS MEETS THE PHANTOM. UK: ATTACK OF THE PHANTOMS)
USA, 1978. Dir: Gordon Hessler. With: KISS (Peter Criss, Ace Frehley, Gene Simmons, Paul Stanley), Anthony Zerbe, Deborah Ryan. Hanna-Barbera Productions/KISS-Aucoin Productions/NBC-TV/Avco Embassy Pictures. Colour.

TV movie set in a financially floundering amusement park, filmed at Magic Mountain in Valencia, California. When the superpowered members of glam rock group KISS (Cat Man, Space Ace, The Demon and Star Child) are hired to boost admissions, they end up battling robot figures in a Chamber of Horrors. Created by vengeful mechanical wizard Abner Devereaux (Zerbe), these include Count Dracula, a Karloffian Frankenstein Monster, a werewolf, the Mummy, Quasimodo, a giant spider, an army of silver-suited beast-men and robot duplicates of the flamboyant heroes. With Brion James as a security guard, disc jockey Don Steele as himself and KISS perform-

ing 'Rock 'n' Roll All Nite', 'Shout it Out Loud' and 'Beth', among other songs.
✦

KISS ME QUICK
(aka DR. BREEDLOVE OR HOW I LEARNED TO STOP WORRYING AND LOVE)
USA, 1964. Dir: Seymour Tuchas (Pete Perry and Max Gardens). With: Mannie Goodtimes (Sexton Friendly), Fatty Beltbuckle (Frank Coe), Natasha, Jackie (Jackie DeWitt), Althea Currier, Claudia Banks. Fantasy Films/Boxoffice International. Colour.
Nudie comedy filmed on a single laboratory set. Sterilox (Beltbuckle, doing a Stan Laurel impression), an alien from the all-male planet Droopiter in the Buttless galaxy, arrives on Earth looking for the 'perfect woman' to breed servants from. He visits the mad Dr Breedlove (Goodtimes, in a spoof of Peter Sellers' Dr Strangelove with a Bela Lugosi accent) who uses his sex machine to create various strippers and topless go-go dancers. In the end, the alien leaves with a vending machine. This includes Dracula, a Karloffian sex-change Monster called Frankie Stein (Beltbuckle/Coe again), Selfish the Mummy and a Peter Lorre-type narration. Lester (Laszlo) Kovacs was the cinematographer, while the direction is often mistakenly attributed to Russ Meyer. All the credits are spoken.
✦✧

THE KISS OF THE VAMPIRE
(aka KISS OF EVIL)
UK, 1962 (1963). Dir: Don Sharp. With: Clifford Evans, Edward De Souza, Noel Willman, Jennifer Daniel, Barry Warren, Brian Oulton. Hammer Films/Universal-International. Colour.
One of Hammer's most stylish films of the sixties. While on a motoring honeymoon in the Carpathian mountains, recently married couple Gerald and Marianne Harcourt (De Souza and Daniel) find themselves stranded at a local inn. The young wife soon attracts the attention of Dr Ravna (Willman), the leader of a pleasure-seeking cult of vampires. Evans gives a solid performance as the drunken Professor Zimmer, waging a fanatical war against the coven, and there are some impressive set pieces: the opening staking of a vampire with a sexton's shovel, a macabre masked ball, and the climax where Zimmer invokes the forces of darkness in the form of a plague of (cartoon) bats to destroy the vampires. In America, the NBC-TV version first broadcast in 1967 cut some scenes and included new sequences filmed at Universal Studios by Irving J. Moore and featuring Virginia Gregg, Carl Esmond and Sheilah Wells, along with clips from Hammer's *The Evil of Frankenstein* (1964).
✦✦✦✧

LEÓN KLIMOVSKY
[1906-1996]

Argentine-born Spanish director of Russian parentage, also billed as Leon Kaminsky and Leon Klim. After working as a dentist for fifteen years, Klimovsky began making short films before moving on to features. Klimovsky is best known for his collaborations with actor Paul Naschy.
qv: *The Dracula Saga* (1972); *Dr. Jekyll and the Werewolf* (1971); *Strange Love of the Vampires* (1974); *The Vampire's Night Orgy* (1972); *Vengeance of the Zombies* (1972); *The Werewolf vs. the Vampire Woman* (1970).

SKELTON KNAGGS
[1911-1955]

Emaciated-looking British-born character actor and former Shakespearean mime, who usually turned up as a scheming provocateur or angry villager in Hollywood movies. He died of cirrhosis of the liver.
qv: *House of Dracula* (1945); *Isle of the Dead* (1945); *Master Minds* (1949).

KNIGHT MOVES
(aka FACE TO FACE)
USA/Germany, 1992. Dir: Carl Schenkel. With: Christopher (Christophe) Lambert, Diane Lane, Tom Skerritt, Daniel Baldwin, Ferdinand (Ferdy) Mayne, Charles Bailey-Gates. Lamb Bear Entertainment/Cinevox. Colour.
This is basically a psycho movie in which a chess master (Lambert) finds himself involved in a bizarre game of cat-and-mouse with a gas-masked killer who drains all the blood from his female victims.
✦✦

KNIGHTS
USA, 1992 (1993). Dir: Albert Pyun. With: Kris Kristofferson, Lance Henriksen, Kathy Long, Scott Paulin, Gary Daniels, Nicholas Guest. Kings Road Entertainment/Moonstone Entertainment. Colour.
Low-budget science fiction adventure filmed in Utah in which the evil Job (Henriksen, going way over the top) leads a race of futuristic vampire cyborgs who prey on the surviving humans. Slave girl Nea (kick-boxing champion Long) teams up with renegade cyborg Gabriel (Kristofferson) to use martial arts against Job and his blood-drinking acolytes. The ending is left open for a sequel. With Tim Thomerson.
✦✧

KNOCK, KNOCK...WHO'S THERE?
Philippines, 1987. Dir: Carlo J. Caparas. With: Joey De Leon, Jimmy Santos, Richard and Raymond, Joe Estrada, Encendencia. Golden Lion Films/Viva Video. Colour.
Low-budget fantasy comedy that features a large demon reviving the local corpses as the walking dead. These include a bride and groom finally reunited after death and a gay zombie.
✦

PATRIC KNOWLES
(Reginald Knowles) [1911-1995]

Lightweight British actor who went to Hollywood in 1936. He played Evelyn Ankers' ineffectual fiancé in *The Wolf Man* (1941) and the misguided scientist who reanimated the Monster in *Frankenstein Meets the Wolf Man* (1943).

KOLCHAK: THE NIGHT STALKER:
Bad Medicine
USA, 1974. Dir: Alex Grasshoff. With: Darren McGavin, Simon Oakland, Ramon Bieri, Richard Kiel, Alice Ghostley, Victor Jory. Universal/Francy Productions/ABC-TV. Colour.
Short-lived, hour-long series (1974-75, twenty episodes) based on the character created by author Jeff Rice (who claimed he never sold the rights for a TV series). Early episodes omitted *Kolchak:* from the title and were just called *The Night Stalker*. In this episode, Chicago reporter Carl Kolchak (McGavin) investigates a series of jewel robberies committed by Diableros (Kiel), a sorcerer from Native American folklore who has the power to transform into different animals. *The Night Stalker Companion* by Mark Dawidziak was published in 1997.
✦✦✧
Demon in Lace
USA, 1975. Dir: Don Weis. With: Darren McGavin, Simon Oakland, Andrew Prine, Keenan Wynn, Jackie Vernon, Carolyn Jones. Universal/Francy Productions/ABC-TV. Colour.
Kolchak discovers that a series of fatal heart attacks among male college students are caused by a succubus. With veteran Milton Parsons as Dr Salem Mozart. This episode was also included in the TV movie compilation *The Demon and the Mummy* (1975).
✦✦✧
The Devil's Platform
USA, 1974. Dir: Allen Baron. With: Darren McGavin, Simon Oakland, Tom Skerritt, Julie Gregg, Ellen Weston, Jack Grinnage. Universal/Francy Productions/ABC-TV. Colour.
In an attempt to defeat incumbent Senator James Talbot (John Myhers) on the road to the White House, crooked politician Robert

D. Palmer (Skerritt) makes a pact with Satanic forces which gives him the power to transform into a murderous Hell Hound.
✦✦✧

Horror in the Heights
(aka The Rakshasa)
USA, 1974. Dir: Michael T. Caffey. With: Darren McGavin, Simon Oakland, Phil Silvers, Benny Rubin, Abraham Sofaer, Jack Grinnage. Universal/Francy Productions/ ABC-TV. Colour.
Elderly residents are being killed by a supernatural creature that can assume the form of someone each victim trusts. Scripted by Hammer veteran Jimmy Sangster.
✦✦

Legacy of Terror
USA, 1975. Dir: Don McDougall. With: Darren McGavin, Simon Oakland, Ramon Bieri, Pippa Scott, Sorrell Booke, Victor Campos. Universal/Francy Productions/ABC-TV. Colour.
Kolchak investigates a series of ritual murders and uncovers a plot to sacrifice young hotel executive Pepe Torres (Erik Estrada) and briefly revive the mummy of an ancient Aztec sorcerer. This episode was also included in the TV movie compilation *The Demon and the Mummy* (1975).
✦✦✧

Primal Scream
USA, 1975. Dir: Robert Scheerer. With: Darren McGavin, Simon Oakland, John Marley, Pat Harrington, Katharine Woodville, Jamie Farr. Universal/Francy Productions/ ABC-TV. Colour.
Kolchak believes that million year-old cells brought back from the Arctic have grown into a prehistoric ape-man that kills at night on the streets of Chicago. This includes clips from *The Mummy's Ghost* (1944) on TV.
✦✦

The Werewolf
USA, 1974. Dir: Allen Baron. With: Darren McGavin, Simon Oakland, Dick Gautier, Henry Jones, Nita Talbot, Eric Braeden. Universal/Francy Productions/ABC-TV. Colour.
While trapped on a Christmas cruise, Kolchak discovers that one of his fellow passengers, Bernhardt Stieglitz (Braeden), is also a murderous werewolf!
✦✦

KONGA
UK, 1960. Dir: John Lemont. With: Michael Gough, Margo Johns, Jess Conrad, Claire Gordon, Leonard Sachs, Austin Trevor. Merton Park/Anglo Amalgamated. Colour.
Producer Herman Cohen (who makes a brief cameo appearance) originally wanted to call this *I Was a Teenage Gorilla*! Gough hams it up as mad botanist Dr Charles Decker, rescued from the African jungle with his pet chimpanzee. Back in England, he uses a growth serum to turn the monkey into a giant ape, which he hypnotises to kill the people he hates. Johns plays Margaret, Decker's jealous live-in assistant who gives the chimp an overdose; Gordon is Sandra Banks, the tight-sweatered object of the Doctor's desires and as Bob Kenton, pop star Conrad ends up as an unfortunate victim. Filmed in so-called 'SpectaMation' for $700,000, the climax has Konga (a man in a monkey suit) attacking Big Ben with a Decker doll clutched in its hand. This also includes some silly-looking giant carnivorous plants. Worth catching for Gough's outrageous performance. There were various *Konga* comic books from Charlton between 1960-65, and Monarch published a paperback novelisation in 1961 by Dean Owen (Dudley Dean McGaughy).
✦✦

MARTIN KOSLECK
(Nicolai Yoshkin) [1907-1994]

Russian character actor and former artist, who appeared on the stage in Germany working under Max Reinhardt before arriving in Hollywood in 1932. Usually cast as Nazis, weaselly killers or homicidal maniacs, he portrayed Joseph Goebbels in three different movies. Poor health forced him into retirement.
qv: *Get Smart: 'Weekend Vampire'* (1965); *The Mummy's Curse* (1944); *Rod Serling's Night Gallery: 'The Devil is Not Mocked'* (1971); *She-Wolf of London* (1946); *The Wild Wild West: 'The Night of the Diva'* (1969).

KRVAVA PANI
Czechoslovakia, 1981. Dir: Viktor Kubal. CFP/Koliba. Colour.

Claire Gordon resists Michael Gough's groping in Konga *(1960).*

Feature-length cartoon version of the Countess Elizabeth Bathory legend.
✦

OTTO KRUGER
[1885-1974]

American stage and screen actor who made his film début in the silent era and was usually cast as a suave leading man during the 1930s and 1940s.
qv: *Dracula's Daughter* (1936); *The Jungle Captive* (1944).

KULL THE CONQUEROR
Slovakia/Croatia/UK/USA, 1997. Dir: John Nicolella. With: Kevin Sorbo, Tia Carrere, Thomas Ian Griffith, Litefoot, Harvey Fierstein, Karina Lombard. Universal/Raffaella de Laurentiis. Colour.
Sorbo (TV's *Hercules the Legendary Journeys* [1995-99]) is fine as the eponymous barbarian warrior from Atlantis, who becomes the king of Valusia in this cut-price fantasy adventure based on the worlds and characters created by Robert E. Howard. When her evil acolyte Enaros (Edward Tudor-Pole) and his beastman slave Zuleki (Pat Roach) reanimate the 3,000 year-old mummy of sorceress queen Akivasha (a red-haired Carrere), she decides to recreate Hell on Earth by regaining the crown to her ancient kingdom. During the climax, Akivasha is transformed into an impressive demon (created by Gianetto De Rossi, Greg Cannom and CGI effects). Charles Edward Pogue's rewritten screenplay apparently began life as *Conan 3*, and L. Sprague de Camp is credited as technical advisor. TV producer/ director Nicolella (who replaced Kevin Hooks before filming) died the following year.
✦✦✧

KUMANDER BAWANG KALABAN NG MGA ASWANG
Philippines, 1988. Dir: Ramje. With: Herbert Bautista, Mat Ranillo III, Matet, Mia Prats, Dick Israel, Jigo Garcia. Viva Films. Colour.
Fantasy comedy in which Conde Regalado (Ranillo III) leads several generations of his family from their graves, where they grow vampire fangs and begin dancing. After a group of mummies and a gorilla join in, those villagers who are watching also sprout fangs.
✦

HARRY KÜMEL
[b 1940]:

Belgian screenwriter and film and theatre director. He began making award-winning short films in his teens before moving into TV and features.
qv: *Daughters of Darkness* (1971).

KUNG FU FROM BEYOND THE GRAVE
(Orig: YIN JI)
Hong Kong, 1979. Dir: Lee Chiu (Li Zhoa). With: Billy Chong (Willy Dohzan), Law Lit (Lo Lieh), Sung Kam-Shing, Hui Piu-Wan, Chui Jong-Shinn, Lai Kim-Hung. Orchids International Video/Ocean Shores. Colour.
When Sonny Sing's (Chong) father returns as a green ghost from Hell, he orders his son to avenge his murder by evil magician Kan Tai-Fu (Lit). During a martial arts battle, the villain calls upon Dracula(!) to aid him, and the Count promptly flies in. This also includes hopping vampires (*gyonsi*), lizard-tongued wizards, occult rays, flying phantoms and a ghost who removes his head and shoulders!
✦✧

KUNG FU THE LEGEND CONTINUES:
Sunday at the Museum with George
Canada/USA, 1994. Dir: Jon Cassar. With: David Carradine, Chris Potter, Robert Lansing, Geordie Johnson, Michele Scarabelli, Patrick Monckton. Warner Bros/UPN. Colour.
Hour-long TV series (1993-97, eighty-eight episodes) that updates the popular 1972-75 show, with co-producer Carradine playing the grandson of the original Kwai Chang Caine, who is reunited with his detective son Peter (Potter). In this sequel to the episode 'Sunday at the Hotel with George' (1993), a cursed archaeological exhibition becomes the target for George Vladpallin (Johnson, the star of *Dracula the Series* [1990-91]), who may just be a vampire. Writer/executive producer Michael Sloan has fun with this *suggested* cross-over show, thanks to various references to the Count, Peter being attacked by bats, and Scarabelli as a woman on the verge of being bitten. With veteran Lansing as police Captain Paul Blaisdell!
✦✦

KUNG FU VAMPIRE BUSTER
(Orig: JIANGSHI FANSHENG/NEW MR. VAMPIRE)
Hong Kong, 1985. Dir: Chung Leung (B. Chan/Xen Lung Ting). With: Xiao Lao Chang, Lu Fang (Leo Fong), Hung Wa. New Ship Film/Focus/Ocean Shores. Colour.
An attempt to duplicate the success of Golden Harvest's popular 'hopping vampire' series of horror comedies. A grave robber finds his soul fused with that of the ghost of a concubine who committed suicide, while a priest uses blood and moonlight to revive a vampire so that he can embarrass his rival.
✦✧

KUNG FU ZOMBIE
(Orig: WU LONG TIAN SHI ZHAO JI GUI)
Hong Kong, 1981 (1982). Dir: Hwa I. Hung. With: Billy Chong (Willy Dohzan), Kwon Young-Moon, Chaing Tao, Cheng Kay-Ying. Eternal Film/Transmedia/Orchids International Video/Ocean Shores. Colour.
Frenetic horror comedy in which Chong stars as magician-priest Pang, who battles the vampiric ghost of a martial arts master and is followed around by a horde of zombies who want to be reincarnated.
✦✧

KURONEKO
(Orig: YABU NO NAKA KURONEKO)
Japan, 1968. Dir: Kaneto Shindo. With: Kichiemon Nakamura, Nobuko Otowa, Kiwako Taichi, Kei Sato, Hideo Kanze, Rokko Toura. Kindai Eiga Kyokai/Nihon Eiga Shinsha/Cinecenta. B&W.
From Shindo, also the writer/director of *Onibaba* (1964), comes a similar horror story, set in the twelfth century. Awaiting her husband's return from the wars, a young woman (Taichi) and her old mother-in-law (Otowa) are raped and murdered by a band of samurai. They return as blood-drinking ghosts who can transform into black cats to destroy any warrior they meet. An imaginative blend of poetic imagery with shock effects that has its moments.
✦✦✧

KUUTAMOSONAATTI 2: KADUNLAKAISIJAT
Finland, 1991. Dir: Olli Soinio. With: Kari Sorvali, Mikko Kivinen, Soli Labbart. Filminor. Colour.
Apparently a comedy(!) about a mother and son who are frozen and burned to death, respectively, and then revived in a sauna.
✦

KYUKETSUKI DORAKYURA KOBE NI ARAWARU: AKUMA WA ONNA WO UTSUKUSHIKU SURU
Japan, 1979. Dir: Hajime Sato. With: Masumi Okada, Kei Taguchi. Toei/Asahi Communications. Colour.
TV movie in which Dracula (Okada) discovers that the reincarnation of his lost love now lives in Kobe. The title translates as 'Vampire Dracula Comes to Kobe: Evil Makes Women Beautiful'!
✦

KYUKETSUKI GA
Japan, 1956. Dir: Nobuo Nakagawa. With: Ryo Ikebe, Akio Kobori, Asami Kuji, Kinuko Ito. Shintoho. B&W.
A somewhat odd vampire film, in which the only clues to a series of murders are teeth marks found in the victims' necks and a blood-stained moth. In the end, the killer turns out not to be one of the undead. This was the first of nine horror movies directed by Nakagawa under the series title *Kaidan Eiga* (ghost story films). Based on the novel by Seishi Yokomizo.
✦✧

THE LADIES' MAN

USA, 1961. Dir: Jerry Lewis. With: Jerry Lewis, Helen Traubel, Kathleen Freeman, Hope Holiday, Pat Stanley, Jack Kruschen. Paramount. Colour.

Lewis directs and stars in this comedy as a handyman in a girls' school run by Mrs Wellenmelon (Traubel). In a dream sequence, he imagines a girl as a beautiful vampire. It includes cameo appearances by Buddy Lester, George Raft and Harry James and His Band.

✦✧

LADY DRACULA

West Germany, 1975 (1977). Dir: Franz-Joseph Gottlieb. With: Brad Harris, Evelyne Kraft, Christine Buchegger, Theo Lingen, Eddi Arent, Walter Giller. TV 13/IFV Produktion. Colour.

Vampire comedy in which Dracula (Ralph Boyd) bites a little girl in 1876. When her coffin is exhumed one hundred years later, she is transformed into a beautiful woman (Kraft) who has to drink five litres of fresh blood a day to survive. After a series of killings she eventually falls in love with the investigating police inspector (Harris, who wrote the original story), and they end up together in her coffin. Special effects created by Colin Chilvers.

✦✧

LADY FRANKENSTEIN

(Orig: LA FIGLIA DI FRANKENSTEIN)
Italy, 1971 (1972). Dir: Mel Well(e)s (Ernst von Theumer). With: Joseph Cotten, Sarah Bay (Rosalba Neri/Rada Rassimov), Mickey Hargitay, Paul Müller, Paul Whiteman, Herbert Fux (Fuchs). Condor International Pictures/New World Pictures. Colour.

'Only the Monster she made could satisfy her strange desires!' enticed the ads. Filmed under the title *Madame Frankenstein*, this crude reworking of Mary Shelley's original has Bay's Lady Tania Frankenstein using the brain of her assistant Charles (Müller) to create a laughable creature (Whiteman, who walks around as if drilling on a parade ground) to battle her father's disfigured Monster. Poor old Cotten is completely wasted in a cameo as Baron Frankenstein, and you know you're in trouble when the best performance in the film comes from Hargitay as a police captain. During the climax, Bay is strangled by her creation as she makes love to it! In 1972 Dario Argento and proposed director Luigi Cozzi scripted an adaptation of *Frankenstein* to star Timothy Dalton. Based on the 1931 version but set in Nazi Germany, it was turned down by both Universal and Hammer. Ten years later, Italian company Filman announced that another film called *Lady Frankenstein*, directed by Alan Cools and starring Antonella Prati and Mark Shannon, was ready for release.

Remake: FRANKENSTEIN (qv; 1973)

✦

LADYHAWKE

UK/Italy/USA, 1985. Dir: Richard Donner. With: Matthew Broderick, Rutger Hauer, Michelle Pfeiffer, Leo McKern, John Wood, Ken Hutchison. Warner Bros/Twentieth Century Fox. Colour.

Overlong and uninvolving medieval fantasy. Placed under a dark curse by a sorcerous Bishop (Wood), the maiden Isabeau of Anjou (Pfeiffer) changes into a hawk during the daytime, returning to human form at sunset when Etienne of Navarre (Hauer), the Captain of the Guards she loves, is transformed into a wolf who watches over her. When a young petty thief, Phillipe Gaston (a miscast Broderick), escapes the Bishop's dungeons, Navarre finally sees a way to enter the heavily guarded fortress and end the evil spell that keeps him and Isabeau always together and eternally apart. The music score by Andrew Powell and Alan Parsons is totally inappropriate.

✦✦✧

LADY MASTER SNAKE

(USA: aka SNAKE WOMAN'S MARRIAGE)
Hong Kong, circa 1980s. Jia's Film/Allstar Film/Tai Seng

As Lady Frankenstein *(1971), Sarah Bay meets her father's creation.*

Video. Colour.
A baby grows up to become queen of a tribe of female were-snakes.
✦

LADY TIGER
Thailand, 1989. Dir: Ry-Man. Colour.
A doctor and his shrill wife discover that their jungle neighbours, a lycanthropic brother and sister, grow fangs and claws when sexually aroused. After a number of killings, the doctor rescues the woman from crucifixion, and she transforms completely into a tiger and is sent to the zoo. This apparently contains plenty of nudity and gratuitous gore.
✦

LADY WOLF
Hong Kong, 1991. Dir: Richard X.C. Tung. With: Joey Wang (Wang Tsu-Hsien/Wang Zu-Xian/Wong Ki-Chang), Wu Ma (Wo Ma/Yuen Wah/Ng Ma-Wu). J&J. Colour.
A trio of sexy female werewolves transform into white-haired fanged creatures with tails to exact vengeance on fur merchant Hsi Wei and his ancestors. Ma plays a hunter who has been relentlessly tracking the creatures for years.
✦✧

CARL LAEMMLE JR
[1908-1979]

Son of Carl Laemmle Sr (1867-1939), the German-born founder of Universal Pictures, he became General Manager in Charge of Production at the studio at the age of twenty-one. After supervising such classics as *Dracula* (1931), *Frankenstein* (1931), *The Old Dark House* (1932), *The Mummy* (1933), *The Invisible Man* (1933), *The Black Cat* (1934), *Bride of Frankenstein* (1935) and *WereWolf of London* (1935), he 'resigned' in 1936 when the studio was sold by his father.

THE LAIR OF THE WHITE WORM
UK, 1988 (1989). Dir: Ken Russell. With: Amanda Donohoe, Hugh Grant, Catherine Oxenberg, Peter Capaldi, Sammi Davis, Stratford Johns. Vestron Pictures. Colour.
Very loosely based on Bram Stoker's novel, this ludicrous contemporary version was somewhat desperately billed as a horror comedy. Donohoe camps it up wonderfully as Lady Sylvia Marsh, a worshipper of the legendary D'Ampton Worm, who turns into a snake woman and seduces boy scouts. However, the rest of the cast are terrible (including a pre-stardom Grant as the hero, Lord James D'Ampton, and *Dynasty*'s Oxenberg, who apparently had to have her Northern accent re-dubbed). Russell's dream sequences are predictably overblown and Image Animation's giant worm effects are used far too sparingly.
✦

THE LAKE OF DRACULA
(Orig: CHI O SUU ME. USA: aka BLOODTHIRTSY EYES) Japan, 1971 (1974). Dir: Michio Yamamoto. With: Choei (Osahide) Takahashi, Sanae Emi, Midori Fujita, Mori Kishida, Kaku Takashina, Suji (Hideji) Ohtaki. Toho/UPA Productions of America/Henry G. Saperstein. Colour.
High school teacher Akiko (Fujita) spends her vacation painting a strange picture and begins to recall a repressed childhood memory. When her dog is killed and her sister Natsuko (Emi) transformed into one of the undead, Akiko and her doctor boyfriend (Takahashi) return to an old house by the sea where they confront a golden-eyed vampire (Kishida) who is eventually impaled on a broken piece of wood by the reanimated corpse of his father. Despite the title, Yamamoto's follow-up to *The Night of the Vampire* (1970) has nothing to do with Dracula.
✦✦✧

LAST FRANKENSTEIN
**(Orig: LASUTO FURANKENSHUTAIN)
Japan, 1991. Dir: Takeshi Kawamura. With: Akira Emoto, Yoshio Harada, Naomasa Musaka, Juro Kara. Bandai/BF Film/Rittor Music/Shochiku. Colour.**
This marked the movie début of theatre director Kawamura. Mad scientist Dr Aleo, convinced that the only way to save the human race is by rebuilding a body totally devoid of emotions, creates a new man and his bride, but comes into conflict with the leader of a religious suicide cult.
✦✧

LAM CHING-YING
(Lin Zheng-Ying) [1952-1997]

Hong Kong Chinese actor who is best known for his portrayals of martial artist vampire hunters in the *Mr. Vampire* series (1985-1992).
qv: *Crazy Safari* (1990); *Encounter of the Spooky Kind* (1980); *Encounter of the Spooky Kind II* (1989); *Exorcist Master* (1992); *The First Vampire in China* (1990); *Forced Nightmare* (1992); *Magic Cop* (1989); *Mr. Vampire* (1985); *Mr. Vampire 1992* (1992); *Mr. Vampire Part III* (1986); *Mr Vampire 2* (1985); *One Eyebrow Priest* (1987); *Red and Black* (1986); *The Spooky Family 2* (1991); *The Ultimate Vampire* (1991); *Vampire Expert* (1995); *Vampire Expert II* (1996).

CHARLES LAMONT
[1898-1993]

American director since the silent era who was responsible for *Francis in the Haunted House* (1956), and Abbott and Costello's final flings together.
qv: *Abbott and Costello Meet Dr. Jekyll and Mr. Hyde* (1953); *Abbott and Costello Meet the Mummy* (1955).

ELSA LANCHESTER
(Elizabeth Sullivan) [1902-1986]

Homely British character actress and former dance instructor who married Charles Laughton in 1929 and moved to Hollywood in 1940. In James Whale's classic *Bride of Frankenstein* (1935) she portrayed both creator Mary Shelley and the memorable shock-haired mate for the Monster. She published two autobiographies, *Charles Laughton and I* (1938) and *Elsa Lanchester Herself* (1983). Rosalind Ayers played her in *Gods and Monsters* (1998).

LEW LANDERS
(Lewis Friedlander) [1901-1962]

American director since the silent days who brought the same level of skill to *The Raven* (1935) and *Return of the Vampire* (1943) as he did to his numerous 'B' movie Westerns.

JOHN LANDIS
[b 1950]

American writer and director who started out working in the mail room at Twentieth Century-Fox. He played an ape in his first feature, *Schlock* (1972), before finding success with the comedies *National Lampoon's Animal House* (1978) and *The Blues Brothers* (1980). A true fan of the genre, he often appears in cameo roles in other directors' films.
qv: *An American Werewolf in London* (1981); *Blues Brothers 2000* (1998); *Coming Soon* (1982); *Death Race 2000* (1975); *Heartstoppers (1992); Innocent Blood* (1992); *Monster by Moonlight: The Immortal Saga of the Wolf Man* (1999); *Night of the Living Dead 25th Anniversary Documentary* (1993); *The Silence of the Hams* (1993); *Sleepwalkers* (1992); *Susan's Plan* (1998); *Thriller* (1983); *Vampirella* (1996).

THE LAST HORROR FILM
USA, 1982 (1984). Dir: David Winters. With: Caroline Munro, Joe Spinell, Glenn Jacobson, Mary Spinell, Sean Casey, June Chadwick. Shere Productions. Colour.

The two stars of *Maniac* (1980) are reunited in another low-budget splatter movie, filmed on location at the 1981 Cannes Film Festival (Marcello Mastroianni, Isabelle Adjani and Karen Black have 'walk ons'). Spinell plays crazy would-be director Vinny Durand who wants horror movie queen Jana Bates (Munro) to star in his project, *The Loves of Dracula*. When she turns him down, he goes on a murder spree, filming his victims until the 'surprise' ending. This even includes Spinell's real-life mother Mary (who won the best actress award for her role at the Sitges Film Festival!) and Munro's husband Judd Hamilton (who co-produced).
✦✧

MICHAEL LANDON
(Eugene Orowitz) [1937-1991]

American TV actor, a regular in such series as *Bonanza* (1959-73), *Little House on the Prairie* (1974-82) and *Highway to Heaven* (1984-88), who played the teen lycanthrope in *I Was a Teenage Werewolf* (1957).
qv: *Highway to Heaven: 'I Was a Middle-Aged Werewolf'* (1987).

PAUL LANDRES
[b 1912]

American director, best known for his musicals and Westerns, who also made two contemporary vampire movies: *The Vampire* (1957) and *The Return of Dracula* (1957).

FRANK LANGELLA
[b 1940]

American actor who portrayed Dracula on Broadway in the 1977 revival and recreated his role as a romantic Count in John Badham's 1979 movie version.
qv: *Dracula* (1982); *Small Soldiers* (1998); *Sphinx* (1980).

JOSÉ RAMÓN LARRAZ
[b 1929]

Spanish director who, after working as a comics artist, moved to England via France during the late 1960s. Despite no formal training as a film-maker, he directed a number of low-budget sex and horror thrillers as Joseph Larraz in the UK before returning to Spain.
qv: *The National Mummy* (1981); *Vampyres* (1974).

THE LAST MAN ON EARTH

(Orig: L'ULTIMO UOMO DELLA TERRA)
Italy/USA, 1961 (1964). Dir: Sidney Salkow (and Ubaldo Ragona). With: Vincent Price, Franca Bettoia, Emma Danieli, Giacomo Rossi-Stuart, Umberto Rali, Christi Courtland. La Regina/Alta Vista/American International. B&W.

Richard Matheson originally scripted his classic novel *I am Legend* for Hammer Films in 1957, and they eventually sold it to producer Robert L. Lippert who shot it on the cheap in Italy for Twentieth Century-Fox, before it was passed on to AIP. Re-written by William P. Leicester, Matheson used the pen-name 'Logan Swanson' on the final screenplay credit. Despite the problems, this is still a pretty effective adaptation. After the world has been decimated by a wind-carried plague, scientist Morgan (Price) is the last human left alive, staking pasty-faced vampires/zombies until he is killed by a group of mutant humans. Price gives a surprisingly restrained performance, and the vampire make-ups were obviously an influence on George Romero's *Night of the Living Dead* (1968). The remake replaced the vampires with blank-eyed mutants. A big-budget version of *I am Legend*, directed by Ridley Scott and starring Arnold Schwarzenegger, was announced by Warner Bros in 1997 but put on hold when the cost spiralled over $100,000,000.
Remake: THE ΩMEGA MAN (1971)
✦✦✦

Vincent Price discovers that he's not quite The Last Man on Earth *(1961).*

LAST RITES
(USA: aka DRACULA'S LAST RITES)
France/USA, 1980. Dir: Domonic Paris. With: Patricia Lee Hammond, Gerald Fielding, Victor Jorge, Michael Lally, Mimi Weddell. New Empire Features/Cannon. Colour.
Lucard, a small town mortician, the sheriff and a local doctor are all vampires who drink the blood of accident victims, then drive a stake through their hearts to avoid unwanted competition. This low-budget horror film, shot in upstate New York, is most notable for its technical incompetence.
✦

THE LAST VAMPIRE
Hong Kong, 1988. HKTV Video. Colour.
A hero seeking a magical sword encounters hopping vampires with detachable heads and elastic arms, plus zombies who are restored to life at the end.
✦✧

THE LAST VAMPYRE
UK, 1992. Dir: Tim Sullivan. With: Jeremy Brett, Edward Hardwicke, Keith Barron, Roy Marsden, Freddie Jones, Maurice Denham. Granada Television/ITV. Colour.
Two-hour TV movie, scripted by Jeremy Paul (*Countess Dracula* [1970], etc) and very loosely based on Sir Arthur Conan Doyle's 1924 story 'The Adventure of the Sussex Vampire'. Sherlock Holmes (an eccentric performance by Brett) and Doctor Watson (Hardwicke) encounter the supernatural when they are summoned by a priest (veteran Denham) to the Sussex village of Lamberley, where the mysterious John Stockton (Marsden) is suspected of being the descendant of a family of vampires. Director Sullivan uses all the genre conventions to keep the audience guessing, while Jones' 'special guest appearance' consists of one very brief scene.
Remake: SHERLOCK HOLMES IN CARACAS (qv; 1992)
✦✦✦✧

LATE NIGHT HORROR:
No Such Thing as a Vampire
UK, 1968. Dir: Paddy Russell. With: Andrew Keir, Meg Wynn Owen, Thomas Gallagher, Peter Blythe, Cynthia Etherington. BBC-TV. Colour.
This contribution to the half-hour anthology TV series (six episodes) was scripted by Richard Matheson, based on his own story. When Alexis (Owen), the beautiful wife of Dr Gheria (Keir), appears to be the victim of a vampire, the young Dr Vares (Blythe) decides to stand guard outside her room...
✦✦

LATIDOS DE PÁNICO
Spain/Japan, 1983. Dir: Jacinto Molina. With: Paul Naschy (Jacinto Molina), Julia Saly, Lola Gaos, Silvia Miró, Pat (Paquita) Ondiviela, Manolo Zarzo. Aconito Films. Colour.
Belated sequel to *Horror Rises from the Tomb* (1972), in which writer/director Naschy recreates his role as the evil fifteenth century knight Alaric de Marnac, who returns from the grave to seek revenge against his murderous descendants in an isolated house. In the end the victims are all revived as zombies in a chapel. The title translates as 'Beats of Panic'.
✦✧

EL LATIGO CONTRA LAS MOMIAS ASESINAS
Mexico, 1979. Dir: Angel Rodriguez. With: 'Tinieblas' (Manuel Leal), Juan Miranda, Rosa Chagoyan, Manuel Leal, Marcko D'Carlo. Peliculas Latinoamericanas/ Novelty Internacional/Mexcinema Video. Colour.
This sequel to *El Latigo contra Satanas* (1977) features giant wrestler 'Tinieblas' ('Darkness') teaming up with the eponymous whip-wielding Zorro impersonator (Miranda, a former Mr Mexico) to battle marauding mummies with glowing eyes who can appear and disappear in an instant.
✦

THE LAUGHING DEAD
USA, 1989. Dir: S.P. Somtow (Somtow Sucharitkul). With: Tim (Timothy Robert) Sullivan, Wendy Webb, Premika Eaton, Patrick Roskowick, Larry Kagan, Krista Keim. Laughing Dead Partners/Archæopteryx/Tercel. Colour.
The direct-to-video début of author and musician Somtow (who also executive produced and composed the score under his real name). Troubled Catholic priest Father O'Sullivan (co-associate producer Sullivan) leads a group of tourists on an archaeological expedition to Mexico, where they are menaced by a Mayan cult of human sacrifice led by the mad Dr Um-tzec (Somtow doing his best George Zucco impression) and encounter basketball-playing zombies (created by John Buechler's Magical Media Industries, Inc) in a subterranean temple. With writers Gregory Frost, Edward Bryant, Arthur Byron Cover, Tim Powers and William F. Wu (the latter three as zombies). Forrest J Ackerman, Bill Warren and Len Wein also turn up briefly as corpses.
✦✧

LAUGHING DEAD
USA, 1996 (1999). Dir: Patrick Gleason. With: Patrick Gleason, John Hammond, Fern Finer, Nancy Rhee, Rico Cymone, Robert Mack. LD Productions/Ishi Entertainment/The Helion Group/EI Independent Cinema. Colour.
Impressive-looking independent feature, written and directed by Gleason. Hunter (Gleason), a young junkie, emerges out of a toxic river into a diseased post-apocalyptic Los Angeles populated by cannibalistic mutants and controlled by Vincent (Hammond), an ages-old vampire who has transformed the city into a human slaughterhouse. With no knowledge of where he is or how he got there, Hunter attempts to stay alive and discover the truth about his own half-human existence.
✦✦

CHARLES LAUGHTON
[1899-1962]

Stout British character actor who moved to Hollywood in 1940. Married to actress Elsa Lanchester but haunted by his own homosexuality. Outstanding as the sadistic, whip-cracking Dr Moreau in *Island of Lost Souls* (1932) and the sympathetic bellringer in *The Hunchback of Notre Dame* (1939), some of his later performances were served up with a lamentable slice of ham.
qv: *The Horror Show* (1979).

LAUREL & HARDY:
Monster Bash
USA, 1966. Dir: Joseph Barbera and William Hanna. Voices: Larry Harmon, Jim MacGeorge, Hal Smith, Don Messick, Doug Young, Paul Frees. Wolper Productions/ Larry Harmon Pictures/Hanna-Barbera Productions. Colour.
Half-hour syndicated cartoon TV series consisting of 130 five minute episodes. In this segment, Stan (Harmon) and Ollie (Mac George) attend a party where they meet the Frankenstein Monster and other creatures.
✦

PHIL LEAKEY
[1908-1992]

British make-up artist who joined Hammer in 1947 and created many of their seminal monsters. He finally became disillusioned with the films and left the studio.
qv: *The Curse of Frankenstein* (1957); *Dracula* (1958); *The Revenge of Frankenstein* (1958); *Vampira* (1974).

LEE AND HERRING'S REASONABLY SCARY MONSTERS
UK, 1998. Dir: Charles Louder. With: Richard Herring, Stewart Lee, Carol Vorderman. BBC Manchester. Colour.
Dire eighteen minute comedy/documentary in which 'comedians' Lee and Herring watch a video of *The World's 9 Scariest Monsters!* introduced by Vorderman. With inane commentary by a motley

bunch of 'celebrities' and occasional brief clips, these are (in reverse order) The Alien, The Cyclops, The Daleks, King Kong (with footage from the 1933 film), Godzilla, Frankenstein's Monster (footage from *Lady Frankenstein* [1971] and Hammer's *The Horror of Frankenstein* [1970]), Sea Monsters, Zombies (footage from Hammer's *The Plague of the Zombies* [1966] and *Night of the Living Dead* [1968]) and Female Monsters. Everybody involved with this rubbish should be ashamed.
✦

REGINALD LeBORG
[1902-1989]

Austrian-born journeyman director best remembered for his work on Universal's *Inner Sanctum* series in the 1940s.
qv: *House of the Black Death* (1965) *Jungle Woman* (1944); *The Mummy's Ghost* (1944); *Voodoo Island* (1957).

FRANCIS LEDERER
[b 1906]

Czechoslovakian leading man who arrived in Hollywood in 1933 following work in films and on the stage in Europe. He portrayed the Count in contemporary California in *The Return of Dracula* (1957).
qv: *100 Years of Horror: 'Dracula and His Disciples'* (1996); *100 Years of Horror: 'Mad Doctors'* (1996); *Rod Serling's Night Gallery: 'The Devil is Not Mocked'* (1971).

CHRISTOPHER LEE
[b 1922]

Commanding British character actor who found stardom through Hammer Films as the Creature in *The Curse of Frankenstein* (1957) and the Count in *Dracula* (1958). Although Lee has appeared in all types of movies, many of which are beneath his talent, he is still best known for the numerous horror roles he often tries to disassociate himself from. His autobiography *Tall, Dark and Gruesome* was published in 1977 and reissued in a revised edition twenty years later.
qv: *Alias John Preston* (1955); *The Avengers: 'Never, Never Say Die'* (1967); *The Blood Demon* (1967); *Bram Stoker's Count Dracula* (1970); *Crypt of Horror* (1964); *Cuadecuc (Vampir)* (1970); *Dracula A.D. 1972* (1972); *Dracula and Son* (1976); *Dracula Has Risen from the Grave* (1968); *Dracula Prince of Darkness* (1965); *Dr. Terror's House of Horrors* (1965); *Fear in the Dark* (1991); *Flesh and Blood: The Hammer Heritage of Horror* (1994); *Gremlins 2 The New Batch* (1990); *Hammer the Studio That Dripped Blood!* (1987); *Hercules in the Haunted World* (1961); *Horror Express* (1972); *The House That Dripped Blood* (1970); *Howling II Stirba — Werewolf Bitch* (1984); *I, Monster* (1971); *In Search of Dracula* (1971); *In Search of Dracula With Jonathan Ross* (1996); *The Magic Christian* (1969); *The Many Faces of Christopher Lee* (1995); *Monsters We've Known and Loved* (1991); *100 Years of Horror* (1996); *The Mummy* (1959); *The Mummy* (1999, documentary); *One More Time* (1970); *Panga* (1990); *The Satanic Rites of Dracula* (1973); *Saturday Night Live* (1978); *Scars of Dracula* (1970); *Scream and Scream Again* (1969); *The South Bank Show: 'Dracula'* (1993); *Talos the Mummy* (1998); *Taste the Blood of Dracula* (1969); *Theatre of Death* (1966); *This is Your Life: 'Christopher Lee'* (1974); *The Tomorrow People: 'The Rameses Connection'* (1995); *The Two Faces of Dr. Jekyll* (1960); *Uncle Was a Vampire* (1959); *The Vampire Interviews* (circa 1990s); *The World of Hammer: 'Hammer Stars: Christopher Lee'* (1990).

ROWLAND V. LEE
[1891-1975]

American director and former actor. Arrived in Hollywood in 1916 and began directing five years later. After various stints at Fox and Paramount, he joined Universal in 1938, where he directed Basil Rathbone and Boris Karloff in both *Tower of London* (1939) and *Son of Frankenstein* (1939).

LEENA MEETS FRANKENSTEIN

USA, 1993. Dir: Scotty Fox. With: Leena (Leena La Bianca), Randy Spears, Tina Tyler, Brittany O'Connell, Madison (Madison Stone), Nicole London. Pinnacle/Odyssey Group Video. Colour/B&W.

Hardcore remake of (Abbott and Costello) *Meet Frankenstein* (1948) which changes from black and white to colour for the sex scenes! When their car breaks down while they are on vacation, two women (London and Leena) are stranded at a time-share condo with the classic monsters — Count Alucard (Mike Horner), his vampire wives (Madison and O'Connell), the Wolfman (Tony Tedeschi) and Frankenstein's creation (Jon Dough). This includes Spears as an inept Steve van Helsing and London also dressed as the Bride of Frankenstein. Written and produced by L.S. Talbot!
✦

LEGACY OF SATAN

USA, 1973. Dir: Gerard Damiano. With: Lisa Cristian, John Francis, Paul Barry, Christ Helm, Deborah Horlen, Ann Paul. Damiano Films. Colour.

Tedious occult thriller, co-produced, written, edited and directed by Damiano, best known for his porn classics *Deep Throat* and *The Devil in Miss Jones* (both 1973). Cristian plays Maya, a New York housewife who is lured into a cult of Satanic blood-drinkers led by Dr Muldavo (Francis). Nothing much more happens until the end when, disowned by the Devil/Lord Rakish, Muldavo is transformed into a horrible-looking corpse. If this ever included any sex scenes they are definitely missing from most prints, which usually run just under an hour!
✦

LEGALLY DEAD

USA, 1923. Dir: William Parke. With: Milton Sills, Margaret Campbell, Claire Adams, Joseph Girard, Edwin Sturgis, Brandon Hurst. Universal. B&W.

In this silent drama, when Will Campbell (Sills) is wrongly hanged for murder, brilliant scientist Dr Gelzer (Hurst) injects a large syringe of adrenaline into the heart of the dead man, bringing him back to life and a happy ending.
✦

LEGEND

UK/USA, 1985. Dir: Ridley Scott. With: Tom Cruise, Mia Sara (Sara Pocciello), Tim Curry, David Bennent, Alice Playten, Billy Barty. Universal/Twentieth Century Fox. Colour.

Although Ridley Scott's magical fantasy looks superb, the short running time hardly allows William Hjortsberg's one-idea script to develop into anything special. As young lovers Jack and Lili, Cruise and Sara are insipid leads compared with Curry's Lord of Darkness (in Rob Bottin's excellent make-up effects), who plans to bring perpetual night to the world by killing the last two unicorns. This includes various fairies, gnomes and elves, Robert Picardo as slimy swamp witch Meg Mucklebones, and Eddie Powell (from *The Mummy's Shroud* [1967], etc) as a mummified guard. The American version was re-edited to simplify the plot even more and provide a different ending, while Jerry Goldsmith's wonderful orchestral score was replaced with one by Tangerine Dream.
✦✦✧

THE LEGENDARY CURSE OF LEMORA

(Orig: LEMORA, THE LADY DRACULA. USA/UK: aka LADY DRACULA/LEMORA A CHILD'S TALE OF THE SUPERNATURAL/LEMORA: A VAMPIRE'S TALE)
USA, 1973 (1974). Dir: Richard Blackburn. With: Lesley Gilb, Cheryl (Rainbeaux) Smith, William Whitton, Hy Pike, Maxine Ballantyne, Steve Johnson. Blackburn Productions/Media Cinema. Colour.

This low-budget supernatural chiller succeeds because of its bizarre atmosphere and Gilb's sensuous performance. Set in 1920s Georgia, thirteen year-old church singer Lila Lee (Smith) has a series of disturbing sexual fantasies and her gangster father (Whitton) is used to lure her to an old village dominated by Lemora (Gilb), a beautiful vampire whose followers include a group of strange children.

John Forbes-Robertson's Dracula possesses his disciple in The Legend of the 7 Golden Vampires *(1974).*

However, the blood-drinking disease has also created many grotesque monstrosities living in the surrounding woods. Director Blackburn turns up as the puritanical Reverend Mueller, who also narrates. The Catholic Film Board gave the movie a condemned rating. The director's own making-of documentary, *Confessions of Lemora*, accompanied the film's 1994 video re-release.
✦✦✦

THE LEGEND OF BLOOD CASTLE

(Orig: CEREMONIA SANGRIENTA/LE VERGINI CAVALCANO LA MORTE. USA: aka BLOOD CEREMONY/ THE FEMALE BUTCHER)
Spain/Italy, 1972 (1973). Dir: Jorge Grau. With: Lucia Bosé, Espartaco Santoni, Ewa Aulin, Ana Farra, Lola Gaos, Franca Grey. X Films/Luis Films/Film Ventures International. Colour.
A serious version of the Countess Elizabeth (Erzsebeth) Bathory legend, given an exploitation release in America ('Schooled in carnage and blood she butchered 610 nubile young virgins'). Former Italian beauty queen Bosé portrays the descendant of the original Countess, who retains her youth by bathing in the blood of virgin victims obtained by her vampire husband. This ponderous, arty movie has the vampires being put on trial for their crimes! Co-writer and director Grau (*The Living Dead at Manchester Morgue* [1974], etc) was a former assistant to Michelangelo Antonioni.
✦✧

LEGEND OF EIGHT SAMURAI

(USA: aka EIGHT SAMURAI)
Japan, 1984. Dir: Kinji Fukasaku. With: Hiroko Yakushimaru, Henry Sanada, Sue Shihomi, Sonny Chiba (Shinichi Chiba), Mickey Narita. Toei Company/Prism Entertainment. Colour.
Fantasy adventure which includes an evil queen who bathes in blood to stay young and lives in a castle protected by magic.
✦✧

THE LEGEND OF THE FRANKENSTEIN MONSTER

USA, 1993 (1994). Simitar Entertainment. B&W/Colour.
Two-part video compilation ('The Creature Is Born'/'The Creature Lives On') of still photographs, excerpts and the usual Universal and Hammer trailers. Slightly more interesting are trailers for *Frankenstein Conquers the World* (1964), *Frankenstein Meets the Spacemonster* (1965), *Frankenstein 1970* (1958), *Frankenstein's Daughter* (1958), *I Was a Teenage Frankenstein* (1957), *Jesse James Meets Frankenstein's Daughter* (1965) and *Lady Frankenstein* (1971), plus clips from *Orlak, El Infierno de Frankenstein* (1960), Hammer's TV *Tales of Frankenstein* (1958) and the creation sequence from the Edison *Frankenstein* (1910). Narrated by Jeffrey Lee.
✦✧

THE LEGEND OF THE 7 GOLDEN VAMPIRES

(USA: THE 7 BROTHERS MEET DRACULA)
Hong Kong/UK, 1974. Dir: Roy Ward Baker (and Chang Cheh). With: Peter Cushing, Julie Ege, David Chiang, Robin Stewart, Shih Szu, Robert Hanna. Hammer Films/Shaw Brothers/Warner Bros. Colour.
Hammer's final Dracula movie to date brings Cushing back for one last time as Van Helsing, but Christopher Lee is replaced by a theatrical John Forbes-Robertson as the Count. This is an enjoyable blend of kung fu and Hammer horror as Van Helsing and companions travel to a Chinese village to protect its inhabitants from a band of masked, marauding vampires. The scenes of the vampires' zombie slaves, rising EC comics-like from their graves, are effective, but

the make-up looks cheap and more care could have been taken with the script. American audiences had to wait six years to see this from Max J. Rosenberg's Dynamite! Entertainment in a version fourteen minutes shorter and re-edited by Jack Rabin, while the Far East version apparently contains an extra twenty minutes of kung fu footage shot by Cheh. The same year Hammer announced *Kali: Devil Bride of Dracula*, scripted by Christopher Wicking and with Cushing again to play Van Helsing, but it was never made. A soundtrack LP was narrated by Cushing and Forbes-Robertson, and this was beautifully adapted into comic strip format by artist Brian Lewis and writer Steve Moore for *The House of Hammer* no.4 (1976).
✦✦✦

LEGEND OF THE WEREWOLF

UK, 1974. Dir: Freddie Francis. With: Peter Cushing, Ron Moody, Hugh Griffith, Roy Castle, David Rintoul, Lynn Dalby. Tyburn Films. Colour.
Producer Kevin Francis' Tyburn Films tried to recreate the heyday of Hammer with this disappointing werewolf thriller, scripted by John Elder (Anthony Hinds), who also wrote Hammer's *The Curse of the Werewolf* (1960), and based on two previously announced projects, *Plague of the Werewolves* by Frederick Warner and Elder's own *Wolf Boy*. Cushing walks through his role as Paul Cataflanque, a police pathologist investigating a series of grisly murders in nineteenth century Paris. Although a wild animal is suspected, the real culprit is Etoile (Rintoul), a young man raised by wolves who transforms into a beast (make-up by Roy Ashton) under the full moon. Made on an obviously minuscule budget, Moody and Griffith contribute eccentric cameos and director Francis seems uninspired by the all-too-familiar material. With Michael Ripper. Sphere Books published the novelisation by Robert Black (Robert Holdstock), while Edward Buscombe's book *Making Legend of the Werewolf* was a record of the production process.
✦✧

THE LEGEND OF THE WOLF WOMAN

(Orig: LA LUPA MANNARA. USA: aka DAUGHTER OF A WEREWOLF/NAKED WEREWOLF WOMAN/SHE WOLF/ TERROR OF THE SHE WOLF. UK: WEREWOLF WOMAN)
Italy, 1976 (1977). Dir: R.D. Silver (Rino [Salvatore] Di Silvestro). With: Anne (Annik) Borel, Howard Ross (Renato Rossini), Dagmar Lassander, Tino Carey (Tino Carrado), Fred (Frederick) Stafford, Ollie Reynolds (Osvaldo Ruggieri). Dialchi Film/Cinestampa/Amanda/ Dimension Pictures. Colour.
Unpleasant blend of softcore sex and horror, supposedly based on an actual case in 1968. Sexually abused as a child, Daniela Messeri (Borel) wanders around the woods naked and is haunted by nightmares of her werewolf ancestor (also Borel), who was burned at the stake. Diagnosed as suffering from psychological lycanthropy, she escapes from a psychiatric hospital and goes on the rampage, tearing the throats out of people who try to have sex with her, stabbing a crazy lesbian with a pair of scissors, beating a doctor's head against a car steering wheel and revenging herself on three rapists. In the end, she is recaptured by the police. The wolf woman is only shown in flashback. The English-language version was directed by Tony La Penna.
✦

THE LEMON GROVE KIDS MEET THE MONSTERS

USA, 1966. Dir: Ray Dennis Steckler. With: Cash Flagg (Ray Dennis Steckler), Carolyn Brandt, Mike Kannon, Larry Byrd, Jim Harmon, Ron Haydock. Morgan-Steckler. Colour.
From the same team that brought you *The Incredibly Strange Creatures Who Stopped Living and Became Mixed-Up Zombies!!?* (1963) comes this homage to The Bowery Boys. Director Steckler stars under the name Cash Flagg, along with his wife (Brandt, as a vampire), friends and neighbours. Set during a car race, this insanity includes a fake mummy and gorilla (both played by Bob Burns), a spaceman and a beatnik spy. It was originally a home-made 16mm short spliced together from *The Lemon Grove Kids Meet the Green Grasshopper and the Vampire Lady from Outer Space* and *Lemon Grove Kids Go to Hollywood*. When shown in America during kiddie matinees, people dressed as monsters ran through the auditorium.
✦

THE LENNY HENRY SHOW

UK, 1984. Dir: Geoff Posner. With: Lenny Henry. BBC-TV. Colour.
The first episode of Henry's episodic TV show (1984-88) features a clever spoof of Michael Jackson's *Thriller* (1983), in which the comedian dreams he is in a graveyard and transforms into a werewolf and dancing zombie (make-up designed by Sally Sutton) until his mother intervenes.
✦✦✧

LEONOR

(aka LEONORE)
France/Italy/Spain, 1974 (1975). Dir: Juan Buñuel. With: Michel Piccoli, Liv Ullmann, Ornella Muti, Antonio Ferrandis, José Maria Caffarel, Angel del Pozo. Goya Films/Arcadie Productions/Transeuropa Films. Colour.
Co-written and directed by the son of director Luis Buñuel, this fourteenth century fairy-tale is based on a story by Ludwig Tieck. Piccoli plays Richard, a knight obsessed with his dead wife Leonor (Ullmann). He makes a deal with the Devil to bring her back to life, but she returns as a plague-carrying vampire. Music by Ennio Morricone.
✦✦

LEPKE

USA/Israel, 1975. Dir: Menahem Golan. With: Tony Curtis, Anjanette Comer, Michael Callan, Warren Berlinger, Gianni Russo, Vic Tayback. Warner Bros/ AmeriEuro. Colour.
Old-fashioned biopic of ruthless Jewish-American gangster Louis 'Lepke' Buchalter (Curtis), who started out as a petty criminal in New York and ended his reign as the head of Murder, Inc in the electric chair in 1944. With Milton Berle, and the wax figure of a Karloffian Frankenstein Monster in a fairground museum.
✦✦✧

LESBIAN VAMPIRE SEX & BONDAGE

USA, 1997. Dir: Geoffrey de Valois. With: Tonya Qualls, Joan A. Teeter, Julie Covarrubias. Digital Entertainment Group/Salt City Home Video. Colour.
One of a series of softcore *Vampire Raw Footage* videos that includes behind-the-scenes nude and erotic sequences. This volume apparently includes bondage scenes between Teeter and Covarrubias, and Qualls undergoing nude electric shock sex torture!
✦

LET'S SCARE JESSICA TO DEATH

USA, 1971. Dir: John Hancock. With: Zohra Lampert, Barton Heyman, Kevin O'Connor, Gretchen Corbett, Alan Manson, Mariclare Costello. Paramount. Colour.
Recovering from a nervous breakdown, Jessica (Lampert) is taken by her husband Duncan (Heyman) and friend Woody (O'Connor) to stay in an old Connecticut farmhouse reputedly haunted by a vampire girl (Corbett). She soon starts seeing and hearing strange things and, from the title, you'd expect that someone is trying to drive her insane. However, the surprise twist is that it's all really happening — there really is a vampire who drowned in the lake and the local community are all undead (although they walk around in daylight). Débuting director Hancock gives the film a slow, dreamlike quality, but is let down by a confused script, ugly photography and weak performances.
✦✦

LET THE BLOOD RUN FREE

Australia, 1992. Dir: John 'Cosmo' Thomson. With: Jean Kittson, Brian Nankervis, Helen Knight, David Swann, Peter Rowsthorn, Lynda Gibson. Media Arts/Primetime/ RPTA/10 Australia. Colour.
Half-hour madcap comedy TV soap opera, with plots involving the reanimated body of dead Nurse Effie (Knight), patient Carla (Paula Gardner) and the Hospital Administrator who are really vampires loose in St. Christopher's Hospital, and Dr Raymond Good's (Nankervis) potion that turns him into the evil Mr Bad.
✦

DIE LEVANDE MUMIEN
Sweden, 1918. With: John Ekman. B&W.
The title of this silent film translates as 'The Living Mummy'.
✦

AL LEWIS
[b 1910]

American actor who played Grandpa (actually Count Dracula himself) on TV's *The Munsters* (1964-66). He now owns and runs a restaurant in New York.
qv: *The ABC Saturday Superstar Movie: 'Mini-Munsters'* (1973); *The Devil's Commandment* (1956); *Grampa's Monster Movies* (1988); *Here Come the Munsters* (1995); *Hi Honey, I'm Home: 'Grey Skies'* (1991); *Moonrise* (1991); *Munster, Go Home!* (1966); *The Munsters' Revenge* (1981); *The Night Strangler* (1972).

HERSCHELL GORDON LEWIS
[b 1926]

Dignified with the title 'godfather of gore', American writer, producer and director Lewis created a whole new horror genre with his crude cult hit *Blood Feast* (1963).
qv: *Doctor Gore* (1972); *A Taste of Blood* (1967).

SHELDON LEWIS
[1868-1958]

American stage and silent serial star. He portrayed a purse-snatching Mr Hyde in the 1920 'spoiler' version of *Dr. Jekyll and Mr. Hyde*, and recreated the role for a 1929 adaptation. Lewis retired from the screen in 1936.
qv: *The Exploits of Elaine* (1914-15).

VAL LEWTON
(Vladimir Ivan Leventon) [1904-1951]

Russian-born American producer, screenwriter (as Carlos Keith) and author, best remembered for the nine low-budget but classy horror films he made for RKO Radio Pictures in the mid-1940s.
qv: *Cat People* (1942); *The Curse of the Cat People* (1944); *Isle of the Dead* (1945); *I Walked With a Zombie* (1943).

LEXX:
Twilight
Canada/Germany, 1999. Dir: Chris Bould. With: Brian Downey, Xenia Seeberg, Michael McManus, Jeffrey Hirschfield, Louise Wischermann, Louis Del Grande. Salter Street Films/TiMe Film-und-TV-Produktions/Vif Filmproduktion/Screen Partners/5/Chum Television. Colour.
Hour-long comedy/SF TV series (1995-) in which the motley crew of coward-turned-reluctant rebel Stanley Tweedle (Downey), cluster lizard/love-slave hybrid Xev (Seeberg), the reanimated corpse of alien assassin Kai (McManus) and disembodied robot head 790 (Hirschfield) travel around the universe in the eponymous intelligent insectoid spaceship. In this episode, when Stan doesn't wake up, Xev puts out a distress signal and they end up on a planet of the walking dead where Xev is also transformed into a yellow-eyed cannibal zombie.
✦✦

LICANTROPO EL ASESINO DE LA LUNA LLENA
Spain, 1996. Dir: Francisco R. Gordillo. With: Paul Naschy (Jacinto Molina), Amparo Muñoz, Jose Maria Caffarell, Javier Loyola, Eva Isanta, Luis Maluenda. Videokine/Television Española. Colour.
Filmed under the title *Lycantropus*, this long-awaited eleventh outing for El Hombre Lobo is yet another origin story, which begins in central Europe in 1944. Sympathetic Nazi SS Colonel Heinrich Wolfstein (Bill Holden) falls in love with cursed gypsy Czinka Tara (Ester Ponce). She becomes pregnant and gives birth to triplets, the third of whom is destined to become a werewolf. Fifty-two years later in Visaria, successful horror novelist Waldemar Daninsky (Naschy, who as usual scripted under his real name) transforms into a savage beast under the influence of the full moon, while a psychopathic priest (Maluenda) is killing young students in the town. As old horror defeats new, a doctor (Muñoz) who loves him shoots the reluctant werewolf to death with silver bullets. This also includes a pair of ghosts and some fun references to classic Universal movies.
✦✦

LIFEFORCE
UK/USA, 1985. Dir: Tobe Hooper. With: Steve Railsback, Peter Firth, Frank Finlay, Nicholas Ball, Mathilda May, Patrick Stewart. Cannon/Tri-Star. Colour.
Loosely based on Colin Wilson's novel *The Space Vampires*, Hooper's lively blend of science fiction and horror begins like *Alien* (1979), turns into a remake of *Quatermass and the Pit* (1967) and ends up looking like a Hammer Gothic! When a gigantic alien spaceship is discovered in the cone of Halley's comet, three humanoid bodies are returned to Earth. Pretty soon an alien vampire woman (May) has turned most of London into rampaging bloodsucking zombies. A wooden cast (Firth's ludicrous SAS officer, Finlay's sub-Van Helsing), laughable script (Dan O'Bannon and Don Jakoby) and unconvincing make-ups are only saved by John Dykstra's impressive optical effects. Originally planned to be filmed in 3-D, this cost $25,000,000 and looks like a 1950s British 'B' movie! With Michael Gothard and Aubrey Morris.
✦✦✧

LIFE RETURNS
USA, 1934 (1935). Dir: Eugen (Eugene) Frenke. With: Onslow Stevens, Lois Wilson, George Breakston, Valerie Hobson, Stanley Fields, Frank Reicher. Universal. B&W.
Based on the real-life exploits of Californian scientist Robert E. Cornish in 1934. Stevens (*House of Dracula* [1945], etc) plays Dr John Kendrick, who is experimenting with a fluid that restores life to the dead. In actual footage of Cornish's operation, Kendrick returns his son's (Breakston) dead dog to life. With Dr Cornish playing himself and future director Richard Quine in a supporting role. The director sued the studio in 1937 for not releasing the film properly, and it was reissued the following year by Scienart Pictures. In Britain it was banned outright for 'bad taste'.
✦

LIFE WITHOUT SOUL
USA, 1915. Dir: Joseph W. Smiley. With: Percy Darrell Standing, William A. Cohill, Lucy Cotton, George DeCarlton, Jack Hopkins, Pauline Curley. Ocean Film Corporation. B&W.
This second silent film version of Mary Shelley's novel (and the first full-length adaptation, in five parts) features English-born actor Standing wearing little or no make-up as the 'Brute Man', the creation of Dr William Frawley (Cohill). When the creature kills his sister on her wedding night, Frawley pursues the Monster across Europe and shoots it before dying from exhaustion. A framing device reveals that the story is being read from a book. This was reissued in a tinted version by Raver Film Corporation the following year, with added scientific documentary footage detailing the reproduction methods of fish.
Remake: IL MOSTRO DI FRANKENSTEIN (qv; 1920)
✦✧

LIGHTS OUT:
The Meddlers
USA, 1951. Dir: William Corrigan. With: John Carradine, E.G. Marshall, Dan Morgan, Robert Hull, Laurence Ryle. NBC-TV. B&W.
Half-hour live anthology TV series (1946-52, 159 episodes), hosted by a floating head (Frank Gallop) and inspired by Arch Oboler's popular radio show, which débuted in 1934. In this episode, based on the story 'Larroes Catch Meddlers' by Manly Wade Wellman, two fortune hunters (Carradine and Marshall) discover a hidden horde of Confederate gold in an old house. They also find that it is guard-

ed by a pair of spooky zombie soldiers (Hull and Ryle).
✦✧

The Men on the Mountain
USA, 1950. Dir: Laurence Schwab Jr. With: Lee Tracy, Bill Free, Vern Collett, Robert Hall, Biff Elliott. NBC-TV. B&W.
A dead soldier returns from the grave during World War Two to save his comrades from a Japanese trap.
Episode remake: LIGHTS OUT: The Men on the Mountain (qv; 1952)
✦

The Men on the Mountain
USA, 1952. Dir: Laurence Schwab Jr. With: Bill Free, Harry Landers, Harry Belaver, Robert Hull, Henry Barnard, Henry Silver. NBC-TV. B&W.
Remake of the 1950 episode from the same director and writer (Harry Muheim).
Series remake: LIGHTS OUT (1972)
✦

EL LIGUERO MAGICO

Spain, 1980 (1981). Dir: Mariano Ozores. With: Andres Pajares, Luis Lorenzo, Antonio Ozores, Adriana Vega, Maria Luisa Ponte, José Carabias. José Frade Producciones. Colour.
Comedy about a pair of werewolves (Pajares and Lorenzo), one of whom (Lorenzo) is gay. Director Ozores filmed this on the same sets used for Jacinto Molina/Paul Naschy's more serious werewolf movie, *The Craving* (1980).
✦

LIMP FANGS THE ADVENTURES OF COUNT MALT LIQUELA

USA, 1996. Dir: Christopher Michael. With: Delbert Howison, John Harwood, Jamie Zozzaro, Charles Napier, Reginald Vel Johnson, Christopher Michael. Creeper Productions. Colour.
A follow-up to the much-plugged *Terror of Blood Gym* (1995). This independent $10,000 comedy stars writer/producer/director Michael as 450 year-old vampire Count Malt Liquela, who returns from his tomb to a very different world when a wino (also Michael) urinates on his coffin. Now wandering the streets of modern-day Transylvania, the Count discovers that he can no longer get his fang hard. With his problem causing embarrassment to vampires everywhere, Liquela finds himself hunted by his old friend and celebrity vampire Count Falstaff (Howison), the National Black Vampires' Alliance and even the police, who all want to destroy him. Narrated by Michael Des Barres. A singing Napier appears briefly in a dream sequence. A sequel, *Count Malt Liquela vs. Blackenstein*, was announced in 1997.
✦

LINDA LOVELACE FOR PRESIDENT

USA, 1975 (1976). Dir: Claudio Guzman. With: Linda Lovelace, Scatman Crothers, Joe E. Ross, Micky Dolenz, Louis Quinn, Chuck McCann. David Winters-Charles Stroud Productions/Selectatape. Colour.
Silly sex comedy, available in various hard- and softcore versions, starring Lovelace, probably the world's most famous porn star. Besides the surprising line-up of guest stars, this also includes a talking chimp, a dwarf, H-bomb footage and a Dracula-like vampire!
✦✧

LINNEA QUIGLEY'S HORROR WORKOUT

USA, 1990 (1991). Dir: Hal Kennedy (Kenneth J. Hall). With: Linnea Quigley, B. Jane Holzer, Amy Hunt, Victoria Nesbitt, Kristine Seeley, Cleve Hall. Cinema Home Video. Colour.
The eponymous scream queen stars as herself in this silly hour-long spoof of workout videos that is interrupted by a mad slasher and several zombies.
✦

LIPS OF BLOOD

(Orig: LE SANG DES AUTRES/LES CHEMINS DE LA VIOLENCE/EL SEGRETTO DE LA MOMIA/PERVERSIONS SEXUELLES)
France/Spain, 1972. Dir: Ken Rudder (Alejandro Marti Gelabert and Pierre Chevalier). With: Frank Brana, Georges Rigaud, Catherine Frank, Patricia Lee, Richard Vitz, Michael Flynn. Les Films de l'Epée/Orbita Films. Colour.
Softcore sex and horror film based on a story by David S. Cooper and set in Dartmoor Castle. Posing as an Egyptologist, detective James Barton (Brana) learns that Lord Dartmoor (Rigaud) has used electricity to successfully revive the perfectly preserved body of an ancient Egyptian boy, who needs fresh blood to survive. This also includes a murderous crawling hand.
✦✧

LIPS OF BLOOD

(Orig: LÈVRES DE SANG)
France, 1975 (1976). Dir: Jean Rollin. With: Jean-Lou Philippe, Anne Briand, Nathalie Perrey, Willy Braque, Paul Biscaglia, Cathy Castel. Off Production/Scorpion 5/ Nordia Films. Colour.
Probably one of Rollin's best films. Co-writer Philippe plays a young man obsessed with a woman in white (Briand) he sees in visions. She leads him to a cemetery, where he opens the coffins and releases a horde of female vampires. In the end he discovers that the woman is his sister, buried by his mother for vampirising his father. This complicated Oedipal fantasy includes some wonderfully poetic images and the siblings finally sail off into the sunset in a coffin. With a scene in a cinema from Rollin's *The Vampire's Thrill* (1970). Out-takes and alternative sequences from this film were used in the sex film *Suck Me, Vampire* (1975).
✦✦✧

LISZTOMANIA

UK, 1975. Dir: Ken Russell. With: Roger Daltrey, Sara Kestelman, Paul Nicholas, Fiona Lewis, Veronica Quilligan, Nell Campbell. Goodtimes Enterprises/Warner Bros. Colour.
Highly fantastic version of the life of nineteenth century Hungarian composer Franz Liszt (Daltrey). This includes a vampire-like Richard Wagner (Nicholas), who rises from the grave as a murderous Frankenstein/Adolf Hitler Monster, and cameos by Ringo Starr as the Pope, John Justin, Rick Wakeman, Oliver Reed and Georgina Hale.
✦✧

LITAN

(aka LA CITÉ DES SPECTRES VERTS)
France, 1982. Dir: Jean-Pierre Mocky. With: Marie-Jose Nat, Jean-Pierre Mocky, Nino Ferrer, Marysa Mocky, Roger Lumont. Mocky Films/Films A2 Productions. Colour.
Co-scripted by Scott Baker. An unknown force transforms the inhabitants of a mountain town into zombies during a macabre local festival.
✦

LITTLE-BOY GHOST

Taiwan, circa 1985. Happy Produce. Colour.
Horror comedy in which little girl Tien-Tien and her grandfather run a boarding house for vampires. When a super-strong member of the undead kills Master Sha Ban-Chu, Tien-Tien and her friends use magic to inadvertently revive his corpse as a big-fanged hopping vampire.
✦✧

LITTLE DRACULA

USA, 1991. Dir: Joe Pearson. Voices: Edan Gross, Joe Flaherty, Jonathan Winters, Kath Soucie, Brian Cummings, Melvyn Hayes. Bandal America/Sachs Family Entertainment/Fox Network. Colour.
The twenty minute cartoon adventures (five episodes) of Count Dracula's green-faced son (voiced by Gross), based on the books by Martin Waddell and Joe Wright. This also includes a character called Werebunny (Joey Camen) and other monsters.
✦✧

The Bite at the Ghoul School Corral
USA, 1991. Dir: Joe Pearson. Voices: Edan Gross, Joe Flaherty, Jonathan Winters, Kath Soucie, Brian Cummings, Melvyn Hayes. Bandal America/Sachs Family Entertainment/Fox Network. Colour.
In this episode, the family's mortal enemy, Garlic Man (Cummings), pits twin Frankenstein Monsters against a swashbuckling Dracula (Flaherty) in an old black and white movie.
✦✧

LITTLE RED RIDING HOOD AND TOM THUMB VS. THE MONSTERS
(Orig: CAPERUCÍTA Y PULGARCÍTO CONTRA LOS MONSTRUOS)
Mexico, 1960 (1965). Dir: Roberto Rodriguez. With: Maria Garcia, Cesarea Quezadas, José Elias Moreno, Manuel 'Loco' Valdés, El Enano Santanon. Peliculas-Rodriguez. Colour.
A sequel to both *Little Red Riding Hood and Her Friends* (1959) and *Tom Thumb* (1958/67). More juvenile weirdness from Mexico as Little Red Riding Hood (Garcia), Tom Thumb and their animal friends battle a Dracula-type vampire and a witch in an evil forest. This was one of three Little Red Riding Hood movies featuring Garcia. The English-language version was produced by K. (Kenneth) Gordon Murray and directed by Manuel San Fernando.
✦

THE LITTLE SHOP OF HORRORS
USA, 1960. Dir: Roger Corman. With: Jonathan Haze, Jackie Joseph, Mel Welles (Ernst von Theumer), Myrtle Vail, Dick Miller, Jack Nicholson. Filmgroup/American International Pictures. B&W.
Corman's cult follow-up to *A Bucket of Blood* (1959), originally titled *The Passionate People Eater* and shot for $27,000 in just over two days from a clever script by Charles B. Griffith. Haze stars as Seymour Krelboined, who works in a skid row florists and grows a talking plant (named Audrey Jr) on a diet of human blood. Great support from Welles as Gravis Mushnik, the flower shop owner, Miller as a customer who eats flowers, and Nicholson as masochistic undertaker Wilbur Force, who enjoys having his teeth pulled! It wasn't released commercially in Britain for thirteen years. 'Feed me, feed me!'
Remakes: PLEASE DON'T EAT MY MOTHER! (1972) and LITTLE SHOP OF HORRORS (qv; 1986)
✦✦✦

LITTLE SHOP OF HORRORS
UK/USA, 1986. Dir: Frank Oz. With: Rick Moranis, Ellen Greene, Vincent Gardenia, Steve Martin, James Belushi, John Candy. Geffen/Warner Bros. Colour.
Big-budget remake of Roger Corman's 1960 cult classic, based on the 1982 off-Broadway hit musical (original screenwriter Charles B. Griffith had to sue for credit). Corman may have filmed his version in two days, but this took over a year to shoot (including a new, happy ending after disastrous previews) at a cost of around $30,000,000! Moranis plays Seymour Krelborn, who works in a skid row florists and grows Audrey II, a talking plant (voiced by Levi Stubbs of The Four Tops) that needs human blood to survive. Martin is great as a sadistic dentist, but the cameos by Belushi, Candy and Bill Murray (in the original Jack Nicholson role) are just thrown away. Directed by the voice of Miss Piggy, this became the basis of a children's TV cartoon.
Remake: LITTLE SHOP (1991-92)
✦✦✦

LITTLEST PET SHOP:
Curse of the Mumsy
USA, 1995. Voices: Lynda Boyd, Gary Chalk, Babs Chula, Tel Cole, Ian James Corlett, Mike Donovan. Sunbow Entertainment/Claster Television. Colour.
Half-hour syndicated cartoon TV series (1995-96, forty episodes) in which the animal inhabitants of eccentric Elwood Funk's (Corlett) pet shop are mysteriously reduced to miniature size. In this episode, Elwood's mother returns from Egypt with a box which transports Stu the sheepdog (Donovan) and Chloe the cat (Chula) back to ancient times. There they must find the mummy which will end a curse.
✦✧

THE LITTLE VAMPIRE
West Germany/UK, 1985. Dir: René Bonnière. With: Joel Dacks, Christopher Stanton, Marsha Moreau, Gert Fröbe, Michael Gough, Lyn Seymour. Norflicks Productions/TVS. Colour.
Children's serial based on the books by Angela Sommer-Bodenburg. A young boy, Anton (Stanton), befriends Rüdiger (Dacks), who is the youngest member of an undead family. Horror veteran Gough turns up as an elder vampire.
Series remake: THE LITTLE VAMPIRE (qv; 1995)
✦✦

THE LITTLE VAMPIRE
Germany, 1995. Dir: Sigmund Grewenig. With: Jan Steilen, Matthias Ruschke, Lena Beyer, Marian Laabuda, Peter Lohmeyer, Nadja Engelbrecht. Polyphor/WDR Cologne/Trube Jatagandzidis. Colour.
Twenty-five minute children's TV series (thirteen episodes) based on the books *Der kleine Vampir verreist* and *Der klein Vampir auf dem Bauerhof* by Angela Sommer-Bodenburg. A young, bespectacled boy, Anton Bohnsach (Ruschke), befriends Rüdiger (Steilen) and Anna (Beyer), the two youngest members of the undead von Schlotterstein family, pursued by vampire-hunter Geiermeirer (Laabuda). The first episode includes a clip from *Nosferatu* (1922) on TV. The English-language version was voiced by George Acock, Tim Bruce, Tim Benton, Dik Cadbury, Regine Candler, Tom Eastwood and others.
Series remake: THE LITTLE VAMPIRE (qv; 2000)
✦✦✧

THE LITTLE VAMPIRE
(Orig: DER KLEINE VAMPIR)
USA/Germany/Holland/UK, 2000. Dir: Uli Edel. With: Jonathan Lipnicki, Rollo Weeks, Jim Carter, Alice Krige, Richard E. Grant. Cometstone International/Comet Film/Avrora Media/Stonewood Communications. Colour.
$20,000,000 children's film based on the book by Angela Sommer-Bodenburg, in which a resourceful young boy (Lipnicki) helps to rescue a dysfunctional vampire family. From the director of *Last Exit to Brooklyn* (1989).
✦✦✧

THE LIVE MUMMY
UK, 1915. Pathé. B&W.
Fifteen minute silent short in which a man disguises himself as an Egyptian mummy to fool a professor.
✦

LIVING A ZOMBIE DREAM
USA, 1996. Dir: Todd Reynolds. With: Amon Elsey, Michelle White, Mike Smith, Frank Alexander. Borderline Entertainment. Colour.
Graphic, low-budget video release. When he finds his brother and his girlfriend together, a young man inadvertently gets his sibling murdered and revenges himself on the psycho responsible. However, the original killer was into voodoo magic and returns from the dead seeking his own vengeance.
✦

THE LIVING DEAD AT MANCHESTER MORGUE
(Orig: NON SI DEVE PROFANARE IL SONNO DEI MORTI/NO PROFANAR EL SUEÑO DE LOS MUERTOS/FIN DE SEMANA PARA LOS MUERTOS/IL SONNO DIE MORTE/ ZOMBI 3 — DA DOVE VIENI? USA: BREAKFAST AT THE MANCHESTER MORGUE/DON'T OPEN THE WINDOW/LET SLEEPING CORPSES LIE)
Italy/Spain/UK, 1974. Dir: Jorge Grau. With: Ray Lovelock, Christine (Cristina) Galbo, Arthur Kennedy, Aldo Massasso, Giorgio Trestini, Roberto Posse. Flaminia Produxioni/Star Films/Newport/Hallmark. Colour.

Effective low-budget chiller, atmospherically directed by Grau, who builds the tension gradually. London art dealer George (Lovelock, like everyone else with a terrible dubbed accent) and Edna (Galbo) travel into the country near Windermere where the radiation from an experimental ultra-sonic farming machine used to destroy insects results in the birth of homicidal babies and causes the dead to rise as frighteningly realistic cannibal zombies. Hollywood veteran Kennedy plays a fascist police sergeant who ends up shooting the hero in the downbeat ending (just as in George Romero's *Night of the Living Dead* [1968]).
✦✦✦✧

THE LIVING DEAD GIRL
(Orig: LA MORTE VIVANTE)
France, 1982. Dir: Jean Rollin. With: Marina Pierro, Françoise Blanchard, Mike Marshall, Carina Barone, Fanny Magier, Patricia Besnard-Rousseau. Les Films ABC/Films Aleriaz/Films Du Yaka/Sam Selsky. Colour.
A chemical waste spillage revives a beautiful dead woman, Catherine Valmont (Blanchard). With the help of her devoted childhood friend and lover Hélène (Pierro), she sticks her fingers into victims' bodies and drinks their blood. As her memories return, the vampiric zombie needs more and more blood until she eventually destroys her companion. Not as visually imaginative as some of his other movies, co-writer/director Rollin still manages to give the film a nicely surreal atmosphere. With French film critic Alain Petit.
✦✧

THE LIVING GHOST
USA, 1942. Dir: William Beaudine. With: James Dunn, Joan Woodbury, Paul McVey, Jan Wiley, J. Farrell MacDonald, Minerva Urecal. Monogram. B&W.
Low-budget comedy thriller in which a private detective (Dunn) is hired to find a missing millionaire and uncovers a serum that paralyses the brain and leaves its victim in a zombie-like state.
✦✧

THE LIVING HEAD
(Orig: LA CABEZA VIVIENTE)
Mexico, 1959 (1961). Dir: Chano Urueta. With: Ana Luisa Peluffo, Abel Salazar, Mauricio Garcés, Germán Robles, Guillermo Cramer, Antonio Raxel. Cinematográfica ABSA/Clasa-Mohme/American International. B&W.
When his tomb is despoiled, the living head of Aztec priest Acatl (Garcés) casts a spell over the mummified body of a warrior (Cramer), who it orders to cut out the hearts of the members of an archaeological expedition led by Professor Mueller (Robles). Meanwhile, the professor's daughter Marta (Peluffo) is hypnotised by the glowing ring belonging to her twin, the Aztec priestess Xochiquetzal. Producer Salazar turns up as the police inspector hero. The English-language version was produced by K. (Kenneth) Gordon Murray.
✦✧

LIVSFARLIG FILM
Sweden, 1987. Dir: Suzanne Osten. With: Etienne Glaser, Stina Ekblad, Henrik Holmborg, Lena T. Hansson, Agneta Ekmanner, Helge Skoog. Sandrew/SVT-1/Film Teknik. Colour.
Comedy set in the near future in which famous horror film director Emil Frankenstein (Glaser) searches for his missing daughter (a star of vampire films) and discovers political refugees hiding in the studio. He decides to make a film about them, but is eventually decapitated. The title translates as 'Lethal Film'.
✦✧

LA LOBA
Mexico, 1964. Dir: Rafael Baledón. With: Kitty de Hoyos, Joaquin Cordero, José Elias Moreno, Adriana Roel, Crox Alvarado, Ramon Bugarini. Producciones Sotomayor/ Columbia. B&W.
Lycanthropic love story about a dark-haired young woman (de Hoyos) who transforms into a blonde werewolf during the full moon and sneaks out of her home through a secret panel in the fireplace to attack victims in the forest. Her fiancé, Dr Lisandro (Cordero), is also a werewolf who is searching for a cure for their mutual affliction. In the end, they die in each other's embrace when she is killed with a special dagger and he is savaged to death by a dog. Filmed under the title *Los Horrores del Bosque Negro* ('The Horrors of the Black Forest').
✦

O LOBISOMEM
Brazil, 1974. Dir: Elyseu Visconti Cavalleiro. With: Wilson Grey, Suzana de Moraes, Paulo Villaça, Jack De Castro, Jacira Silva, Andre Valli. Elyseu Visconti Cavalleiro. Colour.
Experimental horror film from director Cavalleiro, better known for his short films. An eccentric millionaire (Grey) is transformed into a werewolf and rules over a forest of evil bloodsuckers until defeated by a white-robed figure representing the forces of good.
✦

LOCK UP YOUR DAUGHTERS
USA, 1956 (1958). Dir: Phil Rosen. With: Bela Lugosi, Polly Ann Young, The Bowery Boys (Leo Gorcey, Huntz Hall, Bobby Jordan). Monogram/New Realm. B&W.
This is a real rarity, apparently only released in Britain (with an 'X' certificate). Producer 'Jungle' Sam Katzman hired the fading Lugosi to appear in new footage and narrate this fifty minute compilation containing scenes from six of the star's Monogram movies (including *The Ape Man* [1943], *Invisible Ghost* [1941], *Spooks Run Wild* [1941] and *Voodoo Man* [1944]). The seventy-three year-old actor died the year it was made. Has anybody ever seen this?
✦

LOCURA DE TERROR
Mexico, 1960. Dir: Julian Soler. With: Tin-Tan (Germán Valdés), Manuel 'Loco' Valdés, Sonia Furio, Veronica Loyo, Andres Soler, David Silva. Producciones Sotomayor/ Columbia. B&W.
Sometimes gruesome horror comedy in which a giant zombie robs graves for a mad professor and his assistant, who create a machine to melt the flesh off the corpses. They then reconstitute the bodies and produce mindless slaves which are used to kidnap a young boy and his sister, amongst others. In the end, the scientists are defeated by a skeleton with a human head. More madness from South of the Border!
✦✧

LOGAN'S RUN:
Halflife
USA, 1977. Dir: Steve Stern. With: Gregory Harrison, Heather Menzies, Donald Moffat, Randolph Powell, William Smith, Kim Cattrall. Metro-Goldwyn-Mayer/CBS-TV. Colour.
Short-lived, hour-long TV series (1977-78, fourteen episodes) based on the 1976 movie and the novel by William F. Nolan and George Clayton Johnson. Set in a post-apocalyptic twenty-third century, Logan (Harrison), Jessica (Menzies) and android Rem (Moffat) are pursued by Sandman Francis (Powell), who has orders to bring them back to the City of Domes. In this episode, the fugitives discover a society whose people are physically divided into two separate individuals — one peaceful and the other aggressive.
✦✧
Night Visitors
USA, 1978. Dir: Paul Krasny. With: Gregory Harrison, Heather Menzies, Donald Moffat, Randolph Powell, Barbara Babcock, George Maharis. Metro-Goldwyn-Mayer/ CBS-TV. Colour.
The fugitives take shelter from a storm in an apparently haunted house, where the owner wants to sacrifice Jessica in an attempt to bring his wife back from the dead. This episode was not aired during the series' original run in America. With Paul Mantee.
✦✦✧

LOIS & CLARK THE NEW ADVENTURES OF SUPERMAN:
(UK: aka THE NEW ADVENTURES OF SUPERMAN)

Forget Me Not

USA, 1996. Dir: James R. Bagdonas. With: Dean Cain, Teri Hatcher, Lane Smith, Justin Whalin, Eddie Jones, K. Callan. Warner Bros/December 3rd Productions/ABC-TV. Colour.

Hour-long revisionist TV series (1993-97, eighty-eight episodes), based on the DC Comics characters and concentrating on the relationship between Lois Lane (Hatcher) and Clark Kent/Superman (Cain). After Lois loses her memory, she is brainwashed by Dr Elias Mendenhall (Charles Cioffi) into becoming one of his zombie assassins in a plot very similar to the 1942 movie *Fingers at the Window*. The Man of Steel next turned up in a stylised cartoon TV series.

Series remake: SUPERMAN (1996)

✦✦

LOKIS: REKOPILIS DOCTORA WITTENBACHA

Poland, 1970. Dir: Janusz Majewski. With: Józef Duriasz, Edmund Fetting, Gustaw Lutkiewicz, Malgorzata Brannek, Zofia Mrozowska. Tor/Polski State. Colour.

Set in a central European country at the turn of the century, where Doctor Wittembach (Fetting) is summoned to a nobleman's doom-laden castle. Amongst much muttering of curses by the servants, the Baron (Duriasz) transforms (off-screen) into a mythical black bear on his wedding night and cuts his new bride's throat. In the end, the body of the bear is found dead in the snow. Based on the story 'Professor Wittembach's Manuscript' by Prosper Merimée.

✦✧

LOLITA

UK, 1961 (1962). Dir: Stanley Kubrick. With: James Mason, Shelley Winters, Sue Lyon, Peter Sellers, Gary Cockrell, Jerry Stovin. AA Productions/Anya Productions/ Transworld Pictures/Seven Arts Productions/ Metro-Goldwyn-Mayer. B&W.

Adapted (in part) by Vladimir Nabokov from his own 1955 novel. Newcomer Lyon plays Dolores 'Lolita' Haze, a sexually precocious teenager who allows herself to be seduced by Mason's obsessed professor, Humbert Humbert. With Sellers as the bizarre playwright Clare Quilty, and clips from Hammer's *The Curse of Frankenstein* (1957) shown at a drive-in. Produced by James B. Harris (who also appears in the wings during a school play sequence).

Remake: LOLITA (1997)

✦✦✧

HERBERT LOM (Herbert Charles Angelo Kuchacevich ze Schluderpacheru) [b 1917]

Czechoslovakian-born actor who has worked from Britain since 1939. Often cast as a villainous foreigner or an authority figure, such as a doctor or psychiatrist. Lom is best known for his recurring character of Inspector Dreyfus in *The Pink Panther* series, of which only *The Pink Panther Strikes Again* (1976) has any fantasy content.

qv: *Asylum* (1972); *Bram Stoker's Count Dracula* (1970); *Cuadecuc (Vampir)* (1970); *Murders in the Rue Morgue* (1971); *The Phantom of the Opera* (1962); *The Return of the Pink Panther* (1975).

LONDON AFTER MIDNIGHT

(UK: THE HYPNOTIST)

USA, 1927. Dir: Tod Browning. With: Lon Chaney, Marceline Day, Conrad Nagel, Henry B. Walthall, Percy Williams, Polly Moran. Metro-Goldwyn-Mayer. B&W.

Based on director Browning's original story 'The Hypnotist' (which was also the shooting title). Chaney Sr portrays a grotesque vampire prowling the moors with his Bat Girl daughter (Edna Tichenor), but it turns out to be a trick by Scotland Yard Inspector Burke (also played by Chaney) to trap murderer Sir James Hamlin (Walthall) by hypnotising him at the scene of the crime. Chaney's vampire is a masterful creation — he used wire hoops to make his eyes bulge and a bridge of needle-sharp animal teeth which he could only wear for short periods. Browning remade this silent film in 1935 with Chaney's roles split between three actors. Despite rumours of its rediscovery over the years, this still remains apparently lost since the mid-1950s. A novelisation by Mary Coolidge-Rask appeared in 1928, and in 1985 Cornwall Books published Philip J. Riley's photographic reconstruction, which also included the original script.

Remake: MARK OF THE VAMPIRE (qv; 1935)

✦✦✧

Lon Chaney Sr prowls the streets of London After Midnight *(1927).*

LONE WOLF

USA, 1988. Dir: John (P.) Callas. With: Dyann Brown, Kevin Hart, Jamie Newcomb, Anne Douglas, Siren, Jeff Hart. Flash Features/Prism Entertainment. Colour.

Rock video director Callas makes his feature débût with this low-budget thriller, filmed in Denver, Colorado. After a series of gory murders, two small town teenagers, Julie Martin (Brown) and Joel Jessup (Kevin Hart), use a computer programme to predict the next killing and attempt to discover the identity of the werewolf (played Tom Henry) responsible.

✦✧

LORD OF ILLUSIONS

USA, 1995. Dir: Clive Barker. With: Scott Bakula, Kevin J. O'Connor, Famke Janssen, Vincent Schiavelli, Daniel von Bargen, Barry del Sherman. United Artists Pictures/ Seraphim. Colour.

Writer/co-producer Barker's third film as a director shows that he has developed a strong visual style (the death of Swann on stage) but continues to have problems with uneven plotting. This shares almost nothing with his uncredited source novella 'The Last Illusion' as private investigator Harry d'Amour (an impressive Bakula) is caught up in a convoluted mystery involving rival magicians Swann (O'Connor) and Nix (von Bargen), the latter resurrected from the dead by his disciples. The 'Director's Cut' is longer and better. *A Gathering of Magic: Behind the Scenes of Lord of Illusions* (1995) is directed by Robb Humphreys.

✦✦✦

LORD SHANGO

(aka THE COLOR OF LOVE/SOULMATES OF SHANGO)

USA, 1975. Dir: Raymond Marsh. With: Lawrence Cook, Marlene Clark, Avis McCarther, John Russell, Maurice Woods, Stanley Greene. Bryanston. Colour.

A non-exploitation black horror movie, set in Tennessee. Jenny (Clark, also in *Ganja & Hess* [1973]) and her daughter Billie (McCarther) meet African tribal priest Jabo (Cook), who returns to life.

✦

THE LOST BOYS

USA, 1987. Dir: Joel Schumacher. With: Corey Feldman, Jami Gertz, Corey Haim, Edward Herrmann, Barnard Hughes, Jason Patric. Warner Bros. Colour.

Predictable teen horror comedy from *The Omen* (1976) producers Richard Donner (who was originally set to direct, as was Richard Franklin) and Harvey Bernhard. When brothers Sam (Haim) and Michael (Patric) move to the west coastal town of Santa Clara, they soon discover its dark secret — a gang of teenage vampires led by David (Donald Sutherland's son, Kiefer) are preying on the transient crowds. When Michael is infected and begins to turn into one of the undead, it is up to Sam and the bizarre Frog brothers, Edgar (Feldman) and Alan (Jamison Newlander), to confront and destroy the vampires. Some interesting ideas are wasted in this flashy blend of nerds and rock music. With Dianne Wiest. Craig Shaw Gardner wrote the novelisation.

✦✦

THE LOST CITY

(aka CITY OF LOST MEN)

USA, 1935. Dir: Harry (C.) Revier. With: Wm. (William Stage) Boyd, Kane Richmond, Claudia Dell, Josef Swickard, Sam Baker, Geo. F. (George Gabby) Hayes. Sherman Krellberg/Regal Pictures/Super Serial Productions. B&W.

Frenetic twelve chapter serial with such titles as 'Living Dead Men',

'Human Beasts' and 'The Mad Scientist'. Inventor Bruce Gordon (Richmond) uses a magnetic detector to trace a series of world-wide electrical disasters to the lost city of the Ligurians in central Africa. His expedition discovers mad scientist Zolok (former New York bootlegger Boyd, in his last role) and his hunchbacked assistant Gorzo (Wm. Bletcher) using electro-magnetic rays to create an army of giant black zombie slaves with shaggy afros who grunt at each other. Zolok's super-scientific laboratory includes a death ray, TV and electrical effects created by Kenneth Strickfaden. This was later released in two feature versions.
✦✦✧

LOST IN SPACE:
The Space Croppers
USA, 1966. Dir: Sobey Martin. With: Guy Williams, June Lockhart, Billy Mumy, Jonathan Harris, Mark Goddard, Marta Kristen. Irwin Allen Productions/Jodi/Van Bernard/Twentieth Century-Fox/CBS-TV. B&W.
Popular hour-long TV series (1965-68, eighty-three episodes), created by Irwin Allen. After the Robinson family blast off from Earth towards Alpha Centauri in 1997, their spaceship *Jupiter II* is thrown off-course and crash-lands on an unknown world. In this episode, a family of space hillbillies grow a crop that threatens to destroy all life on the Robinson's planet. This also includes an alien werewolf. With Mercedes McCambridge, Sherry Jackson and Dawson Palmer.
Series sequel: THE ABC SATURDAY SUPERSTAR MOVIE: Lost in Space (1973)
Series remake: LOST IN SPACE (1998)
✦

THE LOST ISLAND
USA, 1934. Dir: LeRoy Prinz. Christie Studio. Colour.
Uncompleted live action short, filmed in Technicolor. This was meant to be a musical comedy parody of *King Kong* (1933), using marionettes of famous stars (Mae West, The Marx Brothers, etc, created by Wah [Ming] Chang and others), with Kong played by Charles Gemora in an ape suit. It was abandoned when financial backing ran out.
✦

THE LOST PLATOON
USA, 1989. Dir: David A. Prior. With: William Knight, David Parry, Stephen Quadros, Lew Pipes, Michael Wayne, Sean Heyman. Action International Pictures. Colour.
War correspondent Hollander (Knight) discovers four vampire soldiers — one of whom (Parry) may even be Count Dracula — who have fought in successive conflicts down through the centuries. A clever idea, but not helped by the low budget. Filmed in Alabama.
✦✧

THE LOST SAUCER:
Transylvania 2300
USA, 1976. Dir: Dick Darley. With: Jim Nabors, Ruth Buzzi, Alice Playten, Jarrod Johnson, Larry Larsen, Stan Ross. Sid and Marty Krofft/ABC-TV. Colour.
Half-hour Saturday morning children's TV series (1975-76, sixteen episodes) about two alien androids, Fum (Nabors) and Fi (Buzzi), who land their spacecraft/time machine in Chicago and accidentally take off again with nine year-old Jerry (Johnson) and his fifteen year-old baby-sitter Alice (Playten) on board. In this episode, when a space storm forces the saucer to land, the two Earth children must seek help from Dr Frankenstein XIII who lives in an eerie castle. With Billy Barty. Episodes were subsequently re-edited into *The Krofft Supershow* (1976-77).
✦

LO UCCIDO, TU UCCIDI
Italy/France, 1965. Dir: Gianni Puccini. With: E. Riva, Jean-Louis Trintignant, Dominique Boschero, Margaret Lee, Luciana Paluzzi, Eleonora Rossi Drago. Metropolis Film/Gulliver Films. B&W.
In the first of two stories ('Fullmoon'), a woman (Drago) suffers from 'sexual lycanthropy' and seduces a different man on each of the seven nights of the full moon. In the second story ('Bitter Games'), three children are responsible for the mysterious deaths of those people they didn't like. The title translates as 'I Kill, You Kill'.
✦✧

LE LOUP DES MALVENEUR
France, 1942. Dir: Guillaume Radot. With: Madeleine Sologne, Pierre Renoir, Gabrielle Dorziat, Michel Marsay, Marcelle Geniat, Louis Salou. Union Technique Cinématographique. B&W.
Atmospheric but verbose chiller. The last of his line, Reginald de Malveneur retells the legend of his ancestor, the first Lord of Malveneur, who wanted to use wolves for hunting. The victim of a curse, he becomes a lycanthrope and is locked away in his cellar laboratory. This includes an eerie midnight burial sequence.
✦✧

LE LOUP-GAROU
France, 1923 (1924). Dir: Pierre Bressol and Jacques Roullet. With: Léon Bernard, Jean Marau, Simone Jacquemin, Jeanne Delvair, Madeleine Guitty, Pierre Juvenet. Pathé. B&W.
Silent drama in which the murderer of a priest becomes a 'werewolf' when he is cursed by his victim. In the end, he is killed by a bolt of lightning.
✦

LE LOUP GAROU
Germany, 1932. Dir: Friedrich Feher. With: Magda Sonja, Vladimir Sokolov. B&W.
Based on the novel *Der Schwarze Mann* (aka *The Wolf Man/The Were-Wolf*) by Alfred Machard. An escaped convict explains to his young son that he is always on the run because a werewolf is chasing him.
✦

LE LOUP-GORU DU NORD
Belgium, 1985. Dir: Olivier Appart. With: Patrick Dechesne, Gerald Marti. Institut des Arts de diffusion/Mediadiffusion. Colour.
Seventeen minute short involving a werewolf. Filmed on 16mm.
✦

LOVE, AMERICAN STYLE:
Love and the Vampire
USA, 1970. Dir: Charles R. Rondeau. With: Judy Carne, Robert Reed, Tiny Tim, Julie Newmar. Paramount/Parker-Margolin Productions. Colour.
In this episode of the romantic comedy TV series (1969-74), a couple (Carne and Reed) spend the night in a sinister mansion where they encounter a vampire (played by soprano-voiced singer Tiny Tim). Two hour-long cartoon shows followed.
Series remake: LOVE AMERICAN STYLE (1972)
✦✧

LOVE AND CURSES:
(UK: SHE-WOLF OF LONDON)
Bride of the Wolfman
USA, 1991. Dir: Bruce Seth Green. With: Kate Hodge, Neil Dickson, Dan Gilvezan, Tony Amendola, Gayle Cohen, Roy Abramsohn. MTE/Finnegan-Pinchuk/The Hollywood Premier Network. Colour/B&W.
This series originally started out as *She-Wolf of London* (fourteen episodes), created by Mick Garris and Tom McLoughlin, before changing its title and location for a further six episodes. In this story, werewolf student Randi Wallace (Hodge) and Professor Ian Matheson (Dickson) visit a soon-to-be-demolished haunted movie theatre and find themselves trapped as characters in the old black and white Universal monster movie of the title. Mad scientist Dr Pretorius (Amendola) plans to transfer the brain of Thomas, a Lon Chaney Jr-type Wolf Man, into a Frankenstein-like Monster (Michael Berryman) he has created. With Boris the hunchbacked assistant (Tracy Walter) and clips from *Frankenstein* (1931) and *Bride of Frankenstein* (1935).
✦✦✧

Habeas Corpses

USA, 1991. Dir: Chuck Bowman. With: Kate Hodge, Neil Dickson, Dan Gilvezan, Barry Van Dyke, Marta DuBois, Sandra Kerns. MTE/Finnegan-Pinchuk/The Hollywood Premier Network. Colour.

Randi and Ian investigate a firm of lawyers who are literally bloodsuckers. In the end, the wax-masked vampires are destroyed by sunlight and garlic chicken.

✦✦✧

LOVE AT FIRST BITE

USA, 1979. Dir: Stan Dragoti. With: George Hamilton, Susan Saint James, Richard Benjamin, Dick Shawn, Arte Johnson, Sherman Hemsley. Melvin Simon Productions/ American International. Colour.

Sophisticated Dracula spoof with Hamilton as a suave Count (complete with mock Lugosi accent), who is forced to leave Transylvania when the authorities convert his castle into a gymnasium, and jets to New York in his casket with devoted manservant Renfield (a lunatic Johnson). Good support from Saint James' unusual heroine Cindy Sondheim, who actually enjoys the Count's advances; Benjamin as jealous psychiatrist Dr Jeff Rosenberg, who is a descendant of Van Helsing; and Shawn's baffled police lieutenant Ferguson. Robert Kaufman's script sparkles with witty dialogue and Dragoti (who was later arrested for cocaine possession on his way to the Cannes Film Festival) directs with style and charm. With Barry Gordon, and Michael Pataki as a mobster. The comic-strip Fotonovel appeared in 1979. A sequel, *Love at Second Bite*, was announced but never made.

✦✦✦✦

LOVE AT STAKE

Canada, 1987 (1990). Dir: John Moffitt. With: Patrick Cassidy, Kelly Preston, Bud Cort, Barbara Carrera, Stuart Pankin, Dave Thomas. Hemdale/Tri-Star/Cinemax. Colour.

Filmed under the title *Burnin' Love*, this silly spoof of the Salem witch trials was finally released directly to cable TV. It involves corrupt Puritan officials (Pankin and Thomas) and a sexy witch (Carrera; played by Anne Ramsey in the older incarnation) who denounce an innocent orphan (Preston) as a servant of Satan. With Dr Joyce Brothers (as herself), and a werewolf in the jury box.

✦✧

LOVE BITES

USA, circa 1988. Dir: Marvin Jones. With: Kevin Glover, Christopher Ladd. Campfire Video Productions. Colour.

One hour, gay-oriented (non-porn) vampire horror comedy. After 347 years, the Count is finally ready to settle down. The only problem is that his new amour is West Hollywood's top vampire hunter...

✦

LOVE BITES

USA, 1992. Dir: Malcolm Marmorstein. With: Adam Ant (Stuart Leslie Goddard), Kimberly Foster, Roger Rose, Michelle Forbes, Philip Bruns, Judy Tenuta. Waymar Productions. Colour.

Zachary Simms (Ant), a vampire rock musician, tries to please the woman he loves by reforming and becoming a yuppie. Based on *The Reluctant Vampire*, the writer/director's off-Broadway comedy of the late 1970s.

✦✧

LOVE BOAT THE NEXT WAVE: Don't Judge a Book by Its Lover

USA, 1998 (1999). Dir: Neal Israel. With: Robert Urich, Phil Morris, Stacey Travis, Corey Parker, Randy Vasquez, Joan Severance. Spelling Entertainment/UPN. Colour.

Updated series (1998-99, twenty-five episodes) based on the popular comedy/romance show (1977-86) and suggested by Jeraldine Saunders' *The Love Boat*, set on the cruise liner *Sun Princess*. In this episode, Anne Rice-type author Cassandra Taylor (Harley Jane Kozack) falls under the spell of a mystery man who appears to have stepped out of one of her vampire novels. With Robin Givens, Patrick Cassidy and Nicole Nieth. Co-executive produced by Aaron Spelling.

✦✧

THE LOVE CAPTIVE

USA, 1969. Dir: Larry Crane. With: Charlotte Rouse, Jacqueline Ricardo, Colette Alexander, Alex Mann. Something Weird Video. B&W.

In this 'adult' feature, Jane (Rouse) visits Manzini's Museum of the Macabre in New York's Greenwich Village where she is locked in overnight with a stolen strait-jacket. While sitting in an electric chair she watches a nude vampire woman who climbs out of a coffin and is then attacked by a werewolf. A voodoo priestess dances to bongo music with the vampire and two other naked women, then Jane is tied to a cross and forced to have sex with a man. None of it makes much sense.

✦

LOVE IN THE CITY

(Orig: AMORE IN CITTÀ)

Italy, 1953. Dir: Dino Risi, Michelangelo Antonioni, Federico Fellini, Francesco Maselli, Cesare Zavattini, Alberto Lattuada and Carlo Lizzani. With: Antonio Cifariello, Livia Venturini, Ugo Tognazzi, Maresa Gallo, Caterina Rigoglioso, Silvio Lillo. Faro. B&W.

Omnibus film with six episodes supposedly taken from newspaper reports and filmed in the actual locations they happened with the people involved. Fellini's obviously fictional segment, 'Love Cheerfully Arranged', concerns a reporter at a matrimonial agency claiming to be a doctor and seeking a match for an imaginary patient who turns into a werewolf with the full moon. The episode directed by Lizzani, about prostitution, was cut from prints outside Italy.

✦✧

LOVE ME VAMPIRE

(Orig: KAI XIN GUI JING LING)

Hong Kong, 1985 (1987). Dir: Irene Wang (Hoover Lau/ Kao Wei-Lau). With: Chang Xiao-Hai, Lin Xiao-Ni. Bong Motion Pictures/Rainbow Video/Sunny Video. Colour.

When Ho is murdered by his wife and her lover, he is revived from the dead as a passionate ghost-vampire with a long tongue who can become invisible. The original title of this horror comedy translates as 'Mouth-to-Mouth Resuscitator'.

✦

THE LOVE OF A HUNCHBACK

UK, 1910. Empire/Butcher. B&W.

This silent short was yet another unauthorised remake of the 1906 French film, *Esmeralda*, based on the novel *Notre-Dame de Paris* by Victor Hugo.

Remake: NOTRE-DAME DE PARIS (qv; 1911)

✦

THE LOVE PILL

UK, 1971. Dir: Kenneth Turner. With: Toni Sinclair, Melinda Churcher, Henry Woolf, David Pugh, Kenneth Waller, John Stratton. Mayfair/Target International. Colour.

Silly sex farce in which a grocer's special sugar balls act as an instant contraceptive but also turn the local women into nymphomaniacs.

✦

THE LOVES OF DRACULA

USA, 1979. Dir: Jeffrey Hayden and Kenneth Johnson. With: Michael Nouri, Carol Baxter, Stephen Johnson, Bever-Leigh Banfield, Antoinette Stella, Mark Montgomery. Universal/NBC-TV. Colour.

Following *Dracula '79* (1979), this is a second one hour compilation of the remaining episodes from TV's *Cliffhangers* serial, *The Curse of Dracula*, created by executive producer/co-director Kenneth Johnson. Nouri plays a sophisticated Dracula teaching in San Francisco who is pursued by the grandson of Professor Van Helsing (Johnson) and Mary Gibbons (Baxter). Les Baxter co-composed the music score. *The World of Dracula* (1979) is a feature-length compilation of the TV show.

✦✧

LOVE THAT VAMPIRE
(Orig: UM SONHO DE VAMPIROS. USA: aka A VAMPIRE'S DREAM)
Brazil, 1969 (1971). Dir: Ibere Cavalcanti. With: Ankito, Irma Alvarez, Janet Chermoni, Sonelia Costa, Augusto Mala Filho, Robson Bob. UCB/Ser-Cine/Europix International. Colour.
Comedy in which Dr Pan (Ankito) is visited by Death and given the choice of dying or becoming a vampire. He chooses the latter, and proceeds to put the bite on those in power. Presented in 'Vampcolor'.
✦

LOVE — VAMPIRE STYLE
(Orig: BEISS MICH, LIEBLING!)
West Germany, 1970 (1971). Dir: Helmut Förnbacher. With: Patrick Jordan, Herbert Fuchs, Eva Renzi, Dieter Augustin, Brigitte Skay, Ralf Wolter. New Art Film-UFA/Cinerama/Greenfield/Intent International. Colour.
Softcore sex comedy about a postman (Jordan) with an inexhaustible libido. A psychiatrist grows fangs out of frustration.
✦

LOVE WANGA
(Orig/UK: OUANGA. USA: aka CRIME OF VOODOO/DRUMS OF THE JUNGLE)
USA, 1935. Dir: George Terwilliger. With: Fredi Washington, Sheldon Leonard, Philip Brandon, Marie Paxton, Winifred Harris. JH Hoffberg/Paramount. B&W.
Filmed on location under difficult conditions in Haiti and Jamaica by pioneer writer/director Terwilliger, this obscure roadshow movie was thought lost for many years. Voodoo priestess Cleely (Washington) uses an *ouanga* curse and her powers of hypnotism to create 'zombies' to kidnap the fiancée (Paxton) of her plantation-owner lover Adam (Leonard), who she then plans to sacrifice during a ceremony in the jungle. It wasn't released in America until 1936, and then subsequently reissued under a number of different titles.
Remake: THE DEVIL'S DAUGHTER (qv; 1939)
✦

ROBERT LOWERY
(R.L. Hanks) [1916-1971]

Unmemorable American leading man who was a direct descendant of Abraham Lincoln. He played a belligerent hero in both *The Mummy's Ghost* (1944) and *House of Horrors* (1946), and portrayed a paunchy caped crusader in Columbia's cut-price *Batman and Robin* (1949) serial.
qv: *Revenge of the Zombies* (1943).

ARTHUR LUBIN
[1901-1995]

After his work with Abbott and Costello, Universal entrusted director Lubin with its lavish *Phantom of the Opera* (1943) remake. But despite the added Technicolor, he ensured it was as dull as his horror quickies *Black Friday* (1940) and *The Spider Woman Strikes Back* (1945). Forced by the studio to accept a percentage of the profits to direct *Francis* (1949), about a talking mule, the movie spawned six sequels (five of which he directed) and Lubin successfully reworked the concept into the TV series *Mr. Ed* (1961-65).
qv: *The Addams Family* (1964-66).

LUCI LONTANE
Italy, 1987. Dir: Aurelio Chiesa. With: Thomas Milian, Laura Morante, William Berger, Giacomo Piperno. Reteitalia/Intersound. Colour.
Aliens from outer space invade a cemetery and possess the bodies of the dead. Produced by Claudio Argento.
✦✧

THE LUCY SHOW
USA, 1964. Dir: Jack Donohue. With: Lucille Ball, Vivian Vance, Gale Gordon, Jimmy Garrett, Ralph Hart, George Barrows. Desilu Productions/CBS-TV. Colour.
In this episode of the popular half-hour comedy TV series (1962-68, 156 episodes), Lucy and Viv (Vance) become concerned that horror movies are a bad influence on their children. After experiencing a film for themselves, Lucy has a nightmare in which they visit a spooky castle and encounter Count Dracula (Gordon), a werewolf butler (Robert H. Burns), a gorilla maid (Barrows), a talking head (Jan Arvan), an octopus and a mummy (Sid Haig!). Dracula turns them both into old hags in his laboratory and in the end a costume party Dracula (Shep Sanders) shows up.
Series sequel: HERE'S LUCY (1968-73)
✦✦

BELA LUGOSI
(Belá Ferenc Dezso Blascó) [1882-1956]

Hungarian actor who travelled to America in the 1920s, where he appeared on the stage and in small movie roles. He portrayed the Count in the 1927 Broadway adaptation of *Dracula*, and recreated the role in Universal's 1931 movie. After turning down the part of the Frankenstein Monster the following year, Lugosi quickly lost his crown as the King of Horror to rival Boris Karloff. Despite other such memorable roles as zombie master 'Murder' Legendre in *White Zombie* (1932), and the broken-necked Ygor in *Son of Frankenstein* (1939) and *The Ghost of Frankenstein* (1942), his career floundered amongst poverty-row horrors. Although he successfully overcame drug dependency, he ended his days in such humiliations as *Glen or Glenda* (1953) and *Bride of the Monster* (1954). Martin Landau won an Academy Award for playing him in *Ed Wood* (1995).
qv: *The Ape Man* (1943); *Bela Lugosi Meets a Brooklyn Gorilla* (1952); *Bela Lugosi Spotlight* (1999); *Biography: 'Bela Lugosi Hollywood's Dark Prince'* (1995); *Bowery at Midnight* (1942); *The Corpse Vanishes* (1942); *The Devil Bat* (1940); *Dracula in the Movies* (1992); *Dracula Sucks* (1979); *Ed Wood Look Back in Angora* (1994); *Frankenstein* (1931; test reel); *Frankenstein Meets the Wolf Man* (1943); *Hollywood on Parade No.8* (1933); *The Horror Show* (1979); *Invisible Ghost* (1941); *Der Januskopf* (1920); *Lock Up Your Daughters* (1956); *Lugosi the Forgotten King* (1985); *Mark of the Vampire* (1935); *Meet Frankenstein* (1948); *Mondo Lugosi* (1986); *Mother Riley Meets the Vampire* (1952); *The Mummy* (1999, documentary); *Mysteries & Scandals: 'Bela Lugosi'* (1998); *100 Years of Horror: 'Bela Lugosi'* (1996); *100 Years of Horror: 'Dracula and His Disciples'* (1996); *Plan 9 from Outer Space* (1958); *The Return of Chandu* (1934); *The Return of the Vampire* (1943); *Rivals: 'Frankenstein vs. Dracula'* (1995); *The Saint's Double Trouble* (1940); *The Vampire Interviews* (circa 1990s); *Voodoo Man* (1944); *The Wolf Man* (1941); *The World of Abbott and Costello* (1965); *You Asked for It* (1953); *You'll Find Out* (1940); *Zombies on Broadway* (1945).

LUGOSI THE FORGOTTEN KING
USA, 1985. Dir: Mark S. Gilman Jr and Dave Stuckey. With: Forrest J Ackerman, Carroll (Carol) Borland, Ralph Bellamy, Alex Gordon, John Carradine. Operator 13 Productions/Mediacast TV. Colour/B&W.
Forty-five minute video compilation of rare news clips and interviews with and about Lugosi, hosted by Ackerman and narrated by Carradine. This includes trailers for *Dracula* (1931), *Mark of the Vampire* (1935), (Abbott and Costello) *Meet Frankenstein* (1948), *Plan 9 from Outer Space* (1958) and *White Zombie* (1932), amongst many others. When originally offered through magazine advertisements, buyers received a free Lugosi T-shirt iron-on!
✦✧

LUKE'S DOUBLE
USA, 1916. Phunphilm/Pathé. B&W.
While reading *Strange Case of Dr. Jekyll and Mr. Hyde*, a man falls asleep and dreams he has a double who torments him in this silent short.
✦

LUPIN III
(Orig: LUPIN SANSEI)
Japan, 1983 (1985). Dir: Soji Yoshikawa. Tokyo Movie

Shinsha/Toho. Colour.
One of many anime adventures based on the novels by Maurice Leblanc. In this entry the charming hero-thief of the title (a descendant of French literary character Arsène Lupin) disguises himself as the Count in Castle Dracula and also plays a werewolf whilst battling a giant brain that has cloned itself and others.
Sequel: LUPIN III: GOLDEN LEGEND OF BABYLON (1985)
✦✧

LURK
USA, 1964 (1965). Dir: Rudy Burckhardt. With: Red Grooms, Mimi Grooms, Edwin Denby, Yvonne Burckhardt, Neil Welliver, Jacob Burckhardt. Filmmakers' Cooperative/Canyon Cinema. B&W.
Thirty-eight minute underground spoof of the 1931 *Frankenstein*, shot on 16mm, narrated by Denby and featuring Red Grooms as the Monster.
✦

LUST FOR A VAMPIRE
UK, 1970. Dir: Jimmy Sangster. With: Ralph Bates, Barbara Jefford, Suzanna Leigh, Michael Johnson, Yutte (Jytte) Stensgaard, Helen Christie. Hammer Films/EMI Film Productions. Colour.
Originally announced as *To Love a Vampire*, this was the second in Hammer's Karnstein trilogy and a follow-up to *The Vampire Lovers* (1970). It has almost nothing to do with J. Sheridan Le Fanu's classic story, but instead involves gratuitous nudity and lesbian relationships in a nineteenth century girls finishing school, where one of the students is the reincarnation of a vampire. Bates gives a strong performance as creepy schoolmaster Giles Barton (a role originally intended for Peter Cushing), and Danish actress/model Stensgaard is impressive as the vampiric Mircalla/Carmilla. Radio disc jockey Mike Raven (Austin Churton Fairman) plays Count Karnstein (with his voice dubbed by Valentine Dyall) and the vampires seem happy to wander around in broad daylight. Director Sangster (who replaced Terence Fisher before shooting) brings little style to the film, which utilises the same sets as *Scars of Dracula* (1970) and even close-up shots of Christopher Lee's bloodshot eyes! In one scene the entire camera crew is plainly visible. Hammer's most sexual movie, it was cut for an 'R' rating in America. With Pippa Steel(e), Christopher Neame, Luan Peters and 'Strange Love' sung by Tracy. Sphere Books published the novelisation by William Hughes in 1971.
Sequel: TWINS OF EVIL (qv; 1971)
✦✦

LUST FOR FRANKENSTEIN
Spain, 1997. Dir: Jess (Jesús) Franco. With: Michelle Bauer (Michelle McClellan), Linnea Quigley. Draculina Cine. Colour.
Franco's career hits rock-bottom with this no-budget softcore video release. Frankenstein's daughter is haunted by the ghost of her father while she uses his nude creation (Bauer) to go on a murder spree. This is apparently available in two versions, including a longer 'director's cut'.
✦

LUST IN THE FAST LANE
USA, 1984. Dir: Adam. With: Traci Lords, Ginger Lynn, Tom Byron, Eric Edwards, Crystal Breeze (Lisa Breeze), Peter North. Paradise Visuals. Colour.
Bored and restless, Bill (Byron) and Jackie (an underage Lords) decide to leave town for the weekend. After the inevitable flat tyre on a lonely road, they make their way to the eerie-looking house of swinging couple Jake (Edwards) and his wife Louise (Lynn). After various hardcore combinations with the other guests, the two hosts are revealed to be vampires, and over the course of the weekend the unsuspecting couple have also been turned into the undead — doomed to stay and have sex for eternity.
✦

LUST NEVER DIES
Hong Kong, 1983. Colour.
This apparently includes hopping vampires, hardcore sex and kung fu action.
✦

LUST OF BLACKULA
USA, 1987. Dir: Barry Morrison. With: F.M. Bradley, Jane Daville, Ron Jeremy, Donna-Anne, Ray Victory, Ebony Ayes. Arrow Video. Colour.
Hardcore feature in which a man named Alucard (Bradley) is obsessed with the Dracula legend. In the end, he turns out to be the Count himself.
✦

THE LUST POTION OF DOCTOR F
USA, 1986. Dir: Jerome Tanner. With: Careena Collins, Mike Horner, Krista Lane, John Leslie, Candie Evans, Steve Drake. Jell Productions/Western Visuals. Colour.
Shot on video and available in both hard- and softcore versions. Nerdy Dr Mortimer Lespecker (Horner) is hired by nubile young starlet Phoebe G. Bee (Collins) to create a youth serum. However, when he decides to test the potion on himself, he is transformed into a well-endowed, muscle-bound male dancer who drives women crazy.
Sequel: DR. F PART 2 (1990)
✦

LYCANTHROPE — PRAY FOR SUNRISE
(aka BLOODY MOON)
USA, 1997 (1999). Dir: Bob Cook. With: Robert Carradine, Michael Winslow, Christopher Mitchum, Jeffrey Alan Chase, Dalia Garcia, Bob Cook. BC Entertainment Group/ Spectrum Films. Colour.
Low-budget thriller in which a government team led by Bill Parker (co-producer Carradine) investigate a slaughter at a scientific outpost in the Amazon and discover that the destruction of the ozone layer has created the 'werewolf' responsible.
✦✧

LYKANTROP
Denmark, 1991. Dir: Peder Pedersen. With: Thomas Veng, Marianne Fiil, Peder Pedersen, Peter Nielsen. Inferno/ Lunatic Film. B&W.
Forty-two minute short about a teenage love triangle that turns ugly when one of those involved is bitten by a werewolf. The beast is finally cornered in a warehouse, where it is shot with a bow and arrow. Director Pedersen was also responsible for the make-up effects and was the editor of the Scandinavian horror film magazine, *Inferno*. This was shown on Danish TV and released on video with a seventeen minute making-of featurette.
✦✧

- M -

THE MACABRE TRUNK
(Orig: EL BAÚL MACABRO)
Mexico, 1936. Dir: Miguel Zacarias. With: Esther Fernandez, Ramón Pereda, René Cardona, 'Chaflán' (Carlos López), Manuel Noriega, Enrique Gonce. Produccion Pezet/Distripel. B&W.
Pereda plays the mad Dr del Vialle, who kills young women and uses their blood to keep his paralysed wife (Fernandez) alive. He disposes of his victims by dismembering their bodies. Cardona, who played the hero, went on to become a prolific director.
✦✧

O MACABRO DR SCIVANO
Brazil, 1971. Dir: Raúl Calhado and Rosalvo Caçador. With: Edmundo Scivano (Raúl Calhado), Luis Leme, Oswaldo de Souza, Henricao (Henrique Filipe), Lauro Sawaya, Genésio Aladim. Natus Produçoes Cinematográfica. B&W.
A failed politician, Dr Edmundo Scivano (co-director Calhado, who adopted his character's name in the cast list), dabbles in voodoo and in return for some gold nuggets he is turned into a vampire. He begins preying on the local women until he is finally reduced to dust in front of a crucifix.
✦

EL MACHO BIONICO
Mexico, 1981. Dir: Rodolfo De Anda. With: Isela Vega, Andres Garcia, Roberto Guzmán, Rafael Inclan, Princesa Lea, Wanda Seux. Rodas. Colour.
Silly science fiction comedy based on the novel *El Amor Es una Farsa* by Mauricio Iglesias. When a man (Garcia) is transformed by surgery into a super-strong hero, he later dresses up as Dracula with fake fangs in a failed attempt to attract women.
✦

PATRICK MACNEE
[b 1922]

Sophisticated British actor, best known for playing the dapper John Steed in TV's *The Avengers* (1961-69) and *The New Avengers* (1976-77). Macnee has also portrayed Dr Watson in TV movies opposite both Roger Moore and his old schoolfriend Christopher Lee as the consulting detective. Only limited success as a film actor, more recently in spoofs of the genre.
qv: *Dead of Night* (1976); *The Howling* (1980); *Incense for the Damned* (1970); *Matinee Theater: 'Dr. Jekyll and Mr. Hyde* (1957); *Mysteries, Magic & Miracles: 'Dracula'* (1995); *Mysteries, Magic & Miracles: 'Vampires'* (1996); *This is Your Life: 'Christopher Lee'* (1974); *Thunder in Paradise: 'Strange Bru'* (1994); *The Unforseen: 'The Tintype'* (1960); *Waxwork* (1988); *Waxwork II: Lost in Time* (1991).

MADAME'S PLACE
USA, 1982. Dir: Paul Miller. With: Wayland Flowers, Susan Tolsky, Johnny Haymer, Judy Landers, Bill Kirchenbauer, Carl Balantine. Brad Lachman Productions/Madame, Inc/Paramount. Colour.
Half-hour syndicated adult comedy TV series which combines puppets with live actors. In this episode, after an encounter with vampire Baron Von Leer (Kirchenbauer), the puppet Madame (voiced by Flowers) goes off with Dr Steiner who, with the help of his assistant Igor, transforms her into the Bride of Frankenstein.
✦

Evelyn Ankers is menaced by suitors David Bruce and George Zucco in The Mad Ghoul *(1943).*

MADAM JECKYL
USA, 1994. With: Kaitlyn Ashley (Kelly), Melissa Hill. Colour.
Hardcore feature in which a doctor's experimental serum turns the eponymous character into an insatiable nymphomaniac.
✦

MAD AT THE MOON
USA, 1992. Dir: Martin Donovan. With: Mary Stuart Masterson, Hart Bochner, Steven Blake, Fionnula Flanagan, Cec Verrell, Daphne Zuniga. Cassian Elwes/ Kastenbaum Films/Jaffe Films/Spectacor Films/Republic Home Video. Colour.
Period horror Western in which Jenny Miller (Masterson), the young bride in an arranged marriage, discovers that her new husband James (Blake) suffers from 'moon sickness' and transforms painfully into a werewolf under the influence of the full moon. Only her husband's half-brother, gambler Miller Brown (Bochner), can protect her. With Melissa Anne Moore.
✦✦

THE MAD BAKER
USA, 1972. Dir: Ted Petok. Voices: Len Maxwell. The Crunch Bird Studios/Regency. Colour.
Ten minute cartoon spoof in which a Dracula-like baker creates a Frankenstein Monster made of chocolate cake that terrorises the countryside until it is finally trapped in an old windmill.
✦

THE MADDAMS FAMILY
USA, 1991 (1992). Dir: Herschel Savage. With: Ona Zee, Charisma (Kitty Luv), Kim Angelli (Kim Alexis), Mike Horner, Jon Dough, Diedre (Deidre) Holland. X-Citement Video. Colour.
Hardcore parody of Charles Addams' bizarre characters. The ending of the Cold War financially ruins Cortez (Horner) when the bottom falls out of the munitions market. However, his wife Horticia (Zee) decides to turn their strange house into a brothel to generate extra cash. With Dough as the Frankenstein Monster-like butler Crotch, Ron Jeremy as Uncle Pester, Angelli as Tuesday and Charisma as Cousin Tit.
✦✧

MADE FOR LOVE
USA, 1926. Dir: Paul Sloane. With: Leatrice Joy, Edmund Burns, Ethel Wales, Bertram Grassby, Brandon Hurst, Frank Butler. Cinema Corporation of America/Producers Distributing Corporation. B&W.
Garrett Fort (*Dracula* [1931], *Frankenstein* [1931], etc) scripted this silent drama about a man apparently killed by the curse on an Egyptian tomb. Produced by Cecil B. DeMille.
✦

MADE IN BRITAIN:
Dracula and Frankenstein Make Money for Britain
UK, 1969. Dir: Marcus Davidson and Christopher Riley. With: Michael Sullivan. BBC-TV. B&W.
Ten minute TV series which focuses on British industry and exports. This episode is shot on location with Hammer Films soon after they won the Queen's Award to Industry.
✦✧

THE MAD GHOUL
USA, 1943. Dir: James Hogan. With: David Bruce, Evelyn Ankers, George Zucco, Robert Armstrong, Turhan Bey, Milburn Stone. Universal. B&W.
A neat little 'B' thriller in which the mad Dr Alfred Morris (Zucco on top form) is in love with concert singer Isabel Lewis (Ankers, whose singing voice is dubbed by an uncredited Lillian Cornell) and uses an ancient Inca gas to turn his mistaken rival Ted Allison into a living dead creature (Bruce, in creepy-looking make-up by Jack Pierce). Only the human hearts they steal from freshly buried corpses can temporarily reverse the process. There's good support from Armstrong (*King Kong* [1933], etc) as Ken McClure, a wise-cracking crime reporter who unexpectedly ends up as a victim, but Ankers and Bey disappoint as the insipid lovers. Director Hogan died of a heart attack a week before the film was released. With Rose Hobart and Charles McGraw.
✦✦✧

MADHOUSE
UK, 1974. Dir: Jim Clark. With: Vincent Price, Peter Cushing, Robert Quarry, Adrienne Corri, Natasha Pyne, Linda Hayden. American International/Amicus. Colour.
Originally announced in 1970 as *Devilday* with Robert Fuest directing, this is loosely based on the Angus Hall novel of the same title. When American International wanted to use up their horror stars' contracts, they got Amicus to throw together this old-fashioned but entertaining horror whodunit, announced as *Deathday* and filmed under the much better title *The Revenge of Dr. Death*. Price plays Hollywood film star Paul Toombes, whose career as Dr Death was cut short by the horrific decapitation of his fiancée. Years later, the actor is convinced by scriptwriter Herbert Flay (Cushing) to travel to England to recreate the character in a TV show. But life becomes a nightmare for Toombes when his arrival coincides with a series of brutal murders. Quarry, as an unsympathetic TV producer, recreates his vampiric Count Yorga for a fancy dress party, and Cushing also appears as one of the undead. This includes so many clips from old AIP/Roger Corman movies that both Boris Karloff and Basil Rathbone get a special credit. Price even sings the end song, although this was subsequently replaced on some Orion prints with a synthesizer theme composed by Kendall Schmidt.
✦✦✧

MADHOUSE
USA, 1990. Dir: Tom Ropelewski. With: Kirstie Alley, John Larroquette, Alison LaPlaca, John Diehl, Jessica Lundy, Bradley Gregg. Orion Pictures. Colour.
Alley and Larroquette star as Jessie and Mark Bannister, a couple who find that their lives are being destroyed when their new Los Angeles home is overrun by unwelcome friends and family who refuse to leave. This silly comedy includes a dream sequence in which the house is invaded by zombies and a running gag about a cat that keeps returning from the dead. With Dennis Miller and Robert Ginty.
✦✦

MAD JACK THE PIRATE:
The Horror of Draclia
USA, 1999. Dir: Jeff DeGrandis. Voices: Bill Kopp. Fox Kids Network. Colour.
Half-hour cartoon comedy TV series created by writer Kopp. In this episode, the eponymous pirate and his ratty assistant Snuck are tricked into travelling to Bulgaria to search for vampire Count Draclia's secret treasure of the Golden Wand. In the end, the bat-winged bloodsucker is disintegrated by sunlight.
✦✦✧

MAD LOVE
(UK: THE HANDS OF ORLAC)
USA, 1935. Dir: Karl Freund. With: Peter Lorre, Frances Drake, Colin Clive, Ted Healy, Henry Kolker, Sara Haden. Metro-Goldwyn-Mayer. B&W.
Cinematographer Freund's second (after *The Mummy* [1933]) and last horror film as a director, based on Maurice Renard's often-filmed novel *Les Mains d'Orlac*. Memorable as Lorre's Hollywood début, he stars as creepy bald-headed surgeon Dr Gogol who grafts the hands of a knife murderer onto famous concert pianist Stephen Orlac (a stiff Clive) whose actress wife Yvonne (Drake) he lusts after. The doctor's infatuation finally drives him insane. The most memorable scene has Gogol dressed in a neck brace and steel hands pretending to be the reanimated corpse of the guillotined murderer. With Edward Brophy, Keye Luke, Ian Wolfe (in two roles), Charles Trowbridge and some intrusive comedy relief from Healy as a reporter and May Beatty as a drunken housekeeper. A classic of Grand Guignol cinema. The original trailer includes Lorre, with hair, apparently accepting a fan's phone-call at home.
Remake: THE HANDS OF ORLAC (1961)
✦✦✦✦

THE MAD LOVE LIFE OF A HOT VAMPIRE

USA, 1971. Dir: Sven Christian (Ray Dennis Steckler). With: Jim Parker, Jane Bond (Carolyn Brandt), Rock Heinrich, Will Long, Greta Smith, Fritz King. Something Weird Video. Colour.

Hour-long hardcore horror narrated by the wife of Dracula (Bond). The Count (Las Vegas TV horror host Parker) and his hunchbacked assistant (Heinrich) send out three vampire women to seduce victims and bring back their blood. In the end, they are tracked to their lair by an overweight Van Helsing and Dracula is destroyed by sunlight.

✦

THE MAD, MAD, MAD COMEDIANS

USA, 1970. Dir: Arthur Rankin Jr and Jules Bass. Voices: Jack Benny, George Burns, Groucho Marx, The Smothers Brothers, Flip Wilson, George Jessel. Rankin-Bass Productions/ABC-TV. Colour.

Half-hour cartoon special split into various segments featuring caricatures (by Bruce Stark) of numerous classic comedians. These include W.C. Fields, Chico Marx and Harpo Marx, all voiced by Paul Frees, who also contributes the introductions set on a vaudeville-type stage with an audience that features Dean Martin and Jerry Lewis, Frank Sinatra, Popeye and the Frankenstein Monster, amongst others. Other voices include Phyllis Diller, Jack E. Leonard, Henny Youngman and Joan Gardner. This was apparently Rankin-Bass' highest-rated TV special.

✦✦

THE MAD MONSTER

USA, 1942. Dir: Sam Newfield. With: Johnny Downs, George Zucco, Anne Nagel, Glenn Strange, Sarah Padden, Mae Busch. Producers Releasing Corporation. B&W.

Made in just five days and banned in the UK until 1952 (when it was released with an 'X' certificate and accompanied by a disclaimer about the safety of blood transfusions). Zucco's crazier-than-usual Dr Lorenzo Cameron patriotically injects the blood of a wolf into gentle handyman Petro (Strange, doing his best Lon Chaney Jr simpleton impression), turning him into the prototype for an army of wolfmen to battle the Nazis. However, he then uses the furry-faced giant (make-up by Harry Ross) to kill those men he believes responsible for destroying his reputation. The man-into-wolf transformations are quite well done, but Newfield's direction makes the relatively short running time seem interminable. Director Newfield and stars Zucco and Strange were reunited the following year in PRC's *The Black Raven*.

✦

MAD MONSTER PARTY?

USA, 1966 (1969). Dir: Jules Bass. Voices: Boris Karloff, Alan Swift, Gale Garnett, Phyllis Diller, Ethel Ennis. Embassy/Videocraft International. Colour.

Stop-motion children's puppet film shot in a process dubbed 'Animagic', with character designs by Jack Davis. Karloff voices a puppet version of himself as Baron Von Frankenstein (and even sings one of the better musical numbers), who holds a convention of all the monsters to reveal the secret of total destruction. Among the guests are the Werewolf, Dr Jekyll and Mr Hyde, Frankenstein's Monster Fang and his Mate (Diller), Count Dracula, the Hunchback, the Mummy and It (King Kong). This also includes voice impersonations of Bela Lugosi, Peter Lorre, James Stewart, Charles Laughton and Sydney Greenstreet (as the Invisible Man). Overlong, but often amusing. *Mad* magazine's Harvey Kurtzman co-wrote the script (along with Len Korobkin and an uncredited Forrest J Ackerman). Tie-in T-shirts and a soundtrack CD were available in the late 1990s.

✦✧

MADONNA...BABAENG AHAS

(aka MADONNA...BABAENG AHASSSSSS)

Philippines, circa 1990. Dir: Artemio O. Marquez. With: Snooky Serna, Tirso Cruz III, Eric Quizon, Rosemarie Gil, Luis Gonzales, Caridad Sanchez. Regal Films. Colour.

A cursed woman gives birth to a baby who grows up into the eponymous heroine. When threatened by rapists, she turns into a fanged reptile monster.

✦

THE MAD VAMPIRES

Hong Kong, 1984. Jia's Motion Picture Company/Tai Seng Video. Colour.

Horror comedy involving a pair of hopping vampires, the flying head of another bloodsucker and two zombies in sailor suits.

✦

MA FEMME EST UNE PANTHÈRE

France, 1961. Dir: Raymond Bailly. With: Jean Richard, Jean Poiret, M. Serault, Silvana Blasi, Jean-Max, Marcel Lupovici. UFA Comacuco/Françis Lopez. B&W.

A colonel's wife is reincarnated as a panther who can assume human form at will.

PATRICK MAGEE [1924-1982]

Irish character actor with piercing eyes and sibilant voice. Often cast as a sinister doctor.

qv: *Asylum* (1972); *Beasts: 'What Big Eyes'* (1976); *Bloodbath* (1966); *Bloodlust* (1979); *A Clockwork Orange* (1971); *The Inn of the Flying Dragon* (1978); *The Monster Club* (1980); *Orson Welles' Great Mysteries: 'The Monkey's Paw'* (1973); *Tales from the Crypt* (1972).

MAGIA

Hungary, 1917. Dir: Alexander Korda. With: Mihály Várkonyi. Corvin. B&W.

While gazing into Baron Merlin's magic mirror, the hero learns that his host is an ancient magician who must drink the blood of a young man every thousandth full moon to survive.

✦

THE MAGICAL ADVENTURES OF QUASIMODO

Canada/France, 1995. Dir: Bahram Rohani. Voices: Sonja Ball, Daniel Brochu, A.J. Henderson, Harry Hill, Eleanor Noble, Terrence Scammell. Ciné-Groupe/Arès Films/ France 3/Télé-Images/Hearst Entertainment/Family Channel. Colour.

Half-hour children's cartoon TV series (twenty-six episodes) about a teenage hunchback and his friends, loosely based on Victor Hugo's *Notre-Dame de Paris*.

✦✧

THE MAGIC CHRISTIAN

UK, 1969. Dir: Joseph McGrath. With: Peter Sellers, Ringo Starr, Richard Attenborough, Leonard Frey, Laurence Harvey, Christopher Lee. Grand Film/Commonwealth United Entertainment. Colour.

All-star comedy, based on the novel by co-writer Terry Southern, that badly misfires. Sellers stars as Sir Guy Grand who, along with his adopted son (Beatles drummer Starr), sets out to prove that money corrupts. This includes Lee as a ship's vampire, Raquel Welch as a whip-wielding slave driver, an uncredited Yul Brynner in drag and other embarrassing cameos by Attenborough, Harvey, Spike Milligan, Roman Polanski, Wilfred Hyde White, Graham Chapman, John Cleese, Ferdy Mayne, Dennis Price, John Le Mesurier and Victor Maddern. Music by Badfinger and Thunderclap Newman.

✦✧

MAGIC COP

(Orig: QUMO JINGCHA. USA: aka MR. VAMPIRE V)

Hong Kong, 1989 (1990). Dir: David Lai (Tung Wei/Lai Dai-Wei). With: Lam Ching-Ying (Lin Zheng-Ying), Michiko Nishiwaki, Wilson Lam (Lam Jun-Yin), Billy Chow (Chow Bei-Lei), Lam Jun-Yin. Movie Impact/ Millifame Productions. Colour.

Fifth entry in the popular *Mr. Vampire* series, directed by ex-actor Lai (*Enter the Dragon* [1973], etc). Ching-Ying plays Uncle Fung, an old-fashioned regional police detective, who travels to the big city and teams up with his nephew. Together they investigate a vampire-witch who uses reanimated corpses for drug trafficking.

✦✦

MAGIC CURSE
Hong Kong/Philippines, 1977. With: Jason Pai-Piao, Pinky de Leon, Vic Silayan. Colour.
A man (Pai-Piao) from Hong Kong searching for his uncle in the Borneo jungle encounters the snake princess Philona and helps her battle the wizard Abdullah. This apparently includes flying skulls and a green-faced vampire woman.
✦

THE MAGICIAN
USA/France, 1926. Dir: Rex Ingram. With: Alice Terry, Paul Wegener, Ivan Petrovich, Firmin Gémier, Gladys Hamer, Stowitts. Metro-Goldwyn-Mayer. Tinted.
Based on an early novel by Somerset Maugham, inspired by the exploits of Aleister Crowley, this silent film was thought lost for many years. Wegener plays achemist Dr Oliver Haddo, seeker of the homunculus, which needs the blood of a young maiden's heart to live. He uses magic to seduce the blonde heroine (Terry) on the eve of her wedding and, under hypnosis, she dreams of taking part in an orgiastic rite presided over by Pan (Folies Bergère dancer Stowitts). Michael Powell was the assistant designer and also appears in a supporting role. This was probably an influence on both of James Whale's *Frankenstein* movies.
✦✦✦

THE MAGIC MAN
Thailand, circa 1986. Hong Kong TV Video. Colour.
A holy man gives the hero the power to transform into a super-strong werewolf-like creature to battle the villains.
✦

MAGIC MONGO:
Teenage Werewolf
USA, 1977. With: Lennie Weinrib, Helaine Lembeck, Paul Hinckley, Robin Dearden, Larry Larsen, Bart Braverman. Sid and Marty Krofft/ABC-TV. Colour.
One of a series of sixteen twelve minute episodes, broadcast as part of *The Krofft Supershow* (1977-78). Incompetent genie Mongo (Weinrib) is discovered in a bottle on the beach by teenager Donald (Hinckley), who uses his new-found friend to help him impress girls.
✦

THE MAGIC MUMMY
USA, 1933. Dir: John Foster and George Stallings. Van Beuren Corporation/RKO Radio Pictures. B&W.
Seven minute *Tom and Jerry* cartoon (no connection with the later MGM cat and mouse characters), in which a mysterious cloaked villain steals a female mummy from the museum. After magically removing her bandages, he forces her to perform on stage before an audience of living skeletons.
Sequel: PANICKY PUP (1933)
✦✦

MAGIC STORY
Taiwan, 1985. Dir: I. Yung Tong. With: Bill Tung (Tung Pui) Goodyear Movie Company/New Ship. Colour.
Comedy in which a young boy, Akui, befriends little hopping vampire Ding-Dong who has lost his mother and doesn't fit in with the other ghosts. After being exposed to sunlight, Ding-Dong is revived by a bolt of lightning.
✦✧

MAGIC STORY
(Orig: JIANG SHI SHAO YE. USA: aka YOUNG MASTER VAMPIRE)
Hong Kong, 1986. Dir: Ricky Lau (Ricky Hui/Xu Guanying). With: Sun Kim-Chu, Don Bil, Wong Shi-Kit. Colour.
Cantonese horror comedy in which a young priest attempts to control a group of zombies and a boy tries to win the respect of his girlfriend's father by becoming a vampire-hunter.
✦✧

THE MAGIC SWORD
(UK: ST. GEORGE AND THE SEVEN CURSES)
USA, 1961. Dir: Bert I. Gordon. With: Basil Rathbone, Estelle Winwood, Gary Lockwood, Anne Helm, Jack Kosslyn, Maila Nurmi. Bert I. Gordon Productions/United Artists. Colour.
Filmed under the title *St. George and the Dragon*, this is probably producer/director Gordon's best film, which doesn't mean much. A fairy-tale fantasy with a grim edge, it has witch Sybil (the wonderful Winwood) bringing up dreary foster son George (Lockwood) in the forest. She gives him a magic sword, armour and companions, and he sets out to defy the seven curses of the evil sorcerer Lodac (a nicely villainous Rathbone) and rescue the princess Helene (Helm). Along the way George has to confront a vampire hag (played by Nurmi, aka TV horror host Vampira), a giant wolf-like ogre (Kosslyn) and a two-headed fire-breathing dragon, plus various evil dwarfs and pinheads (who include Richard Kiel and Angelo Rossitto). The special effects (by Bert and Flora Gordon) look cheap and unconvincing, but kids will love it and it's worth catching for Rathbone's performance alone.
✦✦✧

ANG MAHIWAGANG DAIGDIG NI ELIAS PANIKI
Philippines, circa 1989. Dir: Carlo J. Caparas. With: Ramon Revilla, Maria Isabel López, Atong Redillas, Ruel Vernal, Bomber Moran, Tina Godinez. Golden Lions Film. Colour.
A superhero, with a rubber bat on his headband that glows when evil is near, battles an army of outlandish monsters raised by Satanists. These include a bare-chested vampire, a were-pig woman, a huge cackling skeleton, various dwarves and a bat-winged demon.
✦✧

MAHLER
UK, 1974. Dir: Ken Russell. With: Robert Powell, Georgina Hale, Richard Morant, Lee Montague, Rosalie Crutchley, Benny Lee. Goodtimes Enterprises/Visual Programme Systems. Colour.
This typically overblown Russell biography of Gustav Mahler (1860-91) stars Powell as the dying composer, travelling back to Vienna by train with his wife Alma (Hale) and reviewing the events of his life through a series of fantasy flashbacks. These include his affair with vampire-like singer Anna von Mildenburg (Dana Gillespie) and Alma doing a striptease on top of Mahler's coffin in a bizzare homage to Carl Dreyer's *Vampyr* (1931-32). With cameos by George Colouris, Andrew Faulds and an uncredited Oliver Reed.
✦✦✧

MALENKA THE NIECE OF THE VAMPIRE
(Orig: MALENKA, LA SOBRINA DEL VAMPIRO/MALENKA LA NIPOTE DEL VAMPIRO. USA: aka FANGS OF THE LIVING DEAD)
Spain/Italy, 1968 (1971). Dir: Amando de Ossorio. With: Anita Ekberg, John Hamilton (Gianni Medici), Diano (Diana) Lorys, Audrey Amber (Adriana Ambesi), Rosana (Rosanna) Yanni, Julian Ugarte. Victory Films/Cobra Films Production/Triton Film/Europix International. Colour.
First horror film from the director of the *Blind Dead* series, obviously inspired by Hammer's vampire movies and the Italian Gothics of Bava and Freda. When Italian model Sylvia Morrell (Ekberg, who is too old for the role) inherits the title Countess Wolduck, she travels to her ancestral castle where her apparently one hundred year-old vampiric 'uncle' (Ugarte) reveals that she is the image of her grandmother, Malenka (also Ekberg), a seventeenth century biochemist burned as a witch for searching for the secrets of immortality. Warned not to marry because of a family curse, Sylvia is finally rescued by her doctor fiancé Piero (Hamilton) and his comedic friend Max (Guy Roberts). It all turns out to be a plot to drive her insane, but despite the genre clichés there's a nice supernatural twist at the end. With Fernando Bilbao, a very brief appearance by Paul Müller, and some surprisingly strong whipping scenes. This was re-released in America in 1973 as part of Europix's successful 'Orgy of the Living Dead' triple-bill.
✦✦✧

THE MALIBU BEACH VAMPIRES
USA, 1991. Dir: Francis Creighton. With: Kelly Galindo, Christina Walker, Mimi Spivak, Anet Anatelle, Angelyne,

Becky LeBeau. Peacock Films/AMI Entertainment. Colour.
Colonel Ollie West, Congressman Teri Upstart and TV evangelist Rev Timmy Fakker all have secret mistresses in a Malibu beach house who turn out to be vampires (led by Galindo). But instead of drinking blood, these girls inject a truth serum with their bite. This silly horror comedy features the untalented Angelyne of Hollywood Boulevard billboard fame and music by Paul McCarty (*sic*).
✦

MALKOÇOGLU KRALARA KARSI
Turkey, 1967. With: Çüneyt Arkin.
Historical swashbuckler, based on a popular comic strip, in which fifteenth century Ottoman warrior Malkoçoglu (Arkin) battles a bald-headed Vlad the Impaler. The title translates as 'Malkoçoglu vs the Kings'.
✦

MILES MALLESON [1888-1969]
British playwright, screenwriter and character actor since the 1930s. He has scene-stealing cameos in Hammer's *Dracula* (1958), *The Brides of Dracula* (1960) and *The Phantom of the Opera* (1962).

THE MALTESE BIPPY
USA, 1969. Dir: Norman Panama. With: Dan Rowan, Dick Martin, Carol Lynley, Julie Newmar, Mildred Natwick, Fritz Weaver. Metro-Goldwyn-Mayer. Colour.
Filmed under the titles *The Incredible Werewolf Murders, The Strange Case of...!#*%?* and *Who Killed Cock Rubin?* The two stars of the hit TV show, *Rowan and Martin's Laugh-In* (1968-72), unwisely made this horror comedy set in an old dark house on Long Island. When the apparently lycanthropic Ravenwood family move in next door, Sam Smith (Martin) begins to think he's turning into the first American werewolf (which he does in a dream sequence). This includes clips from *Atlantis the Lost Continent* (1960) and *The Time Machine* (1960). With Robert Reed, Dana Elgar and several variant endings.
✦

MAMA DRACULA
Belgium, 1979 (1980). Dir: Boris Szulzinger. With: Louise Fletcher, Maria Schneider, Marc-Henri Wajnberg, Alexander Wajnberg, Jimmy Shuman, Jess Hahn. Valisa Films/Radio Television Belge Française/SND. Colour.
Horror comedy filmed in English and based on the Elizabeth Bathory legend. Fletcher stars as the Countess, who bathes in virgins' blood to preserve her beauty. She brings Professor Van Bloed (Shuman) to her Transylvanian castle to develop artificial blood, aided by the Countess' undead twin sons (comedians the Wajnberg Brothers). Schneider plays policewoman Nancy Hawai, who investigates the vampires' murderous activities and ends up marrying both the twins.
✦✧

THE MAN AND THE MONSTER
(Orig: EL HOMBRE Y EL MONSTRUO)
Mexico, 1958. Dir: Rafael Baledón. With: Abel Salazar, Martha Roth, Henry (Enrique) Rambal, Ofelia Guilmáin, Anita Blanch (Ana Laura Baledón), José Chavez. Cinematográfica ABSA/Clasa-Mohme/American International. B&W.
When pianist Samuel (Rambal) murders his rival Alejandra (Roth) and plays her stolen music in front of her mummified corpse, he is transformed (via photographic dissolves) into a hairy, werewolf-like monster with a bulbous nose. Only his protective mother's caring touch can return him to normality. In the end, he is shot to death by the police when his protégé Laura (also Roth) plays the accursed concerto on stage. With writer/producer Salazar as the hero, a suspicious concert promoter. The English-language version was produced by K. (Kenneth) Gordon Murray and directed by Paul Nagle (Nagel).
✦✧

THE MAN CALLED FLINTSTONE
USA, 1966. Dir: Joseph Barbera and William Hanna (and Charles A. Nichols). Voices: Alan Reed, Mel Blanc, Jean Vander Pyl, Gerry Johnson, Don Messick, Janet Waldo. Hanna-Barbera Productions/Columbia. Colour.
Feature-length musical cartoon version of the popular TV series, inspired by the success of the James Bond films and shot under the title *That Man Flintstone*. Fred (Reed) is the double of caveman secret agent Rock Slag and uses all kinds of ingenious Stone Age gadgets against the villainous Green Goose, the leader of SMIRK. In one scene, Agent Triple-X, master of disguise, transforms himself into a vampire and the Frankenroc Monster. Other voices include Paul Frees, Harvey Korman and June Foray.
✦✦

MILES MANDER (Lionel Mander) [1888-1946]
Lean British character actor and former New Zealand sheep farmer, automobile racer, novelist and playwright, prize-fight promoter, theatre manager and failed entrepreneur. He later moved to Hollywood after unsuccessfully standing for Parliament in 1934. Credited with discovering Merle Oberon and Madeleine Carroll, he was often cast as either victim or villain and portrayed the scheming Richelieu in both the 1935 and 1939 versions of *The Three Musketeers*.
qv: *The Brighton Strangler* (1945); *Fingers at the Window* (1942); *Phantom of the Opera* (1943); *The Return of the Vampire* (1943).

THE MAN FROM ATLANTIS:
C.W. Hyde
USA, 1977. Dir: Dann Cahn. Dir: With: Patrick Duffy, Belinda Montgomery, Alan Fudge, Michele Carey, Val Avery, Pamela Peters-Solow. Solow/NBC-TV. Colour.
Hour-long TV series (1977-78, seventeen episodes) starring Duffy as web-fingered amnesiac Mark Harris, possibly the last survivor of the lost city of Atlantis, who has superhuman powers underwater. After being found washed up on a beach, he teams up with Dr Elizabeth Merrill (Montgomery) of the Foundation for Oceanic Research. In this episode, C.W. Crawford (Fudge), the head of the Foundation, accidentally ingests a mysterious liquid found on the ocean floor and develops a dual personality.
✦✧

THE MAN FROM U.N.C.L.E.:
The Bat Cave Affair
USA, 1965 (1966). Dir: Alf Kjellin. With: Robert Vaughn, David McCallum, Leo G. Carroll, Martin Landau, Joan Freeman, Whit Bissell. Arena Productions/Metro-Goldwyn-Mayer/NBC-TV. Colour.
Hour-long sci-spy TV series (1964-68, 105 episodes), created by Sam Rolfe, about the United Command for Law and Enforcement, an international organisation dedicated to saving the world from THRUSH. In this episode, UNCLE agents Napoleon Solo (Vaughn) and Illya Nikovetch Kuryakin (McCallum) are accompanied by hillbilly clairvoyant Clemency McGill (Freeman) to Europe to stop vampiric THRUSH agent Count Zark (Landau, doing a great Bela Lugosi impression nearly thirty years before *Ed Wood* [1994]) from using his radioactive bats to jam the world's radar systems.
✦✦✧

The Deadly Games Affair
USA, 1964. Dir: Alvin Ganzer. With: Robert Vaughn, David McCallum, Leo G. Carroll, Alexander Scourby, Burt Brinckerhoff, Janine Gray. Arena Productions/Metro-Goldwyn-Mayer/NBC-TV. B&W.
UNCLE agents Solo and Kuryakin discover that a valuable stamp collection leads them to ex-Nazi scientist Professor Amadeus (Scourby), who is continuing his experiments to revive the dead using the body of Adolf Hitler.
✦✦✦

The Very Important Zombie Affair
USA, 1965. Dir: David Alexander. With: Robert Vaughn, David McCallum, Leo G. Carroll, Linda Gaye Scott, Claude Akins, Rodolfo Acosta. Arena Productions/Metro-

Goldwyn-Mayer/NBC-TV. Colour.
Solo and Kuryakin are captured by El Supremo (Akins), the dictator of a Caribbean island who uses voodoo to turn his political rivals into zombies.
Series sequel: THE RETURN OF THE MAN FROM U.N.C.L.E. "THE FIFTEEN YEARS LATER AFFAIR" (1983)
✦✦

MANHATTAN BABY
(aka L'OCCHIO DEL MALE. UK: THE POSSESSED. USA: aka EYE OF THE EVIL DEAD)
Italy/USA/Egypt, 1982 (1983). Dir: Lucio Fulci. With: Christopher Connelly, Martha Taylor, Brigitta Boccoli (Boccole), Giovanni Frezza, Cinzia De Ponti, Laurence Welles. Fulvia Film/Lightning Video. Colour.
Director Fulci (who also appears in a cameo as a doctor) swaps his usual zombies for an ancient Egyptian curse: archaeologist Professor George Hacker (Connelly) is temporarily blinded by a powerful bas-relief shaped like an eye that he discovers beneath a pyramid. At the same time, his daughter Susan (Boccoli) is given an amulet of a similar design by the ghost of an old woman. Once they return to New York, the talisman transports its victims through a portal back to the Egyptian desert and orchestrates a gory attack by stuffed birds. Meanwhile the sands themselves (complete with snakes and scorpions) slowly invade their Manhattan apartment. It doesn't make a lot of sense.
✦✧

MAN HUNTER
(Orig: JUNGFRAU UNTER KANNIBALEN/IL CACCIATORE DI UOMINI/MONDO CANNIBALE/SEXO CANÍBAL. USA: aka MANDINGO MANHUNTER. UK: aka DEVIL HUNTER)
West Germany/Italy/Spain, 1980. Dir: Clifford Brown (Jesús Franco). With: Al Cliver (Pier Luigi Conti), Ursula Fellner (Ursula Buchfellner), Gisela Hahn, Werner Pochath, Burt Altman, Robert Foster (Antonio Mayans). Eurociné/Lisa Films/Filman/JE Films/Trans World Entertainment. Colour.
A pair of adventurers (Cliver and Pochath) travel to the island of Puerto Santo to rescue Hollywood film star Laura Crawford (former *Playboy* Playmate Fellner), who has been kidnapped by gangsters. Along the way they encounter a native tribe making human sacrifices to their pagan god and a bug-eyed cannibal zombie (Altman). Being another Franco film (he took over the direction from Amando de Ossorio, and also composed the score), this is nowhere near as interesting as it sounds.
✦

MANHUNT OF MYSTERY ISLAND
(aka CAPTAIN MEPHISTO AND THE TRANSFORMATION MACHINE)
USA, 1945. Dir: Spencer Bennet, Wallace A. Grissell and Yakima Canutt. With: Richard Bailey, Linda Stirling, Roy Barcroft, Kenne Duncan, Forrest Taylor, Forbes Murray. Republic Pictures. B&W.
For fifteen action-packed episodes, with titles like 'The Sable Shroud' and 'Cauldron of Cremation', Barcroft portrays the villainous Captain Mephisto, one of four owners of Mystery Island who, by means of a transformation chair, can rearrange his molecular structure to resemble that of an ancient pirate ancestor. Mephisto kidnaps a scientist and forces him to build a Radiatomic Power Transmitter which will control the world's transportation networks. But luckily, wooden hero Lance Reardon (Bailey) and plucky Claire Forrest (Stirling) are on hand every episode to get into some incredible fist-fights and end up in outlandish traps for each cliffhanger ending. This serial was re-edited into a feature in 1966.
✦✦✧

MANIAC
(aka SEX MANIAC)
USA, 1934, Dir: Dwain Esper. With: Bill Woods, Horace Carpenter, Ted Edwards, Phyllis Diller, Thea Ramsey, Jennie Dark. Roadshow Attractions Company/Hollywood Producers & Distributors. B&W.
Low-budget, 'adults only' version of 'The Black Cat' by Edgar Allan Poe. A crazed former vaudeville performer (Woods) kills and then impersonates the wild-eyed Dr Meirschultz (silent screen veteran Carpenter), who is experimenting with bringing the dead back to life. This includes the eating of a cat's eye by the doctor's mad assistant, a rapist who believes he's a gorilla, some mild nudity and clips from *Witchcraft Through the Ages* (1918/1921) and *Siegfried* (1923/1924). An unbelievable exploitation movie from the Hollywood husband and wife team of Dwain Esper and Hildegarde Stadie. Some prints add a helpful instructional foreword about mental illness!
✦

MANIAC COP 3: BADGE OF SILENCE
Canada/USA, 1992. Dir: William Lustig and Joel Soisson. With: Robert Davi, Caitlin Dulany, Gretchen Becker, Paul Gleason, Robert Z'Dar, Julius Harris. Footstone/Neo Motion Pictures/First Look Pictures/Home Box Office. Colour.
This cable TV movie was the third and last entry to date in the fun franchise created by Lustig and screenwriter/co-producer Larry Cohen (both of whom distanced themselves from the finished product). Following the events in *Maniac Cop 2* (1990), the homicidal Matt Cordell (Z'Dar) is inexplicably raised from the dead by a voodoo priest (Harris). Detective Sean McKinney (Davi, returning from the previous film) attempts to stop the zombie officer from adding to his list of victims and turning cop-in-a-coma Kate Sullivan (Dulany) into his bride. As usual, the stunts (co-ordinated by second unit director Spiro Razatos) are pretty impressive. With an unbilled Robert Forster and Ted Raimi.
✦✦

MANIMAL
USA, 1983. Dir: Russ Mayberry. With: Simon MacCorkindale, Melody Anderson, Ursula Andress, Glynn Turman, Lloyd Bochner, Ed Lauter. Twentieth Century-Fox/Glen A. Larson Productions/NBC-TV. Colour.
Pilot movie for the short-lived TV series about Jonathan Chase (MacCorkindale), a pompous professor of criminology, who has the power to inexplicably transform into various animals. Stan Winston's man-into-panther effects are over-used and nobody bothers to explain what happens to Chase's clothes during the transformations. Anderson plays Brooke McKenzie, a dumb policewoman, and Andress must have really needed the money to guest star in this routine story about arms smugglers.
Sequel: MANIMAL (qv; 1983)
✦✧

MANIMAL:
Female of the Species
USA, 1983. Dir: Georg J. Fenady. With: Simon MacCorkindale, Melody Anderson, Michael D. Roberts, Reni Santoni, Michael McGuire, Laura Cushing. Twentieth Century-Fox/Glen Larson Productions/NBC-TV. Colour.
Dr Jonathan Chase (MacCorkindale), who has the ability to transform into various animals, helps New York detective Brooke McKenzie (Anderson) fight crime in this short-lived (eight episodes), hour-long TV series. In this episode, Jonathan uses his powers to change into various animals to help protect a woman (Cushing) raised by wolves in India. With Gloria Stuart as a briefly-glimpsed bag lady. Panther and hawk transformations designed and created by Stan Winston. Title sequence narrated by William Conrad.
Series sequel: NIGHTMAN: Manimal (qv; 1998)
✦✧

MAN INTO VAMPIRE!
USA, 1997. Dir: Terrence Smith. With: Terrence Smith, Elizabeth McLaughlin, Sean King, Jason Blasso, Mark Pernice, Michelle Smith. Horror Business Pictures. B&W.
Independent video release with director/writer/editor Smith as a vampire.
✦

MAN MADE MONSTER
(aka THE ATOMIC MONSTER. UK: THE ELECTRIC MAN)

USA, 1941. Dir: George Waggner. With: Lionel Atwill, Lon Chaney Jr, Anne Nagel, Frank Albertson, Samuel S. Hinds, William Davidson. Universal. B&W.
Originally announced in 1937 to co-star Boris Karloff and Bela Lugosi under various titles, including *The Man in the Cab* and *The Mysterious Dr. R.* Instead, it became a neat little 'B' feature, written (under the pseudonym 'Joseph West') and directed by George Waggner, based on a story co-written by Harry J. Essex, which Universal used to launch Chaney Jr's horror film career. He plays 'Dynamo' Dan McCormick, the Electric Man, transformed by Atwill's gleefully insane Dr Paul Rigas into an electric zombie superman whose touch is lethal. Chaney's limited acting ability fails to convey any of the pathos which Karloff might have brought to the role, but his shortcomings are more than made up for by Atwill ('Mad! Of course I'm mad!'), excellent John P. Fulton optical effects and an exciting climax where Chaney's power leaks out along a barbed wire fence. With Byron Foulger.
✦✦✦

MANNEQUIN
USA, 1987. Dir: Michael Gottlieb. With: Andrew McCarthy, Kim Cattrall, Estelle Getty, James Spader, G.W. Bailey, Carole Davis. Gladden Entertainment/Twentieth Century Fox. Colour.
In Ancient Egyptian times, Emmy (Cattrall) disguises herself as a mummy to escape her forthcoming marriage. Calling upon the gods to save her, she is transported through time and ends up in Philadelphia as a mannequin sculpted by Jonathan Switcher (McCarthy). Coming to life only when Jonathan is around, together they create a series of successful shop window displays and fall in love. This dated romantic comedy features songs by Starship, Belinda Carlisle, Alisha and The Temptations.
Sequel: MANNEQUIN II ON THE MOVE (1991)
✦✦✧

DAVID MANNERS
(Rauff de Ryther Duan Acklom) [1901-1998]

Canadian-born actor who claimed to be descended from William the Conqueror. During the 1930s he made a rather bland, if stalwart romantic leading man in several Universal horror classics before retiring from films in 1936 to become a novelist.
qv: *Dracula* (1931); *The Mummy* (1933).

MAN OF A THOUSAND FACES
USA, 1957. Dir: Joseph Pevney. With: James Cagney, Dorothy Malone, Jane Greer, Marjorie Rambeau, Jim Backus, Robert J. Evans. Universal-International. B&W.
This glossy Hollywood biopic about the life of Lon Chaney Sr opens with Irving Thalberg (future producer Evans) giving the eulogy at the silent screen actor's memorial service. Cagney (who doesn't look anything like Chaney) gives a strong performance as the troubled star and he appears as The Hunchback of Notre Dame and the Phantom of the Opera, while his vampire from *London After Midnight* (1927) is tantalizingly glimpsed on a poster. The make-ups recreated by Bud Westmore and Jack Kevin are nowhere near as effective as the originals, but there's good support from Backus as the actor's agent, Celia Lovsky as his deaf mute mother and Roger Smith as a moody Lon Chaney Jr. With Jack Albertson.
✦✦✧

LA MANSION DE LAS 7 MOMIAS
(aka MANSION DE BLUE DEMON)
Mexico/Guatemala, 1975. Dir: Rafael Lanuza. With: Blue Demon (Alejandro Muñoz), Superzán. Colour.
A group of masked wrestlers enter the mansion of the seven mummies, where sixteenth century nobleman De la Garza reputedly made a deal with the Devil in return for riches.
Sequel: SANTO Y BLUE DEMON EN EL MISTERIO DE LAS BERMUDAS (1977)
✦

LA MANSIÓN DE LOS MUERTOS VIVENTES
Spain, 1982. Dir: Jess (Jesús) Franco. With: Candy Coster (Lina Romay/Rosa Maria Almirall), Robert Foster (Antonio Mayans), Mabel Escaño, Eva León, Mamie Kaplan (María del Carmen Nieto), Jasmina Bell (Elisa Valero). Golden Films Internacionál. Colour.
In Franco's semi-sequel to Amando de Ossorio's *Blind Dead* series, four women arrive at a gloomy Mediterranean hotel for a vacation. They discover the ruins of an ancient monastery nearby and soon the undead Templarios Knights are leaving their graves to perform the usual blood sacrifices.
✦✧

MAN SIZE
USA, 1986. Dir: Michael Zen. Colour.
This hardcore feature apparently includes a King Kong scene.
✦

THE MAN THEY COULD NOT HANG
USA, 1939. Dir: Nick Grindé. With: Boris Karloff, Lorna Gray, Robert Wilcox, Roger Pryor, Don Beddoe, Ann Doran. Columbia/Favorite Films. B&W.
The first, and probably best, of five mad doctor movies Karloff starred in for Columbia during the late 1930s and early 1940s. After being unjustly executed for murder, Karloff's Dr Henryk Savaad has his assistant Lang (Byron Foulger) use a mechanical heart to bring him back from the dead. The crazed doctor, his neck broken by the hangman's noose, invites those he believes responsible for his death to a mansion, where he begins killing them off one by one. Karloff gives his usual fine performance, here supported by good production values and imaginative direction. With Charles Trowbridge. This was cut by four minutes when originally released in Britain.
✦✦✦

THE MAN WHO TURNED TO STONE
USA, 1957. Dir: Leslie Kardos. With: Victory Jory, Ann Doran, Charlotte Autin, William Hudson, Paul Cavanagh, Frederick Ledebur. Clover/Columbia. B&W.
Originally titled *The Petrified Man*. Jory underplays his role as the sinister Dr Nurdock, the leader of a group of eighteenth century scientists who retain their youthful appearance after 200 years by stealing the life-force from the inmates of a women's prison. A typically silly low-budget premise from producer Sam Katzman, but the scenes where the scientists' flesh turns to stone when their energy dissipates are quite effective.
✦✦

THE MAN WHO WOULDN'T DIE
USA, 1942. Dir: Herbert I. Leeds. With: Lloyd Nolan, Marjorie Weaver, Helene Reynolds, Henry Wilcoxon, Richard Derr, Jeff Corey. Twentieth Century-Fox. B&W.
Nolan stars as Brett Halliday's wise-cracking private detective Michael (Mike) Shayne in this bizarre murder mystery. Based on the novel *No Coffin for the Corpse* by Clayton Rawson, Shayne becomes involved in a convoluted plot in which a supposedly-dead Swami returns from the grave for revenge. Although it all turns out to be an attempt at blackmail, the scenes involving the walking 'corpse' (LeRoy Mason) are pretty spooky. Corey turns up as a mortician in this fifth entry in the low-budget series. With Billy Bevan.
Sequel: JUST OFF BROADWAY (1942)
✦✦✧

THE MAN WITHIN
(Orig: DER ANDERE. USA: aka DR. HALLERS)
Germany, 1930. Dir: Max Glass. With: Fritz Kortner, Käthe von Nagy, Heinrich George, Hermine Sterler, Ursula von Dieman, Eduard von Winterstein. Terra/Tobis Forenfilms. B&W.
Second film version of the play by Paul Lindau, about a man with a murderous alter-ego.
Remake: LE PROCUREUR HALLERS (qv; 1930)
✦

THE MAN WITHOUT A BODY
UK, 1957. Dir: W. Lee Wilder and Charles Saunders. With: Robert Hutton, George Coulouris, Julia Arnall, Nadja

Regin, Sheldon Lawrence, Michael Golden. Filmways/Eros/Paramount. B&W.
When ruthless New York tycoon Karl Brussard (Coulouris) is diagnosed as suffering from an inoperable brain tumour, he travels to London where he wants Dr Phil Merritt (Hutton) to transplant the revived head of French seer Nostradamus (Golden) onto his body. After the jealous Brussard shoots his romantic rival Lew Waldenhouse (Lawrence), the head is transplanted onto the body of the dying laboratory assistant before the ruined financier plunges to his death and the head hangs itself. This silly thriller was co-directed by Billy Wilder's less-talented brother.
✦✧

THE MAN WITHOUT A SOUL
(USA: I BELIEVE)
UK, 1916 (1917). Dir: George Loane Tucker. With: Milton Rosmer, Edna Flugrath, Barbara Everest, Edward O'Neill, Charles Rock, Frank Stanmore. London/Jury/Cosmotofilm/Sherman Pictures. B&W.
A scientist brings a divinity student back to life, but the latter has no soul. After praying, his soul is restored to him. Scripted by director Tucker, this silent drama is based on a story by Kenelm Foss.
✦

THE MAN WITH 2 HEADS
USA/UK, 1971 (1972). Dir: Andy Milligan. With: Denis De Marne, Julia Stratton, Gay Feld, Jacqueline Lawrence, Laurence Davies, Berwick Kaler. Constitution/Mishkin. Colour.
'Shudder in the House of Degradation!' warned the ads for this laughable version of Robert Louis Stevenson's story, supposedly set in London in 1835. Dr William Jekyll's potion releases his evil alter-ego, Mr Blood, a sex fiend with bushy eyebrows. More inept Milligan madness (he was scriptwriter, cinematographer and director), filmed in 'gory color' under the title *Dr. Jekyll and Mr. Blood.*
Remake: I, MONSTER (qv; 1971)
✦

THE MAN WITH TWO LIVES
USA, 1942. Dir: Phil Rosen. With: Edward Norris, Marlo Dwyer, Eleanor Lawson, Frederick Burton, Addison Richards, Hugh Sothern. Monogram. B&W.
Low-budget thriller in which Norris stars as a doctor's assistant who is killed in a car crash and returned to life by a scientist at midnight. However, the soul of a gangster, electrocuted at the same moment, takes over his mind and body. It all turns out to be a dream. With Kenneth (Kenne) Duncan.
✦✧

THE MANY FACES OF CHRISTOPHER LEE
UK, 1995. With: Christopher Lee. Lumiere. Colour.
Hour-long autobiographical documentary hosted by the actor and featuring numerous clips from his films, home movie footage from *Dracula Prince of Darkness* (1965), and Lee's personal reminiscences of Peter Cushing and Vincent Price.
✦✦✧

FREDRIC MARCH
(Frederick McIntyre Bickel) [1897-1975]

American leading man who won an Academy Award for his portrayal of the title roles in *Dr. Jekyll and Mr. Hyde* (1931).
qv: *Parade of the Award Nominees* (1932).

MARDI GRAS MASSACRE
USA, 1976 (1978). Dir: J. (Jack) Weis. With: Curt Dawson, Gwen Arment, Bill Metzo, Laura Misch, Cathryn Lacey, Nancy Dancer. Weis/Majestic International/Omni Capital Releasing. Colour.
Low-budget chiller set in New Orleans, in which a masked madman who believes he is a 2,000 year-old Aztec priest sacrifices naked prostitutes to an ancient goddess. Weis also directed the voodoo thriller *Crypt of Dark Secrets* (1976), which is sometimes mistakenly listed as an alternative title for this film.
✦

MARERIDT
Denmark, 1987 (1991). Dir: Peter Nielsen. With: Peter Nielsen, Henrik Rytter, Peder Pedersen, Charlotte Nielsen. Colour/B&W.
Eleven minute short, released in Denmark on an anthology video, *Fantavision*, featuring a number of amateur shorts. In a black and white nightmare sequence, two friends visiting the director (who also created the make-up) turn into a werewolf and a Frankenstein Monster. This includes a clip from (Abbott and Costello) *Meet Frankenstein* (1948). The title translates as 'Nightmare'.
✦✧

MARIE-COOKIE AND THE KILLER TARANTULA
Spain, 1998. Dir: Jess (Jesús) Franco. With: Lina Romay (Rosa Maria Almirall), Michelle Bauer (Michelle McClellan), Linnea Quigley, Analia Ivars, Amber Newman. Draculina Cine. Colour.
Romay plays an exotic dancer who can transform herself into a fake-looking tarantula (with clearly visible strings). This also includes a number of lesbian sex scenes between the stars.
✦

MARIE LA LOUVE
France/Spain/Italy, 1991. Dir: Daniel Wronecki. With: Aurélie Gibert, Frédéric Pellegeay, Pierre Debauche, Dora Doll, Etienne Bierry, Sylvie Herbert. FR3/SFP/Beta Taurus/Rete Italia/TVE/RTP. Colour.
TV movie about werewolves and witchcraft, based on the novel *Roc ou la Malédiction* by Claude Seignolle, and originally shown as part of the Spanish series *Sabbath*. Set in the nineteenth century, the beautiful Marie (Gibert) is accused of being a witch by her fellow villagers. When the man who still wants to marry her is murdered, Marie curses his family, who are then terrorised by strange cries from the forest...
✦✧

THE MARK OF DRACULA
USA, 1997 (1998). Dir: Ron Ford. With: Mark Allen, Tim Sullivan, Roxanne Coyne, Ron Ford, Tonja McCoy, Randal Malone. Wildcat Entertainment. Colour.
This very low-budget independent video release appears to be an ill-advised tribute to the type of films Hammer used to make. An undead Lucy Westenra (Coyne) convinces reclusive geneticist Dr Warren (Sullivan) to clone Dracula from blood still on the one hundred year-old wooden stake that destroyed her master. However, the Count (Allen, with a goatee beard) is not at all pleased to be resurrected and orders Warren to find a cure for vampirism by experimenting on two couples who are camping in the area. With director Ford as the portly Sheriff Cobb, and Malone as comedy-relief mortician Mortimer Poe.
✦

THE MARK OF LILITH
UK, 1986. Dir: Bruna Fionda, Polly Gladwin and Islling Mack-Nataf. With: Pamela Lofton, Susan Franklyn, Jeremy Peters, Patricia St. Hilaire, Michael Cudlip, Faye Chang. Rc-Vamp Productions/London College of Printing/Circles. Colour.
Half-hour 16mm experimental short about a black lesbian film-maker (Lofton) researching mythic images of monstrous women. She meets immortal bisexual female vampire Lillia (Franklyn), who wants to escape from her undead male companion. They discuss politics, patriarchy and horror films.
✦

MARK OF THE VAMPIRE
USA, 1935. Dir: Tod Browning. With: Lionel Barrymore, Elizabeth Allan, Bela Lugosi, Lionel Atwill, Jean Hersholt, Donald Meek. Metro-Goldwyn-Mayer. B&W.
Browning's remake of his own *London After Midnight* (1927), originally announced as *Vampires of Prague*, with the multiple roles taken by Lon Chaney Sr in the original here split between Barrymore, Atwill

and Lugosi. When the body of Sir Karell Borotyn (Holmes Herbert) is discovered drained of blood, it is apparently the work of a pair of vampires, Count Mora (Lugosi) and his daughter Luna (Carol [Caroll] Borland). However, disappointingly, it all turns out to be a plot by Barrymore's Professor Zelen and Atwill's police inspector to trap the real killer. Browning gets the chance to re-use a number of ideas from *Dracula* (1931), and such archetypal images as fog-shrouded graveyards, cobwebbed castles, bats and wolves are atmospherically photographed by the great James Wong Howe. Lugosi is effective in a mostly non-speaking role, and the best scene has twenty-one year-old Borland descending through the air on giant bat wings. The original trailer features Lugosi talking to the audience in character and flying shots of Borland not included in the final release print.
✦✦✦✧

MARLEY'S REVENGE: THE MONSTER MOVIE

USA, 1989. Dir: Jet Elle. With: Donnie Broom. Electro. Colour.

Low-budget independent horror movie shot in Charlotte, North Carolina. When two friends are captured by a gang of redneck drug smugglers and a voodoo priestess is murdered, cannibal zombies attack those resposible.
✦

THE MARRIAGE OF THE BEAR

(Orig: MEDVEZHYA SVADBA)

Russia, 1926 (1928). Dir: Vladimir Gardin and Konstantin V. Eggert. With: Konstantin V. Eggert, Vera Malanovskaya, Natalya Rosenel, Yuri Zavadsky, A. Geirot. Mezhrabpom-Russ/Amkino. B&W.

Silent version of the folklore legend, based on the short story by Prosper Merimée. Count Michael Shemet (Eggert) turns into a bear-like brute on his wedding night and bites his bride to death.

Remake: LOKIS: REKOPILIS DOCTORA WITTENBACHA (qv; 1970)
✦✧

WILLIAM MARSHALL
[b 1924]

Sonorously-voiced black American actor who portrayed the dignified Prince Mamuwalde in both *Blacula* (1972) and *Scream Blacula Scream* (1973).

THE MARSUPIALS THE HOWLING III

(USA: HOWLING III)

Australia, 1987. Dir: Philippe Mora. With: Barry Otto, Max Fairchild, Imogen Annesley, Dasha Blahova, Leigh Biolos, Ralph Cotterill. Bancannia Pictures. Colour.

Another low-budget entry in the series, supposedly based on Gary Brandner's novel *The Howling III*. French-born director Mora, who also helmed the awful *Howling II Stirba — Werewolf Bitch* (1984), returns with story, screenwriter, co-producer and director credits (so you know who to blame). This is another mess, about a tribe of sympathetic lycanthropes being hunted down in the Australian outback. Jeroba (Annesley) escapes to the big city, falls in love with an assistant director on horror films (*Shape-Shifters Part 8*), and gives birth to a marsupial werewolf (special effects created by Bob McCarron). With cameos by Frank Thring as a Hitchcock-like director, veteran Michael Pate as the President and Barry Humphries as Dame Edna Everage handing out the Oscars.

Sequel: HOWLING IV THE ORIGINAL NIGHTMARE (qv; 1988)
✦✧

MARSUPILAMI:
Mars Meets Dr. Normanstein

USA, 1993. Voices: Dan Castellaneta, Jim Cummings, Steve Mackall, Tress MacNeille, Danny Mann, Frank Welker. The Walt Disney Company/CBS-TV. Colour.

Half-hour cartoon series (1993-94) based on the Belgian comic book character. In this story, the strange-looking cheetah Marsupilami (Mackall) and his slow-witted ape pal Maurice (Cummings) encounter mad scientist Dr. Normanstein (Cummings) who wants to transfer a brain into his Frankenstein Monster-like ape. In the end, the doctor's brain ends up in a chicken.
✦✧

Caroll Borland as the aptly-named Luna in Mark of the Vampire *(1935).*

MARTIN

USA, 1976. Dir: George A. Romero. With: John Amplas, Lincoln Maazel, Christine Forrest, Elyane Nadeau, Sarah Venable, Tom Savini. Laurel/Libra Films. Colour.

Bleak, downbeat, low-budget vampire movie from the director of *Night of the Living Dead* (1968), etc. After moving to Pennsylvania, eighteen year-old Martin (Amplas, making a powerful screen début) is accused of being a Nosferatu by an elderly relative (Maazel). In fact, the disturbed Martin ignores the traditional methods and kills with a razor blade and syringe, although lyrical flashbacks seem to suggest that his claims to be eighty-four years old are true. Make-up artist Savini, producer Richard Rubinstein and writer/director Romero (as a priest) all appear in cameo roles. The abrupt ending is particularly harrowing. Stein and Day published the novelisation by Romero and Susanna Sparrow in 1977.
✦✦✦✧

MARY, MARY, BLOODY MARY

Mexico, 1975. Dir: Juan López Moctezuma. With: Christina Ferrare, David Young, John Carradine, Helena Rojo, Arthur (Arturo) Hansel, Enrique Lucero. Translor Films/Roala/Cinema Management. Colour.

Ex-model Ferrare (Mrs John DeLorean) plays a bisexual vampire artist pursued by the police and haunted by a mysterious figure in black. It turns out to be her father (Carradine), rotting away as a blood-drinker, out to destroy her and so save her from the family curse. Carradine doesn't have many lines and remains masked (to hide the use of a double) until almost the end.
✦

MARY REILLY

UK, 1996. Dir: Stephen Frears. With: Julia Roberts, John Malkovich, George Cole, Michael Gambon, Kathy Staff, Glenn Close. TriStar Pictures. Colour.

Roman Polanski and Tim Burton were both previously connected with the project until Frears was chosen to direct this $45,000,000 Gothic romance. Production problems resulted in the film being extensively re-edited several times and a number of scenes were re-shot, but it was still a box office flop. Christopher Hampton's downbeat adaptation of Valerie Martin's bestselling novel benefits from atmospheric direction, grim set design and photography, and an evocative score. Despite her dodgy accent, Roberts (who was reportedly paid $10,000,000) gives a strong performance as the eponymous Irish maid who discovers that her employer Dr Jekyll (Malkovich) turns into the younger, murderous Mr Hyde. Only the climactic transformation seems out of place.

Remake: MI NOMBRE ES SOMBRA (qv; 1996)
✦✦✦✧

MARY SHELLEY'S FRANKENSTEIN

UK/USA/Switzerland, 1994. Dir: Kenneth Branagh. With: Robert De Niro, Kenneth Branagh, Tom Hulce, Helena Bonham Carter, Aidan Quinn, Ian Holm. TriStar Pictures/Japan Satellite Broadcasting/The IndieProd Company/American Zoetrope. Colour.

Yet another overblown, overlong, superfluous adaptation of a classic horror novel from co-producer Francis Ford Coppola (*Bram Stoker's Dracula* [1992], etc). It's hard to know what co-star/director Branagh spent the $60,000,000 budget on, particularly given the shoddy script and mis-judged performances. De Niro (in impressive make-up designed by Daniel Parker) attempts to bring some stature to his performance as the horribly scarred Monster, but in the end we've seen it all before. With Richard Briers as the blind Grandfather, John Cleese, Robert Hardy and Cherie Lunghi. Newmarket Press published the illustrated script.
✦✦

THE MASK
USA, 1994. Dir: Charles Russell. With: Jim Carrey, Peter Riegert, Peter Greene, Amy Yasbeck, Richard Jeni, Orestes Matacena. New Line Productions/Dark Horse Entertainment. Colour.
Hugely successful comedy/fantasy based on the Dark Horse comic book. When Edge City bank clerk Stanley Ipkiss (the irritating Carrey) discovers the ancient wooden mask of Loki and puts it on, he is transformed (thanks to Greg Cannom's make-up and the stunning Oscar-nominated CGI effects created by Industrial Light & Magic) into a Tex Avery-inspired green-faced goblin. With his scene-stealing dog Milo, Stanley sets out to revenge himself on those people who wronged him and find the girl of his dreams (newcomer Cameron Diaz). A children's cartoon TV series followed in 1995. 'Smokin'!'
Sequel: THE MASK (qv; 1995-96)
✦✦✦✧

THE MASK
USA, 1995-96. Voices: Rob Paulsen, Tim Curry, Jim Cummings, Tress MacNeille, Mary McDonald-Lewis, Frank Welker. New Line Television/Dark Horse Entertainment/ Film Roman/Sunbow Entertainment/CBS-TV. Colour.
Half-hour children's cartoon TV series (twenty-four episodes) based on the successful 1994 movie, in which Stanley Impkiss (Paulsen) puts on the mask of Loki and transforms into a manic hero to battle the plans of evil scientist Pretorius (Curry) and his Frankenstein Monster-like assistant, Walter. With additional music by Randy Edelman.
✦✦✧

ILONA MASSEY
(Ilona Hajmassy) [1910-1974]

Hungarian actress and singer. A discovery of Louis B. Mayer, she made her Hollywood début in 1937 and appeared in several musicals before playing Baroness Elsa Frankenstein in *Frankenstein Meets the Wolf Man* (1943).

PAUL MASSIE
[b 1932]

Canadian-born stage and screen actor who worked in Britain for many years and played the title role and his alter-ego in Hammer's *The Two Faces of Dr. Jekyll* (1960).

MASTER MINDS
USA, 1949. Dir: Jean Yarbrough. With: Leo Gorcey and The Bowery Boys, Huntz Hall, Gabriel Dell, Alan Napier, Glenn Strange, Jane Adams. Monogram Pictures. B&W.
The Bowery Boys (who started as the Dead End Kids in the classic 1937 gangster thriller *Dead End* and went on to appear [later as the East Side Kids] in series for Warner Bros, Universal and Monogram) had a number of run-ins with the horror genre, including two meetings with Bela Lugosi. In this slightly better-than-usual Bowery Boys comedy, Napier's mad scientist kidnaps carnival fortune teller Satch (Hall) and plans to create a new race of supermen using a serum derived from human lymphatic glands. After transforming an ape into Atlas the beast-man (Strange, in make-up by the great Jack Pierce), he decides that Satch's brain is the perfect fit for his creation. With Skelton Knaggs and Minerva Urecal.
✦✦

MASTER OF HORROR
(Orig: OBRAS MAESTRAS DEL TERROR)
Argentina, 1960 (1965). Dir: Enrique Carreras. With: Narciso Ibañez Menta, Carlos Estrada, Mercedes Carreras, Narciso Ibañez Serrador, Lilian Valmar, Iñez Moreno. Produciones Vicente Marco/Argentina Sono Film/US Films. B&W.
Anthology film based on three stories by Edgar Allan Poe and each starring Menta, Argentina's top horror star. He portrays a sadistic murderer in 'The Cask of Amontillado', and the scheeming mesmerist in 'The Facts in the Case of M. Valdemar' (remade by Roger Corman in *Tales of Terror* [1962]). The English-language version, released by Jack H. Harris, dropped the first and longest episode, 'The Tell-Tale Heart', in which Menta plays an old miser. From the director of *El Fantasma de la Opereta* (1955).
✦✧

MASTER OF MOSQUITON
(USA: aka MOSQUITON PROJECT)
Japan, circa 1998 (1999). Dir: Hiroshi Negishi. Voices: Heather Bryson, Guil Lunde, Carol Matthews. Zero-G-Room/Nippon Columbia/ADV Films. Colour.
Hour-long anime in which Transylvanian teen heiress Innaho (Bryson) resurrects the eponymous vampire (Lunde) in her quest for immortality. While the couple set out on a quest for the O-Part, a legendary device that bestows eternal life upon the holder, alien invaders from a giant pyramid battle mummies, Rasputin and the Count de Saint Germaine for control of 1920s London. The English-language version was produced, written and directed by Matt Greenfield. The undead Mosquiton was voiced by Takehito Koyasu in the original version.
✦✧

RICHARD MATHESON
[b 1926]

Acclaimed American author and screenwriter who began his career working for the science fiction pulp magazines in the 1950s. He made the transition to screenwriter by adapting his 1956 novel *The Incredible Shrinking Man* (1957). In the early 1960s Matheson expanded a quartet of Edgar Allan Poe's works for Roger Corman (*The Fall of the House of Usher* [1960]; *Pit and the Pendulum* [1961]; *Tales of Terror* [1962] and *The Raven* [1963]), and he has written numerous scripts for television. His 1954 vampire novel *I am Legend* has been filmed twice to date (as *The Last Man on Earth* in 1961 and *The Ωmega Man* in 1971), and he adapted another of his own novels as *The Legend of Hell House* (1973).
qv: *Dead of Night* (1977); *Dracula* (1972); *Late Night Horror: 'No Such Thing as a Vampire'* (1968); *The Night Stalker* (1971); *The Night Strangler* (1972); *100 Years of Horror: 'Boris Karloff'* (1996); *Rod Serling's Night Gallery: 'The Big Surprise'* (1971); *Rod Serling's Night Gallery: 'The Funeral'* (1971); *Scream of the Wolf* (1974); *Star Trek: 'The Enemy Within'* (1966); *Trilogy of Terror* (1975); *Trilogy of Terror II* (1996); *Twilight Zone Rod Serling's Lost Classics* (1994).

MATINEE THEATER:
Dracula
USA, 1956. With: John Carradine. NBC-TV. B&W.
Who else but Carradine could have portrayed the first TV Dracula (with a moustache)? Originally broadcast live on 23 November.
Episode remake: DRACULA (qv; 1958)
✦✦

Dr. Jekyll and Mr. Hyde
USA, 1957. With: Douglas Montgomery, Lisa Daniels, Chet Stratton, Lumsden Hare, Patrick Macnee. NBC-TV. B&W.
Live version of Robert Louis Stevenson's story, with simple make-up effects for Montgomery as Dr Jekyll and Mr Hyde.
Episode remake: LE TESTAMENT DU DOCTEUR CORDELIER (qv; 1959)
✦✦

Frankenstein
USA, 1957. With: Primo Carnera, John Conte. NBC-TV. B&W.
Hour-long drama, loosely based on Mary Shelley's novel. Frankenstein is blinded during his experiment, but the Monster (former world heavyweight boxing champion Carnera) visits his creator in hospital and demands a mate, before falling from a castle parapet to his apparent death. Hosted by Conte.
Episode remake: FRANKENSTEIN (qv; 1965)
✦✧

McCLOUD: McCLOUD MEETS DRACULA
USA, 1977. Dir: Bruce Kessler. With: Dennis Weaver, J.D. Cannon, Terry Carter, John Carradine, Diana Muldaur,

Bud Abbott and Lou Costello Meet Frankenstein *(1948), plus the Wolf Man and Dracula.*

Reggie Nalder. Universal/Glen A. Larson Productions/ NBC-TV. Colour.
Made-for-TV movie in the long-running series (1970-77, forty-six episodes) based on *Coogan's Bluff* (1968), originally shown as part of the *NBC Mystery Movie* slot. While the New York police force searches for a sniper (Joe Stone) terrorising the city, veteran Hollywood horror star Loren Belasco (Carradine, in great form), who may or may not be the real Count Dracula, is a suspect when Marshall Sam McCloud (Weaver) is called in to investigate a series of apparent vampire attacks. Nalder plays Morris the creepy butler, and talk show host Tom Snyder appears as himself, along with clips from *House of Dracula* (1945) on TV.
✦✦✦

FRANCIS MATTHEWS
[b 1927]

British film and TV actor who made a somewhat ineffectual hero in such Hammer horrors as *The Revenge of Frankenstein* (1958) and *Dracula Prince of Darkness* (1965).
qv: *Flesh and Blood: The Hammer Heritage of Horror* (1994); *Hammer A-Z* (1997).

MEET FRANKENSTEIN
(aka BUD ABBOTT LOU COSTELLO MEET FRANKENSTEIN. UK: ABBOTT AND COSTELLO MEET THE GHOSTS)
USA, 1948. Dir: Charles Barton. With: Bud Abbott, Lou Costello, Lon Chaney, Bela Lugosi, Glenn Strange, Lenore Aubert. Universal-International. B&W.

Originally entitled *The Brain of Frankenstein* and intended to be a serious entry in the series, this marked Universal's last outing for all its classic monsters. Bud and Lou (in probably their best film) team up with Chaney Jr's Lawrence Talbot/Wolf Man to stop Dr Lahos/Dracula (sixty-five year-old Lugosi, playing the role for the second and last time on screen) and female mad scientist Sandra Mornay (Aubert) from transplanting Lou's brain into the Frankenstein Monster (Strange). For the climactic sequence, it's Chaney under the Frankenstein make-up throwing Aubert's stunt double through a window, after Strange broke his foot. Director Barton plays the horror elements straight, thus emphasising the classic comedy routines, and an uncredited Vincent Price is heard as the Invisible Man. Costello apparently compiled his own collection of 'out-takes'. The script was published in 1990 by MagicImage Filmbooks.
Remake: CASTLE OF THE MONSTERS (qv; 1957)
✦✦✦✦✧

MEN IN BLACK THE SERIES:
The Symbiote Syndrome
USA, 1997. Dir: Nathan Chew. Voices: Keith Diamond, Jennifer Lien, Ed O'Ross, Cameron Clarke, Bob Glouberman, Kurtwood Smith. Adelaide Productions/ Amblin Entertainment/The WB Network. Colour.
Sophisticated half-hour cartoon TV series (1997-) based on the Malibu comics by Lowell Cunningham and inspired by the 1997 hit

movie starring Tommy Lee Jones and Will Smith. K (O'Ross) and J (Diamond) are two members of a secret organisation dedicated to hunting down illegal aliens within Earth's atmosphere. In this episode they encounter a disturbed vampiric alien posing as a New York cab driver who steals the life essence of his victims and shares a symbiotic relationship with K.
✦✦✦

FERDY MAYNE
(Ferdinand Mayer-Boerckel) [1916-1998]

German-born film and TV actor based in Britain. Often cast as a stylish villain, he played vampires in the spoofs *Dance of the Vampires* (1966) and *The Vampire Happening* (1971), and Count Dracula in the TV series *Frankenstein's Auntie* (1986).
qv: *Flesh and Blood: The Hammer Heritage of Horror* (1994); *The Greatest American Hero: 'The Resurrection Of Carlini'* (1982); *The Horror Star* (1981); *Howling II Stirba — Werewolf Bitch* (1984); *Knight Moves* (1992); *The Magic Christian* (1969); *My Lovely Monster* (1990); *100 Years of Horror: 'Blood-Drinking Beings'* (1996); *The Vampire Lovers* (1970).

RODDY McDOWALL
[1928-1998]

British child actor and celebrity photographer in Hollywood since 1940. As a fussy adult performer, his roles often bordered on the bizarre or psychotic. The star of the *Planet of the Apes* film and TV series (playing various intelligent simians), he also portrayed ham horror host Peter Vincent in the vampire comedies *Fright Night* (1985) and *Fright Night Part 2* (1988).
qv: *Biography: 'Boris Karloff the Gentle Monster'* (1995); *The Fantastic Journey: 'Funhouse'* (1976); *Nightmare Classics: 'Carmilla'* (1989); *The Snoop Sisters: A Black Day for Bluebeard* (1973); *The Tick: 'The Tick vs. Dinosaur Neil'* (1994).

DARREN McGAVIN
[b 1922]

American actor who played reporter Carl Kolchak in the TV movies *The Night Stalker* (1971) and *The Night Strangler* (1972) as well as the series *The Night Stalker/Kolchak: The Night Stalker* (1974-75).
qv: *Dead Heat* (1988); *The Demon and the Mummy* (1975); *Happy Hell Night* (1991); *The Night Stalker: Two Tales of Terror* (1974).

GEORGE MELFORD
[1889-1961]

American director who, after starting his career as an actor in 1909, turned to directing two years later. Although his best-known film is probably *The Sheik* (1921), he also directed the Spanish-language *Dracula* (1931) on the same Universal sets as Tod Browning's version. In the 1950s he returned to acting in several Biblical epics.

GEORGES MÉLIÈS
[1861-1938]

Pioneer French film-maker who reputedly 'invented' special effects ('trick films') when a jammed camera transformed an omnibus into a hearse. Forgotten and bankrupt by the First World War, Méliès was reduced to selling toys at a railway station until he was rediscovered in his final years.
qv: *Cleopatra* (1899); *The Haunted Castle* (1896); *The Monster* (1903).

MEN OF ACTION MEET WOMEN OF DRAKULA
Philippines, 1969. Dir: Artemio O. Marquez. With: Dante Varona, Eddie Torrento, Ruben Obligacion, Norman Henson, Ernesto Beren, Angelito Marquez. Villanueva.

A troupe of tumbler/wrestlers apparently battle Dracula and his band of vampire women in this obscure Filipino movie.
✦

ANDREE MELLY
[b 1932]

British actress, the sister of jazz musician George Melly. She portrayed Gina the vampire in Hammer's *The Brides of Dracula* (1960) and spoofed the role in *The Horror of It All* (1963).

FERNANDO MÉNDEZ
[1908-1966]

Mexican director of *The Vampire* (1957) and *The Vampire's Coffin* (1957), both starring Germán Robles as the undead Count Lavud.

MERIDIAN
(aka KISS OF THE BEAST. UK: PHANTOMS)
Italy/USA, 1990. Dir: Charles Band. With: Sherilyn Fenn, Malcolm Jamieson, Hilary Mason, Charlie (Spradling), Alex Daniels, Phil Fondacaro. Full Moon Entertainment. Colour.

Erotic reworking of *Beauty and the Beast*. Young heiress Catherine (Fenn, from TV's *Twin Peaks* [1990-91]) returns to her family estate in Italy. When she invites the players from a travelling carnival to dine at the castle, Catherine becomes involved with the twin Fauvrey brothers, the evil Lawrence and the noble Oliver (both played by Jamieson). The only problem is that Oliver is suffering from a 400 year-old curse that transforms him into a werewolf-like beast (Daniels, in make-up created by Greg Cannom) when he is sexually aroused.
✦✦

LEE MERIWETHER
[b 1935]

American actress and former beauty queen. Best known for playing the Catwoman in the 1966 *Batman* movie, she also portrayed the vampiric Lily on TV's *The Munsters Today* (1988-91).
qv: *Cruise into Terror* (1978); *Murder, She Wrote* (1995).

MESSIAH OF EVIL
(aka DEAD PEOPLE/RETURN OF THE LIVING DEAD/ REVENGE OF THE SCREAMING DEAD/THE SECOND COMING)
USA, 1973 (1975). Dir: Willard Huyck. With: Michael Greer, Mariana Hill, Royal Dano, Elisha Cook (Jr), Joy Bang, Anitra Ford. V-M/International Cinefilm Corporation. Colour.

A low-budget variation on *Night of the Living Dead* (1968), co-scripted by director Huyck and producer Gloria Katz (the team behind *American Graffiti* [1973], etc). Arletty (Hill) is looking for her missing artist-father Joseph Lang (Dano) in the Californian coastal town of Point Dune, where a 'Dark Stranger' returns after one hundred years to spread a mysterious sickness which turns the inhabitants into vampiric zombies. Crude editing and weak performances are offset by some poetic horrors. Veteran Cook Jr has a cameo as a drunken wino, while future film-makers Walter Hill and B.W.L. Norton are also featured down the cast list.
✦✧

METROSCOPIX
USA, 1953. (Dir: George Sidney). With: Pete Smith, Ed Payson. Metro-Goldwyn-Mayer. B&W.

Twenty-four minute 3-D compilation of three Pete Smith's Metroscopix Specials. This includes the novelty short *Third Dimensional Murder* (1940), featuring Payson as the Frankenstein Monster.
✦✦

MEZHPLANETNAYA REVOLUTSIYA
Russia, 1924. SFT. B&W.
Six minute silent propaganda cartoon in which capitalist and national socialist 'ghouls' drink a woman's blood through straws. The title translates as 'Interplanetary Revolution'.
✦

MICKEY'S GALA PREMIERE
USA, 1933. Dir: Bert Gillett. Voices: Walt Disney. Walt Disney/United Artists. B&W.
Seven minute cartoon short, produced by Disney, in which Mickey Mouse dreams he is attending the première of his new movie. It features caricatures of numerous Hollywood stars, including Count Dracula, the Frankenstein Monster and Quasimodo. This also features Pluto and was *Mickey Mouse* no. 15.
✦✦✦

MIDNIGHT
(aka BACKWOODS MASSACRE)
USA, 1980 (1982). Dir: John Russo. With: Lawrence Tierney, John Amplas, Melanie Verlin, Robin Walsh, David Marchick, Greg Besnak. Independent-International Pictures/Congregation. Colour.
An abused teenage runaway (Verlin) and her two companions are captured by a family of backwoods Satanists who drink blood and worship the matriarch's corpse in this low-budget chiller, filmed in Pittsburgh and based on a novel by director Russo. Special make-up effects created by Tom Savini. Samuel M. Sherman was co-executive producer.
Sequel: MIDNIGHT 2: SEX, DEATH AND VIDEOTAPE (1993)
✦✧

MIDNIGHT
USA, 1988 (1989). Dir: Norman Thaddeus Vane. With: Lynn Redgrave, Tony Curtis, Steve Parrish, Rita Gam, Frank Gorshin, Wolfman Jack. SVS Films/Midnight Inc/ Kuys Entertainment Group/Gomillion Studios. Colour.
Comedy murder-mystery in which Redgrave plays Vera, the eponymous vampiric TV horror hostess. Her unscrupulous boss Mr B (Curtis) will do anything to get the copyright to her hit chat show, and soon the bodies start piling up. From the director of *The Black Room* (1981) and *The Horror Star* (1981). With Kathleen Kinmont.
✦✧

THE MIDNIGHT HOUR
USA, 1985. Dir: Jack Bender. With: Jonelle Allen, Shari Belafonte-Harper, LeVar Burton, Peter de Luise, Jonna Lee, Kevin McCarthy. ABC Circle Films/ABC-TV. Colour.
Enjoyable TV movie in which Belafonte-Harper plays high school teen Melissa Cavender who, along with her friends, accidentally resurrects an eighteenth century vampire-witch ancestor on Halloween. Pretty soon the small Massachusetts town of Pitchford Cove is filled with ghouls, demons, the walking dead, a werewolf and a midget zombie (special make-up effects created by Tom Burman Studios). With Lee Montgomery, Dedee Pfeiffer, Dick Van Patten, Kurtwood Smith and the voice of Wolfman Jack.
✦✦✦

MIDNIGHT KISS
(aka IN THE MIDNIGHT HOUR. UK: VAMPIRE COP)
USA, 1992 (1993). Dir: Joel Bender. With: With: Michelle Owens, Michael McMillen, Robert Miano, B.J. Gates, Michael Shawn, Gregory A. Greer. In the Midnight Hour Productions/Academy Entertainment/Overseas Filmgroup. Colour.
Low budget thriller in which a psychotic vampire serial killer (Greer) bites Los Angeles police detective Carrie Blass (Owens), who begins to acquire his strength and hunger for blood. With the help of her partner and ex-husband Dennis (McMillen), she sets out to track down the undead murderer and destroy him before she is fully transformed. With a cameo by Celeste Yarnall, who starred in *The Velvet Vampire* (1971), as one of the evil vampire's first victims.
✦✧

MIDNIGHT MADNESS
USA, 1993. Dir: Eric Edwards. With: Tiffany Minx (Tiffany Mynx), Brittany O'Connell, Tanya Summers, Tony Tedeschi, Peter North, Tina Tyler. Dreamland Entertainment. Colour.
Hardcore feature in which a man (North) is seduced in his dreams by Phaedra (Minx), who is a succubus. Not to be confused with the 1980 Disney movie of the same title!
✦

MIDNIGHTMARE
(Orig: YE BANG GE SHENG)
Hong Kong, 1961. Dir: Yuan Quifeng. Shaw Brothers. B&W.
Reworking of the 1937 film *Song at Midnight*, itself inspired by *The Phantom of the Opera*.
Remake: THE PHANTOM LOVER (qv; 1995)
✦✧

MIDNIGHT RIDERS
USA, 1989. Dir: Jerry K. Jensen. With: Kevin Glover, Tim Lowe, Robert Larkins, Kevin Wiles, Kevin Young, Perry Idol. Video 10. Colour.
Gay porn vampire movie. Glover plays a character named Eripmav, which is 'vampire' spelled backwards.
✦

EL MIEDO NO ANDA EN BURRO
Mexico, 1973. Dir: Fernando Cortes. With: La India Maria (Maria Elena Velasco), Chelelo, Fernando Lujan, Emma Roldan, Oscar Ortiz Pinedo, Gloria Mayo. Diana Films. Colour.
Haunted house comedy in which a group of disgruntled heirs dress up as monsters, including a werewolf, a fanged Cyclops, a frog-man and a mummy-like creature, to scare the heroine and her poodle off the estate which the dog has inherited. This also includes an apparently real hunchbacked ghost, a gorilla and some non-living mummies. The title translates as 'Fear Doesn't Ride a Donkey'. Huh?
✦

THE MIGHTY GORGA
USA, 1969 (1971). Dir: David L. Hewitt. With: Anthony Eisley, Megan Timothy, Kent Taylor, Scott Brady, Lee Parrish, Bruce Kemp. Borelais Enterprises/American General Pictures. Colour.
King Kong (1933)-inspired adventure, filmed on a bottom-of-the-barrel budget in five days. When the money ran out, they ended up shooting at San Diego Zoo! Circus owner Mark Remington (Eisley) leads an expedition into the African jungle, where they discover a giant ape (a prop gorilla head and car coat with hair glued on). This also includes a native witch doctor (Kemp) and a battle between plastic dinosaurs. Advertised as 'The greatest horror monster alive!' It wasn't. With cinematographer Gary Graver, Greydon Clark and director Hewitt in featured roles.
✦

MIGHTY JOE YOUNG
USA, 1949. Dir: Ernest B. Schoedsack. With: Terry Moore, Ben Johnson, Robert Armstrong, Frank McHugh, Douglas Fowley, Nestor Paiva. Arko Productions/RKO Radio Pictures. B&W.
Following the cancellation of Willis O'Brien and Marcel Delgado's *Gwangi* project by RKO in 1942 (after a year of pre-production), producer Merian C. Cooper and director Schoedsack attempted to repeat the success of their classic *King Kong* (1933) with this lightweight adventure. When a giant gorilla is discovered as a household pet in Africa, showman Max O'Hara (Armstrong) takes the animal and its owner Jill Young (Moore) to America as his star nightclub attraction. However, the ape is tormented and runs amok before rescuing several children from a burning orphanage (in a climax that was originally colour-tinted). The excellent stop-motion animation is mostly the work of twenty-eight year-old Ray Harryhausen and Pete Peterson, under the guidance of technical creator O'Brien (who finally won the Academy Award he should have received for *King*

Kong). Co-produced by John Ford, this was filmed under the titles *Mr Joseph Young of Africa* and *The Great Joe Young*. A planned sequel, *Joe Meets Tarzan*, in which the giant ape would meet Lex Barker's jungle king, was never made due to the film's disappointing box office returns. A colourised print appeared in the late 1990s, along with a version restoring the original Technicolor two-negative tinting and toning process. This sequence was later 'recreated' for the 1998 laser disk release.

Remake: MIGHTY JOE YOUNG (qv; 1998)

✦✦✦

MIGHTY JOE YOUNG

USA/Tanzania, 1998. Dir: Ron Underwood. With: Bill Paxton, Charlize Theron, Rade Sherbedgia, Naveen Andrews, Regina King, David Palmer. Disney Enterprises/ Walt Disney Pictures/RKO Pictures/The Jacobson Company. Colour.

Unnecessary, but impressive-looking reworking of the 1949 original, aimed at younger audiences. When both their mothers are killed in Africa by evil poacher Strasser (Sherbedgia), Jill Young (Theron) befriends a young gorilla who because of a recessive gene grows into the eponymous fifteen-foot ape (stunningly created by Dream Quest Images, Rick Baker and others, and nominated for an Academy Award). Along comes friendly zoologist Gregg O'Hara (Paxton) who convices Jill to accompany Joe to a Los Angeles wildlife preserve, where the giant ape escapes onto Hollywood Boulevard before saving a small boy from a blazing Ferris-wheel. Although the set-pieces never match those in the original and the film is overlong at nearly two hours, children should still enjoy it. With Peter Firth as another villain, a nice acknowledgement of the original creators, and a brief cameo by Ray Harryhausen and Terry Moore as party guests.

✦✦✦

THE MIGHTY KONG

Korea/China/USA, 1998. Dir: Art Scott and James A. Simon. Voices: Dudley Moore, Jodi Benson, Randy Hamilton, William Sage III, Jason Gray-Stanford, Richard Newman. The Lana Film Company/Warner Bros. Colour.

Surprisingly serious feature-length children's cartoon, based on the classic *King Kong* story. This includes several forgettable songs by Richard M. Sherman and Robert B. Sherman (*Mary Poppins* [1964], etc), with Moore as the voice of showman C.B. Denham and Benson as heroine Ann Darrow. In the end, after falling from the top of the Empire State Building, Kong opens an eye — proving that even beauty could not kill the beast this time. There was a tie-in comic book.

✦✧

MIGHTY MAX:
Werewolves of Dunneglen

USA, 1993. Voices: Rob Paulsen, Tony Jay, Richard Moll, Tim Curry, Tress MacNeille. Film Roman/Bohbot/ Bluebird Canal/DA. Colour.

Werewolf episode of the young adult half-hour cartoon TV series (1993-94), based on the eponymous pocket toy and originally shown as part of the series *Amazin' Adventures*. Eleven year-old Max (Paulsen) travels through space and time with his talking bird Virgil (Jay) and giant warrior Norman (Moll), while attempting to escape the clutches of the evil Skullmaster (Curry).

✦✧

MIGHTY MORPHIN POWER RANGERS:
(Orig: ZYU RANGER)
Life's a Masquerade

USA/Japan, 1993. Dir: Robert Hughes. With: Austin St. John, Thuy Trang, Walter Jones, Amy Jo Johnson, David Yost, Jason Frank. Saban Entertainment/Renaissance Atlantic Entertainment/Toei Company/MMPR Productions/Fox Kids Network. Colour.

Popular half-hour superhero TV show (1993-96, 156 episodes) that combines special effects action footage from a Japanese *sentai* series with new sequences shot in America. Centuries ago, a legendary inter-dimensional being known as Zordon (Bob Manahan) came to the city of Angel Grove to establish a command centre for his never-ending struggle against evil. With the aid of his trusted assistant Alpha 5 (Romy J. Sharf), Zordon sought out six extraordinary teenagers and gave them the ability to transform into a superhuman fighting force who, in times of great need, could use their powers to also call upon colossal assault vehicles known as Zoids. In this episode, 10,000 year-old evil sorceress Rita Repulsa (Soga Machiko) creates a Karloffian Frankenstein Monster and sends it to destroy the Power Rangers, who are attending a costume party at the local youth centre. The Monster uses his neck bolts as a weapon and transforms into a giant to battle the Rangers' composite robot dinosaur Megazoid/Dragonzoid. This includes a party guest in a vampire costume and Billy (Yost) dressed as Sherlock Holmes.

✦

Trick or Treat

USA/Japan, 1993. Dir: Worth Keeter. With: Austin St. John, Thuy Trang, Walter Jones, Amy Jo Johnson, David Yost, Jason Frank. Saban Entertainment/Renaissance Atlantic Entertainment/Toei Company/MMPR Productions/Fox Kids Network. Colour.

While Kimberly Hart (Johnson) and Eugene 'Skull' Scullowicz (Jason Narvy) play the TV game show *Trick or Treat*, the evil Rita creates the monstrous Pumpkin Rapper to battle the Power Rangers. With Monty the game show host dressed as Count Dracula. 'Zedd's Monster Mash' (1994) was another Halloween episode.

Series sequel: POWER RANGERS ZEO (1996)

✦✧

MIGHTY MORPHIN POWER RANGERS THE MOVIE

Australia/USA, 1995. Dir: Bryan Spicer. With: Karan Ashley, Johnny Yong Bosch, Steve Cardenas, Jason David Frank, Amy Jo Johnson, David Yost. Twentieth Century Fox/Saban Entertainment/Toei Company. Colour.

Better than expected movie version of the popular TV series. This time the six colourful superpowered ninja teens have to battle the evil Ivan Ooze (Paul Freeman) and his monstrous servants, save a dying Zordon and prevent the adults of Angel Grove from becoming zombies. The great-looking special effects include a fight with a reanimated dinosaur skeleton and two gigantic CGI-created insectoid monsters. The music is surprisingly dated.

Sequel: TURBO A POWER RANGERS MOVIE (1997)

✦✦✦

MIGHTY MOUSE MEETS BAD BILL BUNION

USA, 1945. Dir: Mannie Davis. Voices: Tom Morrison. Terrytoons/Twentieth Century-Fox. Colour.

Paul Terry cartoon short starring the super-powered mouse (Morrison), which features Count Dracula.

Sequels: MIGHTY MOUSE IN KRAKATOA (1945) and THE JAIL BREAK (qv; 1946)

✦✧

MIGHTY MOUSE MEETS JEKYLL AND HYDE CAT

USA, 1944. Dir: Mannie Davis. Voices: Tom Morrison. Terrytoons/Twentieth Century-Fox. Colour.

Seven minute Paul Terry cartoon, set in Dr Jekyll's old house. The scientist's cat terrorises the mice also living there, until the super-powered Mighty Mouse arrives and beats him up.

Sequel: ELIZA ON ICE (1944)

✦✧

MIGHTY PEKING MAN
(aka GOLIATHON)

Hong Kong/India, 1977 (1979). Dir: Homer Gaugh (Peter Mak/Mak Yai-Kit/Ho Meng-Hua). With: Danny Lee (Lee Hassen/Li Hsiu-Hsien), Evelyne Kraft, Chen Cheng-Feng, Ah Wei, Huang Tsui-Hua, Chen Ping. Shaw Brothers/ World Northal Corporation. Colour.

$500,000 *King Kong* (1976)-inspired adventure in which blonde jungle woman Samantha (twenty year-old Swiss-born Kraft, also in *Lady Dracula* [1975]) falls in love with oriental hunter Johnny Feng (Lee), who captures a giant prehistoric apeman (special effects by Andrew Ryan [Teisho Arikawa]) and takes it back to Hong Kong to exhibit. The creature, of course, breaks free and goes on the rampage until it

is blown up with gasoline and falls from the island's tallest building, the Connaught Centre. Dino De Laurentiis could have sued. Originally released in a truncated version in America, Kraft's character dies at the end of the European print, entitled *Colossus of the Congo*. In 1999, Quentin Tarantino's Rolling Thunder Pictures reissued an uncut version for midnight screenings in America.
✦✧

DICK MILLER
[b 1928]

American character actor, often a regular in the films of Roger Corman, for whom he played the role of demented beatnik artist Walter Paisley in *A Bucket of Blood* (1959). He has subsequently recreated the character for a variety of directors paying homage to Corman's low-budget masterpiece.
qv: *Dead Heat* (1988); *Dr. Heckyl & Mr. Hype* (1980); *Ghost Writer* (1989); *Gremlins 2 The New Batch* (1990); *The Howling* (1980); *The Little Shop of Horrors* (1960); *Night of the Creeps* (1986); *Not of This Earth* (1957); *100 Years of Horror: 'Blood-Drinking Beings'* (1996); *100 Years of Horror: 'Boris Karloff'* (1996); *100 Years of Horror: 'Mutants'* (1996); *Runaway Daughters* (1994); *Small Soldiers* (1998).

PATSY RUTH MILLER
[1905-1995]

American actress who portrayed Esmeralda the gypsy girl opposite Lon Chaney Sr's Quasimodo in *The Hunchback of Notre Dame* (1923).

ANDY MILLIGAN
[1929-1991]

Untalented low-budget film-maker who began his career in the early 1960s making sex and gore movies on Staten Island and later included sequences shot in Britain in a failed attempt to give his amateurish productions some much-needed class. He died from AIDS.
qv: *Blood!* (1974); *The Body Beneath* (1971); *Guru the Mad Monk* (1970); *The Man With 2 Heads* (1971); *The Naked Witch* (1964); *The Rats Are Coming! The Werewolves Are Here!* (1972).

MILL OF THE STONE WOMEN
(Orig: IL MULINO DELLE DONNE DI PIETRA/LE MOULIN DES SUPPLICES. UK: DROPS OF BLOOD. USA: aka ICON)
Italy/France, 1960. Dir: Giorgio Ferroni. With: Pierre Brice, Scilla Gabel, Danny (Dany) Carrel, Wolfgang Preiss (Lupo Prezzo), Liana Orfei, Marco Guglielmi. Vanguard Film/Faro Film/Explorer Film/CIC/Galatea. Colour.
Filmed in Holland, and based on a story from *Flemish Tales* by Peter Van Weigen. German actor Preiss plays a mad professor who keeps his daughter alive by stealing the blood from young girls and petrifying the corpses into statues for his macabre carousel of death. Ferroni originally dedicated the film to Terence Fisher. Richard McNamara is credited as the director of the English-language version.
✦✦✧

MILTON THE MONSTER
USA, 1965-66. Dir: James 'Shamus' Culhane. Voices: Bob McFadden, Dayton Allen, Larry Best, Dayton Ilen, Bev Arnold, Hettie Galen. Hal Seegar Productions/ABC-TV. Colour.
Half-hour cartoon series (twenty-six episodes), also featuring episodes of *Fearless Fly*, *Penny Penguin*, *Muggy Doo*, *Stuffy Durma* and *Flukey Luke*. These six minute segments star the kindly monster Milton (McFadden), accidentally created by the evil Professor Weirdo (Allen) and Count Kook (Best) in their Horrible Hill laboratory in Transylvania. Co-scripted by Jack Mercer (the voice of Popeye).
✦✧

MIND FUCK
Hong Kong, 1983. Dir: Tu Mah-Wu. With: Yuen Lui, Clare Chan. Colour.
Hardcore horrors about a woman who is poisoned by her unfaithful husband. She returns from the grave as a ghost seeking revenge. This also includes a hopping vampire and a hunchback.
✦

MIND RIPPER
(aka WES CRAVEN PRESENTS MIND RIPPER)
Bulgaria/USA, 1995. Dir: Joe Gayton. With: Lance Henriksen, Claire Stansfield, John Diehl, Natasha (Gregson) Wagner, Giovanni Ribisi, Gregory Sporleder. The Kushner-Locke Company/Outpost Production/Home Box Office. Colour.
Co-written and produced by Jonathan Craven, and executive produced by his father Wes. This low-budget thriller is set in a remote research facility where an experiment with a secret genetic virus results in the creation of Thor (Dan Blom), an acronym for Transmuted Human Organism. When he breaks loose, the reanimated superhuman soldier uses his tongue tentacle to suck the cholestrol out of human brains to survive (shades of *The Braniac* [1961/63]!). Special make-up effects created by Image Animation. Released to cable TV in America and directly to video in Britain, this originally started out as *The Hills Have Eyes III* and was filmed under the title *The Outpost*.
✦✧

MI NOMBRE ES SOMBRA
(aka SR. SOMBRA)
Spain, 1996. Dir: Gonzalo Suarez. With: Javier Bardem, Amparo Larranaga, Eric Francoise Gendrom. Ditirambo/Rocabruno/TVE. Colour.
Another version of Robert Louis Stevenson's *Strange Case of Dr. Jekyll and Mr. Hyde*, produced, directed and scripted by Suarez. In 1998, Al Pacino announced that he was planning to star in a version of the story, to be scripted by David Mamet.
✦✧

IL MIO AMICO JEKYLL
Italy, 1960. Dir: Marino Girolami. With: Ugo Tognazzi, Abbe Lane, Hélène Chanel, Carlo Croccolo, Raimondo Vianello, Linda Sini. MG Cinematográfica/Cei Incom/Union. B&W.
Silly comedy, supposedly based on Robert Louis Stevenson's novel. The ugly Professor Fabius (Vianello) invents a machine which can transfer his personality into the handsome body of girl's schoolteacher Giacinto (Tognazzi). He tries to organise orgies with the girls, but ends up trapped as a chimpanzee at the zoo. The title translates as 'My Friend Dr Jekyll'.
✦

SOLEDAD MIRANDA
(Soledad Redon Bueno) [1943-1971]

Striking Portuguese-Spanish actress best known for her films with Jesús Franco. Also credited as 'Susann Korda' in the director's more explicit movies. She was killed in a car crash.
qv: *Bram Stoker's Count Dracula* (1970); *Cuadecuc (Vampir)* (1970); *Pyro* (1963); *Vampiros Lesbos* (1970).

THE MISSING MUMMY
USA, 1915. With: Bud Duncan, Charles Inslee, Ethel Teare. Kalem. B&W.
Silent short in which a man disguises himself as a mummy.
✦

MISSION GENESIS:
(UK: DWB DEEPWATER BLACK)
Refugee
Canada/USA, 1997. Dir: George Mendeluk. With: Gordon Michael Woolvett, Nicole DeBoer, Jason Cadieux, Julie Khaner, Graig Kirkwood, Sara Sahr. Orbit 1 Productions/

Sunbow Entertainment/YTV/Empire Entertainment/Sci-Fi Channel. Colour.
Half-hour juvenile science fiction TV series, created by Jeff Copeland and Barry Pearson and loosely based on the novels by Ken Catran. The titular spaceship and its crew of six teen clones and a hologram (Khaner) speed towards Earth to restore human life to a home they have never known. In this episode, responding to a lifepod distress signal, the crew of the *Deepwater* bring aboard its only passenger, Kyra (Tara Sloan). However, she turns out to be a genetically-enhanced psychic vampire who uses physical touch to feed upon their emotions.
✦✧

MISSION: IMPOSSIBLE:
The Sands of Seth
Australia/USA, 1990. Dir: Colin Budds. With: Peter Graves (Peter Aurness), Thaao Penghlis, Tony Hamilton, Phil Morris, Jane Badler, Gerard Kennedy. Paramount/Jeffrey Hayes Productions/ABC-TV. Colour.
Belated revival (1988-90, thirty-five episodes) of the popular sci-spy TV series (1966-72) created by Bruce Geller, about a select group of secret government agents. In this final episode, Jim Phelps (Graves) and his IMF (Impossible Missions Force) team must stop Selim (Tim Elliott), the mad leader of an ancient Egyptian cult, who plots to kill the leaders of modern-day Egypt and steal the cursed mummy of the High Priest of Seth so that he can return his country to the rule of the Pharaohs. This uses many of the names and clichés from the old Universal series, plus two fake mummies and the flashback sequence from *The Mummy* (1933) shown in a desert pool. Hit theme music by Lalo Schifrin.
Series remake: MISSION: IMPOSSIBLE (1996)
✦✦✦

MISS JEKYLL AND MADAME HYDE
USA, 1915. Dir: Charles L. Gaskill. With: Helen Gardner, Paul Scardon. Vitagraph. B&W.
Satan (Scardon) sets out to claim the soul of an evil woman. Despite the title, this silent drama has nothing to do with Robert Louis Stevenson's story.
✦

MISS MAGIC
(Orig: LING HUAN XIAO JIE)
Hong Kong, 1988. Rainbow Video. Colour.
Horror comedy about an actress possessed by the ghost of an actor's wife who committed suicide. This includes a scene of performers playing levitating hopping vampires on a movie set.
✦✧

EL MISTERIO DEL CASTILLO ROJO
Spain, 1972. Dir: Jesús Franco. With: Jesús Franco, Alberto Dalbes, Yelena Samarina, Lina Romay (Rosa Maria Almirall), Manuel Pereiro, Mario Alex. Films Manacoa. Colour.
Franco's first film for his own production company apparently remains unfinished. It is a horror comedy in which the writer/director stars as a mad scientist creating a new race of zombies.
✦

CAMERON MITCHELL
(Cameron Mizell) [1918-1994]
American character actor in films and TV, who began as a promising lead but ended his career usually playing villains in low-budget genre movies.
qv: *Blood Suckers* (1965); *Demon Cop* (1990); *Frankenstein Island* (1981); *Island of Mutations* (1979); *The Offspring* (1986); *Raw Force* (1982); *Shadow Chasers: 'Blood and Magnolias'* (1986); *Terror on Tape* (1985); *The Tomb* (1985).

MIXED UP
(Orig: CHI GUI XIAN)
Hong Kong, 1985. Dir: Henry S.K. Chow (Henry Chen). With: Agnes Chan, Deborah Moore, Fanny Cheung, Lo Ho-Gai. World Video. Colour.
A teens-in-peril horror comedy featuring two zombie sailors menacing a group of switchboard operators on a holiday cruise. With a hopping vampire and a fanged Frankenstein-like creature who battle it out on a pleasure yacht during the climax.
✦✧

A MODERN SPHINX
USA, 1916. Dir: Charles Bennett. With: Winifred Greenwood, Edward Coxen, Robert Klein, George Field, Charles Newton, Nan Christy. American. B&W.
Thirty-three minute silent drama. After being put to sleep for 3,000 years, the daughter of an ancient Egyptian astrologer is awakened in modern times but takes poison after a tragic love affair. Her father reawakens her unharmed back in her own era.
✦

MODERN VAMPIRES
(UK: REVENANT)
USA, 1998 (1999). Dir: Richard Elfman. With: Casper Van Dien, Natasha Gregson Wagner, Gabriel Casseus, Kim Cattrall, Craig Ferguson, Natasha Lyonne. Revenant Productions/Muse-Wyman/Storm Entertainment. Colour.
Yet another failed attempt by director/co-producer Elfman (*Shrunken Heads* [1994], etc) to make a coherent movie. As usual the comedy sits uneasily with the nudity and violence when rebellious vampire Dallas (co-executive producer Van Dien) returns to Los Angeles and finds himself looking after undead hooker urchin Nico (Wagner) while confronting The Count (Robert Pastorelli) and evading an obsessed Van Helsing (Rod Steiger!) and his homeboy helpers. Rarely has such an impressive cast given such uniformly terrible performances. Rick Baker was special effects consultant. With Udo Kier as another vampire, a cameo by the director and great theme music by his brother, Danny.
✦✧

MOM
USA, 1989 (1991). Dir: Patrick Rand. With: Mark Thomas Miller, Jeanne Bates, Brion James, Mary McDonough, Art Evans, Stella Stevens. Epic Productions/TransWorld Entertainment. Colour.
Low-budget comedy chiller with James as blind cannibal/vampire Nestor Duvalier who bites his landlady, grey-haired Emily Dwyer (Bates), and turns her into a shades-wearing member of the undead. Her TV newsman son Clay (Miller) is embarrassed by her behaviour and tries to keep her locked up. Stevens has a fun cameo as a drunken hooker, and Claudia Christian turns up as a victim.
✦✧

LA MOMIA AZTECA
Mexico, 1957. Dir: Rafael (López) Portillo. With: Ramón Gay, Rosita Arenas, Crox Alvarado, Luis Aceves Casteñeda, Arturo Martinez, Jorge Mondragón. Cinematográfica Calderón. B&W.
The first in Portillo's popular series about an ugly Aztec mummy, scripted by Alfredo Salazar. Flor (Arenas), who is the reincarnation of Aztec princess Xochitl, leads her scientist fiancé Dr Almada (Gay) and his archeological expedition to an ancient pyramid, where they discover the still-living mummy of her warrior/lover Popoca, who is now the guardian of her tomb. Meanwhile, the evil Dr Krupp/The Bat (Casteñeda) attempts to steal a sacred breastplate and bracelet that hold the secret to a lost Aztec treasure. With Mexican wrestling heroes 'Lobo Negro' (Guillermo Hernández) and 'El Murciélago' (Jesús Velazquez). Scenes from this film were later re-edited into Jerry Warren's terrible *Attack of the Mayan Mummy* (1964).
Sequel: CURSE OF THE AZTEC MUMMY (qv; 1957)
✦✧

LAS MOMIAS DE GUANAJUATO
Mexico, 1970 (1972). Dir: Federico Curiel. With: Blue Demon (Alejandro Muñoz), El Mil Máscaras (Aaron Rodriguez), Santo (Rodolfo Guzmán Huerta or Eric del Castillo), Elsa Cardenas, Juan Gallardo, Jorge Pinqúino.

Presentacion del Niño Julio Cesar/Clasa-Mohme. Colour.
Mexican wrestlers Blue Demon and Mil Máscaras ('Thousand Masks') team up to battle electronically-controlled Aztec mummies in the real-life Mexican town of Guanajuato. With a special appearance by Santo, El Enmascarado de Plata. This is apparently the highest-grossing Mexican wrestling-monster movie to date and spawned two direct sequels.
Sequels: SANTO CONTRA LA HIJA DE FRANKESTEIN (qv; 1971), LA INVASIÓN DE LOS MUERTOS (qv; 1971) and EL ROBO DE LAS MOMIAS DE GUANAJUATO (qv; 1972)
✦✧

LAS MOMIAS DE SAN ANGEL
(aka TERROR EN SAN ANGEL)
Mexico, 1973. Dir: Arturo Martiínez. With: Rogelio Guerra, Alicia Encinas, Mil Máscaras (Aaron Rodriguez), Superzán, Lorena Velázquez, El Fantasma Blanco. Agrasanchez/Mario Cid/Azteca Films. Colour.
When a ghostly hunchback and his horde of mummies haunt an old house, it is up to a group of wrestling heroes led by Mil Máscaras ('Thousand Masks') to battle the mummified remains of priests and nuns in the real-life Mexican town of San Angel.
Sequel: LOS VAMPIROS DE COYOACAN (qv; 1973)
✦✧

MONA THE VAMPIRE
Canada/France, 1999. CINAR Films Inc/Alphanim/YTV/ France 3/Canal J. Colour.
Half-hour cartoon TV series (twenty-six episodes), based on the children's books by Sonia Holleyman, about the eponymous ten year-old who dresses up as a vampire and investigates weird and eerie things along with her quirky friends and her pet cat Fang.
✦✦

MONDO KEYHOLE
(aka THE WORST CRIME OF ALL!)
USA, 1966. Dir: John Lamb (and Jack Hill). With: Cathy Crowfoot, Nick Moriarty, Pluto Felix, V. Wren. Ajay/ Horizon/Boxoffice International. B&W.
'Adults only' sex/horror movie. Pornographer/rapist Howard (Moriarty) is punished by a lesbian karate expert in bondage gear (Crowfoot). His heroin-addicted wife attends a Hollywood costume ball where a man dressed as Dracula (Felix) announces that the punch is spiked with LSD.
✦

MONDO LUGOSI
USA, 1986. With: Bela Lugosi. Rhino Video. B&W/Colour.
Hour-long video compilation of public domain interviews with Lugosi, along with movie clips, trailers and TV appearances. Despite having seen it all before, this is still fascinating.
✦✦✧

MONDO WEIRDO
Austria, circa 1980s. Dir: Carl Andersen. With: Jessica Franco Manera, Soledad Marceignac, Niranda Mariaux, Frank Khunne, David Hollmann, Ron Lourid. Colour.
Over-ambitiously dedicated to Jesús Franco and Jean-Luc Godard, this dream-like underground film features English title cards, a Dutch voice-over and French songs while illustrating the bizarre sexual and homicidal fantasies of fifteen year-old Odile (Manera). In one sequence, the girl meets the blood-drinking Countess Elizabeth Bathory, who is eventually impaled on a pair of antlers. Music by Modell D'oo.
✦

EL MONJE LOCO
Mexico, 1986. Dir: Julio Aldama. With: Julio Aldama, Julio Augurio, Luz Maria Rico, Queta Lavat, Paco Pharrez. Julio Aldama/Videograbaciones. Colour.
Anthology of two very low-budget stories introduced by the cackling mad monk of the title. The first eponymous tale involves a monk who accidentally kills a woman who then appears to come back to life. The second, 'El Talisman Maldito' is another version of 'The Monkey's Paw', in which a man wishes his son back to life.
Remake: GHOST STORIES: GRAVEYARD THRILLER (qv; 1986)
✦

THE MONKEES:
I Was a Teenage Monster
USA, 1966. Dir: Sidney Miller. With: David (Davy) Jones, Micky Dolenz, Michael Nesmith, Peter Tork, John Hoyt, Dick [Richard] Kiel. Raybert Productions/Columbia/NBC-TV. Colour.
In this episode of the popular half-hour musical comedy TV series (1966-68, fifty-eight episodes), the mad Dr Mendoza (veteran Hoyt, having fun) creates an android (Kiel) which looks like the Frankenstein Monster. Mendoza plans to electronically transfer all the group's musical abilities into his creation. With Byron Foulger as Groot the hunchbacked assistant, electrical effects created by Ken Strickfaden, and clips from *Reptilicus* (1962).
✦✦✧

The Monkees Paw
USA, 1968. Dir: James Frawley. With: David (Davy) Jones, Micky Dolenz, Michael Nesmith, Peter Tork, Henry Beckman, Hans Conried. Raybert Productions/Columbia/ NBC-TV. Colour.
More madcap music and comedy, loosely inspired by W.W. Jacobs' story, in which the cursed appendage results in Micky losing his voice.
Episode remake: ORSON WELLES' GREAT MYSTERIES: The Monkey's Paw (qv; 1973)
✦✦

The Monstrous Monkee Mash
USA, 1967. Dir: James Frawley. With: David (Davy) Jones, Micky Dolenz, Michael Nesmith, Peter Tork, Ron Masak, Arlene Martel. Raybert Productions/Columbia/NBC-TV. Colour.
In this episode, Count Dracula (Masak) and his vampiric daughter Lorelei (Martel) want to turn Davy into one of the undead. This also includes a Frankenstein-like Monster (Dick Karp), a werewolf (David Pearl) and a mummy (Bruce Barbour).
✦✦

THE MONKEY'S PAW
UK, 1915. Dir: Sidney Northcote. With: Jack Lawson. Magnet. B&W.
At forty-five minutes, this silent drama was the first screen version of Louis N. Parker's play, based on the classic 1902 story by W. (William) W. (Wymark) Jacobs, about a cursed monkey's paw that can bring the dead back to life, but always at a cost.
Remake: THE MONKEY'S PAW (qv; 1923)
✦

THE MONKEY'S PAW
UK, 1923. Dir: Manning Haynes. With: Moore Marriott, A.B. Imeson, Marie Ault, Charles Ashton, Johnny Butt, George Wynne. Artistic/Selznick. B&W.
Second silent version of the story by W.W. Jacobs, running just under an hour. When a monkey's paw grants a couple three wishes, their son returns from the grave.
Remake: THE MONKEY'S PAW (qv; 1932).
✦✧

THE MONKEY'S PAW
USA, 1932 (1933). Dir: Wesley Ruggles. With: C. Aubrey Smith, Ivan Simpson, Louise Carter, Bramwell Fletcher, Herbert Bunston, Winter Hall. RKO Radio Pictures. B&W.
At under an hour long and now apparently a lost film, this was the first sound version of the story by W.W. Jacobs, based on the play by Louis N. Parker. When a monkey's paw grants a couple three wishes, their mangled son returns from the dead. In the end, it all turns out to have been a dream. Music by Max Steiner.
Remake: THE MONKEY'S PAW (qv; 1948)
✦✦

THE MONKEY'S PAW
UK, 1948. Dir: Norman Lee. With: Milton Rosmer, Megs

Jenkins, Joan Seton, Norman Shelley, Michael Martin Harvey, Alfie Bass. Kay Film/Butcher's Film Distributors. B&W.
Low-budget version of the story by W.W. Jacobs, in which a cursed monkey's paw grants three wishes, but with dire consequences. When a couple wish for wealth, their only son is mangled in machinery and they receive the insurance money. When they wish for the boy to return, he rises from the grave still mangled. With Hay Petrie and Sidney Tafler.
Remake: SUSPENSE: The Monkey's Paw (qv; 1949)
✦✦

THE MONKEY'S PAW
USA, 1982. Dir: Michael Shmulevich and Paul Wolansky. With: Sloane Shelton, William Cain, Jeffrey Garrett, Glen Z. Gress, Herb Peterson, Robert Van Voorst. Stillife Productions/Gryphon Films. Colour.
Low-budget half-hour short based on W.W. Jacobs' classic horror story. Set in the 1890s, an old sailor visits an ex-shipmate now living in upstate New York and leaves behind a cursed monkey's paw, which is able to grant three wishes but with unfortunate results. When his son is crushed in the mill machinery, the paw's new owner wishes the youth would return from the grave but banishes the boy before his twisted features can be seen.
Remake: THE MONKEY'S PAW (qv; 1984)
✦✧

THE MONKEY'S PAW
UK, 1984. Dir: Andrew Barker. With: Alex McAvoy, Patricia Leslie, Derek McLean, George Gabriel, Douglas Milvain. London College of Printing. Colour.
Yet another half-hour short film adapted from W.W. Jacob's story. Mr and Mrs White (McAvoy and Leslie) and their son Herbert (McLean) are visited by Sergeant Major Morris (Gabriel), who has returned home from India with a cursed monkey's paw. When Morris tells them that it has the power to grant three wishes, Mr White insists on keeping it. This appears to have been shot on 16mm.
Remake: EL MONJE LOCO (qv; 1986)
✦✧

THE MONSTER
(Orig: LE MONSTRE)
France, 1903. Dir: Georges Méliès. Star Film. B&W.
Silent trick short involving a living skeleton in an Egyptian setting.
✦

MONSTER BY MOONLIGHT: THE IMMORTAL SAGA OF THE WOLF MAN
USA, 1999. Dir: David J. Skal. With: John Landis, Curt Siodmak, Rick Baker, John Morgan, William T. Stromberg. Universal Studios Home Video. Colour/B&W.
Half-hour documentary, written by Skal and released as a supplement to the DVD of *The Wolf Man* (1941). This includes extensive clips and interviews. Hosted and narrated by Landis.
✦✦✦✧

MONSTER CAFE
UK, 1994-95. Dir: Philippa Langdale. With: Isobel Middleton, David Shimwell, Troy Sedgwick, Peta Lily. BBC-TV. Colour.
Fifteen minute, shot-on-video children's comedy TV series (thirty episodes) about a café in the town of Monster Rock, owned by tyrannical witch Baroness Di Monstro (Lily), and staffed by the female Frankie Monster (Middleton), Igor the cook (Shimwell) and the clumsy 5,000 year-old Mummy (Sedgwick). Written by Simon Davies.
✦

Vinny the Bin
UK, 1994. Dir: Philippa Langdale. With: Isobel Middleton, David Shimwell, Troy Sedgwick, Peta Lily. BBC-TV. Colour.
In this episode, Igor's Aunt Vampira visits the Monster Café in the hope of hiring him away.
✦

THE MONSTER CLUB
UK, 1980. Dir: Roy Ward Baker. With: Vincent Price, Donald Pleasence, John Carradine, Stuart Whitman, Richard Johnson, Barbara Kellerman. Sword & Sorcery Productions/ITC. Colour.
All-star horror vehicle aimed at children by former Amicus producer Milton Subotsky. Based on three stories by R. Chetwynd-Hayes, who is played in the film by Carradine. When he is bitten by the desperate Eramus (Price), the author is taken by the grateful vampire back to meet his friends at The Monster Club (who include the werewolf club secretary [Roger Sloman]). The stories feature a Shadmock with a lethal whistle, a village full of ghouls and a search by the Bleeny for a suburban vampire. With James Laurenson, Simon Ward, Geoffrey Bayldon, Britt Ekland, Anthony Valentine, Patrick Magee and Anthony Steel as film producer Lintom Busotsky. Terrible music (by The Viewers, B.A. Robertson, Night and The Pretty Things) and a silly script, but it's good to see the stars having fun with the material. The unconvincing monster masks were created by milkman Ernie Gasser.
✦✦

MONSTER DOG
(Orig: LEVIATAN/LOS PERROS DE LA MUERTE/IL SIGNORE DEI CANI)
Spain, 1985 (1986). Dir: Clyde Anderson (Claudio Fragasso). With: Alice Cooper (Vince Furnier), Victoria Vera, Carlos Santurio, Pepita James, Emilo Linder, José Sarsa. Continental Motion Pictures/Trans World Entertainment. Colour.
Returning to his old family mansion to shoot a music video, rock star Vince Raven (a dubbed Cooper) and a group of his friends encounter the violent locals who believe that Vince, like his father, is a werewolf controlling the pack of killer dogs terrorising the countryside. A briefly-seen puppet head of the title creature was created by Carlo De Marchis. Cooper wrote the lyrics and sings 'Identity Crises' and 'See Me in the Mirror', and this includes a photo of Lon Chaney Jr as the Wolf Man in a book about werewolves. Produced by Carlos Aured (Carlos A. Alonso).
✦✧

MONSTER FARM
USA, 1998. Dir: Philip A. Reynolds. Voices: Bruce Mahler, Rodger Bumpass, Tifany C. Lenhart, Kevin Killbrew, Robbie Rist. Saban Entertainment/Fox Family Channel. Colour.
Fifteen minute children's cartoon TV series in which Jack inherits a rural farm full of monsters, including vampiric rooster Cluckula, Jekyll and Hyde sheep Dr Woolly, monster pig Frankenswine, living dead bull Zombeef and Egyptian mummy Cowapatra.
✦✧

MONSTER FORCE
Canada/USA, 1994. Lacewood Productions/Universal Cartoon Studios/MCA-TV. Colour.
Half-hour syndicated cartoon TV series in which the high-tech Monster Force (Doc Reed Crawley, Lance McGruder and Tripp Hansen) use their EMACS (Energized Monster Armed Containment Suits) to battle a new breed of Creatures of the Night — Frankenstein's Monster, Luke Talbot the Wolf Man, Ho Tep the Mummy and the Creature from the Black Lagoon, all led by Count Dracula in an attack on mankind. Playmates Toys released a series of tie-in action figures.
✦✦

MONSTER HIGH
USA, 1988 (1989). Dir: Rudiger Poe. With: Dean Iandoli, Diana Frank, David Marriott, Robert M. Lind, Sean Haines, D.J. Kerzner. Eric Bernt/RCA/Columbia. Colour.
Dumb teen comedy in which humanoid alien Mr Armageddon (Marriott) arrives on Earth searching for a stolen explosive doomsday device that could destroy his planet. With rap songs and a basketball game involving such monsters as a mummy (Kim Jones), Art the Gargoyle (Seth Weinstein) and preppie zombie Todd Uppington Smythe III (David Bloch). Even the narration doesn't help.
✦✧

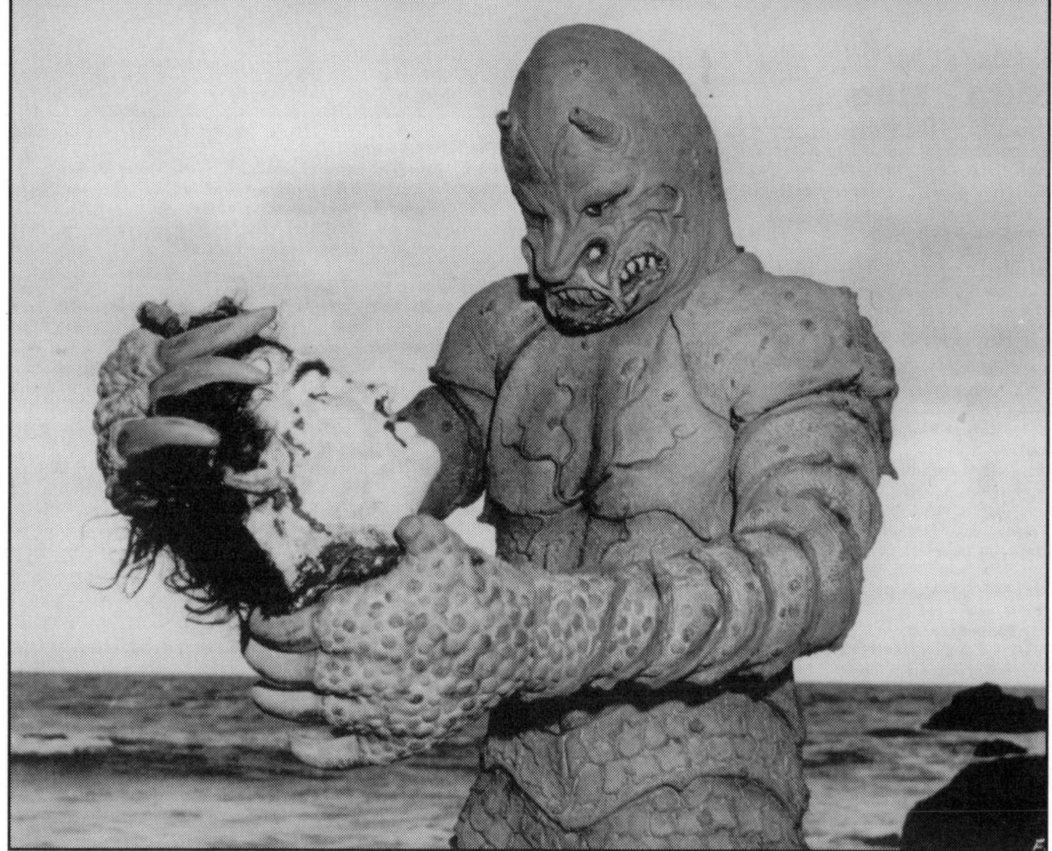

Stuntman Pete Dunn gets a head in The Monster of Piedras Blancas *(1958).*

MONSTER IN MY POCKET: THE BIG SCREAM

USA, 1992. Dir: Don Lusk. Voices: Marvin Kaplan, Mitzi McCall, Rob Paulsen, Stuart K. Robinson, Dina Sherman, B.J. Ward. Hanna-Barbera Productions/Fil-Cartoons/Morrison Entertainment Group/Turner Pictures/Kidmark. Colour.

Half-hour children's cartoon, released on video and based on the line of toys featuring a miniature vampire (Kaplan), mummy, werewolf, Frankenstein Monster and the invisible Dr Henry Davenport (Paxton Whitehead). Other voices include Frank Welker and April Winchell.

✦✧

MONSTER MANIA

USA, 1997. Dir: Kevin Burns. With: Jack Palance. Twentieth Century Fox/Van Ness Films/Foxstar Productions/American Movie Classics. Colour/B&W.

From a mad scientist's laboratory, veteran Palance hosts an hour-long celebration of the classic movie monsters, with many familiar trailers and a few clips from TV's *The Addams Family* (1964-66), *Andy Warhols Frankenstein* (1973), *Asylum* (1972), *Black Sunday* (1960), *Bram Stoker's Dracula* (1992), *Creature from the Black Lagoon* (1954), *The Curse of Frankenstein* (1957), *The Curse of the Werewolf* (1960), *Dracula* (1931 and 1979 versions), *Dracula's Daughter* (1936), *Dr. Jekyll and Mr. Hyde* (1912, 1920 and 1931 versions), *Dr. Jekyll & Sister Hyde* (1971), *Frankenstein* (1910 and 1931 versions), *Frankenstein Meets the Wolf Man* (1943), *Frankenstein 1970* (1958), *House of Dark Shadows* (1970), *House of Dracula* (1945), *House of Frankenstein* (1944), *Horror of Dracula* (1958), *The Hunchback of Notre Dame* (1923, with brief behind-the-scenes footage of Chaney Sr), *King Kong* (1933), *Mark of the Vampire* (1935, with exclusive footage of Bela Lugosi), (Abbott and Costello) *Meet Frankenstein* (1948), *The Mummy* (1933 and 1959 versions), *The Munsters* Cheerios ad! (1964), *Night of the Living Dead* (1968), *Nosferatu* (1922 and 1979 versions), *The Ωmega Man* (1971), *The Phantom of the Opera* (1925, 1943 and 1962 versions), *Phantom of the Paradise* (1974), *The Return of the Vampire* (1943), *The Revenge of Frankenstein* (1958, with exclusive footage of Peter Cushing), *The Rocky Horror Picture Show* (1975), *Tales from the Crypt* (1972), *The Wolf Man* (1941) and *Young Frankenstein* (1974), plus numerous others, along with some impressive monster memorabilia.

✦✦

MONSTER OF CEREMONIES

USA, 1966. Dir: Paul J. Smith. Voices: Grace Stafford. Walter Lantz Productions/Universal. Colour.

Seven minute *Woody Woodpecker* cartoon in which Woody is transformed into a monster robot by a mad scientist trying to create a Frankenstein-like creature.

Sequel: PRACTICAL YOLK (1966)

✦✧

THE MONSTER OF PIEDRAS BLANCAS

USA, 1958 (1961). Dir: Irvin Berwick. With: Don Sullivan, Jeanne Carmen, Les Tremayne, Forrest Lewis, John Harmon, Frank Arvidson. Vanwick/Film Service Distributors/DCA. B&W.

Low-budget monster movie about a lighthouse keeper (Harmon) who puts out food for a legendary sea creature (played by stuntman Pete Dunn) that eventually turns up in town and tears the heads off a few people. Although it's all pretty tedious, the effective looking monster was created by the film's producer, Jack Kevan, who utilised some Universal Studios monster moulds. Veteran Tremayne appears as a local doctor. According to the posters, this was the '1st Place Winner Shock Award from *Famous Monsters of Filmland* Magazine'. There wasn't any such prize.

✦✧

MONSTER ON THE CAMPUS

USA, 1958. Dir: Jack Arnold. With: Arthur Franz, Joanna Moore, Judson Pratt, Nancy Walters, Troy Donahue, Whit Bissell. Universal-International. B&W.

Filmed under the title *Monster in the Night*, this is one of Arnold's worst films, directed as a favour for producer Joseph Gershenson. Campus professor Dr Donald Blake (Franz) turns into a Neanderthal caveman (stuntman Eddie Parker in make-up created by Bud Westmore) when the blood of a prehistoric fish (*coelacanth*) accidentally gets into his pipe. It also causes a friendly dog to revert to its wild state and a silly looking dragonfly to grow to enormous size. This was the director's last monster movie.
✦✦

MONSTERS:
Leavings
USA, 1990 (1991). Dir: John Tillinger. With: Clifton James, John Christopher Jones, Tony Shalhoub, Ken Costigan, John Robert Bloom. Laurel EFX/Tribune Entertainment. Colour.
Low-budget, half-hour syndicated anthology TV series (1988-91, seventy-two episodes), executive produced by Richard P. Rubinstein and shot on video. In this episode scripted by Gahan Wilson and based on his own short story, two New York policemen discover that the homeless are losing body parts so that the city can create people out of the spare limbs. With Bloom as an impressive-looking mutant cop. Dick Smith was the series' special effects make-up consultant.
✦✦✧
My Zombie Lover
USA, 1988. Dir: David Misch. With: Tempestt Bledsoe, Steve Harper, Ed Wheeler, Marcella Lowery, Eugene Byrd. Laurel EFX/Tribune Broadcasting Company. Colour.
This comedy episode is set on the annual Night of the Dead. While the rest of her family are out shooting cannibal zombies, teenager Dottie (Bledsoe) finds herself becoming involved with dead suitor Paul Nichols (Harper).
✦✧
One Wolf's Family
USA, 1989 (1990). Dir: Alex Zamm. With: Anne Mera, Jerry Stiller, Robert Clohessy, Amy Stiller, Karen Shallo. Laurel EFX/Tribune Entertainment. Colour.
Victor Luspian (Stiller), the head of a suburban family of immigrant werewolves, is upset when he learns that his daughter wants to marry a were-hyena.
✦
Pool Sharks
USA, 1988. Dir: Alan Kingsberg. With: Tom Mason, Irving Metzman, Rebecca Downs, Page Johnson. Laurel EFX/ Tribune Entertainment. Colour.
Natasha (Downs), a pool-playing vampire, meets her match when the mysterious Gabe (Mason) challenges her to a game.
✦✦✧
Rerun
USA, 1989. Dir: John Auerbach. With: Mark Nassar, Kay Ballard, Mitchell Whitefield, Rachel Jones, Robert Weil. Laurel EFX/Tribune Entertainment. Colour.
A dead TV star returns to life and moves in with a college student who is his greatest fan.
✦
Shave and a Haircut, Two Bites
USA, 1990. Dir: John Strysik. With: Wil Wheaton, Matt LeBlanc, John O'Leary, Al Mancini. Laurel EFX/Tribune Entertainment. Colour.
Two kids (Wheaton and LeBlanc) think the town's barbers are vampires in this episode, scripted by Dan Simmons and based on his own story.
✦✧
The Vampire Hunter
USA, 1988. Dir: Michael Gornick. With: John Bolger, Page Hannah, Robert Lansing, Jack Koenig, Sylvia Short. Laurel EFX/Tribune Broadcasting Company. Colour.
This episode appears to be a pilot for a psychic detective series. When the beautiful Maura Warren (Hannah) lures his nephew Jack Avery (Koenig) into a trap, veteran vampire hunter Ernest Chariot (Lansing) is forced to confront his arch-nemesis, the undead Charles Poole (Bolger).
✦✦
The Waiting Game
USA, 1990. Dir: Bruno Spandello. With: Doug McKeon, Stephen Burleigh, Carrington Garland, Leo Garcia. Laurel EFX/Tribune Entertainment. Colour.
Following World War Three, vampires invade a deep-level fallout shelter and confront the surviving humans.
✦✧
Werewolf of Hollywood
USA, 1990 (1991). Dir: Tom Whelan. With: Richard Belzer, David Leary, Geraldine Leer, Shelley Berman. Laurel EFX/ Tribune Broadcasting Company. Colour.
A cynical scriptwriter (Belzer) at Pentagram Pictures discovers that the head of the studio turns into an impressive-looking werewolf. Scripted by Ron Goulart and based on his own story.
✦✧
Where's the Rest of Me?
USA, 1988. Dir: Dick Benner. With: Meatloaf (Marvin Lee Aday), Franco Harris, Black-Eyed Susan, Drew Eliot, Frank Tarsia. Laurel EFX/Tribune Entertainment. Colour.
When a doctor (singer Meatloaf) uses a serum to keep a corpse fresh for use in transplant surgery, his victim (Tarsia) comes back to life to regain his stolen body parts.
✦✧

MONSTERS A GO-GO
UK, 1999. Mentorn Barraclough Carey Productions/TV21/ Channel Four Television. Colour.
Half-hour comedy compilation, shown as an introduction to Channel Four's 'Exploitica' season of films, with silly sound effects and dialogue dubbed over extensive clips and trailers from *Frankenstein's Castle of Freaks* (1973), *Guess What Happened to Count Dracula?* (1970), *Horrors of Spider Island* (1959) and *Werewolves on Wheels* (1971). Researched by Frank Henenlotter.
✦

MONSTERS CRASH THE PAJAMA PARTY
USA, 1965. Dir: David L. Hewitt. With: Don Brandon, James Reason, Clara Nagel, Vic McGee, Pauline Hillkirt, Charles Egan. Brandon Films. Colour.
Half-hour novelty short, originally part of a live-action Spook Show stage act, where people in monster masks would invade the theatre and scare the audience (billed on the ads as 'HorrorVision'). A group of teenage girls decide to hold a slumber party in an old dark house inhabited by the Mad Doctor (McGee), who plans to turn them all into gorillas. When the girls' boyfriends crash the party wearing Halloween masks (including one disguised as a werewolf), the fun begins. With the vampire-like Draculina (Hillkirt) and Egan as Ygor. The credits are spoken.
✦

THE MONSTERS DEMOLISHER
(Orig: NOSTRADAMUS Y EL DESTRUCTOR DE MONSTRUOS)
Mexico, 1960 (1962). Dir: Frederick (Federico) Curiel. With: Germán Robles, Julio Aleman, Domingo Soler, Aurora Alvarado, Manver (Manuel Vergara), Rogelio Jimenez Ponz 'Frijolito'. Estudios America/American International. B&W.
A sequel to *The Curse of Nostradamus* (1960), and the second of four features cut down from a twelve-part Mexican serial and released directly to TV in America. Robles stars as a bearded vampire descendant of the prophet Nostradamus who hypnotises a criminal to do his will. Professor Duran (Soler) defeats him with a soundwave machine harmful to bats. This includes the episodes 'El Destructor de Monstruos', 'El Estudiante y la Horca' ('The Student and the Gallows') and 'El Ataud Vacio' ('The Empty Coffin'). The English-language version was produced by K. (Kenneth) Gordon Murray and directed by Stim (Stem) Segar.
Sequel: THE GENII OF DARKNESS (qv; 1960)
✦✧

MONSTERS ON THE MARCH
USA, 1980. Video Yesteryear. B&W.
Twenty-five minute video compilation of mostly re-realease trailers

for the classic Universal horror films.
Sequel: SON OF MONSTERS ON THE MARCH (qv; 1980)
✦✦✧

THE MONSTER SQUAD
USA, 1976-77. Dir: Jim Sheldon, Wes Kenney, Herman Hoffman and William P. D'Angelo. With: Fred Grandy, Henry Polic II, Buck Kartalian, Michael Lane, Paul Smith. D'Angelo Productions/NBC-TV. Colour.
Short-lived (fifteen episodes), half-hour TV series in which the monsters — Count Dracula (Polic II), Frank N. Stein (Lane) and Bruce Wolfman (Kartalian) — pose as wax dummies in a museum by day, and are revived by college student Walter (Grandy) at night to battle outlandish criminals! The guest cast included Alice Ghostley, Billy Curtis, Marty Allen, Edward Andrews, Sid Haig, Jonathan Harris, Julie Newmar, Arthur Mallet, Geoffrey Lewis, Avery Schreiber and Vito Scotti.
✦✧

THE MONSTER SQUAD
USA, 1987. Dir: Fred Dekker. With: Andre Gower, Robby Kiger, Stephen Macht, Duncan Regehr, Tom Noonan, Brent Chalem. Taft Entertainment/Keith Barrish. Colour.
From writer/director Dekker (*Night of the Creeps* [1986], etc) and co-writer Shane Black (*Lethal Weapon* [1987], etc) comes a delightful horror comedy for children that echoes the Universal series of the 1940s. Dracula (an impressive Regehr) is in a small American town to recover an amulet of evil. Only a group of kids, known as The Monster Squad, recognise the danger, and despite the intervention of Van Helsing (Jack Gwillim), the Count teams up with a wolfman (Carl Thibault), the Frankenstein Monster (Noonan), gill man (Tom Woodruff Jr) and mummy (Michael McKay) to create havoc. Make-ups designed by Stan Winston. Great special effects, non-stop action and a nice sense of reverence make this a minor gem. Kids should love it.
✦✦✦✧

MONSTERS WE'VE KNOWN AND LOVED
USA, 1991. Dir: Bryan Cohen. Fireworks Home Video/ Burbank Video. Colour/B&W.
Cheaply produced hour-long video that looks at such classic movie monsters as mummies, vampires and the Creature, with trailers for *Abbott and Costello Meet the Mummy* (1955), *The Alligator People* (1959), *Blacula* (1972), *Blood from the Mummy's Tomb* (1971), *Blood of Dracula* (1957), *The Brides of Dracula* (1960), *Captain Kronos Vampire Hunter* (1972), *Count Yorga, Vampire* (1970), *Creature from the Black Lagoon* (1954), *The Creature Walks Among Us* (1955), *The Curse of the Mummy's Tomb* (1964), *Curse of the Undead* (1959), *Deathmaster* (1972), *Dracula* (1931), *Dracula A.D. 1972* (1972, including behind-the-scenes footage), *Dracula Has Risen from the Grave* (1968), *Dracula Prince of Darkness* (1965), *Dracula's Daughter* (1936), *The Evil of Frankenstein* (1964), *Hollywood on Parade No.8* (1933), *Horror of Dracula* (1958), *House of Dark Shadows* (1970), *House of Dracula* (1945), *House of Frankenstein* (1944), *How to Make a Monster* (1958), *The Kiss of the Vampire* (1962), *Love at First Bite* (1979), *Lust for a Vampire* (1970), *Mark of the Vampire* (1935), (Abbott and Costello) *Meet Frankenstein* (1948), *The Monster of Piedras Blancas* (1958), *Mother Riley Meets the Vampire* (1952), *The Mummy* (1933 and 1959), *The Mummy's Curse* (1944), *The Mummy's Ghost* (1944), *The Mummy's Shroud* (1967), *The Mummy's Tomb* (1942), *Old Dracula* (1974), *Plan 9 from Outer Space* (1958), *The Phantom of the Opera* (1925), *Queen of Blood* (1966), *The Return of Count Yorga* (1971), *The Return of Dracula* (1957), *The Return of the Vampire* (1943), *Revenge of the Creature* (1955), *The Satanic Rites of Dracula* (1973), *Scared to Death* (1947), *Scars of Dracula* (1970, with behind-the-scenes footage), *Scream Blacula Scream* (1973), *The 7 Brothers Meet Dracula* (1974), *Son of Dracula* (1943), *Spooks Run Wild* (1941), *Twins of Evil* (1971), *The Vampire* (1957), *Vampire Circus* (1971), *The Vampire Lovers* (1970), *The Velvet Vampire* (1971) and *The Werewolf* (1956), along with TV's *The Colgate Comedy Hour* (1953) and an excerpt from a 1970s interview with Christopher Lee. Narrated by Derek Crowley.
✦✦✧

EL MONSTRUO RESUCITADO
(aka DR. CRIMEN)
Mexico, 1952 (1955). Dir: Chano Urueta. With: Carlos Navarro, Misroslava, Fernando Wagner, J. (José) M. (María) Linares Rivas, Alberto Mariscal, Estefan Berne. Internacional Cinematografica/Columbia. B&W.
Loosely based on the Frankenstein story and set in the Balkans. Disfigured mad scientist Dr Ling (Rivas) hides his monstrous features behind a mask. He transplants a new brain into the resuscitated body of handsome suicide Ariel (Navarro) and orders the now-ugly monster to kidnap journalist Nora (Misroslava). But when Nora and Ariel fall in love, the zombie turns on his creator before being destroyed. The doctor also has an apeman servant called Crommer (Berne).
✦

MONTY PYTHON'S FLYING CIRCUS
UK, 1969. Dir: Ian McNaughton. With: Graham Chapman, John Cleese, Eric Idle, Terry Jones, Michael Palin, Terry Gilliam. BBC-TV. Colour.
In this half hour episode of the anarchic TV comedy sketch show (1969-74, forty-six episodes), Chapman plays a vampire whose fangs fall out when he tries to bite a woman. This episode also includes a science fiction skit.
Series sequel: MONTY PYTHON AND THE HOLY GRAIL (1975)
✦✦✧

MOONCHILD
USA, 1994. Dir: Todd Sheets. With: Kathleen McSweeney. Screenland/Asylum Home Video/Englewood Entertainment. Colour.
This low-budget independent video is set in the future when an evil totalitarian government has taken control of America. Jacob Stryker breaks out of one of their prisons and attempts to find his son who, like him, was the subject of gene-splicing experiments that have resulted in them being able to transform into 'werewolf' warriors.
✦

MOON LEGEND
(USA: aka A CHINESE LEGEND)
Hong Kong, 1991. Dir: Peter Mak (Mak Yai-Kit/Ho Meng-Hua). With: Jacky Cheung (Cheung Hok-Yau), Joey Wang (Wang Tsu-Hsien/Wang Zu-Xian/Wong Ki-Chang), Cheung Man, Wu Ma (Wo Ma/Yuen Wah/Ng Ma-Wu). Grand March Movies/Tai Seng Video. Colour.
A young swordsman (Cheung) is haunted by recurring dreams of a beautiful vampire, Moon-Cher (Wang), who sucks her victim's blood through a hollow reed and can turn into a fox. Convinced that she is in danger, he sets out on a quest to rescue her.
✦✦

MOON OF THE WOLF
USA, 1972. Dir: Daniel Petrie. With: David Janssen, Barbara Rush, Bradford Dillman, John Beradino, Geoffrey Lewis, Royal Dano. Filmways/ABC-TV. Colour.
Low-budget TV movie, based on the novel by Leslie H. Whitten. Janssen gives his usual fine performance as Sheriff Aaron Whitaker looking for a loup-garou killer in the Louisiana bayous. It turns out to be Andrew Rodanthe (Dillman, in make-up created by William and Tom Tuttle), who suffers from a form of lycanthropy which can be temporarily controlled by drugs. With George Sawaya.
✦✧

MOONRISE
(Orig: GRAMPIRE/MY GRANDPA IS A VAMPIRE. UK: MY GRANDAD'S A VAMPIRE)
New Zealand, 1991 (1992). Dir: David Blyth. With: Al Lewis, Justin Gocke, Milan Borich, Noel Appleby, Pat Evison. Tucker Production Co/Moonrise Productions/ Republic Pictures. Colour.
Likeable children's adventure, starring eighty-one year-old Lewis (TV's *The Munsters* [1964-66], etc) as friendly vampire Vernon T. Cooger. Twelve year-old Lonny (Gocke) arrives in New Zealand from Los Angeles to spend a holiday with his grandfather Cooger, Aunt Leah (Evison), and his friend, Kanziora (Borich). But the boys stumble across an ancient family secret — Cooger is really a 300 year-old member of the undead, and he pleads with them to protect him

from Aunt Leah's unpleasant boyfriend, Ernie (Appleby), who wants to drive a stake through his heart. Family fun from the director of *Death Warmed Up* (1984) and *Red Blooded American Girl* (1990).
✦✦

PHILIPPE MORA
[b 1949]

French-born Australian director, painter and movie historian.
qv: *The Beast Within* (1982); *Brother, Can You Spare a Dime?* (1975); *Howling II Stirba — Werewolf Bitch* (1984); *The Marsupials The Howling III* (1987).

MORBUS
(aka MORBUS, O QUE APROVECHE)
Spain, 1982. Dir: Ignasi P. Ferre Serra. With: Joan Borras, Carla Day, Mon Ferrer, Victor Israel, Montse Calvo, Irene Rives. Producciones Cinematográficas. Colour.
When two prostitutes take their clients into the forest, they are attacked by flesh-eating zombies created by a mad scientist. After another zombie attack on the members of a Satanic cult, the survivors take shelter in the home of a novelist. In the end, everything is revealed to be the writer's drug-induced fantasy.
✦

THE MORECAMBE & WISE SHOW
UK, 1976. Dir: John Ammonds. With: Eric Morecambe, Ernie Wise, Ann Hamilton, Arthur Tolcher, Janet Webb, Grazina Frame. BBC-TV. Colour.
Half-hour TV comedy variety show (1961-83, 169 episodes). In one sketch, Morecambe turns up as Count Alucard, a top-hatted vampire who tries to book a room in a hotel.
✦✧
UK, 1980. Dir: John Ammonds. With: Eric Morecambe, Ernie Wise, Ian Carmichael, Ann Hamilton. Thames Television/ITV. Colour.
This episode of the comedy series includes a sketch in which Baron Frankenstein (Carmichael), with the aid of Igor (Morecambe), creates a Monster (Wise). In another episode, Eric and Ernie team up with Susan Hampshire to search for the giant gorilla in 'The Mighty Kong', and Peter Cushing was a regular guest star in a long-running joke about not being paid for his appearance in 1969 as King Arthur.
✦✦✧

MANTAN MORELAND
[1902-1973]

Black American comedy actor who usually played frightened servants and chauffeurs, including the recurring role of Birmingham Brown in the 1940s *Charlie Chan* series.
qv: *The Chinese Cat* (1944); *The Comic* (1969); *Four Shall Die* (1940); *King of the Zombies* (1941); *Revenge of the Zombies* (1943); *Watermelon Man* (1970).

ANDRÉ MORELL
(Cecil André Mesritz) [1909-1978]

British film and TV actor, best remembered for his portrayal of Professor Quatermass in the BBC TV version of *Quatermass and the Pit* (1958-59) and as solid support in various Hammer horrors, including a dependable Watson in *The Hound of the Baskervilles* (1959).
qv: *The Mummy's Shroud* (1967); *The Plague of the Zombies* (1966).

MORGAN A SUITABLE CASE FOR TREATMENT
(USA: MORGAN!)
UK, 1966. Dir: Karel Reisz. With: David Warner, Vanessa Redgrave, Robert Stephens, Irene Handl, Bernard Bresslaw, Arthur Mullard. Quintra. B&W.
Swinging sixties comedy which made Warner a star. He plays eccentric artist Morgan Delt, an animal-lover obsessed with apes. He upsets his ex-wife Leonie (Redgrave) by putting a skeleton in her bed and dressing up as a gorilla. This includes clips from *King Kong* (1933) and Johnny Weissmuller as Tarzan. With Graham Crowden.
✦✦✦

PAUL MORRISSEY
[b 1939]

American director and writer, associated as a film-maker with Andy Warhol's Factory from the mid-1960s. He made the 3-D camp horrors *Flesh for Frankenstein* (1973) and *Blood for Dracula* (1974) back-to-back in Rome.

HOWARD MORTON
[1926-1997]

American character actor who portrayed the vampiric Grandpa Munster on TV's *The Munsters Today* (1988-91).
qv: *Rod Serling's Night Gallery: 'The Housekeeper'* (1970).

MORTUARY ACADEMY
USA, 1988 (1991). Dir: Michael Schroeder. With: Paul Bartel, Mary Woronov, Perry Lang, Tracey Walter, Christopher Atkins, Lynn Danielson. Landmark Films/ Taurus Entertainment. Colour.
Unfunny black comedy about necrophilia(!). The Grimm Brothers, Sam (Lang) and Max (Atkins), inherit a mortuary and discover they have to learn the business. A heavy metal band managed by Bernie Berkowitz (Wolfman Jack) is revived from the dead. With Cesar Romero and Dona Speir.
✦✧

MORTUARY BLUES
(Orig: SHI JIA ZHONG DI)
Hong Kong, 1990. Dir: Jeffrey Lau (Jeffrey Lau Chan-Wai/ Liu Zhen-Wei). With: Yuen Fui, Sandra Ng, Lowell Lo, Chan Suk-Lan. Bo Ho Films/Golden Harvest/Paragon Films. Colour.
Horror comedy in which an island police chief and three treasure hunters accidentally release a vampire from a pagoda. In the end, the vampire and his treasure disappear in a burst of flames.
✦

MOSQUITO
USA, 1994 (1995). Dir: Gary Jones. With: Gunnar Hansen, Ron Asheton, Steve Dixon, Rachel Loiselle, Tim Lovelace, Mike Hard. Hemdale Communications/Acme Films/ Excalibur Motion Pictures/Antibes. Colour.
Filmed under the titles *Blood Fever*, *Night Swarm* and *Skeeters* in Detroit, Michigan. In this low-budget, old-fashioned monster movie, mosquitos infected with DNA from the pilot of a crashed alien probe grow into gigantic blood-drinking creatures that attack the members of a summer camp community. Hansen plays the leader of a family of bank robbers (and has a nice *Texas Chain Saw* in-joke). Despite too much silly Southern humour, director Jones handles the tension and the bug attacks well, while some of Paul Jessel's stop-motion creatures are quite impressive.
✦✧

IL MOSTRO DI FRANKENSTEIN
Italy, 1920. Dir: Eugenio Testa. With: Luciano Albertini, Umberto Guarracino. Albertini Film/UCI. B&W.
This third silent version of Mary Shelley's novel is now apparently a lost movie. It includes a confrontation in a cave between Frankenstein (played by producer Albertini) and his Monster (Guarracino). Amazingly, this was the last Italian horror film for nearly thirty-six years.
Remake: FRANKENSTEIN (qv; 1931)
✦

MOTHER RILEY MEETS THE VAMPIRE
(USA: MY SON THE VAMPIRE/VAMPIRE OVER LONDON)
UK, 1952. Dir: John Gilling. With: Arthur Lucan, Bela

Lugosi, Dora Bryan, Philip Leaver, Richard Wattis, Graham Moffatt. Renown Pictures. B&W.
The last of Lucan's fourteen Old Mother Riley comedies (this time without partner Kitty McShane) is not quite as awful as expected. Lugosi, looking surprisingly well, was paid only $5,000 to play a mad doctor, Count Von Housen, who thinks he is a vampire (he wears a Dracula cape and sleeps in a coffin). When his prototype robot is delivered by mistake to Irish washerwoman Old Mother Riley, it leads to chaos. Ian Wilson plays Lugosi's maniacal Renfield-like assistant, Hitchcock, and there's a song-and-dance number that includes Hattie Jacques and Dandy Nichols. Moffatt has a brief cameo as a yokel, and Charles Lloyd-Pack and Laurence Naismith also turn up. Released in 1953 in America in a re-edited version, and again in 1963. Yet another version, titled *King Robot*, was apparently never completed.
✦✧

MOTOR MANIA
USA, 1950. Dir: Jack Kinney. Voices: Bob Jackman. Walt Disney/RKO Radio Pictures. Colour.
Nine minute cartoon in which Goofy transforms from Mr Walker, a mild-mannered pedestrian, into Mr Wheeler, a manic motorist.
Sequel: HOLD THAT POSE (1950)
✦✦✧

MOUNTAINTOP MOTEL MASSACRE
USA, 1983 (1986). Dir: Jim McCullough. With: Bill Thurman, Anna Chappell, Will Mitchell, Virginia Loridans, Major Brock, Amy Hills. New World Pictures/ Jim McCullough Productions. Colour.
Evelyn Chambers (Chappell) is a crazy old woman who uses the tunnels beneath her motel cabins to kill the guests with snakes, rats and a scythe. She is driven over the edge by the voice of her young daughter (Jill King), who she accidentally decapitated in a fit of rage, and the girl turns up as a zombie/ghost in the confused climax. Filmed in the South, this low-budget independent movie features amateur performances, ugly photography and unconvincing gore effects.
✦

THE MOUSE AND THE MONSTER
USA, 1996. Saban Entertainment/UPN Network. Colour.
Half-hour cartoon TV series created by Jerry Leibowitz, about Chesbro the big-hearted rodent and his blue monster friend Mo, who are pursued by Mo's mad creator Dr Wackerstein and his bride Olga.
✦✧

MOVING CORPSE IN THE OLD HOUSE
China, 1939. Dir: Maxu Weibang.
This is apparently the cinema's first hopping vampire movie, based on Chinese folklore.
✦

MR & MRS DRACULA
USA, 1980. Dir: Doug Rogers. With: Dick Shawn, Carol Lawrence, Anthony Battaglia, Gail Mayron, Barry

Bela Lugosi is assisted by Ian Wilson when Mother Riley Meets the Vampire *(1952).*

Gordon, Ken Olfson. ABC-TV. Colour.
Shawn and Lawrence play the title characters, driven out of Transylvania, who relocate in the Bronx. Inspired by *Love at First Bite* (1979), this was the twenty-five minute pilot for a proposed sitcom TV series.
✦

MR. MAGOO:
(aka MR. MAGOO AND FRIENDS)
Magoo Meets Frankenstein
USA, 1960. Dir: Gil Turner. Voices: Jim Backus, Daws Butler, Paul Frees, Jerry Hausner, Julie Bennett. Columbia/ UPA. Colour.
Syndicated half-hour cartoon TV series (1960-62, 130 five minute episodes) featuring the near-sighted Mr Quincy Magoo (Backus), created in 1949 by Milfred Kaufman and John Hubley. In this segment, Mr Magoo arrives at Professor Frankenstein's castle thinking it's a European hotel. The Professor, who has given his Monster the brain of a chicken, tries to transfer Magoo's mind into his creation.
Series sequel: THE FAMOUS ADVENTURES OF MR. MAGOO (qv; 1964-65)
✦✦✧

MR. MAGOO, MAN OF MYSTERY
USA, 1967. Voices: Jim Backus. Columbia/UPA. Colour.
Cartoon feature film, re-edited from the NBC-TV series *The Famous Adventures of Mr. Magoo* (1964-65), in which the near-sighted Mr Magoo (Backus) plays Dr Watson to Sherlock Holmes, Dr Frankenstein, the Count of Monte Cristo and appears alongside detective Dick Tracy.
✦✦

MR. MAJEIKA:
Fangs for the Memory
UK, 1990. Dir: Michael Kerrigan. With: Stanley Baxter, Richard Murdoch, Claire Sawyer, Sanjiv Madan, Eve Ferret, Roland MacLeod. ITV. Colour.
Half-hour TV series (1988-90, twenty episodes), based on the children's books by Humphrey Carpenter. The incompetent wizard of the title (Baxter) is banished to Earth, where he gets a job as a teacher in a local school. In this episode, Mr Majeika tries to get rid of a vegetarian vampire (Phillip Herbert), who arrives in the village of Much Barty after having mistaken the Empire Day festivities for Vampire Day.
✦

MR. POSSESSED
(Orig: CHUANG XIE XIAN SHENG)
Hong Kong, 1988. Dir: Wong Jing (Pan Yung-Ee). With: Danny Chan, Wong Jing (Pan Yung-Ee), Kenny Bee (Manny Boo), Do Do-Cheng (Carol Cheng). Colour.
Cantonese horror comedy in which a shy boy (Bee) is possessed by an evil spirit when he becomes sexually aroused. Meanwhile, in a totally separate sub-plot, his friend is transformed into a vampire-werewolf creature that interrupts a girl's slumber party.
✦✧

MRS. AMWORTH
UK/Canada, 1975. Dir: Alvin Rakoff. With: Glynis Johns, Derek Francis, John Phillips, Pip Miller, Ronald Russell, Betty Tucker. Highgate Associates/HTV/OECA/ITV. Colour.
Beautifully photographed half-hour TV movie, based on the classic 1920s vampire story by E.F. Benson. Johns plays Mrs Amworth, a 300 year-old vampire spreading a mysterious sickness through an English village at the height of summer. Only Francis Urcombe (Phillips) isn't taken in by her image of the perfect hostess and he seeks to prove she is one of the undead with the help of Benson (Francis). The scenes of Johns running in slow motion through an old churchyard with the sound of giant wings beating on the soundtrack are particularly effective. This was the pilot for an unproduced TV series to have been called *Classics Dark and Dangerous*.
✦✦✧

MR. STITCH
France/USA, 1995. Dir: Roger Avary. With: Rutger Hauer, Wil Wheaton, Nia Peeples, Ron Perlman, Taylor Negron, Michael Harris. Rysher Entertainment/Studio Megaboom. Colour.
This cable TV movie premièred on the Sci-Fi Channel. Lazarus (a surprisingly impressive Wheaton) is the patchwork creation of Dr Rue Wakeman (an unconvincing Hauer, who was also co-executive producer), whose task is to create a new type of soldier for the tolitarian government of a future America. When he starts remembering his past lives, Lazarus escapes. At least writer/director Avery's low-budget reworking of the Frankenstein story acknowledges its source. With make-up design and effects by Tom Savini, who also has a cameo.
✦✧

MR. VAMPIRE
(Orig: JIANGSHI XIANSHENG. USA: aka MR. DRACULA)
Hong Kong, 1985. Dir: Lau Kun-Wai (Ricky Lau/Ricky Hui/Xu Guan-Ying). With: Ricky Hui (Ricky Lau/Xu Guan-Ying), Moon Lee (Moon Li/Lee Choi-Fung), Lam Ching-Ying (Lin Zheng-Ying), Pauline Lau, Anthony Chan, Wu Ma (Wo Ma/Yuen Wah/Ng Ma-Wa). Bo Ho Films/Golden Harvest/Paragon Films. Colour.
Wonderfully inventive horror comedy involving an evil reanimated vampire, a group of hopping zombies, the hideous ghost of a sexy young woman and plenty of kung fu action. When the time comes for Mr Yan (Wong Ha) to reinter his father's corpse, it suddenly rises from the dead and Mr Yan becomes the first victim of the vampire (Yuen Wah). Ching-Ying plays the titular Taoist priest who has to sort everything out. Star/director Wai/Lau ensures there's never a dull moment, and a likeable cast, good production values and some marvellous effects makes this a classic of Hong Kong fantasy cinema.
✦✦✦✧

MR. VAMPIRE 1992
(Orig: XIN JIANGSHI XIANSHENG)
Hong Kong, 1992. Dir: Lau Kun-Wai (Ricky Lau/Ricky Hui/Xu Guan-Ying). With: Rick(y) Hui (Ricky Lau/Xu Guan-Ying), Lam Ching-Ying (Lin Zheng-Ying), Sandra Ng, Tsien Siu-Ho, Lau Lam-Kwong. Lau Kun-Wai Productions/Grand March Movies/World Video. Colour.
Ching-Ying returns as the One-Eyebrowed Priest in this belated follow-up to the popular horror comedy series. This time he's battling Holy Baby, the vampiric ghost of an aborted foetus, and a horde of (comedic) hopping vampires.
✦✧

MR. VAMPIRE PART III
(Orig: LIANGHUAN XIANSHENG)
Hong Kong, 1986 (1987). Dir: Wong Kee-Hung. With: Lam Ching-Ying (Lin Zheng-Ying), Richard Ng, Yuen Biao, Lui Fong, Billy Lau, Samo Hung (Samo Hung Kam-Po/Hung Kam-Bo/Hong Jin-Baoh). Bo Ho Films/Golden Harvest/ Paragon Films. Colour.
Ching-Ying returns playing a Taoist priest in turn-of-the-century China battling an evil witch and her undead army. Comedy actor Ng is a fake exorcist, caught between the combatants and aided by two friendly ghosts who pretend to be vampires. Darker and gorier than previous entries in the popular series.
✦✦✧

MR. VAMPIRE SAGA 4
(Orig: JIANGSHI SHUSHU)
Hong Kong, 1987 (1988). Dir: Law Lit (Lo Lieh). With: Wu Ma (Wo Ma/Yuen Wah/Ng Ma-Wa), Anthony Chan, Loletta Lee, Chin Kar-Lok. Bo Ho Films/Golden Harvest/Paragon Films. Colour.
Fourth entry in the popular series. While two priests battle each other with magic, a powerful golden-clad vampire wreaks havoc amongst a travelling group of Chinese nobles. More comedy than horror, this also includes a flying woman in white who transforms into a fox-monster.
✦✦

MR VAMPIRE 2
(Orig: JIANGSHI JIAZU/JIANGSHI XIANSHENG XUJI)
Hong Kong, 1985 (1986). Dir: Lao Guan-Wai (Ricky Lau/ Ricky Hui/Xu Guan-Ying). With: Moon Lee (Moon Li/Lee Choi-Fung), Lam Ching-Yin(g) (Lin Zheng-Ying), Lu Nan-Chung, Yuen Biao, Chung Fa. Bo Ho Films/Golden Harvest/Media Asia Distribution/Paragon Films. Colour.
A sequel to *Mr. Vampire* (1985) in name only. Director Wai/Lau injects more slapstick humour into this story about a family of ancient Chinese vampires — father, mother and young son — who are accidentally revived by a trio of incompetent grave robbers. While the undead child is befriended by a young girl and her brother, the hopping adults are tracked down by the vampire hunter descendant (Ching-Ying) of the first films' priest. Although the comedy is too broad at times, the spectacular stunts, creepy-looking vampires and fast-paced direction make this worth catching. This was so successful in Hong Kong that it apparently resulted in a similar-themed TV series.
✦✦✦

MUERTOS DE RISA
Mexico, 1957. Dir: Adolfo Fernandez Bustamante. With: 'Resortes', Maria Victoria, Armando Arriola, Luis Aragon, Renée Damas, José Bigton Castro. Producciones Sotomayor/Columbia. B&W.
Horror comedy that includes mummies, ghosts and a giant spider. The title translates as 'Dead of Laughter'.
✦✧

MUFFY THE VAMPIRE LAYER
USA, 1992. Dir: Jean-Pierre Ferrand. With: P.J. Sparxx (P.J. Carrington), Lacy Rose, Sunset Thomas, Steve Drake, Biff Malibu, Cal Jammer. Las Vegas Video Entertainment. Colour.
Hardcore vampire comedy in which the eponymous cheerleader (Sparxx) and her school friends (Rose and Thomas) investigate a spooky castle and encounter a surfin' bloodsucker (Malibu) and other members of the undead. The similarly titled *Buffy the Vamp* (1992) doesn't feature any vampires.
✦

LAS MUJERES PANTERAS
Mexico, 1966. Dir: René Cardona. With: 'El Angel' Ariadna Welter, Elizabeth Campbell, 'Tongolele' (Yolanda Montes), Eric del Castillo, Manuel 'Loco' Valdés, Eda Lorna. Cinematográfica Calderón/Azteca. Colour.
Following on from *Las Lobas del Ring* (1965), this is the fourth in the series of adventures about Mexican wrestling women El Angel (Welter, the sister of Linda Christian) and The Golden Rubi (Campbell). Satanasa, the Goddess of Evil, creates blood-drinking panther-women with the claws and powers of beasts to destroy the descendant of the man who killed their leader. Scripted by Alfredo Salazar.
Sequel: THE WRESTLING WOMEN VS. THE KILLER ROBOT (qv; 1968)
✦✧

LA MUJER MURCIÉLAGO
Mexico, 1967 (1968). Dir: René Cardona. With: Maura Monti, Roberto Cañedo, Hector Godoy, David Silva, Crox Alvardo, Armando Silvestre. Cinematográfica Calderón. Colour.
Bikini-clad wrestling superheroine the Bat-Woman (Monti) battles the mad Dr Williams and his scaly gill men monsters. With Eric del Castillo.
✦

MUMBLY:
Hyde and Seek
USA, 1976. Voices: Don Messick, John Stephenson. Hanna-Barbera Productions. Colour.
Cartoon TV series (sixteen episodes) featuring the adventures of canine detective Lt Mumbly (Messick) and Shnooker (Stephenson).
✦✧

A MÚMIA KÖZBESZÓL
Hungary, 1967. Dir: Gábor Oláh. With: Éva Ruttkai, István Avar, Tamás Major, János Koltai, Tibor Szilágyi, László Mensáros. Mafilm. B&W.
Koltai plays an Egyptian mummy in this comedy. The title translates as 'The Mummy Interferes'.
✦

MUMMIES ALIVE!
Japan/USA, 1997-98. Dir: Seth Kearsley. Voices: Graeme Kingston, Scott McNeil, Pauline Newstone, Gerard Plunkett, Cree Summer, Bill Switzer. DIC Productions/ Northern Lights Entertainment. Colour.
Syndicated half-hour cartoon TV series (fifty-two episodes). When an archaeological expedition accidentally releases evil sorcerer Scarab (Plunkett) from a sealed Egyptian tomb after 3,500 years, a quartet of transforming mummies with superhuman powers ('With the strength of Ra!') and their sacred cat revive to protect twelve year-old Presley (Switzer), who is the reincarnation of Prince Rapses, the son of Pharaoh Amenhotep. Ivan Reitman was one of the producers. The inevitable action toys followed.
✦✦

MUMMIES ALIVE! THE LEGEND BEGINS
Japan/USA, 1997. Dir: Seth Kearsley. Voices: Graeme Kingston, Scott McNeil, Pauline Newstone, Gerard Plunkett, Cree Summer, Bill Switzer. DIC Productions/ Northern Lights Entertainment. Colour.
Hour-long video compilation, containing two episodes from the TV cartoon series *Mummies Alive!* (1997-98).
✦✦

THE MUMMY
UK, 1911. Dir: A.E. Coleby. Pathé-Britannia. B&W.
Nine minute silent short in which Professor Darnett invents a fluid that can return the dead to life. Meanwhile, his assistant impersonates a mummy as part of a plan to marry the professor's daughter.
✦

THE MUMMY
USA, 1911. Thanhouser. B&W.
Seventeen minute silent short. Electricity brings an ancient mummy to life as a beautiful Egyptian girl.
✦

THE MUMMY
UK, 1911. Urban. B&W.
Sixteen minute silent short in which a professor dreams that a mummy comes to life. This is probably a remake of *The Romance of the Mummy* (1910), based on the book by Theophile Gautier.
Remake: THE MUMMY'S FOOT (qv; 1949)
✦

THE MUMMY
USA, 1933 (1932). Dir: Karl Freund. With: (Boris) Karloff, Zita Johann, David Manners, Arthur Byron, Edward Van Sloan, Bramwell Fletcher. Universal. B&W.
In 1932, Karloff was originally set to star as the 3,000 year-old sorcerer *Cagliostro* for Universal before the studio abandoned the project and used Nina Wilcox Putnam's story as the basis for this slow-moving but atmospheric thriller, which marked the directing début of Freund, the cinematographer on *Dracula* (1931) and *Murders in the Rue Morgue* (1932). Originally announced as *The King of the Dead* and *Im-Ho-Tep*, the film opens in 1921, when a British Museum archaeological expedition to Egypt discovers the Scroll of Thoth and accidentally revives the 3,700 year-old living mummy Imhotep. Ten years later in Cairo, ancient Egyptian priest/sorcerer Ardath Bey (a gaunt Karloff in superb old-age make-up created by Jack Pierce) believes that Helen Grosvenor (Johann, in a role originally considered for Katharine Hepburn) is the reincarnated soul of his lost love, the princess Anck-es-en-Amon. This features some impressive set-pieces, particularly the opening sequence where the mummy is brought to life by Fletcher's young archaeologist ('He went for a little walk!'). Karloff (who is billed by only his last name for the first time) gives a fine performance, but

unfortunately the rest of the cast are stagey and the climax appears rushed and clumsy. With Noble Johnson as the Nubian slave. Several sequences were cut from the film prior to release, mostly illustrating Helen's previous incarnations (Henry Victor's name still appears in the end credits, even though his scenes as a Saxon Warrior are missing). Despite the copyright date, this actually premièred on 22 December 1932. The script was published by MagicImage in 1989, whilst a belated novelisation appeared under the house name 'Carl Dreadstone' in 1977, and there were juvenile adaptations by Ian Thorne the same year and by Parker Smith in 1992.
Sequel: THE MUMMY'S HAND (qv; 1940)
Remakes: THE MUMMY (qv; 1959) and THE MUMMY (qv; 1999)
✦✦✦✧

THE MUMMY

UK, 1959. Dir: Terence Fisher. With: Peter Cushing, Christopher Lee, Yvonne Furneaux, Felix Aylmer, Eddie Byrne, Raymond Huntley. Hammer Films/Universal-International. Colour.
The third of Hammer's big monster remakes once again reunites director Fisher, scriptwriter Jimmy Sangster and stars Cushing and Lee. After the unconvincing opening scenes set around an Egyptian dig, the action moves to England where the reanimated mummy of high priest Kharis (Lee, almost unrecognisable under Roy Ashton's badges) starts murdering the members of the expedition who desecrated the 4,000 year-old tomb of the Princess Ananka (Furneaux). Cushing gives his usual fine performance as archaeologist John Banning, and he's ably supported by veterans Aylmer and Huntley, plus Hammer regulars George Pastell, Michael Ripper, George Woodbridge and stuntman Eddie Powell. Apparently, a Continental version was prepared by producer Michael Carreras containing some mild nudity and extra gore. This was adapted to comic strip format in *Halls of Horror* no.22 (1978).
✦✦✦

THE MUMMY

UK/Morocco/USA, 1999. Dir: Stephen Sommers. With: Brendan Fraser, Rachel Weisz, John Hannah, Arnold Vosloo, Kevin J. O'Connor, Jonathan Hyde. Universal/ Alphaville. Colour.
During the 1990s, Clive Barker, Joe Dante, Mick Garris, George Romero and John Sayles were all linked at various times with a remake of the 1933 Universal movie. Writer/director Sommers finally came up with this action-packed $80,000,000 're-imagining' of the original, with stunning visual effects created by Industrial Light & Magic. Rick O'Connell (a likeable Fraser) is a swashbuckling mercenary hired by British librarian Evelyn Carnarvon (Weisz) and her brother Jonathan (Hannah) to lead an expedition into the Sahara Desert in 1926. Discovering the ancient lost city of Hamunaptra, they unwittingly release Imhotep (Vosloo), a vengeful 3,000 year-old Egyptian High Priest who was sentenced to an eternity of living death for conspiring with royal mistress Anck-Su-Namun (Patricia Velasquez) to murder Pharaoh Seti. An enjoyable combination of adventure and horror, the climax features an army of mummies and a legion of sword-wielding zombies commanded by the revived vampiric sorcerer, who plans to unleash ten plagues upon Egypt. With Oded Fehr as a character named Ardeth Bay, and veteran Bernard Fox as an old RAF pilot. When this was a surprise box office hit, Universal and Sommers quickly began developing a sequel for release in 2001. Max Allan Collins wrote the novelisation and Ebury published a behind-the-scenes tie-in book.
✦✦✦✧

THE MUMMY

USA, 1999. Dir: Ted Newsom. With: Christopher Lee, Boris Karloff, Bela Lugosi. Passport Video. Colour/B&W.
Hour-long compilation video hosted by Lee that looks at mummy and zombie movies including the Universal and Hammer series. Much of the material is apparently recycled from *100 Years of Horror* (1996) and *Flesh and Blood: The Hammer Heritage of Horror* (1994). The DVD version contains half an hour of extra material, including a ten minute featurette on the making of *The Ωmega Man* (1971)!
✦✦

Boris Karloff is wrapped up in his role as The Mummy *(1933).*

THE MUMMY AND THE CURSE OF THE JACKALS

USA, 1969 (1985). Dir: Oliver Drake. With: Anthony Eisley, John Carradine, Robert Allen Browne, Marliza Pons, Maurine Dawson, Saul Goldsmith. Vega International/Academy Home Entertainment. Colour.
Inept feature shot under the title *The Mummy vs. the Were-Jackal*, which, according to star Eisley, was never finished. It was eventually patched together and released directly to video in the mid-1980s. Eisley (in a role originally planned for Scott Brady, who wisely dropped out) plays David Barry, an archaeologist who unearths a pair of 4,000 year-old mummies — a beautiful princess (Pons) and her bandaged guardian, Serac (Goldsmith). When the princess' sarcophagus is opened, Eisley falls under a curse that turns him into a were-jackal (the same mask was used in *Dracula [The Dirty Old Man]* [1969]). This is followed by a lot of wandering around Las Vegas until everyone ends up in a lake, where the princess crumbles to dust. Carradine turns up in a cameo as Professor Cummings. According to the star, director Drake (who associate produced *The Mummy's Curse* [1944], etc) was 'quite senile at the time.' It shows. Wyott Ordung (*Robot Monster* [1953], etc) was assistant director.
✦

MUMMY DEAREST

USA, 1990. Dir: Dick Dumont. With: Nina Hartley, Mike Horner, Cameo (Kelly Page/Katrina Cameo/Kameo), Lynn LeMay, Jamie Gillis, Jacqueline (Jacqueline St. Clair). Las Vegas Video. Colour.
Hardcore comedy in which many characters are named after those in the Universal series. Reanimated in California, the 4,000 year-old mummy of wisecracking Egyptian Princess Akasha (Hartley) is still horny, but every man she has sex with dies due to an ancient curse. Professor Steve Banning (Horner) teams up with Inspector Wimpole (Gillis) to investigate the mysterious deaths. With Cameo as Banning's girlfriend, Helen Grosvenor.
Sequel: MUMMY DEAREST 2 (qv; 1990)
✦✧

MUMMY DEAREST: A HORROR TRADITION UNEARTHED

USA, 1999. Dir: David J. Skal. With: Paul M. Jensen, Gregory W. Mank, David Del Valle, Rick Baker, Sara Karloff, Bill Condon. Universal Studios Home Video. Colour/B&W.
Half-hour documentary, written by Skal and released as a supplement to the DVD of *The Mummy* (1933). This includes an overview of Universal's classic Mummy series, with extensive clips and interviews with various film historians, plus John Balderston, the son of screenwriter John L. Balderston. Hosted and narrated by Rudy Behlmer.
✦✦✦✧

MUMMY DEAREST 3

(aka THE MUMMY III: THE PARTING)
USA, 1991 (1992). Dir: Jean-Pierre Ferrand. With: Nina Hartley, Mike Horner, Kristall (Jenna Wells), Raven (Raven St. James), Marissa Malibu, Ted Wilson. Las Vegas Video. Colour.
Professor Steve Banning (Horner) must decide whether to stay with his girlfriend Helen Grosvenor (Kristall) or accept immortality with ancient Egyptian Princess Akasha (Hartley) in this hardcore comedy.
✦

MUMMY DEAREST 2

(aka MUMMY PART 2: THE UNWRAPPING)
USA, 1990. Dir: Dick Dumont. With: Nina Hartley, Sunny McKay, Raven (Raven St. James), Heather St. Clair, Randy West, Mike Horner. Las Vegas Video. Colour.
Hardcore comedy in which reanimated Egyptian Princess Akasha (Hartley) and now-immortal archaeologist Steve Banning (Horner) travel to Cairo, where they recover the living mummy of Nikara (Raven) and return with her to California. This time McKay plays Banning's girlfriend Helen.
Sequel: MUMMY DEAREST 3 (qv; 1991)
✦

THE MUMMY LIVES

USA/Canada, 1993. Dir: Gerry O'Hara. With: Tony Curtis, Greg Wrangler, Leslie Hardy, Jack Cohen, Muhamed Bakri, Mosko Alkelai. Surge Productions/Cannon Pictures/Global Pictures. Colour.

Unbelievably awful reworking of the usual plot, scripted by Nelson Gidding and supposedly 'suggested' by the story 'Some Words With a Mummy' by Edgar Allan Poe! Curtis keeps his Brooklyn accent as the revived Aziru/Dr Mohassid who revenges himself upon the desecrators of his tomb. Director O'Hara brings no style whatsoever to the low-budget proceedings, produced by the infamous Harry Alan Towers.

✦

MUMMY LOVE

USA, 1926. Dir: Joe Rock. With: Neely Edwards, Alice Ardell. FBO/Standard Cinema Corporation. B&W.

Twenty-two minute silent comedy in which an expedition escape from a tomb dressed as mummies.

✦

THE MUMMY NANNY

(Orig: MOMIE AU PAIR)

France/Germany, 2000. Dir: Luc Vinciguerra. Les Cartooneurs Associés/France 2/EM TV & Merchandising AG. Colour.

Half-hour children's cartoon TV series (twenty-six episodes) created by Claude Prothée and Denis Olivieri about magical Egyptian mummy Amenotop, who is abruptly awakened from a 5,000 year sleep and finds himself in an international airport in the twenty-first century. After narrowly escaping the clutches of Ulysses Catastropholis/Pataquès, the unscrupulous millionaire antique dealer who kidnapped him, the mummy ends up working as the new 'au pair' in the eccentric household of Julius and Dorothy Elsware/Desprairies, thanks to the quick thinking of their children Alex and Samantha.

✦✧

THE MUMMY OF THE KING OF RAMSES

(Orig: LA MOMIE DU ROI)

France, 1909. Dir: Gerard Bourgeois. Lux. B&W.

Ten minute silent short in which an elderly professor brings the mummy of a king back to life.

✦

MUMMY'S BOYS

USA, 1936. Dir: Fred Guiol. With: Bert Wheeler, Robert Woolsey, Barbara Pepper, Moroni Olsen, Frank M. Thomas, Willie Best. RKO Radio Pictures. B&W.

Creaky murder mystery in which the unfunny comedy team of Wheeler and Woolsey encounter a fake 3,000 year-old living mummy as they attempt to return a cursed stolen treasure, already apparently responsible for the death of ten archaeologists, to the ancient Egyptian tomb of the Pharaoh Pharantime.

✦

THE MUMMY'S CURSE

USA, 1944. Dir: Leslie Goodwins. With: Lon Chaney, Virginia Christine, Martin Kosleck, Peter Coe, Kurt Katch, Dennis Moore. Universal. B&W.

Announced as *The Mummy's Return*, this was the fourth and thankfully final film in Universal's series about Kharis (once again played by Chaney Jr in make-up by Jack Pierce). While excavating a New England swamp(!), workers discover the mummy and an inexplicably still-youthful Princess Ananka (both buried there at the end of *The Mummy's Ghost*, made the same year). Soon the high priests of Egypt are at it again until Ilzor Zandaab (Coe) is betrayed by the evil Ragheb (Kosleck) who lusts after the princess (Christine). In the end, Kharis is buried under tons of rock while the magically revived Ananka shrivels up in the sunlight. Bernard L. Schubert's screenplay just rehashes the previous films, while director Goodwins simply goes through the motions. Chaney was tired of the role by this time, and many of his scenes were played by stunt double Eddie Parker. The worst entry in a below-standard series, this includes flashback clips from *The Mummy* (1933) and *The Mummy's Hand* (1940). With Holmes Herbert and silent film star William Farnum.

✦✧

MUMMY'S DUMMIES

USA, 1948. Dir: Edward Bernds. With: The Three Stooges (Moe Howard, Shemp Howard, Larry Fine), Vernon Dent, Ralph Dunn, Phil Van Zandt. Columbia. B&W.

Sixteen minute comedy short set in ancient Rome and involving the Stooges and a mummy.

✦✦

THE MUMMY'S DUNGEON

USA, 1993. Dir: G.W. Lawrence. With: Sal Longo, Dave Castiglione, Michelle Caporaletti, Cristie Clark, Launa Kane (Terri Lewandowski), Dawn Lewis. In Dire Straits Productions. Colour.

Bottom-of-the-barrel independent video in which voyeuristic photographer Rameses Karis (Longo) uses the female models who respond to his newspaper ads as human sacrifices to revive the surprisingly impressive-looking 2,000 year-old living mummy (Castiglione) he keeps in his basement. This New Jersey production includes brief topless nudity, some mild bondage and laughable gore effects. Many of the cast and crew were back in the same director's *Zombie Nightmare* (1993).

✦

THE MUMMY'S FOOT

USA, 1949. Dir: Sobey Martin. Marshall Grant/Realm TV Productions. B&W.

Short 16mm film based on the 1863 story by Théophile Gautier, in which a playwright meets a 3,000 year-old Egyptian princess. An early credit for the director of numerous Irwin Allen TV shows.

✦✧

THE MUMMY'S GHOST

USA, 1944. Dir: Reginald LeBorg. With: Lon Chaney, John Carradine, Ramsay Ames (Ramsey Philips), Barton MacLane, George Zucco, Robert Lowery. Universal. B&W.

The third entry in Universal's lacklustre Kharis series. After failing in *The Mummy's Tomb* (1942), Zucco's High Priest of Arkham is still alive(!) and sends Yousef Bey (Carradine) to New England to help the mummy Kharis (played by a totally wasted Chaney Jr and stuntman Eddie Parker in make-up by Jack Pierce) to discover the reincarnation of the Princess Ananka. It turns out to be college student Amina Mensouri (Ames, who replaced Acquanetta after the first day of shooting), who for no apparent reason gets white streaks in her hair and turns into an old woman as Kharis drags her into the quicksand. Frank Reicher's Professor Norman, a survivor from the previous film, is an early victim, while Yousef Bey's lust for the reincarnated princess gets him killed by the mummy. Despite the impressive cast, this is a tedious reworking of old ideas with cheap production values. With Martha MacVicar (later Vickers) and the voice of David Bruce.

Sequel: THE MUMMY'S CURSE (qv; 1944)

✦✦

THE MUMMY'S HAND

USA, 1940. Dir: Christy Cabanne. With: Dick Foran, Peggy Moran, Wallace Ford, Eduardo Ciannelli, George Zucco, Cecil Kelloway (Kellaway). Universal. B&W.

Universal's long-awaited follow-up to *The Mummy* (1933) turned out to be an entertaining 'B' thriller and the first in a short series. Kept alive for 3,000 years by the High Priests of Egypt with an elixir of Tana leaves, Kharis the mummy (eighth billed cowboy star Tom Tyler) brings death to the members of an archaeological expedition that includes Steve Banning (Foran) and Babe Jenson (Ford), who disturb the tomb of the Princess Ananka. Clips from the previous film are used in flashback (with Karloff identifiable in the long-shots), while the superb set design includes a temple interior borrowed from James Whale's *Green Hell* (1940). Tyler's mummy (in close-up make-up created by Jack Pierce) is a frightening, zombie-like creation with a limp, useless arm and black, undead eyes. Zucco is also on fine form as the mad High Priest of Karnak, Andoheb, who lusts after Marta

Solvani (Moran). With Charles Trowbridge and Harry Stubbs.
Sequel: THE MUMMY'S TOMB (qv; 1942)
✦✦✦

THE MUMMY'S REVENGE

(Orig: LA VENGANZA DE LA MOMIA)
Spain, 1973. Dir: Carlos Aured (Carlos A. Alonso). With: Paul Naschy (Jacinto Molina), Jack Taylor (George Brown Randall/Grek Martin), Maria Silva, Helga Liné (Helga Lina Stern), Rina Otolina, Eduardo Calvo. Lotus Films/ Sara Films. Colour.
Naschy (who also scripted under his real name) portrays the 3,000 year-old living mummy of sadistic Pharaoh Amen-Ho-Tep, restored to life by a mysterious Arab (also Naschy). Searching for a body to contain the soul of his blood-drinking queen (Liné), the mummy is eventually destroyed by an English Egyptologist (Taylor) with fire.
✦✧

THE MUMMY'S SHROUD

UK, 1967. Dir: John Gilling. With: André Morell, John Phillips, David Buck, Elizabeth Sellars, Catherine Lacey, Maggie Kimberley. Hammer Films/Associated British-Pathe. Colour.
Written and directed by Gilling, the third in Hammer's unconnected mummy series is a disappointing collection of clichés as a 1920s archaeological expedition led by Sir Basil Walden (Morell, who is killed off half-way through the film) discovers the long-lost tomb of Kah-to-Bey. However, the guardian of the tomb, Hasmid Ali (Roger Delgado) and his witch-mother Haiti (Lacey), revive the mummy of Prem (Eddie Powell) and send it after the desecrators of the boy Pharaoh's sepulchre. The killings include off-screen head-crushing and death by acid. As the timid valet Longbarrow, Michael Ripper gives a stand-out performance in a larger supporting role than usual. This was the last Hammer film made at Bray Studios. It was adapted into comic strip format in *The House of Hammer* no.15 (1977).
✦✦

THE MUMMY'S TOMB

USA, 1942. Dir: Harold Young. With: Lon Chaney, Dick Foran, John Hubbard, Elyse Knox, George Zucco, Wallace Ford. Universal. B&W.
This atmospheric sequel to *The Mummy's Hand* (1940) cleverly moves the action to America some years later. The High Priest of Karnak, Andoheb (Zucco in old age make-up), returns from the previous film and sends the living mummy Kharis (a wasted Chaney Jr and stuntman Ed[die] Parker in modified make-up by Jack Pierce) to destroy surviving archaeologists Stephen Banning (Foran) and Babe Hanson (Ford). New high priest Mehemet Bey (Turhan Bey) poses as an unlikely cemetery caretaker in New England and makes the usual mistake of falling for Isobel Evans (Knox), the fiancée of John Banning (Hubbard), while in the end the mummy burns again. This includes extensive flashbacks to the previous film and clips from *Frankenstein* (1931). With Mary Gordon, Frank Reicher and Glenn Strange.
Sequel: THE MUMMY'S GHOST (qv; 1944)
✦✦✦

MUNDO DEPRAVADOS (WORLD OF THE DEPRAVED)

USA, 1967. Dir: Herb Jeffries. With: Tempest Storm, (Johnnie) Decker & (Larry) Reed, Bunny Ware. Monique Productions/Boxoffice International. B&W.
Legendary stripper Storm stars as Tango in her first dramatic role in this 'adults only' 'sex murder mystery', in which the well-endowed female clients of her exercise club are targeted by a full moon killer who stabs and then strips his victims. Decker and Reed play comedy cops Ham and Rye, supposedly investigating the crimes.
✦

LAS MUÑECAS DEL KING KONG

Venezuela, 1978. Dir: Alfredo B. Crevenna. Colour.
Obscure Spanish-language movie from the Mexican director of Santo films.
✦

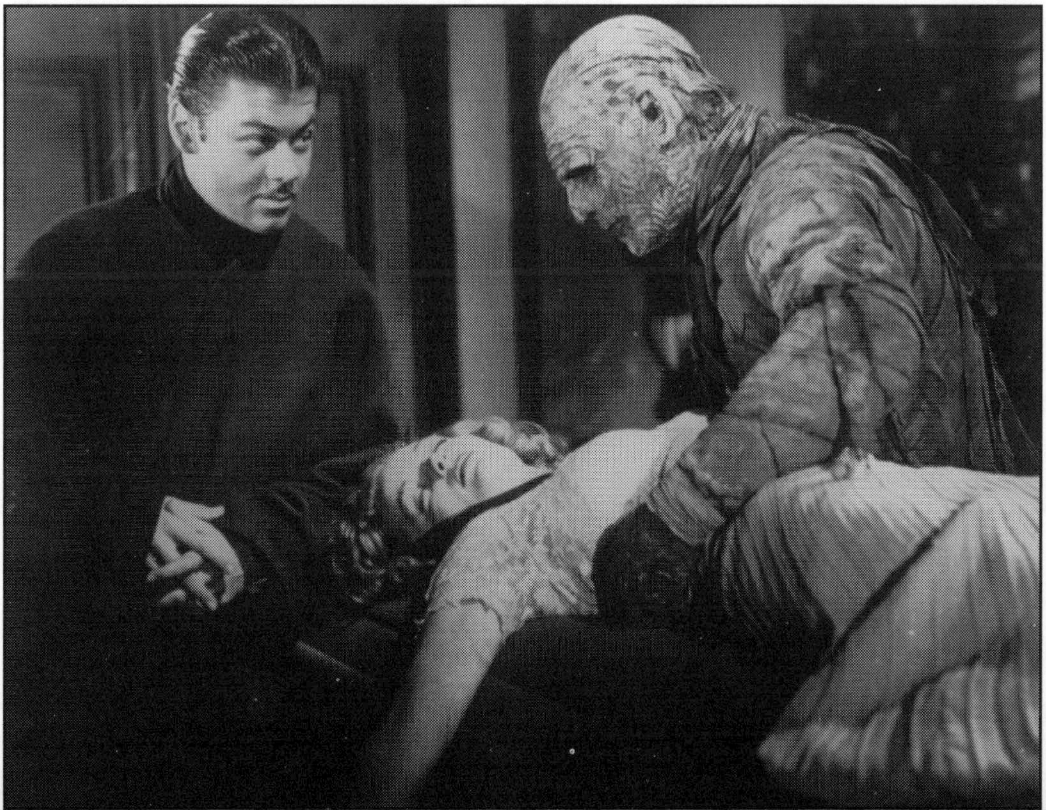

Turhan Bey and Lon Chaney Jr squabble over Elyse Knox in The Mummy's Tomb *(1942).*

CAROLINE MUNRO [b 1951]

British actress, a former Lamb's Navy Rum pin-up and brief Bond girl (*The Spy Who Loved Me* [1977]), whose eclectic genre career has encompassed Hammer vampires, Italian pulp science fiction, low-budget stalk 'n' slash, Paul Naschy, Jesús Franco and playing Vincent Price's dead wife in the two *Dr. Phibes* movies.

qv: *Captain Kronos Vampire Hunter* (1972); *Dracula A.D. 1972* (1972); *Flesh and Blood: The Hammer Heritage of Horror* (1994); *Howl of the Devil* (1988); *The Last Horror Film* (1982); *Night Owl* (1993); *100 Years of Horror: 'Blood-Drinking Beings'* (1996); *100 Years of Horror: 'Dracula and His Disciples'* (1996); *100 Years of Horror: 'Dr. Jekyll and Mr. Hyde'* (1996); *100 Years of Horror: 'Scream Queens'* (1996).

MUNSTER, GO HOME!

USA, 1966. Dir: Earl Bellamy. With: Fred Gwynne, Yvonne De Carlo, Al Lewis, Butch Patrick, Debbie Watson, Terry-Thomas. Universal. Colour.

Based on *The Munsters* TV series (1964-66), this was originally made for TV but released theatrically at the last minute. The weird family travel to Britain to claim Herman's (Gwynne) inheritance. The humour is laboured (although there are a couple of nice *Car 54 Where Are You?* [1961-62] and *Batman* [1966-68] in-jokes), and guest stars like Terry-Thomas and Hermione Gingold just look embarrassed. Only John Carradine, hidden under a red wig and sideburns as Cruikshank, the doddering butler, makes anything out of his small role. The film quickly runs out of steam and ends with a tedious car chase.

Sequel: THE NEW SATURDAY SUPERSTAR MOVIE: The Mini-Munsters (qv; 1973)

✦✧

THE MUNSTERS

USA, 1964-66. Dir: Lawrence Dobkin, David Alexander, Norman Abbott, Seymour Berns, Earl Bellamy, Ezra Stone, Joseph Pevney, Jerry Paris, Charles Barton, Don Richardson, Charles Rondeau and Gene Reynolds. With: Fred Gwynne, Yvonne De Carlo, Al Lewis, Butch Patrick, Beverly Owen, Pat Priest. Kayro-Vue Productions/ Universal/CBS-TV. B&W.

CBS's answer to ABC's slightly better *The Addams Family* (1964-66) features another group of friendly monsters: the Frankenstein Monster-like Herman (Gwynne, who could wear Bud Westmore's Karloff-style make-up because Universal Studios owned the copyright), the vampiric Lily (De Carlo), Grandpa (Lewis, who is revealed to be Count Dracula himself), wolfboy Eddie (Patrick) and the 'horribly' normal Marilyn (played by Owen and, later, Priest). John Carradine originally turned down the role of Herman, but did appear in a couple of episodes ('Herman's Raise' [1965] and 'The Musician' [1966]) as Mr Gateman, the owner of the mortuary where Herman works. A fifteen minute pilot film, 'My Fair Munster' (1964; dir: Norman Abbott. B&W.), with Joan Marshall as Phoebe (instead of Lily) and Happy Derman as Eddie, was never telecast. The series ran for seventy half-hour episodes and has spawned four movies to date. Guest stars included Roger C. Carmel, Robert Cornthwaite, Dom DeLuise, Frank Gorshin, John Hoyt, Harvey Korman, Barton MacLane, Bill Mumy, Don Rickles, Maxie Rosenbloom, Charlie Ruggles and Jesse White. A novelisation by Morton Cooper appeared from Avon Books in 1964, and two juvenile novels by William Johnston were published the following year.

✦✦

Herman's Rival

USA, 1964. Dir: Joseph Pevney. With: Fred Gwynne, Yvonne De Carlo, Al Lewis, Beverley Owen, Butch Patrick, Chet Stratton. Kayro-Vue Productions/Universal/ CBS-TV. B&W.

When Lilly attempts to replace some money taken by her wolf man brother (Irwin Charone), she takes a job as a waitress in a tea-room.

✦✦

Knock Wood, Here Comes Charlie

USA, 1964. Dir: Lawrence Dobkin. With: Fred Gwynne, Yvonne De Carlo, Al Lewis, Beverley Owen, Butch Patrick, Mike Mazurki. Kayro-Vue Productions/ Universal/CBS-TV. B&W.

Herman's untrustworthy twin brother Charlie (also Gwynne) comes to stay with the Munsters and brings with him a machine he claims can extract uranium from sea water.

✦✦

Mummy Munster

USA, 1965. Dir: Ezra Stone. With: Fred Gwynne, Yvonne De Carlo, Al Lewis, Pat Priest, Butch Patrick, Philip Ober. Kayro-Vue Productions/Universal/CBS-TV. B&W.

After taking one of Grandpa's new sleeping pills, Herman falls asleep in an Egyptian sarcophagus while visiting the museum and is mistaken for an ancient mummy.

✦✦

A Visit from Johann

USA, 1965. Dir: Gene Reynolds. With: Fred Gwynne, Yvonne De Carlo, Al Lewis, Pat Priest, Butch Patrick, John Abbott. Kayro-Vue Productions/Universal/CBS-TV. B&W.

Dr Victor Frankenstein IV (Abbott) asks Herman to teach Johann (Gwynne again, looking like Karloff in *Son of Frankenstein* [1939]), his grandfather's monstrous 150 year-old prototype, to become civilised. However, Lily mistakenly takes Johann off for the weekend.

Series sequel: MUNSTER, GO HOME! (qv; 1966)

✦✦

THE MUNSTERS' REVENGE

USA, 1981. Dir: Don Weis. With: Fred Gwynne, Al Lewis, Yvonne De Carlo, K.C. Martel, Jo McDonnell, Bob Hastings. Universal/NBC-TV. Colour.

Terrible TV movie that revives the characters fifteen years after the regular series finished. The Frankenstein Monster-like Herman (Gwynne) and vampiric Grandpa (Lewis) have to prove their innocence when the villainous Dr Dustin Diablo/Emil Hornshymler (an over-the-top Sid Caesar) uses robot doubles of the pair to go on a crime spree. Gwynne and Lewis don't look like they've aged at all and do their best to carry the movie. But Weis' lacklustre direction, an insipid supporting cast (particularly Hastings' irritating Phantom of the Opera) and the awful dubbed laughter make this reunion a sad mistake. With Martel taking over from Butch Patrick as wolfboy Eddie, McDonnell as Marilyn, Howard Morris as Igor, and Charles Macaulay. Amongst the waxwork robots are a werewolf, the Creature from the Black Lagoon, the Hunchback of Notre Dame and another wearing a Tor Johnson mask.

Remake: THE MUNSTERS TODAY (qv; 1988-91)

✦

THE MUNSTERS' SCARY LITTLE CHRISTMAS

Australia/USA, 1996. Dir: Ian Emes. With: Sam McMurray, Ann Magnuson, Bug Hall, Sandy Baron, Mary Woronov, Elaine Hendrix. MTE/Michael R. Joyce Productions/St. Clare Entertainment/Universal/Fox Network. Colour.

TV movie follow-up to *Here Come the Munsters* (1995) in which wolfboy Eddie (Hall) wishes for a Transylvanian Christmas, just like the ones he used to know. So Herman (McMurray), Lily (Magnuson), Marilyn (Hendrix) and the vampiric Grandpa (Baron) attempt to re-create an old-fashioned holiday for the entire family (which includes a mummy [Justin Case], The Creature from the Black Lagoon [Christian Manon], a werewolf [Ben Grieve], The Phantom of the Opera [Jason Taylor], The Invisible Man [Brett Wood], The Hunchback of Notre Dame [Donald Cook], a Moleman [Andrew Windsor] and various zombies). The character make-up effects are once again expertly re-created by Steve Johnson's XFX, Woronov returns as nosy neighbour Edna Dimwitty, and Bruce Spence plays Mr Gateman. John Landis was co-executive producer.

✦✦✧

THE MUNSTERS TODAY

USA, 1988-91. Dir: Russ Petranto, Norman Abbott, Dick Harwood, Bob Claver, Peter Isacksen, Bonnie Franklin,

The cast of TV's The Munsters Today *(1988-91).*

Lee Lochhead, Doug Rogers, Scott Redman, Bruce Bilson, Jerry Ross and Marlena Laird. With: John Schuck, Lee Meriwether, Howard Morton, Hilary Van Dyke, Jason Marsden. The Arthur Company/MCA-TV. Colour.
Ill-conceived attempt to revive the popular 1960s comedy series with an all-new cast. After one of vampire Grandpa's (Morton) experiments causes them to hibernate for more than twenty years, the Munster family — Frankenstein Monster Herman (Schuck), Lily (Meriwether), wolfboy Eddie (Marsden) and normal teenager Marilyn (Van Dyke) — revive in modern times. Incredibly, this shot-on-video travesty survived for seventy-two syndicated episodes — two more than the original TV series! Guest stars included Norman Fell, Ruth Buzzi, Dr Joyce Brothers, Zsa Zsa Gabor, Shelley Berman and Billy Barty.
✦✧

Don't Cry Wolfman
USA, 1989. Dir: Peter Isacksen. With: John Schuck, Lee Meriwether, Howard Morton, Hilary Van Dyke, Jason Marsden, Jerry Hauser. The Arthur Company/MCA-TV. Colour.
A bank robber pretends to be the Munster's long-lost wolfman cousin so that he can recover the stolen loot he hid in their house a decade before.
✦✧

Green-Eyed Munsters
USA, 1989. Dir: Peter Isacksen. With: John Schuck, Lee Meriwether, Howard Morton, Hilary Van Dyke, Jason Marsden, Robert Clary. The Arthur Company/MCA-TV. Colour.
Herman becomes jealous when an old mummy friend of Lily's convinces her to enter the Mrs Transylvania beauty contest.
✦✧

Reunion
USA, 1989. Dir: Scott Redman. With: John Schuck, Lee Meriwether, Howard Morton, Hilary Van Dyke, Jason Marsden, Yetta. The Arthur Company/MCA-TV. Colour.
When their cousin Bella announces her engagement to invisible trapeze artist Boris, the Munsters decide to hold the wedding at Mockingbird Lane. They invite all their in-laws, including Aunt Yetta, Cousin Damien, Igor (Foster Brooks) and Herman's brother Frank (Peter Schuck).
Series sequel: HERE COME THE MUNSTERS (qv; 1995)
✦✧

THE MUPPET SHOW
UK, 1976. Dir: Jim Henson. With: Vincent Price, Jim Henson, Frank Oz, Dave Goelz, Kathy Mullen, Bob Payne. ITC Entertainment/ITV. Colour.
Price, who is the special guest host on this episode of this popular half-hour syndicated puppet show (1976-80, 120 episodes), sings 'You've Got a Friend' and dons vampire fangs to join an equally fanged Kermit the Frog. The semi-regular supporting characters also include Count von Count, a monocled vampiric puppet (voiced by Jerry Nelson) who teaches children how to count on Henson's *Sesame Street* series (1969-). In another first season episode, guest star Twiggy (Lesley Hornby) appeared in a sketch entitled 'Phantom of the Muppet Show'.
Series sequel: THE MUPPET MOVIE (1979)
✦✦

LOS MURCIÉLAGOS
Mexico, 1964. Dir: J. (Juan) Ortega. With: Joaqúin Cordero, Alma Fuentes, William Murray. Sanchez Ramade. B&W.
Horror Western in which the bad guys disguise themselves as vampires. This was released in Spain the following year as *Los Vampiros del Oeste*.
✦

MURDER MANSION
(Orig: LA MANSIÓN DE LA NIEBLA/QUANDO MARTA URLO DALLA TOMBA. USA: aka AMUCK)
Spain/Italy, 1970. Dir: F. (Francisco) Lara Polop. With: Analia Gade, Evelyn Stewart (Ida Galli), Andres Resino, (Anna) Lisa Nardi, Ingrid Garbo, Eduardo Fajardo. Mundial Film/Tritone Filmindustria/Avco-Embassy. Colour.
Lost in the fog, Fred and Laura (Resino and Nardi) encounter terrified heiress Elsie (Gade), who claims to have seen a pair of ghosts in a nearby cemetery. The trio decide to spend the night in an old mansion owned by a strange woman named Marta (Stewart). She reveals that the local village was abandoned because of a mysterious vampire, and in the end, it all turns out to be a plot by Elsie's husband (Fajardo) to drive his wife insane.
✦✧

MURDER, SHE WROTE:
The Legacy of Borbey House
USA, 1993. Dir: Walter Grauman. With: Angela Lansbury, David Birney, Roy Dotrice, Christopher Neame, Madlyn Rhue, William Windom. Universal/Corymore Productions/CBS-TV. Colour.
Popular hour-long TV series (1984-97, 264 episodes) based around the character of successful mystery novelist and amateur sleuth Jessica Fletcher (executive producer Lansbury), created by Peter S. Fischer, and Richard Levinson and William Link. When a mysterious stranger (Birney), suspected of being a vampire, is found staked to death soon after he moves to Cabot Cove, Jessica suspects foul play. With Dotrice as an eccentric vampire-hunter and Neame as a sinister butler. Meanwhile, in the cleverly-titled 1995 episode, 'Death 'n Denial' (dir: Jerry Jameson), veterans Turhan Bey and Lee Meriwether are involved in the smuggling of a 4,000 year-old Egyptian artefact.
✦✦

MURDERS IN THE RUE MORGUE
Spain/France/USA, 1971. Dir: Gordon Hessler. With: Jason Robards, Christine Kaufmann, Herbert Lom, Adolfo Celi, Michael Dunn, Lilli Palmer. American International. Colour.
Although supposedly based on the story by Edgar Alan Poe, the muddled screenplay by Christopher Wicking and Henry Slesar owes more to Gaston Leroux's *The Phantom of the Opera*, with Lom recreating his role from the 1962 Hammer version. Set in turn-of-the-century Paris, Grand Guignol theatre owner César Charron (Robards) discovers that members of his performing troupe are being killed, their faces burned with vitriol. It turns out to be the work of disfigured actor Marot (Lom), a revenge-crazed killer. Hessler's direction is all over the place, thanks to a series of confusing flashbacks and dream sequences, and it's difficult to decide just who we are supposed to sympathise with. Palmer is wasted in a brief cameo and, as usual, only the diminutive Dunn emerges with any style. With Maria Peschy and Peter Arne. Most of the violence was cut from the American print.
Remake: THE MURDERS IN THE RUE MORGUE (1986)
✦✧

F.W. MURNAU (Friedrich Wilhelm Plumpe) [1888-1931]
German Expressionist film-maker, most of whose films are now lost. Winner of the Best Artistic Achievement Academy Award for his 1927 film *Sunrise: A Song of Two Humans* (1927), his major genre credits include *Der Januskopf* (1920), *Nosferatu* (1922) and *Faust* (1926). He was killed in a car crash in California shortly before *Dracula* (1931) was released. Murnau was portrayed by John Malkovich in *Burned to Light* (1999).
qv: *The Twelfth Hour* (1920).

MUSCLE BEACH PARTY
USA, 1964. Dir: William Asher. With: Frankie Avalon, Annette Funicello, Luciana Paluzzi, John Ashley, Don Rickles, Peter Turgeon. Alta Vista/American International Pictures. Colour.
The second in AIP's Beach Party series has an Italian Countess (Paluzzi) trying to turn Frankie (Avalon) into a recording star and take him away from Dee Dee (Funicello). With Jody McCrea, Morey Amsterdam, Buddy Hackett, Dan Haggerty and Rock Stevens (aka

Peter Lupus) as musclemen, Peter Lorre (in his last role) in a cameo as Mr Strangdour, the strongest man in the world, plus Igor, his uncredited werewolf assistant. Music by Dick Dale and the Del Tones, and introducing Little Stevie Wonder. Lancer Books published a novelisation by Elsie Lee.
Sequel: BIKINI BEACH (qv; 1964)
✦✦

EL MUSEO DEL CRIMEN
Mexico, 1944. Dir: René Cardona. With: Fu Manchu (David T. Bamberg), Manuel Medel, Angel T. Sala, Pituka de Foronda, Katy Jurado, Rafael Icardo. Astro/Filmes Mundiales. B&W.
Directed by ex-actor Cardona, this was one of a series of crime thrillers starring British-born stage magician Bamberg, who took the name Fu Manchu because of the oriental make-up he wore for his show. Although it has nothing to do with the rest of this detective story (the title translates as 'The Museum of Crime'), in one scene Bamberg's hero apparently glimpses the face of a werewolf in a hotel room mirror. Based on a story by the star.
✦

MUSEO DEL HORROR
Mexico, 1962. Dir: Rafael Baledon. With: Carlos López Moctezuma, David Reynoso, Emma Roldan, Sonia Infante, Armando Soto la Marina, Julian de Meriche. Producciones Sotomayor/Columbia. B&W.
Mexican version of *Mystery of the Wax Museum* (1932), in which an ex-actor becomes a skull-faced madman who kidnaps women and pours hot wax over their bodies, turning them into exhibits for his museum. The heroine has a nightmare in which rotting corpses return to life.
✦✦

THE MUSICAL VAMPIRE
(Orig: YIN YUE JIANG SHI)
Hong Kong, 1992. Golden Harvest. Colour.
Horror comedy about a hopping vampire that is obsessed with an old-fashioned musical pocket watch. In the end, an eclipse of the moon destroys the undead.
✦

MUTANT SPECIES
USA, 1995. Dir: David A. Prior. With: Leo Rossi, Ted Prior, Powers Boothe, Denise Crosby, Wilford Brimley. Live. Colour.
Set in 2003, a government conspiracy results in a canister of mutated DNA from a crashed spaceship transforming the leader of a Special Forces squad (Rossi) into a killer beast.
✦✧

MY BEST FRIEND IS A VAMPIRE
(aka I WAS A TEENAGE VAMPIRE)
USA, 1986 (1987). Dir: Jimmy Huston. With: Robert Sean Leonard, Cheryl Pollak, Rene Auberjonois, Evan Mirand, Fannie Flagg, David Warner. Kings Road Entertainment/ Icon. Colour.
Better than usual teen horror comedy. When Jeremy Capello (Leonard) is bitten by a female vampire, it causes problems with his home and school life. Luckily he has suave vampire Modoc (Auberjonois) to teach him how to survive and use his new-found talents to outwit rabid vampire hunter Professor McCarthy (Warner, who pulls out all the stops). Director Huston scores with likeable characters, an entertaining script by Tab Murphy and some fun with the clichés.
✦✦✧

MY BOYFRIEND'S BACK
USA, 1993. Dir: Bob Balaban. With: Andrew Lowery, Traci Lind, Danny Zorn, Edward Herrmann, Mary Beth Hurt, Matthew Fox. Buena Vista Pictures/Touchstone. Colour.
Offbeat zombie comedy narrated by murdered teenager Johnny Dingle (Lowery), who returns from the grave to escort his sweetheart Missy McCloud (Lind) to the high school prom. However, when his body starts falling apart, only the consumption of human flesh will hold him together long enough to keep his date. With Austin Pendleton as the mad Dr Bronson, who wants to use Johnny's limbs to create an eternal youth serum, Cloris Leachman as Maggie the zombie expert, and Paul Dooley and Ed Neal as a pair of locals. Produced by Sean S. Cunningham and filmed under the title *Johnny Zombie*.
✦✦

MY COUSIN, THE GHOST
(Orig: BIAO GE DAO)
Hong Kong/UK, 1986. Dir: Wu Ma (Wo Ma/Yuen Wah/Ng Ma-Wu). With: Richard Ng, Kenny Bee (Mamy Boo), Mui Wen-Se, Alam Tam, Wu Ma (Wo Ma/Yuen Wah/Ng Ma-Wu). Colour.
Cantonese comedy. When a man (Ng) sells his restaurant business in Britain and returns to share his profits with his cousins in Hong Kong, he turns out to be a zombie.
✦✧

MY DATE WITH A VAMPIRE
Hong Kong, 1999. Dir: Sin Chi-Wai. With: Wan Tin-Chiu, Meng Yee-Man, Yang Kung-Ru. ATV Enterprises. Colour.
Hour-long TV series (thirty-five episodes) about a battle between two vampires, one of whom is good and the other evil.
✦✧

MY FAVORITE MARTIAN: Miss Jekyll and Hyde
USA, 1964. Dir: Oscar Rudolph. With: Ray Walston, Bill Bixby, Pamela Britton, Ann Marshall, J. Pat O'Malley, Marlo Thomas. CBS-TV. B&W.
Half-hour comedy TV series (1963-66, 107 episodes) in which alien X-Idguis 12 (Walston) crash-lands on Earth and meets up with Los Angeles reporter Tim O'Hara (Bixby), who passes him off as his eccentric Uncle Martin. In this episode, Martin is worried that the landlady's visiting niece will discover his secret. With Tom Skerritt.
Series sequel: MY FAVORITE MARTIANS (1973-75)
Series remake: MY FAVORITE MARTIAN (1999)
✦✦

MY FAVORITE SPY
USA, 1951. Dir: Norman Z. McLeod. With: Bob Hope, Hedy Lamarr (Hedwig Kiesler), Francis L. Sullivan, Arnold Moss, John Archer, Luis Van Rooten. Paramount. B&W.
Comedy thriller in which burlesque comic Peanuts White (Hope) is a double for an international assassin who he has to impersonate to recover a secret microfilm for the American government. In one scene, White is injected by a doctor (Norbert Schiller) with a truth syrum that results in him acting out the part of Dr Jekyll transforming into Mr Hyde during a song. With Morris Ankrum, Mike Mazurki and Nestor Paiva.
✦✦✧

MY LOVELY MONSTER
Germany/USA, 1990 (1991). Dir: Michel Bergmann. With: Silvio Francesco, Forrest J Ackerman, Nicole Fischer, Matthias Fuchs, Marlen Diekhoff, Peter Voss. Xenon Films/WDR/SFB-TV. Colour.
Charming spoof on horror films, featuring additional (pun-filled) dialogue and a cameo appearance by Ackerman as the Master. Francesco plays silent film vampire Maximilian (made-up to look like Lon Chaney Sr in *London After Midnight* [1927]) who is freed from a burning piece of nitrate film and suddenly finds himself in a German cinema. This is filled with horror movie references, and also includes appearances by Ferdinand Mayne, Bobbie Bresee and Boris Karloff's daughter, Sara Jane.
✦✦

MY MOM'S A WEREWOLF
USA, 1988 (1989). Dir: Michael Fischa. With: Susan Blakely, John Saxon, Katrina Caspary, John Schuck, Diana Barrows, Ruth Buzzi. Crown International Pictures. Colour.
Misjudged comedy, scripted by Mark Pirro (*Curse of the Queerwolf*

[1987], etc). Neglected suburban mom Leslie Shaber (Blakely) is seduced and bitten on the toe by smooth werewolf pet shop owner Harry Thropen (Saxon). Soon she's trying to file down her teeth and shave the hair off her legs. In the end, two fully transformed werewolves (in Don Post masks) battle each other. With Buzzi as a gypsy clairvoyant and an uncredited cameo by Forrest J Ackerman at a science fiction convention.
✦✧

MY SECRET IDENTITY:
Two Faces Have I
Canada, 1989. Dir: F. Harvey Frost. With: Derek McGrath, Jerry O'Connell, Wanda Cannon, Marsha Moreau, Elizabeth Leslie, Graham Batchelor. CTV. Colour.
Half-hour syndicated TV series (1988-91, seventy-two episodes) about teenage comic book collector Andrew Clements (O'Connell) who is accidentally exposed to gamma rays by Dr Benjamin Jeffcoate, aka 'Dr J' (McGrath), and develops superpowers which he uses under the guise of Ultraman. In this episode, Dr J invents a device to overcome shyness but when he tests it on himself he develops a Jekyll and Hyde split personality.
✦✧

MY SOUL IS SLASHED
(Orig: DORAKIYURA YORI AI-O/KAMITSUKITAI)
Japan, 1990 (1991). Dir: Shunsuke Kaneko. With: Ken Ogaka, Narumi Yasuda, Hikaru Ishida, Takero Morimoto, Eisei Amamoto. MMI/Castos-Toho. Colour.
Horror comedy in which a doctor (Yasuda) obsessed by vampires discovers that Romanian dictator Ceausecu was experimenting with Dracula's blood before he was overthrown. When some of that blood is mistakenly used during a failed operation, murdered businessman Ishikawa (Ogaka) rises from the dead a year later as a vampire, much to his own confusion and that of his teenage daughter (Ishida). The English-language title song is by French Goth pop star Mylene Farmer.
✦✧

MYSTERIES & SCANDALS:
Bela Lugosi
USA, 1998. Dir: Marian Inova and James 'Bigboy' Medlin. With: A.J. Benza, Forrest (J) Ackerman, Robert Clarke, Robert Wise, Martin Landau, Maila Nurmi. E! Entertainment Television. Colour/B&W.
This sleazy, tabloid-style exposé of 'the tormented life' of Lugosi simply rehashes rumour, innuendo and myths as it concentrates on the end of the actor's career as an alcoholic and drug addict. Hollywood Wax Museum curator Jonathan Morrill, family friends David Dursten and Richard Sheffield, *Cult Magazine* editor Buddy Barnett, and biographers Gary D. Rhodes and Greg Mank are among the interviewees. This is illustrated with re-enactments, still photographs, clips and trailers from *The Black Cat* (1934), *The Body Snatcher* (1945), *The Devil Bat* (1940), *Dracula* (1931), *Frankenstein* (1931), *Frankenstein Meets the Wolf Man* (1943), outtakes from *Glen or Glenda* (1953), *Intimate Interviews* with Dorothy West (1932), (Abbott and Costello) *Meet Frankenstein* (1948), *Plan 9 from Outer Space* (1958), *Spooks Run Wild* (1941), *White Zombie* (1932) and a 1952 newsreel interview. Hosted by Benza.
✦

James Whale
USA, 1998. Dir: Marian Inova. With: A.J. Benza, Greg Mank, Curtis Harrington, Gary D. Rhodes, James Curtis. E! Entertainment Television. Colour/B&W.
A look at director Whale's life and career leading up to and concentrating on his homosexuality, pool parties and eventual suicide. With clips and trailers from *Frankenstein* (1931) and *Bride of Frankenstein* (1935), and Michael White portraying Whale in the reenactment sequences.
✦

MYSTERIES, MAGIC & MIRACLES:
Dracula
USA/UK, 1995. Dir: Susan O'Leary and David McKenzie. With: Patrick Macnee, James Romanovich, Susan O'Leary. Mysteries, Magic & Miracles Productions/Associated Television International. Colour/B&W.
Half-hour TV show in which host Macnee narrates a segment about Bram Stoker and his character Dracula, with clips from *Nosferatu* (1922) and *Dracula* (1931), plus an interview with 'vampire aficionado' Carla Narvy.
✦✧

Vampires
USA/UK, 1996. Dir: Susan O'Leary and David McKenzie. With: Patrick Macnee, Susan O'Leary. Mysteries, Magic & Miracles Productions/Associated Television International. Colour/B&W.
Macnee also narrates an extended version of the above segment that includes numerous clips from the 1931 *Dracula*, black and white scenes from *Dracula Prince of Darkness* (1965), *Nosferatu* (1922 and 1979 versions), the Mexican *The Vampire* (1957), *The Vampire Lovers* (1970) and others, plus comments by 'vampire aficionado' Carla Narvy.
✦✧

THE MYSTERIOUS DEATH OF NINA CHEREAU
Canada, 1988. Dir: Dennis Berry. With: Maud Adams (Maud Wikstrom), Scott Renderer, Alexandra Stewart, László Szabó, Charles Millot, Françoise Brion. Colour.
A ten year-old murder mystery is resurrected when the alleged killer escapes from a mental asylum. This apparently turns out to be another variation on the Countess Elizabeth Bathory legend.
✦✧

MYSTERY AND IMAGINATION:
Carmilla
UK, 1966. Dir: Bill Bain. With: David Buck, Jane Merrow, Joseph O'Connor, Natasha Pyne, Roy Marsden, Sonia Dresdel. Associated British Corporation/ITV. B&W.
Hour-long anthology TV series (1966-68, eighteen episodes) that featured adaptations of classic horror stories. In this version of the 1871 novella by J. Sheridan Le Fanu, Pyne plays the eponymous vampire who insinuates herself into the family of a colonel. Presented by Richard Beckett (Buck).
Episode remake: THE VAMPIRE LOVERS (qv; 1970)
✦✦

Feet Foremost
UK, 1968. Dir: Toby Robertson. With: Neil Stacy, Fiona Hartford, Clive Morton, Timothy West, Fiona Walker. Associated British Corporation/ITV. Colour.
Based on the story by L.P. Hartley. A successful army officer moves into an old country manor which is haunted by vampire/ghost Lady Eleanor (Walker).
Episode remake: SHADES OF DARKNESS: Feet Foremost (qv; 1983)
✦✦

The Flying Dragon
UK, 1966. Dir: Bill Bain. With: David Buck, Ann Bell, John Moffatt, John Phillips, Derek Smith. Associated British Corporation/ITV. B&W.
Based on the 1872 story 'The Room of the Dragon Volant' by J. Sheridan Le Fanu. While on holiday in France, storyteller Richard Beckett (Buck) meets the Countess de St. Valyre who is trying to escape from her aged husband.
✦✦

The Tractate Middoth
UK, 1966. Dir: Kim Mills. With: David Buck, Norman Scace, Jerry Verno, Tim Preece, Giles Block, Edwin Finn. Associated British Corporation/ITV. B&W.
Based on the story by M.R. James. A cobwebbed corpse rises from the dead to prevent Beckett (Buck) from investigating the eponymous volume for one of his customers.
Series sequel: PLAYHOUSE: MYSTERY AND IMAGINATION (qv; 1968-70)
✦✦

THE MYSTERY IN DRACULA'S CASTLE
USA, 1972 (1973). Dir: Robert Totten. With: Johnny Whitaker, Scott Kolden, Mariette Hartley, Clu Gulager. Buena Vista/NBC-TV. Colour.
Juvenile TV movie, originally shown in two parts on the *World of Disney* series. Whitaker plays a fan of Dracula films who, along with

his brother (Kolden), decides to transform an old lighthouse into the location for an amateur horror movie. However, it also turns out to be a hideout for jewel thieves. Scholastic published a novelisation by Vic Crume.
✦✧

MYSTERY OF THE GOLDEN LOTUS

USA, 1989. Dir: Peter Davy and Jean Pierre Ferrano. With: Victoria Paris, Viper (Stephanie Bishop), Jon Martin, Sharon Kane, Eric Edwards, Rick Savage. Pure Class Productions/Hustler Video. Colour.
Hardcore feature which opens in ancient Egyptian times with Aramata (Peter North), the captain of the guards, using the incantation of the gods to return Queen Phaedre (Paris) to life. In 1940, the Nazis are after the scroll containing the secret of eternal life, which archaeologist Dr Roberts (Martin) is attempting to translate.
✦✧

THE MYSTERY OF THE LAMA CONVENT

(aka DR. NICOLA IN TIBET)
Denmark, 1909. Nordisk/Great Northern. B&W.
Silent short in which the dead are returned to life by Tibetan monks.
✦

MYSTERY ON MONSTER ISLAND

(Orig: MISTERIO EN LA ISLA DE LOS MONSTRUOS. USA: aka MONSTER ISLAND)
Spain/USA, 1982. Dir: J. (Juan) Piquer Simon. With: Terence Stamp, Peter Cushing, Ian Sera, David Hatton, Gasphar Ipua, Paul Naschy (Jacinto Molina). Twentieth Century Fox/Almena Films/Fort Films. Colour.
Filmed in 1980, this juvenile comedy/adventure was one of the most expensive films made in Spain and is supposedly based on a story by Jules Verne. The young nephew of a millionaire (Cushing) and his bumbling tutor are tricked into thinking they are shipwrecked on Spencer Island, where they encounter cannibals, rubber dinosaurs, giant worms, seaweed monsters and fake-looking gill men. Naschy has a brief cameo as Flint, a hermit protecting his cave of gold from Stamp's evil crew.
✦✧

MYSTICS IN BALI

(Orig: LEÁK. USA: aka BALINESE MYSTIC)
Indonesia, 1981. Dir: H. Tjut Djalili. With: Ilona Agathe Bastian, Yos Santo, Sofia Wo, W.D. Mochtar. Colour.
While studying folklore on Bali, Australian anthropologist Cathy Dean (Bastian) is transformed by an evil witch into a *penanggalan* — a blood-seeking flying head with its internal organs attached — and ordered to devour a new-born baby. The head is prevented from returning to its body and the witch is defeated in a battle of magic. From the director of *Lady Terminator* (1988).
✦✧

-N-

NADJA

USA, 1994. Dir: Michael Almereyda. With: Suzy Amis, Galaxy Craze, Martin Donovan, Peter Fonda, Karl Geary, Jared Harris. Kino Link Company/October Films. B&W.

Writer/director Almereyda's unofficial remake of *Dracula's Daughter* (1936) is artsy, downbeat and pretentious. The vampiric Nadja (Romanian actress Elina Löwensohn) and her servant Renfield (Geary) wander listlessly around contemporary New York while being pursued by an eccentric Dr Van Helsing (Fonda) and his nephew Jim (Donovan). Dracula is played in flashback by both Fonda and clips of an uncredited Bela Lugosi from *White Zombie* (1932), while executive producer David Lynch (who financed the film) has a cameo as a morgue attendant. Yawn.

✦✧

NAIDRA, THE DREAM WORKER

USA, 1914. Edison. B&W.

Three-reel silent drama in which a man steals a cursed necklace from a mummy and then discovers that he is unable to dispose of it.

✦

J. CARROL NAISH
(Joseph Patrick Carrol Naish) [1900-1973]

Irish-American stage and film actor, often cast as an evil foreigner or mad doctor. He played the eponymous detective in the TV series *The New Adventures of Charlie Chan* (1957).

qv: *Batman* (1943); *Dracula vs. Frankenstein* (1970); *House of Frankenstein* (1944); *Jungle Woman* (1944).

NAKED LOVERS

(Orig: LA FILLE À' LA FOURRURE. USA: PORNO ZOMBIES/ STARSHIP EROS)

France, 1977. Dir: Claude Pierson. With: Ursula White, Alban Ceray, Didier Aubriot, Barbara Moore. Pierson. Colour.

Sex movie in which aliens from the planet Eros reanimate the bodies of the dead and inhabit them. *Starship Eros* is apparently the hardcore version.

✦

THE NAKED WORLD OF HARRISON MARKS

UK, 1967. Dir: (George) Harrison Marks. With: (George) Harrison Marks, Pamela Green, June Palmer, Chris Williams, Annette Johnson, Jukta Goz. Token/Manson Distributing. Colour.

Dated nudie comedy directed, produced and co-scripted by British photographer Marks, who also plays seven roles, including Count Dracula and James Bond. Narrated by Valentine Dyall.

✦

REGGIE NALDER
(Alfred Reginald Natzick) [1912-1991]

Austrian-born character actor with distinctive burn scars on his lower face. He entered films in 1949 and was cast by Hitchcock as the cold-blooded assassin in the remake of *The Man Who Knew Too Much* (1956). After moving to Hollywood in the early 1960s, he began appearing in horror roles, including Dr Van Helsing (under the alias 'Detlef van Berg') in the hardcore *Dracula Sucks* (1979) and the Nosferatu-like vampire Barlow in TV's *Salem's Lot* (1979).

qv: *The Dead Don't Die* (1974); *Dracula's Dog* (1977); *The Hardy Boys* (1977); *McCloud: McCloud Meets Dracula* (1977).

NANBANJI NO SEMUSHI-OTOKO

Japan, 1957. Dir: Torajiro Saito. With: Achako Hanabashi, Shunji Sakai, Naritoshi Hayashi, Kyu Sazanka, Tamao Nakamura. Daiei. B&W.

Too much alcohol transforms a warrior into a hunchback and he becomes a bellringer in this spoof of Victor Hugo's *The Hunchback of Notre Dame*. In the end, he kills his enemy and regains his normal shape. The title translates as 'Return to Manhood'.

✦

ALAN NAPIER
(Alan Napier-Clavering) [1903-1988]

Always dependable British supporting actor, in Hollywood since 1940. Best known for his portrayal of Alfred the butler in the popular TV series *Batman* (1966-68).

qv: *Cat People* (1942); *Isle of the Dead* (1945); *Master Minds* (1949); *Rod Serling's Night Gallery: 'Fright Night'* (1972).

NARCO SATANICO

Mexico, 1988. Dir: Rafael (López) Portillo. With: David Reynoso, Ana Luisa Peluffo, Beatriz Aguirre, Roberto Canedo, Silvia Suarez. Guadalupe Emperatriz. Colour.

Low-budget voodoo sex and horror thriller, with a nightmare sequence involving a graveyard full of grotesque zombies.

✦

PAUL NASCHY
(Jacinto Molina [Alvarez]) [b 1934]

Spanish actor, writer and director. A weightlifting champion, Naschy began working in movies as an extra until he both scripted and starred in *Frankenstein's Bloody Terror* (1967). He recreated his role as the doomed werewolf Waldemar Daninsky in *Nights of the Werewolf* (1968), *Dracula vs. Frankenstein* (1969), *The Fury of the Wolfman* (1970), *The Werewolf vs. the Vampire Woman* (1970), *Dr. Jekyll and the Werewolf* (1971), *Curse of the Devil* (1973), *Night of the Howling Beast* (1975), *The Craving* (1980), *La Bestia y la Espada Mágica* (1983) and *Licantropo el Asesino de la Luna Llena* (1996). The undisputed King of Spanish Horror, he has also portrayed many other classic monsters, including the Count in *Dracula's Great Love* (1972).

qv: *Aquí Huele a Muerto...(¡Pues yo no he Sido!)* (1989); *Buenas Noches, Señor Monstruo* (1982); *La Cruz del Diablo* (1974); *The Hanging Woman* (1972); *Horror Rises from the Tomb* (1972); *Howl of the Devil* (1988); *The Hunchback of the Morgue* (1973); *Latidos de Pánico* (1983); *The Mummy's Revenge* (1973); *Mystery on Monster Island* (1982); *Vengeance of the Zombies* (1972).

NATAS...THE REFLECTION

USA, 1982 (1983). Dir: Jack Dunlap. With: Randy Mulkey, Pat Bolt, Craig Hensley, Kelli Kuhn, Fred Perry, Nino Cochise. West/Arizona. Colour.

Regional thriller in which a reporter investigates an old ghost town and discovers that it is full of real ghosts, a zombie (Richard Aufmuth) and the Prince of Darkness himself.

✦

NATIONAL LAMPOON'S CLASS REUNION

USA, 1982. Dir: Michael Miller. With: Gerrit Graham, Fred McCarren, Miriam Flynn, Stephen Furst, Shelley Smith, Michael Lerner. ABC Motion Pictures/PSO. Colour.

During a ten-year class reunion at the Lizzie Borden High School, maniacal killer Walter Baylor (Blackie Dammett) stalks the corridors and confronts nymphomaniacs, drug addicts, a case of Devil possession (Zane Buzby), vampire Egon von Stoker (Jim Staahl) and Anna Marie Spaniel (Joyce Gittlin), who transforms into a were-poodle (make-up created by veteran Del Armstrong) at inopportune moments. With a hit-and-miss script by John Hughes, director Miller (*Silent Rage* [1982], etc) has trouble keeping all the elements under control, but there are some laughs to be found. Chuck Berry, Misty Rowe and Anne Ramsey are also caught up in the chaos.

✦✦

THE NATIONAL MUMMY

(Orig: LA MOMIA NACIONAL)

Spain, 1981. Dir: José Ramón Larraz. With: Paco (Francisco) Algora, Enrique Camoiras, Azucena Hernández, J. (José) J. (Jaime) Espinosa, Lili Murati, Trini Alonso. Frade/JF Films. Colour.
A mummy comedy set in 1900 from the director of *Vampyres* (1974). When the wrappings from a 1,000 year-old Egyptian princess (Hernández) are removed, she is revived as a beautiful nymphomaniac. This also includes a vampire doctor and a bizarre happy ending.
✦

NATURAL BORN KILLERS

USA, 1994. Dir: Oliver Stone. With: Woody Harrelson, Juliette Lewis, Robert Downey Jr, Tommy Lee Jones, Tom Sizemore, Rodney Dangerfield. Warner Bros/Regency Enterprises/Alcor Films/Ixtlan/New Regency/JD Productions. Colour/B&W.
Loosely based on a story by Quentin Tarantino (who hoped to direct it himself), this controversial two hour satire on celebrity serial killers and media manipulation follows the bloody trail of psychos Mickey (Harrelson) and Mallory Knox (Lewis, the daughter of exploitation star Geoffrey) as they murder their way across the United States. Co-writer/director Stone's dazzling multi-media structure uses stock footage and numerous brief movie clips, including *Frankenstein* (1931). With Edie McClurg and an uncredited Mark Harmon. Songs by Leonard Cohen, Robert Gordon, The Shangri-Las, Duane Eddy, Patti Smith, Cowboy Junkies, Bob Dylan, Patsy Cline, Marilyn Manson and others. John August and Jane Hamshar wrote the novelisation, which includes an introduction by Stone.
✦✦✦✧

LA NAVE DE LOS MONSTRUOUS

Mexico, 1959. Dir: Rogelio A. Gonzalez. With: Lalo Gonzalez 'Piporro' (Eulalio Gonzalaz), Ana Bertha Lepe, Lorena Velázquez, Consuelo Frank, Manuel Alvarado Lodoza, Heberto Davila Jr. Producciones Sotomayor/Azteca/ Columbia. B&W.
A science fiction Western musical comedy, with singing and dancing cowboy 'Piporro' confronting the two female inhabitants of a Venusian spacecraft — the sexy Captain (Lepe), and a fanged vampire-woman (Velázquez) who can fly through the air and controls such talking monsters as a Cyclops, a big brained saucer-man, a spider monster, a living skeleton and Tor the robot. In the end, the vampire woman is impaled on a tree branch. Small kids will probably love it. The title translates as 'The Ship of Monsters'.
✦✧

NAV JAWAN

India, 1937. Dir: Aspi. With: Harishchandra. Wadia. B&W.
Apparently another version of Victor Hugo's *Notre-Dame de Paris*, running more than two hours.
Remake: DHANWAN (qv; 1937)
✦

NAZARENO CRUZ Y EL LOBO

Argentina, 1974. Dir: Leonardo Favio. With: Alfredo Alcon, Juan Jose Camero, Nora Cullen, M. Magali. Choila Productions. Colour.
A seventh son is cursed to transform into a wolf during nights of the full moon. This also includes a shape-changing witch (Cullen) and the Devil (Alcon). Based on a radio play by J.C. Chiappe.
✦✧

NBC STARSHIP RESCUE

USA, 1973. With: Bo Svenson. NBC-TV. Colour.
Half-hour TV special that previews NBC's Saturday morning shows for kids, with a live-action framing sequence involving alien invaders opposed by a heroic Frankenstein Monster (Svenson, who played the creature the same year in the 1973 TV movie *Frankenstein*).
✦

THE NEANDERTHAL MAN

USA, 1953. Dir: E.A. Dupont. With: Robert Shayne, Richard Crane, Doris Merrick, Joyce Terry, Robert Long, Dick Rich. Wisberg-Pollexfen/Global Productions/United Artists. B&W.
An obsessed scientist (Shayne) uses a serum to transform his pet cat into a sabre-tooth tiger and himself into an unconvincing Neanderthal caveman. Low-budget thrills from leading German silent film director Dupont, who handles the transformation scenes effectively, and beautifully photographed by Stanley Cortez (brother of actor Ricardo). Crane (TV's *Rocky Jones, Space Ranger* [1954]) heads a weak supporting cast that includes Beverly Garland as a deaf and dumb servant.
✦✧

NEAR DARK

USA, 1987. Dir: Kathryn Bigelow. With: Adrian Pasdar, Jenny Wright, Lance Henriksen, Bill Paxton, Jenette Goldstein, Tim Thomerson. F/M Entertainment. Colour.
An impressive solo directing début for co-writer Bigelow. Oklahoma farm boy Caleb Colton (Pasdar) becomes involved with the sultry Mae (Wright) and is 'adopted' by her travelling companions — a gang of sleazy, psychopathic, nomad vampires led by Jesse (Henriksen). Despite the low budget, this is beautifully photographed, with an intelligent script and great performances. Two action sequences — a massacre in a bar and a motel shoot-out — are particularly outstanding. Only the weak ending (a simple blood transfusion cures the vampire virus) lets it down.
✦✦✦✦

THE NECKLACE OF RAMESES

USA, 1914. Dir: Charles Brabin. With: Robert Brower, Gertrude Braun, Marc MacDermott, William Betchell, Charles Vernon, Miriam Nesbitt. Edison Film Company. B&W.
Silent drama in which a curse prevents a jewel thief from disposing of a necklace he has stolen from the mummy of Rameses' daughter.
✦

THE NECRO FILES

USA, 1997. Dir: Matt Jaissle. With: Isaac Cooper, Steven Sheppard, Gary Browning, Christian Curmudgeon, Jason McGee, Theresa Bestul. Threat Theatre International. Colour.
Shot on video in Seattle, this extremely gory horror comedy — produced, directed, photographed and edited by Jaissle — is amateurish on every level. A Satanic sacrifice (in broad daylight!) brings serial killer/rapist Logan (Cooper) back from the grave as a blue-faced zombie sex fiend with a (fake-looking) gigantic penis. Soon the living dead cannibal renews his crazed rampage, pursued by a pair of surviving Satanists, a demonic flying foetus (an obvious doll) and a drug-crazed cop (Sheppard). Many of the cast names are obviously pseudonymous. *Fangoria* editor Tony Timpone, Michael Weldon, Forrest J Ackerman and William Lustig are among those thanked in the credits, and the film is dedicated to Joe D'Amato.
✦

NECROMANCY

(aka NECROMANY — A LIFE FOR A LIFE/THE WITCHING)
USA, 1972. Dir: Bert I. Gordon. With: Orson Welles, Pamela Franklin, Michael Ontkean, Lee Purcell, Harvey Jason, Lisa James. Zenith International Pictures/ Cinerama/Premier Productions/Associates Entertainment International. Colour.
Filmed under the title *The Toy Factory*. Welles' career hits close to bottom with this confusing low budget witchcraft thriller, co-written and directed by the legendary Gordon. Welles has little more than a cameo as mumbling toymaker Mr Cato (with a fake nose and silly British accent), who turns out to be the leader of a coven of Satanists in the small town of Lilith. Cato wants newcomer Lori Brandon (Franklin, who appears naked) to use her power to bring his dead son back to life. When Lori finally resurrects the young boy (Terry Quinn), she is forced to take his place in the coffin. In 1982 this was reissued as *The Witching* with added full-frontal nudity and other insert sequences directed by Yakov Bentsvi. It still didn't make a lot of sense.
✦✧

NECROMANIA

USA, 1971 (1975). Dir: Edward D. Wood Jr. With: René Bond, Ric Lutze, Marie Arnold. Pendulum/Something Weird Video. Colour.

Only forty-three minutes of footage apparently remains from this low-budget occult sex film, shot on 16mm by the legendary Ed Wood (in a pink angora sweater!) in just two days for $7,000. Sexually dysfunctional couple Shirley (Bond) and Ben (Lutze) arrive at the house of necromancer Madame Heles (a role originally intended for Maila Nurmi), who turns out to be a zombie who has sex with Ben in one of Criswell's coffins! This also includes a satyr named Carl. The complete version included around three minutes of hardcore footage and Wood himself in a cameo as a wizard. The director subsequently reworked the plot for his novel *The Only House* (1972).

✦

NECROMANIAC

USA, 2000. Dir: Mike Watt. With: Ray Yeo, Kristen Pfeifer, Francis Veltri. Happy Cloud Pictures. Colour.

Independent production shot on 16mm in Pittsburgh. Set in a near future infested by the walking dead, an ex-police detective, a discredited scientist and a pair of exterminators join forces against a large corporation which may hold the secret to stopping the zombie hordes.

✦✧

NECRONOMICON

(USA: aka NECRONOMICON BOOK OF THE DEAD)

USA, 1993. Dir: Brian Yuzna, Christophe Gans and Shusuke Kaneko. With: Jeffrey Combs, Bruce Payne, Belinda Bauer, Richard Lynch, David Warner, Signy Coleman. Necronomicon Films/August Entertainment/ Pioneer LDC Ozla Pictures/New Line. Colour.

Direct-to-video anthology film loosely inspired by the fiction of H.P. Lovecraft. Yuzna's 'The Library' is a fun wraparound story featuring Combs as a great-looking Lovecraft delving into the eponymous cursed book; Gans' 'The Drowned' is the most HPL-inspired segment, with a mother and son revived from the dead by a creepy Cthulu (sic) monster; Kaneko's 'The Cold' is based on the 1928 story 'Cool Air' (previously adapted in 1971 for TV's *Rod Serling's Night Gallery* [1970-73]), in which the mad Dr Madden (Warner) invents a way to cheat death; while the weakest entry is Yuzna's 'Whispers', about a race of monsters living below the city streets. This has problems with the various period settings and too much gore, and its release in America was delayed for three years. With Dennis Christopher, Curt Lowens, Don Calfa and a cameo by Yuzna. Special effects by MMI, Screaming Mad George, Steve Johnson's XFX, Tom Savini, Todd Masters and others. David (L.) Hewitt supervised the opticals.

✦✦

NECROPOLIS

Italy, 1970. Dir: Franco Borcani. With: Viva Auder, Tina Aumont, Carmelo Bene, Pierre Clémenti, Bruno Corazzari, Paul Fabara. Cosmoseion/Q Productions. Colour.

Two-hour art movie which purports to be a 'statement about life'. It includes the Frankenstein Monster, King Kong, Countess Elizabeth Bathory (here called Mathory), Satan, Attila the Hun, Montezuma, the Minotaur and other characters.

✦

NECROPOLIS

(aka NECROPOLIS CITY OF THE DEAD)

USA, 1986 (1987). Dir: Tim Kincaid. With: LeeAnne Baker, Jacquie Fitz, Michael Conte, William K. Reed, Paul Ruben, Andrew Bausili. Empire Pictures/Tycin Entertainment. Colour.

Co-produced/directed by the talentless Kincaid and filmed in New York. Eva (Baker) is a vampiric 300 year-old witch with six breasts who sends out her zombie slaves to find a virgin sacrifice so that she can complete a ritual she began in 1685 and obtain eternal life. Special make-up effects created by Ed French.

✦

ROY WILLIAM NEILL (Roland de Gostrie) [1887-1946]

Irish-born American director/producer, best remembered for his series of atmospheric low-budget Sherlock Holmes films at Universal during the 1940s.

qv: *Black Moon* (1934); *Frankenstein Meets the Wolf Man* (1943).

NEITHER THE SEA NOR THE SAND

UK, 1972. Dir: Fred Burnley. With: Susan Hampshire, Frank Finlay, Michael Petrovitch, Michael Craze, Jack Lambert, David Garth. Tigon British/Portland Film Corporation. Colour.

Low-budget adaptation of the novel by TV news-reader Gordon Honeycombe, whose script was re-written by Rosemary Davies (given an 'additional dialogue' credit). When her lover Hugh (newcomer Petrovitch) unexpectedly dies, Anna Robinson (Hampshire) brings him back by the sheer force of her will-power. However, when she finally accepts that she is unable to stop his body from decomposing, they both walk off into the sea together. Burnley's début film suffers from a leaden pace and banal dialogue, while only the bleak Jersey locations recapture the muted beauty and underlying dread of the original book.

✦✧

NEVERWHERE

UK, 1996. Dir: Dewi Humphreys. With: Gary Bakewell, Laura Fraser, Hywel Bennett, Clive Russell, Paterson Joseph, Tanya Moodie. BBC North/Crucial Films. Colour.

Disappointing TV series of six half-hour shot-on-video episodes, written by Neil Gaiman and devised by Gaiman and comedian Lenny Henry. Richard Mayhew (Bakewell) and the enigmatic Door (Fraser) discover themselves on a quest through a secret world hidden within contemporary London. Bennett and Russell stand out as comic villains Mr Croup and Mr Vandemar, and this also features Freddie Jones, Trevor Peacock, Peter Capaldi as the Angel, Islington, and Tamsin Greig as the vampiric Lamia. Title graphics by Dave McKean. Music by Brian Eno. A companion novel by Gaiman was published by BBC Books.

✦✧

THE NEW ADDAMS FAMILY

Canada/USA, 1998. With: Glenn Taranto, Ellie Harvie, Brody Smith, Nicole (Marie) Fugère, Betty Phillips, Michael Roberds. Shavick Entertainment/Saban International/Fox Family Channel. Colour.

Unfunny half-hour comedy TV series (sixty-five episodes), based on the creepy characters created by Charles Addams: Gomez (Taranto), Morticia (Harvie), Wednesday (the excellent Fugère), Pugsley (Smith), Grandmama (Phillips), Uncle Fester (Roberds), Thing (Steven Fox) and Lurch (former wrestler John De Santis). Shame about the new theme song.

✦✧

Grandpapa Addams Comes to Visit

Canada/USA, 1998. Dir: George Erschbamer. With: Glenn Taranto, Ellie Harvie, Brody Smith, Nicole (Marie) Fugère, Betty Phillips, Michael Roberds. Shavick Entertainment/ Saban International/Fox Family Channel. Colour.

Guest star John Astin (the original Gomez from the 1964-66 series) acts everyone off the screen as Grandpapa Addams, who comes to visit. Fearful that he is going to be sent to a nursing home, Grandpapa starts behaving youthful with the result that the family thinks he has lost his marbles. He returned in the episode 'Fester and Granny vs. Grandpapa Addams' (1998).

✦✦

THE NEW ADVENTURES OF MADELINE:

Madeline and the Hunchback of Notre Dame

Canada, 1995. Dir: Stan Phillips. Voices: Andrea Libman, S. Louise Vallance, Tracey-Lee Smyth, Vanessa King, Veronika Sztopa, David Morse. DIC Productions/ABC-TV. Colour.

Half-hour TV cartoon series (thirteen episodes) aimed at very young

children, narrated in rhyme by Christopher Plummer and based upon characters created by Ludwig Bemelmons. In this episode, French schoolgirl Madeline (Libman) and her friends discover that reading can be fun when they decide to put on a play of *The Hunchback of Notre Dame*. While on a visit to the Paris Cathedral they also witness the filming of a movie based on the novel by Victor Hugo.
Series remake: MADELINE (1999)
✦✧

THE NEW ADVENTURES OF WONDER WOMAN:
Disco Devil

USA, 1978. Dir: Leslie H. Martinson. With: Lynda Carter, Lyle Waggoner, Wolfman Jack, Paul Sand, Michael Delano, Russell Johnson. DC Comics/Warner Bros Television/Bruce Lansbury Productions/The Douglas S. Cramer Co/CBS-TV. Colour.

Hour-long TV series (1977-79, forty-seven episodes) based on the comic book characters created by Charles Moulton and featuring the modern adventures of the superpowered Amazon (Carter) who works for the IADC (the Inter-Agency Defence Command). In this episode, scripted by Alan Brennert, a disco is used as a cover to turn government officials into mindless 'zombies'.
✦✧

Phantom of the Roller Coaster

USA, 1979. Dir: John Newland. With: Lynda Carter, Lyle Waggoner, Joseph Sirola, Jared Martin, Marc Alaimo, Ike Eisenmann. DC Comics/Warner Bros Television/Bruce Lansbury Productions/The Douglas S. Cramer Co/CBS-TV. Colour.

In this two-part adventure, Wonder Woman and the leader of a spy ring both attempt to discover the identity of a mysterious Phantom who guards an old amusement park.
✦✦

THE NEW AVENGERS:
The Eagle's Nest

UK/France, 1976. Dir: Desmond Davis. With: Patrick Macnee, Gareth Hunt, Joanna Lumley, Peter Cushing, Derek Farr, Sydney Bromley. The Avengers (Film & TV) Enterprises/TV Productions/IDTV Paris/ITV. Colour.

Disappointing hour-long revival (1976-77, twenty-six episodes) of the original 1961-69 TV series with John Steed (Macnee) now teamed with partners Purdy (Lumley) and Mike Gambit (Hunt). In this episode, scripted by Brian Clemens, they uncover a plot by Nazis masquerading as monks to kidnap cryogenics scientist Von Claus (Cushing) and start a Fourth Reich on a remote Scottish island by restoring the frozen body of Adolf Hitler to life. John Carter wrote the novelisation.
✦✦✧

SAM NEWFIELD
(Sam Neufeld) [1900-1964]

American director, the brother of Sigmund Neufeld, head of PRC. In a career spanning forty years, he churned out hundreds of quickies in all genres, especially 'B' Westerns, many under pseudonyms.
qv: *Dead Men Walk* (1943); *The Mad Monster* (1942); *Tiger Fangs* (1943).

THE NEW FRED AND BARNEY SHOW:
(aka FRED AND BARNEY MEET THE THING/FRED AND BARNEY MEET THE SHMOO)
Fred and Barney Meet the Frankenstones

USA, 1979. Voices: Henry Corden, Jean Vander Pyl, Mel Blanc, Gay Autterson, Don Messick, John Stephenson. Hanna-Barbera Productions/NBC-TV. Colour.

This half-hour cartoon TV series (thirteen episodes) includes the pilot episode for *The Frankenstones* series (in *The Flintstone Comedy Show* [1980-82]), in which Fred Flintstone (Corden) and Barney Rubble (Blanc) meet the weird family of Frank, Hidea, Freaky and Atrocia.
Series sequel: THE FLINTSTONES' NEW NEIGHBORS (qv; 1980)
✦✦

THE NEW SATURDAY SUPERSTAR MOVIE:
The Mini-Munsters

USA, 1973. Voices: Al Lewis, Richard Long, Bob Diamond. Universal/ABC-TV. Colour.

Series of hour-long cartoon specials (1973-74), retitled from the first season's *The ABC Saturday Superstar Movie* (1972-73). In one of only three new shows, Lewis recreates his role as Grandpa, and Long is the voice of Herman Munster. A Dracula-type relative sends his two teenagers, the Frankenstein-like Igor and the vampiric Lucretia, to stay with the Munster family. The plot involves a hearse that runs on music, thereby eliminating the pollution caused by exhaust fumes.
Episode sequel: THE MUNSTERS' REVENGE (qv; 1981)
✦✧

THE NEW SCOOBY-DOO MOVIES:
Scooby-Doo Meets Sandy Duncan: Sandy Duncan's Jekyll and Hyde

USA, 1972. Dir: William Hanna and Joseph Barbera. Voices: Daws Butler, Don Messick, Casey Kasem, Nicole Jaffe, Heather North, Frank Welker. Hanna-Barbera Productions/CBS-TV. Colour.

TV series of twenty-four forty minute cartoons (1972-74) in which Scooby (Messick), Shaggy Rogers (Casem), Velma Dinkley (Jaffe), Daphne Blake (North) and Fred Jones (Welker) travel around in their van The Mystery Machine and solve ghostly mysteries. They meet such other Hanna-Barbera characters as The Three Stooges, Laurel and Hardy, Josie and the Pussycats, the Harlem Globetrotters plus celebrity guest stars, including Batman and Robin, Davy Jones, Don Knotts, Jerry Reed (in 'The Phantom of the Country Music Hall'), Jonathan Winters, Phyllis Diller, Sonny and Cher, Cass Elliot, Dick Van Dyke, Don Adams, Jeannie, Speed Buggy and Tim Conway. In this episode, Scooby and his friends meet actress Sandy Duncan, who is pursued by a ghostly figure and Mr Hyde while filming a remake of *Dr. Jekyll and Mr. Hyde*, the last film to be shot at Mammoth Studios before it is torn down and replaced by a supermarket. Scooby and Shaggy also encounter a living mummy on another set.
✦✧

Scooby-Doo Meets the Addams Family: Wednesday is Missing

USA, 1972. Dir: William Hanna and Joseph Barbera. Voices: Don Messick, Casey Kasem, John Astin, Ted Cassidy, Jackie Coogan, Carolyn Jones. Hanna-Barbera Productions/CBS-TV. Colour.

In this episode, the friends find themselves acting as housekeepers for The Addams Family (voiced by the original cast members) when a villain known as The Vulture kidnaps Wednesday to force the spooky family to move out of the neighbourhood.
Episode sequel: THE ADDAMS FAMILY (qv; 1973-74)
Series sequel: THE SCOOBY-DOO/DYNOMUTT HOUR (qv; 1976)
✦✧

THE NEW SCOOBY-DOO MYSTERIES:
A Halloween Hassle at Dracula's Castle

USA, 1984. Dir: Ray Patterson, Oscar Dufau and Rudy Zamora. Voices: Rene Auberjonois, Casey Kasem, Kenneth Mars, Don Messick, Heather North, Clive Revill. Hanna-Barbera Productions/ABC-TV. Colour.

TV series of thirteen half-hour cartoon shows comprising twenty-nine episodes (1984-85). After Velma Dinkley (Pat Stevens) becomes an apprentice research scientist with NASA, and Freddie Jones (Frank Welker) becomes an aspiring mystery writer, Scooby-Doo (Messick), Shaggy Rogers (Kasem), Daphne Blake (North) and Scrappy-Doo (Messick) travel around in The Mystery Machine solving weird crimes. The title sequence includes representations of Count Dracula, the Frankenstein Monster, an Igor character, a werewolf and a gill man. Additional voices include Ruth Buzzi, Les Tremayne, and Janet Waldo. Executive produced by William Hanna and Joseph Barbera. In this episode, while shopping for costumes on Halloween night, Scooby and his friends (including Freddy and Velma) win a trip to a spooky castle where they help a Lugosi-voiced Count Dracula and his vampire bride, their assistant Igor (who sounds like

Peter Lorre), a werewolf, a mummy, the Invisible Man, a green gill man and Frankenstein's Monster prevent female magician Chandra and the apparent ghost of Dr Van Helsing from finding the mysterious Moonstone medallion.

✦✦

Scooby's Peep-Hole Pandemonium

USA, 1984. Dir: Ray Patterson, Oscar Dufau and Rudy Zamora. Voices: Rene Auberjonois, Casey Kasem, Kenneth Mars, Don Messick, Heather North, Clive Revill. Hanna-Barbera Productions/ABC-TV. Colour.

When Orson Kane, publisher of *Peep-Hole* magazine, hires Scooby and friends to take a photo of Norma Desmond, the famous horror movie queen who retired after her 1933 werewolf movie *Fangs for the Memories*, they are pursued by the vampiric actress, Franklin Stein the butler, Maid Mummy and Woof Woof the werewolf.

Series sequel: THE 13 GHOSTS OF SCOOBY-DOO (qv; 1985-86)

✦✧

NEW YORK VAMPIRE

USA, 1991 (1998). Dir: Gregory Lamberson. With: Tommy Sweeney, Julie Lynch, Mary Huner, Andrew Lee Barrett, Lee Kayman. Slaughtered Lamb/Video Confidential/EI Independent Cinema. Colour.

Low-budget, direct-to-video release. When suicidal Scott Kelly (Sweeney) meets sexy vampire Carmilla (Lynch), she introduces him into a cult of the undead in New York led by her 500 year-old mentor and former lover Evan (Barrett). These vampires have none of the usual weaknesses and can be killed by normal methods.

✦

JAMES H. NICHOLSON [1916-1972]

Co-founder of American Releasing Corporation with Samuel Z. Arkoff in 1954, the company changed its name to American International Pictures two years later. Throughout the 1950s and 1960s, they churned out hundreds of films aimed at the youth market, most notably Roger Corman's Edgar Allan Poe series starring Vincent Price. Nicholson left AIP in 1971 but produced only *The Legend of Hell House* (1973) before his death.

NICK KNIGHT

(UK: aka MIDNIGHT COP)

USA, 1989. Dir: Farhad Mann. With: Rick Springfield, John Kapelos, Robert Harper, Richard Fancy, Michael Nader. New World/Barry Weitz Films/Robirdie Pictures/ CBS-TV. Colour.

Enjoyable TV movie pilot for the series *Forever Knight* (1992-96). Former teenage heart-throb Springfield plays the eponymous vampire cop who lives in an abandoned movie theatre in San Francisco and, naturally enough, covers the night-shift. While investigating a break-in at an archaeological museum, he is forced to confront Lacroix (an evil-looking Nader), the age-old vampire who originally turned him into one of the undead. Mann directs this like it's a rock video, and Springfield makes a likeable, if unusual, hero.

Sequel: FOREVER KNIGHT (qv; 1992-96)

✦✦✦

NIGHT

USA, 1996. Dir: Glenn Andreiev. With: Jillianne Smith, Glenn Andreiev, Richard Cutler. Kino Andreiev. Joseph Green Pictures. Colour.

Independent release filmed on video in Huntington, Long Island, by the director of *Vampire's Embrace* (1991). Margot (Smith), the widow of a murdered policeman, teams up with a group of vampire hunters (including producer/director/writer/cinematographer/editor Andreiev) to hunt down undead crack dealer Garring (Cutler). This is presented by the legendary Joseph Green (*The Brain That Wouldn't Die* [1960], etc).

✦✧

NIGHT ANGEL

USA, 1989 (1990). Dir: Dominique Othenin-Girard. With: Isa Andersen, Karen Black, Linden Ashby, Debra Feuer, Doug Jones, Phil Fondacaro. Fries Entertainment/ Emerald Pictures/Paragon Arts International. Colour.

Lilith (Andersen) is a vampiric demon who poses as a fashion model and takes human souls during the eclipse of the moon. Narrated by Roscoe Lee Browne.

✦✧

A NIGHT AT THE WAXWORKS

USA, 1990. Dir: Ron Jeremy. With: Stephanie Rage, Debi Diamond, Mandi Wine, Tiarra (Nikki Prince), Jacqueline (Jacqueline St. Clair), Honey Rose (Nikki Wylde). Leisure Time Entertainment/Infinity Film and Video. Colour.

Porn star Jeremy directs this hardcore feature in which Vince (Peter North) celebrates his birthday by spending the night in a spooky house complete with waxworks. A number of wax figures come to life and have sex, including a scene where a woman (Rose) reanimates an Egyptian mummy.

✦

THE NIGHT BOYS

USA, 1990. Dir: Gino Colbert. With: Stewart Copeland. Cinderfella. Colour.

Hardcore gay vampire movie with Copeland as the undead Count Vladimir.

✦

NIGHTBREED

UK/USA/Canada, 1990. Dir: Clive Barker. With: Craig Sheffer, Anne Bobby, David Cronenberg, Charles Haid, Hugh Quarshie, Hugh Ross. Morgan Creek/J&M/ Braveworld/Twentieth Century Fox. Colour.

Author Barker's ambitious second outing as a writer/director (after *Hellraiser* [1987]), based on his own novel *Cabal*. Moody hero Aaron Boone (Sheffer) discovers (after he's dead!) that he is the new messiah for a subterranean city of mythical shape-changers. Masked psycho Dr Philip Decker (Cronenberg) wants them all destroyed. The jumpy storyline is due to studio interference and sequences featuring stop-motion dinosaur-type monsters (animated by Rory Fellowes) were cut prior to release. However, there's still some great action sequences, impressive (if underused) Image Animation make-up effects and genre veteran John Agar turns up in a neat cameo. Barker's original script was published in *Clive Barker's Nightbreed*, while *Clive Barker's The Nightbreed Chronicles* was a tie-in book of photographs.

✦✦✦✧

NIGHT CREATURES

USA, 1992. Dir: Sean Michaels. With: Miss Crystal Wilder, Patricia Kennedy, Lois Ayres, Alicia Rio, Cal Jammer, Marc Wallice. Pleasure Productions. Colour.

Subtitled 'A Real Vampire Tail', this hardcore feature introduces Wilder as Buffy, who is bitten on the neck by a bat that flies out of a graveyard. She soon turns into a vampire and is having sex with everyone she meets before transforming them into bloodsuckers. With a cameo by the director, and a porno actor named Terry Thomas as an uncredited vampire hunter.

✦

NIGHTFALL

USA, 1998 (1999). Dir: Kevin De Lullo. With: Jeff Rector. Troma. Colour.

Direct-to-video release in which an FBI agent (Rector) investigates a series of vampire attacks.

✦✧

THE NIGHT FLIER

USA, 1997. Dir: Mark Pavia. With: Miguel Ferrer, Julie Entwistle, Dan Monahan, Michael H. Moss, John Bennes, Beverly Skinner. New Amsterdam Entertainment/ Stardust International/Medusa Film/Home Box Office/ New Line Cinema. Colour.

Ferrer plays Richard Dees, a ludicrously cynical tabloid photo-journalist on the trail of 'Dwight Renfield' (Moss in special make-up created by KNB EFX group), a classical vampire who flies into remote airfields in his private aeroplane and first hypnotises the inhabitants before slaughtering them. Filmed in Wilmington, North Carolina, and based on an inconsequential story by Stephen King, this was eventually released to cable TV after a short theatrical run. The script (co-written by director Pavia) suffers from a lack of focus and no sympathetic characters. Only the climactic attack at an airport terminal full of the undead has any impact.

✦✧

THE NIGHT HAS EYES
(USA: TERROR HOUSE)
UK, 1942. Dir: Leslie Arliss. With: James Mason, Wilfrid Lawson, Mary Clare, Joyce Howard, Tucker McGuire, John Fermald. Associated British Picture/Pathé Pictures/ Producers Releasing Corporation. B&W.

Effective little chiller, originally awarded an 'A' certificate by the film censor in Britain, but changed to an 'H' (for Horror) after protests. Marian Ives (Howard) is a young teacher who decides to visit the Yorkshire Moors, where her friend Evelyn disappeared a year before. Accompanied by her wise-cracking friend Doris (McGuire), the two women are forced to take shelter in the mysterious house of reclusive, shell-shocked pianist Stephen Deremid (Mason). A veteran of the Spanish Civil War, Deremid suspects he might be an insane full moon killer but, despite the discovery of a secret room and a skeleton, it turns out to be a plot by his scheming companions (Lawson and a creepy Clare) to drive him mad. Based on the novel by Alan Kennington.

✦✦✦

NIGHT HUNTER
USA, 1995. Dir: Rick Jacobson. With: Don 'The Dragon' Wilson, Nicholas Guest, Melanie Smith, Ronald Winston Yuan, Cash Casey, James Lew. Amritraj Premiere Entertainment/New Horizon. Colour.

Okay low-budget action film in which moody Jack Cutter (World Kickboxing Champion Wilson, who also co-produced) uses his martial arts skills to hunt down the last of the vampires (led by Guest) who have gathered in Los Angeles to multiply during an upcoming eclipse. These modern vampires can survive in daylight and are equally adept at fighting. Director Jacobson handles the action scenes well, and many of the characters are named after various horror film directors.

✦✦

NIGHTLIFE
Mexico/USA, 1989. Dir: Daniel Taplitz. With: Ben Cross, Maryam D'Abo, Keith Szarabajka, Camille Saviola, Jesse Corti, Glenn Shadix. MCA/Cine Enterprises/MTE/USA Network. Colour.

Made-for-cable TV vampire comedy. D'Abo looks great as Angelique, a hundred year-old member of the undead, who is chased around Mexico City by her vampiric ex-lover Vlad (a flamboyant Cross) while being wooed by haematologist Dr David Zuckerman (Szarabajka), as he attempts to find a cure for her blood 'disease'. Taplitz's direction is not light enough to carry the black humour, but this still has its moments. Cross returned as a vampire in the TV revival of *Dark Shadows* (1990-91).

✦✦

NIGHT LIFE
(UK: GRAVE MISDEMEANOURS)
USA, 1989. Dir: David Acomba. With: Scott Grimes, Cheryl Pollak, Anthony Geary, Alan Blumenfeld, Kenneth Ian Davis, Darcy DeMoss. Creative Movie Marketing. Colour.

Likeable low-budget horror/comedy in which Grimes plays Archie Melville, a college kid who works part-time in the funeral home owned by his tight-fisted uncle Verlin Flanders (John Astin). When four rich-bitch classmates from his school are involved in a fatal car crash with a toxic container, Archie soon finds himself being pursued by the zombie teens (make-up effects created by Craig Reardon and Ed French) who don't know they're dead yet. Scriptwriter Keith Critchlow was replaced as director by Acomba after the first week's shooting. With Phil Proctor, a nice cameo by Severn Darden, and some discreet zombie sex.

✦✦✧

NIGHTMAN:
Book of the Dead
Canada/USA, 1998. Dir: George Mendeluk. With: Matt McColm, Jayne Heitmeyer, Derwin Jordan, Claudette Mink, Mark Lindsay Chapman, David McNally. Nightman Productions/Glen Larson Entertainment Network/ Tribune Entertainment/Atlantis Films/Crescent. Colour.

Syndicated hour-long TV series (1997-99, forty-four episodes) created by Glen Larson and based on Steve Englehart's Marvel Comics character. Bay City saxophone player Johnny Domino (McColm) uses a secret prototype weapon system to transform himself into the eponymous superhero. In this fun episode, university professor Dr Winslow Sutton (McNally) uses a magician's cursed book of Sumarian magic to raise his wife Lucy (Rebecca Rekhert) from the dead as a vampire and reanimate the body of dark magician Andrei Barzun (Chapman) and an army of scary-looking zombies.

✦✦✧

Constant Craving
Canada/USA, 1997 (1998). With: Matt McColm, Jayne Heitmeyer, Derwin Jordan, Earl Holliman, Lysette Anthony, François Guetary. Nightman Productions/Glen Larson Entertainment Network/Tribune Entertainment/ Atlantis Films/Crescent. Colour.

Johnny's father, Frank Dominus (Holliman), finds himself unwittingly thrust into the middle of a power struggle between the undead Countess (Anthony), who wants to become human once again, and her vampire partner Count Stanislaus Volkov (Guetary), who will do anything for her to remain under his power. When Frank's blood is discovered to hold the DNA sequence that will free the Countess, Volkov kidnaps him to use as bait.

✦✦

Manimal
Canada/USA, 1998. Dir: Simon MacCorkindale. With: Matt McColm, Jayne Heitmeyer, Derwin Jordan, Simon MacCorkindale. Nightman Productions/Glen Larson Entertainment Network/Tribune Entertainment/Atlantis Films/Crescent. Colour.

MacCorkindale, who also directed, recreates his role as animal shape-changer Jonathan Chase (from the short-lived series *Manimal* [1983]), who teams up with NightMan to protect Chase's daughter Teresa from a time-travelling Jack the Ripper.

✦✦✦

NIGHTMARE ASYLUM
USA, 1990 (1991). Dir: Todd Sheets. With: Lori Hassle, Todd Sheets. Cinema Home Video. Colour.

A girl (Hassle) trapped in an amusement park house of horrors is menaced by a group of singing and dancing psychos. A wolfman, a mummy and zombies also turn up, while six-foot four-inch director Sheets (*Zombie Bloodbath* [1993], etc) appears as a butcher in a recreation of a scene from *The Texas Chain Saw Massacre* (1974). A low-budget, direct-to-video gorefest, executive produced by David DeCoteau.

✦

THE NIGHTMARE BEFORE CHRISTMAS
USA, 1993. Dir: Henry Selick. With: Danny Elfman, Chris Sarandon, Catherine O'Hara, William Hickey, Glenn Shadix, Paul Reubens. Touchstone Pictures/Burton-DiNovi. Colour.

Although directed by Selick, it is co-producer Tim Burton who sets his stamp on this wonderfully macabre stop-motion musical fantasy, 'adapted' by Michael McDowell. Set in Halloween Town (filled with vampires, a werewolf, a mummy and numerous other monsters, including a mad scientist [Hickey] and the stitched-together heroine Sally [O'Hara]), Jack Skellington (likeably voiced by Sarandon and sung by composer/lyricist Elfman) is tired of scaring people and decides that Halloween should merge with the Christmas holidays. He then kidnaps Santa Claus with typically bizarre results. Often very funny and endearing, this is probably not suitable for small children.

Hyperion published a juvenile novelisation by Daphne Skinner and a behind-the-scenes book by Frank Thompson entitled *Tim Burton's Nightmare Before Christmas: The Film, The Art, The Vision.*
✦✦✦✦✧

NIGHTMARE CITY
USA, 1997. Dir: Geoffrey de Valois. With: Tonya Qualls. Digital Entertainment Group/Salt City Home Video. Colour.
One of a series of *Vampire Raw Footage* videos that includes behind-the-scenes softcore sequences. Blonde vampire model Qualls dances nude in explicit dungeon sequences from a music video.
✦

NIGHTMARE CLASSICS:
Carmilla
USA, 1989. Dir: Gabrielle Beaumont. With: Ione Skye, Meg Tilly, Armelia McQueen, Roddy McDowall, Roy Dotrice, John Doolittle. Think Entertainment/Showtime Networks. Colour.
Short-lived hour-long cable anthology TV series (four episodes), introduced and executive produced by Shelley Duvall. This surprisingly erotic version of J. Sheridan Le Fanu's classic vampire story is relocated to a Southern plantation just after the American Civil War. While a mysterious plague sweeps the countryside, a lonely Marie (Skye) is befriended by the mysterious and seductive Carmilla (Tilly), who is the only survivor of a coach accident. The opening narration is by Linda Hunt.
Episode remake: CARMILLA (qv; 1994)
✦✦✧
The Eyes of the Panther
USA, 1989. Dir: Noel Black. With: C. Thomas Howell, Daphne Zuniga, John Stockwell, Jeb Brown, Ruth De Sosa, Terry Wills. Think Entertainment/Showtime Networks. Colour.
Based on the title story and 'The Boarded Window' by Ambrose Bierce. A frontier woman in the old West is suspected of turning into a black panther after being cursed when a big cat frightened her pregnant mother.
✦✧
The Strange Case of Dr. Jekyll and Mr. Hyde
USA, 1989. Dir: Michael Lindsay-Hogg. With: Anthony Andrews, Gregory Cooke, Laura Dern, George Murdock, Nicholas Guest, Rue McClanahan. Think Entertainment/ Showtime Networks. Colour.
Halloween episode in which Andrews stars as both the mild-mannered Dr Jekyll and his monstrous alter-ego, Mr Hyde, in J. Michael Straczynski's lacklustre adaptation of Robert Louis Stevenson's story.
Episode remake: JEKYLL & HYDE (qv; 1990)
✦✧

NIGHTMARE IN BLOOD
(UK: HORROR CONVENTION)
USA, 1978. Dir: John Stanley. With: Jerry Walter, Dan Caldwell, Barrie Youngfellow, John H. Cochran, Ray K. Goman, Kerwin Mathews. Xeromega Productions. Colour.
Low-budget chiller, filmed in 1974 and set during a horror movie convention. Malekai (Walter), the star of a number of vampire movies, turns out to be the real thing, while the revived corpses of Burke and Hare are his psychotic assistants! Amateurish nonsense aimed at film buffs and comic fans, co-written, co-produced and directed by the San Francisco TV horror host and author. Special guest star Mathews (*The 7th Voyage of Sinbad* [1958], etc) turns up briefly in one of Malekai's movies and Kathy (Kathleen) Quinlan is also in there somewhere.
✦

NIGHTMARES
USA, 1983. Dir: Joseph Sargent. With: Cristina Raines, Joe Lambie, Emilio Estevez, Mariclare Costello, Lance Henriksen, Tony Plana. Universal/Mirisch-Beaton. Colour.
Unimaginative quartet of tales originally intended for TV. The first story, 'Terror in Topanga', is a routine slasher thriller about an escaped murderer that features *Frankenstein* (1931) on TV. The other episodes are about a video game machine that comes to life ('The Bishop of Battle'), a priest confronted by a demonic car in the desert ('The Benediction') and Veronica Cartwright's whining heroine pursued by a silly-looking giant rat ('The Night of the Rat'). There's not even a linking story to hold it all together. With Richard Masur, Moon Zappa, Billy Jacoby and the voice of James Tolkan.
✦✦

NIGHTMARE THE BIRTH OF HORROR:
Dracula
UK/USA, 1996. Dir: Derek Towers. With: Christopher Frayling, Lord Ruthven The Earl of Gowrie, Trevor St. John Hacker, Eileen Daly, Vida Garman, Vicky Lee. BBC-TV/Wall to Wall Television/A&E Network. Colour.
Second in a series of four hour-long TV shows in which Professor Christopher Frayling takes an academic look at nineteenth century British horror icons. He travels to Romania, America and Switzerland and traces the history of Bram Stoker's 1897 novel. This includes dramatised sequences (featuring the real Lord Ruthven as The Vampyre, Hacker as Stoker, and Daly, Garman and Lee as the Count's vampire brides), trailers for *Dracula* (1931) and *Mark of the Vampire* (1935), and clips from the BBC's *Count Dracula* (1977), Hammer's *Dracula* (1958) and *Nosferatu* (1922).
✦✦✦
Dr Jekyll & Mr Hyde
UK/USA, 1996. Dir: Derek Towers. With: Christopher Frayling, Tim Craig, Tom Forsyth, Alexander John. BBC-TV/Wall to Wall Television/A&E Network. Colour.
Third in the series, in which Professor Frayling travels from Edinburgh to Bournemouth to trace the history of Robert Louis Stevenson's 1886 novel *Strange Case of Dr. Jekyll and Mr. Hyde* (later editions added *The*) and the Jack the Ripper murders. This is illustrated with clips from the 1931 and 1941 movies and the 1980 BBC-TV version, plus *The Body Snatcher* (1945).
✦✦✦
Frankenstein
UK/USA, 1996. Dir: Derek Towers. With: Christopher Frayling, Eileen Daly, Richard Grant, Roy Holder, Chris Mallet, Tony Phillips. BBC-TV/Wall to Wall Television/ A&E Network. Colour.
First in the series, in which Professor Frayling travels to Switzerland and traces the history of Mary Shelley's 1818 novel. This includes dramatised sequences (featuring Grant as The Creature), a trailer for *Frankenstein* (1931) and clips from *Bride of Frankenstein* (1935), *The Curse of Frankenstein* (1957) and the 1910 *Frankenstein*. The fourth and final show looked at *The Hound of the Baskervilles*.
✦✦✦

NIGHTMARE WEEKEND
USA/UK/France, 1985. Dir: Henry Sala. With: Preston Maybank, Wellington Meffert, Andrea Thompson, Kimberly Stahl, Bruce Morton, Lori Lewis. GIG Productions/Vision Communications/English Film Company/Films des Lions/Troma. Colour.
Three teenage girls spend the weekend in a Florida house, where they are turned into drooling 'zombies' by a mad scientist's brain-swapping experiments. This low budget horror film also includes Debbie Laster, Dale Midkiff and a green haired puppet monster.
✦

THE NIGHT OF COUNTING THE YEARS
(Orig: EL MUMIA)
United Arab Republic, 1969 (1972). Dir: Shadi Abdelsalam. With: Ahmed Marei, Zouzou El Hakim, Ahmad Hegazi, Nadia Loutfy, Gaby Karraz, Mohamed Nabih. Egyptian Cinema General Organisation/Contemporary. Colour.
Set in 1881 Thebes, where the two sons of a local chief discover that their tribe has been robbing the tombs of the Pharaohs and selling the treasures to the antiques black market. When his elder brother (Hegazi) refuses to co-operate and is murdered, the equally shocked Wanniss (Marei) contacts a team of archaeologists sent from The Antiquities Department in Cairo and reveals the location of the mummies, even though he knows it will bankrupt his people and destroy his own life.
✦✦✦

A NIGHT OF MAGIC
UK, 1944. Dir: Herbert Wynne. With: Robert Griffith, Billy Scott, Marion Olive, Dot Delavine, Vera Bradley. Berkeley Films. B&W.
This low-budget musical is under an hour long. It includes a dream sequence in which a man is sent an Egyptian sarcophagus and discovers inside the mummy of a 3,000 year-old princess (Olive) who is still alive.
✦

NIGHT OF THE COBRA WOMAN
(aka MOVINI'S VENOM)
Philippines/USA, 1972 (1973). Dir: Andrew Meyer. With: Joy Bang, Marlene Clark, Roger Garrett, Vic Diaz, Slash Marks, Carmen Argenziano. New World Pictures. Colour.
Jungle priestess Lana (Clark) needs sex and snake venom to remain eternally young. Her lover (Garrett) supplies her with various victims who she reduces to skeletons until the venom eventually transforms her into a cobra. Released in 'Slitherama'.
✦

NIGHT OF THE COMET
USA, 1984. Dir: Thom Eberhardt. With: Robert Beltran, Catherine Mary Stewart, Kelli Maroney, Sharon Farrell, Mary Woronov, Geoffrey Lewis. Atlantic 9000/Film Development Fund/Atlantic Releasing. Colour.
Hugely enjoyable post-holocaust exploitation movie, filmed under the title *Teenage Comet Zombies*. When a passing comet reduces most of the inhabitants of Los Angeles to blue dust or turns them into murderous zombies, surviving sisters Regina and Samantha Belmont (Stewart and the wonderful Maroney) set out to enjoy themselves, even if they do need machine guns for protection against the walking dead. Meanwhile, a group of sinister scientists led by Carter (Lewis) and Audrey (Woronov) want the girls' blood as a possible cure. Writer/director Eberhardt uses strong performances, offbeat humour and some nice shock effects to overcome the low budget.
✦✦✦✧

NIGHT OF THE CREEPS
USA, 1986. Dir: Fred Dekker. With: Jason Lively, Steve Marshall, Jill Whitlow, Tom Atkins, Wally Taylor, Bruce Solomon. Tri-Star Pictures. Colour.
Filmed under the title *Creeps*, this self-indulgent pastiche of bad science fiction films opens in 1959 when an alien experiment crashes on Earth and infects a high school student. Twenty-seven years later his frozen body is accidentally thawed out and soon slug-like creatures are leaping down teenagers' throats and turning them into zombies before their heads explode. Despite giving his characters names like Landis and Raimi, writer/director Dekker (*The Monster Squad* [1987], etc) has problems mixing the horror with the humour. Whitlow stands out from among the usual bunch of tedious teens (he uses a flame-thrower on the undead hordes), Atkins has fun with his role as a suicidal cop, and there's a brief cameo by Dick Miller. With a clip from *Plan 9 from Outer Space* (1958). Despite studio interference, this should have been better. Some TV prints feature an alternative ending.
✦✦

NIGHT OF THE CRUEL SACRIFICE
(Orig: LA NUIT DES TRAQUÉES/FILLES TRAQUÉES. USA: aka NIGHT OF THE HUNTED)
France, 1980. Dir: Jean Rollin. With: Brigitte Lahaie, Vincent Garder, Dominique Journe, Bernard Papineau, Marilyn Jess, Cathy Stewart. Impex. Colour.
Gamma rays turn people into zombie-like creatures. This was re-released in 1981 in an alternate French hardcore version.
✦

NIGHT OF THE DAY OF THE DAWN OF THE SON OF THE BRIDE OF THE RETURN OF THE TERROR: THE REVENGE OF THE TERROR OF THE ATTACK OF THE EVIL, MUTANT, HELLBOUND, FLESH-EATING, SUBHUMANOID LIVING DEAD, PART 2
USA, 1968/1991. Dir: Lowell Mason. With: Duane Jones, Judith O'Dea, Karl Hardman, Marilyn Eastman, Keith Wayne, Judith Ridley. Jyvass/Palmer Video. B&W.
Stupid attempt to turn George A. Romero's supposedly public domain *Night of the Living Dead* (1968) into a comedy using new dubbed dialogue, sound effects and music.
✦

NIGHT OF THE DEVILS
(Orig: LA NOTTE DEI DIAVOLI/LA NOCHE DE LOS DIABLOS)
Italy/Spain, 1972. Dir: Giorgio Ferroni. With: John (Gianni) Garko, Teresa Gimpera, Agostina Belli, Mark Roberts (Roberto Maldera), Cinzia de Carolis, Umberto Raho. Filmes Cinematográfica/Due Emme Cinematográfica/Copercines. Colour.
Another reworking of Alexei Constantinovich Tolstoy's story 'The Wurdalak', previously adapted by Mario Bava in *Black Sabbath* (1963). A crazed young man, Nicola (Garko), believes that the peasant family of his girlfriend Sdenka (Belli) has been possessed by vampires. While recovering from his ordeal in hospital, he stakes her in the mistaken belief that she is also one of the undead. From the director of *Mill of the Stone Women* (1960). Check out the Bava version instead.
✦✧

NIGHT OF THE GHOULS
(aka REVENGE OF THE DEAD)
USA, 1959 (1983). Dir: Edward D. Wood (Jr). With: Criswell (Charles Jeron Criswell King), Kenne Duncan, 'Duke' Moore, Valda Hansen, Tor Johnson (Tor Johansson), John Carpenter. Atomic Productions/Crown International. B&W.
Although completed in 1959, writer/director Ed Wood's shoddy sequel to *Bride of the Monster* (1954) was only finally released in 1983. Criswell rises from his coffin to tell the story about a phoney medium, Dr Acula (ex-stuntman Duncan), who lives in the old scientist's house with a fake ghost (Hansen) and the horribly scarred Lobo (Johnson, repeating his role from the first film in make-up by Harry Thomas). Acula fools gullible clients with his séances until, at the end, he succeeds in reviving the dead by accident. With Paul Marco as Kelton the cop, Dr Tom Mason in two roles, plus Hansen and Jeannie Stevens as real ghosts. This is as terrible as you'd expect from one of Wood's films as a director, which incorporates footage from his unfinished *Rock and Roll Hell/Hellborn* (1956, featuring Conrad Brooks) and the TV pilot *Final Curtain* (1957).
✦

NIGHT OF THE HOWLING BEAST
(Orig: LA MALDICIÓN DE LA BESTIA. UK: THE WEREWOLF AND THE YETI. USA: aka HALL OF THE MOUNTAIN KING).
Spain, 1975. Dir: M. (Miguel) I. (Iglesias) Bonns. With: Paul Naschy (Jacinto Molina), Grace Mills, Silvia Solar, Louis (Luis) Induñi, Gil Vidal, Castillo Escalona. Profilmes/Su Arista Exclusivo/Constellation Films/Independent International. Colour.
Following *Curse of the Devil* (1973), Naschy plays reluctant El Hombre Lobo, Waldemar Daninsky, for the eighth time in another new origin story credited to his real name. Joining an expedition to Tibet in search of the legendary yeti, Daninsky discovers a cave containing two exotic cannibalistic sisters. As a result of being bitten by one of them, he turns into a werewolf during the phases of the full moon. After most of the explorers are captured or killed by ruthless bandit Saga Khan and his evil princess, Daninsky battles an Abominable Snowman and rescues the heroine (Mills) before he is cured. This was banned in Britain, probably because of a torture scene involving the skinning of a young girl.
Sequel: THE CRAVING (qv; 1980)
✦

NIGHT OF THE LIVING BABES
USA, 1987. Dir: Jon Valentine. With: Michelle McClellan (Michelle Bauer), Andrew Nichols, Louie Bonnano, Connie Woods, Forrest Witt, Cynthia Clegg. Metropolis Pictures/Magnum Entertainment. Colour.

Barely an hour-long sex comedy. Two sex-starved yuppies (Nichols and Bonnano) pay a visit to Madame Mondo's Fantasy Palace at the Zombie Fantasy Ranch and discover that the girls are actually hypnotised nymphomaniac zombies. In the end, Madame Mondo (Witt) is transformed into a man by a sex-change ray gun. With a clip from *Night of the Living Dead* (1968) on TV.
✦

NIGHT OF THE LIVING BREAD

USA, 1990. Dir: Kevin S. O'Brien. With: Vince Ware, Katie Harris, Robert J. Saunders, Gina Saunders, Wolfgang S. Saunders, Stephen R. Newell. Kevin S. O'Brien/Films From Hell/Ohio University. B&W.

Fun, eight minute student film made at Ohio University which spoofs George A. Romero's 1968 original, with rampaging slices of bread replacing the zombies.
✦✧

NIGHT OF THE LIVING DEAD

USA, 1968. Dir: George A. Romero. With: Duane Jones, Judith O'Dea, Karl Hardman, Marilyn Eastman, Keith Wayne, Judith Ridley. Image Ten/Continental. B&W.

Filmed under the titles *Night of the Flesh Eaters* and *Night of Anubis*, this is one of the most influential horror films ever made, photographed, edited, co-scripted and directed in Pittsburgh by Romero (who also has a cameo as a TV reporter) for just $114,000. A gruesome, low-budget chiller, it has acquired a cult reputation since its original release, thanks to the stark black and white photography, bleak locations and a cast of unknowns, all of which gives the picture a disturbing, documentary-like feel. A Venus probe returning to Earth brings with it an alien contamination that revives the newly dead. A small band of bickering survivors barricade themselves in a farmhouse and attempt to repel the flesh-eating zombies who lay siege to the building. The opening graveyard sequence is a minor masterpiece of atmospheric horror and, despite repeated viewings, the surprise ending still has the power to shock. A print of the film is held in the archives of the New York Museum of Modern Art. This is also available in a terrible colourised version copyrighted in 1986 by Hal Roach Studios. Even worse, a thirtieth anniversary 'special edition' released on video and DVD in 1999 replaced around fifteen minutes with new footage directed by John Russo. These extra scenes included Bill Hinzman returning as the cemetery ghoul in make-up created by Vincent Guastini, plus scream queen Debbie Rochon. Co-writer Russo also belatedly novelised the script in 1974 and published an unauthorised sequel entitled *Return of the Living Dead* in 1978. Russo also wrote the 1985 volume *The Complete Night of the Living Dead Filmbook*, with an introduction by Romero.

Sequels: DAWN OF THE DEAD (qv; 1978) and THE RETURN OF THE LIVING DEAD (qv; 1984)
Remake: NIGHT OF THE LIVING DEAD (qv; 1990)
✦✦✦✦

NIGHT OF THE LIVING DEAD

USA, 1990. Dir: Tom Savini. With: Tony Todd, Patricia Tallman, Tom Towles, McKee Anderson, William Butler, Katie Finneran. 21st Century Productions/Columbia. Colour.

Savini's colour remake of executive producer George A. Romero's 1968 classic is surprisingly faithful and effective, cleverly shifting the emphasis away from Ben (Todd) and on to Barbara (a tough-looking Tallman) as the heroic protagonist. This time the flesh-eating zombies look genuinely dead and scary (thanks to make-up effects by John Vulich and Everett Burrell), and although the director plays down the gore effects, there are some genuinely gruesome scenes. Scripted by Romero, this was produced by John Russo and Russ(ell) Streiner. Unfortunately, it was not the box office success it should have been. 'We're them, and they're us.'
✦✦✦

NIGHT OF THE LIVING DEAD 25TH ANNIVERSARY DOCUMENTARY

USA, 1993 (1994). Dir: Tom (Thomas) Brown. With: George A. Romero, John A. Russo, Russell W. Streiner, Karl Hardman, Fred Olen Ray, Tobe Hooper. The Suburban Tempe Company/Market Square Productions/Tempe Video/Screen Edge. Colour/B&W.

Feature-length video documentary that includes numerous clips

Walking corpses on the Night of the Living Dead *(1968).*

from the 1968 film, plus colour behind-the-scenes stills, a fun round-robin recollection by the four creators, Marilyn Eastman talking about the make-up and music with Hardman, and interviews with such celebrity fans as film-makers David DeCoteau, Sam Raimi, John Landis, Wes Craven and Scott Spiegel.
✦✦✧

NIGHT OF THE LIVING DEBBIES
USA, 1989. Dir: Henri Pachard. With: Nina Hartley, Porsche Lynn, Lynn LeMay, Bionca (Bionica Bradley), Rene Morgan, Robert Bullock. Executive Video Productions. Colour.
Hardcore comedy in the *Debbie* series staring Hartley as the eponymous heroine. In this entry, she is trying to contact her dead husband while mad scientist Dr Finetush and assistant Igor attempt to revive female corpses in a search for the world's best buttocks.
✦

THE NIGHT OF THE LIVING DUCK
USA, 1987. Dir: Greg Ford and Terry Lennon. Voices: Mel Blanc, Mel Tormé. Warner Bros. Colour.
Merrie Melodies cartoon short in which comic book fan Daffy Duck gets hit on the head and finds himself performing for an audience of famous monsters, including a vampire, Frankenstein's Monster and his Bride, a werewolf, mummy, gill man, Cyclops, Leatherface, the Fly and Smogzilla. This subsequently turned up in the feature *Daffy Duck's Quackbusters* (1987) and the TV compilation *Bugs Bunny Creature Features* (1992).
Sequel: DAFFY DUCK'S QUACKBUSTERS (qv; 1987)
✦✦

NIGHT OF THE SEAGULLS
(Orig: LA NOCHE DE LAS GAVIOTAS. USA: aka NIGHT OF THE DEATH CULT/TERROR BEACH)
Spain, 1975. Dir: Amando de Ossorio. With: Victor Petit, Mary (Maria) Kosti, Sandra Mozarosky, Julie James, Julia Saly, José Antonio Calvo. Ancla Century Films/Profilmes. Colour.
Follow-up to *Horror of the Zombies* (1974), and the fourth and last in the *Blind Dead* series. When a young doctor (Petit) and his wife (Kosti) move to a small fishing village, they discover that the taciturn locals sacrifice white-robed virgins to the blind undead Templarios Knights who offer up their hearts to a hideous sea-monster idol. In the end, the blood-drinking zombies turn to dust when the idol is destroyed. As usual, de Ossorio was responsible for the special make-up effects. An unofficial addendum, *La Cruz del Diablo*, was also released in 1974 and directed by John Gilling, and the Templars surfaced again in Jesús Franco's *La Mansión de los Muertos Viventes* (1982).
✦✦

NIGHT OF THE SORCERERS
(Orig: LA NOCHE DE LOS BRUJOS)
Spain/Portugal, 1973. Dir: Amando de Ossorio. With: Simón Andreu, Jack Taylor (George Brown Randall/Grek Martin), Kali Hansa, María Kosti, Lorena Tower (Loretta Tovar), Joseph (José) Thelman. Profilmes/Hesperia/Avco-Embassy. Colour.
In the African jungle, an expedition discovers a voodoo tribe of beautiful vampire women in leopard skins. This also includes zombies, screaming severed heads and cannibalism-in-negative. A disappointment from the director of the *Blind Dead* series.
✦

THE NIGHT OF THE VAMPIRE
(Orig: CHI O SUU NINGYO. USA: aka THE VAMPIRE DOLL)
Japan, 1970. Dir: Michio Yamamoto. With: Kayo Matsuo, Akira Nakao, Yukiko Kobayashi, Yoko Minazake, Atsuo Nakamura, Junya Usami. Toho. Colour.
The first of three vampire films directed by Yamamoto for Toho. After her mother sells the soul of Yuko (Kobayashi) to the Devil to obtain immortality for her daughter, the girl returns as a ghostly vampire who revenges herself on the world she believes treated her unkindly. In the end Yuko kills her father (Usami), which results in her body turning to dust.
✦

Stacie Foster as a flesh-eating zombie in Night of the Living Dead *(1990).*

NIGHT OF THE ZOMBIES
(aka GAMMA 693/NIGHT OF THE WEHRMACHT ZOMBIES/NIGHT OF THE ZOMBIES II. USA/UK: aka THE CHILLING)
USA, 1980 (1981). Dir: Joel M. Reed. With: Jamie Gillis, Ryan Hilliard, Samantha Grey, Ron Armstrong, Joel M. Reed, Ron Dorfman. Bowser/NMD. Colour.
Kept alive in the Bavarian Alps since World War Two by an experimental gas, an SS battalion and a chemical warfare unit of Allied troops continue to battle each other as cannibalistic zombies. In the end, CIA agent Nick (porno star Gillis) decides to join them. Director Reed (*Blood Sucking Freaks* [1978], etc) appears as the ex-Nazi scientist behind the experiment. Despite being in colour, this low-budget, New York City-based production uses black and white stock footage!
✦✧

NIGHT OF VAMPYRMANIA
France, circa 1993. Dir: Richard J. Thompson (Julien Richard). With: Pere Noel. AJC Video. Colour.
Independent comedy made on a low budget that apparently includes a vampiric Santa Claus (Noel).
✦

NIGHT OWL
USA/UK, 1993 (1994). Dir: Jeffrey Arsenault. With: John Leguizamo, Lisa Napoli, David Roya, Ali Thomas, James Raftery, Caroline Munro. Franco Productions/Midnight Movies/Screen Edge. B&W.
Low-budget independent movie, set in the mid-1980s and filmed over a period of three years. Psychopath Jake (Raftery) either imagines or recalls when he was turned into a vampire in 1944. He picks up women in bars in New York's East Village then murders them during sex and drinks their blood. Future star Leguizamo plays Angel, who is looking for his missing sister Zohra (Karen Wexler). This

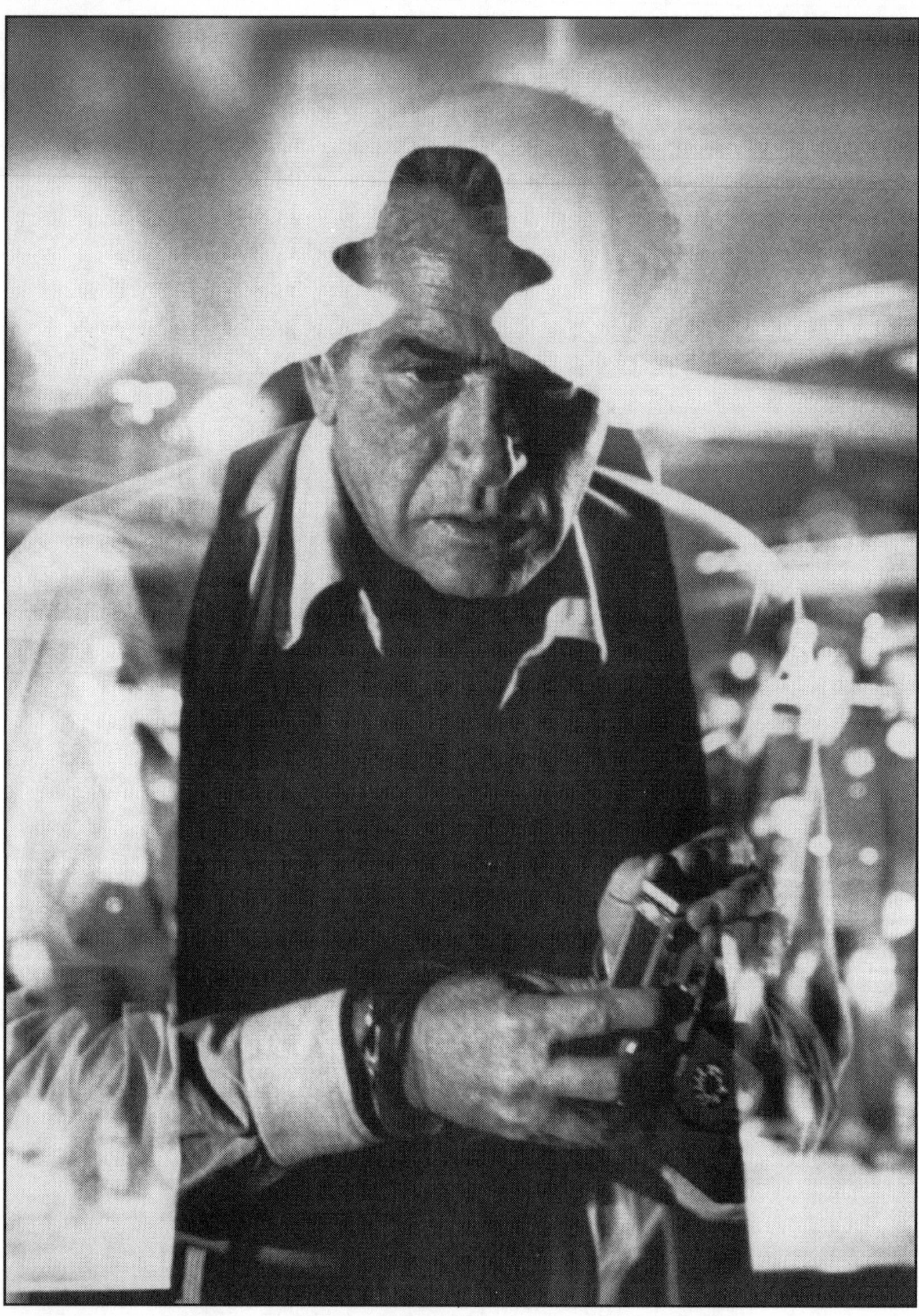

includes a long interview on TV with Munro about her Hammer film appearances and playing a vampire in a Meat Loaf music video.
✦✧

NIGHT SHADE
USA, 1997. Dir: Nicholas Medina (Fred Olen Ray). With: Tim Abell, Tane McClure, Teresa Langley, Ross Hagen, Gabriella Hall, Don Scribner. SC Productions/Playboy Entertainment Group/Royal Oaks Entertainment. Colour.
When recent widower Scott Travers (Abell) goes to a nightclub to forget his grieving, he discovers his dead wife Jennifer (Langley) is one of the dancers. Only now she is also a vampire.
✦

NIGHT SHADOW
USA, 1990. Dir: Randolph Cohlan. With: Brenda Vance, Dana Chan, Tom Boylan, Aldo Ray. Quest. Colour.
A woman returning to her hometown of Danford picks up a hitchhiker. Soon after her arrival, the small community is plagued by a series of murders committed by the wide-eyed drifter, who turns out to be a werewolf.
✦✧

NIGHT SHADOWS
(UK: MUTANT)
USA, 1984. Dir: John 'Bud' Cardos. With: Wings Hauser, Bo Hopkins, Lee Montgomery, Jody Medford, Jennifer Warren, Marc Clement. Film Ventures International. Colour.
Announced as *Toxic Waste*, this is a surprisingly effective low-budget science fiction/horror thriller in which the inhabitants of the Southern town of Goodland are turned into zombies through illegal toxic dumping by the New Era Corporation. Director Cardos (who replaced Mark Rosman after a few days shooting) builds the tension carefully before releasing an army of blood-drinking ghouls on the few survivors. The shock moments work well, thanks to the effective zombie make-up (which owes much to *Invisible Invaders* [1959]). Good production values, a Richard Band score, exciting script and solid performances combine with some genuine chills.
✦✦✦

NIGHTS OF THE WEREWOLF
(Orig: LAS NOCHES DEL HOMBRE LOBO)
Spain/France, 1968. Dir: René Govar. With: Paul Naschy (Jacinto Molina), Monique Brainvillé, Hélèn Vatelle, Peter Beaumont. Kin-Films. Colour.
Filmed in Paris, this first sequel to *Frankenstein's Bloody Terror* (1967) once again stars Naschy (who also scripted under his real name) as El Hombre Lobo. Instead of finding a cure for his condition, the mad Dr Bradoch uses sound waves to control his friend Waldemar Daninsky, the reluctant werewolf, forcing him to destroy the doctor's enemies. The director was killed in a car accident shortly after filming was completed and this is now apparently a 'lost' film.
Sequel: DRACULA VS. FRANKENSTEIN (qv; 1969)
✦

THE NIGHT STALKER
USA, 1971 (1972). Dir: John Llewellyn Moxey. With: Darren McGavin, Carol Lynley, Simon Oakland, Ralph Meeker, Claude Akins, Charles McGraw. American Broadcasting Companies. Colour.
McGavin stars as investigative journalist Carl Kolchak in the first of two made-for-TV pilot movies for the *Kolchak: The Night Stalker* (1974-75) series. Filmed under the title *The Kolchak Tapes*, Richard Matheson's tight script (based on a then-unpublished novel by Jeff Rice, which finally appeared in 1973) has Kolchak hunting a night-time killer in Las Vegas who turns out to be real vampire Janos Skorzeny (Barry Atwater, in a role apparently offered to Robert Quarry). However, nobody wants to publish the story, the police refuse to help and the superhuman killer is prepared to silence the reporter — permanently. With cameos by veterans Kent Smith and Elisha Cook Jr. When first shown, this stylish horror thriller was the highest rated TV movie ever in America.
Sequels: THE NIGHT STRANGLER (qv; 1972) and THE NIGHT STALKER: The Vampire (qv; 1974)
✦✦✦✦

Darren McGavin as reporter Carl Kolchak, TV's The Night Stalker *(1974).*

THE NIGHT STALKER:
The Vampire
USA, 1974. Dir: Don Weis. With: Darren McGavin, Simon Oakland, William Daniels, Suzanne Charny, Larry Storch, Kathleen Nolan. Universal/Francy Production/ABC-TV. Colour.
Hour-long TV series (1974-75, twenty episodes) which subsequently changed its title to *Kolchak: The Night Stalker*. This episode is actually a sequel to the 1971 pilot TV movie. When a series of vampire murders in Las Vegas are blamed on a Satanic cult, Chicago reporter Carl Kolchak (McGavin) investigates and discovers that hooker Catherine Rawlins (Charny), a victim of original vampire Janos Skorzeny, has risen from the grave seeking blood. As usual, no one believes him. The great climax has the vampire destroyed by a giant burning cross. This episode was also included in the video compilation *The Night Stalker: Two Tales of Terror* (1974).
✦✦✦
The Zombie
USA, 1974. Dir: Alex Grasshoff. With: Darren McGavin, Simon Oakland, Charles Aidman, Joseph Sirola, Val Bisoglio, J. Pat O'Malley. Universal/Francy Productions/ABC-TV. Colour.
Kolchak investigates when rival Chicago gangsters are killed off by the corpse of a murder victim, reanimated by an old voodoo Priestess. With Antonio Fargas and Scat Man (*sic*) Crothers.
Series sequel: KOLCHAK: THE NIGHT STALKER (qv; 1974-75)
✦✦✧

NIGHT STALKERS
UK, 1995. Dir: Wayne Hargood. With: Petra Drummond, Michael Mason, Tyron Wolfe, Colyn Walden, Fiona Garfield, Paula Garfield. London Deaf/Shapelondon. Colour.
This was shot on video in London and Liverpool with an all-deaf cast for an incredible $600(!), utilising narration plus sign language and subtitles for the hearing impaired. Set in 1996, private detective Kelly (Drummond) investigates a murder where the victim was found skinned. She discovers that a powerful society of werewolves, headed by the centuries-old Jonathan (Eric Collier), controls London and was responsible for killing her policeman father twenty years earlier. Despite the rock-bottom production values, this is still an impressive achievement from deaf New Zealand-born writer/producer/director Hargood, with imaginative make-up and point-of-view effects of the creatures.
✦

THE NIGHT STALKER: TWO TALES OF TERROR
USA, 1974. Dir: Allen Baron and Don Weis. With: Darren McGavin, Simon Oakland, Beatrice Colen, Kenneth Lynch, William Daniels, Suzanne Charny. Universal/Francy Production/MCA-Universal Home Video. Colour.
Video compilation of two episodes from the short-lived TV series (1974-75). In 'The Ripper', reporter Carl Kolchak (McGavin) believes that a serial killer stalking the streets of Chicago is the original Jack the Ripper. Then, while investigating a series of bizarre murders in Las Vegas, Kolchak discovers that hooker Catherine Rawlins (Charny) has risen from the grave seeking blood in 'The Vampire'. As usual, no one believes him in the end. With Larry Storch and Kathleen Nolan.
✦✦✧

THE NIGHT STRANGLER
USA, 1972 (1973). Dir: Dan Curtis. With: Darren McGavin, Jo Ann Pflug, Simon Oakland, Scott Brady, Wally Cox, Margaret Hamilton. American Broadcasting Companies/ Dan Curtis Productions. Colour.
This atmospheric TV movie sequel to *The Night Stalker* (1971) and second pilot for the short-lived *Kolchak: The Night Stalker* (1974-75) series is once again scripted by Richard Matheson and was filmed

under the title *The Time Killer*. Set in the shadowy streets in the sub-city beneath Seattle, this time investigative reporter Carl Kolchak (McGavin) is hunting down Dr Malcolm (Richard Anderson), a Civil War scientist who has created an elixir of eternal life but needs the blood of young women every twenty-one years for the serum to be effective. The scenes of the corpse-like killer stalking his victims are quite impressive. This was Wally Cox's last film. With veterans John Carradine and Al Lewis. Pocket Books published the novelisation by series creator Jeff Rice in 1974.
Sequel: THE NIGHT STALKER (qv; 1974-75)
✦✦✧

NIGHT TIDE
USA, 1961 (1963). Dir: Curtis Harrington. With: Dennis Hopper, Linda Lawson, Gavin Muir, Luana Anders, Marjorie Eaton, Tom Dillon. Virgo Productions/Phoenix/ American-International. B&W.
Based on his own unpublished story, 'The Secrets of the Sea', writer/director Harrington's theatrical feature début, shot in Santa Monica and Venice, California, is obviously inspired by Val Lewton's *Cat People* (1942). Filmed in four weeks on a budget of $80,000, lonely sailor Johnny Drake (Hopper) is on leave at a seaside resort when he meets orphan Mora (Lawson), a mysterious woman from the Greek island of Mikonos, who plays a mermaid in a pier attraction and believes that she is descended from an ancient race of sea people who kill under the spell of the full moon. With a brief cameo by an uncredited Bruno Ve Sota, who also worked as a make-up artist on the movie.
✦✦✦✦

NIGHT TIME
(Orig: SIEBEN MONDE/NACHTS)
Germany, 1998. Dir: Peter Fratzscher. With: Jan Josef Liefers, Marie Bäumer, Ulrich Mühe, Christoph Waltz, Peter Lohmeyer, Burkhard Driest. Avista Film/Roxy Film/Pro 7/Cinepool. Colour.
Inspired by a series of grisly murders in the vicinity, young writer Thomas Krömer (Liefers) is commissioned to write the story of a werewolf who has no idea who he is. But as the killings escalate and his own grandmother is slaughtered in her cottage in the woods, the writer starts to suspect himself, as reality and fantasy begin to merge.
✦✧

NIGHT TRIPS 2
USA, 1990. Dir: Andrew Blake. With: Paula Price, Randy Spears, Cheri Taylor, Erica Boyer, Bridgette Monroe, Lauren Hall. Caballero. Colour.
Hardcore sequel to the 1989 original in which Price takes over the role (from Tori Welles) of a woman undergoing sex therapy who uses a device to monitor her sexual fantasies. This includes a brief appearance by a couple of vampire-like characters.
✦

NIGHTWING
USA, 1979. Dir: Arthur Hiller. With: Nick Mancuso, David Warner, Kathryn Harrold, Stephen Macht, Strother Martin, George Clutesi. Columbia. Colour.
Based on the début novel by Martin Cruz Smith. When an old Native American medicine man calls on his gods to destroy the world, a plague of deadly vampire bats invades the desert. This interesting blend of Red Indian mysticism and modern science is stylishly directed and beautifully photographed. Henry Mancini supplies an evocative score, and Carlo Rambaldi's mechanical bats look better than the dodgy optical work. Mancuso plays policeman Youngman Duran with an attitude, ably supported by Warner's obsessive bat hunter Phillip Payne (his long soliloquy really imbues the creatures with supernatural menace). With Martin in his last role. A comic-strip Fotonovel was published the same year.
✦✦✦

NIGHT WITH A VAMPIRE
(aka LIFE SUCKS/NIGHT OF THE VAMPIRE)
USA, 1994. Dir: Jace Rocker. Midnight Video. Colour.
More hardcore vampires.
✦

9 AGES OF NAKEDNESS
UK, 1969. Dir: George Harrison Marks. With: George Harrison Marks, Max Wall, Max Bacon, Julian Orchard, Cardew Robinson, Big Bruno Erlington. Token Films. Colour.
Photographer Marks produced, scripted, directed and starred in this nudie comedy in which he reveals to a psychiatrist his family's problems with women throughout history. This involves a Frankenstein spoof (he plays Frankenstein Marks), lesbians in Ancient Egypt, a prehistoric sequence and a futuristic segment. Narrated by Charles Gray.
✦

976-EVIL II
(aka 976-EVIL THE ASTRAL FACTOR)
USA, 1991. Dir: Jim Wynorski. With: Patrick O'Bryan, Rene Assa, Debbie James, Paul Coufos, Leslie Ryan, Brigitte Nielsen. CineTel Films. Colour.
A belated sequel to Robert Englund's 1988 video hit in which motorcycle-riding hero Spike Johnson (O'Bryan, returning from the previous film) helps a young girl (James) battle the evil Mr Grubeck (Assa), who has been turned into a supernatural serial killer by the Satanic horrorscope phone-line. He uses astral projection to hunt his victims down and a Freddy-like pun when the deed is done. The best scene has one of his victims (Ryan) zapped by a hybrid combination of *Night of the Living Dead* (1968) and *It's a Wonderful Life* (1946) on her TV. A mis-cast Nielsen turns up as Agnes, the owner of an occult bookshop. With Wynorski regulars George 'Buck' Flower, Ace Mask and a dubbed Monique Gabrielle. Filmed under the title *Horrorscope*.
✦✧

NINJA, THE VIOLENT SORCERER
Hong Kong, 1986 (1988). Dir: Bruce Lambert. With: Simon Reed, Harry Carter, Joe Nelson, Terry Myers. Filmark International/Trans World Entertainment. Colour.
A murdering gambler who is aided by a pair of 300 year-old hopping vampires is finally defeated by a Ninja warrior and the friendly ghost of his wife.
✦

THE NINTH CONFIGURATION
(aka TWINKLE, TWINKLE, KILLER KANE)
USA, 1979. Dir: William Peter Blatty. With: Stacy Keach, Scott Wilson, Jason Miller, Ed Flanders, Neville Brand, George DiCenzo. The Ninth Configuration Company/ITC Film Distributors. Colour.
Author Blatty (*The Exorcist*) brings his bizarre novel *Twinkle, Twinkle, Killer Kane* to the screen as writer/producer/director. The result is a fascinating failure. Keach gives a strong performance as Colonel Hudson Kane, the new head psychiatrist at a Gothic castle full of disturbed soldiers, who turns out to be crazier than everyone else. Some wonderful moments sit side-by-side with pretentious rubbish. Attempts to create a horror atmosphere (pictures of Bela Lugosi, a man in a Frankenstein Monster mask, the supernatural ending) don't really work, but the impressive cast includes Moses Gunn, Robert Loggia, Joe Spinell, Tom Atkins and Richard Lynch. This exists in various versions, apparently ranging in length from ninety-nine to 140 minutes.
✦✦✦

NOB HILL
USA, 1945. Dir: Henry Hathaway. With: George Raft, Joan Bennett, Vivian Blaine, Peggy Ann Garner, Alan Reed, B.S. Pully. Twentieth Century Fox. Colour.
Impressive-looking Technicolor musical in which a Gold Coast saloon owner (Raft) falls for a wealthy socialite (Bennett). In one brief scene, a Chinese mummy is apparently reanimated by incense in a Chinatown wax museum. With Rory Calhoun (Francis Timothy Durgin).
✦✦

NOCTURNA
USA, 1979. Dir: Harry Tampa (Harry Hurwitz). With: Yvonne De Carlo, John Carradine, Nai Bonet, Tony Hamilton, Brother Theodore (Theodore Gottlieb), Sy

Max Schreck as the deathshead Graf Orlok in Nosferatu *(1922).*

Richardson. Irwin Yablans/Nai Bonet Enterprises/ Compass International. Colour.
Along with *Love at First Bite*, this was the other disco Dracula movie of 1979. It makes *Billy the Kid versus Dracula* (1965) look like a classic as poor seventy-three year-old John Carradine portrays the Count for the last time — he keeps his fangs in a glass of water, and shares a double coffin with Jugulia (De Carlo)! Former belly dancer (and executive producer) Bonet plays Drac's granddaughter, who runs off to New York City with a musician, and Brother Theodore is a werewolf who never transforms. With John Blyth Barrymore and songs by Gloria Gaynor, Vicki Sue Robinson and Moment of Truth.
✦✧

THE NORLISS TAPES

USA, 1973. Dir: Dan Curtis. With: Roy Thinnes, Don Porter, Angie Dickinson, Claude Akins, Michele Carey, Vonetta McGee. Metromedia/Dan Curtis Productions/ ABC-TV. Colour.
This TV movie from producer/director Curtis was apparently what became of his third *Kolchak* pilot. David Norliss (Thinnes) is a writer investigating the supernatural who records his investigations on tape. When he disappears, his publisher (veteran Hurd Hatfield) plays the first tape... Artist James Raymond Cort (Nick Dimitri) returns from the dead with the help of an ancient Egyptian ring to sculpt the demon Sargoth in blood and clay so that he can bring it to life. Scripted by William F. Nolan and based on a story by Fred Mustard Stuart, Cort's yellow-eyed walking corpse is effective, although the caped demon (Bob Schott) looks a little ludicrous. We never do discover what happened to Norliss.
✦✦

NOSFERATO IN BRAZIL

(Orig: NOSFERATO NO BRASIL)
Brazil, 1971. Dir: Ivan Cardoso. With: Torquato Neto, Ciça, Scarlet Moon, Daniel Más, Helena Lustosa. Cardoso/ Quotidianas Kodaks. Colour/B&W.
An early film from director Cardoso (*The Seven Vampires* [1985], etc), shot entirely on Super-8mm. This half-hour silent comedy spoof features a vampire from Budapest preying on bikini-clad beauties on the beaches of Rio de Janeiro. He eventually meets a woman who bites him first.
✦

EDGAR NORTON
[1868-1953]

British stage actor who travelled to America in the late 1800s. He made his film début in 1919 and stayed in Hollywood, usually playing stuffy servants.
qv: *Dracula's Daughter* (1936); *Dr. Jekyll and Mr. Hyde* (1931); *Son of Frankenstein* (1939).

LE NOSFERAT OU LES EAUX GLACEES DU CALCUL EGOÏSTE

Belgium, 1974. Dir: Maurice Rabinowicz. With: Veronique Peynet, Maïté Nahyr, Martine Bertrand, Guy Pion, Quentin Milo. Les Films du Groupe de Chambre. Colour.
Political satire, based on the director's own play. Set in the 1930s, a bourgeois killer drinks the blood of the prostitutes he murders in this mixture of songs and newsreel clips. Originally shot on 16mm.
✦

NOSFERATU

(Orig: NOSFERATU, EINE SYMPHONIE DES GRAUENS/DIE ZWÖLFTE STUNDE, EINE NACHT DES GRAUENS. USA: aka DRACULA/NOSFERATU — A SYMPHONY OF HORROR/NOSFERATU THE FIRST VAMPIRE/NOSFERATU THE VAMPIRE/NOSFERATU THE VAMPIRE (DRACULA). UK: aka NOSFERATU, A SYMPHONY OF HORRORS)
Germany, 1922. Dir: F. (Friedrich) W. (Wilhelm) Murnau.

With: Max Schreck, Alexander Granach, Gustav von Waggenheim (Wangenheim), Greta Schroder (Greta Schröeder-Matray), G. (George) H. (Heinrich) Schnell, Ruth Landshoff. Prana-Film. Tinted.
Early silent version of Bram Stoker's novel *Dracula* which was originally fated for a short commercial life. Although screenwriter Henrik Galeen freely adapted the book, he failed to obtain permission from the copyright holder. The author's widow, Florence Stoker, successfully sued Prana and the company went bankrupt. In July 1925, a court ruled that the negative and all prints of the film should be destroyed. Luckily, some copies survived and it was released in America in 1929. Actor Schreck (whose name literally means 'horror' in German) creates a truly disturbing vampire with the skeletal, taloned Graf Orlok/Nosferatu who is seduced by the heroine Mina/Ellen (Schroder) until the rising sun destroys him. Director Murnau (*Faust* [1926], etc) uses shadows, speeded-up photography and negative images to give the film a dream-like quality. Overlong and dull in places, this still has the power to fascinate. Future director Edgar G. Ulmer contributed to the art direction. Music (by Georg Fliebiger) and sound effects were added in 1930 by Murnau's former student Dr Waldemar Ronger to a re-edited and expanded version entitled *Die Zwölfte Stunde, Eine Nact des Grauens*, from Deutsch Film Produktion. A restored and newly-tinted version was released in 1997 by Channel Four/Photoplay Productions with a specially composed score by Hammer veteran James Bernard, and a 1998 video release featured songs by rock band Type-O Negative along with an introduction by David Carradine.
Remakes: DRACULA (qv; 1931) and NOSFERATU THE VAMPYRE (qv; 1979)
✦✦✧

THE NOSFERATU DIARIES: EMBRACE OF THE VAMPIRE
USA, 1994. Dir: Anne Goursaud. With: Alyssa Milano, Martin Kemp, Harrison Pruett, Charlotte Lewis, Jennifer Tilly, Jordan Ladd. Moving Pictures 1/The Ministry of Film/General Media Entertainment. Colour.
'Directed by the editor of *Bram Stoker's Dracula*'! This often sleazy romantic vampire movie features a laughably inept Kemp as a member of the undead looking for the reincarnation of his long-lost love. The vampire decides he's found her in Charlotte (TV actress Milano [*Charmed* (1998-) etc], trying to change her image), who is an unbelievably naïve student. From his tower aerie he has just three days before his existence ends to seduce Charlotte through her dreams, sowing the seeds of doubt about her relationship with her boyfriend. Tilly turns up in a cameo as a sexy vamp. With lots of nudity.
✦

NOSFERATU THE VAMPYRE
(Orig: NOSFERATU PHANTOM DER NACHT/NOSFERATU FANTÔME DE LA NUIT)
West Germany/France, 1979. Dir: Werner Herzog. With: Klaus Kinski, Isabelle Adjani, Bruno Ganz, Roland Topor, Walter Ladengast, Paul Monette. Werner Herzog Filmproduktion/Gaumont/Twentieth Century Fox. Colour.
Produced, written and directed by Herzog, this remake of F.W. Murnau's 1922 movie is, if anything, even more lethargic than the original. Kinski looks very effective in the Max Schreck-style make-up, but his apathetic vampire just shuffles around the decaying streets, wearily stealing blood from victims. The supporting cast is equally lifeless (excuse the pun), and author Topor (*The Tenant*, etc) gives a bizarre performance as Renfield. This was filmed in simultaneous English- and German-language versions for just $896,000. Paul Monette wrote the Avon novelisation.

Paul Birch as the alien vampire who is Not of This Earth *(1957).*

"NOT OF THIS EARTH" "X"
starring
PAUL BIRCH · BEVERLY GARLAND · MORGAN JONES
AN ALLIED ARTISTS PICTURE
DISTRIBUTED BY ASSOCIATED BRITISH-PATHE LTD

Sequel: VAMPIRE IN VENICE (qv; 1988)
Remake: DRACULA SUCKS (qv; 1979)
✦✧

NOT OF THIS EARTH
USA, 1957. Dir: Roger Corman. With: Paul Birch, Beverly Garland, Morgan Jones, Jonathan Haze, William Roderick, Richard (Dick) Miller. Los Altos/Allied Artists. B&W.
An alien from the dying planet Davanna arrives on Earth to learn whether human blood can be used to replace that of his own race. Soon, the inhabitants of a small American town are being found murdered, with all the blood drained from their bodies... Roger Corman's low-budget science fiction thriller may be short on special effects, but makes up for it with an intelligent script by Mark Hanna and Charles Griffith and a powerful performance by Birch as the shades-wearing alien 'Paul Johnson', who can destroy minds with his bleached-out eyes. This includes a flying bat creature created by an uncredited Paul Blaisdell. According to Dick Miller, when star Birch continued to upset the cast and crew he was replaced by a double for much of the picture. A cult classic.
Remake: NOT OF THIS EARTH (qv; 1988)
✦✦✦✧

NOT OF THIS EARTH
USA, 1988. Dir: Jim Wynorski. With: Traci Lords, Arthur Roberts, Lenny Juliano, Rebecca Perle, Ace Mask, Roger Lodge. Pacific Trust/New Horizons/Concorde. Colour.
Faithful, if inferior, updated remake of Roger Corman's 1957 cult classic, made by Wynorski in response to a challenge that he could not match the original's twelve-day shooting schedule. This time Roberts plays the blood-seeking alien 'Mr Johnson' who is depleting the Earth's bimbo population and transporting suitcases full of their red stuff back to his parched planet. Former under-age porn queen Lords has a nude scene as Nadine Story, the nurse who discovers what he is up to. This is padded out with clips from several other movies, including *Hollywood Boulevard* (1976), *Humanoids from the Deep* (1980), *Galaxy of Terror* (1981), *Piranha* (1978) and even *The Terror* (1963). With Monique Gabrielle, Becky LeBeau and Kelly Maroney. Cheap laughs, cheap production, executive produced by Corman.
Remake: NOT OF THIS EARTH (qv; 1995)
✦✦

NOT OF THIS EARTH
USA, 1995. Dir: Terence H. Winkless. With: Michael York, Parker Stevenson, Richard Belzer, Elizabeth Barondes, Ted Davis, Mason Adams, Julia Mueller. Concorde/New Horizons/Libra Pictures/Showtime. Colour.
The third version of Corman's 1957 film, this made-for-cable TV movie was originally shown as part of the *Roger Corman Presents* series. Based on the original screenplay by Mark Hanna and Charles Griffith, York plays the sunglasses-wearing alien 'Mr Johnson', who hypnotises his victims and burns out their eyes with his power before draining all their blood in an attempt to save his world from an apocalyptic virus. Barondes is the nurse he employs to give him transfusions. Nice CGI effects, but this version fails to improve upon the original despite some oddball humour, gloopy special effects and gratuitous nudity. Johnson also watches a clip from a vampire film on TV. With make-up supervisor John Buechler as another alien.
✦✦

NOTRE-DAME DE PARIS
France, 1911. Dir: Albert Capellani. With: Stacia Napierkowska, Henri Krauss, Claude Garry, René Alexandre, Georges Treville. CGPC/Pathé. B&W.
Forty-five minute silent version of Victor Hugo's novel in which the hunchbacked bellringer Quasimodo (Krauss) becomes handsome when kissed by Esmeralda (Napierkowska), the gypsy dancer he loves. This was apparently released in America in a tinted version in 1913.
Remake: THE DARLING OF PARIS (qv; 1917)
✦

NOT WITHOUT MY HANDBAG
UK, 1997. Dir: Boris Kossmehl. Aardman Animations. Colour.
Surreal stop-motion animation short from the company that created Wallace and Gromit. When a woman discovers that the small print on her washing machine warranty means she has sold her soul to the Devil, she returns from Hell as a zombie to reclaim the precious handbag she left behind.
✦✦✧

LES NOUVELLES BRIGADES DU TIGRE: Le Vampire des Karpates
France, 1982. Dir: Victor Vicas. With: Pinkas Braun, Arthur Brauss, Feodor Atkine, Jacques Buchelier, Claude Carvin, Gerard Couderc. A2/TELEcip. Colour.
Episode of the TV mystery series. With the advent of talking pictures in 1929, many silent stars found themselves unable to adapt to the new technology. One such actor is Lucien Desormes (Brauss), who portrayed the Vampire of the Karpates. Rather than be forgotten by his public, Desormes hangs himself in his apartment. However, after his burial, a frightening silhouette — which looks like the undead monster he played on the screen — prowls the streets of Paris at night. After each sighting, a body is found...
✦✦

NUDE NASTY DRIPPING WET VAMPIRES
USA, 1997. Dir: Geoffrey de Valois. With: Tonya Qualls, Elaine Juliette Williamson. Digital Entertainment Group/ Salt City Home Video. Colour.
Rare scenes and sexy outtakes of the two Vampire Centerfolds in this softcore video in the *Vampire Raw Footage* series.
✦

NUDE SORORITY BITCHES FROM HELL
USA, 1997. Dir: Geoffrey de Valois. With: Heather LeMire, Liddy Roley, Barbara Savage. Digital Entertainment Group/Salt City Home Video. Colour.
This softcore *Vampire Raw Footage* video includes behind-the-scenes nude and erotic sequences from *The Vampire Conspiracy* (1995) and *Vampire Centerfolds* (1995).
✦

THE NUDE VAMPIRE
(Orig: LA VAMPIRE NUE)
France, 1969. Dir: Jean Rollin. With: Christine François, Olivier Martin, Maurice LeMaître, Caroline Cartier, Bernard Musson, Jean Aron. Films ABC/Boxoffice International. Colour.
The second feature film from co-writer, producer and director Rollin has Pierre Radamante (Martin) falling in love with a strange young woman in red (Cartier) he meets being chased through the streets. When she is subsequently captured by a group of men in animal masks, his investigations reveal that she is apparently an immortal vampire being held prisoner by his father's secret suicide sect and that the silver-caped Grand Master (Michel Delahaye) is the leader of a group of other-dimensional mutants who want to rescue her. This tedious mystery from the overrated French director includes more topless nudity and bizarre costumes.
✦✧

NUDE VAMPIRE KILLERS
USA, 1997. Dir: Geoffrey de Valois. With: Mihaella Stoicova, Kathy Arianoff. Digital Entertainment Group/ Salt City Home Video. Colour.
Another softcore *Vampire Raw Footage* video, featuring behind-the-scenes shots of nude kinky killer vampires.
✦

NUDE VAMPIRE MAKEUP EFFECTS
USA, 1997. Dir: Geoffrey de Valois. With: Kim Blair, Elaine Juliette Williamson. Digital Entertainment Group/Salt City Home Video. Colour.
More softcore *Vampire Raw Footage* as Blair attacks topless cheerleader Williamson after being transformed into an alien mutant monster with ten breasts.
✦

NUDE VAMPIRE PHOTO SHOOT PART 2
USA, 1997. Dir: Geoffrey de Valois. With: Joan A. Teeter, Elaine Juliette Williamson, Aileen Frieze. Digital Entertainment Group/Salt City Home Video. Colour.
Vampire Raw Footage video that includes behind-the-scenes nude and erotic sequences. This tape features 1996 Vampire Centrefold of the Year Teeter and nude slave girl Frieze on location for an alien sex and bondage photo shoot.
✦

NUDE VAMPIRES
USA, 1994. Colour.
Softcore video in which a salesman's car breaks down and he discovers an old castle containing three beautiful vampires.
✦

NUDE VAMPIRE STARLET AUDITIONS
USA, 1997. Dir: Geoffrey de Valois. With: Jasmine Jean, Elaine Juliette Williamson. Digital Entertainment Group/Salt City Home Video. Colour.
One of a series of *Vampire Raw Footage* videos that includes softcore behind-the-scenes sequences. A number of girls audition for the vampire sex films *Vampire Centerfolds* (1995) and *The Vampire Conspiracy* (1995).
✦

NUDIST COLONY OF THE DEAD
USA, 1991. Dir: Mark Pirro. With: Deborah Stern, Rachel Latt, Braddon Mendelson, Forrest J Ackerman, Dave Robinson, Bruce Brown. Artistic License Video. Colour.
Musical comedy filmed on Super-8mm by the director of *A Polish Vampire in Burbank* (1983). When religious campaigners close down their camp, a group of nudists vow revenge before they commit suicide. Five years later they return as zombies and attack people at a summer camp. With Ackerman as a judge, and an uncredited Kris Gilpin.
✦✧

THE NUTTY PROFESSOR
USA, 1963. Dir: Jerry Lewis. With: Jerry Lewis, Stella Stevens, Del Moore, Kathleen Freeman, Med Flory, Norman Alden. Jerry Lewis Enterprises/Paramount. Colour.
Better than usual Lewis comedy (he co-scripted, starred and directed) which is an inventive variation on Robert Louis Stevenson's *Strange Case of Dr. Jekyll and Mr. Hyde*. He stars as Julius Kelp, a clumsy, plain-looking college professor who creates a chemical potion that transforms him into the hip, but obnoxious Buddy Love (a dig at Lewis' ex-partner Dean Martin?). Too much pathos, but good support from Moore as the college Principal and Stevens as the gorgeous Stella Purdy, who prefers the awkward Julius. Originally announced as *Dr. Jerkyll and Mr. Hyde*. In 1965, Allied Artists were going to make the comedy musical *Dr. Rock and Mr. Roll* starring Basil Rathbone and Huntz Hall, but thankfully it never appeared.
Remake: THE NUTTY PROFESSOR (qv; 1996)
✦✦✦

THE NUTTY PROFESSOR
USA, 1996. Dir: Tom Shadyac. With: Eddie Murphy, Jada Pinkett, James Coburn, Larry Miller, Dave Chappelle, John Ales. Universal/Imagine Entertainment. Colour.
It took four credited scriptwriters (and numerous others uncredited, including Larry Gelbert who received $1,000,000 for his unused draft) to come up with this lacklustre remake of the 1963 movie starring Jerry Lewis (who co-executive produced this version). Murphy is fine as overweight college professor Sherman Klump, whose experimental formula transforms him into obnoxious lady-killer Buddy Love. But there's far too much Murphy (in Academy Award-winning special make-up effects by Rick Baker), who appears in five other roles. Director Shadyac's idea of comedy revolves more around bodily functions rather than the inherent Jekyll and Hyde situation. This also includes a King Kong-style dream sequence. In 1999 Universal announced *The Nutty Professor II* to be directed F. Gary Gray and again star Murphy.
✦✧

NYLON NOOSE
(Orig: DIE NYLONSCHLINGE)
West Germany, 1963. Dir: Rudolf Zehetgruber. With: Richard Goodman, Laya Raki, Dietmar Schönherr, Helga Sommerfeld, Adi Berber, Gustav Knuth. Monachia/Urania/Medallion. B&W.
Low-budget thriller in which a mad doctor attempts to transfer the substance that preserves mummies into humans.
✦✧

NYMPHO-TEENS OF ROMA MEET SON OF THE WOLFMAN
Italy, 1979. Dir: Robert Paget. With: Angelo Libuty, Karen Meyer, Mark Sinclair, Alex Gordon, Sarah Mensinga, Rod Amador. Colour.
Independent production, filmed in English by writer/director Paget.
✦

NYMPHO ZOMBIE COEDS
USA, 1993. Dir: Toby Dammit. With: Ariel Daye, Thumper (Monique), Tracey Prince, Alicia Rio, Laurie Cameron, Gabriella (Gabriella Portugal). Visual Images. Colour.
This poorly produced hardcore feature doesn't live up to its great title. The director plays a doctor who tests his new formula by pouring it into the punch at a party. Everyone who drinks it is turned into the living dead, which leads to a big orgy until the women are 'cured' with the aid of a transparent dildo.
✦

NYPD BLUE:
NYPD Lou
USA, 1993. Dir: Gregory Hoblit. With: David Caruso, Dennis Franz, James McDaniel, Sherry Stringfield, Amy Brenneman, Nicholas Turturro. Steven Bochco Productions/20th Television/ABC-TV. Colour.
In this episode of the gritty New York police TV series (1993-), created by Steven Bochco, street person Lou (Dan Hedaya) thinks that he is a werewolf, but eventually reveals to Detective John Kelly (Caruso) that he has witnessed the murder of a drug dealer.
✦✦✦✧

THE OASIS OF THE LIVING DEAD

(Orig: LA TUMBA DE LOS MUERTOS VIVIENTES/L'ABÎME DES MORTS VIVANTS/LE TRÉSOR DES MORTS-VIVANTS. USA: aka BLOODSUCKING NAZI ZOMBIES/OASIS OF THE ZOMBIES)

Spain/France, 1981 (1982). Dir: A.M. Frank (Marius Lasoeur and Jesús Franco). With: Manuel Gélin, France Jordan, Jeff Montgomery, Myriam Landson, Eric Saint-Just, Henri Lambert. Marte Films/Diasa/Eurociné. Colour.

Robert Blabert (Gélin) and a group of friends spend their vacation searching for a fortune in gold left behind by Rommel's troops after their defeat in the North African desert during World War Two. Arriving at the oasis where the treasure is buried, they discover that it is protected by flesh-eating Nazi zombies, which rise up from beneath the sand. Originally filmed simultaneously in Spanish and French versions with different casts (including Lina Romay [Rosa Maria Almirall]), this is apparently a re-edited export version that includes sequences from Franco's *La Tumba de los Muertos Vivientes* (1982) and wide-screen stock footage from Alfredo Rizzo's 1971 war film *I Giardini del Diavolo*.

✦

OBAKE NO SAMBA, MON MON MONSTER

Japan, 1980. Dir: Yukito Aizawa. With: Hitoshi Omeae, Minorv Sado, Takeshi Sasano, Midori Fukuhara, Jiro Sakagami. Watanabe Kikaku/Tokyo Hoso 12. Colour.

Half-hour musical sitcom TV series featuring Dracula (Sado), the Frankenstein Monster (Omeae) and the Wolf Man (Sasano), who live in a fake haunted house attraction with the witch Tabasa (Fukuhara) and ghost Baku (Sakagami). Whenever the Monster drinks wine he turns gay!

✦

WILLIS H. O'BRIEN
[1886-1962]

Pioneer American animator Willis Harold O'Brien began experimenting with stop-motion in 1915, and his first short film, *The Dinosaur and the Missing Link*, appeared the same year. His special effects for *The Lost World* (1925) led to the aborted *Creation* (1930-31) before 'Obie' convinced RKO to use stop-motion animation for *King Kong* (1933). He followed it with *The Son of Kong* (1933), *The Animal World* (1955), *The Black Scorpion* (1957), *Behemoth the Sea Monster* (1958) and worked as an advisor on the 1960 remake of *The Lost World*. Although he won an Academy Award for his work on *Mighty Joe Young* (1949), his career was dogged with failed projects and poor luck.

UNA O'CONNOR
[1880-1959]

Irish character actress who made her film début in 1929 and moved to Hollywood three years later. Director James Whale used her as shrieking comic relief in both *The Invisible Man* (1933) and *Bride of Frankenstein* (1935).

OCTAMAN

USA/Mexico, 1971. Dir: Harry (J.) Essex. With: Kerwin Mathews, Pier Angeli, Jeff Morrow, Jerome Guardino, Norman Fields, Robert Warner. Filmers Guild. Colour.

Low-budget science fiction movie about a silly looking octopus-man monster (designed by George Barr and created by a young Rick Baker and Doug Beswick), the result of atomic radiation. Thirty-nine year-old Italian actress Pier Angeli (Anna Maria Pierangeli) made her American film comeback in this directorial début from the co-writer of *Creature from the Black Lagoon* (1954), but died from an overdose of barbiturates during production. With Buck Kartalian.

✦

THE OFFSPRING

(UK: FROM A WHISPER TO A SCREAM)

USA, 1986 (1988). Dir: Jeff Burr. With: Vincent Price, Clu Gulager, Terry Kiser, Harry Caesar, Rosalind Cash, Cameron Mitchell. Manson/Conquest Entertainment. Colour.

Unpleasant, low-budget anthology movie shot in Georgia, Tennessee, in 1985. In a role turned down by Forrest J Ackerman(!), Price portrays a small town historian in the linking sequences who believes that everyone living in Oldfield is cursed by evil: when a man (Gulager in his worst role) violates a corpse, he is killed by its zombie offspring; a small-time crook learns the secret of eternal life as a burned corpse; a carnival glass-eater (Ron Brooks) is destroyed by a voodoo queen (Cash), and a Civil War soldier (veteran Mitchell) is burned alive by cannibal children. In the end, Price's narrator is knifed in the throat by a reporter (Susan Tyrrell). With Angelo Rossitto, Lawrence Tierney and Martine Beswick in a very minor cameo.

✦✧

CHARLES STANTON OGLE
[1865-1940]

American silent movie actor who portrayed the screen's first Frankenstein Monster in Thomas Edison's 1910 version.

OH, BOY!

UK, 1938. Dir: Albert De Courville. With: Albert Burdon, Mary Lawson, Bernard Nedell, Jay Laurier, Robert Cochran, Edmon Ryan. Associated British-Pathé. B&W.

Comedy in which a timid chemist uses a potion that transforms him into a strong and confident character. Unfortunately, it also causes him to regress back to a baby.

✦✧

OIL OF ETERNAL LIFE

Thailand, circa 1987. Thai Video. Colour.

When an old witch shoots rays into her mouth and eyes before exploding, a young woman becomes a vampiric *penanggalan* whose head, glowing heart and lungs detach themselves from her body when she searches for victims.

✦

WARNER OLAND
[1880-1938]

Swedish-born character actor who made his career in Hollywood by playing such oriental characters as Fu Manchu and Charlie Chan. He was Dr Yogami, the other werewolf, in *WereWolf of London* (1935).
qv: *Charlie Chan at the Opera* (1936); *Charlie Chan in Egypt* (1935).

OLD MANOR HOUSE

UK, 1948. Dir: Harold F. Mack. British Animation Productions. Colour.

Seven minute cartoon in which Bubble and his talking taxi Squeak encounter the Frankie Stein monster in a haunted house.

✦✧

O LUCKY MAN!

UK, 1973. Dir: Lindsay Anderson. With: Malcolm McDowell, Ralph Richardson, Rachel Roberts, Arthur Lowe, Helen Mirren, Mona Washbourne. Memorial/Sam/ Warner Bros. Colour.

Optimistic coffee salesman Mick Travis (McDowell, repeating his role from Anderson's *If...* [1968] with more than a nod to Stanley Kubrick's *A Clockwork Orange* [1971]) travels around the North of England and is plunged into a series of bizarre and satirical encounters. As a research volunteer in a private medical clinic, he discovers the mad Dr Millar (the wonderful Graham Crowden) is transplanting human heads onto animal bodies (creating an horrific pig-boy monster). Many of the cast appear in more than one role, and the director turns up as himself. With Dandy Nichols, Peter Jeffrey, pro-

ducer Michael Medwin, Edward Judd, Brian Glover and many others. Music by Alan Price.
Sequel: BRITANNIA HOSPITAL (qv; 1982)
✦✦✦✦

KATE O'MARA
[b 1939]

Glamorous British actress who ended up as a victim in both Hammer's *The Horror of Frankenstein* (1970) and *The Vampire Lovers* (1970).

OMNICRON
Italy, 1963. Dir: Ugo Gregoretti. With: Renato Salvatori, Rosemary Dexter, Dante di Pino, Gaetano Quartaro, Maria Cariso, Ida Serasini. Lux/Ultra/Vides. B&W.
Comedy in which the amorphous alien of the title reanimates the corpse of Italian factory worker Angelo (Salvatori). In the end, the creature decides to invade Venus instead of Earth.
✦✧

ONCE BITTEN
USA, 1985. Dir: Howard Storm. With: Lauren Hutton, Jimmy (Jim) Carrey, Karen Kopins, Cleavon Little, Thomas Ballatore, Skip Lackey. The Samuel Goldwyn Company. Colour.
Embarrassing horror comedy. Teen nerd Mark Kendall (an early film role for Carrey) is seduced by a centuries-old vampire (Hutton) because he's still a virgin. Director Storm includes all the gags you would expect.
✦✧

ONCE UPON A MIDNIGHT DREARY
(aka VINCENT PRICE'S ONCE UPON A MIDNIGHT SCARY)
USA, 1979. Dir: Neil Cox. With: Vincent Price, Rene Auberjonois, Guy Boyd, Severn Darden, Lance Kerwin. CBS-TV. Colour.
Hour-long TV show hosted by Price dressed as Dracula, in which he urges children to read more by introducing extracts from such books as *The Ghost Belonged to Me* by Richard Peck, *The Legend of Sleepy Hollow* by Washington Irving and *The House With a Clock in Its Walls* by John Bellairs. This was released on tape in 1986 as the second in Video Gems' *Video Reading* series.
✦✧

ONCE UPON A PRIME TIME
Canada, 1971.
This apparently includes Count Dracula.
✦

ONCE UPON A TIME:
Frankenstein
UK, 1973. Dir: Gerry Hill. With: John Stride, Geoffrey Bayldon, John Stratton, David Ryall, Derrick O'Connor, Ted Carroll. Granada Television/ITV. Colour.
Clever sequel to Mary Shelley's novel, written by John Stevenson. Although the Monster was last seen clinging to an ice floe, this drama asks what happened to his creator, Baron Frankenstein (Bayldon)? As *The Phoenix* moves further north into the ice packs of the Arctic, the crew want to turn back. But the ship's master, Robert Walton (Stride), has his own secret reasons to press forward...
✦✦✦

ONE-ARMED BANDIT
Sweden, 1974. Dir: Peter Kruse. Svenska. Colour.
Cartoon short in which gamblers are swallowed by Frankenstein fruit machines.
✦

ONE DARK NIGHT
(UK: aka ENTITY FORCE)
USA, 1982 (1983). Dir: Thomas McLoughlin. With: Meg Tilly, Melissa Newman, Robin Evans, Leslie Speights, Donald Hotton, Adam West. The Picture Company/ Comworld Pictures. Colour.
Filmed under the titles *Night in the Crypt* and *Rest in Peace*, this low-budget horror thriller was written and directed by mime actor McLoughlin for just $800,000. As part of a high school initiation, Julie Wells (Tilly) spends the night in a mausoleum and along with a group of other teens is menaced by psychic vampire Karl Raymar. The reanimated corpses (created by the Burman Studio) are not nearly as realistic as they should be, but the electrical effects (filmed live on the set) are quite impressive. With Leo Gorcey Jr and Kevin Peter Hall.
✦✦

ONE EYEBROW PRIEST
(USA: aka VAMPIRE VS. VAMPIRE)
Hong Kong, 1989. Dir: Lam Ching-Ying (Lin Zheng-Ying). With: Lam Ching-Ying (Lin Zheng-Ying), Chin Siu-Ho, Lu Fang, Sandra Ng. Golden Harvest/ Diagonal Pictures. Colour.
Horror comedy in which an exorcist priest (director Ching-Ying) and his vampire child assistant battle a number of ghosts.
✦✧

100 YEARS OF HORROR:
Baron Frankenstein
USA/UK, 1996. Dir: Tom Forrester. With: Christopher Lee, Donald (F.) Glut, Veronica Carlson, Hazel Court, Freddie Francis, Hugh Hefner. Passport International Productions/Jordexx Television. Colour/B&W.
Low-budget, half-hour TV series hosted by Lee from Bray Studios, with incidental music composed by Hans J. Salter. This episode looks at later Frankenstein movies with clips and trailers from Hammer's *The Curse of Frankenstein* (1957), *The Evil of Frankenstein* (1964), *Frankenstein and the Monster from Hell* (1973), *Frankenstein Created Woman* (1966), *The Horror of Frankenstein* (1970) and *The Revenge of Frankenstein* (1958), along with *Frankenstein Conquers the World* (1964), *Frankenstein Meets the Spacemonster* (1965), *Frankenstein 1970* (1958), *Frankenstein's Daughter* (1958), *How to Make a Monster* (1958), *I Was a Teenage Frankenstein* (1957), *Jesse James Meets Frankenstein's Daughter* (1965), *Lady Frankenstein* (1971), *Young Frankenstein* (1974) and TV's *Tales of Frankenstein* (1958), plus interviews with Fred Olen Ray, Richard Cunha, Jimmy Sangster and Kenneth Branaugh (*sic*).
✦✦✧

Bela Lugosi
USA/UK, 1996. Dir: Tom Forrester. With: Christopher Lee, Bela Lugosi Jr, Carol (Caroll) Borland, Hugh Hefner, Ralph Bellamy, John Carradine. Passport International Productions/Jordexx Television. Colour/B&W.
This episode looks at the career of Bela Lugosi and includes clips and trailers from *The Ape Man* (1943), *The Body Snatcher* (1945), *Dark Eyes of London* (1939), *Dracula* (1931), *Hollywood on Parade No.8* (1933), *Invisible Ghost* (1941), *The Invisible Ray* (1936), *Murders in the Rue Morgue* (1932), *Son of Frankenstein* (1939) and *White Zombie* (1932), footage of Lugosi being interviewed by Dorothy West for *Intimate Interviews* in 1932, a 1934 promotional film with Karloff, a brief clip of Lugosi being 'hypnotised' on the set of *Black Friday* (1940), a shipboard interview about *Dracula*, Lugosi interviewed leaving hospital in 1955, TV's *You Asked for It* (1953), plus interviews with producer Mark Gilman Jr, Robert Wise and Sara Karloff.
✦✦✦

Blood-Drinking Beings
USA/UK, 1996. Dir: Tom Forrester. With: Christopher Lee, Brinke Stevens, Roy Ward Baker, Jimmy Sangster, Ferdy (Ferdinand) Mayne, Robert Cornthwaite. Passport International Productions/Jordexx Television. Colour/ B&W.
Episode of the half-hour TV series that looks at non-Dracula vampire movies, with clips and trailers from *Black Sabbath* (1963), *Blood and Roses* (1960), *Captain Kronos Vampire Hunter* (1972), *Countess Dracula* (1970), *Dead Men Walk* (1943), *The Fearless Vampire Killers* (1966), *Isle of the Dead* (1945), *The Last Man on Earth* (1961), *Lust for a Vampire* (1970), *Not of This Earth* (1957), *The Ωmega Man* (1971), *One More Time* (1970), *Planet of the Vampires* (1965), *The Thing from Another World* (1951), *Twins of Evil* (1971), *The Vampire Bat* (1933), *The*

Vampire Lovers (1970), *Vampyr* (1931-32) and *The Werewolf vs. the Vampire Woman* (1970), plus interviews with film historian D.P. Smith, Charlton Heston, Roger Corman, Dick Miller and Caroline Munro.

◆◆◇

Boris Karloff

USA/UK, 1996. Dir: Tom Forrester. With: Christopher Lee, Sara Karloff, Hugh Hefner, Ralph Bellamy, Bela Lugosi Jr, Turhan Bey. Passport International Productions/Jordexx Television. Colour/B&W.

This half-hour episode is dedicated to Karloff, with clips and trailers from *The Black Room* (1935), *The Body Snatcher* (1945), *The Climax* (1944), *The Comedy of Terrors* (1963), *Corridors of Blood* (1958), *Die, Monster, Die!* (1965), *The Invisible Ray* (1936), *The Mask of Fu Manchu* (1932), *Night Key* (1937), *The Raven* (1963), *Snake People* (1968), *The Terror* (1963), and TV's *Carol Burnett Show, Route 66, This is Your Life* and *Thriller*, plus rare colour home movies (including behind-the-scenes footage from *Son of Frankenstein* [1939]) and interviews with Robert Wise, Richard Matheson, Dick Miller, Jack Hill and Roger Corman.

◆◆◆

Dinosaurs

USA/UK, 1996. Dir: Ted Newsom. With: Christopher Lee, Don (Donald F.) Glut, Ray Harryhausen, Robert Cornthwaite, Raquel Welch, Martine Beswick. Passport International Productions/Jordexx Television. Colour/B&W.

This episode looks at dinosaurs with clips and trailers from *The Beast from 20,000 Fathoms* (1953), *Carnosaur* (1993), *Dinosaur Valley Girls* (1996), *The Giant Behemoth* (1958), *Godzilla King of the Monsters!* (1954), *Gorgo* (1961), *King Kong vs. Godzilla* (1963), *The Land Unknown* (1957), *The Lost World* (1960), *One Million Years B.C.* (1966), *Reptilicus* (1962), *The Son of Kong* (1933) and *The Valley of Gwangi* (1969), plus rare footage from the *Creation* (1930-31) screen test, Willis O'Brien's sketches for the unproduced *Gwangi* (1943), Hammer chairman Sir James Carreras behind-the-scenes on *When Dinosaurs Ruled the Earth* (1969), and interviews with *Photon* writer Mark McGee, producer William Alland, Val Guest, Fred Olen Ray and the voice of Victoria Vetri.

◆◆◆

Dracula and His Disciples

USA/UK, 1996. Dir: Tom Forrester. With: Christopher Lee, Bela Lugosi Jr, Hugh Hefner, Carol (Caroll) Borland, Fred Olen Ray, Nina Foch. Passport International Productions/Jordexx Television. Colour/B&W.

Episode of the half-hour TV series that looks at Dracula in the movies, with all the usual clips and trailers from *Billy the Kid Versus Dracula* (1965), *The Brides of Dracula* (1960), *Count Dracula and His Vampire Bride* (1973), both 1931 versions of *Dracula, Dracula A.D. 1972* (1972), *Dracula Has Risen from the Grave* (1968), *Horror of Dracula* (1958), *House of Dracula* (1945), *House of Frankenstein* (1944), *Mark of the Vampire* (1935), (Abbott and Costello) *Meet Frankenstein* (1948), *Nosferatu* (1922), *The Return of Dracula* (1957), *The Return of the Vampire* (1943), *Scared to Death* (1946), *Scars of Dracula* (1970), *Son of Dracula* (1943), and *Valley of the Zombies* (1946), plus rare footage of Edward Van Sloan's screen test for *Dracula* (1931), a 1933 interview with Bela Lugosi, outtakes from (Abbott and Costello) *Meet Frankenstein*, and interviews with John Carradine, Francis Lederer, Peter Cushing, Jimmy Sangster, Veronica Carlson, Freddie Francis, Michael Carreras, Roy Ward Baker and Caroline Munro.

◆◆◆

Dr. Jekyll and Mr. Hyde

USA/UK, 1996. Dir: Tom Forrester. With: Christopher Lee, Don (Donald F.) Glut, Sara Karloff, Gloria Talbott, Fred Olen Ray, John Agar. Passport International Productions/Jordexx Television. Colour/B&W.

Episode of the half-hour TV series hosted by Lee (who is very critical of the 1971 adaptation he appeared in), with clips and trailers from *Abbott and Costello Meet Dr. Jekyll and Mr. Hyde* (1953), *Black Friday* (1940), *Daughter of Dr. Jekyll* (1957), *Dr. Jekyll and Mr. Hyde* (1913, 1920, 1931 and 1941 versions), *Dr. Jekyll & Sister Hyde* (1971), *Hand of Death* (1961), *The Haunted Strangler* (1958), *The Hideous Sun Demon* (1959), *I, Monster* (1971), *The Mad Monster* (1942), *The Manster* (1959), *The Nutty Professor* (1963), *The Two Faces of Dr. Jekyll* (1960) and TV's *Climax!* (1955), plus rare behind-the-scenes footage from *Dr. Jekyll & Sister Hyde* and interviews with Michael Carreras, Roy Ward Baker, Caroline Munro and Martine Beswick.

◆◆◆

Frankenstein and Friends

USA/UK, 1996. Dir: Tom Forrester. With: Christopher Lee, Boris Karloff, David J. Skal, Hugh Hefner, Sarah Karloff, Ralph Bellamy. Passport International Productions/Jordexx Television. Colour/B&W.

This episode looks at early Frankenstein movies, with clips and trailers from *Bride of Frankenstein* (1935), *Frankenstein* (1910 and 1931 versions), *Frankenstein Meets the Wolf Man* (1943), *The Ghost of Frankenstein* (1942), *House of Dracula* (1945), *House of Frankenstein* (1944), (Abbott and Costello) *Meet Frankenstein* (1948) and *Son of Frankenstein* (1939), plus *The Curse of Frankenstein* (1957), rare outtakes from *Bride of Frankenstein* and *Meet Frankenstein*, Karloff's colour home movies on the set of *Son of Frankenstein*, footage of a 1941 baseball game with Karloff in the Monster make-up, plus interviews with writer/film historian Ira Lawson, make-up artist Michael F. Blake, Jack Hill, Bela Lugosi Jr, Robert De Niro and the voice of Glenn Strange.

◆◆◇

Freaks

USA/UK, 1996. Dir: Tom Forrester. With: Christopher Lee, Fred Olen Ray, Robert Wise, David (J.) Skal, Richard Cunha, Beverly Garland. Passport International Productions/Jordexx Television. Colour/B&W.

Episode of half-hour TV series that looks at freaks in the movies, with clips and trailers from *Chained for Life* (1950), *The Day the Earth Stood Still* (1951), *Face Behind the Mask* (1941), *Freaks* (1932), *The Hills Have Eyes* (1977), *The Human Monster* (1939), *The Hunchback of Notre Dame* (1923 and 1956 versions), *Invaders from Mars* (1953), *The Jungle Captive* (1944), *The Magic Sword* (1962), *Man of a Thousand Faces* (1957), *The Man With the Golden Gun* (1974), *Mark of the Devil* (1970), *The Monster Maker* (1944), *She Demons* (1958) and *The Unearthly* (1957), plus TV's *You Asked for It* (1953) and *Route 66*: 'Lizard's Leg and Owlet's Wing' (1962), both with Lon Chaney Jr, and interviews with Lon Chaney biographer and make-up artist Michael F. Blake and Chaney's grandson Gary.

◆◆

Girl Ghouls

USA/UK, 1996. With: Christopher Lee, Brinke Stevens, Gloria Talbott, Nina Foch, Don (Donald F.) Glut, Hazel Court. Passport International Productions/Jordexx Television. Colour/B&W.

This episode looks at female monsters in horror films, with clips and trailers from *Aliens* (1986), *Black Sunday* (1960), *Captive Wild Woman* (1943), *Carrie* (1976, with Stephen King's name misspelled on the credits), *Clash of the Titans* (1981), *Cry of the Werewolf* (1944), *Daughter of Dr. Jekyll* (1957), *Dracula's Daughter* (1936), *The Gorgon* (1964), *Haunting Fear* (1989), *The Hunger* (1983), *The Jungle Captive* (1944), *The Masque of the Red Death* (1964), *The Nanny* (1965), *Nightmare Castle* (1965), *Nightmare Sisters* (1986), *She-Wolf of London* (1946), *Vampyr* (1931-32), *The Velvet Vampire* (1971), *What Ever Happened to Baby Jane?* (1962), and interviews with Roger Corman, Robert Cornthwaite, Pamela Franklin and David DeCoteau. Written and produced by Ted Newsom, no director is credited.

◆◆◇

Gory Gimmicks

USA/UK, 1996. With: Christopher Lee, Don (Donald F.) Glut, Richard Denning, Joe Dante, Roger Corman, Vincent Price. Passport International Productions/Jordexx Television. Colour/B&W.

Episode of the half-hour TV series that looks at various movie gimmicks, with clips and trailers from *The Curse of Frankenstein* (1957), *Doctor X* (1932), *Horror of Dracula* (1958), *How to Make a Monster* (1958), *I Was a Teenage Frankenstein* (1957), *The Phantom of the Opera* (1925 and 1943 versions), *Revenge of the Creature* (1955), *Young Frankenstein* (1975) and numerous others, plus rare colour footage of Boris Karloff's home movies on the set of *Son of Frankenstein* (1939), the colour staking scene from *The Return of Dracula* (1957), the subliminal message trailer for *It! The Terror Beyond Space* (1958), Bela Lugosi in a stage performance of *Dracula*, and interviews with author Mark McGee, producer William Alland, Lori Nelson, Hugh

Hefner and John Carpenter. Written and produced by Ted Newsom, no director is credited.
✦✦✧

Mad Doctors

USA/UK, 1996. Dir: Tom Forrester. With: Christopher Lee, Francis Lederer, Turhan Bey, Fred Olen Ray, Bela Lugosi Jr, Hugh Hefner. Passport International Productions/ Jordexx Television. Colour/B&W.

This episode includes clips and trailers from *The Ape Man* (1943), *Bride of the Monster* (1954), *Doctor X* (1932), *The Frozen Dead* (1967), *The Mad Monster* (1942), *Scream and Scream Again* (1969) and many others, plus rare footage from *Return from the Dead* (1942), an 8mm amateur movie made by Hugh Hefner, and interviews with Hazel Court and directors Richard Cunha and Gordon Hessler.
✦✦✧

Mummies

USA/UK, 1996. Dir: Tom Forrester. With: Christopher Lee, Sara Karloff, Peggy Moran, Turhan Bey, Hugh Hefner, Michael Carreras. Passport International Productions/ Jordexx Television. Colour/B&W.

This episode features clips and trailers from *Abbott and Costello Meet the Mummy* (1952), *Blood from the Mummy's Tomb* (1971), *La Casa del Terror* (1960), *The Curse of the Mummy's Tomb* (1964), *The Ghoul* (1933), *The Mummy* (1933 and 1959 versions), *The Mummy's Curse* (1944), *The Mummy's Ghost* (1944), *The Mummy's Hand* (1940), *The Mummy's Shroud* (1967), *The Mummy's Tomb* (1942), *Pharaoh's Curse* (1956), *The Wrestling Women vs. the Aztec Mummy* (1964) and TV's *Route 66*: 'Lizard's Leg and Owlet's Wing' (1962), plus interviews with make-up artists Michael F. Blake and John Goodwin, writer/ producer Michael T. Gavin, writer/film historian Ira Lawson, and the voices of Boris Karloff and John Carradine.
✦✦✦

Mutants

USA/UK, 1996. Dir: Tom Forrester. With: Christopher Lee, Michael Carreras, John Agar, Richard Denning, Lori Nelson, Beverly Garland. Passport International Productions/Jordexx Television. Colour/B&W.

This episode looks at movie mutants with clips and trailers from *The Abominable Snowman of the Himalayas* (1957), *Beyond the Time Barrier* (1960), *The Black Sleep* (1956), *Creature from the Black Lagoon* (1954), *The Creature Walks Among Us* (1955), *Curucu, Beast of the Amazon* (1956), *Day the World Ended* (1955), *The Little Shop of Horrors* (1960), *Missile to the Moon* (1958), *The Mole People* (1956), *Revenge of the Creature* (1955), *The Snow Creature* (1954), *This Island Earth* (1955), plus interviews with *Photon* writer Mark McGee, producer William Alland, Jonathan Haze, Roger Corman, William Schallert, Richard Cunha, Dick Miller and John Carradine.
✦✦✧

Phantoms

USA/UK, 1996. Dir: Tom Forrester. With: Christopher Lee, Turhan Bey, Sheldon Leonard, Don (Donald F.) Glut. Passport International Productions/Jordexx Television. Colour/B&W.

Episode of the half-hour TV series that looks at all types of 'Phantoms' in the movies, with clips and trailers from *The Phantom of the Opera* (1925, 1943 and 1962 versions), *Phantom of the Paradise* (1974) and several others, rare home movie footage of Lon Chaney Sr in *West of Zanzibar* (1928) and Chaney Jr talking about his father on TV's *You Asked for It* (1953), plus interviews with Lon Chaney's biographer and make-up artist Michael F. Blake, Lon's great-grandson Gary Chaney and Claude Rains' daughter Jessica.
✦✦✧

Scream Queens

USA/UK, 1996. Dir: Ted Newsom. With: Christopher Lee, Linnea Quigley, Carol (Caroll) Borland, Gloria Talbott, Beverly Garland, Roger Corman. Passport International Productions/Jordexx Television. Colour/B&W.

This episode looks at movie heroines, with clips and trailers from *The Alligator People* (1959), *Blood of the Vampire* (1958), *The Curse of Frankenstein* (1957), *The Cyclops* (1958), *Doctor Blood's Coffin* (1961), *Doctor X* (1932), *Dracula A.D. 1972* (1972), *Dracula Prince of Darkness* (1965), *The Fog* (1979), *The Gorgon* (1964), *Halloween* (1978), *Horror Island* (1941), *It Conquered the World* (1956), *King Kong* (1933), *Mark of the Vampire* (1935), *Metropolis* (1926), *The Most Dangerous Game* (1932), *The Mummy's Hand* (1940), *Not of This Earth* (1957), *The Phantom of the Opera* (1925), *The Return of the Living Dead* (1984), *Revenge of the Creature* (1955) and *The Vampire Bat* (1933), plus rare footage behind-the-scenes on *Dracula Prince of Darkness* (1965), and interviews with Lori Nelson, Peggy Moran, Caroline Munro, Hugh Hefner and Hazel Court.
✦✦✦

Werewolves

USA/UK, 1996. Dir: Tom Forrester. With: Christopher Lee, Ralph Bellamy, Richard Denning, Bela Lugosi Jr, Fred Olen Ray, Nina Foch. Passport International Productions/Jordexx Television. Colour/B&W.

This half-hour episode looks at werewolves and includes clips and trailers from *Beauty and the Beast* (1961), *La Casa del Terror* (1960), *Cry of the Werewolf* (1944), *The Curse of the Werewolf* (1960), *Frankenstein Meets the Wolf Man* (1943), *House of Dracula* (1945), *House of Frankenstein* (1944), *I Was a Teenage Werewolf* (1957), (Abbott and Costelo) *Meet Frankenstein* (1948, including rare outtakes), *The Return of the Vampire* (1943), *The Werewolf* (1956), *WereWolf of London* (1935), *The Wolf Man* (1941) and TV's *Route 66*: 'Lizard's Leg and Owlet's Wing' (1962), plus interviews with make-up artist Michael F. Blake, Lon Chaney Jr's grandson Gary and Hugh Hefner.
✦✦✧

Zombies

USA/UK, 1996. Dir: Tom Forrester. With: Christopher Lee, Bela Lugosi Jr, Turhan Bey, Robert Wise, John Agar, Richard Denning. Passport International Productions/ Jordexx Television. Colour/B&W.

This episode of the half-hour TV series features clips and trailers from *Creature With the Atom Brain* (1955), *The Four Skulls of Jonathan Drake* (1959), *Invisible Invaders* (1959), *I Walked With a Zombie* (1943), *The Last Man on Earth* (1961), *The Mad Ghoul* (1943), *Night of the Living Dead* (1968), *The Oblong Box* (1969), *The Plague of the Zombies* (1966), *The Return of the Living Dead* (1984), *Revolt of the Zombies* (1936), *Snake People* (1968), *Sugar Hill* (1974), *White Zombie* (1932), *The Zombies of Mora Tau* (1957) and *Zombies of the Stratosphere* (1952), plus zombie make-up test footage, and interviews with make-up artist John Goodwin, writer/film historian Ira Lawson, screenwriter/producer Bernard Gordon, writer/producers Michael T. Gavin and Anthony Hinds, Gordon Hessler, Linnea Quigley and the voice of George Romero.
✦✦✧

ONE IN A MILLION

USA, 1936. Dir: Sidney Lanfield. With: Sonja Henie, Adolphe Menjou, Don Ameche, Ned Sparks, Jean Hersholt, The Ritz Brothers. Twentieth Century-Fox. B&W.

Début film of skating star Henie, built around the Winter Olympics. Al Ritz impersonates an ice skating Frankenstein Monster and joins brothers Jim and Harry singing 'Horror Boys of Hollywood', a number about movie villains Boris Karloff, Peter Lorre and Charles Laughton.
✦✦

ONE MORE TIME

UK, 1970. Dir: Jerry Lewis. With: Peter Lawford, Sammy Davis Jr, Esther Anderson, Maggie Wright, Leslie Sands, John Wood. Chrislaw/Tracemark/United Artists. Colour.

Unfunny comedy sequel to *Salt and Pepper* (1968), which also starred executive producers Lawford and Davis Jr as Soho nightclub owners who can't stay out of trouble. An uncredited Christopher Lee and Peter Cushing turn up very briefly as Count Dracula and Baron Frankenstein, respectively. This is the only film Lewis directed which he hasn't starred in. He shouldn't have bothered. Popular Library published the novelisation by Michael Avallone.
✦

ONNA KYUKETSUKI

Japan, 1959. Dir: Nobuo Nakagawa. With: Shigeru Amachi, Yoko Mihara, Keinosuke Wada, Junko Ikeuchi. Shintoho. B&W.

Bizarre vampire comedy in which the wife of an atomic scientist is kidnapped by one of the undead (Amachi) and imprisoned in his subterranean castle. The vampire can't stand the light of the moon and wields a pair of swords. This also features a dwarf, a witch and

a bald wrestler. The title translates as 'Vampire Man'. Nakagawa previously tried his hand at a vampire movie with the equally strange *Kyuketsuki Ga* (1956).
✦✧

ON THE TRAIL OF ED WOOD
USA, 1990 (1992). Dir: Michael Copner. With: Conrad Brooks. Videosonic Arts. Colour/B&W.
Interminable hour-long documentary in which the actor from a number of Edward D. Wood Jr films talks about his 'career' and takes the viewer on a guided tour of some of the Hollywood locations where Wood, Bela Lugosi, Tor Johnson and others used to hang out. Unfortunately, what could have been an interesting first-hand reminiscence emerges as simply a self-indulgent interview with Brooks, plus all too few trailers for relief. This looks like a home video.
✦

THE ORBITRONS
USA, 1990. Dir: Christopher C. Frieri. With: Christopher C. Frieri. Ghost Limb Films. B&W.
Low-budget independent spoof, shot in Newark, New Jersey. Writer/director Frieri plays Kubash, a biker who encounters aliens and cannibal zombies in a graveyard.
✦

ORGASMO ESOTICO
Italy, 1982. Dir: Lee Castle (Mario Siciliano). With: Marina Lotar (Marina Hedmann/Marina Frajese), Sonia Bennett, Michel Curie, Peter Brown, Joe Mignano, Mimi Losy. Metheus Film. Colour.
Hardcore horror film in which a woman (Lotar) is turned into a blue-faced zombie sex slave by a black witch (Bennett). After various sexual combinations, it is all revealed to be a dream — or is it?
✦

ORGY OF THE DEAD
USA, 1965 (1966). Dir: A.C. Stephen (Stephen C. Apostoloff). With: Criswell (Charles Jeron Criswell King), Fawn Silver, Pat Barringer, William Bates, Mickey Jines, Barbara Norton. Astra Productions/SCA International. Colour.
'The film that will satisfy every over-sexagesimal adult!' claimed the ads. Softcore supernatural shenanigans scripted by poor old Edward D. Wood Jr, who also wrote the photo novel (with an introduction by Forrest J Ackerman) published by Greenleaf Classics. On the Day of the Dead, horror writer Bob (Bates) and his girlfriend Shirley (Barringer) crash their car while looking for an ancient cemetery in the desert. They wake up in a graveyard where the Emperor of the Dark World (TV psychic Criswell in an unbelievable performance) and the Black Ghoul/Princess of Darkness (Silver) preside over a series of interminable strip acts (including a gold dancer [Barringer again], a topless cat woman [Texas Starr], a murderous bride and a zombie). A talking mummy (Louis Ojena) and wolfman (John Andrews in a Don Post mask) supply the comedy relief. When the sun destroys the ghouls, the whole thing turns out to have been a dream — or was it? Ted V. Mikels was the assistant director. The ads also claimed it was filmed in 'Astravision' and 'Sexicolor'.
✦

ORLAK, EL INFIERNO DE FRANKENSTEIN
Mexico, 1960. Dir: Rafael Baledón. With: Joaquin Cordero, Armando Calvo, Rosa de Castilla, Irma Dorantes, Andres Soler, Pedro de Aguillon. Filmadora Independiente/Columbia. B&W.
At the turn of the century, convicted body snatcher Jaime (Cordero) uses Orlak (also Cordero), the remote-controlled monster of Dr Carlos Frankenstein (Soler), to kill those who found him guilty. Low-budget thrills, filmed in three weeks and comprising four episodes (to get around Mexican union restrictions). The misleading poster art depicts a vampire, a werewolf, an apeman, the Creature from the Black Lagoon and Frankenstein's Daughter! The title translates as 'Orlak, the Hell of Frankenstein'.
✦✧

ALAN ORMSBY
[b 1944]

American writer and make-up effects designer whose uneven career has included such low-budget surprises as *Children Shouldn't Play With Dead Things* (1972) and *Deathdream* (1972).
qv: *Cat People* (1982); *Porky's II The Next Day* (1983); *Shock Waves* (1976).

ORSON WELLES' GREAT MYSTERIES:
(USA: GREAT MYSTERIES)
The Monkey's Paw
UK, 1973 (1974). Dir: Alan Gibson. With: Orson Welles, Cyril Cusack, Megs Jenkins, Patrick Magee, Michael Kitchen, Robert James. Anglia Television/Unicorn Films/ITV. Colour.
Half-hour anthology TV series (1973-75, twenty-six episodes) shot on video and introduced by Welles, dressed in a big cloak and floppy hat. Among its adaptations of famous short stories was this version of W.W. Jacobs' 1902 tale, in which a distraught Mr White (Cusack) uses his third wish to save his wife (Jenkins) from seeing the crushed remains of their resurrected son, Herbert (Kitchen).
Episode remake: THE MONKEY'S PAW (qv; 1982)
✦✦

THE OTHER SELF
USA, 1915. Dir: Leon D. Kent. Lubin. B&W.
Half-hour silent short in which a hypnotised woman develops a split personality.
✦

MARIA OUSPENSKAYA
[1876-1949]

Respected Russian character actress who travelled to America in 1923 on tour with the Moscow Art Theatre. She remained on Broadway, turning to films in 1936. As Maleva the gypsy in both *The Wolf Man* (1941) and *Frankenstein Meets the Wolf Man* (1943) she ensured that Larry Talbot's way was not too thorny. She died as a result of a stroke and burns caused by smoking in bed.

OUTBACK VAMPIRES
(USA: aka THE WICKED)
Australia, 1987 (1989). Dir: Colin Eggleston. With: Brett Climo, Richard Morgan, Angela Kennedy, John Doyle, Maggie Blinco. Somerset/Cine-Funds/Overview/Hemdale Home Video/Select Home Video. Colour.
Dire comedy filmed under the titles *The Prince at the Court of Yarralumla* and *Vampires in the Outback*. Vampire Sir Alfred Terminus (Doyle) and his undead family sleep in upright coffins and rule the outback community of Yarralumla. When their car breaks down, three travellers stumble into town and soon find themselves invited to dinner — as the main course on the menu!
✦

THE OUTER LIMITS:
The Forms of Things Unknown
USA, 1964. Dir: Gerd Oswald. With: Vera Miles, Sir Cedric Hardwicke, Scott Marlowe, David McCallum, Barbara Rush, Wolfe Barzelle. Daystar-Villa di Stefano/United Artists/ABC-TV. B&W.
Hour-long science fiction anthology TV series (1963-65, forty-nine episodes), created by Leslie Stevens and originally produced by Joseph Stefano, who scripted this episode. It was actually a pilot for a proposed series entitled *The Unknown* and filmed in two different versions under the working title 'Lovers and Madmen'. Mad scientist Tone Hobart (McCallum) invents a machine that can change time and bring the dead back to life. Hardwicke's role as the enigmatic blind servant Colas was originally going to be played by Peter Lorre or Joseph Schildkraut, both of whom died before production.
Series remake: THE OUTER LIMITS (qv; 1995-)
✦✦✦✧

THE OUTER LIMITS:
New Lease
Canada/USA, 1997. Dir: Jason Priestley. With: Stephen Lang, Terence Kelly, Nancy Sorel, Michael Ontkean, Brittney Irvin, Jason Priestley. Outer III Productions/ Trilogy Entertainment Group/Atlantis Films/Metro Goldwyn Mayer/CanWest Global System/TMN The Movie Network/CFCF Television/Superchannel/Showtime. Colour.
Surprisingly successful hour-long cable revival (1995-) of the original 1963-65 science fiction anthology TV series. In this episode, when impassionate scientist Dr James Howton (Lang) creates a resuscitation process for temporarily returning the dead to life, little does he realise that he will become the next person it will be used on. Director Priestley appears in a cameo as a young thug. Joseph Stefano was executive consultant and Leslie Stevens the programme consultant. With Kevin Conway as the Control Voice.
✦✦

Second Soul
Canada/USA, 1995. Dir: Paul Lynch. With: Mykelti Williamson, D.W. Moffett, Rae Dawn Chong, Richard Grove, Garry Davey, Kent Campeau. GP V Limited Partnership/Trilogy Entertainment Group/Atlantis Films/ Metro Goldwyn Mayer/CanWest Golbal System/TMN The Movie Network/CFCF Television/Superchannel/Showtime. Colour.
Scripted by Alan Brennert. A group of aliens arrive on Earth and request the use of human corpses as hosts for their dying race. However, Dr Michael Alders (Williamson) suspects that all is not as it appears.
✦✦✧

OUT FOR BLOOD
USA, 1990. Dir: Paul Thomas. With: Tori Wells (Tori Welles), Raquel Darian (Racquel Darrian), Randy Spears, Kelly Royce, Sherry (Cheri) Taylor, Eric Price. Vivid Video. Colour.
Hardcore horror comedy, shot on video, in which Wells plays a woman named Tori who is unaware that she is the offspring of two members of the undead. However, after dark she transforms into a sex-hungry vampire (in a cut-away tuxedo!) who sucks her victims just where you'd expect. Tantala (Tantala Ray) plays her mother, and there's a hunchback named Igor. This is available in both hard- and softcore versions. With Jennifer O'Bryan (Jennifer Stewart).
✦

THE OUTING
(UK: THE LAMP)
USA, 1986 (1987). Dir: Tom Daley. With: Deborah Winters, James Huston, Danny D. Daniels, Andra St. Ivanyi, Scott Bankston, Mark Mitchell. Lamp Productions/Lamp Joint Venture/HIT Films/Moviestore Entertainment. Colour.
Filmed in Texas by the producers of *The Buddy Holly Story* (1978), this begins well with the murder of a strange old woman and the theft of her magic lamp. However, once the ancient artefact finds its way into a local museum and a group of teenagers decide to spend the night there, the script begins to run out of inspiration. There are a number of gruesome deaths, including a boy who has his throat torn out by a magically revived mummified zombie, while an unconvincing twenty-foot demonic Djinn (voiced by Jackson Bostwick) turns up at the end. Actress Winters (who appears in three roles) was also associate producer, and David L. Hewitt designed and supervised the special photographic effects.
✦✧

OUT OF THE UNKNOWN:
Frankenstein Mark II
UK, 1966. Dir: Peter Duguid. With: Rachel Roberts, David Langton, Bernard Archard, Basil Henson, Michael Beint, Wolfe Morris. BBC-TV. B&W
Hour-long anthology TV series (1965-71, forty-nine episodes). In a futuristic space research establishment, Anna Preston (Roberts) discovers that her missing husband George (Henson) has been used in a bizarre experiment.
✦✦

OUT ON A LIMB
USA, 1992. Dir: Francis Veber. With: Matthew Broderick, Jeffrey Jones, Heidi Kling, John C. Reilly, Courtney Peldon, Nancy Lenehan. Universal/Interscope Communications. Colour.
Madcap comedy thriller in which likeable big city businessman Bill (Broderick) comes to the aid of his kid sister Marci (Peldon) and finds himself kidnapped, stripped naked and shot at by his stepfather's evil twin (Jones) in a small town full of screwballs. In the opening scene, Marci watches a clip from *The Wolf Man* (1941) on TV.
✦✦

OVERSEXED
USA, 1974. Dir: Joe Sarno. With: Veronica Parrish, Eric Edwards, Sonny Landham, Cris Jordan, Lisa Beth, Ron Ryan. Scotia American Productions. Colour.
Sex comedy in which Dr Shirley Jekyll (Parrish) experiments with a serum that transforms her into large-breasted Sherry Hyde, who has a greatly increased sexual appetite. In the end, found dying after a mammoth orgy with a number of sailors, Sherry continues to live it up in Hell.
✦

OZONE: THE ATTACK OF THE REDNECK MUTANTS
USA, 1988. Dir: Matt Devlen (Brad McCormick). With: Scott Davis, Blue Thompson, Brad McCormick, Janice Williams, Luther Webb, Lorraine Dowdy. Muther. Colour.
Low-budget independent horror comedy, filmed on Super-8mm. A group of people encounter mutant flesh-eating zombies.
✦

PACTO DIABÓLICO
(USA: JEKYLL & HYDE: PACT WITH THE DEVIL)
Mexico, 1968. Dir: Jaime Salvador. With: Regina Torné, Miguel A. (Angel) Alvarez, Isela Vega, John Carradine, Andrés García, Guillermo Zetina. Filmica Vergara/ Columbia. Colour.
Loosely based on Robert Louis Stevenson's short novel, in which Carradine's aged scientist, Dr Halback (a former colleague of Dr Jekyll), extracts the retina fluids from living female victims to prepare a drug that transforms him into the rejuvenated Frederick (Alvarez). After gouging out the eyes of a local dance hall girl, Frederick turns his attentions to Halback's house guest DiNora (Torné), the daughter of Dr Jekyll. Made back-to-back with Salvador's *La Señora Muerte* (1968), also featuring Carradine. The Mr Hyde from *Abbott and Costello Meet Dr. Jekyll and Mr. Hyde* (1953) was used on the poster design.
✦✧

PAGAN MOON
UA, 1931 (1932). Dir: Rudolf Ising. Warner Bros. B&W.
Seven minute *Merrie Melodies* cartoon set on a South Seas tropical island that includes a pre-Kong giant ape and a monster-toothed fish. This re-uses animation from *Congo Jazz* (1930).
✦✧

ANG PAGBABALIK NI PEDRO PENDUKO
Philippines, 1994. Dir: Erastheo Navoa. With: Janno Gibbs, Chiquito, Vina Morales, Leo Martinez, Donita Rose, Robert Miller. Viva Family Entertainment. Colour.
Comedy fantasy in which winged demons kidnap a group of children. The eponymous superhero from *Captain Barbell* (1986) and alien woman Darna also turn up, along with an army of zombie warriors. This won an award for Best Visual Effects at the 1994 Metro Manila Film Festival.
✦✧

THE PAGEMASTER
USA, 1994. Dir: Maurice Hunt and Joe Johnston. With: Macaulay Culkin, Christopher Lloyd. Voices: Whoopi Goldberg, Patrick Stewart, Frank Welker, Leonard Nimoy. Twentieth Century Fox/Turner Pictures. Colour.
Timid young Richard Tyler (Culkin) becomes lost in a spooky old library during a thunderstorm. There he meets the magical Pagemaster (Lloyd), who transports him to a cartoon fantasy world (created by Hanna-Barbera) where he is aided by three books: the Quasimodo-like *Horror* (Welker), the *Pirate Adventure* (Stewart) and *Magical Fantasy* (Goldberg). Along the way he encounters Dr Jekyll (Nimoy) and Mr Hyde, plus a giant squid, the Hound of the Baskervilles, Moby Dick and a fire-breathing dragon. Scenes featuring the Frankenstein Monster were apparently cut before release. This box office flop cost $35,000,000 and took two years to make. With Ed Begley Jr and Mel Harris.
✦✦

JACK PALANCE
(Vladimir Palanuik) [b 1920]

Rugged American actor, nominated for an Academy Award for his role as the steely-eyed killer in *Shane* (1953). His subsequent career was uneven, and included playing Jack the Ripper in *Man in the Attic* (1953), the title roles in TV's *The Strange Case of Dr. Jekyll and Mr. Hyde* (1967) and an impressive performance as the Count in a TV version of *Dracula* (1972). An Academy Award for his supporting role in *City Slickers* (1991) briefly revived his box office value.
qv: *In Search of Dracula With Jonathan Ross* (1996); *Monster Mania* (1997); *Torture Garden* (1967); *Twilight Zone Rod Serling's Lost Classics* (1994).

PALE BLOOD
USA, 1989 (1991). Dir: V.V. Dachin Hsu. With: George Chakiris, Wings Hauser, Pamela Ludwig, Diana Frank, Darcy DeMoss, Earl Garnes. Noble Entertainment Group/ Alpine Releasing/Leighton-Kaczmarczyk/RCA-Columbia Video. Colour.
During a series of vampire-like killings in Los Angeles, Michael Fury, a real vampire (Chakiris), teams up with obsessed researcher Lori (Ludwig) to solve the murders, hoping to find one of his own kind. Instead, they discover a manic sword-wielding Van Vandameer (Hauser), who wants to capture the undead on videotape. This includes music by Agent Orange and a clip from Murnau's *Nosferatu* (1922).
✦✧

PANDEMONIUM
Australia, 1987 (1988). Dir: Haydn Keenan. With: David Argue, Amanda Dole, Esben Storm, Arna-Maria Winchester, Rainee Skinner, Kery Mack. KFM Pandemonium/Smart Street/Tra La La Films. Colour.
This crude and pretentious comedy is a failed attempt to produce an instant weirdo cult horror movie along the lines of *The Rocky Horror Picture Show* (1975). Escaped lunatic Kales Leadingham/Ding the Dingo (Argue) and a buxom girl (Dole) raised by dingoes stumble into a deserted movie studio and a collection of vampires (Henk Johannes as the Count), lesbian Nazis, drag queens, crippled movie stars, a Hitler clone (Ashley Grenville) and the director as mad scientist Dr Doctor.
✦

PANE VY JSTE VDOVA
Czechoslovakia, 1971. Dir: Vaclav Vorlicek. With: Iva Janzurova, Olga Shoberova (Olinka Berova), Jiri Sovak, Jiri Hrzan, Jan Libieck, Eduard Cupak. Studio Barrandov. B&W.
Gory black comedy about limb and brain transplants. Janzurova portrays Mrs Stub, an artificially-created person, plus two other characters. Shoberova starred in Hammer's *The Vengeance of She* (1967) under the name Olinka Berova.
✦✦

PANGA
(USA: CURSE III BLOOD SACRIFICE)
South Africa, 1990 (1991). Dir: Sean Barton. With: Christopher Lee, Jenilee Harrison, Henry Cele, André Jacobs, Zoe Randall, Olivia Dyer. Panga Management Company/Blue Rock Films/Screen Media/Three's Company/Epic Productions. Colour.
Set in East Africa in 1950. When an American woman disrupts the ritual sacrifice of a goat, the local witch doctor (Dumi Shongwe) curses everyone on a plantation. He calls up the 'Spirit of the Sea', a briefly-seen machete-wielding gill man creature (created by Chris Walas and Peter Greenwood), to hunt down all those involved. Despite the monster, this mostly plays as a slasher movie, while Lee turns up as the enigmatic Dr Pearson, who combines modern medicine with local superstition. Retitled in America, it has nothing to do with the other titles in that direct-to-video series.
✦✦

PARADE OF THE AWARD NOMINEES
USA, 1932. Walt Disney Productions. Colour.
Three minute Technicolor cartoon short, showcasing the nominated talent at the 1932 Academy Awards (at which Walt Disney received a Special Oscar for creating Mickey Mouse). This features the first colour footage of Mickey, who leads a parade that includes Wallace Beery, Helen Hayes, Lynn Fontaine and Alfred Lunt, Marie Dressler and a brief appearance by Frederic March, who transforms from Dr Jekyll into Mr Hyde.
✦✦

PARADE OF THE WOODEN SOLDIERS
USA, 1933. Dir: Dave Fleischer. Voices: Mae Questel. Paramount. B&W.
Eight minute *Betty Boop* cartoon about toys that come to life. With a *King Kong* (1933) parody. Produced by Max Fleischer.
Sequel: SHE WRONG HIM RIGHT (1933)
✦✦

THE PARANORMAL
USA, 1998. Dir: Todd Norris. With: Todd Norris. Englewood Entertainment. Colour.
Shot-on-video release in which the director plays a paranormal researcher investigating a supposedly haunted movie theatre. He ultimately discovers that it is not the building itself, but the film showing there — a gorefest entitled *Z is for Zombie* — that is possessed by supernatural forces.
✦✦

PARIS — WHEN IT SIZZLES
USA/France, 1963 (1964). Dir: Richard Quine. With: William Holden, Audrey Hepburn, Gregoire Aslan, Noël Coward, Raymond Bussieres, Christian Duvallex. Paramount. Colour.
Overindulgent sixties romantic comedy in which a writer (Holden) and his secretary (Hepburn) fall in love while working on a screenplay for a movie producer (Coward) and fantasising about a number of movie clichés. These include Holden as a Dracula-like vampire and Mel Ferrer as Mr Hyde. With uncredited cameo appearances by Marlene Dietrich and Tony Curtis, and a song by Fred Astaire. Filmed under the title *The Girl Who Stole the Eiffel Tower* and based on the film *La Fête à Henriette* (1952). Dell published a novelisation credited to Michael Milner on the cover and Richard Benson on the title page!
✦✧

EDDIE PARKER
(Edwin Parker) [1900-1960]

American stunt man and bit-player at Universal who appeared (often uncredited) as many of the classic monsters in the more strenuous scenes while standing in for the stars. He actually played Mr Hyde in *Abbott and Costello Meet Dr. Jekyll and Mr. Hyde* (1953) and Klaris the mummy in *Abbott and Costello Meet the Mummy* (1955).
qv: *Batman* (1943); *Curse of the Undead* (1959); *Dick Tracy's G-Men* (1939); *Frankenstein Meets the Wolf Man* (1943); *The Ghost of Frankenstein* (1942); *Monster on the Campus* (1958); *The Mummy's Curse* (1944); *The Mummy's Ghost* (1944); *The Mummy's Tomb* (1942); *Son of Frankenstein* (1939); *The WereWolf of London* (1935).

MILTON PARSONS
[1904-1980]

Cadaverous-looking American supporting actor with a Karloff-like lisp. He made his movie début in 1939 and often turned up unbilled playing either a madman or a mortician. Perhaps his finest moment was as escaped homicidal maniac John Channing in *The Hidden Hand* (1942).
qv: *The Cat Creature* (1973); *Cry of the Werewolf* (1944); *The Dead Don't Die* (1975); *The Demon and the Mummy* (1975); *Fingers at the Window* (1942); *Get Smart: 'Shock It to Me'* (1969); *Kolchak: The Night Stalker: 'Demon in Lace'* (1975).

UN PASO AL MAS ACA...
Mexico, 1989. Dir: Gilberto de Anda. With: Sergio Goyri, Luz Maria Jerez, Juan Pelaez, Maria Luisa Alcala, Quintin Bulnes, Alejandro Guce. Radeant Films/Mexcinema Video. Colour.
Horror comedy set in an apartment complex where the landlord turns out to be the Devil. While rehearsing, an actor dressed as Dracula discovers that his victim is a real werewolf, the plumber returns from the dead as a mouldy zombie, and two female tenants are revealed to be ghosts.
✦

PASTEL DE SANGRE
Spain, 1971. Dir: José Maria Vallés, Emilio Martinez Lázaro, Francisco Bellmunt and Jaime Chávarri. With: Carlos Otero, Fernando Rubio, Marta May, Charo López, Marisa Paredes, Julián Ugarte. PC Tiede. Colour.
Four-part horror movie with episodes about medieval witchcraft ('Tarot'), the creation of a beautiful Frankenstein Monster ('Victor Frankenstein'), Romans battling Celtic vampires ('Terror Entre Cristianos') and a ghostly chiller ('The Dance'). The title translates as 'Painting of Blood'.
✦

MICHAEL PATAKI
[b 1938]

American actor and director who portrayed the Count and his descendant in *Dracula's Dog* (1977).
qv: *The Bat People* (1974); *Dead & Buried* (1981); *Death House* (1988); *Grave of the Vampire* (1972); *Love At First Bite* (1979); *The Return of Count Yorga* (1971).

THE PAT BOONE SHOW
USA, circa 1959. With: Pat Boone, Lon Chaney. Channel 9. B&W.
In this episode of the talk and variety TV show, Chaney Jr apparently recreated his Wolf Man role (with the aid of a rubber mask) for a sketch entitled 'The Curse of the Wolf Man', and also performed a specially prepared soliloquy as Lennie from *Of Mice and Men.*
✦

MICHAEL PATE
[b 1920]

Australian-born actor, in Hollywood from the 1950s until the 1980s. He played the gunslinger vampire in *Curse of the Undead* (1959).
qv: *Beauty and the Beast* (1961); *The Marsupials The Howling III* (1987).

JACQUELINE PEARCE
[b 1943]

British actress, who made an impression in Hammer's 'Cornish' duo, *The Reptile* (1966) and *The Plague of the Zombies* (1966), but is best known as the sexy, villainous Servalan in TV's *Blakes 7* (1978-81).

DAVID PEEL
[1920-1982]

British actor best remembered for his role as the Count's vampiric disciple Baron Meinster in Hammer's *Brides of Dracula* (1960), after which he retired from films and became an antiques dealer.

PEE POP 3
Thailand, circa 1989. All Asian Video. Colour.
This third entry in the series once again features zombies, but less gore.
✦

PEE POP 2
Thailand, circa 1988. All Asian Video. Colour.
Comedy-gore movie involving zombies.
Sequel: PEE POP 3 (qv; circa 1989)
✦

PEGGY SUE GOT MARRIED
USA, 1986. Dir: Francis (Ford) Coppola. With: Kathleen Turner, Nicolas Cage, Barry Miller, Catherine Hicks, Don Murray, Barbara Harris. Tri-Star Pictures/Rastar/Paul R. Gurian-Zoetrope Studios. Colour.
Coppola's time-travel fantasy has Oscar-nominated Turner as a housewife who faints at her high school reunion and wakes up back in the early 1960s. How she deals with her friends, family and childhood sweetheart (the irritating Cage, who briefly pretends to be a vampire at a blood drive) makes this witty, romantic, funny and nostalgic. With future stars Jim Carrey and Helen Hunt, and veterans Maureen O'Sullivan, Leon Ames and John Carradine. At one time it was going to be directed by Penny Marshall and star Debra Winger.
✦✦✦✦

PENGABDI SETAN
Indonesia, 1982. Dir: Sisworo Gautama Putra. With: Ruth Pelupessi, W.D. Mochtar, Fachrul Rozy, Simon Cader, Diana Suarkom, J.M. Damsyik. PT Rapi Film. Colour.
When their mother dies, a boy and his elder sister are haunted by various supernatural phenomena, including a couple of gory zombies. In the end, it is revealed that their governess is an evil witch who is subsequently burned to death.
✦

PEOPLE
USA, 1978 (1979). Dir: Gerard Damiano. With: Eric Edwards, Kasey Rodgers, Serena, Jamie Gillis, Susan McBain, Kelly Green. Damiano/Quality X. Colour.
Six hardcore sex stories from the director of *Legacy of Satan* (1973). The third episode is entitled 'Vampires'.
✦

THE PERILS OF PAULINE
USA, 1914. Dir: Louis J. Gasnier and Donald MacKenzie. With: Pearl White, Crane Wilbur, Paul Panzer, Clifford Bruce, Eleanor Woodruff, Edward José. Eclectic/Pathé. B&W.
Twenty chapter silent serial starring White as heroine Pauline, who is the reincarnation of an Egyptian mummy that occasionally comes to life and warns her of danger as she tries to claim her rightful inheritance.
Remake: THE PERILS OF PAULINE (qv; 1934)
✦✧

PERILS OF PAULINE
USA, 1934. Dir: Ray Taylor. With: Evalyn Knapp, Robert Allen, James Durkin, John Davidson, Frank Lackteen, Pat O'Malley. Universal. B&W.
Twelve chapter serial set in Indo-China and involving the search for an ivory disc that is engraved with the formula for a deadly poison that destroyed an ancient civilisation. This also includes a walking mummy and a henchman named Fang.
Remake: THE PERILS OF PAULINE (1967)
✦✦

THE PERILS OF PORK PIE
UK, 1916. Dir: W.P. Kellino. With: Billy Merson, Charles Cohen. Homeland. B&W.
Silent comedy short about a man who dreams he buys a museum where a mummy comes to life and crowns him Pharaoh.
✦

JON PERTWEE
[1919-1996]
British comedy actor and the brother of playwright and screenwriter Michael (1916-1991). He is best remembered as TV's third *Doctor Who* (1970-74).
qv: *Carry on Screaming* (1966); *Doctor Who: 'The Claws of Axos'* (1971); *Doctor Who: 'Inferno'* (1970); *The House That Dripped Blood* (1970); *The Ugly Duckling* (1959).

THE PEST
USA, 1997. Dir: Paul Miller. With: John Leguizamo, Jeffrey Jones, Edoardo Ballerini, Freddy Rodriguez, Tammy Townsend, Aries Spears. TriStar Pictures/The Bubble Factory. Colour.
Witless comedy in which the truly irritating Leguizamo plays Miami con man Pest Vargas and appears in a variety of disguises. In return for $50,000, the energetic Pest is tricked into becoming the human prey of a mad Nazi hunter (Jones). This surprise reworking of *The Most Dangerous Game* (1932) includes a trophy room full of human heads and Leguizamo as a fanged vampire during the rap song credits.
✦

PESTICIDE
(Orig: LES RAISINS DE LA MORT)
France, 1978. Dir: Jean Rollin. With: Marie George Pascal, Felix Marten, Serge Marquand, Mirella Rancelot, Patrice Valota, Patricia Cartier. Rush Productions/Les Films ABC/Off Production. Colour.
This is almost a French *Night of the Living Dead* (1968). Pascal plays Elisabeth, a woman travelling across France to join her lover. She discovers that a pesticide used on the local grape vines has turned most of the country folk into zombies with leaky brains. After being pursued through the countryside, attacked by the living dead, and a witness to all sorts of gruesome events (heads hacked off, bodies impaled with pitchforks, etc), she too becomes infected and goes insane. Filmed in a bleak, washed-out style that mirrors the barren landscape, Rollin (who also appears as a worker in a winery) brings an atmospheric touch to the bloodshed, particularly in the night scenes, as an army of zombies move through the ravaged villages. With French sex star Brigitte Lehaye (Lahaie) as a mad woman. The original title translates as 'The Grapes of Death'.
✦✦✧

PETER CUSHING: A ONE-WAY TICKET TO HOLLYWOOD
UK, 1988 (1989). Dir: Alan Bell. With: Peter Cushing. Tyburn Films/Channel Four Television. Colour.
Fascinating seventy-seven minute TV documentary in which Cushing (who died in 1994) talks to writer Dick Vosburgh about his life and career, illustrated with clips from many of his films and TV appearances (dating back to James Whale's 1939 *The Man in the Iron Mask*). Produced by Kevin Francis.
✦✦✦

PET SEMATARY
USA, 1989. Dir: Mary (Louise) Lambert. With: Dale Midkiff, Fred Gwynne, Denise Crosby, Brad Greenquist, Michael Lombard, Miko Hughes. Laurel/Paramount. Colour.
Stephen King adapts one of his bleakest novels for the screen and gets to play yet another cameo (as a preacher) in this uneven but often genuinely disturbing chiller. Midkiff portrays young Dr Louis Creed, who brings his dead two year-old son Gage (Hughes) back as an evil zombie from an old Native American burial ground. Greenquist's throwaway humour as the ghost of Victor Pascow sits uneasily with the rest of the film, but the scenes involving Rachael Creed's (Crosby) dying sister Zelda (played by a man, Andrew Hubatsek) and the image of the possessed child are terrifying. With Stacy Keach Sr.
Sequel: PET SEMATARY II (qv; 1992)
✦✦✧

PET SEMATARY II
USA, 1992. Dir: Mary (Louise) Lambert. With: Edward Furlong, Anthony Edwards, Clancy Brown, Jared Rushton, Darlanne Fluegel, Jason McGuire. Paramount/Columbus Circle Films. Colour.
Derivative sequel to Lambert's 1989 original, based on the novel by Stephen King (whose name appears nowhere on this follow-up). When his horror movie star mother Renee (Fluegel) is accidentally electrocuted on set, Jeff Matthews (Furlong) and his father Chase (Edwards) move into the house in Maine built near an Native American burial ground that can bring the dead back to life. A dog-headed woman appears to Chase in a dream sequence, and children dress up as vampires and werewolves for Halloween. Brown makes an amusing zombie sheriff (make-up effects by Steve Johnson), and this is an okay chiller up until the ludicrously over-the-top ending.
✦✧

THE PET STORE
USA, 1933. Dir: Wilfred Jackson. Voices: Walt Disney. Walt Disney/United Artists. Colour.
Seven minute *Mickey Mouse* cartoon that includes a spoof of *King Kong* (1933).
Sequel: GIANTLAND (1933)
✦✦

PHANTASM
USA, 1979. Dir: Don Coscarelli. With: (A.) Michael Baldwin, Bill Thornbury, Reggie Bannister, Kathy Lester,

Angus Scrimm (Lawrence Rory Guy), Terrie Kalbus. New Breed/Avco-Embassy. Colour.
This inventive low-budget thriller is a (literally) nightmarish tale about a mysterious funeral home and a plot to reduce dead bodies into three-foot high zombies to work in another dimension. At least, that's what I think it's about, but writer/director Coscarelli doesn't seem to care as he throws in mysterious gateways, hideous dwarves, deadly flying silver spheres and plenty of imagination. As Mike, Baldwin makes a precocious young hero, but there's some nice villainy from Scrimm as The Tall Man. As the ads said: 'If this one doesn't scare you...You're already dead!' It was released as *The Never Dead* in Australia.
Sequel: PHANTASM II (qv; 1988)
✦✦✦

PHANTASM IV OBLIVION
USA, 1998. Dir: Don Coscarelli. With: A. Michael Baldwin, Reggie Bannister, Bill Thornbury, Heidi Marnhout, Bob Ivy, Angus Scrimm (Lawrence Rory Guy). Starway International. Colour.
Confusing direct-to-video sequel which is padded out with numerous flashbacks from the first three films and footage cut from the original 1979 movie. Reggie (Bannister) and Mike (co-producer Baldwin) are still driving around the countryside trying to defeat the nightmare plans of The Tall Man (Scrimm), who is emptying the local towns. There is even an attempt to finally explain the origin of this demonic antagonist by tracing him back to a doctor during the American Civil War. Unfortunately, despite some impressive visuals and a zombie cop (Ivy), Coscarelli's script is a mess.
✦✧

PHANTASM LORD OF THE DEAD
(UK: PHANTASM III)
USA, 1993. Dir: Don Coscarelli. With: Reggie Bannister, A. Michael Baldwin, Bill Thornbury, Gloria Lynne Henry, Kevin Connors, Angus Scrimm (Lawrence Rory Guy). Starway International. Colour.
Released directly to video, this is the third in the enigmatic series from writer, director, producer and executive producer Coscarelli. With the help of the dead Jody (Thornbury), Reggie (Bannister) teams up with a resourceful young boy named Tim (Connors) and tough soldier Rocky (Henry) to rescue his friend Mike (Baldwin, returning from the first film) and confront the demonic Tall Man (Scrimm), who is still wiping out small towns with the help of his murderous dwarves and flying silver spheres (controlled by the brains of the dead). This includes a pair of crawling hand creatures, a trio of zombies and flashbacks to the first two movies. It ends on another cliff-hanger.
Sequel: PHANTASM IV OBLIVION (qv; 1998)
✦✦✦✧

PHANTASM II
USA, 1988. Dir: Don Coscarelli. With: James Le Gros, Reggie Bannister, Angus Scrimm (Lawrence Rory Guy), Paula Irvine, Samantha Phillips, Kenneth Tigar. Spacegate/Universal. Colour.
This disappointing sequel to writer/director Coscarelli's enjoyable 1979 movie is more of a remake with improved special effects. Le Gros portrays the grown-up Mike from the first film, who is released from a sanatorium and teams up with his old friend Reggie (Bannister) and Liz (Irvine), who shares his nightmares, to once again battle Scrimm's menacing Tall Man — this time laying waste to small towns and converting the residents into dwarf zombies before sending them into an alternative dimension. Despite scenes set on another planet and an improved version of the deadly silver spheres, this remains a flashy, if empty, movie. With Felix Silla.
Sequel: PHANTASM LORD OF THE DEAD (qv; 1993)
✦✦

THE PHANTOM FROM 10,000 LEAGUES
USA, 1955 (1956). Dir: Dan Milner. With: Kent Taylor, Kathy (Cathy) Downs, Michael Whalen, Rodney Bell, Phillip Pine, Helene Stanton. Milner Bros Productions/ American Releasing Corporation. B&W.

Jack Cassidy haunts the MGM backlot as TV's The Phantom of Hollywood *(1974).*

Originally double-billed with Roger Corman's *The Day the World Ended* (1955), this low-budget science fiction thriller was one of the first releases from ARC, which became American International Pictures the following year. Whalen plays a scientist who uses an underwater uranium ore deposit to turn a turtle into a silly-looking radioactive gill man. Oceanographer Dr Ted Stevens (Taylor, with a permanent grin on his face) is on hand to track down the creature for the American government and there are plenty of foreign agents around who are also after the secret.
✦

PHANTOM LOVER
USA, circa 1990s. With: Kristi Myst (Tina Harlow/Pamela Sanderson), Laura Palmer, Holly Body, Kimberly Jade, Kimberly Cummings, Kyle Stone. Cinderella Distributors. Colour.
Hardcore version of *The Phantom of the Opera*.
✦

THE PHANTOM LOVER
(Orig: YE BAU GE SHENG)
Hong Kong/Singapore, 1995. Dir: Ronnie Yu (Ronny Yu Yan-Tai). With: Leslie Cheung (Leslie Cheung Kwok-Wing), Wu Chien-Lien (Ng Sin-Lin), Huang Lei, Liu Lin. Tai Seng Video. Colour.
Shot on location in Beijing, this is an overly romantic version of *Song at Midnight*, previously filmed in 1937 and 1961 and loosely based on *The Phantom of the Opera*. Set in 1936, producer Cheung

stars as Song Dan-Ping, a once-famous opera star who lives in the burned-out remains of the opera house he designed and who hides his acid-scarred face behind a mask.
✦✧

THE PHANTOM OF HOLLYWOOD

USA, 1974. Dir: Gene Levitt. With: Jack Cassidy, Skye Aubrey, Jackie Coogan, Broderick Crawford, Peter Haskell, John Ireland. Metro-Goldwyn-Mayer/CBS-TV. Colour.

Filmed under the title *The Phantom of Lot 2*, this TV movie variation on *The Phantom of the Opera* has Cassidy (singer David's father, who was killed in a fire two years later) playing the dual roles of Otto Vonner and his mad brother Karl, a once-famous actor horribly scarred in an accident who lives among the old movie sets dressed as a masked executioner. When Worldwide Studios announces that it plans to sell the backlot, Karl begins to kill. MGM was really tearing down its old backlot at the time, and director Levitt poignantly cuts between the dilapidated sets and film clips of them in their heyday. Although the veteran cast is mostly wasted, this marks the end of a Hollywood era. With Peter Lawford, Corinne Calvet, John Lupton, Kent Taylor, Regis Toomey and special make-up effects created by William Tuttle.
✦✦

PHANTOM OF THE CABARET

USA/France, 1989. Dir: Henri Pachard. With: Jamie Gillis, Bionca (Bionica Bradley), Rick Savage, Sharon Kane, Randy Spears, Barbara Dare. VCA Pictures. Colour.

Hardcore feature in which Gillis portrays Chris Bradley/The Phantom, a janitor in a Paris nightclub, who wears half a mask to cover his scarred face, which was burned with acid by his girlfriend's former lover. Gillis also played The Phantom in *Phantom X* the same year.

Sequel: PHANTOM OF THE CABARET 2 (qv; 1989)
✦

PHANTOM OF THE CABARET 2

USA/France, 1989. Dir: Henri Pachard. With: Jamie Gillis, Bionca (Bionica Bradley), Rick Savage, Sharon Kane, Randy Spears, Barbara Dare. VCA Pictures. Colour.

This hardcore sequel begins with a reprise of the first film, then develops the complicated story further as the masked Phantom (Gillis) unknowingly has sex with his daughter, Missy (Keisha [Melissa Christian]), before she finally finds love with a writer (Spears).
✦

PHANTOM OF THE MALL ERIC'S REVENGE

USA, 1988 (1989). Dir: Richard Friedman. With: Derek Rydall, Jonathan Goldsmith, Rob Estes, Pauly Shore, Kimber Kari Whitman, Morgan Fairchild. Fries Entertainment. Colour.

TV movie-type thrills, inspired by *The Phantom of the Opera*. The new Midwood shopping mall is haunted by masked Eric Matthews (Rydall), who was presumed dead when fire destroyed his home a year before. Now the horribly burned teenager wants to be re-united with his former girlfriend Melody Austin (newcomer Whitman) and have his revenge on the ruthless businessmen who ruined his life. With Fairchild as the corrupt Mayor who gets thrown through a window, Ken Foree as a security guard and Pauly Shore as his usual irritating self.
✦✦

THE PHANTOM OF THE OPERA

USA, 1925. Dir: Rupert Julian and Edward Sedgwick (and Lon Chaney). With: Lon Chaney, Mary Philbin, Norman Kerry, Arthur Edmund Carewe, Gibson Gowland, John Sainpolis. Universal. Tinted/Colour.

Based on the 1911 novel by Gaston Leroux. Chaney gives probably his greatest performance in this silent Gothic fairy-tale as the horribly disfigured Erik, the mad Phantom who hides his ravaged features beneath a mask and haunts the passages below the Paris Opera House (sets designed by Charles D. Hall, Maurice Tourneur, Edgar G. Ulmer and others). Among the most memorable scenes are the journey across the underground lake; the Red Death entering the 'Bal Masque' (in stunning Technicolor!); and the Phantom perched like a maniacal gargoyle on the Opera House roof. Of course, the moment when Christine Daaé (Philbin) unmasks the organ-playing Erik still remains an all-time pinnacle of horror cinema. With comedian Chester Conklin as an orderly. The film was reissued in 1929 cut from 144 to seventy-seven minutes and apparently featured new sequences and added sound (including Philbin and Kerry, but not Chaney) directed by Ernst Laemmle. In this now lost version, Edward Martindel replaced Sainpolis and John Miljan's role was cut entirely. A 1990 re-release included a prologue directed by Michael Armstrong, while a special 'restoration' of the 1929 version was presented in 1996 by Channel Four and Photoplay Productions, with a new music score by Carl Davis.

Remake: PHANTOM OF THE OPERA (qv; 1943)
✦✦✦✦✦

PHANTOM OF THE OPERA

USA, 1943. Dir: Arthur Lubin. With: Nelson Eddy, Susanna Foster, Claude Rains, Edgar Barrier, Leo Carrillo, Jane Farrar. Universal. Colour.

Once again based on the book by Gaston Leroux. Universal originally wanted Deanna Durbin for this $1,750,000 Technicolor remake of its 1925 classic. Charles Laughton, Broderick Crawford and Lon Chaney Jr were all considered for the title role, but instead a sympathetic Rains (who only receives third billing) stars as poor violinist Erique Claudin, who is dismissed from the orchestra at the Paris Opera House after twenty years. Mistakenly believing his music has been stolen, he has acid thrown in his face and escapes into the sewers where he becomes the murderous half-masked Phantom. There's far too much opera from the two leads and not enough horror, while both the classic set-pieces — the falling chandelier and the unmasking (disappointing burn make-up by Jack Pierce) — fail to have the impact they should. Shot on the same Opera House set as the Chaney version, this won Academy Awards for Best Colour Art Direction, Best Colour Photography and Best Set Decoration. With J. Edward Bromberg, Fritz Feld, Hume Cronyn, Fritz Leiber (as Franz Liszt), Miles Mander and 'A Cast of Thousands'. A juvenile novelisation by William R. Sanford (William Reynolds) was published in 1987.

Remake: THE PHANTOM OF THE OPERA (qv; circa 1950s)
✦✦✧

THE PHANTOM OF THE OPERA

Argentina, circa 1950s. With: Narciso Ibañez Menta. B&W.

Popular TV serial based on Gaston Leroux's story, starring Argentina's answer to Boris Karloff. Apparently, on the night the Phantom was unmasked, the streets of Buenos Aires were nearly empty.

Remake: THE PHANTOM OF THE OPERA (qv; 1962)
✦✧

THE PHANTOM OF THE OPERA

UK, 1962. Dir: Terence Fisher. With: Herbert Lom, Heather Sears, Thorley Walters, Michael Gough, Edward De Souza, Martin Miller. Hammer Films/Universal-International. Colour.

Often regarded as one of Hammer's lesser films, this was given an 'A' certificate in Britain when the distributor insisted on the low horror content and director Fisher was temporarily dropped by the studio after the film's poor box office performance. It's not really all that bad, although the script by John Elder (producer Anthony Hinds) transports Gaston Leroux's story from Paris to London and turns the slightly unbalanced Phantom (Lom, in a role originally written for Cary Grant!) into a sympathetic character. The real villain this time is Gough's gleefully nasty Lord Ambrose D'Arcy. Fisher does manage a couple of nice shocks with the hanged body of a stage hand and a rat catcher (Patrick Troughton) stabbed through the eye by a murderous dwarf (Ian Wilson), but the famous unmasking is left until the climax, when Roy Ashton's briefly-glimpsed burn make-up is a disappointment. With Miles Malleson, Miriam Karlin and Michael Ripper. When shown on American TV in 1968, NBC added a six minute sequence set in Scotland Yard's Black Museum, featuring actor Liam Redmond as an Irish detective. Scholastic published a

novelisation by David Bischoff in 1976 based on the various movie adaptations.
Remake: PHANTOM OF THE OPERA (qv; 1982)
✦✦

PHANTOM OF THE OPERA
USA/UK/Hungary, 1982 (1983). Dir: Robert Markowitz. With: Maximilian Schell, Jane Seymour, Michael York, Jeremy Kemp, Diana Quick, Philip Stone. Robert Halmi/Hungarofilm/MA Film/CBS-TV. Colour.
Poor old Gaston Leroux doesn't even get a credit on this made-for-TV movie as the action is moved from Paris to the Budapest Opera House. Schell plays the disfigured Sandor Korvin/The Phantom (in excellent make-up created by Stan Winston), and there's fine support from Kemp and Stone, although Seymour (in two roles) has a dodgy accent and York is stuck in a laughable curly wig. Director Markowitz brings a certain amount of visual flair to all the usual set pieces, including a pointless chandelier sequence.
Remake: THE PHANTOM OF THE OPERA (qv; 1987)
✦✦

THE PHANTOM OF THE OPERA
UK, 1987. Dir: Al Guest and Jean Mathieson. Voices: Aiden Grennell, Daniel Reardon, Collette Proctor, Jim Reid, Joseph Taylor, Virginia Kerr. Emerald City Productions/D.L. Taffner. Colour.
This faithful hour-long cartoon version of the novel by Gaston Leroux suffers from limited animation and stilted characterisation. However, young children may be scared by the skull-like Erik.
Remake: THE PHANTOM OF THE OPERA (qv; 1989)
✦✧

THE PHANTOM OF THE OPERA
Hungary/USA/UK, 1989. Dir: Dwight H. Little. With: Robert Englund, Jill Schoelen, Alex Hyde-White, Bill Nighy, Terence Harvey, Stephanie Lawrence. 21st Century Film Corp/Breton Film/Castle Pictures. Colour.
Surprisingly stylish version of Gaston Leroux's story, produced by the infamous Harry Alan Towers, that adds soprano Christine (Schoelen) being sent back in time to Victorian London, a Phantom (Englund, here far surpassing his Freddy characterisation) who has sold his soul in return for musical genius, and some graphic gore. This includes elements of the Faust legend, and although there is no chandelier scene, the Phantom does turn up as the Red Death and the 'unmasking' involves the character removing the stolen flesh from his face (nice make-up effects by Kevin Yagher with John Buechler). Only the silly framing sequence, set in modern-day New York, and the weak supporting cast let down this handsomely mounted production, filmed for just $6,000,000. A subsequent Warner Bros remake, set in 1940 France, was announced but never made. *Danse Macabre* (1991) was supposed to be a follow-up.
Remake: PHANTOM X (qv; 1989)
✦✦✧

PHANTOM OF THE OPERA
USA, 1990. Dir: Tony Sinclair. Sinclair Blue Productions. Colour.
'Adults only' tickling video from writer/director Sinclair.
✦

THE PHANTOM OF THE OPERA
France/Hungary/USA, 1990. Dir: Tony Richardson. With: Burt Lancaster, Charles Dance, Teri Polo, Adam Storke, Ian Richardson, Andrea Ferreol. Saban/Scherick and Hexatel/NBC-TV. Colour.
Awful three-hour TV movie shown in two parts and scripted by Arthur Kopit, based on his theatrical adaptation of Gaston Leroux's novel. Dance gives a ludicrously camp performance as Erik/The Phantom, while the rest of the cast, except for veteran Lancaster as the Phantom's father(!), act as if they are in a French farce. This

Lon Chaney Sr reveals his face beneath the mask in The Phantom of the Opera *(1925).*

romantic version of the story doesn't even reveal the Phantom's ravaged features. A complete waste of time. The same year Warner Bros announced a version of Andrew Lloyd Webber's musical adaptation starring Michael Crawford and Sarah Brightman, to be directed by Joel Schumacher.
Remake: THE PHANTOM OF THE OPERA (qv; 1998)
✦✧

THE PHANTOM OF THE OPERA
(Orig: IL FANTASMA DELL'OPERA)
Italy/Hungary, 1998. Dir: Dario Argento. With: Julian Sands, Asia Argento, Andrea Di Stefano, Nadia Rinaldi, Coralina Cataldi-Tassoni, Istvan Bubik. Medusa Film/Rete Italia/Cine 2000/Focus Film. Colour.
Following a nationwide survey, this $10,000,000 version of the much-filmed novel by Gaston Leroux was the movie the Italian cinemagoers said they wanted to see from co-writer/director Argento (*Terror at the Opera* [1987], etc). After being found floating in the sewers as a baby and raised by rats, the normal-looking Phantom (the wooden Sands, who took the role after John Malkovich, Tim Roth, Willem Dafoe and Alan Rickman had all turned it down) kills anyone who harms his beloved rodents or comes between him and his attempts to turn his protégé Christine Daaé (Argento's daughter, Asia) into an opera diva. At least they retained the chandelier sequence. Despite being filmed in English, some of the dialogue (co-scripted by long-time Roman Polanski collaborator Gerard Brach) is hilarious. Executive produced by the director's brother, Claudio. Ennio Morricone composed the music score. By 1999, Antonio Banderas and Catherine Zeta Jones were being linked with the long-delayed film adaptation of Andrew Lloyd Webber's musical version, with Shekhar Kapur as director.
✦✦

PHANTOM OF THE PARADISE
USA, 1974. Dir: Brian De Palma. With: Paul Williams, William Finley, Jessica Harper, George Memmoli, Harold Oblong, Archie Hahn. Twentieth-Century Fox. Colour.
De Palma's inventive musical reworking of a number of classic horror themes. Winslow Leach (Finley) has his rock opera version of the Faust legend stolen by ageless music impresario Swan (Williams), who has sold his own soul to the Devil. When Swan decides to open his showcase rock palace, the Paradise, with Winslow's opera, the crazed and disfigured composer seeks revenge. This combines elements of *The Phantom of the Opera*, *The Picture of Dorian Gray*, *Psycho*, *The Cabinet of Dr. Caligari* and *The Manchurian Candidate* with a *Frankenstein* musical number in which outrageous rock star Beef (Gerrit Graham) is assembled from body parts before being electrocuted by the masked Phantom. With great pastiche songs by Williams and an impressive screen début by Harper (*Suspiria* [1976], etc). Announced under the title *The Phantom of Filmore*, all references to Swan Song Records had to be optically removed when Led Zeppelin's company sued. A novelisation by Bjarne Rostaing appeared in 1975.
✦✦✦✦

PHANTOM OF THE RITZ
USA, 1988. Dir: Allan Plone. With: Peter Bergman, Deborah Van Valkenburgh, Russel Curry, Joshua Sussman, B.J. McQueen, Cindy Vincino. Hancock Park/SGE. Colour.
Set in an old movie theatre which has reopened as a 1950s rock venue, a hulking Phantom (Sussman), horribly scarred in a drag race thirty years earlier, kills various patrons. Filmed in Florida, this includes an Elvis impersonator plus The Coasters singing 'Yakity Yak' on stage.
✦✧

PHANTOM QUEST CORP.
(Orig: YOU GEN KAI SYA/YÛGEN KAISHA)
Japan, 1994 (1995). Dir: Morio Asaka, Kôichi Chigira and Takuji Endo. Voices: Kazu Ikura, Yôko Kawanami, Rika Matsumoto, Kotono Mitsuishi, Naoki Tatsuta, Naoko Watanabe. Madhouse/Oniro/Animaze/Pioneer. Colour.
Series of four half-hour anime adventures about the ghost-busting Phantom Quest group set up by the sexy Ayaka Kisaragi and her strange staff to deal with the paranormal and supernatural. Their cases include the secret sale of Dracula's coffin to a Japanese investor, much to the displeasure of the Count and his bride.
✦

PHANTOM X
USA, 1989. Dir: Paul Thomas. With: Shanna McCullough, Aja, Tom Byron, Mike Horner, Jamie Gillis, Ron Jeremy. VCA Pictures. Colour.
Hardcore reworking of *The Phantom of the Opera*, with Gillis as the masked Eric/The Phantom living in the catacombs beneath the Paris Opera House. When he falls in love with young singer Nina (Aja), the Phantom threatens to burn down the building unless she is allowed to replace prima donna Madame Maria De LaTour (McCullough). In the end, the Phantom is shot to death and when his mask is removed it is discovered that he is not scarred at all.
Remake: THE PHANTOM OF THE OPERA (qv; 1990)
✦

PHARAOH'S CURSE
USA, 1956 (1957). Dir: Lee Sholem. With: Mark Dana, Ziva Shapir, Diane Brewster, George Neise, Alvara Guillot, Terence de Marney. Sunrise Pictures/Bel-Air/United Artists. B&W.
Effective low-budget mummy movie from the makers of *The Black Sleep* (1956) and *Voodoo Island* (1957). A turn-of-the-century archaeological expedition into the Valley of the Kings accidentally releases the spirit of a 4,000 year-old royal priest who needs a regular supply of fresh blood to prevent his mummy from rapidly ageing. Jack Rabin and Louis DeWitt created the photographic effects. Music by Les Baxter and produced by Howard W. Koch, who went on to better things. Filmed under the title *Curse of the Pharaoh*.
✦✦✦

PHENOMENAL AND THE TREASURE OF TUTANKAMEN
(Orig: FENOMENAL E IL TESORO DI TUTANKAMEN)
Italy, 1968 (1975). Dir: Roger Rockfeller (Ruggero Deodato). With: Mario Nicola Parenti, Lucretia Love, Gordon Mitchell, John Karlsen, Carla Romanelli, Cyrus Elias. Wizard Video/VCI. Colour.
Parenti stars as Count Norton, aka the eponymous masked superhero, who is on the trail of an Egyptian golden relic with mystical powers.
✦✧

MARY PHILBIN
[1903-1993]

American silent screen actress, a discovery of Erich von Stroheim. She is best remembered for her performance as Christine Daaé, who revealed Lon Chaney Sr's horrific face to the world in *The Phantom of the Opera* (1925). Her career ended with the advent of talkies.

THE PHIL SILVERS SHOW:
(aka YOU'LL NEVER GET RICH)
Bilko's Vampire
USA, 1958. Dir: Aaron Ruben and Al DeCaprio. With: Phil Silvers, Harvey Lembeck, Maurice Gosfield, Allen Melvin, Paul Ford, Joe E. Ross. Columbia Broadcasting System. B&W.
Classic half-hour TV comedy show (1955-59, 143 episodes) created by Nat Hiken and set on an army camp. When his regular poker game is repeatedly called off because of *Shriek Theater* on TV, M/Sgt Ernest Bilko (Silvers) convinces Ritzik (Ross) that he is turning into a vampire and could be the next star of a Dracula series in Hollywood. This was made at the time when Universal's package of *Shock Theater* movies first appeared on American TV.
Series remake: SGT. BILKO (1996)
✦✦✦

THE PINFISH
Thailand, circa 1980s. Thai Video. Colour.
Cursed at birth, a woman removes a magic bracelet and transforms

into a large-finned gill creature whose eyes shoot deadly rays. In the end, she is cured by a mystic and another woman takes her place.
✦

JACK P. PIERCE
[1889-1968]

Greek-born American make-up artist. Between 1926 and 1947 he created all Universal's classic horror make-ups. Considered too old, and his time-consuming techniques obsolete, he was unceremoniously dropped by the studio in 1948. Pierce continued to freelance in films and television but died bitter, bed-ridden and near-forgotten. He was portrayed by James Lecesne in *Gods and Monsters* (1998).
qv: *Beauty and the Beast* (1961); *Bride of Frankenstein* (1935); *The Brute Man* (1946); *Captive Wild Woman* (1943); *The Climax* (1944); *Dracula* (1931); *Dracula's Daughter* (1936); *Frankenstein* (1931, test reel) *Frankenstein* (1931); *Frankenstein Meets the Wolf Man* (1943); *The Ghost of Frankenstein* (1942); *Giant from the Unknown* (1957); *House of Dracula* (1945); *House of Frankenstein* (1944); *I Bury the Living* (1958); *The Jungle Captive* (1944); *Jungle Woman* (1944); *The Mad Ghoul* (1943); *Man Made Monster* (1941); *Master Minds* (1949); *The Mummy* (1933); *The Mummy's Curse* (1944); *The Mummy's Ghost* (1944); *The Mummy's Hand* (1940); *The Mummy's Tomb* (1942); *Phantom of the Opera* (1943); *She-Wolf of London* (1946); *Son of Dracula* (1943); *Son of Frankenstein* (1939); *The Spider Woman Strikes Back* (1945); *Teenage Monster* (1957); *This is Your Life: 'Boris Karloff'* (1957); *WereWolf of London* (1935); *White Zombie* (1932); *The Wolf Man* (1941).

THE PINK CHIQUITAS

Canada, 1986. Dir: Anthony Currie. With: Frank Stallone, Eartha Kitt, Bruce Pirrie, McKinlay Robinson, John Hemphill, Elizabeth Edwards. Mount Pleasant Productions/Prism Entertainment. Colour.
Terrible comedy in which a private detective (Stallone) investigates the sound of a falling meteorite (voiced by Kitt!) that turns women into Amazons who use glowing rays from their eyes to transform men into zombies. This also includes a film titled *Zombie Beach Party II* playing at the local drive-in.
✦

THE PINK PANTHER:
Werewolf in Panther's Clothing

USA, 1993. Dir: Charles Grosvenor and Byron Vaughns. Voices: Matt Frewer, Sheryl Bernstein, Joe Piscopo, John Byner, Charles Nelson Reilly, Dan Castellaneta. Mirisch-Geoffrey DePatie-Freleng/Metro Goldwyn Mayer. Colour.
Half-hour syndicated cartoon TV series (1993-94, fifty-two episodes) based on the character created by creative consultants David H. DePatie and Friz (Isadore) Freleng. In this ten-minute segment, the Pink Panther (Frewer) transforms into a werewolf. With the voices of Wallace Shawn, Joanne Worley, Ruth Buzzi, Kenneth Mars and Gerrit Graham.
✦✧

THE PINK PANTHER STRIKES AGAIN

UK/France/Bavaria, 1976. Dir: Blake Edwards. With: Peter Sellers, Herbert Lom, Lesley-Anne Down, Howard K. Smith, Leonard Rossiter, Colin Blakely. United Artists/ Amjo Productions. Colour.
This fifth entry in the popular comedy series turns into a parody of the James Bond movies, thanks to a larger-than-usual budget. When ex-Chief Inspector Dreyfus (Lom) is finally released from the 'Hopital (*sic*) Psychiatrique', he is once again driven mad by the cause of his breakdown — the bumbling Inspector Jacques Clouseau (Sellers). Moving into a Gothic castle, Dreyfus creates a death ray and threatens to destroy the world unless Clouseau is handed over to him. Although producer/director Edwards allows the humour to collapse into slapstick, Lom obviously enjoys himself and even spoofs his organ-playing Phantom of the Opera role in one scene, while Clouseau disguises himself with a Quasimodo hunchback kit. The impressive supporting cast includes Graham Stark, Richard Vernon, Burt Kwouk as Cato, Geoffrey Bayldon, Robert Beatty, Michael Robbins and 'Howard K. Smith' (Omar Sharif) as an assassin. Richard Williams' cartoon titles include homages to a number of genre film characters, including Alfred Hitchcock, Batman, King Kong and Dracula. Co-writer Frank Waldman was also responsible for the novelisation.
Sequel: REVENGE OF THE PINK PANTHER (1978)
✦✦✦

PINKY AND THE BRAIN:
(aka STEVEN SPIELBERG PRESENTS PINKY & THE BRAIN)
Brain Acres

USA, 1996. Dir: Nelson Recinos. Voices: Maurice LaMarche, Rob Paulsen, Frank Welker, Lauren Tom, Mark Hamill. Warner Bros/Amblin Entertainment/The WB Network. Colour.
In this musical episode of the half-hour cartoon TV show (1995-98), Brain (LaMarche) uses an electrical storm to bring to life a carrot Pinky (Paulsen) names Maurice. The trio then move to a farming community where they create an army of giant vegetables to take over the world. The series was executive produced by Steven Spielberg.
✦✦✧

The Mummy

USA, 1995. Dir: Kirk Tingblad. Voices: Maurice LaMarche, Rob Paulsen. Warner Bros/Amblin Entertainment/The WB Network. Colour.
In this seven minute segment, intelligent laboratory mice Pinky and The Brain, in their latest attempt to take over the world, travel to Egypt. There they wrap themselves in bathroom tissue, pretend to be revived mummies, and encounter a real living mummy.
Series sequel: PINKY, ELMYRA AND THE BRAIN (1998)
✦✦

PINOY DRACULA

Philippines, 1984. Dir: Juan Cairas. With: Kadyo, Sandra, José. R-Video/Transpacific Video. Colour.
Hardcore movie in which a voodoo spell turns one man into Dracula (Kadyo) and another into a vampire, both of whom then fight over a woman they were spying on.
✦

MARK PIRRO
[b 1956]

American director, writer, producer and actor of lame low-budget horror comedies.
qv: *Curse of the Queerwolf* (1987); *My Mom's a Werewolf* (1988); *Nudist Colony of the Dead* (1991); *A Polish Vampire in Burbank* (1983).

INGRID PITT
(Ingoushka Petrov) [b 1944]

Polish-born actress and author. Although her genre début was in the Spanish *Sound of Horror* (1964), she is best remembered for her lesbian Carmilla in Hammer's *The Vampire Lovers* (1970) and the full-frontal blood bath in *Countess Dracula* (1970). Her autobiography *Life's a Scream* was published in 1999.
qv: *Hammer A-Z* (1997); *Hammer the Studio That Dripped Blood!* (1987); *The House That Dripped Blood* (1970); *In Search of Dracula With Jonathan Ross* (1996); *Underworld* (1985).

THE PLAGUE OF THE ZOMBIES

UK, 1966. Dir: John Gilling. With: André Morell, Diane Clare, John Carson, Alex Davion, Jacqueline Pearce, Brook Williams. Hammer Films/Associated British-Pathe. Colour.
Slow-paced voodoo thriller, originally announced as *The Horror of the Zombie* and filmed back-to-back with Gilling's *The Reptile* (1966). Morell plays the snobbish Sir James Forbes, a professor of medicine, investigating a series of bizarre incidents in a remote Cornish village. He finally discovers that the local squire, Clive Hamilton (a stylish Carson), is reviving the dead to work in his tin mine. The

A nightmare member of The Plague of the Zombies *(1966).*

John PEIRCE & Son
IN

supporting cast are weak and Roy Ashton's zombie make-up only really works in long-shot. The one stand-out sequence is a green-tinted nightmare in which the rotting dead burst out of their graves in the churchyard. With Michael Ripper. In America, female audience members received a free pair of cut-out zombie eyes. John Burke novelised this in 1967 as part of *The Second Hammer Horror Film Omnibus*, published by Pan Books, and it was also adapted into comic strip format by writer Steve Moore and artists Trevor Goring and Brian Bolland for *The House of Hammer* no.13 (1977).
✦✦

PLANET OF THE VAMPIRES
(Orig: TERRORE NELLO SPAZIO/TERROR EN EL ESPACIO. USA: aka THE DEMON PLANET)
Italy/Spain, 1965. Dir: Mario Bava. With: Barry Sullivan, Norma Bengell, Angel Aranda, Evi Marandi, Stelio Candelli, Fernando Villena. Italian International/ Castilla/American International Pictures. Colour.
After *Black Sunday* (1960), this is probably Bava's best film. Based on the story 'One Night of 21 Hours' by Renato Pestriniero, the English-language script by Ib Melchior and Louis M. Heyward almost makes sense. Space captain Mark Markary (Sullivan) and his crew crash on Aura, a strange planet where the dead come back to life to kill the living. The 'surprise' ending has the alien-possessed vampiric survivors preparing to land on another alien world — Earth! Bava's chilling images — the living dead tearing themselves out of transparent body bags; the giant inhabitants of another crashed spaceship — influenced everything from *Night of the Living Dead* (1968) to *Alien* (1979). AIP originally wanted Susan Hart as the female lead, and they planned to release the film under the title *Planet of Blood*.
✦✦✦✦

PLAN 9 FROM OUTER SPACE
USA, 1958. Dir: Edward D. Wood Jr. With: Tor Johnson (Tor Johansson), Vampira (Maila Nurmi), Tom Keene, Gregory Walcott, Bela Lugosi, John Breckinridge. Reynolds Pictures. B&W.
Despite its reputation, this is actually a long way from being the worst film of all time. Writer/director/producer/editor Wood was supposed to make a religious film for his Baptist backers, but instead he shot this low-budget story about alien invaders resurrecting the dead under the title *Graverobbers from Outer Space*. There's a hammy introduction by TV astrologist Criswell (Charles Jeron Criswell King), a terrible performance by top-billed Johnson (who speaks!), and three short clips of Lugosi, filmed for the uncompleted *Tomb of the Vampire* prior to his death in 1956, before an unconvincing double (Hollywood chiropractor Dr Tom Mason) takes over. With its papier mâché flying saucer and the worst cardboard graveyard ever, this has become a cult favourite. With Lyle Talbot, Duke Moore and the aptly-named Dudley Manlove. Several scenes were nicely recreated by Tim Burton for *Ed Wood* (1994).
✦

PLAN 69 FROM OUTER SPACE
USA, 1994. Dir: Frank Marino. With: Celeste, Dyanna Lauren, Peter North, Beatrice Valle, Blake Palmer, Woody Long. Caballero. Colour.
This hardcore spoof makes Ed Wood's original look like a classic. Palmer and Long play a pair of aliens from the planet Dworkin who arrive on Earth and send their zombie slave (Brad Armstrong) dressed as Dracula to kidnap a woman (Lauren), so that they can remove her brain and clone her. Narrated by the director.
✦

THE PLASTIC MAN COMEDY-ADVENTURE SHOW: FANGFACE & FANGPUSS
USA, 1979-80. Dir: Rudy Larriva. Voices: Frank Welker, Bart Braverman, Susan Blu, Jerry Dexter. Ruby-Spears Enterprises/Filmways/ABC-TV. Colour.
Two hour (later ninety minute) cartoon TV series that includes the adventures of superhero *Plastic Man*, *Mighty Mann and Yukk*, *Rickety Rocket* and *Fangface & Fangpuss*. In the latter segments, the teen werewolf and his lycanthropic cousin (both voiced by Welker), along with their teenage friends Kim (Blu), Biff (Dexter) and Puggsy (Braverman), investigate such mysteries as 'The Creepy Goon from the Spooky Lagoon', 'The Romantic Plot of the She-Wolf Robot' and 'The Film Fiasco of Director Dosatro'.
Series sequel: THE PLASTIC MAN—BABY PLAS SUPER COMEDY SHOW (1980-81)
✦✧

PLAY FOR TODAY:
Vampires
UK, circa 1970s. Dir: John Goldschmidt. With: Peter Moran, Paul Moran, Tommy White, Linda Beckett, Jimmy Coleman, Bert Edgar. BBC-TV. Colour.
An obsessed young man, Stu (Peter Moran), searches all over Liverpool for a traditional vampire. John G. Heller plays the object of his quest. Written by Dixie Williams.
✦

THE PLAYGIRLS AND THE VAMPIRE
(Orig: L'ULTIMA PREDA DEL VAMPIRO. USA: aka CURSE OF THE VAMPIRE)
Italy, 1960 (1963). Dir: Peter Riethof (Piero Regnoli). With: Lyla Rocco, Walter Brandi (Walter Brandt/Walter Bigari), Maria Giovannini, Alfredo Rizzo, Marisa Quattrini, Leonardo Botta. Nord Film Italiana/Gordon Films/Fanfare Films. B&W.
Writer/director Regnoli, who scripted Riccardo Freda's *The Devil's Commandment* (1956), here reworks the same theme as Renato Polselli's *The Vampire and the Ballerina* (1960). Five sexy showgirls, their manager Lukas (Rizzo) and a pianist shelter from a storm in the castle of Count Gabor Kernassy (Brandi, who was also in Polselli's film), where his undead ancestor (also Brandi) puts the bite on Katya (Giovannini) and believes Vera (Rocco) is the reincarnation of his wife Margherita, who died nearly 180 years before. In the end, the vampire is impaled on the family coat of arms and (via cartoon animation!) disintegrates in the sunlight. The English-language version was presented by Richard Gordon as an 'adults only!' feature in America (one of the girls does a striptease and there's some minor nudity) and copyrighted 1963.
✦✦

PLAYHOUSE: MYSTERY AND IMAGINATION:
Curse of the Mummy
UK, 1970. With: Isobel Black, Patrick Mower, Graham Crowden, Muray Hayne, Donald Churchill. Thames Television/ITV. Colour.
Six episode continuation of the 1966-68 anthology TV series, now ninety minutes long. This episode is based on Bram Stoker's 1903 novel *The Jewel of Seven Stars*. After attempting to revive cursed queen Tera, an eccentric Egyptologist is found dead under mysterious circumstances.
Episode remake: BLOOD FROM THE MUMMY'S TOMB (qv; 1971)
✦✦

Dracula
UK, 1968. Dir: Patrick Dromgoole. With: Denholm Elliott, James Maxwell, Corin Redgrave, Suzanne Neve, Bernard Archard, Susan George. Thames Television/ITV. Colour.
Fairly faithful adaptation of Bram Stoker's novel, with Elliott as a bearded Count Dracula opposed by Archard's Professor Van Helsing. This also includes Marie Legrand, Nina Baden-Semper and Valerie Muller as the Count's vampire brides.
Episode remake: BRAM STOKER'S COUNT DRACULA (qv; 1970)
✦✦✧

Frankenstein
UK, 1968. Dir: Voytek. With: Ian Holm, Richard Vernon, Ron Pember, Neil Stacy, Robert Hunter, Sarah Badel. Thames Television/ITV. Colour.
Written by Robert Muller and loosely based on Mary Shelley's novel, this version develops the doppelgänger theme first explored in *Frankenstein 1970* (1958). When the bandaged Monster's face is revealed, it has the features of its creator (Holm).
Episode remake: FRANKENSTEIN (qv; 1969)
✦✦

DONALD PLEASENCE [1919-1995]

Prolific British character actor who played everything from Pinter to psychopaths. From the early 1960s onwards Pleasence appeared in a wide variety of films of variable quality and in the 1980s was officially listed by *Variety* as the busiest actor in the world. He portrayed the recurring role of psychiatrist Dr Sam Loomis in the *Halloween* films (1978-1995).

qv: *Barry McKenzie Holds His Own* (1974); *Dracula* (1979); *Dr. Jekyll and Mr. Hyde* (1973); *Frankenstein's Great-Aunt Tillie* (1983); *Halloween II* (1981); *The Monster Club* (1980); *Prince of Darkness* (1987); *Terror in the Aisles* (1984); *Vampire in Venice* (1988).

PLEASE SIR!

UK, 1971. Dir: Mark Stuart. With: John Alderton, Deryck Guyler, Noel Howlett, Joan Sanderson, Erik Chitty, Richard Davies. LWI Productions/Leslie Grade/Rank. Colour.

Dire movie version of the popular comedy TV series (1968-72) about naïve teacher Bernard Hedges (Alderton), and the staff and pupils of Fenn Street Secondary School. While away on a camping trip, the other members of Class 5C convince Frankie Abbott (David Barry) that he's a werewolf. 'La La La Lu (I Love You)' sung by Cilla Black.

✦✧

PLENILUNIO

Brazil, 1998. Salt City Home Video. Colour.

Video release in which a group of teenagers working at a local TV station investigate a series of killings and discover that a strange albino man who turns into a furry white werewolf during the full moon is responsible. The lycanthrope then traps them in the studios and hunts them down, one by one.

✦✧

EL POBRECITO DRACULIN

(aka DRACULIN)

Spain, 1976. Dir: Juan Fortuny. With: Joe Rigoli, Losele Roman, Victor Israel. Mezquiriz. Colour.

A Spanish vampire comedy that apparently features Dracula.

✦

ROMAN POLANSKI (Raymond Polanski) [b 1933]

French-born Polish writer, director and actor. His first wife, actress Sharon Tate (1943-69), was murdered by the Manson gang, and he was forced to flee America ten years later after being found guilty of having unlawful sex with a thirteen year-old minor.

qv: *Blood for Dracula* (1974); *Dance of the Vampires* (1966); *The Magic Christian* (1969).

POLICE ACADEMY THE SERIES: Mummy Dearest

Canada/USA, 1997. Dir: Mark Jean. With: Matt Borlenghi, Rod Crawford, Toby Proctor, Jeremiah Birkett, Heather Campbell, Michael Winslow. Warner Bros/Protocol Entertainment/Police Academy Series/Paul Maslansky Productions/Goodman-Rosen Productions/Taurus Film/BetaFilm. Colour.

Stupid hour-long TV show based on the popular comedy movie series about a group of incompetent police cadets. In this episode, when a 2,000 year-old mummy is accidentally delivered to the office of Commandant Hefilfinger (Joe Flaherty), it apparently comes to life. In the end, the mummy is revealed as a clumsy crook attempting to

Vampira (Maila Nurmi) as a graveyard ghoul in Plan 9 from Outer Space *(1958).*

steal a priceless Egyptian statue from the museum. With references to the 1933 Karloff movie. Co-executive produced by Paul Maslansky.
✦

A POLISH VAMPIRE IN BURBANK
(aka POLISH VAMPIRE)
USA, 1983 (1985). Dir: Mark Pirro. With: Mark Pirro, Lori Sutton, Bobbi Dorsch, Hugh O. Fields, Marya Gant, Eddie Deezen. Pirromount Productions/Simitar Entertainment. Colour.
Sacramento-based writer, producer and director Pirro stars in this very silly comedy as Dupar, a Polish vampire who sleeps in a coffin with a Herman Munster doll and a poster of Farrah Fawcett and has never bitten anyone. Kicked out of their castle in the Burbank hills by his father (Fields), Dupar sets off to find his own victims and ends up with vampire fan Delores Lane (Sutton), a health club instructor who is the girl of his dreams. With Gant as Dupar's sexy sister Yvonne, Deezen as the voice of his long-deceased brother Sphincter's skeleton, Conrad Brooks as a bartender, Paul Farbman as the Queerwolf (who doesn't transform), Elvira and the title sequence from *The Fearless Vampire Killers* (1967) on TV, a clip from *Count Yorga, Vampire* (1970) at the movies, and numerous cinematic in-jokes. This was the first feature shot on Super-8mm to be shown on a national cable network, and it ended up grossing over $500,000 on video!
✦✧

POLTERGEIST THE LEGACY:
The Bell of Girardius
Canada/USA, 1996. Dir: Joseph L. Scanlan. With: Derek de Lint, Martin Cummins, Robbi Chong, Helen Shaver, Barbara Tyson, Ryan Michael. Pacific Motion Pictures Productions/Trilogy/Metro Goldwyn Mayer/Showtime Networks. Colour.
Hour-long cable TV series (1995-), created by co-executive producer Richard B. Lewis, about the members of the Legacy, a San Francisco-based secret society led by Dr Derek Rayne (de Lint) and known only to the initiated by its true name, who protect others from the supernatural creatures inhabiting the shadows and the night. This has absolutely nothing to do with the movie series of the same title. In this episode, Miranda Blake (Tyson), the assistant curator of a museum, steals the magical fifteenth century Bell of Girardius and uses it to summon her composer boyfriend back from the dead as a decaying zombie.
✦✦✧
Darkness Falls
Canada/USA, 1998. Dir: Michael Robison. With: Derek de Lint, Robbi Chong, Martin Cummins, Kristin Lehman, Helen Shaver, Anthony Palermo. MGM Worldwide Television Productions/Trilogy/Metro Goldwyn Mayer/Showtime Networks. Colour.
First in a two-part story in which anthropologist Alex Moreau (Chong) is bitten by her old friend Justine (Sarah Strange) while visiting New Orleans, and soon finds herself transforming into a vampire. The Legacy must prevent Alex from making her first kill, or she will become one of the undead for ever.
Episode sequel: POLTERGEIST THE LEGACY: Light of Day (qv; 1998)
✦✦✧
Light of Day
Canada/USA, 1998. Dir: Michael Robison. With: Derek de Lint, Robbi Chong, Martin Cummins, Kristin Lehman, Helen Shaver, Anthony Palermo. MGM Worldwide Television Productions/Trilogy/Metro Goldwyn Mayer/Showtime Networks. Colour.
In this second episode of a two-part story, Alex is taken by the undead Phillipe D'Arcy (Palermo) to his world of vampires beneath San Francisco, where the death of former Navy SEAL Nick Boyle (Cummins) will result in her transforming completely into an immortal bloodsucker.
✦✦
Rough Beast
Canada/USA, 1997. Dir: Garner Simmons. With: Derek de Lint, Martin Cummins, Robbi Chong, Helen Shaver, Chilton Crane, Laura Harris. Pacific Motion Pictures Legacy Productions/Trilogy/Metro Goldwyn Mayer/Showtime Networks. Colour.
While psychiatrist Dr Rachel Corrigan (Shaver) investigates a teenage girl's recurring nightmares, a series of brutal killings lead the Legacy to the correct assumption that a werewolf-like 'Lupin' is loose in San Francisco.
✦✦

POLYMORPH
USA, 1996. Dir: J.R. Bookwalter. With: James Edwards, Ariauna Albright, Sasha Graham. EI Independent Cinema. Colour.
A meteor in the woods brings the dead back to life as glowing-eyed zombies to menace a group of young people and a gang of drug dealers in this low-budget independent release, shot in Ohio.
✦

PONTIANAK
Malaya, 1956. Dir: B.N. Rao. With: Maria Menado, M. Amin, Salmah Ahmed, Dollah Serawak, Aminah Yem, N. Kassim. Keris. B&W.
The first of the popular Pontianak series. Menado plays a hunchbacked girl who is made beautiful by magic. But when her husband is bitten by a snake, she sucks his blood to get the poison out and turns into a vampire (*pontianak*). She then tries to turn her daughter into a bloodsucker as well, but is finally destroyed by having a nail driven into her skull.
Sequel: DENDAM PONTIANAK (qv; 1957)
✦✦

PONTIANAK GUA MUSANG
Malaya, 1964. Dir: B.N. Rao. With: Suraya Haron, Ghazali Sumantri, Malek Siamat, Ummi Kalthoum. Keris. B&W.
A follow-up to *Pontianak Kembali* (1963), this was the sixth and last entry in the popular series. The vampire now lives in a cave.
✦

PONTIANAK KEMBALI
Malaya, 1963. Dir: Ramon Estellia. With: Maria Menado, Malik Selamat. Cathay/Keris. B&W.
Fifth in the popular series and a follow-up to *Anak Pontianak* (1958). Menado returns as the vampire.
Sequel: PONTIANAK GUA MUSANG (qv; 1964)
✦

POPEYE:
Mueller's Mad Monster
USA, circa 1961. Dir: Paul Fennel. Voices: Jackson Beck, Charles Lawrence, Jack Mercer, Mae Questel. King Features. Colour.
Six minute syndicated TV cartoon series (1960-62, 220 episodes). In this episode, Olive Oyle (Questel) is kidnapped by Mueller's Frankenstein Monster. Popeye (Mercer) saves her by knocking it apart and rebuilding it to resemble Elvis Presley.
Series sequel: THE ALL NEW POPEYE HOUR (qv; 1978-81)
✦✧

PORKY'S MOVIE MYSTERY
USA, 1939. Dir: Robert Clampett. Voices: Mel Blanc. Vitaphone/Warner Bros. B&W.
Seven minute *Looney Tunes* cartoon. Porky Pig plays oriental detective 'Mr Motto' on the trail of studio vandal the Phantom, who turns out to be the Invisible Man. This also features a live action sequence and the Frankenstein Monster being given the third degree by police. It was colourised for release to TV in the 1960s and included in the feature compilation *Porky Pig in Hollywood* (1986).
Sequel: CHICKEN JITTERS (1939)
✦✦✦

PORKY'S ROAD RACE
USA, 1937. Dir: Frank Tash (Tashlin). Voices: Mel Blanc. Vitaphone/Warner Bros. B&W.
Seven minute *Looney Tunes* cartoon. Despite the claim that 'Any resemblance to persons living or dead is the bunk', Porky Pig takes

part in a celebrity road race with caricatures of Freddie Bartholomew, Charlie Chaplin, W.C. Fields, Clark Gable, etc. Borax Karoff, looking like the Frankenstein Monster, tries to sabotage the race and Edna May Oliver wins. This was colourised in the late 1960s for release to TV.

Sequel: PICADOR PORKY (1937)

✦✦

PORKY'S II THE NEXT DAY

Canada/USA, 1983. Dir: Bob Clark. With: Dan Monahan, Wyatt Knight, Mark Herrier, Roger Wilson, Cyril O'Reilly, Tony Ganios. Simon-Reeves-Landsburg/Astral Bellevue Pathé/Twentieth Century Fox. Colour.

Sequel to the surprise 1981 box office hit, co-scripted by Alan Ormsby (*Children Shouldn't Play With Dead Things* [1972], etc). An unlikely Shakespeare festival at Florida's Angel Beach high school is opposed by the Reverend Bubba Flavel (Bill Wiley), the city commission and the local chapter of the KKK, until a group of teens tape record a weekly porno night in the Mayor's office, strip the Klan members and publicly discredit Flavel. This dire comedy also includes a lot of full-frontal (male) nudity and a complicated revenge plot hatched by Pee Wee Morris (Monahan) that involves a 'dead' belly dancer and a fake zombie (Rod Bail) in a graveyard. With Eric Christmas and Art Hindle. It was novelised by Ron Renauld for Pocket Books.

Sequel: PORKY'S REVENGE (1985)

✦

LE PORTE DELL'INFERNO

Italy, 1989. Dir: Humphrey Humbert (Umberto Lenzi). With: Barbara Cupisti, Gaetano Russo, M. Luzzi, Giacomo Rossi Stuart. Scena Film. Colour.

A group of scientists battle thirteenth century zombie monks in an ancient underground chapel. The title translates as 'Gates of Hell'.

✦✧

RAFAEL LÓPEZ PORTILLO [1916-1995]

Mexican journeyman director whose credits include more than fifty movies, many of which were belatedly released in America in bowdlerised versions.

qv: *Attack of the Mayan Mummy* (1957/64); *Curse of the Aztec Mummy* (1957); *La Momia Azteca* (1957); *Narco Satanico* (1988); *The Robot vs. the Aztec Mummy* (1957).

POSETITEL MUZEIA

USSR, 1989. Dir: Konstantin Lopushanski. With: Viktor Mikhailov, Irina Rakshina, Vera Maiorova. Lenfilm. Colour.

Overlong, downbeat story set in a dystopian future where the Earth's ice-caps have melted. While travelling to a museum in a waterlogged city, a man (Mikhailov) must evade marauding bands of mutant zombies that have escaped from concentration camps. In the end he becomes their saviour.

✦✧

POSSESSED II

Hong Kong, 1984. Dir: David Lai (Tung Wei/Lai Dai-Wai). With: Wong Siu-Fung, Kong Mei-Pooh, Sui Yuk-Long, Chung Wong. Golden Harvest. Colour.

Unconnected sequel to the 1983 film, about a woman possessed by the vengeful ghost of a 1940s prostitute who turns into a hairy werewolf creature when she kills.

✦✧

POWER RANGERS TURBO: Carlos and the Count

USA/Japan, 1997. Dir: Lawrence L. Simeone. With: Tracy Lynn Cruz, Blake Foster, Patricia Ja Lee, Roger Velasco, Selwyn Ward, Hilary Shepard Turner. Saban Entertainment/Renaissance Atlantic Entertainment/Toei Company/MMPR Productions/Fox Network. Colour.

Half-hour follow-up TV series (forty-five episodes) to *Power Rangers Zeo* (1996). In this episode, inspired by the screening of a vampire movie, the evil Divatox (Turner) changes a lunar bat into Count Nocturne to battle new Power Rangers Ashley (Cruz), Justin (Foster), Cassie (Lee), Carlos (Velasco) and T.J. (Ward). When Carlos is bitten by the Count, he is transformed into one of the undead and Skull (Jason Narvy) and Bulk (Paul Schrier) become vampire hunters.

Series sequel: POWER RANGERS IN SPACE (1998)

✦✦

EDDIE POWELL [b 1927]

British stunt man, long associated with Hammer Films, often as a double for Christopher Lee. He played Prem the living mummy in *The Mummy's Shroud* (1967).

qv: *Dracula* (1979); *Dracula Has Risen from the Grave* (1968); *Dracula Prince of Darkness* (1965); *Howling II Stirba — Werewolf Bitch* (1984); *Legend* (1985); *The Mummy* (1959).

PRACTICAL MAGIC

USA, 1998. Dir: Griffin Dunne. With: Sandra Bullock, Nicole Kidman, Dianne Wiest, Stockard Channing, Aidan Quinn, Goran Visnic. Warner Bros/Village Roadshow Pictures/Di Novi Pictures/Fortis Films. Colour.

Romantic fantasy directed by actor Dunne (*An American Werewolf in London* [1981], etc). Sally (Bullock) and Gillian (Kidman) are disparate orphaned siblings who discover they come from a family of New England witches cursed by an ancestor to have bad things happen to the men they truly love. After Gillian accidentally kills her boyfriend (Visnic), magically raises him from the dead and then kills him again, things begin to get complicated when the investigating cop (Quinn) falls for Sally. The lame Halloween ending makes no attempt to explain things.

✦✦

THE PREVENTERS: Hippy Daze

UK, 1996. Dir: Liddy Oldroyd. With: Morwenna Banks, Robert Harley, Chris England, William Gaunt, Simon Williams, Ed Devereaux. Carlton UK Television/Absolutely/ITV. Colour.

Silly half-hour sci-spy spoof special in which TV has been used to brainwash the population of Britain, with the result that everything has reverted to how it was in the 1960s. Only The Preventers — Penelope Gold (Banks), Craig Sturdy (Harley) and Mike Stallion (England) — can stop the media barons of The Consortium and their zombiefied hippie killers.

✦✦

PREVIEW MURDER MYSTERY

USA, 1936. Dir: Robert Florey. With: Reginald Denny, Frances Drake, Gail Patrick, Rod LaRoque, Ian Keith, George Barbier. Paramount. B&W.

Creaky comedy mystery thriller involving a series of macabre murders on the set of a vampire movie. This includes a super-scientific TV set and silent comedian Chester Conklin.

✦✦

PREVUES FROM HELL

(aka MAD RON'S PREVIEWS FROM HELL)

USA, 1987. Dir: Jim Monaco. With: Nick Pawlow, 'Happy', Michael Townsend Wright, Anthony Kelly, Jim Monaco, ('Mad') Ron Roccia. Off the Wall Video. Colour.

Compiled from the 'Mad Ron' Archives and filmed in Landsdowne, Pennsylvania, this feature-length video compilation is hosted by ventriloquist Pawlow and his bizarre zombie dummy 'Happy' Goldsplatt. A movie theatre full of zombies munching on blood-covered popcorn watch nearly fifty gory trailers for such 1960s and 1970s movies as *The Blood Spattered Bride* (1972)/*I Dismember Mama* (1972), *Children Shouldn't Play With Dead Things* (1972), *Devil's Nightmare* (1971), *Horror of the Zombies* (1974), *Lady Frankenstein* (1971), *Night of the Living Dead* (1968), *Tales from the Crypt* (1972), *Vault of Horror* (1973), and Europix's popular 'Orgy of the Living Dead' triple bill of

Revenge of the Living Dead (aka *The Murder Clinic* [1966]), *Curse of the Living Dead* (aka *Kill, Baby, Kill!* [1966]) and *Fangs of the Living Dead* (aka *Malenka the Niece of the Vampire* [1968]), along with numerous others.
✦✦

DENNIS PRICE (Dennistoun Franklyn John Rose-Price) [1915-1973]

Urbane British leading man, often in light comedies. He played the inventive serial killer in Ealing's *Kind Hearts and Coronets* (1949) and replaced Boris Karloff in *The Haunted House of Horror* (1969). Unfortunately, Price's career hit the skids in the 1970s when he began appearing in increasingly sleazy films, often for director Jesús Franco.
qv: *Dracula Prisoner of Frankenstein* (1972); *The Earth Dies Screaming* (1964); *The Erotic Rites of Frankenstein* (1972); *Go For a Take* (1972); *Helter Skelter* (1949); *Horror Hospital* (1973); *The Horror of Frankenstein* (1970); *The Horror of It All* (1963); *The Magic Christian* (1969); *Son of Dracula* (1973); *Twins of Evil* (1971); *Vampiros Lesbos* (1970).

VINCENT PRICE [1911-1993]

American actor, gourmet cook and art expert who, after a brief flirtation with the genre in the late 1930s and early 1940s, re-invented the modern horror film with his portrayals of madmen and villains from the mid-1950s onwards. Although Price often allowed his performances to topple over into self-parody, roles such as Matthew Hopkins in *Witchfinder General* (1968) proved what a fine actor he could be if given the opportunity. Next to Karloff and Lugosi, no other actor has been so closely linked with the macabre. His autobiography *I Like What I Know* appeared in 1959.
qv: *Annabel Lee* (1969); *Carol Burnett Show* (1972); *City Under the Sea* (1965); *Creepy Classics* (1987); *Cry of the Banshee* (1970); *Dead Heat* (1988); *Edward Scissorhands* (1990); *F Troop: 'V is for Vampire'* (1966); *The Hilarious House of Frightenstein* (1970-72); *The Last Man on Earth* (1961); *Madhouse* (1974); (Abbott and Costello) *Meet Frankenstein* (1948); *The Monster Club* (1980); *The Muppet Show* (1976); *The Offspring* (1986); *Once Upon a Midnight Dreary* (1979); *100 Years of Horror 'Gory Gimmicks'* (1996); *Red Skelton Hour* (1968); *Scream and Scream Again* (1969); *The Snoop Sisters: A Bad Day for Bluebeard* (1973); *Tales of Terror* (1962); *The 13 Ghosts of Scooby-Doo: 'Horror-Scope Scoob'* (1985); *The 13 Ghosts of Scooby-Doo: 'That's Monstertainment'* (1985); *The 13 Ghosts of Scooby-Doo: 'To All the Ghouls I've Loved'* (1985); *This is Your Life: 'Christopher Lee'* (1974); *Thriller* (1983); *Twice-Told Tales* (1963); *Vincent* (1982); *Vincent Price's Dracula* (1982); *Wide World of Entertainment: 'Horror Hall of Fame — A Monster Salute'* (1974).

PRIMITIVE LOVE

(Orig: L'AMORE PRIMITIVO)
Italy, 1964. Dir: Luigi Scattini. With: Jayne Mansfield (Vera Jane Palmer), Franco Franchi, Ciccio Ingrassia. Stan Borden. Colour.
Mondo-style 'adult' movie in which Mansfield (as herself) shows and narrates (often staged) clips of topless women, a live pig sacrifice, witch doctors, a cockfight and a naked Brazilian 'panther woman' to a balding professor in a hotel room. Mansfield also appears in a grass skirt in a dream sequence, and when she does a striptease the professor turns into Dr Jekyll! With the comedy team of Franco and Ciccio (*Dr. Goldfoot and the Girl Bombs* [1966], etc) as a pair of voyeuristic bellboys.
✦

PRINCE OF DARKNESS

USA, 1987. Dir: John Carpenter. With: Donald Pleasence, Lisa Blount, Victor Wong, Dennis Dun, Jameson Parker, Susan Blanchard. Universal/Carolco International/Alive Films. Colour.
This marked a welcome return to medium-budget film-making by director Carpenter, who also composed the pounding music score (with Alan Howarth) and wrote the script under the pseudonym 'Martin Quatermass' (as a tribute to Nigel Kneale). When a Catholic priest (an overacting Pleasence) calls in university professor Howard Birack (veteran Wong) and his team of students to investigate a glowing green entity discovered in the basement of a sixteenth century church in Los Angeles, they eventually discover that the mystery involves messages being transmitted from the future. While members of the team wander off and are turned into zombies, and a creepy-looking Alice Cooper (Vince Furnier) leads an army of psychos, street people and insects, it soon becomes obvious that the secret Brotherhood of Sleep has been guarding the offspring of Satan himself. Despite the illogical behaviour of some characters, this is still great fun.
✦✦✦

PRINCESS OF DARKNESS

USA, circa 1987. With: Samantha Strong, Frankie Leigh, Liza Anne. Video Exclusives. Colour.
This is another hardcore vampire video.
✦

PRINCESS OF THE NIGHT

USA, 1990. Dir: F. (Fred) J. Lincoln. With: Lauren Hall, Madison (Madison Stone), Heather Lere, Viper (Stephanie Bishop), Jamie Gillis, James Lewis. Vidco Entertainment. Colour.
More hardcore vampires. Hall stars as Lauren who, along with her two undead servants (Madison and Gillis), has survived for centuries by drinking the blood of virgins. When Lauren becomes ill after feeding on 'tainted' blood, her sister is called up from the underworld to save her by having sex with three men in coffins. This also includes Viper as another vampire.
✦

ANDREW PRINE [b 1936]

Dependable American leading man, often considered a poor man's Anthony Perkins.
qv: *Crypt of the Living Dead* (1972); *The Demon and the Mummy* (1975); *Kolchak: The Night Stalker: 'Demon in Lace'* (1975); *Weird Science: 'Gary and Wyatt's Bloodsucking Adventure'* (1996).

THE PRIZE PEST

USA, 1951. Dir: Robert McKimson. Voices: Mel Blanc. Warner Bros. Colour.
Seven minute *Looney Tunes* cartoon in which Porky Pig wins Daffy Duck in a radio contest. When Porky tries to get rid of his unwanted house guest, Daffy dons fake fangs and pretends to change into a Mr Hyde-type character.
Sequel: CRACKED QUEST (1952)
✦✦✦

LE PROCUREUR HALLERS

France, 1930. Dir: Robert Wiene. With: Jean Max, Colette Darfeuil, Suzanne Delmas, Georges Colin. Albatros. B&W.
Made the same year as *The Man Within*, this is a French version of Paul Lindau's play *Der Andere*, about a district attorney with a split personality.
✦

THE PROFESSOR

USA, 1958. Dir: Tom McCain. With: John S. Copeland, Irene Barr, Benny McIntyre, Vin Della Rocca, Doug Hobart, Dick Levy. Kent Films/Greg Luce. B&W.
Half-hour pilot TV show about missing atomic scientist Dr Trisler (Hobart, from *Death Curse of Tartu* [1966], etc) who turns into the briefly-seen werewolf that is killing sheep, and later a sheriff and a 'Commie' (Bob Gaus), in the Culver Mountains. Meanwhile, his balding colleague Professor Wilmer (Copeland) attempts to stun the creature with a ray-gun. The producers operated a live spook show in Dayton, Ohio.
✦

PROJECT METALBEAST

(aka PROJECT METALBEAST: DNA OVERLOAD)
USA, 1994 (1995). Dir: Alessandro de Gaetano. With: Barry Bostwick, Brian Brophy, Mario Burgos, T.J. Castronovo, William G. Clark, Kim Delaney. Blue Ridge Entertainment/Prism Entertainment. Colour.

Direct-to-video science fiction/horror thriller. When a top secret government experiment to create the perfect soldier goes wrong, the body of a test subject injected with the blood of a werewolf is cryogenically-suspended for twenty years. Revived by the only surviving team member, villainous CIA Colonel Miller (Bostwick), the werewolf genes are combined with experimental synthetic skin surgery to create an even more indestructible monster. With Kane Hodder under the silly-looking werewolf make-up created by John Carl Buechler.

✦✧

PROJECT VAMPIRE

USA, 1993 (1998). Dir: Peter Flynn. With: Brian Knudson, Mary-Louise Gemmill, Christopher Cho, Paula Randol-Smith, Chris Wolf, Myron Natwick. NBV Productions/ Hicks-Tams/EI Independent Cinema. Colour.

Three young interns led by Victor Hunter oppose the plans of evil vampire Dr Fredrick Klaus (Natwick) to create a world of vampires with his high-tech super-serum. An antidote allows the scientifically created undead to withstand sunlight, thereby enabling them to infiltrate the higher echelons of business and politics. This low-budget independent movie marked the directing début of ex-Corman art director Flynn.

✦✧

PROM NIGHT III THE LAST KISS

Canada, 1989 (1990). Dir: Ron Oliver and Peter R. Simpson. With: Tim Conlon, Cyndy Preston, David Stratton, Courtney Taylor, Dylan Neal, Jeremy Ratchford. Comweb/Famous Players/IVE. Colour.

Follow-up to *Hello Mary Lou Prom Night II* (1987) in which the fire-scarred Mary Lou Maloney (Taylor) returns from Hell to terrorise the students of Hamilton High and seduces student Alex Gray (Conlon) into disposing of the bodies. During the climax, the demonic dance queen raises a Prom Night of the walking dead. The next entry in the direct-to-video series was unconnected.

✦✦

THE PROPHECY

USA, 1995. Dir: Gregory Widen. With: Christopher Walken, Elias Koteas, Virginia Madsen, Eric Stoltz, Amanda Plummer, Viggo Mortensen. Overseas Film Group/Dimension Films/First Look Pictures/Neo Motion Pictures. Colour.

Uneven, but still impressive adult horror thriller shot under the titles *God's Army* and *Daemons* in Arizona by writer/director Widen. Failed priest turned detective Thomas Dagget (a bland Koteas) and Native American schoolteacher Katherine (an impressive Madsen) become embroiled in a war between the angels, led by the psychopathic Gabriel (a nicely over-the-top Walken), who creates zombie slaves from the newly dead. Gabriel is opposed by Simon (Stoltz), who is killed off too early, and a suave Lucifer (Mortensen). Jim Danforth created the angel effects and mesa matte paintings. Walken returned in the post-apocalyptic sequel.

Sequel: THE PROPHECY II: ASHTOWN (1997)

✦✦✦✧

PROTOTYPE

USA, 1983. Dir: David Greene. With: Christopher Plummer, David Morse, Frances Sternhagen, James Sutorius, Stephen Elliott, Arthur Hill. Richard Levinson-William Link Productions/CBS-TV. Colour.

Although credited as an updating of *Frankenstein*, this tedious TV movie is in fact about humanoid robot Michael (Morse), created by Plummer's slightly crazy Dr Carl Forrester. The scientist kidnaps his creation when the Pentagon shows interest in its military capabilities. After watching the 1931 *Frankenstein* on TV and reading Mary Shelley's novel, the creature destroys itself.

✦✧

PROVIDENCE

France/Switzerland, 1977. Dir: Alain Resnais. With: Dirk Bogarde, Ellen Burstyn, John Gielgud, David Warner, Elaine Stritch, Peter Arne. Action-Films/Société Française de Production/FR3/Citel Films Cinéma. Colour.

Pretentious nonsense from screenwriter David Mercer, in which dying novelist Clive Langham (Gielgud) populates his imagination with characters based on his relatives. The result is a rambling, episodic narrative set in a country sliding into anarchy. Accused of murdering an old man (Samson Fainsilber) who was a werewolf, a soldier (Warner) is later transformed into a lycanthrope himself. With a superb music score by Miklós Rózsa.

✦✧

DAVID PROWSE
[b 1935]

British heavyweight weightlifting champion turned actor. He first portrayed the Frankenstein Monster in *Casino Royale* (1967) and recreated the role for Hammer in *The Horror of Frankenstein* (1970) and *Frankenstein and the Monster from Hell* (1973). He also played the body (but not the voice) of Darth Vader in the first three *Star Wars* films.

qv: *A Clockwork Orange* (1971); *Vampire Circus* (1971).

PSI FACTOR CHRONICLES OF THE PARANORMAL:
All Hallow's Eve

Canada, 1998. Dir: Luc Chalifour. With: Matt Frewer, Nancy Anne Sakovich, Barclay Hope, Colin Fox, Nigel Bennett, Peter MacNeill. Paranormal III Productions/ Alliance Atlantis/Eyemark Entertainment/Global/ Endemol Entertainment. Colour.

Hosted by a laughably unconvincing Dan Aykroyd (as himself), each hour-long TV show (1996-), created by executive producers Peter Aykroyd, Christopher Chacon and Peter Ventrella, is supposedly inspired by the actual case files of The Office of Scientific Investigation and Research. Regular OSIR investigators include case managers Connor Doyle (Paul Miller) and Matt Praeger (associate producer Frewer), senior data analyst Lindsay Donner (Sakovich), chief science analyst Peter Axon (Hope), chief of medicine Dr Anton Hendricks (Fox), cryptozoologist L.Q. Cooper (Peter Blais), security co-ordinator Ray Donahue (MacNeill), pathologist Dr Claire Davison (Soo Garay), unofficial advisor Michael Kelly (Michael Moriarty) and enigmatic director of operations Frank Elsinger (Bennett). In this Halloween episode, Rebecca Royce (Linda Blair) is a successful horror novelist with multiple personalities who discovers that her latest best-seller has become all too real. During the climax, Matt Praeger dresses up as Count Dracula at a Halloween dance.

✦✧

The Curse/Angel on a Plane

Canada, 1996 (1997). Dir: Marc Voizard and Ken Girotti. With: Paul Miller, Nancy Anne Sakovich, Barclay Hope, Colin Fox, Maurice Dean Wint, Lindsay Collins. Paranormal Productions/Atlantis Films/Canwest Global System/Eyemark Entertainment. Colour.

In the first segment of this episode, the OSIR begin to suspect that an ancient curse is responsible when archaeologists excavating a 3,000 year-old tomb in Egypt start dying mysteriously and the survivors claim to have seen the god Anubis. In the second part, witnesses claim a plane struck by lightning was landed by an angel.

✦✦

Devolution

Canada, 1997. Dir: Clay Borris. With: Matt Frewer, Nancy Anne Sakovich, Barclay Hope, Colin Fox, Marni Thompson, Lisa Ryder. Paranormal II Productions/ Atlantis Films/Eyemark Entertainment/Global. Colour.

Sixty year-old convict Grey Callwood, who is on life support, is given experimental drug Xaldex which causes her body to devolve on a cellular level. In one scene, Lindsay dresses up as a vampire and goes undercover at a Goth club called The Pentagram looking for a suspect named Lucy Westenra (Nicole Oliver).

✦✦

The Hunter/The Healer

Canada, 1996. Dir: John Bell. With: Paul Miller, Nancy Anne Sakovich, Barclay Hope, Colin Fox, Maurice Dean Wint, John Kalangis. Paranormal Productions/Atlantis Films/Canwest Global System/Eyemark Entertainment. Colour.

In the first of these two half-hour stories, the OSIR team investigate a series of attacks on cattle in Indiana and discover that it is the work of a homeless person who transforms into a werewolf during the full moon. The second segment is about a boy who can heal with the touch of his hands.

✦✧

Night of the Setting Sun

Canada, 1997 (1998). Dir: E. Jane Thompson. With: Matt Frewer, Nancy Anne Sakovich, Barclay Hope, Colin Fox, Peter MacNeill, Lubomir Mykytiuk. Paranormal II Productions/Atlantis Films/Eyemark Entertainment/Global. Colour.

The discovery of an extinct passenger pigeon in the centre of a city leads OSIR case investigator Matt Praeger and his team to the Schulman family, who have survived for more than a century without ageing by drinking fresh blood.

✦✦✧

The Undead/Stalker Moon

Canada, 1996 (1997). Dir: Clay Borris. With: Paul Miller, Nancy Anne Sakovich, Colin Fox, Sten Eirik, Kristin Lehman, John Ralston. Paranormal Productions/Atlantis Films/Canwest Global System/Eyemark Entertainment. Colour.

When an apparently dead body of a homeless man (Eirik) comes back to life and disappears from its own autopsy, OSIR investigators become involved with voodoo and zombies. The second story involves a cult movie actress (Lehman) who is possibly being stalked by an obsessive fan from beyond the grave.

✦✧

Valentine

Canada, 1998 (1999). Dir: Ross Clyde. With: Matt Frewer, Nancy Anne Sakovich, Barclay Hope, Colin Fox, Nigel Bennett, Peter MacNeill. Paranormal III Productions/Alliance Atlantis/Eyemark Entertainment/Global/Endemol Entertainment. Colour.

An investigation into a series of apparent vampire slayings around St. Valentine's Day leads the OSIR's Lindsay Donner into the clutches of husband-and-wife bloodsuckers Reed (Winston Rekert) and Caitlyn Callum (C.J. Fidler).

✦✦

Wish I May

Canada, 1997 (1998). Dir: John Bell. With: Matt Frewer, Nancy Anne Sakovich, Barclay Hope, Colin Fox, Andrew Tarbett, Soo Garay. Paranormal II Productions/Atlantis Films/Eyemark Entertainment/Global. Colour.

The OSIR team travels to swamp country to investigate the case of two murdered brothers who are brought back from the dead by their family as putrefying zombies.

✦✦✦

PSYCHEBLOW

USA, 1999. Dir: Gerald Slota. With: Jacklyn Lick, Dominick Costa, Paige Turner, Barbara Joyce, Charlene Chappee. PushPin Productions. Colour.

Adult film actress Lick stars as Detective Wendy Gore battling alien sex vampires in this independent softcore video shot in six days in Paterson, New Jersey.

✦

PSYCHED BY THE 4-D WITCH

USA, 1972. Dir: Victor Luminera. With: Margo, Esoteria, Tom Yerian. Something Weird Video. Colour.

Obscure underground film shot in Los Angeles, filled with multiple narration, drugs, softcore sex, nightmares and cheap-looking special effects. In one scene, the brother of the possessed Cindy (Margo) goes to Chinatown, becomes the King of the Sex Vampires and bites the breasts of a female victim.

✦

PSYCHOMANIA

(USA: aka THE DEATH WHEELERS)
UK, 1972 (1973). Dir: Don Sharp. With: George Sanders, Beryl Reid, Nicky Henson, Mary Larkin, Roy Holder, Robert Hardy. Benmar/Scotia-International. Colour.

Filmed under the titles *The Living Dead* and *The Frog*, this was Sanders' last film (he committed suicide not long after making it). In a sad career come-down, he plays Shadwell, the Satanic butler who oversees a group of motorcycle hooligans led by Tom Latham (Henson). When the gang kill themselves, they return from the dead as indestructible zombies. Director Sharp (*The Kiss of the Vampire* [1962], etc) almost makes this bizarre blend of horror and humour work, but he is finally defeated by the low budget and uneven script. In the end, medium Mrs Latham (Reid) is turned into a frog.

✦✦✧

A PUP NAMED SCOOBY-DOO:

Chickenstein Lives

USA/South Korea, 1989. Dir: Ray Patterson, Don Lusk, Paul Sommer. Voices: Casey Kasem, Don Messick, Dick Gautier, Kenneth Mars, B.J. Ward, Frank Welker. Hanna-Barbera Productions/ABC-TV. Colour.

Emmy-award winning TV series of half-hour musical cartoon adventures (1988-91, twenty-one episodes), aimed at very young children. In this episode, when Freddie (Carl Stevens) becomes a reporter for his Uncle Eddie's *National Exaggerator*, the childhood friends find themselves trying to prevent a seven-foot tall chicken monster from driving the newspaper out of business. In one scene, Scooby (Messick) disguises himself as a mummy. Executive produced by William Hanna and Joseph Barbera.

✦✧

Night of the Living Burger

USA/South Korea, 1989. Dir: Ray Patterson, Don Lusk, Paul Sommer. Voices: Casey Kasem, Don Messick, Dick Gautier, Kenneth Mars, B.J. Ward, Frank Welker. Hanna-Barbera Productions/ABC-TV. Colour.

The members of the Scooby-Doo Detective Agency investigate a burger monster which is attempting to put restaurant owner O'Greazy out of business. One of the suspects is vampiric TV horror host Count Shockula.

✦

The Were-Doo of Doo Manor

USA/South Korea, 1991. Dir: Ray Patterson, Don Lusk, Carl Urbano. Voices: Rene Auberjonois, Casey Kasem, Don Messick, Rob Paulsen, Robert Picardo, B.J. Ward. Hanna-Barbera Productions/ABC-TV. Colour.

A pup named Scooby-Doo learns that he will apparently turn into a monstrous Were-Doo under the full moon because of a family curse.

Series sequels: ARABIAN NIGHTS (1994) and SCOOBY-DOO ON ZOMBIE ISLAND (qv: 1998)

✦

PUPPETMASTER

USA, 1989. Dir: David Schmoeller. With: Paul Le Mat, Irene Miracle, Matt Roe, Kathryn O'Reilly, Barbara Crampton, William Hickey. Full Moon Productions. Colour.

The first in a very successful low-budget video series executive produced by Charles Band. It opens in an old hotel in Bodega Bay(!), California, in 1939, as Nazi agents close in on mysterious puppet master André Toulon (Hickey). Fifty years later a group of psychics led by Alex (a plump Le Mat) are drawn to the same dilapidated hotel where they discover that one of their number (Jimmie F. Skaggs) has used the puppet master's ancient Egyptian magic to return from the dead and kill his colleagues with the living puppets Pinhead, Leech Woman, Tunneler, Blade and Jester (excellent stop-motion effects by David Allen FX). Much better than you'd expect, thanks to an inventive script and atmospheric direction.

Sequel: PUPPET MASTER II (qv; 1990)

✦✦✦

PUPPET MASTER II

USA, 1990. Dir: David Allen. With: Elizabeth Maclellan, Collin Bernsen, Gregory Webb, Charlie Spradling, Steve Welles, Jeff Weston. Full Moon Entertainment/

Paramount. Colour.
Enjoyable sequel to the 1989 original. The murderous puppets restore André Toulon (Welles) to life. Wrapped in bandages (and looking like Claude Rains' Invisible Man), the mad puppet master uses his creations, constructed through ancient Egyptian magic, to kill off a team of government parapsychologists so that he can claim the leader, Carolyn Bramwell (Maclellan), who he believes to be his lost love, Elsa. The impressive stop-motion and puppet effects were created by director Allen's company. With Nita Talbot and George 'Buck' Flower. Charles Band was executive producer. Three more sequels followed, along with a successful line of toys.
Sequel: PUPPET MASTER III TOULON'S REVENGE (1991)
✦✦✧

PURA SANGRE
Colombia, 1983. Dir: Luís Ospina. With: Florina Lemaitre, Carlos Mayolo, Humberto Arango, Luís Alberto Garcia, Gilberto 'Fly' Forero, Franky Linero. Luís Ospina Productions/Castano. Colour.
When an ailing Howard Hughes-type business tycoon requires fresh blood to survive, a trio of assistants help the man's son supply victims from the country's youngsters in this bizarre political allegory. The title translates as 'Pure Blood'.
✦

PURPLE PLAYHOUSE:
Dracula
Canada, 1973. Dir: Jack Nixon Browne. With: Nehemiah Persoff, Norman Welsh, Blair Brown, Charlotte Hunt. Canadian Broadcasting Company. Colour.
Shot-on-video TV production which closely follows the Bram Stoker novel. Welsh plays a white-haired Count Dracula, thwarted by Persoff's Dr Van Helsing. Hunt portrays the vampiric Lucy.
Remake: COUNT DRACULA (qv; 1977)
✦✦

PUSANG ITEM
Philippines, 1959. Dir: Cirio H. Santiago. With: Johnny Monteiro, Cynthia Zamora, Laura Delgado, Carol Varga. People's Pictures. B&W.
Set in the nineteenth century, when a were-cat creature is cursed to live nine lives unless he performs a sacrificial act. The title translates as 'The Monster Strikes'.
✦

PYASA SHAITAN
India, 1983. With: Kamal Hassan. Colour.
Hassan portrays evil magician Puppet Draculla, who attempts to become immortal by sacrificing seven virgins. The title translates as 'The Thirsty Devil'.
✦✧

PYRAMID TERROR
Cuba, 1983. Dir: Noel Lima and José Reyes. Filminutos. Colour.
Cartoon short about a mummy motivated by music.
✦✧

PYRO
(Orig: FUEGO. UK: WHEEL OF FIRE)
Spain/USA, 1963 (1964). Dir: Julio Coll. With: Barry Sullivan, Martha Hyer, Fernando Hillbeck, Sherry Moreland, Soledad Miranda (Soledad Redon Bueno), Luis Prendes. SWP/American International Pictures. Colour.
Set in Spain, with Sullivan playing an American engineer presumed dead in a fire that killed his family. He returns for revenge, his face hidden behind a life-like mask. Based on a story by co-producer Sidney W. Pink.

QUANTUM LEAP:
Blood Moon
USA, 1993. Dir: Alan J. Levi. With: Scott Bakula, Dean Stockwell, Ian Buchanan, Deborah Maria Moore, Shae D'Lyn, Rod Loomis. Universal/Belisarius Productions/ NBC-TV. Colour.
Popular hour-long TV series (1989-93, ninety-seven episodes) about research scientist Dr Sam Beckett (Bakula) who, during an experiment in time travel in 1999, finds himself forced to leap into the bodies of different people to solve their problems. Sam is aided by Al Calavicci (Stockwell), a hologram only he can see, and the computer Ziggy. In this episode, Sam leaps back to 10 March 1975 and into the body of a famous English artist who Al is convinced is a vampire, about to sacrifice his new wife in a Satanic ritual that will bring his 300 year-old undead ancestor Count Bathory back to life.
✦✦✧
The Curse of Ptah-Hotep
USA, 1992. Dir: Joe Napolitano. With: Scott Bakula, Dean Stockwell, Lisa Darr, John Kapelos, Chaim Jeraffi, Ali Dean. Universal/Belisarius Productions/NBC-TV. Colour.
The time-hopping Sam Beckett leaps into the body of an archaeologist on 2 March 1957, who discovers a fabulous lost tomb of ancient Egypt. But when a series of accidents and unusual deaths occur, is it the curse or is one of the team a murderer? In the end, the long-dead mummy returns to life to kill the villain.
✦✦

ROBERT QUARRY
[b 1923]

American character actor who made his screen début in a part subsequently cut from Hitchcock's *Shadow of a Doubt* (1943). In the early 1970s, American International Pictures put him under a seven-year contract and were grooming him to be their new horror star until a serious car accident resulted in Quarry's forced absence from the screen for nearly a decade. Now he seems trapped in direct-to-video trash.
qv: *Beverly Hills Vamp* (1988); *Count Yorga, Vampire* (1970); *Deathmaster* (1972); *Madhouse* (1974); *The Return of Count Yorga* (1971); *Sugar Hill* (1974); *Teenage Exorcist* (1991).

QUASIMODO D'EL PARIS
France, 1999. Dir: Patrick Timsit. With: Patrick Timsit, Richard Berry, Vincent Elbaz, Mélanie Thierry, Didier Flamand, Dominique Pinon. Hachette Première/TPS Cinéma/Tentative d'Evasion/France 3 Cinéma/M6 Films/ Bac Films. Colour.
Contemporary comedy inspired by Victor Hugo's novel, *Notre-Dame de Paris*, filmed under the title *Quasimodo* and set in the city state of El Paris, where a serial killer is preying upon prostitutes. It turns out to be a plot by the cathedral's fanatical archdeacon Frollo (Berry), who uses his ward, the hunchbacked bell-ringer Quasimodo (co-writer Timsit, making his directorial début), to kidnap the women before turning them into gargoyles. With Thierry as Esméralda.
✦✦

QUEEN KONG
UK/Italy/France, 1976. Dir: Frank (Farouk) Agrama. With: Rula Lenska, Robin Askwith, Valerie Leon. Dexter Films/Gafitti Italiana. Colour.
Silly role reversal of *King Kong* (1933), with a sixty-foot tall female gorilla captured by film producer Luce Habit (Lenska), which escapes in London to search for Ray Fay (Askwith). They finally end up on top of the city's Post Office Tower. Dino De Laurentiis thought this $600,000 spoof was a threat to his $24,000,000 *King Kong* (1976), so he sued, which is probably why you've never seen it. From the director of *Dawn of the Mummy* (1980). A tie-in novel (with photos!) by James Moffatt (Richard Allen) was published in Britain. The same year, the Italians announced *Baby Kong*, to be directed by Mario Bava!
✦

QUEEN OF BLOOD
(aka PLANET OF BLOOD)
USA, 1966. Dir: Curtis Harrington. With: John Saxon, Basil Rathbone, Judi Meredith, Dennis Hopper, Florence Marly (Florence Marly von Wurmbrand), Robert Boon. American International Pictures. Colour.
When Roger Corman acquired special effects footage from the Russian science fiction films *Nebo Zovet* (1959) and *Mechte Navstrechu* (1963), Curtis Harrington wrote a script around it and in 1964 directed this modest thriller in six days for around $50,000. Allan Brenner (Saxon) leads a mission to Mars to rescue a crashed alien spaceship and brings back the green-skinned, glowing-eyed Velena (Marly), who turns out to be a creepy vampire feeding on the crew. Veteran Rathbone plays scientist Dr Farraday back on Earth and Forrest J Ackerman is eleventh billed as his assistant. Stephanie Rothman was associate producer, and *Star Wars* (1977) producer Gary Kurtz the production manager. An 'adult' paperback novelisation by Charles Nuetzel was published in 1966 by Greenleaf Classics. Apparently, Florence Marly herself made a 16mm sequel in the early 1970s entitled *Space Boy*.
✦✦✧

QUEEN VICTORIA AND THE ZOMBIES
USA, 1991. Dir: Steve (J.) Postal. With: Charlotte Leslie, Kendrick Kaufman, Jennifer Tuck, Angela Shepard. Steve Postal Productions. Colour.
Fifth in the terrible amateur horror/comedy series from the Florida-based director, this time involving aliens and the walking dead.
Sequel: BILLY THE KID MEETS THE VAMPIRES (qv; 1991)
✦

QUEM TEM MEDO DE LOBISOMEM
Brazil, 1974. Dir: Reginaldo Faria. With: Reginaldo Faria, Stepan Nercessian, Camila Amado, Carlos Kroeber, Christina Aché, Fatima Freire. Ipanema/Circus/RF Faria/ Embrafilme. Colour.
Odd black comedy in which two men (director Faria and Nercessian) investigating the supernatural and a woman (Amado) searching for her missing husband are captured by a bizarre family. While the pair of heroes are variously seduced by the six daughters before meeting violent deaths, the woman marries the only son, who according to legend can change into a werewolf. This apparently also includes a vampire. The title translates as 'Who's Afraid of the Werewolf?'
✦

LINNEA QUIGLEY
[b 1959]

American actress of little talent who made her movie début in the mid-1970s. Now an archetypal scream queen in numerous direct-to-video horrors.
qv: *The Black Room* (1981); *Bloody Nasty* (1989); *Drive-in Madness!* (1987); *Innocent Blood* (1992); *Linnea Quigley's Horror Workout* (1990); *Lust for Frankenstein* (1997); *Marie-Cookie and the Killer Tarantula* (1998); *100 Years of Horror: Scream Queens* (1996); *100 Years of Horror: 'Zombies'* (1996); *The Return of the Living Dead* (1984); *Sorority Babes in the Slimeball Bowl-O-Rama* (1987).

The titular star of Queen Kong *(1976).*

RABID

Canada, 1976. Dir: David Cronenberg. With: Marilyn Chambers, Frank Moore, Joe Silver, Howard Ryshpan, Patricia Gage, Susan Roman. Dibar Syndicate. Colour.

Porno star Chambers is surprisingly good as Rose, the victim of a skin graft experiment that results in the growth of a phallus-shaped blood-drinking organ. She infects her victims with a rabies-like epidemic that quickly spreads throughout the city of Montreal. Writer/director Cronenberg basically reworks themes from his first feature, *Shivers* (1974), but with more confidence. An effective low-budget thriller with a downbeat ending, this won the awards for Best Screenplay and Best Special Effects at the 1977 Sitges Horror Film Festival. A novelisation by Richard Lewis appeared in Britain in 1977.

✦✦✦

RAGE OF THE WEREWOLF

USA, 1999. Dir: Kevin Lindenmuth. With: Debbie Rochon, Joseph Zaso, Ron Ford. Colour.

Independent video release in which Laslo (Zaso) is a werewolf in contemporary New York.

✦

RAIDERS OF THE LIVING DEAD

Canada/USA, 1985 (1987). Dir: Samuel M. Sherman (and Brett Piper). With: Scott Schwartz, Robert Deveau, Donna Asali, Bob Allen, Bob Sacchetti, Zita Johann. Independent-International Pictures Corp./Cineronde. Colour.

When newspaper reporter Morgan Randall (Deveau) uncovers a plot by mad local coroner Dr Kopek (Leonard Corman) to reanimate corpses at an abandoned prison on Rockmoor Island, New Jersey, two young teens use home-made laser guns to zap a grey-faced army of the dead. Veteran actress Johann (*The Mummy* [1933]) came out of retirement to appear in one scene as an elderly historian. This was originally started in New Hampshire in 1983 by co-writer Piper under the title *Graveyard*. It was later completed in three weeks by writer/producer Sherman. With several clips from a *Three Stooges* short.

✦

SAM RAIMI
[b 1959]

American director, writer and actor who made his name with a trilogy of post-modern horror films: *The Evil Dead* (1982), *Evil Dead II* (1987) and *Army of Darkness* (1992). More recently he has become a successful TV producer with such series as *American Gothic* (1995-96), *Hercules The Legendary Journeys* (1995-99) and *Xena Warrior Princess* (1995-).

qv: *Body Bags* (1993); *The Dead Next Door* (1989); *Filmhouse Fever* (1986); *Flying Saucers Over Hollywood* (1992); *Innocent Blood* (1992); *Night of the Living Dead 25th Anniversary Documentary* (1993).

CLAUDE RAINS
[1889-1967]

British stage actor who made his career in Hollywood, often playing suave villains. Except for the last scene, only his voice was heard in his début feature, *The Invisible Man* (1933). However, despite starring in such films as *The Wolf Man* (1941) and playing the title role in *The Phantom of the Opera* (1943), most of his horror appearances are inferior to his other movie work.

qv: *The Horror Show* (1979).

RAMAR OF THE JUNGLE:
Lady of the Leopards

USA, 1952. With: Jon Hall, Ray Montgomery, Victor Millan, James Fairfax, Nick Stewart, Woody Strode. Incorporated Television Company. B&W.

Half-hour TV series (1952-53, fifty-two episodes) about the jungle adventures of Dr Tom Reynolds (producer Hall), known as Ramar ('white witch doctor') to the local natives. In this episode, Ramar encounters a beautiful woman who may have the power to transform into a leopard during the full moon.

✦

Zombie Terror

USA, 1952. With: Jon Hall, Ray Montgomery, Victor Millan, James Fairfax, Nick Stewart, Woody Strode. Incorporated Television Company. B&W.

Ramar encounters a mad scientist who uses a ray gun to turn natives into 'zombies'.

✦✧

BASIL RATHBONE
(Philip St. John Basil Rathbone) [1892-1967]

South African-born British stage actor, in America since 1922. A memorably urbane villain in such films as *The Mad Doctor* (1940) and *Fingers at the Window* (1942), he will always be remembered as the definitive Sherlock Holmes on stage, screen and radio. His autobiography *In and Out of Character* was published in 1962.

qv: *The Ghost in the Invisible Bikini* (1966); *Hillbillys in a Haunted House* (1967); *The Magic Sword* (1961); *Queen of Blood* (1966); *Son of Frankenstein* (1939); *Suspense: 'Dr. Jekyll and Mr. Hyde'* (1951); *Tales of Terror* (1962).

THE RATS ARE COMING! THE WEREWOLVES ARE HERE!

UK/USA, 1972. Dir: Andy Milligan. With: Hope Stansbury, Jackie Skarvelis, Noel Collins, Joan Ogden, Douglas Phair, Berwick Kaler. William Mishkin Motion Pictures/Constitution. Colour.

Set in 1899, this Milligan monstrosity (he scripted/photographed/directed) is about a woman (Stansbury) and her new husband (Collins) who arrive at the home of her crazy family of incestuous werewolves, ruled over by a 108 year-old patriarch (Phair). They keep her brother Malcolm (Kaler) chained up in a room where he commits graphic cruelty to chickens and mice. The cast of non-actors give hysterical performances with fake British accents, the camera wobbles precariously and the production values are rock-bottom. Legendary producer William Mishkin took Milligan's 16mm film *Curse of the Full Moon*, which was filmed in 1971 and ran for only sixty-seven minutes, and added scenes about flesh-eating rats to cash in on the success of *Willard* (1971) and *Ben* (1972). It still stinks.

✦

MIKE RAVEN
(Austin Churton Fairman) [1924-1997]

A former ballet dancer and British radio disc jockey, who apparently appeared in a few films during the 1940s before he made an unsuccessful attempt to turn himself into a lisping horror star in the early 1970s. Despite looking like a combination of Vincent Price and Christopher Lee, Raven's career fizzled out when it was obvious that he couldn't act, and he later became a sheep farmer and sculptor in Cornwall. He was dubbed by Valentine Dyall (1908-1985) in *Lust for a Vampire* (1970).

qv: *Disciple of Death* (1972); *I, Monster* (1971).

LE RAVISSEMENT DE FRANK N. STEIN

Switzerland, 1982. Dir: Georges Schwizgebel.

Nine minute cartoon about 'the creation of life'.

✦✧

RAW FORCE

Philippines/USA, 1982. Dir: Edward Murphy. With: Cameron Mitchell, Geoff Binney, Jillian Kessner, Vic Diaz, Hope Holiday, Jennifer Holmes. Ansor International/American Panorama. Colour.

Low-budget thrills, filmed under the title *Shogun Island*. A group of charter boat passengers shipwrecked on Warriors' Island in the

South China Seas encounter blue-faced kung fu zombies raised from the dead by Diaz's evil monks. This includes stock footage from *Piranha* (1978).
✦

ALDO RAY
(Aldo DaRe) [1926-1991]

American character actor who, after a promising start in the 1950s, saw his career slide into exploitation and even porno.
qv: *Evils of the Night* (1983); *Frankenstein's Great-Aunt Tillie* (1983); *Night Shadow* (1990).

FRED OLEN RAY
[b 1954]

Prolific American director, producer and writer of low-brow independent films. A former TV station engineer and low-budget make-up artist, his fan-boy mentality results in some fascinating casting of old-timers, but the movies themselves rarely live up to their gimmicky titles.
qv: *Alien Dead* (1978); *Attack of the 60 Foot Centerfold* (1995); *Beverly Hills Vamp* (1988); *Death House* (1988); *Demon Cop* (1990); *Evil Spawn* (1987); *Night of the Living Dead 25th Anniversary Documentary* (1993); *Night Shade* (1997); *100 Years of Horror: 'Baron Frankenstein'* (1996); *100 Years of Horror: 'Dinosaurs'* (1996); *100 Years of Horror: 'Dracula and His Disciples'* (1996); *100 Years of Horror: 'Dr. Jekyll and Mr. Hyde'* (1996); *100 Years of Horror: 'Freaks'* (1996); *100 Years of Horror: 'Mad Doctors'* (1996); *100 Years of Horror: 'Werewolves'* (1996); *Shock Waves* (1976); *Teenage Exorcist* (1991); *The Tomb* (1985); *Vampire Vixens from Venus* (1994); *The Wasp Woman* (1995).

THE RAY BRADBURY THEATER:
The Dead Man

Canada/New Zealand, 1992. Dir: Costa Botes. With: Louise Fletcher, Frank Whitten. Atlantis Films/South Pacific Pictures/Allarcom Pay Television/Bradshaw, MacLeod & Associates/Wilcox Productions/WIC Western International Communications/USA Network/First Choice Canadian Communications Corporation/ Superchannel/Super Ecran/The Global Television Network. Colour.

Half-hour anthology TV series (1985-92, sixty-five episodes), written and presented by co-executive producer Ray Bradbury and based on his stories. In this episode, a woman (Fletcher) is romanced by a dead man (Whitten) who asks her to marry him.
✦✦

The Man Upstairs

Canada/France, 1988. Dir: Alain Bonnot. With: Adam Negley, Feodor Atkine, Micheline Presle, Kate Hardie, Henri Poirier, Michel Winogradoff. RBT Production/ Elipse Programme/Granada Television International/ Atlantis Films/Wilcox Productions/The Global Television Network/The USA Network/First Choice Canadian Communications Corporation. Colour.

Douglas (Negley), a young American boy, believes that Mr Koberman (Atkine), the strange Hungarian man renting a room in his grandmother's boarding house, is the vampire killing women in and around Paris. Koberman is eventually destroyed when his body is filled with silver coins.
✦✦✧

RAZOR BLADE SMILE

UK, 1998. Dir: Jake West. With: Eileen Daly, Christopher Adamson, Jonathan Coote, Kevin Howarth, David Warbeck, Heidi James. Eye Deal Image/Manga Live/Palm Pictures/Beatnik Films. Colour.

Filmed on 16mm in 1996, this woefully cheap-looking thriller simply doesn't have the talent or budget to match the high concepts of twenty-six year-old writer/director West. Vampire Lilith Silver (the awful Daly), a leather cat-suited assassin with a coffin full of weapons, discovers she is being used to kill members of the secret Illuminati sect led by vampire Sir Sethane Blake (Adamson) while being pursued by obsessed Scotland Yard detective Ray Price (Coote). An ill-looking Warbeck (to whom the film is dedicated) appears briefly in his last role as a police forensic expert known as the Horror Movie Man. Despite some impressive visual effects and the sleazy sex and gore, production values and performances are all rock-bottom.
✦

REAL BAD MONSTER RAW

Thailand, circa 1980s. Colour.

Softcore horror comedy in which a Karloffian singing Frankenstein Monster lives in a coffin and has an operation that results in him performing on stage in a club. In the end, he develops a fear of the sun and is staked through the heart. Huh?
✦

THE REAL GHOSTBUSTERS:
No One Comes to Lupusville

USA/Japan, 1986. Voices: Arsenio Hall, Maurice La Marche, Laura Summer, Frank Welker. Columbia Pictures Television/DIC Enterprises/ABC-TV. Colour.

Werewolf episode of the popular children's TV cartoon series (1986-88), based on the *Ghostbusters* (1984) movie.
Series sequel: SLIMER! AND THE REAL GHOSTBUSTERS (1988-89)
✦✧

RE-ANIMATOR

USA, 1985. Dir: Stuart Gordon. With: Bruce Abbott, Barbara Crampton, David Gale, Robert Sampson, Jeffrey Combs, Carolyn Purdy-Gordon. Empire Pictures/Re-Animator Productions. Colour.

Filmed for just $800,000 and based very loosely on H.P. Lovecraft's 1921-22 episodic novella 'Herbert West: Reanimator', this outrageous low-budget horror comedy features medical student West (a nicely sardonic performance by Combs) inventing a glowing liquid which can bring the dead back to life — with horrific results. But the real villain is Dr Carl Hill (Gale), a megalomaniac whose still-living decapitated head unleashes an army of walking corpses in the gory, over-the-top climax. Despite some lapses in logic, Gordon directs with a nice sense of fun. The film was originally released unrated in America because of the violence, and two minutes (including a particularly gross sequence involving Hill's head and heroine Crampton) were cut in Britain. Pocket Books published Jeff Rovin's novelisation in 1987.
Sequel: BRIDE OF RE-ANIMATOR (qv; 1989)
✦✦✦✦

REANIMATOR ACADEMY

USA, 1992. With: Steve Westerheit, Connie Speer. Colour.

Independent, shot-on-video horror/comedy, 'inspired' by H.P. Lovecraft's story, in which a college student discovers that he can restore life with an experimental serum. But when a gangster forces him to revive his dead girlfriend, she turns into a decapitating psycho.
✦

RED AND BLACK

Hong Kong, 1986. Dir: Andrew Kam and Yuen Wah (Wu Ma/Wo Ma/Ng Ma-Wu). With: Joey Wang (Wong Ki-Chang/Wang Tsu-Hsien), Eric Tsang, Leung Chia-Hui, Wu Ma (Wo Ma/Yuen Wah/Ng Ma-Wu), Lam Ching-Ying (Lin Zheng-Ying). Colour.

This political allegory opens in 1941 during the Japanese occupation of the Chinese mainland. A man is infected by a Japanese vampire but manages to impale himself in an underground cavern. Twenty-five years later he is accidentally revived by his son (Chia-Hui) and infects the People's Leader of the Communist Revolution.
✦

RED BLOODED AMERICAN GIRL

Canada, 1990. Dir: David Blyth. With: Andrew Stevens, Heather Thomas, Christopher Plummer, Kim Coates, Lydie Denier, Andrew Jackson. SC Entertainment

International. Colour.
Dr John Alcore (Plummer) and the staff at his Life Research Foundation are infected with an age-prolonging virus that turns them into blood-drinkers. Research volunteer Paula Bukowsky (Thomas) is also affected by the disease and transforms into a superhuman killer, while erratic young scientist Owen Augustus Urban II (Stevens) is employed to find a cure before the virus destroys Alcore and the rest of the scientifically-created vampires. Despite Blyth's flashy direction, Allan Moyle's uneven script owes much to the early films of fellow Canadian David Cronenberg.
✦✦

RED DWARF ~~IIII~~/III: Only the Good...
UK, 1999. Dir: Ed Bye. With: Chris Barrie, Craig Charles, Danny John-Jules, Robert Llewellyn, Chloë Annett, Norman Lovett. Grant Naylor Productions/BBC-TV. Colour.
Cult comedy science fiction TV series (1987-), created by Rob Grant and Doug Naylor, about the misadventures of a group of crewmembers on the Jupiter mining vessel *Red Dwarf* — Rimmer (Barrie), Lister (Charles), the mutated Cat (John-Jules), android Kryten (Llewellyn), Kochanski (Annett) and computer Holly (Lovett). This final episode in the eighth season opens with a clip from a black and white mummy movie on TV. When Rimmer travels to a mirror universe, the clip has noticeably changed. The Grim Reaper turns up at the end.
✦✦✦

REDLINE
Canada/Holland, 1997. Dir: Tibor Takacs. With: Rutger Hauer, Mark Dacascos, Yvonne Scio, Patrick Dreikauss, Randall William Cook, Michael Mehlman. Mondofin/1204019 Ontario/Nu Image. Colour.
In a near-future Russia, American smuggler John Anderson Wade (Hauer) is betrayed and murdered by his partner Merrick (Dacascos). Surgically revived from the dead on the orders of special prosecutor Vanya (special effects designer Cook), Wade becomes involved with a mysterious woman (Scio) as he takes ruthless revenge on Merrick and the organised crime syndicate he works for. Despite the unusual eastern European locations, this is a typical Hauer programmer, with his character's resurrection from the dead soon forgotten in favour of numerous violent shoot-outs.
✦✧

RED LIPS
USA, 1995. Dir: Donald Farmer. With: Ghetty Chasun, Michelle Bauer (Michelle McClellan), Danny Fendley, Jasmine Pond, Mandy Leigh, Bill Randolph, Kitten (Francesca) Natividad. Colour.
Low-budget independent vampire movie filmed in Cookeville, Tennessee. Lisa's (Bauer) new body-pierced girlfriend turns out to be lesbian vampire Caroline (Chasun), created when she sold her blood to a clinic and became infected with a secret test virus. With George Stover as a guy in a bar and a cameo by the director.
Sequel: RED LIPS II (qv; 1996)
✦✧

RED LIPS II
(aka VIRGIN VAMPIRE)
USA, 1996. Dir: Donald Farmer. With: Debbie Rochon, J.J. North, Manon Kelley, George Stover. Colour.
Sequel to writer/director Farmer's 1995 original.
✦

REDNECK ZOMBIES
USA, 1987 (1989). Dir: Pericles Lewnes. With: Lisa M. DeHaven, William E. Benson, Bucky Santini, Tyrone Taylor, Frank Lantz, P. Floyd Piranha. Full Moon Pictures/ColorCast Productions/Troma. Colour.
Low-budget, shot-on-video comedy gore film about a group of campers who are attacked by tobacco chewin', gut chompin' cannibal kinfolk who have been transformed into zombies by a batch of moonshine contaminated with toxic waste. The only way to defeat these backwoods walking dead is by decapitation or deodorant. Filmed on location in Maryland, many of the credits appear to be pseudonymous. This includes a crazy person reading a copy of *Fangoria*. A 'director's cut' was released on video in 1996.
✦

RED SKELTON HOUR
USA, 1968. With: Red Skelton, Boris Karloff, Vincent Price. CBS-TV. Colour.
Hour-long musical comedy TV show starring comedian Skelton. In this episode, mad scientist Dr Nelson (Karloff) and his son (Price!) menace Clem Kadiddlehopper (Skelton). The two horror stars also sing a duet, 'The Two of Us'.
✦✦

OLIVER REED
[1938-1999]

British leading man, the nephew of director Sir Carol Reed (1906-76), who began his film career at Hammer playing handsome young rakes or twitchy psychopaths. Later cast as unruly rebels, he subsequently lived out his life as one. He died of a heart attack while drinking with friends in Malta. Despite notable appearances in such films as *The Devils* (1971) and *The Pit and the Pendulum* (1990), many of his later performances bordered on self-parody. His autobiography was entitled *Reed All About Me*.
qv: *Byron's Evil* (1972); *The Curse of the Werewolf* (1960); *Dr. Heckyll and Mr. Hype* (1980); *Lisztomania* (1975); *Mahler* (1974); *This is Your Life: 'Christopher Lee'* (1974); *Tommy* (1975); *The Two Faces of Dr. Jekyll* (1960); *The World of Hammer* (1990).

THE REFLECTING SKIN
UK/Canada, 1990. Dir: Philip Ridley. With: Viggo Mortensen, Lindsay Duncan, Jeremy Cooper, Shelia Moore, Duncan Fraser, David Longworth. National Film Trustee Company/Fugitive Features/British Screen/BBC Films/Zenith/Live Entertainment. Colour.
Atmospheric drama set in the early 1950s. Eight year-old Seth Dove (Cooper) thinks a mummified baby is an angel and sets out to kill reclusive young widow Dolphin Blue (Duncan) because he believes she's a 200 year-old vampire after the blood of his elder brother Cameron (Mortensen). A stylish and disturbing début by director Ridley, who scripted *Prick Up Your Ears* (1987) and *The Krays* (1990), etc.
✦✦✦

REFLECTIONS
USA, 1977. Dir: Michael Zen. With: Paul Thomas, Annette Haven, Kristine Heller, John Leslie. VCX Video. Colour.
Hardcore sex film, in which a woman (Haven) turns the tables on her childhood friends. The opening scene includes a vampire film at a drive-in.
✦

REGENERATION
Canada, 1988. Dir: Russel Stephens. With: John Anderson, Marek Cieszewski, Suzanne Ristic, Dermot Hennelly, Dennis Shooter, Michael Grandley. International Heliotrope/Howe/Trident Releasing. Colour.
A professor revives the dead in this low-budget thriller.
✦

EL REGRESO DEL MONSTRUO
(aka ZORRO ESCARLATA EN EL REGRESO DEL MONSTRUO)
Mexico, 1958 (1960). Dir: Joselito Rodriguez. With: Luis Aguilar, Teresita Velasquez, Jaime Fernández, Luis Manrique, Antonio Orellana, Fernando Osés. Filmadora Mexicana/Azteca. B&W.
Second in the series, and a sequel to *El Zorro Escarlata* (1958). Mad scientist Dr Kraken and a bizarre talking skeleton bring the bulbous-headed monster back to life in their laboratory and control it through an electronic ring. When masked hero 'El Zorro Escarlata', aka The Scarlet Fox (Aguilar), rescues a young child which the pon-

cho-wearing creature has kidnapped, the laboratory explodes into flames. As the monster collapses and dies, it returns to its human form when the ring is destroyed. The title translates as 'The Return of the Monster'.
Sequel: LA VENGANZA DEL AHORCADO (qv; 1958)
✦✧

FRANK REICHER
[1875-1965]

German-born character actor who emigrated to America in 1899 and enjoyed a long career in Hollywood, originally as a silents director and later as a dependable, often uncredited, supporting player. He will always be remembered as the stolid Captain Englehorn from *King Kong* (1933) and *The Son of Kong* (1933), and his last known credit was *Superman and the Mole Men* (1951).
qv: *The Case of Becky* (1915); *Charlie Chan in Egypt* (1935); *House of Frankenstein* (1944); *Life Returns* (1934); *The Mummy's Ghost* (1944); *The Mummy's Tomb* (1942).

THE REINCARNATION OF ISABEL
(Orig: RITI, MAGIE NERE E SEGRETE ORGE NEL TRECENTO... USA: aka THE GHASTLY ORGIES OF COUNT DRACULA)
Italy, 1973 (1976). Dir: Ralph Brown (Renato Polselli). With: Mickey Hargitay, Rita Calderoni, Raoul, Christa (Krista) Barrymore, Moschera Consolata, William Darni. GRP Cinematográfica/La Primula Cinematográfica. Colour.
Hargitay, a former Mr Universe and husband of Jayne Mansfield, stars in this witchcraft thriller which was thought lost for many years. American businessman Jack Nelson (Hargitay) and his stepdaughter Laureen (Calderoni) move into a cursed Italian castle. Meanwhile, a group of caped Satanists sacrifice young women in a subterranean dungeon and use their victims' blood in an attempt to revive 500 year-old vampire-witch Isabella Drupel (also Calderoni). In the end, Nelson turns out to be the reincarnation of Count Dracula himself, and plans to use his stepdaughter to resurrect his lover on the night of the twenty-fifth moon. Although this doesn't make a lot of sense, there's plenty of nudity and torture from the director of *The Vampire and the Ballerina* (1960) and *The Vampire of the Opera* (1964). The original title translates as 'Rites, Black Magic and Secret Orgies in the Fourteenth Century...'.
✦

THE REINCARNATION OF KARMA
USA, 1912. Vitagraph. B&W.
Thirty minute silent short in which a man transforms into a snake.
✦

THE REJUVENATOR
(aka REJUVENATRIX)
USA, 1988. Dir: Brian Thomas Jones. With: Vivian Lanko, John MacKay, James Hogue, Katell Pleven, Marcus Powell, Jessica Dublin. Jewel Productions/Sony Video. Colour.
Filmed in New York City in 1985, this is apparently a science fiction version of *Sunset Blvd.* (1950), with ageing movie star Elizabeth Warren (Lanko) using a serum distilled from brain matter to transform herself into a young seductress. However, as usual there's a side-effect, which results in her turning into a horrible monster (make-up by Ed French).
✦✧

THE REN & STIMPY SHOW:
Eat My Cookies/Ren's Bitter Half
USA, 1993 (1994). Dir: Ron Hughart and Michael Kim. Voices: Billy West. MTV Networks/Nickelodeon/Games Animations. Colour.
Offbeat half-hour cartoon TV series (1991-95) created by John Kricfalusi. In the second, nine minute segment, Stimpy the cat's experiment with genetic engineering splits his Chihuahua friend Ren into two opposite halves — his evil side and his indifferent side.
✦✦✧

RENDEZVOUS
USA, 1973. Dir: Cortlandt B. Hull. Troc Film Corporation. B&W.
Five minute underground short which uses a montage of clips from Universal's *Bride of Frankenstein* (1935), *Dr. Jekyll and Mr. Hyde* (1931), *Frankenstein* (1931), *House of Dracula* (1945), *House of Frankenstein* (1944), *Son of Frankenstein* (1939), *WereWolf of London* (1935) and *The Wolf Man* (1941) amongst others, set to the music of Frank Sinatra's 'Strangers in the Night'. The director, who is the great-nephew of actor Henry Hull, now runs a horror museum in Connecticut.
Sequel: REVENGE OF RENDEZVOUS (qv; 1975)
✦

REPLIGATOR
USA, 1995. Dir: Bret McCormick. With: Gunnar Hansen, Randy Clower, Keith Kjornes, T.J. Meyers, Brinke Stevens. Group II. Colour.
Independent video release shot in Arlington, Texas. Dr Kildare (Hansen) relates the story of two rival scientists (Clower and Kjornes) at a secret military research laboratory. This comedy includes sex changes, alligator headed people, ray guns, a gay zombie and a topless Stevens experimenting with a sexual thought transfer machine in a flashback sequence.
✦

THE REPTILE
UK, 1966. Dir: John Gilling. With: Noel Willman, Ray Barrett, Jennifer Daniel, Jacqueline Pearce, Michael Ripper, John Laurie. Hammer Films/Associated British-Pathe. Colour.
Plodding Hammer horror, scripted by John Elder (Anthony Hinds). Pearce plays Anna Franklin, a young woman cursed by an Eastern cult, the Ourang Sancto, who changes into a tatty snake monster (make-up created by Roy Ashton). She is finally destroyed in the inevitable fiery climax. Willman gives a solid performance as the enigmatic Dr Franklyn and Ripper gets one of his best roles as a superstitious local. However, Barrett makes a wooden hero, Laurie goes well over the top as Mad Peter and the nineteenth century Cornish setting just doesn't look convincing. Originally announced as *The Curse of the Reptiles* and made back-to-back with Gilling's *The Plague of the Zombies* (1966). With Charles Lloyd Pack and George Woodbridge. This was novelised by John Burke in 1967 as part of *The Second Hammer Horror Film Omnibus*, published by Pan Books, and adapted to comic strip format by writer Steve Moore and artist Brian Lewis for *House of Horror* no.19 (1978).
✦✦

REQUIEM FOR A VAMPIRE
(Orig: REQUIEM POUR UN VAMPIRE. USA: aka CAGED VIRGINS/CRAZED VAMPIRE/DUNGEON OF VIRGINS/ DUNGEONS OF TERROR/SCREAM OF THE CAGED VIRGINS/THE VIRGINS AND THE VAMPIRES)
France, 1971. Dir: Jean Rollin. With: Marie Pirre Castel, Mireille D'Argent, Philippe Gasté, Dominique, Louise Dhour, Paul Bisciglia. Les Films ABC/Boxoffice International. Colour.
The fourth in a series of sex/vampire films by Rollin, filmed under the title *Vierges et Vampires* ('Virgins and Vampires'). After fleeing from the police while dressed as clowns, Marie (Castel) and Michèle (D'Argent) seek shelter in an old castle. There the two young girls are trapped by a sadistic vampire woman (Dominique) belonging to a sect of the undead (led by Gasté) who have sex with their chained-up victims. This was originally rated 'X' in America.
✦✧

RESTLESS NATIVES
UK, 1985. Dir: Michael Hoffman. With: Vincent Friell, Joe Mullaney, Teri Lally, Ned Beatty, Bernard Hill, Robert Urquhart. Oxford Film Company/Thorn EMI Screen Entertainment. Colour.
A pair of Edinburgh teenagers, Will and Ronnie (Friell and Mullaney), ride around on a motorcycle committing a series of highway robberies dressed up as a clown and a wolfman. Armed with

sneezing powder, they hold up tourist coaches in the Scottish countryside and end up becoming folk heroes. In one scene, the police confront a young witness with mug shots of various movie werewolves. With cameo appearances by Bryan Forbes, Nanette Newman, Mel Smith and Ed Bishop. Music performed by Big Country.
✦✧

EL RETORNO DE LOS VAMPIROS
Spain, 1971. Dir: José Maria Zabalza. With: Simon Andreu, Marta Monterrey. Uranzu Films. Colour.
The title of this obscure Spanish film translates as 'The Return of the Vampires'.
✦

RETURN FROM DEATH
(Orig: RITORNO DALLA MORTE)
Italy, 1991 (1993). Dir: David Hills (Joe D'Amato/Aristide Massaccesi). With: Donal O'Brien, Cinthia (Cinzia) Monreale. Filmirage Productions/Eureka Film International. Colour.
Filmed under the title *Frankenstein 2000*. In a coma after suffering a violent assault and rape, Georgia (Monreale) uses her telekinetic powers to revive her murdered friend Ric (O'Brien) with an electric cable so that he can act as the instrument of her revenge.
✦✧

THE RETURN OF CHANDU
(aka CHANDU ON THE MAGIC ISLAND)
USA, 1934. Dir: Ray Taylor. With: Bela Lugosi, Maria Alba, Clara Kimball Young, Lucien Prival, Deane Benton, Phyllis Ludwig. Principal Pictures Corporation. B&W.
Creaky, poverty-row serial in twelve chapters, produced by Sol Lesser and based on the radio serial by Harry A. Earnshaw. A follow-up to *Chandu the Magician* (1932), which featured Lugosi as the villainous Roxor. This time he is mis-cast as Frank Chandler, known in the Orient as Chandu the Magician, who can become invisible and capture minds. He sets out to save the last Egyptian princess, Nadji (Alba), from being sacrificed by Lemurian high priest Vindhyan (Prival) and members of his ancient cat-worshipping sect of Ubasti. They are attempting to resurrect the embalmed body of their long-dead goddess, Ossana, and in one episode Princess Nadji is kidnapped in a mummy case from the Los Angeles Museum. With such episode titles as 'The Evil Eye', 'The Mysterious Island' and 'The Invisible Terror', plus a race of cannibalistic Cat People (including Iron Eyes Cody), this sounds much better than it really is. Filmed on some of the same sets as *King Kong* (1933) and *The Son of Kong* (1933), chapters 1-4 and 5-8 were released the same year as two condensed features with alternative footage. Scenes from this film were also later included in the 1943 compilation *Dr. Terror's House of Horrors*.
✦✧

THE RETURN OF COUNT YORGA
USA, 1971. Dir: Bob Kelljan (Robert Kelljchian). With: Robert Quarry, Mariette Hartley, Roger Perry, Yvonne Wilder, Edward Walsh, George Macready. Peppertree/ American International. Colour.
Improved sequel/remake of *Count Yorga, Vampire* (1970), co-written

Philippe Gasté as the undead sect leader in Requiem for a Vampire *(1971).*

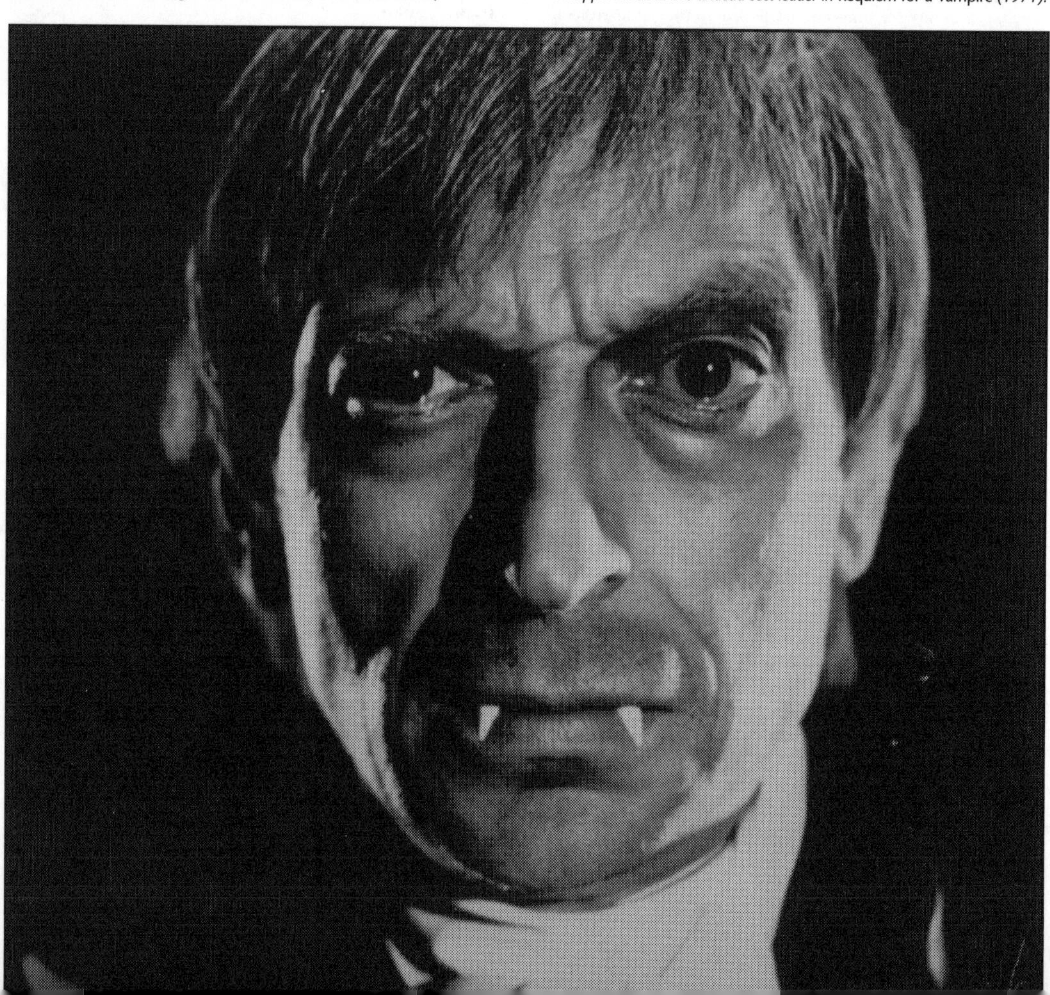

by star Wilder and director Kelljan and filmed under the title *The Abominable Count Yorga*. Quarry gives a splendidly aloof performance as the vampire (with no explanation of how he is revived) preying on an isolated Californian orphanage and falling in love with Cynthia Nelson (Hartley). The direction is more assured, the vampire attacks have greater impact and there's also some amusing comedy relief. Producer Michael Macready even found a cameo role for his veteran father, George (in his last film), as batty vampire hunter Professor Rightstat. This also includes a clip from *The Vampire Lovers* (1970). With Rudy De Luca, Craig Nelson and Mike (Michael) Pataki.
✦✦✦

THE RETURN OF DOCTOR X

USA, 1939. Dir: Vincent Sherman. With: Wayne Morris, Rosemary Lane, Humphrey Bogart, Dennis Morgan, John Litel, Huntz Hall. Warner Bros/First National. B&W.
This was Bogart's only horror film, and he reportedly hated it. Based on the story 'The Doctor's Secret' by William J. Makin, Bogart plays the marble-faced Marshall Quesne, returned to vampiric life with blood transfusions by Dr Francis Flegg (Litel). Although not a sequel to Warner Bros' *Doctor X* (1932), this marked the studio's return to horror after three years' absence and was originally set to star Boris Karloff (in the Bogart role) and Claude Rains. The interesting supporting cast includes Lya Lys as another reanimated corpse, Glenn Langan, William Hopper (husband of Hedda), Ian Wolfe and future Superman George Reeves.
✦✦✦

THE RETURN OF DRACULA

(aka THE CURSE OF DRACULA. UK: THE FANTASTIC DISAPPEARING MAN)
USA, 1957 (1958). Dir: Paul Landres. With: Francis Lederer, Norma Eberhardt, Ray Stricklyn, John Wengraf, Jimmie Baird, Norbert Schiller. Gramercy/United Artists. B&W.
Surprisingly effective low-budget independent Dracula movie, which was released just before Hammer's colour remake made the Count a major box office draw again, is actually an uncredited remake of Alfred Hitchcock's *Shadow of a Doubt* (1943). Lederer is a rather cold Count, forced out of his Transylvanian resting place, who moves in with an ordinary American family as artist 'Bellac Goudal' while preying on the inhabitants of a small California town. He is finally impaled on a wooden stake in an old mine shaft (red-tinted in some prints).
✦✦✧

THE RETURN OF DR. MABUSE

(Orig: IM STAHLNETZ DES DR. MABUSE/FBI CONTRO DOTTORE MABUSE/LE RETOUR DU DOCTEUR MABUSE. USA: aka PHANTOM FIEND)
West Germany/Italy/France, 1961. Dir: Harald Reinl. With: Gert Fröbe, Lex Barker, Daliah Lavi, Wolfgang Preiss (Lupo Prezzo), Joachim Mock, Rudolf Forster. CCC-Film/SPA Cinematográfica/Criterion/Ajay Films. B&W.
The first of five follow-ups to Fritz Lang's superior *The Thousand Eyes of Dr. Mabuse* (1960), once again featuring Preiss as the evil scientist (created by novelist Nobert Jacques), who this time plans to use a narcotic drug to create an army of scientific 'zombies' at a local prison. He is opposed by Inspector Lohmann (Fröbe), FBI agent Joe Como (Barker) and reporter Maria Sabrehm (Lavi), who also happens to be the daughter of the professor (Forster) who invented the drug.
Sequel: THE INVISIBLE DR. MABUSE (1962)
✦✦

THE RETURN OF MAURICE DONNELLY

USA, 1915. Dir: William Humphrey. With: Leo Delaney, Leah Baird, Anders Randolph, Mary Maurice, Denton Vane, Garry McGarry. Broadway Star/Vitagraph. B&W.
When Delaney is electrocuted for a crime he didn't commit, he is restored to life by a machine invented by a physician (Randolph) and tracks down the real culprits. This thirty-five minute silent short was used as a propaganda film by groups advocating the abolition of capital punishment.
✦

RETURN OF THE DEMON

Hong Kong, 1985. Dir: Wong Ching (Wong Ching-Jing/ Lau Sze-Yu). With: Shing Fui-On, Dick Wei. Colour.
Horror comedy in which a slow-witted man is tricked into releasing a monster trapped inside a statue of Buddha. He is soon involved with zombies with spikes in their heads, amorous ghosts and a priest who can transform into a dog.
✦✧

RETURN OF THE EVIL DEAD

(Orig: EL ATAQUE DE LOS MUERTOS SIN OJOS. USA: aka ATTACK OF THE BLIND DEAD/RETURN OF THE BLIND DEAD)
Spain, 1973. Dir: Amando de Ossorio. With: Tony Kendall (Luciano Stella), Fernando Sancho, Esther Ray (Esperanza Roy), Frank Blake (Frank Braña), Loretta Tovar, Lone Fleming. Profilm/Ancla Century Films/Atlas International. Colour.
The first of three sequels to *Tombs of the Blind Dead* (1971). During the annual celebration of the massacre of the Knights Templar (led by Luís Barboo), the blind mummified zombies attack a village, seeking the blood of their victims by sound. A group of fairly unpleasant people take refuge in a church. The slow-motion shots of the Templars on horseback (often taken from the first film) are still quite eerie. As with the original, director de Ossorio was also in charge of the special make-up effects.
Sequel: HORROR OF THE ZOMBIES (qv; 1974)
✦✦

THE RETURN OF THE LIVING DEAD

USA, 1984 (1985). Dir: Dan O'Bannon. With: Clu Gulager, James Karen, Don Calfa, Thom Mathews, Beverly Randolph, John Philbin. Fox Films/Cinema '84/Hemdale. Colour.
Originally to be helmed in 3-D by Tobe Hooper, screenwriter O'Bannon (*Alien* [1979], etc) made his directing début with this gruesome black comedy, based on a story by Rudy Ricci, John Russo and Russell W. Streiner. The film picks up from Russo and Romero's *Night of the Living Dead* (1968) as the zombies that inspired those events are released from army canisters and the local graveyard in Louisville, Kentucky, is soon spitting up rotting corpses screaming 'More brains!' A group of teen punks (including a memorable Linnea Quigley as Trash), a mortician and a group of medical supply workers find themselves under siege by the living dead. Thanks to the offbeat humour and excellent special effects, this is firmly in the EC comics tradition. With the director in a cameo as a police officer who has his brains eaten. John Russo's novelisation is a different book from his unauthorised 1978 sequel of the same title.
Sequel: RETURN OF THE LIVING DEAD PART II (qv; 1987)
✦✦✦

RETURN OF THE LIVING DEAD III

USA/Japan, 1993. Dir: Brian Yuzna. With: Mindy Clarke, J. Trevor Edmond, Kent McCord, Sarah Douglas, James T. Callahan, Basil Wallace. Trimark Pictures/Bandai Visual Co./Ozla Pictures. Colour.
This third entry in the alternative zombie series, from the producer/director of *Bride of Re-Animator* (1989), is serious. When his punk girlfriend Julie Walker (Clarke) is killed in a motorcycle accident, teenager Curt Reynolds (Edmond) sneaks her body into a top-secret military laboratory, where his father (McCord) is supervising a secret programme for raising the dead as bio-mechanical soldiers (special effects make-up by Steve Johnson and others). The only problem is that when she is revived by the Trioxin gas, Julie starts piercing her body like a character from *Hellraiser* (1987) and has a craving for human brains. With Tony (Anthony) Hickox as a zombie doctor.
✦✧

RETURN OF THE LIVING DEAD PART II

USA, 1987 (1988). Dir: Ken Wiederhorn. With: James Karen, Thom Mathews, Dana Ashbrook, Marsha Dietlein, Philip Bruns, Michael Kenworthy. Lorimar/Greenfox. Colour.
Unnecessary sequel/remake to *The Return of the Living Dead* (1984)

which ignores the nuclear climax of that film and has a spilled canister of army gas once again reviving the dead, who lay siege to another town. Only know-it-all twelve year-old Jesse Wilson (Kenworthy) realises what is happening. Karen and Mathews, who were turned into reluctant zombies in the previous film, suffer a similar fate as a pair of comical grave robbers here. Despite the glossy production values, this is neither as classy nor as clever as its predecessor. With Mitch Pileggi, and Forrest J Ackerman as one of the walking dead. From the director of *Shock Waves* (1976).
Sequel: RETURN OF THE LIVING DEAD III (qv; 1993)
✦✧

THE RETURN OF THE PINK PANTHER

UK, 1975. Dir: Blake Edwards. With: Peter Sellers, Christopher Plummer, Catherine Schell, Herbert Lom, Burt Kwouk, Peter Arne. ITC Jewel Productions/Pimlico Films/United Artists. Colour.

The fourth *Pink Panther* film and the third to star Sellers as the bumbling Inspector Clouseau. Not the best in the series, with the plot's elaborate jewel heist lost beneath the slapstick comedy, but the cartoon title sequence (animated by the Richard Williams Studio) includes the Pink Panther imitating the Frankenstein Monster.
Sequel: THE PINK PANTHER STRIKES AGAIN (qv; 1976)
✦✦

THE RETURN OF THE VAMPIRE

USA, 1943. Dir: Lew Landers (Lewis Friedlander). With: Bela Lugosi, Frieda Inescort, Nina Foch, Miles Mander, Matt Willis, Roland Varno. Columbia. B&W.

Filmed under the title *Vampires of London*. Because Universal owned the rights to the Dracula name, Lugosi plays a vampire called Armand Tesla, freed from his stake and tomb during the Nazi blitz of England. Aided by his tatty werewolf assistant, Andreas Obry (Willis), he arrives at the home of Lady Jane Ainsley (Inescort). Lugosi (who was only paid $3,500) brings some dignity to his role, and director Landers piles on the atmosphere with a fog-wreathed graveyard. The werewolf talks and wears a suit, but there's more intentional comedy relief from Billy Bevan. The sequence of Tesla's face melting when exposed to the sunlight was originally cut by the British censor. A proposed sequel, *Bride of the Vampire*, was reworked into *Cry of the Werewolf* (1944). Make-up man Clay Campbell recreated his werewolf design for Matt Willis thirteen years later on Steven Ritch in *The Werewolf* (1956).
✦✦✧

A RETURN TO SALEM'S LOT

USA, 1987. Dir: Larry Cohen. With: Michael Moriarty, Samuel Fuller, Andrew Duggan, Ricky Addison Reed, June Havoc, Evelyn Keyes. Larco Productions/Warner Bros. Colour.

A sequel in name only from co-writer/director Cohen, who had scripted an early version of the 1979 TV mini-series based on Stephen King's novel. After a ludicrous native sacrifice (which looks as if it was filmed in the director's back-yard), anthropologist Joe Weber (Moriarty) and his dysfunctional young son Jeremy (Reed) move to the town of Salem's Lot where head vampire Judge Axel (Duggan) tries to convince them to stay and chronicle the history of the ancient community. However, the intervention of testy Nazi hunter Van Meer (a great performance by veteran director Fuller) convinces them to destroy the undead townsfolk. One of Cohen's most technically inept films, this appears to have been cobbled together from outtakes.
✦

REUNION OF BLOOD

USA, 1999. With: Lila Gagnon. Amalga Films/Black Magic Productions. Colour.

Independent video release in which a military engineer (Gagnon), on her way to an annual high school reunion, discovers that her friends are being transformed into vampires by her ex-boyfriend, an undead anthropologist who studied Vlad the Impaler.
✦

REVENGE IN THE HOUSE OF USHER

(Orig: LOS CRIMINES DE USHER/EL HUNDIMIENTO DE LA

Matt Willis takes orders from Bela Lugosi in The Return of the Vampire *(1943).*

CASA USHER/NÉVROSE. USA: aka THE FALL OF THE HOUSE OF USHER/REVOLT OF THE HOUSE OF USHER/ ZOMBIE 5)
Spain/France, 1983. Dir: J.P. Johnson (Jesús Franco). With: Howard Vernon (Mario Lippert), Lina Romay (Rosa Maria Almirall), Robert Foster (Antonio Mayans), Fata Morgana, Pablo Villa (Daniel J. [Jerome] White). Elite-Film/ Eurociné. Colour.
Loosely inspired by Edgar Allan Poe's story, this mess stars Vernon as the 200 year-old Dr Eric Usher, living out his last days in a secluded cliff-top mansion as his mind slowly descends into madness. A visitor, Dr Alan Harker (Foster), discovers that Usher and his disfigured brother (Olivier Mathot) have murdered a number of women for their blood, including Usher's three wives, and one of his victims now haunts the house as a vampire. This includes black and white clips from Franco's *The Awful Dr. Orlof* (1961) as flashbacks! A hardcore version also reputedly exists.
✦

THE REVENGE OF FRANKENSTEIN
UK, 1958. Dir: Terence Fisher. With: Peter Cushing, Eunice Gayson, Francis Matthews, Michael Gwynn, Lionel Jeffries, John Welsh. Hammer Films/Columbia. Colour.
Good-looking sequel to *The Curse of Frankenstein* (1957), again scripted by Jimmy Sangster (with help from Hurford Janes and an uncredited George Baxt). When a pair of comic grave robbers (Jeffries and Michael Ripper) make the mistake of plundering the 'grave' of Baron Frankenstein (Cushing), he escapes to begin his experiments in another town under the name Victor Stein. With the help of the idealistic Dr Kleve (Matthews), he transplants a dwarf's brain into the body of Karl (Gwynn), who gradually becomes a twisted, murderous cannibal. In the end, the Baron's own brain turns up in a new body. Originally announced as *The Blood of Frankenstein*. With Richard Wordsworth, Charles Lloyd Pack and George Woodbridge. The original trailer features Cushing talking to the audience in character. The film was novelised in 1958 by Sangster and again in 1966 by John Burke as part of *The Hammer Horror Omnibus*.
Sequel: THE EVIL OF FRANKENSTEIN (qv; 1964)
✦✦✦✧

REVENGE OF NINJA
Indonesia, 1987. Dir: Ratno Timoer. With: Barry Prima, Dana Christina, Advent Bangun, W.D. Mochtar. Mount Light/Rapi Films. Colour.
When a magician replaces a zombie's heart, the creature revives an army of the walking dead.
✦

REVENGE OF RENDEZVOUS
USA, 1975. Dir: Cortlandt B. Hull. Troc Film Corporation. B&W.
Five minute underground short which uses a montage of clips, including *Bride of Frankenstein* (1935), *Dr. Jekyll and Mr. Hyde* (1932), *House of Dracula* (1945), *House of Frankenstein* (1944), *Son of Frankenstein* (1939) and *Young Frankenstein* (1974), set to the music of Frank Sinatra's 'Watch What Happens'. A follow-up to the same director's *Rendezvous* (1973).
✦

REVENGE OF THE CREATURE
USA, 1955. Dir: Jack Arnold. With: John Agar, Lori Nelson, John Bromfield, Nestor Paiva, Robert B. Williams, Grandon Rhodes. Universal-International. B&W.
This sequel to *Creature from the Black Lagoon* (1954), once again filmed in 3-D, is almost as good as the original. Director Arnold expertly recaptures the brooding menace of the first film in the opening Amazon sequences, and manages to sustain the tension when the Gill Man (played by Ricou Browning and Tom Hennesy) is captured by Clete Ferguson (Agar) and Joe Hayes (Bromfield) and transported to their Florida oceanarium. There the Creature is tortured by the scientists with electric cattle-prods until he is finally shot and staggers into the sea. Clint Eastwood made his movie début as a technician with a mouse in his pocket. A juvenile novelisation by Carl R. Green and William R. Sanford (William Reynolds) was published by Crestwood House in 1985.
Sequel: THE CREATURE WALKS AMONG US (qv; 1955)
✦✦✦✧

REVENGE OF THE DEAD
(Orig: ZEDER. USA: aka VOICE FROM THE DARKNESS) Italy, 1982 (1984). Dir: Pupi Avati. With: John Stacy, Ann Canovas, Gabriel Lavia, Paola Tanziani, Cesare Barbetti, Bob Tonelli. Motion Picture Marketing. Colour.
When the wife (Canovas) of a young novelist (Lavia) is killed, he buries her body in a mysterious 'K Zone', where the dead are said to rise up and walk. However, she returns from the grave as something unholy.
✦✧

THE REVENGE OF THE LIVING DEAD
(Orig: LA REVANCHE DES MORTES-VIVANTES) France, 1985 (1986). Dir: Peter B. Harsone (Pierre B. Reinhard). With: Veronik Catanzaro (Veronique Catanzaro), Sylvie Novak, Kathryn Charly (Catherine Gourladuen), Anthea Wyler, Laurence Mercier (Henry Jacques Huet), Patrick Guillemin. Tanagra-Samurai Roitfeld. Colour.
Supposedly based on a story by Edgar Wallace (it's not). Toxic waste in milk apparently creates murderous zombies, but it all turns out to be a masquerade at the end.
✦✧

REVENGE OF THE LIVING ZOMBIES
(aka FLESH EATER. UK: ZOMBIE NOSH) USA, 1989. Dir: Bill Hinzman. With: Bill Hinzman, John Mowood, Leslie Ann Wick, Kevin Kindlin, James J. Rutan, Denise Morrone. H&G Films/Hinzman/Magnum Entertainment. Colour.
A farmer uncovers the grave of a Satanic cult in the woods, and he inadvertently releases a cannibal zombie (Hinzman, the graveyard ghoul in George Romero's *Night of the Living Dead* [1968]) that begins attacking a group of teenagers on a Halloween hay ride. As each new victim returns as a flesh-eating corpse, the teens take refuge in an isolated farm house. However, the film quickly runs out of plot, and through a series of disconnected sequences consists of repetitive zombie attacks (including one party victim [Andrew Sands] dressed as a vampire) until the walking dead are hunted down and shot in the head by the locals. Filmed on a low budget in Pittsburgh, this features unconvincing gore effects and some unnecessary nudity, while producer/director/co-writer/co-editor Hinzman blatantly rips off the ending of Romero's original.
✦✧

REVENGE OF THE RADIOACTIVE REPORTER
Canada, 1989 (1990). Dir: Craig Pryce. With: David Scammell, Kathryn Boese, Derrick Strange, Randy Pearlstein, Angelo Celeste, Michael Lubovic. Pryceless Productions/Goldfab Distribution. Colour.
Investigative journalist Mike R. Wave (Scammell) is pushed into a vat of toxic waste and emerges with decomposing features and a lethal touch in this silly comedy. With the director as a power plant guard, and a character (Ron Becker) dressed as an upside-down vampire at a costume party.
✦

REVENGE OF THE ZOMBIES
(UK: THE CORPSE VANISHED) USA, 1943. Dir: Steve Sekely (Istvan Szekely). With: John Carradine, Gale Storm, Robert Lowery, Bob Steele, Mantan Moreland, Veda Ann Borg. Monogram Pictures. B&W.
Set in the Louisiana bayous, where suave Nazi scientist Dr Max Heinrich von Altermann (Carradine) turns his wife Lila (Borg) into a zombie. When her brother Larry Adams (Lowery), Mauritz Hugo (Scott Warrington) and servant Jeff (Moreland) investigate, she leads the living dead to their revenge in the swamp. Director Sekely makes this as atmospheric as he can on a low budget, and although Carradine gives it his best and Borg makes a haunting zombie, the

rest of the cast just walk through their roles. Moreland's tired comedy relief is merely irritating here.
✦✧

REVENGE OF THE ZOMBIES
(Orig: KOU-HUN CHIANG T'OU/BLACK MAGIC PART II. USA: aka BLACK MAGIC 2)
Hong Kong/Thailand/Singapore, 1976 (1981). Dir: Horace Menga (Ho Meng-Hua/Peter Mak/Mak Yai-Kit). With: Ti Lung, Lo Lieh (Law Lit), Liu Hui-Ju (Linda Chu), Lily Li, Liu Wei-Tu (Liu Hui-Tu), Yang Chih-Ching. The Shaw Brothers/World Northal. Colour.
A sequel in name only to the 1975 *Black Magic*, this muddled horror film involves ancient sorcerer Kang Chang (Lieh), who stays young by drinking human milk every day and controls his zombie slaves through metal spikes in their heads. The make-up effects don't look that good, but there's always the kung fu, a fake-looking alligator, magic amulets and the terrible dubbing to keep you fascinated. From the director of *Mighty Peking Man* (1977).
✦

REVOLT OF THE ZOMBIES
(aka REVOLT OF THE DEMONS)
USA, 1936. Dir: Victor Halperin. With: Dorothy Stone, Dean Jagger, Roy D'Arcy, Robert Noland, George Cleveland, E. Alyn (Fred) Warren. Halperin/Academy Pictures Distributing Corporation/Favorite Films Corp. B&W.
Billed as the 'Weirdest Love Story in 2000 years'. After their success with *White Zombie* (1932), director Victor Halperin and his producer brother Edward returned to the theme with this creaky low-budget melodrama. Following the creation of a regiment of invulnerable French Cambodian soldiers on the Franco-Austrian front during the First World War, a military archaeological expedition is dispatched to the 'lost city' of Angkor to destroy the secret of turning living men into zombies. But Armand Louque (Jagger) is driven mad by his obsession with Claire Duval (Stone), the fiancée who rejected him, and he uses the process to establish an army of slaves controlled by his will. Release was delayed when Amusement Securities Corporation, the distributor of *White Zombie*, attempted to sue for $60,000, complaining that a second zombie film was unfair competition! This also includes actors in front of rear-projected photographs and close-up shots of Bela Lugosi's eyes from the earlier film.
✦

SIR RALPH RICHARDSON
[1902-1983]

Dignified British stage actor, also known for his range of eccentric characters on film, including the EC comics Crypt Keeper in *Tales from the Crypt* (1972) and the blind hermit in TV's *Frankenstein: The True Story* (1973).
qv: *The Ghoul* (1933); *O Lucky Man!* (1973).

RIDERS OF THE SKULLS
(Orig: EL CHARRO DE LAS CALAVERAS)
Mexico, 1965 (1966). Dir: Alfredo Salazar. With: Dagoberto Rodriguez, David Silva, Alicia Caro, Pascual Garcia Peña, Laura Martinez, Rosario Montez. Barragan Producciones/Azteca/Columbia. B&W.
Over three episodes, the masked, sombrero-wearing cowboy hero (Rodriguez) battles an ugly, hairy werewolf (Silva) and a cackling old witch ('La Hobo Humano'); a rubber bat that transforms into a caped, hairy-faced vampire with big ears who can vanish at will with his undead female assistant ('El Vampiro Humano'); and a headless sword-fighting horseman, who sets out to reclaim his severed rubber head in a box with the help of two skull-faced slaves ('El Jinete Sin Cabeza'). Incredible!
✦✧

Tom Hennesy tests his chains as he prepares for the Revenge of the Creature *(1955).*

THE RIDERS OF THE WHISTLING SKULL
USA, 1937. Dir: Mack V. Wright. With: The Three Mesquiteers (Bob Livingston, Ray ['Crash'] Corrigan, Max Terhune), Mary Russell, Yakima Canutt, Roger Williams. Republic Pictures. B&W.
Fourth in the light-hearted Western series, and loosely based on the books *Riders of the Whistling Skull* and *The Singing Scorpion* by William Colt MacDonald. Cowboy heroes The Three Mesquiteers — Stoney (Livingston), Tucson (Corrigan) and comic relief Lullaby (Terhune) with his ventriloquist dummy Elmer — help an archaeological expedition investigate a mysterious lost cult of Native Americans who conduct sacrificial rituals in a valley at the base of a gigantic skull-shaped rock formation. A mummy in the skull cave apparently comes to life and speaks. However, it turns out to be a live Indian and another case of ventriloquism. With Native American actors Iron Eyes Cody and Chief Thunder Cloud. This was later remade as a Charlie Chan mystery featuring Livingston as the villain!
Remake: THE FEATHERED SERPENT (1948)
✦✦

MICHAEL RIPPER
[b 1913]

Dependable British character actor, in films since the mid-1930s and a staple of Hammer Films for more than a decade, playing body-snatchers, innkeepers and policemen. One of his most significant roles is as a superstitious local in *The Reptile* (1966).
qv: *The Brides of Dracula* (1960); *The Curse of the Mummy's Tomb* (1964); *The Curse of the Werewolf* (1960); *Dracula Has Risen from the Grave* (1968); *Fog for a Killer* (1962); *Hammer A-Z* (1997); *In Search of Dracula With Jonathan Ross* (1996); *Legend of the Werewolf* (1974); *The Mummy* (1959); *The Mummy's Shroud* (1967); *The Phantom of the Opera* (1962); *The Plague of the Zombies* (1966); *The Revenge of Frankenstein* (1958); *Scars of Dracula* (1970); *Taste the Blood of Dracula* (1969); *Torture Garden* (1967); *The Ugly Duckling* (1959).

RIPTIDE:
Curse of the Mary Aberdeen
USA, 1985. Dir: Ron Satlof. With: Perry King, Joe Penny, Thom Bray, Ken Olandt, Jack Ging, Richard Lynch. Stephen J. Cannell Productions/Twentieth Century Fox/NBC-TV. Colour.
Light-hearted hour-long adventure TV series (1984-86, fifty-five episodes), created by executive producers Stephen J. Cannell and Frank Lupo. In this episode, the members of the Riptide Detective Agency, ex-army buddies Cody Allen (King) and Nick Ryder (Penny), along with electronics expert Murray 'Boz' Bozinsky (Bray) and his robot Roboz, are employed by the apparent ghost of magician Martin Stonewall (Lynch) to find a supposedly haunted boat and a map that leads to the location of Harry Houdini's diary. This includes the climax from *The Wolf Man* (1941) on TV, and the theme music from *The Twilight Zone* (1959-64).
✦✦

IL RISVEGLIO DI DRACULA
Italy, circa 1960s. Dir: U. Paolessi. With: Gabby Paul, Gill Chadwich.
The title of this obscure Italian film translates as 'The Revival of Dracula'.
✦

RIVALS:
Frankenstein vs Dracula
USA, 1995. With: Gerald McRaney, Sara Karloff. Hearst Entertainment Television/Discovery Channel/Jaffe Productions. Colour.
Hour-long documentary hosted by actor McRaney, which compares the two very different careers of Boris Karloff and Bela Lugosi. With many rare photographs, clips and trailers from *Bela Lugosi Meets a Brooklyn Gorilla* (1952), *Black Friday* (1941), *The Body Snatcher* (1945), *Dracula* (1931), *Frankenstein* (1931), *Frankenstein Meets the Wolf Man* (1942), *Glen or Glenda* (1953), *The Invisible Ray* (1936), (Abbott and Costello) *Meet Frankenstein* (1948), *The Mummy* (1933), *Nosferatu*

(1922), *Son of Frankenstein* (1939) and *The Terror* (1963), plus TV's *This is Your Life* and newsreel footage. Other interviewees include authors Gary Don Rhodes and Gregory Mank, and Lugosi's friend Richard Sheffield.
✦✦✧

ROAD ROVERS: A Hair of the Dog That Bit You

USA, 1996. Voices: Jess Harnell, Tress MacNeille, Frank Welker, Joseph Campanella, Jim Cummings, Sheena Easton. Warner Bros/The WB Network. Colour.
Werewolf episode of the half-hour cartoon series (1996-97, thirteen episodes) about a group of six crime-fighting canines owned by the world's leaders.
✦✧

THE ROAD TO DRACULA

USA, 1999. Dir: David J. Skal. With: Bela Lugosi Jr, David J. Skal, Nina Auerbach, Clive Barker, Gary Don Rhodes, Scott MacQueen. Universal Studios Home Video. Colour/B&W.
Forty-five minute documentary, written by Skal and released as a supplement to the DVD of *Dracula* (1931). This includes numerous clips, plus interviews with *Dracula* archivist/curator Michael Barsanti and original stage company member Ivan Butler. Hosted and narrated by Carl Laemmle's niece Carla (Rebecca Beth Laemmle), the actress who spoke the first lines of dialogue in the 1931 movie.
✦✦✦✧

ROBERT MONTGOMERY PRESENTS: The Hunchback of Notre Dame

USA, 1954. With: Robert Ellenstein, Hurd Hatfield, Celia Lipton, Bramwell Fletcher, Frederic Worlock, Mary Sinclair. B&W.
Two-part TV adaptation of Victor Hugo's novel, with Ellenstein as Quasimodo.
Remake: BADSHAH (qv; 1954)
✦

GERMÁN ROBLES
[b 1929]

Spanish-born actor who moved to Mexico in 1946, where he later became the Mexican answer to Christopher Lee. Among nearly one hundred film appearances, Robles played the undead Count Karol de Lavud in *The Vampire* (1957) and *The Vampire's Coffin* (1957), and starred as a vampiric Nostradamus in a series of four films before eventually becoming a stage actor.
qv: *The Blood of Nostradamus* (1960); *Castle of the Monsters* (1957); *The Curse of Nostradamus* (1960); *The Genii of Darkness* (1960); *The Living Head* (1959); *The Monsters Demolisher* (1960); *El Vampiro Aechecha* (1962); *Los Vampiros de Coyoacan* (1973).

EL ROBO DE LAS MOMIAS DE GUANAJUATO

Mexico, 1972. Dir: Tito Novaro. With: Mil Máscaras (Aaron Rodriguez), Blue Angel, Mabel Luna, Tito Novaro, El Niño Júlio César, El Rayo de Jalisco. Producciones Filmicas Agrasanchez/Tikai Internacional de Guatemala/Clasa-Mohme. Colour.
In this sequel to *Las Momias de Guanajuato* (1970), a number of wrestling heroes, including Mil Máscaras ('Thousand Masks') and Blue Angel, battle the evil Count Cagliostro (director Novaro) who, together with a mad scientist, has electronically resurrected the zombie-like mummies of Guanajuato in his attempt to rule the world.
Sequels: EL CASTILLO DE LAS MOMIAS DE GUANAJUATO (qv; 1972) and VUELVEN LOS CAMPEONES JUSTICIEROS (1972)

John Carradine is about to experience Revenge of the Zombies *(1943).*

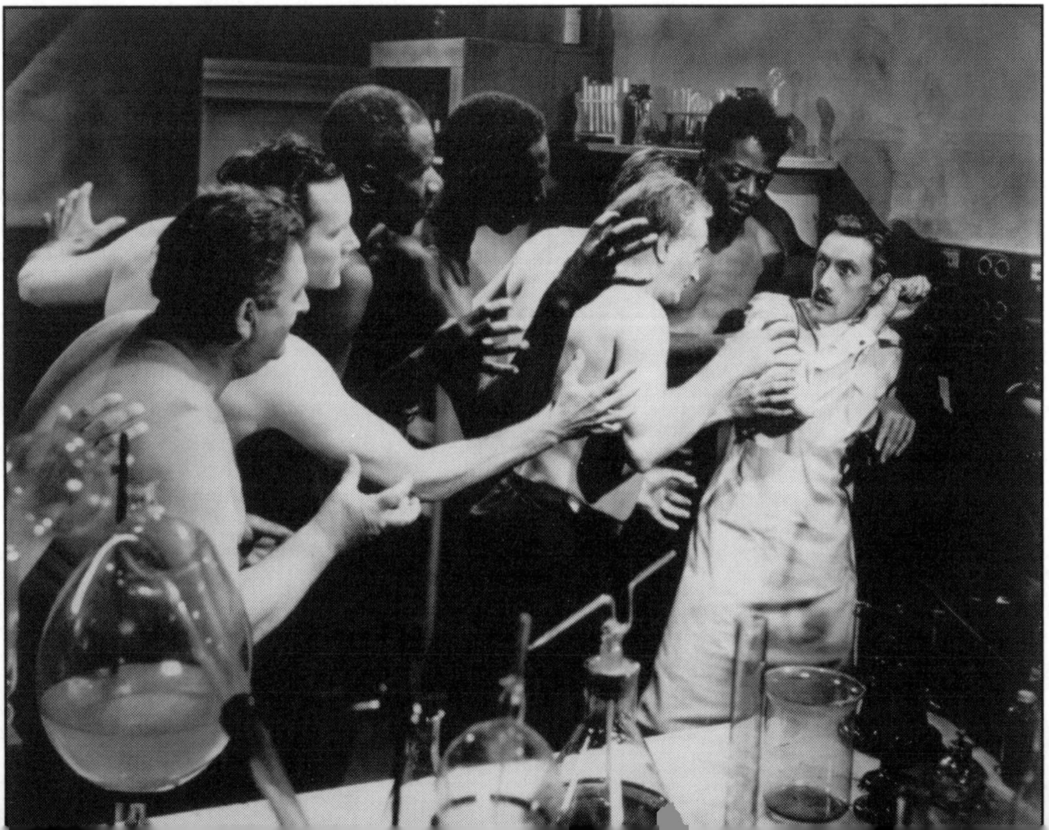

THE ROBOT VS THE AZTEC MUMMY

(Orig: LA MOMIA AZTECA CONTRA EL ROBOT HUMANO) Mexico, 1957 (1964). Dir: Rafael (López) Portillo. With: Ramón Gay, Rosita Arenas, Crox Alvarado, Luis Aceves Castañeda, Jorge Mondragón, Arturo Martinez. Cinematica Calderón/Azteca Films/Young America Productions/K. Gordon Murray Productions. B&W.

The third in Portillo's Aztec Mummy series, again scripted by Alfredo Salazar. After using a hypnotised Flora (Arenas) to discover the whereabouts of the ugly zombie/mummy Popoca, mad scientist Dr Krupp/The Bat (Castañeda) creates a silly-looking robot with a human brain to recover the breastplate and bracelet which will reveal the location of the hidden treasure from the cursed tomb of Xochitl. This includes lengthy flashbacks from the first two films plus Mexican wrestlers 'Lobo Negro' (Guillermo Hernández) and 'Murciélago Velazquez' (Jesús Velazquez). The English language version, released in 'Hypnoscope', was produced by K. (Kenneth) Gordon Murray and directed by Paul Nagel (but is credited to Manuel San Fernando). Star Gay was shot to death in 1960 by a jealous husband.

Sequel: THE WRESTLING WOMEN VS THE AZTEC MUMMY (qv; 1964)

✦✧

ROBO VAMPIRE

Hong Kong, 1988. Dir: Joe Livingstone. With: Robin Mackay, Nian Watts, Harry Myles, Joe Browne, Nick Norman, George Tripos. Dallie Yeung/Filmark International/Magnum Video. Colour.

Hopping vampires are used to battle a flying android in this action movie that also includes a female ghost.

✦✧

MARK ROBSON [1913-1978]

American director and editor. After working (uncredited) with Orson Welles on *Citizen Kane* (1941), he found himself exiled by RKO to Val Lewton's 'B' movie unit, where he cut *Cat People* (1942), *I Walked With a Zombie* (1943) and *The Leopard Man* (1943) before being promoted to director for such grim thrillers as *The Seventh Victim* (1943), *The Ghost Ship* (1943), *Isle of the Dead* (1945) and *Bedlam* (1946). He later directed Hollywood mainstream features like *Peyton Place* (1957), *Valley of the Dolls* (1967) and *Earthquake* (1974).

ROCKABILLY VAMPIRE

(Orig: BURNIN' LOVE) USA, 1996 (1997). Dir: Lee Bennett Sobel. With: Margaret Lancaster, Paul Stevenson, Stephen Blackehart. Garage Rock Pictures/Troma. Colour.

Independent comedy from writer/director Sobel in which tortured 1950s vampire Eddie Vincent (Stevenson) meets Elvis fan Iris (Lancaster) in contemporary New York and they fall in love.

✦

THE ROCKFORD FILES: Never Send a Boy King to do a Man's Job

(aka The Return of Richie Brockelman) USA, 1979. Dir: William Wiard. With: James Garner, Noah Beery (Jr), Joe Santos, Robert Webber, Trisha Noble, Stuart Margolin. Universal/Roy Huggins-Public Arts/ Cherokee Productions/NBC-TV. Colour.

One of three original TV movies in the popular detective series (1974-80, 120 episodes) created by Roy Huggins and Stephen J. Cannell. Ex-con turned Los Angeles private detective Jim Rockford (Garner) teams up with fellow investigator Richie Brockelman (Dennis Dugan, whose own show had been cancelled) to avenge the cheating of Brockelman's father (Harold Gould) by ruthless sports promoter Harold Jack Coombs (Webber). Rockford sets up a complicated scam involving a King Tut exhibit and a curse that will fall upon anyone involved in the enterprise. The ancient Egyptian props were apparently left over from Universal's Mummy series. With Kim Hunter.

Series sequel: THE ROCKFORD FILES: I STILL LOVE L.A. (1994)

✦✦✦✧

ROCK N' ROLL FRANKENSTEIN

USA, 1999. Dir: Brian O'Hara. With: Barry Feterman, Jayson Spence, Hiram Jacob Segarra, Craig Guggenheim. R&R Productions. Colour.

Independent sex comedy shot on Super-16mm and blown up to 35mm. New York music producer Bernie (Feterman) uses his nephews' regeneration process on body parts taken from the corpses of rock 'n' roll legends to create the ultimate rock star, King (Guggenheim).

✦

ROCK 'N' ROLL VAMPIRE SEX

USA, 1997. Dir: Geoffrey de Valois. With: Tonya Qualls, Elaine Juliette Williamson, Julie Covarrubias, Kathy Presgrave, Eugenie Bondurant, Marie Brent. Digital Entertainment Group/Salt City Home Video. Colour.

One of a series of softcore *Vampire Raw Footage* videos that includes behind-the-scenes nude and erotic sequences. This features clips from vampire music videos (probably from *The Vampire Conspiracy* [1995]), with nude bathroom scenes and rare bondage footage.

✦

ROCKO'S MODERN LIFE: (aka ROCKO'S LIFE) Popcorn Pandemonium

USA, 1995. Dir: Joe Murray. Voices: Carlos Alazraqui, Tom Kenny, Doug Lawrence, Charlie Adler, Linda Wallem. Nickelodeon Productions/Games Animation. Colour.

Half-hour cartoon TV series (1993-95, thirty-nine episodes) created by Joe Murray, about Australian wallaby Rocko (Alazraqui), his friends Heffer the cow (Kenny) and Filbert the turtle (Lawrence), and his dog Spunky. In this episode Rocko and Hefer go to the movies and watch a trailer for a Dracula movie. However, when the two heroes on screen open the Count's coffin, they discover that he is already dead and decide to go and do something else.

✦✦

ROCKULA

USA, 1990. Dir: Luca Bercovici. With: Dean Cameron, Tawny Feré, Susan Tyrrell, Bo Diddley, Thomas Dolby, Toni Basil. Cannon Pictures. Colour.

Would you believe a vampire musical from the director of *Ghoulies* (1984)? Actually, it's not as bad as it sounds, thanks to stylish production values and likeable performances. 400 year-old teen vampire Ralph (Cameron) is cursed to fall in love with the reincarnation of the same girl, Mona (Feré), every twenty-two years. He must save her before she is killed by a pirate with a peg-leg wielding a gigantic ham-bone! The musical numbers may be uneven, but you can't help liking a film that includes a vampire who argues with his wise-cracking mirror(!) image and ends with an Elvis impersonation. With Tamara DeTreaux as Bat Dork and the director as the pirate chieftain.

✦✦✧

THE ROCKY HORROR PICTURE SHOW

UK, 1975. Dir: Jim Sharman. With: Tim Curry, Susan Sarandon, Barry Bostwick, Richard O'Brien, Patricia Quinn, Little Nell (Nell Campbell). Twentieth Century-Fox. Colour.

Based on O'Brien's long-running stage musical, this originally flopped at the box office before becoming a surprise cult hit. Director Sharman doesn't try to open up the film version too much and wisely allows the bizarre sets, offbeat characters and great pastiche rock 'n' roll songs to carry the movie. When their car breaks down during a storm, newly-weds Brad and Janet Majors (Bostwick and Sarandon) seek help at a nearby spooky mansion. They soon discover they've stumbled on the annual convention of aliens from the planet Transylvania, and sweet transvestite Dr Frank N. Furter (an outrageous Curry) is about to reveal his latest creation: blond, blue-eyed Rocky (Peter Hinwood). Great support from O'Brien as the rebellious butler Riff Raff (a handyman), plus Meatloaf (Marvin Lee

Aday) as the doomed Eddie and Charles Gray as the deadpan narrator. With Koo Stark, Henry Woolf and Christopher Biggins. It was reissued with various re-edited endings. A sequel first announced in 1979 as *Rocky Horror II* and *The Rocky Horror Show Again* still remains unmade. 'Let's do the Time Warp again!'
Sequel: SHOCK TREATMENT (1981)
✦✦✦✦

THE ROCKY PORNO VIDEO SHOW
USA, 1986. Dir: Loretta Stirling. With: Mistress Tantala (Tantala Ray), Bionca (Bionica Bradley), Kristara Barrington, Tom Byron, Karen Summer, Marc Wallice. Loretta Sterling Productions/4-Play Video. Colour.
In this hardcore spoof, young honeymooners (Byron and Bionca) end up at the home of a strange woman (Tantala) and her white-haired hunchback (François Papillon), really aliens from the planet Sexylvania, who give the newly-weds a guided tour of sexual perversions and wanton desires through their hypersex machine.
✦

ROD BROWN OF THE ROCKET RANGERS:
The Monkey That Couldn't Stop Growing
USA, 1954. Dir: George Gould. With: Cliff Robertson, Bruce Hall, Jack Weston, John Boruff. CBS-TV. B&W.
Half-hour live science fiction TV series (1953-54, fifty-eight episodes), set in the twenty-second century, about Rocket Rangers Rod Brown (Robertson), Frank Boyd (Hall) and Wilbur 'Wormsey' Wormser (Weston) who patrol space in their ship the *Beta* from Omega Base. In this episode, a rogue planet causes a pet chimp to grow to gigantic proportions.
✦

ROD SERLING'S NIGHT GALLERY:
(Orig: FOUR IN ONE: NIGHT GALLERY/NIGHT GALLERY)
The Big Surprise
USA, 1971. Dir: Jeannot Szwarc. With: Vincent Van Patten, Marc Vehanian, Eric Chase, John Carradine. Universal/NBC-TV. Colour.
Anthology TV series (1970-73, ninety-seven stories of varying lengths) with each episode represented by a macabre painting (by Tom Wright) and introduced by creator/host Rod Serling. Old eccentric farmer Mr Hawkins (Carradine) summons three boys and tells them where to dig for a big surprise. When they find a coffin, the surprise soon follows. Scripted by Richard Matheson and based on his own story in a 1959 issue of *Ellery Queen's Magazine*.
✦✦
Cool Air
USA, 1971. Dir: Jeannot Szwarc. With: Barbara Rush, Henry Darrow, Beatrice Kay, Larry Blake, Karl Lukas. Universal/NBC-TV. Colour.
Rod Serling's adaptation of the short story by H.P. Lovecraft, set in 1923. Every time it is cool or windy, Agatha (Rush) recalls that final, terrible moment of her relationship with Dr Juan Munos (Darrow), who managed to cheat death for ten years with the aid of a refrigeration machine and the strength of his own will, until his mechanism failed during a heatwave. Lovecraft's 1928 story was remade as part of *Necronomicon* (1993).
✦✦✦
The Dead Man
USA, 1970. Dir: Douglas Heyes. With: Carl Betz, Jeff Corey, Louise Sorel, Michael Blodgett, Glenn Dixon. Universal/NBC-TV. Colour.
Based on the 1950 *Weird Tales* story by Fritz Leiber. Dr Miles Talmadge (Corey) is presented by his colleague Dr Max Redford (Betz) with a man (Blodgett) who, under hypnosis, can exhibit the physical symptoms of numerous diseases, including death. However, when the latter is given the wrong signal to revive, he returns from the tomb as a vengeful corpse.
✦✦✧
Death on a Barge
USA, 1973. Dir: Leonard Nimoy. With: Lesley Ann Warren, Lou Antonio, Brooke Bundy, Robert Pratt, Jim Boles, Artie Spain. Universal/NBC-TV. Colour.
Atmospheric adaptation of the 1927 *Weird Tales* story by Everil Worrell. When Ron (Pratt) becomes obsessed with Hyacinth (Warren), a beautiful woman who lives on a barge, he discovers that she is a vampire unable to cross over flowing water. Then Ron's jilted girlfriend, Phyllis (Bundy), decides to confront her rival...
✦✦✦
The Devil is Not Mocked
USA, 1971. Dir: Gene Kearney. With: Helmut Dantine, Francis Lederer, Hank Brandt, Martin Kosleck, Gino Gottarelli, Mark De Vries. Universal/NBC-TV. Colour.
Based on the story by Manly Wade Wellman, originally published in the June 1943 *Unknown Worlds*. During World War Two, Nazi General von Grunn (Dantine) invades an old Transylvanian castle which he suspects houses the leader of the local resistance movement. Instead, he discovers it belongs to Dracula (Lederer, who also played the Count in *The Return of Dracula* [1957]).
✦✦✧
Fright Night
USA, 1972. Dir: Jeff Corey. With: Stuart Whitman, Barbara Anderson, Ellen Corby, Alan Napier, Larry Watson, Michael Laird. Universal/NBC-TV. Colour.
When Tom and Leona Ogilvy (Whitman and Anderson) move into an old house, evil goblin spirits from a trunk attempt to possess them on Halloween. With veteran Napier as zombie warlock Zachariah Ogilvy.
✦✦
The Funeral
USA, 1971 (1972). Dir: John Meredyth Lucas. With: Joe Flynn, Werner Klemperer, Harvey Jason, Charles Macaulay, Jack Laird, Laara Lacey. Universal/NBC-TV. Colour.
Scripted by Richard Matheson and based on his 1955 short story. Ludwig Asper (Klemperer), a visitor to Silkline's Cut Rate Catafalque, turns out to be a vampire wanting to experience his own funeral service. But funeral director Morton Silkline (Flynn) doesn't count on the mourners being Ygor the hunchbacked servant (Laird), Jenny the witch (Lacey), Bruce the werewolf (Jerry Summers), Morrow the psychopath (Jason) and various other members of the undead (Leonidas D. Ossetynski and Diana Hale), including the Count (Macaulay). In the end, the monsters begin fighting with each other and an alien turns up, having been recommended.
✦✦
The Girl With the Hungry Eyes
USA, 1972. Dir: John Badham. With: James Farentino, John Astin, Joanna Pettet, Kip Niven, Bruce Powers. Universal/NBC-TV. Colour.
Based on the 1949 short story by Fritz Leiber. Struggling photographer David Faulkner (Farentino) discovers that his successful new model (Pettet) is really a psychic vampire who has the power to seduce men with her eyes before feeding on their life-force.
Episode remake: THE GIRL WITH THE HUNGRY EYES (qv; 1993)
✦✦✦
The Housekeeper
USA, 1970. Dir: John Meredyth Lucas. With: Larry Hagman, Suzy Parker, Jeanette Nolan, Cathleen Cordell, Howard Morton. Universal/NBC-TV. Colour.
Scripted by Matthew Howard (Douglas Heyes). When scheming husband Cedric Acton (Hagman) uses magic to swap the personalities of his shrewish wife Carlotta (Parker) with that of homely old Miss Wattle (Nolan), who is employed as his housekeeper, he discovers that nothing has changed. Various red-tinted clips from *Frankenstein* (1931) are used to illustrate the old woman's thoughts.
✦✦
How to Cure the Common Vampire
USA, 1973. Dir: Jack Laird. With: Richard Deacon, Johnny Brown, George Carlin. Universal/NBC-TV. Colour.
Comedy short in which a group of vampire hunters enter a crypt and prepare to stake their prey.
✦
Junior
USA, 1971. Dir: Theodore J. Flicker. With: Wally Cox, Barbara Flicker, Bill Svanoe. Universal/NBC-TV. Colour.
Comedy short in which a couple are woken up in the night to get a drink of water for their 'baby' — who turns out to be the Universal

Frankenstein Monster (Svanoe)!

✦

A Matter of Semantics
USA, 1971. Dir: Jack Laird. With: Cesar Romero, E.J. Peaker, Monie Ellis. Universal/NBC-TV. Colour.
Comedy short in which Count Dracula (Romero) expects to make a withdrawal from a blood bank.

✦✦✧

A Midnight Visit to the Neighborhood Blood Bank
USA, 1971. Dir: William Hale. With: Victor Buono, Journey Laird. Universal/NBC-TV. Colour.
Comedy short in which a vampire (Buono) discovers his intended victim (Laird) already 'gave at the office'.

✦

Miss Lovecraft Sent Me
USA, 1971. Dir: Gene Kearney. With: Sue Lyon, Joseph Campanella. Universal/NBC-TV. Colour.
When a vampire (Campanella) hires blonde babysitter Betsy (Lyon), the latter ends up fleeing in terror.

✦✧

The Painted Mirror
USA, 1971. Dir: Gene Kearney. With: Zsa Zsa Gabor, Arthur O'Connell, Rosemary DeCamp. Universal/NBC-TV. Colour.
Based on the 1937 short story by Donald Wandrei. Mrs Moore (Gabor), the ruthless co-owner of a run-down thrift shop, is transported through an old mirror into a prehistoric world filled with dinosaurs. This is padded with clips from *Dinosaurus!* (1960), *The Animal World* (1955) and *The Lost World* (1960), this also features the Creature from the Black Lagoon's claws!

✦

The Phantom Farmhouse
USA, 1971. Dir: Jeannot Szwarc. With: David McCallum, Linda Marsh, David Carradine, Ivor Francis, Ford Rainey, Bill Quinn. Universal/NBC-TV. Colour.
Based on the 1923 *Weird Tales* story by Seabury Quinn. After a patient from his private asylum turns up dead, psychiatrist Dr J (McCallum) falls in love with the ghostly Mildred (Marsh), who is cursed with lycanthropy.

✦✦

The Phantom of What Opera?
USA, 1971. Dir: Gene Kearney. With: Leslie Nielsen, Mary Ann Beck. Universal/NBC-TV. Colour.
When a masked Phantom (Nielsen) kidnaps a beautiful young girl (Beck), he discovers she has a secret of her own.

✦

Smile Please
USA, 1971 (1972). Dir: Jack Laird. With: Cesare Danova, Lindsay Wagner. Universal/NBC-TV. Colour.
Comedy short in which a photographer (Wagner) visits an underground crypt to find a vampire (Danova).

✦

With Apologies to Mr. Hyde
USA, 1971. Dir: Jeannot Szwarc. With: Adam West, Jack Laird. Universal/NBC-TV. Colour.
Short vignette in which Dr Jekyll (West) drinks a potion prepared by his assistant (played by writer/producer Laird), but pauses in mid-transformation to complain that it needs more vermouth!

✦✧

You Can Come Up Now, Mrs. Millikan
USA, 1972. Dir: John Badham. With: Ozzie Nelson, Harriet Nelson, Roger Davis, Michael Lerner, Don Keefer, Margaret Muse. Universal/NBC-TV. Colour.
When inventor Henry Millikan (Ozzie Nelson) poisons his absent-minded wife Eleanor (Harriet Nelson) and attempts to bring her back to life, she's late again as usual.

✦✧

THE ROMANCE OF THE MUMMY

France, 1910. Pathé. B&W
In this fourteen minute silent short, Lord Evandale falls asleep in front of a mummy and dreams that he loves an ancient Egyptian queen. When he awakens he meets and subsequently marries a woman who looks exactly like her. Based on the book by Théophile Gautier.
Remake: THE MUMMY (qv; 1911, Urban)

✦

JEAN ROLLIN
(Jean-Michel Rollin le Gentil) [b 1938]

French writer and director (also known as Michel Gand, Michel Gentil, J.A. Lazar and Peter Chevalier), noted for his erotic, although often incomprehensible, vampire movies. The Gothic chic he brought to such films as *The Nude Vampire* (1969), *Sex and the Vampire* (1969) and *Requiem for a Vampire* (1971) just looks woefully dated in his 1995 comeback *Les deux Orphelines Vampires*. As well as directing a number of pseudonymous hardcore projects between 1973 and 1980, he also inherited *Zombie Lake* (1980) from Jesús Franco.
qv: *Amours Collectives* (1976); *Fascination* (1979); *The Hunchback of Notre-Dame* (1956); *Lips of Blood* (1975); *The Living Dead Girl* (1982); *Night of the Cruel Sacrifice* (1980); *Pesticide* (1978); *The Vampire's Rape* (1967); *The Vampire's Thrill* (1970); *Virgin Among the Living Dead* (1971).

YVONNE ROMAIN
(Yvonne Warren) [b 1938]

Exotic-looking British actress who brought some sex appeal to a number of horror films during the early 1960s, notably as the mute servant girl who gives birth to the lycanthropic Leon in Hammer's *The Curse of the Werewolf* (1960). She later married composer and lyricist Leslie Bricusse (b 1931).
qv: *Double Trouble* (1967).

THE ROMANCE OF THE VAMPIRES

(Orig: KAP NGOH YAT GOH MAN/XI WO YI GE WEN)
Hong Kong, 1994. Dir: Lau Kun-Wai (Ricky Lau/Ricky Hui/Xu Guan-Ying). With: Yau Yu-Ching (Ching Fung/Ben Lam Kwok-Pun), Yum Hum (Yvonne Yung-Hung), Usang Yeong-Fang (Mondi Yau Yuet-Ching), Lin Go-Bin (Louie Yuen Siu-Cheung), Ip Wing-Cho. Sunton Films/Tai Seng Video/Ocean Shores Video. Colour.
This features a Western-style vampire couple, Ching Fung and Ming Yuet (Yu-Ching and Yeong-Fang), who sleep together in a crystal coffin. The undead husband uses drops of his own blood to cure blind prostitute Rainbow (Hum), who looks like his long-lost love.

✦✧

THE ROMANTIC AGONY

(Orig: VAARWHEL)
Holland, 1973. Dir: Guido Pieters. With: Pieke Dassen, Nettie Blanken, Rik Bravenboer. Cinema Film. Colour.
A near-immortal man travels through time from the Stone Age to the twenty-ninth century. In one era, Blanken plays a vampire who steals plasma from the local blood bank. Music by Ennio Morricone.

✦

ROSEANNE:

Halloween IV
USA, 1992. Dir: Andrew D. Weyman. With: Roseanne Arnold, John Goodman, Laurie Metcalf, Sara Gilbert, Michael Fishman, Lecy Goranson. The Carsey-Werner Company/ABC-TV. Colour.
Half-hour sitcom (1988-97, 220 episodes) created by Matt Williams and executive produced by Roseanne Arnold and Tom Arnold. Depressed about the Halloween festivities, Roseanne is visited by the ghosts of Halloween past, present and future. With Sandra Bernhard dressed as the Bride of Frankenstein at a party.

✦✦

Trick Me Up, Trick Me Down
USA, 1991. Dir: Andrew D. Weyman. With: Roseanne Arnold, John Goodman, Laurie Metcalf, Natalie West, Michael Fishman, Sara Gilbert. The Carsey-Werner Company/ABC-TV. Colour.
Halloween episode in which Roseanne and Dan (Goodman) scare

their new neighbour and attend a costume party where they perform a zombie ventriloquist act. This includes someone wearing a Dracula mask, Jackie (Metcalf) dressed as Morticia Addams and Crystal (West) in an Elvira costume. With Tom Arnold, and George Clooney as a moose.
✦✦✧

GEORGE A. ROMERO [b 1940]

American writer and director who began his career in television commercials and industrial films. He transformed the entire zombie movie genre with his début feature, *Night of the Living Dead* (1968), which he followed with two sequels, *Dawn of the Dead* (1978) and *Day of the Dead* (1985), plus a 1990 remake of the original directed by Tom Savini.
qv: *Clive Barker's A-Z of Horror: 'The Kingdom of the Dead'* (1997); *Creepshow* (1982); *Creepshow 2* (1987); *Document of the Dead* (1989); *Drive-In Madness!* (1987); *Heartstoppers* (1992); *Martin* (1976); *Night of the Day of the Dawn of the Son of the Bride of the Return of the Terror: The Revenge of the Terror of the Attack of the Evil, Mutant, Hellbound, Flesh-Eating, Subhumanoid Living Dead, Part 2 (1968/1991); Night of the Living Dead 25th Anniversary Documentary* (1993); *100 Years of Horror: 'Zombies'* (1996); *Tales from the Darkside: 'The Circus'* (1986); *Tales from the Darkside The Movie* (1990); *Two Evil Eyes* (1989).

ANGELO ROSSITTO [1901-1991]

Dwarf newspaper seller in Los Angeles who occasionally appeared in acting roles. He was discovered by John Barrymore and featured as a character in Nathanael West's 1939 novel *Day of the Locust*. His career spanned an incredible six decades in films of wildly variable quality.
qv: *Brain of Blood* (1971); *The Corpse Vanishes* (1942); *Dracula vs. Frankenstein* (1970); *Hellzapoppin'* (1941); *The Magic Sword* (1961); *The Offspring* (1986); *The Snoop Sisters: A Black Day for Bluebeard* (1973).

STEPHANIE ROTHMAN [b 1936]

The first female exploitation director, a graduate from the Roger Corman school of budgetary restriction.
qv: *Blood Bath* (1966); *Queen of Blood* (1966); *The Velvet Vampire* (1971).

LE ROUGE DE CHINE

France, 1977. Dir: Jacques Richard. With: Jacques Richard, Agathe Vannier, Bernard Dubois. Les Films Elementaires. Colour/B&W.
Written, directed, edited by and featuring Richard, this minimalist art film is supposedly a homage to vampires. The title translates as 'Chinese Red'.
✦

ROUTE 66: Lizard's Leg and Owlet's Wing

USA, 1962. Dir: Robert Gist. With: Martin Milner, George Maharis, Peter Lorre, Lon Chaney, Martita Hunt, Boris Karloff. Lancer Productions/Screen Gems/ABC-TV. B&W.
Classic Halloween episode of the hour-long TV series (1960-64), scripted by Sterling Silliphant, in which Tod Styles (Milner) and Buzz Murdoch (Maharis) get jobs at Chicago's O'Hare Inn and become involved with a competition between horror stars Karloff (as the Frankenstein Monster), Chaney Jr (as the Hunchback, Mummy and Wolf Man) and a sinister Lorre to prove that the old-style scares are still effective. With Conrad Nagel and Jeannie Riley. Jack Pierce's original make-ups were disappointingly recreated by Ben Lane.
Series remake: ROUTE 66 (1993)
✦✦✦

ROWING WITH THE WIND

(Orig: REMANDO AL VIENTO)
Spain/Switzerland/Italy/Norway, 1988. Dir: Gonzalo Suarez. With: Hugh Grant, Lizzy McInnerny, Valentine Pelka, Elizabeth Hurley, José Luis Gomez, Virginia Mataix. Ditirambo Films/Viking Films/Iberoamericana de TV. Colour.
Writer/director Suarez's fictional account of the events which led up to Mary Shelley writing *Frankenstein*. In June 1816, Percy Bysshe Shelley (Pelka) and Mary Shelley/Godwin (McInnerny) visit the home of Lord Byron (a miscast Grant) in Switzerland with Dr Polidori (Gomez) and Claire Clairmont (Hurley). Mary's life and those of her dysfunctional friends are subsequently haunted by tragic death and her monstrous literary creation (José Carlos Rivas). The unusual locations can't overcome the plodding storyline and uneven performances. This was apparently a big hit in Spain.
✦✧

RUBY FRUIT

Japan/Indonesia, circa 1990s. Dir: Takumi Kimizuka. Colour.
Following the death of her husband, artist Maiko travels to Bali to track down the vampire-like Shirani, who lives with three female lovers on an estate deep in the jungle. Eventually Maiko joins the group and discovers that sex is the source of these women's energy.
✦✧

RUGRATS: The Mysterious Mr. Friend

USA, 1993. Dir: Jim Duffy. Voices: Michael Bell, Christine Cavanaugh, Melanie Chartoff, Cheryl Chase, E. (Elizabeth) G. Daily, Phil Proctor. Nickelodeon Network/ Klasky-Csupo. Colour.
Half-hour cartoon TV series (1991-), created by Arlene Klasky, Gabor Csupo and Paul Germain, about a group of small children and their somewhat skewed view of the adult world. In this episode, Tommy Pickles' father Stu (Jack Riley) invents the eponymous new doll which is brought to life by electricity and behaves like the Frankenstein Monster.
Series sequel: THE RUGRATS MOVIE (1998)
✦✦✧

THE RULING CLASS

UK, 1971. Dir: Peter Medak. With: Peter O'Toole, Alastair Sim, Arthur Lowe, Harry Andrews, Coral Browne, Michael Bryant. Keep Films/United Artists/Avco-Embassy. Colour.
Anarchic fantasy scripted by Peter Barnes and based on his own play. O'Toole stars as Jack Gurney, the fourteenth Earl, recently released from a mental institution and convinced that he is the God of Love. When he returns to claim his inheritance, through a combination of music, comedy, satire and horror we discover that Jack may just be the sanest member of the British aristocracy. Towards the end, the film takes a dark turn when Jack becomes the Ripper, a God of Hate, and as such is readily accepted by the zombiefied members of The House of Lords. The superb supporting cast includes Graham Crowden, Nigel Green (in his final role before his 1972 suicide), Carolyn Seymour, James Villiers and Hugh Burden.
✦✦✦✦

RUMPELSTILTSKIN

USA, 1996. Dir: Mark Jones. With: Kim Johnston-Ulrich, Max Grodenchik, Tommy Blaze, Allyce Beasley. Spelling Entertainment. Colour.
Financed by an uncredited Dino De Laurentiis, this low-budget horror film from co-writer/director Jones (*Leprechaun* [1992], etc) is another attempt to create a franchise character. Loosely based on the classic fairy-tale, Grodenchik plays the eponymous monster (in make-up designed by Kevin Yagher), who is accidentally released from his stone prison and sets out to steal the baby son of the recently widowed Shelley (Johnston-Ulrich). In one scene, the young mother encounters a zombie in a graveyard.
✦✦

RUNAWAY BRAIN

France/USA, 1995. Dir: Chris Bailey. Voices: Wayne Allwine, Russi Taylor, Kelsey Grammer, Jim Cummings, Bill Farmer. Walt Disney. Colour.

Seven minute *Mickey Mouse* cartoon. When Mickey (Allwine) forgets his and Minnie's anniversary and accidentally promises to take her on a Hawaiian cruise, he applies to a want ad in the newspaper from Dr Frankenollie (Grammer) to earn the money he needs. However, when the apeish mad scientist swaps Mickey's brain with that of his gigantic creation, Julius (Cummings), the monstrous mouse must save his girlfriend from the clutches of the homicidal impostor. With Pluto, and a Snow White and the Seven Dwarfs computer game!

✦✦✧

RUNAWAY DAUGHTERS

USA, 1994. Dir: Joe Dante. With: Julie Bowen, Holly Fields, Jenny Lewis, Paul Rudd, Chris Young, Dick Miller. Drive-In Classics/Showtime Networks. Colour.

Using only the title from a 1956 AIP release, this made-for-cable TV movie was originally shown as part of Showtime's *Rebel Highway* series. A trio of teenage girls (Fields, Bowen and Lewis) steal a car and drive across country to find the sailor who got one of them pregnant. With cameos by Roger Corman, Dee Wallace Stone, Christopher Stone, Robert Picardo, Joe Flaherty, Belinda Balaski, Julie Corman, Wendy Schaal, Rance Howard, Don Steele, John Astin, Fabian (Forte), Samuel Z. Arkoff, an uncredited Cathy Moriarty, and a clip from *I Was a Teenage Werewolf* (1957). Co-produced by Debra Hill.

✦✦

RUNAWAY NIGHTMARE

USA, 1982 (1984). Dir: Michael Cartel. With: Michael Cartel, Al Valletta, Sutske Vandenberg, Cindy Donlan, Judy Lee, Cheryl Gamson. Pepperbox Productions/All Seasons Entertainment. Colour.

A case of plutonium explodes, giving the members of a Death Valley cult of women increased sexual appetites. This group includes Vampiria (Alexis Alexander), who likes to dress up as one of the undead, and another who is into witchcraft. The radiation also transforms insect farmer Ralph (director Cartel) into a bloodsucker in this offbeat comedy.

✦

THE RUNESTONE

USA, 1990 (1992). Dir: Willard Carroll. With: Peter Riegert, Joan Severance, William Hickey, Tim Ryan, Lawrence Tierney, Alexander Godunov. Hyperion Pictures/Signature Communications/The Movie Group. Colour.

Surprisingly stylish and fun horror thriller, adapted from the novella by Mark E. Rogers. When an ancient runic stone is unearthed in a Pennsylvania mine, it attracts the notice of a group of aged Scandinavian 'watchers'. As New York archaeologist Martin Almquist (Mitchell Laurence) is transformed into Feneir (Dawan Scott), a demonic wolf-creature of Norse legend, only the god Tyr, represented by clockmaker Sigvaldson (Godunov), can defeat the creature and avert the predicted apocalypse. With Arthur Malet.

✦✦✦

ELIZABETH RUSSELL
[b 1916]

Distinctive American actress best remembered for her supporting roles in Val Lewton's *Cat People* (1942) and *The Curse of the Cat People* (1944). Although she only appeared in a small number of genre movies, she is memorable in every one.

qv: *The Corpse Vanishes* (1942).

JOHN A. RUSSO
[b 1939]

American writer and director who co-scripted *Night of the Living Dead* (1968), which he's been living off ever since. *The Return of the Living Dead* (1984) is loosely based on his 1978 book, which Russo also re-novelised.

qv: *Clive Barker's A-Z of Horror: 'The Kingdom of the Dead'* (1997); *Drive-In Madness!* (1987); *Heartstopper* (1989); *House of Frankenstein* (1997); *Midnight* (1980); *Night of the Living Dead* (1990); *Night of the Living Dead 25th Anniversary Documentary* (1993); *Voodoo Dawn* (1989).

-S-

SABRINA AND THE GROOVIE GOOLIES
USA, 1970-71. Dir: Hal Sutherland. Voices: Jennifer Darling, Alan Dexter, Larry D. Mann, Mel Blanc, Jane Webb, Don Messick. Filmation Associates/Mark Goodson-Bill Todman Productions/Columbia/CBS-TV. Colour.
Hour-long cartoon TV series, based on the Archie comic book character Sabrina Spellman the teenage witch (Webb), first introduced in *The Archie Show* (1968-69) and *The Archie Comedy Hour* (1969-70). While attempting to keep her supernatural powers secret, Sabrina is supported by Tom Dracula (Larry Storch), Franklin 'Frankie' Frankenstein, Wolfgang 'Wolfie' Wolfman, Orville Mummy (all voiced by Howard Morris) and other members of the Groovie Goolies. Dr Jekyll and Mr Hyde (Mann) also turns up.
Series sequels: SABRINA, THE TEENAGE WITCH (1971-74) and THE ABC SATURDAY SUPERSTAR MOVIE: Daffy Duck and Porky Pig Meet the Groovie Goolies (qv; 1972)
✦✧

LE SADIQUE AUX DENTS ROUGES
Belgium, 1970 (1971). Dir: Jean-Louis van Belle. With: Jane Clayton, Albert Simono, Daniel Moosmann. Cinévision Productions/CPF Colour.
Billed as 'Un film de sex horreur' and apparently inspired by AIP's monster movies of the 1950s. A scientist transforms an obsessed teenager into a toothy vampire, who then runs amok at a fancy dress party.
✦

THE SAINT'S DOUBLE TROUBLE
USA, 1940. Dir: Jack Hively. With: George Sanders, Helene Whitney, Jonathan Hale, Bela Lugosi, Donald McBride, John E. Hamilton. RKO Radio Pictures. B&W.
The fourth of nine low-budget films from RKO based on Leslie Charteris' enigmatic hero. In this adventure, Sanders plays both Simon Templar (nicknamed 'The Saint') and Boss, a murderous smuggler who has hidden a fortune in gems inside an old mummy. Things get confusing for the crooks and the police (not to mention the audience!) when Templar starts switching identities with the villain. With Hale as series regular Detective Fernack and a fourth-billed Lugosi, in a brief cameo as a gangster who spends most of his time in a basement hideout.
Sequel: THE SAINT TAKES OVER (1940)
✦✧

ABEL SALAZAR
[1917-1995]

Producer and actor who was Mexico's answer to Peter Cushing. He played the vampire hunter in *The Vampire* (1957) and *The Vampire's Coffin* (1957).
qv: *The Curse of the Crying Woman* (1961); *The Living Head* (1959); *The Man and the Monster* (1958); *El Vampiro Aechecha* (1962); *The World of the Vampires* (1960).

SALEM'S LOT
(aka BLOOD THIRST)
USA, 1979. Dir: Tobe Hooper. With: David Soul, James Mason, Lance Kerwin, Bonnie Bedelia, Lew Ayres, Elisha Cook (Jr). Warner Bros. Colour.
Three hour TV mini-series, based on Stephen King's sprawling vampire novel. Paul Monash's script remains surprisingly faithful to the book while condensing the plot and characters. When writer Ben Mears (Soul) returns to his home town of Salem's Lot he relives his childhood fears of the Marsten House, now occupied by vampire Kurt Barlow (Reggie Nalder, in impressive Nosferatu-type make-up) and his human agent Mr Straker (the excellent Mason). Pretty soon the whole town is infected by the undead. Although director Hooper handles the vampire attacks effectively, he has trouble with the more intimate scenes. The film's major change/flaw has Straker as the chief villain while reducing Barlow to only a supporting role. Veterans Ayres, Cook Jr and Marie Windsor are wasted. The shorter theatrical version includes more gore.
Sequel: A RETURN TO SALEM'S LOT (qv; 1987)
✦✦✦

HANS J. SALTER
[1896-1994]

Austrian-born composer and arranger, in Hollywood since 1938. He created most of the classic scores for Universal's monster movies during the 1940s.
qv: *Abbott and Costello Meet Dr. Jekyll and Mr. Hyde* (1953); *Abbott and Costello Meet the Mummy* (1955); *The Brute Man* (1946); *Captive Wild Woman* (1943); *Creature from the Black Lagoon* (1954); *The Creature Walks Among Us* (1955); *Frankenstein Meets the Wolf Man* (1943); *The Ghost of Frankenstein* (1942); *House of Frankenstein* (1944); *The Mad Ghoul* (1943); *Man Made Monster* (1941); *The Mummy's Ghost* (1944); *The Mummy's Hand* (1940); *The Mummy's Tomb* (1942); *100 Years of Horror* (1996); *Son of Dracula* (1943); *Son of Frankenstein* (1939); *The Wolf Man* (1941).

SALVAGE-1:
Dark Island
USA, 1978 (1979). Dir: Gene Nelson. With: Andy Griffith, Joe Higgins, Trish Stewart, Richard Jaeckel, Jacqueline Scott, J. Jay Saunders. Bennett-Katleman Productions/Columbia/ABC-TV. Colour.
Hour-long TV series (twenty episodes) about junk dealer Harry Broderick (Griffith) who builds his own spaceship, the *Vulture*, to salvage equipment NASA has abandoned on the moon. In this episode, while on a trip to survey Antarctic icebergs, Harry and his companions encounter a giant ape on a deserted island. With Henry Jones.
✦✧

SAM & MAX FREELANCE POLICE!!!:
The Tell Tale Tail
Canada/Philippines, 1997. Dir: Steve Whitehouse. Voices: Harvey Atkin, Robert Tinkler, Tracey Moore. Nelvana. Colour.
Half-hour cartoon TV series, created by Steve Purcell, about freelance police Sam (Atkin), a six-foot suit-wearing dog, and Max (Tinkler), a vicious naked rabbit. In this episode, the detective duo relate a story to Mary Shelley, John Keats and Lord Byron about Max's amputated bunny tail. When they agree to help the mad Dr Disfunctio Cerebri and his grey-skinned Monster, Max's tail is re-animated and escapes, terrorising the countryside.
✦✦✧

SAMSON IN THE WAX MUSEUM
(Orig: SANTO EN EL MUSEO DE CERA)
Mexico, 1963 (1964). Dir: Alfonso Corona Blake. With: Samson (Santo/Rodolfo Guzmán Huerta), Claudio Brook, Rubén Rojo, Norma Mora, Roxana Bellini, Fernando Osés. Filmadora Panamericana/Azteca/Clasa-Mohme/American International. B&W.
Santo the silver masked wrestler (called Samson in this English dubbed version) battles mad scientist Dr Karol (Brook), who transforms sleepwalkers into monsters and displays them in his spooky wax museum. On show are figures of a Frankenstein Monster, a werewolf, the Phantom of the Opera, Quasimodo, Landru (Bluebeard) and a yeti. The English-language version was produced by K. (Kenneth) Gordon Murray.
Sequel: SANTO CONTRA EL ESTRANGULADOR (qv; 1963)
✦

SAMSON VS. THE VAMPIRE WOMEN
(Orig: SANTO VS. LAS MUJERES VAMPIRO)
Mexico, 1961. Dir: Alfonso Corona Blake. With: Samson (Santo/Rodolfo Guzmán Huerta), Lorena Velázquez, María Duval, Jaime Fernandez, Augusto Benedico, Ofelia Montesco. Filmadora Panamericana/Tele-Cine-Radio/

American International. B&W.
One of the better movies featuring Santo, the silver masked wrestling hero (re-named Samson in this English dubbed version and Superman in the French version), who sets out to save doctor's daughter Diana (Duval) from becoming queen to a group of vampire women led by resurrected priestess Zorina (Velázquez). In one scene, Santo wrestles with a black-masked opponent (Fernando Osés) who is revealed to be a hairy werewolf. When the police open fire, the wolfman transforms into a bat and flies away. With wrestlers 'Lobo Negro' (Guillermo Hernández), 'Frankenstein' (Nathaniel Leon) and 'Black Shadow' (Alejandro Cruz). Producer K. (Kenneth) Gordon Murray's English-language version was directed by Manuel San Fernando.
Sequel: SAMSON IN THE WAX MUSEUM (qv; 1963)
Remake: ATACAN LAS BRUJAS (1964)
✦✧

SAMURAI VAMPIRE BIKERS FROM HELL
USA, 1996. Dir: Scott Shaw. With: Scott Shaw, Kenneth H. Kim, Selina Jayne. No Mercy Productions. Colour.
Independent shot-on-video release in which kickboxer Alexander Hell (co-writer/director Shaw) teams up with Sir Katana (co-writer Kim) and Octavia (Jayne) to battle a gang of undead bikers controlled by a vampire businessman in Los Angeles.
✦

SANGRE DE VÍRGENES
Argentina, 1967 (1968). Dir: Emilio Vieyra. With: Ricardo Bauleo, Gloria Prat, Susanna Beltrán, Rolo Puente, Walter Kliche, Orestes A. Trueco. Azteca. Colour.
Argentina's first vampire movie which, because of its sex scenes, was banned for many years in its native country. This includes long dialogue sequences, topless go-go dancers, shots of people skiing and close-ups of the vampire's eyes. The budget was so low that red-tinted footage of seagulls stood in for shots of bats.
✦

JIMMY SANGSTER
[b 1924]

British writer, director and producer who began working at Hammer in the late 1940s as an assistant director. With his scripts for *The Curse of Frankenstein* (1957), *Dracula* (1958), *The Revenge of Frankenstein* (1958) and *The Mummy* (1959), Sangster established the tone for the studio's output for the next decade. He briefly turned director in 1970 for two Hammer projects, *The Horror of Frankenstein* and *Lust for a Vampire*. His autobiography *Do You Want It Good or Tuesday?* was published in 1997.
qv: *Blood of the Vampire* (1958); *The Brides of Dracula* (1960); *Dracula Prince of Darkness* (1965); *Flesh and Blood: The Hammer Heritage of Horror* (1994); *Hammer the Studio That Dripped Blood!* (1987); *Kolchak: The Night Stalker: 'Horror in the Heights'* (1974); *100 Years of Horror: 'Baron Frankenstein'* (1996); *100 Years of Horror: 'Blood-Drinking Beings'* (1996); *100 Years of Horror: 'Dracula and His Disciples'* (1996).

SANTO CONTRA EL CEREBRO DEL MAL
(Orig: CEREBRO DEL MAL)
Cuba/Mexico, 1958 (1961). Dir: Joselito Rodriguez and Enrique J. Zambrano. With: Joaquin Cordero, Norma Suarez, Santo (Rodolfo Guzmán Huerta), El Incógnito (Fernando Osés), Zambrano, Alberto Insua. Besne-Garduno-Alvarino/ATICCA. B&W.
Despite a 1952 serial entitled *El Enmascarado de Plata* directed by René Cardona, this low-budget movie actually marked the début of silver-masked wrestling hero Santo. He helps 'El Incógnito' (Osés, who co-scripted with fellow wrestler Zambrano) to defeat the plans of a mad scientist using electrodes to turn his victims into docile 'zombies'. It remained unreleased for three years, when it finally appeared under a new title which reflected the growing popularity of its co-star.
Sequel: SANTO CONTRA HOMBRES INFERNALES (1958)
✦

SANTO CONTRA EL CEREBRO DIABOLICO
Mexico, 1961 (1962). Dir: Federico Curiel. With: Fernando Casanova, Ana Bertha Lepe, Santo (Rodolfo Guzmán Huerta), Beto Boticario, Luis Aceves Castañeda, Celia Viveros. Peliculas Rodriguez. B&W.
Frankenstein-type mad scientist Dr Zuko creates a monster to battle Santo, the silver-masked wrestling hero. In the end, the creature turns on its creator and destroys him. Filmed in three parts ('Santo contra el Cerebro diabolico', 'Pueblo Sin Ley' and 'La Lucha Final'), the title translates as 'Santo vs the Diabolical Brain'.
Sequel: SANTO CONTRA EL REY DEL CRIMEN (1961)
✦

SANTO
(Rodolfo Guzmán Huerta) [1917-1984]

The most popular of Mexico's masked wrestling heroes, Santo el Enmascarado de Plata was created and essentially played by Huerta. He became a star of the ring following World War Two and, as Santo, never appeared without his silver mask. His first movie was *Santo contra el Cerebro del Mal* (1958), filmed in Cuba just prior to the revolution and co-starring another masked hero, El Incógnito (Fernando Osés). It was shot back-to-back with *Cargamento Blanco* (1958), which utilised footage from the previous film. However, neither movie was released until 1961, after the success of a weekly *Santo* comic-book had furthered the character's popularity and led to a series of low-budget movies. Many of these were originally shot in three twenty minute segments to get around government and union regulations about making feature films. Whether in the persona of a simple wrestler, super-scientist or secret agent, Santo battled vampires, werewolves, zombies, mad scientists, aliens and numerous other outlandish monstrosities until his final brief appearances in *Chanoc y el Hijo del Santo contra los Vampiros Asesinos* (1981) and *El Hijo del Santo en Frontera Sin Ley* (1982), when he passed the baton and some words of wisdom on to his superhero son. In later years wrestler Eric del Castillo may also have worn the silver mask.
qv: *El Baron Brakola* (1965); *¡Las Bestias del Terror!* (1972); *El Hacha Diabolica* (1964); *Las Momias de Guanajuato* (1970); *Samson in the Wax Museum* (1963); *Samson vs. the Vampire Women* (1961); *Santo contra el Cerebro Diabolico* (1961); *Santo contra el Espectro del Estrangulador* (1963); *Santo contra el Estrangulador* (1963); *Santo contra la Hija de Frankenstein* (1971); *Santo contra la Magia Negra* (1972); *Santo contra los Cazadores de Cabezas* (1969); *Santo en la Venganza de la Momia* (1969); *Santo vs. las Lobas* (1974); *Santo vs. the Zombies* (1961); *Santo y Blue Demon contra Dracula y el Hombre Lobo* (1971); *Santo y Blue Demon contra el Dr. Frankenstein* (1973); *Santo y Blue Demon vs. los Monstruos* (1968); *Santo y el Tesoro de Dracula* (1967); *Son of Incredibly Strange Film Show* (1989); *La Venganza de las Mujeres Vampiro* (1969).

SANTO CONTRA EL ESPECTRO DEL ESTRANGULADOR
Mexico, 1963. Dir: René Cardona. With: Santo (Rodolfo Guzmán Huerta), Alberto Vazquez, Maria Duval, Begoña Palacios, Carlos López Moctezuma, Roberto Cañedo. Clasa-Mohme. B&W.
Made back-to-back with *Santo Contra el Estrangulador* (1963), Santo once again battles the disfigured Phantom of the Opera-type mad strangler (Cañedo) who returns from the dead and uses the corpses of his victims to create a macabre tableau.
Sequel: BLUE DEMON VS. EL PODER SATANICO (1964)
✦

SANTO CONTRA EL ESTRANGULADOR
Mexico, 1963. Dir: René Cardona. With: Santo (Rodolfo Guzmán Huerta), Alberto Vazquez, Maria Duval, Begoña Palacios, Ofelia Montesco, Carlos López Moctezuma. Clasa-Mohme. B&W.
Santo, the silver-masked wrestler, battles a scarred mad strangler (Roberto Cañedo) who is a master of disguise. Loosely based on *The Phantom of the Opera* by Gaston Leroux, this was filmed in three episodes ('Santo contra el Estrangulador', 'La Pantera Negra' and 'El Fantasma del Teatro') to circumvent Mexican union rules.
Sequel: SANTO CONTRA EL ESPECTRO DEL ESTRANGULADOR (qv; 1963)
✦

SANTO CONTRA LA HIJA DE FRANKESTEIN
(aka SANTO VS. LA HIJA DE FRANKESTEIN)
Mexico, 1971 (1972). Dir: Miguel M. Delgado. With: Santo (Rodolfo Guzmán Huerta or Eric del Castillo), Gina Romand, Roberto Cañedo, Carlos Suarez, Carlos Agosti, Gerardo Zepeda. Cinematográfica Calderón/Azteca Films. Colour.
Frankenstein's daughter (Romand) uses the blood of her female victims to remain young. She creates a Karloffian Monster called Ursus, transforms her aunt (Lucy Gallardo) into a mummy and tries to obtain the 'powerful' blood of Santo, the silver-masked hero. In the end, Santo wrestles Frankenstein's apeman to the death and teams up with the acid-scarred Ursus to defeat the mad offspring's plans.
Sequel: SANTO CONTRA LOS ASESINOS DE OTROS MUNDOS (1971)
✦✧

SANTO CONTRA LA MAGIA NEGRA
Mexico/USA, 1972. Dir: Alfredo B. Crevenna. With: Santo (Rodolfo Guzmán Huerta or Eric del Castillo), Elsa Cardenas, Sasha Montenegro, Gerty Jones, Cesar del Campo, Fernando Osés. Peliculas Latinoamericanas/ Cinematográfica Flama. Colour.
Filmed on location in Haiti. Santo the silver-masked wrestler becomes involved with black magic (featuring apparently authentic voodoo ceremonies) and battles more pasty-faced zombies and a wrestling opponent who appears to transform into a tiger. The titles translates as 'Santo vs Black Magic'.
Sequel: SANTO CONTRA LOS SECUESTRADORES (1972)
✦

SANTO CONTRA LOS CAZADORES DE CABEZAS
Mexico, 1969. Dir: René Cardona. With: Santo (Rodolfo Guzmán Huerta), Nadia Milton, René Cardona, Freddy Fernández, Enrique Lucero. Zacarias/Azteca. Colour.
Santo, the silver-masked wrestler, sets out to stop the mad Dr Mathus using the blood of the living to revive the dead. The title translates as 'Santo vs the Head Hunters'.
Sequel: SANTO CONTRA LOS ASESINOS DE LA MAFIA (1969)
✦

SANTO EN LA VENGANZA DE LA MOMIA
(aka LA VENGANZA DE LA MOMIA)
Mexico, 1969 (1971). Dir: René Cardona. With: Santo (Rodolfo Guzmán Huerta), Eric del Castillo, Carlos Ancira, Mary Montiel, Cesar del Campo, Alma Rojo. Cinematográfica Calderón/Azteca Films. Colour.
Santo, the silver-masked wrestler, helps an expedition and confronts a fake Aztec mummy that kills its victims with a bow and arrow.
Sequel: SANTO CONTRA LA MAFIA DEL VICIO (1970)
✦✧

SANTO VS. LAS LOBAS
(aka SANTO CONTRA LAS LOBAS)
Mexico, 1974. Dir: Jaime Jiménez Pons and Rúben Galindo. With: Santo (Rodolfo Guzmán Huerta or Eric del Castillo), Rudolfo De Anda, Gloria Mayo, Jorge Russek, Nubia Marti, Federico Falcon. Jiménez Pons Hermanos. Colour.
Possibly filmed in 1972. Santo the silver-masked wrestler teams up with a professor to defend a town against a tribe of werewolves (actually Alsatian dogs), led by a female white wolf. In one scene, Santo and his companions are invited to a party, where the other guests transform into wolves and attack them. However, the film ends abruptly when Santo throws the male leader of the lycanthropes over a cliff. As usual, this is padded with plenty of boring wrestling footage.
Sequel: SANTO EN ORO NEGRO (1974)
✦✧

SANTO VS THE ZOMBIES
(Orig: SANTO CONTRA LOS ZOMBIES. USA: aka INVASION OF THE ZOMBIES)
Mexico, 1961. Dir: Benito Alazraki. With: Santo (Rodolfo Guzmán Huerta), Armando Silvestre, Lorena Velázquez, Jaime Fernandez, Dagoberto Rodriguez, Carlos Agosti. Pelicula Mexicana/Trabajadores Miembros/Filmadora Panamericana/Azteca Films. B&W.
The first true starring vehicle for Santo, the silver-masked wrestler. Here he helps the police track down a masked mad scientist who is using an army of radio-controlled living dead strongmen to go out and steal. This has all the production value of a 1930s serial! With the usual interminable wrestling sequences (including Santo battling a zombie opponent [Fernando Osés]) and former Miss Mexico Velázquez as the heroine searching for her missing father.
Sequel: SANTO CONTRA EL CEREBRO DIABOLICO (qv; 1961)
✦✧

SANTO Y BLUE DEMON CONTRA DRACULA Y EL HOMBRE LOBO
Mexico, 1971 (1972). Dir: Miguel M. Delgado. With: Santo (Rodolfo Guzmán Huerta or Eric del Castillo), Blue Demon (Alejandro Muñoz), Aldo Monti, Augustin Martinez Solares, Nubia Marti, Ma. (María) Eugenia San Martin. Cinematográfica Calderón/Azteca Films. Colour.
Dracula (Monti) and Rufus Rex, his wolfman assistant, are restored to life when a hunchbacked villain named Eric spills the blood of Professor Cristaldi over their skeletons. Masked wrestling heroes Santo and the Blue Demon battle numerous vampires, werewolves and zombies before the two lead monsters fall into a pit of wooden stakes and vanish.
Sequels: SANTO Y EL AGUILA REAL (1971) and NOCHE DE MUERTE (1972)
✦✧

SANTO Y BLUE DEMON CONTRA EL DR. FRANKENSTEIN
Mexico, 1973. Dir: Miguel M. Delgado. With: Santo (Rudolfo Guzmán Huerta or Eric del Castillo), Blue Demon (Alejandro Muñoz), Sasha Montenegro, Jorge Russek, Ivonne Govea. Cinematográfica Calderón. Colour.
During the late 1960s and early 1970s, as their respective series reached a peak of popularity, Mexico's two greatest wrestling heroes, Santo and the Blue Demon, teamed up for a number of adventures. This time they battle male and female monsters created by Dr Frankenstein.
Sequels: SANTO Y MANTEQUILLA NÁPOLES EN LA VENGANZA DE LA LLORONA (1973) and SANTO Y BLUE DEMON EN EL MISTERIO DE LAS BERMUDAS (1977)
✦

SANTO Y BLUE DEMON VS. LOS MONSTRUOS
(aka CONTRA LOS MONSTRUOS/SANTO CONTRA LOS MONSTRUOS DE FRANKENSTEIN/SANTO Y BLUE DEMON CONTRA LOS MONSTRUOS)
Mexico, 1968 (1969). Dir: Gilberto Martinez Solares. With: Santo (Rodolfo Guzmán Huerta), Blue Demon (Alejandro Muñoz), Jorge Rado, Carlos Ancira, Raul Martinez Solares Jr, Hedy (Heidi) Blue. Cinematográfica Sotomayor/ Azteca/Clasa-Mohme. Colour.
Mexico's masked wrestling heroes, Santo and the Blue Demon, team up for probably their wildest adventure (from the original director of *Face of the Screaming Werewolf* [1960], etc). They not only have to confront the mad Dr Bruno Halder (Ancira), who is revived by his evil dwarf assistant, but also battle El Vampiro (David Alvizu) with pointy ears and a top hat, La Mujer Vampiro (Elsa Maria Tako and Yolanda Ponce as two vampire women), the bearded Franquestain/Frankestein (*sic*) Monster (Manuel Leal), a black El Hombro Lobo (Vincente Lare 'Cacama'), a quartet of zombies, La Momia (Fernando Rosales), a glowing-eyed El Ciclope (Gerardo Cepeda), a big-brained blue alien and a deadly double of the Blue Demon! It ends in an incredible battle between the wrestlers and all the monsters that has to be seen to be believed. They sure loved multi-monster movies in Mexico.
Sequels: SANTO CONTRA LOS CAZADORES DE CABEZAS (1969) and LOS CAMPEONES JUSTICIEROS (1970)
✦✧

SANTO Y EL TESORO DE DRACULA
(aka SANTO CONTRA DRACULA/EL TESORO DE DRACULA/EL VAMPIRO Y EL SEXO)
Mexico, 1967 (1968). Dir: René Cardona. With: Santo (Rodolfo Guzmán Huerta), Aldo Monti, Noelia Noel, Roberto G. Rivera, Carlos Agosti, Alberto Rojas. Cinematográfica Calderón/Azteca Films. Colour.
Comic strip-style wrestling/horror movie. Female scientist Luisa (Noel) travels back in time and space to discover where the legendary gold of vampire Count Alucard/Dracula (Monti) is hidden. Santo, the silver-masked hero ('El Enmascarado de Plata'), watches it all from his secret laboratory. He follows his beautiful ally through his time tunnel in an attempt to save her from the Satanic orgies of the Count and his thirteen topless priestesses of sex. An export version, featuring more nudity, was released as *El Vampiro y el Sexo.*
Sequel: SANTO CONTRA CAPULINA (1968)
✦✧

PETER SASDY
[b 1934]

Hungarian-born director who arrived in Britain in 1956 and later joined the BBC. His début feature was Hammer's *Taste the Blood of Dracula* (1969).
qv: *Countess Dracula* (1970); *Hammer House of Horror: 'Visitor from the Grave'* (1980).

SATANIC
(Orig: SATANIK)
Italy/Spain, 1968. Dir: Piero Vivarelli. With: Magda Konopka, Julio Peña, Umi Raho, Luigi Montini, Armando Calvo, Umberto Raho. Rodiancines/Copernices. Colour.
Yet another variation on Robert Louis Stevenson's story, based on a popular Italian comic book. The scarred Dr Marnie Bannister (Konopka) murders a scientist colleague and drinks his serum which regenerates her cells and makes her younger and more beautiful. She becomes a sexy cabaret performer and a seductive serial killer, but discovers she needs more of the drug to prevent her features from reverting to their original ugly appearance. After escaping the pipe-smoking Inspector Trent from Scotland Yard, Marnie is killed in an automobile accident and reverts to her beautiful self.
✦

THE SATANIC RITES OF DRACULA
(USA: COUNT DRACULA AND HIS VAMPIRE BRIDE/THE RITES OF DRACULA)
UK, 1973 (1974). Dir: Alan Gibson. With: Christopher Lee, Peter Cushing, Michael Coles, William Franklyn, Freddie Jones, Joanna Lumley. Hammer Films/Warner Bros. Colour.
Originally announced as *Dracula is Dead and Well and Living in London.* This enjoyable sequel to *Dracula A.D. 1972* (1972) was the last in Hammer's series to feature Lee as the Count. A fast-paced blend of sci-spy and horror, Dracula is now a Howard Hughes-type property tycoon, D.D. Denham, living in seclusion in contemporary London and planning to release a deadly new bubonic plague virus to hasten Armageddon. Lee and Cushing's Dracula/Van Helsing confrontation recalls their earlier films together, and the Count's destruction in a hawthorn bush adds a new twist to the mythology. Lee even gets to do a mock-Lugosi accent! It wasn't released in America for five years, and then by Max J. Rosenberg's independent distributor Dynamite! Entertainment (who gave away 'Count Dracula' Halloween posters free to the first 1,000 patrons). With Richard Vernon, and Patrick Barr as Lord Carradine!
Sequel: THE LEGEND OF THE 7 GOLDEN VAMPIRES (qv; 1974)
✦✦✦

SATAN'S BLACK WEDDING
USA, 1974 (1976). Dir: Philip Miller (Steve Millard). With: Greg Braddock, Ray Myles, Lisa Milano, Barrett Cooper, Zarrah Whiting, Lisa Pons. Irmi Films Corporation. Colour.
When historical novelist Nina Gray (Whiting) dies under mysterious circumstances, her brother Mark (Braddock) returns to Monterey, California. He discovers a monastery filled with 150 year-old Satanic vampires and his sister, now a big-fanged blood-drinker. Hour-long low-budget thrills (there is no ending), originally co-billed with the same director's *Criminally Insane* (1973).
✦

SATURDAY NIGHT LIVE
USA, 1978. Dir: Dave Wilson. With: Christopher Lee, Dan Aykroyd, John Belushi, Jane Curtin, Bill Murray, Laraine Newman. NBC-TV. Colour.
Long-running (1975-) live TV comedy sketch show. This episode was guest hosted in March 1978 by Lee, who appeared in a vampire sketch with Belushi and Curtin.
✦✦

SATURDAY THE 14TH
USA, 1981. Dir: Howard R. Cohen. With: Richard Benjamin, Paula Prentiss, Jeffrey Tambor, Severn Darden, Kari Michaelson, Stacy Keach Sr. New World/Embassy. Colour.
Despite the misleading title, this is not a spoof on slasher films but a parody of old dark house/monster movies. Along with their two children, Debbie (Michaelson) and Billy (Kevin Brando), John and Mary (real-life married couple Benjamin and Prentiss) move into a spooky old house they have inherited and which a pair of vampires, Waldemar (Tambor) and Yolanda (Nancy Lee Andrews), also want to own. When Billy uses the *Book of Evil* to unwittingly conjure up a number of creatures (left over from *Galaxina* [1980]), strange things begin to happen — including a scaly gill man which turns up in the bath! Despite the low budget, this often silly comedy features some imaginative gags. Darden is great as Van Helsing, who in fact turns out to be the real villain, and the vampires save the day! Produced by Julie Corman; Aaron Lipstadt was second unit production manager.
Sequel: SATURDAY THE 14TH STRIKES BACK (qv; 1988)
✦✦

SATURDAY THE 14TH STRIKES BACK
USA, 1988. Dir: Howard R. Cohen. With: Ray Walston, Avery Schreiber, Patty McCormack, Jason Presson, Julianne McNamara, Rhonda Aldrich. Pacific Trust/Concorde. Colour.
Director Cohen's quirky sequel-of-sorts to his 1981 original. Young Eddie Baxter (the likeable Presson) is about to turn sixteen when he discovers that a fissure in the basement of his weird family's creepy old house is releasing the forces of evil into the world. These include sexy singing vampire Charlene (Pamela Stonebrook) and her vampirettes (Dorissa Curry, Kathryn O'Reilly and Victoria Morsell), a werewolf (Tommy Rall), Egyptian Kharis (Joe Ruskin) and the Mummy (Michael Berryman), grave robber Burke (Peter Frankland) and Lizzie Borden (Lauren Petersen). When Eddie learns that he has been chosen by The Evil One (Leo V. Gordon) to help them in their conquest of the Earth, only the wizard pretending to be his Gramps (Walston) can save him. With a cameo appearance by the director as Mr Bleckner. Produced by Julie Corman.
✦✧

SAU SAAL BAAD
India, 1989. Dir: Mohan Bhakri. With: Hemant Birje, Sahila Chadha, Joginder, Narinder Nath, Huma Khan, Shobhni Singh. Aarti Pictures/Bombino Video. Colour.
Horror musical, apparently a remake of *So Saal Baad* (1967). A revived sorcerer conjures up a hairy monster and zombies. When he is bitten by a cobra and dies, the monsters fade away.
✦

SCARAB
Spain, 1982. Dir: Steven-Charles Jaffe. With: Rip Torn, Robert Ginty, Cristina Hachuel, Donald Pickering, Sam Chew Jr, Isabel Garcia Lorca. Tesauro/Alloi. Colour.
After an opening title that makes very little sense, a professor (Torn) raises a briefly-glimpsed demon. Some years later he is using his ancient Egyptian powers to kill world leaders in an attempt to bring about a lasting peace! While Torn smirks his way through the film,

Ginty is a surprisingly likeable reporter who uncovers the supernatural plot. This includes plenty of naked women.
✦✧

TOM SAVINI
[b 1947]

American special effects make-up designer, actor and director. Best known for his inventive stalk 'n' slash deaths, his long collaboration with George Romero (*Martin* [1976]; *Dawn of the Dead* [1978]; *Creepshow* [1982]; *Day of the Dead* [1985]; *Two Evil Eyes* [1989], etc) led to him directing the 1990 colour remake of *Night of the Living Dead.*
qv: *Bloodsucking Pharaohs in Pittsburgh* (1988); *Creepshow 2* (1987); *Deathdream* (1972); *The Demolitionist* (1995); *Document of the Dead* (1989); *Drive-In Madness!* (1987); *Eyes Are Upon You* (1997); *From Dusk Till Dawn* (1995); *Heartstopper* (1989); *Innocent Blood* (1992); *Killing Zoë* (1993); *Midnight* (1980); *Mr. Stitch* (1995); *Necronomicon* (1993); *Tales from the Darkside: 'The Family Reunion'* (1988).

PAUL SAWTELL
[1906-1971]

Polish-born American composer and musical director, at Universal during the mid-1940s.
qv: *It! The Terror from Beyond Space* (1958); *The Jungle Captive* (1944); *Jungle Woman* (1944); *The Last Man on Earth* (1961); *The Mummy's Curse* (1944); *Son of Dr. Jekyll* (1951).

JOHN SAXON
(Carmen Orrico) [b 1935]

American leading man, formally a model, who began his career in the mid-1950s portraying teenage rebels and ended up usually playing cops or other authority figures.
qv: *The Arrival* (1990); *Death House* (1988); *From Dusk Till Dawn* (1995); *My Mom's a Werewolf* (1988); *Queen of Blood* (1966); *Starsky & Hutch: 'The Vampire'* (1976).

SCARECROWS

USA, 1988. Dir: William Wesley. With: Ted Vernon, Victoria Christian, Richard Vidan, B.J. Turner, David Campbell, Michael Simms. Effigy Films/Manson International/Forum Home Video. Colour.
When a paramilitary unit steals the payroll from a military base and lands a hijacked plane near a remote abandoned farm in southern California, they soon encounter one of their number (Turner) as an eviscerated walking corpse and are then attacked by a trio of demonic scarecrows who kill them off one by one. This was filmed in Florida.
✦✦✧

SCARED STIFF

USA, 1953. Dir: George Marshall. With: Dean Martin, Jerry Lewis, Lizabeth Scott, Carmen Miranda, George Dolenz, Dorothy Malone. Paramount. B&W.
Director Marshall's disappointing remake of his own, superior, *The Ghost Breakers* (1940), in which night club performers Larry Todd (Martin) and Myron Mertz (Lewis) escape from gangsters by helping heiress Mary Carroll (Scott) uncover the secret of a hidden treasure in a supposedly haunted Cuban castle. Lewis is his usual irritating self, and there are far too many musical numbers, especially from the ageing Miranda. Jack Lambert makes an unimpressive zombie and even an uncredited appearance by Bob Hope and Bing Crosby can't save this dire comedy, based on the play *The Ghost Breaker* by Paul Dickey and Charles W. Goddard. Not to be confused with the 1945 old dark house mystery *Scared Stiff*, starring Jack Haley.
✦✧

SCARE THE LIVING

Hong Kong, 1991. Dir: Lee Leung (Xen Chu-Lung). With: Hui Ying-Hong, Ku Fan. Colour.
When the ancient Chinese mummy of a witch is unearthed during an excavation project, the reanimated torso goes looking for its head. In the meantime, the missing head has taken possession of a woman (Ying-Hong) who is killing the descendants of those who originally decapitated the sorceress.
✦✧

SCARS OF DRACULA

UK, 1970. Dir: Roy Ward Baker. With: Christopher Lee, Dennis Waterman, Jenny Hanley, Christopher Matthews, Patrick Troughton, Michael Gwynn. Hammer Films/EMI Film Productions. Colour.
Hammer's fifth Dracula movie has no connection with any other entry in the series. The script by John Elder (Anthony Hinds) returns Lee's Count to his Transylvanian castle, where he is revived by a rubber bat vomiting blood. When a young rake (Matthews) spends the night at the castle, his brother and girlfriend (Waterman and Hanley) go looking for him. It's all been done before, and despite using a number of ideas from Bram Stoker's original novel (Dracula crawling up the castle wall), this is just an attempt by Hammer to introduce more nudity (Anoushka [Anouska] Hempel's sensuous vampire Tania) and some mild S&M (the Count whipping his servant, Klove [Troughton]) into the series. This time Dracula is impaled on a metal spike and fried by a lightning bolt. With Michael Ripper, Bob Todd and future writer/director David Leland (*Mona Lisa* [1986], etc) as a comic-relief policeman. It cost just £480,000 to make. Sphere Books published a novelisation in 1971 by Angus Hall (the author of *Devilday*, which was filmed as *Madhouse* [1974])
Sequel: DRACULA A.D. 1972 (qv; 1972)
✦✦

SCHALCKEN THE PAINTER

UK, 1979. Dir: Leslie Megahey. With: Jeremy Clyde, Maurice Denham, Cheryl Kennedy, John Justin, Charles Gray, Anthony Sharp. BBC/RM Productions. Colour.
Short TV movie, based on the 1839 story by J. Sheridan Le Fanu and originally shown as part of the *Omnibus* series. A horrifying experience is revealed in a painting by Dutch artist Godfried Schalcken (1643-1706). While still a student, Schalcken's love Rose (Kennedy) was sold by her father to a rich and sinister nobleman, Vanderhausen (Justin, from *The Thief of Bagdad* [1940], etc), who turns out to be a living corpse. This is beautifully photographed by John Hooper in a series of tableaux that mirror the style of the Dutch Masters.
✦✦✦✧

SCHOOL FOR VAMPIRES

Hong Kong, 1988. Pan-Asia Video. Colour.
Comedy about an academy for hopping vampires. These undead students wear uniforms, sing communal songs and receive diplomas.
✦

MAX SCHRECK
[1879-1936]

German actor (his name literally means 'horror') immortalised for his portrayal of the rat-like Graf Orlok in *Nosferatu* (1922). He was played by Willem Dafoe in *Burned to Light* (1999).

JOHN SCHUCK
[b 1944]

American TV and film actor who played Herman Munster in the TV series *The Munsters Today* (1988-91).
qv: *The Halloween That Almost Wasn't* (1979); *Holmes and Yoyo: 'The Last Phantom'* (1976); *My Mom's a Werewolf* (1989).

SCIENCE FICTION THEATER:
Before the Beginning

USA, 1955. Dir: Alvin Ganzer. With: Dane Clark, Judith Ames, Phillip Pine, Ted de Corsia, Emerson Treacy. ZIV Productions. Colour.
Half-hour syndicated anthology TV series (1955-57, seventy-eight

episodes), hosted by Truman Bradley, supposedly based on science fact. Young bio-chemist Dr Ken Donaldson (Clark) uses an experimental photon gun designed to create life to save the wife (Ames) he neglected.

✦✧

Beyond Return

USA, 1955. Dir: Eddie Davis. With: Zachary Scott, Peter Hansen, Joan Vohn, Toni Carroll, Kay Faylen, Dennis Moore. ZIV Productions. Colour.

When timid Kyra Zelas (Vohn) is saved from death by a new drug created by Dr Erwin Bach (Scott), she turns into a seductive beauty with a Jekyll and Hyde personality. Based on the story 'The Adaptive Ultimate' by John Jessel (Stanley G. Weinbaum), which was filmed again the following year.

Episode sequel: SHE DEVIL (qv; 1956)

✦✧

THE SCI-FI FILES:
Children of Frankenstein

UK, 1997. Dir: Peter Swain. With: Brian Aldiss, Stephen Baxter, Arthur C. Clarke, Marge Piercy, William Gibson, Terry Gilliam. A Satel Doc Production/The Learning Channel/Canal+/Dogstar/NHK/Channel Four Television. Colour.

This first hour-long episode in a four-part documentary TV series takes a very dry look at how biological experimentation has influenced or been influenced by science fiction ever since Mary Shelley wrote *Frankenstein; or, The Modern Prometheus*. With commentary by Professor of Genetics Steve Jones and nuclear physicist Lawrence Krauss, plus archive footage and many clips from *Back to the Future* (1985), *Barbarella* (1967), *Blade Runner* (1982), *Brazil* (1985), *Bride of Frankenstein* (1935), *The Creation of the Humanoids* (1962), *The Fly* (1986), *Frankenstein* (1931), *Futureworld* (1976), *Ghost in the Shell* (1995), *Island of Lost Souls* (1932), *Metropolis* (1926), *Planet of the Apes* (1968), *Sleeper* (1973), *Terminator 2 Judgment Day* (1991), *Time Bandits* (1981), *The Time Machine* (1960), *Twelve Monkeys* (1995), *2001: A Space Odyssey* (1968) and TV's *The Outer Limits* and *Doctor Who*. Narrated by Heather Couper.

✦✧

SCOOBY-DOO AND SCRAPPY-DOO:
(aka THE NEW SCOOBY AND SCRAPPY-DOO SHOW/ SCOOBY'S MYSTERY FUNHOUSE)
Canine to Five

USA, 1979 (1980). Dir: Ray Patterson, Carl Urbano, Oscar Dufau and George Gordon. Voices: Joe Baker, Pat Fraley, Bob Hastings, Casey Kasem, Don Messick, Frank Welker. Hanna-Barbera Productions/ABC-TV. Colour.

Continuing the cartoon adventures (1979-80, sixteen thirty minute episodes, followed by a further twenty-one shows comprising sixty seven minute episodes) of Scooby-Doo (Messick) and Shaggy Rogers (Kasem), who are joined by Scooby's over-confident nephew Scrappy (Lennie Weinrib and later Messick), who gets them into trouble with supernatural encounters, both real and fake. The opening sequence includes a living mummy. In this episode, while working for research scientist Dr Werner Wolf, the trio discover that their employer's experiments have transformed him into a werewolf. Joseph Barbera and William Hanna were executive producers.

✦

A Fit Night Out for Bats

USA, 1979 (1980). Dir: Ray Patterson, Carl Urbano, Oscar Dufau and George Gordon. Voices: Joe Baker, Pat Fraley, Bob Hastings, Casey Kasem, Don Messick, Frank Welker. Hanna-Barbera Productions/ABC-TV. Colour.

When The Mystery Machine gets a flat tyre, Scooby-Doo, Shaggy and Scrappy take refuge in a spooky old house belonging to Sylvester the vampire.

✦✧

The Ghoul, the Bat and the Ugly

USA, 1979. Dir: Ray Patterson, Carl Urbano, Oscar Dufau and George Gordon. Voices: Joe Baker, Pat Fraley, Bob Hastings, Casey Kasem, Don Messick, Frank Welker. Hanna-Barbera Productions/ABC-TV. Colour.

Scooby and the gang investigate a shadow creature that appears during a horror movie convention at Hillside Manor and encounter a pair of suspicious horror film actors dressed as a vampire and a werewolf, plus a real estate developer disguised as the Bride of Frankenstein. This also includes people in classic movie monster costumes at The Batty Awards and a Hall of Horror Fame featuring The Mummy and Frankenstein's Monster.

✦✦

Hard Hat Scooby

USA, 1979 (1980). Dir: Ray Patterson, Carl Urbano, Oscar Dufau and George Gordon. Voices: Joe Baker, Pat Fraley, Bob Hastings, Casey Kasem, Don Messick, Frank Welker. Hanna-Barbera Productions/ABC-TV. Colour.

While working nights as hard hats on a construction site building the Vampire State Building, Scooby, Scrappy and Shaggy have problems with an undead foreman.

✦

I Left My Neck in San Francisco

USA, 1979. Dir: Ray Patterson, Carl Urbano, Oscar Dufau and George Gordon. Voices: Maria Frumkin, Casey Kasem, Don Messick, Pat Stevens, Lennie Weinrib, Frank Welker. Hanna-Barbera Productions/ABC-TV. Colour.

Scooby, Scrappy and the rest of the gang visit Alcatraz, where they encounter the legendary Lady Vampire of the Bay and uncover a plot to recover some stolen jewels.

✦✧

Moonlight Madness

USA, 1979 (1980). Dir: Ray Patterson, Carl Urbano, Oscar Dufau and George Gordon. Voices: Joe Baker, Pat Fraley, Bob Hastings, Casey Kasem, Don Messick, Frank Welker. Hanna-Barbera Productions/ABC-TV. Colour.

When Shaggy visits his ancestral Moonlight Castle, he wears a medallion that periodically transforms him into a werewolf under the full moon.

✦✧

Mummy's the Word

USA, 1979 (1980). Dir: Ray Patterson, Carl Urbano, Oscar Dufau and George Gordon. Voices: Joe Baker, Pat Fraley, Bob Hastings, Casey Kasem, Don Messick, Frank Welker. Hanna-Barbera Productions/ABC-TV. Colour.

While looking for an oasis in the Egyptian desert, Scooby, Shaggy and Scrappy discover a pyramid and encounter a marauding mummy.

✦✧

Soggy Bog Scooby

USA, 1979 (1980). Dir: Ray Patterson, Carl Urbano, Oscar Dufau and George Gordon. Voices: Joe Baker, Pat Fraley, Bob Hastings, Casey Kasem, Don Messick, Frank Welker. Hanna-Barbera Productions/ABC-TV. Colour.

Scooby, Shaggy and Scrappy are fishing in a swamp, when they encounter a green gill man-type monster.

✦✧

Stuntman Scooby

USA, 1979 (1980). Dir: Ray Patterson, Carl Urbano, Oscar Dufau and George Gordon. Voices: Joe Baker, Pat Fraley, Bob Hastings, Casey Kasem, Don Messick, Frank Welker. Hanna-Barbera Productions/ABC-TV. Colour.

While taking the Gigantic Studios tour, Scooby, Shaggy and Scrappy are mistaken by a director for stuntmen and find themselves being put in dangerous situations, including being menaced by a giant robot ape in *Bing Bong the Monster*.

Series sequels: THE RICHIE RICH—SCOOBY-DOO SHOW—AND SCRAPPY, TOO! (1980-81) and THE SCOOBY-DOO AND SCRAPPY-DOO—PUPPY HOUR (qv; 1982-83)

✦✧

THE SCOOBY-DOO AND SCRAPPY-DOO—PUPPY HOUR
(aka SCOOBY'S MYSTERY FUNHOUSE)

USA, 1982-83. Dir: Charles A. Nichols and Rudy Larriva. Voices: Casey Kasem, Don Messick, Frank Welker, Michael Bell, Billy Jacoby, Peter Cullen. Hanna-Barbera Productions/Ruby-Spears Enterprises/ABC-TV. Colour.

Thirteen cartoon shows comprising thirty-nine seven minute episodes featuring Scooby-Doo (Messick), Shaggy Rogers (Kasem) and Scrappy-Doo (Messick) along with Scooby's uncle Yabba-Doo

(Messick) and Deputy Dusty (Welker) encountering criminals in the Wild West. Episode titles include 'Vild Vest Vampire' and 'Where's the Werewolf'. Additional voices include Leon Askin, Ed Begley Jr, Virginia Christine, Keene Curtis, Bernard Fox, Darryl Hickman, Keye Luke, Alan Oppenheimer, Henry Polic, Philip Proctor, Larry Storch and Alan Young.
Series sequels: THE ALL-NEW SCOOBY AND SCRAPPY-DOO SHOW (1983-84) and THE NEW SCOOBY-DOO MYSTERIES (qv; 1984-85)
✦

SCOOBY-DOO AND THE GHOUL SCHOOL
USA, 1988. Dir: Ray Patterson and Charles A. Nichols. Voices: Hamilton Camp, Glynis Johns, Casey Kasem, Don Messick, Pat Musick, Frank Welker. Hanna-Barbera Productions. Colour.
Syndicated cartoon TV movie, a follow-up to *Scooby-Doo Meets the Boo Brothers* (1987). When Scooby (Messick), Shaggy (Kasem) and Scrappy-Doo (Messick) arrive at Miss Grimwood's (Johns) spooky Finishing School for Ghouls to teach gym, they meet Count Dracula's daughter Sibella (Susan Blu), Elsa Frankenstein (Musick), Winnie the werewolf (Marilyn Schreffler), the Mummy's daughter Tannis (Patty Maloney), and Phantasma the ghost (Russi Taylor). While Shaggy and his pals coach the girls for a volleyball tournament against a team of young military cadets, Revolta the Witch of the Web (Ruta Lee) and her companion Matches the dragon (Welker) use hypnosis to kidnap the famous offspring and turn them into a fiendish team of their own. Shaggy's evil double escapes from a mirror, and the monster fathers turn up for a school open house.
Sequel: SCOOBY-DOO AND THE RELUCTANT WEREWOLF (qv; 1988)
✦✧

SCOOBY-DOO AND THE RELUCTANT WEREWOLF
USA, 1988. Dir: Ray Patterson. Voices: Don Messick, Casey Kasem, Hamilton Camp, Jim Cummings, Joanie Gerber, Ed Gilbert. Hanna-Barbera Productions. Colour.
Syndicated musical cartoon TV movie based on the *Scooby-Doo* series. A green-faced Count Dracula (Camp) turns Scooby and Scrappy's (both voiced by Messick) pal Shaggy (Kasem) into a werewolf so that he can take part in the Transylvanian monster road race. This also includes a Frankenstein Monster (Cummings) and his bride Repulsa (B.J. Ward), Vana Pira (Pat Musick), the Mummy (Alan Oppenheimer), Dr Jekyll and Mr Snyde (Gilbert), the giant ape Genghis Kong and the Hunch Bunch duo (Rob Paulsen and Frank Welker). Executive produced by William Hanna and Joseph Barbera.
Sequel: A PUP NAMED SCOOBY-DOO (qv; 1988-91)
✦✧

THE SCOOBY-DOO—DYNOMUTT HOUR:
(aka THE BEST OF SCOOBY-DOO/SCOOBY-DOO CLASSICS/THE SCOOBY-DOO—DYNOMUTT SHOW)
Everyone Hyde!
USA, 1976. Dir: Charles A. Nichols. Voices: Bob Holt, Allan Melvin, Casey Kasem, Don Messick, Gary Owens, Frank Welker. Hanna-Barbera Productions/ABC-TV. Colour.
TV series of twelve poorly produced hour-long cartoon shows, each containing two half-hour episodes featuring Scooby-Doo (Messick) and the usual gang plus, occasionally, Scooby-Doo's backwoods cousin Scooby-Dum (Daws Butler), and the adventures of superhero Radley Crowne/The Blue Falcon (Owens) and his dumb mechanical Dog Wonder, Dynomutt (Welker). In this episode, The Blue Falcon and Dog Wonder team up with Scooby and the gang to track down Mr Hyde, alias Willie the Weasel who, along with his Hyde Dog, threatens to transform the inhabitants of Big City with his formula unless he becomes mayor. Additional voices include Micky Dolenz, Virginia Gregg and Alan Oppenheimer. Executive produced by Joseph Barbera and William Hanna.
✦✧

A Frightened Hound Meets Demons Underground
USA, 1976. Dir: Charles A. Nichols. Voices: Bob Holt, Allan Melvin, Casey Kasem, Don Messick, Gary Owens, Frank Welker. Hanna-Barbera Productions/ABC-TV. Colour.
Scooby and his friends investigate various sightings of sulphurous winged demons from beneath the ground in Seattle, Washington. While exploring an underground city, they discover an old horror museum containing stone statues of werewolves, a mummy, a witch and other monsters.
✦✧

Mamba Wamba and the Voodoo Hoodoo
USA, 1976. Dir: Charles A. Nichols. Voices: Bob Holt, Allan Melvin, Casey Kasem, Don Messick, Janet Waldo, Heather North. Hanna-Barbera Productions/ABC-TV. Colour.
Scooby and his pals are special guests at a concert given by their old friend Alex Cooper (Dolenz) and his band, whose new song based on an ancient voodoo chant apparently summons up the ghosts of witch doctor Mamba Wamba and his zombie slave. This also includes a comedy relief frog.
✦✧

The No-Face Zombie Chase Case
USA, 1976. Dir: Charles A. Nichols. Voices: Bob Holt, Allan Melvin, Casey Kasem, Don Messick, Janet Waldo, Heather North. Hanna-Barbera Productions/ABC-TV. Colour.
The theft of a valuable cursed coin leads Scooby and his teenage friends to the Dilly Dally Dolly Factory where they encounter a no-faced zombie who turns out to be a robot.
Series sequel: THE SCOOBY-DOO—DYNOMUTT SHOW (qv; 1976-77)
✦✧

THE SCOOBY-DOO—DYNOMUTT SHOW:
(aka THE BEST OF SCOOBY-DOO)
Vampires, Bats and Scaredy Cats
USA, 1976. Dir: Charles A. Nichols. Voices: Bob Holt, Allan Melvin, Casey Kasem, Don Messick, Janet Waldo, Heather North. Hanna-Barbera Productions/ABC-TV. Colour.
TV series of ninety minute cartoon shows (1976-77) featuring Scooby-Doo (Messick) and his friends, plus the adventures of superhero Radley Crowne/The Blue Falcon (Gary Owens) and Dynomutt/Wonder Dog (Frank Welker). In this episode, Scooby and the gang investigate the Vampire of Skull Island.
✦✧

Who Was That Cat Creature I Saw You With Last Night
USA, 1976. Dir: Charles A. Nichols. Voices: Bob Holt, Allan Melvin, Casey Kasem, Don Messick, Janet Waldo, Heather North. Hanna-Barbera Productions/ABC-TV. Colour.
While visiting New York, Scooby and his friends discover that a magical medallion apparently transforms Daphne's (North) Aunt Olivia into a cloaked cat-creature that commits robberies.
Series sequels: SCOOBY'S ALL STARS LAFF-A-LYMPICS (1977-78) and SCOOBY'S ALL-STARS (qv; 1978-79)
✦✧

SCOOBY-DOO ON ZOMBIE ISLAND
USA, 1998. Dir: Jim Stenstrum (and Hiroshi Aoyama and Kazumi Fukushima). Voices: Adrienne Barbeau, Mary Kay Bergman, Jim Cummings, Scott Innes, Mark Hamill, B.J. Ward. Hanna Barbera Cartoons/Warner Bros. Colour.
Impressive-looking, direct-to-video cartoon feature in which TV reporter Daphne (Bergman) and her producer/cameraman Fred (Frank Welker) are reunited with mystery bookshop owner Velma (Ward) and the always-hungry Scooby (Innes) and Shaggy (Billy West) in an attempt to finally discover a real ghost. They travel in a new Mystery Machine to Moonscar Island, in the heart of haunted bayou country, where they investigate the ghost of a pirate and meet up with some scary EC comics-style zombies and a trio of vampiric were-cat creatures. This also includes some fun in-jokes for the fans and a fake gill man and vampire. Third Eye Blind perform the famous theme song, and the film is dedicated to Don Messick, the original voice of Scooby-Doo, who died in 1997. A live-action version of *Scooby-Doo* with comedian Michael Myers was announced in 1998.
Sequel: SCOOBY-DOO AND THE WITCH'S GHOST (1999)
✦✦✦

SCOOBY DOO WHERE ARE YOU!:
(aka THE BEST OF SCOOBY-DOO/SCOOBY-DOO CLASSICS)
A Gaggle of Galloping Ghosts
USA, 1969. Dir: Joseph Barbera and William Hanna.

Voices: Nicole Jaffe, Casey Kasem, Don Messick, Stefanianna Christopherson, Jean Vander Pyl, Frank Welker. Hanna-Barbera Productions/CBS-TV. Colour.
Popular half-hour cartoon TV series (1969-72, twenty-five episodes) developed by story editors Ken Spears and Joe Ruby under the titles *Mysteries Five* and *Who's Scared*. The eponymous cowardly dog (voiced by Messick, and apparently named after a line in the Frank Sinatra song 'Strangers in the Night') and his teenage friends Norville 'Shaggy' Rogers (Kasem), Freddie Jones (Welker), Daphne Blake (Christopherson or Heather North) and Velma Dinkley (Jaffe) investigate all kinds of supernatural manifestations, most of which turn out to be the work of human criminals. Over thirty years, Scooby-Doo has appeared in around 340 cartoons and Gold Key published a successful tie-in comic book. In this episode, while searching for hidden jewels in the Franken castle (imported stone-by-stone from Transylvania), a criminal disguises himself as Dracula, the Frankenstein Monster and a werewolf to scare people away.
✦✦

Mystery Mask Mix-Up
USA, 1969. Dir: Joseph Barbera and William Hanna. Voices: Nicole Jaffe, Casey Kasem, Don Messick, Heather North, Jean Vander Pyl, Frank Welker. Hanna-Barbera Productions/CBS-TV. Colour.
While celebrating the Chinese New Year, Daphne involves Scooby and the gang with the ghost of Zen Tuo and his zombie henchmen, who are searching for a stolen golden mask.
✦✧

Nowhere to Hyde
USA, 1970. Dir: Joseph Barbera and William Hanna. Voices: Nicole Jaffe, Casey Kasem, Don Messick, Heather North, Jean Vander Pyl, Frank Welker. Hanna-Barbera Productions/CBS-TV. Colour.
Dr Jekyll's new vitamin formula may be turning him into the jewel-stealing ghost of his great-grandfather's green-faced Hyde, although Scooby and the gang suspect that Helga the acrobatic housemaid may be the real culprit.
✦✦

Scooby Doo and a Mummy, Too
USA, 1969. Dir: Joseph Barbera and William Hanna. Voices: Stefanianna Christopherson, Nicole Jaffe, Casey Kasem, Don Messick, Vic Perrin, Jean Vander Pyl. Hanna-Barbera Productions/CBS-TV. Colour.
The 2,000 year-old mummy of Ankh apparently comes to life in a museum and turns its victims to stone. However, Scooby and his friends discover that the living mummy is really a criminal after an ancient Egyptian coin which reveals the hiding place of a diamond scarab.
✦✧

Which Witch is Which?
USA, 1969. Dir: Joseph Barbera and William Hanna. Voices: Nicole Jaffe, Casey Kasem, Don Messick, Vic Perrin, Stefanianna Christopherson, Jean Vander Pyl. Hanna-Barbera Productions/CBS-TV. Colour.
Scooby and the gang are taking a short cut through a swamp when they encounter a zombie and learn about the legend of an old witch who created him with her voodoo magic.
✦✦

Who's Afraid of the Big Bad Werewolf
USA, 1970. Dir: Joseph Barbera and William Hanna. Voices: Nicole Jaffe, Casey Kasem, Don Messick, Heather North, Jean Vander Pyl, Frank Welker. Hanna-Barbera Productions/CBS-TV. Colour.
While on a camping trip, Scooby and his pals investigate a ghostly green werewolf, Silas Long, and uncover a sheep smuggling ring in an old abandoned mill.
Series sequel: THE NEW SCOOBY-DOO MOVIES (qv; 1972)
✦✧

SCOOBY'S ALL-STARS: South America/Transylvania

USA, 1978. Voices: Mel Blanc, Daws Butler, Casey Kasem, Don Messick, Gary Owens, Frank Welker. Hanna-Barbera Productions/ABC-TV. Colour.
Ninety minute cartoon TV show (1978-79, eight episodes) that includes segments of *Captain Caveman and the Teen Angels* plus *Scooby's All Star Laff-a-Lympics*, a series of half-hour episodes featuring races around the world between three teams of various Hanna-Barbera characters — The Scooby-Dooby's (including Scooby, Shaggy, Scooby-Dum, The Blue Falcon, Dynomutt, and Captain Caveman and the Teen Angels), The Yogi-Yahooey's and The Really Rotten's (featuring Mr and Mrs Creeply and Mumbly). This episode involves the teams racing to Transylvania. Additional voices include Joe Besser and Scatman Crothers.
Series sequels: THE SCOOBY-DOO SHOW (1979-80) and SCOOBY-DOO AND SCRAPPY-DOO (qv; 1979-80)
✦✧

SCORPIO

USA, 1998. Dir: Ron Atkins. Colour.
Independent feature, filmed in Florida, about two couples menaced in a graveyard by reanimated corpses.
✦

SCREAM

USA, 1995. Dir: Wes Craven. With: David Arquette, Neve Campbell, Courteney Cox, Matthew Lillard, Rose McGowan, Skeet Ulrich. Miramax/Woods Entertainment/ Dimension Films. Colour.
Filmed under the title *Scary Movie*, this was a surprise box office hit from director Craven (who has an uncredited cameo). Following an impressive opening sequence (featuring Drew Barrymore as the victim), screenwriter Kevin Williamson's recreation of the 1980s stalk 'n' slash cycle follows all the expected genre conventions, despite its annoying use of movie references and the surprise revelation of two psychos working together. As the list of suspects grows, the teenage friends of Woodsboro High School student Sidney Prescott (Campbell) are gruesomely killed off while she receives taunting telephone calls from the ghost-masked murderer. With an uncredited Henry Winkler as the school principal and clips from *Frankenstein* (1931) and *Halloween* (1978) on TV.
Sequel: SCREAM 2 (qv; 1997)
✦✦✦

SCREAM AND SCREAM AGAIN

UK, 1969. Dir: Gordon Hessler. With: Vincent Price, Christopher Lee, Peter Cushing, Judy Huxtable, Alfred Marks, Michael Gothard. American International/ Amicus. Colour.
A cult classic of the science fiction/horror genre, which benefits from a clever and amusing performance by Marks as harassed police superintendent Bellaver, investigating a series of savage murders where each of the bodies has been sucked dry of blood. Christopher Wicking's confused screenplay, based on Peter Saxon's 1966 novel *The Disorientated Man*, finally leads to a plot by Price's Dr Browning to create a new race of superbeings. The three horror stars are grievously wasted (particularly Cushing, who shares no scenes with the other two and is killed off early on). With Anthony Newlands, Yutte (Jytte) Stensgaard and Peter Sallis. David Whittaker's original jazz music and two songs by The Amen Corner were subsequently replaced on some Orion prints by an inferior synthesiser score from Kendall Schmidt. 'But what of the dream?' asks Price. 'There is only nightmare,' replies Lee.
✦✦✦✧

SCREAM BLACULA SCREAM

USA, 1973. Dir: Bob Kelljan (Robert Kelljchian). With: William Marshall, Don Mitchell, Pam Grier, Michael Conrad, Richard Lawson, Bernie Hamilton. American International Productions. Colour.
Disappointing sequel to *Blacula* (1972), filmed under the title *Blacula II* and made towards the end of AIP's blaxploitation period by *Count Yorga* director Kelljan. When Marshall's dignified Prince Mamuwalde is resurrected through black magic, he attempts to convince voodoo priestess Lisa (Grier) to 'cure' his vampirism until she finally destroys him through a fetish doll. This includes flashbacks to the first film, featuring an uncredited Charles Macauley as Dracula, and some nice cartoon vampire-into-bat transformations. Samuel Z. Arkoff was executive producer.
✦✦

SCREAM OF THE DEMON LOVER
(Orig: IL CASTELLO DALLE PORTE DI FUOCO/IVANNA. USA: aka BLOOD CASTLE)
Italy/Spain, 1970 (1971). Dir: J. (José) L. (Luis) Merino. With: Jeffrey Chase (Charles Quinney), Jennifer Harvey (Erna Schurer), Agostina Belli, Cristiana Galloni, Antonio Gimenez Escribano, Mariano Vidal Molina. Prodimex Films/Hispaner Films/New World Pictures. Colour.
Nineteenth century horror drama in which beautiful biochemist Ivanna (Harvey) arrives at Dalmar Castle, where the local Baron Janos Dalmar (Chase, dubbed by Richard Johnson) is trying to reanimate the charred remains of his brother Igor. He needn't have bothered, as his horribly-scarred sibling is running around the village killing off the local women. Merino's direction includes some imaginative touches, and Belli gives a stand-out performance as Olga, the evil housekeeper.
✦✦

SCREAM OF THE WOLF
USA, 1974. Dir: Dan Curtis. With: Peter Graves, Clint Walker, Jo Ann Pflug, Philip Carey, Don Megowan, Brian Richards. Metromedia/Dan Curtis/ABC-TV. Colour.
TV movie scripted by Richard Matheson, based on the story 'The Hunter' by David Case. Moody big game hunter Douglas Byron (an interesting performance by Walker) pretends to be a murderous werewolf and forces his friend John Wetherby (Graves) to exert his masculinity while hunting him down. Curtis' pedestrian direction and the plot's bizarre gay subtext hardly do justice to the excellent source material.
✦✧

SCREAM 2
USA, 1997. Dir: Wes Craven. With: David Arquette, Neve Campbell, Courteney Cox, Sarah Michelle Gellar, Jamie Kennedy, Laurie Metcalf. Miramax/Dimension Films/ Konrad Pictures/Craven-Maddalena Films. Colour.
Following the surprise box office success of *Scream* (1995), director Craven and screenwriter Kevin Williamson were again teamed for this slick but implausible follow-up, filmed under the title *Scream: The Sequel*. Set two years after the original, Sidney Prescott (Campbell) is now in her freshman year at a midwest college when she finds herself being stalked by a copycat ghost-masked murderer. Meanwhile, pushy TV reporter Gale Weathers (Cox) has written a best-selling book about the earlier killings, which has been made into a movie called *Stab* (with Tori Spelling playing Sidney). Jada Pinkett appears as the killer's first victim while attending the film's unbelievable première. A ludicrous number of suspects and a hysterical ending didn't stop this from becoming another box office smash. With a wasted Gellar (TV's *Buffy the Vampire Slayer* [1996-], etc) as a victim who watches *Nosferatu* (1922) on TV, Jerry O'Connell, Liev Schreiber, David Warner and a cameo by writer Williamson.
Sequel: SCREAM 3 (1999)
✦✦✧

ANGUS SCRIMM (Lawrence Rory Guy) [b 1938]

Cadaverous American character actor, best known for playing the demonic Tall Man in *Phantasm* (1979), *Phantasm II* (1988), *Phantasm Lord of the Dead* (1993) and *Phantasm IV Oblivion* (1998).
qv: *Subspecies* (1990); *Transylvania Twist* (1989); *Vampirella* (1996).

SCROOGED
USA, 1988. Dir: Richard Donner. With: Bill Murray, Karen Allen, John Forsythe, Bobcat Goldthwait, Carol Kane, Robert Mitchum. Mirage/Paramount. Colour.
Irreverent black comedy 'suggested' by Charles Dickens' *A Christmas Carol*. Murray plays Frank Cross, a wonderfully despicable network TV president who hates Christmas. He is visited by three very strange ghosts who teach him to change his ways. Along with Forsythe (who returns from the dead as a grey-faced rotting zombie), veteran Mitchum, Michael J. Pollard and John Glover, there are also cameos by Jamie Farr, Robert Goulet, Buddy Hackett, Lee Majors, Anne Ramsey (it was one of her last films) and Logan Ramsey, with John Houseman (in his last film) playing himself. Only the overly-sentimental ending spoils the fun. Music score by Danny Elfman.
✦✦✦

THE SECRET FILES OF THE SPYDOGS:
Spin or the Secret File of the Television Taboo
USA, 1998. Dir: Dave Simons. Voices: Micky Dolenz, Adam West, Mary Kay Berghan, Jim Cummings, Michael Donovan, Jess Harnell. Saban Entertainment/Fox Kids Network/YTV. Colour.
Fun half-hour cartoon TV series (1998-), based upon characters created by co-executive producer Jim Benton, in which all dogs belong to a secret organisation controlled by Dog Zero (West) dedicated to keeping mankind safe from really bad stuff. In this twelve minute segment, a TV station controlled by spin (witch) doctors is turning its human viewers into TV zombies. Series guest voices include Clancy Brown, Robert Culp, Eddie Deezen, Ami Dolenz, Michael Gough, Lou Rawls and Frank Welker.
✦✦
Twilight or the Secret File of the Meowing Mummies
USA, 1998. Dir: Dave Simons. Voices: Micky Dolenz, Adam West, Mary Kay Berghan, Jim Cummings, Michael Donovan, Jess Harnell. Saban Entertainment/Fox Kids Network/YTV. Colour.
Twelve minute segment in which the undercover hounds battle master villain Catastrophe, the world's smartest feline, who has reanimated an army of Egyptian mummy cats to complete his plans for immortality and world domination.
✦✦

THE SECRET OF THE MUMMY
(Orig: LAGO MALDITO/EL SECRETO DE LA MOMIA/ O SEGREDO DA MÚMIA)
Brazil, 1982. Dir: Ivan Cardoso. With: Anseilmo Vasconcelos, Clarice Piovesan, Wilson Grey, Tania Boscoli, Felipe Falcáo, Regina Casé. Mapa Filmes/Super 8 Produçoes. Colour.
Horror comedy set in 1954. After murdering the owners of a map that has been divided into eight parts, the mad professor Expedito Vitus (who looks like Boris Karloff!) travels to Egypt and discovers the 3,000 year-old mummy of Runamb (Daniel Stambovsky), which he takes back to Brazil. A student of Dr Arthur Frankenstein, the professor uses his elixir of life to bring the psychopathic mummy back to life. However, Vitus' devoted servant Igor sends the mummy out to kidnap women and bring them back to a dungeon full of bestial lesbians. When radio station reporter Miriam searches for a missing colleague, Runamb believes she is the reincarnation of his lost love, Nasha. This low-budget insanity features lots of nudity, a bloody severed head, old newsreel footage, several well-known songs (including a Portuguese cover of The Beatles!), music from *The Egyptian* (1954), and the special participation of the director's mentor José Mojica Marins (aka 'Coffin Joe').
✦

SECRETS OF SEX
(USA: BIZARRE/EROTIC TALES FROM THE MUMMY'S TOMB)
UK, 1969 (1970). Dir: Antony Balch. With: Yvonne Quenet, Kenneth Benda, Mike Briton, Cathy Howard, Maria Frost, Sue Bond. Richard Gordon/Noteworthy Films. Colour.
Softcore sex anthology that marked the feature début of thirty-two year-old co-writer/director Balch (*Horror Hospital* (1973), etc). A 1,000 year-old mummy, cursed to wander the world observing tormented lovers, relates a number of stories. These involve a sadistic photographer, the birth of a freak, a seductive cat burglar, a silent movie-style secret agent, a reptile voyeur and a woman searching for the soul of a previous lover. Narrated by veteran Valentine Dyall; Richard Gordon was the executive producer. It was heavily cut in Britain.
✦

SEDUCED BY EVIL

USA, 1994. Dir: Tony Wharmby. With: Suzanne Somers, James B. Sikking, John Vargas, Mindy Spence, Nancy Moonves, Julie Carmen. Wilshire Court Productions/USA Network. Colour.

While experiencing a series of psychic dreams, tourist magazine writer Lee Lindsay (Somers) interviews a mysterious healer (Vargas) in the desert. He turns out to be a seventeenth century Brazilian shape-shifter who believes her body contains the soul of his long-lost love. When he begins harming those close to her, Lindsay discovers her own spirit powers and briefly transforms into a wolf to defeat the evil sorcerer. Based on the book *Brujo* by Ann Arrington Wolcott, this romantic TV movie was filmed in Tucson, Arizona.

✦✧

SEEDING OF A GHOST

(Orig: ZHONG GUI)

Hong Kong, 1983 (1986). Dir: Yang Chuan. With: Phillip Ko (Kao Fei), Chuan Chi-Hui, Chu Shao-Chiang (Tsu Sui-Kung). Shaw Brothers/Ocean Shores Video. Colour.

This was originally intended to be the third entry in the gory *Black Magic* trilogy. Falsely accused of murdering his unfaithful wife Irene, taxi driver Chou Li (Kao) asks for help from a sorcerer he saved and together they dig up the woman's mummified body. She is brought back to life as a *plazawa* — a zombie that sucks the life-force out of its victims — and sets out to supernaturally revenge herself on the two men responsible for raping and killing her. During the climax, a woman gives birth to a tentacled monster.

✦✧

SEE HEAR!:

The Monkey's Paw

UK, circa 1989. Dir: Carol Winton. With: John Lee, Maureen Denmark, Clive Mason, Doug Alker, Craig Flynn. BBC-TV. Colour.

Half-hour TV adaptation of W.W. Jacobs' classic story performed in a British sign language translation.

Episode remake: TALES FROM THE CRYPT: Last Respects (qv; 1996)

✦

SEEING THINGS:

The Eyes of Ra

Canada, 1986. Dir: George McCowan. With: Louis Del Grande, Martha Gibson, Janet-Laine Green, Frank Adamson, Ivan Beaulieu, Murray Westgate. CBC-TV. Colour.

Hour-long TV series (1981-87, forty-three episodes) set in Toronto, about middle-aged newspaper reporter Louie Ciccone (Del Grande) who has psychic visions of murders being committed. In this episode, while visiting a museum, Louie has an image of an ancient Egyptian murder that is similar to a series of contemporary killings occurring in the city.

✦✦✧

EIN SELTSAMER FALL

Germany, 1914. Dir: Max Mack. With: Alwin Neuss, Hanni Weisse, Lotte Neumann. Vitascope. B&W.

Although unofficial, this fifty minute silent drama was the first German version of Robert Louis Stevenson's short novel *Strange Case of Dr. Jekyll and Mr. Hyde*. From the director of *The Other* (1913).

Remake: DR. JEKYLL AND MR. HYDE DONE TO A FRAZZLE (qv; 1914)

✦

LA SEÑORA MUERTE

Mexico, 1968. Dir: Jaime Salvador. With: Regina Torne, John Carradine, Elsa Cardenas, Miguel Angel Alvarez, Isela Vega, Victor Junco. Filmica Vergara/Columbia. Colour.

Carradine's smirking mad scientist, Dr Diabolo, forces a beautiful fashion designer (Torne) to murder young women and then use their blood to stop her features from periodically reverting into those of an ugly hag. One of her victims is stabbed to death in a spooky wax museum that features figures of a mangy werewolf and the Frankenstein Monster. This also includes a love-sick hunch-backed assistant and gratuitous fashion parade footage. It was made back-to-back with *Pacto Diabólico* (1968), also featuring Carradine.

✦

THE SERPENT AND THE RAINBOW

USA/Dominican Republic/Haiti, 1987 (1988). Dir: Wes Craven. With: Bill Pullman, Cathy Tyson, Zakes Mokae, Paul Winfield, Brent Jennings, Conrad Roberts. Universal. Colour.

This was director Craven's attempt to make a serious zombie thriller based on Wade Davis' non-fiction book about voodoo in pre-revolutionary Haiti. The film certainly benefits from the genuine locations and an opening sequence that is breathtaking. The problem is that Pullman's Harvard anthropologist Dr Dennis Alan is not a particularly strong character, and once he discovers the deadly powder that turns men into the walking dead, there's nowhere else for the film to go. With Mokae as the evil zombie master Dargent Peytraud, a ludicrous haunted chair, and a brief cameo by horror veteran Michael Gough.

✦✦✧

SERPENT'S LAIR

Romania/USA, 1995. Dir: Jeffrey Reiner. With: Jeff Fahey, Lisa B., Heather Medved, Patrick Bachau. Warnervision. Colour.

Direct-to-video erotic thriller, filmed in Bucharest. After moving into a new apartment in an old building, Tom (Fahey) is seduced by a succubus named Lilith (Lisa B.) who can transform into a cat.

✦✧

THE SERVANTS OF MIDNIGHT

USA, 1992. Dir: Jack Stephen. With: Alexis DeVall, Cindy Lee (Sonja), Ona Zee, Tianna Taylor, Shauna Rose, Steve Drake. Conderella/CDI Home Video. Colour.

Hardcore feature in which a woman (DeVall) in a strait-jacket hallucinates a number of sexual encounters that include herself and a vampire-like woman (Zee), who is the descendant of the Count himself, on a coffin.

✦

SEVEN DEAD IN THE CAT'S EYES

(Orig: LA MORTE NEGLI OCCHI DEL GATTO/LES DIABLESSES. USA: aka 7 DEATHS IN THE CAT'S EYE)

Italy/France/West Germany, 1972 (1973). Dir: Anthony M. Dawson (Antonio Margheriti). With: Jane Birkin, Hiram Keller, Françoise Christophe, Venantino Venantini, Serge Gainsbourg, Anton Diffring. Starkiss-Falcon International/Capitol Films/Roxy Film. Colour.

When Corringa MacGrieff (Birkin) joins a group of relatives for a family reunion at a spooky Scottish castle, a detective (Gainsbourg) investigates a series of gory murders linked with an ancient curse about a woman changing into a vampiric cat. This old-fashioned murder mystery was filmed under the title *Corringa*. With Alan Collins (Luciano Pigozzi).

✦✧

SEVEN FOXES

Hong Kong, 1984 (1985). Dir: Yin-Ping Chu. Ocean Shore Video. Colour.

Cantonese horror comedy set in an old dark house, where a knife-wielding killer wears a Frankenstein Monster mask. It turns out to be another plot to gain an inheritance.

✦✧

SEVEN MAIDENS

(USA: aka HOLY WEAPON)

Hong Kong, 1993. Dir: Wong Ching (Wong Ching-Jing/Lau Sze-Yu). With: Michelle Yeoh, Maggie Cheung, Chung Man, Simon Yam, Sandra Ng, Ng Man-Tat. Regal Films. Colour.

Action comedy in which seven female virgins are needed to combat the evil Super Sword (Yam), who can become a blade of light to decapitate his opponents. Among the women who team up to battle the villain are a beautiful maiden (Man) who can change into a

spiderwoman to trap her male pursuers, and a peasant boy, who transforms into a girl to complete the line-up of heroines. This confusing fantasy also includes a green-haired zombie vampire and Super Sword's flying henchmen.
✦✦

THE SEVEN VAMPIRES
(Orig: AS SETE VAMPIRAS. USA: 7 VAMPIRES)
Brazil, 1985. Dir: Ivan Cardoso. With: Nicole Puzzi, Simone Carvalho, Lucelia Santos, Nuño Leal Maia, Andrea Beltrao, Leo Jaime. Embrafilme/Superoito Productions. Colour.
Low-budget horror/musical that is an odd mixture of bad comedy and gratuitous nudity. When a carnivorous plant from Africa is imported into 1950s Rio de Janiero, it eats the face off dedicated botanist Frederico Rossi and infects his wife Silvia with a mysterious malady that produces rapid ageing. Pretty soon she is staging a cabaret act titled 'The Dance of the Seven Female Vampires', while a masked killer terrorises the city, draining the blood from victims. Introduced by Alfred Hitchcock (re-dubbed from his TV series)!
✦✧

SEVIMLI FRANKESTAYN
Turkey, 1975. Dir: Nejat Saydem. With: Savas Basar, Bülent Kayabas, Meral Orhonsay, Sevda Karaca, Yuksel Gozen, Mualla Firat. Acar Films. Colour.
Comedy spoof that apparently owes much to *Young Frankenstein* (1974). The title translates as 'My Friend Frankenstein'.
✦

LES SEXANDROIDES
(aka LA DAGYDE LES SEXANDROIDE/SEXANDROIDE)
France, 1987. Dir: Michel Ricaud. With: Daniel Dubois, Le Petit Mescal Company. Video Self. Colour.
Three-part hardcore horror anthology shot on video. The final story involves vampires.
✦

SEX AND THE SINGLE VAMPIRE
USA, 1970 (1971). Dir: Modunk Phreezer. With: John C. Holmes, John Dallahan, L.G. Allard, Jesse Moreno, Sandy Dempsey, Stephanie Sarver. Xcalibre Motion Picture Company. Colour.
Hardcore horror comedy in which Holmes plays Count Spatula (with plastic fangs and a mock-Lugosi accent), whose home is invaded by seven swingers who want to have sex in a haunted house. The Count observes their various couplings until, after tying up the three men, he beds the four women before turning into a skeleton.
✦

SEX & ZEN II
(Orig: YU PUI TSUEN ER ZHI YU NU XIN JING/YUK PO TUEN YI JI YUK NUI SAM GING)
Hong Kong, 1996. Dir: Chin Man-Kei. With: Loletta Lee (Loletta Lee Lai-Chun), Shu Qi (Hsu Chi/Shu Kei), Xu Jin-Jiang (Elvis Tsui Kam-Kong), Ben Ng (Ben Ng Ngai-Cheung), Lok Tak-Wah. Golden Movies International/ Jing's Production/Golden Harvest/Tai Seng Video. Colour.
Softcore sequel in name only to Michael Mak's successful 1991 original. The chaste Yau (Lee) is appalled by the sexual behaviour of her father Simon Khan (Jin-Jiang) and decides to attend school disguised as a boy. When Siu-Tsui (Qi), a demonic vampire also known as Mirage Lady, marries into her family, Yau teams up with swordsman Ironman (Ng) to battle the supernatural hermaphrodite who drains the life-force from her victims during sex.
✦✦✧

SEX EXPRESS
UK, 1975. Dir: Derek Ford. With: Heather Deeley, James Lister, Derek Martin, Jack Rigby, Terry Walsh, Tim Burr. Blackwater. Colour.
Four adult fantasies, one featuring Lister as a vampire and another involving ghosts.
✦

SEX SCIENTIST
USA, 1993. With: Pearl Madison, Carl Jammer, Nasty Natasha, Buffy Ho, Don Fernando, Tony Martino. Fat Dog Productions. Colour.
Hardcore comedy in which Dr Spankingtime and his assistant create the most beautiful and sensual nymphomaniac in the world. They then conduct a lengthy series of sex tests to determine their creation's levels of erotic pleasure and sexual performance.
✦

THE SEXUAL LIFE OF FRANKENSTEIN
France/USA, 1970. Dir: Harry Novack. Novack. Colour.
Another sex film apparently featuring Frankenstein's creation.
✦

SEXY PROIBITISSIMO
(Orig: SUPER SEXY INTERDIT. USA: aka FORBIDDEN FEMININITY)
Italy, 1963 (1964). Dir: Marcello Martinelli (Gino Mordini). With: Karmela, Lilli de Saigon, Monique, Joan Clair, Diana West, Poppy Scott. Gino Mordini Produzioni Cinematografiche/Atlantis Films/Olympic International. Colour.
Nudie musical with a history of striptease that includes the Frankenstein Monster pursuing the doctor's laboratory assistant, a female astronaut surrounded by moon men with antennas, and the victim of a peeping vampire. The American version apparently includes new footage of New York strip acts and an exterior shot of Dracula's castle. With narration scripted by Bob Cresse.
✦

SHADA KALO
India, 1953. Dir: Amal Bose. With: Sipra, Sisir, Gurudas, Pahari Sanyal, Biren Chatterjee. Mitra. B&W.
Based on Robert Louis Stevenson's *Strange Case of Dr. Jekyll and Mr. Hyde*. The title translates as 'Black and White'.
Remake: ABBOTT AND COSTELLO MEET DR. JEKYLL AND MR. HYDE (qv; 1953)
✦

SHADES OF DARKNESS:
(USA: MYSTERY! UK: aka HAUNTED)
Feet Foremost
UK, 1983. Dir: Gordon Flemyng. With: Jeremy Kemp, Joanna Van Gyseghem, Peter Machin, Heather Chasen, Carol Royle. Granada UK/ITV. Colour.
Hour-long TV series (seven episodes) based on classic supernatural stories. In this episode, scriptwriter Alan Plater updates L.P. Hartley's story to a contemporary setting. Guests at a house-warming party discover that the ghost haunting a fourteenth century country manor is a vampire seeking revenge.
✦✦

SHADOW CHASERS:
Blood and Magnolias
USA, 1986. Dir: Chuck Bowman. With: Dennis Dugan, Trevor Eve, Nina Foch, Hermione Baddeley, Cameron Mitchell, Mary-Margaret Humes. Warner Bros/Kenneth Johnson Productions/ABC-TV. Colour.
Short-lived, hour-long TV series (1985-86, fourteen episodes), created by Kenneth Johnson, in which tabloid reporter Edgar 'Benny' Benedek (Dugan) teams up with professor of anthropology Jonathan MacKenzie (Eve) to investigate the paranormal. Veteran Foch (*The Return of the Vampire* [1943], etc) plays Jonathan's boss, Dr Julianne Moorhouse. In this episode, while investigating a strange death, Benny and Jonathan discover a vampire living in a Southern Gothic mansion.
✦✦✧
Curse of the Full Moon
USA, 1986. Dir: Bob Sweeney. With: Dennis Dugan, Trevor Eve, Nina Foch, Hannah Cutrona, Mike Preston. Warner Bros/Kenneth Johnson Productions/ABC-TV. Colour.
Benny and Jonathan investigate reports of a werewolf and discover a girl who has been raised by wolves.
✦✦

Parts Unknown
USA, 1985. Dir: Bob Sweeney. With: Dennis Dugan, Trevor Eve, Nina Foch, Avery Schreiber, Robert F. Lyons, Hermione Baddeley. Warner Bros/Kenneth Johnson Productions/ABC-TV. Colour.
While investigating reports about modern-day zombies and grave robbing, Benny and Jonathan discover a suspicious health club and a man who has been buried alive.
✦✦

Phantom of the Galleria
USA, 1985. Dir: Alan Myerson. With: Dennis Dugan, Trevor Eve, Nina Foch, Patricia Duff, Michael McManus, David Welch. Warner Bros/Kenneth Johnson Productions/ABC-TV. Colour.
Benny and Jonathan are on the trail of a hideous figure, rumoured to be a 148 year-old ghost, who is terrorising a shopping mall.
✦✦

Spirit of St. Louis
USA, 1985. Dir: Victor Lobl. With: Dennis Dugan, Trevor Eve, Nina Foch, Laurie O'Brien, Vincent Schiavelli, Richard Romanus. Warner Bros/Kenneth Johnson Productions/ABC-TV. Colour.
Benny and Jonathan investigate a bizarre death that leads them to an ancient Egyptian cult worshipping King Tut.
✦✦

SHADOWMAN

(Orig: L'HOMME SANS VISAGE/NUITS ROUGE)
France/Italy, 1973 (1976). Dir: Georges Franju. With: Jacques Champreux, Gayle Hunnicutt, Josephine Chaplin, Gert Fröbe, Raymond Bussières, Ugo Pagliai. Terra Film/SOAT/Connoisseur Films/New Line Cinema. Colour.
Feature version of an eight-hour TV serial. Red-hooded criminal mastermind The Shadowman (Champreux) uses zombie slaves created by the mad Dr Dutrueil (Clement Harari) as assassins in his search for the missing half of a map revealing the location of the lost treasure of the Knights Templar. With his penultimate film, Franju (who was also responsible for the music) once again pays homage to the serials of Louis Feuillade (who was Champreux's grandfather).
✦✦

SHADOW OF DRACULA

Canada, 1973. Colour.
Hour-long amateur production, filmed in Toronto under the government's Opportunities for Youth Program.
✦

SHADOWS IN THE CITY

USA, 1990. Dir: Ari Roussimoff. With: Craig Smith, Nick Zedd, Brinke Stevens, Taylor Mead, Joe Coleman, Annie Sprinkle. B&W/Colour.
Underground feature filmed over five years and originally set to star Joe Spinnell. A suicidal carnival barker (Smith) returns to New York and finds himself among pasty-faced zombies.
✦

SHADOWS IN THE DARK

USA, 1989 (1990). Dir: Bruce Seven. With: Tianna (Tara Collins), Randy Spears, Bionca (Bionica Bradley), Victoria Paris, Randy West, Cherri Bush. 4-Play Video. Colour.
The plot of this hardcore vampire movie sounds similar to *Dance of the Damned* (1988). Spears plays an alien vampire who watches various sex acts performed in a moody nightclub. Afterwards, he asks the participants some personal questions before he is destroyed by sunlight.
✦

SHADOW WARRIORS

USA, 1994. Dir: Lamar Card. With: Evan Lurie, Terry O'Quinn, Russ Tertyask, Ashley Anne Graham, Timothy Patrick Cavanaugh. SGE/SAK/New Horizons Home Video. Colour.
Evil security expert Connors (O'Quinn) and doctor Natalie (Graham) use corpses to create enhanced cyborg bodyguards.
✦✧

SHADOW ZONE: THE UNDEAD EXPRESS

Canada/USA, 1996. Dir: Stephen Williams. With: Chauncey Leopardi, Natanya Ross, Tony T. Johnson, Ron White, Wes Craven, Ron Silver. Showtime Networks/Hallmark Entertainment/Lynch Entertainment. Colour.
Introduced by The Reaper (Stephen Russell), this fun cable TV movie is based on the young adult book series by J.R. Black. Young Zach (Leopardi) and his friends Gabe (Ross) and J.T. (Johnson) encounter turn-of-the-century vampire Valentine (a suave and subdued Silver) and his fellow undead travellers on a 'lost' train on the New York subway. Horror director Craven portrays a strange counsellor, while Zach watches a film entitled *Blood Curse of the Vampire* on video. The impressive make-up effects were created by Paul Jones.
✦✦✦✧

THE SHAGGY DOG

USA, 1994. Dir: Dennis Dugan. With: Ed Begley Jr, Sharon Lawrence, Jon Polito, James Cromwell, Jeremy Sisto, Scott Weinger. The Walt Disney Company/Zaloom Mayfield Productions/ABC-TV. Colour.
TV movie remake of the 1959 Disney film, based on characters from *The Hound of Florence* by Felix Salten. Teenage amateur inventor Wilbur Daniels (Weinger) is periodically transformed into a talking sheepdog by the magical ring of Lucrezia Borgia. This also features a sub-pot involving an international jewel thief (Cromwell), while actor-turned-director Dugan manages to incorporate various *Lady and the Tramp* (1955), *Beethoven* (1992) and werewolf in-jokes, including clips from Hammer's *The Curse of the Werewolf* (1960)! With Natasha Gregson Wagner.
✦✦

SHAITANI ILAAKA

India, 1990. Dir: Kiran Ramsay. Colour.
After being shot, a shape-shifting witch transforms into a hairy wolf-like creature.
✦✦

SHAKE RATTLE & ROLL IV

Philippines, 1992. Dir: Peque Gallaga and Lore Reyes. With: Janice de Belen, Edu Manzano, Manilyn Reynes. Regal Films. Colour.
Another compilation of three short films. A chemical potion turns a man into a super-strong monster in 'Ang Guro', and 'Ang Kapitbahay' is about a sympathetic tree creature. 'Ang Madre' features a large bat-winged vampire called a *manananggal* that splits itself horizontally in half and then the top part flies off in search of victims.
✦✧

SHAKE, RATTLE & ROLL 2

Philippines, 1990. Dir: Peque Gallaga and Lore Reyes. With: Janice de Belen, Eric Quizon, Caridad Sanchez, Eddie Guiterrez, Isabel Granada, Joey Marquez. Regal Films/Springtowne Home Video. Colour.
Compilation of three short films. In 'Multo' a man is possessed by a ghost when he puts his wedding ring on, while 'Kulam' involves a witch's voodoo doll that raises the dead in a hospital. The final episode, 'Aswang', is about villagers who drink blood and transform into the vampiric liver-eating creatures of the title.
Sequel: SHAKE, RATTLE & ROLL III (1991)
✦✧

SHANKS

USA/Canada, 1974. Dir: William Castle (and Marcel Marceau and Jack Hill). With: Marcel Marceau, Philippe Clay, Tsilla Chelton, Cindy Eilbacher, Helena Kallianiotes, Larry Bishop. Paramount. Colour.
Announced as *Shock*, this was the last film to be directed by 'Showman of Shock' Castle, who died in 1977. French mime artist Marceau plays mute puppeteer Malcolm Shanks who uses the electrical invention of wrinkled scientist Old Walker (also played by Marceau) to bring the dead back to life. A strange, uneven film in which it's never clear whether the revived corpses are merely imagined by Shanks. With minimal dialogue, old-fashioned title cards, a gang of bikers, an unhealthy relationship between the puppeteer

and a young girl (Eilbacher), and Castle making his usual cameo appearance as a grocer. Alex North's terrible music score was nominated for an Academy Award.
✦✧

SHATTER DEAD

USA, 1993 (1994). Dir: Scooter McCrae. With: Stark Raven, Flora Fauna, Daniel 'smalls' Johnson, Robert Wells, Marina Del Rey, John Weiner. Seeing Eye Dog Productions/Tempe Video/Screen Edge. Colour.

Shot on video over eleven days in Middletown, New York, for $4,000, this independent horror thriller is set in the near future when the dead have stopped dying. The gun-toting Susan (Raven) attempts to get home to her boyfriend Dan (Johnson) through a countryside populated by religious fanatics and the walking dead. With special effects supervised by Pericles Lewnes (*Redneck Zombies* [1987], etc). This was winner of a Best Independent Film award at the 1995 FantaFestival in Rome.
✦

SHE

Spain/Italy, 1983. Dir: Avi Nesher. With: Sandahl Bergman, Quin Kessler, David Goss, Harrison Muller, Gordon Mitchell, David Brandon. Eduardo Sarlui/ Continental Motion Pictures/American National Enterprises. Colour.

Despite being 'inspired' by H. Rider Haggard's famous novel, this is just another terrible post-holocaust barbarian fantasy/comedy with a heavy-metal soundtrack by the likes of Motorhead, Rick Wakeman, Justin Hayward and Maggie Bell. The eponymous warrior queen (Bergman) teams up with wanderers Tom (Goss), Dick (Muller) and Hari (Elena Wiedermann) to battle radioactive mutants, mad scientists, vampires and the warrior Norks. With cheap-looking sets and unconvincing special effects, this is one to miss at all costs.
✦

SHE DEVIL

USA, 1956 (1957). Dir: Kurt Neumann. With: Mari Blanchard, Jack Kelly, Albert Dekker, John Archer, Blossom Rock, Paul Cavanagh. Regal Films/Twentieth Century-Fox. B&W.

Based on the short story 'The Adaptive Ultimate' by John Jessel (Stanley G. Weinbaum), previously adapted in 1955 for TV's *Science Fiction Theater* (1955-57). Blanchard plays a terminally ill woman suffering from tuberculosis who is cured by a serum distilled from fruit flies. As a side-effect, she can change her hair colour and has super-strength. She kills anyone who gets in her way until, in the end, the antidote kills her. From the director of *The Fly* (1958). Filmed in Regalscope.
✦

BARBARA SHELLEY [b 1933]

British actress and former model. Although she made her genre début in *Cat Girl* (1957), she is best remembered for her roles in Hammer's *The Gorgon* (1964), *Dracula Prince of Darkness* (1965), *Rasputin the Mad Monk* (1965) and *Quatermass and the Pit* (1967).
qv: *Blood of the Vampire* (1958).

PATY SHEPARD [b 1945]

American-born actress (also known as Patty Sheppard) who has lived in Spain since she was eighteen. After work as a model and in TV commercials, she appeared with Paul Naschy in *Dracula vs. Frankenstein* (1969), *The Werewolf vs. the Vampire Woman* (1970) and *Curse of the Devil* (1973), portraying a vampiric Countess in the latter two.
qv: *Crypt of the Living Dead* (1972).

SHERLOCK HOLMES: The Laughing Mummy

France/UK/USA, 1954. Dir: Steve Previn With: Ronald Howard, H. (Howard) Marion Crawford, Barry Mackay, Paul Bonifas, June Cranford, Lois Marechal. Guild Films/ SH Television/MPTV Television. B&W.

Episode of the half-hour syndicated TV series (thirty-nine episodes) filmed in France and on location in England, with thirty-six year-old Howard as a youthful Sherlock Holmes and Crawford as his faithful Doctor Watson. In this episode, the detective duo investigate a mummy belonging to their old friend Taunton (Mackay) which apparently laughs at certain times. In the end, the solution turns out to be much more prosaic than expected.
Series sequel: THE HOUND OF THE BASKERVILLES (1959)
✦✧

SHERLOCK HOLMES IN CARACAS

Venezuela, 1992. Dir: Juan E. Fresan. With: Jean Manuel Montesinos, Gilbert Dacournan, Carolina Luzardo, Maria Eugenia Cruz, Giles Bickford, Richard Cumming. Big Ben Productions/Tiuna Films/Foncine. Colour.

Shot in English, this low-budget slapstick comedy is loosely based on Sir Arthur Conan Doyle's story 'The Sussex Vampyre' (also filmed as *The Last Vampyre* the same year). Montesinos stars as Sherlock Holmes, who merely travels through Caracas on his way to Maracaibo to help an old friend married to an ex-Miss Venezuela (Cruz). Late in the plot, she turns out to be a vampire who threatens the lives of her children. This includes numerous hit-or-miss gags, silly subtitles, a pagan-worshipping governess and Watson (Dacournan) filming everything with an anachronistic video camera!
✦

SHE'S ALIVE: CREATING THE BRIDE OF FRANKENSTEIN

USA, 1999. Dir: David J. Skal. With: Paul M. Jensen, Scott MacQueen, Gregory W. Mank, Bob Madison, Rick Baker, Sara Karloff. Universal Studios Home Video. Colour/B&W.

Forty minute documentary, written by Skal and released as a supplement to the DVD of *Bride of Frankenstein* (1935). This includes numerous clips, plus interviews with Dwight D. Frye, *Father of Frankenstein* novelist Christopher Bram, and writer/director Bill Condon. Hosted and narrated by Joe Dante.
✦✦✦✧

SHE-WOLF OF LONDON

(UK: THE CURSE OF THE ALLENBYS)
USA, 1946. Dir: Jean Yarbrough. With: Don Porter, June Lockhart, Sara Haden, Jan Wiley, Lloyd Corrigan, Eily Malyon. Universal. B&W.

Set in turn-of-the-century London, where Phyllis Allenby (twenty-one year-old Lockhart) is convinced she suffers from the family curse and has nightmares that she is a werewolf. Although the evidence points to her being responsible for a series of murders where the victims are clawed to death, the real killer is exposed as using a garden tool to mark her victims (a similar concept turned up in the 1944 Sherlock Holmes adventure, *The Scarlet Claw*, also from Universal). This used some of the sets from Universal's *The Wolf Man* (1941), but is nowhere near the same quality as that classic. Originally released on a double bill with *The Cat Creeps* (1946). With Corrigan (who replaced Forrester Harvey, who died before production began) as a police inspector, Dennis Hoey (from Universal's *Sherlock Holmes* series) as another detective, a miscast Martin Kosleck, Frederic Worlock and veteran comedian James Finlayson.
✦✧

SHE-WOLF OF LONDON

UK/USA, 1990-91. Dir: Dennis Abey, Roger Cheveley, Brian Grant, Gerry Mill, Chuck Bowmen, Bruce Seth Green and Gary Walkow. With: Kate Hodge, Neil Dickson, Scott Fults, Jean Challis, Arthur Cox, Dorothea Phillips. MTE/ HTV International/Finnegan-Pinchuk/The Hollywood Premier Network. Colour.

Hour-long TV series (twenty episodes) created by Tom McLoughlin and executive consultant Mick Garris. After fourteen episodes, the title was changed in America to *Love and Curses* and the show relocated to California for the remaining six episodes. Irritating American college student Randi Wallace (Hodge) is bitten by a gypsy werewolf on the moors(!) outside London. She teams up with her teacher, Professor Ian Matheson (Dickson), to research the occult in an attempt to discover a cure for her lycanthropy. The transformed Randi was played by Diane Youdale and the silly-looking creature effects were created by Christopher Tucker. This has nothing to do with the 1946 movie of the same title.

✦✦

The Bog Man of Letchmoor Heath

UK/USA, 1990. Dir: Roger Cheveley. With: Kate Hodge, Neil Dickson, Scott Fults, Jean Challis, John Hallam, Pamela Duncan. MTE/HTV International/Finnegan-Pinchuk/The Hollywood Premier Network. Colour.

Randi and Ian travel to a peaceful country village where Ian's aunt has been murdered by a mummy she uncovered in a bog.

✦✧

Can't Keep a Dead Man Down

UK/USA, 1990. Dir: Roger Cheveley. With: Kate Hodge, Neil Dickson, Scott Fults, Rolf Saxon, Sally Faulkner, Gary Olsen. MTE/HTV International/Finnegan-Pinchuk/The Hollywood Premier Network. Colour.

Two-part story in which Randi is drugged and taken back to America by sleazy producer Charlie Beaudine (Saxon) who she was once engaged to, while Ian is left behind to battle some scary-looking flesh-eating zombies that are being raised by a witch.

✦✦✧

Moonlight Becomes You

UK/USA, 1990. Dir: Brian Grant. With: Kate Hodge, Neil Dickson, Scott Fults, Jean Challis, Ingrid Lacey, Christopher Guard. MTE/HTV International/Finnegan-Pinchuk/The Hollywood Premier Network. Colour.

Randi and Ian discover that the mad Dr Nigel Hatchard (Guard) is using the blood of a captured male werewolf to experiment on the patients of an insane asylum.

✦✧

Nice Girls Don't

UK/USA, 1990. Dir: Roger Cheveley. With: Kate Hodge, Neil Dickson, Scott Fults, Rachel Robertson, Stuart Linden, April Olrich. MTE/HTV International/Finnegan-Pinchuk/The Hollywood Premier Network. Colour.

Ian has the youth drained out of him when he becomes the victim of an escort agency run by succubi.

✦✦

She-Devil

UK/USA, 1990. Dir: Dennis Abey. With: Kate Hodge, Neil Dickson, Scott Fults, Natalie Forbes, Kevin Drinkwater, Tony Hughes. MTE/Finnegan-Pinchuk/Hollywood Premier Network. Colour.

Much to the disgust of Randi, an old scientist girlfriend of Ian's is experimenting with an aphrodisiac that turns people into sex-crazed fanged monsters.

Series sequel: LOVE AND CURSES (qv; 1991)

✦✧

SHINDIG

USA, 1965. With: Jimmy O'Neill, Boris Karloff, Ted Cassidy. ABC-TV. Colour.

For the Halloween episode of this teen pop music TV show, first broadcast on 30 October, Karloff plays a mad scientist and sings 'The Monster Mash' with Cassidy, who is lying on a slab made-up as Lurch from TV's *The Addams Family* (1964-66). Cassidy also débuts a new dance based on his recently released single 'The Lurch'.

✦✧

SHOCK WAVES

(UK: ALMOST HUMAN)

USA, 1976 (1977). Dir: Ken Wiederhorn. With: Peter Cushing, John Carradine, Brooke Adams, Fred Buch, Jack Davidson, Luke Halpin. Zopix Company/Joseph Brenner Associates/Cinema Shares. Colour.

Low-budget, independent horror thriller filmed on 16mm as *Death Corps* in Miami, Florida, in 1975. Top-billed Cushing really only appears in an extended cameo as a scarred SS commander discovered on a deserted island by a group of shipwreck survivors. They soon find themselves being stalked by an army of blond Nazi zombies (make-up effects created by Alan Ormsby) who rise from underneath the water to slay their victims. In the end, only Rose (Adams)

Lloyd Corrigan is clawed to death by the She-Wolf of London *(1946).*

survives (the film is told in flashback). Although Carradine turns up as the crusty captain of the doomed ship who becomes the zombies' first victim, the two horror stars share no scenes together. An uncredited Fred Olen Ray was one of the production crew.
✦✦✧

SHOPPING FOR FANGS
USA, 1998. Dir: Quentin Lee and Justin Lin. With: Radmar Jho, Jeanne Chin, Clint Jung. Margin Films. Colour.
Offbeat 'Generasian X' comedy/drama in which mail room worker Phil (Jho) thinks he is changing into a werewolf who has to shave every hour, but even his brother-in-law who is studying lycanthropy doesn't believe him.
✦

THE SHORT STORIES OF CONAN DOYLE:
(aka CONAN DOYLE/SIR ARTHUR CONAN DOYLE)
Lot No. 249
UK, 1967. Dir: Richard Martin. With: Michael Latimer, Keith Buckley, Christopher Matthews, Philip Manikum. BBC-TV.
Hour-long TV series (thirteen episodes) created by John Hawkesworth and based on the non-Sherlock Holmes stories of Conan Doyle. In this episode, based on the 1892 tale, undergraduates Philip Hardacre (Latimer), Tom Crabbe (Buckley) and Monkhouse 'Monkey' Lee (Matthews) encounter an Egyptian mummy.
Episode remake: TALES FROM THE DARKSIDE THE MOVIE (qv; 1990)
✦✧

SHRUNKEN HEADS
USA, 1994. Dir: Richard Elfman. With: Aeryk Egan, Becky Herbert, A.J. Damato, Bo Sharon, Meg Foster, Julius Harris. Full Moon Entertainment/Paramount. Colour.
Quirky fantasy/horror/comedy from director Elfman (*Forbidden Zone* [1980], etc). This begins like a 1960s Disney movie, but it soon turns dark and mean-spirited when teenager Tommy Larson (Egan) and his two pals are murdered by a gang of youths and reanimated by weird Haitian voodoo priest Mr Sumatra (Harris) as flying shrunken heads. They then use their super powers to turn the villains into tidy zombies! Foster has fun as Big Moe, a bizarre lesbian gangster. The main title theme is by the director's brother, Danny.
✦✦✧

SI BALELENG AT ANG GINTONG SIRENA
Philippines, circa 1988. Dir: Chito Rono. With: Charito Solis, Eddie Garcia, Laurice Guillen, Melissa Perez Rubio, Cheche Sta. Ana, Frank Crisostomo. Lea Productions/Viva Video. Colour.
The title of this children's fantasy film translates as 'You Baleleng and the Golden Mermaid'. It features a number of monsters, including a vampire baby and a pair of shambling zombies (Cecil Inigo and Carlos Ding). With Rubio as Perlita, the mermaid.
✦

SIGMUND AND THE SEA MONSTERS:
Frankenstein Drops In
USA, 1973. Dir: Richard Dunlap. With: Johnny Whitaker, Scott Kolden, Billy Barty, Mary Wickes, Bill Germain, Fred Spencer. Sid and Marty Krofft/NBC-TV. Colour.
Half-hour children's TV series (1973-75, twenty-nine episodes) about Johnny and Scott Stuart (Whitaker and Kolden), two brothers who befriend Sigmund Ooz, a green sea monster with six arms (played by veteran Barty) who has run away from home. In this episode, Sigmund's family kidnap Scott, and Johnny disguises himself as the Frankenstein Monster in order to get his brother back.
✦

THE SILENCE OF THE HAMS
USA/Italy, 1993. Dir: Ezio Greggio. With: Ezio Greggio, Dom DeLuise, Billy Zane, Joanna Pacula, Charlene Tilton, Martin Balsam. Thirtieth Century Wolf/Silvio Berlusconi Communications. Colour.
Silly spoof of *Psycho* (1960) and numerous other movies, executive produced, co-produced, written, directed and starring the talentless Greggio. While on the trail of serial killer Antonio Motel (Greggio) and some stolen money, clumsy FBI agent Jo Dee Fostar (Zane) encounters Dr Animal Cannibal Pizza (Deluise) dressed up as Gary Oldman's Dracula, a spoof of Michael Jackson's *Thriller* (1983) complete with barn-dancing zombies, a fake mummy (Jeff Bright) and Alfred Hitchcock as the shower murderer. With John Astin (nice *Addams Family* gag), Phyllis Diller, Bubba Smith, Larry Storch, Rip Taylor and Shelley Winters (as 'Mother') among the has-been cast, plus surprise cameos from Henry Silva, Joe Dante, John Carpenter, Eddie Deezen, Rudy De Luca, John Landis, an uncredited Mel Brooks and lots of lookalikes. Julie Corman was co-producer.
✦✧

THE SILENT MYSTERY
USA, 1918-19. Dir: Francis Ford. With: Francis Ford, Rosemary Theby, Mae Gaston, Elsie Van Neame, Grace Cunard. Silent Mystery Corporation/Hiller & Wilk/ Burston Films. B&W.
Fifteen chapter silent serial, starring both the director and screenwriter (Van Neame), that involves the supernatural power surrounding a cursed gem stolen from an Egyptian mummy.
✦✧

SILENT NIGHT, LONELY NIGHT
USA, 1969. Dir: Daniel Petrie. With: Lloyd Bridges, Shirley Jones, Lynn Carlin, Carrie Snodgress, Robert Lipton, Cloris Leachman. Universal. Colour.
TV movie based on the play by Robert Anderson. A chance Christmas meeting at a New England inn turns into a short-lived romance for troubled middle-agers John Sparrow (Bridges) and Katherine Johnson (Jones). With a young Jeffrey (Jeff) Bridges and a clip from *Bride of Frankenstein* (1935) on TV.
✦

SILENT RAGE
USA, 1982. Dir: Michael Miller. With: Chuck Norris, Ron Silver, Steven Keats, Toni Kalem, William Finley, Brian Libby. Anthony B. Unger/Topick Productions/Columbia. Colour.
Entertaining action thriller in which martial arts expert Norris plays a small town Texas sheriff confronted with axe-murderer John Kirby (Libby), who has been transformed by super-serum Monogen 35 into an indestructible zombie killer. In the end, the scientific superman is thrown down a well.
✦✦

SILVER BULLET
(aka STEPHEN KING'S SILVER BULLET)
USA, 1985. Dir: Daniel Attias. With: Gary Busey, Everett McGill, Corey Haim, Megan Fellows, Terry O'Quinn, Lawrence Tierney. Famous Films/Dino De Laurentiis/ Paramount. Colour.
Scripted by Stephen King and based on his illustrated novella *Cycle of the Werewolf.* What might have been an atmospheric short is expanded into a tedious thriller in which thirteen year-old wheelchair-bound Marty Coslaw (a nice performance by Haim) tries to convince his unpredictable Uncle Red (Busey) and older sister Jane (Fellows) that the werewolf laying waste to the locals of Tarker's Mills is the Reverend Lester Lowe (McGill), the town's minister. During a hallucination sequence, the entire congregation at a funeral service transform into leaping werewolves (make-up by Michael McCracken Jr). Disappointing creature effects created by Carlo Rambaldi.
✦✧

THE SILVER SPEAR
(USA: aka SILVER HERMIT FROM SHAOLIN VALLEY MEETS BLOODY FANGS OF DEATH)
Hong Kong, 1985. Dir: Roc Tien. With: Roc Tien, Men Fei, Tien Ho, Chung Hwa, Doris Chen, Chan Sing. IFD Films/ Ocean Shores Video. Colour.
Based on the novel by Ku Lung. Persian vampire Wu Shih-San

returns to China after twenty years, seeking revenge on the inhabitants of the Green Jade Villa.
✦✧

SIMONE SIMON
[b 1910]

French actress and former fashion designer and model who played Irena Dubrovna, who believes she will turn into one of the *Cat People* (1942) if sexually aroused. She reprised the role as a ghost in *The Curse of the Cat People* (1944) and played Satan's sexy seductress in *All That Money Can Buy* (1941).

THE SIMPSONS:
The Simpsons Halloween Special V

USA/South Korea, 1994. Dir: Jaundiced Jim Reardon. Voices: Ro-Dan Castellaneta (Dan Castellaneta), Jooooolie (Julie) Kavner, Nancy Heart-Fright (Nancy Cartwright), Grave-Yeardley (Yeardley) Smith, The Shaws-Hank Azaria (Hank Azaria), Harry (O.J.) Shearer. Twentieth Century Fox/Gracie Films/Fox Network. Colour.

Halloween episode of the popular half-hour cartoon TV series (1990-) about a dysfunctional family. After an *Outer Limits* opening, the Simpsons become the caretakers of an old lodge where Bart (Cartwright) learns he has the power of 'The Shinning' and Homer (Castellaneta) goes crazy when he discovers there is no TV or beer. This features a brief appearance by a mummy, a werewolf, Count Dracula, Jason, Freddy and Pinhead! In a reworking of a classic Ray Bradbury story, 'Time and Punishment', Homer is sucked into a vortex and transported back in time to a prehistoric jungle while fixing a toaster. After killing a mosquito, he returns to the present to find that Ned Flanders (Shearer) is the Unquestioned Lord and Master of the World. In 'Nightmare Cafeteria', Bart and Lisa (Smith) discover that the cannibalistic staff of Springfield School are eating the students. With special guest voice James Earl Boggins Jones and theme by Danny Skellingelfman.
✦✦✧

The Simpsons Halloween Special IV

USA/South Korea, 1993. Dir: David 'Dry Bones' Silverman. Voices: Dysfunctional Dan Castellaneta, Jooooolie (Julie) Kavner, Nasty Nancy Cartwright, Scabby Yeardley Smith, Boo! Boo! Scare Ya Hank Azaria, Frighticious Harry Shearer. Twentieth Century Fox/Gracie Films/Fox Network. Colour.

In a spoof of *Rod Serling's Night Gallery*, Bart introduces 'The Devil and Homer Simpson', in which Homer sells his soul for a donut, spends a day in Hell and faces a jury of the damned. In 'Terror at 5 $^1/_2$ Feet', Bart sees a gremlin on the side of his school bus, while in 'Bart Simpson's Dracula', a spoof on the 1992 Coppola film, a vampiric Montgomery Burns (Shearer) invites the Simpsons to a midnight dinner at his castle in Pennsylvania and turns Bart into one of the undead. Theme by Red Wolf Elfman.
✦✦✦✦

The Simpsons Halloween Special IX

USA/South Korea, 1998. Dir: Steven 'Demon' Moore. Voices: ? (Dan Castellaneta), Ghoulie (Julie) Kavner, Nancy 'Killer Actor' Cartwright, The Canker (Yeardley Smith), Yank My Area (Hank Azaria), Harry (Dead Til 2005) Shearer. Twentieth Century Fox/Gracie Films/Fox Network. Colour.

In 'Hell Toupee', Homer's new hairpiece is possessed by the revenge-seeking spirit of executed criminal Snake. 'The Terror of Tiny Toon' is introduced by a fanged Krusty the clown (Castellaneta), dressed as a vampire, while Bart and Lisa are sucked into an Itchy and Scratchy cartoon on their TV. Finally, Maggie turns out to be the offspring of alien commander Kang in 'Starship Poopers'. With a live-action Kathie Lee Gifford and Regis Philbin, guest voices Robert Englund, Ed McMahon and Jerry Springer, and an appearance by Freddy and Jason on the couch. Theme by Danny 'Hell'fman.
✦✦✦

The Simpsons Halloween Special III

USA/South Korea, 1992. Dir: Bloodcurdling Carlos Baeza. Voices: Decaying Dan Castellaneta, Julie Kadaver Kavner, Nocturnal Nancy Cartwright, Yeardley Psycho Smith, Scare Ya'Hank Azaria, Fearsome Harry Shearer. Twentieth Century Fox/Gracie Films/Fox Network. Colour.

At a Simpsons Halloween costume party, Lisa narrates the tale of 'Clown Without Pity', about a cursed Krusty doll. Grandpa (Castellaneta) tells the story of 'King Homer' (in black and white), about a fifty-foot prehistoric ape captured and returned to civilisation, where it escapes and runs amuck in downtown Springfield. Finally, Bart relates 'Dial "Z" for Zombies', in which an incantation from a *Book of Magick and Spelles* raises the dead of Springfield Cemetery who are looking for brains. Theme by Red Wolf Elfman.
✦✦✦✧

SINBAD OF THE SEVEN SEAS

(Orig: SINBAD IL MARINAIO)
Italy, 1986 (1989). Dir: Enzo G. Castellari (Enzo Girolami) (and Luigi Cozzi). With: Lou Ferrigno, John Steiner, Leo Gullotta, Teagan, Haruhiko Yamanouchi, Stefania Girolami. Cannon Productions. Colour.

Fantasy adventure with a story by 'Lewis Coates' (Cozzi), supposedly based on Edgar Allan Poe's 'The Thousand-and-Second Tale of Scheherazade'. Sinbad (Ferrigno) battles an evil Jaffar (Steiner) with hypnotic powers who creates a double of Sinbad, psychic vampire Farida (Melonee Rodgers), a stone monster on Skull Island, plus a zombie king (Attilio Lo Pinto) and his living-dead followers. Narrated by Daria Nicolodi, this was originally intended for TV.
✦✧

SING, BABY, SING

USA, 1936. Dir: Sidney Lanfield. With: Alice Faye, Adolphe Menjou, Gregory Ratoff, Ted Healy, Patsy Kelly, Tony Martin. Twentieth Century-Fox. B&W.

Madcap musical comedy with Menjou playing a wonderfully drunken Shakespearean actor. In their feature début, the irritating Ritz Brothers (Al, Jim and Harry) perform a comedy skit (supposedly for radio!) in which Dr Jekyll's Mr Hyde meets the Frankenstein Monster.
✦✦

CURT SIODMAK
(Kurt Siodmak) [b 1902]

German writer and director, brother of Robert Siodmak (1900-1973), who began his long career as an extra in Fritz Lang's *Metropolis* (1926). Fleeing the Nazis in 1937, Siodmak arrived in Hollywood the following year. Hired to script *The Wolf Man* (1941), he created a memorable new monster in lycanthrope Larry Talbot. A joke made by Siodmak in the Universal commissary resulted in *Frankenstein Meets the Wolf Man* (1943), and he came up with the initial concept for *House of Frankenstein* (1944). Siodmak's directing credits include the half-hour pilot for Hammer's unsold TV series *Tales of Frankenstein* (1958). His 1943 novel *Donovan's Brain* has been filmed many times. Siodmak's autobiography is titled *Even a Man Who is Pure in Heart*.

qv: *Bride of the Gorilla* (1951); *The Climax* (1944); *Creature With the Atom Brain* (1955); *I Walked with a Zombie* (1943); *In Search of History: 'Legends of the Werewolves'* (1998); *Monster by Moonlight: The Immortal Saga of the Wolf Man* (1999); *Son of Dracula* (1943); *Universal Horror* (1998).

SISTERS OF SATAN

(Orig: ALUCARDA, LA HIJA DE LAS TINIEBLAS. USA: aka INNOCENTS FROM HELL/MARK OF THE DEVIL PART 3)
Mexico, 1975. Dir: Juan López Moctezuma. With: Tina Romero, Susana Kamini, Claudio Brook, David Silva, Lily Garza, Martin Lasalle. Films 75/Yuma Films. Colour.

Despite the almost anagrammatic original title, this mix of sex and gore from the director of *Mary, Mary, Bloody Mary* (1975) is about nineteenth century possessed nuns. Justine (Kamini) is sent to a monastery and quickly succumbs to the evil influence of Alucarda (Romero). This leads to them drinking each other's blood, biting other nuns on the neck, participating in a black magic orgy with a

Dieter Eppler rises from his coffin during *The Slaughter of the Vampires (1962).*

goat-headed demon (Brook) and Justine rising naked from a blood-filled coffin.
✦✦

SIX HOURS TO LIVE
USA, 1932. Dir: William Dieterle. With: Warner Baxter, Miriam Jordan, John Boles, George Marion, Beryl Mercer, Irene Ware. Fox. B&W.
Slow-moving drama based on the story 'Auf Wiedersehen' by Gordon Morris and Morton Barteaux. When stubborn Sylvarian diplomat Captain Paul Onslow (Baxter) is murdered at an international trade conference, eccentric scientist Professor Otto Bauer (Marion) uses a new ray to bring him back to life for just six hours, giving him time to catch his murderer and destroy the life-giving machine before dying a second time. With Halliwell Hobbes.
✦

SIXTH SENSE:
Five Widows Weeping
USA, 1972. Dir: Allen Baron. With: Gary Collins, Mary Ann Mobley, Barry Sullivan, Ellen Weston, Hank Brandt, William Jordan. Universal/ABC-TV. Colour.
Hour-long TV series (twenty-six episodes) created by Anthony Lawrence and developed and produced by Stan Shpetner. In this episode, while parapsychologist Dr Michael Rhodes (Collins) investigates an apparent kidnapping, the wife of the missing man experiences nightmare hallucinations of zombies and a phantom knight in armour. When shown in syndication, these original episodes were cut down to an incomprehensible half-hour length as part of *Rod Serling's Night Gallery* (1970-73), with new introductions by Serling (who charged Universal $200,000 for the day's work).
✦✧

SKEETER
USA, 1993 (1994). Dir: Clark Brandon. With: Tracy Griffith, Jim Youngs, Charles Napier, Jay Robinson, William Sanderson, Michael J. Pollard. Team Players Productions/KAR Films/New Line Cinema/August Entertainment. Colour.
Fun low-budget B movie thrills when illegal toxic waste dumping results in enlarged blood-drinking mutant mosquitoes (created by Makeup and Effects Labs, Inc) that attack the inhabitants of the small south-western desert community of Clear Sky. The dream exploitation cast also includes (George) 'Buck' Flower and executive-in-charge-of-production Don Edmunds (*Ilsa She Wolf of the SS* [1973], etc) in an uncredited cameo.
✦✦

SKOLOVANJE
Yugoslavia, 1970. Dir: Zlatko Bourek and Zlatko Sacer. Zabreb. Colour.
Nine minute cartoon about odd-looking birds spreading discord which apparently also includes an appearance by the Frankenstein Monster. The title translates as 'Schooling'.
✦

SLAPSTICK OF ANOTHER KIND
(Orig: SLAPSTICK)
USA, 1982 (1984). Dir: Steven Paul. With: Jerry Lewis, Madeline Kahn, Marty Feldman, John Abbott, Jim Backus, Samuel Fuller. The S. Paul Company/ Entertainment Releasing. Colour.
Written, produced and directed by twenty-four year-old former child actor Paul, based on the satirical novel by Kurt Vonnegut (Jr). Veteran Abbott (*The Vampire's Ghost* [1945], etc) portrays Dr Frankenstein, who delivers two monstrous babies, Wilbur and Eliza Swain (Lewis and Kahn, who also play the twins' parents). Although they appear to be morons to outsiders, when together the brother and sister are, in fact, alien geniuses capable of solving the world's problems. With Merv Griffin, a miniaturised Pat Morita, the director in a cameo and the uncredited voice of Orson Welles. This originally opened in Germany and was then subsequently re-edited.
✦✧

THE SLAUGHTER OF THE VAMPIRES
(Orig: LA STRAGE DEI VAMPIRI. USA: aka CURSE OF THE BLOOD-GHOULS)
Italy, 1962 (1967). Dir: Roberto Mauri. With: Walter Brandy (Walter Brandi/Walter Bigari), Dieter Eppler, Graziella Granata, Paolo Solvay (Luigi Batzella), Gena Gimmy (Gimmi), Alfredo Rizzo. Mercur-Roma/Pacemaker Pictures. B&W.
After an exciting pre-credits sequence with two vampires being pursued by an angry mob of villagers, it's all downhill. When his new wife and other members of his household fall prey to a pasty-faced vampiric descendant (Eppler), nobleman Wolfgang (Brandy) teams up with a vampire-hunting doctor to save a little girl. In the end, the vampire is staked with a section of pointed railing and turns into a skeleton. Writer/director Mauri drags out the skimpy storyline with gratuitous coach driving sequences and too much (badly dubbed) dialogue.
✦✧

SLAVE GIRLS FROM BEYOND INFINITY
USA, 1987. Dir: Ken Dixon. With: Elizabeth Cayton, Cindy Beal, Brinke Stevens, Don Scribner, Carl Horner, Kirk Graves. Titan Productions/Troma. Colour.
Writer/producer/director Dixon rips off *The Most Dangerous Game* (1932) without any credit. Daria (Cayton) and Tisa (Beal) are two slave girls who escape captivity on a space ship and crash land their shuttle on a mysterious planet where Scribner's mad Zed (for Zaroff?) and his two android servants (created by John Buechler's MMI Inc) are hunting down his 'guests' for sport. The heads of his prey are displayed in a gruesome trophy room. This includes a mutant (Fred Tate) and a zombie (Jacques Schardo). You know a film's in trouble when Stevens gives the best performance.
✦✧

SLEDGE HAMMER!:
Last of the Red Hot Vampires
USA, 1987. Dir: Bill Bixby. With: David Rasche, Anne-Marie Martin, Harrison Page, Bernie Kopell, Deborah Wakeham, Bud Cort. New World Television/Alan Spencer Productions/ABC-TV. Colour.
Half-hour comedy detective TV series (1986-88, thirty-three episodes), created by Alan Spencer. In this episode, Sledge (Rasche) and his partner Detective Dori Doreau (Martin) investigate a series of vampire murders which are apparently the work of recently-dead horror movie star Vincent Lagarski (Kopell), who was fired from his comeback film *Touch of the Vampire* by Monogamy Pictures. With 'clips' from an old Lagarski film in which he plays Dracula. Theme music by Danny Elfman.
✦✦

SLEEPOVER MASSACRE
USA, 1989. Dir: Gary Whitson. WAVE Productions. Colour.
Very obscure amateur vampire movie from the New Jersey company who will videotape your script for money. It's apparently not much of a showreel.
✦

SLEEPWALKERS
USA, 1992. Dir: Mick Garris. With: Brian Krause, Mädchen Amick, Alice Krige, Jim Haynie, Cindy Pickett, Ron Perlman. Columbia/Ion Pictures/Victor & Grais. Colour.
After an intriguing opening (set in Hitchcock's Bodega Bay and featuring an uncredited Mark Hamill), it's all downhill as incestuous mother and son, Mary and Charles Brady (Krige and Krause), move to Travis, Indiana, and stir up the local cat population. It turns out that they are ancient feline shape-changers, who need to suck the life-force from local popcorn sales girl Tanya (Amick, from TV's *Twin Peaks* [1990-91]) to survive. Only the town's cats can see through the human disguise of the creatures who inspired the vampire legends. Despite good performances, competent direction and clever special effects, this is one of the dumbest movies ever made. It's based on an original screenplay by Stephen King, who makes a pointless cameo appearance along with horror directors John Landis, Joe Dante, Clive Barker and Tobe Hooper.
✦✧

SLIDERS:
The Alternateville Horror
USA, 1998. Dir: David Grossman. With: Jerry O'Connell, Cleavant Derricks, Kari Wuhrer, Charlie O'Connell, Elyse Mirto, Lance Wilson-White. Universal/St. Clare Entertainment/Sci-Fi Channel. Colour.
Hour-long TV series (1995-99), created by Tracy Tormé and Robert K. Weiss, about a group of people forced to travel ('slide') between parallel Earths using a device created by young inventor Quinn Mallory (Jerry O'Connell). In this episode, the Sliders land on a world of acid rain storms and end up staying in the apparently haunted Chandler Hotel. This includes clips from *Frankenstein* (1931) on TV and some bizarre alternative versions of the Sliders. John Landis was one of the executive consultants for the 1995-97 seasons.
✦✦✧

Data World
USA, 1998. Dir: Jerry O'Connell. With: Jerry O'Connell, Cleavant Derricks, Kari Wuhrer, Charlie O'Connell, Roy Dotrice, Phil Fondacaro. Universal/St. Clare Entertainment/Sci-Fi Channel. Colour.
The Sliders land on a world where they are trapped by Archibald Chandler (Dotrice) inside digitised versions of themselves, while their real bodies wander around outside as zombie-like 'Empties'.
✦✦

Sole Survivors
USA, 1997. Dir: David Peckinpah. With: Jerry O'Connell, Sabrina Lloyd, Cleavant Derricks, Kari Wuhrer, Stephanie Niznik, Jay Acovone. Universal/St. Clare Entertainment/ Fox Network. Colour.
Still pursuing Rickman, the Sliders arrive on a devastated world where most of the population has been transformed by a weight-loss bacteria into glowing-eyed cannibalistic zombies. When Quinn is bitten, he is also changed into one of the walking dead.
✦✦✦

Stoker
USA, 1997. Dir: Jerry O'Connell. With: Jerry O'Connell, Sabrina Lloyd, Cleavant Derricks, Kari Wuhrer, Ryan Alosio, Neil Dickson. Universal/St. Clare Entertainment/ Fox Network. Colour.
Following Rickman (Dickson), the Sliders land on a world where Wade (Lloyd) becomes involved with Goth rock band Stoker, which is made up of centuries-old vampires (named after characters in *Dracula*). With Tommy Chong as an obsessed vampire hunter.
✦✦

SMALL SOLDIERS
USA, 1998. Dir: Joe Dante. With: Kirsten Dunst, Gregory Smith, Jay Mohr, Phil Hartman, Kevin Dunn, Denis Leary. DreamWorks Pictures/Universal/Amblin Entertainment. Colour.
A dark comedy from Dante about the perils of consumerism. When young Alan Abernathy (Smith) takes delivery of a shipment of voice-activated toys to be sold in his father's store, he discovers they have been accidentally fitted with munitions chips supplied by the multinational Globotech company. The small town of Winslow, Ohio, soon becomes a battleground between Chip Hazard (voiced by Tommy Lee Jones) and his Commando Elite (voiced by original cast members of *The Dirty Dozen* [1967] Ernest Borgnine, Jim Brown, George Kennedy and Clint Walker, plus Bruce Dern) and the gentle Gorgonites (voiced by Christopher Guest, Michael McKean and Harry Shearer from *This is Spinal Tap* [1984]), led by Archer (Frank Langella). This includes impressive CGI effects from Industrial Light & Magic and animatronic figures designed by the Stan Winston Studio. Amongst the in-jokes, one of the Gorgonites watches a clip from *Frankenstein* (1931) on TV, and there's also a nod to *The Hunchback of Notre Dame*. With Robert Picardo, Dick Miller, Belinda Balaski and Rance Howard, plus Sarah Michelle Gellar and Christina Ricci as the voices of the homicidal Gwendy dolls. The film is dedicated to Phil Hartman, who was shot to death by his wife in a murder-suicide the same year.
✦✦✦

DICK SMITH
[b 1922]

Pioneer American make-up artist who joined NBC-TV in 1945. Although working in movies since the late 1950s, he came to prominence in the early 1970s for his make-ups in *Little Big Man* (1970), *The Exorcist* (1973) and others. He won an Academy Award for his work on *Amadeus* (1984).
qv: *Dark Shadows* (1966-71); *Death Becomes Her* (1992); *House of Dark Shadows* (1970); *The Hunger* (1983); *Monsters* (1988-91); *The Strange Case of Dr. Jekyll and Mr. Hyde* (1967); *Tales from the Darkside The Movie* (1990); *Way Out* (1961).

MADELINE SMITH
[b 1949]

Big-eyed and big-busted British actress, a 1970s glamour girl who appeared in Hammer's *Taste the Blood of Dracula* (1969), *The Vampire Lovers* (1970) and *Frankenstein and the Monster from Hell* (1973).

SMOGGIES:
(USA: STOP THE SMOGGIES)
Zombies of Coral Island
Canada, 1988. Global/CINAR. Colour.
Half-hour cartoon series about a group of environmentally friendly creatures living on a coral island.
✦

THE SNAKE MAN
(aka THE SERPENT MAN)
France, 1910. Lux. B&W.
Silent short in which a man has the ability to transform into a snake.
✦

THE SNAKE WOMAN
UK, 1961. Dir: Sidney J. Furie. With: John McCarthy, Susan Travers, Geoffrey Danton, Arnold Marle, Elsie Wagstaff, John Cazabon. Caralan Productions/United Artists. B&W.
Low-budget chills from the team that made *Doctor Blood's Coffin* (1961). Set in nineteenth century England, Dr Adderson (Cazabon) injects his insane pregnant wife with snake venom. This results in the birth of a daughter, Atheris (Travers), who transforms into a cobra and uses her lethal bite on those she holds responsible for her father's death. Scripted by Orville H. Hampton (*The Alligator People* [1959], etc) and filmed under the title *The Lady is a Snake*.
✦✧

SNIFFLES AND THE BOOKWORM
USA, 1939. Dir: Charles M. (Chuck) Jones. Voices: Bernice Hansen. Vitaphone/Warner Bros. Colour.
Seven minute *Merrie Melodies* cartoon in which Sniffles the mouse enters a bookstore where various literary characters come to life and perform the song 'Mutiny in the Nursery' (from *Going Places* [1938]). He is then chased by a Monster (beautifully animated by Robert McKimson) that steps out from the pages of Mary Shelley's *Frankenstein*.
Sequel: SNIFFLES TAKES A TRIP (1940)
✦✦✧

THE SNOOP SISTERS: A BLACK DAY FOR BLUEBEARD
USA, 1973 (1974). With: Helen Hayes, Mildred Natwick, Lou Antonio, Bert Convey, Vincent Price, Roddy McDowall. Universal/NBC-TV. Colour.
One of four TV movies originally shown as part of *The NBC Wednesday/Thursday Mystery Movie* (1973-74), featuring veterans Hayes and Natwick as spinster sleuths Ernesta and Gwendolyn Snoop. Price gives a delightful performance as old-time horror film star Michael Bastian, who is accused of murdering his wife at a comeback film festival held in his honour. With McDowall in the cast, it's not difficult to guess the identity of the real killer. This includes scenes from a fictional Bastian movie, *Gravely Yours* (incorporating clips from *Bride of Frankenstein* [1935]), plus Angelo Rossitto, Mort Sahl and William Devane.
✦✦

SODA SQUIRT
USA, 1933. Dir: Ub Iwerks. Celebrity Pictures/Metro-Goldwyn-Mayer. B&W.
Six minute cartoon in which Flip the Frog's potion turns a man into a Mr Hyde-type character. Last in the series.
✦✧

I SOGNI DEL SIGNOR ROSSI
Italy, 1978. Dir: Bruno Bozetto. Colour.
Cartoon short in which the Frankenstein Monster appears in the dreams of Mr Rossi.
✦✧

SOLE SURVIVOR
USA, 1982 (1984). Dir: Thom Eberhardt. With: Anita Skinner, Kurt Johnson, Caren Larkey, Robin Davidson, Andrew Boyer, Daniel Cartmell. Larkey/IFM. Colour.
Low-budget supernatural mystery. Advertising executive Denise Watson (Skinner) is the only survivor of a plane crash and discovers herself in a city surrounded by zombies. With Brinke Stevens.
✦✧

LA SOMBRA DEL MURCIÉLAGO
Mexico, 1966 (1968). Dir: Federico Curiel (and Luís Enrique Vergara and Fernando Rivero). With: Blue Demon (Alejandro Muñoz), Jaime Fernandez, Marta Romero, Fernando Osés, (Jesús) 'Murciélago' Velazquez, Cesar Silva. Filmica Vergara/Columbia. B&W.
Reworking of *The Phantom of the Opera*, with Velazquez (who also scripted) as the organ-playing, wrestling villain El Murciélago/The Bat, who kidnaps women and imprisons them in his castle dungeon. When his girlfriend (Romero) is abducted, the hero (Fernandez) calls upon the Blue Demon for help. The title translates as 'The Shadow of the Bat'.
Sequel: ARAÑAS INFERNALES (1966)
✦

SOMETHING ELSE — ENTIRELY
(Orig: NOE HELT ANNET/SOMETHING QUITE DIFFERENT — OR THE VAMPIRE MOVIE)
Norway, 1985 (1986). Dir: Morten Kolstad. With: Trond Kirkvaag, Knut Lystad, Lars Mjoen, Linn Stokke. Oslo Film Association/Norsk Film/Media Vision. Colour.
An adopted boy, Buffalo Bull (Kirkvaag), dies and revives at his funeral as a vampire — possibly a descendant of Dracula. In the end, he decides to become a comedian.
✦

SOMETHING IS OUT THERE:
In His Own Image
USA, 1988. Dir: Larry Shaw. With: Joe Cortese, Maryam D'Abo, Gregory Sierra, Mitchell Laurance, Lise Hilboldt, J.E. Freeman. Columbia/NBC-TV. Colour.
Short-lived, hour-long TV series (eight episodes), based on the 1988 four-hour mini-series. In this episode, homicide detective Jack Breslin (Cortese) and telepathic alien Ta'ra (D'Abo) investigate a mysterious wax museum run by mad axe murderer Andrew Pike (Laurance) who is killing off the jurors who convicted him. The opening sequence features a briefly-glimpsed werewolf figure. Executive produced by Frank Lupo and John Ashley.
✦✦

SOMETIMES THEY COME BACK
(aka STEPHEN KING'S SOMETIMES THEY COME BACK)
USA, 1991. Dir: Tom McLoughlin. With: Tim Matheson,

Lon Chaney Jr passes himself off as Son of Dracula *(1943).*

Brooke Adams, Robert Rusler, Chris Demetral, Robert Hy Gorman, William Sanderson. Paradise Films/Dino De Laurentiis/CBS-TV. Colour.
Based on the 1974 short story by Stephen King, this effective little TV movie is atmospherically directed by McLoughlin. It features a strong performance by Matheson as teacher Jim Norman, who returns to his home town with his family only to find himself haunted by the ghosts of a trio of sadistic thugs who murdered his older brother Wayne (Demetral) in 1963. After three of his students are killed, Jim discovers that only by confronting the past can he hope to change his future. With clips from De Laurentiis' terrible 1976 *King Kong* on TV and a posthumous co-producer credit for Milton Subotsky. Two unrelated direct-to-video sequels followed. In 1992, King's story was remade by Danish director Martin Schmidt as *Snake Eyes*, an award-winning feature-length amateur video.
Sequel: SOMETIMES THEY COME BACK...AGAIN (1996)
✦✦✦

SOMEWHERE IN EGYPT

USA, 1943. Dir: Mannie Davis. Voices: Arthur Kay. Terrytoons/Twentieth Century-Fox. Colour.
Six minute Paul Terry cartoon, in which Gandy Goose dreams he is in Egypt and encounters a floating sarcophagus, a ghostly dancing cat and a living skull.
Sequel: ALADDIN'S LAMP (1943)
✦✧

GALE SONDERGAARD (Edith Sondergaard) [1899-1985]

Sinister-looking American actress who usually played menacing housekeepers (*The Cat and the Canary* [1939], etc). She won the first ever Academy Award for Best Supporting Actress in 1936 for her début film, but was blacklisted through association by Joseph McCarthy's anti-communist witch-hunt of the early 1950s. Her career never really recovered.
qv: *The Cat Creature* (1973); *The Climax* (1944); *The Spider Woman Strikes Back* (1945).

SONG AT MIDNIGHT

(Orig: YE BANG GE SHENG)
China, 1937. Dir: Maxu Weibang. B&W.
An obscure reworking of *The Phantom of the Opera*, about an actor/director who has acid thrown in his face by thugs when he attempts to elope with the daughter of a rich Shanghai merchant. Now hiding his horribly deformed features beneath a thick cloak, he haunts the burned-out ruin of a theatre, singing the song he composed for his lost love each midnight. A sequel followed in 1941.
Remake: MIDNIGHTMARE (qv; 1961)
✦✧

THE SONNY AND CHER COMEDY HOUR

USA, 1972. With: Sonny Bono, Cher Bono, Jerry Lewis, Ted Ziegler, Clark Carr, Peter Cullen. Paul Bowenstein Productions/CBS-TV. Colour.
Halloween episode of the musical comedy TV series (1971-74) featuring the singing duo which includes Dracula as a guest.
✦
USA, 1972. With: Sonny Bono, Cher Bono, Ted Ziegler, Tom Solari, Clark Carr, Murray Langston. Paul Bowenstein Productions/CBS-TV. Colour.
In this episode, Sonny plays Dr Jekyll who serves his Mr Hyde potion to his guests.
Series sequels: THE SONNY COMEDY REVUE (1974) and CHER (1975-76)
✦

SON OF DARKNESS TO DIE FOR II

USA, 1991. Dir: David F. Price. With: Rosalind Allen, Steve Bond, Scott Jacoby, Michael Praed, Jay Underwood, Amanda Wyss. Son of Darkness Productions/Trimark Pictures/Arrowhead Entertainment/Lee Caplin. Colour.
This vampire soap opera is a sequel to the 1988 original. Praed (replacing Brendan Hughes) stars as Dr Max Schreck/Vlad Tepish; a vampire working in a small town hospital. While he tries to curb his blood-drinking habits with plasma bags and protect his adopted son, his evil undead brother Tom (Bond) once again attempts to ruin things. Most of the original cast return, and make-up effects are again created by Magical Media Industries.
✦✧

SON OF DRACULA

USA, 1943. Dir: Robert Siodmak. With: Lon Chaney, Louise Allbritton, Robert Paige (David Carlyle), Evelyn Ankers, Frank Craven, J. Edward Bromberg. Universal. B&W.
A stylish blend of vampires and witchcraft, set in the American bayous. Based on an idea by Curt (*Donovan's Brain*) Siodmak and directed by his brother, Universal's follow-up to *Dracula's Daughter* (1936) features beautifully detailed sets, a good cast of contract players and John P. Fulton's impressive man-into-bat-and-mist transformations. The title is a misnomer — Chaney Jr's moustachioed Count Alucard (spell it backwards) is really Dracula himself, who travels to Louisiana to turn willing Katherine Caldwell (Allbritton) into his vampire bride. Because of a knee injury, Alan Curtis was replaced as the hero by Paige after the first week of shooting. One of the most atmospheric sequences has the Count's coffin rise from the swamp water and magically glide towards the shore where a victim eagerly awaits his embrace. A dark, Gothic fairy-tale, which is much better than most forties horror movies.
Sequel: HOUSE OF FRANKENSTEIN (qv; 1944)
✦✦✦✧

SON OF DRACULA

(USA: aka YOUNG DRACULA)
UK, 1973 (1974). Dir: Freddie Francis. With: Harry Nilsson, Ringo Starr (Richard Starkey), Rosanna Lee, Freddie Jones, Suzanna Leigh, Dennis Price. Apple/Cinemation Industries. Colour.
Filmed under the title *Count Downe*, this incomprehensible musical horror comedy stars singer/songwriter Nilsson as Dracula's son (who can turn into a cartoon bat). He travels to London, where he is about to be crowned king of the Netherworld — whose inhabitants include Frankenstein's Monster (Morris Bush), a gorgon (Nita Larraine), a werewolf (Derek Woodward), a shape-shifting cat woman (Shakira Baksh), a mummy and various cobweb-covered zombies. When the reluctant vampire falls in love with a human woman (Leigh), he turns to a wheelchair-bound Dr Van Helsing (a dubbed Price, who died the same year) and the scheming Baron Frankenstein (Jones) to make him mortal. With producer Starr as Merlin the Magician, Dan Meaden as a Nosferatu-like Count Dracula, Lorna Wilde as Countess Dracula, Skip Martin as Igor, Jenny Runacre, and rock stars John Bonham, Peter Frampton, Keith Moon and Klaus Voorman. No wonder director Francis went back to being a cinematographer!
✦

SON OF DR. JEKYLL

USA, 1951. Dir: Seymour Friedman. With: Louis Hayward, Jody Lawrance, Alexander Knox, Gavin Muir, Lester Matthews, Paul Cavanagh. Columbia. B&W.
Edward Jekyll (Hayward), the illegitimate son of Mr Hyde, tries to prove that his father was a serious scientist. Experimenting with the formula, he only turns into Mr Hyde in a dream sequence (Clay Campbell's make-up was revealed through the use of filters). The film opens with a flashback to the death of the original Dr Jekyll/Mr Hyde, and the sword cane carried by actor Hayward is the same used by John Barrymore in the 1920 version. Blacklisted as a communist, screenwriter Edward Huebsch's name was removed from the credits.
✦✧

SON OF FRANKENSTEIN

USA, 1939. Dir: Rowland V. Lee. With: Basil Rathbone, Boris Karloff, Bela Lugosi, Lionel Atwill, Josephine Hutchinson, Donnie Dunagan. Universal. B&W.

Bela Lugosi watches over his friend Boris Karloff in Son of Frankenstein *(1939).*

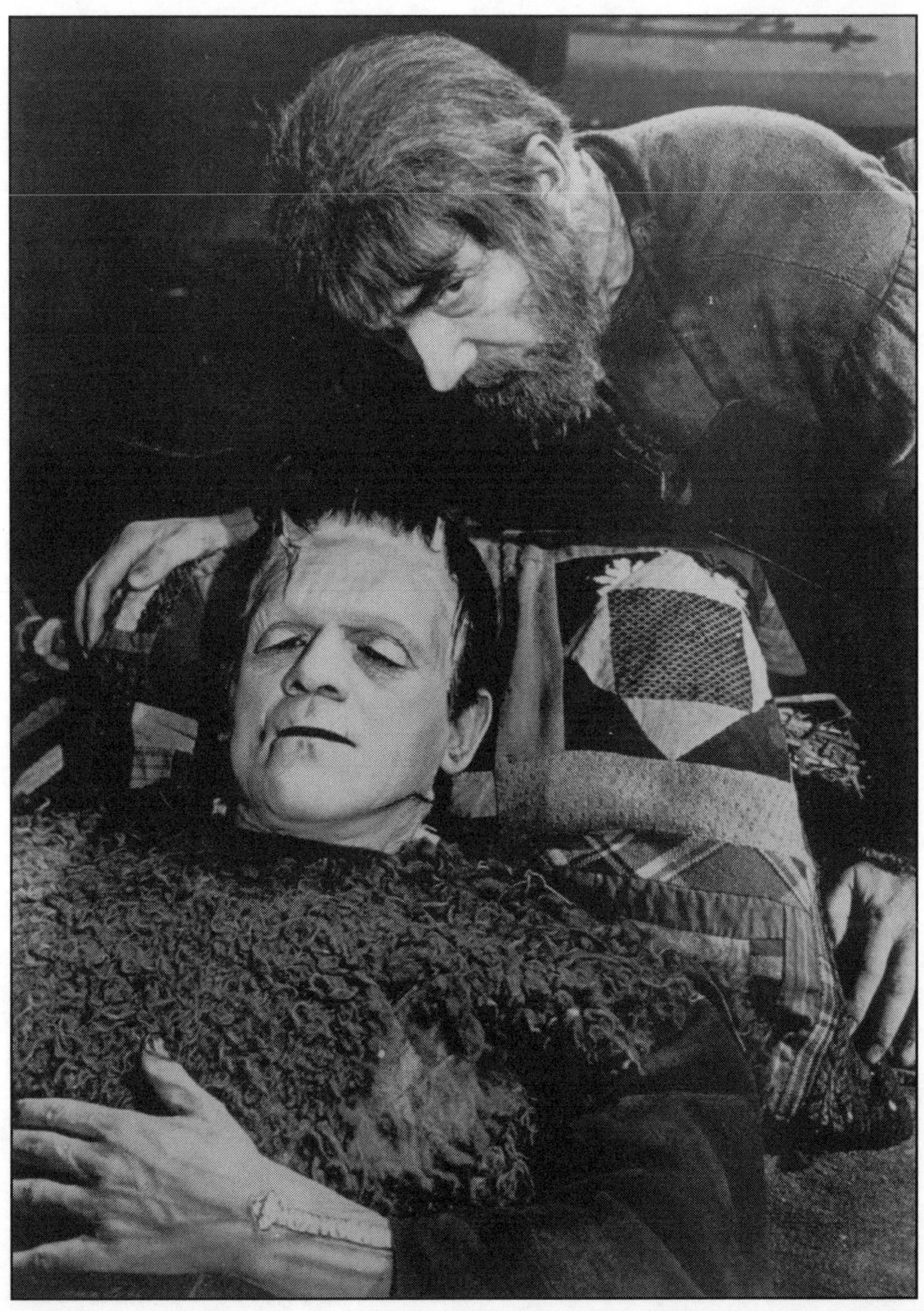

Stylish follow-up to *Bride of Frankenstein* (1935). Rathbone (in a role originally planned for Peter Lorre) plays the eponymous Baron Wolf von Frankenstein, who returns to his ancestral castle with his family. There, at the bidding of the broken-necked shepherd Ygor (Lugosi, in one of his finest roles), he once again resurrects his father's creation (fifty-one year-old Karloff in his third and final film appearance as the Monster, now reduced to little more than a killing machine). In one scene, Rathbone's obsessive scientist complains that the name of his father and the Monster have become synonymous. With Atwill's memorable one-armed Inspector Krogh and strong support from Lionel Belmore, Gustav von Seyffertitz, Edgar Norton and Lawrence Grant. This was to be Universal's first Technicolor production, but after tests began in October 1938, it was discovered that Karloff's make-up didn't photograph well in colour and the footage (which included Dwight Frye as an angry villager) was abandoned and reshot in black and white. The same year Universal announced a sequel, *After Frankenstein*, which was never made. The script was published by MagicImage in 1990.
Sequel: THE GHOST OF FRANKENSTEIN (qv; 1942)
✦✦✦✦

THE SON OF KONG
USA, 1933. Dir: Ernest B. Schoedsack. With: Robert Armstrong, Helen Mack, Frank Reicher, John Marston, Victor Wong, Noble Johnson. RKO Radio Pictures. B&W.
Ill-conceived, quickie sequel to the great *King Kong* (1933), originally announced as *Jamboree*. Subtitled 'A serio-comic phantasy', it was filmed for just $250,000 — less than half the budget of the original. With a short running time of only seventy minutes, Ruth Rose's thin script has showman Carl Denham (Armstrong) returning to Skull Island after being sued for the damage the original giant ape did to New York. There he discovers Kiko, a white, smaller version of Kong (mostly used for comedy relief), various dinosaurs, an impressive sea serpent and a giant cave bear. On the plus side are Willis O'Brien's superb stop-motion animation and effects (although he tried to have his name removed from the credits), Marcel Delgado's models, another brilliant Max Steiner score, and Armstrong, Reicher, Wong and Johnson all recreating their roles from the original film.
✦✦✧

SON OF MONSTERS ON THE MARCH
USA, 1980. Video Yesteryear. B&W.
This twenty-five minute video compilation is a follow-up to *Monsters on the March* (1980) and also consists of mostly re-release trailers for the classic Universal horror films.
✦✦✧

SON OF THE INCREDIBLY STRANGE FILM SHOW
UK/Mexico, 1989. Dir: Andy Harries. With: Jonathan Ross, Johnny Legend, El Hijo del Santo (Jorge Guzmán), Lorena Velásquez (Velázquez), Blue Demon (Alejandro Muñoz), Blue Demon Jr. Channel X/Sleeping Partners/ Channel Four Television. Colour/B&W.
The Incredibly Strange Film Show (1988) is a series of forty-minute TV documentaries hosted by co-producer Ross. Segments are devoted to Herschell Gordon Lewis, Ted V. Mikels, Ray Dennis Steckler and Edward D. Wood Jr, amongst others. In this episode of the follow-up series, Ross travels to Mexico to look at the career of El Santo, the silver-masked hero ('El Enmascarado de Plata'). It includes unique interviews and numerous clips from *Doctor of Doom* (1962), *Las Momias de Guanajuato* (1970), *Samson vs. the Vampire Women* (1961), *Santo contra la Magia Negra* (1972), *Santo y Blue Demon contra Dracula y el Hombre Lobo* (1971), *The Wrestling Women vs. the Aztec Mummy* (1964) and many other wrestling/horror movies. This also features a reunion between Velázquez and the Aztec Mummy. Other episodes are devoted to Stuart Gordon, Sam Raimi, Fred Olen Ray, George A. Romero, Tom Savini and Doris Wishman. The cartoon title sequence includes Ross encountering a masked Mexican wrestler, a zombified Tor Johnson and a Chinese hopping vampire.
✦✦✦✧

SON OF TICKLESTEIN
USA, 1990. Dir: Tony Sinclair. Sinclair Blue Productions. Colour.
'Adults only' tickling video which is a sequel to writer/director Sinclair's *Doctor Ticklestein* (1989).
✦

SONS OF SATAN
USA, 1973. Dir: Lancer Brooks. With: Robert McKay, Tom Payne, Ned Burke, Carl Ford, Bill North, Tex Neeley. Blue & Brooks. Colour.
Gay pastiche of 1940s horror films, featuring black magic rituals and McKay as a vampire.
✦

SORCERESS
Mexico/USA, 1982. Dir: Brian Stuart (Jack Hill). With: Lynette Harris, Leigh Anne Harris, Robert Ballesteros, Martin La Salle, Bob Nelson, David Milbern. New World Pictures. Colour.
Written by Jim Wynorski, this silly sword and sorcery movie features the Harris twins as Mora and Mira, two warrior women disguised as boys (sure!). They set out on a quest to find their father, the resurrected evil wizard Traigon (Ballesteros) who is responsible for killing their mother and their foster family. Aided by a Viking (La Salle), a horned satyr and others, the sexy siblings encounter a guardian winged lion, fighting gorillas with fruit bombs and an army of sword-wielding zombies. Executive producer Roger Corman had the film re-edited and the director's name removed from the credits.
✦✧

SORORITY BABES IN THE SLIMEBALL BOWL-O-RAMA
USA, 1987. Dir: David DeCoteau. With: Linnea Quigley, Andras Jones, Robin Rochelle, Hal Havins, Brinke Stevens, Michelle McClellan (Michelle Bauer). Titan Productions/Urban Classics. Colour.
Filmed under the title *The Imp* in two weeks for just $190,000. Lisa and Taffy (McClellan and Stevens), a pair of college girls on a sorority initiation, along with three nerdy boys and lively punk thief Spider (Quigley), all find themselves trapped in a shopping mall where an evil imp (an unconvincing puppet voiced by 'Dukey Flyswatter' [Michael Sonye]) has been accidentally released from a bowling trophy(!) after thirty years. While the supernatural creature starts killing off the teenagers, two other girls, Rhonda and Frankie (Kathi Obrecht and Carla Baron), are possessed by demons and transformed into a crusty-faced zombie and the Bride of Frankenstein, respectively. As usual, co-producer/director DeCoteau is unable to raise the fun storyline above its low-budget origins and the gratuitous nudity. With 'C.D. LaFleur' (George 'Buck' Flower).
✦✧

SORORITY HOUSE VAMPIRES
(aka SORORITY HOUSE VAMPIRES FROM HELL)
USA, 1992. Dir: Geoffrey de Valois. With: Kathy Presgrave, Eugenie Bondurant, Natalia Bondurant, Rachel A. Wolkow, Shay Moore, Kenny Gibbs. Digital Entertainment Group/Digital Doom/Desire. Colour.
Low-budget comedy in which 200 year-old shape-changing vampire Natalia (Eugenie Bondurant) is accidentally awakened during a sorority house initiation ceremony. A busty college girl (Presgrave) must rescue her boyfriend and save the world from environmental disaster before the Queen of Darkness can claim ten victims (who she turns into zombies) and become human again. With Robert Bucholz as the bumbling Count Vlad trying to escape from a locked wine cellar.
✦

SORORITY HOUSE VAMPIRES
USA, 1997. Dir: Geoffrey de Valois and Eugene James. With: Kathy Presgrave, Eugenie Bondurant. Digital Vision Entertainment/Bovine Productions/Cinematrix Releasing. Colour.
Approximately half the running time of this independent video release includes footage from de Valois' 1992 film of the same title. The remainder is new, and the story has been changed significantly. Samantha attempts to discover what happened to her sister Buffy after her sibling joined a sorority and encountered a redneck stalker, a kinky pledge sister, her gang-banger room-mate and blood-

sucking vampires. This includes some mild S&M with paddles.
✦

SORORITY SLUMBER PARTY MASSACRE
USA, 1997. Dir: Geoffrey de Valois. With: Heather LeMire, Liddy Roley, Barbara Savage. Digital Entertainment Group/Salt City Home Video. Colour.
One of a series of softcore *Vampire Raw Footage* videos that includes behind-the-scenes nude and erotic sequences from *The Vampire Conspiracy* (1995). Sorority girls become involved in a nude vampire blood orgy during college Hell Week.
Sequel: SORORITY SLUMBER PARTY MASSACRE 2 (qv; 1997)
✦

SORORITY SLUMBER PARTY MASSACRE 3
USA, 1997. Dir: Geoffrey de Valois. With: Heather LeMire, Liddy Roley, Barbara Savage. Digital Entertainment Group/Salt City Home Video. Colour.
Third in the series of *Vampire Raw Footage* videos. Nude college girls struggle to survive the horror of their own bloodlust.
✦

SORORITY SLUMBER PARTY MASSACRE 2
USA, 1997. Dir: Geoffrey de Valois. With: Heather LeMire, Liddy Roley, Barbara Savage. Digital Entertainment Group/Salt City Home Video. Colour.
More softcore clips as college students attempt to escape the evil of their sorority house from Hell in this *Vampire Raw Footage* video.
Sequel: SORORITY SLUMBER PARTY MASSACRE 3 (qv; 1997)
✦

S.O.S. INVASION
Spain, 1969. Dir: Silvio F. Balbuena. With: Jack Taylor (George Brown Randall/Grek Martin), Mara Cruz, Diana Sorel, José María Tasso, Titania Climent, Catherine Ellison. Internacional de Mercados Turisticos. Colour.
A group of strange women turn corpses into electronic zombies in their castle laboratory.
✦✧

THE SOUL OF A MONSTER
USA, 1944. Dir: Will Jason. With: Rose Hobart, George Macready, Jim Bannon, Jeanne Bates, Erik Rolf, Ernest Hilliard. Columbia. B&W.
This attempt by Columbia to create an atmospheric Val Lewton-type 'B' chiller fails because of Edward Dein's risible script and Jason's tedious direction. Macready plays a wonderfully kind doctor who is dying. In desperation, his wife calls upon the powers of darkness to save him and Hobart's supernatural dragon lady turns up. She allows the doctor to live on, but as a soulless zombie.
✦✧

THE SOUND OF LAUGHTER
USA, 1963. Dir: John O'Shaughnessy. With: F. Chase Taylor, Wilbur Budd Hulick. Union. B&W.
Feature-length compilation of clips from short films, including *The Inventors* (1934), in which radio stars Colonel Lemuel Q. Stoopnagle (Taylor) and Budd (Hulick) use various spare parts collected by the students at a girls' school to build a 'Stoopenstein' (Frankenstein's second cousin).
✦✦

THE SOUTH BANK SHOW:
Dracula
(USA: BIOGRAPHY: Dracula)
UK, 1993. Dir: Daniel Wiles. With: Prof Leonard Wolf, Prof Christopher Frayling, Winona Ryder, Stephen Jones, Christopher Lee, James V. Hart. London Weekend Television/A&E Television Networks/ITV. Colour.
Long-running hour-long arts and entertainment series (1978-). In this episode, editor and presenter Melvyn Bragg takes a look at the history of Bram Stoker's character, from the inspirations for the original novel up to and including Francis Ford Coppola's version of *Bram Stoker's Dracula* (1992). This also includes clips from the BBC's *Count Dracula* (1977), *Dracula* (1958), *Dracula Has Risen from the Grave* (1968), *Dracula Prince of Darkness* (1965), *Nosferatu* (1922), *The Satanic Rites of Dracula* (1973), *Scars of Dracula* (1970) and *The Vampire Lovers* (1970), plus interviews with Stoker's great-nephew Daniel Farson, Professor Elaine Showalter of Princeton University, Carroll Borland, Francis Ford Coppola, Gary Oldman, Sadie Frost, The Rt Reverend Sean Manchester and members of The Vampyre Society. The *Biography* version is introduced by Peter Graves.
✦✦✦✧

SPACE MASTER X-7
USA, 1957. Dir: Edward Bernds. With: Bill Williams, Lyn Thomas, Robert Ellis, Paul Frees, Rhoda Williams, Joan Barry. Twentieth Century-Fox. B&W.
Low-budget documentary-style science fiction thriller, co-scripted by George Worthing Yates. A returning space probe brings back to Earth a vampiric alien fungus dubbed 'blood rust'. Government agents Hand (Williams) and Radigan (Ellis) attempt to track down the infected girlfriend (Thomas) of scientist Charles Palmer (Frees). Fourteenth-billed Moe Howard plays a cab driver for regular Three Stooges director Bernds. Filmed in Regalscope.
✦✦

SPACE PRECINCT:
Predator and Prey
USA/UK, 1994. Dir: Sidney Hayers. With: Ted Shackelford, Rob Youngblood, Simone Bendix, Nancy Paul, Jerome Willis, Rolf Saxon. The Space Precinct LP/Mentorn Films/GTV/Sky Television. Colour.
Hour-long syndicated TV series (1994-95, twenty-four episodes), created by producer Gerry Anderson and set in the year 2040. New York cops Lieutenant Patrick Brogan (Shackelford) and Officer Jack Haldane (Youngblood) are part of an exchange programme, based in Demeter City, a sprawling metropolis on the planet Altor. In this episode, Brogan and Haldane team up with a cop with a bad attitude to try to stop one hundred year-old bogeyman Kmada (Richard James), a Nosferatu-looking alien serial killer, who possesses other bodies and takes the life-force of his victims to sustain himself. From the director of *Circus of Horrors* (1960).
✦✧

SPACE SHIP SAPPY
USA, 1957. Dir: Jules White. With: The Three Stooges (Moe Howard, Larry Fine, Joe Besser), Doreen Woodbury, Benny Rubin, Marilyn Hanold. Columbia. B&W.
Sixteen minute comedy short in which Moe, Larry and Joe are launched into space and land on a planet populated by fanged vampire women.
✦✦

SPACE ZOMBIE BINGO!!!
USA, 1993. Dir: George F. Ormrod. With: Bill Darkow, Hugh Crawford, Ramona Provost, Michael Wood, Jim Wark, Steve Younker. George F. Ormrod/Troma. Colour.
Woefully amateurish low-budget spoof of Ed Wood's *Plan 9 from Outer Space* (1958), with flesh-eating robot zombies from outer space (wearing welding masks, flippers and ping pong antenna) invading the Earth. Only Major Kent Bendover (Darkow) of Earth's Zombie Defence Corp can defeat them with atomic bombs, but the radioactivity turns the zombies into giants until they are finally destroyed by 'Solarnite'. Padded with stock footage, this unfunny comedy is narrated by psychic Crisko (Wood).
✦

SPERMULA
France, 1975. Dir: Charles Matton. With: Dayle Haddon, Udo Kier, François Dunoyer, Jocelyne Boisseau, Georges Géret, Ginette Leclerc. Film and Co/PPFC. Colour.
Written and directed by former fashion photographer and illustrator Matton. Having disappeared from America during the late 1930s, Spermula (Haddon) and her hedonistic sect of beautiful vampire women return to civilisation in a huge flying boat. These women

live in a lavish art deco mansion, communicate telepathically, and drink sperm instead of blood. When Spermula falls in love with an artist (Kier), she sacrifices her immortality for him.
✦✧

SPHINX
USA/UK/Hungary/Egypt, 1980. Dir: Franklin J. Schaffner. With: Lesley-Anne Down, Frank Langella, Maurice Ronet, Sir John Gielgud, Martin Benson, John Rhys-Davies. Orion Pictures/S & L Films/Warner Bros. Colour.
Based on the novel by Robin Cook, this daft romantic thriller stars Down as an unlikely Boston Egyptologist, Dr Erica Baron, who discovers a solid gold statue of Seti in the home of Cairo antiques dealer Abdu Hamdi (a cameo by Gielgud). When the shopkeeper is murdered and the statue stolen, she begins to realise that someone is plundering a previously undiscovered tomb in The Valley of the Kings. With Saeed Jaffrey, William Hootkins, and James Cossins and Victoria Tennant as Lord and Lady Carnarvon. Despite the talent involved, this is laughable hokum.
✦✧

SPIDER-MAN:
Blade, the Vampire Hunter/The Immortal Vampire
USA/Japan, 1995. Dir: Bob Shellhorn. Voices: Christopher Daniel Barnes, Linda Gary, Edward (Ed) Asner, Saratoga Ballantine, Jennifer Hale, Gary Imhoff. Marvel Entertainment Group/Marvel Films/New World Entertainment/Fox Kids Network. Colour.
Superhero Spider-Man (Barnes) and obsessed half-human vampire hunter Blade (J.D. Hall) team-up to track down scientifically-created vampire Michael Morbius (Nick Jameson) in Chapters IX and X of the 'Neogenic Nightmare' sequence of this half-hour cartoon TV series (1994-98) based on the Marvel Comics characters. With the voices of Joseph Campanella and Malcolm McDowell. Co-executive produced by Stan Lee.
Sequel: BLADE (qv; 1998)
✦✦✧

THE SPIDER WOMAN STRIKES BACK
USA, 1945 (1946). Dir: Arthur Lubin. With: Brenda Joyce, Gale Sondergaard, Kirby Grant, Rondo Hatton, Milburn Stone, Hobart Cavanaugh. Universal. B&W.
The year before, Sondergaard played a woman who used poison to drive her victims to suicide in Universal's Sherlock Holmes adventure *The Spider Woman*. She returns in this shoddy sequel-in-name-only as a totally different character, the evil Zenobia Dollard, who uses the blood of her female companions to feed the carnivorous Drochenema plants in her basement. Real-life acromegalic Hatton portrays her ugly mute servant, Mario the Monster Man, while Joyce's insipid heroine nearly ends up as plant food because she keeps drinking drugged milk. Director Lubin (the 1943 *Phantom of the Opera*, etc) totally botches the fiery climax, and despite a running time of just under an hour, it seems much longer.
✦✧

SPIRITISM
(Orig: ESPIRITISMO)
Mexico, 1961. Dir: Benito Alazraki. With: Joseph L. Jimenez (José Luis Jiménez), Nora Veryán, Beatriz Aguirre, Alice Caro, Carmen (Carmelita) Gonzalez, Anthony (Antonio) Bravo. Cinematográfica Calderón/Young-America Productions/American International. B&W.
Based on the uncredited story 'The Monkey's Paw' by W.W. Jacobs. Calling upon the Devil to aid her when the family's finances fail, a mother (Gonzalez) is granted three wishes upon a crawling human hand inside Pandora's Box. When she wishes that her mangled son returns from the grave, he almost does. The English-language version was produced by K. (Kenneth) Gordon Murray and directed by Manuel San Fernando. With Eugenia San Martin and future director René Cardona Jr.
Remake: GREAT GHOST TALES: The Monkey's Paw (qv; 1961)
✦

SPIRITUAL LOVE
Hong Kong, circa 1992. With: Ju Bao-Yih, Guh Guan-Jong, Guu Feng, Roan Pey-Jong. Film Line Entertainments/Lucky Star Film. Colour.
Not to be confused with the 1985 film of the same title. This horror comedy involves a trio of vampire sisters and a ghostly little boy.
✦✧

SPIRIT VS. ZOMBI
Taiwan/Hong Kong, 1989. Dir: Yao Feng-Pan. World Video. Colour.
Sentimental tale about a one hundred year-old vampire father and his undead son resurrected in modern Taiwan. They become separated, and the father bites an actor playing a vampire and takes his place in a movie. In the end, the father is destroyed and the young vampire boy disappears into the mist. Despite the title, there are no spirits or zombies.
✦

SPLIT IMAGE
USA, 1982. Dir: Ted Kotcheff. With: Michael O'Keefe, Karen Allen, Peter Fonda, James Woods, Elizabeth Ashley, Brian Dennehy. Orion Pictures/PolyGram. Colour.
A middle-class teenager (O'Keefe) is brainwashed into joining a cult (whose leader is played by Fonda). This includes clips from the 1941 version of *Dr. Jekyll and Mr. Hyde* and a post-screening discussion on 'the duality of human nature'. Strong performances, particularly from Woods as a deprogrammer and Dennehy as the boy's father.
✦✦

SPOOKED!
USA, 1989. With: Samantha Strong, Jessica Longe, Dana Lynn. Video Exclusives. Colour.
Hardcore comedy in which two jealous classmates conduct a scientific experiment that turns a handsome stud into a monster.
✦

SPOOKIES
USA, 1985. Dir: Eugenie Joseph, Thomas Doran and Brendan Faulkner. With: Felix Ward, Dan Scott, Alec Nemser, Maria Pechukas, A.J. Lowenthal, Peter Dain. Miggles Corporation/Twisted Souls. Colour.
Filmed in upstate New York, *Twisted Souls* (1984) was an unreleased horror comedy designed to hold together a number of special effects showreels. Editor Joseph took her co-directors' film and added a new framing sequence in which ancient sorcerer Kreon (Ward) attempts to raise his dead wife Isabelle (Pechukas) with the help of his cat-boy servant (Scott) and the souls of a dumb group of teens trapped in his old mansion. This also includes a spider woman (Soo Paek), the Grim Reaper (James M. Glen), and a climatic chase involving numerous zombies.
✦

SPOOKS!
USA, 1952 (1953). Dir: Jules White. With: The Three Stooges (Moe Howard, Shemp Howard, Larry Fine), Phil Van Zandt, Tom Kennedy, Norma Randall. Columbia. B&W.
Sixteen minute 3-D short in which the Three Stooges explore a spooky haunted house and encounter a mad scientist named Dr Jekyll, who is attempting to transplant a woman's brain into a gorilla. This includes a custard pie fight and the usual slapstick comedy routines.
✦✦

SPOOK WARFARE
(Orig: YOKAI DAISENSO)
Japan, 1968. Dir: Yoshiyuki Kuroda. With: Yoshihiko Aoyama, Akane Kawasaki, Osamu Okawa, Tomoo Uchida, Hajme Kimuru. Daiei. Colour.
A governor of Izu province is possessed by Daimon, a 4,000 year-old blood-sucking Babylonian demon. The creature is finally defeated by a local water spirit and various other monsters.
✦

THE SPOOKY FAMILY
(Orig: ZHUO GUI HE JIA HUAN)
Hong Kong, 1990. Dir: Chin Yue Sang (and Kent Cheng/Cheng Jut). With: Kent Cheng (Cheng Jut), Nina Li-Chi, Pauline Wong, Wu Kwan-Yu, Billy Lau, Lau Sze-Yu (Wong Ching/Wong Ching-Jing). Samico Films/Newport Entertainment/World Video. Colour.
From the creators of the popular *Mr. Vampire* series, this horror comedy is filled with non-stop action and special effects. A group of evil magicians revive the blue-faced Copper Vampire, the most evil being in the world, by mixing their tainted blood with the creature's own. Ghost hunter/wizard Master Chu Kor (Cheng), his strange smiling family and a couple of friendly ghosts are hired to destroy the undead monster.
Sequel: THE SPOOKY FAMILY 2 (qv; 1991)
✦✦

THE SPOOKY FAMILY 2
Hong Kong, 1991. Dir: Ricky Lau (Ricky Hui/Xu Guan-Ying). With: Kent Cheng (Cheng Jut), Lam Ching-Ying (Lin Zheng-Ying), Lau Sze-Yu (Wong Ching/Wong Ching-Jing). Colour.
Slightly disappointing sequel to the 1990 original, from the creators of the *Mr. Vampire* series. Ching-Ying (who plays One-Eyebrow Priest from that series) joins the cast of this Cantonese horror comedy.
✦✧

SPOOKY KAMA SUTRA
(USA: aka BEAUTIFUL DEAD BODIES)
Taiwan, 1987. Dir: Xin Ren. With: Sun Chi Sun (Cheryle Chung), Tiajia Han. Suiki. Colour.
Sex/horror film in which a woman (Sun) kills herself after being drugged and raped by evil wizard Tong (Han). However, the sorcerer brings her back to life and uses a trio of hopping vampires to battle a good magician.
✦

SPOOKY, SPOOKY
(Orig: GUI MENG JIAO/GWAI MAANG GEUK)
Hong Kong, 1988. Dir: Lon Weng-Tung (Lo Wei-Don) and Samo Hung (Samo Hung Kam-Po/Hung Kam-Bo/Hong Jin-Baoh). With: Joyce Godenzi (Ko Lai-Hung), Wu Ma (Wo Ma/Yuen Wah/Ng Ma-Wu), Jacob Cheung, Richard Ng, Corey Yuan, Billy Lau. Golden Harvest/Bo-Jon Films/ Paragon Films/Rainbow Video. Colour.
Horror comedy in which the ghost of a female adulterer is pulling swimmers underwater to their death. When the phantom falls in love with rookie policeman Wang (Alfred Cheung Kin-Ting), he is accidentally drowned and returns from the dead as a blue-faced zombie.
✦✦

STARFIGHTERS
(Orig: LUCHADORES DE LAS ESTRELLAS)
Mexico/USA, 1992. Dir: Rodolfo López Real. With: Gloria Mayo, Nitron, Blue Demon Jr, El Misterioso, El Volador, Mascarita Sagrada. Arena Films. Colour.
Low-budget attempt to recreate the wrestling/horror movies of the 1960s and 1970s. When a spaceship crash-lands on Earth, a group of masked heroes battle its inhabitants — a big space vampire (Nitron) and his trio of comic-relief alien midgets.
✦

STARSKY & HUTCH:
The Vampire
USA, 1976. Dir: Bob Kelljan (Robert Kelljchian). With: David Soul, Paul Michael Glaser, Antonio Fargas, Bernie Hamilton, John Saxon, G.W. Bailey. Spelling-Goldberg Productions/ABC-TV. Colour.
In this episode of the hour-long TV series (1975-79, eighty-eight episodes) created by William Blinn, the two eponymous undercover cops (Soul and Glaser) track down mad ballet instructor René Nadasy (Saxon), who commits a series of vampire attacks in an attempt to resurrect his dead wife before falling to his death in a theatre. With Suzanne Somers and Colleen Camp. From the director of the *Count Yorga* films and the *Blacula* sequel.
✦✦

STAR TREK:
Catspaw
USA, 1967. Dir: Joseph Pevney. With: William Shatner, Leonard Nimoy, DeForrest Kelley, Antoinette Bower, Theo Marcuse, James Doohan. Desilu Productions/Norway Corporation/NBC-TV. Colour.
Halloween episode of the popular hour-long science fiction TV series (1966-68, seventy-nine episodes), written by Robert Bloch and D.C. Fontana. Beaming down to Pyris VII, Kirk (Shatner), Spock (Nimoy) and McCoy (Kelley) are captured by Sylvia and Korob (Bower and Marcuse), two magical alien creatures who have turned Sulu (George Takei) and Scotty (Doohan) into zombies and can transform their own shapes, including changing into a giant black cat. This episode was adapted by James Blish in the collection *Star Trek 8* (1972).
✦✦✦
The Enemy Within
USA, 1966. Dir: Leo Penn. With: William Shatner, Leonard Nimoy, DeForrest Kelley, Jim Goodwin, James Doohan, Nichelle Nichols. Desilu Productions/Norway Corporation/ NBC-TV. Colour.
Scripted by Richard Matheson, a transporter malfunction splits Captain Kirk into two beings — one evil and the other good. As they battle for supremacy, it becomes obvious that they need each other to survive. James Blish adapted this episode in the collection *Star Trek 8* (1972).
✦✦✦
The Man Trap
USA, 1966. Dir: Marc Daniels. With: William Shatner, Leonard Nimoy, Jeanne Bal, Alfred Ryder, DeForrest Kelley, Grace Lee Whitney. Desilu Productions/Norway Corporation/NBC-TV. Colour.
The dynamics of the regular characters had not quite been worked out yet in this, the first televised episode of *Star Trek*, scripted by George Clayton Johnson. Assigned to make a medical examination of the only two inhabitants of planet M-113, the crew of the *Enterprise* discover that archaeologist Dr Nancy Crater (Bal), a former girlfriend of Dr McCoy's, is really the last of a race of alien shape-changing salt vampires (played by Francine Pyne), able to seduce its victims by assuming the form of someone they know. With George Takei and Nichelle Nichols. This was adapted in the collection *Star Trek 1* (1967) by James Blish.
Series sequel: STAR TREK (1973-74)
✦✦✧

STAR VIRGIN
USA, 1979. Dir: Linus Gator. With: Kari Klark, Tracy Walton, Jeanette Harlow, Maureen O'Hara, Trisha Cole, Brenda Leggs. Gail/VCX. Colour.
Hardcore science fiction film in which a penial robot (Kevin Thompson) shows a test tube-created woman (*Hustler* centrefold Klark) various sex scenes involving the now defunct human race. These include a 1950s Garden of Eden sequence with a human-headed snake (J.C. Phillips), and a silent black and white Dracula spoof, with an Igor character wearing a Richard Nixon mask and the Count (Johnny Harden) sinking more than his teeth into his victim. It's not anywhere near as interesting as it sounds. This was *Hustler*'s 1979 'Picture of the Year'.
✦

STEPPENWOLF
USA/Switzerland/UK, 1974 (1976). Dir: Fred Haines. With: Max Von Sydow, Dominique Sanda, Pierre Clementi, Carla Romanelli, Roy Bosier, Alfred Baillou. D/R Films/ Peter J. Sprague. Colour.
Surreal fantasy based on the 1927 novel, *Der Steppenwolf*, by Nobel Prize winner Herman Hesse. Von Sydow portrays the suicidal Harry Haller, who thinks he is a werewolf and embarks on a voyage of self-discovery through The Magic Theatre (created with electronic video effects and the early use of a Dolby sound system), where the only

price of admission is his imagination.
✦✧

BARBARA STEELE
[b.1938]

British-born actress who escaped Rank's Charm School in the late 1950s and became an icon in Italian horror movies, thanks to her expressive eyes, distinctive cheekbones and the obsessive sexual undertones of many of her films. She was a regular on the briefly-revived TV series *Dark Shadows* (1990-91).
qv: *Black Sunday* (1960); *Castle of Blood* (1964); *Clive Barker's A-Z of Horror* (1997); *Fear in the Dark* (1991); *The Horrible Dr. Hichcock* (1962); *Terror Creatures from the Grave* (1965).

PIPPA STEELE
[1948-1992]

British character actress (also known as Pippa Steel) who appeared in Hammer's *The Vampire Lovers* (1970) and *Lust for a Vampire* (1970) before her untimely death from cancer.

MAX STEINER
[1888-1971]

Austrian composer who scored more than 300 films in Hollywood and was nominated for numerous Academy Awards, winning three of them. He will always be remembered for his exuberant symphonic score for *King Kong* (1933).
qv: *The Monkey's Paw* (1932); *The Son of Kong* (1933).

YUTTE STENSGAARD
(Jytte Stensgaard) [b 1946]

Danish-born actress and former au pair and model. In Britain since the early 1960s, she appeared in a number of small roles on TV and in movies before playing the bisexual Mircalla/Carmilla in Hammer's *Lust for a Vampire* (1970).
qv: *Hammer the Studio That Dripped Blood!* (1987); *Scream and Scream Again* (1969).

STEPS FROM HELL
USA, 1992. Dir: James Tucker. With: Bernardo Rosa, Rocky Tucker, Ron Odell, Philip Cable, Liz Stoeckel, Steve Quimby. Coast to Coast Video. Colour.
Low-budget independent video release. Evil immortal Vlad Tempest and his female zombie servants have stolen a sacred map that reveals the location of a gateway which, when opened, will unleash the ultimate evil upon the world.
✦

ONSLOW STEVENS
(Onslow Ford Stevenson) [1902-1977]

American stage actor who occasionally appeared in film roles, most notably as the vampiric Dr Franz Edelmann, infected with the Count's blood in *House of Dracula* (1945). He died, a victim of institutional abuse, at a nursing home where he was convalescing from a heart ailment.
qv: *The Creeper* (1948); *Life Returns* (1934).

STING OF DEATH
USA, 1966 (1967). Dir: William Grefé. With: Joe Morrison, Valerie Hawkins, John Vella, Jack Nagle, Sandy Lee Kane, Deanna Dund. Essen Productions/Thunderbird International. Colour.
More low-budget madness from Florida. Vella plays a disfigured marine biologist experimenting with a Portuguese man-of-war in his underwater laboratory. Instead of curing his scarred features, he transforms himself into a giant jellyfish monster (played by Doug Hobart). Neil Sedaka is the special musical guest.
✦

THE STORY OF THE DRAGON AND THE LION HUNCHBACK
Hong Kong, 1962. B&W.
This is apparently inspired by Victor Hugo's *The Hunchback of Notre Dame*.
✦

A STORY OF TUTANKHAMUN
UK/Egypt, 1976. Dir: Kevin Scott. With: Domini Blyth, Barbara Bilton, E. Elalaily. Colour.
Apparently filmed in 1973, this is under an hour long! The discoverers of a cursed Pharaoh's tomb are plagued by visions.
✦

GLENN STRANGE
(George Glenn Strange) [1899-1973]

Bulky American character actor, formally a fiddle player, professional heavyweight boxer and rodeo rider, who mainly appeared as a villain in cowboy films. He was coached by Boris Karloff to play the Frankenstein Monster in *House of Frankenstein* (1944), and recreated the role in *House of Dracula* (1945), *Meet Frankenstein* (1948) and on TV's *Colgate Comedy Hour* with Abbott and Costello in 1953. Strange unsuccessfully tested for the title roles of *Tarzan the Ape Man* (1932) and the *Creature from the Black Lagoon* (1954), and in later years portrayed Sam the bartender on TV's *Gunsmoke* (1960-73).
qv: *The Adventures of the Spirit* (1963); *The Mad Monster* (1942); *Master Minds* (1949); *The Mummy's Tomb* (1942); *100 Years of Horror: 'Frankenstein and Friends'* (1996); *The Tex Williams Show* (circa 1951).

THE STRANGE CASE OF DR. JEKYLL AND MR. HYDE
Canada/USA, 1967 (1968). Dir: Charles Jarrott. With: Jack Palance, Denholm Elliott, Billie Whitelaw, Leo Genn, Oscar Homolka, Tessie O'Shea. Dan Curtis/Canadian Broadcasting Company/ABC-TV. Colour.
Two-hour videotaped adaptation of Robert Louis Stevenson's 1886 novel, produced by Dan Curtis (TV's *Dark Shadows* [1966-71], etc) for TV. Palance's timid Dr Jekyll is transformed into a satyr-like Mr Hyde thanks to Dick Smith's excellent make-up effects. Original star Jason Robards (in sequences directed by John Llewellyn Moxey from a script by Rod Serling) looked more monstrous as Hyde, but was replaced because of delays caused by an actor's strike in London. Palance fractured his arm while attempting a stunt during production and was made up in his hospital bed. With Torin Thatcher and Duncan Lamont. In 1971, Dan Curtis announced he would make another version of Stevenson's story, but it was never filmed.
Remake: THE ADULT VERSION OF JEKYLL & HIDE (qv; 1971)
✦✦✧

STRANGE DEAD BODIES
(Orig: KOESI)
Republic of Korea, 1981. Dir: Kang Bum-Koo. With: Kang Myung, Yoo Kwang-Ok. Han Lim Cinema Corporation. Colour.
Scientific experiments with a new insecticide accidentally cause the dead to rise as white-faced zombies with red rings around their eyes. In the end, the hero and heroine destroy the scientists' laboratory, and the walking corpses return to their resting places.
✦✧

STRANGE LOVE OF THE VAMPIRES
(Orig: EL ESTRAÑO AMOR DE LOS VAMPIROS/LA NOCHE DE LOS VAMPIROS. USA: aka NIGHT OF THE WALKING DEAD)
Spain, 1974. Dir: León Klimovsky. With: Emma Cohen, Carlos Ballesteros, Vicky Lusson, Barta Barry, Mari Paz Pondal, Rafael Hernandez. Richard Films. Colour.

A young woman (Cohen) falls in love with an undead aristocrat (Ballesteros) and they sleep together for a night. Afterwards, she finds herself called to a sinister castle populated by his orgiastic vampire followers. Finally a group of angry villagers, including her own father, kill her along with the rest of the bloodsuckers, while her living dead lover commits suicide.
✦

STRANGE PARADISE
Canada, 1969-70. Dir: Herb Kenwith, Herbert Roland, Vladimir Handera, William Glenn and George Gorman. With: Colin Fox, Tudi Wiggins, Bruce Gray, Dawn Greenhalgh, Jon Granik, Sylvia Feigel. Canadian Broadcasting Company/ABC-TV. Colour.
Half-hour daily supernatural soap opera (195 episodes) that boasts even cheaper production values than *Dark Shadows* (1966-71), the TV series it attempted to emulate. Set on Maljarin Island in the Caribbean, rich industrialist Jean Paul Desmond (Fox) revives his dead pregnant wife Erica (Wiggins) through black magic, which results in the release of his own 300 year-old French ancestor (also Fox), who decrees that no one may leave the island alive.
✦

THE STRANGERS
USA, 1998. Dir: Sergei Ivanov and Yuri Ivanov. With: Richard Bent, Shana Betz, Victoria Hunter, Jennifer Marks, Matt Martin, Jimmy Lord. Rotten Pictures/Vista Street Entertainment. Colour.
Low budget erotic horror thriller, shot on video by co-writers/producers/directors Sergei and Yuri Ivanov. Reluctant werewolf Trent (Bent) discovers that evil lycanthropes Jade (Hunter) and Carson (Lord) are responsible for a number of deaths in a small Californian mountain community. When transformed, these werewolves look like man-bats with big ears and are killed by a stake through the heart.
✦

STRANNAYAR ISTORIYAR DOKTORA DZEHEKILA I MISTERA KHAIDA
USSR, 1986. Dir: Alexander Orlov. With: Innokenti Smoktunovsky, Alexander Feklistov, Anatoly Adoskin, Alexander Lazarev, Bruno Frienlich, Alla Budnitskaya. Mosfilm. Colour.
This is apparently a very faithful adaptation of Robert Louis Stevenson's *Strange Case of Dr. Jekyll and Mr. Hyde*, with Smoktunovsky playing an elderly, conscientious Dr Jekyll/Dzehekila and (thanks to some impressive transformation sequences) Feklistov as a sadistic young Mr Hyde/Khaida. Most of the story is told in flashback, with the lawyer Utterson (Adoskin) attempting to discover the link between the two characters.
Remake: EDGE OF SANITY (qv; 1988)
✦✧

STRASEK — DER VAMPIR
West Germany, 1982. Dir: Theodor Boder. With: Oscar Olano, Beat Bangerter, Simone Haenggi, Jackie Steel. Boder. B&W.
Strange things begin to happen around a boy in a very disturbed state in a small Serbian village.
✦

FRANK STRAYER
[1891-1964]

American director, best remembered for his low-budget variations of the vampire theme, *The Vampire Bat* (1933) and *Condemned to Live* (1935).

STREETS
USA, 1990. Dir: Katt Shea Ruben. With: Christina Applegate, David Mendenhall, Eb Lottimer, Starr Andreeff, Patrick Richwood, Kady Tran. Concorde. Colour.
Los Angeles teenage junkie hooker Dawn (Applegate) is stalked by vampiric psycho cop Lumley (Lottimer) in this low-budget thriller directed by Ruben (*Dance of the Damned* [1988], etc), who also co-scripted with her husband, Andy. Shot in nineteen days, Roger Corman was executive producer. With Kay Lenz.
✦✧

KENNETH STRICKFADEN
[1896-1984]

American special effects technician best remembered for his electrical laboratory set in *Frankenstein* (1931) and numerous other films and serials (often uncredited).
qv: *The Atomic Brain* (1963); *Blackenstein* (1972); *Bride of Frankenstein* (1935); *Dracula vs. Frankenstein* (1971); *Frankenweenie* (1984); *The Lost City* (1935); *The Monkees: 'I Was a Teenage Monster'* (1966); *The Phantom of the Opera* (1925); *Son of Frankenstein* (1939); *Young Frankenstein* (1974).

STRIKER BOB
Belgium/Holland. Dir: Lars Damoiseaux. With: Tom De Wispelaere, Stijn Van Opstael, Ben Segers, Stefan Perceval, Coen Van Impe, Jan Blonde. Striker Production. Colour.
Sixteen minute short in which a pair of bowling brothers drown their rival. Unfortunately, a professor has also dumped his life-giving serum into the water, and the murder victim returns from the dead as a flesh-eating zombie.
✦✧

HERBERT L. STROCK
[b 1918]

American hack director, responsible for AIP's drive-in teenage trio *I Was a Teenage Frankenstein* (1957), *Blood of Dracula* (1957) and *How to Make a Monster* (1958).

STRUCK BY LIGHTNING
USA, 1979. Dir: Joel Zwick. With: Jeffrey Kramer, Jack Elam, Millie Slavin, Bill Erwin, Jeff Cotler, Richard Stahl. The Fellows-Keegan Company/Paramount/CBS-TV. Colour.
Short-lived (three episodes!), half-hour sitcom TV series featuring veteran Elam as Frank, the ageing Monster, who is inherited along with a rustic inn by Ted Stein (Kramer), the great-great grandson of the original Frankenstein. Frank needs Ted to recreate a serum so that he may survive. In the third episode, 'The Movie', Frank becomes mixed up in the making of a horror film at the inn. He thinks the actor playing Count Dracula (Jonathan Goldsmith) is really a vampire and tries to stake him. Several other episodes were apparently shot but never telecast.
✦✧

STURMTRUPPEN
Italy/France, 1977. Dir: Salvatore Samperi. With: Renato Pozzetto, Lino Toffolo, Cochi Ponzoni, Teo Teocoli, Jean Pierre Marielle, Corinne Clery. Achille Manzotti. Irrigazione/Les Film Jacques Leitienne. Colour.
Based on the Italian anti-war comic strip by Bonvi, this includes a sequence in a hospital room with a vampire and the Frankenstein Monster.
✦

SUBSPECIES
Romania/USA, 1990 (1991). Dir: Ted Nicolaou. With: Michael Watson, Laura Tate, Anders Hove, Michelle McBride, Irina Movila, Angus Scrimm (Lawrence Rory Guy). Full Moon Entertainment/Paramount. Colour.
Despite being executive produced by Charles Band, this is a pretty good vampire thriller, shot on location in Romania. Michelle (Tate) and Lillian (McBride) are two American college students studying folklore who become involved in a struggle between half-brothers Radu (Hove as the evil vampire) and Stefan Vladislas (Watson as the

hero vampire) for the powers of a Transylvanian blood-stone. David Allen supplied the stop-motion demons.
Sequel: BLOODSTONE SUBSPECIES II (qv; 1993)
✦✦✦

MILTON SUBOTSKY
[1921-1991]

American-born producer and screenwriter who lived and worked in Britain from the late 1950s onwards. He teamed up with financier Max J. Rosenberg and, following *City of the Dead* (1960), they created Amicus Productions, which along with AIP became the only serious rival to the House of Hammer. He successfully revived the anthology format with *Dr. Terror's House of Horrors* (1965), but the partnership broke up acrimoniously in the mid-1970s. Subotsky's subsequent genre projects are variable at best, and he is posthumously credited on a number of Stephen King adaptations.
qv: *Asylum* (1972); *The Beast Must Die* (1974); *Cat People* (1982); *The House That Dripped Blood* (1970); *I, Monster* (1970); *Madhouse* (1974); *The Monster Club* (1980); *Sometimes They Come Back* (1991); *Tales from the Crypt* (1972); *Torture Garden* (1967); *Vault of Horror* (1973); *The World of Abbott and Costello* (1964).

SUBSPECIES 4 BLOODSTORM
Romania/USA, 1998. Dir: Ted Nicolaou. With: Anders Hove, Denice Duff, Jonathon Morris, Ilinka Goya. Tanna Productions/Full Moon Pictures. Colour.
Writer/director Nicolaou's fourth entry in the direct-to-video series is a sequel to both his *Bloodlust Subspecies III* (1993) and *Vampire Journals* (1996). Having escaped the clutches of evil vampire Radu Vladislas (Hove), the undead Michelle (Duff) travels to Bucharest to seek out a vampire slayer/doctor who promises relief from her unquenchable thirst for blood. Meanwhile, Radu is searching for his beloved and has decided to reclaim the riches that his protégé Ash (Morris) has amassed over more than a century of power and decadence in the Vladislas name.
✦✦✧

SUCKER
USA, 1997 (1998). Dir: Hans Rodionoff. With: Yan Birch, Monica Baber, P.K. Phillips, Alex Erkiletian, Colleen Moore, Greg Fawcett. Seed Productions/Troma. Colour.
Written, co-produced and directed by Rodionoff, this offbeat no-budget comedy stars Erkiletian as Reed Buccholz, the strangely likeable assistant to undead rocker Anthony (Birch), who has sex with the corpses of the vampire's nubile victims before disposing of them. When Anthony is infected with the AIDS virus by Vanessa van Helsing (Baber), who has staked his bloodsucking band members in revenge for the death of her family, the vampire decides that it is time to end his immortal existence by watching the sun come up. With Phillips as the undead Lenore and Gail Harris as one of Anthony's victims.
✦✧

SUCK ME, VAMPIRE
(Orig: SUCE-MOI, VAMPIRE)
France, 1975 (1976). Dir: Maxime Debest. Off. Colour.
Hardcore horror film that includes out-takes and alternative scenes from Jean Rollin's *Lips of Blood* (1975).
✦

SUCKULA
USA, 1973. Dir: Anthony Spinelli. Boccaccio 100.
The title sums up this 'adults only' release.
✦

SUFFER LITTLE CHILDREN
UK, 1984 (1985). Dir: Alan Briggs. With: Colin Chamberlain, Ginny Rose, John Hollandz, Nicola Diana, Mark Insull, Joanna Bryant. Exciting Spectacular Pictures/FGL. Colour.
Made on an incredibly low budget and shot on video, this abysmal independent feature actually received a video release in Britain. A demonic child abandoned at a children's home possesses the youngsters and forces them to chop the adults to pieces until she is zapped by Jesus Christ! In a dream sequence, the children turn into zombies at a tea party. This cheap-looking production is amateurish in every respect.
✦

SUGAR HILL
(aka THE ZOMBIES OF SUGAR HILL. UK: VOODOO GIRL)
USA, 1974. Dir: Paul Maslansky. With: Marki Bey, Robert Quarry, Don Pedro Colley, Betty Anne Rees, Richard Lawson, Zara Cully. American International Productions. Colour.
Enjoyable, low-budget blaxploitation chiller. When a nightclub owner is murdered, his girlfriend Diana 'Sugar' Hill (Bey) calls upon the powers of voodoo god Baron Samedi (Colley) to send some creepy cobweb-covered zombie hit men (actually drowned seventeenth century slaves) after white gangster Mr Morgan (Quarry) and his thugs. The Originals sing 'Supernatural Voodoo Woman'.
✦✦

SULOCHANA
India, 1934. Dir: Chaudhury. With: Sulochana, D. Billimoria, Chandra, Zilloo, Hadi, Gulam Mahomed. Imperial. B&W.
A man invents an elixir that brings a dead girl back to life. The title translates as 'Temple Bells'.
✦

SUMMER OF SECRETS
Australia, 1976. Dir: Jim Sharman. With: Arthur Dignam, Rufus Collins, Nell Campbell, Kate Fitzpatrick, Andrew Sharp. Secret Picture Productions. Colour.
Dignam plays a mad scientist living on an island who uses revolutionary brain surgery to revive his dead wife (Fitzpatrick). Not a big hit from the director of *The Rocky Horror Picture Show* (1975).
✦✧

SUMPAH PONTIANAK
Malaya, 1958. Dir: B. Narayan Rao. With: Maria Menado, Mustaffa Maarof, Salmah Ahmad. Keris. B&W.
The third entry in the popular series, and a follow-up to *Dendam Pontianak* (1957). Menado returns as the cursed vampire, along with various ghosts and monsters.
Sequel: ANAK PONTIANAK (qv; 1958)
✦✧

SUNDOWN THE VAMPIRE IN RETREAT
USA, 1988 (1990). Dir: Anthony Hickox. With: David Carradine, Maxwell Caulfield, Morgan Brittany, Bruce Campbell, Jim Metzler, John Ireland. Vestron Pictures. Colour.
Inventive horror comedy co-written and stylishly directed by Hickox, who dedicated it to his late father, director Douglas. Carradine plays Mardulak (really Count Dracula), the leader of a group of vampires living peacefully in the community of Purgatory, somewhere in the American West. When the Harrison family (led by Metzler) arrive in town, followed by a manic descendant of Van Helsing (Campbell, mugging outrageously), villains Shane (Caulfield) and Jefferson (Ireland) lead a vampire revolt. Great fun, and a chance to see Carradine recreate one of his father's most famous roles. With M. Emmet Walsh, Dana Ashbrook, Elizabeth Gracen, Deborah Foreman, Dabbs Greer, Bert Remsen and George 'Buck' Flower. Not released in America until 1991.
✦✦✦

SUPERBOY:
Brimstone
USA, 1989 (1990). Dir: Andre R. Guttfreund. With: Gerard Christopher, Stacy Haiduk, Ilan Mitchell-Smith, Philip Michael Thomas, Carlos Cestero, Marc Macaulay. Cantharus Productions/Alexander and Ilya Salkind. Colour.
Syndicated (1988-92, one hundred episodes) half-hour adventures

of the Boy of Steel/campus reporter Clark Kent (John Haymes Newton/Christopher), Lana Lang (Haiduk), photographer T.J. White (Jim Calvert) and Clark's new roommate Andy McAlister (Mitchell-Smith) at Schuster College. Gerard Christopher replaced John Haymes Newton for the final three seasons (with seasons three and four retitled *The Adventures of Superboy*). In this episode, when Superboy is attacked by a zombie-like madman under the spell of evil sorcerer Prodo (Cestero), only a magical stranger named Brimstone (Thomas) can save him. Filmed in Florida; Ilya Salkind (the *Superman* movies, etc) was executive producer.

✦✦

Johnny Casanova and the Case of Secret Serum

USA, 1990. Dir: David Nutter. With: Gerard Christopher, Stacy Haiduk, Ilan Mitchell-Smith, Mark Holton, Glenn Maska, Robert Reynolds. Cantharus Productions/ Alexander and Ilya Salkind. Colour.

The titular tennis player (Holton) drinks a serum sent to him by his late brother and becomes irresistible.

✦✦

Run, Dracula, Run

USA, 1989 (1990). Dir: Richard J. Lewis. With: Gerard Christopher, Stacy Haiduk, Ilan Mitchell-Smith, Kevin Bernhardt, Louis Seeger Crume, Ivan Green. Cantharus Productions/Alexander and Ilya Salkind. Colour.

When his serum is stolen, Dracula's doctor son Byron Shelley (Bernhardt) reverts to his vampire state, transforming Lana Lang into a sexy member of the undead to bite Superboy.

✦✦

Succubus

USA, 1989. Dir: David Nutter. With: John Haymes Newton, Stacy Haiduk, Jim Calvert, Sybil Danning, Rita Rehn, T.J. Kelly. Cantharus Productions/Alexander and Ilya Salkind. Colour.

Best-selling novelist Pamela Dare (Danning) is secretly an ancient succubus who retains her youth and beauty by feeding on the life-force of others. After seducing T.J. White and capturing Lana, she chooses Superboy as her next victim.

✦✦✧

Young Dracula

USA, 1989. Dir: David Nutter. With: Gerard Christopher, Stacy Haiduk, Ilan Mitchell-Smith, Kevin Bernhardt, Lloyd Bochner, Dennis Neal. Cantharus Productions/ Alexander and Ilya Salkind. Colour.

When an old vampire (Bochner) attacks Lana, she is saved by Dracula's doctor son Byron Shelley (Bernhardt), who uses a daily injection of a serum he has created to control his 'disease'.

Episode sequel: SUPERBOY: Run, Dracula, Run (qv; 1989)
Series sequel: THE ADVENTURES OF SUPERBOY (qv; 1990-92)

✦✦✧

SUPER FRIENDS:

The Monster of Dr. Droid

USA, 1973. Dir: Charles A. Nichols. Voices: Sherry Alberoni, Danny Dark, Casey Kasem, Shannon Farnon, Ted Knight, Franklin (Frank) Welker. National Periodical Publications/Hanna-Barbera Productions/ABC-TV. Colour.

Half-hour cartoon TV series (1973-74, sixteen episodes) in which DC Comics' Justice League of America characters Superman (Dark), Batman (Olan Soule) and Robin (Kasem), Wonder Woman (Alberoni) and Aquaman (Norman Alden) team up with teenagers Wendy (Alberoni) and Marvin (Welker) and their pet Wonderdog (Welker) to battle crime from the Hall of Justice. In this episode, the Superfriends confront a Frankenstein-like monster created in the laboratory of Dr Droid (a caricature of Boris Karloff). Narrated by Knight. Executive produced by William Hanna and Joseph Barbera.

✦✦

The Super Friends Meet Frankenstein

USA, 1973. Dir: Charles A. Nichols. Voices: Sherry Alberoni, Danny Dark, Casey Kasem, Shannon Farnon, Ted Knight, Franklin (Frank) Welker. National Periodical Publications/Hanna-Barbera Productions/ABC-TV. Colour.

Dr Frankenstein revives his ancestor's Monster, which captures Batman and steals the superpowers from Superman and Wonder Woman until it is defeated by Robin with Kryptonite.

Series sequel: THE ALL-NEW SUPER FRIENDS HOUR (1977-78)

✦✦

THE SUPERGRASS

UK, 1985. Dir: Peter Richardson. With: Adrian Edmondson, Jennifer Saunders, Peter Richardson, Dawn French, Keith Allen, Nigel Planer. Michael White/The Comic Strip/Recorded Releasing. Colour.

Comedy feature inspired by *The Comic Strip Presents*... (1982-93) TV series. After inventing a story about being involved with an international drugs ring to impress his girlfriend Andrea (French), the hapless Dennis (Edmondson) is arrested by the police and forced to play out his fantasy as he encounters a pair of real dope smugglers (Allen and Planer). With Ronald Allen as the vampiric police Commander Robertson, Robbie Coltrane, Alexei Sayle and Michael Elphick.

✦✦

EL SUPERHOMBRE

Mexico, 1946. Dir: Chano Urueta. With: Enrique Herrera, Luis Manrique, Susana Cora. Manrique. B&W.

A blow on the head gives a man a dual personality and at night he turns into a criminal.

✦

EL SUPERLOCO

Mexico, 1936. Dir: Juan José Segura. With: Leopoldo Ortin, Carlos Villarías (Carlos Villarías Llano), Consuelo Frank, Ramùn Armengod, Raul Urquijo, 'Indian' Fernandez. PCE. B&W.

Obscure comedy reworking of Mary Shelley's *Frankenstein*, in which the mad Dr Dyenis (Villarías, star of the Spanish-language *Dracula* [1931]) performs bizarre brain experiments on his Monster (Urquijo) and attempts to discover the secret of eternal youth. This also apparently includes elements of *Strange Case of Dr. Jekyll and Mr. Hyde* and *The Picture of Dorian Gray*.

Remake: FRANKENSTEIN (qv; 1940)

✦

SUPERMAN: TERROR ON THE MIDWAY

USA, 1942. Dir: Dave Fleischer. Voices: Clayton 'Bud' Collyer, Joan Alexander. Paramount/Max Fleischer. Colour.

The last of nine *Superman* cartoon shorts producer Max Fleischer was coerced to make by Paramount before production was handed over to Famous Studios. Gigantic, a giant ape, escapes from its circus cage. When it kidnaps reporter Lois Lane (Alexander), only the Man of Steel (Collyer) can save her from the ensuing chaos.

Sequel: SUPERMAN: JAPOTEURS (1942)

✦✦

SUPERMAN: THE MUMMY STRIKES

USA, 1943. Dir: Seymour Kneitel. Voices: Clayton 'Bud' Collyer, Joan Alexander. Paramount/Famous Studios. Colour.

One of seventeen great-looking *Superman* cartoon shorts produced by Paramount between 1940 and 1943. Reporters Clark Kent (Collyer) and Lois Lane (Alexander) are investigating the mysterious death of an Egyptologist when they open a cursed tomb and release an ancient power source that brings to life the pharaoh's giant guardians.

Sequel: SUPERMAN: JUNGLE DRUMS (1942)

✦✦✧

SUPERNATURAL:

Countess Ilona/The Werewolf Reunion

UK, 1977. Dir: Simon Langton. With: Billie Whitelaw, Ian Hendry, John Fraser, Charles Kay, John Stuart, Edward Hardwicke. BBC-TV. Colour.

Short-lived (eight episodes) anthology TV series, shot on video and set in Victorian times. Each guest star has to recount a personal tale of the supernatural to gain entrance to the Club of the Damned. If their membership is rejected, they are then killed. Fontana pub-

lished a collection of novellas based on the series by Brian Leonard Hayles. In this two-part story (scripted by series creator Robert Muller), the beautiful widowed Countess Ilona (Whitelaw) invites four old friends to her castle in Transylvania. Following the death of one of the Countess' guests, another visitor arrives... With Sandor Elès as 'He', a werewolf.
✦✦

Dorabella
UK, 1977. Dir: Simon Langton. With: Jeremy Clyde, David Robb, Ania Marson, John Justin, Esmond Knight, Jonathan Hyde. BBC-TV. Colour.
Scripted by Robert Muller, this story involves two young men travelling in Eastern Europe. They fall in love with Dorabella (Marson), a beautiful vampire woman who lures them to the castle of her undead father (veteran Justin).
✦✦✧

Night of the Marionettes
UK, 1977. Dir: Alan Cooke. With: Gordon Jackson, Kathleen Byron, Vladek Sheybal, Andre Van Gyseghem, Pauline Moran, Sydney Bromley. BBC-TV. Colour.
Writer Howard Lawrence (Jackson) and his family stay at an inn in the Swiss Alps and witness a bizarre entertainment featuring life-size puppets. These turn out to be living creatures created from corpses by mysterious innkeeper Hubert (Sheybal), a descendant of Frankenstein. Lawrence learns that a century before, Mary Shelley and her companions stayed at the same inn. Scripted by Robert Muller.
✦✦✧

THE SUPERNATURALS
USA, 1985 (1987). Dir: Armand Mastroianni. With: Maxwell Caulfield, Nichelle Nichols, Talia Balsam, Bradford Bancroft, LeVar Burton, Bobby di Cicco. Republic Entertainment International. Colour.
Low-budget supernatural thriller shot in the American south. Nichols (TV's *Star Trek* [1966-68], etc) plays the leader of a group of young soldiers on manoeuvres in the Alabama backwoods who encounter a platoon of Civil War zombies seeking revenge (make-up effects created by Mark Shostrom). The haunting music score is by Maurice Gibb, who also turns up in a brief uncredited cameo as a Yankee soldier. With Scott Jacoby.
✦✦✧

SUPERSEXY '64
Italy, 1963. Dir: Mino Loy. Documento Film. Colour.
Mondo-style film in which Marika the stripper performs on stage with a mummy.
✦

SURF II
USA, 1983 (1984). Dir: Randall Badat. With: Eric Stoltz, Jeffrey Rogers, Corinne Bohrer, Lucinda Dooling, Eddie Deezen, Linda Kerridge. Frank D. Tolin Productions/ Braunstein. Colour.
Despite the title, this unfunny comedy is actually not a sequel to anything. While a group of Californian teens are preparing for a big surfing contest, mad scientist Menlo Schwartzer (the insufferable Deezen) creates a soft drink called Buzzz Cola that turns the clean-cut surfers he hates into punk zombies. With Lyle Waggoner, Terry Kiser, Ruth Buzzi, Eric Stoltz and Cleavon Little. Brinke Stevens was an extra. Where are Frankie and Annette when you need them?
✦

SUR LES TRACES DE FRANKENSTEIN
France, 1968.
While researching Mary Shelley in Geneva, a young student fears that she is being followed by the Frankenstein Monster.
✦✧

SUSAN'S PLAN
USA, 1998. Dir: John Landis. With: Natassja (Nastassia) Kinski, Billy Zane, Michael Biehn, Rob Schneider, Lara Flynn Boyle, Dan Aykroyd. The Kushner-Locke Company. Colour.
Comedy thriller co-produced, written and directed by Landis, in which the plans of Susan (Kinski) and her lover (Zane) to hire a hitman (Aykroyd) to kill her husband Paul (Adrian Paul) for a huge insurance policy go disastrously wrong. In a nightmare sequence, Betty Johnson (Boyle) sees Paul's desiccated corpse return as a zombie. With Sheree North and Randal Kleiser.
✦✦

SUSPENSE:
Dr. Jekyll and Mr. Hyde
USA, 1949. With: Ralph Bell. CBS-TV. B&W.
Early live TV series (1949-54). This adaptation of Robert Louis Stevenson's story features Bell in the dual roles.
Episode remake: SUSPENSE: Dr. Jekyll and Mr. Hyde (qv; 1951)
✦

Dr. Jekyll and Mr. Hyde
USA, 1951. With: Basil Rathbone. CBS-TV. B&W.
The second live version of Stevenson's story to be produced on this series, transmitted on 5 March, and starring Rathbone as both Jekyll and Hyde.
Episode remake: EL HOMBRE Y LA BESTIA (qv; 1951)
✦✧

The Monkey's Paw
USA, 1949. With: Boris Karloff, Mildred Natwick. CBS-TV. B&W.
Live version of the 1902 short story by W.W. Jacobs, about a couple who are given a mummified monkey's paw and granted three wishes. When they wish for their son to come back from the dead, he returns mangled.
Episode remake: SUSPENSE: The Monkey's Paw (qv; 1950)
✦

The Monkey's Paw
USA, 1950. With: Mildred Natwick, Stanley Ridges. CBS-TV. B&W.
Yet another live version of the story by W.W. Jacobs, featuring Natwick who was also in the 1949 adaptation.
Episode remake: SPIRITISM (qv; 1961)
✦

Vamp til Dead
USA, 1951. With: Mary Sinclair. CBS-TV. B&W.
Vampire episode of this early TV fantasy series.
✦

DONALD SUTHERLAND [b 1935]

Canadian actor and the father of Kiefer Sutherland (b 1967). After establishing himself in a number of European horror films, Sutherland briefly became fashionable in the late 1960s and early 1970s. He has now settled down as a superior character actor.
qv: *Buffy the Vampire Slayer* (1992); *Dr. Terror's House of Horrors* (1965); *Great Books: 'Dracula'* (1998).

THE SWAMP OF THE LOST MONSTERS
(Orig: EL PANTANO DE LAS ANIMAS)
Mexico, 1958 (1964). Dir: Rafael Baledón. With: Gaston Santos, Manola Saavedra, Manuel Dondi, Sarah Cabera, Salvador Rodrigues, Lupe Carriles. Young America Productions/American International. Colour.
This is one of a series featuring cowboy Santos and his performing horse, Moonlight. This time they uncover the mystery of a disappearing body and a very unconvincing gill man which lives in a local pond and kills the peons. It turns out to be a plot to swindle $1,000,000 in insurance, and the silly creature is revealed as the missing 'corpse' in a monster suit. Far too much comedy relief and not enough thrills. The English-language version was produced by K. (Kenneth) Gordon Murray and directed by Stem Segar.
✦

SWAMP THING:
The Curse
USA, 1992. Dir: Chuck Bowman. With: Mark Lindsay Chapman, Carrell Myers, Scott Garrison, Dick Durock,

David Ackroyd. MTE/Batfilm Productions/DIC Enterprises/BBK Productions/USA Network. Colour.
Durock recreates his role from the two low-budget movies as the titular DC Comics character (in a bodysuit designed by Carl Fullerton and Neal Martz) still battling the evil Dr Anton Arcane (Chapman) in this half-hour TV series (1990-93, seventy-two episodes) filmed in Florida and developed for TV by Joseph Stefano. In this episode, Arcane leads an expedition into the swamp to recover a cursed Egyptian mummy that was aboard a plane that crashed forty years before. Director Bowman is one of the guest stars.
✦✦

Powers of Darkness
USA, 1992. Dir: Chuck Bowman. With: Mark Lindsay Chapman, Carrell Myers, Scott Garrison, Dick Durock, Jeremy Licht, Larry Manetti. MTE/Batfilm Productions/DIC Enterprises/BBK Productions/USA Network. Colour.
Swamp Thing's young friend Will (Garrison) meets a boy accused of murder who believes he is a vampire.
✦✧

Touch of Death
USA, 1991. Dir: Walter Von Huene. With: Mark Lindsay Chapman, Carrell Myers, Scott Garrison, Kari Wuhrer, Dick Durock, Mark McCracken. MTE/Batfilm Productions/DIC Enterprises/BBK Productions/USA Network. Colour.
Will encounters Abraham MacCyrus (McCracken), a man with a deadly touch who Arcane has revived from the dead. Swamp Thing next turned up in a children's cartoon TV series.
Series sequel: SWAMP THING (1991)
✦✧

SWEET CHARITY

USA, 1969. Dir: Bob Fosse. With: Shirley MacLaine, John McMartin, Ricardo Montalban, Sammy Davis Jr, Chita Rivera, Stubby Kaye. Universal. Colour.
Fosse made his début as a film director with this energetic musical about a prostitute with a heart of gold. Adapted from the Broadway show written by Neil Simon, which in turn was based on Federico Fellini's *Nights of Cabiria* (1957). It includes the songs 'Big Spender', 'If They Could See Me Now' and 'Rhythm of Life', plus clips from *Frankenstein* (1931).
✦✦✦✧

SWEET SPIRITS OF THE NIGHTER

USA, 1941. Dir: Del Lord. With: El Brendel, Tom Kennedy, Frank Lackteen, Duke York, Vernon Dent, Hank Mann. Columbia. B&W.
This twenty minute remake of *Midnight Blunders* (1936) was given an 'H' (for horror) certificate in Britain. The terrible comedy duo of Brendel and Kennedy investigate an old dark house where they uncover a mad doctor's experiments to revive the dead and encounter a scary-looking zombie.
✦✦

SWINGING THE LEAD

UK, 1935. Dir: David MacKane. With: Billy (William) Hartnell, Moira Lynd, Gibb McLaughlin, Marie Ault, George Rogers, Nita Harvey. Weiner, MacKane & Rogers. B&W.
Comedy about a drug which changes the personality of those who take it.
✦

WILLIAM SYLVESTER
[1922-1996]

American leading man who appeared in British films since 1949. He starred in several low-budget horror movies during the 1960s and played Dr Heywood Floyd in *2001: A Space Odyssey* (1968) before moving back to America, where he was a regular on the TV series *Gemini Man* (1976-77).
qv: *Devils of Darkness* (1964); *The Hand of Night* (1966).

TABITHA:
The Post-Halloween, Pre-Thanksgiving Special
USA, 1977. Dir: Charles Rondeau. With: Lisa Hartman, Robert Urich, Mel Stewart, David Ankrum, Karen Morrow, Mary Wickes. Columbia/ABC-TV. Colour.
Short-lived, half-hour spin-off TV series (1977-78, twelve episodes) about the grown-up adventures of young witch Tabitha Stevens (Hartman) and her brother Adam (Ankrum) from *Bewitched* (1964-72). In this episode, when TV newscaster Paul Thurston (Urich) upsets Tabitha and her relatives by insulting witches on his show, Aunt Minerva (Morrow) turns him into a werewolf.
✦✦

TAINTED
USA, 1998 (1999). Dir: Brian Evans. With: Greg James, Caryn Hottle, Sean Farley, Tina Kaprousi, Tony Lucchi, Brian Evans. 'Am I Wrong?' Productions/Troma. Colour.
$35,000 independent comedy from director/cinematographer/co-editor Evans in which good vampire Alex (Dunsan Cechvla) and his two friends end up battling the undead Slain.
✦✧

TAKBO..., BILIS...TAKBOOOOOO!
(aka TAKBO...! BILIS...! TAKABOOOO)
Philippines, 1987. Dir: Carlo J. Caparas. With: Herbert Bautista, Matet, Ana Margarita, Ronel Victor, Ruffa Gutierrez, Charito Solis. Golden Lion Films/Regal International. Colour.
Comedy in which the lighting of candles in a spooky old mansion revives a Dracula-like vampire and his undead wives, a Frankenstein Monster, a big-eared wolf creature, an ape and other monsters and demons.
✦✧

TAKBO...PETER...TAKBO!
Philippines, 1984. Dir: Augusto V. Pangan. With: Chiquito, C. Reyes Mumar, George Estregan, Baby Delgado, Martha Sevilla, Rodolfo 'Boy' Garcia. Archer Productions/Trigon Video. Colour.
Horror comedy set in the Vampire Disco House, situated amongst the ruins outside a small town. When the vampires he commands go on strike, Count Dracula raises the dead from their graves to battle the bloodsuckers. It all turns out to be a dream in the end.
✦✧

TAKE IT EASY!
Thailand, circa 1987. All Asian Home Video. Colour.
Comedy that includes a scene where two students dress up as a vampire and a mummy to scare some newcomers.
✦

TALE OF A VAMPIRE
(aka A TALE OF VAMPIRE)
UK/Japan, 1992. Dir: Shimako Sato. With: Julian Sands, Suzanna Hamilton, Kenneth Cranham, Marian Diamond, Michael Kenton, Catherine Blake. State Screen Productions/Tsuburaya Ezio/Furama. Colour.
Slow but impressive-looking début feature by Japanese film-maker Sato. This was shot on a very low budget in London, and is loosely based on Edgar Allan Poe's poem 'Annabel Lee'. Sands stars as Alex, a melancholic blood-drinker attracted to Anne (Hamilton), a librarian who is the image of Virginia, the lover he lost more than a century ago. Cranham's mysterious immortal vampire hunter Edgar turns out to be Poe himself!
✦✧

TALES FROM THE CRYPT
UK, 1972. Dir: Freddie Francis. With: Joan Collins, Peter Cushing, Roy Dotrice, Richard Greene, Ian Hendry, Sir Ralph Richardson. Amicus/Andromeda. Colour.
All-star anthology horror movie, scripted by producer Milton Subotsky and based on the EC comics of the 1950s. When five tourists become separated from their group in the catacombs beneath Highgate Cemetery, they encounter the hooded Crypt Keeper (Richardson) who relates a story about each of them: In 'And All Through the House', Joanne Clayton (Collins) has just murdered her husband when a psychopath dressed as Santa Claus turns up. Carl Maitland (Hendry) discovers he has returned from the grave after a fatal car crash two(!) years before in the weakest story, 'Reflection of Death'. 'Wish You Were Here' is a gruesome reworking of 'The Monkey's Paw' by W.W. Jacobs as Ralph Jason (Greene) is wished back to life in his coffin. Cushing gives one of his most sympathetic performances as old Mr Grimsdyke, who is hounded to death and returns from the grave to enact a grisly revenge in 'Poetic Justice'. The longest episode is 'Blind Alleys', in which a group of blind people plan a nasty retribution on their contemptuous keeper William Rogers (Nigel Patrick). In the end, The Crypt Keeper reveals to his audience that they are all dead and destined for Hell. With Patrick Magee, Barbara Murray and Robert Hutton. Bantam Books published a novelisation by Jack Oleck.
✦✦✦✧

TALES FROM THE CRYPT:
(aka HBO'S TALES FROM THE CRYPT)
Cold War
UK/USA, 1996. Dir: Andy Morahan. With: Ewan McGregor, Jane Horrocks, Colin Salmon, John Salthouse, Willie Ross, Peter Lee. Tales From the Crypt Holdings/New World Entertainment/Home Box Office. Colour.
Made-for-cable, half-hour anthology TV series (1989-96, ninety-three episodes) based on the EC horror comics *Tales from the Crypt, The Vault of Horror, The Haunt of Fear, Shock SuspenStories, Crime SuspenStories* and *Two-Fisted Tales* from the 1950s; executive produced by Richard Donner, David Giler, Walter Hill, Joel Silver and Robert Zemeckis, and introduced by the animatronic Crypt Keeper (created and directed by Kevin Yagher and voiced by John Kassir). Series theme composed by Danny Elfman. This pointless episode is set in London and based on a story in *Tales from the Crypt* no.43. Zombie petty crooks Ford (McGregor) and Cammy (Horrocks) meet their match in black vampire Jimmy. Robin Vidgeon (*Hellraiser* [1987], etc) was director of photography.
✦✧

Comes the Dawn
USA, 1994 (1995). Dir: John Herzfeld. With: Bruce Payne, Vivian Wu, Susan Tyrrell, Michael Ironside, Kaitlyn Walker, John Kassir. Tales From the Crypt Holdings/New World International/Home Box Office. Colour.
Originally published in *The Haunt of Fear* no.26. Two ex-army poachers (Payne and Ironside) are lured by a mysterious hunter (Wu) into a den of vampires and discover that for six months each year the sun never rises in Alaska.
✦✦

Creep Course
USA, 1993. Dir: Jeffrey Boam. With: Jeffrey Jones, Anthony Michael Hall, Nina Siemaszko, John Kassir, Julius Carry, Rae Norman. Tales From the Crypt Holdings/New World International/Home Box Office. Colour.
Originally published in *The Haunt of Fear* no.23. A professor of Egyptology (Jones) teams up with an unpleasant student (Hall) to lure a bookish maiden (Siemaszko) to his basement tomb as a sacrifice to 'The Mummy That Wouldn't Die' (Ivan E. Roth).
✦✦

Fitting Punishment
USA, 1990. Dir: Jack Sholder. With: Moses Gunn, Jon Clair, Teddy Wilson, Al Fann, Nick La Tour, Joanne Jackson. Tales From the Crypt Holdings/New World International/Home Box Office. Colour.
Originally published in *The Vault of Horror* no.16. When orphan teenager Bobby is murdered by his Uncle Ezra (Gunn), the miserly funeral director trims off the boy's feet so that he will fit into an extra coffin. However, the nephew uses crutches to return as a zombie and get his revenge.
✦✦

Half Way Horrible
USA, 1993. Dir: Greg Widen. With: Clancy Brown, Martin Kove, Costas Mandylor, Charles Martin Smith, Jon Tenney, Cheech Marin. Tales From the Crypt Holdings/ New World International/Home Box Office. Colour.
Originally published in *The Vault of Horror* no.26. When chemical manufacturer Roger Lassen (Brown) buries his friend alive in the South American jungle, his victim returns as a revenge-seeking zombie. After decapitating the living-dead corpse, Lassen is offered a deal by a mysterious voodoo priest (Marin) which leaves him only half the man he used to be.
✦✦

House of Horror
USA, 1993. Dir: Bob Gale. With: Kevin Dillon, Keith Coogan, Michael DeLuise, Courtney Gains, Brian Krause, Jason London. Tales From the Crypt Holdings/New World International/Home Box Office. Colour.
Based on a story in *The Haunt of Fear* no.15. When three young pledges are forced to spend the night in a supposedly haunted house, they discover a group vampire sorority sisters wielding a chainsaw in the attic.
✦✦✧

Judy, You're Not Yourself Today
USA, 1990. Dir: Randa Haines. With: Frances Bay, Carol Kane, Brian Kerwin, David Dunard, Todd Field, Shari Maier. Tales From the Crypt Holdings/New World International/Home Box Office. Colour.
Originally published in *Tales from the Crypt* no.25. Weird reclusive couple Donald (Kerwin) and Judy (Kane) kill an old witch (Bay) who tries to switch bodies with Judy. Months later, the old woman rises from her grave in the cellar seeking revenge.
✦✦

Last Respects
UK/USA, 1996. Dir: Freddie Francis. With: Emma Samms, Kerry Fox, Julie Cox, Michael Denison, Dulcie Gray, Peter Waddington. Tales From the Crypt Holdings/New World Entertainment/Home Box Office. Colour.
Another reworking of 'The Monkey's Paw' from the veteran horror director (*Tales from the Crypt* [1972], etc), based on a story in *Tales from the Crypt* no.23. Three sisters attempt to use the magical item to get themselves out of financial difficulties. In the end, one of them (Fox) returns from the dead as a zombie.
✦✧

Lower Berth
USA, 1990. Dir: Kevin Yagher. With: Lewis Arquette, Stefan Gierasch, Mark Rolston, Jeff Yagher, John Kassir, Cindy Riegel. Tales From the Crypt Holdings/New World International/Home Box Office. Colour.
Scripted by Fred Dekker and based on a story in *Tales from the Crypt* no.33. The owner of a failing carnival makes a bargain to acquire a stolen 4,000 year-old Egyptian mummy wearing a fabulous necklace. Enoch (Yagher), a two-headed freak, falls in love with the mummy, and the bizarre offspring of their relationship is revealed to be the Crypt Keeper himself.
✦✦

The New Arrival
USA, 1992. Dir: Peter Medak. With: David Warner, Joan Severance, Zelda Rubenstein, Twiggy Lawson (Twiggy), Robert Patrick, John Kassir. Tales From the Crypt Holdings/New World International/Home Box Office. Colour.
Originally published in *The Haunt of Fear* no.25. A pompous radio child psychologist (Warner) investigates a haunted house and meets his match in a murderous zombie.
✦✦✧

The Reluctant Vampire
USA, 1991. Dir: Elliot Silverstein. With: Malcolm McDowell, Sandra Searles Dickinson, George Wendt, Michael Berryman, Paul Gleason, Gloria Dawson. Tales From the Crypt Holdings/New World International/ Home Box Office. Colour.
Originally published in *The Vault of Horror* no.20. Donald Longtooth (McDowell) is a squeamish vampire who gets a job working as a night watchman in The Sunnyside Memorial Blood Bank. However, he has to replace the blood he steals when his sleazy boss Mr Crosswaite (Wendt) notices the shortage. Berryman turns up as creepy vampire-hunter Rupert Van Helsing.
✦✦

The Secret
USA, 1990. Dir: Michael Riva. With: Larry Drake, Grace Zabriskie, Mike Simmrin, Georgann Johnson, Stella Hall, William Frankfather. Tales From the Crypt Holdings/New World International/Home Box Office. Colour.
Based on a story in *The Haunt of Fear* no.24. Young orphan boy Theodore is adopted by the Colberts (Drake and Zabriskie), a wealthy, reclusive couple, who turn out to be vampires fattening him up for dinner. In the twist ending, the potential victim is revealed to be a werewolf.
✦✦✧

The Thing from the Grave
USA, 1990. Dir: Fred Dekker. With: Miguel Ferrer, Teri Hatcher, Kyle Secor, John Kassir, Laird MacIntosh, Cindy Riegel. Tales From the Crypt Holdings/New World International/Home Box Office. Colour.
Originally published in *Tales from the Crypt* no.22. The unbalanced Mitch (Ferrer) becomes jealous when a young photographer (Secor) falls for his model girlfriend Stacey (Hatcher). When Mitch murders her lover and plans to kill Stacey as well, the photographer rises from the grave as a zombie seeking revenge.
✦✦

The Third Pig
USA/Canada, 1996. Dir: Bill Kopp and Pat Ventura. Voices: John Kassir, Bobcat Goldthwait, Cam Clarke, Charlie Adler, Brad Garrett, Cory Barton. Tales From the Crypt Holdings/Nelvana/New World Entertainment/ Home Box Office. Colour.
Gruesome 'adult' cartoon version of 'The Three Little Pigs'. When his brothers Smokey and Drinky are eaten, Dudley Pig (Clarke) revives their remains to create a Zombie Pig Monster to revenge himself on the Big Bad Wolf (Goldthwait). Narrated by the Crypt Keeper (Kassir).
✦✦✧

'Til Death
USA, 1990. Dir: Chris Walas. With: D.W. Moffett, Pamela Gien, Aubrey Morris, John Kassir. Tales From the Crypt Holdings/New World International/Home Box Office. Colour.
Directed by make-up effects designer Walas, and based on a story in *The Vault of Horror* no.28. When a greedy plantation owner (Moffett) discovers the land he owns is nothing but quicksand, he uses a magic potion to make a wealthy young Englishwoman (Gien) his for life. However, when she suddenly dies, the woman returns from beyond the grave as a rotting zombie to drive him to suicide, and the couple are reunited after death by a voodoo priestess.
✦✦

Werewolf Concerto
USA, 1992. Dir: Steve Perry. With: Timothy Dalton, Dennis Farina, Walter Gotell, Charles Fleischer, Reginald VelJohnson, Beverly D'Angelo. Tales From the Crypt Holdings/New World International/Home Box Office. Colour.
It's the old vampire versus werewolf plot, based on a story in *The Vault of Horror* no.16, as hunter Mr Loki (Dalton) investigates a number of suspicious guests in a remote hotel who are being killed off by a murderous shape-changer. With Andre P. Bustanoby as the transformed lycanthrope and Wolfgang Puck as a chef. Two *Tales from the Crypt* spin-off movies followed in 1995 and 1996.
Series sequel: TALES FROM THE CRYPTKEEPER (qv; 1993-95)
✦✦

TALES FROM THE CRYPTKEEPER:
All the Gory Details!
USA/Canada, 1994. Dir: Laura Shepherd. Voices: John Kassir, David Hemblen, Harvey Atkin, Paulina Gillis, Stuart Stone, Keith Knight. Tales from the Crypt Holdings/Nelvana/ABC-TV. Colour.
Half-hour children's cartoon TV series (1993-95) introduced by

Kassir's The Cryptkeeper (and also The Vaultkeeper and The Old Witch). In this episode, when *City Tribune* newspaper reporter Sally investigates the mad Doctor Kromwell's gruesome experiments in creating artificial life back in the early 1940s, she discovers that some of his monstrous creations have survived. Executive produced by Richard Donner, David Giler, Walter Hill, Joel Silver and Robert Zemeckis, this series has little to do with the original EC comics.
✦✦✧

The Avenging Phantom/Myth Conceptions
USA/Canada, 1994. Dir: Laura Shepherd. Voices: John Kassir, David Hemblen, Paulina Gillis, Colin Fox, Lawrence Bayne, Daniel Desanto. Tales from the Crypt Holdings/Nelvana/ABC-TV. Colour.
In the introduction to this two-story episode (about a timid young boy who accidentally calls up an evil phantom to get even with his enemies, and a fortune hunter who discovers the temple of the Gorgon, Medusa), The Cryptkeeper and The Vaultkeeper attempt to upstage each other at shadowplay, creating images of a werewolf and the Frankenstein Monster.
✦

Fare Tonight
USA/Canada, 1993. Dir: Laura Shepherd. Voices: John Kassir, Valentina Cardinalli, Marsha Moreau, Robert Bockstael, David Hemblen. Tales from the Crypt Holdings/Nelvana/ABC-TV. Colour.
Teenage girls Camille and Mildred are two imaginative vampire movie fans who go looking for a bloodsucker and end up meeting the real thing.
✦✧

Gorilla's Paw
USA/Canada, 1993. Dir: Laura Shepherd. Voices: John Kassir, Jamieson Boulanger, Robert Budd, Christopher Redman, Jason Armstrong, Robert Bockstael. Tales from the Crypt Holdings/Nelvana/ABC-TV. Colour.
Yet another uncredited reworking of 'The Monkey's Paw' by W.W. Jacobs, in which the unpopular Lewis (Boulanger) steals the eponymous magical item from The Crypt of Curios to try and impress three other boys. When he uses the paw's powers to make himself more accepted, Lewis discovers he should be careful about what he wishes for.
✦✧

Hyde and Go Shriek
USA/Canada, 1993. Dir: Laura Shepherd. Voices: John Kassir, Michael Barry, Noah Zylberman, Justin Louis, Andrew Sabiston, Barry Flatman. Tales from the Crypt Holdings/Nelvana/ABC-TV. Colour.
When school wimp Wendell (Barry) drinks some magic tea, he transforms into a fearsome werewolf to revenge himself on the school bully.
✦✧

Pleasant Screams
USA/Canada, 1993. Dir: Laura Shepherd. Voices: John Kassir, Tara Charendoff, Roger Dunn, Marlow Vella. Tales from the Crypt Holdings/Nelvana/ABC-TV. Colour.
Trapped in a series of nightmares, Mr Purdy (Dunn) and Jenny (Charendoff) find themselves in a graveyard being pursued by green-faced zombies; menaced in Tokyo by two-headed fire-breathing monster Godan; captured by living gargoyles; chased by a green swamp blob, and attacked by a golem.
✦✧

This Wraps It Up
USA/Canada, 1993. Dir: Laura Shepherd. Voices: John Kassir, Marion Bennett, Elva Mai Hoover, Daniel Stemer, Daniel Cummings, Nathaniel Moreau. Tales from the Crypt Holdings/Nelvana/ABC-TV. Colour.
On a class field trip to the Egyptian pyramids, gangly schoolgirl Naomi (Bennett) and her classmates are caught in a sandstorm and discover two unscrupulous researchers about to uncover the tomb of Ikah Mu Kahma. Following a series of prophetic dreams, Naomi and the tomb robbers encounter the living mummy of Egypt's first woman ruler.
✦✦

Transylvania Express
USA/Canada, 1994. Dir: Laura Shepherd. Voices: John Kassir, Elizabeth Hanna, Damon D'Oliveira, Rob Stefaniuk, Colin Fox, John Stoker. Tales from the Crypt Holdings/Nelvana/ABC-TV. Colour.
Two Californian surfing dudes stowaway aboard the midnight Transylvanian Express and encounter vampires, a werewolf and the Frankenstein Monster.
✦✦✧

Uncle Harry's Horrible House of Horrors
USA/Canada, 1994. Dir: Laura Shepherd. Voices: John Kassir, David Hemblen, Elizabeth Hanna, Diane Fabian, Harvey Atkin, Kevin Zegers. Tales from the Crypt Holdings/Nelvana/ABC-TV. Colour.
While visiting the funfair on his birthday, six year-old Jeremy convinces his miserable Uncle Harry to go with him on the Horrible House of Horrors ride where they travel into a nightmare graveyard full of zombies.
✦✦

While the Cat's Away
USA/Canada, 1993. Dir: Laura Shepherd. Voices: John Kassir, Don Dickinson, Lorna Wilson, Noam Zylberman, Daniel De Santo. Tales from the Crypt Holdings/Nelvana/ABC-TV. Colour.
When brothers Stu and Dwight attempt to steal something from a spooky old mansion, they discover an old map and encounter a chained-up werewolf, a mad scientist's laboratory with a Frankenstein Monster, a trio of vampires, a room full of zombies and various other horrors before they discover the hidden 'treasure' — a copy of *Tales from the Crypt* no.1! The title sequence for this first episode, written by Manny Coto, features a vampire, Frankenstein Monster, werewolf, zombie, mummy and a gargoyle.
✦✦

The Works....In Wax
USA/Canada, 1993. Dir: Laura Shepherd. Voices: John Kassir, Stuart Stone, George Buza, Cedric Smith, John Stocker. Tales from the Crypt Holdings/Nelvana/ABC-TV. Colour.
The story of a young boy who saves an old wax museum from a scheming developer, with some help from the exhibits of a vampire Count, a werewolf and the Frankenstein Monster.
Series sequel: SECRETS OF THE CRYPT KEEPER'S HAUNTED HOUSE (1996-97)
✦✧

TALES FROM THE DARKSIDE:
Beetles
USA, 1987. Dir: Frank De Palma. With: Rod McCary, Sirri Murad, Donald McKechnie, Colm Meaney, Angelo Grisanti, Neil Kinsella. Laurel Entertainment/Jaygee. Colour.
Half-hour, shot-on-video syndicated anthology TV series (1983-88, ninety episodes). In this episode scripted by Robert Bloch, and based on his 1938 *Weird Tales* story, archaeologist Arthur Hartley (McCary) ignores the warnings and opens a cursed mummy case. Title sequence narrated by Paul Sparer. Executive produced by Richard P. Rubinstein, George A. Romero and Jerry Golod.
✦✦

A Case of the Stubbons
USA, 1984. Dir: Jerry Smith. With: Eddie Bracken, Barbara Eda Young, Christian Slater, Brent Spiner, Bill McCutcheon, Tresa Hughes. Laurel Entertainment/Jaygee. Colour.
Another episode written by Robert Bloch. Grandpa (Bracken) just will not accept that he is dead — despite the smell!
✦✧

The Circus
USA, 1986. Dir: Michael Gornick. With: Kevin O'Connor, William Hickey, Jacques Sandulescu, David Thorton, Ed French. Laurel Entertainment/Jaygee. Colour.
George A. Romero scripted this episode, based on a story by Sydney J. Bounds. Cynical reporter Arnold Bragg (O'Connor) discovers that carnival showman Dr Nis (Hickey) keeps a werewolf (Thorton), a mummy (Sandulescu) and a Nosferatu-like vampire (played by make-up creator French) amongst his attractions.
✦✧

The Family Reunion
USA, 1988. Dir: Tom Savini. With: Stephen McHattie, Daniel Terrence Kelly, Patricia Tallman, Marilyn Rockafellow. Laurel Entertainment/Jaygee. Colour.
In this episode, Robert Perry (McHattie) flees from his wife and home with his son Bobby (Kelly), who is a werewolf.
✦✧
The Grave Robber
USA, 1987. Dir: Jeff Schiro. With: Arnold Stang, Polly Draper, Daren Kelly, Ed Kovens. Laurel Entertainment/Jaygee. Colour.
Comedy episode in which ancient Egyptian mummy Tapok (Stang) comes to life to revenge itself on those who desecrated its tomb, and ends up playing a game of strip poker with them.
✦✧
My Ghostwriter, the Vampire
USA, 1987. Dir: Frank de Palma. With: Jeff Conaway, Roy Dotrice, Jillie Mack, Chi Chi Navarro. Laurel Entertainment/Jaygee. Colour.
Hack horror writer Peter Prentis (Conaway) gets a best-selling book out of the life of 900 year-old vampire Count Draco (Dotrice) who wants a safe place to hide his coffin. Based on a story by Scott Edelman.
✦✧
Strange Love
USA, 1986. Dir: Ted Gershuny. With: Patrick Kilpatrick, Harsh Nayyar, Marcia Cross. Laurel Entertainment/Jaygee. Colour.
Set in the 1930s, about young doctor Philip Carrol (Kilpatrick) helping married couple Edmund and Marie Alcott (Nayyar and Cross), who turn out to be vampires. However, the undead wife falls in love with him. This was also one of four episodes included in a two hour video compilation, *Tales from the Darkside*, introduced by Rich Little.
✦✧

TALES FROM THE DARKSIDE THE MOVIE
USA, 1990. Dir: John Harrison. With: Deborah Harry, Christian Slater, David Johansen, William Hickey, James Remar, Rae Dawn Chong. Laurel Entertainment/Paramount. Colour.
Anthology spin-off movie from the low-budget TV series (1983-88). The linking story has a captured young boy, Timmy (Matthew Lawrence), telling three scary stories to modern witch Betty (Harry) to delay her from cooking him. In 'Lot (No.) 249', scripted by Michael McDowell and based on the 1892 story by Sir Arthur Conan Doyle (previously adapted for TV's *The Short Stories of Conan Doyle* [1967]), college student Andy Smith (Slater) uses a creepy 3,000 year-old mummy (Michael Deak) to revenge himself on his classmates. Stephen King's 'Cat from Hell', scripted by George Romero, is a routine tale of supernatural revenge when aged tycoon Drogan (Hickey) hires hitman Halston (Johansen) to kill a cat. An impressive-looking gargoyle allows Preston (Remar) to live if he can keep a secret in Michael McDowell's original 'Lover's Vow'. Dick Smith was the make-up consultant for all the episodes. With Steve Buscemi.
✦✦✧

TALES FROM THE HOOD
USA, 1995. Dir: Rusty Cundieff. With: Corbin Bernsen, Rosalind Cash, Rusty Cundieff, David Allen Grier, Anthony Griffith, Wings Hauser. Savoy Pictures/40 Acres and a Mule Filmworks. Colour.
Fun black horror anthology, executive produced by Spike Lee. In the wraparound episode, 'Welcome to My Mortuary', a trio of boys (Joe Torry, D'Aundre Bonds and Samuel Monroe Jr) caught breaking into the funeral home belonging to the spooky Mr Simms (Clarence Williams III) are forced to listen to him tell four stories. A zombie policeman revenges himself upon the racist colleagues who killed him in 'Rogue Cop Revelation'. An abusive father (Grier) suffers a terrible fate in 'Boys Do Get Bruised'. 'KKK Comeuppance' is about a white politician (Bernsen) who is haunted by some deadly (stop-motion) dolls. The mad Dr Cushing (Cash) messes with a gang member's mind in 'Hard Core Convert'. In the end, Mr Simms reveals his true demonic form to the boys.
✦✦✦

TALES OF FRANKENSTEIN
USA/UK, 1958. Dir: Curt Siodmak. With: Anton Diffring, Helen Westcott, Don Megowan, Ludwig Stossel, Richard Bull, Raymond Greenleaf. Hammer Films/Screen Gems. B&W.
Half-hour pilot episode for an unsold TV series of twenty-six shows, scripted by Catherine (C.L. Moore) and Henry Kuttner and filmed under the title 'The Face in the Tombstone Mirror'. When Christine Halpert (Westcott) pleads with Baron Frankenstein (Diffring), he transplants the brain of her dead husband into the Karloff-like Monster (Megowan, in make-up created by Clay Campbell) he has created. Based on a story by associate producer/director Siodmak, this was finally shown as part of *Target*, a syndicated anthology series. Five more episodes, written by A.R. Rawlinson, Hugh Woodhouse, Cyril Kersh, Edward Dryhurst and Peter Bryan, were developed but never made.
✦✦

TALES OF TERROR
USA, 1962. Dir: Roger Corman. With: Vincent Price, Peter Lorre, Basil Rathbone, Debra Paget, Maggie Pierce, Joyce Jameson. American International Pictures. Colour.
An entertaining trilogy of Edgar Allan Poe stories, scripted by Richard Matheson and each starring Price in a different role. 'Morella' is the first and weakest as Locke (Price) discovers that the vengeance-seeking spirit of his first wife, Morella (Leona Gage), has risen from her mummified corpse and possessed his daughter Leonora (Pierce). The two stars ham it up in 'The Black Cat' (which also incorporates themes from Poe's 'The Cask of Amontillado') when Fortunato (Price) realises that the drunken Montresor (Lorre) is having an affair with his wife Annabel (Jameson) and entombs them both alive in the cellar wall of his house. It is Rathbone who stands out in the final episode, 'The Case of Mr. Valdemar' — as the unscrupulous mesmerist Carmichael, he uses hypnotism to hold the body of the dying Valdemar (Price) in a zombie-like state. In the end, Valdemar rises from his trance and scares Carmichael to death before his long-dead body liquefies. A sequence featuring Valdemar in Hell was cut by Corman before release. Music by Les Baxter. Lancer Books published a novelisation by Eunice Sudak.
Remake: TWO EVIL EYES (qv; 1989)
✦✦✦

TALES OF THE THIRD DIMENSION
USA, 1983 (1985). Dir: Earl Owensby, Thom McIntyre, Worth Keeter and Todd Durham. With: Robert Bloodworth, Kevin Campbell, William Hicks, Kate Hunter, Terry Loughlin, Kathy O'Toole. Earl Owensby Studios/Regency/Shapiro Entertainment. Colour.
Introduced by the Crypt Keeper-like Igor, this three-story horror anthology was filmed in 3-D, during the height of the process' brief revival, at Owensby's North Carolina studios. The episode entitled 'Young Blood', directed by McIntyre, involves a vampire couple and their fourteen year-old werewolf son (Kent Raiteri). The other episodes are entitled 'The Guardians' (about grave robbers) and 'Visions of Sugar-Plum' (featuring a murderous grandmother). A planned fourth story was dropped before release.
✦✧

TALES OF THE UNEXPECTED:
(UK: TWIST IN THE TALE)
The Nomads
USA, 1977. Dir: Allen Reisner. With: David Birney, Eugene Roche, David Huddleston, Katherine Justice, Lynne Marta, Read Morgan. Quinn Martin/NBC-TV. Colour.
Short-lived anthology TV series (nine episodes). In this remake of the pilot episode of *The Invaders* ('Beachhead', 1967), a Vietnam veteran (Birney) recovering from a mental breakdown tries to convince anyone that he has seen a UFO piloted by vampiric aliens who are about to take over the Earth. Title sequence narrated by William Conrad.
✦✦

TALES OF THE URBAN WEREWOLF
USA, 1996 (1997). Dir: Ian Black, Francesco Pagnelli and Roberto Crocitti. With: Johnny LaFleche, Nancy-Ann

Michaud, Tim Armstrong, Julie Menard, Fabio Cicirello, Oreste Crispino. Black Magic/Brain Escape Pictures/EI Independent Cinema. Colour.
Independent, shot-on-video release in which Johnny Schaeffer (LaFleche) is transformed through Native American magic and his heroin addiction into an unconvincing werewolf (created and played by co-director Black). The title on the end credits and the video box is *Tale of the Urban Werewolf.*
✦

TALES OF TOMORROW:
The Evil Within
USA, 1953. Dir: Don Medford. With: Rod Steiger, James Dean, Margaret Phillips. George F. Foley, Inc/ABC-TV. B&W.
Broadcast live, this half-hour anthology series (1951-53, eighty-four episodes) was TV's first successful adult science fiction show. In this episode, scripted by A.E. van Vogt, the wife of an inventor accidentally swallows the serum he designed to bring out a person's evil nature.
✦✧
Frankenstein
USA, 1952. With: Lon Chaney, John Newland, Mary Alice Moore, Farrell Pelly, Peggy Allenby, Michael Mann. George F. Foley, Inc/ABC-TV. B&W.
Updated version of Mary Shelley's novel, in which Dr Victor Frankenstein (Newland) brings to life his bald-headed Monster (Chaney Jr, who was apparently so drunk he went through the entire live transmission believing it was a rehearsal!). When the creature goes berserk, it stumbles around the painted castle sets, falls through a window and strangles the housekeeper before being electrocuted. Chaney's scarred make-up was effectively created by Vincent Kehoe.
Episode remake: THE CURSE OF FRANKENSTEIN (qv; 1957)
✦✧
The Tomb of King Tarus
USA, 1952. With: Walter Abel, Charles Nolte, Richard Purdy. George F. Foley, Inc/ABC-TV. B&W.
In this Halloween episode, while searching a Pharaoh's tomb for treasure and the secret of eternal life, an archaeologist is confronted by a group of ancient Egyptian scientists.
✦✧
Youth on Tap
(aka Young Blood)
USA, 1952. Dir: Don Medford. With: Robert Alda, Harry Townes, Mary Alice Moore, Bernard Burke, Ralph Porter. George F. Foley, Inc/ABC-TV. B&W.
When Dr Platan (Townes) offers truck driver Jeff (Alda) $1,000 for a pint of his blood, the scheming scientist turns out to be 160 years old and using his victims' blood to periodically rejuvenate himself.
✦✦

TALOS THE MUMMY
(USA: TALE OF THE MUMMY)
Luxembourg/UK/USA, 1998 (1999). Dir: Russell Mulcahy. With: Jason Scott Lee, Louise Lombard, Sean Pertwee, Lysette Anthony, Michael Lerner, Jack Davenport. The Pharaohs Company/The Carousel Picture Company/ Muraglia Sladek Productions/7th Voyage/Imperial Entertainment Group/KNB EFX Group/Brimstone Entertainment/Telepool/Miramax/Dimension. Colour.
$10,000,000 'B' movie co-written, co-produced and directed by Mulcahy as a tribute to Hammer's *The Mummy* (1959) and the work of Ray Harryhausen. After an atmospheric prologue (only let down by some shoddy visual effects) set in 1948, the story jumps ahead to the present day. The unlikely-named Detective Riley (Lee) investigates a string of gruesome murders and discovers they are connected by the 3,000 year-old spirit of evil Egyptian sorcerer Talos (depicted as shape-changing CGI bandages and by seven-foot, four-inch stuntman Roger Morrissey) that has been unwittingly unleashed on an unsuspecting London as it retrieves its missing organs and searches for the reincarnation of the Princess Nefriama. Almost everyone ends up dead at the end except the mummy. With Honor Blackman wasted as a police captain, Shelley Duvall as a psychic, and seventy-five year-old Christopher Lee playing famed archaeologist Sir Richard Turkel, who meets a gruesome death in the Valley of the Kings.
✦✧

TAMERE CHAMPONE AME KEL
India, 1978. Dir: Chandrakant Sangani. With: Naresh Kumar, Snehalata, A. Joshi, Rajanibala. Kanodia. Colour.
A Gujarati film in which a vampire woman marries a man on the condition that they never sleep together.
✦

TAMMY AND THE T-REX
USA, 1993 (1994). Dir: Stewart Raffill. With: Terry Kiser, Denise Richards, Ellen Rubin, John Franklin, Paul Walker. Image. Colour.
Direct-to-video comedy from the director of *The Ice Pirates* (1984). Mad scientist Dr Wachenstein (Kiser) transplants the brain of dying teenager Michael (Franklin) into a mechanical dinosaur he has created. The unwitting donor's girlfriend, high-school cheerleader Tammy (twenty-one year-old Richards), rides the revenge-seeking dinosaur. With George 'Buck' Flower.
✦✧

TANYA'S ISLAND
Canada/USA, 1980. Dir: Alfred Sole. With: D.D. Winters (Denise Matthews/Vanity), Richard Sargent, Don McCleod. Filmplan International. Colour.
Filmed in Puerto Rico. When her artist boyfriend (Sargent) abruptly ends their relationship, a top model (Winters) fantasises that she falls in love with a blue-eyed missing link creature (designed by Rick Baker and operated by Rob Bottin) on a tropical island. With clips from *Mighty Joe Young* (1949).
✦✦

TARKAN ALTIN MADALYON
(aka TARKAN)
Turkey, 1972. Dir: Mehmet Aslan. With: Kartal Tibet, Eva Bender, Birsen Ayda, Zeki Alasya. Sabri Demirdögen. Colour.
One of a series of five films made between 1969 and 1972 about Asian swordsman Tarkan (Tibet), who was raised by wolves, and his faithful wolf-dog companion Kurt. This time they team up with a troupe of acrobats to rescue the kidnapped son of a warlord and battle a nude vampire sorceress (Swedish ex-stripper Bender, who also appeared in *Tarkan Gümüs Eyer* [1970]), resurrected from a skeleton through the sacrifice of a naked nun and a topless belly dancer. The blonde vampire woman has a Cyclops servant and uses a life-size wax effigy to control Tarkan before falling to her death into a burning chamber. The title translates as 'Tarkan and the Golden Medallion'.
✦

TARZAN AND KING KONG
India, 1963. Dir: A. Shamsheer. With: Mumtaz, Bela Bose, Dara Singh, Master Bhagwan, Shyam Kumar, Siddhu. Sargaam Chittra/Amrit. B&W.
Part of the Hindi Tarzan series which ran from 1963 to 1965, in which the unofficial Ape Man (wrestler Singh) battles a big gorilla.
Sequel: TARZAN COMES TO DELHI (1964).
✦

TARZAN ESCAPES
USA, 1936. Dir: Richard Thorpe (and James McKay and John Farrow). With: Johnny Weissmuller, Maureen O'Sullivan, John Buckler, Benita Hume, William Henry, Herbert Mundin. Metro-Goldwyn-Mayer. B&W.
Scripted by O'Sullivan's husband Cyril Hume and based on the characters created by Edgar Rice Burroughs, this third movie in MGM's series starring Weissmuller was filmed under the title *The Capture of Tarzan* as the Ape Man is abducted by a safari searching for Jane. Sequences involving huge vampire bats (shown in stills) were cut by the studio prior to release because they were considered too horrific, although a bubbling swamp full of man-eating lizards and

Bill Rogers uses his vampire powers on another victim in A Taste of Blood *(1967).*

Tarzan's underwater battle with a giant crocodile are still included. With E.E. Clive and Darby Jones.
Sequel: TARZAN FINDS A SON! (1939)
✦✦✧

A TASTE OF BLOOD
(aka THE SECRET OF DR. ALUCARD)
USA, 1967. Dir: Herschell Gordon Lewis. With: Bill Rogers, Elizabeth Wilkinson, Thomas Wood (William Kerwin), Lawrence Tobin, Ted Schell, Otto Schlesinger. Creative Film Enterprises. Colour.
A two hour vampire movie filmed in Miami by producer/director Lewis of *Blood Feast* (1963) fame! Rogers stars as John A. Stone, a successful businessman who drinks some old British brandy tainted with Dracula's blood and turns into a pasty-faced member of the undead. He travels to foggy London to avenge the death of his ancestor, the Count, and then returns to America where he kills a stripper. Dr Howard Helsing (Schlesinger) turns up in time to stake Stone before he can transform his wife Helene (Wilkinson) into a bloodsucker as well. Lewis himself appears in a cameo as an unconvincing cockney sailor, and Wood/Kerwin was also the production manager.
✦✧

TASTE THE BLOOD OF DRACULA
UK, 1969. Dir: Peter Sasdy. With: Christopher Lee, Linda Hayden, Anthony Corlan, Geoffrey Keen, Peter Sallis, John Carson. Hammer Films/Warner Bros. Colour.
The fourth in Hammer's Dracula series and one of the best. A salesman named Weller (Roy Kinnear) is travelling through Europe when he witnesses the climax of *Dracula Has Risen from the Grave* (1968). Collecting up the Count's cape, ring and dried blood, he returns to Victorian London where he sells the artefacts to the depraved Lord Courtley (Ralph Bates, in his movie début). Secretly a disciple of Dracula, Courtley calls upon the powers of darkness and revives the Count, who then revenges himself on three families through their children. The literate script by John Elder (Anthony Hinds) explores the repressed sexuality of Victorian values, while Lee's suave vampire is used as a catalyst for sex and death. The climax apparently has God destroying Dracula in church! With Michael Ripper
Sequel: SCARS OF DRACULA (qv; 1970)
✦✦✦✧

TATTOO VAMPIRE
UK, circa 1995. The Wildcat Collection. Colour.
Independent specialist video in which American tattooist 'Spider Web' illustrates his skills on various parts of human anatomy while portraying himself as a vampire prince biting his female victims. For tattooing and piercing fans only.
✦

TEENAGE CAT GIRLS IN HEAT
USA, 1991 (1994). Dir: Scott Perry. With: Gary Graves, Carrie Vanston, Dave Cox, Helen Griffiths, Marissa Mireur. MPG/Troma. Colour.
Low-budget comedy filmed in Austin, Texas. Keshra, a 4,000 year-old Egyptian Cat Sphinx, transforms cats into topless women with feline characteristics. They have sex with men and then kill them in an attempt to rule the world. It's terrible.
✦

TEENAGE EXORCIST
USA, 1991 (1993). Dir: Grant Austin Waldman. With: Brinke Stevens, Eddie Deezen, Michael Berryman, Robert Quarry, Jay Richardson, Tom Shell. Austin Entertainments/Wald-Way Films. Colour.
Woeful comedy in which Diane (Stevens, who is also credited with writing the script) rents a creepy house from a weird real estate agent (Berryman). After a series of nightmares, she is possessed by a chainsaw-wielding demon (Oliver Darrow). When her family telephone for an exorcist, they mis-dial and get a pizza delivery nerd (the irritating Deezen, in a role originally offered to Traci Lords!). With Hoke Howell as Baron DeSade, Quarry reduced to doing card tricks, and a bit with a zombie (Joe Zimmerman). Executive produced by Fred Olen Ray, who also came up with the story. Previously-shot footage of the late John Carradine as a sorcerer was considered too outdated to use.
✦

TEENAGE MONSTER
(aka METEOR MONSTER)
USA, 1957. Dir: Jacques Marquette. With: Anne Gwynne, Stuart Wade, Gloria Castillo, Charles Courtney, Gilbert Perkins, Norman Leavitt. Howco International/Marquette. B&W.
Low-budget horror Western, filmed under the title *Monster on the Hill*. When young Charles Cannon (Stephen Parker) is struck by a meteorite, he grows up as a hairy psychopath (Perkins, who doubled for Spencer Tracy in *Dr. Jekyll and Mr. Hyde* [1941]). Protected by his mother (Universal veteran Gwynne), he is used by a blackmailing servant (Castillo) to kill anyone who upsets her. Despite having make-up designed by Jack P. Pierce (*The Wolf Man* [1941], etc), the monster is a laughable creation.
✦

TEENAGERS BATTLE THE THING
(aka THE CURSE OF BIGFOOT)
USA, 1958. Dir: Don Fields. With: William Simonsen, Robert Clymire, Ruth Ann Mannella, Jan Swihart, Ken Kloepfer. Etiwanda/Monument Entertainment/Program Power Entertainment. B&W.
A professor takes six students on a field trip and they discover a mummy in an ancient Native American burial ground that comes to life, kills a babysitter and is finally destroyed with fire. In 1972, Universal Entertainment/Gold Key TV changed the title and added new colour framing sequences to this obscure hour-long movie that played the midnight drive-in circuit between 1958 and 1961. Producer Hugh Thomas was also responsible for funding Ed Wood's infamous *Plan 9 from Outer Space* (1958).
✦

TEENAGE ZOMBIES
USA, 1957 (1960). Dir: Jerry Warren. With: Don Sullivan, Katherine Victor, Steve Conte, Paul Repper, Bri Murphy, Mitzie Albertson. GBM Productions/Governor Films. B&W.
'Young pawns thrust into pulsating cages of horror in a sadistic experiment!' enticed the ads. Female mad scientist Dr Myra (Victor), along with her helper Ivan the Ape Man (Chuck Niles), kidnaps four teenage water-skiers on a deserted island and plans to expose them to a nerve gas she has created for a foreign power that will transform them into mindless zombies. Who would know the difference? More incompetence from producer/director Warren.
✦

TEEN MONSTER
USA, 1998 (1999). Dir: Mitch Marcus. With: Judge Reinhold, Shelley Duvall, Charles Fleischer, Richard Moll, Matthew Lawrence, Christine Lakin. Regent Entertainment. Colour.
Horror comedy scripted by Dave Payne (*Addams Family Reunion* [1998], etc). When brilliant but nerdy teenager Frank Stein (Lawrence) reanimates the corpse of fellow high school student Karl (Ryan Reynolds), accidentally murdered by popular jocks Lance (Justin Walker) and Tuttle (Christian Payne), he unknowingly replaces the brain with that of a notorious murderer.
✦✧

TEEN VAMP
USA, 1988. Dir: Samuel Bradford. With: Clu Gulager, Karen Carlson, Angie Brown, Beau Bishop, Mick Lane, Evans Dietz. Jim McCullough Productions/New World International. Colour.
Filmed on a shoestring budget in Tennessee. This predictable horror comedy features Murphy (Bishop), another teen nerd whose life is changed when he is bitten by a vampire hooker. It's the usual plot, helped here by a good script from writer/director Bradford. Unfortunately, the film suffers from dark, ugly photography and amateurish performances. Star Gulager is obviously slumming in a cameo as a vampire-hunting priest.
✦✧

TEEN WOLF
USA, 1985. Dir: Rod Daniel. With: Michael J. Fox, James Hampton, Scott Paulin, Susan Ursitti, Jerry Levine, Jay Tarses. Wolfkill Productions/Atlantic Releasing Corporation. Colour.
Enjoyable comedy in which average high school student Scott Howard (Fox, making his starring début) discovers that, like his father Harold (Hampton), he is a werewolf (unconvincing make-up effects created by the Burman Studios). With his new-found lycanthropic skills Scott becomes a local celebrity, a big hit with girls and a basketball star. However, when he starts to lose his real friends, he decides to remain as himself. Fox's likeable personality dominates the film, which grossed over $50,000,000 and led to an inferior sequel and a children's cartoon TV series.
Sequels: TEEN WOLF (qv; 1986) and TEEN WOLF TOO (qv; 1987)
✦✦✦

TEEN WOLF
Australia/USA, 1986-87. Dir: Gordon Kent. Voices: Sheryl Bernstein, June Foray, James Hampton, Stacy Keach Sr, Craig Schaefer, Frank Welker. Atlantic Entertainment Group/Southern Star/Hanna-Barbera Australia/ Clubhouse Pictures/CBS-TV. Colour.
Half-hour children's cartoon TV series loosely based on the hit 1985 movie. Scott Howard (Townsend Coleman) lives in Wolverton (the werewolf capital of the world) with his lycanthropic family — his father Howard (Hampton, returning from the movie), sister Lupy, his Transylvanian grandparents (Foray and Keach Sr) and their housekeeper Freda. Along with his friends, entrepreneur Styles (Donny Most) and girlfriend Boof (Jeannie Elias), who both know his secret, Scott must overcome his unique problem of being both a teenager and a werewolf.
✦✧

TEEN WOLF TOO
USA, 1987. Dir: Christopher Leitch. With: Jason Bateman, Kim Darby, John Astin, Paul Sand, James Hampton, Mark Holton. Atlantic Entertainment. Colour.
Not so much a $3,000,000 sequel as a remake of the 1985 box office hit, with the producer's son replacing the now too famous Michael J. Fox as the cousin of the original Teen Wolf. When Todd Howard (Bateman) starts college, he learns from Harold Howard (Hampton, returning from the previous film) that he has inherited the family's lycanthropic curse (make-up once again created by the Burman Studios). As in the first film, he soon becomes a popular over-achiever and must eventually decide whether to enter a boxing championship as his nerdy self or as the popular wolfboy. Despite the presence of veterans Darby and Astin, this is neither clever nor amusing.
✦✧

THE TEMPTATIONS OF JOSEPH
UK, 1914. Dir: Langford Reed. Kineto. B&W.
Twenty-two minute silent short in which an amorous mummy comes to life and hugs its terrified antiquarian owner.
✦

TENDER DRACULA
(Orig: LA GRANDE TROUILLE/TENDRE DRACULA. USA: aka FLESH RIPS RED)
France, 1974. Dir: Pierre Grunstein. With: Peter Cushing, Alida Valli, Miou-Miou, Nathalie Courval, Bernard Menez, Stephanie Shandor. Renne Productions/Les Filmes Ch Fechner/VM Productions/AMLF/Scotia. Colour.
Black comedy in which Cushing plays an eccentric vampire movie actor named MacGregor who wants to abandon horror films for more romantic roles. His producer sets up a series of fake murders in the actor's castle home to convince MacGregor to return to the genre. In French prints, Cushing's voice was dubbed by Jean Rochefort.
✦✦

THE TENDERNESS OF WOLVES
(Orig: DIE ZAERTLICHKEIT DER VOELFE)
West Germany, 1973. Dir: Ulli Lommel. With: Kurt Raab, Jeff Roden, Margit Carstensen, Wolfgang Schenk, Rainer

Werner Fassbinder, Ingrid Caven. Tango Film. Colour.
Arty but disturbing version of the true-life case of Fritz Haarman (Raab), a homosexual murderer and blood-drinker, who killed around twenty-five young boys in pre-Nazi Germany. Producer Rainer Werner Fassbinder turns up in a supporting role. Director Lommel's career went downhill after this.
✦✦✦

TENGKORAK HIDUP
Indonesia, 1941. B&W.
Apparently inspired by Universal's *Dracula* (1931), the title translates as 'The Living Skull'.
✦

TERROR AT THE OPERA
(Orig: OPERA)
Italy, 1987 (1989). Dir: Dario Argento. With: Cristina Marsillach, Ian Charleson, Urbano Barberini, William McNamara, Daria Nicolodi, Antonella Vitale. Cecchi-Gori Gruppo Tiger Cinematográfica/ADC Produzione/RAI Radio Televizione/Orion. Colour.
Style wins out over substance in co-writer/director Argento's $8,000,000 *giallo* variation on *The Phantom of the Opera*. A hooded maniac terrorises a modern production of Verdi's *Macbeth* so that understudy Betty (Spanish model Marsillach) can take over the role of Lady Macbeth (Vanessa Redgrave was apparently dropped as diva Mara Cecova when she demanded more money, and the role was cut from the film). The various murders are handsomely designed set-pieces but, as usual in Argento's later productions, the script (by Argento and Franco Ferrini) lets the side down. Michelle Soavi directed the second unit, and behind-the-scenes footage turned up in Luigi Cozzi's 1991 documentary *Dario Argento: Master of Horror*.
✦✦✧

TERROR CREATURES FROM THE GRAVE
(Orig: 5 TOMBE PER UN MEDIUM. UK/USA: aka CEMETERY OF THE LIVING DEAD/THE TOMBS OF HORROR)
Italy, 1965. Dir: Ralph Zucker. With: Barbara Steele, Walter Brandt (Walder Brandi/Walter Bigari), Marilyn Mitchell, Alfred Rice (Alfredo Rizzo), Richard Garret (Riccardo Garrone), Alan Collins (Luciano Pigozzi). International Entertainment Corporation/MRS Cinematográfica/GIA Cinematográfica. B&W.
Often erroneously credited to Massimo Pupillo, American Zucker's only directing credit is supposedly based on a story by Edgar Allan Poe and set in a small village in Central Europe at the turn of the century. A young lawyer, Albert Kovaks (Brandt), arrives at the home of the late Dr Jeronimus Hauff, who died a year earlier. With a series of horrible deaths occurring in the neighbourhood, it becomes apparent that the victims were among the five people who helped the doctor's wife Cleo (Steele) kill her husband. Dr Hauff dabbled in the occult, and with his last breath he invoked the victims of the black plague to rise from their graves to avenge his murder. This is worth catching for Steele's bubble bath scene.
✦✧

TERRORE A AMITYVILLE PARK
(Orig: PREY. USA: ALIEN PREY)
Italy/UK, 1984 (1977). Dir: Ferruccio Casacci (and Norman J. Warren). With: Barry Stokes, Sally Faulkner, Glory Annen, Sandy Chimney, Eddie Stacey, Jerry Crampton. Tymar Film Productions. Colour.
Italian director Casacci took Warren's softcore science fiction/horror movie *Prey* (1977), about two lesbians (Faulkner and Annen) menaced by a flesh-eating alien in human guise (Stokes), and significantly re-edited it, adding new sequences involving a mummy. It didn't help.
✦

TERRORGRAM
USA, 1985 (1988). Dir: Stephen M. Kienzle. With: James Earl Jones, Jerry Anderson, Michael Hartson, J.T. Wallace, Linda Carol Toner, Steven Field. Blue Moon/Monarch. Colour.
Independent horror anthology in which three people receive mysterious packages from a delivery man (Field). 'Heroine Overdose' is about misogynistic horror movie director Alan Smythee (Anderson), who finds himself in a female-dominated version of one of his own movies. Responsible for a hit-and-run death, ambitious TV reporter Angela Pandorus (Toner) imagines that her victim returns as a talking corpse in 'Pandora'. 'Veteran's Day' features an abusive husband who is restored to the Vietnam war zone by the zombie (Paul Perme) of a dead comrade. Narrated by Jones as the Voice of Retribution.
✦✧

TERROR IN THE AISLES
USA, 1984. Dir: Andrew J. Kuehn. With: Donald Pleasence, Nancy Allen, Fred Asparagus, Lainie Cook, Joel S. Rice, Angel Salazar. Universal/Kaleidoscope Films. Colour/B&W.
Compilation hosted by Pleasence and the somewhat bland Allen seated amidst a 'typical' sleazoid film audience, talking pretentious nonsense while the clips (often brief, muddled and uncredited) range from the classic Universal horrors of the 1940s through to the slasher genre of the 1980s. *An American Werewolf in London* (1981), *Bride of Frankenstein* (1935), *Cat People* (1982), *Dawn of the Dead* (1978), *The Howling* (1980), *Konga* (1960), (Abbott and Costello) *Meet Frankenstein* (1948), *Night of the Living Dead* (1968), *Nightwing* (1979), *Phantom of the Paradise* (1974), *Saturday the 14th* (1981) and *The Wolf Man* (1941) are just some of the titles on show. This also features a few odd non-genre inclusions such as *Marathon Man* (1976), *To Catch a Thief* (1955) and *Klute* (1971), and although Gregory McClatchy's editing and John Beal's music score are often inspired, the linking scenes with the two stars are simply pathetic.
✦

TERROR OF BLOOD GYM
USA, 1995. Dir: Christopher Michael. With: Christopher Michael. Creeper Productions. Colour.
Half-hour, shot-on-tape spoof that was used as a lighting and character test for *Limp Fangs The Adventures of Count Malt Liquela* (1996). A group of people exercising in a Los Angeles gym are killed for no apparent reason by the psychopathic Creeper played by writer/producer/director Michael, who also shows up as a vampire who gives the orders to kill and bites a girl's neck at the end.
✦

TERROR ON TAPE
USA, 1985. Dir: Robert A. Worms III. With: Cameron Mitchell, Mark Fenske, Tim Noyes, Micheule Bauer (Michelle Bauer/Michelle McClellan). Comet/Continental Video. Colour.
Feature-length compilation, shot on video and featuring poor old Mitchell as the weird-looking owner of the 'Shoppe of Horrors Video Store' who gives three customers a preview of various horror tapes released by Continental. These include *City of the Walking Dead* (1980), *The Eerie Midnight Horror Show* (1978), *Vampire Hookers* (1979) and the *Bloodiest of H.G. Lewis* series, amongst others. Mitchell and Bauer were both in *The Tomb* the same year.
✦

TERRORVISION
USA, 1985. Dir: Jonathan Heap, Mark Esposito, John Auerbach and A. Merrill. With: Margaret Johnson, Philip Morton, Jonathan Gabriel, Bill Reilly, Will Buchanan, Lynette Perry. Excel Telemedia International. Colour.
This compilation of six short horror films includes 'The Craving', directed by Auerbach, in which dentist Dr A. Cula (Ron Darvan) turns out to be you-know-who. The other stories involve a young boy's nightmares ('The Closet Monster'), a killer who sees his victim in a mirror ('Reflections of Murder'), a shop owner who turns models into mannequins ('One of a Kind'), a mysterious bathroom shower ('A Cold Day in July') and the body parts of a surgeon returning to life ('Rosemary's Lot'). Not to be confused with the 1986 film with the same title.
✦✧

LE TESTAMENT DU DOCTEUR CORDELIER
(UK: EXPERIMENT IN EVIL. USA: THE DOCTOR'S HORRIBLE EXPERIMENT)
France, 1959 (1961). Dir: Jean Renoir. With: Jean-Louis

Barrault, Teddy Bilis, Michel Vitold, Jean Topart, Micheline Gary, Gaston Modot. Consortium Pathé/RTF/SOFIRAD/Compagnie Jean Renoir. B&W.
This begins with writer/director Renoir arriving at a French TV station and introducing his contemporary film inspired by Robert Louis Stevenson's *Strange Case of Dr. Jekyll and Mr. Hyde*. The respected Dr Cordelier (Barrault) reveals to his friend Maître Joly (Bilis) that he has created a potion that frees him from his inhibitions and transforms him into the brutish Mr Opale (also Barrault, in a nicely comedic performance as a teddy boy from Hell). In the end, Opale kills himself by drinking poison and changes back to his true self.
Remake: THE UGLY DUCKLING (qv; 1959)
✦✦✧

EL TESTAMENTO DEL FRANKENSTEIN
Spain, 1964. Dir: José Luis Madrid. With: Gerard Landry, George Vallis.
A descendant of Frankenstein (Landry) creates yet another Monster (Vallis) in this obscure Spanish production.
✦

THE TEX WILLIAMS SHOW
USA, circa 1951. With: Tex Williams, Glenn Strange. NBC-TV. B&W.
Strange recreates his role as the Frankenstein Monster during the singer's musical/comedy TV show.
✦

THEATRE OF DEATH
(USA: aka BLOOD FIEND)
UK, 1966. Dir: Samuel Gallu. With: Christopher Lee, Lelia Goldoni, Julian Glover, Evelyn Laye, Jenny Till, Ivor Dean. London Independent Producers/Pennea Productions. Colour.
Lee stars as Phillipe Darvas, an egotistical playwright/director with hypnotic powers, who is suspected of a series of vampire murders around the Theatre de Mort in modern-day Paris. The plot is filled with false clues and red herrings that will keep you guessing the killer's identity until the surprise revelation. Glover plays the police surgeon hero and Dean is an unlikely French police inspector. Director Gallu has a flair for weird camera angles, and this includes still shots from Hammer's *Dracula* (1958), *The Golem* (1920) and *Dr. Jekyll and Mr. Hyde* (1931).
✦✦✧

ERNEST THESIGER [1879-1961]

Prissy, emaciated-looking British stage actor who appeared in several bizarre film roles, including the cowardly Horace Femm in *The Old Dark House* (1932) and the memorable Dr Septimus Pretorius toasting a new world of gods and monsters in *Bride of Frankenstein* (1935). An exhibited artist and accomplished crochet expert (he wrote a book on the subject), Thesiger was also apparently a skilled female impersonator. In 1960 he was awarded the Order of the British Empire. Arthur Dignam played him in *Gods and Monsters* (1998).
qv: *The Ghoul* (1933).

THEY BITE
USA, 1990 (1993). Dir: Brett Piper. With: Ron Jeremy, Christina Veronica, Donna Frotscher, Blake Pickett, Susie Owens, Vince Camiti. Trio Entertainment. Colour.
Independent softcore spoof shot in Florida and New Hampshire for $130,000. The makers of a porn monster movie featuring humanoid fish creatures encounter gill men monsters from outer space. In a nightmare sequence, cut by the MPAA in America, a woman (1988 *Playboy* centrefold Owens) surprises her boyfriend with her own toothy mutation during sex. This includes clips from *The Beach Girls and the Monster* (1964).
✦

THEY SAVED HITLER'S BRAIN
(aka MADMEN OF MANDORAS)
USA, 1963. Dir: David Bradley. With: Audrey Caire, Walter Stocker, Carlos Rivas, John Holland, Dani Lynn, Nestor Paiva. Sans/Crown International. B&W.
Originally titled *The Amazing Mr H* and *The Return of Mr H*, this was filmed on an almost-nothing budget, with some sequences apparently shot in Mexico or the Philippines and an impressive car crash lifted from *Thunder Road* (1958). The incoherent plot has an American secret agent taking his wife to Mandoras to stop a group of Nazis from wiping out the world's population with a secret toxic gas. When the only scientist with an antidote is kidnapped along with his daughter, it turns out that Adolf Hitler's head (kept alive in a glass container but unable to do much more than raise its eyebrows) is behind the whole silly plot! Photographed by Stanley Cortez. Director Bradley made his début in 1941 directing a teenage Charlton Heston in an amateur version of *Peer Gynt*.
✦

THE THING FROM ANOTHER WORLD
USA, 1951. Dir: Christian Nyby. With: Margaret Sheridan, Kenneth Tobey, Robert Cornthwaite, Douglas Spencer, James Young, Dewey Martin. RKO Radio Pictures/Winchester. B&W.
Classic science fiction/horror thriller based on John W. Campbell's 1938 pulp story 'Who Goes There?'. When a crashed flying saucer is discovered beneath the Arctic ice, a research team rescues the frozen alien inhabitant which is unfortunately allowed to thaw out. The original story's shape-changing monster here becomes an eight-foot tall vegetable (played by James Arness, later the star of TV's *Gunsmoke* [1955-75], and midget Billy Curtis during the climax) which needs human blood to germinate its seeds. The movie develops into a remarkable exercise in prolonged claustrophobic terror, as Captain Hendry (Tobey) and his crewmen track the creature with Geiger counters through the corridors of the snowbound camp. Militarism, not science, wins in the end and the final Cold War message is to 'Keep watching the skies!' With Eduard Franz, John Dierkes and Paul Frees. Film editor Nyby received his first director's credit, but the film is heavily influenced by producer Howard Hawks, who prepared the script and 'supervised' the production. This was originally titled simply *The Thing*, but changed prior to release because of the novelty song of the same name. John Carpenter's dazzling remake returned to the theme of an alien shape-changer.
Remake: THE THING (1982)
✦✦✦✦✦

THINGS 3: OLD THINGS
(aka DEAD TIME TALES)
USA, 1998. Dir: Ron Ford. With: Ron Ford. Fat Free Features. Colour.
Contemporary anthology movie based on three classic stories by H.G. Wells, Mary Shelley and Rudyard Kipling. In 'Crystal Gazing' an antique dealer discovers a mysterious crystal that reveals the surface of a distant planet and the hungry creatures who live there. 'Cold Feet' is about a man who is obsessed by the picture of a leather-clad woman he saw on an old postcard. 'Beastiality', based on Kipling's 1891 story 'The Mark of the Beast', is about a film star who is cursed by a tribal shaman and periodically transforms into a werewolf (special effects created by Anna Futrell and Tim Thomson).
✦✧

THE THING THAT COULDN'T DIE
USA, 1958. Dir: Will Cowan. With: William Reynolds, Andra Martin, Jeffrey Stone, Carolyn Kearney, Peggy Converse, Robin Hughes. Universal-International. B&W.
'B' movie thrills from veteran producer/director Cowan as farm girl Jessica Burns (Kearney), a water-diviner with psychic powers, discovers a chest buried by Sir Francis Drake in California in 1579. Inside is the still-living head of Elizabethan sorcerer Gideon Drew (Hughes) who uses his hypnotic powers to uncover another chest containing his headless corpse. This is all pretty silly, although the film does have one genuine scare moment as the headless body steps

Ed Payson plays the Monster in the 3-D short Third Dimensional Murder *(1940).*

out of its container before being abruptly reduced to a skeleton by a magic amulet. Based on his story 'The Water Witch' by screenwriter David Duncan.
✦✧

THIRD DIMENSIONAL MURDER
USA, 1940 (1941). Dir: George Sidney. With: Pete Smith, Ed Payson. Metro-Goldwyn-Mayer. B&W.
One of narrator Pete Smith's Metroscopix Specials, this seven minute short was originally released in 3-D. When a man enters the old Smith Mansion at midnight, he encounters ghosts, a witch, a skeleton, a masked archer and the Frankenstein Monster (Payson, in Jack Kevan's make-up inspired by Universal's *Son of Frankenstein* [1939]). This was later included in the 1953 compilation *Metroscopix*.
✦✦

THIRST
Australia, 1979. Dir: Rod Hardy. With: Chantal Contouri, Shirley Cameron, Max Phipps, Henry Silva, Rod Mullinar, David Hemmings. FG Film Productions/New South Wales Film Corporation. Colour.
Hemmings plays Dr Fraser, one of the leaders of the international Hyma Brotherhood (named after the Greek symbol for human blood). They kidnap Kate Davis (Contouri) because they believe her to be the descendant of their founder, Countess Elizabeth Bathory, and attempt to convince her to join their cult of scientific blood-drinkers. Despite such unnecessary genre trappings as fake fangs, glowing red eyes and a rotting corpse, this is an unusual psychological variation on the theme, made with style by director Hardy.
✦✦✦✧

THE THIRSTY DEAD
(aka BLOOD CULT OF SHANGRI-LA/BLOOD HUNT)
Philippines, 1974. Dir: Terry Becker. With: Jennifer Billingsley, John Considine, Judith McConnell, Tani Guthrie, Fredricka Myers, Chiqui da Rosa. De & Be Productions/International Amusement Corporation. Colour.
Laura (Billingsley) is one of four young women kidnapped from the city by members of a hidden jungle civilisation led by evil High Priestess Ranu (Guthrie) and romantic High Priest Baru (Considine), who worship a 500 year-old severed head that talks. They also mix the leaves of a rare plant with human blood to create an elixir that gives them eternal life. When she refuses to drink the blood of her friend, Laura is thrown into a dungeon with their shrivelled-up victims. This low-budget Filipino movie looks like a bad *Star Trek* episode and has to be seen to be believed. Vic Diaz turns up as a police lieutenant and was also production co-ordinator.
✦

THE THIRTEEN CHAIRS
(Orig: UNA SU TREDICI/DOUZE ET UN. USA: aka 12+1)
Italy/France/UK, 1969 (1970). Dir: Nicolas Gessner. With: Vittorio Gassmann, Sharon Tate, Orson Welles, Vittorio De Sica, Terry-Thomas, Tim Brooke-Taylor. CEF/COFCI. Colour.
Comedy based on the Russian novel *Twelve Chairs* by Ilya Ilf and Evgeny Petrov about the search for a set of antique chairs, one of which contains a hidden fortune. Welles plays the proprietor of a Grand Guignol theatre show based on *Dr Jekyll and Mr Hyde*. Sharon Tate was murdered just after this was completed. With John Steiner and Lionel Jeffries.
Remake: THE TWELVE CHAIRS (1970)
✦✧

THE 13 GHOSTS OF SCOOBY-DOO:
Horror-Scope Scoob
USA, 1985. Dir: Ray Patterson. Voices: Susan Blu, Arte Johnson, Casey Kasem, Don Messick, Heather North, Vincent Price. Hanna-Barbera Productions/ABC-TV. Colour.
Cartoon TV series comprising thirteen half-hour episodes (1985-86).

John Considine reverts to his true age at the end of The Thirsty Dead *(1974).*

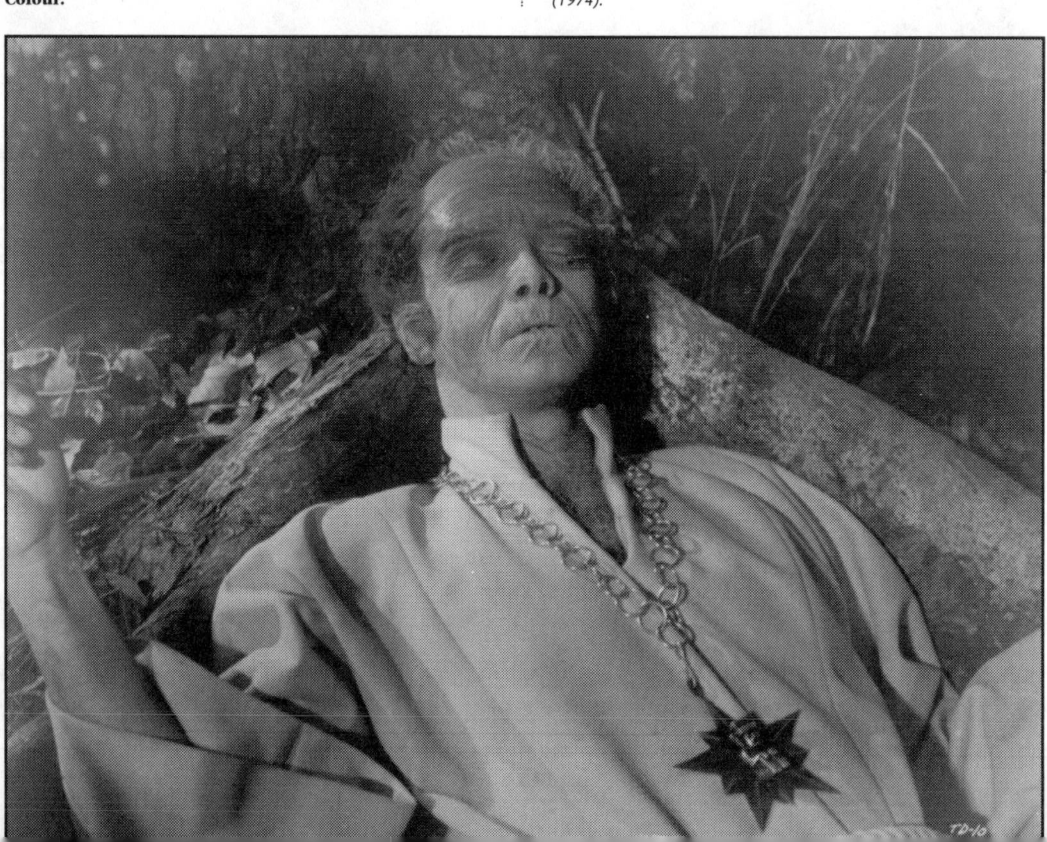

In this episode, TV horror host Boris Kreepoff (based on you-know-who) attempts to steal the chest of demons and open it live on air, while Scooby-Doo (Messick) and Shaggy Rogers (Kasem) are chased by zombies in a graveyard. Additional voices include Hamilton Camp, Kenneth Mars, Edie McClurg, Alan Oppenheimer, Les Tremayne, B.J. Ward and Frank Welker. Executive produced by William Hanna and Joseph Barbera.

✦✦

That's Monstertainment

USA, 1985. Dir: Ray Patterson. Voices: Susan Blu, Arte Johnson, Casey Kasem, Don Messick, Heather North, Vincent Price. Hanna-Barbera Productions/ABC-TV. Colour.

Scooby-Doo and his pals are magically transported by the evil Zomba into an old black and white horror movie on TV, where Scooby becomes the mad scientist Dr Frankenscoob who, with the aid of Scrappy-Doo (Messick) as his hunchbacked assistant, brings his Monster to life. With Daphne (North) as the Bride of Frankenscoob and a homage to (Abbott and Costello) *Meet Frankenstein* (1948).

✦✦

To All the Ghouls I've Loved

USA, 1985. Dir: Ray Patterson. Voices: Susan Blu, Arte Johnson, Casey Kasem, Don Messick, Heather North, Vincent Price. Hanna-Barbera Productions/ABC-TV. Colour.

In this first episode, Scooby-Doo and his friends Shaggy Rogers, Daphne Blake, Scrappy-Doo and Flim Flam (Blu) crash their plane in a remote mountain village in Tibet. There they not only discover a town full of werewolves, but are tricked by Weerd (Johnson) and Bogel (Howard Morris), a pair of scheming phantoms, into opening an ancient chest of demons, thus releasing thirteen of the most terrifying ghosts upon the face of the earth. Only with the aid of sorcerer Vincent Van Ghoul (Price) can they return the demons to the chest.

Series sequels: THE FLINTSTONES 25TH ANNIVERSARY CELEBRATION (1986), SCOOBY-DOO MEETS THE BOO BROTHERS (1987) and SCOOBY-DOO AND THE GHOUL SCHOOL (qv; 1988)

✦✦

THIS IS YOUR LIFE:
Boris Karloff

USA, 1957. Dir: Richard Gottlieb. With: Ralph Edwards, Boris Karloff, Jack Pierce. Ralph Edwards Productions/ NBC-TV. B&W.

Karloff is genuinely surprised and delighted as he becomes the subject of this popular half-hour TV show (1952-), first broadcast on 13 November. He meets an old school friend, people he acted with early in his career, make-up artist Pierce, the producers of *Arsenic and Old Lace*, Surrey cricketer Jim Laker, his wife Evelyn and daughter Sarah Jane.

Series remake: THIS IS YOUR LIFE (qv; 1955-)

✦✦✧

THIS IS YOUR LIFE:
Christopher Lee

UK, 1974. With: Eamonn Andrews, Christopher Lee, Peter Cushing, Vincent Price, Oliver Reed, Veronica Carlson. Thames Television/ITV. Colour.

First broadcast on 3 April, the British version of the half-hour TV show (1955-) surprises Lee during a sword fight rehearsal. Along with the actor's family, guests include Joanna Lumley, Valerie Van Ost, Trevor Howard, and filmed tributes from Charlton Heston, Patrick Macnee and Sammy Davis Jr. With clips from Hammer's *The Curse of Frankenstein* (1957) and *Dracula* (1958).

✦✦✧

THOSE CRUEL AND BLOODY VAMPIRES

(Orig: LAS ALEGRES VAMPIRAS DE VOGEL)

Spain, 1974. Dir: Julio Pérez Tabernero. With: Agata Lys, Maria José Cantudo, Germán Cobos, Rafael Conesa. Titanic. Colour.

Two beautiful women visit a European village in search of vampires.

✦

HARRY THOMAS
[1909-1996]

Cut-price American make-up artist who began his career as an apprentice at MGM in the late 1930s. According to his own estimate, he worked on more than 400 films and TV shows, many of them in the horror and exploitation genre.

qv: *The Bride and the Beast* (1957); *Flying Saucers Over Hollywood* (1992); *Frankenstein's Daughter* (1958); *The Haunted World of Ed Wood* (1996); *House on Bare Mountain* (1962); *Killers from Space* (1954); *Little Shop of Horrors* (1960); *The Mad Monster* (1942); *The Munsters* (1964-66); *The Neanderthal Man* (1953); *Night of the Ghouls* (1959); *Plan 9 from Outer Space* (1956).

THOSE FEEDY ON BLOOD

(Orig: PYUSHCHYE KROVY. UK: aka BLOOD-SUCKERS)

Russia, 1991 (1992). Dir: E. Tatarskiy (Eugeny Tatarsky). With: Marina Vladi (Vlady), Andrey Sokolov, Marina Maiko, Donatas Banionis. Lenfilm/Printex. Colour.

Yet another adaptation of Count Alexei Tolstoy's story 'The Wurdalak', which suffers from some terrible subtitling (the above title is from the print). Rather than confuse you more, I'll just quote from the plot synopsis: 'At a high society party of a young officer, Runevsky (Sokolov), meets Dashenka, who is the company of her grandmother Sugrobina. Runevsky falls in love with Dashenka at first glance. A strange young man, Rybarenko, tells him that Sugrobina is a vampire, and reveals the mystery of the ever-lasting monster Sugrobina. A preposterous duel between Runevsky and Dashenka's cousin delays the outcome. However, Runevsky is not aware that Sugrobina had managed to prolong her life by merging it in Dashenka.' I'm glad that's clear! This also includes a particularly eerie sequence where a portrait of Dashenka's dead mother comes to life.

✦✧

THE 3-D ARMY

Hong Kong, circa 1992. Kinco. Colour.

3-D horror comedy involving Hing Kun, a hopping vampire who can become invisible, and Elder Ho, a magician who attempts to raise an army of the dead.

✦✧

3 MEN AND A LITTLE LADY

USA/UK, 1990. Dir: Emile Ardolino. With: Tom Selleck, Steve Guttenberg, Ted Danson, Nancy Travis, Christopher Cazenove, Fiona Shaw. Touchstone Pictures/Jean François Lepetit/Interscope Communications. Colour.

Slightly improved sequel to the hit comedy *3 Men and a Baby* (1987). The unorthodox three-father family is thrown into turmoil when mother Sylvia Bennington (Travis) announces that she is marrying her English lover Edward (Cazenove) and taking five year-old Mary (Robin Wiseman) with her. Danson's hammy actor Jack Holden turns up to meet his daughter's school board dressed as the vampiric Count Cholesterol from a TV commercial.

✦✧

THREE'S A CROWD

USA, 1932 (1933). Dir: Rudolf Ising. Vitaphone/Warner Bros. B&W.

Seven minute *Merrie Melodies* cartoon in which book cover characters come to life. These include Mr Hyde (drawn by Bob Clampett and based on the Fredric March performance), who tries to kidnap Alice in Wonderland but is foiled by such heroes as Tarzan, the Three Musketeers and Robin Hood. This features the title song, plus 'I've Got the South in My Soul' and 'One Step Ahead of My Shadow'. Footage from this cartoon was later reused in Ising's MGM short *Good Little Monkeys* (1935).

✦✦

THRILLER:

(UK: BORIS KARLOFF PRESENTS)

The Incredible Doktor Markesan

USA, 1962. Dir: Robert Florey. With: Boris Karloff, Dick York, Carolyn Kearney, Richard Hale, Henry Hunter,

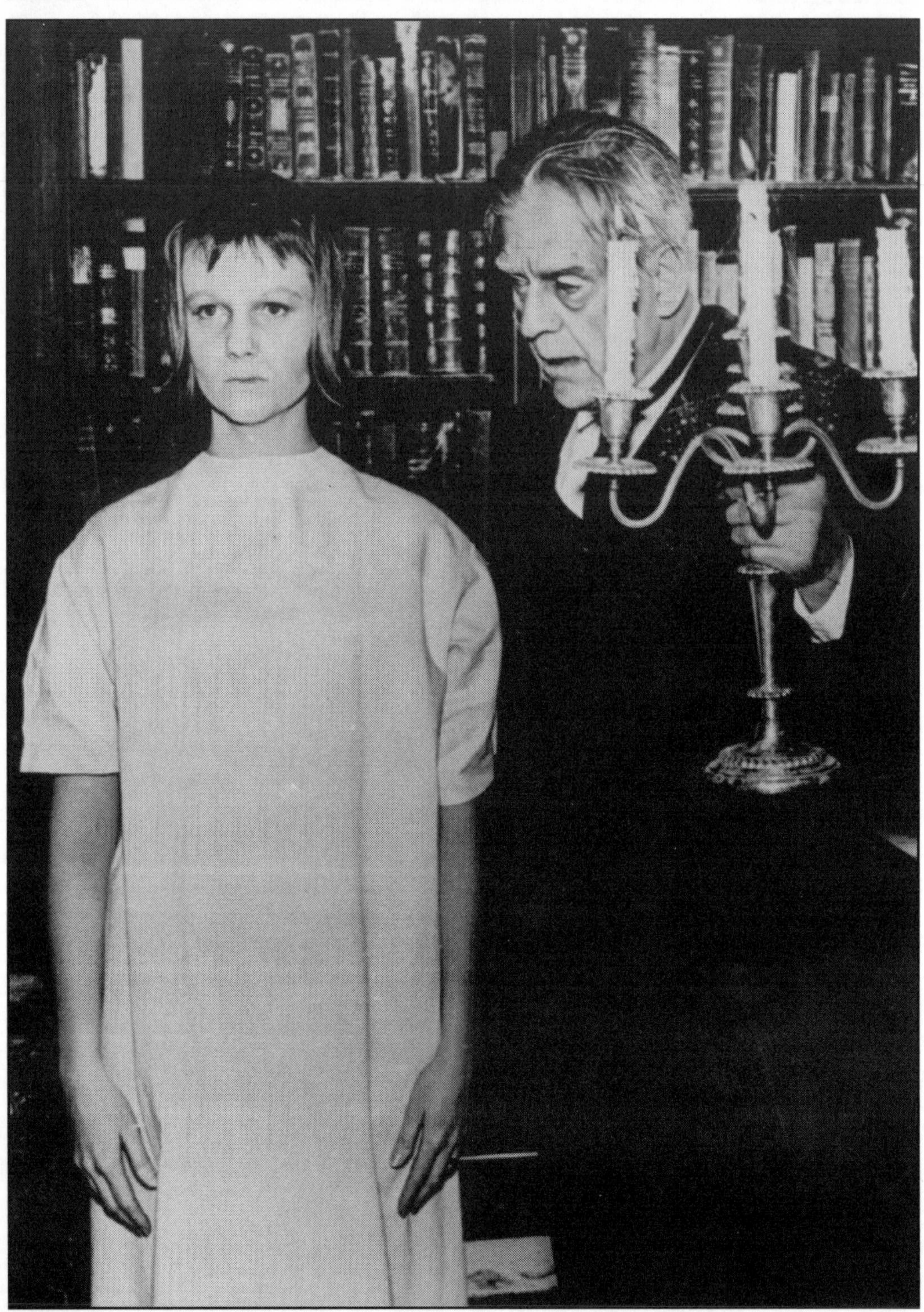

Basil Howes. Hubbell Robinson Productions/MCA-TV/ NBC-TV. B&W.
Superior hour-long anthology TV series (1960-62, sixty-seven episodes) hosted by and occasionally starring Karloff. In this classic episode, based on the short story by August Derleth and Mark Schörer, Karloff plays deceased scientist Doktor Konrad Markesan who has discovered a chemical method of bringing the dead back to life to exact a terrible revenge upon his former colleagues. Director Florey was originally set to helm *Frankenstein* (1931).
✦✦✦✧

Masquerade
USA, 1961. Dir: Herschel Daugherty. With: Elizabeth Montgomery, Tom Poston, John Carradine, Jack Lambert, Dorothy Neumann. Hubbell Robinson Productions/MCA-TV/NBC-TV. B&W.
Ghoulishly funny Halloween episode, based on a short story by Henry Kuttner. Modern honeymooners (Montgomery and Poston) take refuge for the night in a run down old dark house belonging to a trio of creepy hillbillies (Carradine, Lambert and Neumann). The latter scare their guests with tales of local vampire attacks, but in the twist ending it is the young couple who turn out to be undead. This was filmed on the *Psycho* (1960) sets.
✦✦✦✧

Pigeons from Hell
USA, 1961. Dir: John Newland. With: Brandon deWilde, Crahan Denton, Ken Renard, David Whorf, Guy Wilkerson, Ottola Nesmith. Hubbell Robinson Productions/MCA-TV/NBC-TV. B&W.
Based on the short story by Robert E. Howard. When their car becomes stranded in the swamp, Tim (deWilde) and his brother John (Whorf) come upon a dilapidated old Southern mansion, inhabited by the hatchet-wielding *zuvembi* of an old servant woman, Eula Lee (Nesmith), who can control the living and the dead.
✦✦✦✦

The Weird Tailor
USA, 1961. Dir: Herschel Daugherty. With: Henry Jones, George Macready, Abraham Sofaer, Sondra Kerr, Stanley Adams, Iphigenie Castiglioni. Hubbell Robinson Productions/MCA-TV/NBC-TV. B&W.
Scripted by Robert Bloch and based on his own story. When his son Arthur (Gary Clarke) accidentally dies during an occult ceremony, Mr Smith (Macready) uses his fortune to purchase a book of black magic which reveals how to make a suit that will bring his only offspring back from the dead. In the end, the tailor's wife Anna (Kerr) puts the strange suit on a creepy-looking dummy that comes to life. Bloch adapted this story again as one of the tales in *Asylum* (1972).
✦✦✦

THRILLER
USA, 1983. Dir: John Landis. With: Michael Jackson, Ola Ray, Vincent Price, Forrest J Ackerman, Rick Baker. Optimum Productions/Epic Records. Colour.
Fourteen minute music video that cost $2,000,000 and begins with a silly disclaimer stating that Jackson has no belief in the occult. Supposedly also released as a short film to qualify for an Oscar nomination, it is based on the title track of the multi-million selling music album which features a 'rap' by Price, recorded in a day for a flat fee. When a couple's car breaks down in a dark forest, the moon appears and the boy (Jackson) transforms into a very hairy werewolf (make-up created by Rick Baker). It all turns out to be a clip from a movie, with audience members including Jackson, *Playboy* centrefold Ray and Ackerman. But when the couple leave the theatre, the boy turns into a zombie and leads the shambling dead (one of whom is wearing a Tor Johnson mask!) in an energetic dance routine. With creepy music by Elmer Bernstein. Jerry Kramer's hour-long *Michael Jackson: Making the 'Thriller'* (1983) was released on video and included clips from *An American Werewolf in London* (1981).
✦✦✦✧

Boris Karloff returns from the dead in TV's Thriller: 'The Incredible Doktor Markesan' *(1962).*

THROUGH THE CENTURIES
USA, 1914. Dir: Fred W. Huntley. With: Harold Lockwood, Mabel Van Buren, Henry W. Otto. Selig Polyscope Company. B&W.
Silent short in which ancient Egyptian Princess Merza (Van Buren) is scientifically returned to life after 2,000 years by archaeologists Truxton (Lockwood) and Willing (Otto) who are the reincarnations of her rival lovers.
✦

THUNDER IN PARADISE:
Strange Bru
USA, 1994. Dir: Lyndon Chubbuck. With: (Terry) Hulk Hogan, Chris Lemmon, Carol Alt, Ashley Gorrell, Patrick Macnee, Kiki Shepard (D.J. 'Trelawny' Moran). Walt Disney Television/Metro-Goldwyn-Mayer/Rysher Entertainment. Colour.
Hour-long syndicated adventure show (twenty-two episodes) in which former Navy SEALS Randolph J. 'Spence' Spencer (professional wrestler-turned-actor Hogan) and Martin 'Bru' Brubaker (Lemmon) hire themselves and their high-tech speedboat *Thunder* out for $5,000 a day, plus expenses. In this episode, an old girlfriend of Spence's comes to the Paradise Beach Resort searching for her missing husband, and Spence is apparently attacked by scuba-diving zombies.
✦✦

THUNDER KIDS 3 HUNT FOR DEVIL BOXER
(USA: aka THE THUNDER NINJA KIDS THE HUNT FOR THE DEVIL BOXER)
Hong Kong, 1991. Dir: Alton Cheung. With: Mark Hougton, Vince Parr, Sophia Warhol, Tsui Po-wah, Steven Tee, David Frank Hallet. IFD Films & Arts. Colour.
This comedy features a group of hopping vampire children from a cemetery who only drink blood from criminals, and a thug who is transformed into a half-zombie.
✦✧

THE TICK:
The Tick vs. Dinosaur Neil
USA, 1994. Dir: Dorie Rich. Voices: Townsend Coleman, Micky Dolenz, Kay Lenz, Hamilton Camp, Rob Paulsen, Roddy McDowall. Fox Kids Network/Sunbow Productions/Graz Entertainment. Colour.
Fun half-hour TV cartoon superhero spoof (1994-97), based upon characters created by Ben Edlund. In this adventure, the titular blue-clad costumed hero (Coleman) and his faithful sidekick Arthur, aka The Moth (Dolenz), visit Dinosaur Grotto, an archaeological dig. Palaeontologist and tour guide 'Dinosaur' Neil inadvertently eats some regenerated dinosaur tissue and is transformed into a seventy-foot green scaly monster. This includes *The Mummy Speaks* on TV. 'May Evil beware, and may Good dress warmly and eat plenty of fresh vegetables.'
✦✦✦

TICKLE ME
USA, 1965. Dir: Norman Taurog. With: Elvis Presley, Julie Adams (Julia Adams/Betty May Adams), Jack Mullaney, Merry Anders, Bill Williams, Allison Hayes. Allied Artists. Colour.
Lightweight comedy/musical in which Elvis plays singing rodeo star Lonnie Beale, hired by Adams (*Creature from the Black Lagoon* [1954], etc) to work on her health ranch full of beautiful women. During a thunderstorm in a ghost town's 'haunted' inn, comedy relief Mullaney and heroine Jocelyn Lane are scared by a crook wearing a werewolf mask. In the end, Lonnie foils a kidnap plot and finds a hidden fortune. Elvis sings 'Dirty, Dirty Feeling' and 'Slowly But Surely'. Co-scripted by regular Three Stooges director Edward Bernds.
✦✧

TICKLING VAMPS
USA. Vid Tech Films. Colour.
Low-budget 'adults only' tickling video. In their castle dungeon, a female vampire tickles another cute bloodsucker bound to a cross

until they are interrupted by a pair of nerdy male vampire-hunters, who proceed to tie up both undead women and tickle them.
✦

TICKS
(aka INFESTED)
USA/Japan, 1993 (1995). Dir: Tony Randel. With: Rosalind Allen, Ami Dolenz, Seth Green, Virginya Keehne, Ray Oriel, Alfonso Ribiero. Ticks United/First Look Pictures/ Daiei/Overseas Filmgroup/Republic Pictures. Colour.
Director Randel (*Hellbound Hellraiser II* [1988], etc) handles this extremely gory low-budget chiller with style. Two social workers take a group of dysfunctional inner city teens on a backwoods camping project where they encounter crazy rednecks plus oversized blood-drinking ticks (impressive special visual effects supervised by associate producer Doug Beswick, who also came up with the original idea) mutated through accidental contact with an experimental marihuana growth steroid. With Clint Howard as a pot grower and his father Rance as the local sheriff. Brian Yuzna was executive producer.
✦✦✦

TIEMPOS DUROS PARA DRACULA
Spain/Argentina, 1976. Dir: Jorge M. Darnell. With: José Ruiz Lifante, Miguel Ligero, Maria Noel, Adolfo Linvel, Alfonso de Grazia. Aitor/Espacio. Colour.
The Count's grandson returns to Transylvania.
✦

TIGER FANGS
USA, 1943. Dir: Sam Newfeld. With: Frank Buck, June Duprez, Duncan Renaldo, Howard Banks, J. Farrell MacDonald, Pedro Regas. Producers Releasing Corporation. B&W.
Superstitious rubber-plant workers blame a series of killings on mythical *T'jindaks* — men with the ability to take on tiger form. Unfortunately, in the end it turns out to be the work of real tigers, driven mad through a drug created by insane Nazi Dr Lang (Arno Frey). At least this slice of PRC hokum is less than an hour long!
✦

TILL DEATH
USA, 1978. Dir: Walter Stocker. With: Keith Atkinson, Belinda Balaski, Bert Freed, Marshall Reed, Jonathan Hole. Cougar/Cinema Shares International. Colour.
Locked inside a mausoleum, a husband's (Atkinson) love appears to bring his young bride (Balaski) back from the dead. She then tries to seduce him into joining her.
✦

THE TIME OF VAMPIRES
(Orig: VRIJEME VAMPIRA)
Yugoslavia, 1971. Dir: Nikola Majdak. Dunav/Zagreb. Colour.
Nine minute cartoon comedy about vampires' midnight visits to a haunted graveyard.
✦

TIME TRAX:
Night of the Savage
Australia/USA, 1993. Dir: Colin Budds. With: Dale Midkiff, Elizabeth Alexander, Peter O'Brien, Elaine Smith, Steven Grives, John Dicks. Lorimar Productions/ Gary Nardino Productions/Warner Bros. Colour.
Syndicated TV series (1993-94, forty-four episodes) about straight-laced futuristic cop Darien Lambert (a likeable Midkiff) who pursues evil scientist Sahmbi (Peter Donat) on a one-way time trip from 2193 back to the twentieth century. With his holographic helper Selma (Alexander, in a role originally offered to Maggie Smith) he begins hunting down those criminals who Sahmbi helped escape into the past. In this episode, Darien travels to a quaintly foggy London, where he teams up with a female reporter (Smith) to pursue the Soho 'Savage', a serial killer who drains his victims of blood. Co-created and developed for TV by executive producer Harve Bennett.
✦✧

TIME WALKER
(aka BEING FROM ANOTHER PLANET)
USA, 1982 (1983). Dir: Tom Kennedy. With: Ben Murphy, Nina Axelrod, Kevin Brophy, James Karen, Austin Stoker, Shari Belafonte-Harper. Dimitri Villard/Wescom Productions/Byzantine/New World Pictures. Colour.
This low-budget science fiction/horror thriller begins well when the recently-discovered mummy of Ankh-Venharis (Jack Olson) from Tutankhamen's tomb is revived by X-rays and begins spreading a bone-eating green fungus amongst a group of college kids. However, the film changes direction towards the end as the deadly fungus is ignored and the mummy turns out to be a friendly 3,000 year-old alien who just wants to go home. With Antoinette Bower and co-producer Jason Williams (*Flesh Gordon* [1974], etc). The music score is by Richard Band.
✦

TIMON & PUMBAA:
(aka THE LION KING'S TIMON & PUMBAA)
Jamaica Mistake?
USA, 1996. Dir: Tony Craig and Roberts Gannaway. Voices: Jeff Bennett, Quinton Flynn, Nathan Lane, Ernie Sabella, Frank Welker. Disney Enterprises/Walt Disney Television Animation/Buena Vista Television/CBS-TV. Colour.
Half-hour children's cartoon series (1995-97) featuring the misadventures of the eponymous meerkat and warthog from *The Lion King* (1994). In this ten minute segment, Timon (Flynn or Lane, who shared the role) and Pumbaa (Sabella) are trapped in a strange mansion where they are invited to dinner by the bloodthirsty Mr Pire Bat and his batty assistant. However, they soon discover that *they* are next on the menu at midnight.
✦✦✧

TINTIN ET LE TEMPLE DU SOLEIL
Belgium/France, 1969. Dir: Eddie Lateste. Raymond Le Blanc/Belvision/Dargaud Films. Colour.
Feature-length cartoon based on the book by Belgian cartoonist Hergé (Georges Remi). The discovery of a cursed Inca mummy results in seven archaeologists falling into a deep sleep. Boy adventurer Tintin travels to Peru to solve the mystery and rescue his friend Professor Tournesol.
Remake: THE ADVENTURES OF TINTIN: Prisoners of the Sun (qv; 1992)
✦✦

TINY TOON ADVENTURES: TINY TOONS' NIGHT GHOULERY
(aka STEVEN SPIELBERG PRESENTS TINY TOON ADVENTURES: TINY TOONS' NIGHT GHOULERY)
USA/Japan, 1995. Dir: Michael Gerard, Rusty Mills, Rich Arons and Greg Reyna. Voices: Joe Alaskey, Tress MacNeille, John Kassir, Don Messick, Cree Summer, Maurice LaMarche. Warner Bros/Amblin Entertainment/ Fox Kids Network. Colour.
Emmy Award-nominated special of the cartoon TV series (1990-93, one hundred episodes) executive produced by Steven Spielberg that spoofs TV's *Rod Serling's Night Gallery* (1970-73). Hosted by Babs Bunny (MacNeille), among the best of the eight stories featured are 'The Tell-Tale Vacuum', 'The Devil and Daniel Webfoot' (with Ron Perlman voicing Mr Scratch), 'Frankenelmyra', 'Gremlin on a Wing' and the black and white pastiche 'Hold That Duck', in which Buster Bunny (Kassir) and Plucky Pig (Alaskey) recreate some classic Abbott and Costello routines and encounter Count Dracula, the Frankenstein Monster, a werewolf, a mummy and a devil dog. With June Foray as the voice of Witch Hazel, numerous William Shatner/*Star Trek* gags, and an appearance by the original Warner Bros gremlin.
✦✦✦

TITANIC 2000: VAMPIRE LUST
USA, 1999. Dir: John P. Fedele. With: Tammy Parks, Tina Krause, Roxanne Michaels, Michael Thomas, Joe Who, Suzanne Lenore. EI Independent Cinema Studios. Colour.
Supposedly based on the story 'Dracula's Daughter & the Titanic

2000' by producer Michael L. Raso, this independent erotic horror spoof was shot on 16mm and released directly to video. Set at the turn of the century aboard the new cruise ship Titanic 2000, lesbian vampire Vladamina (Parks) attempts to seduce Shari O'Carey (Krause) into becoming her eternal soulmate. However, Vladamina and her dim-witted henchmen Eegor and Mareem are opposed by the ship's helmsman turned vampire-hunter Willy (John Link).
✦✧

TO DIE FOR

USA, 1988 (1989). Dir: Deran Sarafian. With: Brendan Hughes, Sydney Walsh, Amanda Wyss, Scott Jacoby, Micah Grant, Duane Jones. Academy Entertainment/Arrowhead Entertainment/Lee Caplin/Skouras Pictures. Colour.

Filmed under the title *Dracula: The Love Story*, this romantic horror film features vampires with telepathic powers and one impressive staking sequence (make-up effects created by John Buechler and Magical Media Industries). Undead Vlad Tepish (Hughes) tries to put the bite on beautiful estate agent Kate Wooten (Walsh) who sold him his Californian home, but he's opposed by his evil undead brother, Tom (Steve Bond). In the end, Vlad stakes his brother on a bedpost and then commits suicide by exposing himself to sunlight. *Night of the Living Dead* (1968) star Jones turns up briefly in his last role.

Sequel: SON OF DARKNESS TO DIE FOR II (qv; 1991)
✦✦

THE TOMB

USA, 1985 (1986). Dir: Fred Olen Ray. With: Cameron Mitchell, John Carradine, Susan Stokey, Richard Alan Hench, Michelle Bauer (Michelle McClellan), Sybil Danning (Sybelle Denninger). Trans World Entertainment. Colour.

Low-budget homage to the Universal Mummy series from Ray, with characters named after those in the original movies. A pair of fortune hunters break into an Egyptian tomb and release ancient vampire witch-queen Nefratis (Bauer). She follows her stolen treasure to America, where she zaps her victims with magic powers and feeds a lesbian (Dawn Wildsmith) to a bed full of snakes. Carradine turns up in one scene as Egyptian expert Mr Andoheb. Great cast, low concept. With Kitten (Francesca) Natividad as a stripper (cut from some prints).
✦✦

TOMBS OF THE BLIND DEAD

(Orig: LA NOCHE DEL TERROR CIEGO. USA: aka THE BLIND DEAD/NIGHT OF THE BLIND DEAD)
Spain/Portugal, 1971. Dir: Amando de Ossorio. With: Maria Silva (Sylva), Lone Fleming, Oscar (Cesar) Burner, Helen Harp (Helen Hay/Maria Elena Arpon), Joseph Thelman (José Telman), Rufino Ingles. Plata Films/Interfilme/Hallmark/Atlas International. Colour.

Popular horror film that spawned three sequels. A group of people stumble upon an abandoned monastery where the skeletal corpses of an evil cult of thirteenth century Templarios Knights, executed for killing women as part of their blood rituals and whose eyes were pecked out on the gallows by crows, rise from the grave seeking human blood to prolong their unholy existence. Writer/director de Ossorio also designed and supervised the special effects make-up (with José Luis Campos). The opening torture scenes (featuring an uncredited Britt Nichols) are missing from some prints. An original uncut version was digitally remastered in 1997 from a new 35mm print, struck from the original negative.

Sequel: RETURN OF THE EVIL DEAD (qv; 1973)
✦✦

TOMCAT: DANGEROUS DESIRES

(UK: DANGEROUS DESIRE)
Canada, 1993. Dir: Paul Donovan. With: Richard Grieco, Natalie Radford, Maryam D'Abo, Serge Houde, Sean Orr, David McLeod. Tomcat Productions/Entertainment Securities/Saban Entertainment/Den Pictures/Republic Home Video. Colour.

Silly erotic thriller written and directed by Donovan. In an attempt to cure a rare degenerative brain condition, Tom (Grieco) becomes the subject of a secret cross-species gene transfer experiment by Dr Jacki Eddington (D'Abo). After his recovery, he takes on the heightened senses, predatory instincts and increased sexual appetite of the donor animal — a cat. He starts killing everyone who can reveal his secret as he plays cat-and-mouse with a colleague (Radford). This also includes some mild nudity and a couple of bizarre dance sequences.
✦

TOMMY

UK, 1975. Dir: Ken Russell. With: Roger Daltrey, Oliver Reed, Ann-Margret, Elton John, Eric Clapton, John Entwistle. The Robert Stigwood Organisation/Hemdale. Colour.

Russell's often exhilarating musical, based upon the rock opera by Pete Townshend. When he witnesses the murder of his father, Group-Captain Walker (Robert Powell), by his mother Nora (Ann-Margret) and her new husband Frank Hobbs (the excellent Reed), young Tommy (Barry Winch) is so traumatised that he becomes deaf, dumb and blind. However, when the boy grows up he becomes the Pinball Champion of the World (Daltrey). In one scene, Sally Simpson (the director's daughter, Victoria) marries an American rock musician (Gary Rich) who looks just like the Frankenstein Monster. With John as The Pinball Wizard, Clapton as The Preacher, Tina Turner as The Acid Queen, Daltrey's fellow members of The Who (Entwistle, Townshend and Keith Moon), plus Paul Nicholas and Jack Nicholson. Originally shown in cinemas in quintaphonic sound, the soundtrack was released by Polydor Records.
✦✦✦✧

THE TOMORROW PEOPLE: Castle of Fear

UK, 1978. Dir: Vic Hughes. With: Nicholas Young, Elizabeth Adare, Mike Holoway, Misako Koba, Nigel Rhodes, Dominic Allan. Thames Television/ITV. Colour.

Half-hour children's TV series (1973-79, twenty-two serials comprising sixty-eight episodes) about a group of young people who are the next stage in human evolution. In this two-part story ('Ghosts and Monsters'/'Fighting Spirit'), a strange dream about a headless highlander leads the Homo Superior teens to Scotland where they search for the Loch Ness monster, meet Frankenstein's creation and discover a boy with the power to make ghosts appear.

Series sequel: THE TOMORROW PEOPLE (qv; 1992-95)
✦✧

THE TOMORROW PEOPLE: The Rameses Connection

UK, 1995. Dir: Roger Gartland. With: Kristian Schmid, Christian Tessier, Naomie Harris, Christopher Lee, Elizabeth Spriggs, Robert Lang. Tetra Films/Thames Television/ITV/Nickelodeon. Colour.

Updated revival half-hour TV series (1992-95, five serials comprising twenty-five episodes) about a new group of Homo Superior children with supernatural powers, this time based on an alien spacecraft on an uncharted Pacific island. Seventy-two year-old horror veteran Lee stars as the anagrammatic Sam Rees, a 4,000 year-old immortal Egyptian sorcerer who plans to harness the power of the stars to make himself all-powerful. Only Adam Neuman (Schmid), Marmaduke 'Megabyte' Damon (Tessier), Ami Jackson (Harris) and the bizarre forces of good can stop him.
✦✦✦

TOO MUCH ELIXIR OF LIFE

USA, 1915. Dir: Bruce Mitchell. Alhambra. B&W.

A professor believes that his new elixir has revived a mummy in this silent film.
✦

TOONSYLVANIA

(aka STEVEN SPIELBERG PRESENTS TOONSYLVANIA)
USA, 1998. Dir: Jeff DeGrandis. Voices: Nancy Cartwright, Jim Cummings, Matt Frewer, Wayne Knight, David

Warner, Billy West. DreamWorks/Fox Family Channel. Colour.

Gruesome half-hour comedy cartoon TV series, featuring the adventures of Igor (Knight), Dr Frankenstein (Warner) and his dumb Monster Phil, along with such segments as *Night of the Living Fred*, *Igor's Science Minute*, *Melissa Screetch's Morbid Morals* and *B-Movie* spoofs of 1950s sci-fi films. Steven Spielberg was executive producer.

✦✦✦

Family Plot

USA, 1998. Dir: Jeff DeGrandis. Voices: Jocelyn Blue, Nancy Cartwright, Matt Frewer, Wayne Knight, Valery Pappas, David Warner. DreamWorks/Fox Family Channel. Colour.

While clearing out the attic, Igor discovers a bottle of reanimation juice and uses it to bring Dr Frankenstein's ex-wife Gretchen and her in-laws back from the dead.

✦✦

Love Hurts

USA, 1998. Dir: Jeff DeGrandis. Voices: Nancy Cartwright, Matt Frewer, Wayne Knight, Valery Pappas, David Warner, April Winchell. DreamWorks/Fox Family Channel. Colour.

Igor, Dr Frankenstein and Phil appear on the TV dating show *Love Hurts*, hosted by a suave Dracula. A werewolf, gill man and the zombie family from *Night of the Living Fred* are in the audience.

✦✦✧

Weregranny

USA, 1998. Dir: Jeff DeGrandis. Voices: Charlie Adler, Jocelyn Blue, Nancy Cartwright, Wayne Knight, David Warner, Billy West. DreamWorks/Fox Family Channel. Colour.

When Dr Frankenstein's old granny arrives to stay at the castle, Phil accidentally gives her wolfbane instead of tea, and she periodically transforms into a werewolf whenever she sees a moon.

✦✦

TOOTHLESS VAMPIRES

Hong Kong, 1987. Dir: Lu Wong-Tu (Lee Hun Yu). With: Che Bao-Luo, Chan Yi-Xin. World Video. Colour.

Horror comedy about a family of vampires who, in a blue-tinted flashback sequence, were de-fanged by vampire hunter 'Peter Camshing'. They are therefore forced to try various ludicrous schemes for getting blood out of a dentist.

✦✦

TOPPER:

Topper's Egyptian Deal

USA, 1955. Dir: Leslie Goodwins. With: Anne Jeffreys, Robert Sterling, Leo G. Carroll, Lee Patrick, Thurston Hall, Benny Rubin. CBS-TV. B&W.

TV's first fantasy sitcom (1953-55, seventy-eight half-hour episodes), based on the books by Thorne Smith. The ghosts of a fun-loving couple, George and Marion Kirby (Sterling and Jeffreys), along with their alcoholic St. Bernard, Neil, haunt stuffy bank vice-president Cosmo Topper (Carroll) who lives with his wife Henrietta (Patrick) in their former house. In this episode, the Kirbys and Topper are worried about the curse attached to an ancient Egyptian mummy given to the bank by an archaeologist who is subsequently killed.

Series remake: TOPPER (1979)

✦✦

TORE NG DIYABLO

Philippines, 1969. Dir: Lauro Pacheco. With: Jimmy Morato, Pilar Pilapil, Rodolfo Garcia, Lucita Soriano, Ramon D'Salva, Diana Dean. Santiago. Colour.

Based on the comic strip by Nela Morales published in Lagim Komiks, the title translates as 'Tower of the Devil'. A pregnant woman who sucks the life out of lizards is sought by a Dracula-like vampire (D'Salva) to bear his blood-drinking offspring. In the end, the vampire and his undead followers battle an army of lycanthropes led by a powerful werewolf (Garcia) before both sets of monsters are destroyed by a convenient earthquake.

✦

TORTICOLA CONTRE FRANKENSBERG

France, 1952. Dir: Paul Paviot. With: Roger Blin, Michel Piccoli, Véra Norman, François Patrice, Helena Menson, Marc Boussac. Les Films Marceau. B&W.

Thirty-six minute short, comprising three segments ('Le laboratoire de l'epouvante', 'La proie du maudit' and 'Le monstre avait un coeur'). Dr Frankensberg (Blin), with the help of his assistant Furrespiegel (Boussac), plans to drain the blood of his niece, Lorelei (Norman). She is saved by Torticola (Piccoli), a monster the doctor has created from corpses. The title translates as 'Twisted Neck vs Frankensberg'.

✦✧

TORTURE GARDEN

UK, 1967. Dir: Freddie Francis. With: Jack Palance, Burgess Meredith, Beverly Adams, Peter Cushing, Maurice Denham, Michael Bryant. Amicus/Columbia. Colour.

Yet another anthology film from Amicus, scripted by Robert Bloch and based on his own short stories. In the linking sequences, Meredith hams it up nicely as the sinister Dr Diabolo, who promises five visitors to a fairground a glimpse of what the future has in store for them. Colin Williams (Bryant) becomes the victim of the titular head-eating cat-demon in 'Enoch'. A producer (Robert Hutton) reveals that most movie stars are robots in 'Terror Over Hollywood'. 'Mr Steinway' is the name of Leo's (John Standing) laughably jealous piano that pushes his girlfriend out of the window. In 'The Man Who Collected Poe', Wyatt (a mugging Palance) and Canning (Cushing) are rival collectors who both want to own the resurrected Edgar Allan Poe (Hedger Wallace)! With Barbara Ewing, Michael Ripper, Bernard Kay and Niall McGinnis. In America, audiences were given their own packet of Fright Seeds.

✦✦✦

THE TORTURE ZONE

(Orig: LA CAMARA DEL TERROR. USA: aka FEAR CHAMBER/THE TORTURE CHAMBER)

Mexico/USA, 1968 (1974). Dir: John (Juan) Ibañez (and Jack Hill). With: Boris Karloff, Julissa, Charles (Carlos) East, Isela Vega, Yerye Beirute, Eva Muller. Filmica Vergara/Columbia/Azteca Films/Parasol. Colour.

The third of four Mexican movies Karloff (confined to a wheelchair with only one lung) made just before his death. This one involves the discovery of a stone creature in a volcano which needs human blood to survive. Karloff's kindly but obsessed scientist Dr Mantell creates a chamber to scare kidnapped women before drawing their blood, but his assistant Helga (Vega) and her mad hunchback servant (Beirute) feed the creature with more victims until it grows out of control. Eighty-one year-old Karloff's scenes were filmed in Los Angeles by co-writer/director Hill. Not released in Britain until 1988 (and then heavily cut on video), it includes some mild scenes of sex and sadism and marks a tragic end to Karloff's career.

✦

TO SLEEP WITH A VAMPIRE

USA, 1992 (1993). Dir: Adam Friedman. With: Scott Valentine, Charlie Spradling, Richard Zobel, Ingrid Void, Stephanie Hardy, Kristine Rose. Concorde Pictures/New Horizons Home Video. Colour.

Low-budget remake of the 1988 movie *Dance of the Damned*, released directly to video. A tortured, lonely, 1,000 year-old vampire (Valentine) spends the evening with suicidal Los Angeles stripper Nina (Spradling). Roger Corman was executive producer.

✦✧

TOTAL ECLIPSE FIRST CONTACT

UK, 1999. Dir: David Coleman. With: Michael Buerk, Philippa Forrester, Jamie Theakston, Patrick Moore, Dr Mark Porter, Helen Young. BBC- TV. Colour.

Half-hour show, hosted live from Cornwall on 10 August which previews Britain's total eclipse of the sun the following day. It includes Theakston investigating the legends surrounding eclipses with a brief shot of a mythical Romanian vampire (not Dracula).

✦✧

A TOUCH OF SWEDEN
(aka PASTRIES)
USA, 1971. With: Uschi Digart, Sandy Dempsey, Maria Arnold, Sandi Carey, Peggy Church. Something Weird Video. Colour.
Softcore feature in which 'famous actress' Jerry (Digart) recalls a series of sexual flashbacks that include comedians dressed as Dracula and Groucho Marx.
✦

JACQUES TOURNEUR
[1904-1977]

French-born American director, the son of director Maurice Tourneur (1876-1961). He joined Val Lewton's 'B' movie unit at RKO Radio Pictures for *Cat People* (1942), *I Walked With a Zombie* (1943) and *The Leopard Man* (1943) and brought a European sensibility to low-budget Hollywood horrors.
qv: *City Under the Sea* (1965); *The Hunchback of Notre Dame* (1939).

TOWER OF THE SCREAMING VIRGINS
(Orig: DER TURM DER VERBOTENEN LIEBE/LA TOUR DE NESLE. USA: aka THE SWEETNESS OF SIN)
West Germany/France/Italy, 1968 (1971). Dir: Leo Joannon (François Legrand). With: Terry Torday, Jean Piat, Ursula Glass (Uschi Glas), Veronique Vendell, Marie Anies, Dada Galoff. EGE/Rapid Films/Maron Films. Colour.
Marquerita, the wife of King Louis X, is suspected of being a vampire-witch when the many young noblemen she shares with her courtesans are found in the river, killed by an arrow which leaves the mark of the vampire on their throats. Colourful historical 'adult' feature, based on the play *The Tower of Nesle* by Alexander Dumas. This includes a hunchback and an incongruous jazz and bongo score.
✦

HARRY ALAN TOWERS
[b 1920]

British producer and writer (the latter usually under the pseudonym Peter Welbeck) who travels the world setting up some pretty terrible films and always manages to somehow get away with it. After working in radio (with Orson Welles) and early TV, he was arrested in America in 1961 for allegedly running a call-girl racket. Jumping bail, he produced numerous movies before ending up in Canada in the early 1970s. He gave himself up to the authorities in 1981 and was fined $4,200 before all charges were dropped. Samuel Z. Arkoff described him as 'The blandest guy I ever met'.
qv: *Bram Stoker's Count Dracula* (1970); *Edge of Sanity* (1988); *Howling IV The Original Nightmare* (1988); *The Mummy Lives* (1993); *The Phantom of the Opera* (1989).

TOYLAND PREMIERE
USA, 1934. Dir: Walter Lantz. Walter Lantz Productions/ Universal. Colour.
Six minute cartoon in the *Walter Lantz Cartune Specials* series, set in a department store at Christmas. A toy Frankenstein Monster comes to life and scares the Laurel and Hardy toys.
✦✦

SPENCER TRACY
[1900-1967]

Craggy-looking American actor who had a long relationship with frequent co-star Katharine Hepburn (b 1907). After eight years stage experience, he arrived in Hollywood in 1930 and subsequently won two Academy Awards. He played the eponymous *Dr. Jekyll and Mr. Hyde* in MGM's psychological version of 1941.

THE TRAIL
(Orig: PAO DAN FEI CHE)
Hong Kong, 1982. Dir: Ronnie (Ronny) Yu. With: Ricky Hui (Ricky Lau/Xu Guan-Ying), Zhang Zeshi, Cheung Fat, Miao Tian, Tin Liang, Hsu Siu. Golden Harvest. Colour.
Atmospheric horror comedy which involves a hopping vampire and a group of opium smugglers disguised as zombies.
✦✦

TRAILERS ON TAPE: HAMMER HORROR THE CLASSIC SERIES "MONSTERS"
USA, 1987. San Francisco Rush Video. Colour/B&W.
Chronological compilation video of classic Hammer trailers, including all the studio's Dracula, Frankenstein, Mummy and Quatermass entries, plus *The Curse of the Werewolf* (1960), *The Hound of the Baskervilles* (1959), *The Gorgon* (1964), etc. Kate Bush sings 'Hammer Horror'.
✦✦

TRAIN RIDE TO HOLLYWOOD
USA, 1973 (1975). Dir: Charles Rondeau. With: Charles Love, Willis Draffen, Harry Williams, Charles McCormick, Roberta Collins, Jay Robinson. Arista Films/CJFC. Colour.
Filmed under the title *Night Train*. The lead singer of a soul group called The Sinceres (actually 'Bloodstone') dreams that they are on a train to Heaven filled with many famous Hollywood film stars (played by doubles). This also includes a gorilla and a funeral with Count Dracula dancing in a deserted Western street.
✦

LA TRAITE DU VAMPIRE
France, 1960. Dir: Pierre Boursons. With: Jean Boullett, Michele Vian.
A short film featuring vampires.
✦

TRAMPIRE
USA, 1987. Dir: C.C. Williams. With: Angela Baron, Jodi (Nikki Knights), Angel Kelly, Carol Hall, Titian, Randy West. C.C. Williams/Fantasy Home Video. Colour.
Hardcore comedy in which Baron plays the eponymous 400 year-old vampire queen, the daughter of Dracula, who sucks the life out of her victims during sex. A doctor (West) who has vowed to defeat her hires two detectives (Joey Silvera and Tom Byron) to sexually exhaust the vampire and her minions (Jodi and Kelly) and so save the male population.
✦

TRANCERS
(aka FUTURE COP)
USA, 1984 (1985). Dir: Charles Band. With: Tim Thomerson, Helen Hunt, Michael Stefani, Art Le Fleur, Telma Hopkins, Richard Heard. Lexyn Productions/ Empire Pictures. Colour.
Scripted by Danny Bilson and Paul De Meo. Stand-up comic Thomerson is great as twenty-third century post-holocaust trooper Jack Deth, sent back to 1980s Los Angeles in a race against time to stop futuristic madman Martin Whistler (Stefani) from creating homicidal zombies called 'Trancers' to destroy the ancestors of the Ruling Council of Angel City. Unused to the twentieth century, Jack teams up with the street-wise Leena (Hunt), who is attacked by a rabid Santa Claus. With Anne Seymour.
Sequel: TRANCERS II (qv; 1990)
✦✦✦✧

TRANCERS 5 SUDDEN DETH
Romania/USA, 1994. Dir: David Nutter. With: Tim Thomerson, Stacie Randall, Ty Miller, Terri Ivens, Mark Anold, Clabe Hartley. Full Moon Entertainment/ Paramount. Colour.
Fifth and final entry in the direct-to-video series, filmed back-to-back with the previous episode. When Lord Caliban (Hartley) is revived, Jack Deth (Thomerson, who is obviously tiring of the role) leads the rebels in an attack on the vampiric Trancers' castle. With

Alan Oppenheimer and Stephen Macht. This is once again based on an original idea by executive producer Charles Band.
✦✧

TRANCERS 4 JACK OF SWORDS
Romania/USA, 1993. Dir: David Nutter. With: Tim Thomerson, Stacie Randall, Ty Miller, Terri Ivens, Mark Arnold, Clabe Hartley. Full Moon Entertainment/ Paramount. Colour.
A drop in budget results in a drop in quality in this direct-to-video entry as Jack Deth (Thomerson) travels to a mystical medieval world where he teams up with a group of rebels to battle psychic vampire Trancers, led by the sword-wielding Lord Caliban (Hartley), who are preying on the local humans. With Alan Oppenheimer and Stephen Macht. Filmed back-to-back with the sequel, and based on an original idea by executive producer Charles Band.
Sequel: TRANCERS 5 SUDDEN DETH (qv; 1994)
✦✧

TRANCERS III
USA, 1992. Dir: Courtney Joyner. With: Tim Thomerson, Melanie Smith, Andrew Robinson, Tony Pierce, Dawn Ann Billings, Ed Beechner. Full Moon Entertainment/ Paramount. Colour.
Titled *Trancers 3 Deth Lives* on the direct-to-video publicity material. Twenty-fourth century Android Shark (R.A. Mihailoff) transports Jack Deth (Thomerson) back to 2005 AD to stop Colonel Daddy Muthah (Robinson) from creating his army of zombie-like Trancer troops. With special appearances by Helen Hunt, Megan Ward, Stephen Macht and Telma Hopkins. Produced by Albert Band (Alfredo Antonini) and music by Richard Band.
Sequel: TRANCERS 4 JACK OF SWORDS (qv; 1993)
✦✦

TRANCERS II
USA, 1990 (1991). Dir: Charles Band. With: Tim Thomerson, Helen Hunt, Megan Ward, Biff Manard, Martine Beswicke, Jeffrey Combs. Full Moon Entertainment/Paramount. Colour.
The three-part *Pulsepounders Vol.1* (1988) was originally supposed to include a follow-up episode to *Trancers* (1984) scripted by creators Danny Bilson and Paul De Meo, but although filmed (with Thomerson, Hunt, Grace Zabriskie and Telma Hopkins), that anthology film was never released. So this low-budget adventure (subtitled *The Return of Jack Deth* on publicity material only) became the disappointing direct-to-video sequel. Futuristic trooper Jack Deth (Thomerson) has to deal with his dead wife Alice (Ward), sent back in time from the future to help him defeat a trio of villains (Beswicke, Combs and Richard Lynch, who are given too little to do) and the psychopathic Trancers. Made with none of the style of the first film, this is a waste of the talent involved. With Art La Fleur and Barbara Crampton. Co-edited by Ted Nicolaou.
Sequel: TRANCERS III (qv; 1992)
✦✧

TRANSYLVANIA 6-5000
USA, 1963. Dir: Chuck (Charles M.) Jones. Voices: Mel Blanc. Warner Bros. Colour.
Inventive seven minute *Merrie Melodies* cartoon short, made towards the end of Warner Bros' original series (1938-63). Bugs Bunny enters a spooky Transylvanian castle to use the phone and is menaced by the resident top-hatted vampire, Count Bloodcount. As usual, Bugs manages to turn the tables on the bloodsucker. This is also included on the laserdisc compilation *Looney Tunes After Dark*.
Sequel: DR. DEVIL AND MR. HARE (qv; 1964)
✦✦✦

TRANSYLVANIA 6-5000
USA/Yugoslavia, 1985. Dir: Rudy De Luca. With: Jeff Goldblum, Joseph Bologna, Ed Begley Jr, Carol Kane, Jeffrey Jones, John Byner. New World Pictures/Dow Chemical Company/Lakeshore Entertainment/Jadran Film. Colour.
A good cast is wasted in this low-budget comedy, scripted and directed by De Luca, that steals its title from a (much better) 1963 Bugs Bunny cartoon. Goldblum and Begley Jr play investigative journalists Jack Harrison and Gil Turner, who are sent by the editor (Norman Fell) of a sleazy tabloid newspaper to Transylvania to write an exposé on the Frankenstein legend. When they arrive, they encounter the schizophrenic Dr Malavaqua (Bologna), a Frankenstein Monster-like accident victim (Petar Buntic), wolfman Lawrence Malbot Jr (Donald Gibb), a plastic surgery mummy (Ksenija Prohaska), the hunchback Radu (Byner), nymphomaniac vamp Odette (Geena Davis) and the twisted man (Dusko Valentic). The director turns up as Malbot Sr.
✦✧

TRANSYLVANIA TWIST
USA, 1989. Dir: Jim Wynorski. With: Robert Vaughn, Teri Copley, Steve Altman, Ace Mask, Angus Scrimm (Lawrence Rory Guy), Steve Franken. Miracle/Concorde/ New Horizons. Colour.
Silly but inventive horror comedy, with numerous in-jokes for film buffs and H.P. Lovecraft fans. Altman plays Dexter Ward, who must recover the ancient *Book of Ulthar*, stolen from Arkham Library and hidden in the castle of vampire Lord Byron Orlok (Vaughn). He's aided by Orlok's niece Marisa (Copley) and a descendant of Professor Van Helsing (Mask). This includes fun pastiches of Fisher's *Dracula* (1958), *Phantasm* (1979) and the AIP Poe films, and cameo appearances by Pinhead (make-up designer Dean C. Jones), Freddy Krueger, Leatherface and Jason, plus Kelli Maroney, Brinke Stevens, Deanna Lund, Monique Gabrielle, Jay Robinson and an uncredited Forrest J Ackerman. Twenty years after his death, Boris Karloff makes a special appearance as himself (courtesy of unused footage from *The Terror* [1963]). It was shot in nineteen days on a $1,000,000 budget. Roger Corman was executive producer.
✦✦✧

TRASHI
USA, 1980 (1981). Dir: Louie Lewis. With: Lisa DeLeeuw, Sharon Mitchell, Paul Thomas, Joey Silvera, Loni Sanders, Dorothy LeMay. Artimi/Caballero. Colour.
Hardcore movie in which the mad Dr Schtup (Michael Morrison) creates a 'perfect' woman, Trashi (DeLeeuw), out of dead bodies. He then programmes her for sex. Also featuring Serena.
✦

TREMPLIN
France, 1969. Dir: Henri Dassa and Bernard Soulie. With: Bernard Soulie.
Soulie portrays Count Dracula in this French TV production.
✦

TRE PIGER OG EN GRIS
Denmark, 1971 (1972). Dir: Per Kirkeby. With: Lene Adler-Petersen, Ursula Reuter Christiansen, Elisabeth Therkelsen. Kortfilmradet. Colour.
Tedious experimental feature, shot on 16mm in three days and originally intended as a film version of Bram Stoker's *Dracula*. A trio of frustrated women living alone with their pets pass the time by making wreaths of garlic and battling a symbolic male vampire. In one scene they really castrate a piglet with a razor and feed its testicles to their cat! Described as 'a metaphor for the modern woman's state of mind', the title translates as 'Three Girls and a Pig'.
✦

TRES ERAN TRES
Spain, 1954 (1955). Dir: Eduardo G. Maroto. With: Manolo Morán, Antonio Riquelme, Gustavo Re, Manuel Arbó, Antonio Riquelme. Cooperative dei Cinema/Victory Films. B&W/Colour.
Anthology of three stories based around the creation of a film company called Tiacapa. In the episode entitled 'Una de Miedo' ('A Horror Story'), Dr Salsamendi (Riquelme) creates his own Frankenstein-type monster (Arbó). The title translates as 'Three Are Three'.
✦✧

LE TRIBUNAL DE L'IMPOSSIBLE:
La Bête du Gévaudan

France, 1967. Dir: Yves-André Hubert. With: André Valmy, Georges Chamarat, René Dary, Pierre Hatet, Guy Tréjan, Maria Meriko. 1re Chaîne.
Episode of the French fantasy TV series. Set during the eighteenth century, featuring a huge beast (reported to be a wolfman) killing people. The creature is never shown, although the murders are depicted from its point-of-view.
✦✧

THE TRIGGER EFFECT
USA, 1996. Dir: David Koepp. With: Kyle MacLachlan, Elizabeth Shue, Dermot Mulroney, Bill Smitrovich, Michael Rooker. Amblin Entertainment/Universal. Colour.
Inspired by the BBC TV series *Connections* (1979) directed by Mick Jackson, this tense drama shows how a middle-class Los Angeles neighbourhood begins to fall apart when a passing meteor causes a city-wide blackout on a sweltering hot summer night. With a brief clip from *Night of the Living Dead* (1968) on TV.
✦✦

TRILOGY OF FEAR
USA, 1991. Dir: Richard L. Fox Jr, Steve Maier and Kevin Nunan. With: Claude Akins, Louise Le Tourneau, James Coffey, Larry Silver, Frank Cummings, Peter Zaff. Trilogy Group. Colour.
Anthology of three half-hour supernatural tales about a mass murderer ('Saved by the Spell'), a vampire ('Hubert's Homecoming') and a modern-day witch who helps the police stop a demented doctor ('Midnight Date').
✦✧

TRILOGY OF TERROR
USA, 1975. Dir: Dan Curtis. With: Karen Black, Robert Burton, John Karlin, Kathryn Reynolds, George Gaynes, James Storm. Dan Curtis Productions/ABC-TV. Colour.
Based on three stories by Richard Matheson, this anthology TV movie is made up of scripts from the proposed *Dead of Night* series, the first two written by William F. Nolan and the final one by Matheson himself. Each stars Black as a different character. As the eponymous 'Julie', she uses her psychic powers to make people act out her sexual fantasies. This episode includes a nice Dracula in-joke and *The Night Stalker* (1971) showing at a drive-in. 'Millicent and Therese' involves voodoo and two sisters (both played by Black) who appear to be opposites. The third and best episode is 'Amelia' (based on Matheson's story 'Prey', and released separately on video in America as *Terror of the Doll*), in which Amelia (Black) is pursued around her apartment by a murderous Zuni fetish doll with a big knife.
Sequel: TRILOGY OF TERROR II (qv; 1996)
✦✦✧

TRILOGY OF TERROR II
Canada/USA, 1996. Dir: Dan Curtis. With: Lysette Anthony, Geraint Wyn Davies, Matt Clark, Geoffrey Lewis, Blake Heron, Richard Fitzpatrick. Wilshire Court Productions/Power Pictures/Dan Curtis/USA Network. Colour.
Belated cable TV movie follow-up to director/executive producer Curtis' 1975 film. This time the awful Anthony stars in three different roles. In Henry Kuttner's 'The Graveyard Rats', scripted by William F. Nolan and Curtis, fake-looking giant rats prevent her from getting her murdered husband's fortune. She attempts to bring her drowned son back from the dead and calls up something evil from the depths in the Richard Matheson-scripted 'Bobby' (previously filmed by Curtis as part of *Dead of Night* [1976]). Finally, she plays a museum doctor who is pursued by the silly Zuni fetish doll in 'He Who Kills', also scripted by Nolan and Curtis, and a sequel to the story in the first film.
✦✧

A TRIP WITH DRACULA
USA, 1970.
Underground film.
✦

TROLLKINS:
Dr. Frankentroll, I Presume
USA, 1987. Dir: Ray Patterson, George Gordon, Carl Urbano and Rudy Zamora. Voices: Mel Blanc, Scatman Crothers, Ken (Kenneth) Mars, Frank Welker, Paul Winchell, Alan Young. Hanna-Barbera Productions/CBS-TV. Colour.
Half-hour young children's cartoon TV series. In this episode, the mad Dr. Frankentroll creates his monster Lumpkinstein, who looks just like Mayor Lumpkin (Winchell) of Trolltown.
✦

EL TROÑO DEL INFERNO
Mexico, 1992. Dir: Sergio Goyri. With: Sergio Goyri, Jorge Luke, Telly Filippini, Roberto Ballesteros, Ernesto Gomez Cruz, Agustín Bernal. Goyri/López Asociados. Colour.
A mystical warrior (played by director Goyri) battles a demon-possessed archaeologist (Ballesteros) who transforms into a werewolf-like creature (Bernal) during the climax. The title of this low-budget, direct-to-video release translates as 'The Throne of Hell'.
✦✧

PATRICK TROUGHTON
[1920-1987]
British character actor, often in supporting roles in Hammer films. Best known as TV's second *Doctor Who* (1966-69), he died while guest of honour at a convention.
qv: *Frankenstein and the Monster from Hell* (1973); *The Phantom of the Opera* (1962); *Scars of Dracula* (1970).

LA TUMBA DE LOS MUERTOS VIVIENTES
(aka LE TRÉSOR DES MORTS VIVANTS)
Spain/France 1981 (1982). Dir: Jess (Jesús) Franco. With: Manuel Gélin, Eduardo Fajardo, Antonio Mayans (Robert Foster), Lina Romay (Rosa Maria Almirall), Javier Maiza, Albino Graziani. Eurociné/Marte Films/Diasa. Colour.
After pulling out of *Zombie Lake* (1980), Franco made his own contribution to the Nazi zombie sub-genre with this low-budget mess. Two former soldiers searching for Rommel's hidden treasure in the North African desert discover that it is guarded by an army of the living-dead. Footage from this film also turned up in *The Oasis of the Living Dead* (1981).
✦

IL TUNNEL SOTTO IL MONDO
Italy, 1969. Dir: Luigi Cozzi. With: Alberto Moro, Bruno Salviero, Ivana Monti, Anna Mantovani, Luigi Cozzi, Lello Maraniello. Idea Film. Colour.
Based on the short science fiction story 'The Tunnel Under the World' by Frederik Pohl. A man discovers that his life and his entire town are being electronically controlled by a giant corporation, which uses them to test new advertising campaigns. The film also includes homages to science fiction writers Kurt Vonnegut, Ray Bradbury and J.G. Ballard. In the Bradbury-inspired sequence, the director turns up as a Martian and Pietro Rosati appears as an evil alien vampire. This also incorporates a longer sequence (with additional footage) from Cozzi's *Isabell, A Dream* (1968).
✦✧

TURIST ÖMER UZAY YOLUNDA
Turkey, 1973. Dir: Hulki Saner. With: Sadri Alisik, Cemil Sahbaz, Erol Amaç, Ferdi Merter, Kayhan Yildizoglu, Elif Pektas. Saner Film/Renkli. Colour.
Unofficial *Star Trek* spoof, with bumbling tramp Ömer (Alisik) rescued from a shotgun wedding and transported to an alien planet. There he helps Kaptan Kirk (Sahbaz), Mr Spak (Amaç), Dr Makkoy (Merter) and Uhura (Füsun Olgaç) battle a mad professor (Yildizoglu), his muscle-man robots and a shape-changing psychic vampire monster. The title translates as 'Ömer the Tourist in Star Trek'.
✦

TUT-TUT AND HIS TERRIBLE TOMB
UK, 1923. Dir: Bertram Phillips. With: Queenie Thomas, Frank Stanmore. Butcher. B&W.
Twenty-five minute silent comedy apparently involving revived mummies.
✦

THE TWELFTH HOUR
(Orig: DIE ZWÖLFTE STUNDE)
Germany, 1920. Dir: F. (Friedrich) W. (Wilhelm) Murnau. With: Alfred Abel, Margarethe Schlegel. B&W.
In his 1989 book *The Hidden Cinema: British Censorship in Action 1913-1972*, author James C. Robertson claims that Murnau directed, at least in part, this faithful but still unauthorised silent adaptation of Bram Stoker's *Dracula*, which preceded by two years his much more famous *Nosferatu* (itself re-edited and expanded in 1930 as *Die Zwölfte Stunde, Eine Nacht des Grauens*). According to Robertson's unsubstantiated account, Abel played Count Dracula and Schlegel was cast as heroine Ellen Harker. If this ever existed, it is now lost along with many of the director's other early films.
Remake: DRAKULA (qv; 1921)
✦

21 JUMP STREET:
Old Haunts in the New Age
USA, 1989. Dir: Jefferson Kibbee. With: Steve Williams, Johnny Depp, Peter DeLuise, Holly Robinson, Dustin Nguyen, Pamela Segall. Columbia/Stephen J. Cannell Productions/Fox Network. Colour.
This episode of the popular hour-long teen crime TV series (1987-91, 105 episodes), created by Patrick Hasburgh and Stephen J. Cannell, is scripted by Glen Morgan and James Wong (*The X Files* [1993-], etc). The premonitions of a psychic (Segall) may prefigure the death of undercover Officer Doug Penhall (DeLuise), while a mysterious skeleton is unearthed in a haunted chapel and a student dressed as Dracula starts fires.
✦✦

TWICE-TOLD TALES
USA, 1963. Dir: Sidney Salkow. With: Vincent Price, Sebastian Cabot, Brett Halsey, Beverly Garland, Richard Denning, Joyce Taylor. Admiral Pictures/United Artists. Colour.
Filmed under the title *The Corpse Makers* and re-titled *Nights of Terror* in Australia. Despite being billed on the credits as 'A Trio of Terror', these adaptations of Nathaniel Hawthorne's stories fail to chill: 'Dr Heidegger's Experiment' features Cabot as the titular doctor who discovers life-restoring water dripping into the crypt of his long-dead fiancée, Sylvia Ward (Mari Blanchard). Having used the liquid to bring back youth to himself and his old friend Alex Medbourne (Price), Heidegger injects the water into Sylvia's corpse and she returns to life, as beautiful as ever. However, when the naïve doctor discovers that Sylvia and Alex were once secret lovers, he is killed in a struggle and Sylvia reverts to a skeleton. In 'Rappaccini's Daughter' Price's crazed scientist ensures that his beautiful daughter Beatrice (Taylor) is poisonous to all, while a cut-down version of 'House of the Seven Gables' features Price (who was also in the 1940 version) as Gerald Pyncheon, haunted by a family curse and the ghost of a man executed for witchcraft. Price makes the most of the substandard material and director Salkow at least ensures that it looks good. With Abraham Sofaer.
✦✦

THE TWILIGHT ZONE:
Mr. Garrity and the Graves
USA, 1964. Dir: Ted Post. With: John Dehner, J. Pat O'Malley, Stanley Adams, Percy Helton, Norman Leavitt, John Mitchum. Cayuga/CBS-TV. B&W.
Fantasy anthology TV series (1959-64, 156 episodes) created and hosted by co-producer Rod Serling. In this half-hour episode scripted by Serling and based on a story by Mike Korologos, the eponymous con man (Dehner) in the Old West convinces the inhabitants of a small town that he can raise the dead from the local cemetery at midnight.
✦✦✧

Queen of the Nile
USA, 1964. Dir: John Brahm. With: Ann Blyth, Lee Philips, Celia Lovsky, Ruth Phillips, Frank Ferguson, James Tyler. Cayuga/CBS-TV. B&W.
Half-hour episode scripted by Charles Beaumont and an uncredited Jerry Sohl. A magazine reporter attempts to discover the secret behind a glamorous film star's apparent immortality.
Series remake: THE TWILIGHT ZONE (qv; 1985-89)
✦✦✧

THE TWILIGHT ZONE:
Cat and Mouse
Canada/USA, 1989. Dir: Eric Till. With: Pamela Bellwood, Page Fletcher, Gwynyth Walsh, John Blackwood, Peg Christopherson. CBS Broadcast International/Atlantis/London Films/MGM-UA. Colour.
Revival (1985-89, sixty-five episodes containing 110 stories) of the classic 1960s anthology TV show. In this syndicated half-hour episode, the new black cat belonging to mousy pharmacist Andrea Moffitt (Bellwood) transforms at night into a cursed Prince Charming, Guillaume De Marchaux (Fletcher). However, when he turns out to be unfaithful, she has him fixed by the vet. Narration by Robin Ward.
✦✧

Father & Son Game
USA/Canada, 1989. Dir: Randy Bradshaw. With: Ed Marinaro, Eugene Robert Glazer, Patricia Phillips, George Touliatos, Richard Monette, Mark Melymick. CBS Broadcast International/Atlantis/London Films/MGM-UA. Colour.
Set in the future, when Michael Stevens (Glazer) attempts to take over the family company after his seventy-nine year-old father Darius (Marinaro) is resurrected in an artificial body with an electronic brain implant.
✦✧

Monsters!
Canada/USA, 1986. Dir: B.W.L. Norton. With: Ralph Bellamy, Oliver Robins, Kathleen Lloyd, Bruce Solomon, Lewis Dauber, Mary Margaret Lewis. CBS Entertainment Productions/London Films/Persistence of Vision/MGM-UA/CBS-TV. Colour.
During a lonely summer, young horror film fan Toby (Robins) discovers his new neighbour Emile Francis Bendictson (Bellamy) is a strange old man who claims to be a 147 year-old vampire who is tired of his undead existence and has returned home to die. A nicely sentimental horror story, with a wonderful performance by veteran Bellamy and a clip from *Reptilicus* (1962) on TV. Harlan Ellison was creative consultant. Originally narrated by Charles Aidman.
✦✦✦✧

Red Snow
Canada/USA, 1986. Dir: Jeannot Szwarc. With: George Dzundza, Barry Miller, Vladimir Skomarovsky, Victoria Tennant, Rod Colbin, Andrew Divoff. CBS Entertainment Productions/London Films/Persistence of Vision/MGM-UA/CBS-TV. Colour.
Ordered to investigate the unusual deaths of two Party members near the Arctic circle, sympathetic KGB Colonel Ulyanov (Dzundza) travels to a Siberian village where it remains dark for most of the year. His investigations uncover a community of vampires dating back to Stalin's rule who live in symbiosis with the exiled dissidents. A clever script (by Michael Cassutt), strong performances and good special effects help make this one of the better new episodes. Originally narrated by Charles Aidman.
✦✦✦✧

TWILIGHT ZONE ROD SERLING'S LOST CLASSICS
USA, 1994. Dir: Robert Markowitz. With: James Earl Jones, Amy Irving, Gary Cole, Patrick Bergin, Jenna Stern, Jack Palance. O'Hara Horowitz Productions/CBS-TV. Colour.
Hosted by Jones, this TV movie features two stories: 'The Theatre', scripted by Richard Matheson and based on a story by Serling (1924-1975), is about sculptor Melissa Sanders (Irving) who keeps returning to a movie theatre showing *His Girl Friday* (1940), where she sees

Paul Massie exposes the less interesting of The Two Faces of Dr. Jekyll *(1960).*

terrifying visions of her future. Although talky, 'Where the Dead Are' is much better, adapted from Serling's final movie script. Set in 1868, ex-army surgeon Dr Benjamin Ramsey (Bergin) is obsessed with defying death. He travels to Shadow Island, where he discovers that crazed chemist Jeremy Wheaton (Palance) has created a serum from an Egyptian plant that can return the dead to life. When all the potion is gone, the locals turn into scary-looking zombies. Carol Serling was supervising producer.

✦✦✧

TWINS OF EVIL

UK, 1971. Dir: John Hough. With: Peter Cushing, Dennis Price, Madeleine Collinson, Mary Collinson, Isobel Black, Kathleen Byron. Hammer Films/Rank Film Distributors. Colour.

When Hammer rejected the idea of *The Vampire Virgins/Village of the Vampires* (which would have starred Peter Cushing as Count Karnstein), this became the third and probably best of Hammer's Karnstein trilogy, loosely based on characters created by J. Sheridan Le Fanu. Damien Thomas is the pleasure-seeking Count who is transformed into a vampire (who can walk around in daylight) by his ancestor, Countess Mircalla (Katya Wyeth). He is opposed by Cushing's Gustav Weil, the fanatical leader of a group of sadistic Puritan witch hunters. The eighteen year-old Collinson sisters (who are dubbed) were *Playboy*'s first twin playmates (October 1970) and, despite some mild sex scenes and some serious gore, Hough's careful direction makes this one of Hammer's better later efforts. With David Warbeck and Luan Peters. It was cut by more than five-and-a-half minutes in America and re-titled *Twins of Dracula* in Australia. This was adapted into comic strip format in *The House of Hammer* no.7 (1977).

✦✦✧

TWISTED ISSUES

USA, 1988. Dir: Charles Pinion. With: Paul Soto, Steve Antczak, Lisa Soto, Chuck Speta. Twisted Films. Colour.

Low-budget horrors shot on video in Florida. When a skateboarder is killed by a car, he is brought back to life by a mad doctor (Speta), who he promptly murders with a stake before seeking revenge on his persecutors.

✦

TWISTED TALES

USA, 1991. Dir: Rita Klus, Mick McCleery and Kevin J. Lindenmuth. With: Arija Bareikis, Monica Baxavanis, John Collins, Freddie Ganno, Brett Heniss, John Innocenzo. One by One Film & Video/Brimstone Productions/Screen Edge. Colour.

Low-budget, independent shot-on-video anthology set in the same apartment over a period of years. After being mugged, Joey (Ganno) is pursued by his own outrageous lies in 'Nothing But the Truth', while Tommy (Heniss) murders his brother (Collins) and then meets him again in 'The Shooting'. In the final story, 'Hungry Like a...Bat?', Charlie (co-director McCleery) is a reluctant vampire-werewolf hybrid who explains to a psychiatrist why he doesn't want to kill his attractive new neighbour Allison (Laura McLauchlin), who turns out to be a succubus. With film critic Joe Mauceri as Charlie's brother, plus numerous outtakes under the end credits. The video also includes ten minutes of interviews with the three directors, actress McLauchlin, and quotes from various reviews.

✦

TWO EVIL EYES
(aka DUE OCCHI DIABOLICI)

Italy/USA, 1989 (1990). Dir: George (A.) Romero and Dario Argento. With: Adrienne Barbeau, Ramy Zada, E.G. Marshall, Harvey Keitel, Madeleine Potter, John Amos. ADC/Gruppo Bema/Taurus Entertainment. Colour.

Writers/directors Romero and Argento (who also co-produced) remake two-thirds of Roger Corman's *Tales of Terror* (1962) while updating Edgar Allan Poe's stories. Romero's 'The Facts in the Case of M. Valdemar' looks like an average TV movie, with only Bingo O'Malley's living corpse Ernest Valdemar and Barbeau as his scheming wife Jessica to keep it watchable. But even this is better than Argento's dire version of 'The Black Cat', which except for some impressive body parts (created by Tom Savini, who has a cameo as a

murderer) and several Poe in-jokes, is almost destroyed by Keitel's bizarre performance as news photographer Rod Usher and a confusing script. With Tom Atkins, Sally Kirkland, Martin Balsam in a nice *Psycho* (1960) gag and a cameo by Kim Hunter. Luigi Cozzi was second unit director for the Argento episode.
✦✧

THE TWO FACES OF DR. JEKYLL

(USA: HOUSE OF FRIGHT)
UK, 1960. Dir: Terence Fisher. With: Paul Massie, Dawn Addams, Christopher Lee, David Kossoff, Francis De Wolff, Norma Marla. Hammer Films/Columbia. Colour.
After making *The Ugly Duckling*, a humorous adaptation of Robert Louis Stevenson's novel, the previous year, Hammer decided to produce a more serious version, directed with style by Fisher. It was a box office flop, despite a clever script by Wolf Mankowitz which features a reversal of the usual story as the dull Dr Henry Jekyll (Canadian actor Massie, in make-up created by Roy Ashton) is transformed into the young and handsome Mr Hyde. With solid support from Lee (who is crushed to death by a snake), and Oliver Reed in a brief cameo as a guest in a nightclub. Originally announced as *Jekyll's Inferno*, American-International's version was cut by eight minutes and re-dubbed by the actors themselves.
Remake: THE STRANGE CASE OF DR. JEKYLL AND MR. HYDE (qv; 1967)
✦✦

TWO HEARTS IN WAX TIME

USA, 1935. With: Shirley Ross, Sid Saylor, Sam McDaniels. Metro-Goldwyn-Mayer. Colour.
Twenty minute Technicolor short in MGM's *A Musical Revue* series. A drunk imagines a number of wax figures coming to life in a store window displaying 'The Greatest Menace of Them All'. These include Frankenstein's Monster, Mr Hyde and Fu Manchu. Filmed under the title *The Department Store*.
✦✧

200 MOTELS

UK/USA, 1971. Dir: Frank Zappa and Tony Palmer. With: Frank Zappa, The Mothers of Invention (Mark Volman, Howard Kaylan, Ian Underwood, Aynsley Dunbar, George Duke). Murakami Wolf/Bizarre/United Artists. Colour.
Concert docudrama, shot on videotape. This includes a spoof of Dr Jekyll taking his elixir. With Theodore Bikel, Ringo Starr (Richard Starkey), Keith Moon and a cartoon Devil. For Zappa fans only.
✦

THE TWO NATURES WITHIN HIM

USA, 1915. Dir: Thomas Santschi. With: Thomas Santschi, Bessie Eyton, Franklin Paul. Selig Polyscope Company. B&W.
Forty minute silent drama. After a blow on the head, a man develops a dual personality until he is cured by an operation.
✦

THE TWO-SOUL WOMAN

USA, 1918. Dir: Elmer Clifton. With: Priscilla Dean, Joseph Girard, Ashton Dearholt, Evelyn Selbie. Bluebird/ Universal. B&W.
Silent drama, based on the novel *The White Cat* by Gelette Burgess. An evil doctor hypnotises a woman and gives her a dual personality.
Remake: THE UNTAMEABLE (qv; 1923)
✦

TWO WEEKS TO LIVE

USA, 1942 (1943). Dir: Mal St. Clair. With: Lum 'n' Abner (Chester Lauck and Norris Goff), Franklin Pangborn, Irving Bacon, Kay Linaker, Herbert Rawlinson, Rosemary LaPlanche. Jack Wm. Votion Productions/RKO Radio Pictures. B&W.
Based on the popular radio series. Comedy duo Lum 'n' Abner are in debt, so when Abner mistakenly believes that he only has two weeks to live, Lum finds him a variety of dangerous jobs to raise money. These involve a Jekyll and Hyde potion, a supposedly haunted house with a tame gorilla, and testing a rocket ship to Mars. With Charles Middleton.
✦

TOM TYLER
(Vincent Markowsky) [1903-1954]

American actor who appeared in numerous 'B' westerns and serials. He portrayed the title role in *The Adventures of Captain Marvel* (1941) and was the first to play Kharis in Universal's Mummy series of the 1940s.
qv: *The Mummy's Hand* (1940).

- U -

U.F.O.

UK, 1993. Dir: Tony Dow. With: Roy 'Chubby' Brown, Sara Stockbridge, Amanda Symonds, Roger Lloyd Pack, Shirley Ann Field, Sue Lloyd. PolyGram Video/George Forster. Colour.

Offensive softcore sci-fi comedy in which explicit stand-up comedian Brown is kidnapped during a live show in Blackpool by spaceship captain Zoe (model Stockbridge) and her fellow feminists from the twenty-third century. They put the sexist singing comic on trial for his crimes against women and scientifically impregnate him as a punishment. This includes various *Star Trek* and *Doctor Who* spoofs, and a 'chemically reduced' Dracula (midget Anthony Georghiou) living with other famous historical characters in the bowels of the alien's craft. With Kenny Baker.

✦

THE UGLY DUCKLING

UK, 1959. Dir: Lance Comfort. With: Bernard Bresslaw, Reginald Beckwith, Jon Pertwee, Maudie Edwards, Jean Muir, Richard Wattis. Hammer Films/Columbia. B&W.

Hammer's first version of Robert Louis Stevenson's story is a silly comedy in which the stupid Henry Jekyll (six-foot, five-inch Bresslaw, who was originally considered for the role of the Creature in the studio's *The Curse of Frankenstein* [1957]) discovers his grandfather's long-lost formula and transforms himself into jewel thief and terror of the dance halls Teddy Hyde. With David Lodge, Michael Ripper, Jess Conrad and Joe Loss and his Orchestra. Hammer abandoned a serious Jekyll and Hyde film to also star Bresslaw when this failed at the box office.

Remake: THE TWO FACES OF DR. JEKYLL (qv; 1960)

✦

THE ULTIMATE LOVER

USA, 1986. Dir: Thomas Paine. With: Tracey Adams, Nina Hartley, Amber Lynn, Eric Edwards, Ron Jeremy. Broad Appeal/Vidco. Colour.

Hardcore film in which Dr Shelly Franklin (Adams) and Dr Mary Stein (Hartley) create a man (Edwards) in their laboratory. This includes another penis transplant.

✦

THE ULTIMATE VAMPIRE

(Orig: JIANG SHI ZHI ZUN.USA: aka SPIRITUAC FAMILY)

Hong Kong, 1987 (1991). Dir: Andrew Lau (Ricky Lau/ Ricky Hui/Xu Guan-Ying). With: Lam Ching-Ying (Lin Zheng-Ying), Chin Siu-Ho (Chen Siu-Ho), Wong Pan, Carrie Ng (Ng Kar Lee). Eagle Films/Pan-Asia Video. Colour.

Lam Ching-Ying once again portrays vampire hunter extraordinaire the One Eyebrow Priest in this unofficial sequel to the popular *Mr. Vampire* series. This time he must save his loyal student Hsi (Siu-Ho) from the love of an undead beauty (Ng). It also features a quartet of undead Hell Police and outtakes under the end credits.

✦✦

ULTRAVIOLET

UK, 1998. Dir: Joe Ahearne. With: Jack Davenport, Susannah Harker, Idris Elba, Philip Quast, Colette Brown, Fiona Dolman. World/Channel Four Television/ ITV. Colour.

Moody six-part serial written and directed by Ahearne. When his partner Jack (Stephen Moyer) disappears on the eve of his wedding, Detective Sergeant Michael Colefield (Davenport) finds himself recruited by a covert organisation led by the enigmatic Pearse (Quast), Dr Angie March (Harker) and Vaughan Rice (Elba) that is dedicated to eradicating modern-day vampires in a secret war being fought on the streets of contemporary London. With Corin Redgrave as vampire leader 'John Doe'.

✦✦✧

ULVETID

Denmark, 1981. Dir: Jens Ravn. With: Ghita Nørby, Frits Helmuth, Jannie Faurschou, Henning Rohde. Det Danske Filmstudie. Colour.

Based on the novel by Helle Stangerup. Married couple Tom (Helmuth) and Anna (Nørby) live in the woods where Tom is studying a caged pack of wolves for a book he is writing. When a teenage girl, Ellinor (Faurschou), arrives and is allowed to stay with them, the pregnant Anna becomes increasingly neurotic and is convinced that there is something wolf-like about the newcomer. The title translates as 'Wolftime'.

✦✧

UNCLE SAM

USA, 1996 (1998). Dir: William Lustig. With: Timothy Bottoms, Isaac Hayes, Bo Hopkins, Robert Forster, Ann Tremko, P.J. Soles. A-Pix Home Video. Colour.

Director Lustig and scriptwriter Larry Cohen (the team behind the *Maniac Cop* series) are reunited for this direct-to-video release. A deranged soldier, killed by 'friendly fire' in Operation Desert Storm, returns home as a zombie. Dressed as Uncle Sam, he starts killing off anyone he considers un-American during the fourth of July celebrations. With William Smith, who reads poetry over the end credits.

✦✧

UNCLE WAS A VAMPIRE

(Orig: TEMPI DURI PER I VAMPIRI. UK: HARD TIMES FOR VAMPIRES)

Italy, 1959. Dir: Pio Angeletti. With: Renato Rascel, Sylva Koscina, Christopher Lee, Lia Zoppelli, Kay Ficher, Franco Scandurra. Maxima Film/Cei Incom/Mountflour Films/ Embassy Pictures. Colour.

Following the success of Hammer's *Dracula* (1958), Lee went to Italy to play another vampire in this horror comedy, originally conceived by six screenwriters. Although dubbed by someone else, he looks great as the 400 year-old undead Baron Rodrigo, who travels from Germany and bites his bankrupt nephew (comedian Rascel), now reduced to working as a hotel porter in his own ancestral castle. In the end, the love of gardener Lilli (Koscina) cures the nephew's periodical transformations and the Baron goes off with two beautiful models. The song 'Dracula Cha Cha Cha' was composed by Rascel and Bruno Martino, and sung by Martino.

✦✦

THE UNDERSTUDY: GRAVEYARD SHIFT II

Canada, 1988 (1989). Dir: Gerard Ciccoritti. With: Wendy Gazelle, Mark Soper, Silvio Oliviero, Ilse Von Glatz, Timothy Kelleher, Lesley Kelly. Cinema Ventures. Colour.

This odd sequel to *Graveyard Shift* (1986) has real vampire Baissez (Oliviero) resurrected on the set of low-budget horror movie *The Blood Lover*, about a pool-playing(!) vampire. There's not much in the way of scares in this arty and pretentious Canadian production, as the often confusing plot meanders its way through to the inevitable ending where fiction and reality merge with the vampire impaled on a pool cue. The film-within-a-film scenario might have worked in better hands, but the cast of unknowns and director Ciccoritti's reliance on style over content doom this to failure.

✦✧

UNDERWORLD

(USA: TRANSFORMATIONS)

UK, 1985. Dir: George Pavlou. With: Denholm Elliott, Steven Berkoff, Larry Lamb, Miranda Richardson, Art Malik, Nicola Cowper. Alpine Pictures/Green Man Productions. Colour.

Co-scripted by Clive Barker and based on his original story, this low-budget horror movie manages to fumble every interesting idea it contains. Tough hero Roy Bain (a wooden Lamb) tries to save a young girl with remarkable powers (Cowper) from London's criminal underworld (controlled by a ludicrously over-the-top Berkoff) and an underground society of mutated monsters. The latter are the result of the mad Dr Savary's (Elliott) experimental drug that allows the user to transform into their wildest dream (or nightmare). Director Pavlou handles the action sequences adequately, but the rest

of the film looks like a bleak rock video. With Ingrid Pitt.
✦✧

UNDER WRAPS

USA, 1997. Dir: Greg Beeman. With: Adam Wylie, Mario Yedidia, Clara Bryant, Ken Campbell, Ed Lauter, Bill Fagerbakke. RHI Entertainment/Mummy Entertainment/ Hallmark Entertainment/Disney. Colour.

Enjoyable children's adventure. When the rays of the full moon accidentally fall upon a scary-looking 3,000 year-old mummy (created by KNB EFX Group), it comes to life and is discovered by young teenager Marshall (Wylie) and his friends Amy (Bryant) and the timid Gilbert (Yedidia). They name the mummy 'Harold' (Fagerbakke) and set out to find his stolen sarcophagus and return him to it before midnight on Halloween, or he will turn to dust and his soul will be lost forever.
✦✦✦

THE UNDYING FLAME

USA, 1917. Dir: Maurice Tourneur. With: Olga Petrova, Mahlon Hamilton, Edward Mordant, Herbert Evans, Warren Cook, Charles W. Martin. Lasky/Paramount. B&W.

Silent drama in which an ancient Egyptian is reincarnated in the body of an English girl.
✦

UNDYING LOVE

USA, 1991. Dir: Greg Lamberson. With: Lee Kayman. Colour.

When a man is seduced by Carmilla, a New York City vampire who has been around since the French Revolution, he becomes one of the undead. Unfortunately, her vampire boyfriend gets jealous.
✦✧

THE UNDYING MONSTER

(UK: THE HAMMOND MYSTERY)

USA, 1942. Dir: John Brahm. With: James Ellison, Heather Angel, John Howard, Bramwell Fletcher, Heather Thatcher, Aubrey Mather. Twentieth Century-Fox. B&W.

Slow-paced werewolf thriller, stylishly directed by Brahm and based on the novel *The Hammond Mystery* by Jessie Douglas Kerruish. Scotland Yard doctor Bob Curtis (Ellison) and his perky assistant 'Cristy' Christopher (Thatcher) investigate a mysterious legend ('When stars are bright, on a frosty night/Beware thy bane, on the rocky lane') which appears to warn that a member of the Hammond family will be killed by an unknown monster. In the end, Oliver Hammond (Howard) is revealed to have inherited the lycanthropic curse from his ancestors and changes into a briefly-glimpsed werewolf in a wobbly travelling matte shot. With Halliwell Hobbes and Holmes Herbert. It was not released in Britain until 1946.
✦✧

THE UNEARTHING

(Orig: ASWANG)

USA, 1993 (1994). Dir: Wyre Martin and Barry Poltermann. With: Norman Moses, Tina Ona Paukstelis, John Kishline, Flora Coker, Mildred Nierras, Victor Delorenzo. Purple Onion/YAF/Prism. Colour.

Low-budget, direct-to-video release, based on Filipino legend and filmed in Wisconsin. A pregnant girl (Paukstelis) discovers that members of the wealthy but strange Null family are really *aswangs* — vampire creatures with long tongues who feed on the unborn.
✦✧

THE UNFORSEEN:
The Tintype

Canada, 1960. Dir: John Ashby. With: Patrick Macnee, Eileen Seaton, Sean Mulcahy. Canadian Broadcasting Company. B&W.

Half-hour syndicated anthology TV series (1958-60, fifty-eight episodes), based on published stories of science fiction and the supernatural. In this episode, set in the nineteenth century, a woman has a photograph which she believes proves that her husband has returned from the dead to prevent her from marrying again.
✦✧

THE UNHOLY QUEST

UK, 1934. Dir: R.W. Lotinga. With: Claude Bailey, Terence de Marney, Cristine Adrien, John Milton, Harry Terry, Ian Wilson. Newman-Wyer-Hopkins. B&W.

This is only fifty-six minutes long. When an ex-convict butler kills a blackmailer, a doctor uses the body to revive an embalmed Crusader.
✦

UNIVERSAL HORROR

USA, 1998. Dir: Kevin Brownlow. With: Ray Bradbury, Nina Foch, James Karen, Carla Laemmle, Sara Karloff, Forrest (J) Ackerman. Universal Television Enterprises/ Photoplay Productions/Turner Classic Movies. Colour/B&W.

The title of this slightly disappointing two-hour cable TV documentary, directed and edited by Brownlow, is something of a misnomer as it also includes material from several other studios. A look at the creators of some of the classic horror movies, this concentrates on the silent years and the 1930s with good-looking clips from *The Black Cat* (1934), *Bride of Frankenstein* (1935), *The Cabinet of Dr. Caligari* (1919), *The Cat and the Canary* (1927), *The Cat Creeps* (1930), *Dracula* (both 1931 versions), *Dracula's Daughter* (1936), *Dr. Jekyll and Mr. Hyde* (1913, 1920 and 1931), *Frankenstein* (1910 and 1931), *The Golem* (1920), *The Hunchback of Notre Dame* (1923), *The Invisible Man* (1933), *Island of Lost Souls* (1932), *J'Accusé* (1938), *King Kong* (1933), *The Last Warning* (1929), *The Magician* (1926), *The Man Who Laughs* (1927), *Mark of the Vampire* (1935), (Abbott and Costello) *Meet Frankenstein* (1948), *Metropolis* (1926), *The Mummy* (1933), *Murders in the Rue Morgue* (1932), *Mystery of the Wax Museum* (1932), *Nosferatu* (1922), *The Old Dark House* (1932), *The Penalty* (1920), *The Phantom of the Opera* (1925), *The Raven* (1935), *The Red Spectre* (1907), *Son of Frankenstein* (1939), *Tower of London* (1939), *The Unknown* (1927), *The Wolf Man* (1941), and mostly familiar behind-the-scenes footage, stills and sketches, plus interviews with historical consultant David J. Skal, Gloria Stuart, Fay Wray, Anne Carré, Gavin Lambert, Nicholas Webster, Lupita Tovar, James Curtis, George (E.) Turner, Gloria Jean, Curtis Harrington, Turhan Bey, Rose Hobart, Rouben Mamoulian, Arianne Ulmer Cipes, Curt Siodmak and others. With original music by James Bernard, and narrated by Kenneth Branagh, this is dedicated to David Gill (1928-97).
✦✦✦

UNIVERSAL HORROR CLASSICS

USA, 1987. Sinister Cinema. B&W/Colour.

Excellent hour-long video compilation of trailers from classic Universal monster movies. As you would expect, this includes *Dracula* (1931), *Frankenstein* (1931), (Abbott and Costello) *Meet Frankenstein* (1948), *Phantom of the Opera* (1943), *The Wolf Man* (1941) and many other familiar titles.
✦✦✧

UNIVERSAL SOLDIER

USA, 1992. Dir: Roland Emmerich. With: Jean-Claude Van Damme, Dolph Lundgren, Ally Walker, Ed O'Ross, Jerry Orbach, Leon Rippy. Carolco. Colour.

Big-budget science fiction adventure in which the corpses of American soldiers killed in Vietnam are revived years later by a secret military unit as unstoppable zombie warriors. However, for two of the bio-mechanical soldiers, old habits die hard. When Luc Devreux (Van Damme) starts to recall his previous life, psychotic killer Andrew Scott (Lundgren) does as well. Pretty soon the two enemies are tearing up the countryside trying to kill each other while TV reporter Veronica Roberts (Walker) is caught in the middle. Despite the simple plot, German-born director Emmerich (who replaced Andrew Davis before shooting) stages some impressive action sequences and great stunts. With Rance Howard. Jove Books published the novelisation by Robert Tine. Confusingly, two TV

John Howard is revealed as The Undying Monster *(1942).*

movie sequels followed before Van Damme returned in a feature sequel.
Sequels: UNIVERSAL SOLDIER II: BROTHERS IN ARMS (qv; 1998) and UNIVERSAL SOLDIER THE RETURN (qv; 1999)
✦✦✦

UNIVERSAL SOLDIER THE RETURN

USA, 1999. Dir: Mic Rodgers. With: Jean-Claude Van Damme, Michael Jai White, Kiana Tom, Daniel Von Bargen, Bill Goldberg. TriStar Pictures. Colour.
Ignoring the two cable TV movie spin-offs, Van Damme returns in his first sequel as zombie soldier Luc Devreux in this belated theatrical follow-up to the 1992 film. When single father Devreux returns to the UniSol programme as a technical advisor, he finds himself teaming up with reporter Erin (Heidi Schanz) to battle renegade super-computer SETH (White), which controls a new breed of reanimated warrior being developed by the military.
✦✧

UNIVERSAL SOLDIER III UNFINISHED BUSINESS

Canada, 1998. Dir: Jeff Woolnough. With: Matt Battaglia, Chandra West, Burt Reynolds, Richard McMillan. Catalyst Entertainment/Showtime. Colour.
In this second cable TV movie based on the 1992 film, sinister military officer Mentor (Reynolds) unleashes a new generation of zombie fighting machine while Luc Devreux (Battaglia) learns a secret concerning his tour of Vietnam. Jean-Claude Van Damme returned in a theatrical sequel next.
✦✧

UNIVERSAL SOLDIER II BROTHERS IN ARMS

Canada, 1998. Dir: Jeff Woolnough. With: Matt Battaglia, Chandra West, Jeff Wincott, Gary Busey, Burt Reynolds, Von Flores. Catalyst Entertainment/Showtime. Colour.
Made-for-cable TV movie, based on the 1992 film starring Jean-Claude Van Damme. Resurrected from the dead by UniSol as a robotic killing machine, Vietnam casualty Luc Devreux (ex-pro football linebacker Battaglia) teams up again with reporter Veronica Roberts (West) and his long-lost brother Eric (Wincott) to stop a madman (Busey) from selling other zombie warriors to the highest bidder. Filmed back-to-back with the sequel as possible pilots for a TV series.
Sequel: UNIVERSAL SOLDIER III: UNFINISHED BUSINESS (qv; 1998)
✦✧

THE UNIVERSAL STORY

USA, 1995. Dir: David Heeley. With: Richard Dreyfuss. Top Hat Productions/Universal. B&W/Colour.
Two-hour self-promotional TV documentary, hosted by Dreyfuss from the Universal backlot, that looks at the often turbulent history of the oldest studio in Hollywood, from the silent days up to the latest blockbusters. This gives due credit to the importance of Universal's horror and fantasy output and features good-looking clips and rare behind-the-scenes footage and stills from, amongst others, *Back to the Future* (1985), *The Birds* (1963), *Bride of Frankenstein* (1935), *Casper* (1995), *The Cat and the Canary* (1927), *Conan the Barbarian* (1982), *Creature from the Black Lagoon* (1954), *Duel* (1971), *Dracula* (1931), the Spanish-language *Dracula* (1931), *Dr. Jekyll and Mr. Hyde* (1913), *E.T. The Extra-Terrestrial* (1982, with alien test footage), *Field of Dreams* (1989), *Flash Gordon* (1936), *The Flintstones* (1994), *Frankenstein* (1931), *Harvey* (1950), *The Hunchback of Notre Dame* (1923), *The Invisible Man* (1933), *Jaws* (1975), *Jurassic Park* (1993, including stop-motion tests), *Man of a Thousand Faces* (1957), (Abbott and Costello) *Meet Frankenstein* (1948), *The Mummy* (1933), *Murders in the Rue Morgue* (1932), *Night Gallery* (1969), *The Phantom of the Opera* (1925, containing the colour sequences) and *Waterworld* (1995), plus commentary by Boris Karloff, Lupita Tovar, Orson Welles, Alfred Hitchcock, Arnold Schwarzenegger, Steven Spielberg and others.
✦✦✦

THE UNTAMEABLE

(aka THE TWO-SOULED WOMAN)
USA, 1923. Dir: Herbert Blaché. With: Gladys Walton, Malcolm McGregor, John Sainpolis, Etta Lee. Universal. B&W.
Silent film based on the novel *The White Cat* by Gelette Burgess (previously filmed in 1918 as *The Two-Soul Woman*). Under a hypnotic trance, a woman is given a dual personality. In the end, the evil hypnotist is killed by her own hounds.
✦

UPIOR

Poland, 1967. Dir: Stanislaw Lenartowicz. With: Jan Machulski, Aleksandra Zawieruszanka, Jadwiga Chojnacka, Zdzislaw Karczewski, Ryszard Ronczewski, W. Pyrkosz. KADR Film Unit. Colour.
Half-hour short, based on 'The Wurdalak' by Alexei Tolstoy (previously filmed as part of *Black Sabbath* [1963]). A young man (Machulski) at a ball rescues the heroine from other guests who are vampires. It apparently has a rational explanation with a twist ending. The title translates as 'Vampire'.
Remake: THOSE FEEDY ON BLOOD (qv; 1991)
✦

MINERVA URECAL
[1896-1966]

Hard-faced American supporting actress who usually played a weird housekeeper or suspicious relation in poverty-row horrors.
qv: *The Ape Man* (1943); *The Corpse Vanishes* (1942); *The Living Ghost* (1942); *Master Minds* (1949).

L'URLO DEL VAMPIRO

Italy, 1960. Dir: Theodora Fec. With: Milion Chery, Peppino Spoletini, Gianna Giacchi, Franco Vietri, Angela Cavalli, Antonio D'Agostino. Pao International. B&W.
Apparently a traditional-looking vampire disintegrates at the end of this obscure Italian movie. The title translates as 'The Cry of the Vampire'.
✦

URUSEI YATSURA 2: BEAUTIFUL DREAMER

Japan, 1984 (1992). Dir: Mamoru Oshii. Voices: Takuya Fujioka, Shigeru Chiba, Machiko Washio, Akira Kamiya. Toho/Kitty Films/Central Park Media. Colour.
Anime in which bizarre events surround the Tomobiki High School's annual festival. They are caused by Mujaki, the evil Dream Demon (Fujioka), who traps Ataru in a succession of nightmares. These include turning him into Franken-Ataru and he recreates the scene with the little girl from the 1931 movie. With a cartoon Godzilla film showing at a movie theatre.
Sequel: URUSEI YATSURA 3: REMEMBER MY LOVE (1985)
✦✧

-V-

VALERIE

USA, 1991. Dir: Jay Lind. With: Austin Pendleton, Maria Pechukas, Debbie Rochon. Colour.

Ten minute promotional short designed to interest backers in a full-length feature. Pechukas plays the eponymous character who fantasises about vampires and transforms into one of the undead. Writer/director Lind apparently wanted to combine elements of *The Legendary Curse of Lemora* (1973) with the lesbianism of J. Sheridan Le Fanu's story 'Carmilla'.

✦

VALERIE AND HER WEEK OF WONDERS

(Orig: VALERIE A TYDEN DIVN)

Czechoslovakia, 1970. Dir: Jaromil Jires. With: Jaroslava Schallerová, Helena Anýzová, Petr Kopriva, Jüiri Prymek, Jan Klusák, Libuse Komancová. Barrandov/Janus. Colour.

The thirteen year-old Valerie (Schallerová) believes she owns a pair of magic earrings and lives in a dream world that includes masked priest the Weasel (Prymek), her incestuous brother Eagle (Kopriva), and grandmother Elsa (Anysková) who turns into a vampire ancestor to regain her youth.

✦✧

THE VALIANT VARNEYS:

The Incredible Adventures of Dr. Henry Varney and Mr. Hyde

UK, 1964. Dir: Peter Whitmore. With: Reg Varney, Ronald Adam, Grace Arnold, Roger Avon, Gwenda Ewen, Scot Finch. BBC-TV. B&W.

Half-hour childrens' sitcom (1964-65, fifteen episodes) in which comedian Varney portrays various fictional ancestors. This episode is a spoof on the Robert Louis Stevenson story.

✦

THE VALLEY OF BEES

(Orig: ÚDOLI VCEL)

Czechoslovakia, 1968. Dir: Frantisek Vlácil. With: Petr Cepek, Jan Kacer, Vera Galatíková, Zdenek Sedlácek, Zdenek Kryzánek, Jana Hájková. Barrandov Film Studios/ L. Novotny-B. Kubala. B&W.

The image of the werewolf haunts co-writer/director Vlácil's tale about Ondres (Cepek), a thirteenth century Bohemian knight, who escapes his monastic order and returns home to the cursed Wolfenburg Castle, pursued by his friend Armin von Heide (Kacer). In the end, Armin murders Ondres' new bride Leonora (Galatíková) and transforms into a werewolf before being torn apart by hounds. This was filmed on 16mm and not released in Britain until 1974.

✦✧

VALLEY OF THE ZOMBIES

USA, 1946. Dir: Philip Ford. With: Robert Livingston, Adrian Booth (Lorna Gray), Ian Keith, Thomas Jackson, Charles Trowbridge, Earl Hodgins. Republic. B&W.

Short, low-budget chiller starring a spooky-looking Keith (who was originally considered for the title role in *Dracula* [1931]) as mad undertaker Ormand Murks, who returns from the dead after several years to strangle and then embalm those he holds responsible. After visiting the eponymous valley, he also needs to regularly drink blood to stay alive. In the end, the zombie-vampire is shot by the police and plunges off a rooftop. Atmospherically directed by the nephew of John Ford, this was originally co-billed with *The Catman of Paris* (1946).

✦✦

VAMP

USA, 1986. Dir: Richard Wenk. With: Chris Makepeace, Sandy Baron, Robert Rusler, Dedee Pfeiffer, Gedde Watanabe, Grace Jones. Baker Films/New World Pictures. Colour.

A teen horror comedy which is actually stylish, witty and scary. Three college kids, looking to find a stripper for an upcoming fraternity house party, stumble across the After Dark club run by model-turned-actress Jones' mute Egyptian Queen, Katrina, and her undead slaves. The humour is often grim (comedy relief Watanabe is burned to death as a vampire), but Greg Cannom's bloodsucker make-ups are excellent. There's great support from Baron as a vampire emcee who dreams of moving to Las Vegas, Pfeiffer as the scatty young heroine and Billy Drago as a punk. The role of Katrina was written by first-time director Wenk for Tina Turner, who apparently turned it down.

✦✦✦✦

VAMPIRA
(Maila Nurmi) [b 1921]

Finnish-born actress who was TV's first horror host on Los Angeles' KABC-TV (1954-55). She appeared as a non-speaking ghoul in Edward D. Wood Jr's infamous *Plan 9 from Outer Space* (1958), and was portrayed by Lisa Marie in *Ed Wood* (1994).
qv: *The Haunted World of Ed Wood* (1996); *The Magic Sword* (1961).

VAMPIRA

(USA: OLD DRACULA)

UK, 1974. Dir: Clive Donner. With: David Niven, Teresa Graves, Jennie Linden, Nicky Henson, Peter Bayliss, Bernard Bresslaw. Columbia/World Film Services. Colour.

Filmed under the title *Vampirella*, even Niven's urbane Vladimir Dracula can't save this terrible vampire spoof. The Count reads *Playboy* and shows tourists around his castle. But when his lost love, Vampira, Countess Dracula, is revived as a jive-talking black woman (Graves), he is appalled and sets out for swinging London to 'cure' her. In the end, he turns black as well! Jeremy Lloyd's screenplay might have been funnier if it didn't rely so heavily on crude slapstick humour and tired old vampire jokes. Bayliss gets all the best scenes as Maltravers, Dracula's faithful servant, and the cast includes Hammer horror veterans Linda Hayden, Veronica Carlson, Luan Peters and Freddie Jones.

✦

VAMPIRA

Philippines, 1994. Dir: Joey Romero. With: Christopher De Leon, Maricel Soriano, Jayvee Gayoso, Nida Blanca, Joanne Quintas. Regal Films. Colour.

A number of people transform into vampires during the full moon and attack rapists and muggers.

✦

LAS VAMPIRAS

Mexico, 1968. Dir: Frederico Curiel. With: John Carradine, Mil Mascaras (Aaron Rodriguez), Maria Duval, Marta Romero, Maura Monti, Pedro Armendariz Jr. Filmica Vergara/Columbia. Colour.

Another entry in Mexico's wrestling/horror movie stakes. Carradine plays the Dracula-like leader of a group of female vampires who are defeated by wrestling heroes Mil Mascaras ('Thousand Masks') and Duval. This was the third of four horror movies Carradine made in Mexico for producer Luis Enrique Vergara in 1968.

Sequel: LOS CANALLAS (1969)

✦✧

VAMPIRASS

USA, 1992 (1993). Dir: Michael Black. With: Madison (Madison Stone), Teddi Austin, Gail Force, Ashley Dunn, Brandy Blaxx, Don Fernando. VCA Pictures. Colour.

Hardcore feature which begins with a real estate agent (Force) trying to sell a multi-million dollar property to a woman (Dunn) and her bodyguard (Ted Wilson). Entering the dungeon, they are confronted by the vampire (Madison) who has bitten the original owner of the house (Austin).

✦

THE VAMPIRE

USA, 1913. Dir: Robert Vignola. With: Harry Millarde,

Alice Hollister, Marguerite Courtot, Bert French, Alice Eis. Kalem. B&W.
An artist is lured to his death by a seductive wood nymph (Eis) in this silent drama.
✦

THE VAMPIRE
UK, 1913. Searchlight. B&W.
Apparently a lost silent film, set in India. When a native woman kills a hunter, his friend shoots her. But she transforms into a were-snake and kills him as well.
✦

THE VAMPIRE
USA, 1914. Éclair. B&W.
In this thirty-two minute silent drama, a psychologist who is a member of a mysterious organisation is bound by an oath to kill his second wife with drugs and a huge vampire bat.
✦

LE VAMPIRE
France, 1945. Dir: Jean Painlevé. La Cinégraphie Documentaire. B&W.
Nine minute natural history documentary, filmed between 1939 and 1945, in which the pioneer surrealistic scientific film-maker looks at real vampire bats with the use of clips from *Nosferatu* (1922) and music by Duke Ellington.
✦

THE VAMPIRE
(aka THE MARK OF THE VAMPIRE)
USA, 1957. Dir: Paul Landres. With: John Beal, Coleen Gray, Kenneth Tobey, Lydia Reed, Dabbs Greer, Herb Vigran. Gramercy Pictures/United Artists. B&W.
This contemporary reworking of the Jekyll and Hyde and vampire themes, from the same team who brought you *The Return of Dracula* (also 1957), was billed as 'A new kind of horror!'. It wasn't. When kindly small town doctor Paul Beecher (Beal) mistakenly takes some experimental pills extracted from vampire bats, he periodically regresses into a scaly blood-drinking monster whose victims die from a rare virus that destroys their body tissue. In the end, he realises that he is responsible for the killings and is shot to death by the police. With Paul Brinegar.
✦✦✧

THE VAMPIRE
(Orig: EL VAMPIRO)
Mexico, 1957. Dir: Fernando Méndez. With: Abel Salazar, Ariadne Welter, Alicia Montoya (Carmen Montejo), José Luis Jimenez, Germán Robles, Mercedes Soler. Cinematográfica ABSA/American International. B&W.
About the same time Riccardo Freda was reviving the vampire movie in Italy, Méndez was doing the same thing south of the border. In this classic Mexican horror movie, Spanish actor Robles (in a role originally intended for veteran screen villain Carlos López Moctezuma) stars for the first time as Hungarian Count Karol de Lavud who puts the bite on various supporting players until staked by Dr Enrique (producer Salazar). An inferior English-language version, with Robles dubbed by Matt King, was produced by K. (Kenneth) Gordon Murray and directed by Paul Nagel (who also dubbed Salazar's role).
Sequel: THE VAMPIRE'S COFFIN (qv; 1957)
✦✦✦✧

THE VAMPIRE
Poland, 1968.
Half-hour short in which vampires attend a dance.
✦

THE VAMPIRE
Austria, 1976. Dir: Karin Brandaner.
Short satire on horror movies.
✦

VAMPIRE
USA, 1979. Dir: E.W. Swackhamer. With: Jason Miller, Richard Lynch, E.G. Marshall, Kathryn Harrold, Jessica

Maria Luisa Rolando deals with more unwelcome guests in The Vampire and the Ballerina *(1960).*

Walter, Barrie Youngfellow. Company Four/MTM/ABC-TV. Colour.
Modern day vampire thriller with no blood in sight. That's because it was made by Mary Tyler Moore's company as a TV pilot. When work begins on converting an old San Francisco family estate into a church and park, police are soon confronted with several gruesome killings, reminiscent of a thirty year-old series of unsolved murders. Former policeman Harry Kilcoyne (Marshall) believes a vampire has been released and teams up with architect John Rawlins (Miller) to destroy the monster. Lynch is marvellously evil as the undead Anton Voytek, and the imaginative script by Steven Bochco and Michael Kozoll ends with the vampire vowing to return. Unfortunately, no series followed. With Joe Spinell.
✦✦✦

VAMPIRE

USA, 1998. Dir: Steve Sayre. With: Steve Sayre, Angelina Servi, Edward Samuels. Broadstar Entertainment. Colour.
A forensics expert and the local police track down an apparent vampire serial killer.
✦✧

THE VAMPIRE AND THE BALLERINA

(Orig: L'AMANTE DEL VAMPIRO)
Italy, 1960 (1962). Dir: Renato Polselli. With: Helene Remy, Tina Gloriani, Walter Brandi (Walter Bigari), Isarco Ravaioli, John Turner (Gino Turini), Ugo Gragnani. CIF Consorzio Italiano Films/United Artists. B&W.
Remy and Gloriani play two blonde members of a modern dance group (hardly 'ballerinas'!) staying at the country home of a professor who are preyed upon from a nearby castle by the vampiric Contessa Alda (Maria Luisa Rolando) and her undead servant Herman (Brandi), who reverts to his ugly form when he needs

Lionel Atwill and Fay Wray share a look over comedy relief Maude Eburne in The Vampire Bat *(1933).*

blood. In the end, the vampires are forced into the sunlight where they disintegrate into dust. Director Polselli creates some atmospheric moments, and this features a great 'improvised' vampire dance by women in leotards and a music score by Aldo Piga.
✦✦✧

VAMPIRE AT MIDNIGHT

USA, 1987 (1988). Dir: Gregory McClatchy. With: Jason Williams, Gustav Vintas, Lesley Milne, Esther Alise, Jeanie Moore, Ted Hamaguchi. Vampire Limited Partners/ Skouras International/Key Video. Colour.
Low-budget thriller in which co-producer/second unit director Williams (*Flesh Gordon* [1974], etc) plays maverick Los Angeles detective Roger Sutter, who is investigating a series of murders in which all the victims are drained of blood. Could charismatic hypnotherapist Dr Viktor Radkoff (Vintas) be a real vampire? Actually, despite his hypnotic powers and the fact that he sleeps during the day and drinks blood, he is a human psychopath who is eventually shot to death.
✦✧

UN VAMPIRE AU PARADIS

France, 1992. Dir: Abdelkrim Bahloul. With: Bruno Cremer, Brigitte Fossey, Farid Chopel, Laure Marsac, Helene Sugere, Abdel Kechicho. Les Films Auramax/Canal Plus/CNC/MC-4. Colour.
Comedy about the friendship between bourgeois French businessman Mr Belfond (Cremer) and Nosfer Arbi (Chopel), an escaped lunatic who thinks he's a vampire. Winner of the Chamrousse

Comedy Film Festival and the Grand Prix at the annual Paris Festival of Films for Children and Young People, which also voted Marsac best actress. The title of this deft blend of everyday life and the supernatural translates as 'A Vampire in Paradise'. Algerian-born director Bahloul has a bit part as a grocer.
✦✧

THE VAMPIRE BAT

USA, 1933. Dir: Frank Strayer. With: Lionel Atwill, Fay Wray, Melvyn Douglas, Maude Eburne, George E. Stone, Dwight Frye. Majestic Pictures. B&W.

Stars Atwill and Wray are teamed for the third time (after *Doctor X* [1932] and *Mystery of the Wax Museum* [1932]) in this low-budget independent chiller, filmed on the Universal backlot. Atwill plays the mad Dr Otto van Niemann who uses hypnotism to create fake vampire deaths and obtain blood to feed the synthetic creature he has created. Douglas is miscast as the stiff police inspector, but there's always Lionel Belmore, recreating his Burgomaster role from *Frankenstein* (1931), and a sleazy Frye as Herman, the idiot bat-lover.
✦✦

VAMPIRE BRIDES

USA, 1994. Dir: Gary Whitson. With: Aven Warren, Amanda Madison (Christine Cavalier), Dave Castiglione, Michelle Caporaletti, Launa Kane (Terri Lewandowski), Cristie Clark. WAVE Productions. Colour.

Independent shot-on-video production from the makers of *Zombie Nightmare* (1993). Nina (Madison) is a young girl who is kidnapped by Anton the ugly zombie (Warren, who also created the make-up) to become the bride of 500 year-old big-fanged vampire Dominic (Castiglione). In the end, the troubled vampire exposes himself to the sun's rays and destroys himself. Made in New Jersey, this contains semi-nudity and some mild bondage.
✦

VAMPIRE BUSTER

(Orig: ZHUO GUI DASHI)
Hong Kong, 1989 (1990). Dir: Norman Law and Stanley Siu (Law Man/Stanley Wing Siu/Siu Ka-Wing). With: Nick Chan, Simon Cheng, Stanley Fung (Fung Chui-Fen), Jacky Cheung (Cheung Hok Yau), May Law, Vivian Leung. In-Gear Film Production. Colour.

Despite the title, there are no real vampires in this violent horror comedy, just a green-faced body-hopping demon accidentally released from an ancient urn and pursued by an exorcist. With plenty of action and slapstick humour. The title on the video box is *Ninja Vampire Buster.*
✦✧

VAMPIRE CALL GIRLS

USA, 1998. Dir: Everette Hartsoe. With: Everette Hartsoe, Glori-Anne Gilbert, Lilith Stabs, Roxanne Micheals, Lisa Ann DeVaul, Harold Keller. Full Metal Films/EH! Productions. Colour/B&W.

Hour-long independent shot-on-video softcore release. Producer/director/writer Hartsoe plays Bill Simons, who orders a girl from the Night Vamps Escort Service and ends up introducing his friends to some big-breasted bloodsuckers.
✦

VAMPIRE CARMILLA

(aka J. SHERIDAN LE FANU'S CARMILLA)
USA, 1999. Dir: Tom LePine and Denise Tempelton. With: Stacia Crawford, Marina Morgan, Bootsie Cairns. Scorpio Pictures/Hellish Experience/Salt City Home Video. Colour.

This independent erotic video is an updated version of J. Sheridan Le Fanu's novella. Crawford stars as Laura, a young woman who arrives at an isolated town looking for answers to the mysterious death of her estranged sister, Monique (Morgan). When she discovers Monique's hidden diary, she learns of her sister's dark infatuation with the vampiric Carmilla (Cairns).
✦

VAMPIRE CENTERFOLDS

USA, 1995 (1996). Dir: Geoffrey de Valois. With: Jasmine Jean, Tonya Qualls, Joan A. Teeter, Kim Blair, Barbara Savage, Liddy Roley. Digital Entertainment Group/Salt City Home Video. Colour.

Independent vampire video in which college cheerleader Elaine is cast in a Hollywood cult film and soon discovers a secret coven of former *Playboy* and *Penthouse* models and actresses who are transformed into sex-obsessed vampires. Behind-the-scenes nude and erotic sequences from this film were released on a number of *Vampire Raw Footage* videos in 1997.
✦

VAMPIRE CHILD

Hong Kong, 1987. Dir: Wang Chung-Kuan. With: Chuan Chuan, Wang Chiang, Chai Yu-Niang. Colour.

When a good sorceress gives them the opportunity to embrace Buddhism, a vampire child (Chuan) and his family help her to defeat the King of Evil.
✦

VAMPIRE CIRCUS

UK, 1971 (1972). Dir: Robert Young. With: Adrienne Corri, Laurence Payne, Thorley Walters, John Moulder-Brown, Anthony Corlan (Anthony Higgins), Lynne Frederick. Hammer Films/Rank Film Distributors. Colour.

Unusual vampire chiller from Hammer, set in 1825. Director Young was apparently allotted a very short production schedule (six weeks) and, when he ran over, shooting simply stopped and he had to assemble what he had. This probably explains the film's tight editing, occasional dream-like atmosphere and abrupt storyline. When the Circus of the Night sets up camp in the small Serbian village of Schtettel, plague breaks out and the villagers blame the curse of vampire Count Mitterhouse (Robert Tayman), staked in his castle years before. In fact, the Count's cousin Emil (Corlan), a were-panther, and an evil gypsy woman (Corri) are the leaders of the undead troupe and they plan to revive Mitterhouse, who has vowed to revenge himself on Professor Mueller (Payne, who replaced Anton Rodgers) and the other townsfolk who destroyed him. The circus includes a tiger woman (Serena), twin acrobats (Lalla Ward and Robin Sachs) who transform into bats, a magical hall of mirrors, Skip Martin as a murderous dwarf and Dave Prowse as a strongman. It ends with almost the entire cast being slaughtered. This was adapted into comic strip format by writer Steve Parkhouse and artist Brian Bolland for *The House of Hammer* no.17 (1978).
✦✦

VAMPIRE CLUB

USA, 1998. Dir: Ulli Lommel. With: Michelle Bonfils, Peter Sean, Ulli Lommel, Christopher Rogers, Samantha Scully, George 'Buck' Flower. Milky Way Pictures/Million Wishes Productions/Black Cat Enterprises. Colour.

Low-budget movie from the German-born director of *The Tenderness of the Wolves* (1973) and *The Boogeyman* (1980), announced under the titles *I Want to Be a Vampire* and *Nothing Generation.* A bored teenage girl decides to join the ranks of the undead but is dissuaded by a real vampire.
✦

THE VAMPIRE CONSPIRACY

USA, 1995 (1996). Dir: Geoffrey de Valois. With: Heather LeMire, Floyd Irons, Barbara Savage, Liddy Roley, Joan A. Teeter, Tonya Qualls. Digital Entertainment Group/Sierra Sky Entertainment/Digital Doom/Desire Release/Salt City Home Video. Colour.

Low-budget independent softcore video involving a group of female college students who discover during 'Hell Week' that a high-tech group of cyber-vampires intent on world domination are kidnapping young women and using them as sex slaves for breeding purposes. The birth of the resulting mutant offspring apparently only takes a few hours. Meanwhile, the vampires also plan to create an army of teenage bloodsuckers through erotic music videos which introduce Jasmine Jean as the Vampire Centerfold. Behind-the-scenes nude and erotic sequences from this film were released on a number of *Vampire*

Raw Footage videos in 1997, and the *Vampire Conspiracy Photo Book* includes the story plus one hundred nude pictures from the movie.
✦

Robert Tayman is about to get his revenge, thanks to the Vampire Circus (1971).

VAMPIRE COP
USA, 1988 (1991). Dir: Donald Farmer. With: Melissa Moore, Ed Cannon, Terence Jenkins, R.J. McKay, Michelle Berman, Phil Newman. Donald Farmer Productions/ Panorama Entertainment/Atlas Entertainment Corporation. Colour.
Filmed on 16mm in Atlanta and Florida. Cannon plays big blond vampire cop Officer Lucas, who sleeps upside-down like a bat. TV reporter Melanie Roberts (Moore) is trying to stop him from vampirising the local drug dealers. Mal Arnold (who starred in *Blood Feast* [1963], etc) appears as a police lieutenant who is killed with a chainsaw. This includes plenty of nudity, slow motion action and close-ups of fangs.
✦

THE VAMPIRE DANCER
(Orig: VAMPYRDANSERINDEN)
Denmark, 1911 (1912). Dir: August Blom. With: Robert Dinesen, Clara Wieth, Otto Lagoni, Henry Seemann, Svend Bille, Birger von Cotta Schonberg. Nordisk Film. B&W.
Oscar Borch (Dinesen) is chosen as the new partner for famous 'vampire dancer' Silvia Lafont (Wieth). During rehersals, the young man falls passionately in love with her, but when his advances are rejected, he drinks from a mysterious bottle on the night of their public début. At the end of their climactic dance routine — in which Oscar is lured to the vampire's lair, where a mysterious, beautiful woman hypnotises and kills him in vampire-like fashion — he lies motionless on the stage, dead from poisoning. This silent film now exists only as a 'paper print', made for copyright purposes.
✦

LE VAMPIRE DE DÜSSELDORF
(aka EL ASESINO DE DÜSSELDORF)
France/Italy/Spain, 1964. Dir: Robert Hossein. With: Robert Hossein, Marie-France Pisier, Roger Dutoit, Annie Andersson, Michel Dacquin, Anne Carrere. Georges de Beauregard Productions/Benito Perojo/Mega Films. B&W.
Fourth film version of the true-life crimes of child murderer Peter Kürten, known as the Vampire of Düsseldorf. Previously filmed as *M* in 1931 and 1953 and *La Vampiro Negro* in 1953.
✦

LE VAMPIRE DE LA CINÉMATHÈQUE
Belgium, 1971. Dir: Roland Lethem. B&W.
16mm experimental short made by Belgian writer Lethem. This apparently caused one Paris audience to break up the seats!
✦

VAMPIRE DUNGEON OF HORRORS
USA, 1997. Dir: Geoffrey de Valois. With: Heather LeMire, Joan A. Teeter, Liddy Roley. Digital Entertainment Group/Salt City Home Video. Colour.
One of a series of softcore *Vampire Raw Footage* videos that includes behind-the-scenes nude and erotic sequences from *The Vampire Conspiracy* (1995) and *Vampire Centerfolds* (1995). Vampire killers, sex slaves and sorority girls are driven mad by torture in a bondage dungeon from Hell.
✦

VAMPIRE EXPERT
Hong Kong, 1995. With: Lam Ching-Ying (Lin Zheng-Ying). ATV. Colour.
TV series (forty episodes) about an evil Taoist priest who raises Count Dracula from the dead and controls the vampire's will. After being beaten to death in prison, the priest himself returns from the grave and commands an army of corpses, until he is defeated by another holy man (veteran Ching-Ying) and a police detective.
Sequel: VAMPIRE EXPERT II (qv; 1996)
✦✧

VAMPIRE EXPERT II

Hong Kong, 1996. With: Lam Ching-Ying (Lin Zheng-Ying). ATV. Colour.

Ching-Ying (who died in 1997) returns in this TV series (seventy episodes) as a Taoist priest who, along with two assistants, becomes involved with a haunted Chinese opera house, a trio of female demons, an evil sect of Buddhist monks and an underground kingdom of hopping vampires.

✦✧

VAMPIRE FAMILY

(Orig: YI WU SHAO YA GUI)

Hong Kong, 1993. Dir: Eric Tsang. With: Eric Tsang, Jimmy Lin, Cheung Man, Chan Hi-Lung. Chang-Hong Channel Film/Regal/Tai Seng Video. Colour.

Cantonese horror comedy about a family of vampires. An undead couple can produce a child every 1,000 years, and have two toothy offspring, Jimmy (Lin) and Linda (Man), who are ageing faster than their parents because of a weakening bloodline.

✦✧

VAMPIRE FANTASIES

USA, circa 1998. With: Mario Cimadevilla, Savannah (Shannon Wilsey), Tonia Ayers, Jamela. Colour.

Forty-five minute erotic video in which lesbian vampires put the bite on willing young victims.

✦

A VAMPIRE FOR TWO

(Orig: UN VAMPIRO PARA DOS)

Spain, 1965. Dir: Pedro Lazaga. With: Gracita Morales, José Luis Lopez Vazquez, Fernando Fernan Gomez, Trini Alonso, Adriano Dominguez, Goyo Lebreros. Rosa Film Production/Belmar. B&W.

The comedy duo of Morales and Vazquez play Spanish servants Gracita and José Luis, who are menaced by German vampire Baron De Rosenthal (Gomez) and his undead family. This is supposedly not very funny.

✦

THE VAMPIRE HAPPENING

(Orig: GEBISSEN WIRD NUR NACHTS — DAS HAPPENING DER VAMPIRE)

West Germany, 1971 (1974). Dir: Freddie Francis. With: Pia Degermark, Thomas Hunter, Ivor Murillo, Ingrid van Bergen, Ferdie (Ferdinand) Mayne, Joachim Kemmer. Acquila Film Enterprises. Colour.

Francis' uneven career as a director hits rock-bottom with this dire sex/horror comedy. Degermark (also the producer's wife) stars in the dual roles of Hollywood actress Betty Williams and her vampire ancestor Clarimonde, with predictable results. A dubbed Mayne turns up as Count Dracula ('Just call me Christopher'), parodying his role in *Dance of the Vampires* (1966), as he arrives in a helicopter for an orgy of the undead in an old Transylvanian castle! It's not very funny or sexy.

✦

VAMPIRE HOLOCAUST

USA, 1997. Dir: Shane Hatfield. With: Nick Stodden, Coelle Peck, Brandy Gordon, Rico Love, Pat Stodden, Shawna Jones. Englewood Entertainment. Colour.

Low-budget independent video based on a script by producer Todd Sheets. When his car breaks down in a bad part of town, Dave (Nick Stodden) and his friends decide to walk to the nearest police station. However, street gang leader Tommy (Love) uses a spell from an occult book to revive a group of vampires, and soon both the living and the undead are battling each other on the city streets.

✦

VAMPIRE HOOKERS

(USA: aka CEMETERY GIRLS/NIGHT OF THE BLOODSUCKERS/SENSUOUS VAMPIRES. USA/UK: aka TWICE BITTEN)

Philippines, 1978 (1979). Dir: Cirio H. Santiago. With: John Carradine, Bruce Fairbairn, Trey Wilson, Karen Stride, Lenka Novak, Katie Dolan. Cosa Nueva Productions/ Capricorn Three Films/Saturn International. Colour.

A frail-looking seventy-two year-old Carradine (dressed in a white suit, wide-brimmed hat and cape) plays the leader of a trio of sexy vampires (Stride, Novak and Dolan) who lure victims back to their graveyard crypt. In the end, they are destroyed by a group of sailors with a bag of garlic. Despite Vic Diaz's farting vampire servant Pavo, some reviewers couldn't decide if this was meant to be a comedy or not.

✦

VAMPIRE HUNTER

(USA: aka NIGHTWARRIORS: DARKSTALKERS' REVENGE)

Japan, 1997. Voices: Unshô Ishizuka, Akiko Yajima, Akio Ôtsuka, Rei Sakuma, Yukana Nogami, Yûko Miyamura. VIZ Video. Colour.

Four-part anime loosely based on the 1994 video arcade game and CD-ROM, previously adapted on American TV as *Darkstalkers* (1996). Vampire hunter Donovan (Ishizuka) becomes involved with the Darkstalkers — vampire Demitri Maximoff (Ôtsuka), succubus Morrigan Aensland (Sakuma), cat woman Felicia (Nogami), Chinese ghost Lei Lei (Miyamura), werewolf Gallon (Fumihiko Tachiki) and the emotionless little girl Anita (Yajima) — and their battle to stop evil alien Pyron from conquering the Earth.

✦✧

VAMPIRE HUNTER D

(Orig: BAMPAIA HANTA "D")

Japan, 1985 (1992). Dir: Toyoo Ashida. Voices: Michael McConnohie, Barbara Goodson, Jeff Winkless, Edie Mirman, Kerrigan Mahan, Steve Kramer. Epic/Sony Inc/ Movie Inc/CBS Sony Group Inc/Ashi Productions/ Streamline Pictures/Manga Entertinment. Colour.

Billed as 'the first animated horror film for adults!', this futuristic anime adventure is set in 12,090 AD on an Earth which has been overrun by vampires. When a young girl, Doris Ran, is kidnapped, enigmatic bounty hunter 'D' (who turns out to be the half-human son of Dracula) sets out to destroy the 9,000 year-old vampire Count Magus Lee. This includes a giant werewolf, a three-headed female snake monster and a mutant dinosaur. Original voices by Michie Tomizawa and Kaneto Shiozawa. The English-language version was adapted and directed by Carl Macek.

✦✦✧

VAMPIRE IN BROOKLYN

USA, 1995. Dir: Wes Craven. With: Eddie Murphy, Angela Bassett, Allen Payne, Kadeem Hardison, John Witherspoon, Zakes Mokae. Paramount. Colour.

Maximillian (a surprisingly effective Murphy, who also co-produced, in make-up created by KNB EFX) is the last of a race of ancient Egyptian vampires living in the Bermuda Triangle. He travels to New York City seeking a half-human mate, who turns out to be policewoman Rita (Bassett). Along the way street-wise Julius (Hardison) is turned into his ghoul, with the unfortunate side-effect that his limbs start to drop off. A sometimes uneasy blend of horror and humour, Murphy's tiresome comedy make-ups weaken an otherwise effectively scary movie from director Craven. With Joanna Cassidy, Wendy Robie and an unbilled Mitch Pileggi.

✦✦✦

THE VAMPIRE INTERVIEWS

USA, circa 1990s. With: Bela Lugosi, Christopher Lee, John Carradine, Peter Cushing. Colour/B&W.

Video compilation that includes a look at vampire mythology, the movies and interviews with some of the stars of vampire films.

✦✦

VAMPIRE IN THE HIGH RISE

(Orig: UPIR VE VEZAKU)

Czechoslovakia, 1979 (1983). Dir: Ludvik Raza. With: Thomas Holy, Miroslav Batik, Josef Abrham, Dagmar Veskrnova. Praha-TV. Colour.

Forty-seven minute comedy TV film in which a pair of young brothers (Holy and Batik) read a magazine story, 'The Vampire in the Tower', and become convinced that their sister's boyfriend Mr

Ruzicka (Abrham) is one of the undead. At the end, the two boys start reading *The Hound of the Baskervilles*...
✦✧

VAMPIRE IN VENICE
(Orig: NOSFERATU A VENEZIA. UK/USA: aka VAMPIRES IN VENICE)
Italy, 1988. Dir: Augusto Caminito (and Klaus Kinski and Luigi Cozzi). With: Klaus Kinski, Barbara de Rossi, Yorgo Voyagis, Anne Knecht, Donald Pleasence, Christopher Plummer. Scena/Reteitalia/Vestron. Colour.
Visually striking sequel to *Nosferatu the Vampyre* (1979). Kinski returns as the weary vampire (with hair this time) to modern-day Venice to find love and death during the Carnival. Plummer plays the Van Helsing-type Catalano, who tries to destroy him. Like the original, this plods along and, with Caminito's dull direction and confusing script, it has only the evocative photography to recommend it. Kinski apparently refused to wear the vampire make-up from the earlier film and ended up directing much of the production himself. Cozzi was then brought in to try and make some sense of it all.
✦✧

VAMPIRE JOURNALS
Romania/USA, 1996 (1997). Dir: Ted Nicolaou. With: Jonathon Morris, Kirsten Cerre, David Gunn, Ilinka Goya, Dan Condurache, Starr Andreeff. Full Moon Studios. Colour.
Renegade vampire Zachary (Gunn) has spent the centuries hunting down and destroying the members of his bloodline. While pursuing evil vampire Ash (British actor Morris), a follower of Radu (from Nicolaou's *Subspecies* series), he attempts to rescue beautiful concert pianist Sofia (Cerre) from the lair of the music-loving master of the undead. This direct-to-video release features more romantic vampires in the Anne Rice/Goth tradition. Executive produced by Charles Band.
Sequel: SUBSPECIES 4 BLOODSTORM (qv; 1998)
✦✦

VAMPIRE KIDS
(Orig: JIANG SHI FU XING ZI)
Hong Kong, 1991. With: Amy Yip (Yip Chi-May). High Grow Films/World Video. Colour.
Horror comedy in which a group of survivors shipwrecked on a desert island encounter hopping vampire children who collect blood for their leader in a cave.
✦✧

VAMPIRE KILLERS
Hong Kong, circa 1980s. Hong Kong Man Wah Film Company/World Video. Colour.
Softcore horror/sex film about Lisa, a ghostly vampire who sucks blood from her lover's neck and cries tears of blood.
✦✧

VAMPIRE KNIGHTS
USA, 1987. Dir: Daniel M. Peterson. With: Ken Abraham, Billy Frank, Daniel M. Peterson, Robin Rochelle, Thomas Kingsley, Ann Michaels. Mezcal Films/Filmtrust. Colour.
Yet another low-budget vampire comedy. Tazar, Zanetet and Elissa are a trio of beautiful vampire women in modern Transylvania who are hunted by a TV horror host (director Peterson) and the single member (Abraham) of his club, the Vampire Knights, committed to the destruction of the undead.
✦

VAMPIRE KUNG-FU
Hong Kong, 1972. Dir: Li Fai-Mon. Colour.
Martial arts meets the undead.
✦

VAMPIRELLA
USA, 1996. Dir: Jim Wynorski. With: Talisa Soto, Roger Daltrey, Richard Joseph Paul, Lee de Broux, Robert Clotworthy, Brian Bloom. Sunset Films International/Concorde/New Horizons/Showtime. Colour.
First announced by Hammer Films in 1975 as a project to star Barbara Leigh, Peter Cushing and Sir John Gielgud, this low-budget cable TV movie stars a mis-cast Soto as Forrest J Ackerman's eponymous comic book character. She pursues four renegade vampires, including Daltrey's ludicrous Vlad (Dracula), from her own world Drakulon to Earth where, thirty centuries later, she meets teenager Forry (David B. Katz) and teams up with an elite army of vampire-hunters led by Adam Van Helsing (Paul). With cameos by Angus Scrimm (Lawrence Rory Guy) as the High Elder of Drakulon and John Landis as an astronaut. Many of the crew names appear to be fake. Mark Patrick Carducci and Ackerman (whose cameo appearance was cut) were co-associate producers, and Roger Corman was executive producer.
✦✧

THE VAMPIRE LOVERS
UK, 1970. Dir: Roy Ward Baker. With: Ingrid Pitt, George Cole, Kate O'Mara, Peter Cushing, Ferdy (Ferdinand) Mayne, Douglas Wilmer, Dawn Addams. Hammer Films/American International. Colour.
The first of three Hammer films based on J. Sheridan Le Fanu's 1871 novella 'Carmilla'. Tudor Gates' screenplay remains fairly faithful to the original story, but with greater emphasis on vampire Carmilla/Mircalla/Marcilla's lesbian seductions. However, Polish-born Pitt looks too old for the role. When the household of Roger Morton (Cole) begin to succumb to Carmilla's advances, only General Spielsdorf and Baron Hartog (veterans Cushing and Wilmer) realise that decapitation will destroy the undead. This had a higher budget than most Hammer vampire films, reflected in the excellent production values. With Madeline Smith, Jon Finch, Pippa Steele, Kirsten Betts and John Forbes Robertson.
Sequel: LUST FOR A VAMPIRE (qv; 1970)
Remake: THE BLOOD SPATTERED BRIDE (qv; 1972)
✦✦✧

VAMPIRE LOVERS
USA, 1997. Dir: Geoffrey de Valois. With: Elaine Juliette Williamson, Kim Blair, Mihaella Stoicova. Digital Entertainment Group/Salt City Home Video. Colour.
Another in the series of softcore *Vampire Raw Footage* videos of various lengths that include behind-the-scenes nude and erotic sequences. This tape apparently features an orgy of lesbian vampires.
✦

VAMPIRE LUST
USA, circa 1970s. Dir: Vladimir. With: John Leslie, Alexandra, Luda Diva. Pacific Coast/Roger Wald. Colour.
More hardcore vampires, scripted by 'Al Hazrad'!
✦

VAMPIRE NIGHT
USA, 1999. Dir: Jason Robert Stephens. With: Jimmy Jerman, Heather Metcalfe, Robert Ryan, Les Sekely, Kat Facchino. Unknown Productions. Colour.
Low-budget vampire movie filmed in Los Angeles by writer/producer/director/editor Stephens.
✦✧

THE VAMPIRE OF THE DESERT
USA, 1913. With: Helen Gardner, Flora Finch, Tefft Johnson. Vitagraph. B&W.
Silent film based on the poem 'The Vampire' by Rudyard Kipling, about a vamp who uses her hypnotic power.
✦

THE VAMPIRE OF THE OPERA
(Orig: IL MOSTRO DELL'OPERA/IL VAMPIRO DELL'OPERA)
Italy, 1964. Dir: Renato Polselli. With: Mac Maryan (Marco Mariani), Vittoria Prada, Barbara Howard, John McDouglas (Giuseppe Addobbati), Albert Archett (Alberto Archetti), Carla Cavalli. Produzione NIF/Nord Industrial Film. B&W.

Director Polselli started filming *Il Vampiro dell'Opera* the year after he completed *The Vampire and the Ballerina* (1960). This low-budget Italian sexploitation movie was finally finished in 1964 and released as *Il Mostro dell'Opera*. Loosely based on Gaston Leroux's novel, ravenous vampire Stefano (McDouglas) preys on a troupe of ballet dancers who are rehearsing in an old opera house. He falls in love with the star of the show (Prada), who is the reincarnation of the countess who cursed him a century before.
✦✧

VAMPIRE ON BIKINI BEACH

USA, 1987 (1988). Dir: Jerry Brady. With: Jennifer Badham, Todd Kaufmann, Stephen Mathews, Nancy Rogers, Amanda Hughes, Jennifer Jostyn. Richard A. Jones/Beacon Films. Colour.

This low-budget, direct-to-video release was filmed under the title *Vampire at Death Beach*. Very old vampire Falto (Mariusz Olbrychowski) is searching for an undead bride, while his monstrous assistant Demos (Michael Hao) attempts to revive an army of ghouls. In the end, they are defeated by Gnordron (Robert Ankers), High Priest of the Undead.
✦

VAMPIRE ORGASMS

USA, 1997. Dir: Geoffrey de Valois. With: Jasmine Jean, Joan A. Teeter, Kathy Arianoff, Shyler. Digital Entertainment Group/Salt City Home Video. Colour.

This tape in the *Vampire Raw Footage* video series apparently features exactly what the title says!
✦

VAMPIRE PARTNER

Hong Kong, 1987. Dir: Peter Chan. Sheng Hong Film/Golden Harvest/Rainbow Video. Colour.

Horror comedy about a pair of vampires who become involved with gangsters.
✦

VAMPIRE PHOTO SHOOT

USA, 1997. Dir: Geoffrey de Valois. With: Jasmine Jean, Elaine Juliette Williamson, Kim Blair, Doria Rone, Alexandre Scully. Digital Entertainment Group. Colour.

More behind-the-scenes softcore clips in the *Vampire Raw Footage* video series. A group of Vampire Centrefolds pose nude outdoors for the camera.
✦

VAMPIRE PRINCESS MIYU

(Orig: KYÛKETSUKI MIYU)

Japan, 1988-89 (1992). Dir: Toshihiro Hirano and Eri Tsukamoto. Voices: Anne Marie Zola, Louise Thompson, Spacey Jefferson, Ian MacKinnon, Laura Davis. Soeishinsha/Pony Canyon/AnimEigo/Manga Entertainment. Colour.

Anime series which consists of four half-hour episodes (American/British titles are 'Unearthly Kyoto'/'Capital of Mystery', 'A Banquet of Marionettes'/'Puppet Festival', 'Brittle Armor'/'Fragile Armour' and 'Frozen Time'). Female medium Himiko (Thompson) suspects that the child-like Miyu (Zola) and her mysterious cowled companion Laba (MacKinnon) are responsible for a series of vampire attacks in modern-day Kyoto. Together they oppose the diabolical forces of the sleep demon Raen, battle the demon-god Ranka (Jefferson) who turns her victims into dolls, rescue Laba from the Abyss, and discover something about each of their own origins. The original Japanese voices include Naoko Watanabe, Koyama Mami, Kobayashi Kiyoko, Toriumi Katsumi, Nakamura Hidetoshi and Matsuoka Yooka. The English language version is directed by Michael House.
✦✦

Ingrid Pitt and Madeline Smith as The Vampire Lovers *(1970).*

VAMPIRE RAIDERS — NINJA QUEEN

USA, 1989. Dir: Bruce Lambert. With: Agnes Chan, Chris Petersen. Trans-World Entertainment. Colour.

White ninjas versus black ninjas who are trying to take over the hotel business.
✦

VAMPIRE RETURNS

Hong Kong, 1993. Colour.

TV series (twenty-six episodes) in which a young policeman must defeat a female demon who leads an army of hopping vampires.
✦✧

LES VAMPIRES

(UK/USA: aka VAMPIRES, THE ARCH CRIMINALS OF PARIS)

France, 1915-16. Dir: Louis Feuillade. With: Juliet Musidora, Edouard Mathé, Florense Simoni, Marcel Levesque, Jean Aymé, Jacques Hermann. Gaumont Studios. Tinted.

Ten-part, seven hour silent serial about a secret society of supercriminals. Crusading reporter Philippe Guèrande (Mathé) and his bumbling friend Oscar-Cloud Mazamette (Levesque) set out to destroy the eponymous organisation led by master of disguise Le Grand Vampire (Aymé) and Satanas (Louis Leubas). Chapter titles include 'The Ghost', 'The Dead Man's Escape' and 'The Poison Man', and they involve hypnotism, a fake psychic, a severed head, poisoned paper, revived corpses and an electric cannon attack on Paris. Musidora's anti-heroine is named Irma Vep (an anagram of 'vampire'). Olivier Assayas' *Irma Vep* (1996) is about a director's attempt to remake the serial exactly as Feuillade made it, with Maggie Cheung in the title role.
✦✦

LES VAMPIRES

France, 1947. Dir: Henri Gruault. With: Boris Vian.

Short film with vampires.
✦

VAMPIRES

(aka ABADON/FRIGHT HOUSE)

USA, 1988. Dir: Len Anthony. With: Duane Jones, Orly Benyair, Kit Jones, Jackie Harmon, John Bly, Robin Michaels. Len Anthony Studios. Colour.

Okay, pay attention because this is going to be confusing. Originally released in 1988, this stars Duane Jones (from *Night of the Living Dead* [1968] and *Ganja & Hess* [1973], etc) as Dr Charles Harmon in a muddled occult chiller about a machine that drains the youth from students and keeps its female owner Madeline Abadon (Kit Jones) immortal. An abbreviated version of this film then turned up in *Fright House* (1989), also produced and directed by Anthony, which has Al Lewis (Grandpa from TV's *The Munsters* [1964-66], etc) investigating mysterious suicides in an old house on campus. You probably won't care.
✦

VAMPIRES

(aka JOHN CARPENTER'S VAMPIRES)

USA/Mexico, 1998. Dir: John Carpenter. With: James Woods, Daniel Baldwin, Sheryl Lee, Thomas Ian Griffith, Maximilian Schell, Tim Guinee. Largo Entertainment/ Storm King/Columbia Pictures. Colour.

Based on John Steakley's 1990 novel *Vampire$*, this is one of Carpenter's worst movies, thanks to a dumb script (Don Jakoby), laughable performances, unconvincing special effects and the obvious low budget. Jack Crow (another out-of-control performance from Woods) leads a crack team of mercenary vampire hunters on the payroll of the Roman Catholic Church. When most of his group are killed in a surprise attack by the undead, Jack and his surviving sidekick Tony Montoya (an unconvincing Baldwin) team up with young priest Father Adam Guiteau (Guinee) and Katarina (Lee, who is totally wasted as a hooker who has been bitten and is transforming), to destroy 600 year-old master vampire Valek (Griffith) before the latter can lay claim to a fourteenth century cross that will enable him

and his bloodsucking followers to survive in sunlight. Despite his obvious attempt to emulate Sergio Leone's 'spaghetti Westerns', Carpenter's film is overlong and lacks any style. It premièred in France. With Cary-Hiroyuki Tagawa.
✦✧

VAMPIRES ALWAYS RING TWICE
USA, 1990. Dir: Steve J. Postal. With: Alan Ramey, Jennifer Tuck, Angela Shepard, Charlotte Leslie, Daisy Meeker, Maurice Postal. Steve Postal Productions/Cinevue. Colour.
Fourth in the low-budget horror comedy series from Florida *auteur* Postal who edited, photographed, directed, co-executive produced and co-scripted! When her husband Don is seduced by a pair of vampires, his wife Helen and her loony friend Regina get into trouble in the haunted honeymoon cottage belonging to monster landlord B.J. Smith (Maurice Postal).
Sequel: QUEEN VICTORIA AND THE ZOMBIES (qv; 1991)
✦

VAMPIRES AND OTHER STEREOTYPES
(aka HELL'S BELLES)
USA, 1992. Dir: Kevin J. Lindenmuth. With: William White, Ed Hubbard, Wendy Bednarz, Rick Poli, Anna DiPace, Mick McCleery. Brimstone Productions/Screen Edge/EI Independent Cinema. Colour.
Low-budget, independent video shot in two weeks by writer/director/producer/editor Lindenmuth. Three girls (Bednarz, DiPace and Suzanne Scott) looking for a late-night party in New York find themselves trapped with a pair of 150 year-old vampires (White and Hubbard) in Hell, where they encounter demons, a talking severed hand, zombie heads, a giant rat, and even monstrous versions of Elvis and Jim Morrison, as they attempt to survive until daylight. With the voice of critic J.B. Macabre (Joe Mauceri).
✦✧

VAMPIRESAS 1930
(aka CERTAINS L'AIMENT NOIRE)
Spain/France, 1960. Dir: Jesús Franco. With: Mikaela (Mikaela Wood), Antonio Ozores, Lina Morgan, Yves Massard, Antonio Garisa, Juan Riqueime. Hispamer/Cifesa/Eurociné. Colour.
Filmed under the title *Volando Hacia la Fama*, this early musical comedy from Franco is basically a Spanish reworking of *Singin' in the Rain* (1952), set in France during the silent era. The opening sequence takes place in Paris during the making of a sequel to Louis Feuillade's *Les Vampires* (1915-16), and Mikaela stars as a 1920s movie vamp.
✦✧

THE VAMPIRE'S BITE
USA, 1972.
Hardcore vampire movie.
✦

VAMPIRE'S BREAKFAST
(Orig: LING CHEN WAN CAN)
Hong Kong, 1986 (1987). Dir: Wong Chung. With: Kent Cheng, Emily Chu, Wong Pak-Man, Ng Ma-Wu (Wo Ma/Wu Ma/Yuen Wah). Dennis Yu/Cinema City/Rainbow Video. Colour.
Horror comedy in which Hong Kong newspaper reporter Fat Piao (Cheng) investigates a series of brutal murders and discovers that a super-strong vampire is responsible. In the end, he drives a mahogany nail into the back of the undead killer.
✦

THE VAMPIRE'S COFFIN
(Orig: EL ATAUD VAMPIRO)
Mexico, 1957 (1964). Dir: Fernando Méndez. With: Abel Salazar, Ariadne Welter, Germán Robles, Yerye Beirute, Alicia Montoya (Carmen Montejo), Carlos Ancira. Cinematográfica ABSA/Young America Productions. B&W.
Director Méndez made this sequel to his own *The Vampire* (1957) just six months after the original, using the same cast and crew. Robles (dubbed by Matt King) returns as the suave Count Karol de Lavud when the stake piercing his heart is removed by a body snatcher. It's then up to producer/hero/comedy relief Salazar as Dr Enrique to hunt the vampire down to his waxworks lair, finally spearing the Count while he is transformed into a bat. Much of the plot is chaotic, but Robles makes an impressive vampire and the scenes of Lavud's shadow(!) stalking a victim through the night-time streets are heightened by imaginative lighting effects. The English-language version, produced by K. (Kenneth) Gordon Murray and directed by Paul Nagel (who also dubbed Salazar's role), was released in 'Hypnoscope'.
✦✦✧

THE VAMPIRE'S CURSE
USA, 1998. Dir: Gary Whitson. With: Tina Krause, Michelle Caporaletti, Dean Paul Fragola, Laura Giglio, Kassie Karr, Dawn Murphy. WAVE Productions/Salt City Home Video. Colour.
Amateurish independent video from New Jersey, written, produced, edited and directed by Whitson. In the linking sequence, the talentless Krause (who talks incessantly to herself and gets naked in every scene she's in) plays Chris, a young woman who ignores a warning not to read two stories from a old book in a single sitting. In the first tale, a gypsy girl (Murphy) puts a curse on the soldier (Fragola) who murdered then raped her sister (Giglio) and the wife (Karr) who lied to protect him. This also includes a green-skinned zombie. The second story involves two female explorers (Murphy and Caporaletti) and their guide (G.W. Lawrence) who discover more than they expected while searching for a legendary treasure in the tomb of vampire Vlad the Impaler. In the end, the ancient tome transforms its reader into one of the undead.
✦

VAMPIRES D'ALFAMA
France, 1963. Dir: Pierre Kast.
Short cartoon film.
✦

VAMPIRE'S EMBRACE
USA, 1991 (1993). Dir: Glenn Andreiev. With: Paul Borgese, Sarah Watchman, Edna Boyle, Mimi Stuart. NJF Productions/Panorama Entertainment/EI Independent Cinema. Colour.
Two vampire sisters return from the dead after one hundred years. The undead Angela is ruled by the good spirit of her past life, but when she meets a man (Borgese) at a horror movie in New York, her evil sibling attempts to wreck the growing love affair. Low-budget thrills from Westport, Long Island, co-produced, written and directed by Andreiev.
✦

VAMPIRE SETTLE ON POLICE-CAMP
Hong Kong, 1990 (1991). Dir: Chan Chi-Wah (Lo Wei-Lang). With: Eddie Ko (Kou Sheng), Sandra Ng, Kong Yan Yin, Billy Lau, Anglie Leung. World Power Film/Top Sun Film/D&B Films Distribution/World Video. Colour.
Behind the unwieldy title is another horror comedy, inspired by the popular *Haunted Cop Shop* series. A young vampire-like ghost torments Inspector Chan because of who he was in a former life. Meanwhile, a group of teenagers, studying to join the police force, save the day when they are attacked by vampires.
✦✧

VAMPIRE SEX & DEATH
USA, 1997. Dir: Geoffrey de Valois. With: Heather LeMire, Kathy Arianoff, Leslie Hunt. Digital Entertainment Group/Salt City Home Video. Colour.
Another in the behind-the-scenes series of *Vampire Raw Footage* videos. This one involves *The Vampire Conspiracy* (1995) star LeMire and Arianoff as an alien vampire.
✦

VAMPIRES FROM OUTER SPACE
USA, 1990. Dir: Steve J. Postal. With: Alan Ramey, Jennifer Tuck, Angela Shepard, Maurice Postal. Steve Postal Productions/Cinevue. Colour.

Third in the low-budget horror comedy series from Florida *auteur* Postal who photographed, directed, co-executive produced and co-scripted! British professor Bob Spencer (Ramey) marries Tanya (Shepard), a vampire from outer space. When they honeymoon at the haunted cottage belonging to monster-landlord B.J. Smith (Maurice Postal), they are disturbed by extra-terrestrial vampires from the planet Sirius II, situated 8.7 light years from Earth.
Sequel: VAMPIRES ALWAYS RING TWICE (qv; 1990)
✦

THE VAMPIRE'S GHOST

USA, 1945. Dir: Lesley Selander. With: John Abbott, Charles Gordon, Peggy Stewart, Grant Withers, Adele Mara, Emmett Vogam. Republic. B&W.
Surprisingly faithful reinterpretation of John Polidori's tale 'The Vampyre', co-scripted by science fiction writer Leigh Brackett and based on her original story. English character actor Abbott plays Webb Fallon, an unlikely looking 400 year-old vampire posing as a nightclub owner on the west coast of Africa. When Julie Vance (Stewart) discovers his real identity, he tries to burn her to death at the stake. Even with a running time of just under an hour, director Selander (better known for his 'B' movie Westerns) struggles to make it interesting.
✦✦✧

THE VAMPIRE SHOWS HIS TEETH

Taiwan, 1986. Silver Bird Films/Sunny Video. Colour.
Period horror comedy involving hopping vampires and a woman on a bicycle who turns out to be a flying ghost. This TV mini-series has also been released on video as a single movie.
Sequel: THE VAMPIRE SHOWS HIS TEETH II (qv; circa 1986)
✦✧

THE VAMPIRE SHOWS HIS TEETH III

Taiwan, 1986. Silver Bird Films/Sunny Video. Colour.
In the conclusion to this series, the ghost woman returns and a needle through the top of his skull stops an apparently invulnerable vampire.

THE VAMPIRE SHOWS HIS TEETH II

Taiwan, 1986. Silver Bird Films/Sunny Video. Colour.
In this sequel, a flying vampire captures the ghost woman on a bicycle and a wizard leads a regiment of hopping vampires.
Sequel: THE VAMPIRE SHOWS HIS TEETH III (qv; 1986)
✦✧

VAMPIRES IN THE CLOSET

USA, 1990. Dir: Steve J. Postal. With: Laurie Gregg, Angela Shepard, Dawn Chappel, Maurice Postal. Steve Postal Productions. Colour.
Low-budget horror comedy from Florida *auteur* Postal who edited, photographed, directed, co-executive produced, co-scripted and co-wrote the original book! When two sisters (Gregg and Shepard) hire a honeymoon cottage to write their horror stories in, a seance raises a female vampire (Chappel). This is the first in a regional series featuring Maurice Postal as monster-landlord B.J. Smith.
Sequel: EVIL SPIRITS IN THE HOUSE (qv; 1990)
✦

VAMPIRE'S KISS

USA, 1988 (1989). Dir: Robert Bierman. With: Nicolas Cage, Maria Conchita Alonso, Jennifer Beals, Kasi Lemmons, Bob Lujan, Elizabeth Ashley. Magellan Pictures/Hemdale. Colour.
A typically bizarre performance by Cage as Peter Loew, a yuppie literary agent who believes that he has been bitten by sexy vampire Rachel (Beals) while making love. After watching a clip from *Nosferatu* (1922) on TV he becomes a different person, shunning the sunlight, fearing the cross and eating beetles until, wearing plastic fangs and impersonating Max Schreck, he begins attacking women. This doesn't make a whole lot of sense. See George Romero's *Martin* (1976) instead.
✦✧

Two surprise guests at The Vampire's Night Orgy *(1972).*

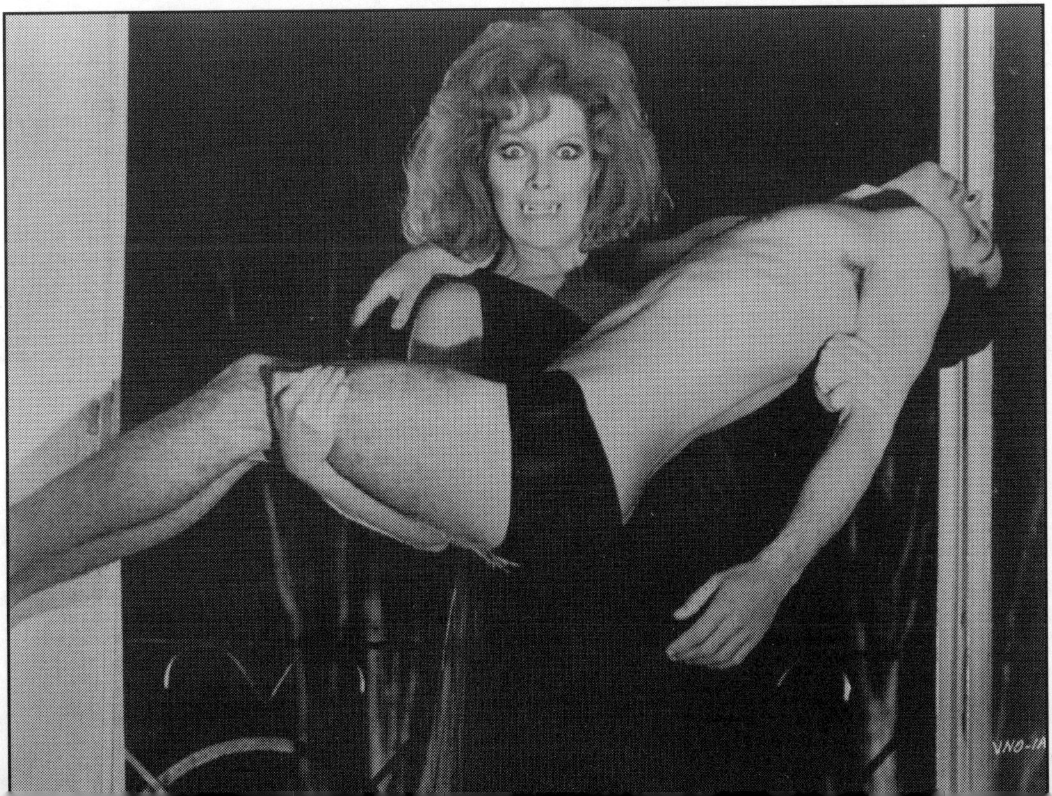

VAMPIRE'S KISS
USA, 1993. Dir: Scotty Fox. With: Nikki Dial, Jonathon Morgan, Lacy Rose, Alex Jordan, Rebecca Wild, Chaz Vincent. Oasis Productions/AVICA Entertainment. Colour.
In this hardcore feature, vampire author Anna Price (Dial), based on you-know-who, has sex at a costume party with a mysterious stranger (Morgan) who turns out to be one of the undead. Now a vampire herself, she hires a private detective (Steve Drake) to hunt down the handsome bloodsucker. In the end, the two lovers turn into bats and fly away together.
✦

VAMPIRES LIVE AGAIN
Hong Kong, 1987 (1988). Dir: Kam-Yoo Tu. With: Bok Yuen, Loretta Ying. Ocean Shores Video. Colour.
Shot-on-video story about mother and father vampires who attack humans and animals when their coffins are unearthed, and their undead little boy who plays with other children in the woods. In the end, the two adult vampires are destroyed and their offspring re-buried.
✦

THE VAMPIRE'S MILK
USA, 1997. Dir: Geoffrey de Valois. With: Jamine Jean, Anastasia Alexander. Digital Entertainment Group/Salt City Home Video. Colour.
One of a series of softcore *Vampire Raw Footage* videos of various running times that include behind-the-scenes nude and erotic sequences. Jean, the 1997 Vampire Centerfold of the Year, auditions nude in the studio, is tied to a stake at a ruined castle and stars in the eponymous fetish scenes. With Alexander as the Vampire Priestess.
✦

THE VAMPIRE'S NIGHT ORGY
(Orig: EXTRANO AMOR DE LOS VAMPIROS/LA NOCHE DE LOS VAMPIROS/LA ORGIA NOCTURNA DE LOS VAMPIROS/LOS VAMPIROS TAMBIEN DUERMEN. USA: aka ORGY OF THE VAMPIRES)
Spain, 1972 (1973). Dir: León Klimovsky. With: Dianik Zurakowska, Jack Taylor (George Brown Randall/Grek Martin), Charo Soriano, John Richard, Helga Liné (Helga Lina Stern), Manuel de Blas. Atlantida Films/ International Amusement. Colour.
When their mini-bus breaks down, a group of six tourists spend the night in the Transylvanian town of Tonia. They soon discover that it is populated entirely by flesh-eating vampires with long fangs.
✦✦

THE VAMPIRE'S RAPE
(Orig: LA REINE DES VAMPIRES/LE VIOL DU VAMPIRE. USA: QUEEN OF THE VAMPIRES)
France, 1967 (1968). Dir: Jean Rollin. With: Solange Pradel, Bernard Letrou, Ursule Pauly, Nicole Romain, Catherine Deville, Jacqueline Sieger. Les Films ABC/Sam Selsky. B&W.
Originally made as a thirty minute short to pad out the belated release of *Dead Men Walk* (1943) in France, then expanded to feature length with a second part, Rollin's first major film is about two crazy blood-drinking sisters who think they are cursed by a sword-wielding vampire. This amateurish blend of arty imagery, narrative incoherence and mild eroticism set the tone for many of the director's later movies. Although highly admired by some critics, Rollin's work only occasionally rises to the lyrical heights he so obviously aims for. With a brief appearance by comic-strip artist Druillet.
✦

THE VAMPIRE'S ROPE
Commonwealth of Independent States, 1992. Dir: Nikolai Gibu. The Nord Company. Colour.
Obscure Russian vampire movie, scripted by Clara Luchko and Zinaida Chirkova.
✦

THE VAMPIRE'S SEDUCTION
USA, 1998. Dir: John Bacchus. With: Tina Krause, Paige Turner, Kiki Michaels, John Paul Fedele, Zachary W. Snygg, Debbie Rochon. Brain Escape Pictures/EI Independent Cinema. Colour.
Krause stars as Dracula's lesbian vampire daughter, who hypnotises Wally, a descendant of Van Helsing, to become her mindless servant and bring her the women she needs to satisfy her erotic bloodlust. After spying on a number of lesbian encounters, Wally is visited by the ghost of his great-great grandfather and the vampire eats a garlic salt sandwich and dies. With a cameo by Rochon.
✦

VAMPIRES STRIKE BACK
(USA: aka HEY GHOST! II/VAMPIRES)
Hong Kong, 1988. Dir: Kam Yoo-Tu. With: Bok Yuen, Cheung Yu, Amy Yip (Yip Chi-May). World Video. Colour.
Unfunny TV horror comedy about the friendship between a little girl and a hopping vampire boy. The boy's putrefying undead father escapes from his coffin and burns people with his hands.
✦

THE VAMPIRE'S THRILL
(Orig: LE FRISSON DES VAMPIRES. UK: SEX AND THE VAMPIRE/SHIVER OF THE VAMPIRES. USA: aka THRILL OF THE VAMPIRE)
France, 1970. Dir: Jean Rollin. With: Sandra Julien, Jean-Marie Durand, Jacques Robiolles, Michèl Delahaye, Marie-Pierre, Dominique. Les Films Modernes/Les Films ABC. Colour.
One of Rollin's more imaginative films, with some moments of striking imagery. Honeymooning couple Ise (Julien) and Antoine (Durand) decide to stay in an old castle where the new bride is seduced by beautiful vampire Isolde (Dominique) and other members of the undead household. Some of the most memorable sequences include the female vampire emerging from a grandfather clock on the stroke of midnight and Antoine being attacked by a room full of books. Additional erotic footage found in the American print was shot by Rollin and an uncredited production associate. Rollin was supposed to direct Sandra Julien again in a follow-up movie entitled *Docteur Vampire*, but the producer died before production could begin.
✦✦

VAMPIRE STRANGLER
USA, 1999. With: Bill Hellfire, Misty Mundae. WAVE Productions/Video Outlaw/EI Independent Cinema. Colour.
Independent video release in which a voodoo priest turns a young couple (Hellfire and Mundae) into sexy bloodsuckers.
✦

VAMPIRE TIME TRAVELERS
USA, 1998. Dir: Les Sekely. With: J.J. Rodgers, Jillien Weisz, Lynne Baker, Jimmy Jerman, Ali Elk, Kat Facchino. Scarborough Films/Cinematrix Releasing. Colour.
Written and directed by Sekely, this independent shot-on-video production is subtitled *Bite Her in the Butt!* on publicity material. Sue Anne (Rodgers) and her three friends become involved with time travel, psycho-nerds, flesh-eating blobs, a sadistic sorority leader and a vengeful vampire in their attempts to get into the Alpha Omega Sorority.
✦

VAMPIRE TRAILER PARK
USA, 1991. Dir: Steve Latshaw. With: Robert Shurtz, Cathy Moran, Patrick Moran, Blake Pickett, Bentley Little, Michael Street. Cinemondo. Colour.
Low-budget vampire comedy filmed in Florida. An undead eighteenth century plantation owner (scriptwriter Patrick Moran) and his creepy Aunt Hattie move into a trailer park and invite guests over for dinner. Unfortunately, the bulimic vampire spends most of his time vomiting up blood after every meal. Meanwhile, a drunken private eye (Shurtz) and an epileptic psychic (Cathy Moran) cruise the topless bars looking for the vampire who drained her grandmother.
✦

VAMPIRE VIXENS FROM VENUS

USA, 1994. Dir: Ted A. Bohus. With: Leon Head, Theresa Lynn, J.J. North, Leslie Glass, John Knox, Michelle Bauer (Michelle McClellan). Austin/Filmline/4-Front Video. Colour.

Low-budget direct-to-video comedy filmed in New Jersey. A trio of ugly, tentacled drug-smuggling aliens (special make-up effects created by Vincent Guastini) arrive on Earth and transform into beautiful women (Lynn, North and *Penthouse* Pet Glass) who drain men of their life essence when they are sexually aroused. With Charlie Callas and Fred Olen Ray. Producer Daniel Provenzano, a New Jersey businessman and the nephew of Mafia boss Anthony (Tony Pro) Provenzano, was indicted by a state grand jury in 1999 for racketeering and charged with heading an organised crime ring.

✦

VAMPIRE VS. SORCERER

Hong Kong, 1988. World Video. Colour.

Horror comedy about a sorcerer who raises a horde of vampires from beneath the ground. In the end, the undead turn on the wizard.

✦

VAMPIRE WARS

Japan, 1991 (1998). Dir: Kazuhisa Takenouchi and Yukio Katayama. Voices: Roger May, Alan Blyton, Johnathan Keeble, Lesley Rooney, Julia Brahms, Frank Rozelaar Green. Yasuaki/Kadota/Toei Video/Promise/Manga Entertainment. Colour.

Hour-long adult anime based on an original story by Katsuyoshi Kasai (published by Kadaokawa Shoten). Set in a near-future Paris, ex-KGB agent Kousaburo Kuki (aka 'Bat') is recruited by the Western Intelligence Network Group (WING) to investigate a CIA project code named 'D' (for 'Dracula'). He soon finds himself involved with young female film star Lamia Vindaw (whose rare blood type contains alien DNA), a group of vampire terrorists and an interplanetary war. The English-language version was directed by John Wolskel.

✦✦✧

THE VAMPIRE WEDDING

(Orig: SVATBA UPÍRÙ)

Czech Republic, 1993. Dir: Jaroslav Soukup. With: Rudolf Hrusínsky III, Jiri Bratoská. JS Film/Servex Pilsen/Ceska Pojistovna Production Company. Colour.

An Englishman meets a vampire in eighteenth century Prague.

✦✧

VAMPIRE WOMAN

(Orig: XI XUEFU)

Hong Kong, 1962. Dir: Li Tie. With: Bak Yin (Bai Yang), Cheng Wo-Yau (Zhang Huo-You), Wong Manlee (Huang Manli), Rong Xiaoyi, Keung Chung-Ping (Jiang Zhong-Ping). Zhong Lian. B&W.

Family melodrama with horror overtones. When a woman (Yin) is seen sucking the blood of her baby, she is accused of vampirism and punished by being buried alive. It turns out that the child had been poisoned by an evil servant (Chung-Ping) and she was trying to save it.

✦

VAMPIRISME

France, 1967. Dir: Patrice Duvic and Bernard Chaouat. With: Michel Beaune, Guy Mineur, Jean-Pierre Bouyxou, Alain Le Bris, Bernard Chaouat, Bernard Tretton. Films du Cosmos. B&W.

Twelve minute comedy short showing vampires going about their daily business: drinking blood, a baby vampire sucking its mother's blood, advertising for vampires, etc.

✦

EL VAMPIRO AECHECHA

Mexico, 1962. With: Germán Robles, Nestor Zarvade, Blanca del Prado. B&W.

The title of this apparently lost film translates as 'The Lurking Vampire'. In a dream sequence, a young boy opposes a vampire-killer who preys on small children around a creepy carousel. Based on a story by William Irish (aka Cornell Woolrich), this might actually be a 1959 Argentinian film.

✦

LA VAMPIRO NEGRO

Argentina, 1953. Dir: Román Viñoly Barreto. With: Olga Zubarry, Roberto Escalada, Nathán Pinzon, Nelly Panizza, George Rivier, Pascual Pelliciotta. Argentina Sono Film. B&W.

Hallucinatory version of Fritz Lang's *M* (1931) and the Peter Kürten case, with Pinzon as the child serial killer. The title translates as 'The Black Vampire'.

Remake: LE VAMPIRE DE DÜSSELDORF (qv; 1964)

✦

LOS VAMPIROS DE COYOACAN

Mexico, 1973. Dir: Arturo Martínez. With: Germán Robles, Mil Máscaras (Aaron Rodriguez), Sasha Montenegro, Superzán, Carlos López Moctezuma, Mario Cid. Producciones Filmicas Agrasánchez/Azteca Films. Colour.

Mexican wrestling/horror movie which marks the return of star Robles (*The Vampire* [1957], etc), this time playing a hero who, along with masked wrestlers Mil Máscaras ('Thousand Masks') and Superzán, battles Transylvanian vampire Baron Braddock, his two undead sons and a trio of fanged dwarves who have kidnapped a doctor's daughter (Montenegro) and transformed her into a hungry bloodsucker. In the end, the heroes burn the vampires' coffins, and the undead creatures fade away with the rising sun. With bald Nathaniel Leon 'Frankenstein' as a wrestling vampire.

Sequel: LA MANSION DE LAS 7 MOMIAS (qv; 1975)

✦✧

LOS VAMPIROS DEL OESTE

Mexico, 1963. Dir: Juan Oetega. With: Joaquin Cordero, Alma Fuentes, William Murray, José Elias Moreno. B&W.

A series of mysterious deaths in a small village are investigated by a government agent.

✦

¡VAMPIROS EN LA HABANA!

Cuba, 1985. Dir: Juan Padrón. With: Manuel Marín, Margarita Agüero, Frank González. Voices: Irela Bravo, Carlos González, Mirella Guillot. Icaic TV Española/Durniok Producciones. Colour.

Feature-length cartoon comedy set in 1933, when Cuba was under the tyranny of General Machado. Two rival gangs, Chicago's Capa Nostra and Europe's The Vampire Group, arrive in Havana to squabble over the formula for Vampisol, a cream invented by Dracula's son, Werner Amadeus, which enables the undead to survive in daylight. His nephew, Joseph 'Pepe' Emmanuel, is a trumpet player (dubbed by Arturo Sandoval) and part-time revolutionary who doesn't even know he's a vampire thanks to his uncle's invention. In one scene, Pepe hides in a cinema showing a tinted live-action vampire movie. This also includes Lupus, a werewolf working for Capa Nostra, who is pursued by amorous street dogs and eventually run over by a police car.

✦✦✦

VAMPIROS LESBOS

(Orig: VAMPYROS LESBOS DIE ERBIN DES DRACULA/LAS VAMPIRAS)

West Germany/Spain/Turkey, 1970. Dir: Franco Manera (Jesús Franco). With: Susann Korda (Soledad Miranda/Soledad Redon Bueno), Dennis Price, Paul Müller, Ewa Ströemberg, Heidrun Kussin, Michael Berling. TeleCine Film-Fernsehproduktion/Fénix-Film/Hispano-Allemande. Colour.

Filmed in Turkey, this combines elements of the Countess Elizabeth Bathory legend with J. Sheridan Le Fanu's 'Carmilla'. Soledad Miranda (who was killed in a car crash before this was released) plays Count Dracula's heir, exotic dancer Countess Nadine Carody, who entices lawyer Linda Westinghouse (Ströemberg) to her secluded island, where she seduces her guest and drinks her blood. The German version (released in 1971) apparently includes a great deal

more sex and violence than the version which finally appeared in Spain in 1974. With English actor Price as occult expert Dr Aldon Seeward, director Franco as Memmet, a sadistic murderer, and José Martinez Blanco playing Morpho, Nadine's servant.
Remake: MACUMBA SEXUAL (1981)
✦✧

EL VAMPIRO TEPOROCHO
Mexico, 1989. Dir: Rafael Villaseñor Kuri. With: Pedro Weber 'Chatanuga', Charly Valentino, Humberto Herrera, Gabriela Goldsmith, Rebeca Silva, Guillermo de Alvarado 'Condorito'. Galáctica Films. Colour.
'Inspirado en el personaje de Bran-Stocker' (*sic*). When three scientists remove the stake from the heart of a fat Dracula (comedian 'Chatanuga') in 'Transilvania' (*sic*), they send him into space in a test rocket and he crash-lands in Mexico. There he teams up with a trio of drunken street entertainers and is transformed into a turkey(!) when he eats hot chili. He eventually turns his nurse into a vampire as well. This is a very bizarre musical comedy. The title translates as 'The Wino Vampire'.
✦✧

VAMPIRO 2000
Italy, 1972. Dir: Riccardo Ghione. With: Nino Castelnuevo, Dominique Boschero, Lucio Dalla, Carlo de Leyo, Rada Rassimov (Sarah Bay/Rosalba Neri), Francisco Rabal. Canguro. Colour.
There is some doubt that this was ever completed or released.
✦

VAMPS DEADLY DREAMGIRLS
USA, 1996 (1997). Dir: Mark Burchett and Michael D. Fox. With: Lorissa McComas, Jennifer Huss, Paul Morris, Jenny Wallace, Charles Cooper, Stacey Sparks. B+ Productions/ EI Independent Cinema. Colour.
Independent video production about Heather (Huss), who begins working at the eponymous striptease club run by 500 year-old vampire queen Tasha (Wallace) and her undead lap dancers. When she meets old school friend Seamus McConnel (Morris), only the disillusioned priest can save her soul from the bloodsucking showgirls.
✦✧

VAMPYR
(Orig: VAMPYR OU L'ETRANGE ADVENTURE DE DAVID GRAY/VAMPIR/DER TRAUM DES ALLAN GRAY. UK: aka THE STRANGE ADVENTURES OF DAVID GRAY. USA: aka CASTLE OF DOOM/THE VAMPIRE)
France/Germany, 1931-32. Dir: Carl Theodore Dreyer. With: Julian West (Baron Nicolas de Gunzberg), Henriette Gérard, Jan Hieronimko, Rena Mandel, Sybille Schmitz, Maurice Schultz. Tobis/Klangfilm. B&W.
Danish-born Dreyer co-wrote, produced and directed this ponderous vampire mystery, loosely based on J. Sheridan Le Fanu's story 'Carmilla'. It was filmed silently in Paris in 1931 and a German soundtrack was added in Berlin the following year. Baron Nicolas de Gunzberg financed the project and, under the name of Julian West, played David Gray (Allan Gray in the German version), who arrives at a strange inn in the Carpathians. There he discovers a book about vampires, an old woman (Gérard) who is one of the undead and the evil doctor (Hieronimko) who aids her. In a dream, he watches his own funeral. Dreyer uses such camera effects as filming through gauze, double exposure and reverse photography to create a sense of unreality, but it remains often incomprehensible due to the dream-like narrative and hilariously misspelled title cards. Austrian cinematographer Rudolf (Rudolph) Maté later became a director in Hollywood (*When Worlds Collide* [1951], etc). Scenes from this film were later included in the 1943 compilation *Dr. Terror's House of Horrors*.
✦✧

THE VAMPYR — A SOAP OPERA
(USA: THE VAMPYR)
UK, 1992. Dir: Nigel Finch. With: Omar Ebrahim, Fiona O'Neill, Philip Salmon, Richard Van Allan, Willemijn Van Gent, Roberto Salvatori. BBC-TV/Arts & Entertainment Network/Virgin Classics. Colour.
Musical production in which modern-day lyrics are set to the 1828 opera by German composer Heinrich Marschner. Ripley (Ebrahim) is a 200 year-old yuppie vampire living in 1990s London. Unless he can find a trio of female victims within three days, he is condemned to eternal damnation. This features plenty of sex and blood. Narrated by Robert Stephens and produced by Janet Street-Porter. Originally shown in six half-hour episodes on TV, this is available on video in America in a feature-length version.
✦✧

VAMPYRE
USA, 1990 (1991). Dir: Bruce G. Hallenbeck. With: Randy Scott Rozler, Cathy Seyler, Jack Brent, Marilyn Semerad, Greg Boggia, John L. Gilson. Pagan Productions/Panorama Entertainment/EI Independent Cinema. Colour.
A mysterious stranger confonts a topless, leather-clad vampiress and her nubile disciples who are out to destroy the inhabitants of an eighteenth century village in this amateurish movie, written, edited, co-produced and directed by Hallenbeck. Only worth catching to see the self-styled 'King of Splatter', book author John McCarty, as a victim of the undead. Filmed under the title *Vampyr* and inspired by Carl Dreyer's 1931-32 movie, this was shot on video in New Jersey for just $20,000.
✦

VAMPYRES
(USA: BLOOD HUNGER/MIDNIGHT SLAUGHTER/SATAN'S DAUGHTERS/VAMPYRES DAUGHTERS OF DRACULA)
UK, 1974 (1976). Dir: Joseph (José Ramón) Larraz. With: Marianne Morris, Anulka, Murray Brown, Brian Deacon, Sally Faulkner, Michael Byrne. Essay/Rank Films. Colour.
Filmed in three weeks for £40,000. Despite the title, Fran (*Mayfair* pin-up Morris) and Miriam (May 1973 *Playboy* centrefold Anulka) are not really vampires but a pair of bisexual ghosts who seduce visitors to their old mansion and drink their blood. They have no fangs, can move around in daylight and don't sleep in coffins. Despite the sex and gore, director Larraz manages to reduce the plot to a lethargic exercise. When released on video in America as *Satan's Daughters*, a new title sequence included footage from Hammer's *The Vampire Lovers* (1970)!
✦✧

VAN PIRES
USA, 1997-98. Dir: John Gentile and Anthony Gentile. With: Carikayi Mutambirwa, Melissa Marsala, Marc Schwarz, Jason Hayes, Van He'll Sing. Abrams Gentile Entertainment/MSH Entertainment Corporation/The Summit Media Group/Fremantle. Colour.
Half-hour syndicated live-action/computer animation TV series (thirteen episodes), created by John and Anthony Gentile. When a mysterious meteor crashes into the Sunrise Salvage junkyard, derelict vehicles take on a life of their own, led by their evil king, Trackula. The Van Pires suck the gasoline from other cars to feed their need for speed and drain the planet of all its fuel. Only four teenagers — Snap (Mutambirwa), Reve (Marsala), Nuke (Schwarz) and Axle (Hayes), able to transform at night into the heroic Motorvators — stand between the vehicular parasites and a world sucked dry and running on empty. The Who's John Entwistle was one of the show's musical supervisors.
✦✧

DALE VAN SICKEL
[1906-1976]

American actor-stunt man who portrayed the Frankenstein Monster in a gag cameo in *Hellzapoppin'* (1941).
qv: *Zombies of the Stratosphere* (1952).

VASCO, THE VAMPIRE
USA, 1914. Independent Motion Picture Company. B&W.
A detective is hypnotised and taken to the eponymous villain's lair in this silent drama.
✦

EDWARD VAN SLOAN
[1882-1964]

American character actor of Dutch origins who often played elderly doctors and scientists. As Professor van (and von) Helsing, he confronted the Count in *Dracula* (1931) and his vampiric offspring in *Dracula's Daughter* (1936), after originating the role on Broadway. He retired in 1946.
qv: *Before I Hang* (1940); *Frankenstein* (1931, test reel); *Frankenstein* (1931); *The Mummy* (1933).

VAULT OF HORROR

(USA: aka TALES FROM THE CRYPT II)
UK, 1973. Dir: Roy Ward Baker. With: Dawn Addams, Tom Baker, Michael Craig, Denholm Elliott, Glynis Johns, Edward Judd. Amicus/Metromedia. Colour.

After the success of *Tales from the Crypt* (1972), Amicus followed it up with this second all-star anthology of horror stories adapted by producer Milton Subotsky from the EC comics of the 1950s. Unfortunately, the film aims more for laughs than chills, which ruins 'Midnight Mess', in which Rogers (Daniel Massey) murders his sister Donna (the actor's real-life sibling Anna Massey) and then stumbles upon a very special restaurant for vampires, where he ends up on the menu. The other stories involve an insufferably tidy husband ('The Neat Job'), a macabre double-cross ('Bargain in Death'), a stolen Indian rope trick ('This Trick'll Kill You') and an artist's voodoo revenge ('Drawn and Quartered'). In the framing story, five people trapped in an underground vault recount their recurring dreams to each other while waiting for the elevator to be repaired. Of course, as usual it turns out that they are already dead. With Curt Jurgens, Terry-Thomas, Arthur Mullard, Mike Pratt and John Forbes-Robertson. Bantam Books published a novelisation by Jack Oleck in 1972. A third Amicus anthology based on EC comics, *Tales of the Incredible*, was announced in 1973 as a 3-D project but never made.
✦✧

VEERANA

India, 1985 (1988). Dir: Tulsi Ramsay and Shyam Ramsay. With: Jasmin, H. Birje, Satish Shah, Sahila Chadha, Kulbushan. Sai Om Productions/Shiva. Colour.

Veerana (Jasmin) is a young girl who is possessed by the spirit of a dead witch. When her bat necklace is removed, she is forced to seduce men and then suck their blood after having sex with them. In the end, she is captured by torch-wielding villagers who seal her up in a coffin. The comedy relief is supplied by Shah as a horror film director obsessed with Alfred Hitchcock. The Hindi title translates as 'Loneliness'.
✦✦

VEGGIE TALES: TALES FROM THE CRISPER

USA, 1993. Dir: Phil Vischer. Voices: Dan Anderson, Gail Freeman, Michael Nawrocki, Lisa Vischer, Phil Vischer. Big Idea Productions/Lyrick Studios. Colour.

Eleven minute children's cartoon from a Chicago-based Christian organisation. After five year-old Junior Asparagus watches a black and white Frankencelery movie on TV, he is too afraid to sleep. So Archibald Asparagus and Larry the Cucumber teach him a lesson by singing the song 'God is Bigger' (than the boogeyman), which helps when the bolt-necked vegetable appears in Junior's bedroom. This cartoon and another, 'Daniel and the Lion's Den', are both available on the 1998 video compilation *Veggie Tales: Where's God When I'm S-Scared?*
✦✧

THE VELVET VAMPIRE

(UK: aka THE WAKING HOUR)
USA, 1971. Dir: Stephanie Rothman. With: Michael Blodgett, Sherry Miles, Celeste Yarnall, Paul Prokop, Gene Shane, Bob (Robert) Tessier. New World Pictures. Colour.

From the co-director of *Blood Bath* (1966) comes this slow-moving vampire movie, filmed under the title *Through the Looking Glass* for just $165,000. Yarnall stars as centuries-old Diane LeFanu, who moves around in sunlight and sleeps with her dead husband in his coffin. She invites young married couple Lee and Susan Ritter (Blodgett and Miles) to her home in the Mojave desert and seduces them both, until she is finally destroyed by hippies with crosses in downtown Los Angeles. This was not released in Britain until 1984.
✦✧

THE VENETIAN AFFAIR

USA/Italy, 1966 (1967). Dir: Jerry Thorpe. With: Robert Vaughn, Elke Sommer, Felicia Farr, Karl Boehm (Boëm), Boris Karloff, Roger C. Carmel. Metro-Goldwyn-Mayer/ Jerry Thorpe Productions. Colour.

Complex sci-spy thriller based upon the novel by Helen MacInnes. At the height of his popularity in TV's *The Man from U.N.C.L.E.* (1964-68), Vaughn stars as alcoholic news reporter and ex-CIA agent Bill Fenner, who is sent to Venice to investigate the killing of a group of world leaders at a conference. He soon becomes involved in the deadly hunt for a secret report and a plot by the ruthless Robert Wahl (Boehm, from *Peeping Tom* [1960], etc) to use mind-control drugs to create invulnerable robotic assassins, including Karloff's political scientist Dr Pierre Vaugiroud. Several major characters are surprisingly killed off. With Edward Asner and Luciana Paluzzi.
✦✦✧

LA VENGANZA DE HURACÁN RAMÍREZ

Mexico, 1967. Dir: Josélito Rodríguez. With: Pepe Romay, Titina Romay, David Silva (Daniel Garcia), Carmelita Gonzalez, Jean Safont, Fredy Fernandez 'Pichi'. Cinematográfica Roma. Colour.

Masked wrestling hero Huracán Ramírez made his screen début in 1952, and appeared in several movies during the 1960s and 1970s. This one is a bizarre mix of family drama, musical comedy and horror movie. Between several Mexican go-go songs, a mad professor uses a serum to turn himself and his two assistants into super-strong wrestlers. The mad doctor battles the heroic Huracán Ramírez (Silva) under the names 'Professor Landru' and 'El Vampiro Sangrento' until, in the final minutes, prolonged use of the drug turns him into a werewolf before he dies. Very nicely directed by Rodríguez, this also features a slapstick food fight!
Sequel: HURACÁN RAMÍREZ Y LA MONJITA NEGRA (1972)
✦✧

LA VENGANZA DEL AHORCADO

(aka ZORRO ESCARLATA EN LA VENGANZA DEL AHORCADO)
Mexico, 1958 (1959). Dir: Rafael Baledón. With: Luis Aguilar, Fernando Fernández, Irma Dorantes, Jaime Fernández, Pascual Garcia Peña, Fanny Shiller. Clasa-Mohme. B&W.

Sequel to *El Regreso Del Monstruo* (1958) and the third and final entry in the series, in which the cackling old witch revives the bulbous-headed monster and sends it out to kidnap a young woman so that she can have a new body. After destroying the local gallows, the ugly creature carries a girl back to the duo's subterranean lair. But before the witch can ritually stab the girl, masked hero 'El Zorro Escarlata', aka The Scarlet Fox (Aguilar), shoots the old woman, who disintegrates, and the monster's fear of fire results in it being blown up with dynamite. The title translates as 'The Vengeance of the Hanged'.
✦

LA VENGANZA DE LAS MUJERES VAMPIRO

(aka SANTO EN LA VENGANZA DE LAS MUJERES VAMPIRO/SANTO Y LA MALDICIÓN DE LAS VAMPIRAS)
Mexico, 1969 (1970). Dir: Federico Curiel. With: Santo (Rodolfo Guzmán Huerta or Eric del Castillo), Norma Lazareno, Gina Romand, Aldo Monti, Victor Junco, Patricia Ferrer. Cinematográfica Flama/Peliculas Latinoamericanas. Colour.

Despite the title, this is not really a sequel to *Samson vs. the Vampire Women* (1961), but an uncredited remake of *Atacan Las Brujas* (1964). Using the blood of a nightclub dancer, mad Dr Brancor (Junco) revives the undead Countess Mayra (Romand), who believes that Santo, the silver masked wrestler, is the descendant of the man

who staked her vampire ancestors. The doctor also creates the Frankenstein Monster-like Razos (Nathaniel Leon) from spare cadavers. *Santo Contra las Diabolicas*, announced in 1969 and directed by René Cardona Jr, was cancelled before completion.
Sequel: SANTO CONTRA LOS JINETES DEL TERROR (1970)
✦

THE VENGEANCE OF EGYPT
UK, 1912. Gaumont. B&W.
Forty-five minute silent short in which Napoleon Bonaparte digs up an Egyptian mummy. When the mummy's cursed scarab ring is stolen, each owner of the ring dies. Finally an Egyptologist returns it to the mummy, whose eyes glow in triumph.
✦

VENGEANCE OF THE ZOMBIES
(Orig: LA REBELIÓN DE LAS MUERTAS/LA VENDETTA DEI MORTI VIVENTI. USA: aka WALK OF THE DEAD) Spain/Italy, 1972. Dir: León Klimovsky. With: Paul Naschy (Jacinto Molina), Romy (Carmen Romero), Mirta Miller, Vic Winner (Victor Alcazar), Maria Kosti, Aurora de Alba. Profilmes/ZIV International/Independent Artists. Colour.
Set in London, a mysterious black-cloaked figure uses voodoo to raise a trio of unimpressive zombie women so that he can revenge himself on three English families. Naschy (who also scripted under his real name) stars as both the horribly burned zombie master Kantaka Fanatim and his brother, the Hindu mystic Krishna. He also turns up briefly as a horned Devil in a dream sequence. When this was re-released in America in the late 1970s, several cast and crew names were Anglicised.
✦✧

VENGEFUL VAMPIRE GIRL
(Orig: HUPHYOKWI YANYO) Republic of Korea, 1980. Dir: Kim In-Soo (Kim Si-Hyo). With: Choi Bong, Chong Hi-Jung. Han Jin Enterprises. Colour.
Set in the middle ages. When a woman is raped by a wealthy governor, she bites her own tongue off and bleeds to death. Ten years later a pair of grave robbers dig her up and she returns as a ghostly vampire seeking revenge, but is finally dispatched by the governor's son, a martial arts expert. This was a gory remake of one of the stories in Park Yoon-Kyo's (non-vampire) *Myonuriui Han* (1971).
✦✧

HOWARD VERNON
(Mario Lippert) [1914-1996]

Swiss-American actor, best known for his more than thirty-five films with Jesús Franco, notably the Dr Orloff series (1961-88). He portrayed a green-faced Dracula for the director in *Dracula Prisoner of Frankenstein* (1972) and *The Erotic Rites of Frankenstein* (1972).
qv: *The Awful Dr. Orlof* (1961); *Bloodlust* (1979); *Castle of Bloody Lust* (1967); *Daughter of Dracula* (1972); *Dr. Crippen Lebt* (1957); *Howl of the Devil* (1988); *Revenge in the House of Usher* (1983); *Virgin Among the Living Dead* (1971); *Zombie Lake* (1980).

BRUNO VE SOTA
(William Ve Sota) [1922-1976]

A low-budget jack-of-all trades, often for AIP or Jerry Warren, who co-scripted and co-directed *Dementia* (aka *Daughter of Horror*, 1952/56) in which he also appeared and is credited as associate producer. Ve Sota also provided the make-up for Curtis Harrington's *Night Tide* (1961), directed *The Brain Eaters* (1958) and *Invasion of the Star Creatures* (1962), and made a substantial heavy in such films as *Attack of the Giant Leeches* (1959), *The Wasp Woman* (1959), *Creature of the Walking Dead* (1960/63), *Attack of the Mayan Mummy* (1957/64) and *The Wild Wild World of Batwoman* (1966). He died from a heart attack.

IL VICINO DI CASA
Italy, 1973. Dir: Luigi Cozzi. With: Aldo Reggiani, Laura Belli, Pino Mangogna, Mimmo Palmara, Dario Argento. Seda Spettacoli/RAI. Colour.
The first in a series of four hour-long TV movies, produced by Dario Argento (who also hosted) and Salvatore Argento and shown under the umbrella title *La Porta sul Buio* ('The Door Into Darkness'). A couple with an infant rent an isolated house by the coast and discover that their upstairs neighbour is a maniacal killer. While the couple watch Cozzi's *Il Tunnel Sotto il Mondo* (1969) and (Abbott and Costello) *Meet Frankenstein* (1948) on TV, the murderer is calmly dispatching more victims in his room. The title translates as 'The Man Upstairs'.
✦✧

KATHERINE VICTOR
(Katena Ktenavea) [b 1928]

American actress and singer who appeared in a number of low-budget movies during the 1950s and 1960s, mostly for producer/director Jerry Warren.
qv: *Cape Canaveral Monsters* (1960); *Creature of the Walking Dead* (1960/63); *Frankenstein Island* (1981); *House of the Black Death* (1966); *Teenage Zombies* (1957); *The Wild World of Batwoman* (1966).

VICTOR FRANKENSTEIN
(USA: aka TERROR OF FRANKENSTEIN) Sweden/Ireland, 1976. Dir: Calvin Floyd. With: Leon Vitali, Per Oscarsson, Nicholas Clay, Stacey Dorning, Jan Ohlsson, Olof Bergström. Aspekt Film/National Film Studios of Ireland. Colour.
Numbingly faithful adaptation of 'the classic by Mary Shelly' (*sic*), with Vitali as the doomed Victor Frankenstein. Despite a botched creation sequence, Oscarsson's articulate Monster is a tragic and truly disturbing creation with its death-like pallor and childish rage. Co-written, produced and directed by Floyd, this includes footage of the actual killing of a cow.
Remake: FRANKENSTEIN (qv; 1981)
✦✦

THE VIDEO DEAD
USA, 1987. Dir: Robert Scott. With: Roxanna Augesen, Rocky Duvall, Vickie Bastel, Sam David McClelland, Michael St. Michaels, Jennifer Miro. Interstate 5/ Highlight/Manson International. Colour.
Low-budget chiller written, produced and directed by the talentless Scott. When a haunted TV set is delivered to the wrong house, the walking dead that are featured in a film entitled *Zombie Blood Nightmare* materialise in the real world and start tearing people apart. A human character in the TV world is sadly never exploited, and instead we are treated to a group of no-talent teen actors trying to defend themselves against some unconvincing zombies (mostly played for laughs).
✦✧

VIDEO VIOLENCE
USA, 1986 (1987). Dir: Gary P. Cohen. With: Art Neill, Jackie Neill, William Toddie, Bart Sumner, Lisa Cohen. Little Zach Productions/Camp Video. Colour.
Shot-on-video horror comedy set in Frenchtown, where the crazed local video store owner makes his own snuff movies and rents them out. These include *The Vampire Takes a Bride* with a Dracula-like character (David Christopher) and his bride (Mavis Harris).
Sequel: VIDEO VIOLENCE PART 2...THE EXPLOITATION! (1987)
✦

VIJ
(aka VIY/VII) Russia, 1967. Dir: K. Ierchova (Konstantin Yershov/De Constantin Erchov) and G. (Giorgio) Kropacheva (Georgui Kropatchov). With: Leonid Kuravlev (Leonide Kouravliev), N. Varley (Natalia Varlei), A. Glazyrin, N.

Kutuzov, N. Zakharchenko, P. Veskliarov. Mosfilm Productions/Creative Union 'Lutch'/Sovexportfilm. Colour.

Based on Nicholas (Nikolai) Gogol's 1833 story 'The Vij', which was first filmed as a stop-motion feature in 1914 and also formed the basis for *Black Sunday* (1960) and several other films. When he kills a hideous old hag (male actor Kutuzov), young priest Khoma Brut (Kuravlev) is forced to spend three nights watching over her now-beautiful corpse (Varley). She returns to life each night in a flying coffin, and calls up ghosts and demons from Hell to torment him. Obviously inspired by the paintings of Hieronymus Bosch, the impressive special effects at the climax were created by Aleksandr Ptushko.

✦✦✧

CARLOS VILLARÍAS
(Carlos Villarías Llano) [circa 1893-19??]

Spanish stage actor who (credited as Carlos Villar) was a hot-blooded Count in Universal's Spanish-language version of *Dracula* (1931). He occasionally turned up in small English-speaking roles in other American movies during the 1930s and 1940s before presumably returning to Spain.

qv: *El Superloco* (1936).

VINCENT

USA, 1982. Dir: Tim Burton. Voice: Vincent Price. Walt Disney Productions. B&W.

Financed by Disney for $60,000, this delightful six minute short is not really aimed at children. Designer/director Burton and creative producer Rick Heinrich use model animation to tell the story of a young boy who sets out to emulate his hero — Vincent Price. He creates a zombie dog, boils his aunt in wax, waits for his wife to return from the tomb and reads Edgar Allan Poe to himself. Price's rhyming narration is a perfect complement to this beautifully created dark fable.

✦✦✦✦

VINCENT PRICE'S DRACULA

(USA: DRACULA: THE GREAT UNDEAD)

UK, 1982. Dir: John Muller. With: Vincent Price. M&M Film Productions/Atlantis. Colour.

Hour-long drama/documentary in which Price makes the most of the tedious script and sends himself up as the sinister host and narrator explaining the legend of Count Dracula and real-life Vlad the Impaler. This is similar to *In Search of Dracula* (1971) with Christopher Lee, and includes footage from the Romanian *Vlad Tepes* (1978), as well as clips from *Mark of the Vampire* (1935), *The Return of Dracula* (1957) and *The Return of the Vampire* (1943). It was released directly to video in America in 1985.

✦✧

THE VINDICATOR

(Orig: FRANKENSTEIN 88)

Canada, 1984 (1986). Dir: Jean Claude Lord. With: Terri Austin, Richard Cox, Maury Chaykin, Pam Grier, David McIlwraith, Denis Simpson. Michael T. Levy Enterprises/Telefilm Canada/Twentieth Century Fox. Colour.

Filmed under the title *The Frankenstein Factor.* At the high-tech laboratories of the Aerospace Research Corporation (ARC), ruthless scientist Alex Whyte (Cox) murders colleague Carl Lehman (McIlwraith) and transplants his brain and mutilated body into an indestructible gold spacesuit (created by the Stan Winston Studio). The monster escapes and goes on a murderous rampage, pursued by Hunter (Grier), a tough female samurai.

✦✧

THE VINEYARD

USA, 1989. Dir: Bill (William) Rice and James Hong. With: James Hong, Karen Witter, Michael Wong, Cheryl Madsen, Lars Wanberg, Cheryl Lawson. Vineyard Partners/Northstar Entertainment. Colour.

This is the 1980s equivalent of a Monogram movie! Hong (who also co-wrote the story, co-scripted and co-directed) stars as Dr Elson Po, an immortal sorcerer who invites a group of attractive starlets to his secluded island. He soon begins killing them off one-by-one, adding more body to his wine vats, or chaining them up in the basement with his other half-naked captives. While his martial arts guards patrol the grounds, his zombiefied victims, buried in the sacred vineyard, rise for revenge. This ludicrous horror melodrama is actually pretty funny in places. The whipping scenes were cut in Britain.

✦✦

A VIRGEM DA COLINA

Brazil, 1977. Dir: Celso Falcao. With: Jofre Soares, Christina Amaral, Edson Seretti, Marcos Lyra, Joel Barcellos, Wagner Tadeu. Dragao Filmes. Colour.

A woman (Amaral) is given an antique ring by her new husband (Soares) which results in her developing a dual personality. She becomes a prostitute during the day, while remaining the perfect wife in the evening. Her uninhibited personality begins to show on her face, and she is forced to wear a mask to hide her monstrous features. An exorcist called in by the husband eventually discovers that the ring once belonged to a witch. When it is thrown into the water, the curse is broken.

✦

VIRGIN AMONG THE LIVING DEAD

(Orig: CHRISTINA PRINCESSE DE L'ÉROTISME/HOLOCAUSTE DE ZOMBI/UNE VIERGE CHEZ LES MORTS-VIVANTS/I DESIDERI EROTICI DI CHRISTINA/EXORCISMO PER UNA VERGINE/UNA VERGINE FRAI I MORTI VIVENTI. USA: aka ZOMBIE 4)

France/Italy, 1971. Dir: Jess (Jesús) Franco. With: Christina von Blanc, Britt Nichols, Howard Vernon (Mario Lippert), Ann(e) Libert (Josiane Gibert), Rose Kiekens, Paul Müller. JK Films/Prodif Ets/Brux International Pictures/Cinema Shares International. Colour.

When the father she has never met dies, Christina (von Blanc) returns to the family mansion in the British Honduras for the reading of the will. There she meets the members of her strange family and is soon experiencing a number of bizarre nightmares and ghostly apparitions. With director Franco as Basilio, a murderous mad mute. Softcore inserts were added by the original French distributor, while in 1979 Eurociné hired director Jean Rollin to replace these erotic sequences with fifteen minutes of gap-toothed zombie footage. In Italy, yet another re-edited version apparently includes material from one of Rollin's vampire films.

✦

VIRTUAL MURDER:
A Dream of Dracula

UK, 1992. Dir: Philip Draycott. With: Nicholas Clay, Kim Thomson, Ronald Fraser, Jill Gascoine, Alfred Marks, Peggy Mount. BBC Pebble Mill. Colour.

Is Dracula really kidnapping young women and draining their blood? Or are criminal psychologist Dr John Cornelius (Clay) and Samantha Valentine (Thomson) hunting someone with a vampire fixation? Julian Clary plays a flamboyant coffin-maker and Fraser turns up as Van Helsing in this episode of the shot-on-video comedy/thriller TV series.

✦✧

V IS FOR VAMPIRE

USA, 1998. Dir: Paul Knop. With: Greg Dukes, Amy Luciano, Tony McDowell, Amy Schauder, Josalyn Steele, Robert Schultz. Kryptic K/Salt City Home Video. Colour.

Independent video release. There is a good reason why Laura Manning is the number one bestselling vampire author, and now she is sponsoring a contest which has the most beautiful girls in town lining up.

✦

I VITELLONI

Italy/France, 1953. Dir: Federico Fellini. With: Alberto Sordi, Franco Interlenghi, Franco Fabrizi, Leopoldo Trieste, Eleonora Ruffo. Peg/Cité. B&W

Drama about five adolescents growing up in a small Italian resort.

Pat McKee and John Carradine deliver Louise Currie to Bela Lugosi's Voodoo Man *(1944).*

This includes a reveller wearing a Frankenstein Monster mask.
✦✦✧

VIVIR MATA
Argentina, 1991. Dir: Bebe Kamin. With: Maurico Dayub, Alejandro Urdapilleta, Osvaldo Sanforo, Cecilia Roth, Soledad Villamil, Cecilia Biagini. La Maga Films SRL. Colour.
Blas, a promising young diplomat in Buenos Aires at the turn of the century, is sent on a mission to Central Europe where he is vampirised by Princess Mircalla (Biagini), the daughter of Vlad the Impaler. Returning to Argentina, Blas has his brother bury him in the local cemetery to save his bride-to-be from his uncontrollable bloodlust. After several decades, he emerges into modern times, where he is horrified by contemporary pop culture manifestations. A stylish satire of recent Argentinian social and political trends (Blas is initiated into drug abuse by inhaling cocaine through his fangs!), the film is let down by Biagini's hammy performance and the irritating disco soundtrack.
✦✧

VLAD TEPES
(USA: THE TRUE LIFE OF DRACULA)
Romania, 1978. Dir: Doru Nastase. With: Stefan Sileanu, George Constantin, Teofil Vilcu. Romaniafilm. Colour.
The story behind the real Dracula, Vlad Tepes, the fifteenth century Romanian prince who impaled his enemies.
✦

VOODOO
USA, 1995. Dir: Rene Eram. With: Corey Feldman, Joel J. Edwards, Diana Nadeau, Ron Melendez, Sarah Douglas, Jack Nance. Planet Productions/Image Organization/ A-Pix Entertainment. Colour.
Neat little horror thriller released directly to video. Feldman stars as new student Andy Chadway, who must rescue his girlfriend Rebecca (Nadeau) from a sacrificial ritual when he discovers that the five other members of his Ωmega college fraternity are actually 'undead' zombies. They are under the control of evil voodoo priest Marsh (Edwards), who is seeking eternal life from the snake goddess Ezili.
✦✦✧

VOODOO BLACK EXORCIST
(Orig: LOA VUDÚ/VUDÚ SANGRIENTO)
Spain/USA, 1972 (1974). Dir: M. (Manuel) Caño. With: Aldo Sambrell, Eva Leon, Ferdinand (Fernando) Sancho, Julia Peña, Tanyeka Stadler, Alexander (Kurd) Abrahan. Mingyar/Rosgard/Horizon. Colour.
With a title that attempts to cash-in on both the blaxploitation genre and the success of *The Exorcist* (1973), this obscure, low-budget co-production was filmed in Jamaica, Haiti and Santo Domingo and apparently inspired by *The Mummy* (1933). The 1,000 year-old mummy of African voodoo priest Guede Nibo (Sambrell) returns to life on board a Caribbean cruise ship. Periodically transforming into its human guise through a magic ring, the creature seeks out scientist's secretary Silvia (Stadler), the reincarnation of his decapitated lost love Kenya (also Stadler). In the end, both the mummy and the heroine are destroyed in a cave by police with flame-throwers. 'See It At Your Own Risk' warned the ads.
✦

VOODOO DAWN
(aka STRANGE TURF)
USA, 1989 (1990). Dir: Steven Fierberg. With: Raymond St. Jacques, Theresa Merritt, Gina Gershon, Kirk Baily, Billy 'Sly' Williams, Tony Todd. Stillwell Productions/Academy Entertainment. Colour.
Filmed in Charleston, South Carolina, and co-scripted by John Russo (*Night of the Living Dead* [1968], etc). A pair of NYCU students (Baily and Williams) travel to a Southern plantation and discover that mute voodoo priest Makoute (Todd), who is also head of the Haitian secret police, has transformed their friend (J. Grant Albrecht) into a patchwork zombie.
✦✧

VOODOO HEARTBEAT
USA, 1972 (1975). Dir: Charles Nizet. With: Ray Molina, Philip Ahn, Ern Dugo, Forrest Duke, Ebby Rhodes, Mike Zapata. Ray Molina Productions/TWI National. Colour.
The ads warned that you had to be 'mature enough to witness the shocking detail' of this low-budget horror movie shot in Las Vegas. Producer Molina stars as an Elvis lookalike who is transformed into a hideous blood-drinking monster after swallowing a stolen voodoo formula for restoring youth. A sequel, *Dr. Blake's Revenge*, was announced but thankfully never made.
✦

VOODOO ISLAND
(aka SILENT DEATH)
USA, 1957. Dir: Reginald Le Borg. With: Boris Karloff, Beverley Tyler, Murvyn Vye, Elisha Cook (Jr), Rhodes Reason, Jean Engstrom. Bel-Air/United Artists. B&W.
This low-budget thriller, filmed on the Hawaiian island of Kauai, marked sixty-nine year-old Karloff's return to movies after a four year absence. This time he plays the hero, Dr Phillip Knight, who is sent to a remote island by a group of businessmen who want to develop it as a vacation resort. Karloff does the best he can with the weak script, but even dressed in a baseball cap and flowered shirt he can't help looking sinister as he investigates a series of black magic deaths and discovers a single zombie (Vye), some unconvincing man-eating plants and a mild voodoo cult. With good support from Cook Jr, and featuring the movie début of an uncredited Adam West, this was apparently made in both American and European versions. A photo comic was published in France in 1962.
✦✦

VOODOO MAN
USA, 1944. Dir: William Beaudine. With: Bela Lugosi, John Carradine, George Zucco, Michael Ames (Tod Andrews), Wanda McKay, Ellen Hall. Monogram/Banner Productions. B&W.
Wonderfully daft low-budget horror film, produced by 'Jungle' Sam Katzman (who turns up as a character name) and directed by 'One Shot' Beaudine (who replaced William Nigh and Philip Rosen before shooting) under Monogram's even cheaper Banner company. Apparently based on Andrew Colvin's story 'The Tiger Man', Lugosi's demented scientist Dr Richard Marlowe kidnaps beautiful blondes and uses the voodoo rituals of garage owner Nicholas (Zucco) to steal their souls in an attempt to revive his wife who has been dead for twenty-two years. Carradine plays his idiot assistant Toby who looks after the cellar full of zombie women. In the end, Ralph (Ames), a screenwriter from Banner Productions, defeats them all and suggests that Bela Lugosi should star in the movie version!
✦✦✧

ZANDOR VORKOV
(Roger Engell)

Former New York stockbroker re-named by Forrest J Ackerman for his role as a hammy Count in *Dracula vs. Frankenstein* (1970).
qv: *Brain of Blood* (1971).

VOODOO SOUP
USA, 1994 (1996). Dir: Greg Lewolt. With: Phebe Mansur, Pete Mahar, J. Scott Bovitz, Joanna Taylor, Lucia Mortato, Ernie Orosco. K-Beech/EI Independent Cinema. Colour.
Horror/comedy video from writer/director/editor Lewolt featuring *Playboy* lingerie model Corrie Singer as a trainee vampire, Roberta Martinez as an exploding vampire, and Brian Gusner as a wolfman. It doesn't make a lot of sense, but that is apparently not the point.
✦

VOYAGE TO THE BOTTOM OF THE SEA:
The Brand of the Beast
USA, 1966. Dir: Justus Addiss. With: Richard Basehart, David Hedison, Bob Dowdell, Del Monroe, Paul Trinka, Richard Bull. Irwin Allen Productions/Twentieth Century-Fox/ABC-TV. Colour.
Popular hour-long TV series (1964-68, 110 episodes), created and produced by Irwin Allen and based on his 1961 movie of the same title. In this silly sequel to the 1966 episode 'Werewolf', Admiral Harriman Nelson (Basehart) is exposed to a radiation leak and suffers a recurrence of the werewolf virus.
✦

Man-Beast
USA, 1968. Dir: Jerry Hopper. With: Richard Basehart, David Hedison, Bob Dowdell, Del Monroe, Paul Trinka, Lawrence Montaigne. Irwin Allen Productions/Twentieth Century-Fox/ABC-TV. Colour.
After making a descent in an experimental diving bell, Captain Lee Crane (Hedison) is transformed into a monstrous beast-creature.
✦✧

The Mummy
USA, 1967. Dir: Harry Harris. With: Richard Basehart, David Hedison, Bob Dowdell, Del Monroe, Paul Trinka, Richard Bull. Irwin Allen Productions/Twentieth Century-Fox/ABC-TV. Colour.
When a 3,000 year-old sarcophagus is transported aboard the *Seaview*, the mummy it contains awakens and attacks the crew.
✦✦

Werewolf
USA, 1966. Dir: Justus Addiss. With: Richard Basehart, David Hedison, Bob Dowdell, Del Monroe, Charles Aidman, Douglas Bank. Irwin Allen Productions/ Twentieth Century-Fox/ABC-TV. Colour.
When volcanic radioactivity turns a scientist into a werewolf, it results in Admiral Nelson and some of the crew of the *Seaview* also being transformed into beasts.
Episode sequel: VOYAGE TO THE BOTTOM OF THE SEA: The Brand of the Beast (qv; 1966)
✦✧

- W -

WACKY RACES:
Real Gone Ape
USA, 1968. Dir: William Hanna and Joseph Barbera. Voices: Daws Butler, Don Messick, John Stephenson, Janet Waldo, Dave Willock, Paul Winchell. Hanna-Barbera Productions/Heatter-Quigley/CBS-TV. Colour.
Half-hour cartoon TV series (1968-70, fifty-two episodes) involving a group of characters (including the Creepy Kook with the Gruesome Twosome [Butler and Messick]) competing with each other during a cross-country automobile race. In this ten minute segment, the scheming Dick Dastardly (Winchell) and his sniggering dog Muttley (Messick) release King Klong, the largest gorilla in captivity. Narrated by Willock.
Series sequels: DASTARDLY AND MUTTLEY (1969), MAGNIFICENT MUTTLEY (1969) and THE PERILS OF PENELOPE PITSTOP (1969-70)
✦✧

GEORGE WAGGNER
[1894-1984]

American producer, director and screenwriter, who began his career as a silents actor. Best remembered for his Universal horrors of the 1940s, ranging from *The Wolf Man* (1941) and *The Ghost of Frankenstein* (1942) to entertaining programmers like *Man Made Monster* (1941) and *Frankenstein Meets the Wolf Man* (1943). He ended up directing episodes of the *Batman* TV series (1966-69).
qv: *The Climax* (1944); *Phantom of the Opera* (1943).

WAKE, RATTLE AND ROLL: MONSTER TAILS
(aka JUMP, RATTLE AND ROLL)
USA, 1990-91. With: R.J. Williams, Ebonie Smith, Terri Ivens, Avery Schreiber, Tim Lawrence, Rob Paulsen. Hanna-Barbera Productions/Four Point Entertainment. Colour.
Daily half-hour TV series, created by David Kirschner, in which Sam Baxter (Williams) and his magical Grandpa Quirk (Schreiber) watch two cartoon shows on his robot DECKS (Lawrence): *Fender Bender 500* is another race-car series featuring classic Hanna-Barbera characters, while *Monster Tails* (voiced by Charlie Adler, Tim Curry, Dick Gautier, Pat Musick, Frank Welker and Jonathan Winters) is about the pets of Hollywood's famous movie monsters, left behind in a creepy old castle.
✦✧

THE WALKING DEAD
USA, 1936. Dir: Michael Curtiz (Mihaly Kertesze). With: Boris Karloff, Ricardo Cortez, Edmund Gwenn, Marguerite Churchill, Warren Hull, Barton MacLane. Warner Bros. B&W.
Combining both the horror and gangster genres, this is one of Karloff's best movies. He plays John Ellman, an ex-convict framed and executed for murder. When scientist Dr Beaumont (Gwenn) uses electricity to revive him, Ellman returns from the dead to seek revenge on those who framed him. The execution scene was originally cut from British prints. During shooting, author H.G. Wells visited the set and met Karloff and Gwenn.
Remake: INDESTRUCTIBLE MAN (qv; 1955)
✦✦✦✧

WANDA DOES TRANSYLVANIA
USA, 1990. Dir: Ken Gibbs. With: Kitty Luv (Charisma), Rene Morgan, Ashley Wagner (Ashley Winger), Tony Montana, Jerry Butler. Venus 99. Colour.
Shot on video back-to-back with *Wanda Whips the Dragon Lady* (1990), Luv returns as the eponymous heroine, who is involved with more hardcore vampires.
✦

THORLEY WALTERS
[1913-1991]

Bumbling British character actor who gave solid support in a number of Hammer horrors, notably as the Count's crazed servant Ludwig in *Dracula Prince of Darkness* (1965) and the Baron's compassionate assistant Dr Hertz in *Frankenstein Created Woman* (1966). He also portrayed Dr Watson in films and on TV.
qv: *The Earth Dies Screaming* (1964); *Frankenstein Must Be Destroyed* (1969); *The Phantom of the Opera* (1962); *Vampire Circus* (1971).

WANDA WHIPS THE DRAGON LADY
USA, 1990. Dir: Ken Gibbs. With: Fetish (Heather Lere), Kitty Luv (Charisma), Rene Morgan, Sade (Elissa Vanderbilt), Ashley Wagner (Ashley Winger), T.T. Boy. Venus 99. Colour.
This shot-on-video hardcore feature involves Wanda (Luv) and her rival The Dragon Lady (Sade) in a minimal plot that revolves around the inheritance of Dracula's treasure. Filmed back-to-back with the sequel.
Sequel: WANDA DOES TRANSYLVANIA (qv; 1990)
✦

WANTED — A MUMMY
UK, 1910. Cricks & Martin. B&W.
Nine minute silent short in which a man pretends to be a mummy.
✦

DAVID WARBECK
[1942-1997]

New Zealand-born British actor who ended up as an all-purpose hero in Italian horror movies.
qv: *The Beyond* (1981); *Breakfast With Dracula: A Vampire in Miami* (1993); *Razor Blade Smile* (1998); *Twins of Evil* (1971).

DAVID WARNER
[b 1941]

British actor who, after a promising career in the 1960s and 1970s, moved to Hollywood and has subsequently wasted his talent walking through numerous exploitation movies.
qv: *Batman: The Animated Series: 'Avatar'* (1994); *Beastmaster The Eye of Braxus* (1995); *Body Bags* (1993); *Cast a Deadly Spell* (1991); *The Company of Wolves* (1984); *Frankenstein* (1984); *Grave Secrets* (1989); *Morgan a Suitable Case for Treatment* (1966); *My Best Friend is a Vampire* (1986); *Necronomicon* (1993); *Nightwing* (1979); *Providence* (1977); *Scream 2* (1997); *Tales from the Crypt: 'The New Arrival'* (1992); *Toonsylvania* (1998); *Waxwork* (1988).

WARNING SIGN
USA, 1985. Dir: Hal Barwood. With: Sam Waterson, Kathleen Quinlan, Yaphet Kotto, Jeffrey DeMunn, Richard Dysart, G.W. Bailey. Barwood-Robbins/Twentieth Century Fox. Colour.
Originally filmed under the title *Biohazard*, this classy horror film was scripted by Matthew Robbins and director Barwood (*Dragonslayer* [1981], etc). A leak at a germ warfare laboratory turns those exposed into homicidal zombies. This well-made exploitation concept is given added class by Waterson's local sheriff, Quinlan as his security guard wife and Kotto as a government contamination expert. There's a nice sense of paranoia and conspiracy, but the film ultimately cops out when a cure is discovered for the zombies. Stylishly photographed by Dean Cundey.
✦✦✦✧

WAR OF THE GARGANTUAS
(Orig: FURANKENSHUTAIN NO KAIJU — SANDA TAI GAILAH)
Japan/USA, 1966 (1970). Dir: Inoshiro Honda. With: Russ Tamblyn, Kumi Mizuno, Kenji Sahara, Kipp Hamilton,

Jun Tazaki. Toho/American International Pictures. Colour.
Intended as a sequel to *Frankenstein Conquers the World* (1964), all references to the earlier film were deleted during shooting by the American producer. A friendly (brown) giant Frankenstein Monster and his evil (green) brother battle each other in the middle of Eiji Tsuburaya's miniature Tokyo. This also includes shots of a giant octopus attacking a ship, cut from the 1964 film. It was apparently based (uncredited) on one of Willis O'Brien's yeti stories.
✦✦

WAR OF THE ZOMBIES

(Orig: ROMA CONTRO ROMA. USA: aka NIGHT STAR, GODDESS OF ELECTRA)
Italy, 1963 (1965). Dir: Giuseppe Vari. With: Suzy (Susi) Andersen, Ettore Manni, Ida Galli, Philippe Hersent, John Drew Barrymore, Nino Doro. Galatea Film/American International. Colour.
Mad magician Aderbal (Barrymore) uses the giant idol of a bloodthirsty goddess to raise an army of zombie soldiers to overthrow ancient Rome and rule the world. His power is destroyed when hero Centurion Gaius (Manni) stabs the cyclopean eye of the golden idol.
✦✦

JERRY WARREN [1923-1988]

American producer and director who was responsible for re-editing and adding new footage to Mexican monster movies during the 1960s. Incredibly, his own films are even worse.
qv: *Attack of the Mayan Mummy* (1957/64); *Creature of the Walking Dead* (1960/63); *Face of the Screaming Werewolf* (1960); *Frankenstein Island* (1981); *Ghost Catchers* (1944); *House of the Black Death* (1966); *Teenage Zombies* (1957); *The Wild World of Batwoman* (1966).

THE WASP WOMAN

USA, 1959. Dir: Roger Corman. With: Susan Cabot, Fred (Anthony) Eisley, Barboura Morris, William Roerick, Michael Mark, Frank Gerstle. Santa Cruz Productions/ Filmgroup/Allied Artists. B&W.
The first major movie from producer/director Corman's own Filmgroup company, shot in six days for just $50,000. Cabot plays Janice Starlin, the wealthy head of a cosmetics firm, who uses a serum created by Eric Zinthrop (Mark) from wasp enzymes to reverse the effects of ageing. Although the serum works, Starlin periodically turns into a wasp woman and kills her victims for their blood. With Bruno Ve Sota. When released to American TV in 1962, Corman hired Jack Hill to shoot an extra eleven minutes, including a long prologue featuring Mark. Hill and actors Carl Schanzer and Aron Kincaid all turn up uncredited in the new footage.
Remake: THE WASP WOMAN (qv; 1995)
✦✦

THE WASP WOMAN

(aka FINAL SEDUCTION)
USA, 1995. Dir: Jim Wynorski. With: Jennifer Rubin, Doug Wert, Maria Ford, Melissa Brasselle, Daniel J. Travanti, Jay Richardson. Concorde/New Horizons/ Showtime Networks. Colour.
Low-budget cable TV remake of the 1959 original, shown as part of *Roger Corman Presents* and co-executive produced by Corman (who should have known better). Rubin stars as cosmetics tycoon Janice Starlin, who uses a serum created from wasp enzymes by Dr Zinthorp (Travanti, slumming here) to regain her youthful looks. The only problem is that she periodically transforms into a ludicrous giant wasp (created by Greg Aronowitz). With Gerrit Graham and Fred Olen Ray.
✦

WATERMELON MAN

USA, 1970. Dir: Melvin Van Peebles. With: Godfrey Cambridge, Estelle Parsons, Howard Caine, D'Urville Martin, Mantan Moreland, Kay Kimberly. Bennett-Mirell-Van Peebles Productions/Columbia. Colour.
When bigoted white insurance salesman Jeff Gerber (comedian Cambridge) discovers that he has turned black overnight, he has to adjust to his new life. An uneven comedy, filmed under the title *The Night the Sun Came Out on Happy Hollow Lane* by director Van Peebles (the father of actor Mario).
✦✧

FRANZ WAXMAN (Franz Wachsmann) [1906-1967]

German composer who joined UFA in 1930 but soon fled the rise of anti-Semitism, arriving in Hollywood in 1934. He won Academy Awards for *Sunset Blvd.* (1950) and *A Place in the Sun* (1951).
qv: *Bride of Frankenstein* (1935); *Dr. Jekyll and Mr. Hyde* (1941).

WAXWORK

USA, 1988. Dir: Anthony Hickox. With: Zach Galligan, Deborah Foreman, Michelle Johnson, Dana Ashbrook, Miles O'Keeffe, Charles McCaughan. Vestron Pictures. Colour.
After a group of teenagers are invited to a private midnight showing of a creepy new waxwork museum by its mysterious owner, Mr Lincoln (David Warner), they are each magically transported into the exhibits, where they encounter backwoods werewolf Anton Weber (John Rhys Davies), Count Dracula (former Tarzan O'Keeffe with long blond hair and designer stubble) and his vampire brides (Merle Stronck, Joanne Russell and Ann Sophie Noblet), The Phantom of the Opera, Raoul the Mummy (Paul Badger), the Marquis de Sade (J. Kenneth Campbell) and a monochrome graveyard full of zombies. With the help of wheelchair-bound Sir Wilfred (Patrick Macnee), Mark Loftmore (Galligan) and Sarah Brightman (Foreman) must stop the eighteen most evil people in history rising from the dead and destroying the world. The climactic battle between the forces of Good and Evil also features Frankenstein's Monster, Mr Hyde, Jack the Ripper, the Invisible Man, a witch, a voodoo priest, a snake man, a mutant baby, an alien, a pod person, an axe murderer and a crawling hand. The special make-up effects by second unit director Bob Keen and Image Animation (*Hellraiser* [1987], etc) are the best thing in this shoddy horror comedy. With writer/director Hickox as an English prince, and comedian Joe Baker.
Sequel: WAXWORK II: LOST IN TIME (qv; 1991)
✦✧

WAXWORK II: LOST IN TIME

(UK: LOST IN TIME)
USA, 1991 (1992). Dir: Anthony Hickox. With: Zach Galligan, Alexander Godunov, Monika Schnarre, Martin Kemp, Sophie Ward, Bruce Campbell. Electric Pictures. Colour.
Great-looking comedy sequel to *Waxwork* (1988), in which the surviving severed hand from the first film frames Sarah (model Schnarre) for a murder it commits. To prove her innocence, Mark (Galligan) takes her through the time doors into alternate worlds where Good battles Evil using characters from horror films and fiction. These include clever pastiches of *Frankenstein* (with Kemp as the Baron and Stefanos Miltsakakis as his Monster), *The Haunting* (1963; in black and white), *Alien* (1979) and an original story inspired by Edgar Allan Poe, in which a sacrificial victim is transformed into a were-panther (Shanna L. Teare). During the climactic battle, the time-travelling teens also encounter Nosferatu (Steve Painter), the zombies from *Dawn of the Dead* (1978), Mr Hyde (Michael Viela), Jack the Ripper (Alex Butler), Godzilla and such guest stars as Marina Sirtis, Juliet Mills, David Carradine, John Ireland (his last role), George 'Buck' Flower, Joe Baker, Patrick Macnee (as a raven!), Alexander Godunov, Maxwell Caulfield, Drew Barrymore and director Hickox. Special make-up effects again created by Bob Keen's Image Animation.
✦✦✧

WAYNE AND SHUSTER TAKE AN AFFECTIONATE LOOK AT THE MONSTERS

Canada, 1966. With: Johnny Wayne, Frank Shuster. CBC/CBS-TV. Colour.

This TV special features the comedy team looking at the 1960s monster craze and includes clips from silent films, the classic Universal series, 1950s mutated monsters and comedy horror on TV.
✦✧

WAY OUT:
Dissolve to Black
USA, 1961. Dir: William Corrigan. With: Kathleen Widdoes, Richard Morse, James Patterson, Mark Lenard, Leonardo Cimino, Moultrie Patton. CBS-TV. B&W.
Short-lived, half-hour anthology TV series (fourteen episodes) created by host Roald Dahl and shot on videotape. An inexperienced actress (Widdoes) is hired to play the victim of a murderer in a TV play. After rehearsing with the day crew, she finds herself filming the scene for real with a zombie-like night crew.
✦✦✧

The Down Car
USA, 1961. Dir: Marc Daniels. With: Frank Overton, Ray Walston. CBS-TV. B&W.
A man returns from the grave to revenge himself on the business partner who framed him for embezzlement and then murdered him, making it look like a suicide.
✦✧

False Face
USA, 1961. Dir: Paul Bogart. With: Alfred Ryder, Martin E. Brooks, Gerry Jedd, Laster Rawlins, Dana Elcar. CBS-TV. B&W.
In this episode, scripted by Larry Cohen, a theatre actor (Ryder) preparing to play Quasimodo in *The Hunchback of Notre Dame* searches for a horribly disfigured man on whom to base his make-up (created by series regular Dick Smith).
✦✧

WAY...WAY OUT
USA, 1966. Dir: Gordon Douglas. With: Jerry Lewis, Connie Stevens, Robert Morley, Dennis Weaver, Brian Keith, Dick Shawn. Coldwater/Twentieth Century-Fox. Colour.
Dire science fiction comedy set in 1984 and featuring the romantic misadventures of American and Soviet astronauts in weather stations on the Moon. This includes clips from *Frankenstein* (1931) on a giant TV screen. With Alex D'Arcy, Linda Harrison, Sig Ruman, James Brolin and Milton Frome.
✦✧

ROY WEBB
[1888-1982]

Prolific American composer who joined RKO Radio Pictures in 1929 and worked on most of Val Lewton's films for the studio.
qv: *Cat People* (1942); *The Curse of the Cat People* (1944); *I Walked With a Zombie* (1943); *Mighty Joe Young* (1949); *Zombies on Broadway* (1945).

WEB OF THE SPIDER
(Orig: NELLA STRETTA MORSA DEL RAGNO/DRACULA IM SCHLOß DES SCHRECKENS/PRISONNIER DE L'ARAIGNÉE) Italy/West Germany/France, 1970. Dir: Anthony M. Dawson (Antonio Margheriti). With: Anthony Franciosa, Michèle Mercier, Peter Carsten, Silvano Tranquilli, Karen (Karin) Field, Klaus Kinsky (Kinski). Produzione DC7/ Paris Cannes Production/Terra Filmkunst/ Panta Cinematográfica/Cinema Shares International. Colour.
Director Margheriti's colour remake of his own *Castle of Blood* (1964). Sceptical American reporter Foster (Franciosa) accepts a bet by Edgar Allan Poe (an uneven cameo by Kinski, whose name is misspelled on the credits) that he can't survive the night in Lord Blackwood's deserted old mansion haunted by vampiric ghosts. The muddled script trots out all the old supernatural clichés. Supposedly based on Poe's *Night of the Living Dead*!
✦✧

WEEKEND AT BERNIE'S II
USA, 1992 (1993). Dir: Robert Klane. With: Andrew McCarthy, Jonathan Silverman, Terry Kiser, Tom Wright, Steve James, Barry Bostwick. D&A Partnership/TriStar Pictures. Colour.
In this sequel to the superior 1989 black comedy, Larry (McCarthy) and Richard (Silverman) try to discover where their still-dead boss Bernie (Kiser) has hidden his stolen $2,000,000 in the US Virgin Islands. Unfortunately for them, voodoo priestess Mobu (Novella Nelson) has the same idea and casts a spell on Bernie that turns him into a zombie whenever he hears music. The result is a likeable, if slight comedy.
✦✧

WEIRD SCIENCE
USA, 1985. Dir: John Hughes. With: Anthony Michael Hall, Ilan Mitchell-Smith, Kelly LeBrock, Bill Paxton, Suzanne Snyder, Robert Downey. Universal. Colour.
This has nothing to do with the EC comics title it borrowed. Instead, it's an often tasteless fantasy comedy in which a pair of teenage nerds, Gary and Wyatt (Hall and Mitchell-Smith), create Lisa (LeBrock, looking like a teenage boy's wet dream) when their computer overloads. After taking a quick shower together, the trio set out to pay back all those people who made the boys' lives hell. The results are unfunny and often quite nasty. With Michael Berryman as a mutant biker, a slimy monster and colourised clips from the 1931 *Frankenstein* on TV. Theme song by Danny Elfman, performed by Oingo Boingo. This became the basis for a belated TV series in 1994.
Remake: WEIRD SCIENCE (qv; 1994-)
✦✦

WEIRD SCIENCE:
Gary and Wyatt's Bloodsucking Adventure
USA, 1996. Dir: Les Landau. With: Michael Manasseri, John Mallory Asher, Lee Tergesen, Vanessa Angel, Bruce Jarchow, Andrew Prine. Universal/St. Clare Entertainment/USA Network. Colour.
Surprisingly successful half-hour comedy TV series (1994-), based on the 1985 John Hughes movie. Two teenage nerds, Wyatt Donnelly (Manasseri) and Gary Walter Wallace (Asher), use their computer to create Lisa (Angel), their perfect woman. In this episode, Lisa turns Gary and Wyatt into the undead so that they can party all night. But then they meet a group of real vampires... Co-executive produced by John Landis. This uses clips from *Bride of Frankenstein* (1935) in the title sequence.
✦✦

Searching for Boris Karloff
USA, 1995 (1996). Dir: Tom Spezialy. With: Michael Manasseri, John Mallory Asher, Lee Tergesen, Vanessa Angel, Gerrit Graham, Richard Moll. Universal/St. Clare Entertainment/USA Network. Colour.
When Gary and Wyatt want to meet someone who will appreciate them, Lisa introduces them to Dr Frankenstein.
✦✦

She's Alive
USA, 1994. Dir: Max Tash. With: Michael Manasseri, John Mallory Asher, Lee Tergesen, Vanessa Angel, Richard Fancy, Melendy Britt. Universal/St. Clare Entertainment/USA Network. Colour.
Première episode in which Lisa makes Wyatt and Gary irresistible to girls at the school dance. With clips from *Bride of Frankenstein* (1935) on TV.
✦✦

MEL WELLES
(Ernst von Theumer) [b 1924]

American character actor and director who became a Corman regular. A memorable Gravis Mushnik in *The Little Shop of Horrors* (1960).
qv: *Abbott and Costello Meet the Mummy* (1955); *Blood Suckers* (1965); *Dr. Heckyl and Mr. Hype* (1980); *Lady Frankenstein* (1971); *Wolfen* (1981).

Lester Matthews finds himself beneath the claws of Henry Hull, alias the WereWolf of London *(1935).*

WERE TIGER

USA, circa 1918. With: Hedda Nova, Jules Cowles, George Carrossella, J. Frank Glendon. Searles Cinevision. B&W.

Twenty-two minute silent two-reeler. Set in the Malaya jungle, Cynthia Trevor (Nova) is the daughter of the manager of a mining operation. On her way to Singapore, she crosses the path of a tiger that is attacking the locals. When the natives see her covered in the blood of one of the beast's victims, they suspect that she is a weretiger.

✦

THE WEREWOLF

USA, 1913. Dir: Henry McRae. With: Clarence F. Burton, Marie Walcam, Lule Warrenton, Phyllis Gordon, Sherman Bainbridge, William Clifford. 101 Bison/Universal. B&W.

Eighteen minute silent drama. According to Navajo legend, Watuma (Gordon), the daughter of wronged Native American witch Kee-On-Ee (played at different ages by both Walcam and Warrenton), has the power to take the form of a wolf, until she is confronted by a Friar with a cross. One hundred years later, the sweetheart of a reincarnated prospector (Clifford) is killed by the wolfwoman. The transformation scenes were achieved through simple camera dissolves. Loosely based on Henry Beaugrand's story 'The Werewolves', all prints were apparently destroyed by a fire in 1924.

✦

THE WEREWOLF

USA, 1956. Dir: Fred F. Sears. With: Don Megowan, Joyce Holden, Steven Ritch, Eleanore Tanin, Kim Charney, Harry Lauter. Clover/Columbia. B&W.

Duncan Marsh (Ritch) is a car accident victim who is given an experimental serum containing mutant wolf blood by two scientists. Unfortunately, it has the side effect of turning him into a remorseful werewolf. He is finally shot to death by a posse. Produced by 'Jungle' Sam Katzman. The reason Ritch's werewolf resembles Matt Willis' in *The Return of the Vampire* (1943) is because both were created by make-up man Clay Campbell.

✦✦✧

THE WEREWOLF

Thailand, circa 1980s. AAE. Colour.

Bizarre blend of sex and monsters as two campers are chased by zombies which later attack a village and a man is transformed into a werewolf by rays that shoot from a wolf's eyes.

✦

WEREWOLF

USA, 1987. Dir: David Hemmings. With: John J. York, Lance LeGault, Chuck Connors, Raphael Sbarge, Michelle Johnson, Ethan Phillips. Tri-Star/Columbia. Colour.

Slow-moving pilot movie for the short-lived syndicated TV series (1987-88), executive produced by creator Frank Lupo and John Ashley. After his best friend pleads for death by a silver bullet, Eric Cord (York) discovers that he has been infected with lycanthropy and must track down and destroy the creator of the werewolf blood line to be free of the curse. With a nice cameo by Connors as the evil one-eyed werewolf master Janos Skorzeny (named after the character in *The Night Stalker* [1971]), and the climax has two Rick Baker-designed, Greg Cannom-created creatures battling each other. However, actor-turned-director Hemmings makes the mistake of holding back the horror until the final twenty minutes and the film ultimately can't overcome its small screen origins.

Sequel: WEREWOLF (qv; 1987-88)

✦✦

WEREWOLF

USA, 1987-88. Dir: David Hemmings, Larry Shaw, James Darren, Guy Magar, Lyndon Chubbuck, Rob Bowman, Robert Bralver, Sidney Hayers, Richard Colla and John Pare. With: John J. York, Lance LeGault, Chuck Connors, Brian Thompson. Tri-Star/Columbia/Fox Network. Colour.

Half-hour TV series (twenty-seven episodes) based on the 1987 TV movie, executive produced by creator Frank Lupo and John Ashley. Good werewolf Eric Cord (York) continues his hunt for evil werewolf Janos Skorzeny (Connors), still pursued by bounty hunter Alamo Joe Rogan (LeGault). Guest stars include R.G. Armstrong, Larry Drake, Howard Duff, Sid Haig, Richard Lynch, W. Morgan Sheppard, Guy Stockwell and Tony Todd. Special make-up effects created by Greg Cannom and Rick Baker.

✦✦

WEREWOLF

(aka ARIZONA WEREWOLF)

USA/Mexico, 1995 (1996). Dir: Tony Zarindast. With: George Rivero, Fred Cavalli, Adrianna Miles, Joe Estevez,

Jules Desjarlais, Richard Lynch. Tony Zarindast/Tozart Publishing/A-Pix Entertainment. Colour.
An archaeological expedition in the Arizona desert discovers the bizarre skeleton of a shape-shifter from Navajo legend. When a workman cuts himself on the bones, scheming scientists Yuri (Rivero) and Noel (Lynch, who disappears for much of the running time) set out to create their own tatty-looking lycanthropes. These include an author (Cavalli) who is new in town. With co-writer/producer/director Zarindast as a security guard. In America this direct-to-video release came in an impressive-looking 3-D box, but terrible performances, an incomprehensible script and clichéd direction make it one to miss at all costs.
✦

WEREWOLF IN A GIRLS' DORMITORY
(Orig: LYCANTHROPUS/BEI VOLLMOND MORD. UK: I MARRIED A WEREWOLF)
Italy/Austria, 1961 (1963). Dir: Richard Benson (Paolo Heusch). With: Barbara Lass, Carl Schell, Curt Lowens, Maurice Marsac, Mary McNeeran, Grace Neame. Royal Film/Metro-Goldwyn-Mayer. B&W.
'Beauties! The prey of a Monster's Desires!' enticed the ads for this slow-moving mystery. Mr Swift (Lowens) is the superintendent of a British reform school for over-age girls that happens to be surrounded by wolves! He is also the reluctant human-looking lycanthrope preying on the pupils, including the beautiful Brunhilde (Lass, then Mrs Roman Polanski). In the end, he is shot to death by Julian Olcott (Schell), a new teacher with a shady past. With Alan Collins (Luciano Pigozzi) as the creepy caretaker. The much-hyped theme song 'The Ghoul in School', sung by Marilyn Stewart and Frank Owens and released on Cub Records, is apparently not included in any version of the film! However, some lucky American cinemagoers did receive a 'Do-It-Yourself' Werewolf Kit!
✦✧

WEREWOLF OF LONDON
USA, 1935. Dir: Stuart Walker. With: Henry Hull, Warner Oland, Valerie Hobson, Lester Matthews, Spring Byington, Lawrence Grant. Universal. B&W.
Following the success of *Frankenstein* (1931), Universal announced *The Wolf Man* the following year, to star Boris Karloff and be directed by Robert Florey. In fact, this became the studio's first werewolf movie. Travelling to the Valley of Spirits in Tibet in search of a rare flower, the *Mariphasa lupina lumino* which blooms only in moonlight, Dr Wilfrid Glendon (a theatrical Hull) is bitten by a briefly-glimpsed werewolf. Returning to London with a specimen of the plant, Glendon discovers from the villainous Dr Yogami (Oland, in a role originally considered for Bela Lugosi) that only the uncommon bloom can prevent one of them from transforming into a werewolf (courtesy of John P. Fulton's special photographic effects). Hull refused to wear Jack Pierce's original make-up design (used six years later on Lon Chaney Jr) because it was too time-consuming, while scenes of the hairy creature putting on his hat and coat before going out are simply laughable. This includes a wonderful frog-eating plant, comedy relief from Zeffie Tilbury and Ethel Griffies as two gin-sodden Cockney landladies, and Edwin Parker doubling for Matthews. Director Walker replaced the originally announced Kurt Neumann. It was re-titled *The Unholy Hour* in Canada. The film was belatedly novelised in 1977 by Carl Dreadstone (Walter Harris), and a juvenile adaptation by Carl R. Green and William R. Sanford (William Reynolds) was published in 1985.
✦✦✧

THE WEREWOLF OF WASHINGTON
USA, 1973. Dir: Milton Moses Ginsberg. With: Dean Stockwell, Biff McGuire, Clifton James, Michael Dunn, Jane House, Beeson Carroll. Millco Productions/Diplomat Pictures. Colour.
This low-budget horror comedy begins well, with Presidential press aide Jack Whittier (Stockwell) bitten by a werewolf in a middle European country straight out of the old Universal films, but it never really lives up to its promise of a wolfman loose in the White House. In one scene, the lycanthrope encounters a dormant Frankenstein Monster in the secret laboratory of Dunn's sinister dwarf scientist, Dr Kiss. Writer/director Ginsberg's attempts at social commentary — particularly the Watergate scandal — never really hit the mark.
✦✧

THE WEREWOLF OF WOODSTOCK
USA, 1975. Dir: John Moffitt. With: Michael Parks, Harold J. Stone, Meredith MacRae, Tige Andrews, Ann Doran, Belinda Balaski. Dick Clark/ABC-TV. Colour.
Silly TV movie shot on video and originally shown as part of the *Wide World of Mystery* series. Set several days after the Woodstock festival has finished, a disgruntled farmer (Andrews) who hates rock music is struck by lightning and the resulting cellular disruption turns him into a hairy werewolf. It's up to a pair of young, vacationing detectives (Parks and MacRae) to track down the murderous creature. The werewolf is eventually killed in broad daylight with silver bullets. With Andrew Stevens.
✦

WEREWOLF REBORN!
Romania/USA, 1998. Dir: Jeff Burr. With: Ashley Cafagna, Bogdan Cambera, Len Lesser, Robin Downes, Lucia Maier, Serban Cellea. Tanna Productions/Full Moon Pictures. Colour.
The first in executive producer Charles Band's proposed series of thirteen *Filmonsters!* movies aimed at teenagers. While her parents are attending a conference, fourteen year-old Eleanor Crane (Cafagna) visits her uncle Peter (Downes) in Eastern Europe, only to discover that he is suspected by the locals of being the werewolf (make-up created by Mark Rappaport Creature FX) that is terrorising the countryside. They're right, and Eleanor finally kills the lycanthrope with silver bullets. At just forty-five minutes long, not much else happens. From the director of *Leatherface The Texas Chainsaw Massacre III* (1989).
✦✧

WEREWOLF TOM
(Orig: OBOROTEN' TOM)
USSR, circa 1980s. Dir: Eric Latsis. With: Gunnar Tsylinsky, Uldis Vazdiks, Helmuts Kalnynsh, Olga Drage. Riga Film Studio. Colour.
Folk tale about three brothers, Tom, Andr and Mikelis, who tame a pack of wolves and use the legends of the werewolf in their struggle against the local robber barons.
✦

DER WERWOLF VON W.
West Germany, 1988. Dir: Manfred Müller. With: Henry Hübchen, Michael Gwisdek, Martina Schieber, Werner Brehm, Horst Fechner, Erwin Brunn. Reinery/ZDF. Colour.
Investigating the death of a night watchman at a factory, a girl (Schieber) discovers that the building has been constructed on a site associated with mysterious happenings dating back over four centuries. Despite more bloody deaths, the film never bothers to solve the mystery and the unseen lycanthrope of the title is only one of several possible explanations.
✦

THE WEREWOLF VS. THE VAMPIRE WOMAN
(Orig: LA NOCHE DE WALPURGIS/NACHT DER VAMPIRE. USA: aka BLOOD MOON/WEREWOLF SHADOW. UK: SHADOW OF THE WEREWOLF/WEREWOLF'S SHADOW)
Spain/West Germany, 1970 (1972). Dir: Leon Klim (León Klimovsky). With: Paul Nash (Paul Naschy/Jacinto Molina), Gaby Fuchs, Andrew Reese (Andrés Resino), Barbara Capell, Patty (Paty) Shepard, Julio Peña. Plata Films/HI-FI Stereo 70/Intent International/Ellman Enterprises. Colour.
Fifth in the El Hombre Lobo series and a sequel to *The Fury of the Wolfman* (1970). When the silver bullets are removed by a doctor from the body of werewolf Count Waldemar Daninsky (Naschy who, as usual, also scripted under his real name), he returns to life and goes in search of vampire/witch Countess Wandesa de Nadasdy

(Shepard) and her silver cross. In the end, he is impaled on the crucifix by the woman who loves him. The ads suggested you 'See it with someone you hate' and warned, 'Those easily nauseated approach with caution'. A novelisation by Arthur N. Scarm appeared from Guild-Hartford Publishers in 1972.
Sequel: DR. JEKYLL AND THE WEREWOLF (qv; 1971)
✦✧

WEREWOLVES ON WHEELS
USA, 1971. Dir: Michel Levesque. With: Stephen Oliver, D.J. Anderson, Deuce Berry, William Gray, Barry McGuire, Severn Darden. South Street Productions/The Fanfare Corporation. Colour.
This low-budget thriller is actually better than you'd expect from the title. The Devil's Advocates are a gang of southern Californian bikers led by Adam (Oliver) who invade the temple of Satanic cult leader One (Darden). As revenge, a number of gang members are cursed and one turns into a werewolf on a motorcycle, who kills his companions. In the end, the effective-looking lycanthrope is destroyed by fire. With singer Barry ('Eve of Destruction') McGuire as Scarf and a better-than-average soundtrack.
✦✦

BUD WESTMORE
(Hamilton Adolph Westmore) [1918-1973]

American make-up artist, one of the Westmore dynasty founded by his father George (1879-1931). After a brief stint with PRC in the mid-1940s, he succeeded Jack P. Pierce at Universal.
qv: *Abbott and Costello Meet Dr. Jekyll and Mr. Hyde* (1953); *Abbott and Costello Meet the Mummy* (1955); *Creature from the Black Lagoon* (1954); *The Creature Walks Among Us* (1955); *Curse of the Undead* (1959); *Devil Bat's Daughter* (1946); *Man of a Thousand Faces* (1957); *Meet Frankenstein* (1948); *Monster on the Campus* (1958); *Munster, Go Home!* (1966); *The Munsters* (1964-66); *Revenge of the Creature* (1955).

PERC WESTMORE
(Percival Herry Westmore) [1904-1970]

American make-up artist and Bud's older brother. He created the make-ups for the TV series *The Munsters* (1964-66).
qv: *The Hunchback of Notre Dame* (1939); *The Return of Doctor X* (1939).

WALLY WESTMORE
(Walter James Westmore) [1906-1973]

American make-up artist, the brother of Bud and Perc, who was long associated with Paramount.
qv: *Dr. Jekyll and Mr. Hyde* (1931); *The Nutty Professor* (1963).

WET AND DRY
UK, 1996. Dir: John McKay. With: Kathryn Hunter, David Bamber, Marcello Magni, Geoffrey Rose, Paul Rogan, Jane McDowell. Channel Four Films/BBC Films/Pipedream Pictures. Colour.
Eleven minute comedy short in which the decaying mummy of an Egyptian princess (Hunter), living a lonely life in suburban London, drinks the blood of a scheming cosmetic surgeon (Bamber) to regain her mobility.
✦✧

WET SCIENCE
USA, 1986. Dir: Flesh Flasher. With: Candice (Candie) Evans, Bunny Bleu, Erica Boyer, Marc Wallice, Tom Byron, Tony Montana. Essex/Playtime. Colour.
Hardcore feature in which a couple (Wallice and Evans) lose their way and arrive at the home of a female mad scientist (Boyer) who has created her own man (Byron) to have sex with.
✦

WE WANT OUR MUMMY
USA, 1938. Dir: Del Lord. With: The Three Stooges (Jerry 'Curly' Howard, Larry Fine, Moe Howard), Bud Jamison, James C. Morton, Dick Curtis. Columbia. B&W.
Eighteen minute short in which the Stooges play inept detectives searching for a missing Egyptologist who end up being chased around a lost tomb by the mummy of ancient Pharaoh Rutentuten. It turns out to be a plot by a gang of crooks, but there are some hilarious moments in this slapstick farce that preceded Universal's Mummy series of the 1940s.
✦✦✧

JAMES WHALE
[1889-1957]

British director and former cartoonist who arrived in Hollywood with R.C. Sherriff's anti-war play *Journey's End* (1930). Although he brought a black humour to such seminal Universal horrors as *Frankenstein* (1931), *The Old Dark House* (1932), *The Invisible Man* (1933) and *Bride of Frankenstein* (1935), he retired in 1941 to paint and apparently committed suicide by drowning himself in his swimming pool after suffering a minor stroke. He was portrayed in an Academy Award-nominated performance by Ian McKellen in *Gods and Monsters* (1998).
qv: *Mysteries & Scandals: 'James Whale'* (1998); *The World of Gods and Monsters: A Journey With James Whale* (1999).

WHAT'S COOKIN' DOC?
USA, 1944. Dir: Robert Clampett. Voices: Mel Blanc. Warner Bros. Colour.
Seven minute *Merrie Melodies* cartoon set on Academy Awards night, in which Bugs Bunny does impressions of Edward G. Robinson, Jerry Colonna, Bing Crosby and the Frankenstein Monster to convince the committee he deserves an Oscar more than James Cagney. With clips from *Hiawatha's Rabbit Hunt* (1941) and the live-action *A Star is Born* (1937). This was later included in the feature compilation *Bugs Bunny Superstar* (1975).
Sequel: BUGS BUNNY AND THE THREE BEARS (1944)
✦✦✦

WHEN QUACKEL DID HYDE
USA, 1920. With: Charlie Joy. Aywon. B&W.
Silent comedy short based on *Strange Case of Dr. Jekyll and Mr. Hyde* by Robert Louis Stevenson.
Remake: DER JANUSKOPF (qv; 1920)
✦

WHEN SOUL MEETS SOUL
USA, 1912. Dir: J. Farrell McDonald. With: Francis X. Bushman, Dolores Cassinelli, Fred Wolf. Essanay. B&W.
Fifteen minute silent short in which the mummy of an Egyptian princess is acquired by her reincarnated lover.
✦

WHEN THE MUMMY CRIED FOR HELP
USA, 1915. With: Lee Moran, Eddie Lyons. Nestor/Universal. B&W.
A man masquerades as a mummy in this silent short featuring the comedy team of Moran and Lyons.
✦

WHERE TIME BEGAN
(Orig: VIAJE AL CENTRO DE LA TIERRA. USA: aka JOURNEY TO THE CENTER OF THE EARTH)
Spain, 1976. Dir: J. (Juan) Piquer Simon. With: Kenneth More, Pep Munne, Yvonne Sentis, Jack Taylor (George Brown Randall/Grek Martin), Frank Braña, Lone Fleming. Almena International. Colour.
Low-budget fantasy adventure, loosely based on the novel *Journey to the Centre of the Earth* by Jules Verne (previously filmed in 1959 and 1963). More plays Professor Lindenbrock, who discovers a strange manuscript detailing a route to the centre of the Earth. Good support from Taylor as the mysterious Olsen, but a futuristic under-

ground city and hints of space and time travel are more interesting than the passable dinosaurs, giant turtles and a Kong-like giant ape.
Remake: JOURNEY TO THE CENTER OF THE EARTH (1987)
✦✧

WHISTLING IN THE DARK
USA, 1941. Dir: S. Sylvan Simon. With: Red Skelton, Conrad Veidt, Ann Rutherford, Virginia Grey, 'Rags' Ragland, Eve Arden. Metro-Goldwyn-Mayer. B&W.
Remake of *Scared* (1933), also based on the play *Whistling in the Dark* by Lawrence Gross and Edward Childs Carpenter. This radio/old dark house murder mystery features Veidt as Joseph Jones, the sinister leader of a phoney cult of moon worshippers who kidnap bumbling radio sleuth Wally Benton, alias The Fox (Skelton), to plan the perfect murder. Featuring secret passages and fake mummies, it relies heavily on Skelton's comedy antics. The first in a three film series. With Lloyd Corrigan.
Sequel: WHISTLING IN DIXIE (1942)
✦✦

WHITE TO BLACK
UK, 1909. Dir: W. Wormald. London Cinematograph Company. B&W.
Silent comedy short in which a young boy uses a professor's serum to turn his sister from white to black while she is having a bath.
✦

THE WHITE WOLF
(aka THE WHITE HUNTER)
USA, 1914. Nestor/Universal. B&W.
Silent short in which a wolf caught in a trap transforms into a Native American medicine man who desires a woman betrothed to another.
✦

WHITE ZOMBIE
USA, 1932. Dir: Victor Halperin. With: Bela Lugosi, Madge Bellamy (Margaret Philpott), Joseph Cawthorn, Robert Frazer, John Harron, Brandon Hurst. Halperin/Amusement Securities Corporation/United Artists. B&W.
This low-budget independent thriller, produced by Edward Halperin and directed by his brother Victor, was the first zombie movie. Jealous Haitian plantation owner Charles Beaumont (Frazer) uses a voodoo powder to transform new bride Madeline Short (Bellamy) into one of the living dead. It is a dark, Gothic fairy-tale, and although Lugosi (in striking make-up designed by Carl Axcelle and Jack Pierce) goes over the top as the zombie master 'Murder' Legendre, it remains one of his most memorable roles. In later years the actor said he couldn't watch the film because he was paid just $800 and it made a fortune for the Halperins. According to Bela Lugosi Jr and others, his father also claimed to have directed some sequences, and unsubstantiated rumours also credit Edgar G. Ulmer with having a hand in the direction. Suggested by William B. Seabrook's 1929 book *The Magic Island* and the short-lived 1932 Broadway play *Zombie*, this was apparently shot in two weeks on many of the sets left over from Universal's *The Hunchback of Notre Dame* (1923), *Frankenstein* (1931) and *Dracula* (1931). Scenes from this film were later included in the 1943 compilation *Dr. Terror's House of Horrors*.
✦✦✦

THE WHIZ KID AND THE CARNIVAL CAPER
USA, 1976. Dir: Tom Letch. With: Jack Kruschen, John Colicos, Jaclyn Smith, Dick Bakalyan, Eric Shea, John Lupton. Walt Disney Productions. Colour.
TV movie shown in two parts on *The Wonderful World of Disney*. Boy inventor Alvin Fernald (Shea) attends a carnival where a man claiming to be Dr Frankenstein is exhibiting his robot monster. Alvin creates his own 'Whangdoogle Monster' which helps foil a bank robbery before exploding. Pyramid Books published a novelisation by Vic Crume under the title *Frankenstein and the Whiz Kid* in 1975.
✦✦

WHO IS AFRAID OF DRACULA
(Orig: FRACCHIA CONTRO DRACULA/FRACCHIA VS

Bela Lugosi introduces Brandon Hurst to one of his angels of death (John Peters) in White Zombie *(1932).*

DRACULA)
Italy, 1985. Dir: Neri Parenti. With: Paolo Villaggio, Edmund (Edmond) Purdom, Gigi Reder, Ania Pieroni, Federica Brion, Isabella Fearrare (Ferrari). Faso Film/ Titanus/Maura International Film. Colour.
Horror spoof in which star and co-writer Villaggio (*Dr. Jekyll Likes 'em Hot* [1978], etc) recreates his comic character Fantozzi as Giandomenico Fracchia, an unsuccessful estate agent who tries to sell a cheap Transylvanian castle to a myopic client (Reder). Purdom plays a Lugosi-like Dracula and Pieroni turns up as his undead sister, Countess Oniria. The knockabout climax also throws in the Frankenstein Monster and a group of zombies.
✦✧

WHY RUSSIANS ARE REVOLTING
USA, 1970. Dir: Neil Sullivan. With: Neil Sullivan, Ed Mayhood, George Badera, Seneca Ames, D.F. Barry, Herbert Boland. Mutual Releasing. B&W.
Satire about an American travelling salesman (looking and sounding like W.C. Fields) touring pre-revolutionary Russia. He meets such historical characters as Trotsky, Stalin, Lenin and Rasputin (Wes Carter). This includes clips from the John Barrymore version of *Dr. Jekyll and Mr. Hyde* (1920).
✦

THE WICKED CARESSES OF SATAN
(Orig: LA CARESSE DE SATAN/LA PERVERSA CARICIA DE SATAN. USA: aka DEVIL KISS/THE PERVERSE KISS OF SATAN)
France/Spain, 1973 (1977). Dir: Georges (Jordi) Gigo. With: Sylvia Solar (Silva Solar/Genevieve Couzain), Oliver Matthau (Olivier Mathot), Evelyn Scott (Evelyn Deher), Daniel Martin, José Nieto, Victor Israel. Boxoffice International/Home Cinema Corporation. Colour.
The usual blend of sex and horror as vengeful clairvoyant Countess Claire Grandier (Solar), the mad Professor Gruber (Matthau) and their dwarf assistant (Ronnie Harp) are invited to a château to conduct a séance. These guests then use a cellular regeneration serum and a book of black magic to reanimate the corpse of the Countess' husband (Jack Rocha) and send the blue-skinned zombie out to avenge his suicide on their host, the Duke de Haussemont (Nieto), and his wealthy friends.
✦✧

WICKED, WICKED
USA, 1973. Dir: Richard L. Bare. With: David Bailey, Tiffany Bolling, Randolph Roberts, Scott Brady, Edd Byrnes, Diane McBain. Metro-Goldwyn-Mayer. Colour.
Horror thriller set in the rambling Grandview Hotel, where psychotic handyman Rick Stewart (Bailey) wears a monster mask to murder blonde women. He then embalms them and hides their bodies in the attic. Most of the film is presented in 'Duo Vision' ('A New Concept'), which is simply a split-screen effect. Even more confusing is a strange old woman (Maryesther Denver) playing the entire original score from the 1925 *The Phantom of the Opera* on a harpsichord! With Arthur O'Connell.
✦✦

WIDE WORLD OF ENTERTAINMENT:
Horror Hall of Fame — A Monster Salute
USA, 1974. With: Vincent Price, Raymond T. McNally. ABC-TV. Colour.
Documentary in which Price performs a brief scene from *Dracula* and vampire expert and author McNally appears wearing a Dracula cape. This also includes clips from *Blacula* (1972), *Dracula Has Risen from the Grave* (1968) and *Mark of the Vampire* (1935).
✦✧

WILDERNESS
UK, 1996. Dir: Ben Bolt. With: Amanda Ooms, Owen Teale, Michael Kitchen, Gemma Jones, Catherine Holman, Johanna Benyon. Carlton UK Television/Red Rooster Film and Television Entertainment. Colour.
Three-hour TV mini-series shown in three parts, based on the novel by Dennis Danvers. Swedish-Dutch actress Ooms stars as Alice White, a sensuous university librarian living in London who, once a month, gets naked in her basement and changes into a werewolf, much to the consternation of her psychotherapist (Kitchen, who gets progressively loonier) and her new boyfriend (Teale). This includes some graphic sex scenes, nightmare sequences and optical transformations. In the end, Alice decides to remain as a wolf in the Scottish Highlands.
✦✦

THE WILD WILD WEST:
The Night of the Big Blast
USA, 1966. Dir: Ralph Senensky. With: Robert Conrad, Ross Martin, Ida Lupino, Mala Powers, Patsy Kelly, Robert Miller Driscoll. Columbia Broadcasting System/ Michael Garrison Productions. Colour.
Hour-long sci-spy Western TV series (1965-69, 104 episodes), created by executive producer Michael Garrison and set in the 1870s. In this episode, the evil Dr Faustina (Lupino) and her hunchback servant Miklos (Michael McCloud) create deadly exploding duplicates of special government agents Captain James T. West (Conrad) and Artemus Gordon (Martin) from corpses they bring to life with their electrical apparatus. This includes clips from Roger Corman's *The Fall of the House of Usher* (1960).
✦✦✧
The Night of the Cadre
USA, 1967. Dir: Leon Benson. With: Robert Conrad, Ross Martin, Richard Jaeckel, Donald Gordon, Sheilah Wells, Vince Howard. Columbia Broadcasting System/Michael Garrison Productions. Colour.
While posing as a convicted murderer, Jim West discovers that General Titus Trask (Gordon) is implanting crystals into the brains of criminals to create scientific zombies that will help him take control of President Grant and become dictator of the United States.
✦✦
The Night of the Diva
USA, 1969. Dir: Herb Wallerstein. With: Robert Conrad, Ross Martin, Patrice Munsel, Patrick Hogan, Patricia Dunne, Martin Kosleck. Columbia Broadcasting System/ Michael Garrison Productions. Colour.
Filmed under the title *The Return of Artemus Gordon* (marking Martin's return to the series after suffering a serious heart attack). When Jim and Artie rescue Italian opera star Rosa Montebello (Munsel) from a kidnapping attempt, they discover that two other singers who previously performed her role in *Lucia di L'Amour* have already disappeared. With horror veteran Kosleck as Igor the manservant.
✦✦
The Night of the Undead
USA, 1968. Dir: Marvin Chomsky. With: Robert Conrad, Ross Martin, Hurd Hatfield, Priscilla Morrill, Joan Delaney, John Zaremba. Columbia Broadcasting System/ Michael Garrison Productions. Colour.
In the swamps of the deep South, Jim West encounters voodoo sacrifices and scientific zombies created by missing mad scientist, Dr Articulus (Hatfield).
✦✦✧
The Night of the Wolf
USA, 1967. Dir: Charles Rondeau. With: Robert Conrad, Ross Martin, Joseph Campanella, Lorri Scott, John Marley, Jonathan Lippe. Columbia Broadcasting System/ Michael Garrison Productions. Colour.
While guarding King Stefan IX (Marley), the royal heir to a central European empire, and his daughter, Leandra (Scott), government agents Jim West and Artemus Gordon must stop a series of assassination attempts by the evil Talamantes (a Lugosi-like Campanella), who apparently controls a pack of werewolves that can only be killed by silver bullets.
Series sequel: THE WILD WILD WEST REVISITED (1979)
✦✦✧

THE WILD WILD WORLD OF BATWOMAN
(aka SHE WAS A HIPPY VAMPIRE)
USA, 1966. Dir: Jerry Warren. With: Katherine Victor,

George Andre, Steve Brodie, Lloyd Nelson, Richard Banks, Bruno Ve Sota. ADP International Pictures/Medallion Television. Colour.
Writer/producer/director Warren unwisely attempted to cash-in on the TV *Batman* (1966-68) craze with Victor as a cheap-looking costumed crimefighter. Along with her Bat Girls, who are equipped with wrist radios, she battles Professor Neon, Ratfink and the hunchbacked Heathcliff, who are on the trail of an atomic-powered hearing aid(!). When he was sued by National Periodical Publications for using the name 'Batwoman', Warren added a new introduction about drinking blood and changed the title in the early 1970s. It still didn't help. With Steve Conte and a few brief clips of the monsters from *The Mole People* (1956).
✦

WILLIE'S MAGIC WAND
UK, 1907. Dir: W.R. Booth. Urban. B&W.
Silent comedy short in which Willie, a magician's son, plays tricks with his father's wand. These include turning himself into a little girl.
✦

NOEL WILLMAN [1918-1988]
Solid British actor and stage director best remembered as suave vampire Dr Ravna in Hammer's *The Kiss of the Vampire* (1962) and the enigmatic Dr Franklyn in *The Reptile* (1966).

WILL VINTON'S CLAYMATION COMEDY OF HORRORS
USA, 1991. Dir: Barry Bruce. Will Vinton/FHE/CBS-TV. Colour.
Half-hour clay animation Halloween short for TV, in which fortune hunter Wilshire Pig and his assistant Sheldon Snail visit a long-deserted castle in search of the miniature Monster created by Doctor of Mad Science Victor Frankenswine. This also includes a mummy that uses its head as a bowling ball.
✦✧

WINDWALKER
USA, 1980. Dir: Keith Merrill. With: Trevor Howard, Nick Ramus, Rudy Diaz, James Remar, Serene Hedin, Dusty Iron Wing McCrea. Windwalker Productions. Colour.
Mystical adventure in which the eponymous Cheyenne chief (an unlikely role for veteran Howard) is resurrected to unite his family and aid their revenge upon the members of the Crow tribe who stole away his son. Much of the dialogue is spoken in Native American dialect and subtitled in English.
✦✦✧

WINGS OF DEATH
UK, 1985. Dir: Nichola Bruce and Michael Coulson. With: Dexter Fletcher, Kate Hardie, Tony Haygarth, Paula Jacobs, Lynne Radford, Adam French. A BFI Production. Colour.
Twenty-two minute low-budget independent short in which dying heroin addict Alex (Fletcher) is holed up in a bizarre hotel where he suffers from a series of horrific hallucinations (including zombies and some impressive gore effects). Genuinely disturbing, this won a number of awards at festivals.
✦✦✧

WINTER WITH DRACULA
Romania/UK, 1971 (1972). Dir: John Dooley. Polonius/ Border. Colour.
Despite the title, this tedious twenty-seven minute travelogue about winter sports in Romania only makes a passing reference to Vlad Tepes, the inspiration for Bram Stoker's *Dracula*. Narrated by Patrick Allen.
✦

THE WISDOM OF CROCODILES
UK, 1998. Dir: Po-Chih Leong. With: Jude Law, Elina Löwensohn, Timothy Spall, Kerry Fox, Jack Davenport, Colin Salmon. Zenith Productions/Goldwyn Films International/Foundry Film Partners/Entertainment Film Distributors. Colour.
This arty post-modern vampire thriller, set in a surreal London, was made for just $1,500,000 by Hong Kong director Leong. Law (who replaced James Woods before shooting) plays the oddly named Steven Griscz, a Bulgarian medical researcher who seduces women and feeds off the positive emotions that exist in their blood streams. When the body of his previous victim (a wasted Fox) turns up in the sea, Detective Roche (Davenport) and Inspector Healey (Spall) suspect that Griscz's new girlfriend, unlikely asthmatic structural engineer Anna Levels (Löwensohn, from *Nadja* [1994]), may become the next target of this different type of vampire. In a unique twist to the mythology, Griscz coughs up crystals of emotion from his victims, and then files them away under their names and the feelings they invoke. The title comes from a Francis Bacon quote.
✦✧

WISHBONE:
Frankenbone
USA, 1995. Dir: Allen Mondell and Jackie Martin Kaptan. With: Larry Brantley, Jordan Wall, Christie Abbott, Adam Springfield, Mary Chris Wall, Angee Hughes. Big Feats! Entertainment/Southern Star/PBS. Colour.
Half-hour children's TV show (1995-) about the Jack Russell dog who day-dreams himself into great works of literature. In this episode, when the robot David (Springfield) creates for the school science fair goes out of control, Wishbone the dog (voiced by Brantley) imagines himself as Victor Frankenstein in pursuit of the horribly scarred Monster (Matthew Tompkins) he has created.
✦✦✦

The Hunchdog of Notre Dame
USA, 1995. Dir: Ben Vaughn and Jackie Martin Kaptan. With: Larry Brantley, Jordan Wall, Christie Abbott, Adam Springfield, Mary Chris Wall, Angee Hughes. Big Feats! Entertainment/Southern Star/PBS. Colour.
While Sam (Abbott) helps Nathanial (Justin Reese) learn to play roller hockey, Wishbone imagines himself as Quasimodo, the hunchbacked bellringer of Notre Dame who is befriended by the dancing gypsy girl Esmeralda (Lanell Peña).
✦✦✧

Mixed Breeds
USA, 1995. Dir: Ken Harrison and Jackie Martin Kaptan. With: Larry Brantley, Jordan Wall, Christie Abbott, Adam Springfield, Mary Chris Wall, Angee Hughes. Big Feats! Entertainment/Southern Star/PBS. Colour.
Wanda (Hughes) and Mr Pruitt (Rick Perkins) learn to be themselves, and the day-dreaming dog imagines himself as the lawyer Utterson in the strange case of Dr Jekyll and Mr Hyde (Joe Nemmers).
✦✦

Pantin' at the Opera
USA, 1995. Dir: Ben Vaughn and Jackie Martin Kaptan. With: Larry Brantley, Jordan Wall, Christie Abbott, Adam Springfield, Mary Chris Wall, Angee Hughes. Big Feats! Entertainment/Southern Star/PBS. Colour.
A series of bizarre thefts at the public library result in Wishbone imagining himself as Viscount Raoul de Chagny, who must save singer Christine (Lisa-Gabrielle Greene) from the horribly disfigured Erik (Kevin Page), the Phantom of the Opera.
✦✦✧

WITCHCRAFT MISTRESS OF THE CRAFT
UK/USA, 1998 (1999). Dir: Elisar Cabrera. With: Wendy Cooper, Eileen Daly, Kerry Knowlton, Stephanie Beaton, Sean Harry, Frank Scantori. Vista Street Entertainment/ Armadillo Films. Colour.
The tenth episode in the low-budget, softcore video franchise and the first to be shot outside America. Celeste Sheridan (Cooper) is a supernatural being from another dimension who works in London as a consultant for Interpol's Bureau 17 and uses her magical powers to battle the forces of evil. She teams up with Detective Lucy Luntz (Beaton), who has travelled from Los Angeles to hunt down a serial killer Satanist named Hyde (Knowlton). However, Hyde has joined

forces with the undead Raven Daminelli (the awful Daly) and her cult of female vampires to bring the bloodsucker's Demon Master to Earth.
✦

WITCHCRAFT 7 A TASTE FOR BLOOD
(aka WITCHCRAFT 7 JUDGEMENT HOUR)
USA, 1995. Dir: Michael Paul Girard. With: David Byrnes, April Brenenman, Alisa Christensen, John Cragen, Loren Schmalle, Ashley Rhey. Vista Street Entertainment. Colour.
Seventh in the sometimes-connected, direct-to-video series that began in 1988. Modern-day warlock/lawyer Will Spanner (Byrnes) teams up with Los Angeles detectives Luntz and Gardner to stop a vampire turning women into indestructible killers. In the end, he is forced to sacrifice his earthly existence to destroy the bloodsucker.
Sequel: WITCHCRAFT VIII SALEM'S GHOST (1995)
✦✧

WITCHCRAFT III THE KISS OF DEATH
USA, 1991. Dir: R.L. Tillmans. With: Charles Solomon, Lisa Toothman, Domonic Luciano, Leana Hall, William L. Baker, Sha Bennett. Marketing Media/Vista Street Entertainment. Colour.
Third in the direct-to-video series. Los Angeles attorney William Spanner (Solomon) returns from *Witchcraft II The Temptress* (1989) and uses his warlock powers to stop the vampiric Louis Daminelli (Luciano), who threatens Spanner's girlfriend Charlotte (Toothman) with a kiss of death. *Witchcraft IV Virgin Heart* (1991) is an unconnected follow-up.
✦✧

WITCHDOCTOR OF THE LIVING DEAD
Nigeria, circa 1980s. Dir: Charles Abi Enonchong. With: Joe Layode 'Garuba', St. Mary Enonchong, Victor Eriabie, Larry Williams. Enonchong-O'Reilly Cinema Productions/ Film Video. Colour.
Shot on video in English. A trendy police detective investigates the witch doctor who is terrorising an African village. The Ju-Ju man turns into a goat, conjures up a rubber snake to kill a victim on the toilet, and commands an army of gaping pasty-faced zombies. In the end, his hut burns to the ground as he is destroyed by a priest.
✦

WITCH FROM NEPAL
(Orig: KEI YUEN/QI YUAN. USA: aka THE NEPAL AFFAIR/ A TOUCH OF LOVE)
Hong Kong, 1985 (1986). Dir: Ching Siu-Tung (Cheng Xiu-Dong). With: Chow Yun-Fat, Emily Chu (Chu Bo-Yee/ Cherie Chung), Nam Kit-Ying, Dick Wei (Tik Wai), Ng Kong-Sang, Chu Bao Yi. Golden Harvest/Paragon/ Rainbow Video/Tai Seng Video. Colour.
Good witch Sheila (Chu), pursued by a cat-like demon (Wei), travels from the Himalayas to Hong Kong to inform artist Joe Wong (Yun-Fat) that it is his destiny to become the new leader of her sect. In one scene, the evil creature raises the rotting dead from their graves to attack Wong and a car full of children.
✦✦✧

WITCH HUNT
USA, 1994. Dir: Paul Schrader. With: Dennis Hopper, Penelope Ann Miller, Eric Bogosian, Sheryl Lee Ralph, Valerie Mahaffey, Lypsinka. Home Box Office/LC Dynamic. Colour.
Slightly disappointing sequel to HBO's *Cast a Deadly Spell* (1991). A mis-cast Hopper replaces Fred Ward as private investigator H. Philip Lovecraft in a Hollywood where magic really works. The script cleverly reworks the communist witch-hunts of the 1950s, with Lovecraft's friend Hypolita Kropotkin (Ralph) as one of those accused. However, this cable TV movie is let down by Schrader's (*Cat People* [1982], etc) uninspired direction. With Julian Sands, a police lieutenant named Bradbury, William Shakespeare as a scriptwriter and a zombie (Michael 'Bear' Taliferro).
✦✦✧

WITCH'S NIGHT OUT
USA, 1978. Dir: John Leach. Voices: Gilda Radner, Bob Church, John Leach, Naomi Leach, Tony Molesworth, Gerry Salsberg. Leach-Rankin/Rankin-Bass Productions/ NBC-TV. Colour.
Half-hour cartoon TV special in which has-been witch The Godmother (Radner) transforms two children on Halloween into a werewolf and a ghost, and their babysitter Bazooey (Salsberg) into Frankenstein's Monster.
✦✦

THE WITCH WITH THE FLYING HEAD
Hong Kong, 1979. Dir: Woo Lian-Sing. With: Tsang Yin, Fariney Chang. Tai Seng Video. Colour.
Hong Kong horror movie that involves a vampire who can detach her head and entrails (a *penanggalan*), spit snakes and centipedes, and breath fire.
✦✧

WITCH WORLD:
(Orig: GRAND MÉRE EST UNE SORCIÈRE)
Monsterland
France, 1997. Dir: Alexis Lavillat. Voices: Jean-Marie Boyer, Jean-François Kopf, Richard Leblond, Christine Pâris, Charlyne Pestel, Natacha Sapey. France 2/ Goldvision/Canal +/Nickelodeon. Colour.
Twenty minute cartoon TV series aimed at very young children and based on characters created by Colin Hawkins. Young witch Zarina and her friend Einstein travel through a library book to Monsterland where they deliver a TV to the Bogeyman, much to the delight of the other monstrous inhabitants — including a werewolf, a zombie, a hunchback and a Frankenstein Monster. However, the vampiric Uncle Drac does not approve. A mummy and a vampire also appear in the opening sequence.
✦✧

WITHOUT A SOUL
(aka LOLA)
USA, 1916. Director: James Young. With: Clara Kimball Young, Alec B. Francis, Edward M. Kimball, Irene Tams, Mary Moore. Young Pictures/World Film Corporation. B&W.
Silent drama based on the play *Lola* by Owen Davis. When his daughter Lola (the director's wife, Young) is killed in a car accident, her scientist father (Kimball) creates an electric ray which brings her back from the dead. However, when the girl's behaviour becomes selfish and wanton, her father realises that his daughter has been revived without her original soul. In the end, she dies on the laboratory floor from a heart attack and he destroys his equipment.
✦✧

WITH THE MUMMIES' HELP
USA, 1917. With: Eddie Barry, Ethel Lynne, George French, Margaret Gibson. Christie. B&W.
Eleven minute silent comedy in which a wife decides to cure her husband's obsession for collecting antiques by getting two friends to disguise themselves as mummies and give him a scare.
✦

WIZARDS AND WARRIORS:
Vulkar's Revenge
USA, 1983. Dir: Kevin Connor. With: Jeff Conaway, Walter Olkewicz, Duncan Regehr, Julia Duffy, Clive Revill, Ian Wolfe. Warner Bros/CBS-TV. Colour.
Short-lived (eight episodes) hour-long sword and sorcery TV series, set in the mythical kingdom of Camarand. In this final episode, while taking shelter in Baaldorf's castle, Wizard Vector (Revill) creates a zombie killer to hunt down the evil Prince Dirk Blackpool (Regehr) so that he can reclaim the source of his power. At the time, this was the most expensive series on TV.
✦✦✧

WOHI BHAYAANAK RAAT
India, 1989. Dir: Vinod Talwar. With: Kiran Kumar, Neeta

Puri. Talwar Productions. Colour.
Hindi horror film inspired by *Fright Night* (1985). A young student returns home from college and is convinced that a suave vampire (Kumar) is living in the empty mansion opposite. His girlfriend (Puri) turns out to be the reincarnation of the vampire's lost love. The title translates as 'That Same Horrifying Night'.
✦✦

WOLF

USA, 1994. Dir: Mike Nichols. With: Jack Nicholson, Michelle Pfeiffer, James Spader, Kate Nelligan, Richard Jenkins, Christopher Plummer. Columbia. Colour.
Uneven and often ludicrous, this was originally announced as *Woolf.* Nicholson plays Will Randall, a Manhattan book editor about to lose his job. While driving along a remote country road at night, he is attacked and bitten by a giant wolf. From that point on his life begins to change. The transformation is subtle at first, with his senses becoming more acute, but as his powers increase, so the animal in him is released (Rick Baker's special make-up effects make Nicholson look like Henry Hull in *WereWolf of London* [1935]). Spader's Stewart Swinton also transforms into a yuppie lycanthrope, while Nelligan replaced the originally cast Mia Farrow as Randall's wife. An uncredited Elaine May contributed to the script. With a lush music score by Ennio Morricone.
✦✦✧

WOLF BLOOD

USA, 1925. Dir: George Chesebro and George Mitchell. With: George Chesebro, Marguerite Clayton, Ray Hanford, Roy Watson, Milburn Morante, Frank Clark. Ryan Brothers/Lee-Bradford Corporation. B&W.
Silent drama. Following a series of unexplained deaths, Dick (Chesebro) fears that he is turning into a wild beast after he receives an emergency transfusion of wolf's blood from Dr Horton.
✦

IAN WOLFE [1896-1992]

Dependable American character actor who appeared in more than 200 films in a career spanning seven decades, often playing officious little men.
qv: *The Brighton Strangler* (1945); *Mad Love* (1935); *The Return of Doctor X* (1939); *Wizards and Warriors: 'Vulkar's Revenge'* (1983); *Zombies on Broadway* (1945).

WOLFEN

USA, 1981. Dir: Michael Wadleigh (and John Hancock). With: Albert Finney, Diane Venora, Edward James Olmos, Gregory Hines, Tom Noonan, Dick O'Neill. Orion Pictures/ King-Hitzig. Colour.
Based on the best-selling novel by Whitley Strieber, this cost an incredible (at the time) $15,000,000. When a rich industrialist, his wife and bodyguard are found with their throats torn out (gore effects created by Carl Fullerton), the investigation by New York detective Dewey Wilson (a strong performance by Finney) uncovers an ancient race of shape-shifters co-existing with man. To produce the creatures' unique point-of-view, the film-makers created the over-hyped 'Alienvision' process, combining Stedicam techniques with various visual effects. Optically-enhanced real wolves were mostly used to depict the Wolfen. Documentary film-maker Wadleigh (*Woodstock* [1970], etc) was replaced by an uncredited Hancock, but despite a muddled screenplay involving terrorists and Native American mythology, this is still a very impressive thriller.
✦✦✦✧

WOLFEN NINJA

(USA: aka WOLF DEVIL WOMAN)
Hong Kong, 1982 (1986). Dir: Pearl Cheung (Pearl Cheong/ Chang Ling). With: Pearl Cheung (Pearl Cheong/Chang Ling), Shek Fong (Shih Fong), Shek Ying. Chang I-Shiang/ Trans-World Entertainment/Ocean Shores Video. Colour.
Based on the 1954 novel *Jiang-Hu* by Leung Yu-Sang (also the basis for *The Bride With White Hair* [1992]). A woman raised by wolves (director Cheung) becomes a mystic Ninja warrior and uses her powers to battle the followers of the evil Red Devil. After eating a ginseng root, whenever she gets angry or drunk her hair turns pure white, and when her boyfriend is set on fire by the villain, she savages her own arm and uses the blood to douse the flames. This includes a pair of hopping vampires, a green-faced werewolf, and zombies whose souls are imprisoned in golden needles. The first in a trilogy starring Cheung as the Wolf Devil Woman.
Sequel: VENUS THE NINJA (1983)
Remake: WHITE HAIR DEVIL LADY (1985)
✦✦

WOLFEN TICKLE

USA, 1990. Dir: Tony Sinclair. With: Saki St. Jermaine. Sinclair Blue Productions. Colour.
Hour-long 'adults only' tickling video, presented 'in furry color'! Bondage queen St. Jermaine is tied up and tickled relentlessly by a silly-looking werewolf. You've got to laugh!
✦

THE WOLF GIRL

Hong Kong/Thailand, 1981. Dir: Chen Tung-Man and Chin Weng. With: Ai Lan-Yeh, Chin Weng, Sung Pa, Huoy Dyng, Su Szu. Ocean Shores. Colour.
Escaping a murderous mystic, a woman gives birth to twin girls in the woods. One is left in the care of a peasant family, while the other is raised by wolves. The latter grows up as a topless furry beast with long claws, who leads her pack of wolves (actually German shepherds) in raids on the local farming community. As the plot progresses, the hero manages to get the twins' identities confused, while a demonic little boy turns up and starts decapitating people with his magic powers. This apparently re-uses howls from a Paul Naschy werewolf movie and steals its title song from *Rosemary's Baby* (1968)!
✦✧

THE WOLF MAN

USA, 1941. Dir: George Waggner. With: Lon Chaney, Claude Rains, Warren William, Ralph Bellamy, Patric Knowles, Bela Lugosi. Universal. B&W.
This was originally considered as a 1932 project for director Robert Florey, to star Boris Karloff. Scripted by Curt Siodmak and filmed under the title *Destiny*, it introduced the cursed Lawrence Stewart Talbot (Chaney Jr, giving one of his best performances), who returns to his ancestral home in Wales. While going to the rescue of a young woman, he is attacked and bitten by a werewolf and soon discovers that only silver can destroy the beast he changes into beneath the full moon (make-up by Jack P. Pierce, originally created for Henry Hull in *WereWolf of London* [1935], and special visual effects by John P. Fulton). The impressive supporting cast includes Rains as Sir John Talbot, Lugosi in a cameo as Bela the werewolf gypsy, Evelyn Ankers, Fay Helm, Forrester Harvey, Harry Stubbs, silent film star Gibson Gowland (*Greed* [1924], etc) and Maria Ouspenskaya as the wise old gypsy woman, Maleva. Scenes of Talbot wrestling a bear (which escaped on set during filming) in the gypsy encampment were cut from most prints but appear in the original trailer. It was novelised twice in 1977, by Carl Dreadstone/E.K. Leyton (Ramsey Campbell) and in a juvenile edition by Ian Thorne, while Jeff Rovin's sequel *Return of the Wolf Man* appeared in 1998. Editor Philip J. Riley published the script in his MagicImage Filmbooks series in 1993, and Siodmak included his own script as part of a commemorative package to tie-in with the release of the Classic Movie Monsters stamps in America in 1997. 'Even a man who is pure in heart...'
Sequel: FRANKENSTEIN MEETS THE WOLF MAN (qv; 1943)
✦✦✦✦✧

WOLFMAN

(aka WOLFMAN — A LYCANTHROPE)
USA, 1978 (1979). Dir: Worth Keeter III. With: Earl Owensby, Kristina Reynolds, Edward L. Grady, Maggie Lauterer, Richard Dedmon, Sid Rancer. EO Corporation/

Lon Chaney Jr has a howling good time with Evelyn Ankers in The Wolf Man *(1941).*

Omni. Colour.
Set in Georgia in 1910. Through a black magic ceremony, the Reverend Leonard (Grady) passes on a family curse to Colin Glasgow (Owensby, who was also the producer), causing him to transform into a werewolf during the phases of the full moon. He is finally stabbed to death with a silver dagger. Filmed in North Carolina by twenty-two year old Keeter, Owensby's movies mostly played drive-in circuits in the southern United States.
✦

THE WOLFMAN CHRONICLES
USA, 1991. Dir: Ted Newsom. Robert T. Newsom/ Heidelberg Films/Rhino Video. Colour/B&W.
Hour-long documentary about movie werewolves that also includes Dr Jekyll and Mr Hyde, illustrated with numerous stills, lobby cards, clips and trailers from, amongst others, Chaney Jr's *The Wolf Man* (1941), all the Universal sequels plus *Abbott and Costello Meet Dr. Jekyll and Mr. Hyde* (1953), *An American Werewolf in London* (1981), *The Ape Man* (1943), *The Beast Must Die* (1974), *La Casa Del Terror* (1960), *Cry of the Werewolf* (1944), *The Curse of the Werewolf* (1960), *Daughter of Dr. Jekyll* (1957), *Dr. Jekyll and Mr. Hyde* (1931 and 1941 versions), *Frankenstein's Bloody Terror* (1967), *The Howling* (1980), *How to Make a Monster* (1958), *I Was a Teenage Werewolf* (1957), *The Mad Monster* (1942), *The Return of the Vampire* (1943), *She-Wolf of London* (1946), *The Werewolf* (1956), *Werewolf in a Girls' Dormitory* (1961), *WereWolf of London* (1935), *The Werewolf vs. the Vampire Woman* (1970) and *Werewolves on Wheels* (1971). Although it contains nothing unusual, this value-for-money compilation includes a great selection of material. Titled *Wolfman A Cinematic Scrapbook* on the American video box.
✦✦✦

WOLFMAN JACK
(Robert Smith) [1939-1995]

American radio disc jockey, famous for his deep-throated howl, who made numerous cameo appearances in movies and on TV.
qv: *Conquest of the Earth* (1980); *Galactica 1980: 'The Night the Cylons Landed'* (1980); *The Hilarious House of Frightenstein* (1970-72); *Midnight* (1988); *The Midnight Hour* (1985); *Mortuary Academy* (1988); *The New Adventures of Wonder Woman: 'Disco Devil'* (1978).

WOLNYOUI HAN
Republic of Korea, 1980. Dir: Kim In-Soo. With: Chin Bong-Chin, Huh Chin. Han Jin Enterprises. Colour.
Folk tale fantasy set in a medieval Korean village. After losing the man she loves to another woman, a young girl takes refuge in a swamp and is possessed by an evil spirit in the form of a vampiric white cat. She then returns to revenge herself on those who betrayed her.
✦

EDWARD D. WOOD JR
[1924-1978]

Cult American director and writer who is unfairly remembered as the worst film-maker of all time and whose life and career have now become something of a mini-industry. A fan and friend of Bela Lugosi during the actor's final years, Edward Davis Wood Jr apparently had more enthusiasm than talent (or budget), so he surrounded himself with a loyal stock company that included a post-drug addicted Bela, Swedish wrestler Tor Johnson, television psychic Criswell, and would-be actors Paul Marco and Conrad Brooks. As a result, films like *Glen or Glenda* (1953), *Bride of the Monster* (1954), *Plan 9 from Outer Space* (1958) and *Night of the Ghouls* (1959) now have a certain naïve charm, which Tim Burton acknowledged in his affectionate tribute *Ed Wood* (1994), starring Johnny Depp as the eponymous cross-dresser.
qv: *The Bride and the Beast* (1957); *Ed Wood Look Back in Angora* (1994); *Final Curtain* (1957); *Flying Saucers Over Hollywood* (1992); *The Haunted World of Ed Wood* (1996); *Necromania* (1971); *On the Trail of Ed Wood* (1990); *Orgy of the Dead* (1965).

GEORGE WOODBRIDGE
[1907-1973]

British character actor notable for playing portly innkeepers and irate villagers in various Hammer horrors.
qv: *The Curse of the Werewolf* (1960); *Dracula* (1958); *Dracula Prince of Darkness* (1965); *Fog for a Killer* (1962); *The Mummy* (1959); *The Reptile* (1966); *The Revenge of Frankenstein* (1958).

WOOF!
(USA: WOOF! IT'S A DOG'S LIFE)
UK, 1988- . Dir: David Cobham. With: Liza Goddard, Edward Fidoe, Adam Roper, Sebastian Mahjouri, Monty Allan. Central Independent Television/Carlton UK Television/ITV. Colour.
Popular half-hour comedy/drama for TV, inspired by the children's book by Alan Ahlberg. Over the course of several series, linked by Goddard as schoolteacher Miss Victoria Jessop, a number of young schoolboys — Eric Banks (Fidoe), Rex Thomas (Roper) and Jim Walters (Mahjouri) — discover that they periodically transform into an intelligent dog whenever they get an itchy feeling. Guest stars include Nigel Davenport, Anita Dobson, Stephen Fry, Leslie Grantham, Nigel Havers, Lionel Jeffries, Freddie Jones, Bill Pertwee, Leslie Phillips and Michael Troughton.
✦✦

RICHARD WORDSWORTH
[1915-1993]

British actor, the great-great-grandson of the poet William Wordsworth. On the stage since 1938, he made his film début as metamorphic astronaut Victor Caroon in Hammer's *The Quatermass Experiment* (1955).
qv: *The Curse of the Werewolf* (1960); *The Revenge of Frankenstein* (1958).

WORKING STIFFS
USA, circa 1990s. Dir: Michael Legge. With: Beverly Epstein, Bruce Harding, Tony Ferreira, Alan Kennedy, Michael McInnis, James O'Brien. Sideshow Cinema Production/Wham! USA. Colour.
Shot on video in Massachusetts by writer/director Legge, this independent comedy is just over an hour long. A woman discovers her brother has become a workaholic from beyond the grave when an unscrupulous employment agency uses voodoo spells to revive dead employees as cheap labour.
✦

THE WORLD OF ABBOTT AND COSTELLO
USA, 1964 (1965). Dir: Sidney Meyers. With: Bud Abbott, Lou Costello, Lon Chaney, Marjorie Main, Tom Ewell, Bela Lugosi. Universal/Vanguard. B&W.
Produced by Max J. Rosenberg and Milton Subotsky of Amicus, this compilation of numerous sequences from Abbott and Costello's Universal comedies features classic clips and redundant commentary by Jack E. Leonard and Gene Wood. The most memorable excerpts are from the team's fantasy movies, including *Abbott and Costello Go to Mars* (1953), an uncredited *Abbott and Costello Meet Dr. Jekyll and Mr. Hyde* (1953), *Abbott and Costello Meet the Mummy* (1955), *Hold That Ghost* (1941), (Abbott and Costello)...*Meet the Invisible Man* (1952) and, best of all, (Abbott and Costello) *Meet Frankenstein* (1948), featuring Lugosi's Count Dracula, Chaney Jr's Wolf Man and Glenn Strange's Frankenstein Monster. Music supervision by Joseph Gershenson.
✦✦

THE WORLD OF DRACULA
USA, 1979. Dir: Jeffrey Hayden, Sutton Roley and Kenneth Johnson. With: Michael Nouri, Carol Baxter, Stephen Johnson, Bever-Leigh Banfield, Louise Sorel, Antoinette Stella. Universal. Colour.
TV movie cobbled together from episodes of the *Cliffhangers* serial,

The Curse of Dracula, created by executive producer Kenneth Johnson. Padded with flashbacks within flashbacks, an urbane and sophisticated Dracula (Nouri) teaches night-school in San Francisco while Van Helsing's grandson Kurt (Johnson) and Mary Gibbons (Baxter) track down the Count's boxes of sacred earth and destroy them along with his undead followers. The film has no ending because the series was cancelled after ten episodes. Les Baxter co-composed the music score. *Dracula '79* (1979) and *The Loves of Dracula* (1979) were other TV movies derived from the same material.
✦✦

THE WORLD OF GODS AND MONSTERS: A JOURNEY WITH JAMES WHALE

USA, 1999. Dir: David J. Skal and Sam Irvin. With: Ian McKellen, Brendan Fraser, Lynn Redgrave, Bill Condon, Clive Barker, Gloria Stewart. Lions Gate Films/Universal Studios Home Video. Colour/B&W.

Half-hour documentary, written by Skal and released as a supplement to the DVD of *Gods and Monsters* (1998). This behind-the-scenes look at the making of the film is interwoven with a candid examination of the life and career of director James Whale and includes interviews with Curtis Harrington and novelist Christopher Bram. Narrated by Clive Barker.
✦✦✦

THE WORLD OF HAMMER

UK, 1990 (1994). Hammer Film Productions/Best of British Films/Channel Four Television. Colour.

Half-hour series (thirteen episodes) written and created by editor Ashley Sidaway and producer Robert Sidaway and narrated by Oliver Reed. Episode titles include 'The Curse of Frankenstein', 'Dracula & the Undead', 'Hammer Stars: Christopher Lee', 'Hammer Stars: Peter Cushing', 'Mummies, Werewolves & the Living Dead' and 'Vamp'. Each show is devoted to a specific theme and illustrated with lengthy sequences from several Hammer films, including *Brides of Dracula* (1960), *Captain Kronos Vampire Hunter* (1972), *Dracula* (1958), *Dracula Prince of Darkness* (1965), *Kiss of the Vampire* (1962), *The Legend of the 7 Golden Vampires* (1974), *Lust for a Vampire* (1971), *Scars of Dracula* (1970), *Twins of Evil* (1971), *Vampire Circus* (1972) and *The Vampire Lovers* (1970), amongst many others.
✦✦✧

THE WORLD OF THE VAMPIRES

(Orig: EL MUNDO DE LOS VAMPIROS)
Mexico, 1960 (1962). Dir: Alfonso Corona Blake. With: Mauricio Garcés, Erna Martha Bauman, Silvia Fournier, Guillermo Murray, José Baviera, Yolanda Margain. Cinematográfica ABSA/Clasa-Mohme/American International. B&W.

Atmospheric vampire thriller scripted by Alfred (Alfredo) Salazar and produced by Abel Salazar. Vampire Count Sergio Subotai (Argentinean actor Murray) rises from his coffin to play music on an organ made out of human skulls and bones in his secret subterranean caverns. The big-fanged Count's victims become werewolves, he has a hunchbacked assistant, and his undead disciples are either women wearing too much make-up or ugly pop-eyed bat-men. When Subotai puts the bite on Professor Kolman's niece Leonor and kidnaps her sister Mirta, piano-playing occult expert Rodolfo (Garcés) uses a special tune to overcome the Count before hurling him into a pit of wooden stakes. The English-language version was produced by K. (Kenneth) Gordon Murray and directed by Paul Nagle (Nagel).
✦✦✧

WORLD PREMIERE TOONS:

(aka WORLD PREMIERE TOON-IN/WHAT A CARTOON! SHOW)

Mina and the Count Interlude with a Vampire

USA/Philippines, 1995. Dir: Chris Cuddington. Voices: Michael Bell, Mark Hamill, Jeff Bennett, Ashley Johnson. Hanna-Barbera Cartoons/Fil-Cartoons/The Cartoon Network. Colour.

Ten minute TV series (1995-96) which premièred numerous new cartoons, including *Dexter's Laboratory*, *The PowerPuff Girls*, *Cow and Chicken* and *Johnny Bravo*. Just when he thinks he's found the perfect victim with Mina (Johnson), a little girl, the vampire Count (Hamill) discovers he's found a new friend instead in this delightful segment.
✦✦✦

WORLDS BEYOND:

The Black Tomb

UK, 1986 (1988). Dir: John Jacobs. With: Eli Wallach, Anne Jackson, John Vine, Derek Benfield, Rosalie Crutchley. Brent Walker/ITV. Colour.

Half-hour anthology TV series (thirteen episodes), supposedly based on true-life cases from the Archives of the Society for Psychical Research. In this episode, an American couple visiting an old graveyard discover a tomb with no inscription, which they later learn belongs to a vampire.
✦✦

Guardian of the Past

UK, 1986 (1988). Dir: Adrian Cooper. With: Paul Freeman, Terence Alexander, Mary Tamm. Brent Walker/ITV. Colour.

A cursed piece of bone from the tomb of a princess brings death and terror to the inhabitants of an English country house.
✦✦

WOWSER:

Dracula Meets the Wowser

Belgium/Japan, 1988. Telecable Benelux/Saban Entertainment/The Family Channel. Colour.

In this episode of the half-hour cartoon TV series, the eponymous white sheepdog and his eccentric owner Professor Dinghy meet the vampire Count.
✦

THE WRAITH OF THE TOMB

(aka THE AVENGING HAND)
UK, 1915. Dir: Charles Calvert. With: Dorothy Bellew, Sydney Vautier, Douglas Payne. Cricks & Martin. B&W.

Silent short in which the ghost of an ancient Egyptian princess curses an archaeologist who has stolen her mummified hand.
✦

FAY WRAY
[b 1907]

Canadian-born American actress immortalised as the object of the giant ape's affections in *King Kong* (1933). She also exercised her lungs by screaming her way through *Doctor X* (1932), *Mystery of the Wax Museum* (1932), *The Most Dangerous Game* (1932) and *The Vampire Bat* (1933). Her autobiography *On the Other Hand* was published in 1989.

qv: *Black Moon* (1934); *Universal Horror* (1998).

THE WRESTLING WOMEN VS. THE AZTEC MUMMY

(Orig: LAS LUCHADORAS CONTRA LA MOMIA. USA: aka ROCK 'N ROLL WRESTLING WOMEN VS. THE AZTEC MUMMY)
Mexico, 1964 (1965). Dir: René Cardona. With: Lorena Velázquez, Armand (Armando) Silvestre, Elizabeth Campbell, Eugenia Saint Martin (Maria Eugenia San Martin), Chucho Salinas, Raymond (Ramón) Bugarini. Cinematográfica Calderón/Clasa-Mohme/Azteca/Young America Productions/American International. B&W.

As usual scripted by Alfred (Alfredo) Salazar, this is a sequel-of-sorts to both *The Robot vs the Aztec Mummy* (1957) and *Doctor of Doom* (1962). This time Mexican wrestling women Loreta — formerly Gloria — Venus (Velázquez) and The Golden Rubi (Campbell) battle sinister oriental villain the Black Dragon and his crime syndicate, who are attempting to discover the location of a golden necklace belonging to Princess Xochitl. However, the cursed Aztec tomb is guarded Tezomoc, the living mummy of a sorcerer who can magically transform himself into a vampire bat and tarantula spider during the hours of darkness. The English language version was produced by K. (Kenneth) Gordon Murray and directed by Manuel San Fernando. In 1986 Rhino Video released a version remixed with new

rock 'n' roll songs and produced by Johnny Legend.
Sequel: LAS LOBAS DEL RING (1965)
✦✧

THE WRESTLING WOMEN VS. THE KILLER ROBOT

(Orig: EL ASESINO LOCO Y EL SEXO/LAS LUCHADORAS CONTRA EL ROBOT ASESINO)
Mexico, 1968 (1969). Dir: René Cardona. With: Joaquin Cordero, Regina Torné, Hector Lechuga, Malu Reyes, Carlos Agosti, Gerado Moreno. Cinematográfica Calderón. Colour.

Following on from *Las Mujeres Panteras* (1966), a new set of Las Luchadoras appear in this fifth and final film in the series, as wrestling women Gaby (Torné) and Gema (Reyes) battle mad scientist Professor Orlak (Cordero), his assistant Waldo and his monster creations Carfax (Gerardo Cepeda) and Electra, who are using special bracelets to transform their victims into human robots. An export version, featuring more nudity and violence, was also released.
✦

JIM WYNORSKI
(Jim Wnorski) [b 1950]

American director, producer and writer, a former contributor to *Fangoria* and publicist for Roger Corman. The William Beaudine of his generation, he continues to churn out derivative direct-to-video trash and instantly forgettable sequels and remakes.
qv: *Attack of the 60 Foot Centerfold* (1995); *Dark Universe* (1993); *Deathstalker II Duel of the Titans* (1986); *Heartstoppers* (1992); *976-Evil II* (1991); *Not of This Earth* (1988); *Sorceress* (1982); *Transylvania Twist* (1989); *Vampirella* (1996); *The Wasp Woman* (1995).

- X -

XENA WARRIOR PRINCESS:
Girls Just Wanna Have Fun
USA/New Zealand, 1996. Dir: T.J. Scott. With: Lucy Lawless, Renee O'Connor, Ted Raimi, Matthew Chamberlain, Anthony Ray Parker, Kym Krystaly. MCA Television/Renaissance Pictures. Colour.
Popular hour-long syndicated TV series (1995-), a spin-off from *Hercules the Legendary Journeys* (1994-99), about the titular female warrior (Lawless) and her companion Gabrielle (O'Connor). In this Halloween episode, Xena, Gabrielle, Joxer (Raimi) and the talking severed head of Orpheus (Chamberlain) team up to battle the demonic Bacchus and his fanged female followers. This includes some great-looking Driads (*sic*) — CGI-created flying skeletons (supervised by Doug Beswick) — and Xena and Gabrielle transformed into bloodsucking Bacchae. Sam Raimi was co-executive producer.
✦✦✦
The Xena Scrolls
USA/New Zealand, 1996. Dir: Charlie Haskell. With: Lucy Lawless, Renee O'Connor, Ted Raimi, Kevin Smith, Mark Ferguson, Ajay Vasisht. MCA Television/Renaissance Pictures. Colour.
This jokey Indiana Jones-style episode is set in Macedonia in 1940. While looking for the legendary Xena Scrolls (an excuse to show excerpts from several other episodes, including Xena battling harpies), an archaeological dig led by whip-carrying Dr Janice Covington (O'Connor) discovers Ares, God of War (Smith), imprisoned for centuries in an ancient tomb. The three leads play the descendants of their original characters, while the whole story turns out to be a pitch fifty years later to co-executive producer Robert Tapert (playing himself). With surprise clips from *The Wrestling Women vs. the Aztec Mummy* (1964) and a Paul Naschy werewolf movie, plus a poster for *The Mummy* (1933)!
✦✦✧

XENIA
USA, 1990. Dir: Dennis Edwards and Dana M. Reeves. With: Dana M. Reeves, Dennis Edwards, Herb A. Lightman, Timothy Gray, Sharie-Marie Jonsin, Bob Wilkins. Edwards-Reeves/Cetus. Colour/B&W.
Low-budget spoof of horror movies that includes a film-within-a-film, mysterious director Andre W. Wiers' *Xenia, Priestess of the Night*, about a belly-dancing vampire with a lisp. With San Francisco Bay Area TV horror host Wilkins in a cameo.
✦

THE X FILES:
Alpha
USA, 1999. Dir: Peter Markle. With: David Duchovny, Gillian Anderson, Melinda Culea, Thomas Duffy, Michael Mantell, David Starwalt. Twentieth Century Fox/Ten Thirteen Productions/Fox Network. Colour.
Phenomenally popular hour-long TV series (1993-), created by executive producer Chris Carter, which gets its title from the FBI records pertaining to unresolved and bizarre cases. In this episode, Fox William Mulder (Duchovny) and Dana Catherine Scully (Anderson) suspect that cryptozoologist Dr Ian Detweiler (a wasted Andrew J. Robinson) was bitten by an apparently extinct Chinese dog and has become a murderous shapeshifter who turns into a glowing-eyed werewolf. The story doesn't make a great deal of sense, but there is a very nice transformation sequence in a basement corridor.
✦✦✧
Bad Blood
Canada/USA, 1998. Dir: Cliff Bole. With: David Duchovny, Gillian Anderson, Mitch Pileggi, Luke Wilson, Patrick Renna, Forbes Angus. Twentieth Century Fox/Ten Thirteen Productions/Fox Network. Colour.
This great comedy episode, written by Vince Gilligan, is told from the conflicting viewpoints of FBI special agents Mulder and Scully. Mulder is accused of staking pizza delivery boy and serial bloodsucker Ronnie Strickland (Renna), an inhabitant of Chaney, Texas, because he believes he was a vampire. As the surprise scary ending proves, the whole trailer park community is made up of the glowing-eyed undead. Meanwhile, in the episode 'The Pine Bluff Variant' (dir: Rob Bowman, 1998), Mulder wore a Dracula mask while undercover with a group of terrorist bank robbers in monster masks.
✦✦✦✧

David Duchovny and Gillian Anderson investigate The X Files *(1993-).*

Eve
Canada/USA, 1993. Dir: Fred Gerber. With: David Duchovny, Gillian Anderson, Harriet Harris, Erika Krievins, Sabrina Krievins, Jerry Hardin. Twentieth Century Fox/Ten Thirteen Productions/Fox Network. Colour.
Mulder and Scully investigate two exsanguinated murder victims and uncover a conspiracy involving a group of genetically-created children who have developed into super-intelligent psychopaths.
✦✦✦✧
Folie a Deux
Canada/USA, 1998. Dir: Kim Manners. With: David Duchovny, Gillian Anderson, Mitch Pileggi, Brian Markinson, John Apicella, Roger R. Cross. Twentieth Century Fox/Ten Thirteen Productions/Fox Network. Colour.
Chicago tele-marketing employee Gary Lambert (Markinson), who is holding his colleagues as hostages, tries to convince Mulder that his boss Greg Pincus (Apicella) is really a mind-clouding insectoid monster that for ten years has been turning its victims into bloodless, blank-eyed zombies which it controls through mental telepathy. It turns out he's right.
✦✦✦
Fresh Bones
Canada/USA, 1995. Dir: Rob Bowman. With: David Duchovny, Gillian Anderson, Bruce Young, Daniel Benzali, Jamil Walker Smith, Steven Williams. Twentieth Century Fox/Ten Thirteen Productions/Fox Network. Colour.
Mulder and Scully investigate the bizarre deaths of two soldiers at a

US Marine processing centre holding Haitian refugees and discover themselves at the cross-roads between the worlds of voodoo, ghosts and zombies.

✦✦

Post-Modern Prometheus

Canada/USA, 1997. Dir: Chris Carter. With: David Duchovny, Gillian Anderson, John O'Hurley, Pattie Tierce, Stewart Gale, Chris Giacoletti. Twentieth Century Fox/Ten Thirteen Productions/Fox Network. B&W/Colour.

Filmed in black and white, this humorous comic strip horror episode, written and directed by series creator Carter, is loosely based on the Frankenstein story. Mulder and Scully investigate sightings of The Great Mutato (Chris Owens, in special make-up created by Toby Lindala), the grotesque result of illegal genetic experiments by the mad Dr Pollidori (O'Hurley). With Jerry Springer, who appears on his TV talk show with the mother of a werewolf baby, clips from *Mask* (1985) and music by Cher (who refused to appear).

✦✦✦✧

Shapes

Canada/USA, 1994. Dir: David Nutter. With: David Duchovny, Gillian Anderson, Ty Miller, Michael Horse, Donnelly Rhodes, Jimmy Herman. Twentieth Century Fox/Ten Thirteen Productions/Fox Network. Colour.

FBI agents Mulder and Scully investigate the killing of a Native American on a reservation in Montana and discover that a series of recurrent murders are committed by legendary shape-changers.

✦✦✦✧

3

Canada/USA, 1994. Dir: David Nutter. With: David Duchovny, Gillian Anderson, Justina Vail, Perrey Reeves, Frank Military, Tom McBeath. Twentieth Century Fox/Ten Thirteen Productions/Fox Network. Colour.

While Scully has become an X-file herself, a depressed Mulder investigates a series of attacks in Los Angeles by a trinity of modern-day bloodsuckers (possibly supernatural in origin) and has a relationship with one of them, Kristen Kilar (Reeves). With a clip from *M* (1931) projected on a wall in 'Club Tepes'.

✦✦✧

2Shy

Canada/USA, 1995. Dir: David Nutter. With: David Duchovny, Gillian Anderson, Timothy Carhart, Catherine Paolone, James Handy, Kerry Sandomirsky. Twentieth Century Fox/Ten Thirteen Productions/Fox Network. Colour.

Mulder and Scully track down vampiric serial killer Virgil Incanto (Carhart), who uses the Internet to meet lonely women on blind dates and then sucks all the body fat out of his victims to survive.

✦✦✦

-Y-

KEVIN YAGHER
[b 1962]

American special effects make-up artist and director. Responsible for the Crypt Keeper wraparounds on TV's *Tales from the Crypt* (1989-96), he made his feature début under the credit 'Alan Smithee' on the troubled *Hellraiser: Bloodline* (1996).
qv: *Bride of Chucky* (1998); *Dr. Jekyll and Ms. Hyde* (1995); *The Phantom of the Opera* (1989); *Rumpelstiltskin* (1996); *Tales from the Crypt: 'Lower Berth'* (1990).

JEAN YARBROUGH
[1900-1975]

Prolific American director (sometimes credited as Jean Yarborough) and former prop man whose poverty-row horrors are slightly more imaginative than those of his contemporaries, usually the result of interesting casting.
qv: *The Addams Family* (1964-66); *The Brute Man* (1946); *The Creeper* (1948); *The Devil Bat* (1940); *Hillbillys in a Haunted House* (1967); *King of the Zombies* (1941); *Master Minds* (1949); *She-Wolf of London* (1946).

Y...DONE ESTA EL MUERTO?
Peru, 1985. Dir: Joaquin Vargas. With: Yvonne Frayssinet, Ricardo Fernandez, Nilda Muñoz, Teddy Guzman, Pablo Fernandez, Flor de Maria Andrade. Futuro Films/Madera CineVideo. Colour.
Peruvian old dark house comedy that features a reanimated mouldy corpse that leaves its coffin to scare a gathering of heirs. The title translates as 'And...Where is the Dead Man?'
✦

YE BANG GE SHENG
Hong Kong, 1962. Dir: Yuan Quifeng. With: Betty Loh-Tih (Le Di), Zhou Lai, Fang Li, Zhang Chong. Shaw Brothers. Colour.
Apparently inspired by *The Phantom of the Opera*. A revolutionary actor in the Chinese Republic is arrested and has his face horribly scarred by acid. Following his release, he retreats to the disused wing of an old theatre, where he gains a reputation as a ghost. Years later, he is befriended by a young actor who reunites him with his lost love (Loh-Tih), and he revenges himself upon the official who disfigured him before being drowned in the struggle. Star Loh-Tih committed suicide in 1968, aged thirty-one.
✦

YELLOW SUBMARINE
UK, 1968. Dir: George Dunning. With: The Beatles (John Lennon, Paul McCartney, George Harrison, Ringo Starr [Richard Starkey]). Voices: John Clive, Geoffrey Hughes. Apple Films/King Features/Subafilms/United Artists. Colour.
Cartoon musical fantasy based around fourteen songs performed by The Beatles. The Fab Four escape a grey Liverpool and travel to Pepperland to save their alter-egos, Sergeant Pepper's Lonely Hearts Club Band, from the music-hating Blue Meanies. With brief glimpses of the Frankenstein Monster and King Kong, voices by Paul Angelus, Dick Emery and Lance Percival, and a contrived live-action epilogue featuring the boys themselves.
✦✦✦✧

YOU ASKED FOR IT
USA, 1953. With: Art Baker, Bela Lugosi. ABC-TV. B&W.
At a viewer's request, a sick-looking Lugosi plays Dracula, summoned by his servant to rise from his coffin. He then performs his 'Vampire Bat Illusion' on a hypnotised blonde woman. Out of character, he tells host Baker that he will soon star in a TV series called *Dr. Acula*. It was never made.
✦✦

YOU'LL FIND OUT
USA, 1940. Dir: David Butler. With: Kay Kyser, Boris Karloff, Peter Lorre, Helen Parrish, Dennis O'Keefe, Bela Lugosi. RKO Radio Pictures. B&W.
Enjoyable musical horror comedy in which Kyser and his Band are invited to a mysterious old mansion full of secret passages, where a trio of con men are using the supernatural to cover-up their attempts to murder a young heiress (Parrish). Filmed under the title *The Old Professor*, this marked the only teaming of Karloff, Lorre and Lugosi, who are given the opportunity to send themselves up wonderfully in this typical Kyser programmer, complete with six songs written by John(ny) Mercer. In the end, the band leader explains that the three horror stars are really nice guys! With Alma Kruger, singer Ginny Simms, Jeff Corey as himself in an uncredited cameo as a quiz show contestant, and several models left over from *King Kong* (1933) in the villains' lair — including Kong himself and one of the legendary giant spiders!
✦✦

YOUNG FRANKENSTEIN
USA, 1974. Dir: Mel Brooks. With: Gene Wilder, Peter Boyle, Marty Feldman, Cloris Leachman, Teri Garr, Kenneth Mars. Twentieth Century-Fox/Gruskoff-Venture Films/Crossbow Productions/Jouer. B&W.
A wonderful parody of the heyday of Universal's Frankenstein series, beautifully recreated in black and white and hilariously scripted by star Wilder and director Brooks (reunited from *Blazing Saddles* [1974]). Wilder plays eccentric brain surgeon Dr Frederick Frankenstein ('that's Frahnkensteen'), who travels to Transylvania to receive a family legacy. With the help of Feldman's Igor ('Hump? What hump?') and Garr's beautiful laboratory assistant Inga, he soon begins building his own Monster (Boyle in make-up created by William Tuttle) with which to astound the medical profession. With Mars as the one-armed Inspector Kemp, Madeline Kahn as Elizabeth, Gene Hackman playing a blind hermit and Kenneth Strickfaden's original laboratory equipment from the 1931 *Frankenstein*. This is worth catching for the 'Puttin' on the Ritz' routine alone. A will-reading scene, which included the voice of John Carradine as Baron Frankenstein, was deleted before release but appears on the laserdisc as part of seventeen minutes of deleted scenes. A novelisation by Gilbert Pearlman (William Johnston) was published by Ballantine Books.
Remake: FRANKENSTEIN — ITALIAN STYLE (qv; 1975)
✦✦✦✦

YOUNG HERCULES:
Fame
New Zealand/USA, 1998. Dir: Chris Graves. With: Ryan Gosling, Dean O'Gorman, Chris Conrad, Kevin Smith, Kieren Hutchison, Morgan Fairhead. Studios USA Television/Renaissance Pictures/Fox Kids Network. Colour.
Half-hour spin-off TV series (1998-99, fifty episodes) from *Hercules the Legendary Journeys* (1994-99) featuring the adventures of the son of Zeus (Gosling), his friend Iolaus (O'Gorman) and Jason (Conrad), the future King of Corinth. In this episode, when young minstrel Orpheus (Hutchison) performs a concert in front of a sell-out audience, the music from his lyre transforms those listening into fanged followers of the evil god Bacchus (Smith). Sam Raimi was co-executive producer.
Episode sequel: YOUNG HERCULES: Lyre, Liar (qv; 1998)
✦✦

A Lady in Hades
New Zealand/USA, 1998. Dir: Chris Graves. With: Ryan Gosling, Dean O'Gorman, Chris Conrad, Erik Thomson, Morgan Fairhead, Michael Hurst. Studios USA Television/ Renaissance Pictures/Fox Kids Network. Colour.
Hercules and Jason travel to the Underworld to convince Hercules' uncle Hades (Thomson) that Eurydice deserves to be forgiven for being a vampiric Bacchae and her soul should be allowed to spend

Gene Wilder and Teri Garr prepare to bring Peter Boyle to life in Young Frankenstein *(1974).*

eternity in the Elysian Fields. With Hurst as a comic Charon.
✦✦✧

The Lure of the Lyre

New Zealand/USA, 1998. Dir: Chris Graves. With: Ryan Gosling, Dean O'Gorman, Chris Conrad, Jodie Rimmer, Kevin Smith, Kieren Hutchison. Studios USA Television/ Renaissance Pictures/Fox Kids Network. Colour.

Orpheus and his girlfriend Eurydice (Morgan Fairhead) lure Hercules, Lilith (Rimmer) and Iolaus to a bizarre club where Lilith is bitten by one of the vampiric followers of Bacchus.

Episode sequel: YOUNG HERCULES: Fame (qv; 1998)
✦✦✧

Lyre, Liar

New Zealand/USA, 1998. Dir: Chris Graves. With: Ryan Gosling, Dean O'Gorman, Chris Conrad, Jodie Rimmer, Kevin Smith, Kieren Hutchison. Studios USA Television/ Renaissance Pictures/Fox Kids Network. Colour.

Hercules discovers that Orpheus never destroyed his lyre, and when the fanged Bacchae attack, Eurydice sacrifices her life.

Episode sequel: YOUNG HERCULES: A Lady in Hades (qv; 1998)
✦✦

YOUNG INDIANA JONES AND THE CURSE OF THE JACKAL

USA/UK/Spain/Egypt/Mexico, 1992. Dir: Carl Schultz and Jim O'Brien. With: Sean Patrick Flanery, Corey Carrier, Margaret Tyzack, Ronny Coutteure, Mike Moroff, Francesco Quinn. Lucasfilm/Amblin Television/ Paramount/ABC-TV. Colour.

Two hour pilot movie for the TV series. Old Indy (George Hall) relates how, when he was a young boy (Carrier), he became involved in a murder and a missing mummy in Egypt while meeting Lawrence of Arabia (Joseph Bennett) and Howard Carter (Pip Torrens). Years later, as a teenager (Flanery), he solves the case during the Mexican war while running into Pancho Villa (Moroff) and George Patton (Stuart Milligan). Despite being based on a story by executive producer George Lucas, like the series that followed this is heavy on history and light on the fantasy elements that made the movie trilogy so successful. It was novelised as *Young Indiana Jones #1: The Mummy's Curse* by Megan Stine and H. William Stine, and as a 'Choose Your Own Adventure' *#1: The Valley of the Kings* by Richard Brightfield.

Sequel: THE YOUNG INDIANA JONES CHRONICLES (1992-93)
✦✦✧

THE YOUNG ONES:
Nasty

UK, 1984. Dir: Paul Jackson. With: Adrian Edmondson, Rik Mayall, Nigel Planer, Christopher Ryan, Alexei Sayle, Terry Jones. BBC-TV. Colour.

Half-hour comedy sitcom (1982-84, twelve episodes), co-scripted by Ben Elton, about Vyvyan (Edmondson), Rik (Mayall), Neil (Planer) and Mike (Ryan), four very different friends who share a house. In this horror-themed episode, a package is delivered to the boys apparently containing a South African vampire (Sayle). After they think they have destroyed the bloodsucker by opening their curtains and exposing him to sunlight, the vampire turns out to be Harry the Bastard, who is owed £500 for a video recorder. With Christopher Barrie, Dawn French, Gareth Hale, Norman Pace and music by The Damned.
✦✧

YOUNG SHERLOCK HOLMES
(UK: YOUNG SHERLOCK HOLMES AND THE PYRAMID OF FEAR)

UK/USA, 1985. Dir: Barry Levinson. With: Nicholas Rowe, Alan Cox, Sophie Ward, Anthony Higgins, Susan Fleetwood, Freddie Jones. Amblin Entertainment/ Paramount. Colour.

Steven Spielberg executive produced this box office flop from the director of *Rain Man* (1988). Chris Columbus' wonderful script hypothesises what might have happened if Sherlock Holmes (Rowe) and John Watson (Cox) had first met as schoolboys. He then throws in an ancient Egyptian death cult operating in 1870s London. There are good performances from the young leads, an excellent supporting cast that includes Nigel Stock (his last film), Patrick Newell, Willoughby Goddard and the voice of Michael Hordern as an older Watson, plus some impressive stop-motion nightmare effects by

Industrial Light & Magic. Make sure you sit through the final credits for a neat surprise twist. This was novelised by Alan Arnold.
✦✦✦✧

THE YOUNG TAOISM FIGHTER

Hong Kong, circa 1986. Ocean Shores Video. Colour.
Action comedy that includes several fantasy sequences, including one where a mummy is revived by a magic amulet.
✦✧

YOUR JEWELER'S SHOWCASE:
The Monkey's Paw

USA, 1963. With: Una Merkel. B&W.
TV adaptation of W.W. Jacobs' 1902 short story.
Episode remake: THE ALFRED HITCHCOCK HOUR: The Monkey's Paw: A Retelling (qv; 1965)
✦

YSANI THE PRIESTESS

UK, 1934. Dir: Gordon Sherry. With: Raven Wood, Vivienne Bell, Charles Hay. International Productions. B&W.
Half-hour novelty short in which a mummified Egyptian princess tells the audience's fortune with the aid of a live actor on the stage.
✦

BRIAN YUZNA
[b 1949]

Philippines-born American producer and director. Having scored a hit with Stuart Gordon's *Re-Animator* (1985), he directed the sequel, *Bride of Re-Animator* (1989), himself. Since then Yuzna's usually direct-to-video credits have included *Society* (1989), *Return of the Living Dead III* (1993) and *Necronomicon* (1993).
qv: *Fear in the Dark.*

-Z-

ZEE HORROR SHOW:
Tantrik
India, 1993. Dir: Deepak Ramsay. Zee TV. Colour.
Serial-like thrills from India's 'No. 1 Popular Horror Show', broadcast in six twenty-five minute weekly episodes and featuring a vampire. Produced by Tulsi Ramsay and Shyam Ramsay.
✦✧

ZEGUY
(Orig: UNKAI NO MEIKYU)
Japan, 1993 (1994). Dir: Shigenori Kageyama. Kageyama/ KSS Films/CPM/Manga Corps/Manga Video. Colour.
Confused juvenile anime, originally released in two forty minute segments, that includes a character's friend being kidnapped by werewolves on a school bus.
✦

LE ZOMBI DE CAP-ROUGE
Canada, 1997. Dir: Alan Smithee (Simon Robidoux). With: John T. Carter (Francois O. Hamel), Luc Langevin, Alexandre Coté, Floyd Levine (J.F. Perras), Simon Robidoux, Michael Deak (Dominic Drouin). Solaris Entertainment. Colour.
Low-budget independent horror thriller set in the small Québec town of Cap-Rouge. When serial killer Jason Vohrees (Deak) is revived from the dead by a lightning bolt, Sheriff Marc Bannerman (Carter) attempts to prevent the zombie killer from going on a murderous rampage.
✦

ZOMBIE
(Orig: ZOMBI 2. UK: ZOMBIE FLESH-EATERS. USA: aka THE ISLAND OF THE LIVING DEAD/ZOMBIE 2 THE DEAD ARE AMONG US)
Italy/USA, 1979. Dir: Lucio Fulci. With: Ian McCulloch, Tisa Farrow, Richard Johnson, Al Cliver (Pier Luigi Conti), Auretta Gay, Stefania D'Amario. Variety Film/ Jerry Gross Organization/Miracle Films. Colour.
Announced as *The Island of the Living Dead*, this was originally titled *Zombi 2* to cash-in on the success of George Romero's *Dawn of the Dead* (1978) which was released in Italy as *Zombie*. In fact, Fulci's film was probably much more influential, spawning an entire sub-genre of low-budget, gory zombie movies. Two couples travel to the remote island of Mantoul in the Antilles, where they team up with Dr David Menard (Johnson) and his assistants to defend themselves against the contagious flesh-eating dead. This includes an underwater battle between a zombie and a shark, and grimly effective scenes of the walking corpses invading New York City (special make-up effects created by Gianetto de Rossi). The film received a self-imposed 'X' rating in America, and two minutes of violence (including Olga Karlatos' eye being impaled on a wooden splinter) were cut from the British print.
✦✦✧

ZOMBIE APOCALYPSE
(Orig: CEMENTERIO DEL TERROR)
Mexico, 1985. Dir: Ruben Galindo Jr. With: Hugo Stiglitz, Usi Velasco, Erika Buenfil, Edna Bolkan, Maria Rebeca, René Cardona III. Dynamic/Torrente. Colour.
When a group of teens revive a corpse through a Satanic ceremony, other zombies leave their graves to attack the living.
✦✧

THE ZOMBIE ARMY
USA, 1991 (1993). Dir: Betty Stapleford. With: Eileen Saddow, Jody Amato, Steven Roberts, John C. Kalinowski, Betty Stapleford. Video Outlaw/Tempe Video/Movies Unlimited. Colour.
Low-budget independent feature, shot on video in Delaware and Pennsylvania. A group of female military cadets on a training exercise in a former insane asylum are trapped in the subterranean tunnels by inmates who were left behind and turned into killer zombies.
✦

ZOMBIE BLOODBATH
USA, 1993. Dir: Todd Sheets. Asylum Home Video/ Englewood Entertainment. B&W.
Independent, shot-on-video feature written, produced and directed by twenty-five year-old Sheets. An ex-soldier and a group of teens battle slow-moving cannibal zombies in a closed Kansas City nuclear power plant. This also includes melting bodies and plenty of gore.
Sequel: ZOMBIE BLOODBATH 2: RAGE OF THE UNDEAD (qv; 1995)
✦

ZOMBIE BLOODBATH 2: RAGE OF THE UNDEAD
USA, 1995 (1996). Dir: Todd Sheets. With: Kathleen McSweeney, Dave Miller, Nick Stodden, Jerry Angell, Matthew Jason Walsh. Extreme Video/Asylum Home Video/Englewood Entertainment. B&W.
Donna (McSweeney) and her friends return to a small town to revisit their childhood homes but encounter escaped convicts, psycho killers and cannibal zombies in this independent video release.
Sequel: ZOMBIE BLOODBATH 3: ZOMBIE ARMAGEDDON (1999)
✦

ZOMBIE BRIGADE
(USA: aka NIGHT CRAWL)
Australia, 1988. Dir: Carmelo Musca and Barrie Pattison. With: John Moore, Khym Lam, Geoff Gibbs, Adam A. Wong, Maggie Wilde West, Bob Faggetter. Smart Egg Cinema/CEA/CM Films. Colour.
In an attempt to convince Japanese investors to build a theme park on the site, the greedy Mayor Ransom (Gibbs) has the local monument to Vietnam veterans in his small Outback town blown up. That night a horde of blood-drinking vampire/zombie soldiers crawl out of the rubble and attack the community. Eventually, a local Aborigine sorcerer calls up the ghosts of the town's World War Two veterans to battle the walking dead.
✦✧

ZOMBIE COP
USA, 1991. Dir: J.R. Bookwalter. With: Michael Kemper, Ken Jarosz, James R. Black Jr, Bill Morrison, James L. Edwards, Christina M. Bookwalter. Tempe Video/Cinema Home Video. Colour.
This amateurish direct-to-video release runs just over an hour. A serial killer voodoo sorcerer, Doctor Death (Black Jr), murders a police officer (Kemper) and then inexplicably brings him back to life. With the aid of his old partner, the zombie detective sets out to stop the evil priest from claiming his vengeance against the city. Rock-bottom production values, executive produced by David DeCoteau.
✦

ZOMBIE CREEPING FLESH
(Orig: VIRUS — L'INFERNO DEI MORTI-VIVENTI/ APOCALIPSIS CANIBAL. USA: CANNIBAL VIRUS/NIGHT OF THE ZOMBIES)
Italy/Spain, 1980 (1983). Dir: Vincent Dawn (Bruno Mattei). With: Margi Evelyn Newton, Frank Garfield (Franco Giraldi), Selan Karay, Robert O'Neil, Gaby Renom, Luis Fonoll. Beatrice Film/Films Dara/Motion Picture Marketing. Colour.
Set in Papua New Guinea, where a TV reporter (Newton) and a commando team (led by Garfield) investigate a radioactive leak at a chemical research centre that turns the locals into cannibalistic zombies. It turns out to be a plot to solve the world's overpopulation problem, and in the end the zombie virus sweeps the world. This reuses the Goblin soundtrack from *Dawn of the Dead* (1978) and the

Wrestler Karl 'Killer' Davis and Rube Schaffer are just two Zombies of Mora Tau *(1957).*

jungle stock footage is apparently taken from a 1974 Japanese movie directed by Takira Ida.
✦✧

ZOMBIE HIGH
(aka THE SCHOOL THAT ATE MY BRAIN)
USA, 1987 (1988). Dir: Ron Link. With: Virginia Madsen, Richard Cox, Kay E. Kuter, James Wilder, Sherilyn Fenn, Paul Feig. Priest Hill Productions/Cinema Group. Colour.
Thematically closer to *The Stepford Wives* (1974) than the zombie movies of George Romero, this was filmed under the title *Prep School*. A student (Madsen) arrives at the exclusive Ettinger Academy and discovers that her classmates are being turned into 'perfect' pupils by the teachers — members of a secret society who have survived for over a century by stealing the brain fluid of their victims. Director Link's use of the clichéd material is fun and entertaining and, despite the almost mandatory heavy metal soundtrack, this is a surprisingly stylish little thriller. With Paul Williams.
✦✦✧

ZOMBIE ISLAND MASSACRE
USA, 1983 (1984). Dir: John N. Carter. With: David Broadnax, Rita Jenrette, Tom Cantrell, Diane Clayre Holub, George Peters, Ian McMillian. Picnic Productions/ Troma. Colour.
Filmed under the titles *Picnic* and *The Last Picnic*. Former congressional wife and *Playboy* model Jenrette plays the big-busted Sandy, one of a group of holiday-makers who take a boat cruise to the Caribbean island of San Marie, where they witness a voodoo ceremony and the creation of a briefly-seen zombie (Oscar Lawson) before being killed off one by one by a hit squad of Colombian drug dealers. Despite the obvious low budget and a cast of non-actors, director/editor Carter manages to include at least one genuine shock moment and a surprise plot twist. Producer/star Broadnax also co-wrote the original story.
✦✧

ZOMBIE LAKE
(Orig: EL LAGO DE LOS MUERTOS VIVIENTES/LE LAC DES MORTS VIVANTS. UK: ZOMBIES LAKE).
Spain/France, 1980 (1986). Dir: J.A. Lazar/Peter Chevalier (Jean Rollin). With: Howard Vernon (Mario Lippert), Peter Escourt (Pierre Escourrou), Anouchka, Anthony May (Robert Foster/Antonio Mayans), Marcia Sharif, Nadine Pascal (Nadine Pascale). Eurociné/JE Films/ Wizard Video. Colour.
Originally to be directed by Jesús Franco, who pulled out because the budget was too low! A platoon of Nazi soldiers, killed by local villagers during World War Two, rise from the lake as green-faced zombies and attack numerous naked women. In the end, the flesh-eating dead are trapped in a barn and set on fire. The director turns up in a cameo as a detective.
✦

ZOMBIE NIGHTMARE
Canada, 1986 (1987). Dir: Jack Bravman. With: Adam West, Jon-Mikl Thor, Tia Carrere, Manuska Rigaud, Frank Dietz, Linda Singer. Filmworld/Gold-Gems/New World Pictures. Colour.
When baseball loving Tony Washington (ex-Mr Canada and heavy metal rock star Thor) is killed in a hit-and-run incident, his grieving mother has Haitian voodoo priestess Molly Mokembe (Rigaud) revive her son as a green-faced zombie. Using his beloved baseball bat as a lethal weapon, he sets out to revenge himself on the delinquent teens who ran him down. With Carrere making her film début and West (TV's *Batman* [1966-68], etc) as the local police chief, who shoots the priestess before being dragged down to Hell by the rotting corpse of Tony's father. With music by Motorhead, Death Mask and Jon-Mikl Thor.
✦✧

ZOMBIE NIGHTMARE
USA, 1993. Dir: G.W. Lawrence. With: Aven Warren, Sal Longo, Alex Reed, Cristie Clark, Amanda Madison (Christine Cavalier), Clancey McCauley. In Dire Straits Productions/WAVE Productions. Colour.
Independent video from the makers of *The Mummy's Dungeon* (1993), featuring many of the same cast, crew and locations. A mad professor (Longo) sends his electric-brained zombie Hector (Warren, who was also responsible for the make-up) out to kidnap women who he then uses in experiments to revive his terminally-ill wife from suspended animation. In the end, the ugly, living-dead servant turns on his creator. This contains mild bondage. Some of the cast from this New Jersey production returned in *Vampire Brides* (1994).
✦

ZOMBIE '90: EXTREME PESTILENCE
West Germany, 1990. Dir: Andreas Schnaas. With: Matthias Kerl, Ralf Hess, Matthias Abbes, Marc Trinkhaus, Christian Biallas, Wolfgang Hinz. Blood Pictures/Reel Gore/Tempe Video. Colour.
Amateur direct-to-video production from the director of *Violent Shit* (1988). After a toxic substance leaks from a plane crash, murderous zombies wander around a European landscape. Writer/director Schnaas, who was also responsible for the make-up effects, fills his film with plenty of low-budget gore but little imagination.
✦

ZOMBIE NINJA GANGBANGERS
(aka BANGERS/THE ZOMBIE NINJA)
USA, 1997. Dir: Jeff Emralino. With: Ross Marshall, Stephanie Beaton, Kitten (Francesca) Natividad, Maureen Shawaf, James Riley. Plutonium Film. Colour.
Low-budget independent video release in which Hollywood hooker Alice Hudson (Beaton) claims that she has been raped by zombies. When she teams up with a teenage boy who has also been attacked, they discover that Dr Alexander Mondo (Marshall, with a Peter Lorre-type voice) is creating the walking dead in his laboratory in the basement of a video store. Natividad (as herself) plays a bar owner and does a topless dance.
✦

ZOMBIE RAMPAGE
USA, 1989. Dir: Todd Sheets. Cinema Home Video. Colour.
Another low-budget, direct-to-video release in which a young man attempts to meet his friend in a train station but instead encounters inner-city gangs, serial killers and zombies.
Sequel: ZOMBIE RAMPAGE 2 (qv; 1992)
✦

ZOMBIE RAMPAGE 2
USA, 1992. Dir: Todd Sheets. Slime Time Home Video. Colour.
Direct-to-video sequel to the 1989 original.
✦

ZOMBIES OF MORA TAU
(UK: THE DEAD THAT WALK)
USA, 1957. Dir: Edward (L.) Cahn. With: Gregg Palmer, Allison Hayes, Autumn Russell, Joel Ashley, Morris Ankrum, Marjorie Eaton. Clover Productions/Columbia. B&W.
George Harrison (Ashley) is the greedy leader of a group of treasure hunters, attempting to recover a horde of sunken diamonds off the African coast, who encounter a number of spooky-looking zombie pirates that can move around underwater. Director Cahn creates a few creepy moments with the zombies emerging from their coffins, and Hayes' sexy Mona livens things up until she is inexplicably turned into one of the living dead and trapped in her bed by candles. More low-budget nonsense produced by 'Jungle' Sam Katzman and scripted by Raymond T. Marcus (blacklisted writer Bernard Gordon). With Ray 'Crash' Corrigan.
✦

ZOMBIES OF THE STRATOSPHERE
(aka SATAN'S SATELLITES)
USA, 1952. Dir: Fred C. Brannon. With: Judd Holdren, Aline Towne, Wilson Wood, Lane Bradford, John

Crawford, Craig Kelly. Republic. B&W.
Twelve-chapter serial in which Larry Martin/Commando Cody (Holdren) battles a trio of Martians who have invaded the Earth, secretly helped by a renegade scientist (Stanley Waxman), and plan to blast the planet out of orbit with a giant bomb. With flying footage from *King of the Rocket Men* (1949), Republic's usual tin-can robots (dating from *Mysterious Dr Satan* [1940]), and an early appearance by Leonard Nimoy as Narab, one of the evil aliens. A *Commando Cody* TV series starring Holdren and Towne followed in 1955. This sequel to *Radar Men from the Moon* (1952) was also released in a feature version in 1958, which was later colourised on video.
Sequel: COMMANDO CODY SKY MARSHALL OF THE UNIVERSE (1955)
✦✦

ZOMBIES ON BROADWAY

(UK: LOONIES ON BROADWAY)
USA, 1945. Dir: Gordon Douglas (and Ben Stoloff). With: Wally Brown, Alan Carney, Bela Lugosi, Anne Jeffreys, Sheldon Leonard, Frank Jenks. RKO Radio Pictures. B&W.
The unfunny comedy team of Brown and Carney play press agents Jerry Miles and Mike Strager, who work for ex-gangster Ace Miller (Leonard) and have to produce a real zombie to open his 'Zombie Hut' night club. They travel to the tropical island of San Sebastian, where the mad Dr Paul Renault (a wasted Lugosi, who has an embarrassing comedy scene with a monkey!) temporarily turns Mike into a pop-eyed scientific zombie. With Ian Wolfe as a professor who talks to a mummy, Robert Clarke, Jason Robards (Sr) and Rosemary La Planche, plus Darby Jones as Kolaga the zombie and uncredited calypso singer Sir Lancelot both repeating their roles from RKO's *I Walked With a Zombie* (1943).
✦✧

ZOMBIETHON

USA, 1986. Dir: Ken Dixon. With: K. Janyll Caudle, Tracy Burton, Paula Singleton, Janelle Lewis, Janessa Lester, Randolph Roehbling. Taryn Productions/Wizard Video/Lightning. Colour.
Compilation of nudity and gore scenes from low-budget movies available on Wizard Video. The sometimes arty linking sequences (produced and directed by Dixon of *Slave Girls from Beyond Infinity* [1987] fame) involve various women in peril and a living dead audience (in make-up by Joe Reader and David Lady) in the El Rey movie theatre. This includes edited highlights from *The Astro-Zombies* (1968), *Fear* (1980), *The Invisible Dead* (1970), *Oasis of the Zombies* (1981), *Virgin Among the Living Dead* (1971), *Zombie* (1979) and *Zombie Lake* (1980). Guess which two of the above titles don't include any zombies...?
✦✦

ZOMBIE 3

(Orig: LA NOTTI DEI TERRORE/ZOMBI HORROR/ZOMBI 3. USA: aka BURIAL GROUND/ZOMBIE HORROR/ZOMBIE III: THE NIGHTS OF TERROR. UK: NIGHTS OF TERROR)
Italy, 1980. Dir: Andrea Bianchi. With: Karin Well, Gian Luigi Chirizzi, Simone Mattioli, Antonietta Antinori, Roberto Caporali, Maria Angela (Mariangela) Giordano. Esteban Cinematográfica/FCG. Colour.
This was released in Italy as an unofficial follow-up to Lucio Fulci's *Zombie* (1979), which itself was an unofficial sequel to George Romero's *Dawn of the Dead* (1978). A group of unsympathetic guests are trapped in a country villa by a horde of skull-faced cannibal zombies who have shuffled up from the crypts below. After much sex and gratuitous gore, none of them survive. This includes the decapitation of a maid by a zombie wielding a scythe and a weird-looking living dead boy incestuously eating the breast of his mother (Giordano). Gino (Gianetto) de Rossi created the special effects, while Rosario Prestopino was responsible for the quite effective zombie make-ups.
✦✧

Darby Jones watches Bela Lugosi turn Alan Carney into one of the Zombies on Broadway *(1945).*

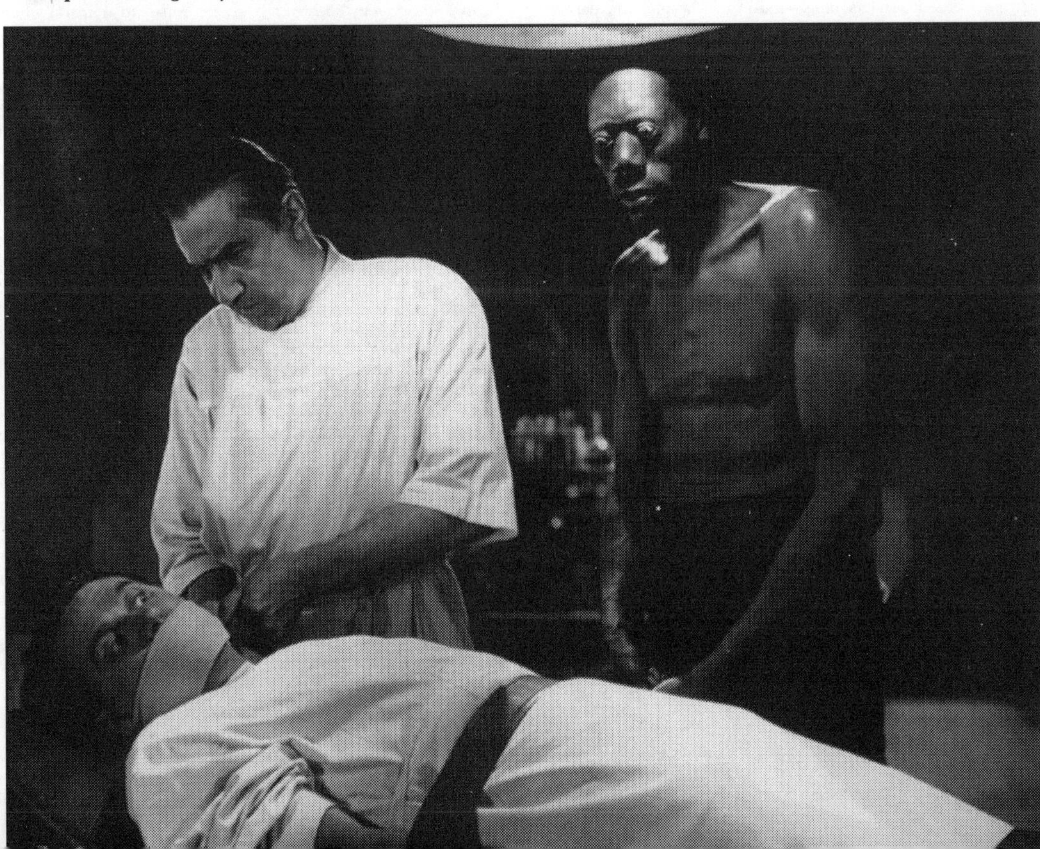

ZOMBIE 3
(Orig: ZOMBI 3)
Italy/Philippines, 1987 (1988). Dir: Lucio Fulci (and Bruno Mattei). With: Deran Serafian, Beatrice Ring, Richard Raymond, Alex McBride, Ulli Reinthaler, Alan Collins (Luciano Pigozzi). Flora Film Productions/Variety. Colour.
A follow-up of sorts to his successful *Zombie* (1979), an ailing Fulci was replaced during production by Mattei (*Zombie Creeping Flesh* [1980], etc). When a secret government virus is stolen and accidentally released into the countryside, a group of off-duty soldiers and three women find themselves battling the local population who have been transformed into a horde of flesh-hungry zombies.
✦✧

ZOMBIE TOXIN
(Orig: HOMEBREW)
UK, 1993-96 (1998). Dir: Tom J. Moose. With: Robert Taylor, Adrian Ottiwell, Tom J. Moose, Lee Simpson, Nestus Forsythe, Russell Ottiwell. Viscera Films/Viscera International Pictures/Brain Escape Pictures/EI Independent Cinema. Colour.
Billed as 'Monty Python meets Dawn of the Dead!', this extremely gory low budget zombie comedy/musical(!) was shot on video in Greater Manchester. Scripted by Taylor and Adrian Ottiwell, an Adolf Hitler look-a-like (editor/producer/director Moose) uses toxic waste in wine to create flesh-eating zombies and living bottles of 'home brew'.
✦

ZOMBIE! VS MARDI GRAS
USA, 1996 (1997). Dir: Mike Lyddon. With: Dale Ashmun, Loreli Fuller, Jeannette Hauser, John Sinclair. Carnavale Productions. B&W/Colour.
Independent video release shot in New Orleans during Mardi Gras. After being crippled by drunken revellers, a child grows up studying the occult and plans his revenge. During the city's festivities he raises a group of zombies, including a naked female zombie who dances in a graveyard.
✦

ZOMBIE VS NINJA
(USA: aka ZOMBIE REVIVAL: NINJA MASTER)
Hong Kong, 1987. Dir: Charles Lee (Godfrey Ho). With: Pierre Kirby, Dewey Bosworth, Renato Sala, Sean Odell, Meike Blischloe, Wei Ping-Ao. Joseph Lai-Betty Chan/IFD Films/IEC. Colour.
Comedy about a buck-toothed coffin-maker who rescues a young man from being beaten by robbers. This also features a kung fu fighter (Kirby) wearing a golden headband and an opening sequence that includes a brief appearance by hopping vampire/zombies who must return to their coffins before dawn.
✦

ZOMBI HOLOCAUST
(Orig: LA REGINA DEI CANNIBALI. USA: DOCTOR BUTCHER M.D./MEDICAL DEVIATE/QUEEN OF THE CANNIBALS)
Italy/USA, 1979 (1981). Dir: Frank Martin (Franco Martinelli/Marino Girolami). With: Ian McCulloch, Alexandra Cole (Alexandra delli Colli), Sherry Buchanan, Peter O'Neal, Donald O'Brien, Walter Patriarca. Flora Film/Fulvia Cinematográfica/Gico Cinematográfica/ Aquarius Releasing. Colour.
This begins in a Manhattan morgue, where the hearts are being stolen from corpses (apparently a tagged-on sequence taken from Roy Frumkes' unreleased NYU film *Tales That Will Rip Your Heart Out*), but the action soon shifts to a remote Indonesian island as Peter Chandler (McCulloch) and Lori Ridgeway (Cole) discover that the mad Dr Abrero (O'Brien) is turning the local natives into misshapen zombies. When most of their party are killed, Lori is captured by cannibals who strip her and hail her as a goddess. The climax features an all-out battle between cannibals and zombies — thus effectively combining Italy's two most popular movie themes at that time. With its bloody scalping, cannibalism and minor nudity, this was released on video in the early 1980s and then banned in Britain. A 'Butchermobile' toured the New York City area to promote the film.
✦✧

EL ZORRO ESCARLATA
Mexico, 1958. Dir: Rafael Baledón. With: Luis Aguilar, Fernando Fernández, Irma Dorantes, Jaime Fernandez, Pascual Garcia Peña, Fanny Schiller. Importadora. B&W.
Masked hero 'El Zorro Escarlata', aka The Scarlet Fox (Aguilar), and his assistant arrive in a village plagued by a series of mysterious disappearances. They discover that mad scientist Dr Kraken has brought a cackling old witch back from the dead and created his own bulbous-headed monster which is impervious to bullets.
Sequel: EL REGRESO DEL MONSTRUO (qv; 1958)
✦

A ZSARNOK SZIVA, AVAGY BOCCCCIO MAGYARORSZAGON
Hungary/Italy, 1981. Dir: Miklós Janscó. With: Ninetto Davoli, Laszlo Galffy, Theresa-Ann Savoy. Mafilm/ Radiotelevision Italiana/Leone. Colour.
Based on stories by Boccaccio. A woman apparently remains young by drinking the blood of virgins.
✦

GEORGE ZUCCO
[1886-1960]

British stage actor who became the poor man's mad doctor. Despite a successful Hollywood career as a supporting player in major films, Zucco also starred in numerous poverty-row productions, often alongside Bela Lugosi and John Carradine. A memorable Professor Moriarty in *The Adventures of Sherlock Holmes* (1939), even he had the career sense to pull out of *Return of the Ape Man* (1944), although he still shared star billing and can be glimpsed in a few scenes as the thawed-out caveman. After becoming ill in the early 1950s, he was committed to a sanatorium for the remainder of his life.
qv: *Dead Men Walk* (1943); *House of Frankenstein* (1944); *The Hunchback of Notre Dame* (1939); *The Mad Ghoul* (1943); *The Mad Monster* (1942); *The Mummy's Ghost* (1944); *The Mummy's Hand* (1940); *The Mummy's Tomb* (1942); *Voodoo Man* (1944).

FAMOUS MONSTERS

TOP TWENTY MONSTER MOVIES

The following list is based on the ratings given in this volume and reflects my own personal opinions. You are welcome to disagree with me!

1 King Kong (1933)
2 Bride of Frankenstein
3 Dracula (1958)
4 The Phantom of the Opera (1925)
5 Dr. Jekyll and Mr. Hyde (1931)
6 Black Sunday
7 The Thing from Another World
8 The Wolf Man
9 Creature from the Black Lagoon
10 Cat People (1942)
11 (Abbott and Costello) Meet Frankenstein
12 The Howling
13 Isle of the Dead
14 Frankenstein (1931)
15 Mad Love
16 I Walked With a Zombie
17 Dracula (1931; Spanish-language version)
18 Son of Frankenstein
19 Night of the Living Dead (1968)
20 The Night Stalker (1971)

TWENTY CLASSIC MONSTER MOVIE BOOKS

These volumes contain the stories of the classic monsters and deserve to be on the bookshelf of every serious horror film fan.

1 *Bride of Frankenstein* (1936) by Michael Egremont (Michael Harrison).
2 *Bride of Frankenstein* (1977) by Carl Dreadstone (Ramsey Campbell).
3 *Dracula* (1897) by Bram Stoker.
4 *Dracula's Daughter* (1977) by Carl Dreadstone/E.K. Leyton (Ramsey Campbell).
5 *Creature from the Black Lagoon* (1954) by Vargo Statten (John Russell Fearn).
6 *Creature from the Black Lagoon* (1977) by Carl Dreadstone/ E.K. Leyton.
7 *Frankenstein; or, The Modern Prometheus* (1816) by Mary W. Shelley.
8 *The Hammer Horror Omnibus* (1966) by John Burke.
9 *In a Glass Darkly* (1872, includes 'Carmilla') by J. Sheridan Le Fanu.
10 *The Jewel of Seven Stars* (1903) by Bram Stoker.
11 *King Kong* (1932) by Delos W. Lovelace.
12 *The Mummy* (1977) by Carl Dreadstone.
13 *Notre-Dame de Paris* (1831) by Victor Hugo.
14 *The Phantom of the Opera* (1911) by Gaston Leroux.
15 *Return of the Wolf Man* (1998) by Jeff Rovin.
16 *The Second Hammer Horror Film Omnibus* (1967) by John Burke.
17 *Strange Case of Dr. Jekyll and Mr. Hyde* (1886) by Robert Louis Stevenson.
18 *The WereWolf of London* (1977) by Carl Dreadstone (Walter Harris).
19 *The Werewolf of Paris* (1933) by Guy Endore.
20 *The Wolf Man* (1977) by Carl Dreadstone/E.K. Leyton (Ramsey Campbell).

PRIMARY TITLES

The following titles are the first film appearances of these classic characters, stories and series. Use them as the starting point to trace through the chain of remakes and sequels.

The Aztec Mummy:
La Momia Azteca (1957)

Carmilla:
Blood and Roses (1960)

Creature from the Black Lagoon:
Creature from the Black Lagoon (1954)

Dracula:
The Twelfth Hour (1920)

Dr Jekyll and Mr Hyde:
Dr. Jekyll and Mr. Hyde (1908)

Frankenstein:
Frankenstein (1910)

El Hombre Lobo (Waldemar Daninsky):
Frankenstein's Bloody Terror (1967)

The Hunchback of Notre Dame:
Esmeralda (1906)

The Jewel of Seven Stars:
Playhouse: Mystery and Imagination: 'Curse of the Mummy' (1970)

King Kong:
King Kong (1933)

The Monkey's Paw:
The Monkey's Paw (1915)

The Mummy:
The Mummy (1933)

Paula Dupree 'The Gorilla Girl':
Captive Wild Woman (1943)

The Phantom of the Opera:
The Phantom of the Opera (1925)

The Wolf Man (Lawrence Talbot):
The Wolf Man (1941)

PERSONALITY PROFILE INDEX

ALTERNATE TITLE INDEX

BLOOD OF DR. JEKYLL: see BLOODLUST (1979)
BLOOD OF FRANKENSTEIN: see DRACULA VS. FRANKENSTEIN (1970)
BLOOD OF THE MAN-DEVIL: see HOUSE OF THE BLACK DEATH
BLOOD SUCKERS, THE (1966): see DR. TERROR'S GALLERY OF HORRORS
BLOODSUCKERS (1970): see INCENSE FOR THE DAMNED
BLOOD-SUCKERS (1991): see THOSE FEEDY ON BLOOD
BLOODSUCKING NAZI ZOMBIES: see OASIS OF THE LIVING DEAD, THE
BLOOD THIRST: see SALEM'S LOT
BLOODTHIRTSY EYES: see LAKE OF DRACULA, THE
BLOODY FIANCEE: see BLOOD SPATTERED BRIDE, THE
BLOODY MOON: see LYCANTHROPE — PRAY FOR SUNRISE
BLUE DEMON VS. EL CRIMEN: see BLUE DEMON CONTRA CEREBROS INFERNALES
BLUE DEMON Y ZOVEK EL LA INVASIÓN DE LOS MUERTOS: see INVASIÓN DE LOS MUERTOS, LA
BLUE LIGHTS: see CURSE OF THE BLUE LIGHTS
BLUT AN DEN LIPPEN: see DAUGHTERS OF DARKNESS
BODY SHOP, THE: see DOCTOR GORE
BODY SNATCHER FROM HELL: see GOKE, BODY SNATCHER FROM HELL
BON APPETIT, MAMA: see ED AND HIS DEAD MOTHER
BONDAGE REVENGE: see CLEOPATRA'S BONDAGE REVENGE
BORIS KARLOFF PRESENTS: see THRILLER (1960-62)
BOSQUE DE ANCINES, EL: see ANCINES WOODS, THE
BOSQUE DEL LOBO, EL: see ANCINES WOODS, THE
BOYS FROM BROOKLYN, THE: see BELA LUGOSI MEETS A BROOKLYN GORILLA
BRACULA — THE TERROR OF THE LIVING DEAD!: see HANGING WOMAN, THE
BRAIN, THE: see BRAIN OF BLOOD
BRAM STOKER'S DRACULA (1972): see DRACULA (1972)
BRAM STOKER'S THE MUMMY: see BRAM STOKER'S LEGEND OF THE MUMMY
BREAKFAST AT THE MANCHESTER MORGUE: see LIVING DEAD AT MANCHESTER MORGUE, THE
BROADWAY ON SHOWTIME: FRANKENSTEIN: see FRANKENSTEIN (1984)
BUBBLE GUM CRISIS 5: see BUBBLE GUM CRISIS 5: MOONLIGHT RAMBLER
BUCK ADAMS' FRANKENSTEIN: see FRANKENSTEIN (1994)
BUD ABBOTT LOU COSTELLO MEET FRANKENSTEIN: see MEET FRANKENSTEIN
BUQUE MALDITO, EL: see HORROR OF THE ZOMBIES
BURIAL GROUND: see ZOMBIE 3 (1980)
BURNIN' LOVE: see ROCKABILLY VAMPIRE
BYE BYE MONKEY: see CIAO MASCHIO
CABEZA VIVIENTE, LA: see LIVING HEAD, THE
CACCIATORE DI UOMINI, IL: see MAN HUNTER
CAGED VIRGINS: see REQUIEM FOR A VAMPIRE
CAMARA DEL TERROR, LA: see TORTURE ZONE, THE
CANNIBAL VIRUS: see ZOMBIE CREEPING FLESH
CAPERUCÍTA Y PULGARCÍTO CONTRA LOS MONSTRUOS: see LITTLE RED RIDING HOOD AND TOM THUMB VS. THE MONSTERS
CAPTAIN MEPHISTO AND THE TRANSFORMATION MACHINE: see MANHUNT OF MYSTERY ISLAND
CAPULINA CONTRA LOS MONSTRUOS: see CAPULINA VS. LOS MONSTRUOS
CAPULINA ENTRE LAS MOMIAS: see CAPULINA CONTRA LAS MOMIAS
CARESSE DE SATAN, LA: see WICKED CARESSES OF SATAN, THE
CARESS OF THE VAMPIRE 3: VAMPIRE LUST: see CARESS OF THE VAMPIRE 3 LUST OF THE NIGHT STALKER
CARNE PER FRANKENSTEIN: see FLESH FOR FRANKENSTEIN (1973)
CARTAS BOCA ARRIBA: see ATTACK OF THE ROBOTS
CARTES SUR TABLE: see ATTACK OF THE ROBOTS
CASA DEL TEMPO, LA: see HOUSE OF CLOCKS
CASA DEL TERROR, LA: see FACE OF THE SCREAMING WEREWOLF
CASE OF THE MISSING BRIDES, THE: see CORPSE VANISHES, THE
CASE OF THE SMILING STIFFS: see CASE OF THE FULL MOON MURDERS
CAS ÉTRANGE DE DR. JEKYLL ET DE MISS OSBOURNE, LE: see BLOODLUST (1979)
CASTELLO DALLE PORTE DI FUOCO, IL: see SCREAM OF THE DEMON LOVER
CASTELLO DELLA PAURA, IL: see FRANKENSTEIN'S CASTLE OF FREAKS
CASTILLO DE LOS MONSTRUOS, EL: see CASTLE OF THE MONSTERS
CASTLE OF DOOM: see VAMPYR (1931-32)
CASTLE OF TERROR: see CASTLE OF BLOOD
CASTLE OF THE CREEPING FLESH: see CASTLE OF BLOODY LUST
CASTLE OF THE WALKING DEAD: see BLOOD DEMON, THE
CAZADOR DE DEMONIOS: see DEMON HUNTER
CAZADOR II, EL: see DEATHSTALKER II DUEL OF THE TITANS
CEMENTERIO DEL TERROR: see ZOMBIE APOCALYPSE
CEMETERY GIRLS (1972): see DRACULA'S GREAT LOVE
CEMETERY GIRLS (1978): see VAMPIRE HOOKERS
CEMETERY OF THE LIVING DEAD: see TERROR CREATURES FROM THE GRAVE
CENA CON IL VAMPIRO, A: see DINNER WITH A VAMPIRE
CEREBRO DEL MAL: see SANTO CONTRA EL CEREBRO DEL MAL
CEREBRO INFERNAL, EL: see BLUE DEMON CONTRA CEREBROS INFERNALES
CEREMONIA SANGRIENTA: see LEGEND OF BLOOD CASTLE, THE
CERTAINS L'AIMENT NOIRE: see VAMPIRESAS 1930
CHABELO Y PEPITO CONTRA LOS MONSTRUOS: see CHABELO Y PEPITO VS. LOS MONSTRUOS
CHANDU ON THE MAGIC ISLAND: see RETURN OF CHANDU, THE
CHARLIE CHAN IN MURDER IN THE FUN HOUSE: see CHINESE CAT, THE
CHARLIE CHAN IN THE CHINESE CAT: see CHINESE CAT, THE
CHARLOTS CHEZ DRACULA JUNIOR, LES: see CHARLOTS CONTRE DRACULA, LES
CHARRO DE LAS CALAVERAS, EL: see RIDERS OF THE SKULLS
CHEMINS DE LA VIOLENCE, LES: see LIPS OF BLOOD (1972)
CHI GUI XIAN: see MIXED UP
CHILDREN OF THE NIGHT: see DAUGHTERS OF DARKNESS
CHILLING, THE: see NIGHT OF THE ZOMBIES
CHINESE LEGEND, A: see MOON LEGEND
CHI O SUU BARA: see EVIL OF DRACULA
CHI O SUU ME: see LAKE OF DRACULA, THE
CHI O SUU NINGYO: see NIGHT OF THE VAMPIRE, THE
CHRISTINA PRINCESSE DE L'ÉROTISME: see VIRGIN AMONG THE LIVING DEAD
CHUANG XIE XIAN SHENG: see MR. POSSESSED
CHU NU DE YOU HUO: see EVIL BLACK MAGIC
CHU SHI QI BING: see FIGURES FROM EARTH
CHUT SI KEI BING: see FIGURES FROM EARTH
5 TOMBE PER UN MEDIUM: see TERROR CREATURES FROM THE GRAVE
CIRCLE OF FEAR: see GHOST STORY
CITE DES FEMMES, LA: see CITY OF WOMEN
CITÉ DES SPECTRES VERTS, LA: see LITAN
CITTÀ DELLE DONNE, LA: see CITY OF WOMEN
CITY OF LOST MEN: see LOST CITY, THE
CLEOPATRA'S TOMB: see CLEOPATRA
CLÉOPÂTRE: see CLEOPATRA
CLOSE ENCOUNTER OF THE VAMPIRE: see DRAGON AGAINST VAMPIRE
CLUTCH — IL BOSCO: see EVIL CLUTCH
COLOR OF LOVE, THE: see LORD SHANGO
COMEDY DRACULLA: see COMEDY DRACULA
COMPUTER KILLERS: see HORROR HOSPITAL
COMTESSE AUX SEINS NUS, LA: see BARE BREASTED COUNTESS, THE
COMTESSE NOIRE, LA: see BARE BREASTED COUNTESS, THE
CONAN DOYLE: see SHORT STORIES OF CONAN DOYLE, THE
CONDE DRÁCULA, EL: see BRAM STOKER'S COUNT DRACULA
CONDE FRANKENHAUSEN, EL: see BLOODY VAMPIRE, THE
CONDEMNED MEN: see FOUR SHALL DIE
CONQUISTA DE LA TIERRA PERDIDA, LA: see CONQUEST
CONQUISTATORE DELL'ATLANTIDA, IL: see KINGDOM IN THE SAND
CONTE DRACULA, IL: see BRAM STOKER'S COUNT DRACULA
CONTES IMMORAUX: see IMMORAL TALES
CONTRA LOS MONSTRUOS: see SANTO Y BLUE DEMON VS. LOS MONSTRUOS
CORPSE VANISHED, THE: see REVENGE OF THE ZOMBIES (1943)
CORRIDORS OF EVIL: see CARNIVAL OF SOULS (1962)
COUNT DRACULA (1970): see BRAM STOKER'S COUNT DRACULA
COUNT DRACULA AND HIS VAMPIRE BRIDE: see SATANIC RITES

OF DRACULA, THE
COUNT DRACULA'S GREAT LOVE: see DRACULA'S GREAT LOVE
CRAZED VAMPIRE: see REQUIEM FOR A VAMPIRE
CREATURE OF THE DEVIL: see DEAD MEN WALK
CREATURES OF THE PREHISTORIC PLANET: see HORROR OF THE BLOOD MONSTERS
CREATURES OF THE RED PLANET: see HORROR OF THE BLOOD MONSTERS
CREATURE'S REVENGE, THE: see BRAIN OF BLOOD
CRIME OF VOODOO: see LOVE WANGA
CRIMINES DE USHER, LOS: see REVENGE IN THE HOUSE OF USHER
CRIPTA E L'INCUBO, LA: see CRYPT OF HORROR
CROCE DALLE 7 PIETRE, LA: see CROSS OF SEVEN JEWELS, THE
CROCIFISSO DI SETTE GIOIELLOS: see CROSS OF SEVEN JEWELS, THE
CRUCIBLE OF HORROR: see CORPSE, THE
CULT OF THE DEAD: see CULT OF THE DAMNED
CURSED SHIP, THE: see HORROR OF THE ZOMBIES
CURSE OF BIGFOOT, THE: see TEENAGERS BATTLE THE THING
CURSE OF DEATH: see DEATH CURSE OF TARTU
CURSE OF DRACULA, THE: see RETURN OF DRACULA, THE
CURSE OF FRANKENSTEIN, THE (1972): see EROTIC RITES OF FRANKENSTEIN, THE
CURSE OF KING TUT'S TOMB, THE: see CURSE OF KING TUTANKHAMEN'S TOMB, THE
CURSE OF THE ALLENBYS, THE: see SHE-WOLF OF LONDON (1946)
CURSE OF THE BLOOD-GHOULS: see SLAUGHTER OF THE VAMPIRES, THE
CURSE OF THE CANNIBAL CONFEDERATES: see CURSE OF THE SCREAMING DEAD
CURSE OF THE VAMPIRE: see PLAYGIRLS AND THE VAMPIRE, THE
CURSE OF THE VAMPIRES: see CREATURES OF EVIL
CURSE OF THE WALKING DEAD: see BLOOD DEMON, THE
CURSE III BLOOD SACRIFICE: see PANGA
CYBER CITY OEDO 808 DATA-3 KURENAI NO BAITAI: see CYBER CITY OEDO 808 FILE-3 BLOODLUST
CYBER CITY OEDO 808 FILE-3: see CYBER CITY OEDO 808 FILE-3 BLOODLUST
DAGYDE LES SEXANDROIDE, LA: see SEXANDROIDES, LES
DAI HADO ENJERUSU: KIKEN NI DAKARETA ONNATACHI: see DIE HARD ANGELS: PROJECT ZOMBIE ANNIHILATION
DAI HADO ENJERUSU: see DIE HARD ANGELS
DALLA NUBE ALLA RESISTENZA: see FROM THE CLOUD TO THE RESISTANCE
DANCE MACABRE: see DANSE MACABRE
DANGEROUS DESIRE: see TOMCAT: DANGEROUS DESIRES
DANZA MACABRA: see CASTLE OF BLOOD
DARK EYES OF THE ZOMBIES: see KILLING BIRDS
DARKNESS THE VAMPIRE CUT: see DARKNESS
DAUGHTER OF A WEREWOLF: see LEGEND OF THE WOLF WOMAN, THE
DEAD ALIVE: see BRAINDEAD
DEAD COME HOME, THE: see HOUSE ON TOMBSTONE HILL, THE
DEAD DUDES IN THE HOUSE: see HOUSE ON TOMBSTONE HILL, THE
DEADLY NEIGHBOR: see FIEND
DEADLY STING: see EVIL SPAWN
DEAD OF NIGHT (1972): see DEATHDREAM
DEAD PEOPLE: see MESSIAH OF EVIL
DEAD THAT WALK, THE: see ZOMBIES OF MORA TAU
DEAD TIME TALES: see THINGS 3: OLD THINGS
DEATH WHEELERS, THE: see PSYCHOMANIA
DE LA CHAIR POUR FRANKENSTEIN: see FLESH FOR FRANKENSTEIN (1973)
DELLAMORTE DELLAMORE: see CEMETERY MAN
DEMON APOCALYPSE: see BACK FROM HELL
DEMON DOCTOR, THE: see AWFUL DR. ORLOF, THE
DEMONIO AZUL, EL: see BLUE DEMON EL DEMONIO AZUL
DEMONI 3: see BLACK DEMONS
DEMON PLANET, THE: see PLANET OF THE VAMPIRES
DEMONS '95: see CEMETERY MAN
DEMONS OF THE SWAMP: see ATTACK OF THE GIANT LEECHES
DEN SKÆBNESVANGRE OPFINDELSE: see DR. JEKYLL AND MR. HYDE (1909)
DENTRO IL CIMITRIO: see GRAVEYARD DISTURBANCE
DESIDERI EROTICI DI CHRISTINA, I: see VIRGIN AMONG THE LIVING DEAD
DESTINATION SATURN: see BUCK ROGERS
DEVIL BATS: see DEVIL BAT, THE
DEVIL CAT: see CAT LIVING TEN TIMES
DEVIL HUNTER: see MAN HUNTER
DEVIL HUNTER YOKO: see DEVIL HUNTER YOHKO
DEVIL KISS: see WICKED CARESSES OF SATAN, THE
DEVIL'S CASTLE, THE: see HAUNTED CASTLE, THE
DEVIL'S MANOR, THE: see HAUNTED CASTLE, THE
DIABLESSES, LES: see SEVEN DEAD IN THE CAT'S EYES
DINNER WITH THE VAMPIRE: see DINNER WITH A VAMPIRE
DOCTOR BLOODBATH: see HORROR HOSPITAL
DOCTOR BUTCHER M.D. [MEDICAL DEVIATE]: see ZOMBI HOLOCAUST
DOCTOR JEKYLL Y EL HOMBRE LOBO: see DR. JEKYLL AND THE WEREWOLF
DOCTOR MANIAC: see HOUSE OF THE LIVING DEAD
DOCTOR SATAN, EL: see DR. SATAN
DOCTOR'S HORRIBLE EXPERIMENT, THE: see TESTAMENT DU DOCTEUR CORDELIER, LE
DON'T OPEN THE WINDOW: see LIVING DEAD AT MANCHESTER MORGUE, THE
DORAKIYURA YORI AI-O: see MY SOUL IS SLASHED
DOTTORE JEKILL JR., IL: see DR. JEKYLL LIKES 'EM HOT
DOTTOR JEKYLL E IL GENTILE SIGNORA: see DR. JEKYLL LIKES 'EM HOT
DOUBLE POSSESSION: see GANJA & HESS
DOUZE ET UN: see THIRTEEN CHAIRS, THE
DRACULA (1922): see NOSFERATU (1922)
DRACULA (1990): see DRACULA CINEMATIC SCRAPBOOK
DRACULA AND THE BOYS: see DOES DRACULA REALLY SUCK?
DRACULA CERCA SANGUE DI VERGINE E...MORI DI SETE!!!: see BLOOD FOR DRACULA
DRACULA CONTRA EL DOCTOR FRANKENSTEIN: see DRACULA PRISONER OF FRANKENSTEIN
DRACULA CONTRA FRANKENSTEIN: see DRACULA PRISONER OF FRANKENSTEIN
DRACULA...DOES HE?: see DOES DRACULA REALLY SUCK?
DRACULA '87: see DINASTIA DRACULA, LA
DRACULA FATHER & SON: see DRACULA AND SON
DRACULA IM SCHLOß DES SCHRECKENS: see WEB OF THE SPIDER
DRACULA JAGT FRANKENSTEIN: see DRACULA VS. FRANKENSTEIN (1969)
DRACULA LE PRISONNIER DE FRANKENSTEIN: see DRACULA PRISONER OF FRANKENSTEIN
DRACULA, PÈRE ET FILS: see DRACULA AND SON
DRACULA'S BRIDE: see DRACULA SUCKS
DRACULA'S CASTLE: see BLOOD OF DRACULA'S CASTLE
DRACULA'S LAST RITES: see LAST RITES
DRACULA'S SAGA, THE: see DRACULA SAGA, THE
DRACULA SUCKS (1969): see DOES DRACULA REALLY SUCK?
DRACULA SUCKS (1979, West Germany): see DRACULA BLOWS HIS COOL
DRACULA'S VIRGIN LOVERS: see DRACULA'S GREAT LOVE
DRACULA TAN EXARCHIA: see DRACULA & COMPANY
DRACULA — THE BLOODLINE CONTINUES: see DRACULA SAGA, THE
DRACULA: THE GREAT UNDEAD: see VINCENT PRICE'S DRACULA
DRACULA — UP IN HARLEM: see GANJA & HESS
DRACULA: VAMPIRE EMPEROR OF DARKNESS: see DRACULA: SOVEREIGN OF THE DAMNED
DRACULA VUOLE VIVERE...CERCA SANGUE DI VERGINE!: see BLOOD FOR DRACULA
DRACULIN: see POBRECITO DRACULIN, EL
DRAGON VS VAMPIRE: see DRAGON AGAINST VAMPIRE
DRAKULA HALÁLA: see DRAKULA (1921)
DR. BREEDLOVE OR HOW I LEARNED TO STOP WORRYING AND LOVE: see KISS ME QUICK
DR. CRIMEN: see MONSTRUO RESUCITADO, EL
DR. HALLERS: see MAN WITHIN, THE
DR. JEKYLL AND HIS WOMEN: see BLOODLUST (1979)
DR. JEKYLL AND MR. HYDE (1920, Germany): see JANUSKOPF, DER
DR. JEKYLL ET LES FEMMES: see BLOODLUST (1979)
DR. LOVE: see DR. LOVE AND HIS HOUSE OF PERVERSIONS
DR. NICOLA IN TIBET: see MYSTERY OF THE LAMA CONVENT, THE

DROPS OF BLOOD: see MILL OF THE STONE WOMEN
DRUMS OF THE JUNGLE: see LOVE WANGA
DUEL OF THE SPACE MONSTERS: see FRANKENSTEIN MEETS THE SPACEMONSTER
DUE OCCHI DIABOLICI: see TWO EVIL EYES
DUGO NG VAMPIRA: see CREATURES OF EVIL
DUNGEON OF VIRGINS: see REQUIEM FOR A VAMPIRE
DUNGEONS OF TERROR: see REQUIEM FOR A VAMPIRE
DWB DEEPWATER BLACK: see MISSION GENESIS
ÉCHENME AL VAMPIRO: see BRING ME THE VAMPIRE
ED WOOD STORY: THE PLAN 9 COMPANION, THE: see FLYING SAUCERS OVER HOLLYWOOD
EIGHT SAMURAI: see LEGEND OF EIGHT SAMURAI
ELECTRIC MAN, THE: see MAN MADE MONSTER
ENTITY FORCE: see ONE DARK NIGHT
ERCOLE AL CENTRO DELLA TERRA: see HERCULES IN THE HAUNTED WORLD
EROTIC TALES FROM THE MUMMY'S TOMB: see SECRETS OF SEX
EROTIKILL: see BARE BREASTED COUNTESS, THE
ESPANTO SURGE DE LA TUMBA, EL: see HORROR RISES FROM THE TOMB
ESPIRITISMO: see SPIRITISM
ESTRAÑO AMOR DE LOS VAMPIROS, EL: see STRANGE LOVE OF THE VAMPIRES
ETAIT UNE FOIS..LE DIABLE, IL: see DEVIL STORY
...E TU VIVRAI NEL TERRORE! L'ALDILA: see BEYOND, THE
EVA, LA VENERE SELVAGGIO: see KING OF KONG ISLAND
EVENING WITH BATMAN AND ROBIN, AN: see BATMAN
EVE THE WILD WOMAN: see KING OF KONG ISLAND
EXORCISMO PER UNA VERGINE: see VIRGIN AMONG THE LIVING DEAD
EXPÉRIENCES ÉROTIQUES DE FRANKENSTEIN, LES: see EROTIC RITES OF FRANKENSTEIN, THE
EXPERIMENT, THE: see BLOODLUST (1979)
EXPERIMENT IN EVIL: see TESTAMENT DU DOCTEUR CORDELIER, LE
EXTERMINADOR NOCTURO, EL: see CHIQUIDRACULA
EXTRANO AMOR DE LOS VAMPIROS: see VAMPIRE'S NIGHT ORGY, THE
EXTRAÑO CASO DEL HOMBRE Y LA BESTIA, EL: see HOMBRE Y LA BESTIA, EL (1951)
EYE OF THE EVIL DEAD: see MANHATTAN BABY
FACE TO FACE: see KNIGHT MOVES
FALL OF THE HOUSE OF USHER, THE: see REVENGE IN THE HOUSE OF USHER
FANGS OF THE LIVING DEAD: see MALENKA THE NIECE OF THE VAMPIRE
FANTASMA DELL'OPERA, IL: see PHANTOM OF THE OPERA, THE (1998)
FANTASTIC DISAPPEARING MAN, THE: see RETURN OF DRACULA, THE
FANTASTIC PUPPET PEOPLE: see ATTACK OF THE PUPPET PEOPLE
FA SEMPRE, FINO ALLA MORTE: see CHANGELING 2: THE REVENGE
FBI CONTRO DOTTORE MABUSE: see RETURN OF DR. MABUSE, THE
FEAR CHAMBER: see TORTURE ZONE, THE
FEARLESS FOSDICK IN: see FEARLESS FOSDICK PUPPET SHOW
FEARLESS VAMPIRE KILLERS, THE: see DANCE OF THE VAMPIRES
FEI SHI: see BLOOD THIRSTY DEAD, THE
FEMALE BUTCHER, THE: see LEGEND OF BLOOD CASTLE, THE
FENOMENAL E IL TESORO DI TUTANKAMEN: see PHENOMENAL AND THE TREASURE OF TUTANKAMEN
FIEND WITH THE ELECTRONIC BRAIN, THE: see BLOOD OF GHASTLY HORROR
FIGLIA DI FRANKENSTEIN, LA: see LADY FRANKENSTEIN
FILHA DE DRACULA, LA: see DAUGHTER OF DRACULA
FILLE À' LA FOURRURE, LA: see NAKED LOVERS
FILLE DE DRACULA, LA: see DAUGHTER OF DRACULA
FILLES TRAQUÉES: see NIGHT OF THE CRUEL SACRIFICE
FINAL SEDUCTION: see WASP WOMAN, THE (1995)
FIN DE SEMANA PARA LOS MUERTOS: see LIVING DEAD AT MANCHESTER MORGUE, THE
FLESH CREATURES, THE: see HORROR OF THE BLOOD MONSTERS
FLESH CREATURES OF THE RED PLANET: see HORROR OF THE BLOOD MONSTERS
FLESH EATER: see REVENGE OF THE LIVING ZOMBIES
FLESH RIPS RED: see TENDER DRACULA
FLINTSTONES COMEDY HOUR, THE: see FLINTSTONES, THE
FLINTSTONES FAMILY ADVENTURE HOUR, THE: see FLINTSTONE COMEDY SHOW, THE: THE FRANKENSTONES
FLINTSTONES SHOW, THE: see FLINTSTONES, THE
FLUCH DER GRÜNEN AUGEN, DER: see CAVE OF THE LIVING DEAD
FLUCH DER SCHWARZEN SCHWESTERN, DER: see DEVIL'S PLAYTHING, THE
FOOTSTEPS IN THE SAND: see BLACK LIMELIGHT
FORBIDDEN FEMININITY: see SEXY PROIBITISSIMO
FOREST OF FEAR: see BLOODEATERS
FOUR IN ONE: NIGHT GALLERY: see ROD SERLING'S NIGHT GALLERY
FRACCHIA CONTRO DRACULA: see WHO IS AFRAID OF DRACULA
FRACCHIA VS DRACULA: see WHO IS AFRAID OF DRACULA
FRANKENSTEIN (1973): see FLESH FOR FRANKENSTEIN (1973)
FRANKENSTEIN A CINEMATIC SCRAPBOOK: see FRANKENSTEIN (1990)
FRANKENSTEIN ALL'ITALIANA: see FRANKENSTEIN — ITALIAN STYLE
FRANKENSTEIN 88: see VINDICATOR, THE
FRANKENSTEIN EXPERIMENT, THE: see FLESH FOR FRANKENSTEIN (1973)
FRANKENSTEIN JR. SHOW: see FRANKENSTEIN JR. AND THE IMPOSSIBLES
FRANKENSTEIN ON CAMPUS: see DR. FRANKENSTEIN ON CAMPUS
FRANKENSTEIN SYNDROME, THE: see FRANKENSTEIN COMPLEX, THE
FRANKENSTEIN — THE REAL STORY: see FRANKENSTEIN (1992)
FRANKENSTEIN, UNE HISTOIRE D'AMOUR: see FRANKENSTEIN (1974)
FREAKY FAIRY TALES: see DEADTIME STORIES
FRED AND BARNEY MEET THE THING: see NEW FRED AND BARNEY SHOW, THE
FRED AND BARNEY MEET THE SHMOO: see NEW FRED AND BARNEY SHOW, THE
FRED FLINTSTONE AND FRIENDS: see FLINTSTONES, THE
FREUDSTEIN: see HOUSE BY THE CEMETERY, THE
FRIGHT HOUSE: see VAMPIRES (1988)
FRIGHTMARE: see HORROR STAR, THE
FRISSON DES VAMPIRES, LE: see VAMPIRE'S THRILL, THE
FROM A WHISPER TO A SCREAM: see OFFSPRING, THE
FUEGO: see PYRO
FURANKENSHUTAIN NO KAIJU — SANDA TAI GAILAH: see WAR OF THE GARGANTUAS
FURANKENSHUTAIN TAI BARAGON: see FRANKENSTEIN CONQUERS THE WORLD
FURIA DEL HOMBRE LOBO, LA: see FURY OF THE WOLFMAN, THE
FUTURE COP: see TRANCERS
GALLERY OF HORROR: see DR. TERROR'S GALLERY OF HORRORS
GAMMA 693 (1980): see NIGHT OF THE ZOMBIES
GAMMA 693 (1989): see CHILLING, THE
GANDY GOOSE IN FORTUNE HUNTERS: see FORTUNE HUNTERS
GANDY GOOSE IN G-MAN JITTERS: see G-MAN JITTERS
GATES OF HELL, THE: see CITY OF THE LIVING DEAD
GEBISSEN WIRD NUR NACHTS — DAS HAPPENING DER VAMPIRE: see VAMPIRE HAPPENING, THE
GEBURT DES HOMUNCULUS, DIE: see HOMUNCULUS
GEHEIMNIS DER TODESINSEL, DAS: see BLOOD SUCKERS (1965)
GHASTLY ORGIES OF COUNT DRACULA, THE: see REINCARNATION OF ISABEL, THE
GIANT LEECHES, THE: see ATTACK OF THE GIANT LEECHES
GLI ORRORI DEL CASTELLO DI NORIMBERGA: see BARON BLOOD
GOLIATHON: see MIGHTY PEKING MAN
GRAF DRACULA BEIßT JETZT AUCH IN OBERBAYERN: see DRACULA BLOWS HIS COOL
GRAF DRACULA IN OBERBAYERN: see DRACULA BLOWS HIS COOL
GRAMPIRE: see MOONRISE
GRAN AMOR DEL CONDE DRACULA, EL: see DRACULA'S GREAT LOVE
GRANDE TROUILLE, LA: see TENDER DRACULA
GRAND MÉRE EST UNE SORCIÈRE: see WITCH WORLD
GRAVE MISDEMEANOURS: see NIGHT LIFE
GRAVEROBBERS: see DEAD MATE

GRAVEYARD TRAMPS: see INVASION OF THE BEE GIRLS
GREAT MYSTERIES: see ORSON WELLES' GREAT MYSTERIES
GRITOS EN LA NOCHE: see AWFUL DR. ORLOF, THE
GROOVIE GOOLIES AND FRIENDS: see GROOVIE GOOLIES, THE
GU: see BEWITCHED (1981)
GUI DA GUI: see ENCOUNTER OF THE SPOOKY KIND
GUI MENG JIAO: see SPOOKY, SPOOKY
GUI YAO GUI: see ENCOUNTER OF THE SPOOKY KIND II
GWAI CHUK GWAI: see ENCOUNTER OF THE SPOOKY KIND
GWAI MAANG GEUK: see SPOOKY, SPOOKY
GYONSI YIM TAM: see GHOUL SEX SQUAD
HALF LIFE: see DANCE OF THE DAMNED
HALL OF THE MOUNTAIN KING: see NIGHT OF THE HOWLING BEAST
HALLOWEEN WITH THE NEW ADDAMS FAMILY: see HALLOWEEN WITH THE ADDAMS FAMILY
HAMMOND MYSTERY, THE: see UNDYING MONSTER, THE
HANDS OF ORLAC, THE: see MAD LOVE
HANNAH QUEEN OF THE VAMPIRES: see CRYPT OF THE LIVING DEAD
HAPPY HOOLIGAN IN DR. JEKYL AND MR. ZIP: see DR. JEKYL AND MR. ZIP
HARD TIMES FOR VAMPIRES: see UNCLE WAS A VAMPIRE
HAUNTED: see SHADES OF DARKNESS
HAUNTED STRANGLER, THE: see GRIP OF THE STRANGLER
HAUNTED WORLD OF EDWARD D. WOOD JR., THE: see HAUNTED WORLD OF ED WOOD, THE
HAVING A WILD WEEKEND: see CATCH US IF YOU CAN
HAVING SUPPER WITH A VAMPIRE: see DINNER WITH A VAMPIRE
HBO'S TALES FROM THE CRYPT: see TALES FROM THE CRYPT (1989-96)
HEAD OF JANUS, THE: see JANUSKOPF, DER
HEAVEN WIFE, HELL WIFE: see HAPPY GHOST
HECKLE AND JECKLE, THE TALKING MAGPIES, IN KING TUT'S TOMB: see KING TUT'S TOMB
HELLO, DRACULAR: see HELLO, DRACULA
HELL'S BELLES: see VAMPIRES AND OTHER STEREOTYPES
HELL'S CREATURES: see FRANKENSTEIN'S BLOODY TERROR
HERCULES IN THE CENTER OF THE EARTH: see HERCULES IN THE HAUNTED WORLD
HEY, GHOST!: see CLOSE ENCOUNTER OF THE VAMPIRE
HEY GHOST! II: see VAMPIRES STRIKE BACK
HIDEOUS MUTANT: see A*P*E
HIJOS DE LA NOCHE: see CHILDREN OF THE NIGHT (1997)
HITLER, EIN FILM AUS DEUTSCHLAND: see HITLER, A FILM FROM GERMANY
HOLOCAUSTE DE ZOMBI: see VIRGIN AMONG THE LIVING DEAD
HOLY WEAPON: see SEVEN MAIDENS
HOMBRE QUE VINO DEL UMMO, EL: see DRACULA VS. FRANKENSTEIN (1969)
HOMBRE Y EL MONSTRUO, EL: see MAN AND THE MONSTER, THE
HOMEBREW: see ZOMBIE TOXIN
HOMME SANS VISAGE, L': see SHADOWMAN
HOR B'LEVANA: see HOLE IN THE MOON
HORRIBLE DOCTEUR ORLOF, L': see AWFUL DR. ORLOF, THE
HORROR CONVENTION: see NIGHTMARE IN BLOOD
HORROR CREATURES OF THE PREHISTORIC PLANET: see HORROR OF THE BLOOD MONSTERS
HORROR OF DRACULA: see DRACULA (1958)
HORROR QUEEN: see EVIL CLUTCH
HOUSE OF CRAZIES: see ASYLUM
HOUSE OF FRANKENSTEIN 1997: see HOUSE OF FRANKENSTEIN (1997)
HOUSE OF FREAKS: see FRANKENSTEIN'S CASTLE OF FREAKS
HOUSE OF FRIGHT: see TWO FACES OF DR. JEKYLL, THE
HOUSE OF TERROR: see HANGING WOMAN, THE
HOWLING VII MYSTERY WOMAN: see HOWLING NEW MOON RISING, THE
HOWLING III: see MARSUPIALS THE HOWLING III, THE
HOWLING II YOUR SISTER IS A WEREWOLF: see HOWLING II STIRBA — WEREWOLF BITCH
HUA GUI LU XING TUAN: see FORCED NIGHTMARE
HUAGUI YOUXIAN GONGSI: see GHOST BUSTING
HUMAN EXPERIMENTS: see DEAD KIDS
HUNCHBACK (1981): see HUNCHBACK OF NOTRE DAME, THE (1981)
HUNCHBACK HAIRBALL OF L.A., THE: see BIG MAN ON CAMPUS
HUNCHBACK OF NOTRE DAME, THE (1997): see HUNCHBACK, THE (1997)
HUNCHBACK OF UCLA, THE: see BIG MAN ON CAMPUS
HUNDIMIENTO DE LA CASA USHER, EL: see REVENGE IN THE HOUSE OF USHER
HUPHYOKWI YANYO: see VENGEFUL VAMPIRE GIRL
HYDRA: see BLOOD WATERS OF DR. Z
HYPNOTIST, THE: see LONDON AFTER MIDNIGHT
I BELIEVE: see MAN WITHOUT A SOUL, THE
ICON: see MILL OF THE STONE WOMEN
IE: see HOUSE (1977)
I MARRIED A WEREWOLF: see WEREWOLF IN A GIRLS' DORMITORY
IM SCHLOSS DER BLÜTEN BEGIERDE: see CASTLE OF BLOODY LUST
IM STAHLNETZ DES DR. MABUSE: see RETURN OF DR. MABUSE, THE
INCUBO SULLA CITTÀ CONTAMINATA: see CITY OF THE WALKING DEAD
INFESTED: see TICKS
INHUMAINE, L': see INHUMAN WOMAN, THE
INMA DAITOSHI: see BEAST CITY
INNOCENTS FROM HELL: see SISTERS OF SATAN
INSAAN SHAITANI: see INSAAN BANA SHAITAN
IN SEARCH OF THE REAL DRACULA: see IN SEARCH OF DRACULA
INSOMNIE: see INSOMNIA
IN THE MIDNIGHT HOUR: see MIDNIGHT KISS
INVASIÓN DE LOS VAMPIROS, LA: see INVASION OF THE VAMPIRES, THE
INVASIÓN DE LOS ZOMBIES ATOMICOS, LA: see CITY OF THE WALKING DEAD
INVASION OF THE ZOMBIES: see SANTO VS THE ZOMBIES
INVENCIÓN DE CRONOS, LA: see CRONOS
ISLA DE LA MUERTE, LA: see BLOOD SUCKERS (1965)
ISLA DE LOS MUERTOS, LA: see CULT OF THE DAMNED
ISLAND OF DEATH: see BLOOD SUCKERS (1965)
ISLAND OF THE DOOMED: see BLOOD SUCKERS (1965)
ISLAND OF THE LIVING DEAD, THE: see ZOMBIE
ISLE OF THE FISHMEN: see ISLAND OF MUTATIONS
ISLE OF THE SNAKE PEOPLE: see CULT OF THE DAMNED
ISOLA DEGLI UOMINI PESCI, L': see ISLAND OF MUTATIONS
IT FELL FROM THE SKY: see ALIEN DEAD
IVANNA: see SCREAM OF THE DEMON LOVER
I WAS A TEENAGE VAMPIRE: see MY BEST FRIEND IS A VAMPIRE
JASON LIVES FRIDAY THE 13TH PART VI: see FRIDAY THE 13TH PART VI JASON LIVES
JEKYLL AND HYDE (1909): see DR. JEKYLL AND MR. HYDE (1909)
JEKYLL & HYDE: PACT WITH THE DEVIL: see PACTO DIABÓLICO
JEKYLL AND HYDE UNLEASHED: see JEKYLL AND HYDE PORTFOLIO, THE
JEU DE MASSACRE: see KILLING GAME, THE
JEUX DE LA COMTESSE DOLINGEN DE GRATZ, LES: see GAMES OF THE COUNTESS DOLINGEN OF GRATZ, THE
JIANGSHI FANSHENG: see KUNG FU VAMPIRE BUSTER
JIANG SHI FU XING ZI: see VAMPIRE KIDS
JIANGSHI JIAZU: see MR VAMPIRE 2
JIANGSHI PAPA: see CLOSE ENCOUNTER OF THE VAMPIRE
JIANG SHI SHAO YE: see MAGIC STORY (1986)
JIANGSHI SHUSHU: see MR. VAMPIRE SAGA 4
JIANGSHI XIANSHENG: see MR. VAMPIRE
JIANGSHI XIANSHENG XUJI: see MR VAMPIRE 2
JIANGSHI YANTAN: see GHOUL SEX SQUAD
JIANG SHI YI SHENG: see DOCTOR VAMPIRE
JIANG SHI ZHI ZUN: see ULTIMATE VAMPIRE, THE
JOHN CARPENTER PRESENTS BODY BAGS: see BODY BAGS
JOHN CARPENTER'S VAMPIRES: see VAMPIRES (1998)
JONATHAN, VAMPIRE STERBEN NICHT: see JONATHAN
JONNY QUEST THE NEW ADVENTURES: see JONNY QUEST THE REAL ADVENTURES
JOROBADO DE LA MORGUE, EL: see HUNCHBACK OF THE MORGUE, THE
JOURNEY TO THE CENTER OF THE EARTH: see WHERE TIME BEGAN
J. SHERIDAN LE FANU'S CARMILLA: see VAMPIRE CARMILLA
JUMP, RATTLE AND ROLL: see WAKE, RATTLE AND ROLL: MONSTER TAILS
JUNGFRAU UNTER KANNIBALEN: see MAN HUNTER

JUNGLE VIRGIN: see JAWS OF THE JUNGLE
KAI XIN GUI JING LING: see LOVE ME VAMPIRE
KAMITSUKITAI: see MY SOUL IS SLASHED
KAP NGOH YAT GOH MAN: see ROMANCE OF THE VAMPIRES, THE
KEI YUEN: see WITCH FROM NEPAL
KILL AND GO HIDE!: see CHILD, THE
KILLER BATS: see DEVIL BAT, THE
KILLER BIRDS: see KILLING BIRDS
KILLING BOX, THE: see GHOST BRIGADE, THE
KING KONGS FAUST: see KING KONG'S FIST
KING KONG VS. MECHA-KONG: see KING KONG ESCAPES
KINGU KONGU NO GYAKUSHU: see KING KONG ESCAPES
KINGU KONGU TAI GOJIRA: see KING KONG VS. GODZILLA
KISMET KI BHOOL: see KALKUT
KISS MEETS THE PHANTOM: see KISS MEETS THE PHANTOM OF THE PARK
KISS OF EVIL: see KISS OF THE VAMPIRE, THE
KISS OF THE BEAST: see MERIDIAN
KLEINE VAMPIR, DER: see LITTLE VAMPIRE, THE
KOESI: see STRANGE DEAD BODIES
KOMMISSAR X: JAGD AUF UNBEKANNT: see KISS KISS, KILL KILL
KOU-HUN CHIANG T'OU: see REVENGE OF THE ZOMBIES (1976)
KYOFU DENSETSU: KAIBUTSU! FRANKENSTEIN: see FRANKENSTEIN (1981)
KYÛKETSUKI GOKEMIDORO: see GOKE, BODY SNATCHER FROM HELL
KYÛKETSUKI MIYU: see VAMPIRE PRINCESS MIYU
LAC DES MORTS VIVANTS, LE: see ZOMBIE LAKE
LADY DRACULA: see LEGENDARY CURSE OF LEMORA, THE
LAGO DE LOS MUERTOS VIVIENTES, EL: see ZOMBIE LAKE
LAGO MALDITO: see SECRET OF THE MUMMY, THE
LAMP, THE: see OUTING, THE
LASUTO FURANKENSHUTAIN: see LAST FRANKENSTEIN
LEÁK: see MYSTICS IN BALI
LEGEND OF THE ZAAT MONSTER, THE: see BLOOD WATERS OF DR. Z
LEMORA A CHILD'S TALE OF THE SUPERNATURAL: see LEGENDARY CURSE OF LEMORA, THE
LEMORA: A VAMPIRE'S TALE: see LEGENDARY CURSE OF LEMORA, THE
LEMORA, THE LADY DRACULA: see LEGENDARY CURSE OF LEMORA, THE
LEONORE: see LEONOR
LET SLEEPING CORPSES LIE: see LIVING DEAD AT MANCHESTER MORGUE, THE
LEVIATAN: see MONSTER DOG
LÈVRES DE SANG: see LIPS OF BLOOD (1975)
LIANGHUAN XIANSHENG: see MR. VAMPIRE PART III
LIAO ZHAI JIN PING MEI: see GHOST STORY OF KAM PIN MUI
LIFE SUCKS: see NIGHT WITH A VAMPIRE
LING CHEN WAN CAN: see VAMPIRE'S BREAKFAST
LING HUAN XIAO JIE: see MISS MAGIC
LION KING'S TIMON & PUMBAA, THE: see TIMON & PUMBAA
LIVING DEAD MAN, THE: see INHUMAN WOMAN, THE
LLAMADA DEL VAMPIRO, LA: see CURSE OF THE VAMPIRE, THE
LOA VUDÚ: see VOODOO BLACK EXORCIST
LOCK YOUR DOORS: see APE MAN, THE
LOLA: see WITHOUT A SOUL
LOONIES ON BROADWAY: see ZOMBIES ON BROADWAY
LOST IN NEW YORK: see DEUX ORPHELINES VAMPIRES, LES
LOST IN TIME: see WAXWORK II: LOST IN TIME
LOST ON ADVENTURE ISLAND: see KING DONG
LOVE AT FIRST GULP: see DRACULA EXOTICA
LOVE'S MOCKERY: see JANUSKOPF, DER
LOVES OF COUNT IORGA, VAMPIRE, THE: see COUNT YORGA, VAMPIRE
LOVES OF IRINA, THE: see BARE BREASTED COUNTESS, THE
LOVES OF THE LIVING DEAD: see HAPPY GHOST
LOVE STORIES OF THE LIVING DEAD: see GHOUL SEX SQUAD
LOVE TRAP: see CURSE OF THE BLACK WIDOW
LUBIE NIETOPERZE: see I LIKE BATS
LUCHADORAS CONTRA EL ROBOT ASESINO, LAS: see WRESTLING WOMEN VS. THE KILLER ROBOT, THE
LUCHADORAS CONTRA LA MOMIA, LAS: see WRESTLING WOMEN VS. THE AZTEC MUMMY, THE
LUCHADORES DE LAS ESTRELLAS: see STARFIGHTERS
LUNGA NOTTE DEL TERRORE, LA: see CASTLE OF BLOOD
LUPA MANNARA, LA: see LEGEND OF THE WOLF WOMAN, THE
LUPIN SANSEI: see LUPIN III
LUST AT FIRST BITE: see DRACULA SUCKS
LUST OF DRACULA, THE: see GUESS WHAT HAPPENED TO COUNT DRACULA?
LUST OF THE VAMPIRE: see DEVIL'S COMMANDMENT, THE
LYCANTHROPUS: see WEREWOLF IN A GIRLS' DORMITORY
MACE IL FUORILEGGE: see CONQUEST
MACISTE CONTRO IL VAMPIRO: see GOLIATH AND THE VAMPIRES
MADMEN OF MANDORAS: see THEY SAVED HITLER'S BRAIN
MADONNA...BABAENG AHASSSSSS: see MADONNA...BABAENG AHAS
MAD RON'S PREVIEWS FROM HELL: see PREVUES FROM HELL
MALDICIÓN DE FRANKENSTEIN, LA: see EROTIC RITES OF FRANKENSTEIN, THE
MALDICIÓN DE LA BESTIA, LA: see NIGHT OF THE HOWLING BEAST
MALDICIÓN DE LA LLORONA, LA: see CURSE OF THE CRYING WOMAN, THE
MALDICIÓN DE LA MOMIA AZTECA, LA: see CURSE OF THE AZTEC MUMMY
MALDICIÓN DE LOS KARNSTEIN, LA: see CRYPT OF HORROR
MALDICIÓN DE NOSTRADAMUS, LA: see CURSE OF NOSTRADAMUS, THE
MALENKA LA NIPOTE DEL VAMPIRO: see MALENKA THE NIECE OF THE VAMPIRE
MALENKA, LA SOBRINA DEL VAMPIRO: see MALENKA THE NIECE OF THE VAMPIRE
MAMONO HUNTER YOHKO: see DEVIL HUNTER YOHKO
MANDINGO MANHUNTER: see MAN HUNTER
MAN-EATER OF HYDRA: see BLOOD SUCKERS (1965)
MANGLED ALIVE: see FATAL EXPOSURE
MANOIR DU DIABLE, LE: see HAUNTED CASTLE, THE
MANOR OF THE DEVIL, THE: see HAUNTED CASTLE, THE
MANSION DE BLUE DEMON: see MANSION DE LAS 7 MOMIAS, LA
MANSIÓN DE LA NIEBLA, LA: see MURDER MANSION
MAN WITH THE SYNTHETIC BRAIN: see BLOOD OF GHASTLY HORROR
MAO SHAN XIAO TANG: see FIRST VAMPIRE IN CHINA, THE
MARCA DEL HOMBRE LOBO, LA: see FRANKENSTEIN'S BLOODY TERROR
MARCA DEL MUERTO, LA: see CREATURE OF THE WALKING DEAD
MARK OF THE DEVIL PART 3: see SISTERS OF SATAN
MARK OF THE VAMPIRE, THE: see VAMPIRE, THE (1957, USA)
MARK OF THE WEST: see CURSE OF THE UNDEAD
MARK OF THE WOLFMAN: see FRANKENSTEIN'S BLOODY TERROR
MARQUISE DE SADE, DIE: see BILDNIS DER DORIAN GRAY, DAS
MARTE INVADE A PUERTO RICO: see FRANKENSTEIN MEETS THE SPACEMONSTER
MÁS ALLA DEL TERROR: see BEYOND TERROR
MASCHERA DEL DEMONIO, LA (1960): see BLACK SUNDAY
MASCHERA DEL DEMONIO, LA (1960): see DEMONS 5: DEVIL'S VEIL
MASK OF SATAN, THE (1960): see BLACK SUNDAY
MASK OF SATAN, THE (1990): see DEMONS 5: DEVIL'S VEIL
MASTER OF THE DUNGEON, THE: see GUESS WHAT HAPPENED TO COUNT DRACULA?
MATRIARCH, THE: see GRANNY, THE
MAZDOOR KI BETI: see DHANWAN
MEDVEZHYA SVADBA: see MARRIAGE OF THE BEAR, THE
MENG GUI CHA GUAN: see HAUNTED COP SHOP, THE
MENG GUI XUE TANG: see HAUNTED COP SHOP II, THE
MENG GUI ZHOU: see DEVIL CURSE
METAMORPHOSIS: see EVIL SPAWN
METEOR MONSTER: see TEENAGE MONSTER
MIDNIGHT COP: see NICK KNIGHT
MIDNIGHT SLAUGHTER: see VAMPYRES
MIGHTY MOUSE IN FRANKENSTEIN'S CAT: see FRANKENSTEIN'S CAT
MIGHTY MOUSE IN THE JAILBREAK: see JAILBREAK, THE
MIGHTY MOUSE MEETS JEKYLL AND HYDE CAT: see JEKYLL AND HYDE CAT
MISTERIO EN LA ISLA DE LOS MONSTRUOS: see MYSTERY ON MONSTER ISLAND
MODERN DR. JEKYLL, THE: see DR. JEKYLL AND MR. HYDE (1908)

MOMIA AZTECA CONTRA EL ROBOT HUMANO, LA: see ROBOT VS THE AZTEC MUMMY, THE
MOMIA NACIONAL, LA: see NATIONAL MUMMY, THE
MOMIE AU PAIR: see MUMMY NANNY, THE
MOMIE DU ROI, LA: see MUMMY OF THE KING OF RAMSES, THE
MONDO CANNIBALE: see MAN HUNTER
MONSTER FROM THE SURF: see BEACH GIRLS AND THE MONSTER, THE
MONSTER [HUMANOIDS FROM THE DEEP]: see HUMANOIDS FROM THE DEEP (1980)
MONSTER ISLAND: see MYSTERY ON MONSTER ISLAND
MONSTER MASH THE MOVIE: see FRANKENSTEIN SINGS
MONSTER MEETS THE GORILLA, THE: see BELA LUGOSI MEETS A BROOKLYN GORILLA
MONSTRE, LE: see MONSTER, THE
MONSTROSITY: see ATOMIC BRAIN, THE
MONSTRUOS DEL TERROR, LOS: see DRACULA VS. FRANKENSTEIN (1969)
MORBUS, O QUE APROVECHE: see MORBUS
MORGAN!: see MORGAN A SUITABLE CASE FOR TREATMENT
MORTE HA SORRISO ALL'ASSASSINO, LA: see DEATH SMILES ON A MURDERER
MORTE NEGLI OCCHI DEL GATTO, LA: see SEVEN DEAD IN THE CAT'S EYES
MORTE VIVANTE, LA: see LIVING DEAD GIRL, THE
MOSAICO: see FRANKENSTEIN '80
MOSQUITO DER SCHAENDER: see BLOODLUST (1976)
MOSQUITON PROJECT: see MASTER OF MOSQUITON
MOSTRO DELL'OPERA, IL: see VAMPIRE OF THE OPERA, THE
MOSTRO É IN TAVOLA...BARONE FRANKSTEIN, IL: see FLESH FOR FRANKENSTEIN (1973)
MOULIN DES SUPPLICES, LE: see MILL OF THE STONE WOMEN
MOURIR DE PLAISIR, ET: see BLOOD AND ROSES
MOVINI'S VENOM: see NIGHT OF THE COBRA WOMAN
MR. DRACULA: see MR. VAMPIRE
MR. MAGOO AND FRIENDS: see MR. MAGOO
MR. MAGOO LITERARY CLASSICS: see FAMOUS ADVENTURES OF MR. MAGOO
MR. VAMPIRE V: see MAGIC COP
MUERTE VIVIENTE, LA: see CULT OF THE DAMNED
MUJERES DE DRACULA, LAS: see IMPERIO DE DRACULA, EL
MULINO DELLE DONNE DI PIETRA, IL: see MILL OF THE STONE WOMEN
MUMIA, EL: see NIGHT OF COUNTING THE YEARS, THE
MUMIA MA, DIE: see EYES OF THE MUMMY MA, THE
MUMMY PART 2: THE UNWRAPPING: see MUMMY DEAREST 2
MUMMY III: THE PARTING, THE: see MUMMY DEAREST 3
MUNDO DE LOS VAMPIROS, EL: see WORLD OF THE VAMPIRES, THE
MUÑECOS INFERNALES, LOS: see CURSE OF THE DOLL PEOPLE
MURDER IN THE FUN HOUSE: see CHINESE CAT, THE
MUTANT: see NIGHT SHADOWS
MY GRANDAD'S A VAMPIRE: see MOONRISE
MY GRANDPA IS A VAMPIRE: see MOONRISE
MY SON THE VAMPIRE: see MOTHER RILEY MEETS THE VAMPIRE
MYSTERY! (1983): see SHADES OF DARKNESS
MYSTERY! (1993): see AGATHA CHRISTIE'S POIROT
MYSTERY!: DR. JEKYLL AND MR. HYDE: see DR. JEKYLL AND MR. HYDE (1980)
MYSTERY! FRANKENSTEIN — LEGEND OF TERROR: see FRANKENSTEIN (1981)
MYSTERY OF KING TUT-ANKH-AMEN'S EIGHTH WIFE, THE: see KING TUT-ANKH-AMEN'S EIGHTH WIFE
NACHT DER VAMPIRE: see WEREWOLF VS. THE VAMPIRE WOMAN, THE
NACHTS: see NIGHT TIME
NACHTS, WENN DRACULA ERWACHT: see BRAM STOKER'S COUNT DRACULA
NACKTE UND DER SATAN, DIE: see HEAD, THE
NAKED WEREWOLF WOMAN: see LEGEND OF THE WOLF WOMAN, THE
NAO MO: see BLACK MAGIC WITH BUTCHERY
NATTENS ENGEL: see ANGEL OF THE NIGHT
NECROMANY — A LIFE FOR A LIFE: see NECROMANCY
NECROPOLIS CITY OF THE DEAD: see NECROPOLIS
NELLA STRETTA MORSA DEL RAGNO: see WEB OF THE SPIDER
NEPAL AFFAIR, THE: see WITCH FROM NEPAL
NÉVROSE: see REVENGE IN THE HOUSE OF USHER
NEW ADVENTURES OF SUPERMAN, THE: see LOIS & CLARK THE NEW ADVENTURES OF SUPERMAN
NEW ADVENTURES OF TINTIN, THE: see ADVENTURES OF TINTIN, THE
NEW MR. VAMPIRE: see KUNG FU VAMPIRE BUSTER
NEW SCOOBY AND SCRAPPY-DOO SHOW, THE: see SCOOBY-DOO AND SCRAPPY-DOO
NIGHT CRAWL: see ZOMBIE BRIGADE
NIGHT FEAST: see HUNGRY PART 2
NIGHT GALLERY: see ROD SERLING'S NIGHT GALLERY
NIGHT LEGS: see FRIGHT
NIGHTMARE CITY (1980): see CITY OF THE WALKING DEAD
NIGHT OF THE BLIND DEAD: see TOMBS OF THE BLIND DEAD
NIGHT OF THE BLOODSUCKERS: see VAMPIRE HOOKERS
NIGHT OF THE DEATH CULT: see NIGHT OF THE SEAGULLS
NIGHT OF THE HUNTED: see NIGHT OF THE CRUEL SACRIFICE
NIGHT OF THE VAMPIRE: see NIGHT WITH A VAMPIRE
NIGHT OF THE WALKING DEAD: see STRANGE LOVE OF THE VAMPIRES
NIGHT OF THE WEHRMACHT ZOMBIES: see NIGHT OF THE ZOMBIES
NIGHT OF THE ZOMBIES: see ZOMBIE CREEPING FLESH
NIGHT OF THE ZOMBIES II: see NIGHT OF THE ZOMBIES
NIGHTS OF TERROR: see ZOMBIE 3 (1980)
NIGHT STALKER, THE (1974): see KOLCHAK: THE NIGHT STALKER
NIGHT STAR, GODDESS OF ELECTRA: see WAR OF THE ZOMBIES
NIGHTWARRIORS: DARKSTALKERS' REVENGE: see VAMPIRE HUNTER
976-EVIL THE ASTRAL FACTOR: see 976-EVIL II
NOCHE DE LAS GAVIOTAS, LA: see NIGHT OF THE SEAGULLS
NOCHE DE LOS BRUJOS, LA: see NIGHT OF THE SORCERERS
NOCHE DE LOS DIABLOS, LA: see NIGHT OF THE DEVILS
NOCHE DE LOS VAMPIROS, LA: see STRANGE LOVE OF THE VAMPIRES
NOCHE DE LOS VAMPIROS, LA: see VAMPIRE'S NIGHT ORGY, THE
NOCHE DEL TERROR CIEGO, LA: see TOMBS OF THE BLIND DEAD
NOCHE DE WALPURGIS, LA: see WEREWOLF VS. THE VAMPIRE WOMAN, THE
NOCHES DEL HOMBRE LOBO, LAS: see NIGHTS OF THE WEREWOLF
NOE HELT ANNET: see SOMETHING ELSE — ENTIRELY
NON SI DEVE PROFANARE IL SONNO DEI MORTI: see LIVING DEAD AT MANCHESTER MORGUE, THE
NO PROFANAR EL SUEÑO DE LOS MUERTOS: see LIVING DEAD AT MANCHESTER MORGUE, THE
NOSFERATO NO BRASIL: see NOSFERATO IN BRAZIL
NOSFERATU — A SYMPHONY OF HORROR: see NOSFERATU
NOSFERATU, A SYMPHONY OF HORRORS: see NOSFERATU
NOSFERATU A VENEZIA: see VAMPIRE IN VENICE
NOSFERATU, EINE SYMPHONIE DES GRAUENS: see NOSFERATU
NOSFERATU FANTÔME DE LA NUIT: see NOSFERATU THE VAMPYRE
NOSFERATU PHANTOM DER NACHT: see NOSFERATU THE VAMPYRE
NOSFERATU THE FIRST VAMPIRE: see NOSFERATU
NOSFERATU THE VAMPIRE (DRACULA): see NOSFERATU
NOSFERATU THE VAMPIRE: see NOSFERATU
NOSTRADAMUS, EL GENIO DE LAS TINIEBLAS: see GENII OF DARKNESS, THE
NOSTRADAMUS Y EL DESTRUCTOR DE MONSTRUOS: see MONSTERS DEMOLISHER, THE
NOTRE-DAME DE PARIS (1956): see HUNCHBACK OF NOTRE-DAME, THE (1956)
NOTTE DEI DIAVOLI, LA: see NIGHT OF THE DEVILS
NOTTE EROTICHE DEI MORTE VIVENTI, LE: see EROTIC NIGHTS OF THE LIVING DEAD
NOTTE NEL BOSCO: see EVIL CLUTCH
NOTTE NEL CIMITERO, UNA: see GRAVEYARD DISTURBANCE
NOTTI DEI TERRORE, LA: see ZOMBIE 3 (1980)
NOVIA ENSANGRENTADA, LA: see BLOOD SPATTERED BRIDE, THE
NUIT DES TRAQUÉES, LA: see NIGHT OF THE CRUEL SACRIFICE
NUITS ROUGE: see SHADOWMAN
NYAI BLORONG: see HUNGRY SNAKE WOMAN, THE
NYLONSCHLINGE, DIE: see NYLON NOOSE
OASIS OF THE ZOMBIES: see OASIS OF THE LIVING DEAD, THE
OBOROTEN' TOM: see WEREWOLF TOM

OBRAS MAESTRAS DEL TERROR: see MASTER OF HORROR
OBSESSION: see JUNOON
OBSZÖNITÄTEN: see CONFESSIONS OF A MALE ESCORT
OCCHIO DEL MALE, L': see MANHATTAN BABY
OLD DRACULA: see VAMPIRA (1974)
OLTRA LA MORTE: see AFTER DEATH: ZOMBIE 4
ONDSKANS VÄRDSHUS: see INN OF THE FLYING DRAGON, THE
OOKAMI-OTOKO TO SAMURAI: see BESTIA Y LA ESPADA MÁGICA, LA
OPERA: see TERROR AT THE OPERA
ORGIA DEI MORTI, L': see HANGING WOMAN, THE
ORGIA DE LOS MUERTOS, LA: see HANGING WOMAN, THE
ORGIA NOCTURNA DE LOS VAMPIROS, LA: see VAMPIRE'S NIGHT ORGY, THE
ORGY OF THE VAMPIRES: see VAMPIRE'S NIGHT ORGY, THE
ORIGINAL GHOSTBUSTERS, THE: see GHOSTBUSTERS
ORIGINAL TV ADVENTURES OF KING KONG: see KING KONG SHOW, THE
ORRIBILE SEGRETO DEL DR. HICHCOCK, L': see HORRIBLE DR. HICHCOCK, THE
OSAMU TEZUKA'S DON DRACULA: see DON DRACULA
O SEGREDO DA MÚMIA: see SECRET OF THE MUMMY, THE
OUANGA: see LOVE WANGA
OUT OF THE FOG: see FOG FOR A KILLER
PA JAKT EFTER DRACULA: see IN SEARCH OF DRACULA
PANICO EN EL TRANSIBERIANO: see HORROR EXPRESS
PANTANO DE LAS ANIMAS, EL: see SWAMP OF THE LOST MONSTERS, THE
PAO DAN FEI CHE: see TRAIL, THE
PARTY GIRLS FOR THE CANDIDATE: see CANDIDATE, THE
PASTRIES: see TOUCH OF SWEDEN, A
PAUL NORMAN'S HUNCHBACK OF NOTRE DAME: see HUNCHBACK OF NOTRE DAME, THE (1991)
PAURA NELLA CITTÀ DEI MORTI VIVENTI, LA: see CITY OF THE LIVING DEAD
PEEPING PHANTOM, THE: see HOW TO SUCCEED WITH GIRLS
PERROS DE LA MUERTE, LOS: see MONSTER DOG
PERVERSA CARICIA DE SATAN, LA: see WICKED CARESSES OF SATAN, THE
PERVERSE KISS OF SATAN, THE: see WICKED CARESSES OF SATAN, THE
PERVERSIONS SEXUELLES: see LIPS OF BLOOD (1972)
PHANTASM III: see PHANTASM LORD OF THE DEAD
PHANTOM FIEND: see RETURN OF DR. MABUSE, THE
PHANTOM OF MANHATTAN: see DANSE MACABRE
PHANTOMS: see MERIDIAN
PLANET OF BLOOD: see QUEEN OF BLOOD
PLANET OUTLAWS: see BUCK ROGERS
PLENILUNIO DELLE VERGINI, IL: see DEVIL'S WEDDING NIGHT, THE
POCOMANIA: see DEVIL'S DAUGHTER, THE
POLISH VAMPIRE: see POLISH VAMPIRE IN BURBANK, A
PORNO ZOMBIES: see NAKED LOVERS
POSSESSED, THE: see MANHATTAN BABY
PRANZO CON VAMPIRO: see DINNER WITH A VAMPIRE
PRENDIMI, STRAZIAMI, CHE BRUCIO DI PASSIONE!: see FRANKENSTEIN — ITALIAN STYLE
PRESA TENACE: see EVIL CLUTCH
PRESENCE, THE: see DANGER ISLAND
PREY: see TERRORE A AMITYVILLE PARK
PRISONNIER DE L'ARAIGNÉE: see WEB OF THE SPIDER
PROJECT METALBEAST: DNA OVERLOAD: see PROJECT METALBEAST
PSYCHO-A-GO-GO: see BLOOD OF GHASTLY HORROR
PUBLIC EYE, THE: see FOLLOW ME
PYUSHCHYE KROVY: see THOSE FEEDY ON BLOOD
QIAN NU YOU HUN: see CHINESE GHOST STORY, A
QIAN NU YOU HUN II: REN JIAN DAO: see CHINESE GHOST STORY II, A
QIAN YUNYU QING: see GHOSTLY LOVE
QI YUAN: see WITCH FROM NEPAL
QUANDO MARTA URLO DALLA TOMBA: see MURDER MANSION
QUEEN OF THE CANNIBALS: see ZOMBI HOLOCAUST
QUEEN OF THE GORILLAS: see BRIDE AND THE BEAST, THE
QUEEN OF THE VAMPIRES: see VAMPIRE'S RAPE, THE
QUELLA VILLA ACCANTO AL CIMITERO: see HOUSE BY THE CEMETERY, THE
QUMO JINGCHA: see MAGIC COP
RACHE DES HOMUNCULUS, DIE: see HOMUNCULUS
RAGEWAR: see DUNGEONMASTER, THE
RAISINS DE LA MORT, LES: see PESTICIDE
RAPTORS: GLI UCCELLI ASSASSINI: see KILLING BIRDS
RAPTUS: THE SECRET OF DR. HICHCOCK: see HORRIBLE DR. HICHCOCK, THE
RAPTUS: THE TERROR OF DR. HICHCOCK: see HORRIBLE DR. HICHCOCK, THE
RE-ANIMATOR 2: see BRIDE OF RE-ANIMATOR
REBELIÓN DE LAS MUERTAS, LA: see VENGEANCE OF THE ZOMBIES
RED HOOD CHACHA: see AKAZUKIN CHACHA
REGINA DEGLI ZOMBI, LA: see EROTIC NIGHTS OF THE LIVING DEAD
REGINA DEI CANNIBALI, LA: see ZOMBI HOLOCAUST
REINE DES VAMPIRES, LA: see VAMPIRE'S RAPE, THE
REJUVENATRIX: see REJUVENATOR, THE
REMANDO AL VIENTO: see ROWING WITH THE WIND
REQUIEM POUR UN VAMPIRE: see REQUIEM FOR A VAMPIRE
RETORNO DEL HOMBRE LOBO, EL: see CRAVING, THE
RETORNO DE WALPURGIS, EL: see CURSE OF THE DEVIL
RETOUR DU DOCTEUR MABUSE, LE: see RETURN OF DR. MABUSE, THE
RETURN FROM THE PAST: see DR. TERROR'S GALLERY OF HORRORS
RETURN OF THE BLIND DEAD: see RETURN OF THE EVIL DEAD
RETURN OF THE LIVING DEAD (1973): see MESSIAH OF EVIL
RETURN OF THE ZOMBIS, THE: see HANGING WOMAN, THE
REVANCHE DES MORTES-VIVANTES, LA: see REVENGE OF THE LIVING DEAD, THE (1985)
REVE DE SINGE: see CIAO MASCHIO
REVENANT: see MODERN VAMPIRES
REVENGE OF DRACULA: see DRACULA VS. FRANKENSTEIN (1970)
REVENGE OF THE BLACK SISTERS: see DEVIL'S PLAYTHING, THE
REVENGE OF THE CORPSE: see BLOOD THIRSTY DEAD, THE
REVENGE OF THE DEAD: see NIGHT OF THE GHOULS
REVENGE OF THE LIVING DEAD (1972): see CHILDREN SHOULDN'T PLAY WITH DEAD THINGS
REVENGE OF THE SCREAMING DEAD: see MESSIAH OF EVIL
REVENGE OF THE VAMPIRE: see BLACK SUNDAY
REVENGE OF THE ZOMBIE: see KISS DADDY GOODBYE
REVOLT OF THE DEMONS: see REVOLT OF THE ZOMBIES
REVOLT OF THE HOUSE OF USHER: see REVENGE IN THE HOUSE OF USHER
RICK MORANIS IN GRAVEDALE HIGH: see GRAVEDALE HIGH
RITES OF DRACULA, THE: see SATANIC RITES OF DRACULA, THE
RITI, MAGIE NERE E SEGRETE ORGE NEL TRECENTO...: see REINCARNATION OF ISABEL, THE
RITORNO DALLA MORTE: see RETURN FROM DEATH
ROBBING CLEOPATRA'S TOMB: see CLEOPATRA
ROCK 'N ROLL WRESTLING WOMEN VS. THE AZTEC MUMMY: see WRESTLING WOMEN VS. THE AZTEC MUMMY, THE
ROCKO'S LIFE: see ROCKO'S MODERN LIFE
ROMA CONTRO ROMA: see WAR OF THE ZOMBIES
ROMAN'S AWAKENING, THE: see BACK TO LIFE AFTER 2000 YEARS
ROUGE AUX LÈVRES, LE: see DAUGHTERS OF DARKNESS
RUE MORGUE MASSACRES, THE: see HUNCHBACK OF THE MORGUE, THE
SABBAH, LA MASCHERA DEL DEMONIO: see DEMONS 5: DEVIL'S VEIL
SAGA DE LOS DRÁCULA, LA: see DRACULA SAGA, THE
SAGA OF THE DRACULAS: see DRACULA SAGA, THE
SANG DES AUTRES, LE: see LIPS OF BLOOD (1972)
SANGRE DE NOSTRADAMUS, LA: see BLOOD OF NOSTRADAMUS, THE
SANGUE E LA ROSA, IL: see BLOOD AND ROSES
SANTO CONTRA DRACULA: see SANTO Y EL TESORO DE DRACULA
SANTO CONTRA EL BARON BRAKOLA: see BARON BRAKOLA, EL
SANTO CONTRA EL HACHA DIABOLICA: see HACHA DIABOLICA, EL
SANTO CONTRA LAS BESTIAS DEL TERROR: see BESTIAS DEL TERROR!, LAS
SANTO CONTRA LAS LOBAS: see SANTO VS. LAS LOBAS
SANTO CONTRA LOS MONSTRUOS DE FRANKENSTEIN: see SANTO Y BLUE DEMON VS. LOS MONSTRUOS
SANTO CONTRA LOS ZOMBIES: see SANTO VS THE ZOMBIES
SANTO EN EL MUSEO DE CERA: see SAMSON IN THE WAX

MUSEUM
SANTO EN LA VENGANZA DE LAS MUJERES VAMPIRO: see VENGANZA DE LAS MUJERES VAMPIRO, LA
SANTO VS. LA HIJA DE FRANKESTEIN: see SANTO CONTRA LA HIJA DE FRANKESTEIN
SANTO VS. LAS MUJERES VAMPIRO: see SAMSON VS. THE VAMPIRE WOMEN
SANTO Y BLUE DEMON CONTRA LOS MONSTRUOS: see SANTO Y BLUE DEMON VS. LOS MONSTRUOS
SANTO Y LA MALDICIÓN DE LAS VAMPIRAS: see VENGANZA DE LAS MUJERES VAMPIRO, LA
SATANIK: see SATANIC
SATAN'S BLOOD FREAKS: see DRACULA VS. FRANKENSTEIN (1970)
SATAN'S DAUGHTERS: see VAMPYRES
SATAN'S SATELLITES: see ZOMBIES OF THE STRATOSPHERE
SCHLANGENGRUBE UND DAS PENDEL, DIE: see BLOOD DEMON, THE
SCHOOL THAT ATE MY BRAIN, THE: see ZOMBIE HIGH
SCOOBY-DOO CLASSICS (1969-72): see SCOOBY DOO WHERE ARE YOU!
SCOOBY-DOO CLASSICS (1976): see SCOOBY-DOO—DYNOMUTT HOUR, THE
SCOOBY-DOO—DYNOMUTT SHOW, THE (1976): see SCOOBY-DOO—DYNOMUTT HOUR, THE
SCOOBY'S MYSTERY FUNHOUSE (1979-80): see SCOOBY-DOO AND SCRAPPY-DOO
SCOOBY'S MYSTERY FUNHOUSE (1982-83): see SCOOBY-DOO AND SCRAPPY-DOO—PUPPY HOUR, THE
SCREAMERS: see ISLAND OF MUTATIONS
SCREAMING DEAD, THE: see DRACULA PRISONER OF FRANKENSTEIN
SCREAM OF THE CAGED VIRGINS: see REQUIEM FOR A VAMPIRE
SCREEN SCARIES: see DRIVE-IN MADNESS!
SECOND COMING, THE: see MESSIAH OF EVIL
SECRETO DE LA MOMIA, EL: see SECRET OF THE MUMMY, THE
SECRETO DEL DR. ORLOFF, EL: see DR. ORLOFF'S MONSTER
SECRET OF DR. ALUCARD, THE: see TASTE OF BLOOD, A
SECTE DE L'HORREUR, LA: see DEVIL'S PLAYTHING, THE
SEDDOK: see ATOM AGE VAMPIRE
SEDDOK L'EREDE DI SATANA: see ATOM AGE VAMPIRE
SEED OF TERROR: see GRAVE OF THE VAMPIRE
SEGRETTO DE LA MOMIA, EL: see LIPS OF BLOOD (1972)
SENSACIONAL Y EXTRAÑO CASO DEL HOMBRE Y LA BESTIA, EL: see HOMBRE Y LA BESTIA, EL (1951)
SENSUOUS VAMPIRES: see VAMPIRE HOOKERS
SERPENT MAN, THE: see SNAKE MAN, THE
SESAME STREET PRESENTS: FOLLOW THAT BIRD: see FOLLOW THAT BIRD
SETE VAMPIRAS, AS: see SEVEN VAMPIRES, THE
7 BROTHERS MEET DRACULA, THE: see LEGEND OF THE 7 GOLDEN VAMPIRES, THE
7 DEATHS IN THE CAT'S EYE: see SEVEN DEAD IN THE CAT'S EYES
7 DOORS OF DEATH: see BEYOND, THE
7 VAMPIRES: see SEVEN VAMPIRES, THE
SEXANDROIDE: see SEXANDROIDES, LES
SEX AND THE VAMPIRE: see VAMPIRE'S THRILL, THE
SEX MANIAC: see MANIAC
SEXO CANÍBAL: see MAN HUNTER
SEX ON THE GROOVE TUBE: see CASE OF THE FULL MOON MURDERS
SEXY EROTIC LOVE: see EROTIC NIGHTS OF THE LIVING DEAD
SHADOW OF THE VAMPIRE: see BURNED TO LIGHT
SHADOW OF THE WEREWOLF: see WEREWOLF VS. THE VAMPIRE WOMAN, THE
SHE WAS A HIPPY VAMPIRE: see WILD WILD WORLD OF BATWOMAN, THE
SHE WOLF: see LEGEND OF THE WOLF WOMAN, THE
SHE-WOLF OF LONDON: see LOVE AND CURSES
SHI JIA ZHONG DI: see MORTUARY BLUES
SHIVER OF THE VAMPIRES: see VAMPIRE'S THRILL, THE
SIEBEN MONDE: see NIGHT TIME
SIEN NUI YAU WAN: see CHINESE GHOST STORY, A
SIEN NUI YAU WAN II: YAN GAAN DO: see CHINESE GHOST STORY II, A
SIGNORE DEI CANI, IL: see MONSTER DOG
SILENT DEATH: see VOODOO ISLAND
SILVER HERMIT FROM SHAOLIN VALLEY MEETS BLOODY FANGS OF DEATH: see SILVER SPEAR, THE
SINBAD IL MARINAIO: see SINBAD OF THE SEVEN SEAS
SIR ARTHUR CONAN DOYLE: see SHORT STORIES OF CONAN DOYLE, THE
SIU-SIN: see CHINESE GHOST STORY: THE TSUI HARK ANIMATION, A
SKADUWEES OOR BRUGPLAAS: see HOUSE OF THE LIVING DEAD
SLAPSTICK: see SLAPSTICK OF ANOTHER KIND
SLEEP OF DEATH, THE: see INN OF THE FLYING DRAGON, THE
SMALL TOWN MASSACRE: see DEAD KIDS
SNAKE PEOPLE: see CULT OF THE DAMNED
SNAKE WOMAN'S MARRIAGE: see LADY MASTER SNAKE
SOMETHING QUITE DIFFERENT — OR THE VAMPIRE MOVIE: see SOMETHING ELSE — ENTIRELY
SOMETHING WAITS IN THE DARK: see ISLAND OF MUTATIONS
SONNO DIE MORTE, IL: see LIVING DEAD AT MANCHESTER MORGUE, THE
SORORITY HOUSE VAMPIRES FROM HELL: see SORORITY HOUSE VAMPIRES (1992)
SOULMATES OF SHANGO: see LORD SHANGO
SPACE GHOST, THE: see FRANKENSTEIN JR. AND THE IMPOSSIBLES
SPACE MISSION OF THE LOST PLANET: see HORROR OF THE BLOOD MONSTERS
SPACE MONSTERS: see EVILS OF THE NIGHT
SPACE ORGAN, THE: see EROTIC ENCOUNTERS OF THE FOURTH KIND
SPACE VAMPIRES, THE: see ASTRO-ZOMBIES, THE
SPACE ZOMBIES: see ASTRO-ZOMBIES, THE
SPIRITUAC FAMILY: see ULTIMATE VAMPIRE
SPIRIT OF THE BEEHIVE, THE: see ESPIRITU DE LA COLMENA, EL
SPOOKY ENCOUNTER: see ENCOUNTER OF THE SPOOKY KIND
SPOOKY ENCOUNTERS 2: see ENCOUNTER OF THE SPOOKY KIND II
SR. SOMBRA: see MI NOMBRE ES SOMBRA
STARSHIP EROS: see NAKED LOVERS
STEPHEN KING'S SILVER BULLET: see SILVER BULLET
STEPHEN KING'S SOMETIMES THEY COME BACK: see SOMETIMES THEY COME BACK
STEVEN SPIELBERG PRESENTS ANIMANIACS: see ANIMANIACS
STEVEN SPIELBERG PRESENTS PINKY & THE BRAIN: see PINKY AND THE BRAIN
STEVEN SPIELBERG PRESENTS TOONSYLVANIA: see TOONSYLVANIA
STEVEN SPIELBERG PRESENTS TINY TOON ADVENTURES: TINY TOONS' NIGHT GHOULERY: see TINY TOON ADVENTURES: TINY TOONS' NIGHT GHOULERY
ST. GEORGE AND THE SEVEN CURSES: see MAGIC SWORD, THE
STONE BOY: see BOY GOD
STOP THE SMOGGIES: see SMOGGIES
STRAGE DEI VAMPIRI, LA: see SLAUGHTER OF THE VAMPIRES, THE
STRANGE ADVENTURES OF DAVID GRAY, THE: see VAMPYR (1931-32)
STRANGE BEHAVIOUR: see DEAD KIDS
STRANGE CASE OF DR. JECKEL & MS. HIDE, THE: see DR. JECKEL & MS. HIDE
STRANGE TURF: see VOODOO DAWN
SUCE-MOI, VAMPIRE: see SUCK ME, VAMPIRE
SUPER DICK: see CRY UNCLE
SUPERMAN: see ADVENTURES OF SUPERMAN, THE
SUPER SEXY INTERDIT: see SEXY PROIBITISSIMO
SUPERSIMIAN: see KING DONG
SVATBA UPÍRŮ: see VAMPIRE WEDDING, THE
SWEETNESS OF SIN, THE: see TOWER OF THE SCREAMING VIRGINS
TAKAISIN RYSSIIN: see BACK TO THE USSR
TAKBO...! BILIS...! TAKABOOOO: see TAKBO..., BILIS... TAKBOOOOOO!
TALE OF THE MUMMY: see TALOS THE MUMMY
TALE OF VAMPIRE, A: see TALE OF A VAMPIRE
TALES FROM THE CRYPT II: see VAULT OF HORROR
TALES FROM THE CRYPT PRESENTS BORDELLO OF BLOOD: see BORDELLO OF BLOOD
TARKAN: see TARKAN ALTIN MADALYON
TEENAGE FRANKENSTEIN: see I WAS A TEENAGE FRANKENSTEIN
TEENAGE PSYCHO MEETS BLOODY MARY: see INCREDIBLY STRANGE CREATURES WHO STOPPED LIVING AND BECAME MIXED-UP ZOMBIES!!?, THE

TEMPI DURI PER I VAMPIRI: see UNCLE WAS A VAMPIRE
TENDRE DRACULA: see TENDER DRACULA
TERROR BEACH: see NIGHT OF THE SEAGULLS
TERROR DE GUANAJUATO, EL: see CAPULINA CONTRA LAS MOMIAS
TERROR EN EL ESPACIO: see PLANET OF THE VAMPIRES
TERRORE NELLO SPAZIO: see PLANET OF THE VAMPIRES
TERROR EN SAN ANGEL: see MOMIAS DE SAN ANGEL, LAS
TERROR HOUSE: see NIGHT HAS EYES, THE
TERROR! IL CASTELLO DELLE DONNE MALEDETTE: see FRANKENSTEIN'S CASTLE OF FREAKS
TERROR IN THE CRYPT: see CRYPT OF HORROR
TERROR OF DR. HICHCOCK, THE: see HORRIBLE DR. HICHCOCK, THE
TERROR OF FRANKENSTEIN: see VICTOR FRANKENSTEIN
TERROR OF MANHATTAN: see DANSE MACABRE
TERROR OF THE SHE WOLF: see LEGEND OF THE WOLF WOMAN, THE
TESORO DE DRACULA, EL: see SANTO Y EL TESORO DE DRACULA
TETSUWAN ATOM: see ASTRO BOY (1980)
TETSUWAN ATOMA: Franken: see ASTRO BOY: Colosso
THAT THEY MAY LIVE: see J'ACCUSÉ (1938)
THEY'RE COMING TO GET YOU: see DRACULA VS. FRANKENSTEIN (1970)
THINK DIRTY: see EVERY HOME SHOULD HAVE ONE
THIS VAMPIRE SUCKS: see DRACULA SUCKS
THRILL OF THE VAMPIRE: see VAMPIRE'S THRILL, THE
THUNDER NINJA KIDS THE HUNT FOR THE DEVIL BOXER, THE: see THUNDER KIDS 3 HUNT FOR DEVIL BOXER
TILL DEATH DO US PART: see BLOOD SPATTERED BRIDE, THE
TOMB OF THE UNDEAD: see GARDEN OF THE DEAD
TOMBS OF HORROR, THE: see TERROR CREATURES FROM THE GRAVE
TORTURE CHAMBER, THE: see TORTURE ZONE, THE
TORTURE CHAMBER OF BARON BLOOD, THE: see BARON BLOOD
TORTURE CHAMBER OF DR. SADISM, THE: see BLOOD DEMON, THE
TOUCH OF LOVE, A: see WITCH FROM NEPAL
TOUR DE NESLE, LA: see TOWER OF THE SCREAMING VIRGINS
TOXIC ZOMBIES: see BLOODEATERS
TRACK OF THE VAMPIRE: see BLOOD BATH
TRANSFORMATIONS: see UNDERWORLD
TRAUM DES ALLAN GRAY, DER: see VAMPYR (1931-32)
TRÉSOR DES MORTS-VIVANTS, LE (1981, Dir: A.M. Frank): see OASIS OF THE LIVING DEAD, THE
TRÉSOR DES MORTS VIVANTS, LE (1981, Dir: Jess Franco): see TUMBA DE LOS MUERTOS VIVIENTES, LA (1981, Dir: Jess Franco)
TRE VOLTI DELLA PAURA, I: see BLACK SABBATH
TRIO INFERNAL, LE: see INFERNAL TRIO, THE
TROIS VISAGES DE LA PEUR, LES: see BLACK SABBATH
TRUE LIFE OF DRACULA, THE: see VLAD TEPES
TUMBA DE LA ISLA MALDITA, LA: see CRYPT OF THE LIVING DEAD
TUMBA DE LOS MUERTOS VIVIENTES, LA (1981, Dir: A.M. Frank): see OASIS OF THE LIVING DEAD, THE
TURM DER VERBOTENEN LIEBE, DER: see TOWER OF THE SCREAMING VIRGINS
12+1: see THIRTEEN CHAIRS, THE
TWICE BITTEN: see VAMPIRE HOOKERS
TWINKLE, TWINKLE, KILLER KANE: see NINTH CONFIGURATION, THE
TWISTED BRAIN: see HORROR HIGH
TWIST IN THE TALE: see TALES OF THE UNEXPECTED
TWO-SOULED WOMAN, THE: see UNTAMEABLE, THE
ÚDOLI VCEL: see VALLEY OF BEES, THE
ULTIMA PREDA DEL VAMPIRO, L': see PLAYGIRLS AND THE VAMPIRE, THE
ULTIMATE GOOSEBUMPS: see GOOSEBUMPS
ULTIMO UOMO DELLA TERRA, L': see LAST MAN ON EARTH, THE
UM SONHO DE VAMPIROS: see LOVE THAT VAMPIRE
UNA SU TREDICI: see THIRTEEN CHAIRS, THE
UNDYING BRAIN, THE: see BRAIN OF BLOOD
UNKAI NO MEIKYU: see ZEGUY
UNTIL DEATH: see CHANGELING 2: THE REVENGE
UPIR VE VEZAKU: see VAMPIRE IN THE HIGH RISE
UPIR Z FERATU: see FERAT VAMPIRE
UPON A FRIGHTMARE: see HORROR STAR, THE
URSUS E IL TERRORE DEI KIRGHISI: see HERCULES, PRISONER OF EVIL
VAARWHEL: see ROMANTIC AGONY, THE
VALERIE A TYDEN DIVN: see VALERIE AND HER WEEK OF WONDERS
VAMPIR: see CUADECUC (VAMPIR)
VAMPIR: see VAMPYR (1931-32)
VAMPIRAS, LAS (1970): see VAMPIROS LESBOS
VAMPIRE, THE (1931-32): see VAMPYR (1931-32)
VAMPIRE-BEAST CRAVES BLOOD, THE: see BLOOD BEAST TERROR, THE
VAMPIRE COP: see MIDNIGHT KISS
VAMPIRE DOLL, THE: see NIGHT OF THE VAMPIRE, THE
VAMPIRE ECSTASY: see DEVIL'S PLAYTHING, THE
VAMPIRE MEN OF THE LOST PLANET: see HORROR OF THE BLOOD MONSTERS
VAMPIRE NUE, LA: see NUDE VAMPIRE, THE
VAMPIRE OVER LONDON: see MOTHER RILEY MEETS THE VAMPIRE
VAMPIRE PEOPLE: see BLOOD DRINKERS, THE
VAMPIRE PLAYGIRLS: see DRACULA'S GREAT LOVE
VAMPIRES (1988): see VAMPIRES STRIKE BACK
VAMPIRE'S DREAM, A: see LOVE THAT VAMPIRE
VAMPIRES EN ONT RAS LE BOL, LES: see BLOOD RELATIONS
VAMPIRES IN VENICE: see VAMPIRE IN VENICE
VAMPIRES, THE ARCH CRIMINALS OF PARIS: see VAMPIRES, LES (1915-16)
VAMPIRE THAT CAME FROM SPACE, THE: see GOKE, BODY SNATCHER FROM HELL
VAMPIRE VS. VAMPIRE: see ONE EYEBROW PRIEST
VAMPIRE WOMAN (1972): see CRYPT OF THE LIVING DEAD
VAMPIRI, I: see DEVIL'S COMMANDMENT, THE
VAMPIRO, EL: see VAMPIRE, THE (1957, Mexico)
VAMPIRO DE LA AUTOPISTA, EL: see HORRIBLE SEXY VAMPIRE, THE
VAMPIRO DELL'OPERA, IL: see VAMPIRE OF THE OPERA, THE
VAMPIRO PARA DOS, UN: see VAMPIRE FOR TWO, A
VAMPIRO SANGRIENTO, EL: see BLOODY VAMPIRE, THE
VAMPIROS TAMBIEN DUERMEN, LOS: see VAMPIRE'S NIGHT ORGY, THE
VAMPIRO Y EL SEXO, EL: see SANTO Y EL TESORO DE DRACULA
VAMPYR, THE: see VAMPYR — A SOAP OPERA, THE
VAMPYRDANSERINDEN: see VAMPIRE DANCER, THE
VAMPYRES DAUGHTERS OF DRACULA: see VAMPYRES
VAMPYROS LESBOS DIE ERBIN DES DRACULA: see VAMPIROS LESBOS
VAMPYR OU L'ETRANGE ADVENTURE DE DAVID GRAY: see VAMPYR (1931-32)
VEIL OF BLOOD: see DEVIL'S PLAYTHING, THE
VENDETTA DEI MORTI VIVENTI, LA: see VENGEANCE OF THE ZOMBIES
VENGANZA DE LA MOMIA, LA (1969): see SANTO EN LA VENGANZA DE LA MOMIA
VENGANZA DE LA MOMIA, LA (1973): see MUMMY'S REVENGE, THE
VENGEANCE OF THE DEAD: see KISS DADDY GOODBYE
VENGEFUL DEAD, THE: see KISS DADDY GOODBYE
VERGINE FRAI I MORTI VIVENTI, UNA: see VIRGIN AMONG THE LIVING DEAD
VERGINI CAVALCANO LA MORTE, LE: see LEGEND OF BLOOD CASTLE, THE
VIAJE AL CENTRO DE LA TIERRA: see WHERE TIME BEGAN
VIERGE CHEZ LES MORTS-VIVANTS, UNE: see VIRGIN AMONG THE LIVING DEAD
VII: see VIJ
VINCENT PRICE'S ONCE UPON A MIDNIGHT SCARY: see ONCE UPON A MIDNIGHT DREARY
VIOL DU VAMPIRE, LE: see VAMPIRE'S RAPE, THE
VIRGINS AND THE VAMPIRES, THE: see REQUIEM FOR A VAMPIRE
VIRGIN VAMPIRE: see RED LIPS II
VIRUS — L'INFERNO DEI MORTI-VIVENTI: see ZOMBIE CREEPING FLESH
VIY: see VIJ
VOICE FROM THE DARKNESS: see REVENGE OF THE DEAD
VOODOO GIRL: see SUGAR HILL
VRIJEME VAMPIRA: see TIME OF VAMPIRES, THE
VUDÚ SANGRIENTO: see VOODOO BLACK EXORCIST

BIBLIOGRAPHY & FURTHER READING

I am indebted to the authors and editors of the following books and magazines which were consulted in the compilation of this work:

Absurd 1-3.
Adam Film World Guide 1997 Directory of Adult Films.
The Addams Chronicles (HarperPerennial, 1991) by Stephen Cox.
Adult Video News The 1997 Adult Video Guide.
Aka Joe D'Amato.
All Hallows 8.
Alternate Cinema.
The Anime! Movie Guide (Titan Books, 1996) by Helen McCarthy.
Asian Cult Cinema 23.
Asian Cult Cinema (Boulevard Books, 1997) by Thomas Weisser.
The Aurum Film Encyclopedia: Horror (Aurum Press, 1993) edited by Phil Hardy.
The A-Z of Horror Films (B.T. Batsford, 1996) by Howard Maxford.
Bare-Bones 2.
Batman: Animated (Titan Books, 1998) by Paul Dini and Chip Kidd.
Best New Horror Volumes 1-5 (Robinson Publishing/Carroll & Graf, 1990-94, five volumes) edited by Stephen Jones and Ramsey Campbell.
Best New Horror Volumes 6-10 (Robinson Publishing/Carroll & Graf, 1995-99, five volumes) edited by Stephen Jones.
The BFI Companion to Horror (Cassell/British Film Institute, 1996) edited by Kim Newman.
Bizarre Sinema! Wildest Sexiest Weirdest Sleaziest Films: Horror All'Italiana 1957-1979 (Glittering Images, 1996) edited by Stefano Piselli and Riccardo Morrocchi. Text by Antonio Bruschini.
Book of the Dead nos 1-4.
The Boxtree Encyclopedia of TV Detectives (Boxtree, 1992) by Geoff Tibballs.
British Television (Oxford University Press, 1994) by Tise Vahimagi.
The Carry On Companion (B.T. Batsford, 1996) by Robert Ross.
Cinefantastique.
Clive Barker's A-Z of Horror (BBC Books, 1997) compiled by Stephen Jones.
The Complete Directory to Science Fiction, Fantasy and Horror Television Series: A Comprehensive Guide to the First 50 Years 1946 to 1996 (Other Worlds Books, 1997) by Alan Morton.
Ze Craignos Monsters (Éditions Vents D'Ouest, 1991) by Jean-Pierre Putters.
Ze Craignos Monsters Le Retour (Éditions Vents D'Ouest, 1995) by Jean-Pierre Putters.
Ze Craignos Monsters Le Re-Retour (Éditions Vents D'Ouest, 1998) by Jean-Pierre Putters.
Creature Features (Boulevard Books, 1997) by John Stanley.
Crimson.
Cult Movies & Video.
Cult TV A Viewer's Guide to the Shows America Can't Live Without!! (St Martin's Press, 1985) by John Javna.
The Dark Side.
Daughters of the Night: Carmilla on the Screen.
Delirium A Guide to Italian Exploitation Cinema 1975-1979 (Media Publications, 1997) edited by Adrian Luther-Smith.
Doctor Who: The Eighties (Doctor Who Books/Virgin Publishing, 1996) by David J. Howe, Mark Stammers and Stephen James Walker.
Doctor Who: The Seventies (Doctor Who Books/Virgin Publishing, 1994) by David J. Howe, Mark Stammers and Stephen James Walker.
Dracula: The Vampire Legend on Film (Fantasma Books, 1992) by Robert Marrero.
Dreadfull Pleasures.
Drums of Terror: Voodoo in the Cinema (Midnight Marquee Press, 1998) by Bryan Senn.
Elliot's guide to Films on Video Third Edition (Boxtree, 1993) by John Elliot.
The Encyclopedia of Animated Cartoons, second edition (Checkmark Books, 1999) by Jeff Lenburg.
Encyclopedia of Indian Cinema (BFI Publishing/Oxford University Press, 1994) by Ashish Rajadhyaksha and Paul Willemen.
The Essential Guide to Hong Kong Movies (Eastern Heroes Publications, 1994) by Rick Baker and Toby Russell.
Eyeball.
Famous Monsters of Filmland.
Fangoria.
Fantastic Cinema Subject Guide: A Topical Index to 2500 Horror, Science Fiction, and Fantasy Films (McFarland & Company, 1992) by Bryan Senn and John Johnson.
Fantastic Television (Titan Books, 1987) by Gary Gerani with Paul H. Schulman.
Le Fantastique Français (Monster Bis) by Vince Rogers.
Femme Fatales.
Films Into Books: An Analytical Bibliography of Film Novelizations, Movie, and TV Tie-Ins (The Scarecrow Press, 1995) by Randall D. Larson.
The Films of Boris Karloff (The Citadel Press, 1974) by Richard Bojarski and Kenneth Beals.
Flesh & Blood.
Foreign Film Guide (Bloomsbury, 1988) by Ronald Bergen and Robyn Karney.
Forgotten Horrors: Early Talkie Chillers from Poverty Row (A.S. Barnes and Company, 1979) by George E. Turner and Michael H. Price.
Les Grands Films: Dracula (Editions J'ai lu, 1990) by Philippe Ross.
Graven Images: The Best Horror, Fantasy, and Science-Fiction Film Art from the Collection of Ronald V. Borst (Grove Press, 1992) edited by Ronald V. Borst, Keith Burns and Leith Adams.
Halliwell's Film and Video Guide 1998 Edition (Harper Collins, 1997) edited by John Walker.
Halliwell's Filmgoer's Companion (Paladin/Granada, 1980) by Leslie Halliwell.
Halliwell's Television Companion Third Edition (Grafton Books, 1986) by Leslie Halliwell and Philip Purser.

The Hammer Story (Titan Books, 1997) by Marcus Hearn and Alan Barnes.
Hollywood Gothic: The Tangled Web of Dracula from Novel to Stage to Screen (W.W. Norton & Company, 1990) by David J. Skal.
Hong Kong Babylon (Faber & Faber, 1997) by Frederic Dannen and Barry Long.
Hong Kong Films 1989-1990 (Hong Kong, Kowloon and New Territories Motion Picture Industry Association Ltd, 1991).
Hong Kong Films 1992 (Hong Kong, Kowloon and New Territories Motion Picture Industry Association Ltd, 1993).
Horror and Science Fiction Films (The Scarecrow Press, 1972, 1982, 1984, 1997; four volumes) by Donald C. Willis.
Horror Film Stars (McFarland & Company, 1981) by Michael R. Pitts.
Horror in Silent Films: A Filmography, 1896-1929 (McFarland & Company, 1995) by Roy Kinnard.
Horrors From Screen to Scream (Futura Publications, 1976) by Ed Naha.
The House of Horror: The Complete Story of Hammer Films (Lorrimer Publishing, 1981) edited by Allen Eyles, Robert Adkinson and Nicholas Fry.
The Illustrated Dinosaur Movie Guide (Titan Books, 1993) by Stephen Jones.
The Illustrated Frankenstein Movie Guide (Titan Books, 1994) by Stephen Jones.
The Illustrated Vampire Movie Guide (Titan Books, 1993) by Stephen Jones.
The Illustrated Werewolf Movie Guide (Titan Books, 1996) by Stephen Jones.
Images in the Dark An Encyclopedia of Gay and Lesbian Film and Video (Titan Books, 1998) by Raymond Murray.
Immoral Tales: Sex and Horror Cinema in Europe 1956-1984 (Titan Books, 1995) by Cathal Tohill and Pete Tombs.
Inferno.
Inside Gilligan's Island (St. Martin's Press, 1994) by Sherwood Schwartz.
Into the Twilight Zone: The Rod Serling Programme Guide (Virgin Books, 1995) by Jean-Marc and Randy Lofficier.
It's Alive! The Classic Cinema Saga of Frankenstein (A.S. Barnes & Company, 1981) by Gregory Willaim Mank.
Leonard Maltin's Movie and Video Guide (Signet, 1994) edited by Leonard Maltin.
Mad Doctors, Monsters and Mummies!: Lobby Card Posters from Hollywood Horrors! (H.C. Blossom, 1991) by Denis Gifford.
Made in Hell Volume One.
Manga Max 4.
Merveilleux, Fantastique et Science-fiction: à la télévision française (Huitième Art Editions, 1995) by Jacques Baudou and Jean-Jacques Schleret.
The Mexican Film Bulletin.
Mondo Macabro: Weird & Wonderful Cinema Around the World (Titan Books, 1997) by Pete Tombs.
Monster! International.
Monthly Film Bulletin.
The Movie Tie-In Book (Nostalgia Books, 1994) by Moe Wadle.
Nightmare of Ecstasy The Life and Art of Edward D. Wood, Jr. (Feral House, 1992) by Rudolph Grey.
Obsession: The Films of Jess Franco (Graf Haufen & Frank Trebbin, 1993) by Lucas Balbo, Peter Blumenstock, Christian Kessler and Tim Lucas.
Of Mice and Magic (Plume, 1980) by Leonard Maltin.
Oriental Cinema 15
The Outer Limits: The Official Companion (Ace Science Fiction Books, 1986) by David J. Schow and Jeffrey Frentzen.
Outré.
The Phantom's Ultimate Video Guide (Dell Publishing, 1989) by The Phantom of the Movies.
Photon 20.
The Psychotronic Encyclopedia of Film (Ballantine Books, 1983) by Michael Weldon.
The Psychotronic Video Guide (Titan Books, 1996) by Michael Weldon.
Pufnstuf & Other Stuff The Weird and Wonderful World of Sid & Marty Krofft (Renaissance Books, 1998) by David Martindale.
Radio Times.
Reference Guide to Fantastic Films (Chelsea-Lee Books, 1972, 1973, 1974; three volumes) compiled by Walt Lee.
Saturday Morning Fever (St. Martin's Friffin, 1999) by Timothy Burke and Kevin Burke.
Science Fiction, Horror & Fantasy Film and Television Credits Supplement 2: Through 1993 (McFarland & Company, 1994) by Harris M. Lentz, III.
A Separate Cinema Fifty Years of Black Cast Posters (The Noonday Press, 1992) by John Kisch and Edward Mapp.
Shivers.
Sight and Sound.
Slimetime: A Guide to Sleazy, Mindless, Movie Entertainment (Critical Vision/Headpress, 1996) by Steven Puchalski.
Something Weird Catalog.
Tales from the Crypt: The Official Archives (St. Martin's Press, 1996) by Digby Diehl.
Things, Its and Aliens!: Lobby Card Posters from Sci-fi Shockers! (H.C. Blossom, 1991) by Denis Gifford.
TV Guide.
TV Tie-Ins A Bibliography of American TV Tie-In Paperbacks (Neptune Publishing, 1997) by Kurt Peer.
TV Times.
TV Zone Special 25.
Universal Horrors: The Studio's Classic Films, 1931-1946 (McFarland & Company, 1990) by Michael Brunas, John Brunas and Tom Weaver.
The Vampire Film (The Tantivy Press, 1975) by James Ursini and Alain Silver.
Videoguía X (Midons Editorial S.L, 1994) by Manuel Valencia.
Video Hound's Golden Movie Retriever (Visible Ink Press).
Videooze 6-7.
Video Wasteland Rental, Reference and Review Guide #6 (Video Wasteland, 1997) by Ken Kish.
Video Watchdog.
The Video Watchdog Book (Video Watchdog, 1992) by Tim Lucas.
Virgins & Vampires (Crippled Publishing, 1997) by Jean Rollin.
The Warner Brothers Cartoons (The Scarecrow Press, 1981) by Will Friedwald and Jerry Beck.
The Whole Toon Catalog.
Who's Who of the Horrors and Other Fantasy Films (The Tantivy Press, 1981) by David J Hogan.
The Wild Wild West The Series (Arnett Press, 1988) by Susan E. Kesler.
The X-Rated Videotape Guide I-II (Prometheus Books, 1993, 1991; two volumes) by Robert H. Rimmer.
The X-Rated Videotape Guide III-IV (Prometheus Books, 1993, 1994; two volumes) by Robert H. Rimmer and Patrick Riley.
The X-Rated Videotape Star Index (Prometheus Books, 1994) by Patrick Riley.

ABOUT THE AUTHOR

STEPHEN JONES discovered *Famous Monsters of Filmland* magazine around the time he first saw the 1933 *King Kong* on television. He has never been the same since. One of Britain's most acclaimed anthologists of dark fantasy and horror, he has had more than fifty books published and is the winner of two World Fantasy Awards, three Horror Writers Association Bram Stoker Awards and two International Horror Guild Awards as well as being a twelve-time recipient of the British Fantasy Award and a Hugo Award nominee. As a genre movie publicist he worked on the first three *Hellraiser* movies, *Night Life, Nightbreed, Split Second, Mind Ripper, Last Gasp*, etc, and his books include *The Illustrated Vampire Movie Guide, The Illustrated Dinosaur Movie Guide, The Illustrated Frankenstein Movie Guide, The Illustrated Werewolf Movie Guide, Clive Barker's A-Z of Horror, Clive Barker's The Nightbreed Chronicles* and *The Hellraiser Chronicles*. He lives in London.

Photo credits

All the photographs used in this book are from private collections and picture libraries and are used solely for the advertising, promotion, publicity and review of the specific motion pictures they illustrate. They have not been reproduced for advertising or poster purposes, nor to create the appearance of a specially licensed or authorised publication. Grateful acknowledgement is made to the following for the use of their material. All rights reserved. While every effort has been made to trace and acknowledge all copyright holders, the publisher apologises for any errors or omissions and, if informed, will be glad to make corrections in any subsequent editions.

Frontispiece illustration copyright © 1999 by Randy Broecker; p2 Universal City Studios, Inc; pp6-21 The Forrest J Ackerman Imagi-Movie Archives; p23 Universal City Studios, Inc; p24 RKO Pictures, Inc/Turner Broadcasting System, Inc.; p25 Universal City Studios, Inc; p26 Universal City Studios, Inc; p33 PolyGram Pictures/Lycanthrope Films Ltd; p39 Hesperia Films/Grand National Pictures; p44 American Academy; p52 Galatea/American International Pictures; p62 Towers of London; p64 Universal City Studios, Inc; p73 Producciones Sotomayor, S.A./Columbia Pictures Industries, Inc; p78 Geneni Film Distributing; p85 BBC Worldwide Ltd; p87 Universal City Studios, Inc; p91 Hammer Film Productions Ltd; p95 Hammer Film Productions Ltd; p101 Dawn Associates/United Film Distribution Co; p112 Universal City Studios, Inc; p114 Universal City Studios, Inc; p116 Hammer Film Productions Ltd; p123 Paramount Pictures Corp; p124 Metro-Goldwyn-Mayer, Inc; p126 BBC Worldwide Ltd; p129 Allied Vision Ltd; p135 Hammer Film Productions Ltd; p137 Monogram Pictures; p144 Edison Films; p147 Universal City Studios, Inc; p150 Universal City Studios, Inc; p157 Avco Embassy Pictures Corp; p162 Universal City Studios, Inc; p164 Gaumont-British; p170 Producers Associates/Richard Gordon Films; p176 S.F. Film Distributors; p186 Universal City Studios, Inc; p187 Universal City Studios, Inc; p190 RKO Pictures, Inc/Turner Broadcasting System, Inc.; p197 Geffen Pictures; p200 United Artists Corp; p202 RKO Pictures, Inc/Turner Broadcasting System, Inc.; p210 RKO Pictures, Inc/Turner Broadcasting System, Inc.; p211 Toho Co., Ltd; p212 Monogram Pictures; p215 American International Film Distributing Corp; p217 Condor International Pictures; p219 American International Pictures; p222 Hammer Film Productions Ltd; p228 Metro-Goldwyn-Mayer, Inc; p234 Universal City Studios, Inc; p242 Metro-Goldwyn-Mayer, Inc; p245 Universal City Studios, Inc; p253 Film Service Distributors; p257 Renown Pictures; p260 Universal City Studios, Inc; p263 Universal City Studios, Inc; p265 MCA Communications, Inc; p278 Image Ten, Inc; p279 Columbia Pictures Industries, Inc; p280 Universal City Studios, Inc; p283 Prana-Film; p284 Los Altos Productions, Inc; p296 CBS Television Network; p298 Universal City Studios, Inc; p301 Hammer Film Productions Ltd; p303 Wade Williams Productions; p311 Dexter Films; p316 Boxoffice International Pictures; p318 Columbia Pictures Industries, Inc; p320 Universal City Studios, Inc; p322 Monogram Pictures/World Northal Corp; p341 Universal City Studios, Inc; p344 Pacemaker Pictures; p347 Universal City Studios, Inc; p349 Universal City Studios, Inc; p365 Paramount Pictures Corp; p369 Metro-Goldwyn-Mayer, Inc; p370 International Amusement Corp; p372 Universal City Studios, Inc; p381 Hammer Film Productions Ltd; p385 Twentieth Century Fox Film Corp; p388 United Artists Corp; p389 Majestic Pictures; p391 Hammer Film Productions Ltd; p394 Hammer Film Productions Ltd; p397 International Amusement Corp; p404 Monogram Pictures; p409 Universal City Studios, Inc; p412 United Artists Corp; p417 Universal City Studios, Inc; p421 Twentieth Century Fox Film Corp; p424 Twentieth Century Fox Film Corp; p427 Columbia Pictures Industries, Inc (courtesy of Ronald V. Borst/Hollywood Movie Posters); p429 RKO Pictures, Inc/Turner Broadcasting System, Inc. (courtesy of Ronald V. Borst/Hollywood Movie Posters); p447 photograph by Jo Fletcher.